LAW for RECREATION and SPORT MANAGERS

Fifth Edition

Doyice J. Cotten

John T. Wolohan

Kendall Hunt
publishing company

Book Team

Chairman and Chief Executive Officer   Mark C. Falb
President and Chief Operating Officer   Chad M. Chandlee
Vice President, Higher Education   David L. Tart
Director of National Book Program   Paul B. Carty
Editorial Manager   Georgia Botsford
Developmental Editor   Melissa Tittle
Vice President, Operations   Timothy J. Beitzel
Assistant Vice President, Production Services   Christine E. O'Brien
Senior Production Editor   Charmayne McMurray
Permissions Editor   Colleen Zelinsky
Cover Designer   Heather Richman

Cover images:
Books and Gavel © Stieglitz, 2010.
Biker © Jonathan Larsen, 2010.
Baseball © Stephen McSweeny, 2010.
Swimmer © T-Design, 2010.
All under license from Shutterstock, Inc.

Kendall Hunt
publishing company
www.kendallhunt.com
Send all inquiries to:
4050 Westmark Drive
Dubuque, IA 52004-1840

Copyright © 1997, 2001, 2003, 2007, 2010 by Kendall Hunt Publishing Company

ISBN 978-0-7575-7180-0
Special Edition ISBN 978-0-7575-7176-3

Printed in the United States of America
10 9 8 7 6 5 4 3 2 1

In Memoriam

Betty van der Smissen

December 27, 1927–November 6, 2008

CONTENTS

1.00 INTRODUCTION TO SPORT LAW

2.00 NEGLIGENCE LAW

3.00 INTENTIONAL TORTS AND CRIMINAL ACTS

4.00 RISK MANAGEMENT

5.00 CONTRACT LAW

6.00 CONSTITUTIONAL LAW

7.00 SPORT AND LEGISLATION

PREFACE

WHAT IS THE SAME?

About the only things that are the same are the goals of the text. The goals of the book never change. They are:

1. To provide an **easy-to-read, user-friendly source** of accurate legal information appropriate for recreation majors, sport management majors, and recreation and sport managers in the field. We try to make every section understandable to both undergraduate and graduate students;

2. To provide **current information** regarding recreation and sport law. Every section is updated in each edition. We accomplish this by providing a new edition every three years. It would be near impossible for one or two authors to do this, but we are able to keep the book up-to-date because we have more than 35 persons involved in each revision;

3. To address a **wide range of topics** so that the professor can select the sections and topics he or she feels are most important for his or her students. This edition has 56 sections from which to select—including sections on negligence law, intentional torts and criminal acts, risk management, contract law, constitutional law, and sport-related legislation.

WHAT IS NEW?

Change in the law is constant and the same is true for *Law for Recreation and Sport Managers*. In this edition, in addition to many new authors, we have two major changes.

1. **All sections have been updated.** Some sections had minor changes (updates, to add clarity, and/or new sections added); some had major changes (usually due to substantial changes in the case law); sometimes two sections have been merged into one; and some sections have been totally rewritten by new authors.

2. The major change, however, is the inclusion of a **Supplemental CD containing 150 court cases.** Many users of the text have been pleased with the inclusion of a significant case in most of the sections, but have expressed regret that there are not more. We have included a CD with three or more cases for every section (except for 3 sections where cases would not be applicable—Legal Research, Business Structures, and Audits in Risk Management).

OUR HOPE!

It is our hope that professors adopting the text and students using the text will find it even more helpful than previous editions. We further welcome any comments or suggestions that would make the text more useful to you.

Doyice and John

ACKNOWLEDGMENTS

This is the fifth edition of *Law for Recreation and Sport Managers*. Like all editions, there have been some unexpected bumps along the way. Even though this edition, surprisingly, had more such challenges than any previous edition, I believe this fifth edition is the best so far. I want to thank my partner, John Wolohan, for helping to smooth the bumps and making sure the revision was a success. Many characteristics make me appreciate John as a partner. Some of them include (1) his sound advice and sympathetic ear when things do not go as planned and tough decisions must be made; (2) his willingness to do whatever needs to be done; and (3) his patience and tact—which I sometimes lack.

I would like to thank the many contributors who shared their knowledge throughout the book, worked diligently on writing and revising their sections, and submitted quality sections in time for us to meet our deadlines. Special thanks go to contributors who stepped in to author excellent sections when unexpected circumstances necessitated last minute changes.

As usual, the professionals at Kendall Hunt have done an excellent job in preparing the materials for this new edition. Particular thanks are due Melissa Tittle and Charmayne McMurray for their efforts and their patience while working with John and me in proofreading the sections, and her suggestions and comments were invaluable.

Finally, thanks go to my wife, Mary, for her support in the endeavor, and her assistance.

Doyice

I would like to express my appreciation to all of the contributing authors for their hard work and dedication to this project, without them this book would not be possible.

In addition, I would also like to acknowledge all the administrative support and help I received from Ithaca College and my administrative assistant Cindy Turo. I would also like to acknowledge all the students in my sports law classes, who are constantly challenging and amazing me.

I also need to give a special acknowledgement to two people that have worked almost nonstop since the fourth edition hit the press to get this fifth edition out. They are Doyice Cotten and Melissa Tittle. Doyice, when not off visiting some exotic place, is always looking for ways to improve the text and is constantly sending authors current information.

Melissa, on the other hand, has the unenviable job of coordinating and keeping both Doyice and me organized and on task, not an easy task yet one which Melissa does with remarkable ease.

Finally, special thanks and love to my family, Nicole, J.T. and Katie.

John

ABOUT THE AUTHORS

DOYICE J. COTTEN

Doyice J. Cotten is an emeritus professor of sport management at Georgia Southern University where he taught graduate and undergraduate courses in sport law and risk management. He manages his own writing and risk management consulting business, Sport Risk Consulting.

During his professional career, Dr. Cotten has been active in many professional organizations in the areas of sport management and physical education. He has served as president of the Sport and Recreation Law Association and as president of the Georgia Association for Health, Physical Education, and Recreation as well as the editor of the GAHPERD Journal.

Dr. Cotten speaks on legal issues at such conferences as the North American Society for Sport Management (NASSM), the American Alliance for Health, Physical Education, Recreation and Dance (AAHPERD), the Athletic Business Conference; the Sports Business Workshop, the International Conference on Sport Business, the International Health, Racquet & Sportsclub Association (IHRSA), the National Intramural-Recreational Sports Association (NIRSA), the Resort and Commercial Recreation Association (RCRA), the American College of Sports Medicine (ACSM), and the National Equine Law Conference.

Dr. Cotten has published more than 150 articles on legal liability and risk management in such publications as *Journal of Legal Aspects of Sport, Journal of Sport Management, Sports Parks & Recreation Law Reporter, Exercise Standards and Malpractice Law Reporter, Athletic Business,* and *Fitness Management.* He wrote a bi-monthly column on risk management for *Fitness Management* for seven years. His major area of interest is in waivers and releases of liability. He has collected and analyzed about 900 sport- and recreation-related waiver cases and has co-authored two books on the subject. They are *Waivers & Releases of Liability* (7th ed.) and *Legal Aspects of Waivers for Sport, Recreation and Fitness Activities.*

Readers are invited to visit Dr. Cotten's website, www.sportwaiver.com. The site features current information regarding both risk management and liability waivers.

JOHN T. WOLOHAN

John Wolohan is a Professor and Department Chair of the Sport Management & Media Department at Ithaca College, Ithaca, New York. He teaches undergraduate and graduate courses in Sports Law and Labor Relations in Sports.

Professor Wolohan writes a monthly article in *Athletic Business* called the "Sports Law Report." He has published numerous articles and book chapters in the areas of intellectual property, athlete's rights, and antitrust issues in sport in such journals as the *Marquette Sports Law Journal, Seton Hall Journal of Sports Law, Villanova Sports & Entertainment Law Journal, University of Missouri-Kansas City Law Review, Educational Law Reporter, International Sports Law Journal, Journal of the Legal Aspects of Sport,* and the *Journal of Sport Management.* In addition, he has made numerous presentations in the area of sports law to such organizations as the American Bar Association, International Sports Lawyers Association, Athletic Business, the Sport and Recreation Law Association, the North American Society of Sport Management, the European Association for Sport Management and the Asser Sports Law Institute.

Professor Wolohan, who is a member of the American and Massachusetts Bar Associations, received his B.A. from the University of Massachusetts-Amherst, and his J.D. from Western New England College.

CONTRIBUTING AUTHORS

Stacey Altman

Stacey R. Altman is an Associate Professor and Chairperson of the Department of Exercise and Sport Science at East Carolina University. She currently teaches courses in Legal Issues in Sport and Intercollegiate Athletic Administration. She received a B.S. in Political Science from Coastal Carolina University, a M.Ed. in Sport Management from the University of Georgia, and a J.D. from the University of Alabama. Her research interests include the study of constitutional provisions and certain legislative initiatives as they relate to participation in sport and physical activity.

Robin Ammon, Jr.

Robin Ammon, Jr. is a Professor and Chair of the Department of Sport Management at Slippery Rock University, Slippery Rock, PA. He received his B.S. degree from the University of Colorado in Physical Education, his M.S. degree from Louisiana State University in Exercise Science and his doctorate from the University of Northern Colorado in Sport Administration. Dr. Ammon currently teaches classes in Sport Law and in Facility and Event Management at both the undergraduate and graduate levels. His areas of research include: legal liabilities in sport, risk management in sport and athletics, and premises liability. He is a co-author of three Sport Facility and Event Management textbooks, plus he has authored chapters in many other edited texts. In addition, Dr. Ammon has 33 years of practical experience working with crowd and event management as a consultant and manager.

Paul M. Anderson

Paul M. Anderson is the Associate Director of the National Sports Law Institute of Marquette University Law School, where he is also an Adjunct Professor of Law. Professor Anderson teaches courses in amateur sports law, current issues in sports law, selected topics in sports law, advanced legal research- sports law, and entertainment law. He is the author of three books, editor of two books, and author of several book chapters and numerous articles. He is the Editor of the Journal of Legal Aspects of Sport and the Faculty Advisor and Supervisor of the Marquette Sports Law Review. He coordinates all events and the student internship program for the Sports Law Program at Marquette University Law School, the nation's most extensive sports law program. He is a practicing attorney most recently associated with The Leib Group, LLC, advisors to the sports and entertainment industry, and is the Vice-Chair and Program Coordinator for the Sports & Entertainment Law Section of the State Bar of Wisconsin. Professor Anderson received his B.A. Phi Beta Kappa from Marquette University and his J.D. from Marquette University Law School.

Thomas A. Baker III

Thomas A. Baker III is an assistant professor in sport management at the University of Georgia. Baker has a Ph.D. from the University of Florida (sport management), a J.D. from Loyola University New Orleans School of Law, and a B.A. in Journalism from the University of Southern Mississippi. He also completed a comparative law program at the University of Vienna in Austria. At the University of Florida, Baker was a Charles W. LaPradd Ph.D. fellow. He graduated from Loyola University New Orleans School of law in the top 10 percent of his class, with honors, earning the distinction of William L. Crowe, Sr. Scholar. He is a member of the Louisiana Bar Association and his areas of practice include sport law and commercial litigation. At the University of Georgia, Baker teaches graduate and undergraduate classes in sport law, sport ethics, and sport facilities. He has coauthored two books, several book chapters, and multiple articles on the topic of sport law.

Paul J. Batista

Paul J. Batista, Associate Professor, Texas A&M University; B.S., Trinity University, 1973; J.D., Baylor Law School, 1976. Professor Batista is admitted to practice before the United States Supreme Court, is licensed to appear in all of the courts in Texas, is a former County Judge of Burleson County, Texas, and is a certified Mediator and Arbitrator. He has taught sport law at Texas A&M since 1991, has received the Texas A&M Association of Former Students Distinguished Achievement Award in Teaching and the Student Led Award for Teaching Excellence, and has been named a Montague Center for Teaching Excellence Scholar. His primary research interest is sports related liability issues in school settings, with particular emphasis on First Amendment religion and free speech issues. He has delivered research presentations at numerous conferences throughout the United States, as well as in Canada, Germany, Slovenia and South Korea.

Linda Carpenter

Linda Jean Carpenter, Ph.D., J.D. Professor Emerita of Physical Education and Exercise Science at Brooklyn College of the City University of New York is also a member of the New York State and United States Supreme Court Bars. She has published numerous books and articles as well as speaking at many national and international professional meetings. Her research, including the national longitudinal study on the status of women in sport, coauthored with Vivian Acosta and now it its 31st year, is frequently cited in scholarly writing as well as the lay press and has been used often in Senate and Congressional hearings on Title IX and equity in sport. She holds the B.S. and M.S. from Brigham Young University, the Ph.D. from the University of Southern California and the J.D. from Fordham Law School.

Rodney L. Caughron

Rod Caughron, Ph.D., is an Associate Professor in the KNPE/Sport Management department at Northern Illinois University, and serves as Director of Graduate Studies in Sport Management. He received both his B.A. in Political Science and M.S. in Exercise Physiology from Iowa State University and his Ph.D. from The University of Iowa in Athletic Administration. Previous to his current position, Caughron served as Coordinator of Fitness for the Saudi Air Force and worked in the Student Services and ticket office at The University of Iowa. Professor Caughron currently teaches graduate courses in sport law and sport management and leadership.

Margaret E. Ciccolella

Margaret E. Ciccolella is a Professor in the Department of Sport Sciences at the University of the Pacific. She received an Ed.D. in exercise physiology from Brigham Young University and a J.D. from Humphreys College. Currently, she teaches graduate and undergraduate course work in sports law and higher education law. Additionally, she is a board member for WorkWell, an organization specializing in research on chronic fatigue syndrome.

Colleen Colles

Colleen Colles is an Associate Professor and Chair of the Sport Management Program at Nichols College. She received her bachelor's degree in Health and Fitness Management from Northern Michigan University, her master's degree in Physical Education from Eastern Kentucky University and her doctorate in Sport Administration from the University of Northern Colorado. She has experience as a collegiate volleyball coach, campus recreation director and employee wellness coordinator. She is an active member of SRLA and NASSM and her research interests include gender equity in sport and collegiate athletics.

Daniel P. Connaughton

Dan Connaughton is an Associate Professor in the Department of Tourism, Recreation and Sport Management at the University of Florida (UF). He received a B.S. in Exercise and Sport Sciences and a M.S. in Recreation from the UF, a M.S. in Physical Education (Administration) from Bridgewater State College, and an Ed.D. in Sport Administration from the Florida State University. Dr. Connaughton has held management positions in campus and public recreation departments, aquatic programs, and health/fitness facilities. At the UF,

Connaughton conducts research and teaches classes in sport law and risk management. He is an author/ co-author of three textbooks, several book chapters and journal articles, and is a Fellow with the Research Consortium of the AAHPERD.

Windy Dees

Windy Dees is an Assistant Professor in the Department of Hospitality, Tourism, and Family and Consumer Sciences at Georgia Southern University. She currently teaches undergraduate Legal Issues in Sport and graduate Sport Law and Risk Management. She also teaches undergraduate and graduate courses in Sport Marketing. She received a B.A. in Psychology and Communications from Rollins College, an M.S. in Sport Management from the University of Florida, and a Ph.D. in Sport Management from Texas A&M University. Her research interests include the study of constitutional law as it relates to the organization and operation of private clubs in sport and recreation.

JoAnn Eickhoff-Shemek

JoAnn M. Eickhoff-Shemek is a Professor and the Coordinator of the Exercise Science program at the University of South Florida in Tampa. Her research in recreation and sport law has focused on standards of practice and legal liability/risk management issues in the exercise/fitness field. Dr. Eickhoff-Shemek is the lead author of a new, ground-breaking text entitled *Risk Management for Health/Fitness Professionals: Legal Issues and Strategies* published by Lippincott Williams and Wilkins in 2009. (David L. Herbert, J.D. and Daniel P. Connaughton, Ed.D. are co-authors). Since 2000, Dr. Eickhoff-Shemek has served as an associate editor and the legal columnist for *ACSM's Health & Fitness Journal*. She is an ACSM Health/Fitness Director certified and an ACSM Exercise Test Technologist certified and a Fellow of ACSM and AWHP.

Sarah K. Fields

Sarah K. Fields is an Associate Professor in the Sport Humanities program at the Ohio State University where she teaches, among others, courses on Sports Law. She received her undergraduate degree from Yale University, her juris doctorate from Washington University in St. Louis, her master's degree from Washington State University, and her doctorate in American Studies from the University of Iowa. She is the author of *Female Gladiators: Gender, Law, and Contact Sport in America* (2005) as well as articles in scholarly journals including the *Journal of Sport History*, the *Journal of College and University Law*, the *American Journal of Sports Medicine*, and *Pediatrics*.

Susan Brown Foster

Susan Brown Foster is a Professor of Sport Business and coordinates the MBA specialization in Sport Business in the School of Business at Saint Leo University in Saint Leo, Florida. She has taught undergraduate/graduate legal issues courses at four post-secondary institutions. She received her Bachelor's degree from Florida State University, her Master's from Eastern Illinois University, her Doctorate from The Ohio State University, and has additional coursework in legal research. Dr. Foster has authored ten book chapters, is co-editor of two books and has published legal articles in several journals including the Journal of the Legal Aspects of Sport, the International Journal of Sport Management, and the Journal of Sport Management. She was also profiled in the book Profiles of Sport Management Professionals: Making the Games Happen. She is currently co-authoring a book on experiential learning in sport business with a 2010 copyright date. She was a co-winner of the 2006 Sport and Recreational Law Association Honor Award for her support of undergraduate legal research. Dr. Foster has also dedicated most of her 20+ years in higher education to quality curriculum development and served the Sport Management Program Review Council (SMPRC) for 11 years including five years as Chair and is now a site reviewer for the Council on Sport Management Accreditation (COSMA). Dr. Foster started her own company, Sport Business Consulting, Inc., in 2007.

Gil Fried

Gil Fried is a Professor and Chair of the Sport/ Hospitality and Tourism Management Department at the University of New Haven. Professor Fried received a joint law and sport management degree from the Ohio

State University. He is a practicing attorney who represents several national and international sports organizations. He consults on sport facility and finance issues, and has served as the director of risk management for a large facility management company. He has written six books and numerous articles. His primary emphases are sports law, finance and facility administration.

Lynne P. Gaskin

Lynne Gaskin is the Associate Dean of the College of Education and Professor Emerita of Physical Education at the University of West Georgia. She received her B.S. degree from Wesleyan College and her M.S. and Ed.D. degrees from the University of North Carolina at Greensboro. Dr. Gaskin has written and spoken extensively at the national and international levels in the area of sport law. She is a member of 15 professional societies and serves as an officer and as a member of the Board of Directors for a number of professional organizations. She received the Ethel Martus Lawther Award and the Research Excellence Award from the University of North Carolina at Greensboro; the Honor Award from the North Carolina Alliance for Health, Physical Education, Recreation and Dance; the Service Award from Phi Delta Kappa; the Presidential Citation for Meritorious Service from the Georgia Association of Health, Physical Education, Recreation and Dance; and the honor award and meritorious service award from the Sport and Recreation Law Association. Dr. Gaskin teaches graduate and undergraduate courses in sport law, marketing, and facility management.

Michael Gibbons

Michael Gibbons is an Associate Professor and Chair of the Sport Studies Department at St. John Fisher College. He received his law degree from Suffolk University Law School and his Masters in Sport Management from the University of Massachusetts. His primary teaching and research interests are in the legal aspects of sport.

Genevieve Gordon

Genevieve Gordon, LLB, LLM currently teaches International Sports Law, Sports Law and Sports Marketing at various undergraduate and postgraduate programs in the UK. In addition to being invited to give lectures in a number of different countries, Ms. Gordon has also published numerous articles in the area of sports law. Her research mainly focuses on legal issues surrounding the sport of polo, drug testing sport and sport marketing.

John Grady

John Grady is an Assistant Professor in the Department of Sport & Entertainment at the University of South Carolina. He received a B.S. in Management with Honors in Finance from Penn State University. Both his law degree and Ph.D. are from Florida State University. Dr. Grady's research interests focus primarily on legal issues in the sport industry. This includes concentrations in the implementation of the Americans with Disabilities Act in sport and entertainment venues, sponsorship protection from ambush marketing, as well as intellectual property protection for professional and collegiate sport properties. At the University of South Carolina, he teaches graduate and undergraduate courses in the areas of sport law and risk and security management.

Curt Hamakawa

Curt Hamakawa is an assistant professor of sport management at Western New England College in Springfield, Massachusetts, where he teaches courses in sport management, sport law, and international sport policy. He is also the founding director of the Center for International Sport Business (CISB), a forum for the study of the business of sport, but with an international focus. Prior to joining Western New England College, Mr. Hamakawa served the United States Olympic Committee (USOC) as associate general counsel (1990–1992), director of athlete services (1992–2000), and director of international relations (2000–2006). From 1987 to 1990, he worked for the National Collegiate Athletic Association in its compliance and enforcement department. Mr. Hamakawa is a law graduate of Western New England College, and holds a master's degree from Springfield College, and a bachelor's degree from the University of Hawaii.

Mary A. Hums

Mary A. Hums, Ph.D. is a Professor of Sport Administration at the University of Louisville. A Past President of the Society for the Study of Legal Aspects of Sport and Physical Activity (SSLASPA), and recipient of numerous outstanding teaching awards, her extensive national and international research focuses primarily on in sport management issues related to sport for people with disabilities as well as sport and human rights. In 2009, Hums was named the Earle F. Zeigler Lecturer by NASSM. She was a co-contributor to Article 30.5 (Participation in Cultural Life, Recreation, Leisure and Sport) of the 2006 United Nations Convention on the Rights of Persons with Disabilities. She is an active member of the International Olympic Academy Participants Association, and an inductee into the ASA Indiana Softball Hall of Fame and the Mishawaka (IN) Marian High School Hall of Fame.

Jim Masteralexis

Jim Masteralexis is an Assistant Professor of Sport Law at Western New England College in Springfield, Massachusetts. His research focuses on professional baseball, and labor and employment issues in sport. He is a graduate of the University of New Hampshire and Suffolk University Law School and is a partner in a professional athlete management firm.

Lisa Pike Masteralexis

Lisa Pike Masteralexis is the Department Head and an Associate Professor of Sport Law in the Department of Sport Management at the Isenberg School of Management at the University of Massachusetts. She holds a J.D. from Suffolk University School of Law and a B.S. in Sport Management from the University of Massachusetts. Professor Masteralexis' teaching and research interests are in legal issues and labor relations in the sport industry. She is the lead editor of *Principles and Practice of Sport Management,* now in its third edition and has also written book chapters for *Sport Law: A Managerial Approach, Sport Marketing, Sport in the Global Village,* and *Management for Athletic/Sport Administration.* She is an Advisory Board member of the Marquette University Law School's National Sports Law Institute and consults with a professional athlete management firm.

John D. McMillen

John McMillen is an Associate Professor of Sport Administration at California State University, Fresno. He received his law degree from Drake University Law School and his B.A., M.Ed. and Ph.D. from the University of Nebraska-Lincoln. His primary research area is the legal aspects of sport art.

Merry Moiseichik

Merry Moiseichik is currently a Full Professor at the University of Arkansas in Recreation and Sport Management. She received her doctorate from Indiana University in Recreation Administration and Bachelors and Masters from SUNY Cortland in Recreation, and a Juris Doctorate from the University of Arkansas. Dr. Moiseichik has worked in recreation administration in central New York. Her research interests are in community development and legal aspects both as they affect recreation and sport. She teaches courses in Legal Aspects of Sport and Recreation Services, Sport and Recreation Risk Management as well as other recreation and sport administration courses.

Anita M. Moorman

Anita M. Moorman, J.D. is an Associate Professor in Sport Administration at the University of Louisville where she teaches Sport Law and Legal Aspects of Sport. She joined the faculty at the University of Louisville in 1996. Professor Moorman has a law degree from Southern Methodist University and prior to her academic pursuits, she practiced law in Oklahoma City, Oklahoma in the areas of commercial and corporate litigation for ten years. Professor Moorman also holds an M.S. in Sport Management from the University of Oklahoma, and a B.S. in Political Science from Oklahoma State University. Professor Moorman's research interests include commercial law issues in the sport industry; and legal and ethical issues related to sport marketing practices, brand protection, and intellectual property issues in sport. She has published more than twenty articles in academic journals/proceedings and has given more than forty presentations at national and international conferences.

Rebecca J. Mowrey

Rebecca J. Mowrey is Coordinator for the Graduate Sports Management program and Professor of Sport Management at Millersville University of Pennsylvania. She teaches graduate and undergraduate courses in the areas of sport law, risk management, professional ethics, and additional sport management courses. Dr. Mowrey is Past-President of the Sport and Recreation Law Association and Past President of the Sport Management Council of the National Association for Sport and Physical Education. Her professional contributions include serving as a member of the editorial boards of the Journal of Legal Aspects of Sport, and the Recreational Sports Journal, and as a reviewer for the Sport Management Program Review Council (SMPRC).

Bridget Niland

Bridget Niland is an Assistant Professor of Business Administration at Daemen College in Amherst, New York. She currently serves as Coordinator of the Sport Management Specialization and teaches courses in Sport Law, Sport Management, Labor Relations and Business Law. She earned a B.S. in History, Political Science and Legal Studies and an M.Ed in Higher Education Administration from the State University of New York at Buffalo, and a J.D. from the University of Buffalo School of Law. Prior to joining the Daemen faculty, she served as a trial attorney for the United States Department of Justice in Washington, D.C. and was an Associate Director of Legislative Services at the National Collegiate Athletic Association. Her research focuses on legal issues in intercollegiate athletics.

Barbara Osborne

Barbara Osborne, J.D. is currently the Coordinator for the Undergraduate Program in Sport Administration and an Associate Professor in the Department of Exercise and Sport Science at the University of North Carolina at Chapel Hill. Prior to her appointment at UNC, she worked for 14 years as an administrator in intercollegiate athletics. Osborne has an undergraduate degree in communications from the University of Wisconsin-Parkside, a master's degree in sport administration from Boston University, a law degree from Boston College, and is licensed to practice law in Massachusetts and North Carolina. She has also had experience as a competitive athlete, coach, public relations coordinator, television sports commentator, publisher and sports information director. She has served on the Board of Directors of the Sport and Recreation Law Association and chaired the North Carolina Bar Association Sport and Entertainment Law Section. Osborne's current research focuses on legal issues in intercollegiate sport and gender issues in sport.

Gary Rushing

Gary Rushing, Full Professor, received his Ed.D. from the University of Northern Colorado; B.S. and M.S. from the University of Arizona. Currently, he is the Human Performance Department Chair at Minnesota State University, Mankato. His research and teaching areas include a variety of sport management courses such as Legal Aspects of Sport and Physical Activity. He has published in several law reporters and coaching journals and has over twenty-five years of experience in athletics as a coach and administrator.

Kristi Schoepfer

Kristi L. Schoepfer is an Assistant Professor in the Department of Physical Education, Sport and Human Performance at Winthrop University in Rock Hill, S.C. She currently serves as Program Director for the undergraduate Sport Management Program and teaches Legal Issues in Sport courses at the undergraduate and graduate level. Additionally, she teaches Sport Marketing, Sport Public Relations and Introduction to Sport Management at the undergraduate level. She received a B.S. in Secondary Education from the University of Dayton and a J.D. from Marquette University. Additionally, she earned a certificate in Sport Law from the National Sport Law Institute. Prior to assuming her current position, she taught for five years at the University of Wisconsin-Parkside in Kenosha, W.I.

Linda L. Schoonmaker

Linda L. Schoonmaker is currently an Assistant Professor in the Department of Health, Exercise, and Sport Science at The Citadel. Dr. Schoonmaker has twenty years experience teaching a variety of undergraduate and graduate sport management courses. She also has ten years administrative experience in campus recreation, seven of those years as Director of Campus Recreation and Facilities at the University of Wisconsin-Whitewater. A Past President of the Sport and Recreation Association, Dr. Schoonmaker earned her undergaduate and graduate degrees from SUNY, Brockport and earned her PhD from The Ohio State University. Dr. Schoonmaker's research focus is in the area of gender equity and interscholastic athletics.

Todd L. Seidler

Todd Seidler is an Professor and coordinator of the graduate program in Sport Administration at the University of New Mexico, one of only a few programs that offer both the Master's and Doctorate in Sport Administration. He received his Bachelor's degree in Physical Education from San Diego State University and taught and coached in high school. He then went to graduate school and earned his Master's and Ph.D. in Sports Administration from the University of New Mexico. Prior to returning to U.N.M., Dr. Seidler spent six years as the coordinator of the graduate Sports Administration program at Wayne State University and then coordinated the undergraduate Sport Management Program at Guilford College. He is currently interim Executive Director and a Past President of the Society for the Study of the Sport and Recreation Law Association, contributing editor to *From The Gym To The Jury* newsletter, past chair of the Sport Management Council and of the Council on Facilities and Equipment within AAHPERD.

David L. Snyder

David Snyder is a Professor of Sport Management at the State University of New York College at Cortland, and a part-time Associate Professor of Sport Management at Tompkins Cortland Community College. Professor Snyder received his J.D. from the University of Tennessee and has been licensed to practice law in New York since 1986. Prior to accepting his current position at Cortland, he served as president of an international sports marketing company headquartered in Tokyo, Japan. He is currently pursuing his doctoral degree in sports management at the Deutsche Sporthochsule Köln in Germany. His doctoral research focuses upon the relationship between Japanese socio-cultural values and the business of professional baseball in Japan.

Ellen J. Staurowsky

Ellen J. Staurowsky is Professor and Graduate Chair in the Department of Sport Management & Media at Ithaca College, Ithaca, NY. Dr. Staurowsky received her undergraduate degree in health and physical education from Ursinus College, master's degree in sport psychology from Ithaca College, and doctorate in sport management from Temple University. In addition to publications in scholarly journals such as the American Indian Quarterly, Journal of Sport and Social Issues, Sociology of Sport Journal, Quest, Journal of Sport Management, the International Journal of Sport Sociology, and the International Journal of Sport History, her critiques and analyses on a variety of issues have appeared in *The New York Times, The Chronicle of Higher Education, Street & Smith's Sports Business Journal, The NCAA News, Athletic Business, Athletic Management,* and *News From Indian Country.* In 1998, she co-authored a book along with Allen Sack from the University of New Haven entitled *College Athletes for Hire: The Evolution and Legacy of the NCAA Amateur Myth.*

Stephanie A. Tryce

Stephanie A. Tryce earned a juris doctorate from Temple University School of Law, completed M.S. course work in Sport Management at the University of Massachusetts and earned a B.S. in Business Administration from Drexel University. Ms. Tryce has taught *Introduction to Sport Law, Amateur Sport and the Law* and *Professional Sport and the Law* for the Sport Management Department of the University of Massachusetts. Formerly, Ms. Tryce lectured at the Wharton School of the University of Pennsylvania teaching courses in Introduction to Law and the Legal Process and The Sport Industry. Ms. Tryce is currently an Assistant City Solicitor in the Major Tax Enforcement Unit of the Law Department for the City of Philadelphia.

Nita Unruh

Nita Unruh is currently the Chair of the HPERLS Department, and Degree Coordinator for the Sport Administration program at the University of Nebraska-Kearney. She received her Ed.D. in HPER from the

University of Arkansas, M.S. in Leisure Studies from Florida State University and her B.S. from Henderson State University. Nita is an active member of SRLA and currently teaches the Sports Law Course at UNK.

Jo Williams

Jo Williams is an Associate Professor at the University of Southern Maine. She received her bachelor's degree from West London Institute of Higher Education (Brunel University) and her master's degree and doctorate from Springfield College, MA. Her research interests include sport marketing, particularly the use of digital media, and collegiate athletics. Additional interests focus on curricula innovation and student engagement. Williams teaches sport management and marketing courses and has previous experience as an event director in professional golf. She is an active member of NASSM and COSMA.

Sarah J. Young

Sarah J. Young is an Associate Professor with the Department of Recreation, Park & Tourism Studies at Indiana University-Bloomington. She earned her B.S. degree in Recreation and Park Administration from Illinois State University, and earned both her Ph.D. in Leisure Behavior with a minor in Law, and her M.S. in Recreational Sport Administration from Indiana University. Sarah also worked as an Assistant Director of Intramural Sports for nine years with the Division of Recreational Sports at Indiana University. Sandwiched between her IU experiences, Sarah was an Assistant Professor with the Leisure Studies program in the College of Hotel Administration at University of Nevada, Las Vegas for four years. Sarah is an active member of NIRSA, NRPA, and SRLA, and teaches legal aspects of sport and recreation management courses.

1.00

INTRODUCTION TO SPORT LAW

In today's litigious society, it is important that sport and recreation administrators have a sound understanding of the law. The *Introduction to Sport Law* section consists of three sections covering a wide range of legal areas, intended to provide administrators with a basic introduction to legal principles as they apply to the sport and recreation industry.

The first section addresses the foundations of the legal system, both federal and state, as well as the process involved in the evolution of a lawsuit. It is intended to help the reader to better understand how the legal system functions.

The second section introduces the reader to the tools that are available for conducting legal research. Additionally, the author provides guidance to the reader regarding the basic steps to be used in conducting legal research.

The third section provides an overview of the business structures and legal authority found in the sport and recreation industry. Guidance is given regarding the type of protection provided by a number of popular business structures.

1.10   The Legal System

—Gil B. Fried

University of New Haven

If one asked what the term **law** means, one would probably receive a different answer from each person one asked. One definition defines the law as a system of regulations designed to govern the conduct of people living in a society and these regulations are often developed through the body of human experience and values (Hill, 2009). Law implies a multitude of definitions and concepts. Law is abstract, living, constantly changing and evolving. At the same time, laws provide predictability, accountability, justice, protection, and even compassion. Law consists of the entire conglomeration of rules, values, and principles that govern daily conduct that can be enforced by either the government or individual citizens through courts.

Individuals often confuse the law with **justice**. The law normally provides for one specific interpretation. Justice, however, does not necessarily mean the same thing to all people. Justice varies based on one's education, upbringing, social class, and related factors. Thus, although the law protects one's freedom of speech, many people might not think justice is served by letting a hate group demonstrate on public property. However, our society has determined that laws are often required to protect certain rights or people that the rest of society might not cherish or approve.

The Significant Case highlights an injury to a hockey player who sought to use the "law" through the legal system to obtain a remedy for his injury. However, based on the injured player's failure to properly write his complaint, he was prevented from obtaining the justice he thought he deserved. Some might think this is unfair, since the injured player did not receive his day in court. However, it is important for people to know if they are possibly going to be sued. Thus, legislators developed a concept requiring timely filing of cases.

FUNDAMENTAL CONCEPTS

Types of Law

Three primary areas of law will be discussed in this section—**common law, statutory law**, and **Constitutional law**. Because laws passed by legislative bodies (statutory laws) can never cover all potential circumstances, conditions, or occasions, common law can be used to provide specific guidance for interpreting the laws.

Common law refers to cases that have been resolved by various courts. The decisions of numerous courts over hundreds of years are combined to form our common law system. For example, numerous principles concerning the liability of an individual who fails to live up to a certain standard of conduct have been developed over the past five centuries. These cases comprise common law and serve as a precedent for future cases involving the same or similar facts. **Precedent** serves to create boundaries by which future cases must be decided. Once a case becomes precedent at a higher court (such as an appellate court), all future analyses by lower courts in that jurisdiction (of the same or similar facts) must rely on the prior decision. In sport cases, foul-ball cases follow precedent, which is why court decisions in foul-ball cases often refer to cases from almost 100 years ago to help establish the principle of assumption of risk and the limited duty rule. Common law can transcend state borders. Thus, while the law in New York or California is not precedent for a court in Nevada, in 2008 the Nevada Supreme Court relied on cases from many other jurisdictions to reach a decision on a foul-ball case in Nevada. Since the Supreme Court of Nevada had not yet reached a decision on foul-ball liability in that state, the court relied upon decisions (precedent) from other states to establish the new law to apply throughout Nevada. (*Turner v. Mandalay Sports Entertainment*, 2008).

Constitutional law refers to laws embodied in the U.S. Constitution. In addition, each state has its own constitution. An example of Constitutional law in recreation or sport involves prayer in a locker room. Although most athletes are familiar with pregame prayers, the Constitution prohibits states from endorsing any religion. Thus, if a public high school coach required players to pray before a game, the coach would be violating the constitutionally required separation of church and state. Other Constitutional law issues seen in sport include search and seizure issues in athlete lockers and due process rights, such as when the NCAA investigated Jerry Tarkanian and did not have to give him any rights to face his accusers.

Statutory law is law originating from and passed by legislative bodies. All levels of government adopt statutory law, including national, state, municipal, county, and city entities. This body of law is only valid for the area governed by that entity and can cover such topics as zoning, advertising, taxes, or building a recreation or sport facility. Statutory law and Constitutional law are analogous in that both types of law are adopted or changed by a voting system and form the framework of laws that guide our everyday actions. Examples of sport-related legislation are the various laws being passed to control the interaction between agents and college athletes. Examples of recreation-related legislation are the recreational user statutes that provide immunity protection for landowners who allow recreational users to use the property for free.

There are numerous subcategories of the law including tax, tort, contract, employment, real estate, and sport law, to name a few. One of the broader categories worth mentioning is administrative law. **Administrative law** refers to the body of laws, rules, and regulations that are developed, adopted, and enforced by government units responsible for managing specific government agencies. Although administrative law is not as widely applied as statutory or common law, it still affects a variety of recreation or sport issues. Large portions of the economy are governed by federal administrative agencies. The regulations adopted by national administrative agencies such as the National Labor Relations Board (NLRB) or the Occupational Safety and Health Administration (OSHA) have the force of law. In 1972, Congress passed the law commonly referred to as Title IX. This law requires equal treatment of men and women in programs receiving federal funds. Colleges receiving federal funds are required to provide similar funding to both men's and women's athletic programs. The law is enforced by the Department of Justice, which can help develop and interpret how the law should be enforced, and can prosecute those schools that do not comply. Administrative law concerns are not relegated to just federal agencies, but can be seen at the state and local level as well. State administrative agencies have jurisdiction over issues such as workers' compensation, facility rentals, and fair employment practices.

How Statutory Laws Are Enacted

Understanding the process by which a bill becomes law is critical for understanding statutory law and how individuals and politicians can identify a problem and then develop an appropriate legal solution. Most state legislatures and the U.S. Congress enact laws using substantially the same procedures. To illustrate this general procedure, the following scenario outlines the revision of the Indiana recreational user statute—from the initial bill to the final adoption.

Indiana had an existing statute that provided liability protection for those landowners who opened their property to individuals for free recreational use. However, it was unclear whether the law applied to hunting and related activities. The primary focus of the bill was the revision of the existing law to clarify the protection afforded to landowners who open their land, including caves, for recreational users involved in hunting, fishing, trapping, or preparing to engage in any of those three activities.

Introducing the Bill

Initially someone approached a state representative and indicated a desire to amend the existing law. Although this bill started in the House of Representatives, it could just as easily have been introduced in the Senate. In this case, the representative authored the revisions and introduced the bill on January 6, 1998. It was read into the record and then referred to the appropriate House committee (Committee on Natural Resources). On January 28, after study and testimony regarding the effects of the act, the committee returned a report to the House analyzing the potential impact that changes in the existing law might have on land use, recreational users, government entities, and other affected parties. The committee could recommend, reject, or be neutral regarding the proposed changes. In this case, the committee recommended adoption of the changes. After being debated in the House, a vote was taken on February 3, with the bill passing 61 to 36. After passing the House, the bill was immediately referred to the Indiana Senate.

Moving from the House to the Senate

Some bills are introduced simultaneously in the House and the Senate; however, in this case, the bill was introduced and passed in one body prior to introduction in the other chamber. After being referred to the Senate, the bill was sponsored by several state senators and referred to the Senate's Committee on Natural Resources. (A **sponsor** is someone who introduces the bill to the chamber. If a bill passes one chamber, but does not have a sponsor in the second chamber, it dies despite the fact that it has already passed in the other chamber.)

While in the Senate's committee, the bill was amended to address some concerns the senators had. After the changes were made, the revised bill was sent to the Senate floor on February 23, 1998. Although there were 232 senators present, the bill passed by a 49 to 1 vote. Generally, a simple majority of votes is all that is needed to pass a bill. In some cases (e.g., impeachment votes, overriding a governor's veto), a two-thirds majority might be required to pass a bill. Because there were changes in the bill, it had to be referred back to the House of Representatives.

Compromise

If the House accepts the amendments, then they vote to approve the bill, and the appropriate leaders sign it. However, there often is a conflict between the exact languages of the two bills. In this case the House did not accept the revised wording, and on February 25, the House and the Senate leaders appointed a joint committee containing representatives and senators to confer on the two versions and try to reconcile the different versions. In a relatively short time, two days, they were able to work out the differences, and both the Senate and the House unanimously adopted the combined Conference Committee Report. Sometimes the process can take several days or several months.

To the Governor

On March 3, the senate president signed the bill. It was signed two days later by the speaker of the house and sent to the governor for his signature. When the governor receives the bill, he has three choices: (1) he can sign the bill and it becomes law; (2) he can decline to sign the bill and it becomes law in ten days (in most states); or (3) he can veto the bill. If he vetoes the bill, it returns to the originating chamber and requires a two-thirds vote of that body to override. In this case, the governor signed the bill and it became a law on March 16, 1998. Even though it was enacted in March, the law was not to take effect until July 1, 1998.

It should be noted that not all bills are passed this quickly. In fact, numerous bills die each year because the legislature does not have time to act on the bill. Also, even if a bill requiring funding is passed, that bill may be not be implemented if the necessary financial support is not appropriated.

Court System

When a dispute arises involving either the application of a statute or an individual's rights, the dispute is traditionally resolved through an appropriate **court** system. A court is a tribunal established by governments to hear certain cases and administer justice. There are three primary court systems: state, federal, and administrative courts. Legal authority, procedures, and the types of disputes heard are different in each court system.

A **state court** has jurisdiction (authority) to hear a case if the case involves an event or activity that occurred within the state. In addition, the parties to the lawsuit have to reside or conduct significant business activities in the state. Typical cases brought in state court include breach of contract claims, personal injury suits, and suits involving real estate located in the state.

State court systems traditionally consist of general or superior jurisdiction courts, which are referred to by various names in different states. They are commonly called circuit courts, district courts, superior courts, or courts of common pleas. Some states have other special courts such as probate (to handle the estates of deceased persons), juvenile, family law, municipal, city, and small claims courts.

If a party to a suit does not feel the law was properly applied, he or she can appeal the case to an appellate court. An appeal is the process by which a party to a suit can challenge the legal decision rendered by a court. The appeals process is designed to guarantee that the court cannot exercise unchecked or abusive power. If the appellate court's decision is also disputed, the litigant can file another appeal to the state's supreme court. State supreme court decisions are final unless the decision impacts federal laws, treaties, or the Constitution. Appellate courts and the state supreme court can only review issues of law. They cannot review the facts or reanalyze evidence. A trial court has to follow decisions reached by their immediate appellate court. Other appellate courts in the same jurisdiction do not have to follow the decision reached by a different appellate court in the same state. All state courts (trial and appellate) must follow all state supreme court decisions in that state.

A majority of cases are brought in state courts. However, if a dispute involves over $75,000, citizens of different states, or a question involving the Constitution or a federal law question, the case is brought in **federal court.** Federal courts also hear patent, tax, copyright, maritime, and bankruptcy matters. If a party believes that the federal court misapplied the law, the party can petition a federal court of appeals. The United States is divided into twelve judicial districts, each with a federal appellate court. The last resort for any party is to request that the U.S. Supreme Court review a case. The process of applying for review by the Supreme Court involves filing a **writ of certiorari.** A writ of certiorari is sent from the Supreme Court to a lower level court when at least four of the nine Supreme Court justices vote to hear the case. The writ requires the lower court to turn the case over to the Supreme Court.

Administrative courts or agencies are created by Congress or state legislatures, and both create and enforce their own rules. All other courts only enforce or interpret rules made by other courts or legislatures. For example, the National Labor Relations Board (NLRB) is a lawmaker, an executive agency that enforces the law, and a court that interprets and applies the law. If a professional league decided to lock its unionized players out of training camp, the players could file a complaint with the NLRB. The NLRB would investigate and reach a decision concerning the players' complaint. A federal administrator has the power to investigate violations of agency rules and to force individuals to appear before the agency and answer charges against the individuals. Because administrative agencies make, enforce, and judge their own laws, most associations have established separate judicial branches removed from the law-making and enforcing divisions and directed by an administrative law judge. An administrative law judge helps ensure some degree of independence.

A court can only hear a case if it has **jurisdiction** over the people involved or if the issue involved in the case occurred or is located within the court's jurisdiction. Jurisdiction refers to a court's authority to hear and decide a certain case. If a court does not have jurisdiction, then the court cannot hear the case. A court having jurisdiction over a person or company or the subject matter of the dispute can obtain jurisdiction. Thus, federal courts have subject matter jurisdiction over a case if the case involves issues under the federal Constitution, the amount in controversy is over $75,000, or the disputing parties are located in different states. On the other hand, a state court only has jurisdiction if a disputant lives in that state or has significant contacts within the state. Noted track star Butch Reynolds sued the International Amateur Athletic Federation (IAAF) in an Ohio state court. The case centered on IAAF's failure to overturn a competition suspension imposed on Reynolds after an inaccurate drug test. The IAAF did not attend the state court trial, which resulted in a $28.3 million verdict against the IAAF. The case was appealed to a federal court, which overturned the state court's decision. The federal court's decision was based on the fact that the IAAF was not based in Ohio and did not conduct a significant amount of business in Ohio. Therefore, the Ohio court did not have jurisdiction to hear a case involving a non-Ohio-based organization. In a recent case involving two professional hockey players, a Colorado judge dismissed a case brought by former Avalanche forward Steve Moore against Vancouver Canuck's Todd Bertuzzi. Bertuzzi hit Moore in a March 8, 2004, game, fracturing three vertebrae in his neck. The case was dismissed in Colorado because the hit occurred in Canada, and the judge suggested the parties pursue the matter there because Canada was the proper jurisdiction.

Typically, courts are distinguished by the types of cases they can hear. **Criminal courts** only resolve criminal matters in which the people, represented by a public prosecutor, bring charges against individual(s) who violate the law through the commission of a misdemeanor or felony. Cases between individuals, corporations, business entities, organizations, and government units involving noncriminal matters are resolved primarily in **civil courts**. The O. J. Simpson murder cases provide an excellent distinction between criminal and civil courts. Simpson was first tried by the State of California for allegedly harming state citizens. The criminal case resulted in a not guilty verdict. The double jeopardy rule prohibits Simpson from ever being tried again on the same charges in a criminal case. However, the victims' families subsequently sued Simpson in civil court. The criminal court decision has no bearing on the civil court case because the two courts require a different burden of proof. In order to convict someone in criminal court, the prosecutors must prove beyond a reasonable doubt the accused committed the crime. On the other hand, a person suing in civil court only has to prove by a preponderance of the evidence that the other side is the guilty party. The criminal standard requires a jury to find the person 100 percent guilty, whereas the civil standard only requires the jury to find the defendant 51 percent guilty.

Legal Process

Detailed rules specify the how, when, and where questions associated with bringing a lawsuit. These rules differ in each court and are often very complex. An example provides the best method of discussing the structure and processes involved in a lawsuit. The following is a fictitious example of such a case.

Sarah Jones was a high school student and interscholastic volleyball star in Houston, Texas. While playing in a sanctioned interscholastic event, Jones attempted to spike a ball, but slipped on a water puddle. Jones tore her knee ligaments. She acquired over $10,000 in medical bills, missed the remainder of the volleyball season, lost $4,000 from not being able to work, and missed her chance to possibly receive a volleyball scholarship from the University of New Haven.

After Jones left the hospital, her father set up an interview with a lawyer to discuss their legal options. The lawyer was Ruth Smith, a young lawyer fresh out of law school. Smith asked numerous questions and discovered from Mr. Jones that he heard one official tell a coach immediately after the accident that the school had failed to sweep the floor prior to the match and the roof had been leaking for over two months. Utilizing her legal prowess, Smith thought she had a great negligence case and accepted the Joneses as clients. Both were clients because Sarah was a minor (under 18) and could not bring the suit herself. Her father had to bring the case on her behalf.

Smith initially performed research and discovered that the likely parties that should be sued included the school, the school district, the volleyball officials, the athletic director, the coach, and the high school athletic association. Jones, who brought the suit to recover her damages, was called the **plaintiff**, while all parties being sued were called **defendants**. Jones and all the defendants lived or operated in Texas. Because there was no federal question, or litigants from different states, Smith's only option was to bring the suit in a Texas state court. Based on the medical expenses and potential future damages, Smith had to bring the case in a specific court with proper jurisdiction.

Smith remembered that special rules applied whenever a governmental entity is sued. Thus, after some initial research, Smith filed a **governmental claim** against the school district. Smith filed the claim specifically to avoid a statute of limitations issue. The **statute of limitations** required the suit to be filed within a certain time period, or Jones would have been forever barred from filing suit. *Each state has its own rules concerning filing a claim against the state. These governmental claim rules are designed to provide the state with notice it might be sued. Some states require the filing of a claim, whereas others allow a party just to name the state in a lawsuit.*

Smith prepared a **complaint** that described key facts available to Jones and provided enough information for the opposing side to know why they were being sued. The complaint specifically identified all known defendants, the reason why jurisdiction was proper, and a statement setting forth what remedies Jones demanded. Smith had a specified amount of time within which she had to serve the defendants with a copy of the complaint that she had already filed with the chosen court. Smith was required to personally serve each defendant with the complaint. *Some states allow a party to mail a complaint or to serve the complaint through a sheriff. A complaint indicates the title of the case, identifies all the parties, designates in which court the case is being filed, and tells the story of the dispute in a specified legal form.*

Within a specified time after receiving the complaint, the defendants filed an **answer** indicating why they were not liable for Jones' injuries. Along with their answer, the defendants served Jones (through her attorney) with several discovery requests. **Discovery** was used as a means to find out what Jones knew about the incident and her damages. The discovery requests included a request to produce all relevant documents in Jones' possession (e.g., medical bills), a request for admissions (e.g., admitting she did not miss any work or she did not receive lower grades as a result of the injury), interrogatories or specific questions (e.g., her age, her address, whether she had a driver's license), and a request to take Jones' deposition. Smith responded by serving similar discovery requests on all the defendants. Jones was required to attend a **deposition**, where she had to answer numerous questions, under oath, asked by the defendants' attorneys. Smith had the right to request the same types of discovery from the defendants. *Discovery is the process used to discover information about the opposing parties in a suit. Answers have to be given under oath or the penalty of perjury. Additional discovery tools not specifically addressed earlier could include: a request to inspect the gym, an independent medical examination of Jones, and possibly an independent psychological evaluation if Jones was claiming severe or extreme emotional distress.*

After several months of discovery, the defendants filed a **motion for summary judgment.** Summary judgment motions are brought when a party concludes that, as a matter of law, the undisputed facts are in their favor and they should win without having to go to trial. These motions are solely based on applicable case law and the facts uncovered through the discovery process. After all the parties have uncovered the basic facts, the party who thinks he/she/they can win on summary judgment files a summary judgment motion. The motion contains all the critical facts and a legal memorandum indicating what the applicable law should be as applied to the facts. A court will only grant a summary judgment motion if there are no contested facts. Thus, if there is a "fact" question on which the two parties disagree, the court would not grant the motion. The case would require a jury to determine the "truth." By pursuing summary judgment, a party can reduce the amount of discovery required and save tens of thousands of dollars. If summary judgment fails, then the case will either go to trial or be voluntarily dismissed through settlement. In the Sarah Jones example, the judge determined that there were still issues of fact that were in dispute and, as such, the judge denied the defendants' summary judgment motion. The parties tried to settle the case, but when they were unable to reach a mutually acceptable settlement, they started preparing for trial. Each side obtained witnesses on its own behalf. The court chose a trial date that was approximately two years after Jones was first injured.

Summary judgment is one of several possible pretrial motions. Other such motions include a **demurrer**, **motion to sever**, **motion to strike**, motion to remove for lack of subject matter jurisdiction, and other motions that attack the complaint or require the production of requested discovery material. Such motions are brought when, as a matter of law, one party is or should be required to alter its case. For example, an injured high school athlete might have suffered a great injury, but due to governmental immunity bestowed to the high school principal, the principal could bring a summary judgment motion to be dismissed from the case as a matter of law.

Smith thought the facts favored her client. Her client made a good witness. Thus, Jones demanded a trial by **jury.** The plaintiff in a civil case always has the choice of whether or not he or she wants a jury. The twelve-member jury was required to decide who was telling the truth and ultimately what were the facts. Each side prepared a trial memorandum explaining its case and provided the memorandum to the judge. After resolving some disputes concerning what evidence would be allowed at trial, the judge allowed the parties to pick a jury. Utilizing a process called **voir dire,** each side interviewed prospective jurors and had the right to dismiss all biased jurors or a limited number of jurors that they just did not want. *The size and role of a jury varies in different states. Some juries only examine facts or certain components of a case, whereas other juries are responsible for analyzing all facts and determining damages.*

Smith provided an eloquent **opening statement** that Perry Mason would have envied. The defendants also had a strong opening statement on their own behalf. The trial proceeded with Smith calling Jones as the first witness. After answering all the questions asked by Smith, Jones was **cross-examined** by defendants' attorneys, who were attempting to refute Jones' testimony or highlight any inconsistencies. Jones' father was **a fact witness** because he had specific facts concerning the accident and injuries. Both sides also acquired the services of **expert witnesses** to testify about the standard of care for schools, doctors to testify about Jones' injuries, and several high school volleyball coaches. The trial continued with each side presenting its witnesses and the other side having the opportunity to cross-examine each witness. Each side also introduced documentary evidence. Throughout the trial, each side repeatedly made **objections** to certain questions or the introduction of some evidence. The judge was forced to determine, as a matter of law, which side was correct and which questions or evidence were legally allowable. *The plaintiff always presents his or her case first in civil cases.*

Each side concluded its questioning and then made its final **closing statement**. The closing statements provided a summary of the facts and law espoused by each side during the trial. The jury was given specific instructions by the judge concerning the law and how the jury was to apply the facts to the law. Based on the evidence presented, the jury returned a verdict in Jones' favor. The jury awarded Jones $14,000 for **actual damages** (medical expenses and lost wages) and $40,000 for **pain and suffering**. The lost scholarship was too speculative, thus the jury was barred from awarding damages for that loss.

The defendants were not happy with the jury's conclusion. The defendants' attorneys knew they could not challenge the jury's evidentiary conclusion, but felt the judge gave the jury an incorrect instruction concerning the school's duty to Jones. The judge could have overturned the jury's decision if the judge felt neither the law nor the facts supported it. However, the judge affirmed the jury's decision. Defendants filed a **notice of appeal**, which is the first step in the appeals process. Each side was required to submit a "brief" that outlined its legal analysis and then argue its case in front of the appellate judges. The appellate court, after carefully reviewing the lower court's actions, determined that the lower court made a **procedural mistake** in using an incorrect jury instruction. Therefore, the appellate court **remanded** (sent back) the case to the lower court to retry the case using the correct instruction. *The number of judges hearing an appeal varies in different courts. An appellate court can remand a case, uphold the lower court's decision, or reverse the lower court's decision.*

Before the new trial began, the sides reached a **settlement** in which the school paid Jones $30,000. By the time Jones finally settled the case, she was in college and three years had elapsed since she brought the suit. The appellate court's reasoning was published in the state's official case registry and became precedent for any future cases dealing with the appropriate jury instruction to give concerning a school's duty to its students. However, from reading the published appellate court's decision, a reader would not know that the case was settled once it was remanded to the lower court. The appellate court report only indicated that it was remanding the case to be retried. Rarely does one discover what happens to cases, because lower court decisions are not officially published. Furthermore, most cases are settled, and the settlement terms are often confidential. Although Jones' fictitious case went to trial, it is estimated that less than 5 percent of all cases filed ever reach a trial. Most cases are dismissed prior to trial, settled, or defeated through summary judgment or other defensive maneuvers. Only state appellate and state supreme court cases are officially published. All federal cases are published. Cases are commonly found in the following reporters: federal district court cases can be found in *Federal Supplement* volumes (cases are cited using the initials F. Supp.), federal appellate cases can be found in the *Federal Reporter* ("F." or "F.2d," the second volume), U.S. Supreme Court cases can be found in three different reporters—*United States Supreme Court Reports* (U.S.), *Supreme Court Reporter* (S. Ct.), and *Supreme Court Reports, Lawyer's Edition* (L. Ed.). Nine different reporters exist for various state courts or regional groupings of courts. These cases are found in the following reporters: *Atlantic Reporter* (A. or A.2d), *Northeastern Reporter* (N.E. or N.E.2d), *Northwestern Reporter* (N.W. or N.W.2d), *Pacific Reporter* (P. or P.2d), *Southeastern Reporter* (S.E. or S.E.2d), *Southern Reporter* (So. or So.2d), *Southwestern Reporter* (S.W. or S.W.2d), *New York Supplement* (N.Y.S.), or *California Reporter* (Cal.Rptr.). (See Section 1.20, *Legal Research*).

SIGNIFICANT CASE

This case involves a legal action taken by a hockey player who was injured by a hockey puck shot by another player. Throughout the case, terms presented in this section are shown in bold print. This should help to illustrate the usage of the terms and to clarify their legal meaning.

SAVINO V. ROBERTSON

Appellate Court of Illinois, First District, Second Division
273 Ill. App. 3d 811; 652 N.E.2d 1240; 1995 Ill. App. LEXIS480; 210 Ill. Dec. 264
June 30, 1995, Decided

Opinion: Justice McCormick

Plaintiff John Savino brought a **negligence action** against **defendant** Scott Robertson after plaintiff was struck and injured in the eye by a hockey puck shot by defendant. The **trial court** granted defendant's subsequent motion for **summary judgment**, but allowed plaintiff to amend the complaint to allege that defendant's conduct was wilful and wanton. Upon another motion by defendant, the trial court granted summary judgment in favor of defendant on the amended complaint. On **appeal** from both orders, plaintiff raises the following issues for our consideration: (1) whether a plaintiff must plead and prove wilful and wanton conduct in order to recover for injuries incurred during athletic competition; and (2) whether there was a genuine issue of material fact as to whether defendant's conduct was wilful and wanton in injuring plaintiff. We **affirm**.

Plaintiff and defendant were teammates in an amateur hockey league sponsored by the Northbrook Park District. Plaintiff and defendant also had met in various "pick-up" games prior to playing in the Northbrook league, but they were neither friends nor enemies. On April 20, 1990, plaintiff and defendant were warming up prior to a game. During warm-up, teams skate around and behind their goal on their half of the ice. Plaintiff was on the ice, "to the right of the face off circle in front of the net." Defendant shot a puck that missed the goal and hit plaintiff near the right eye. Plaintiff lost 80 percent vision in that eye.

On September 11, 1990, plaintiff filed a one-count **complaint** against defendant alleging that defendant was negligent and failed to exercise ordinary care in shooting the puck. Specifically, plaintiff alleged that defendant (a) failed to warn plaintiff that he was going to shoot the puck toward plaintiff; (b) failed to wait until a goalie was present before shooting the puck; (c) failed to warn others that he was shooting the puck; (d) failed to follow the custom and practice of the Northbrook Men's Summer League which required the presence of a goalie at the net before shooting; and (e) failed to keep an adequate lookout.

Defendant filed his **answer to the complaint** and, after **interrogatories** and **discovery depositions** were taken, defendant moved for summary judgment. (735 ILCS 5/2-1005 (West 1992).) Defendant argued that he was entitled to judgment as a matter of law because plaintiff alleged ordinary negligence. To be entitled to relief for injuries incurred during athletic competition, defendant argued, plaintiff had to plead and prove wilful and wanton conduct or conduct done in reckless disregard for the safety of others. The trial court granted defendant's motion for summary judgment and denied plaintiff leave to amend count I of the complaint. Upon reconsideration, the trial court granted plaintiff leave to file an **amended complaint** to allege a count II based on wilful and wanton conduct.

Defendant filed his **answer to plaintiff's subsequent amended complaint** and the parties engaged in discovery as to count II of that complaint. Defendant later filed another **motion for summary judgment**. Defendant argued that, due to plaintiff's admission that his injury was caused by an accident, plaintiff's case presented no genuine issue of material fact with regard to defendant's alleged wilful and wanton conduct. Defendant further argued that plaintiff could not show that defendant's action was anything more than an ordinary practice shot normally taken during warm-up sessions.

Plaintiff, on the other hand, argued in his **response to defendant's motion** that ordinary negligence should be the standard applied to his case rather than wilful and wanton conduct, because, since the hockey game had not officially begun, he was not a participant at the time of his injury. Plaintiff attached the affidavit of Thomas Czarnik, a hockey coach at Deerfield High School, to his response. According to Czarnik, it was the custom of amateur hockey leagues to wait until the goalie was present in the net before any practice shots were taken.

Czarnik had no knowledge of the rules and usages of the Northbrook Hockey League and had no firsthand knowledge of the incident.

Czarnik also stated that he had seen players in adult hockey leagues take shots at open goals, that is, goals without a goalie present, during the warm-up period and that he had taken shots at open goals. According to Czarnik, the warm-up period was a part of the game of hockey even though the players are not technically playing a game. Czarnik considered plaintiff's injury an accident.

Defendant attached excerpts of Czarnik's deposition in support of his reply to plaintiff's **response to the motion for summary judgment**. Defendant argued that Czarnik's responses demonstrated that plaintiff could not show, as a matter of law, that defendant's conduct was wilful or wanton. Defendant also contended that Czarnik was not a proper **expert** to render an opinion in this case, given his lack of familiarity with adult hockey leagues and lack of knowledge of the rules and usages of the Northbrook Summer Men's Hockey League. The trial court granted defendant's motion for summary judgment. Plaintiff now **appeals** from both orders of the trial court granting summary judgment in favor of defendant.

Our review of the trial court's grant of summary judgment is de novo. (*Superior Investment & Development Corp., Inc. v. Devine* (1993), 244 Ill. App. 3d 759, 767, 614 N.E.2d 302, 185 Ill. Dec. 168.) The granting of summary judgment is proper when the pleadings, depositions and affidavits show that no genuine issue of material fact exists and the moving party is entitled to judgment as a matter of law. (*Estate of Henderson v. W.R. Grace Co.* (1989), 185 Ill. App. 3d 523, 527, 541 N.E.2d 805, 133 Ill. Dec. 594.) In determining whether summary judgment is proper, the court must construe the evidence in a light most favorable to the non-movant and strongly against the movant. (*Schroth v. Norton Co.* (1989), 185 Ill. App. 3d 575, 577, 541 N.E.2d 855, 133 Ill. Dec. 644.)

Plaintiff first argues that he should not have been required to plead wilful and wanton conduct in this case because he was not actually "playing" the game of hockey at the time his injury occurred, but rather was participating in the warm-up practice.

The seminal case on this issue is *Nabozny v. Barnhill* (1975), 31 Ill. App. 3d 212, 334 N.E.2d 258. In *Nabozny*, the plaintiff was the goalkeeper for a teenage soccer league and the defendant was a forward from an opposing team. The game's rules prevented players from making contact with the goalkeeper while he is in possession of the ball in the penalty area. (*Nabozny*, 31 Ill. App. 3d at 214.)

During the game, the ball was passed to the plaintiff while he was in the penalty area. The plaintiff fell onto his knee. The defendant, who had been going for the ball, continued to run towards the plaintiff and kicked the plaintiff in the head, causing severe injuries. (*Nabozny*, 31 Ill. App. 3d at 214.) The trial court directed a verdict in favor of the defendant, holding that as a matter of law the defendant was free from negligence (owed no duty to the plaintiff) and that the plaintiff was contributorily negligent.

In reversing the trial court, the *Nabozny* court held that when athletes engage in organized competition, with a set of rules that guides the conduct and safety of the players, then "a player is charged with a legal duty to every other player on the field to refrain from conduct proscribed by a safety rule." (*Nabozny*, 31 Ill. App. 3d at 215.) The court then announced the following rule:

> *It is our opinion that a player is liable for injury in a tort action if his conduct is such that it is either deliberate, wilful or with a reckless disregard for the safety of the other player so as to cause injury to that player, the same being a question of fact to be decided by a jury. Nabozny, 31 Ill. App. 3d at 215.*

Illinois courts have construed Nabozny to hold that a plaintiff-participant injured during a contact sport may recover from another player only if the other's conduct was wilful or wanton. (*Novak v. Virene* (1991), 224 Ill. App. 3d 317, 586 N.E.2d 578, 166 Ill. Dec. 620; *Keller v. Mols* (1987), 156 Ill. App. 3d 235, 509 N.E.2d 584, 108 Ill. Dec. 888; *Oswald v. Township High School District No. 214* (1980), 84 Ill. App. 3d 723, 406 N.E.2d 157, 40 Ill. Dec. 456.) Plaintiff contends, however, that decisions subsequent to *Nabozny* have misconstrued the court's holding in that case. According to plaintiff, *Nabozny* is to be applied only to conduct during a game because *Nabozny* "involved an injury that occurred during a game and therefore, it implicitly recognizes a distinction with pre-game injuries."

In the case at bar, we believe that plaintiff was no less a participant in a team sport merely because he was engaged in "warm-up" activities at the time of his injury. However, assuming arguendo that we were to view plaintiff's action using an ordinary negligence standard, we must find that plaintiff knowingly and voluntarily assumed the risks inherent in playing the game of hockey. Plaintiff's own testimony bears out this fact. Plaintiff was an experienced hockey player, playing from the time he was eight years old. He had played in organized adult leagues for approximately 10 years prior to his accident. Plaintiff testified that while it was "customary" for players to wait for a goalie to be present prior to taking practice shots, in his experience he had seen players take shots at open nets. There was no written rule against taking shots at open nets. Plaintiff was also aware, at the time he stepped onto the ice, that there was a risk of being hit with a puck during "warm-ups." Indeed, according to plaintiff, that risk "always" existed. Nonetheless, plaintiff chose not to wear a protective face mask, since it was not required, even though in his estimation 65–70 percent of his teammates were wearing protective masks during "warm-up" and despite the inherent risk of being hit with a puck, irrespective of the goalie's presence at the net. Based on plaintiff's testimony, we believe that plaintiff voluntarily consented, understood and accepted the dangers inherent in the sport or due to a co-participant's negligence.

We find no reason to abandon the well-established **precedent** of this court, and that of a majority of **jurisdictions**, that a participant in a contact sport may recover for injury only where the other's conduct is wilful or wanton or in reckless disregard to safety.

It is undisputed that plaintiff and defendant were teammates in an organized hockey league. There were rules and usages. Reviewing the evidence in a light most favorable to plaintiff, there appears to be no genuine issue of material fact that practice shots were often taken at an open net and such was the custom of the team.

For the foregoing reasons, we **affirm** both orders of the circuit court granting summary judgment in defendant's favor.

Affirmed.

SCARIANO, P.J., and DiVITO, J., concur.

CASES ON THE SUPPLEMENTAL CD

Reynolds v. IAAF, 23 F.3d 1110; 28 Fed.R.Serv.3d 1455. Notice that this case illustrates the importance of jurisdiction.

Roman v. Liberty University, Cal.App.4th 670; 75 Cal.Rptr.3d 828. Notice that in this case the appellate court upheld the trial court ruling concluding that the trial court properly granted Liberty's motion regarding jurisdiction.

Boucher v. Syracuse University, F.3d 113 (2nd Cir. 1999). This case addresses an allegation that Syracuse University was in violation of Title IX.

QUESTIONS YOU SHOULD BE ABLE TO ANSWER

1. Compare the impact and importance of common law, statutory law, and Constitutional law.
2. What is a summary judgment and what is its impact on the legal action?
3. What are some types of cases that would involve administrative law?
4. What is the impact of precedence on current rulings?
5. Discuss what issues are addressed by an appellate court.

REFERENCES

Cases

Turner v. Mandalay Sports Entertainment, LLC, 180 P.3d 1172 (Nevada 2008).

Publications

Anderson, R., Fox, I., & Twomey, D. (1984). *Business law* (12th ed.). Cincinnati: South-Western Publishing Co.

Cheeseman, H. (1998). *Business law* (3rd ed.). Upper Saddle River, NJ: Prentice Hall.

Coughlin, G. G. (1983). *Your introduction to law* (4th ed.). New York: Barnes & Noble Books.

Fried, G. (1999). *Safe at first.* Durham, NC: Carolina Academic Press.

Hill, G. and Hill, K. (2009). Law.com. Retrieved February 3, 2009 from http://dictionary.law.com/default2.asp?selected=1111&bold=||||.

Useful Websites

http://caselaw.lp.findlaw.com/cgi-bin/getcase.pl?court=US&navby=case&vol=000&invol=99-62

http://web2.westlaw.com/signon/default.wl

www.archives.state.al.us/legislat/billmap.gif (2000)

www.law.cornell.edu/statutes.html

www.lexis.com

1.20 Legal Research

—Anita M. Moorman
UNIVERSITY OF LOUISVILLE

Many sport organizations have legal counsel on staff, or have ready access to outside legal counsel who can certainly assist as legal issues arise. However, recreation and sport managers should also have the ability to perform and analyze legal research for themselves either in an effort to proactively anticipate legal issues or to respond to a legal issue once it has arisen. In addition, the ability to conduct legal research will allow the recreation and sport manager to obtain information about current and emerging legal developments. A meaningful understanding of current legal developments is as critical to the recreation and sport manager as is a firm understanding of current developments in communication, marketing, finance, sponsorship, ethics, and many other areas. This section will introduce future recreation and sport managers to the variety of legal resources available in the traditional law library as well as from electronic and Internet sources.

Locating legal information is much easier if the searcher has a comfortable understanding of how the legal system works. Thus, it is imperative for the recreation and sport manager to understand that the U.S. judicial system is divided into distinctly separate federal and state systems. Also, what exactly is "the law"? The "law" can mean different things to different people, but for the purposes of conducting legal research, "the law" refers to a source that actually establishes a legal standard, principle, or mandate. For example, to govern a democratic society such as the United States, that society typically will create a governing document that will define how it will govern itself. Typically, this governing document is called a Constitution and it will define the powers and authority of the various branches of the government as well as limitations on governmental powers and authority. Thus, both the United States Constitution and the various state constitutions are examples of primary sources of law. Another example of the law can be found in legislation or statutes. Legislation or statutes are enacted by the state and federal legislatures, which in turn rely on state and federal agencies to enforce the statutes. Thus, administrative agencies tend to be primarily responsible for writing or promulgating rules and regulations to enforce the statutes. Lastly, the courts must interpret the statutes or rules and fill any gaps left by the legislatures or administrative agencies. Thus, **Constitutions, Statutes, Administrative Regulations/Rules**, and **Court Decisions** make up the four primary sources of law. All the activities described above are recorded, catalogued, stored, indexed, and housed in thousands of volumes. And while the sheer volume of this legal information can appear daunting to a beginning researcher, because it is catalogued and indexed so thoroughly, a well-planned research project can be managed effectively.

The purpose of this section is to help the reader understand legal research. First, we will look at the legal resources available to the researcher. These include the four **primary sources** listed above (the actual law), **secondary sources** (explanations/definitions/summaries of the law), and certain **research tools** (digests, electronic databases, computerized legal research). Then we will look at two important techniques to use in conducting legal research. These are **Developing the Research Plan** and **Summarizing Cases**.

LEGAL RESOURCES

Primary Legal Resources

Primary legal sources include constitutions, statutes, rules and regulations, and court decisions. Primary legal sources represent the actual law, whether it is a decision of the U.S. Supreme Court or a state statute enacted by the State of Oklahoma. *Regardless of the type of legal research being conducted, ultimately only primary legal sources can be relied on in determining what the law is and what the law requires.*

Constitutions/Statutes/Rules/Regulations

The U.S. Constitution is the supreme law of the land. It both authorizes and restricts conduct of the federal and state governments, as well as conduct of private citizens. Each of the fifty states will similarly have a state constitution governing conduct of the state government and citizens of that state. The U.S. Congress and fifty state legislatures enact laws known as statutes addressing issues ranging from the enforceability of contracts, to ticket scalping, to registration of trademarks. The federal statutes are codified (or published) in a series of volumes known as the *United States Code* (U.S.C.). Each of the fifty states also codifies its state statutes, which are often called civil codes, public laws, session laws, or revised statutes. Both the *United States Code* and the state statutes are bound and published. Many of the bound volumes contain **annotations** that categorize court decisions interpreting the statute in question. These annotations are similar to an index and will assist the researcher in locating specific court decisions and understanding how the statute has been interpreted and applied by the courts. For example, if you were trying to determine whether a federal district court in your state had ruled in a case involving the *Olympic and Amateur Sports Act* (this is the act that created and empowered the U.S. Olympic Committee), you could use the annotations to locate specific cases decided by courts in your state.

Rather than republish the hardback editions of the *U.S. Code* each year, the publishers of these volumes instead print supplements to the hardback volume that contain any amendments or modifications that have been made to statutes. This supplement is called a "**pocket part**," which is a softbound pamphlet that is inserted in a sleeve located inside the back cover of each hardback volume. The publisher will use this process for a number of years before publishing a new series of the hardback volumes. Thus, the most recent amendments or changes to laws will be in the pocket part, so you must always look in the pocket part for any changes passed by Congress or the state legislature since the printing of the original hardback volume. One example of this is the Sport Agent Responsibility and Trust Act (SPARTA), which is a federal law regulating athlete agents' activities with student athletes and was passed by Congress in September 2004. This law would be cited as the *Sports Agent Responsibility and Trust Act*, 15 U.S.C. § 7801 et seq. (2005). This citation tells us that this act can be found beginning at Section 7801 in Title 15 of the *U.S. Code*. Title 15 of the *U.S. Code* will be published in several volumes as explained earlier. Because the publisher is not going to reprint all of Title 15 every time Congress passes new laws or amends existing laws, you would have to look in the pocket part to find SPARTA.

Another example is the recent amendment to the Americans with Disabilities Act (ADA). On September 24, 2008, the ADA Amendments Act of 2008 (ADAAA) was signed into law and became effective on January 1, 2009. The ADAAA amends several significant provisions in the ADA and will naturally be of interest to sport and recreation organizations, most of which are subject to the ADA. So the official statutory language and legislative history for The Americans with Disabilities Act of 1990, 42 U.S.C. § 12101 et seq. will initially be included in the pocket part until the bound volumes are reprinted. Sport and recreation managers can also gain immediate access to information about these types of developments from Internet-based information sources which will be explored later in this section.

Congress and the state legislatures also create regulatory bodies such as the Federal Aviation Administration, Environmental Protection Agency, and Equal Employment Opportunity Commission. These regulatory bodies often are required to create rules and regulations to fulfill their assigned purpose. These rules and regulations for federal agencies are codified in the *Code of Federal Regulations* (C.F.R.) and can be a useful resource for research related to a particular agency's activities. Most state and federal agencies also maintain up-to-date information concerning rules, regulations, and policies on the Internet to permit easy access to this information. A partial list of constitutional and statutory resources is as follows:

U.S. Constitution	State Constitutions
Treaties	Federal Statutes (the *U.S. Code* [U.S.C.])
State Statutes	Municipal Ordinances
Rules of Court	Executive Orders and Promulgations
Rules/Regulations of Federal Administrative Agencies (C.F.R.)	
Rules/Regulations of State Administrative Agencies	
Attorney General Opinions—federal and state	

Court Decisions

A court decision results from a jury verdict or court order that resolves a case or an issue in a case. For example, Tiger Woods may have sued John Brown Company based on the company's unauthorized use of Tiger Woods' name in an advertisement. Tiger Woods' lawsuit or case will probably include several different legal claims such as trademark infringement, violation of the right of publicity, and misappropriation of goodwill. It is possible that John Brown would file a motion for summary judgment (remember this was discussed in the previous section) asking the court to dismiss Tiger Woods' trademark infringement claim. When the court either grants or denies the motion for summary judgment, it will enter an order to that effect. This order represents a court decision. Ultimately, if the case goes to trial, another court decision will be entered reflecting the outcome of the trial. Either or both of these court decisions may be published. Thus, if we want to be able to find and read this decision, we must understand when and where these court decisions are published.

Understanding the court system (which was covered in the previous section) aids us in locating these decisions. You may recall that court systems are hierarchical in structure, that is, that some courts are superior to others. The highest court is usually a supreme or superior court, followed by an intermediate appellate court, and ending with a district or trial court at the bottom. Most cases will originate at the trial or district court level and work their way *up* through the court system. This process can take years for a case to move through all levels of the court system. Any number of court decisions may be entered in a case as it winds its way through the court system to its ultimate conclusion, so to find court decisions, you need to understand how those decisions are reported. First, we will explore the federal court system and then the state court system.

Federal Courts

In the federal court system, the vast majority of federal cases originate in the U.S. District Court. The U.S. District Court is the federal trial court and the first level within the federal court system. Any appeal from a U.S. District Court decision would be made to the appropriate U.S. Court of Appeals. Any party to the district court action may appeal to the U.S. Court of Appeals. The U.S. Courts of Appeals represent the second level or the intermediate appellate level in the federal court system. As explained in the previous section, the court of appeals only exercises appellate jurisdiction. That means cases do not originate in the court of appeals; instead, a case would only reach the court of appeals after a decision has been made in a lower court (such as the district court) and a party appeals from that decision. That appeal requests the appellate court to review a portion of the lower court's decision to determine whether the lower court made a mistake. After the U.S. Court of Appeals renders its decision, a party can still request another appellate review by the U.S. Supreme Court. However, the U.S. Supreme Court is not required to hear these appeals. The appellate jurisdiction of the U.S. Supreme Court is considered discretionary and, as such, requests for appeal (known as petitions for **certiorari**) are rarely granted. The U.S. Supreme Court is the highest court in the land, and its decisions are considered the supreme law of the land, which must be followed by all lower federal and state courts. As the federal courts make these decisions regarding cases, they are published or reported in the reporters listed following.

U.S. District Courts. Federal Supplement and *Federal Supplement Second Series* (cited F. Supp., or F. Supp. 2d). (Note: These reporters are a continuing series of cases reported by the U.S. District Courts from 1932 to the present date. This reporter is in its second series or edition now).

Sample Citation: *Hoopla Sports and Entertainment, Inc. v. Nike, Inc.*, 947 F. Supp. 347 (N.D. Ill. 1996). This citation tells us that this court decision can be located in volume 947 at page 347 in the Federal Supplement. It further tells us that the decision was made by the U.S. District Court for the Northern District of Illinois in 1996.

U.S. Courts of Appeals. Federal Reporter, Federal Reporter Second Series, Federal Reporter Third Series (cited F., F.2d, or F.3d). (Note: These reporters are a continuing series of cases reported by the U.S. Courts of Appeals from 1880 to the present date. This reporter is in its third series or edition now).

Sample Citation: *National Basketball Association v. Motorola, Inc.*, 105 F.3d 841 (2nd Cir. 1997). This citation tells us that this court decision can be found in volume 105 at page 841 in the Federal Reporter Third Series. It further tells us that the decision was made by the U.S. Court of Appeals for the Second Circuit in 1997.

U.S. Supreme Court. U.S. Supreme Court Reports (cited U.S.); Supreme Court Reporter (cited S. Ct.); Lawyer's Edition (cited L.Ed.2d). (Note: These three reporters all report the same Supreme Court cases. *U.S. Supreme Court Reports* is the official Supreme Court reporter, but *Supreme Court Reporter* is most commonly used and more user-friendly).

Sample Citation: *PGA Tour, Inc. v. Martin*, 532 U.S. 661, 121 S. Ct. 1879, 149 L. Ed. 2d 904 (2001). You will often see all three reporters cited; this is called a **string cite**. The first part of the string is the citation to the U.S. Supreme Court Reports (532 U.S. 661), followed by the citation to the Supreme Court Reporter (121 S. Ct. 1879), and ending with the citation to the Lawyer's Edition (149 L. Ed. 2d 904). You may also see a Supreme Court case cited with only one of these three possible citations, such as *PGA Tour, Inc. v. Martin*, 121 S. Ct. 1879 (2001). This citation tells us that this decision can be found at volume 121 at page 1879 in the Supreme Court Reporter. It further tells us that this decision of the U.S. Supreme Court was made in 2001.

State Courts

The state court systems are organized in a similar fashion to the federal courts. Most states will have several trial or district courts located in the various counties in the state. Most cases will originate in the trial or district courts and then follow a similar path as federal cases with appeals going to an intermediate appellate court or directly to the state supreme court. Typically, only decisions made by a state's Supreme Court are selected for publication in the **state reporters.** These decisions, once published, are organized in a reporter system in two different ways. Each state's decisions can be found in its separate state reporter such as the *California Reporter.* However, many law libraries only carry the individual state reporter for the state in which they are located. For all other states' court decisions, the library will likely have the **regional reporter** that publishes the same state court decisions but grouped together in a specific region. The regional reporters are broken down as follows.

Atlantic Reporter (cited A. and A.2d)
[Pennsylvania, Vermont, New Hampshire, Maine, Rhode Island, Connecticut, New Jersey, Delaware, and Maryland]

North Eastern Reporter (cited N.E. and N.E.2d)
[New York, Massachusetts, Ohio, Indiana, and Illinois]

North Western Reporter (cited N.W. and N.W.2d)
[North Dakota, South Dakota, Minnesota, Wisconsin, Michigan, Nebraska, and Iowa]

Pacific Reporter (cited P. and P.2d)
[Kansas, Oklahoma, New Mexico, Colorado, Wyoming, Montana, Arizona, Utah, Idaho, Nevada, Washington, Oregon, California, Hawaii, and Alaska]

South Eastern Reporter (cited S.E. and S.E.2d)
[West Virginia, Virginia, North Carolina, South Carolina, and Georgia]

Southern Reporter (cited So. and So.2d)
[Louisiana, Mississippi, Alabama, and Florida]

South Western Reporter (cited S.W. and S.W.2d)
[Kentucky, Tennessee, Missouri, Arkansas, and Texas]

The following sample citations to state reporters follow a similar format to those we examined in the federal courts:

Maisonave v. Newark Bears Professional Baseball Club, 881 A.2d 700 (N.J. 2005). This case can be found in volume 881 at page 700 in the Atlantic Reporter, Second Series. This is a 2005 decision of the New Jersey Supreme Court.

Rowe v. Pinellas Sports Auth., 461 So. 2d 72 (Fla. 1984). This case can be found in volume 461 at page 72 in the Southern Reporter, Second Series and is a 1984 decision of the Florida Supreme Court.

Kelly v. Marylanders for Sports Sanity, Inc. 530 A.2d 245 (Md. Ct. App. 1987). This case can be found in volume 530 at page 245 of the Atlantic Reporter, Second Series; however, notice that it is a 1987 decision of the Maryland Court of Appeals. This is one of those instances where an intermediate appellate court decision was published and the use of the term "App." or "Ct. App." in the parenthesis with the date is how you can distinguish between decisions of the court of appeals and those of the various state supreme courts. If the citation does not contain "App" or "Ct. App," but instead just the state abbreviation as in the first two sample citations, that means the decision was made by the state's highest court (either a supreme court or superior court).

Secondary Resources

Secondary resources include articles, journals, papers, and other written sources that summarize, explain, interpret, or analyze certain issues or topics of the law. In addition to making a scholarly contribution to the understanding of legal issues and topics, they provide the sports and/or recreation manager with an overview or insight into a particular area. Secondary resources also can be a valuable source for locating additional or related primary sources; however, only primary resources represent the actual law. *Thus, secondary resources should never be solely relied on as legal authority.* Following is a listing of several secondary resources by type and description.

Legal Dictionaries. *Black's Law Dictionary* provides definitions of legal terms. It is a must for studying and researching law. Many paperback, condensed versions are available.

Lawyer Directories. Martindale-Hubbell is useful for locating attorneys in any state in the United States.

American Law Reports. A.L.R. contains commentary and summary on areas of law. It covers both state and federal courts. The annotation usually includes a case summary together with commentary about the case and how it may or does affect other cases or the current status of the law. ALR is very useful if you have a specific case for which you wish to study the impact it has had on the law.

Legal Encyclopedias. *Corpus Juris Secundum* and *American Jurisprudence* (Am. Jur.). A legal encyclopedia functions like a standard encyclopedia and includes topical summaries of numerous legal issues. The summary will also include supporting references to cases, statutes, and other primary and secondary resources. This is a good place to start if you know little or nothing about a topic and want a jumping-off point. These will not provide much analysis and may not contain the latest developments.

Restatement of Law. Torts, contracts, etc. Restatements are comprehensive surveys of a specific and major category of law. For example, the **Restatement of Contracts** summarizes the origin, development, and current application of contract law in the United States, noting differences among individual states, majority positions, and the general rule of law for all issues related to contracts. These can be useful to develop a better understanding of the principle and theory of law if the reader has some familiarity with the law already.

Treatises. Textbooks, casebooks, and hornbooks. Treatises are written by scholars and experts on a particular legal issue or topic. These resources are usually very comprehensive, and provide an in-depth examination of the issue or topic. Note, however, that a treatise represents the author's interpretation of the law—a treatise is not the actual law. Treatises can provide the reader with substantial references and resources on a specific topic. Most law libraries have extensive collections of treatises. The preeminent publication in the field is the three-volume set by Betty van der Smissen entitled *Legal Liability and Risk Management for Public and Private Entities.* Some sport law treatises include: *Sports Law* by Michael J. Bailiff, Tim Kerr, and Marie Dimitri; *Torts and Sports: Legal Liability in Professional and Amateur Athletics* by Raymond L. Yasser; *Sports Law* by George W. Schubert, Rodney K. Smith, and Jesse C. Trended; *Sports and Law: Contemporary Issues* by Herb Appenzeller; *Fundamentals of Sports Law* by Walter T. Champion, Jr.; *Sports and the Law: Major Legal Cases* by Charles E. Quirk; *The Law of Sports* by John C. Weistart and Cym H. Lowell; *Essentials of Amateur Sports Law, Essentials of Amateur Sports Law*, 2nd ed., and *Essentials of Sports Law*, 3rd ed. by Glenn M. Wong; and *Sports Law* by Michael E. Jones.

Shepard's Citations. Shepard's Citations is a publication that allows the researcher to track a court decision or statute through a citation index. The citation index lists court decisions that have cited previous court decisions and court decisions interpreting specific statutory sections. This resource is useful to locate additional cases once the research has located a major or dispositive case. But more importantly, this index tracks any "treatment" of a particular case. Thus, the index identifies whether a case the researcher is relying on has been questioned, criticized, followed, reversed, or otherwise interpreted by later court decisions. This is extremely important to ensure that court decisions relied on are indeed still representative of the current legal standard.

Legal Indexes. *Index to Legal Periodicals* (**ILP**). The ILP allows the researcher to locate law review articles by topic and/or author. Now the ILP is available both in the traditional book form and electronically. The researcher can conduct a topical electronic search and will be provided with citation and location information for law review articles on that topic.

Law Review Articles. Published primarily by law schools or professional law associations throughout the United States. To date there are numerous law reviews/journals regularly addressing sport law issues. Some of these include: *Marquette Sports Law Review*; *Villanova Sports & Entertainment Law Journal*; *Univ. Miami Entertainment & Sports Law Review*; *Seton Hall Journal of Sport Law*; *American Bar Association Entertainment & Sports Lawyer*; and *Sports Lawyers Journal*.

Academic Legal Journals. Several academic associations publish journals focused on legal issues. In sport, the Society for the Study of the Legal Aspects of Sport and Physical Activity publishes the *Journal of Legal Aspects of Sport* containing scholarly papers related to legal issues in sport and recreation. Other scholarly publications include *From the Gym to the Jury*; *Sports in the Courts*; *Sports, Parks and Recreation Law Reporter*; and *The Exercise Standards and Malpractice Reporter*.

Business or Academic Journals. Many current legal issues related to sport may be covered in business and academic journals. Many academic business journals also contain special sections for legal developments. For example, the *Sport Marketing Quarterly* has a column entitled Marketing and the Law featured in each issue. *Journal of Marketing & Public Policy* also has a similar feature.

Business Magazines and Newspapers. The sport industry is often the subject of articles in business magazines and daily newspapers. Often current developments in the sport industry have a legal impact. For example, the filing of a case will often be reported in major newspapers both in their print and electronic versions. Street and Smith's *SportsBusiness Journal* and *Athletic Business* often report on recent legal developments and issues. These articles can help sport managers identify the issues and stay current with legal developments in the sport industry.

Additional Research Tools

The preceding secondary sources are especially helpful in locating topical and/or general information. However, ultimately the researcher must locate primary legal resources. Although the secondary sources will normally identify many useful primary resources, often the primary resources identified are not exhaustive or not the most current. At this point several additional research tools are available, including printed digests and a number of electronic databases.

Digests

Digests are particularly useful for locating court decisions on a particular topic. Digests are basically subject indexes to the federal and state reporters described earlier. For each state reporter there is a corresponding digest, and for federal cases there is a *Federal Practice Digest*, as well as several general digests that contain state and federal cases grouped by year. To make it even easier, remember that the fifty states are grouped by region, so those court decisions that were published together in a regional state reporter also have a corresponding regional digest (for example, the Atlantic Reporter has a corresponding Atlantic Digest).

For example, if the researcher does not know the citation for a specific case but would like to find cases pertaining to a promoter's liability for an injury to a spectator during a wrestling match in the state of Vermont, the researcher could locate the Vermont or Atlantic Digest and topically search for key words such as "spectator," "wrestling," and "assumption of the risk." The digest will contain a listing of all cases in Vermont or the Atlantic region related to that topic. Now this sounds a bit easier than it actually is, because the law is not always indexed in the manner that an ordinary person may think. Consider the injured spectator example: the actual key word used by the digest to index these cases is "theatres and shows." The digests have indexes to help find the appropriate key word, but the researcher will have to explore many variations and be persistent in his or her search. Nevertheless, the digests provide a great wealth of information once the appropriate key word is found.

Electronic and Web-based Research

Electronic Search Engines and Databases. The availability and efficiency of electronic and Web-based research continues to expand and improve. Now the researcher can accomplish a great deal of his or her research via computer. Although electronic and Web-based sources may never replace a trip to the law library, growth in this area has been tremendous. Many law schools provide students with access to electronic databases known as **WESTLAW** and **LEXIS**, which allow the researcher to search topically or for a specific case or statute. Some law libraries restrict access to these databases to law students. In that case, **LexisNexis Academic Universe**, available through most college and university libraries, is also a valuable research tool and provides for searching top news; general news topics; company, industry, and market news; legal news; company financial information; law reviews; federal case law; *U.S. Code*; and state legal research. In the event that your library does not have or allow access to any of these resources, there are several additional Web-based research sites.

In addition to using electronic databases, we also have many electronic subscription services available to keep us abreast of current legal developments specific to the sport industry. Many of these services are free, such as the *FindLaw* Website, which offers a free subscription to a weekly e-mail listing current developments in sport law. An excellent paid subscription is available from *Sports Litigation Alerts*. Students are offered reduced subscription rates and will receive a bi-weekly, detailed summary of recent sport law developments. A listing and description of several other excellent electronic resources is contained at the end of the section.

Legal Blogs and Internet Searches. Thanks to Google and Yahoo and other Internet-based search engines, legal information often can be accessed with just a click of the mouse. For example, if you enter the search term "sport law" into Google, Google's search engine will return more than 92,000 results from your search if you happened to put "sport law" in parenthesis to limit the number of hits. If you didn't put "sport law" in parentheses, Google will actually return more than 131,000,000 hits instantly. This capability can be both a benefit and a detriment. The speed and ease of such a search is a great benefit, but obviously, it could take days or even weeks to sort through 92,000 results, and tackling more than one hundred thirty million results is nearly impossible. So for maximum effectiveness, our searches need to be as specific and detailed as possible.

Google and other search engines can also be used very effectively to locate current relevant developments in sport law. For example, assume you are a sport or recreation manager and have been following a pending lawsuit. In the past, it could take days, even weeks, after a final decision was made in that pending case for you to be able to learn of the decision and access a copy of the court's order or opinion. Today, often the notification of the final decision is made almost simultaneously with the decision itself and the actual written decision or order is available within just a few minutes or hours. Almost every major news outlet delivers the news via the Internet, and enables you to receive instant notifications of breaking news stories. A good example of just how useful these services are to a sport and/or recreation manager can be found related to a pending case in which a collegiate baseball player, Andrew Oliver, sued the NCAA. This case was being watched with great interest by most college athletic administrators and the NCAA since it challenges the authority of the NCAA to enforce its eligibility rules and regulations. If you had been following this case, and subscribed to one of the many daily email news updates available today, you would have been notified immediately when the Ohio state court invalidated the NCAA rule which restricts the manner in which athletes who are considering a professional offer may use legal representation. In addition, within just a few hours a great deal of legal commentary was also accessible, interpreting, analyzing, and criticizing the court's decision. This kind of immediate information concerning legal developments can be very useful to a sport and/or recreation manager.

In addition to the search engines and news alerts, a number of legal blogs also exist that can be a valuable resource for practitioners. Blogs (which is short for Weblogs) originally began as Websites where individuals posted commentary or personal diaries. In the past, a blog was not a very useful research source, particularly for legal research because it primarily represented the personal opinion of the blogger and contained anonymous and/or random comments by the blog's readers. It was very difficult to discern whether the blogger possessed any particular expertise or knowledge and whether the blogger's posts were credible and reliable. Thus, the Web made it possible for any person who has an opinion or knowledge about anything, to post that opinion or share that knowledge on the Internet. Like Google searches, not every post on a blog is credible, particularly when one is conducting legal research. Legal research must lead to verifiable and credible conclusions. For example, a post by a blogger that Andrew Oliver "is the Curt Flood of college athletics" may be interesting conversation, but is not useful or reliable when trying to understand the Andrew Oliver decision, the court's reasoning, or the legal impact of the decision going forward. Thus, while blogs generally should still be viewed with some skepticism when conducting legal research, a number of "credible legal authorities" provide their opinions, commentary, and legal analysis via Weblogs. These legal blogs, such as the Sports Law Blog, are a useful legal resource for tracking current legal developments, reviewing credible commentary concerning legal issues, and linking to additional resources related to legal developments. The researcher still should exercise caution when citing to these sources unless he or she is able to satisfy himself or herself that the information is credible and reasonable to rely upon to support his or her conclusions. And if the researcher is going to rely upon these sources, he or she needs to take care to cite the sources properly to assure that the reader understands that a particular statement or conclusion is based upon a **secondary source** (not a primary source) and represents the opinion or analysis of another, not necessarily the opinion or analysis of a court or legal expert or authority. If used cautiously and properly, however, legal blogs are quite effective research tools.

Electronic and Internet Resources

Provided below are a number of Websites, search engines, electronic resources, and sport and recreation law blogs that should help you rapidly locate current developments in sport law, as well as conduct more in-depth research.

General Legal Research. Searchable databases that cover a broad range of topics including general federal and state law information, federal and state court decisions:

FindLaw Search Database. www.findlaw.com/

Internet Reference Desk Website. www.refdesk.com

Law Library Resource Xchange. www.llrx.com

Law Journal EXTRA! Federal Courts. http://lawonline.ljx.com/federal/

Where to Find Court Opinions. www.legalonline.com/courts.htm

National Center for State Courts. www.ncsc.dni.us/

Law Crawler-Legal Search. www.lawcrawler.com/

The 'Lectric Law Lexicon. www.lectlaw.com//ref.html

American Law Source On-Line. www.lawsource.com/also/

Government Research Sources. Websites, some searchable, that provide information about government agencies, governmental functions, Congress, and general information

United States Patent and Trademark Office. http://trademarks.uspto.gov/

United States Geological Survey. http://mapping.usgs.gov/www.gnis

State and Local Government on the Net. www.piperinfo.com/state/states.html

United States Federal Trade Commission. www.ftc.gov

United States Department of Labor. www.dol.gov.

United States Congress. www.congress.org.

United States Library of Congress. http://thomas.loc.gov/

United States Supreme Court. http://www.supremecourtus.gov/

University Sponsored Research Sites. Searchable databases and links that include general research of state and federal court decisions, the constitution, and state and federal statutes as well as Websites focused on a single topic, such as Title IX and hazing

The Legal Information Institute of Cornell Law School. www.law.cornell.edu

University of Iowa Gender Equity in Sports Project. http://bailiwick.lib.uiowa.edu/ge/

Alfred University Hazing Study. www.alfred.edu/news/html/hazing_study.html

The Legal Education Network at the University of Pittsburgh. http://jurist.law.pitt.edu/

Indiana State University Sport Law Links. http://library.indstate.edu/level1.dir/lio.dir/sportslaw.htm#Sports

Law Journals and Associations Sites. Websites with sport law links and general information about sport law studies and research.

Emory Law School. www.law.emory.edu/FEDCTS/

Marquette Law School. www.marquette.edu/law/sports/links.html

National Sport Law Institute publications. http://law.marquette.edu/cgi-bin/site.pl?2130&pageID=463 #YMTC

Sport and Recreation Law Association. www.srlaweb.org

Miscellaneous Private Sites. Dozens of individuals and companies offer sport law information and links.

Mark's Sports Law News. www.sportslawnews.com/

Insurance Information Website. www.insure.com

Court TV Glossary of Legal Terms. www.courttv.com/legalterms/glossary.html

Sport Law Blogs:

http://www.sportslawblog.com

http://thesportslawprofessor.blogspot.com/

http://blog.willamette.edu/wucl/journals/sportslaw/

http://abajournal.com/blawgs/entertainment+sports+law

http://ctsportslaw.com/

http://athleteagent.blogspot.com/

http://www.sportsagentblog.com/

http://rec-law.blogspot.com/

RESEARCH TECHNIQUES

Developing the Research Plan

Once the researcher is comfortable with the court system and how legal information is codified and reported, it is time to begin the actual research. Having a clearly defined research plan is vital to locating legal information efficiently. Otherwise, the researcher could spend countless hours in the law library with little to show for it. The following six steps represent a good approach to conducting legal research.

Step One: Identify the Problem or Issue

Step One is by far the most important step in the research process. If the issue or problem is not clearly identified, it will be impossible to narrow your search enough to produce meaningful results. A clearly defined issue will also help to discover key words, phrases, and terms that may facilitate the research. However, before you can identify the legal issue involved, you must search current business and professional literature to stay on top of industry activities. For example, when the University of Kentucky terminated head men's basketball coach, Billy Gillispie at the end of the 2008–2009 season a number of questions were raised as to what, if any, buy-out would be paid to Gillispie since he had never executed a formal, extensive contract with UK, but instead had been employed for the previous two years pursuant to a simple three-page Memorandum of Understanding (MOA) (Tipton, 2009). Even though no lawsuit had yet been filed, the actual legal issues which would be raised in that case may have implications that extend beyond the University of Kentucky and could impact all future college coaches' contract negotiations. Thus, from this current development in the business of collegiate sport, numerous legal issues may emerge.

Several good sources of recent developments in the sport industry are available. The *Chronicle of Higher Education* has sections on college athletics, which report recent educational, administrative, business, and legal developments. Several industry publications such as Street and Smith's *SportsBusiness Journal* also will report emerging business and legal issues. In addition, any current news source will be a good place to locate current trends and issues. Once the general issue has been identified, it then becomes easier to identify the legal issues. However, if instead of a specific recent development, a familiar topic or subject in the sport industry is to be the focus of our research, such as Title IX (Gender Equity), then the *Index to Legal Periodicals* and **LexisNexis Academic Universe** are helpful to track down previous law review articles on the subject. Also, remember electronic sources such as **www.findlaw.com** and **www.law.com** have subject sections available with links to numerous other information sources.

Step Two: Consult an Encyclopedia or Treatise

Once the issue is identified, legal encyclopedias, treatises, and digests will help the researcher gain familiarity with the general area of the law implicated by the current problem or issue. For example, consider the situation where you are interested in researching whether coaches can be terminated from their jobs for violent behavior. Determine what area of law is implicated: labor relations, assault and battery, teacher rights, or some other area. **Encyclopedias** and **treatises** will help to sift through the information to narrow the search to what ultimately may be a simple question of either contract law (Does the coach have a contract, and if so, what does it say about termination?), or employer/employee relations (Is the coach an employee at will, or must the school demonstrate just cause to terminate?). **Digests** will provide references to court decisions related to your issue or subject. If you have discovered that your issue relates to a specific state or federal statute, most statutes contain **annotations** that identify other related statutes, legislative history, law review articles, and court decisions relating to that specific statutory provision. Step Two will also help to refine the problem or issue defined in Step One as more information becomes available to the researcher.

Step Three: Read and Summarize Cases

Cases identified in Step Two need to be read thoroughly and then summarized according to their importance and relevance to the issue. A sample summary for a key case is provided at the end of this section. Any relevant literature such as law review articles, business journal articles, or other literature must be summarized to help frame the importance of the issue to the sport industry.

Step Four: Locate Additional Cases and Shepardize

Once a few key cases are located, locating more recent or relevant cases is fairly simple. For this task the **West's Key Number System** together with the **digests** is critical. Each case published in the West's Reporter System will contain several short summaries indexed by topic and key number throughout the West's Digest System. Basically, once you have found a major case relevant to your problem, finding other similar cases from the same jurisdiction or from other states or federal cases is easy to accomplish using the West's Digest. Shepard's Citations is the most available updating service. *Shepard's Citations* will also help to locate additional cases and verify whether the cases the researcher is relying on are still good law. This process is usually referred to as "Shepardizing." If the cases you are relying on have been reversed, overruled, or somehow disregarded by later courts, your position can be severely weakened. Although the service is a bit cumbersome to use, it is important to make the effort. Most law librarians will demonstrate how to use the service once you have a particular case citation that you would like to update.

Step Five: Determine Any Constitutional or Statutory Connections

Not every problem or issue requires an examination of constitutional and statutory law; however, if a particular article of a constitution or a statute, state or federal, is implicated, it needs to be located and thoroughly read and updated. It is not uncommon for Congress or state legislatures to frequently amend and modify existing statutory laws; thus, the researcher must find the most current version of any statutory provisions. Always be sure to consult the "pocket part" of any statutory volume for the latest amendments or modifications.

Step Six: Organize Your Information

Organizing all the general information, cases, and statutes can be a daunting task, but it is critical to effectively answer your question or problem identified in Step One. It is recommended that you summarize every case, define and redefine your issue as you gain a better understanding of the issue, search other jurisdictions for similar or dissimilar cases, and then locate any relevant statutory laws. After that, you will be able to integrate all the information together. For example, if your issue deals with gender equity in sports, you will soon learn that not only is there a specific federal statute to consider (Title IX), but numerous court decisions have also been published that help to interpret and understand the statute. Also, you will find that some rules or regulations issued by the Office of Civil Rights help in understanding the scope and impact of Title IX. In addition, scholars are frequently writing treatises and law review articles on this subject. A researcher could literally find hundreds of pages of information about Title IX.

So how does a researcher organize hundreds of pages of information? Simple—look back to the original problem or question. Limit or narrow the inquiry to only those bits of information that actually provide an answer to the original problem or question. Once that is completed, it is recommended that you then organize the information as follows:

Statement of Facts. Identify the facts or circumstances that created the need to study the problem.

Statement of the Issue/Problem. State the actual issue, question, or problem that will be answered.

Identification of the Relevant Law. Identify the cases, statutes, or other information needed to understand this issue. This should include a brief summary of relevant cases, relevant statutory language, and other information needed to understand the law.

Application of the Law. This section should include a detailed analysis of the law identified in the *Identification of the Relevant Law* section and how it applies to the *Statement of Facts* section to answer the question identified in the *Statement of the Issue/Problem* section.

Conclusion. Discuss the anticipated effect of your analysis in the *Application of the Law* section. How are recreation and sports managers or the industry affected by this legal issue?

SUMMARIZING CASES

As mentioned earlier, planning and organization are critical to the research plan. Court decisions must be read, summarized, and applied to answer the original research question. Following is an excerpt of a tort case involving an injury received by a fan at a wrestling match.

SIGNIFICANT CASE

This case presents a good opportunity to demonstrate how to condense a case into its most important elements: citation, key facts, issues to be decided, decision of the court, and reasoning of the court. If every important case revealed during your research is summarized in this fashion, you will be able to quickly and efficiently incorporate this information into any report or written findings.

DUSCKIEWICZ V. JACK CARTER, D/B/A/, JACK CARTER ENTERPRISES

Supreme Court of Vermont
52 A.2d 788 (1947)

This is a tort action. The complaint is based upon the alleged negligence of the defendant in conducting a wrestling match, resulting in injury to the plaintiff, a spectator at that contest. The plaintiff had a verdict and judgment below in the sum of $150. . . .

* * *

We first consider the defendant's motion for a directed verdict. Material to this issue the jury could reasonably find the following facts from the evidence, viewed in the light most favorable to the plaintiff.

The defendant does business under the name "Jack Carter Enterprises". As one of his enterprises, Carter put on a show at the armory in Rutland on the evening of June 6, 1945. The principal feature of his show was a wrestling match. Through a booking office in Montreal, Carter engaged as contestants in this match two men skilled in the art of wrestling, one by the name of Savoli and the other's name is Ryan. Ryan had performed for Carter three times previous to this engagement and Savoli, once. At some time before June 6, 1945, Carter went to Rutland and made the necessary arrangements for putting on this show. Compensation for each wrestler, as arranged by Carter through the booking office, was a guaranty that each should receive a certain flat sum with a percentage option. That is, if the agreed percentage of the gate receipts amounted to more than the sum guaranteed, then the wrestler concerned could elect to receive such percentage in lieu of the flat sum named in the guaranty. Compensation paid by Carter did not include payment of hotel bills or other expenses, in addition to payment as above stated.

On the evening of the show Carter saw the wrestlers and made sure that they were ready for the contest, but gave them no instructions as to the manner of their behavior during the contest. Savoli then weighed about 230 lbs., and Ryan about 225 lbs. A "ring" was erected in the armory as the arena where the contest was staged. This arena

platform was at an elevation of about four feet from the floor and was enclosed by three ropes extending around the outsides of it. Carter inspected this "ring" after it had been set up. Folding chairs fastened together in sets of three or four were provided as seats for spectators. The four or five rows nearest the "ring" were called "ring side seats" and sold for $1.50 each and the others were general admission seats and were cheaper. The chairs were not fastened to the floor.

The plaintiff resides in West Rutland and, at the time in question, was running a barbershop there. The owner of this shop was in service of the United States Armed Forces and it was agreed between him and the plaintiff that when the owner returned he was to take over this shop. The owner returned sometime in October or December of 1945 and then took over that business. The plaintiff made about seventy-five dollars per week from his barbering business and he also got about $20 per week as his part of the proceeds of a licensed pin ball machine then in the shop. As stated by the plaintiff in cross examination, he was "a wrestling fan". He invited two of his friends to attend this match with him and at the armory entrance he purchased three tickets for ring-side seats. These seats were in the front row nearest the ring. A person in the employ of the defendant ushered them to their seats, which were numbered to correspond with numbers on their tickets. The plaintiff paid $1.50 each for the seats. After the match had been going on for some time, one of the wrestlers threw the other through the ropes in the direction where the plaintiff was seated. When the plaintiff saw the wrestler coming he put up his right hand to protect himself from the oncoming wrestler landing on him and as a result he received a sprained hand and wrist. It is for this injury and resulting alleged damages that the plaintiff seeks to recover.

The defendant based his motion for a directed verdict on grounds that may be briefly stated as follows. The plaintiff assumed the risk of the danger, which resulted in his alleged injury; the wrestlers were independent contractors and not employees of the defendant and the evidence does not show any negligence on the part of the defendant.

As to the question of assumption of risks, the evidence shows that the plaintiff was a business visitor of the defendant at the time and place in question. He had paid $1.50 for his seat and was occupying it for the purpose as intended by the defendant. " " " An invitee at a place of amusement ordinarily assumes the risk of an obvious danger or of one that is a matter of common knowledge; conversely, such a person does not assume the risk of a hidden or undisclosed danger, not of common knowledge, in the absence of warning or personal knowledge. * * * That the danger which resulted in the plaintiff's injury was not an obvious danger is self-evident. However, the defendant contends that the plaintiff must be taken to have assumed the risks of the danger which resulted in his injury, because he had personal knowledge of it and also because such danger is a matter of common knowledge, and he cites several baseball cases in support of this contention. These cases hold that an invitee, familiar with the game of baseball, buying a seat in a part of the stands not protected by screens, who is hit by a batted ball during the progress of a ball game proceeding in a normal manner, can not recover, because it is a matter of common knowledge that chance is an important factor in determining the direction a batted ball may take as it leaves the bat. Such spectator assumes the risks of dangers of which he has personal knowledge and also he assumes the risks of those dangers, which are matters of common knowledge.

The defendant in his brief makes the following statement. "The intent and purpose of a baseball game is to hit the ball as far as possible, and apparently one of the purposes of a wrestling match is to throw a wrestler as far as possible." It is to be noted that while the defendant makes a positive assertion as to the purpose and object of baseball, he is less positive and more cautious in speaking of the purposes and objects of wrestling. If it is true that one of the objects of wrestling is to throw a wrestler as far as possible from the ring, such purpose can not be said to be a matter of common knowledge, and we so hold. The number of people who know how a wrestling match is conducted and what may reasonably be expected to happen there is small when compared with the great number who know what may reasonably be expected to happen at a baseball game played in the normal manner.

While the record shows that the plaintiff stated in cross examination that he is a "wrestling fan", there is nothing therein showing the rules under which this contest was conducted nor whether such rules permit one wrestler to throw the other from the ring and neither does it appear that the plaintiff had ever seen that done previous to the occasion in question. From what has been hereinbefore stated, it follows that it cannot be held as a matter of law that the plaintiff assumed the risks of the danger which resulted in his injury.

Whether the wrestlers were employees of the defendant or were independent contractors is not important in determining the questions before us. The defendant was putting on a show and as a feature of this he engaged these wrestlers to put on this match. It was his business to know the kind and type of performance that he was exhibiting and to use reasonable care as to location of seats and all other matters connected with this enterprise, for the reasonable protection of his invitees. Whether he performed this duty was, under the circumstances, a jury question.

* * *

Judgment reversed. Plaintiff's motion for a new trial on all issues raised by the pleadings is granted, and cause remanded.

SAMPLE CASE SUMMARY

Dusckiewicz v. Jack Carter, d/b/a/, Jack Carter Enterprises, 52 A.2d 788 (Vt. 1947).

Key Facts

(**Teaching Note:** *In this section, you should select only those facts that directly relate to the court's final decision. Which facts were relevant to the court in reaching its conclusion?*).

The Plaintiff, a spectator at a wrestling match, sued Jack Carter *dba* Jack Carter Enterprises for negligence in his presentation of the wrestling match. The Plaintiff purchased ringside seats to watch a professional wrestling match being presented by Carter. Carter selected which wrestlers would be featured and hired two men who were considered skilled in the art of wrestling. Both men had performed for Carter previously. The ring was elevated four feet from the floor and was enclosed by three ropes around the entire ring. During the course of the match one wrestler threw the other through the ropes toward the Plaintiff's seat. The Plaintiff used his right hand to protect himself from the airborne wrestler. The Plaintiff received a sprained hand and wrist.

Issues to Be Decided

(**Teaching Note:** *In this section, you should identify the specific legal question that the court is being asked to decide. It should be stated in the form of a question and should incorporate enough of the facts involved in the case so that it is distinctive. This question will be answered in the next section*).

1. Whether a spectator at a professional wrestling match has assumed the risk of injury associated with the likelihood that one of the contestants will be thrown from the ring?

2. Whether the risks associated with throwing a wrestler as far as possible from the ring is a matter of common knowledge to ordinary spectators of wrestling events?

Decision of the Court

(**Teaching Note:** *In this section, you should simply answer the question posed in the previous section. Your answer should be an affirmative or negative restatement of the question posed above*).

1. A spectator at a wrestling match does not assume the risk of injury associated with the likelihood that one of the contestants will be thrown from the ring absent evidence of personal knowledge on the part of the spectator of such risks.

2. Risks associated with throwing a wrestler as far as possible from the ring during a wrestling match are not a matter of common knowledge to ordinary spectators.

Reasoning of the Court

(**Teaching Note:** *This section summarized the reasoning or rationale of the court. It answers the "why" question. Why did the court answer the legal question in the way that it did? This section is critical to being able to apply the decision of case to future cases and vital to an in-depth understanding of the legal question and outcome*).

With regard to whether *Dusckiewicz had assumed the risk of being injured by a thrown wrestler,* the court initially observed that *Dusckiewicz* was a business visitor of Carter Enterprises during the match. As such, an invitee at a place of amusement only assumes the risk of an **obvious danger** or of dangers that are a **matter of common knowledge.** Dangers that are hidden or undisclosed are not assumed unless there is evidence of warning or personal knowledge on the part of the injured party. In concluding that the risk of being injured by a thrown wrestler was not a matter of common knowledge, the court rejected Carter Enterprises reliance on several baseball cases. Carter argued that the risk of a wrestler being thrown as far as possible from the ring is as common to wrestling as the risk of having a baseball being hit as far as possible from the baseball field. The court rejected the Defendant's comparison because Carter was not able to demonstrate that throwing a wrestler as far as possible from the ring is a purpose associated with wrestling. Further, the court concluded that even if it had been shown that such purpose was associated with wrestling, it was still not reasonable to expect that many spectators would have known such purpose. Even though the Plaintiff identified himself as a wrestling fan, there was no evidence that he was aware of any such purpose. The Defendant's other arguments concerning whether the wrestlers were independent contractors were rejected as unimportant to the court's decision.

QUESTIONS YOU SHOULD BE ABLE TO ANSWER

1. Explain the difference between primary legal sources and secondary legal sources.

2. Identify and provide an example of each of the four primary legal sources.

3. Summarize the steps in the research process.

4. Why should researchers exercise caution when relying on secondary legal sources especially Internet based sources or blogs?

5. What is the legal "issue" and "rationale of the court" in a court decision and why is it important to be able to properly identify the legal issue and the court's reasoning in a court decision?

REFERENCES

Larsen, S., & Bourdeau, J. (1997). *Legal research for beginners.* Hauppauge, NY: Barron's Educational Series, Inc.

Tipton, J. (2009, March 29). Coach's buyout a sticking point. Attorney, UK don't agree. *Lexington Herald-Leader*, p. A1.

West Publishing Co. (1991). *Sample pages* (3rd ed.). St. Paul, MN: West Publishing Co.

Useful Books on Legal Research

Delaney, S. (2002). *Electronic legal research: An integrated approach.* Albany, NY: West/Thomson Learning.

Elias, S., & Levinkind, S. (2002). *Legal research: How to find and understand the law.* Berkeley, CA: Nolo.

Journal of International Law & Economics. (2002). *Guide to international legal research.* Newark, NJ: LexisNexis/Matthew Bender.

Manz, W. H. (2002). *Guide to state legislative and administrative materials.* Buffalo, NY: William S. Hein.

Redfield, S. E. (2002). *Thinking like a lawyer: An educator's guide to legal analysis and research.* Durham, NC: Carolina Academic Press.

1.30 Business Structure and Legal Authority

—**John T. Wolohan**

ITHACA COLLEGE

One of the first, and perhaps most important, decisions a sport or recreation business owner must make is how to organize or structure the new business. For example, should the new sport and recreation organization use one of the traditional common business structures, such as a sole proprietorship, partnership, or corporation, or a newer one, like a limited liability corporation (LLC). Although each business structure has some distinct advantages and disadvantages, such as federal, state, and local taxes, as well as the limited legal liability of the business owners, the type of structure a new sport and recreation organization chooses should depend in large part on the nature of the business. This section examines the legal issues surrounding new businesses, and identifies some of the advantages and disadvantages of the different business structures used in the sport and recreation industry.

FUNDAMENTAL CONCEPTS

Three of the most common business structures in sport and recreation include sole proprietorships, partnerships, and corporations. In selecting the business structure or form that is appropriate for your business, sport and recreation administrators should be aware of the following factors: limited legal liability; federal, state, and local tax laws; flexibility; access to capital; cost and ease of formation; and transferability of ownership in the business (Hamilton, 2001).

Sole Proprietorships

The most common business structure in the United States, and the easiest one for an individual to start and maintain, is the sole proprietorship. A sole proprietorship is an unincorporated business, owned by one individual, which has no legal existence apart from the owner (Eisenberg, 2005). The courts will automatically view the business as a sole proprietorship, unless the individual starting the business files articles of incorporation with the secretary of state in the state in which the business is located.

The sole proprietorship is one of the most popular business structures in the sport and recreation industry because of the low costs and ease involved in its formation. The cost of formation is low because there are no legal papers to file, thus eliminating legal expenses. In addition, because the income and expenses of the business are attributed to the owner, there are no business or corporate taxes to be paid or additional tax forms to file.

The sole proprietorship does have some disadvantage over other business forms, however. First, because the business has no legal existence apart from the owner, the owner has unlimited personal liability for all the financial and legal risks of the business. Other disadvantages are that the life of the business is limited to the life of the owner; when he or she dies, the business ends. In addition, the business's ability to raise large amounts of capital is limited to the owner's assets or borrowing power (Miller, 1997).

Partnerships

Another common form of business in the sport and recreation industry is the general partnership. A partnership is created when two or more people, each contributing one or more of: money, property, labor, or skill, enter into a business with the expectation that each will share proportionally in the profits and losses (Crane & Bromberg, 1968). Because a partnership is basically a creation of contract law, no formal written agreement is necessary to create a valid partnership. However, like any good contract, to help avoid future disagreements, it is important that there be a formal written partnership agreement so that all partners understand their rights and obligations, and how profits and losses will be shared (Hamilton, 2001). For example, unless otherwise stated in a partnership agreement, the partners will share in the profits and losses of the business equally.

Partnerships enjoy many of the same benefits of the sole proprietorship, such as low costs, ease of formation, and single taxation. Partnerships have conduit or pass-through taxation, in that income or loss of the partnership is passed on to personal income taxes of the partners. While the IRS requires the partnership to file an annual informational tax return to document profits and losses among the partners, the partnership pays no tax (Crane & Bromberg, 1968).

The major disadvantage of the partnership over other forms of business is that each partner has a fiduciary duty toward the other partners, through which they are legally bound by each other's actions. As a result of this fiduciary duty, each of the partners has unlimited joint and several liability for the acts of each of the other general partners, regardless of whether the partner consented or had notice of such acts (Miller, 1997). Therefore, it is essential that partners trust each other and are aware of each other's activities. Another disadvantage of the partnership is that, because it is created by contract, partners are prohibited from selling or transferring their share in the partnership, even with the consent of the other partners. In order for one to sell or transfer their share in the partnership, the partners must dissolve the first partnership and create a second separate partnership (Miller, 1997).

Limited Partnerships

The only real difference between a limited partnership and a general partnership is that the limited partner(s) enjoys limited legal and financial liability for the debts and legal obligations of the partnership. To receive limited liability, however, the limited partner must not have any involvement in the day-to-day operations of the business (Hamilton, 2001). Once a limited partner becomes involved in the management of the business, he or she forfeits their status as a limited partner and becomes a general partner, assuming unlimited joint and several liability for the acts of the partnerships (Crane & Bromberg, 1968).

Limited Liability Company

Another unincorporated business structure is the Limited Liability Company (LLC). The LLC structure is attractive to businesses because it provides greater flexibility in management of the business and has less-restrictive ownership requirements, by combining the best aspects of both the partnership and the corporation forms (Soderquist, 2005). For example, like a partnership, the LLC usually qualifies for pass-through taxation. In other words, the LLC's profits pass through to the company's members, who report their share of the profits on their personal federal tax returns. The company itself does not pay a federal tax before the money is distributed to the members, as in the case of C corporations (see the following page). However, as a separate legal entity, like a corporation, the LLC provides all the members with limited liability protection from business debts (Callison & Sullivan, 2008).

Another advantage of the LLC is that, unlike S corporations (see below), there can be an unlimited number of members, and membership is not limited to individuals, but may include partnerships, corporations, other LLCs and foreign entities. Most states also permit "single member" LLCs, those having only one owner. Finally, because it is designed as a single entity, the LLC also provides the business with important protection from federal antitrust law. (For more information on single entities and antitrust law see Section 7.31, *Antitrust Law: Professional Applications*). In fact, the LLC is so attractive as a new business form that Major League Soccer established themselves as an LLC.

The sports or recreation business may be managed either by its members or by a designated group of managers, who may or may not be members of the company. If the members, as in a partnership, manage the business, each of the members has the same ability as a partnership to bind the entire business through their acts. However, as mentioned earlier, the LLC provides each member limited liability. If a designated group, as in a corporation, manages the business, members do not have the ability to bind the entire business unless they are in the designated group managing the business (Soderquist, 2005).

Corporations

Although there are a number of different types of corporations, all corporations share some basic characteristics. First, to do business as a corporation, the business must file "Articles of Incorporation" with the secretary of state in the state of incorporation. The state of incorporation is usually the state in which the business is located. A business, however, can incorporate in any state it chooses. Once the Articles of Incorporation are filed, the laws of the state of incorporation govern the corporation. Second, all corporations are treated as separate legal entities, with many of the same legal rights as an individual. For example, corporations can sue or be sued, carry on business activities, enter into contracts, and own property and other tangible and intangible assets (Eisenberg, 2005). Third, because a corporation is a separate legal entity, the business can be sold or transferred through the sale of stock, making changes in ownership simple. Fourth, the life of a corporation is unlimited. Because a corporation is a separate legal entity, the life of the business extends beyond the illness or death of the owners, individual officers, managers, or shareholders. Finally, and most importantly, all corporations provide the owner or shareholders with limited liability for corporate obligations. In other words, because corporations are treated as individual entities, separate from the owner or shareholders, the only legal and financial liability of the owner or shareholder is the money they invested into the company (Eisenberg, 2005).

In addition to the preceding benefits of corporations, there are a number of disadvantages involved in incorporating; these include the cost, the formal legal requirements, state and federal rules and regulations, and double taxation. First, because to form a corporation, an individual must file articles of incorporation with the secretary of state, a corporation requires more paperwork and record-keeping than other business forms. Also, unlike other forms of business, corporations must pay taxes on the income of the business, rather than passing it through to the owner's personal income tax (Hamilton, 2001). In addition, individual shareholders must also pay taxes on any dividends the corporation distributes. As a result, the corporation's profits are taxed twice, once at the corporate rate and again at the individual shareholder's rate (Hamilton, 2001). Finally, because an attorney is needed to help file all the necessary forms and meet all the requirements and formalities, there is a higher cost associated with the formation of a corporation.

Due to the inherent physical risks associated with most sports and recreation activities, it might seem that the advantages of limited liability are so great that all businesses in the sports and recreation industry should be conducted as corporations (Hamilton, 2001). However, the nature of the business is only one factor that a new business should consider when selecting a business form. For example, you should also consider the tax consequences, cost of formation, the formal requirements, flexibility, and simplicity.

Although all corporations share some of the same characteristics; Congress has created certain tax benefits or other advantages that distinguish different corporations. The following section examines some of the differences among corporate forms.

C Corporations

C corporations are the most common form of corporation. C corporations get their name because the tax rate these corporations use is found in subchapter C of the Internal Revenue Code. C corporations may have an unlimited number of shareholders, and may issue more than one class of stock (Hamilton, 2001). In deciding whether to form a new business as a C corporation, it is important to understand that all corporate income that is distributed to shareholders under C corporations is subject to double taxation. For example, as indicated previously, if at the end of the year the business has taxable income, the corporation must pay a corporate income tax. If any income is distributed to the shareholders, each individual shareholder must declare the income on his or her individual tax return and pay a second tax on the same money.

S Corporations

Instead of electing to be taxed under subchapter C of the Internal Revenue Code, a corporation can elect to be taxed under subchapter S; therefore, the choice is more of a tax election. Corporations making this selection are called S corporations. To be eligible for S corporation status, corporations must have fewer than seventy-five shareholders, may not have shareholders who are nonresident aliens, and may only issue one class of stock (Hamilton, 2001). Although S corporations have the same basic features as C corporations, S corporations have the benefit of allowing shareholders to elect to be taxed under a conduit or pass-through taxation approach that is similar to a partnership or proprietorship (Lind, Schwarz, Lathrope & Rosenberg, 2008).

Publicly Traded Corporations

The main reason for "going public" with your business is financial. For example, in 1998, the Cleveland Indians raised $55 million by selling four million shares of stock in the team. However, besides the financial benefit, there are a number of other issues to consider. First, the organization must comply with all Security and Exchange Commission (SEC) rules and regulations. Second, the corporation must make full financial disclosures concerning profits and losses. Third, because common shareholders are owners of the corporation, they have certain rights, such as voting on the makeup of the board of directors and attending annual meetings. Therefore, there are more legal formalities, and organizations have less control. Finally, there are the added costs to the organization. The corporation must have annual board of director meetings, create and mail annual financial reports, assign staff for investor relations, and incur added legal costs (Eisenberg, 2005).

Nonprofit Corporations

Some organizations, due to their special nature or mission, are nonprofit corporations. The major difference between a nonprofit and a regular for-profit corporation is that, unlike regular corporations, nonprofit corporations do not have shareholders or owners of any kind (Soderquist, 2005). Instead, nonprofit corporations are run by the members of the organization or people in the community (van der Smissen, 1999). No matter who is running the nonprofit corporation, the members or the people in the community, none of the income or property generated by the nonprofit can be distributed as a dividend (Soderquist, 2005). It should be noted, however, that this does not mean that nonprofit corporations cannot make a profit. It only means that none of the profits can be distributed to the members.

There are generally two types of nonprofit corporations: **eleemosynary** (or charitable) and **mutual benefit**. In distinguishing the two types, the courts look at whether the purpose of the corporation is to benefit its members or to benefit some other group (Soderquist, 2005). Private schools and universities are generally classified as eleemosynary, whereas private clubs would generally be considered mutual benefit nonprofit corporations.

No matter which type of nonprofit corporation (eleemosynary or mutual benefit) the business is classified as, because nonprofit corporations serve a public purpose, they receive a number of benefits or privileges not available to other types of corporations. Some of these benefits include being exempt from most federal and state taxes, special postage rates, and exemption from certain labor law requirements (van der Smissen, 1999). At the federal level, nonprofit corporations are known as having 501 (c)(3) tax status. Even if a corporation is nonprofit, however, it is also important to note that any profits that arise from essentially commercial activities will be taxable in the same manner they would be in a business corporation (Soderquist, 2005).

For a business to be recognized as a nonprofit corporation, it must file the required forms and meet the established legal requirements. Currently every state has legislation establishing nonprofit corporations, and the incorporation process usually follows the same procedure as business corporations.

Public Corporations

Another type of corporation that is involved in providing sports and recreational activities is a public corporation. Public corporations are usually municipalities such as cities, towns, and villages (Soderquist, 2005). In addition to municipalities, public corporations are sometimes formed by special legislative acts to perform some special purpose. For example, the National Park Service was formed by Congress and has administrative control over all national parks and forests. In forming a public corporation, like the National Park Service, Congress hopes to take the organization, operation, and finances of the organization from the governmental sphere of influence and place them in a more businesslike structure (Soderquist, 2005).

SIGNIFICANT CASE

The following case examines the decision of Major League Soccer to organize as a limited liability company and whether the league is a single entity for antitrust purposes.

FRASER V. MAJOR LEAGUE SOCCER

United States District Court for the District of Massachusetts
97 F. Supp. 130 (2000)

MEMORANDUM AND ORDER

The individual plaintiffs are the representatives of the certified class of professional soccer players who are or who have been employed by the defendant Major League Soccer, L.L.C. ("MLS"). MLS is a limited liability company ("LLC") organized under Delaware law. The defendant United States Soccer Federation, Inc. ("USSF") is the national governing body for professional and amateur soccer in the United States.

The plaintiffs assert a number of antitrust claims. In Count I, they allege that MLS and several of its investors who operate MLS teams (hereafter "operator-investors" or "operators") have unlawfully combined to restrain trade or commerce in violation to § 1 of the Sherman Anti-Trust Act, 15 U.S.C. § 1, by contracting for player services centrally through MLS, effectively eliminating the competition for those services that would take place if each MLS team were free to bid for and sign players directly. . . . Count III alleges that all defendants have jointly exercised monopoly power in violation of § 2 of the Sherman Act, 15 U.S.C. § 2. In Count IV, the plaintiffs allege that the transaction which brought MLS into existence violated § 7 of the Clayton Act, 15 U.S.C. § 18.

* * *

The plaintiffs have moved for summary judgment as to the defendants' so-called "single entity" defense. The gist of their argument is that although MLS appears to be a single business entity, so that its method of hiring players centrally can be characterized as the act of a single economic actor for antitrust purposes, the organizational form is really just a sham that should be considered ineffective to insulate from condemnation what are in substance illegal horizontal restraints on the hiring of players resulting from the unlawful concerted behavior of the several MLS team operators. . . .

I. RELEVANT FACTS

At the time MLS was formed, no "Division I" or "premiere" professional outdoor soccer league operated in the United States. The last premiere soccer league to operate in this country had been the North American Soccer League ("NASL"), which led a turbulent existence from 1968 until the mid-1980s, when it collapsed. In 1988, Federation Internationale de Football Association ("FIFA") awarded to the United States the right to host the 1994 World Cup, soccer's illustrious international competition. In consideration for that award, the organizers of the event promised to resurrect premiere professional soccer in the United States.

In the early 1990s, Alan Rothenberg, the President of USSF and of World Cup USA 1994, with assistance from others began developing plans for a Division I professional outdoor soccer league in the United States. Rothenberg and others at the USSF consulted extensively with potential investors in an effort to understand what type of league structure and business plan they might find attractive. He also consulted antitrust counsel in the hope of avoiding the antitrust problems that which other sports leagues such as the National Football League ("NFL") had encountered. Eventually the planners settled on the concept of organizing a limited liability company to run the league, and in 1995 MLS was formed.

The structure and mode of operation of MLS is governed by its Limited Liability Company Agreement ("MLS Agreement" or "Agreement"). The MLS Agreement establishes a Management Committee consisting of representatives of each of the investors. The Management Committee has authority to manage the business and affairs of MLS. Several of the investors have signed Operating Agreements with MLS which, subject to certain conditions and obligations, give them the right to operate specific MLS teams. There are also passive investors in MLS who do not operate teams. None of the passive investors is a defendant here.

Operator-investors do not hire players for their respective teams directly. Rather, players are hired by MLS as employees of the league itself and then are assigned to the various teams. Each player's employment contract is between the player and MLS, not between the player and the operator of the team to which the player is assigned. MLS centrally establishes and administers rules for the acquisition, assignment, and drafting of players, and all player assignments are subject to guidelines set by the Management Committee. Among other things, the guidelines limit the aggregate salaries that the league may pay its players.

Under applicable player assignment policies, MLS centrally allocates the top or "marquee" players among the teams, aiming to prevent talent imbalances and assure a degree of comparability of team strength in order to promote competitive soccer matches. These assignments are effective unless disapproved by a two-thirds vote of a subcommittee of the Management Committee. Most of the rest of the players—the non-"marquee" players—are selected for teams by the individual operator-investors through player drafts and the like. The league allows player trades between teams, but MLS's central league office must approve (and routinely does approve) such trades. Team operators are not permitted to trade players in exchange for cash compensation.

MLS distributes profits (and losses) to its investors in a manner consistent with its charter as a limited liability company, not unlike the distribution of dividends to shareholders in a corporation. Revenues generated by league operations belong directly to MLS. MLS owns and controls all trademarks, copyrights, and other intellectual property rights that relate in any way either to the league or to any of its teams. MLS owns all tickets to MLS games and receives the revenues from ticket sales. There are central league regulations regarding ticket policies, even including limits on the number of complimentary tickets any team may give away. Team operators do retain the ability to negotiate some purely local matters, including local sponsorship agreements with respect to a limited array of products and services and local broadcast agreements, but they do so as agents of MLS.

Under the Operating Agreement, each team operator receives from MLS a management fee. As of the time this action was filed, the management fee consisted of (a) 100% of the first $1.24 million, and 30% of the excess over $1.24 million, of local television broadcast and sponsorship revenues, the latter percentage subject to some specified annual increase; (b) 50% of ticket revenues from home games, increasing to 55% in year six of the league's operation; and (c) 50% of stadium revenues from concessions and other sources.

Expenses are allocated in a way similar to the allocation of revenues. MLS is responsible for most expenses associated with league operations. For example, MLS pays all player acquisition costs, player salaries, and player benefits. It also pays the salaries of all league personnel (including referees), game-related travel expenses for each team, workers' compensation insurance, fees and expenses of foreign teams playing in exhibition games promoted by MLS within the U.S., league-wide marketing expenses, and 50% of each individual team's stadium rental expense.

The team operators are responsible for the other half of their stadium rents, costs of approved local marketing, licensing, and promotion, and general team administration, including salaries of the team's management and coaching staff.

Passive investors do not pay any team operating expenses or receive any management fee. They share in the general distribution of profits (and losses) resulting from league operations.

Team operators cannot transfer their MLS interests or operational rights without the consent of the Management Committee. That consent may be withheld without cause, but the league is required to repurchase the team operator's interest at its fair market value if approval is withheld. Team operators derive whatever rights they may have exclusively from MLS, and the league may terminate these rights if a team operator violates these provisions or fails to act in the best interest of the league.

* * *

III. THE OPERATION OF MLS

Section 1 of the Sherman Act forbids contracts, combinations, and conspiracies in restraint of trade or commerce. See 15 U.S.C. § 1. Agreements between separate economic actors that have the effect of substantially and unreasonably reducing competition in a particular market violate § 1. The plaintiffs argue that MLS player policies constitute an unlawful agreement among the various team operators to limit or eliminate competition in the market for players' services.

Though the language of § 1 is sweeping, there are some limits to its reach. One critical limitation for the purposes of this case is that the statute does not prohibit single economic entities from acting unilaterally in ways that may, in some manner, decrease competition. . . . Because it is directed against contracts, combinations or conspiracies, § 1 only prohibits collective activity by plural economic actors, which unreasonably restrains competition. See *Copperweld Corp. v. Independence Tube Corp.*, 467 U.S. 752 (1984). The MLS defendants contend that MLS is a "single entity" and that even if its policies and practices have the effect of substantially reducing competition for players' salaries, they do not—*cannot* as a matter of law—violate § 1.

MLS is a limited liability company organized under Delaware law. An LLC is a form of statutory business organization that combines some of the advantages of a partnership with some of the advantages of a corporation. Under Delaware law, an LLC is a separate legal entity distinct from its members. Del. Code Ann. tit. 6, § 18-201(b). As in a corporation, investors (shareholders in a corporation, members in an LLC) have limited liability (*Id.*, § 18-303), own undivided interests in the company's property (§ 18-701), are bound by the terms of their Agreement (like the corporate Articles), and share in the overall profits and losses ratably according to their investment or as otherwise provided by the organizing Agreement (§ 18-503). The Federal Trade Commission has treated LLCs like corporations. . . . In the present context, there is little reason to treat an LLC such as MLS differently from a corporation.

MLS's operations should therefore be analyzed as the operations of a single corporation would be, with its operator-investors treated essentially as officers and shareholders. There can be no § 1 claim based on concerted action among a corporation and its officers, nor among officers themselves, so long as the officers are not acting to promote an interest, from which they would directly benefit, that is independent from the corporation's success. . . . If an LLC should be considered like a corporation for these purposes, as I conclude it should, then there can be no § 1 violation by reason of concerted action between the LLC as an entity and its members, or between the individual members themselves, unless the members are acting not in the interest of the entity, but rather in their own separate self-interest. The "independent personal stake" exception has not yet been squarely addressed in this Circuit; recognizing the risk that this exception, if left unchecked, might swallow the rule, courts that employ it have done so conservatively.

* * *

The plaintiffs argue that even if MLS is deemed a single entity, the divergent self-interests of the operator-investors provides sufficient cause to invoke the independent personal stake exception. The plaintiffs base this argument largely on their assertion that the operator-investors do not truly share in MLS's profits and losses. Instead of owning undivided interests in the league that are not attached to the operation of any given team, they pay certain operating expenses individually and receive management fees from MLS that are calculated in large part according to their local team-generated revenues. Also, they are able to harvest the value of the particular teams they operate by selling their operational rights or, if the Management Committee vetoes the sale, by requiring the league to pay them the fair market value of their investment.

The management fee arrangement exists in addition to, not in place of, the overall profit and loss sharing specified in the Agreement. Indeed, the fact that there are passive investors in MLS is strong evidence that the payment of management fees and assignment of local expenses do not account for all economic risks and benefits associated with the league's operation.

Furthermore, successful local operation of a team benefits the entire league. The league's net revenues, not just the local operator's management fees, increase when more local revenues are generated.

A similar effect is foreseeable in the market for operator-investor shares. Admittedly, unlike undifferentiated shares of stock, the market value of a team operator's investment will not simply reflect an aliquot share of the whole enterprise, but will also reflect in certain respects the success of the local operation. Nonetheless, unlike competition in most markets, where the value of an enterprise would usually be enhanced if its competitors grew weaker, the value of the right to operate an MLS team would be diminished, not enhanced, by the weaknesses of other teams, their operators, and the league as a whole. Management fees and operational rights notwithstanding, every operator-investor has a strong incentive to make the league—and the other operator-investors—as robust as possible. Each operator-investor's personal stake is not independent of the success of MLS as a whole enterprise.

The plaintiffs point to other ways in which the operator-investors compete on and off the field. That teams (and, by extension, their operators) compete playing soccer, and that operators directly hire certain staff, such as coaches, to make teams more capable of on-field heroics, does nothing to assist the plaintiffs. Exciting on-field competition between teams is what makes MLS games worth watching. *Chicago Prof'l Sports*, 95 F.3d at 598-99 ("a league with one team would be like one hand clapping"). Game competition, without doubt, is part of the league's entertainment product, not an indicator of divergent economic interests among operators.

On balance, the business organization of MLS is quite centralized. The league owns the teams themselves; disgruntled operators may not simply "take their ball and go home" by withdrawing the teams they operate and forming or joining a rival league. MLS also owns all intellectual property related to the teams. It contracts for local-level services through its operators, who act on its behalf as agents. Operators risk losing their rights to operate their teams if they breach the governing Agreement. The Management Committee exercises supervisory authority over most of the league's activities. It may reject, without cause, any operator's individual attempt to assign the rights to operate a team.

It is true that MLS is run by a Management Committee that can be controlled by the operator-investors, who constitute the majority of the members of the Committee. It is not remarkable that principal investors can collectively control the governing board of an LLC (or of a corporation). That fact hardly proves that the investors are pursuing economic interests separate from the interests of the firm. The notion that the members of the Management Committee of a single firm violate the antitrust laws when they vote together to maximize the price or minimize the cost of the firm's product is easily rejected.

As a factual matter, therefore, there is insufficient basis in the record for concluding that operators have divergent economic interests within MLS's structure. Even if one draws the most favorable inference on the plaintiffs' behalf, there is no reasonable basis for imposing § 1 liability.

MLS's player policies, in particular, do not call for application of the independent personal stake exception. The operator-investors benefit from those policies because centralized contracting for player services results in lower salaries. However, that benefit is, in the MLS structure, a derivative one. No operator has an individual player payroll to worry about; the league pays the salaries. Moreover, the MLS investor gets the lower-cost benefit in exchange for having surrendered the degree of autonomy that team owners in "plural entity" leagues typically enjoy. The reason an individual team owner in one of those other leagues is willing to bid up players' salaries to get the particular players it wants is because by paying high salaries to get desirable players, the owner can achieve other substantial benefits, such as increased sales of tickets and promotional goods, media revenues, and the like. The MLS operator-investors have largely yielded that opportunity to the central league office. Plainly, there are trade-offs in the different approaches. The MLS members have calculated that the surrender of autonomy, together with the attendant benefit of lower and more controlled player payrolls and greater parity in talent among teams, will help MLS to succeed where others, notably NASL, failed. That is a calculation made on behalf of the entity, and it does not serve only the ulterior interests of the individual investors standing on their own. It is not an occasion for application of the independent personal stake exception to the general single-entity rule described in *Copperweld*.

The plaintiffs also argue that the structure of MLS is a sham designed to allow what is actually an illegal combination of plural actors to masquerade as the business conduct of a single entity. The plaintiffs do not argue that the structure of MLS as established by the its organizing Agreement is legally defective so that it should not be recognized as a lawful entity under Delaware law. Rather, they say that even if MLS is a legitimate LLC—a legitimate single entity for state law purposes—a court should disregard that legal form in evaluating under antitrust principles whether the operator—investors are engaged in a horizontal restraint in the market for players' services. To make the argument, the plaintiffs put a reverse spin on the *Copperweld* holding.

Copperweld held that a corporation could not conspire with its wholly owned subsidiary in violation of § 1 because, though the parent and subsidiary were distinct legal entities, the economic reality was that they functioned as a single business enterprise. Cases following *Copperweld* have mainly addressed the question whether to disregard formal distinctions among entities in order to find economic singularity for the purposes of § 1. See, e.g., *Sullivan v. NFL*, 34 F.3d 1091, 1099 (1st Cir. 1994) (NFL, composed of separately owned clubs, not a single entity in the market for ownership of teams); *Chicago Prof'l Sports Ltd. Partnership v. NBA*, 95 F.3d 593, 597-600 (7th Cir. 1996) (characterizing NBA, composed of separately owned clubs, as a single entity for the purpose of league-wide limitations on locally televising games through "superstations," though expressly withholding judgment as to whether NBA was single entity in other markets, such as player contracting)....

The plaintiffs propose that the "economic reality" test should be applied not only to *ignore* formal legal distinctions between separate corporations as the court did in *Copperweld*, but conversely to *envision* distinctions in what is formally a single legal entity when doing so would accurately describe how the business of the entity actually operates. The argument may have some superficial appeal, but on close examination it appears that it rests on a misconception of the scope of the *Copperweld* principle.

It was noted above that the courts have not given the sweeping language of § 1 its broadest possible effect. The "rule of reason" is an obvious example of a limitation on the literal scope of the statutory language....

The *Copperweld* rule similarly limits the reach of the statute's broad language. While concerted action between two separate corporations, one the parent and the other a subsidiary, could literally be described as a "combination" that restrains trade, the Supreme Court concluded that it was not the kind of combination that § 1 was intended to forbid. Like the coordination between a corporation and its unincorporated division, an agreement between a parent and its subsidiary did not represent "a sudden joining of two independent sources of economic power previously pursuing separate interests." *Copperweld*, 467 U.S. at 770. The plaintiffs are correct that the Court was looking to substance, not merely form.

But that does not mean that form is irrelevant. Copperweld does not support the proposition that a business organized as a single legal entity should have its form ignored, or its "veil" pierced, so that courts could examine whether participants in the firm have conducted concerted activity that would violate § 1. Merely posing that proposition suggests how troublesome it would be as a practical matter. It would permit the atomization of firms into their constituent parts, then to have the relationships of those parts examined to see if they produced anticompetitive effects that, had they been brought about by independent economic actors, would have violated § 1. The number of companies that could be vulnerable to examination of internal business decisions under such an approach would be mind-boggling. No case has suggested that it would be appropriate to deconstruct a corporate entity in that way.

Practical objections aside, the theory is also fundamentally incompatible with the axiom the *Copperweld* Court's analysis started with—that coordination of business activities within a single firm is not subject to scrutiny under § 1. *Copperweld* cannot be understood to authorize an "economic reality" analysis that would require rejection of the very premise the holding of the case depended on. Moreover, the plaintiffs' proposition would plainly interfere with the objective of the antitrust laws. "Subjecting a single firm's every action to judicial scrutiny for reasonableness would threaten to discourage the competitive enthusiasm that the antitrust laws seek to promote." *Copperweld*, 467 U.S. at 775.

In sum, the plaintiffs' deconstruction efforts are unavailing. MLS is what it is. As a single entity, it cannot conspire or combine with its investors in violation of § 1, and its investors do not combine or conspire with each other in pursuing the economic interests of the entity. MLS's policy of contracting centrally for player services is unilateral activity of a single firm. Since § 1 does not apply to unilateral activity—even unilateral activity that tends to restrain trade—the claim set forth in Count I cannot succeed as a matter of law.

IV. THE FORMATION OF MLS

In addition to the claim that the player policies of MLS are an unlawful horizontal restraint of trade, the plaintiffs also claim that the very formation of MLS in the first place violated § 7 of the Clayton Act, which prohibits acquisitions or mergers the effect of which "may be substantially to lessen competition, or to tend to create a monopoly" in any line of commerce or activity affecting commerce, 15 U.S.C. § 18, as well as § 1 of the Sherman Act. The two theories are related.

* * *

2. Existing Market
. . . There can be no § 7 liability because the formation of MLS did not involve the acquisition or merger of existing business enterprises, but rather the formation of an entirely new entity which itself represented the creation of an entirely new market. The relevant test under § 7 looks to whether competition in *existing* markets has been reduced. . . . Where there is no existing market, there can be no reduction in the level of competition. There are no negative numbers in this math; there is nothing lower than zero. Competition that does not exist cannot be decreased. The creation of MLS did not reduce competition in an existing market because when the company was formed there was no active market for Division I professional soccer in the United States.

* * *

B. The Sherman Act Claim
In addition to the Clayton Act theory, the plaintiffs urge that the formation of MLS, by which multiple operator-investors combined to create the single entity, also violated the Sherman Act's prohibition of contracts, combinations or conspiracies in restraint of trade.

It is generally held that a coming together that does not violate § 7 of the Clayton Act does not violate § 1 of the Sherman Act either. See *White Consol. Indus. v. Whirlpool Corp.*, 781 F.2d 1224, 1228 (6th Cir. 1986) (failure to show Clayton § 7 violation precluded Sherman § 1 violation for same conduct). A merger of market participants that does not lessen competition and thus does not offend § 7 ordinarily would not constitute a combination in restraint of trade in violation of § 1. Though the statutory provisions present slightly different modes of analysis, when those modes are applied to the same constellation of facts, the answer will ordinarily be the same.

Here, the pertinent facts are that the founding investors of MLS created both a new company and simultaneously a new market, in effect increasing the number of competitors from zero to one. As explained above, that did not represent a lessening of actual or potential competition in an existing market. Similarly, it did not represent a "sudden joining of . . . independent sources of economic power previously pursuing separate interests," see *Copperweld*, 467 U.S. at 770, which is what is forbidden by § 1.

V. CONCLUSION AND ORDER

For all the reasons set forth above, the defendants' motion for summary judgment in their favor under Counts I and IV of the Amended Complaint is GRANTED. It follows that the plaintiffs' motion for summary judgment on the defendants' "single entity" defense is DENIED.

IT IS SO ORDERED.

QUESTIONS YOU SHOULD BE ABLE TO ANSWER

1. What are the advantages of forming a corporation rather than a partnership?

2. What are the disadvantages of forming a corporation rather than a partnership?

3. What happens when a limited partner becomes active in managing the business?

4. For sport organizations, what are some of the major benefits of a LLC?

5. Since publicly traded businesses are able to generate additional revenue by selling stock, why are there not more publicly traded sports organizations?

REFERENCES

Cases

Fraser v. Major League Soccer, 97 F. Supp. 130 (2000).

Publications

Callison, J. W., & Sullivan, M. A. (2008). *Limited Liability Companies: A State-By-State Guide to Law and Practice.* Eagan, MN: Thomson/West Publishing.

Crane, J. A., & Bromberg, A. R. (1968). *Law of Partnership.* St. Paul, MN: West Publishing.

Eisenberg, M. A. (2005). *Corporations and other Business Organizations* (9th ed.). New York, NY: Foundation Press.

Hamilton, R. W. (2001). *Corporations: Including partnerships and limited partnerships* (7th ed.). St. Paul, MN: West Publishing.

Lind, S. A., Schwarz, S., Lathrope, D. J., & Rosenberg, J. D. (2008). *Fundamentals of Corporate Taxation* (7th ed.). New York, NY: Foundation Press.

Miller, L. K. (1997). *Sport business management.* Gaithersburg, MD: Aspen Publishers.

Soderquist, L. B. et al. (2005). *Corporations and other business organizations* (6th ed.). Newark, NJ: LexisNexis Publishing Group.

Van der Smissen, B. et al. (1999) *Management of park and recreation agencies.* Ashburn, VA: National Recreation and Park Association.

2.00

NEGLIGENCE LAW

Negligence law is that law which deals with unintentional torts committed by individuals or organizations. *Negligence* is an unintentional tort that injures an individual in person, property, or reputation. The negligence section is divided into three sections. The first section addresses negligence theory, which includes and examines both the elements of negligence and which parties are liable in Section 2.10. This section serves as a foundation for each of the two succeeding sections.

It is important that the recreation or sport manager understand that being sued for negligence does not necessarily mean that one will lose that suit. Section 2.20 addresses many of the defenses available to recreation and sport providers. Some of these defenses are based in common law, some in contract law, and some in statutory law.

Section 2.30 addresses some of the many recreation and sport management applications of negligence theory. Some of the major applications addressed relate to premises liability, property law, supervision, and hospitality/tourism law.

* * *

The reader is cautioned, however, regarding a limitation of this or any other text. *Negligence law is primarily state law and, as such, may vary considerably from state to state. It is impossible to cover all of the quirks and variations in the various laws and court rulings for each state. It is, therefore, necessary to utilize generalizations or "general rules" when discussing most topics. The reader must understand that these generalizations are not necessarily true in every state and that certain exceptions may exist.*

2.11 Negligence

—Doyice J. Cotten
SPORT RISK CONSULTING

Almost everyone associated with the wide-ranging fields of sport, recreation, and fitness is somewhat aware that litigation frequently occurs in these fields. In every state, case law is replete with legal actions against sport, recreation, and fitness service providers. Defendants include a diversity of providers including universities, public schools, professional sports teams, recreation departments, state and national parks, vehicle racing providers, ski resorts, country clubs, equine activity providers, adventure outfitters, bowling alleys, personal trainers, and health clubs.

The majority of these lawsuits involves injuries to a participant, and allege negligence on the part of the defendant. **Negligence** is an unintentional tort that causes injury to a person in the form of physical injury, property loss, or reputation. In negligence, there is no intent to cause injury or harm. Negligence may be in the form of an **act of omission** (something one should have done, but did not) or in the form of an **act of commission** (something that one did do, but should not).

Authorities have defined negligence in many ways. *Black's Law Dictionary* offers the following definitions, which help one to better understand the concept:

- Negligence is the failure to use such care as a reasonably prudent and careful person would use under similar circumstances; it is the doing of some act which a person of ordinary prudence would not have done under similar circumstances or failure to do what a person of ordinary prudence would have done under similar circumstances.

- Conduct which falls below the standard established by law for the protection of others against unreasonable risk of harm.

- The term refers only to that legal delinquency which results whenever a man fails to exhibit the care which he ought to exhibit, whether it be slight, ordinary, or great. (p. 1032)

There are four elements of negligence. To prove negligence against the service provider, the plaintiff must show that all four of the elements are present. *If all four of the elements are present, there is negligence–and subsequent liability. If any one of the elements is not met, there is no negligence* and the service provider is not liable. The elements are:

1. **Duty.** The service provider must owe a duty (created by a special relationship between the service provider and the participant) to protect the participant from unreasonable risk of harm.

2. **Breach of Duty.** The service provider must breach its duty to protect the participant from unreasonable risk of harm.

3. **Damage or Injury.** The participant must suffer physical damage to person or property or emotional damage.

4. **Proximate Cause.** The breach of duty must have been the proximate cause (or the reason) the injury occurred.

FUNDAMENTAL CONCEPTS

Duty

The first requirement for liability is that one must have owed the plaintiff a legal duty of care. van der Smissen said that **duty** (as an element of negligence) refers to a responsibility toward others (arising from a relationship between parties) **to protect them from unreasonable risk of injury.** She said "Duty is a particular status or a special relationship to others." (1990, Part A, p. 2–3)

van der Smissen frequently distinguished between the term duty (the first element of negligence) and what she often referred to as **obligations** to parties to whom a duty is owed. These obligations are the means by which one fulfills the duty to protect them from unreasonable risk of injury. In fact, she frequently stated that calling these obligations "duties" (e.g., duty to warn, duty to inspect, duty to supervise) is a misnomer. They should be referred to as obligation to warn, obligation to inspect, and obligation to supervise. She emphasized that there is no duty to inspect, duty to warn, or duty to supervise unless one first has a duty based on a status or special relationship to others.

Courts have traditionally imposed certain obligations (often referred to as duties) on those who have a duty to protect another from unreasonable risk of injury. The particular obligations required in any specific situation vary depending upon such factors as the nature of the activity, the nature of the participants, the nature of the facility, and the location of the activity. Some examples of obligations include:

Obligation to warn	Obligation to inspect facilities and equipment
Obligation to supervise	Obligation to provide a safe environment
Obligation to instruct	Obligation to provide safe vehicles
Obligation to match competitors	Obligation to provide safety equipment
Obligation to hire qualified staff	Obligation to provide first aid & emergency care
Obligation to provide fit staff	Obligation to evaluate for injury or incapacity

For any specific situation, a service provider might have additional obligations not listed here; conversely, many of these obligations might not apply in some situations. For example, a health club might have no obligation to match competitors or to provide safe vehicles, but might have an obligation to screen participants for certain health problems. *It is important to remember that if the provider has no duty to protect participants from unreasonable risk of injury, the provider has no obligations.*

> *To illustrate, suppose Happy Holiday Stables rents a horse to a novice rider for a trail ride. Due to their relationship of equine provider and client, Happy Holiday has the duty to protect the rider from unreasonable risk of injury. To fulfill this duty, the stable has many obligations to the novice rider. Some obligations required to fulfill the provider's duty to protect might include providing a properly trained horse, matching the rider to the appropriate horse, providing proper tack, correctly saddling of the horse, warning the rider of the inherent risks, providing basic instruction if needed, and providing a competent, qualified employee to supervise and lead the ride. If the stable met all of its obligations and the client fell from the horse and broke a leg when the horse was startled by a nearby lightning strike (an inherent risk of a trail ride), Happy Holiday would not be liable because (1) it fulfilled its duty to protect the rider from the unreasonable risk of injury and (2) the stable is not required to protect the rider from the inherent risks of the activity.*

Sources of Duty

There are three sources or origins of *duty as an element of negligence*. They are (1) from a relationship inherent in the situation, (2) from the voluntary assumption of a duty, and (3) from duties mandated by statutes.

Inherent Relationship. A duty arises when one has an inherent relationship with another party. Examples of such relationships include that of a parent and child, a coach and athlete, a health club and its patrons, a school and its students, a scoutmaster and scouts, a bus driver and passengers, and a service provider and its users. The general duty owed is to protect the other from exposure to unreasonable risks that may cause injury; however, the specific duties (or obligations) owed depend upon many factors (van der Smissen, 2007).

For example, a vacationer casually walking down the beach has no *legal* duty to rescue a stranger in the water shouting for help, because there is no special relationship between them. On the other hand, the lifeguard on duty at the time does have a legal duty to do all that he or she can to rescue the drowning party, because of the lifeguard-swimmer relationship.

Voluntary Assumption. There are occasions when one has no duty, but voluntarily assumes such a duty. When one voluntarily assumes a duty, a special relationship is established, bestowing an obligation to perform the act with the appropriate standard of care. For example, if the vacationer walking on the beach, upon hearing the shouts for help from the swimmer in distress, rushes into the water, swims out, and tries to rescue the swimmer, he voluntarily assumes the duty of rescue and an obligation to do all that he or she can to rescue the drowning party.

Voluntary assumption of a duty is often associated with a decision to aid one in need (e.g., a passerby administering CPR, rescuing a swimmer in difficulty, or assisting at an automobile accident). In cases such as these, there might be a moral duty to rescue or assist, but there is generally no legal duty. A few states have very limited "duty to rescue" statutes, but they often carry insignificant penalties and are seldom enforced.

The voluntary assumption of a duty is not limited to one administering emergency care. A parent who volunteers to serve as a little league coach creates a relationship with the team members and assumes the duty to protect them from unreasonable risk of injury. As the coach, he then has the responsibility to act as a reasonable, prudent coach and perform the obligations of such a coach (e.g., to instruct, to supervise, to inspect, to warn, etc.). Other examples of parties who voluntarily assume a duty include persons who volunteer to direct traffic before a game, physicians who volunteer to be the team doctor, teachers who volunteer to sponsor a club, and sport management majors who volunteer time to work with a professional team.

Statutes. Statutes or laws often specify duties of one party to another. If the state legislature passes a statute requiring that an ambulance and a physician be present at every high school football game, an athletic director failing to provide both might be found to be in breach of his statutory duty. West Virginia has a statute that specifies that whitewater guides and ski operators owe their patrons a duty of ordinary care (W.Va.C. 20-38-1 to 8.). Since this duty is a statutory duty, operators may not shield themselves from liability for negligent conduct by using a liability waiver.

Violations of statutes and ordinances are frequently associated with negligence *per se*. **Negligence *per se*** has been described as negligence attached to acts that are deemed negligent without having to prove negligence or investigate the reasonableness of the conduct (van der Smissen, 1990). The act is so opposed to common prudence that it is obvious that no reasonable person would have done it. However, violation of a statute or ordinance does not always constitute negligence *per se*. One must show that a statute was broken, that it was a safety statute, and that the violation of the statute was the actual proximate cause of the injury.

Foreseeability

There are certain situations in which there is no duty to protect the participant, even when a special relationship exists. Since no conduct can be considered to be unreasonable when there is no foreseeable risk, the scope of liability is governed by whether the risk of injury is foreseeable. The question then becomes "what is foreseeable?" Whether something is **foreseeable** "is established by proof that the actor, as a person of ordinary intelligence and circumspection, should reasonably have foreseen that his or her action would imperil others, whether by the event that transpired or some similar occurrence, and regardless of what the actor surmised would happen in regard to the actual event or the manner of causation of injuries" (http://legal-dictionary .thefreedictionary.com). van der Smissen (1990) concludes that when negative results of an act cannot be reasonably anticipated by reasonable people, it cannot be said that the result was foreseeable; hence, there is no duty to protect against it. It is important, then, to understand that one can have a special relationship and owe a duty to protect, but because the risk was unforeseeable, there is no liability for the injury.

Another situation where no proactive action to protect is necessary in spite of a duty created by a special relationship is when there is an "open and obvious" environmental hazard. Since the hazard is open and obvious, it is generally not foreseeable that an individual would ignore the hazard and continue the activity. So, in spite of the special relationship, one generally has no duty to protect (van der Smissen, 2007).

The key to foreseeability is foresight, and the reasonable, prudent professional must be able to anticipate or foresee dangers or risks faced by the participant. *One is not required to be able to foresee the exact nature of the accident or of the injury—one need only foresee that injury is likely.* Of course, reasonable people can disagree as to what is or should have been foreseeable. When this occurs, it is the job of the jury to resolve the question.

Breach of Duty

The second requirement for liability is that the defendant must have breached his duty to the plaintiff. Black (1990) describes breach of duty as "any violation or omission of a legal or moral duty. More particularly, [it is] the neglect or failure to fulfill in a just and proper manner the duties of an office or fiduciary employment" (p. 189).

> *In the Happy Holiday Stables illustration, the business relationship between Happy Holidays and the novice rider imposes the duty to protect the rider from unreasonable risk of injury. Two obligations of the stable include the provision of good tack and proper saddling of the horse. If the novice rider falls and breaks a leg because worn and faulty tack breaks or because the Happy Holiday employee failed to tighten the saddle adequately resulting in a slipping saddle, Happy Holiday could be liable for negligence because the stable failed to meet its obligations and breached its duty to protect the rider from unreasonable risk of injury.*

There are three components used to determine if the duty has been breached. These three components may be addressed by asking three questions: What are the risks of injury? What is reasonable care? Was the risk foreseeable?

What Are the Types of Risk?

The first question asked to determine if there is a breach of duty is "What type of risk caused the injury?" Risk may be placed into three categories. These categories are (1) inherent risks, (2) risks arising from negligent behavior, and (3) risks arising from extreme behavior that goes beyond ordinary negligence. Generally, the service provider has no duty to protect one from the inherent risks of an activity. Providers do, however, have a duty to protect participants from unreasonable risks of injury, which includes risks created by both negligent behavior and extreme behavior.

Inherent Risks. **Inherent risks** are those risks that are integral to the activity; risks that if removed would essentially alter the nature of the sport (van der Smissen, 2007). *The provider of an activity generally has no duty to protect one from the inherent risks of the activity.* Some examples of inherent risks include: a softball player pulling a hamstring while running the bases; a college football player suffering an ACL injury when tackled; a raft striking a rock and capsizing during a whitewater rafting expedition; a hiker in the mountains encountering a dangerous animal; and thunder or lightning spooking one's horse while on a trail ride. These risks are inherent to the activity and cannot be eliminated. In fact, if whitewater rafting were done on a stream with no rocks or rapids, it is no longer "whitewater" rafting and loses much of its excitement and appeal.

Under the doctrine of primary assumption of risk (see Section 2.21, *Defenses Against Negligence* for information regarding primary assumption of risk), a participant generally assumes the inherent risks of the activity. Thus, "[T]here is no liability for injury that occurs due to inherent risks of which the injured participant is knowledgeable or should have been knowledgeable." (van der Smissen, 2007, p. 38) Roxane Harting was distracted by the San Diego Chicken (*Harting v. Dayton Dragons Professional Baseball Club, LLC*, 2007) when she was struck in the head by a foul ball and knocked unconscious during a baseball game. She argued that the mascot was not an inherent risk of a baseball game but the court ruled that it was perfectly reasonable for a spectator at a baseball game to observe mascots, such as the Chicken, during the course of the game.

It is important to note, however, the qualifying phrase " . . . of which the injured participant is knowledgeable or should have been knowledgeable." It is vital that participants understand the inherent risks to which they are exposing themselves, so in the whitewater rafting example above, it is important that the provider adequately warn the participant of the inherent risks of whitewater rafting. Otherwise, the provider may be found liable for injury resulting from inherent risks unknown to the participant. One can inform participants of the risks through (1) oral instructions, (2) detailed risk information in documents such as applications, assumption of risk agreements, or liability waivers, and (3) detailed printed risk information in brochures, handouts, and signs. It is crucial that the information regarding the inherent risks provide the participant with adequate information to know, understand, and appreciate the inherent risks of the activity (van der Smissen, personal communication, 1996).

Ordinary Negligence. Negligent acts fall below the required standard of care and constitute a breach of the duty to protect one from unreasonable risk of injury. The California Supreme Court stated "[A]lthough defendants generally have no legal duty to eliminate (or protect a plaintiff against) risks inherent in the sport itself, it is well established that *defendants generally do have a duty to use due care not to increase the risks to a participant over and above those inherent in the sport*" (*Knight v. Jewett*, 1992, p. 14). When a provider increases the risks by negligent actions, these risks are not assumed by the participant, and the provider can be found liable for any resulting injuries.

van der Smissen (1996) has described **negligence** as "an unintentional breach of duty, an act of omission or commission that exposes the person with whom one has a special relationship to an unreasonable risk of injury, causing damage" (p. 165). Acts of ordinary negligence are illustrated in the following two cases. A girl collided with an unpadded metal pole supporting a basketball backboard and suffered injury. The school district was found negligent because the school increased the risk by allowing students to play basketball around poles that they knew to be dangerous. (*Gill v. Tamalpais Union High School District*, 2008) Sisino, a motorcyclist, was injured when his motorcycle was struck by an all-terrain vehicle (ATV). The court said that by allowing ATVs to use the track at the same time as the motorcyclists, the owners were negligent since they increased the risk of injury beyond those inherent in the sport (*Sisino v. Island Motocross of N.Y., Inc.*, 2007).

Risks Arising from Extreme Behavior. Several types of behaviors involve an extreme breach of duty. These behaviors are most often labeled as **gross negligence, reckless misconduct, and willful and wanton misconduct**, though there is considerable inconsistency in terminology among states. Some states do not recognize gross negligence, failing to distinguish between ordinary and gross negligence. Some use the terms "gross negligence" and "recklessness" synonymously. Some recognize reckless conduct, but not willful and wanton conduct. California defines wanton misconduct, reckless misconduct, and willful and wanton negligence identically (*City of Santa Barbara v. Superior Court*, 2007).

Distinguishing among the types of behavior is important because the type of behavior affects the effectiveness of a number of common defenses. First, in most states, the immunity provided by immunity legislation (e.g., governmental immunity, state tort claims acts, recreational user statutes, Good Samaritan statutes, AED statutes, volunteer statutes, sport safety statutes) applies only to acts of ordinary negligence and does not protect those who have been grossly negligent, reckless, or wanton (See Section 2.21, *Defenses Against Negligence* and Section 2.22 *Immunity*). Second, in most states, liability waivers do not effectively protect against liability resulting from gross negligence or reckless misconduct. Further, waivers do not protect against liability for willful and wanton actions in any state (See Section 2.23, *Waivers and Releases*). Third, exemplary or punitive damages are generally not awarded for injury unless gross negligence, reckless conduct, or willful and wanton actions are involved (see the Damage section later in this section).

Gross Negligence is defined by Black (1990) as the "intentional failure to perform a manifest duty in reckless disregard of the consequences as affecting the life or property of another" (p. 1033). Gross negligence is more than the failure to exercise ordinary care, but is an act of indifference to or a heedless and palpable violation of a legal duty. It differs from ordinary negligence as to the degree of inattention. California courts have defined gross negligence as "a want of even scant care" or "an extreme departure from the ordinary standard of conduct" (*City of Santa Barbara v. Superior Court,* 2007 p. 6), while van der Smissen (1990, Part A p. 51) describes it as "failure to exercise even that care which a careless person would use." Gross negligence is generally thought to fall short of reckless conduct and to differ from ordinary negligence only in degree.

A Utah case (*Milne v. USA Cycling Inc.,* 2007) involving a bicycle race helps to illustrate the distinction between gross negligence and ordinary negligence. One participant was seriously injured and another was killed during a bicycle race when struck by a truck/trailer. The race was an "open-course" race in which racers and regular traffic shared the roadway. Plaintiffs alleged gross negligence on the part of USA Cycling Inc. The defense showed that a sign was used to advise passersby of the event, that motorists were notified of the race, racers were warned orally and in writing of the dangers of the event, and marshals and parking attendants were stationed at the start of the race for purposes of traffic control. The court stated that gross negligence is: (1) a gross deviation from the standard of care of an ordinary person in the given circumstances; (2) failure to observe even slight care; and (3) is a degree of carelessness that shows utter indifference to the possible consequences. The court stated that the defendants were not grossly negligent because there was no evidence that the defendant failed to exercise even slight care or showed utter indifference to the safety of the participants.

Some examples of cases in which gross negligence was ruled illustrate the difference between ordinary negligence and gross negligence. A racecar driver was seriously injured when he was trapped in his burning racecar after a crash. The court found gross negligence because only two firefighters were present, they had not trained together, they were not familiar with the car design, there was no extrication equipment except pry bars, some of the extinguishers were not designed for methanol fires, and it took 8–10 minutes before he was finally rescued by other drivers (*Wolfgang v. Mid-America Sports, Inc.,* 1997). In a Missouri case (*Hatch v. V.P. Fair Foundation, Inc.,* 1999), a bungee jumper was seriously injured at a fair and sued alleging reckless misconduct (Missouri courts do not recognize the concept of gross negligence). The bungee operator arrived late, used an 18-year-old controller when the company policy manual called for age 25 or older, operated the attraction with five workers when the manual called for six, failed to inspect the equipment, failed to conduct a test jump, and failed to attach the bungee cord to the crane. The court ruled that the conduct of the operator was reckless.

Reckless misconduct is defined by Black (1990) as when one "intentionally does an act or fails to do an act which it is his duty to another to do, knowing or having reason to know of facts which would lead a reasonable man to conclude that such conduct creates an unreasonable risk of bodily harm to the other." (p. 1271) The California courts define reckless misconduct (as well as "wanton" and "willful and wanton negligence") as "conduct by a person who may have no intent to cause harm, but who intentionally performs an act so unreasonable and dangerous that he or she knows or should know it is highly probable that harm will result"(*City of Santa Barbara v. Superior Court,* 2007 p. 6). Recklessness and gross negligence are thought by some to be closely related or even synonymous, but reckless misconduct "denotes a greater degree of misconduct, bordering on intent, for the tortfeasor is aware that one's conduct may cause injury to others, yet proceeds to act heedlessly, willfully, and wantonly" (van der Smissen, 1990, Part A p. 52).

Willful and wanton misconduct is defined by Black (1990) as "conduct which is committed with an intentional or reckless disregard for the safety of others or with an intentional disregard of a duty necessary to the safety of another's property."(p. 1600) In Michigan, to prove a willful and wanton misconduct claim, the plaintiff must prove that the defendant "(1) knew of a situation *requiring* [emphasis added] the exercise of due care and diligence to avert an injury to another, (2) had the ability to avoid the resulting harm by ordinary care and diligence in the use of the means at hand, and (3) failed to use such care and diligence to avert the threatened danger, when to the ordinary mind it must be apparent that the result is likely to prove disastrous to another" (*Lamp v. Reynolds,* 2002 p. 4–5). It seems that willful and wanton conduct is somewhat more extreme than recklessness; some even suggest that willful and wanton misconduct is an intentional tort (van der Smissen, 1990).

What Is Reasonable Care?

The second component of breach of duty can only be evaluated after determining "what is reasonable care?" The **standard of care** is determined by the reasonable and prudent person concept, that is, one is required to act as a reasonable and prudent person would act under the circumstances. *One should note, however, that when one is a professional in a field (e.g., sport management, coaching, recreation, athletic training), it is not enough to act as the imaginary reasonable and prudent "person," but one must act as a* **reasonable** *and* **prudent** *"professional" would act under the given circumstances* (van der Smissen, 1990).

A service provider is not required to be an insurer of the safety of its patrons, but to provide reasonably safe premises and conditions for the activity. In a Maine case involving the standard of care required of an athletic trainer, the court held that the defendant trainer "has the duty to conform to the standard of care required of an ordinary, careful trainer." (*Searles v. Trustees of St. Joseph College*, 1997) Likewise, in *Cerny v. Cedar Bluffs Junior/Senior High* (2004), the Nebraska Supreme Court ruled that a football coach returning a football player to play after an injury is held to the standard of conduct of a reasonably prudent person holding a Nebraska teaching certificate with a coaching endorsement.

A Single Standard of Care. Since the required standard of care is that of a reasonable and prudent professional, this means that an inexperienced physical educator, sport manager, or park ranger is held to the same standard of care required of an experienced, reasonable, and prudent physical educator, sport manager, or park ranger. In other words, there is only one standard of care for a given situation. van der Smissen (1990) stresses that "*the standard is not that of a person with the actual qualification of the individual, but of a person competent for the position for which the individual holds oneself to be qualified*" (Part A, p. 43).

Was the Risk Foreseeable?

The third component of breach of duty is to determine "was the risk foreseeable by a reasonable and prudent professional?" As discussed in the Duty section of this section, there is liability only if the risk was foreseeable. The reasonable prudent professional needs only to have foreseen that an injury was likely and need not have been able to foresee the exact nature of the incident or of the injury.

Proximate Cause

The fact that a duty exists and is breached does not necessarily mean that there is liability. The injured party must show that the breach of duty was the cause-in-fact of the injury, that is, the proximate cause. Black (1990) defines **proximate cause** or **cause-in-fact** as "[T]hat particular cause which produces an event and without which the event would not have occurred." (p. 221) In other words, proximate cause refers to an act from which an injury is the natural, direct, uninterrupted consequence.

> *Returning to the Happy Holiday Stables illustration, one of the obligations of the stable is to consider the ability and experience of the rider when assigning a horse. If the stable employee fails to assign a disciplined, easy-to-handle horse to a novice rider, the undisciplined horse is too headstrong for the novice rider to control, and the novice falls from the horse, breaking a leg, Happy Holiday might be liable for negligence. On the other hand, suppose the employee fails to properly match the horse to the rider and the horse bolts when struck by a snake, causing the rider to be thrown, breaking a leg, Happy Holiday would not be liable because the breach of duty had nothing to do with the injury because even a properly matched horse would have bolted under the circumstances. Happy Holiday would not be liable because the breach of duty was not the proximate cause of the injury.*

Southwest Key Program, Inc. v. Gil-Perez (2000), illustrates an instance in which a negligent act was the proximate cause of the injury (see the Supplemental CD). Gil-Perez was injured when employees of the Southwest Key Program allowed the boys to play tackle football without pads, instruction, or supervision. On the other hand, *Rutecki v. CSX Hotels* (2007), is a case in which the negligent act was not determined to be the proximate cause of injury. In *Rutecki*, the resort operator conducted a horseback ride and violated a statute by failing to determine the riding skill of the plaintiff. During the ride, the guide's horse misbehaved and fell, startling the plaintiff's horse and causing the plaintiff to fall. The court ruled that the violation of the statute was not causally related to the injury and ruled for the defendant.

Many states use the **probable consequences rule**, which holds the defendant liable for injuries that are the natural and probable consequences of one's negligent act. A Texas court stated that the elements of proximate cause may be inferred from the circumstances of the event and that the jury should be allowed latitude in determining proximate cause. Other jurisdictions have adopted the **substantial factor test.** Under this theory, the law does not require that a negligent act be the only causal factor, but may be a substantial factor among several factors that caused the injury. In a Kentucky case (*Figure World v. Farley*, 1984), a bar sold alcohol to six minors in violation of a state statute. The boys drank most of the alcohol, went swimming in a pond, and one of the boys drowned. The court ruled that a jury could find that injury was foreseeable and that the sale of the alcohol to the minors was a substantial factor in the death and remanded the case for trial.

Many plaintiffs name **failure to supervise** as the proximate cause of an injury. Most jurisdictions, however, require that supervision must be the actual proximate cause (i.e., show that the injury was a consequence of the lack of supervision and would not have occurred had there been adequate supervision).

On occasion two parties commit two separate negligent acts prior to an injury. It is then the duty of the court to determine which act was the proximate cause. *Cirillo v. City of Milwaukee* (1967), illustrates such a situation. When a teacher left a physical education class of 49 adolescent boys unsupervised shooting baskets, the boys, including the plaintiff, soon began participating in roughhousing and rowdy behavior. After 25 minutes Cirillo was injured, and his parents subsequently sued, alleging negligence on the part of the teacher. Here, both the action of the teacher and the rowdy behavior of the plaintiff were instrumental in causing the injury. The question was, which act constituted the proximate cause of the injury—the failure to supervise which allowed the roughhousing or the intervening act of roughhousing indulged in by the student.

When a negligent act is followed by a second unforeseeable and independent negligent act by another party, the second negligent act can be deemed the proximate cause—thereby intervening and averting liability from the doer of the first negligent act. Such an act is called an **intervening act** or **intervening cause.** The intervening act must be independent of the original act, must be capable in itself of creating the injury, and must not have been foreseeable by the party committing the first act.

Damage

The fourth element of negligence is damage. If there is no damage, then there is no negligence and hence, no compensation. **Damage** is "injury, loss, or deterioration caused by the negligence, design, or accident of one person to another in respect to the latter's person or property" (Black, 1996, p. 389). Although the damage that is compensable varies from state to state, it commonly includes: (1) economic losses; (2) physical pain and suffering; (3) emotional distress; and (4) physical impairment (van der Smissen, 1990).

Economic loss can include medical expenses, lost wages, rehabilitation expenses, custodial care, and much more. The court determines the economic loss based upon actual expenses and projected expenses by expert witnesses. Monetary award for **pain and suffering** is determined by the jury. The amount of such awards depends on many factors, such as the credibility of witnesses; whether the plaintiff's actions are consistent with one in pain; pre-existing injuries; whether the plaintiff can do what he or she could do in everyday life; the plaintiff's pain tolerance; the plaintiff's occupation; whether the plaintiff makes a sympathetic witness; and the skill of the attorney (http://injury-law.freeadvice.com). **Emotional distress** is not always compensable in negligence cases. In states that allow awards for emotional distress, the distress is generally in the form of fright, anxiety, humiliation, and loss of being able to enjoy a normal life. **Physical impairments** may constitute damage and may be considered in lieu of emotional distress. The award may be made for temporary and permanent impairments as well as for partial or total impairments (van der Smissen, 1990).

Damages

Damage and damages are sometimes confused. Where **damage** is the actual element of negligence (injury or loss), **damages** is the monetary compensation sought or awarded as a remedy for a tortious act. There are two major types of damages—compensatory and punitive. **Compensatory damages** is a monetary award intended to compensate the injured party for injury or loss caused by the wrong. These damages are intended to restore the injured party to his or her position prior to the injury. **Punitive** or **exemplary damages** is an award beyond the compensatory damages, generally where the action involved violence, oppression, malice, fraud, or wanton and wicked conduct by the defendant. These damages are intended (1) to punish the wrongdoer for outrageous conduct and (2) to deter such acts in the future.

Punitive or exemplary damages vary greatly from state to state. Some states do not permit them, while others limit the amount of the award. Generally, these awards are made only when the tortfeasors acted from a wrongful motive or knowing indifference for the safety and rights of others. Thus, these awards are generally available when the act was gross negligence (rarely), reckless misconduct, or willful and wanton acts (varying by state), and then, are generally at the discretion of the jury (van der Smissen, 1990).

In *Borne v. Haverhill Golf and Country Club, Inc.* (2003), Borne and eight other women sued the club alleging that the club, a place of public accommodation, discriminated unfairly against them on the basis of their sex. The trial judge instructed the jury that punitive damages could be awarded only if there had been extraordinary misconduct by the defendant–"for malicious, wanton or oppressive conduct done in reckless disregard of the plaintiff's rights or in callous indifference to the plaintiff." (p. 28). After a 22-day trial, the court ruled in favor of the plaintiffs and awarded $1,967,400 in damages, including $1,430,000 in punitive damages. The appellate court affirmed the trial court verdict.

> *Finally, in the Happy Holiday Stables illustration, the novice rider suffered a broken leg due to the fall from the horse. A physical injury such as this constitutes damage and creates the possibility of monetary recovery if a negligent act by the Happy Holidays was the proximate cause of the injury. In the event of negligence, the court can award compensatory damages (e.g., medical expenses, pain and suffering, lost wages in the case of an adult). The plaintiff would not be eligible for punitive damages because the conduct of the stables was ordinary negligence and involved no outrageous conduct. If the injury results from an inherent risk of horseback riding (e.g., horse bolting because of a snake or nearby lightning strike), Happy Holidays would not be liable and there would be no damages awarded.*

SIGNIFICANT CASE

This is a case that illustrates the necessity that all four elements of negligence be present in order to show negligence. Each of the three allegations—negligent supervision, negligent instruction, and negligence in failing to inspect the plaintiff's shoes prior to play—fail because the plaintiff did not provide evidence showing that negligence in any of the three areas was a causative factor in producing the injury.

SANDERS V. KUNA JOINT SCHOOL DISTRICT

Court of Appeals of Idaho
125 Idaho 872; 876 P.2d 154; 1994 Ida. App. LEXIS 77
June 16, 1994, Filed

Opinion: Perry, J.

Josh Sanders appeals from a district court order granting summary judgment in favor of the respondents, Kuna Joint School District and Ron Emry. For the reasons stated below, we affirm the judgment.

FACTS AND PROCEDURE

The underlying facts of this lawsuit are generally agreed upon by all of the parties. On May 15, 1990, Josh Sanders, a student at Kuna High School, attempted to slide into first base during a softball game and broke his ankle. Sanders had been enrolled in a specialized physical education class which provided instruction in weight lifting. On the date of the incident, the instructor, respondent Ron Emry, decided to have the class play softball outside instead of weight lifting. The students were not informed of this decision until after they appeared in the school's weight room. According to Sanders, on that particular day he was wearing a pair of "Saucony Shadows," a shoe designed specifically for running. Once on the softball field, Emry did not give instruction in the game of softball and supervised the game from behind a backstop. During one particular sequence of play, Sanders attempted to slide into first base in order to avoid being tagged out. During the slide, Sanders broke his ankle.

Following proper notice as required by I.C. @@ 6-901 et seq., Sanders filed suit against Emry and the school district as Emry's employer. Sanders claimed that Emry had been negligent by requiring the students to play softball, by failing to adequately supervise the students, including inspecting their footwear, and by failing to properly instruct the students on how to play softball.

After initial discovery was completed, the respondents filed a motion for summary judgment on grounds that, accepting the truth of Sanders' evidence, it did not prove a claim of negligence as a matter of fact. The district court granted the respondents' motion. Sanders now appeals to

this Court, claiming that the district court improperly granted the summary judgment.

ANALYSIS

In this case, Sanders would bear the burden of proof at trial to establish the elements of negligence. In Idaho, a cause of action in negligence requires proof of the following: (1) the existence of a duty, recognized by law, requiring the defendant to conform to a certain standard of conduct; (2) a breach of that duty; (3) a causal connection between the defendant's conduct and the resulting injury; and (4) actual loss or damage. *Black Canyon Racquetball Club, Inc. v. Idaho First Nat'l Bank, N.A.*, 119 Idaho 171, 175–76, 804 P.2d 900, 904–05 (1991).

The respondents contended in their summary judgment motion that Sanders had failed to offer sufficient proof of causation. In order to properly analyze the evidence of causation, we must look separately at the negligent instruction and negligent supervision claims.

As to the negligent instruction claim, we agree with the district court that the record reveals a lack of evidence as to causation. Sanders simply claims that Emry failed to instruct the students in the game of softball and that such a failure caused the injury. Sanders does not, however, offer any evidence as to what the instructions should have been, how such instructions would have prevented the injury, or how Sanders improperly slid. We agree with the conclusion of the district court that a rational jury could not find a causal connection between the failure to instruct and the resulting injury on the evidence presented. Therefore, the district court did not err in granting summary judgment as to Emry's alleged negligent instruction.

With respect to the negligent supervision claim, there are two separate issues we must consider—the actual supervision of the game as it was being played and the failure to inspect the footwear of the students. Again, as with the negligent instruction claim, Sanders' allegation of negligent supervision during the actual game must fail for lack of proof of causation. Sanders alleges that Emry failed to supervise the game and that such a failure caused the injury. Sanders does not offer any evidence, however, as to what the supervision of the game should have entailed, how that supervision was related to sliding or how such supervision would have prevented the injury. The only causal connection offered is the naked inference that if Emry had been standing on the field giving instruction to each student as the class played, this injury would not have occurred. Such an implausible inference does not rise to the level of evidence, however. In short, Sanders has failed to offer sufficient evidence of the causal connection between Emry's alleged negligent supervision and the injury. The district court's conclusion that no reasonable jury, on this evidence, could find a causal connection between the two was correct and, therefore, the summary judgment was properly granted as to this issue.

As to the issue of whether Emry was negligent in failing to inspect Sanders' shoes and should have prevented Sanders from playing in them, there is a mere scintilla of evidence presented. Sanders offered his own deposition testimony that he was playing in shoes that were designed for running. In response to the summary judgment motion, Sanders submitted the affidavit of the owner/manager of an athletic shoe store. The witness states that, "from a safety standpoint I would not recommend the use of the Saucony Shadow Shoe for use as a baseball or softball shoe." No evidence was offered, however, beyond the post hoc inference that because this was a running shoe with a wide sole, it must have caused the injury. Further, there was no evidence how a different shoe would have prevented the injury. Offering the mere coincidence that Sanders was injured and that he was wearing running shoes at the time is not sufficient to establish a causal connection. There must be some evidence that the shoe caused the injury. The evidence offered, the testimony of Sanders and the owner/manager of the shoe store, is not a sufficient basis upon which a jury could base a verdict for Sanders.

Jurors may draw inferences of causation where such inferences are within the common experience of the average person. In this case, however, we do not believe that the common experience of the average person includes knowledge of the properties of specialized running shoes versus other types of footware. Nor do we think the average person possesses knowledge in the mechanics of sliding or injuries from sliding. Without sufficient evidence on the differences in design, purpose, and function of the shoes worn by Sanders and other shoes, no reasonable jury could infer causation under the facts as presented in this case. Likewise, with no evidence as to the actual mechanics of this injury, a jury should not be left to speculate as what might have been the cause. Sanders has simply failed to offer any competent evidence as to the cause of this injury. Alleging temporally coincidental events is not a sufficient basis upon which a jury could find or infer causation. Therefore, the district court did not err by granting the summary judgment.

As an alternative basis for its summary judgment argument, the respondents asserted that Sanders had failed to offer sufficient evidence as to the existence of a duty. Having decided that the summary judgment was proper on the issue of causation, we need not consider this issue here.

CONCLUSION

The respondents in this case properly carried their burden on their motion for summary judgment by showing that Sanders was unable to present sufficient evidence on the causal connection between the alleged negligence and the injury. The burden then shifted to Sanders to show that a genuine issue did exist. Sanders failed to meet this burden and therefore the summary judgment was properly granted.

Costs on this appeal are awarded to respondents; no attorney fees are awarded.

WALTERS, C. J., and LANSING, J., concur.

CASES ON THE SUPPLEMENTAL CD

Craig v. Amateur Softball Association of America, 2008 PA Super 123; 951 A.2d 372; 2008 Pa. Super. LEXIS 1108. The primary issue in this case is whether or not a duty was owed.

Spotlite Skating Rink, Inc. v. Barnes, 988 So. 2d 364; 2008 Miss. LEXIS 322. This case illustrates the need for the plaintiff to show a duty, a breach of duty, and causation. Notice that there is conflicting testimony regarding the facts of the case, so the court must judge who is telling the truth.

Southwest Key Program, Inc. v. Gil-Perez, 2000 Tex. App. LEXIS 7851; 79 S.W.3d 571. The court established that a duty was owed to the plaintiff, that the duty was breached, and that the breach was the proximate cause of injury. Further, they found that the injury was foreseeable.

QUESTIONS YOU SHOULD BE ABLE TO ANSWER

1. What is the difference in duty *as an element of negligence* and duty *as a requirement of actions*?

2. Compare the duty based on an inherent relationship to the duty of a volunteer.

3. What are three reasons why the distinction between ordinary negligence and gross negligence is important?

4. Compare the standard of care owed by a first-year coach, a coach with 10 years of experience, and a coach with 30 years of experience.

5. Explain proximate cause and the effect of an intervening act. Give a clear example.

REFERENCES

Cases

Borne v. Haverhill Golf and Country Club, 2003 Mass App. LEXIS 642.

Cerny v. Cedar Bluff's Junior/Senior Public School, 679 N.W.2d. 198 (Neb. 2004).

Cirillo v. City of Milwaukee, 1967 Wisc. LEXIS 1123.

City of Santa Barbara v. Superior Court, 2007 Cal. LEXIS 7603.

Figure World v. Farley, 680 S.W.2d 33 (Tex. App. 1984).

Gill v. Tamalpais Union High School District, 2008 Cal. App. Unpub. LEXIS 3928.

Harting v. Dayton Dragons Professional Baseball Club, LLC, 2007 Ohio App LEXIS 1956.

Hatch v. V.P. Fair Foundation, Inc., 990 S.W.2d 126 (Mo. App. 1999).

Knight v. Jewett, 3 Cal.4th 296; 834 P.2d 696 (1992).

Lamp v. Reynolds, 2002 Mich. App. LEXIS 123.

Milne v. USA Cycling Inc., 2007 U.S. Dist. LEXIS 42579.

Rutecki v. CSX Hotels, Inc., 2007 U.S. Dist. LEXIS 3181.

Searles v. Trustees of St. Joseph College, 695 A2d. 1206 (Me 1997).

Sisino v. Island Motocross of N.Y., Inc., 2007 WL 1629958 (N.Y. App. Div. June 5, 2007).

Southwest Key Program v. Gil-Perez, 2000 Tex. App. LEXIS 7851; 79 S.W.3d 571.

Wolfgang v. Mid-America Sports, Inc., 1997 U.S. App. LEXIS 8817.

Publications

Black, H. C. (1990). Black's Law Dictionary, (6th Ed.) St. Paul: West Publishing Co.

van der Smissen, B. (1996). Tort Liability and Risk Management. In Parkhouse, B. L. The Management of Sport (2nd Ed.) C.V. Mosby Company: St. Louis.

van der Smissen, B. (1990). Legal Liability and Risk Management for Public and Private Entities. Cincinnati: Anderson Publishing Company.

van der Smissen, B. Elements of Negligence. In Cotten, D. J. and Wolohan. J. T. Law for Recreation and Sport Managers (4th Ed.) Dubuque, Iowa: Kendall/Hunt Publishing Co.

Websites

http://injury-law.freeadvice.com/injury-law/pain_and_suffering_factors.htm

Legislation

W.Va.C. 20-38-1 to 8.

—Doyice J. Cotten
SPORT RISK CONSULTING

Recreation and sport law students often ask, "Why did they sue the school system or the recreation department when it was the teacher or the employee who was negligent?" or "If I am the supervisor, will I be liable if someone in my charge is negligent?" These questions represent just two of the many issues to be considered in answering the question of which parties may be liable when an injury occurs. Where in the past, the party sued was usually the corporate entity or the "deep pocket," today the trend is to sue everyone associated with the incident leading to the injury. For instance, suppose an aerobics instructor at a health club conducts an aerobics class in a room where speakers have been placed very near the participants. A participant loses his or her balance, falls into the speaker, and suffers injury. The participant might well name as individual defendants not only the aerobics instructor, but the manager of the health club, the program director, the person responsible for room setup and maintenance, the owner of the health club, as well as the health club corporate entity.

The question to be addressed in this section is: Who is liable when a negligent act results in an injury? The reader should remember, however, that since the laws regarding liability in such situations differ somewhat from state to state, the discussion will be general in nature. State law in any one state may differ somewhat from these general concepts.

FUNDAMENTAL CONCEPTS

There are three categories of parties that may be liable in any given situation. The first category consists of the **employee** or service personnel involved. This is usually the person who committed the negligent act. This category includes persons who generally have actual contact with the participants (e.g., teacher, coach, weight room attendant, referee, aerobics instructor, scout master). Also included in this category are the maintenance personnel or custodians who are often in direct contact with the participant.

The second category is the **administrative or supervisory personnel**. These are generally individuals who have some sort of administrative or supervisory authority over the service personnel. Examples include a director of recreation and intramurals, city recreation director, a principal, a head coach, a school superintendent, a manager of a health club, or a general manager of a professional baseball club. It is important to remember, however, that the classification of this individual can vary with the act being performed. For instance, the department head would be categorized as service personnel when teaching a class, but as administrative when performing scheduling duties.

The third category is the **corporate entity**. This category includes the governing body of the organization. Examples include the county school board, the municipal recreation board, the university board of regents, the corporation board of directors, or the local health club corporation.

Who Is Liable?

The liability of three categories or groups is addressed here—employees or service personnel, administrative/supervisory personnel, and the corporate entity. In general, both employees and administrative/supervisory personnel are liable for their own negligence. In addition, under the doctrine of *respondeat superior,* the employer or corporate entity is liable for injury to person or property when the injury results from the negligent acts of the employee—so long as the injury occurs while the employee is acting within the scope of his or her authority. While each can be liable under certain circumstances, state immunity statutes (intended to help protect them from liability in certain situations) affect that liability.

Immunity. Sovereign or governmental immunity, still in effect in some states, generally protects the public corporate entity but not its employees. However, officials of public entities are generally immune from liability for discretionary acts performed within the scope of their authority (see Section 2.21, *Defenses Against Negligence* and Section 2.22 *Immunity*) and a few states do provide the employee with immunity from liability for any act as long as it is in performance of the employee's duties and is not willful and wanton (van der Smissen, 1990). In addition, many states have passed limited liability statutes that provide immunity to certain individuals under selected circumstances. These statutes include recreational use statutes (landowners), Good Samaritan statutes (those who come to the aid of the injured), various sport volunteer statutes (volunteer coaches and officials), and assumption of risk statutes for specific activities, for general activities, and for hazardous recreational activities (providers of recreational activities and sports). Most states also have passed laws which allow either for the indemnification of a public employee or for liability insurance coverage of the employee (see Section 2.21, *Defenses Against Negligence* and Section 4.25 *Managing Risk Through Insurance*).

Employees

In the absence of immunity, employees are individually liable for their own negligent conduct. The employee who performed the negligent act is generally the person in close contact with the participant (e.g., a teacher, a lifeguard, a camp counselor, an assistant coach, an athletic trainer, or a maintenance person). If the employee has a duty, breaches that duty by failing to meet the required standard of care, and that breach is the proximate cause of injury to the plaintiff, the employee is negligent and is legally liable. Sometimes employees think they are not liable because they have insurance coverage. Insurance does not prevent or bar liability; however, it may pay the damages in the event of an award.

The aerobics instructor in the example at the beginning of this section would fall into the service personnel category. If the instructor breaches a duty to the aerobics class by allowing participation too close to a hazard (the speaker), and that breach is shown to be the proximate cause of the injury, then the instructor is negligent and can be legally liable for damages.

Administrative/Supervisory Personnel

Whereas the question regarding liability of service personnel is relatively simple, the question of liability of the administrative or supervisory personnel for the negligence of subordinates is much more complex. *When there is no immunity, the general rule is that administrative/supervisory personnel are individually liable for their own negligent conduct, but are not liable for the negligence of subordinates. The administrator/supervisor is liable, however, if the administrator owes a duty and acts (or omissions) of the administrator enhanced the likelihood of injury* (van der Smissen, 1990).

Administrative obligations fall into five categories (van der Smissen, 1990). These obligations are:

1. To employ competent personnel and discharge those unfit;
2. To provide proper supervision and to have a supervisory plan;
3. To direct the services or program in a proper manner;
4. To establish safety rules and regulations and to comply with policy and statutory requirements;
5. To remedy dangerous conditions and defective equipment or to warn users of dangers involved.

In the example involving the aerobics instructor, the health club manager would fall into the administrative/supervisory personnel category. Normally the manager is not liable for the negligence of the aerobics instructor unless the manager did something that enhanced the likelihood of injury. In this case the manager hired a qualified, certified instructor, supervised the program adequately, and the aerobics program was conducted according to standards suggested by a national association. The manager may have breached an administrative/supervisory obligation, however, by failing to establish or enforce safety rules regarding hazards on the floor or minimal clear space requirements or by failing to identify and remedy or warn of dangerous conditions. On the other hand, if the presence of the speaker on the floor was a one-time occurrence and the manager had safety rules regarding hazards and space and regularly enforced them, then the manager would not likely be liable since the manager breached no obligation or duty and did not increase the likelihood of injury.

The administrative or supervisory personnel are, however, liable for human resources or employment torts committed by their employees. They are liable when the administrator or supervisor is negligent in the employment process.

The Corporate Entity

The next question regards the liability of the corporate entity for the negligence of an employee, whether that employee is classified as service personnel or administrative/supervisory personnel. The answer to this question is governed by the **doctrine of *respondeat superior*** (also referred to as **vicarious liability**) which states that *the negligence of an employee is imputed to the corporate entity if the employee was acting within the scope of the employee's responsibility and authority and if the act was not grossly negligent, willful/wanton, and did not involve malfeasance* (van der Smissen, 1990). So, according to this doctrine, if an employee commits ordinary negligence while engaged in the furtherance of the employer's enterprise, the employer as well as the employee can be liable.

In the foregoing example, the aerobics instructor instructing the class was acting within the scope of responsibility and authority and was engaged in the furtherance of the employer's enterprise. If it is shown that allowing activity too near the speakers was ordinary negligence, then not only is the instructor liable, but liability is also imputed to the health club corporate entity.

Ultra Vires Acts. Acts that are beyond the scope of responsibility and authority of the employee are considered ***ultra vires* acts** and, generally, such an act relieves the corporate entity of liability via *respondeat superior*. The city in *Myricks v. Lynnwood Unified School District* (1999) was not liable for an accident transporting a team since the trip was not within the scope of the driver's responsibility. Exceptions to this rule occur when the corporate entity benefited from, had notice of, or condoned the act.

Respondeat Superior* in Human Resources Law.** When employment torts are concerned, the corporate entity is liable for the intentional torts and criminal acts of its employees. Traditionally, under the doctrine of ***respondeat superior, an employer is liable for injuries to the person or property of third persons resulting from actions by an employee that were within the scope of employment, but the employer carried no liability for unauthorized acts by employees including willful acts to injure another. In recent years, however, many jurisdictions have extended the doctrine of *respondeat superior* to include workplace torts (i.e., the wrongdoing of those in positions of authority such as sexual assaults, sexual harassment, and abuse by a party in a position of authority over children) (Carter, 1995; van der Smissen, 1996; *Williams v. Butler,* 1991). The concept of "acting within the scope of authority" continues to apply, but is more broadly interpreted to mean any activities which carry out the objectives of the employer (van der Smissen, 1996) and those during which the employer was or could have been exercising control of the activities of the employee (*Longin v. Kelly,* 1995).

The employer may also be held liable for acts of the employee in cases of **employment process negligence** (i.e., when the employer in the employment process negligently allows the assignment of an unfit employee or fails to use reasonable care to discover the unfitness of an employee). Liability of the employer can result from negligent hiring, negligent supervision, negligent training, negligent retention, and negligent referral of an employee that is unfit (van der Smissen, 1996; Carter, 1995).

Board Members. *Board members are not individually liable for the actions of the board or for the negligence of employees of the organization.* Board members are, however, individually liable for (1) collective acts of the board or individual acts that are outside the scope of authority; (2) breaches of statutory duty or violation of participant/employee Constitutional rights; and (3) intentional torts (e.g., assault and battery, slander, libel) (Kaiser & Robinson, 1999).

Intentional Torts or Willful Acts by an Employee. Many employers believe that they are not the employer is vicariously liable for intentional acts by the employee depends upon whether the action (1) was within the scope of employment (required by or was incidental to employment) or liable for intentional acts committed by their employees. This commonly held belief is not always true. In fact, courts generally look at whether there is social justification for holding the employer liable, rather than at whether the conduct of the employee was intentional or negligent. So whether (2) was reasonably foreseeable by the employer. If either prong of the test is met, the employer can be held liable even if the employee's act was willful or malicious.

Three cases in which an employee assaulted a patron while on duty resulted in rulings in favor of the victim (*Glucksman v. Walters*, 1995; *Rogers v. Fred R. Hiller Company of GA., Inc.*, 1994; *Pelletier v. Bilbiles*, 1967). Each court stated that a master is liable for the willful torts of his servant if the tort was committed within the scope of the servant's employment and in furtherance of his master's business. The *Glucksman* court further stated that the fact that the specific method employed to accomplish the master's orders is not authorized does not relieve the master of liability. One fact that employers should remember is that the court determines what falls "within the scope of employment" and there is little consistency among courts.

Employers, however, can be found liable in some cases even when the employee's action was not within the scope of employment if the employer ratifies the employee's action. Ratification may be either express or implied and can include such factors as failing to investigate the complaint, failing to redress the harm done, and failing to discharge the employee.

So there is no simple rule of thumb that the employer is not liable for intentional or willful acts of an employee. Each case is different and the result will turn on the facts of the particular case.

Volunteers, Trainees, and Interns. The question often arises as to whether the acts of a **volunteer**, a **trainee**, or an **intern** fall under the doctrine of *respondeat superior*. In general, volunteers, trainees, and interns are liable individually for their own negligence. If they were under the control of the corporate entity and were acting within the scope of "employment," authority, and responsibility, the corporate entity is liable under the doctrine of *respondeat superior*. Volunteers of public or nonprofit organizations are immune from liability for their own negligence if they qualify under the federal Volunteer Protection Act of 1997 or a state volunteer immunity statute (see Section 2.21, *Defenses Against Negligence* and Section 2.22, *Immunity*). In those instances, the corporate entity is still liable for the negligence of the volunteer (van der Smissen, 1990; Manley, 1995). It is worth noting that the volunteer, trainee, or intern *is held to the same standard of care as that of an experienced, competent professional.*

University Athletes. An issue that sometimes arises is whether a university is liable under *respondeat superior* for the negligent acts of a university varsity athlete (*Townsend v. The State of California*, 1987; *Hanson v. Kynast*, 1986; *Brown v. Day*, 1990). Courts have ruled the applicability of the doctrine requires an individualized determination of whether a master-servant relationship exists between the tortfeasor and the university (*Townsend v. The State of California*, 1987). The Townsend court concluded that whether on scholarship or not, the athlete is not an employee and the university is not vicariously liable for the athlete's negligent acts.

Joint and Several Liability and Uniform Contribution among Joint Tortfeasors. The **joint and several liability doctrine** holds that one defendant can be held liable for the tot amages even though other defendants were also at fault. If more than one party is found liable, the al d court does not limit the injured party's recovery against each to a proportionate share of fault. A classic example of this can be found in *Walt Disney World Co. v. Wood* (1987) where Disney was found 1 percent at fault, plaintiff was 14 percent at fault, and other defendants were 85 percent at fault. Under joint and several liability, Disney was ordered to pay the entire 86 percent of damages. However, in the 1980s, most states enacted statutes that provide for **uniform contribution among joint tortfeasors** in equitable portions, but not necessarily equal portions. When one tortfeasor has paid a disproportionate share of damages, that tortfeasor can file suit against the other tortfeasor in a separate action.

In *Universal Gym Equipment, Inc. v. Vic Tanny International, Inc.* (1994), the plaintiff was injured while working on a Universal machine. She had signed a waiver that protected Tanny from litigation, so she sued Universal and obtained a settlement of $225,000. Universal then commenced action against Tanny, alleging failure to maintain safe premises and that Tanny had an obligation to indemnify or contribute to any settlement between the injured plaintiff and Universal. Michigan law allowed Tanny to use any defense that would have been valid against liability for the injury to exonerate it from liability for contribution. Thus, the waiver signed by the injured party protected Tanny from liability for contribution to Universal. The court remanded the case to determine if Tanny was grossly negligent—in which case, the waiver would not protect Tanny from liability for the injury, nor from liability for the contribution.

Limiting Corporate Liability by Contract

Corporate entities frequently limit their liability through the use of various types of contractual arrangements. The following are four methods in common use.

Leasing Facilities

The use of sport and recreational facilities by another group or organization is a common practice. The details of these transactions can range from free use by oral agreement to a formal lease with a rental charge. In any case, the question is: What is the liability of the owner of the premises when an injury occurs on the premises while being used by another organization? To determine such liability, one must first determine whether the injury was premise-related (resulting from unsafe premises) or activity-related (resulting from the conduct of the activity) (van der Smissen, 1990). Unless specified in the contract, the owner generally remains liable for premise-related injuries. Second, if the injury is activity-related, one must determine if the owner retained *control* over the activity or the use of the premises. Essentially, the liability for activity-related injury generally lies with the party that had control over the activity. Thus, if a university leases an arena to a promoter of an ice-skating event and retains no control over how the activity is conducted, the university would not be liable for activity-related injuries, but might be liable if the injury resulted from an unsafe facility.

Facility owners generally require that the leasing party provide a certificate of insurance showing adequate liability insurance for the event. Many require that the owners be named as a co-insured on the policy (see Section 2.21, *Defenses Against Negligence* and Section 2.31, *Premises Liability*).

Independent Contractors

An **independent contractor** is an individual or a company that contracts to perform a particular task using his own methods, and is subject to the employer's control only as to end product or final result of his work (Black's Law Dictionary, 1990). Examples of persons that are often classified as independent contractors include referees for a contest, an aerobics specialist at a health club, a team physician, or a diving business that teaches scuba diving for a municipal recreation department.

A major reason that employers use independent contractors is to reduce the amount of liability faced by the service provider. *The general rule is that if an injury results from the negligence of the independent contractor, the liability for negligence is shifted from the employer to the independent contractor* (see Table 2.21.1 in Section 2.21, *Defenses Against Negligence*). Thus, the employer avoids much of the potential liability posed by offering the activity. However, the employer does retain some responsibilities. The employer is responsible (1) for using reasonable care in selecting a competent independent contractor and for inspection after completion; (2) for keeping the premises reasonably safe for invitees and employees; and (3) for "inherently dangerous activities" (e.g., activities presenting substantial harm unless precautions are taken such as fireworks displays, keeping of dangerous animals, ultra hazardous activities).

In *Hatch v. V.P. Fair Foundation, Inc.* (1999), a patron was injured when an independent contractor at a fair failed to attach the bungee cord to the platform prior to the jump. The court ruled that a landowner who hires an independent contractor to perform an "inherently dangerous activity" has a non-delegable duty to take special precautions to prevent injury from the activity. The landowner remains liable for the torts of the contractor even though the landowner was not negligent.

Often, whether one is an employee or an independent contractor is at issue. Courts generally rule that one is an **employee** if one is hired, paid a set wage or salary, is often trained by the employer, works on an ongoing basis, must perform the work as directed by the employer, and is paid by the hour, week, or month. An **independent contractor** is one who is generally engaged for a specific project, usually for a set sum, often paid at the end of the project, may do the job in one's own way, often furnishes one's own equipment, is subject to minimal restrictions, and is responsible only for the satisfactory completion of the job (*Jaeger v. Western Rivers Fly Fisher*, 1994). The distinction is important from a financial standpoint because the classification can affect the amount owed for (1) unemployment contributions, (2) workers' compensation, (3) FICA, and (4) federal and state income tax withholding. The IRS and other relevant agencies can levy heavy fines for failure to pay sufficient taxes or fees when companies have been improperly classified as independent contractors.

Unfortunately, there is no specific number of these conditions that must be met and no magic formula for weighting these conditions to determine if, indeed, one is an independent contractor. A review board or court may determine that failure, to some degree, to meet any one of the conditions is sufficient to invalidate the claim for independent contractor status. The difficulty in determining whether the person is properly classified as an employee or an independent contractor is illustrated in a case dealing with fitness instructors. Fitness Plus provided fitness classes for corporate clients on the premises of the client (*In the Matter of Fitness Plus, Inc.*, 2002). Fitness Plus would assess the needs of the client, contact one of about 30 instructors, negotiate a fee, bill the client, pay the instructor regardless of profit or loss, pay the instructor every two weeks, and report their income on a 1099 form. Most of these procedures fit the conditions for an independent contractor. In selecting the instructors, Fitness Plus conducted interviews, checked background, training, certification, and experience, and usually observed them in a class—seemingly meeting the requirement that they select qualified contractors. Instructors worked generally one to six hours weekly and signed an agreement that their status was that of an independent contractor. The court determined that there was sufficient evidence that Fitness Plus exercised sufficient direction and control over the services of the instructors to support the Unemployment Insurance Appeal Board ruling that they were employees.

Indemnification

An **indemnification agreement** is an agreement by which one party agrees to indemnify, reimburse, or restore a loss of another upon the occurrence of an anticipated loss. They are sometimes referred to as **hold harmless agreements** or **save harmless agreements**. Indemnification agreements can be very effective when one business indemnifies another business against loss; however, they are not always enforceable when used as a waiver of liability in which the user of the service must agree to indemnify the service provider for loss resulting from the negligence of the provider (see also Section 2.21 *Defenses Against Negligence*).

Waivers

The corporate entity may protect itself and its employees from liability by use of waivers of liability in which the participant or service user contractually releases the business from liability for negligence by the corporate entity or its employees (see also Section 2.23 *Waivers and Releases*).

Corporate Liability in Other Situations

Financial Sponsorship

Many organizations provide financial sponsorship for recreational activities or teams. **Financial sponsorship** exists when the sponsoring organization provides financial support, but exercises no control over the activity. An example of this type of sponsorship would be a civic club or private business sponsoring a recreation department softball team. Financial sponsorship of this sort generally carries with it no liability. Whether the sponsoring organization is liable for injuries that occur due to negligence depends upon several things: (1) was the person in charge an agent of the organization?; (2) did the organization have control over the activity?; and (3) was a duty owed to the participant? (van der Smissen, 1990).

In *Wilson v. United States of America* (1993), the issue was whether an agency relationship existed between the Boy Scouts of America and adult volunteers of a troop so as to provide for vicarious liability for the negligence of the adult troop leaders. The court stated that liability based upon *respondeat superior* requires evidence of a master-servant relationship. In this case, there was no liability since the national organization exerts no direct control over the leaders or the activities of individual troops. In an older case, Boy Scouts of America was found liable for the negligence of an adult volunteer at a Scout-o-Rama controlled by the regional council. The key difference was control (*Riker v. Boy Scouts of America*, 1959). In *Fazzinga v. Westchester Track Club* (2008), PepsiCo was named in a negligence suit involving a death in a 5K run. The court ruled that PepsiCo was not liable because it did not supervise or control the event and was a "mere sponsor" of the race. By way of contrast, in *Williams v. City of Albany* (2000) the defendant Capital District Flag Football, Inc. claimed to be only a sponsor of a flag football game in which Williams was injured. The court rejected this contention because the organization organized the league in question, arranged for the use of six fields, provided referees for league play, and acquired insurance for its protection.

Program Sponsorship and Joint Programming

Program sponsorship exists when an organization or entity organizes an event or maintains control over an event. An example would be when a recreation department organizes and conducts a Fourth of July slate of special activities. **Joint programming** is when more than one entity is involved in program sponsorship. Examples of such sponsorship or programming include an NCAA championship event, an event sponsored and conducted by the University of Georgia and the Southeastern Conference, and a high school game under the auspices of the state high school athletic association.

When leagues or athletic associations exert control over the conduct of the game and the eligibility of the participants, a duty is created and liability for negligence emerges. When two organizations are involved in joint programming or joint sponsorship of an activity, each is responsible and liable for injuries resulting from negligence.

Governing Organization Sponsorship

Governing organizations of sports or other activities often sponsor events or lend their name to such events. If the organization has no hand in the actual conduct of the event, it owes no duty to the participants. Of course, there is no liability when there is no duty.

In *Lautieri v. Bai v. USA Triathlon, Inc.* (2003), the liability of a governing organization was at issue. The governing organization was USA Triathlon, Inc. (USAT), the program sponsor was William Fiske d/b/a Fiske Independent Race Management. Fiske was found to be grossly negligent, however, the court held that for USAT to be liable, it must be established that USAT owed a duty of care to the plaintiff. To accomplish this, the plaintiff would have to show that such a duty has a source (1) existing in social values and customs, or that (2) USAT voluntarily, or for consideration, assumed a duty of care to the plaintiff. Evidence indicated that USAT's only involvement was its approval of the application of the organizer of the event. There was no evidence to indicate that USAT was obligated to or was expected to participate in the planning, operation, or supervision of the race.

Joint Ventures

A **joint venture** is "an agreement between two or more persons, ordinarily, but not necessarily limited to a single transaction for the purpose of making a profit" (*Jaeger v. Western Rivers Fly Fisher*, 1994, p. 1224). Some essential elements for classification as a joint venture include: (1) combining of property, money, time, or skill in a common undertaking; (2) joint proprietorship and control over the matter; (3) sharing of profits (but not necessarily of losses); and (4) an express or implied contract showing a joint venture was entered into (*Catalano v. N.W.A. Inc.*, 1998). A group of college students who wanted to go whitewater rafting, put up notices informing other students of the proposed trip, met, planned the trip, shared resources, and went on the trip would form a joint venture. It would not be a joint venture if the campus recreation department conceived the idea of the trip, publicized the proposed trip, helped them plan the trip, and supplied equipment for the trip. In the latter case, the university would be a sponsor of the activity and would be liable in the event of negligence. In a true joint venture, there is no group sponsorship and, hence, no liability for the corporation.

Apparent Authority

Apparent authority is a legal doctrine that describes a situation in which the principal (a person or organization) treats a second party is such as way as to lead a third party to think that the second party is an agent of the principal or has the authority to bind the principal. Under agency law, the principal is responsible for or liable for the acts of a second party that the principal allows to appear to have authority. Those in the recreation and tourism industries, in particular, need to take steps to insure that the relationship between the organization and independent contractors creates no confusion that might cause the client to rely on the appearance of an agency relationship between the principal and the apparent agent.

In a 2004 case (*Cash v. Six Continents Hotels*), two tourists were injured while climbing Dunn's River Falls in Jamaica. While the tour was provided by Harmony Tours (which had a desk in the hotel lobby), the plaintiffs had booked the tour through their hotel. They claimed the hotel was liable for Harmony Tours' negligence under the doctrine of apparent authority since the hotel allowed it to appear that the company was an agent of the hotel. The court found for the hotel since the hotel did not make representations of an affiliation, had a large sign stating "Harmony Tours" near the desk, and included a statement on the ticket informing that the company was an independent contractor and that the hotel was not responsible.

This significant case was chosen because it addresses the duties and liability of several categories of defendants—vicarious liability of the team sponsor of the player who committed the act resulting in injury, the other financial (or team) sponsor, the softball league hosting the tournament, a national softball association that sponsors the league, the owner of the property, and the insurer of some of the defendants. Also included is a discussion of assumption of risk and participant responsibilities.

ALLEN V. DOVER CO-RECREATIONAL SOFTBALL LEAGUE

The Supreme Court of New Hampshire
2002 N.H. LEXIS 145
Opinion Issued: September 30, 2002

duggan, J. * * *

Facts

The plaintiffs allege the following facts. On September 13, 1998, Carol Allen was injured while participating in a recreational softball game when an errantly thrown softball struck her in the head as she ran to first base. The game was part of an adult, co-recreational, slow-pitch softball tournament.

The defendants are all organizations associated with the softball tournament. The teams playing in the tournament were part of defendant Dover Co-Recreational Softball League (league), which is sponsored by defendant Amateur Softball Association, Inc. (ASA). The ASA promulgates rules that govern the play of its member leagues. The teams playing in this particular game were sponsored by defendant Daniel's Sports Bar and Grill (Daniel's) and defendant Thompson Imports (Thompson). Team sponsors provided t-shirts for the players. The game was played on a field owned by defendant Martel-Roberge American Legion Post #47 (American Legion). Defendant Bollinger Fowler Company (Bollinger) provided liability insurance coverage for the league, ASA, the American Legion, the Daniel's team and the Thompson team.

On the day the plaintiff was injured, she was playing for the Daniel's team in a one-pitch tournament. As set forth in ASA official rules, the softball used when women batted was smaller than the softball used when men batted. This use of different balls is intended to allow the women to hit more competitively with the men. The defendants did not recommend, require or provide helmets for players. Although a slow-pitch game under the ASA official rules is played with five men and five women for each team, the game on September 13 was played with seven men and three women on each team.

Facts

When batting for the first time on September 13, Carol Allen hit a ball toward shortstop. A male player for the Thompson team fielded the ball and threw it toward first base. His throw, however, was inaccurate and struck Carol Allen in the head. * * *

Procedural History

The plaintiffs subsequently filed a writ alleging several counts of negligence. First, the plaintiffs allege that **the league** and **Daniel's** acted negligently when they conducted the softball game "without utilizing all reasonable safety precautions including but not limited to recommending, requiring, or providing batting helmets for the players, using less dangerous softballs, and maintaining proper male/female player ratios." The plaintiffs further allege that **ASA** breached its duty to promulgate and enforce rules that required batting helmets to be worn in softball games, use of a less dangerous softball and each team to play with five men and five women, and to otherwise minimize the risk of injury to participants in co-recreational softball games. The plaintiffs also allege that ASA "had a duty to warn, advise, inform and instruct its members regarding the risk of injury to participants in co-recreational softball games and the manner in which such risks could be minimized." As for the **American Legion**, the plaintiffs claim that as the owner of the softball field, it "had a duty to require that softball games played on its field were played pursuant to rules and in a manner which minimized the risk of injury to participants." The plaintiffs further allege that **Thompson** "is vicariously liable for the negligence of its shortstop in errantly throwing the softball." Finally, the plaintiffs allege that because Bollinger provided risk management services to its insureds—the league, ASA, the American Legion, the Daniel's team and the Thompson team—"**Bollinger** had a duty to warn, advise, inform, and instruct its insureds regarding the risk of injury to participants in co-recreational softball games and the manner in which such risks could be minimized." (bold added)

All of the defendants moved to dismiss the case arguing, among other things, that they owed no duty to protect Carol Allen from the inherent risks of injury that arose out of her participation in the softball game. * * *

* * * The court ruled that participants do not owe a duty to other participants to refrain from "injury-causing events which are known, apparent or reasonably foreseeable

consequences of the participation" but rather participants "in recreational sporting events owe a duty to other participants to refrain from reckless or intentional conduct [that may injure the other participants]." Because the plaintiffs alleged that Thompson's shortstop acted negligently, not recklessly or intentionally, when he errantly threw the ball, the court concluded, "Thompson Imports cannot be held vicariously liable under the circumstances of this case."

* * * The court ruled that the league, ASA, Daniel's, and Thompson, as sponsors, and the American Legion, as owner of the field, owed the plaintiffs "a duty to refrain from reckless[ly] or intentional[ly causing injury to a participant]." Rather than acting recklessly or intentionally to create a risk of injury, the court observed that the defendants' alleged conduct involved the ordinary risks of injury inherent in playing recreational softball. * * * Accordingly, the trial court dismissed all counts of the plaintiffs' writ.

On appeal, the plaintiffs argue that the trial court erred by applying the doctrine of assumption of the risk. Applying the doctrine, the plaintiffs contend, was error because under New Hampshire common law, the doctrine was historically applied only to employer-employee relationships and supplanted altogether when the legislature enacted the comparative fault statute. *See* RSA 507:7-d (1997).

* * *

The comparative fault statute does not apply in this case because the defendants do not claim that Carol Allen acted negligently in causing her own injury; rather, they argue that they owed no duty to protect her against the risk that she would be injured by an errantly thrown softball.

ASSUMPTION OF THE RISK

We next determine the applicability of the doctrine of assumption of the risk. The defendants and the plaintiffs disagree on what the term "assumption of the risk" means and how it should be applied in this case. To resolve this issue, we must examine the history and various uses of the term "assumption of the risk."

The term "assumption of the risk" has been used to express distinct common law theories, derived from different sources, which apply when a plaintiff has knowingly exposed herself to particular risks The three distinct legal concepts encompassed by the term are: (1) a plaintiff's consent in exposing herself to a defendant's negligence; (2) a defendant's negligence together with a plaintiff's negligence which causes the plaintiff injury; and (3) a plaintiff's voluntary participation in a reasonable activity with known risks such that a defendant owes no duty to the plaintiff to protect against harm arising from those risks.

* * *

The third theory, the doctrine of primary implied assumption of the risk, applies when a plaintiff voluntarily and reasonably enters into some relation with a defendant, which the plaintiff reasonably knows involves certain obvious risks such that a defendant has no duty to protect the plaintiff against injury caused by those risks. * * * This primary implied assumption of risk doctrine, the defendants argue, applies to this case. The plaintiffs, however, contend that this doctrine applies only where there is an employer-employee relationship.

* * *

When, however, a defendant owes no duty to a plaintiff in light of a particular risk, the defendant cannot be held accountable to a plaintiff who is injured upon the plaintiff's voluntary encounter with that risk. * * * In other words, a defendant who has no duty cannot be negligent. Moreover, contrary to the plaintiffs' contention, the comparative fault statute does not supplant this common-law doctrine because a plaintiff's fault is irrelevant in determining whether a defendant has a duty. It is this third theory that is applicable here.

DEFENDANTS' DUTY

Under this theory, we must determine what duty if any the defendants owed to Carol Allen to protect her against the risk that she would be injured when she participated in the softball game. The defendants argue that they owed no duty to protect her against the risk that she might be injured when a softball struck her head because that was an ordinary risk of playing co-recreational softball, a reasonable activity in which she voluntarily participated. We conclude that when Carol Allen voluntarily played softball—a reasonable activity that she knew involved obvious risks—the defendants had no duty to protect her against injury caused by those risks.

However, even if there is no duty to protect a plaintiff against ordinary risks, we must address the standard of care that co-participants, sponsors, and organizers owe to participants in recreational sports activities when extraordinary risks are alleged. Generally, "persons owe a duty of care only to those who are foreseeably endangered by their conduct and only with respect to those risks or hazards whose likelihood made the conduct unreasonably dangerous."

* * *

"We believe that the negligence standard, properly understood and applied, is suitable for recreational athletic activities because the conduct of a participant, sponsor or organizer is measured against the conduct that a reasonable participant, sponsor or organizer would engage in under the circumstances. *See Lestina v. West Bend Mut. Ins. Co.*, 501 N.W.2d 28, 33 (Wis. 1993); * * * When one creates an unreasonable risk under the circumstances, however, he has breached the standard of care. *Crawn*, 630 A.2d at 373.

To determine the appropriate standard of care to be applied to participants, sponsors and organizers of recreational athletics, we consider: (1) the nature of the sport involved; (2) the type of contest, *i.e.*, amateur, high school, little league, pick-up, etc.; (3) the ages, physical characteristics and skills of the participants; (4) the type of equipment involved; and (5) the rules, customs and practices of the sport, including the types of contact and the level of violence generally accepted. *See Lestina*, at 33. "A defendant may be held liable to the plaintiff for [unreasonably] creating or countenancing risks other than risks inherent in the sport, or for increasing inherent risks, and in any event will be held liable for reckless] or intentional injurious conduct totally outside the range of ordinary activity involved in the sport, but liability should not place unreasonable burdens on the free and vigorous participation in the sport." A defendant, however, may not be held liable for negligent, or even reckless or intentional injurious conduct that is *not* outside the range of ordinary activity involved in the sport.

In this case, we first consider the nature of the sport of softball. The sport of softball is a reasonable activity, commonly played by men, women and children of varying skill levels. Consistent with this wide variety of players, a wide variety of rules are applied. Whether played by men, women or children, skilled or unskilled, participation in a softball game generally gives rise to the risk that a player may be struck by a ball that has been hit by a batter or thrown by a fielder.

* * *

Under the circumstances of this game, the only duty the defendants had was not to act in an unreasonable manner that would increase or create a risk of injury outside the range of risks that flow from participation in an adult co-recreational softball game. The plaintiffs argue the defendants' duty specifically included taking the following actions: (1) participants had a duty to not make errant throws when fielding the ball; (2) the league, Daniel's and Thompson had a duty to utilize all reasonable safety precautions in their conduct of the games; (3) the American Legion and ASA had a duty to promulgate or enforce rules that would minimize the risk of injury; and (4) ASA and Bollinger had a duty to warn, advise, inform and instruct the league regarding the risk of injury to participants and the manner in which such risks could be minimized. We examine each act the plaintiffs contend was required of the defendants in turn.

The plaintiffs first argue that the shortstop had a duty to not make an errant throw when fielding the ball. Participants in an adult co-recreational slow-pitch softball game have a duty to not create an unreasonable risk of injury. When fielding the ball, therefore, a fielder has a duty to not act unreasonably. In other words, the fielder has a duty to not act in a manner outside the range of the ordinary activity involved in playing softball. A fielder, however, does *not* have a duty to make only accurate throws.

Because reasonable fielders commonly make errant throws, being injured by an errant throw is a common risk inherent in and arising out of a softball game. A fielder therefore cannot be held liable for errant throws that reasonably flow from participation. * * * Accordingly, the plaintiffs' claim based upon the shortstop's errant throw does not constitute a legal basis for relief.

The plaintiffs next argue that the league, Daniel's and Thompson had a duty to utilize all reasonable safety precautions in their conduct of the games. * * * Because we assume the facts as pled by the plaintiffs are true, we will assume that Daniel's and Thompson as team sponsors, in fact, conducted the game. To the extent a team sponsor conducts a game, it has a duty to conduct the game in a manner that does not unreasonably increase the risks that flow from the ordinary play of the game. *See Hacking*, 143 N.H. at 553.

The plaintiffs' complaint alleges that the team sponsors had a duty to conduct this game using certain equipment, specifically batting helmets and "less dangerous softballs." While the plaintiffs allege that batting helmets should have been used when conducting this game, they do not allege that batting helmets are ordinarily worn by players in adult co-recreational slow-pitch softball games. The ASA rules the plaintiffs allege applied to this game do not require batting helmets to be worn. Further, the plaintiffs do not allege that reasonable teams use batting helmets when playing in adult co-recreational softball games. They have thus failed to make an allegation that gives rise to a duty for these team sponsors to recommend, require or provide helmets when conducting an adult co-recreational softball game. Thus, under the circumstances of this game, not recommending, requiring or providing batting helmets did not unreasonably increase or create a new risk outside of the range of ordinary activity.

The plaintiffs further allege that the softball manufactured for use when adult men play softball is less dangerous than the softball manufactured for use when children and women play softball. * * * Because the risk that a player may suffer an injury upon being struck by a ball is an ordinary risk incident to playing softball, using the smaller softball manufactured for use by women to allow the women in a co-ed game to hit more competitively with men did not unreasonably increase the ordinary risks inherent in the game. Therefore, the team sponsors' duty to Carol Allen did not include using the least "dangerous" softball available when conducting an adult co-recreational softball game. * * *

Finally, the plaintiffs allege that the defendants had a duty to adhere to a strict five-male to five-female ratio * * *. Being struck by a ball thrown by a male player is an ordinary risk inherent in co-ed softball. The ratio rule did not unreasonably increase or conceal the risk that Carol Allen would be struck by a ball thrown by a male player. * * *

Thus, by not using a strict five-female to five-male ratio the defendants did not unreasonably increase her risk of injury or create a new risk outside the range of risks that ordinarily flow from participation in an adult co-recreational softball game. Therefore the defendants did not owe a duty to Carol Allen to adhere to the five-male to five-female ratio.

* * *

The plaintiffs' writ also alleges that defendants American Legion, as owner of the softball field, and ASA, as sponsor of the league, had a duty to promulgate or enforce rules that would minimize the risk of injury. * * *. The defendants thus have a duty to promulgate or enforce rules that minimize the risk of injury, if without those rules the game is otherwise unreasonably dangerous. While the plaintiffs allege that promulgating and enforcing rules that required batting helmets, a larger, softer softball, or a certain male-female ratio would make the game safer, they do not allege that failing to promulgate and enforce such rules created risks outside the risks ordinarily involved in softball and made the game unreasonably dangerous. Consequently, the plaintiffs' writ does not allege facts that, if true, would show that the defendants breached the duty they owed to Carol Allen to promulgate and enforce rules that were necessary to minimize injury in an otherwise unreasonably dangerous sport. Therefore, it does not allege a basis for legal relief.

Finally, the plaintiffs allege ASA and Bollinger had a duty to warn, advise, inform and instruct the league regarding the risk of injury to participants and the manner in which such risks could be minimized. As we have previously stated, the defendants may not be held liable to the plaintiffs for creating or countenancing those risks inherent in the sport of softball. * * * Thus, the defendants may be held liable if the plaintiffs allege that a reasonable person would customarily warn, advise, inform and instruct the league regarding the risk of injury to participants and the manner in which such risks could be minimized and their failure to do so caused the plaintiff's injuries. The plaintiffs, however, do not allege that reasonable sponsors and insurers customarily warn or instruct leagues regarding the risk of injury to participants. Therefore the defendants, in this case, had no duty to warn and instruct the league regarding the risk of injury.

In sum, the plaintiffs' writ does not allege any facts from which one could reasonably infer that the standard of care required the defendants to recommend, require or provide helmets, use a less dangerous softball or maintain a ratio of five men and five women on each team, and therefore, the writ does not allege sufficient facts that the defendants unreasonably created a new risk outside the ordinary risks or unreasonably increased the inherent risk that Carol Allen would be injured when struck by a softball while participating in an adult co-recreational softball game. * * * Because the plaintiffs' allegations do not constitute a legal basis for relief, the trial court properly dismissed the case.

Affirmed.

BROCK, C. J., and DALIANIS, J., concurred.

CASES ON THE SUPPLEMENTAL CD

Rostai v. Neste Enterprises, 2006 Cal. App. LEXIS 476. In this case, both the club and the independent contractor personal trainer were sued for the alleged negligence of the trainer.

Avenoso v. Mangan, 2006 Conn. Super. LEXIS 489. Under agency theory, the agency (the soccer club) is not liable if the agent (the coach) is not negligent. Why, then, didn't the court rule that the soccer club was not liable?

Eastman v. Yutzy, 2001 Mass. Super. LEXIS 157. Note the number of defendant, their positions in the camp, and what the court says about their duties.

QUESTIONS YOU SHOULD BE ABLE TO ANSWER

1. Under what circumstances is the administrator or supervisor liable for the negligence of employees whom they supervise?

2. When is the corporate entity liable for willful acts by employees?

3. Why is it necessary to determine if a party is an independent contractor or an employee?

4. When an injury results from negligence at an event, who is most likely to be held liable, a financial sponsor, the program sponsor, or a national governing organization? Why?

5. When a teacher is negligent, who is liable, the teacher or the school district? Explain.

REFERENCES

Cases

Cash v. Six Continents Hotels, 2004 U.S. Dist. LEXIS 2901.

Catalano v. N.W.A. Inc., 1998 Minn. Tax. LEXIS 68.

Doe v. Taylor Independent School District, 15 F.3d 443 (Texas 1994).

Glucksman v. Walters, 659 A.2d 1217 (Conn. 1995).

Hanson v. Kynast, 494 N.E.2d 1091 (Ohio 1986).

Hatch v. U.P. Fair Foundation, Inc., 1999 MO. App. LEXIS 315.

In the Matter of Fitness Plus, Inc., 2002 N.Y. App. Div. LEXIS 3830.

Jaeger v. Western Rivers Fly Fisher, 855 F. Supp. 1217 (Utah 1994).

Lautieri v. Bai v. USA Triathlon, Inc., 2003 Mass. Super. LEXIS 290.

Longin v. Kelly, 875 F. Supp. 196 (NY 1995).

Myricks v. Lynnwood Unified School District, 87 Cal. Rptr. 2d 734 (Cal. App. 2 Dist. 1999).

Pelletier v. Bilbiles, 227 A.2d 251 (Conn. 1967).

Riker v. Boy Scouts of America, 183 N.Y.S.2d 484 (1959).

Rogers v. Fred R. Hiller Company of Georgia, Inc., 448 S.E.2d 46 (Ga. 1994).

Townsend v. The State of California, 237 Cal. Rptr. 146 (Cal. 1987).

Universal Gym Equipment, Inc. v. Vic Tanny International, Inc., 526 N.W.2d 5 (Mich. 1994).

Walt Disney World Co. v. Wood, 489 So.2d 61 (1986); 515 So.2d 198 (Fla. 1987).

Williams v. Butler, 577 So.2d 1113 (La. App. 1 Cir. 1991).

Wilson v. United States of America, 989 F.2d 953 (Mo. 1993)

Publications

Carter, P. (1995). Employer's Liability for Assault, Theft, or Similar Intentional Wrong Committed by Employee at Home or Business of Customer, 13 A.L.R.5th 217.

Creason, J. and Dunlap L. Evaluating Employers' Liability for Intentional Torts of Employees. http://www.creasonandaarvig.com/CM/Articles/Articles2.asp

Kaiser, R., & Robinson, K. (1999). Risk Management. In van der Smissen, B., Moiseichik, M., Hartenburg, V., & Twardgik, L. (Eds.). *Management of park and recreation agencies* (pp. 713–741). Ashuba, VA: National Recreation and Parks Association.

Manley, A. (1995). Liability of Charitable Organization Under *Respondeat Superior* Doctrine for Tort of Unpaid Volunteer, 82 *A.L.R.* 3d 1213.

van der Smissen, B. (1990). *Legal liability and risk management for public and private entities.* Cincinnati: Anderson Publishing Co.

van der Smissen, B. (1996). *Legal liability and risk management for public and private entities.* Cincinnati: Anderson Publishing Co. (Prepublication supplement).

2.20 Defenses

2.21 Defenses Against Negligence

—Doyice J. Cotten
SPORT RISK CONSULTING

In today's litigious society, lawsuits against recreation and sport businesses are common. The fact that a recreation or sport business is sued, however, does not necessarily mean that loss of the suit is inevitable. There are many effective defenses that may be used by the defendant. Most common defenses are presented in this and the three subsequent sections (see Section 2.22 *Immunity*, Section 2.23 *Waivers and Releases*, and Section 2.24 *Agreements Related to the Inherent Risks*).

But one should not wait until one is sued to consider defenses! One must plan ahead. Knowing the type of risks one anticipates or which have previously resulted in injury is critical in selecting an appropriate defense. Through effective risk management, potential and existing risks can be identified. Once identified, positioning oneself to ameliorate or transfer liability by allocation of risk can prepare one to defend against the risks.

There are essentially two types of risk—inherent risks and negligence risks. The **inherent risks** are those that are a normal, integral part of the activity—risks that cannot normally be eliminated without changing the nature of the activity itself. Such injuries as an athlete pulling a hamstring while running wind sprints, a person spraining an ankle while hiking over rough terrain, or a football player breaking his collarbone while throwing a block may exemplify the inherent risks of the activity. On the other hand, some injuries result from the **negligence** of the service provider or its employees. The following are some examples where the injury might have been due to negligence: a player injuring a knee when he steps in one of many outfield holes while running for a fly ball; a tumbler injured doing a handspring when no spotter is provided; or a player suffering additional injury when the coach fails to secure proper medical treatment for an injury (see Section 2.11 *Elements of Negligence*).

FUNDAMENTAL CONCEPTS

The allocation of risk to other parties may be accomplished by recreation and sport businesses through the utilization of several defenses. All of these defenses come from one of three sources—common law, contract law, and statutory law. **Common law** is that body of principles and rules of action that derive their authority solely from the prior judgments and decrees of the courts. It is the body of law that develops and derives through judicial decisions—as distinguished from legislative enactments. **Contract law** is that body of law that governs the rules regarding binding agreements between parties. Several means by which risk can be allocated derive from this body of law. **Statutory law** is that body of law that is created by acts of a legislative body. Such law requiring or prohibiting specific acts or actions may apply to individuals, public recreation and sport entities, or private recreation and sport entities—depending upon the intent and wording of the legislation. *The reader is cautioned that there is significant disparity among states and that the defenses discussed in this section do not apply in all states.*

The reader is directed to Table 2.21.1, which outlines the allocation of risk in terms of (1) to whom the risk is allocated, (2) who is eligible for the defense, (3) which risks are allocated, (4) the effect upon the standard of care required, and (5) the impact on the liability of the service provider. To use the table effectively, one must consider the facts of any given situation. By way of illustration, suppose a skateboarder is injured in a skateboard competition. Applying this situation to the table, one of the defenses available to the business conducting the competition would be primary assumption of risk. The risk would be allocated to the player and from the recreation or sports business—assuming the player consented to the activity, participated voluntarily, and understood the risks of the activity. From the table, one can see that this defense could protect the business from liability for the inherent risks of the activity, but does not affect the required standard of care. The business would still be liable for its own ordinary negligence. If the business was negligent, but could show that fault-related conduct by the skateboarder contributed to the injury, then the defense of secondary assumption of risk would apply. Additionally, under comparative-fault statutes, this secondary assumption of risk would ameliorate the financial liability by barring or reducing the negligence award to the skateboarder.

However, suppose the management had required that the skateboarder sign a waiver of liability prior to the event, thus releasing the recreation or sport business from liability for its own negligence. From Table 2.21.1, one can see that if the participant is of majority age, the waiver allocates the risk of ordinary negligence from the business to the participant skateboarder.

Defenses Based on Common Law

Elements of Ordinary Negligence Not Proven

Perhaps the best defense against a claim of negligence is that one or more of the elements required for negligence is not present. As discussed in Section 2.11 *Negligence*, to be liable, one must have a legal duty to the plaintiff, must breach that duty, and the breach of duty must be the proximate cause of an injury to the plaintiff. If one of these elements is missing (duty, breach, proximate cause, or injury), then no other defense is necessary—no negligence, no liability.

Primary Assumption of Risk

Primary assumption of risk is a legal theory by which a plaintiff may not recover for an injury received when the plaintiff voluntarily exposed himself or herself to a known and appreciated danger. Primary assumption of risk involves the assumption of well-known risks that are inherent to the activity. In other words, when one knows the inherent dangers involved and voluntarily participates, one assumes those risks inherent in the activity (but not risks of negligence) and the service provider is not liable for injuries resulting from those inherent risks. In *Daigle v. West Mountain* (2001), the court held that while participants assume those risks that are known, apparent or reasonably foreseeable, they do not assume risks that are unique and result in a dangerous condition over and above the usual dangers inherent in the activity.

Primary assumption of risk is presumed when an individual has voluntarily participated in an activity that involves inherent or well-known risks. One is held to have consented, by virtue of one's voluntary participation, to those injury-causing events that are known and reasonably foreseeable (*Truett v. Fell*). Primary assumption of risk acts as a defense, in that it relieves the defendant of a duty that might otherwise be owed to the plaintiff. The organizer of an event has a duty to produce a reasonably safe event and is required to use ordinary care not to increase the risk beyond what is inherent in the activity.[1] For example, if a man attends a YMCA, knows and appreciates the risks involved in weight lifting, chooses to lift weights, and injures his back, the YMCA has no duty and bears no responsibility, absent negligence on its part, because of primary assumption of risk (or more specifically, implied assumption of risk—see following page).

The doctrine of primary assumption of risk embodies the legal conclusion that the defendant has "no duty" to protect the plaintiff from a particular risk. In sport-related cases, however, the issue of whether a duty is owed depends upon (1) the nature of the activity or sport involved, and (2) the relationship of the defendant and the plaintiff to that activity or sport (*Knight v. Jewett*, 1992). The service provider generally has no duty to protect

---

[1]However, a California court (*Saffro v. Elite Racing, Inc.*, 2002) held that the organizer of a marathon has a duty to "take reasonable steps to minimize the risks without altering the nature of the sport, including the provision of sufficient water and electrolyte replacement drinks" (at 1.)

Table 2.21.1 Allocation of Risk[1,2]

Authority and Defenses	To Whom Risk is Allocated	Eligibility for Defense	Which Risks Are Allocated	Effect on Standard of CareProvider	Impact on Liability of Provider
COMMON LAW					
Elements of Ordinary Negligence Not Proven	participant	any service provider	injuries not due to provider negligence	none	provider not liable
Primary Assumption of Risk	participant	consent/voluntary; inherent risks; know, understand, & appreciate risks	inherent risks	none	provider not liable for inherent risks
Secondary Assumption of Risk	participant	fault-related conduct; understands dangers; usually age 6 or older	participant fault that enhances chance of injury	none	bars or reduces award
Sovereign & Gov't. Immunity (See Statutory Codification below)	participant	public entity only	all risks related to governmental function	reduces duty to wilful/wanton	bars provider from liability for ordinary or gross negligence.
Ultra Vires Acts	employee	action outside scope of responsibility or authority	ordinary negligence	none	liability shifts from employer to employee alone
CONTRACT LAW					
Waivers	participant	participant of majority age	ordinary negligence	reduces duty to gross negligence	not liable for ordinary negligence
Inherent Risk Agreements					
Informed Consent (ADA, rehab, research, fitness regimen, therapy)	participant or subject	adequately informed of treatment risk; majority age or parental signature	treatment risks	none	stronger primary & secondary assumption of risk defenses
Agreement to Participate (Including Assumption of Risk Agreement)	participant	adequately informed of activity risks and behavioral expectations	inherent risks	none	stronger primary & secondary assumption of risk defenses
Facility Lease Agreements	lessee	authorization for lease by corporate entity; lessee of majority age	activity risks to lessee; facility risks to lessee & lessor	none	not liable for activity risks; lessee & provider share facility risk as per contract
Equipment Rental Agreements	user (renter)	user of majority age	inherent risks; risks from equipment misuse or user misconduct; provider retains risk of equipment failure; may include a waiver	none	not liable for inherent risks or risks from misuse or misconduct
Indemnity Agreements	indemnitor	appropriate relationship	financial loss of indemnitee	none	indemnitee losses pass to indemnitor
Independent Contract for Services	independent contractors	authorization of entity; check contractor credentials	all risks of provider except for "inherently dangerous" activities	none	all liability transfers to indep. contractor (except "inherently dangerous" activities)

[1]Table was adapted with the permission and assistance of Dr. Betty van der Smissen from a chart on allocation of risk in a handout entitled "How to Defend Yourself and Your Program," SSLASPA, 1997.

[2]The reader is cautioned that a table is simply an outline of the subject, and that it is impossible to include all elements of the subject or all exceptions. This table is meant as an overview of Allocation of Risk and the reader is directed to this section as well as Section 2.22 *Immunity*, Section 2.23 *Waivers and Releases*, and Section 2.24 *Inherent Risk-Related Defenses* for more detail regarding the subject.

Table 2.21.1 Allocation of Risk[1,2] (continued)

Authority and Defenses	To Whom Risk is Allocated	Eligibility for Defense	Which Risks Are Allocated	Effect on Standard of CareProvider	Impact on Liability of Provider
STATUTORY LAW					
Comparative Fault	shared with participant based on % fault	fault-related conduct; participant usually age 6 or older; all providers eligible	risk shared for damages allocation based on % of fault	none	reduces damages by % participant at fault
Legislation-Based Immunity Charitable Immunity	participant	charitable, educational, and religious organizations	ordinary negligence	reduces duty to gross negligence	not liable for ordinary negligence
Tort Claims Acts	participant	public entities qualified by specific state statutes	discretionary acts; negligence except dangerous physical conditions usually	reduced to w/w; retain duty for dangerous physical conditions	provider liable for dangerous physical conditions and for wilful/wanton acts
Recreational User Immunity	user	owners of natural, undeveloped area; no fee for use of land; specified by state statute	open & obvious premise risks & all activity risks; retain ultra hazardous environmental risks	only duty: to warn of ultra-hazardous & of known, hidden hazards	no liability except for ultra-hazardous; retains liability for wilful/ malicious (sometimes gross)
Volunteer Immunity (State)	participant	charitable & educational organization volunteers; safety training in some states	ordinary negligence in most states	volunteer to gross negligence	no effect on liability of provider
Federal Volunteer Protection Act	participant	volunteers of public and non-profit organizations within scope of responsibility who hold appropriate certifications	ordinary negligence	volunteer to gross negligence	no effect on liability of provider
Good Samaritan (First Aid) Immunity	injured party	In good faith; gratuitous	usually ordinary negligence	caregiver to gross negligence	not available to provider
Good Samaritan (AED) Immunity	injured party	in good faith, gratuitous aid; training in some states	usually ordinary negligence	caregiver to gross negligence	immunity in many states
Rec & Sport Provider Immunity Specific Activity Statutes (Equine, Ski, skating, & other specified activities)	inherent to participant, sometimes negligence	usually all providers & participants in specified activities	inherent activity risk to participant; provider retains operational, facility & premise risks	participant assumes inherent risks; sometimes reduces to gross	not liable for inherent activity-related risks; sometimes not liable for negligence
General Rec & Sport Statutes Applies to numerous sports & activities in one statute)	inherent to participant	all providers & participants in specified activities	inherent activity risk to participant; provider retains operational, facility & premise risks	none; participant assumes inherent risks	not liable for inherent activity-related risks; liable for negligence
Hazardous Recreational Activity (Applies to numerous activites in one statute)	participant	public entities & employees w/o fee for activity	inherent activity risks & secondary assumption of risk to participant; provider must warn of dangerous conditions and maintain premises	reduces activity duty to gross; no effect on duty to warn, construct/maintain facility/equipment	not liable for inherent risk or activity-related negligence; liable for operational, facility, & premise risks & failure to warn
Procedural Noncompliance Statute of Limitations	participant	all providers	all risks	none	limits the time during which suit can be filed
Notice of Claim (Tort Claims Act)	participant	only public entities	all risks	none	limits time during which notice of intent to sue must be given

the client against the inherent risks of the sport; however, sometimes the relationship between provider and client creates a *duty to not increase the risks* inherent in the activity. For instance, in *El-Halees v. Chaucer* (2002), the court found Chaucer liable for injury to a six-year-old client due to a fall from a gymnastic apparatus because Chaucer left the child unattended on the uneven parallel bars, thereby violating the duty to not increase the risk of injury.

Courts have ruled that three elements must exist for a successful primary assumption of risk defense. They are: (1) the risk must be inherent to the sport; (2) the participant must voluntarily consent to be exposed to the risk; and (3) the participant must know, understand, and appreciate the inherent risks of the activity. However, this varies somewhat from state to state (e.g., under Missouri law, a skier assumes the inherent risks of or incidental to skiing, regardless of his or her subjective knowledge of those risks [*Bennett v. Hidden Valley Golf and Ski, Inc.*, 2003]).

It is important that the recreation or sport manager understand that the participant assumes only the risks that are **inherent** to the sport or activity. Examples of inherent risks might include falling while skiing, falling from a horse while horseback riding, or pulling a muscle while putting the shot. The participant does not normally assume risks incurred as a result of the negligence of the service provider. Examples of negligence risks might include being struck by a bat with an untaped handle when it slipped from the batter's hand during a swing; being struck in the face by an elbow in an excessively rough basketball game when the officials failed to control the game; or a football player suffering a facial injury when supplied with a helmet with no face guard.

A person who is playing recreation league softball, a person in a pickup basketball game, or a person on the varsity football team is participating by choice and thus meets the second requirement for primary assumption of risk—**voluntary consent.** Voluntary consent is sometimes at issue in cases regarding injuries in required physical education classes. If the plaintiff is a student in a required class where gymnastics is a required activity and is injured performing a mandatory back handspring, the voluntary consent requirement would be difficult to meet. On the other hand, if the student elected from among several choices to take weight training to meet the physical education requirement, there might be a degree of voluntary participation.

Thirdly, one cannot assume a risk of which one has no **knowledge, understanding, or appreciation**. Courts have ruled that one must not only know of the facts creating the danger, but also must comprehend and appreciate the nature of the danger to be confronted. Whether one is held to know, understand, and appreciate the risks usually depends upon the age of the plaintiff, experience of the plaintiff, and opportunity of the plaintiff to become aware of the risks. Courts have held that it is not necessary that the injured plaintiff foresee the exact manner in which his or her injury occurred (*Tremblay v. West Experience Inc.*, 2002). In some jurisdictions, however, knowledge and appreciation are measured by an objective test, and can be determined by law when "any person of normal intelligence in [the plaintiff's] position must have understood the danger" (*Leakas v. Columbia Country Club*, 1993).

One way to strengthen the primary assumption of risk defense is to ensure that participants know, understand, and appreciate the risks of the activity. An effective way to accomplish this is through the use of participant agreements (see Section 2.23 *Waivers and Releases*), informed consent agreements, and agreements to participate (see Section 2.24 *Agreements Related to Inherent Risks*). Use of these documents provides documentation that the participant was aware of the risks.

Implied Primary Assumption of Risk and Express Assumption of Risk

There are two types of primary assumption of risk—implied primary assumption of risk and express assumption of risk. **Implied primary assumption of risk** is that form of primary assumption of risk where it is evident by the conduct or actions (i.e., participation) of the individual that the participant has voluntarily taken part in an activity that involves inherent or well-known risks. The participant has signed no document by which he or she assumes the risk.

Express assumption of risk is that form of primary assumption of risk in which the participant sets forth in words (either verbally or in writing) that he or she assumes the **inherent risks** of the activity.[2] Participant agreements (see Section 2.23), informed consent agreements, and agreements to participate (see Section 2.24) are instruments that can be used to obtain this type of assumption of risk. In these agreements, the participant explicitly agrees to assume the *inherent risks* (or the **treatment risks**) of the activity. Understanding of the concept of express assumption of risk, however, is complicated by the fact that courts vary as to its definition.

Secondary Assumption of Risk

Secondary assumption of risk (formerly called contributory negligence and contributory fault) involves the voluntary choice or conduct of the participant to encounter a known or obvious risk created by the negligent conduct of the service provider, or to fail to follow rules or heed warnings set down by the provider (*Riddle v. Universal Sport Camp*, 1990). The following are three types of situations where secondary assumption of risk may occur. In the first, the participant voluntarily participates when there is a substantial risk that the defendant will act in a negligent manner (e.g., going up in a plane with someone who has a reputation for wild or careless acts). The second is when the service provider has already been negligent and the participant takes part anyway (e.g., playing softball in an outfield that has obvious rocks and holes scattered about). The third is when the participant fails to follow rules or heed warnings. In each case, the conduct of the participant (electing to participate) falls below the standard to which one is required to conform for one's own protection.

Sovereign and Governmental Immunity

Sovereign and governmental immunity are judicial doctrines that prevent one from filing suit against the government and its political subdivisions without their consent (see Section 2.22 *Immunity*).

Ultra Vires Act

A defense that can be very helpful to the corporate entity is the defense that the act by the employee was an *ultra vires* act—one that is not within the authority or scope of responsibility of the employee. Normally under the doctrine of *respondeat superior*, the employer is liable for the negligent acts of the employee (see Section 2.12 *Which Parties Are Liable?*). A major exception to this rule, however, is when the employee had no authority or responsibility to perform the act in question. In such a case, only the employee is liable for the negligent act. If a coach injured a youngster while administering corporal punishment when the school had a strict rule prohibiting corporal punishment, the act would be outside the authority of the coach and the school system would probably escape liability. The coach would still be liable for the act. Note, however, that if the school is aware of the fact that the coach uses corporal punishment and has failed to act upon this knowledge, the school will also be liable for the action. In essence, by not taking action in knowing of the coach's behavior, the school is in fact condoning the act.

Defenses Based on Contract Law

Waivers

A **waiver** is a contract in which the participant or user of a service agrees to relinquish the right to pursue legal action against the service provider in the event that *negligence* of the provider results in an injury to the participant (see Section 2.23 *Waivers and Releases*).

Informed Consent

An informed consent agreement is a formal contract or agreement document used to protect the provider from liability for the informed treatment risks of a treatment or program to which the signer is subjected. The agreement is designed to provide full disclosure to the individual regarding both the known risks and the anticipated outcome or benefits of the treatment, thereby enabling the participant to make an informed decision regarding acceptance of the treatment. *By signing the agreement, the signer is agreeing to assume the treatment*

---

[2]In some jurisdictions, express assumption of risk refers specifically to contractual agreements (i.e., waivers of liability) in which the participant releases the provider from liability for negligence.

risks of which he or she is informed. The signer is not agreeing to relieve the entity from liability for injury resulting from negligent acts of the entity or its employees (see Section 2.24 Agreements Related to the Inherent Risks).

Agreement to Participate

The **agreement to participate** is a document which helps to inform participants in recreation, sport, or educational activities of (1) the nature of the activity, (2) the risks to be encountered through participation in the activity, and (3) the behaviors expected of the participant. It is designed to help protect the provider from liability for injuries resulting from the inherent risks of the activity, but is informative rather than contractual in nature. The **assumption of risk agreement** is a statement whereby the signer (1) explicitly asserts that the signer knows the nature of the activity, understands the physical and skill demands of the activity, and appreciates the types of injuries that may result from participation; (2) asserts that participation is voluntary; and (3) agrees to assume those risks that are inherent to the activity. *It is essentially the same as the agreement to participate, but in a different format* (see Section 2.24 Agreements Related to the Inherent Risks.)

Facility Leases Agreements

Owners of facilities often permit groups or other businesses to make use of their facilities. A recreational softball team might sign up for a field and conduct a team practice, a facility owner might lease an arena to a promoter for a concert, or a facility owner might lease the entire facility or a part of the facility for a matter of months or years (a university might lease its dressing facilities and practice fields to a professional football team for several months for preseason practice). When an injury occurs at the facility, it is not unlikely that the facility owner will be named as a defendant in a lawsuit regarding the injury. A defense against such litigation may be provided to owners of property/lessors by virtue of their status as lessors or by contractual provisions.

To determine the extent of the liability of the facility owner, one must determine if the injury was **activity-related** or **premise-related**. Generally, injuries that are activity-related are the responsibility of the lessee. When injuries are premise-related, liability may rest on both the entity conducting the activity and the facility owner. Generally, the facility owner is responsible for structural-type problems and the entity conducting the activity is often responsible for maintenance-type problems. In the instance of the softball team using the field, the facility owner would retain liability. In the case of the football team leasing the facility for preseason practice, the responsibility would probably be shared by lessor and lessee depending on the nature of the hazard unless the lease contract includes provisions that assign sole responsibility for certain types of hazards to the lessee football team (see Section 2.31 *Premises Liability*).

Equipment Rental Agreements

When individuals rent equipment, rental agreements are often used to help protect the rentor. Rental agreements often include a waiver of liability signed by the renter (user) of the equipment as well as an indemnification agreement. By using the waiver in the rental agreement, the provider is passing the liability for a negligence-related injury on to the renter. An indemnification agreement is usually included to have the renter promise to repay the provider for loss due to litigation resulting from accidents to the renter or to a third party (see the next section).

Rental agreements also function much like an agreement to participate (see also Section 2.24 *Agreements Related to Inherent Risks*) in that they can inform the renter of behavior expected and his responsibility for third-party injuries, and gain affirmation that the renter is knowledgeable regarding the use of the equipment. The provider then passes along much of the responsibility for injury to the renter and enhances the position of the provider when comparative negligence is determined. The provider, however, retains liability for injury relating to defective equipment.

Indemnification Agreements

An **indemnification agreement** is an agreement by which one party agrees to indemnify or reimburse another upon the occurrence of an anticipated loss. The agreement creates a contractual right under which the loss is generally shifted from a tortfeasor who is passively at fault to one that is actively responsible. Indemnification agreements are commonly included in facility leases to protect the property owner from loss resulting from litigation by the lessee or by a patron naming the owner as a defendant. For instance, a municipality leasing an arena to a wrestling promoter for an event would generally include within the lease a provision by which the promoter agrees to indemnify or reimburse the municipality for any loss resulting from the event. Then, if an injury occurs to a spectator and the municipality is named as a codefendant, the promoter is responsible for the municipality's legal fees, any award, and any other related expenses. In *Auburn School District No. 408 v. King County* (1999), the school district agreed to indemnify the county for loss due to the district's use of the county swimming pool. A student injured in the pool sued both the county and the school district. The school district was ordered to reimburse the county for its financial loss. This defense is summarized in Table 2.21.1.

The law regarding the enforcement of indemnification agreements is more exacting in some states than in others. For instance, in Georgia the public policy is reluctant to cast the burden for negligent actions upon one who is not actually at fault. Unless a contract for indemnification explicitly and expressly states that the negligence of the indemnitee is covered, courts will not enforce the contract against the indemnitor. In *Pride Park Atlanta v. City of Atlanta* (2000), the agreement was not enforced because the agreement said ". . . agrees to protect and hold harmless . . . from any and all claims . . ." and did not explicitly refer to negligence by the indemnitee.

While most indemnity agreements involve two corporate entities, some involve a corporate entity and an individual. Some courts have held that indemnification agreements used with consumers and intended to perform much like a waiver are not enforceable, but indemnification law varies from state to state. A rafting company (*Madsen v. Wyoming River Trips, Inc.*, 1999) required that a father agree to indemnify the company on behalf of himself and his family. When the wife was injured due to negligence of the rafting company, the Wyoming court refused to enforce the agreement stating that such contracts are enforced when the indemnitor is assuming liability for an act that was no fault of the indemnitee. The court ruled that the agreement, which sought to hold an innocent party liable for the negligence of the indemnitee, was void as against public policy.

In *Yang v. Voyagaire Houseboats, Inc.* (2005), Voyagaire had rented a houseboat to Yang and required that Yang sign an indemnity agreement. After six members of Yang's party suffered injury from carbon monoxide poisoning, Yang and others filed suit against Voyagaire; however, Voyagaire claimed protection by the waiver and indemnity agreement signed by Yang. The Supreme Court of Minnesota ruled that the waiver and indemnity agreement were against public policy since Voyagaire was, in effect, a resort providing a public service by furnishing sleeping accommodations to the public. It also stated that the indemnity clauses were unenforceable because they do not contain language that (1) specifically refers to negligence, (2) expressly states that the renter will indemnify Voyagaire for Voyagaire's negligence, or (3) clearly indicates that the renter will indemnify Voyagaire for negligence occurring before the renter took possession of the houseboat. This ruling suggests that parties relying on indemnity agreements take care to clearly state the intent of the clause.

On the other hand, courts in some states have upheld such agreements (*Beaver v. Foamcraft, Inc.*, 2002). In a 2005 Wisconsin case, a man was injured during a tractor-pull contest after signing a waiver and indemnification agreement. The waiver protected against the plaintiff's claims, but did not protect against a loss of consortium claim by the wife. The indemnity language within the document stated clearly and without ambiguity that the plaintiff agreed to indemnify the provider for all claims–thus the indemnity agreement protected the provider from the loss of consortium claim (*Walsh v. Luedtke*, 2005).

In several cases, corporate entities (in an effort to bypass the law in some states that disallows liability waivers signed by parents on behalf of minors) have attempted to gain liability protection by having parents sign indemnity agreements in order for the child to be able to participate in an activity. Some courts have said that such agreements are enforceable because they involve a contract between two adults (*Eastman v. Yutzy*, 2001).

Other courts have ruled such an agreement invalid as against public policy, since it is inconsistent with the parent's duty to the child (*Hawkins v. Peart*, 2001; *Cooper v. The Aspen Skiing Company*, 2002).

Independent Contract for Services

An independent contract for services involves an agreement between the corporate entity and an individual or companies that contract to perform a service for the corporate entity (see Section 2.12 *Which Parties Are Liable?*). When one contracts with an independent contractor, the corporate entity generally avoids liability for injuries resulting from the negligence of the independent contractor. However, the employer retains the responsibility: (1) to use reasonable care in selecting a competent independent contractor and to inspect after completion of the project; (2) to keep the premises reasonably safe for invitees and employees; and (3) for "inherently dangerous activities" (e.g., fireworks displays, keeping of dangerous animals, and ultra-hazardous activities) (see Section 2.12 *Which Parties Are Liable?*).

Defenses Based On Statutory Law

Comparative Fault

Comparative fault is not a true defense against liability for negligence. More precisely, it is a method for apportioning damages awarded based on the fault or blame or the relative degree of responsibility for the injury. Comparative fault is based on the fact that both plaintiff and defendant are at fault. The jury compares the fault of each party and generally allocates the fault by percentage.[3] Comparative fault was enacted to ameliorate the harsh effect of contributory negligence where, if the plaintiff contributes at all, regardless of the extent, the plaintiff receives no award. **Pure comparative fault** has been adopted by a number of states. In this form, the award to the plaintiff is reduced by the percentage of fault assigned to the plaintiff. For example, suppose the award is $100,000 and the fault is apportioned 75 percent to the plaintiff and 25 percent to the defendant. Since the plaintiff is 75 percent to blame, the plaintiff's award would be reduced by 75 percent and the plaintiff would receive $25,000. **Modified comparative fault** operates on the theory that the plaintiff is not entitled to recovery if the plaintiff is substantially at fault. State statutes vary, but, in essence, if the fault of the plaintiff is 50 percent or more, the plaintiff is barred from recovery and receives no award. When the fault exceeds these limits, modified comparative fault has the same effect as contributory negligence or fault—acting as a complete bar to recovery.

Legislation-based Immunity

There are several forms of legislation-based immunity that affect recreation and sport managers as well as the business entity. **Charitable immunity** is a doctrine that relieves or immunizes charitable organizations from liability for tort. **Federal** and **state tort claims acts** rescinded sovereign/governmental immunity and enumerated the areas or acts for which immunity was retained. **Recreational user immunity** was passed to protect certain landowners who gratuitously allow others to use their property for recreational purposes. **Volunteer immunity** was enacted to aid in the recruitment of volunteers for public, charitable, and nonprofit entities. **Good Samaritan statutes** protect those utilizing AEDs and rendering aid to victims in cases of medical emergency. **Shared responsibility and statutory assumption of risk statutes** are intended to help protect providers

---

[3] **Contributory fault** (formerly called contributory negligence) exists when the conduct of the plaintiff in any way helps to cause or aggravate the plaintiff's injury. In the past, this was a major defense against negligence claims because in states adhering to the contributory fault doctrine, any contributory fault by the plaintiff, regardless of how slight, served as a complete bar to recovery. Now, however, only four states (Alabama, Maryland, North Carolina, and Virginia) and the District of Columbia hold to this doctrine. In **comparative fault** states, contributory fault serves to reduce the award to the plaintiff by the proportion of fault allotted to the plaintiff. Even under the comparative fault theory, however, most states bar recovery if the fault of the plaintiff is 50 percent or greater.

Regarding age, the general rule has been that children over the age of fourteen are capable of negligence and children under seven are incapable of negligence. Those between seven and fourteen are judged capable of negligence in certain circumstances. These lines of demarcation seem to be weakening in recent years as cases in various jurisdictions have begun to allocate contributory fault to children six years of age and under (*Grace v. Kumalaa*, 1963; *Lash v. Cutts*, 1991; *Robertson v. Travis*, 1980).

of recreation and sport activities from liability for injuries resulting from the inherent risks (and negligence in a few statutes) of the activity or sport. These are discussed in detail in Section 2.22 *Immunity*.

Procedural Noncompliance

A **statute of limitations** is a restriction on the length of time an injured party has in which to file suit. The law differs from state to state, and also with the nature of the claim. In tort claims, states allow one to four years in which to file suit with most allowing two or three years. When minors are involved, the statute of limitations does not begin running until the minor has reached the age of majority. So, if a child is injured at age 11 due to the negligence of an employee at a recreation department, the youngster would have one to four years (the length of the statute of limitations in that state) after reaching the age of 18 in which to file suit.

Notice of claim statutes relate usually to tort claim statutes and provide that the plaintiff must provide the defendant *public entity* with a notice of intent to file suit. This notice must be filed within a period of time (ranging from 90 days to 2 years) following the accident or the right to sue is lost. In essence, the notice of claim is a form of statute of limitations with a similar effect. Not all states have a notice of claim provision in their tort law statutes and the notice of claim requirements apply only when the defendant is a public entity.

In this case, the defendant claims that the school district is not liable because of recreational user immunity and because of implied primary assumption of risk. The opinion presents an enlightening discussion of each of the defenses.

HOME V. NORTH KITSAP SCHOOL DISTRICT

2 Wn. App. 709; 965 P.2d 1112; 1998 Wash. App. LEXIS 1405
October 2, 1998, Filed

OPINION:

In 1993, Home was a teacher in the Central Kitsap School District, an organization not related to the North Kitsap School District. He taught at Central Kitsap Junior High, where he was also a part-time assistant football coach. Ken Anderson was the head football coach.

On November 3, 1993, Home's Central Kitsap team played an away game on the football field at North Kitsap Junior High. * * * The football field is a permanent facility with football goal posts at each end and a track around the perimeter. It is available for public use when not being used for school events or activities. On November 3, it was being used exclusively for the North Kitsap-Central Kitsap football game, a school-sponsored event to which parents and other spectators were admitted without charge.

When Home and Anderson arrived at the North Kitsap field, they saw a curb "raised several inches above ground level," separating the football area from the track area. The curb ran along the outside of the football field's sideline area, not far from the sideline itself. Home and Anderson thought it was a hazard to any player who might be propelled out of bounds by momentum or by another player. After discussing several courses of action, they decided that Home would station himself in front of the curb, so he could stop any player who might be heading for it. Later, during the game, Home was standing in front of the curb when the Central Kitsap team ran a "sweep" play toward his side of the field. As he testified later: I saw the kid coming to the sideline, I saw the tackler coming and saw imminent collision.

* * * My kid was a full stride out of bounds and starting a second stride when he was impacted. He was going into the cement. And using both hands, I took him to the ground. And the North Kitsap player with most of his weight came across my left thigh. Home was injured, he alleges, as a result of this impact.

In July 1996, Home sued the North Kitsap School District for negligence. North Kitsap moved for summary judgment, contending (1) that it was immune under RCW 4.24.210, the recreational land use statute; (2) that Home was a licensee who could not prove a breach of the duty owed to licensees; and (3) that Home knowingly and voluntarily assumed the risk that culminated in the accident. The trial court granted the motion, and this appeal followed.

I.

North Kitsap argues that RCW 4.24.210 renders it immune from liability to Home. * * * The purpose of RCW 4.24.210(1) is "to encourage owners or others in lawful possession and control of land and water areas or channels to make them available to the public for recreational purposes." RCW 4.24.210(1) provides in pertinent part:

*Any public or private landowners or others in lawful possession and control of any lands whether designated resource, rural, or urban, or water areas or channels and lands adjacent to such areas or channels, who allow members of the public to use them for the purposes of outdoor recreation, which term includes, but is not limited to, the cutting, gathering, and removing of firewood by private persons for their personal use without purchasing the firewood from the landowner, hunting, fishing, camping, picnicking, swimming, hiking, bicycling, * * * boating, nature study, winter or water sports, viewing or enjoying historical, archaeological, scenic, or scientific sites, without charging a fee of any kind therefor, shall not be liable for unintentional injuries to such users.*

According to Division One, the proper approach when applying this statute is to analyze the purpose for which the landowner was using the land, as opposed to the purpose for which the plaintiff was using the land. We agree, although we observe that a landowner may use the land for different purposes at different times. Here, then, it is necessary to focus on the nature of the landowner's use at the time of the accident being litigated.

* * *

Turning to this case, a North Kitsap school administrator testified that the North Kitsap field, "including the area used for football games, is available for public use when school is not in session and when it is not being used for a scheduled sport, such as a junior high school football game." Thus, it is undisputed that North Kitsap was not holding the football field open for use by members of the public when Home was injured, and North Kitsap is not immune by virtue of RCW 4.24.210.

II.

We next consider whether Home was an invitee or licensee. As we explained in Thompson v. Katzer, "An invitee is either a public invitee or a business visitor." "A public invitee is a person who is invited to enter or remain on land as a member of the public for a purpose for which the land is held open to the public." "A business visitor is a person who is invited to enter or remain on land for a purpose directly or indirectly connected with business dealings with the possessor of the land." In contrast, a "licensee" enters the occupier's premises with the occupier's permission or tolerance, either (a) without an invitation or (b) with an invitation but for a purpose unrelated to any business dealings between the two. * * * Here, Home was an assistant football coach invited to North Kitsap's field so that a school-sponsored football game could be played. His presence was related to North Kitsap's business of running its schools, and he was an invitee as a matter of law.

III.

North Kitsap claims that Home assumed the specific risk that culminated in the accident. Home disagrees, arguing primarily that he had no reasonable alternative course of action. Traditionally, the doctrine of assumption of risk has four facets: (1) express assumption of risk; (2) implied primary assumption of risk; (3) implied reasonable assumption of risk; and (4) implied unreasonable assumption of risk. The third and fourth facets, implied reasonable and implied unreasonable assumption of risk, are nothing but alternative names for contributory negligence, and neither is pertinent here. The first and second facets, express assumption of risk and implied primary assumption of risk, raise the same question: Did the plaintiff consent, before the accident or injury, to the negation of a duty that the defendant would otherwise have owed to the plaintiff? If the answer is yes, "the defendant does not have the duty, there can be no breach and hence no negligence." Thus, when either facet applies, it bars any recovery based on the duty that was negated. Although the first and second facets involve the same idea—the plaintiff's consent to negate a duty the defendant would otherwise have owed to the plaintiff—they differ with respect to the way in which the plaintiff manifests consent. With express assumption of risk, the plaintiff states in so many words that

he or she consents to relieve the defendant of a duty the defendant would otherwise have. With implied primary assumption of risk, the plaintiff engages in other kinds of conduct, from which consent is then implied. Here, we focus on implied consent, which we alternatively refer to as assumption of risk.

To invoke assumption of risk, a defendant must show that the plaintiff knowingly and voluntarily chose to encounter the risk. Thus, "the evidence must show the plaintiff (1) had full subjective understanding (2) of the presence and nature of the specific risk, and (3) voluntarily chose to encounter the risk." Put another way, the plaintiff "must have knowledge of the risk, appreciate and understand its nature, and voluntarily choose to incur it." Knowledge and voluntariness are questions of fact for the jury, except when reasonable minds could not differ. Whether a plaintiff decides knowingly to encounter a risk turns on whether he or she, at the time of decision, actually and subjectively knew all facts that a reasonable person in the defendant's shoes would know and disclose, or, concomitantly, all facts that a reasonable person in the plaintiff's shoes would want to know and consider. Thus, "The test is a subjective one: Whether the plaintiff in fact understood the risk; not whether the reasonable person of ordinary prudence would comprehend the risk." The plaintiff must "be aware of more than just the generalized risk of [his or her] activities; there must be proof [he or she] knew of and appreciated the specific hazard which caused the injury." And a plaintiff "appreciates the specific hazard" or risk only if he or she actually and subjectively knows all facts that a reasonable person in the defendant's shoes would know and disclose, or, concomitantly, all facts that a reasonable person in the plaintiff's shoes would want to know and consider when making the decision at issue. Whether a plaintiff decides voluntarily to encounter a risk depends on whether he or she elects to encounter it despite knowing of a reasonable alternative course of action. Thus, Division One has said that in order for assumption of risk to bar recovery, the plaintiff "must have had a reasonable opportunity to act differently or proceed on an alternate course that would have avoided the danger." The Restatement comments:

> Since the basis of assumption of risk is the plaintiff's willingness to accept the risk, take his chances, and look out for himself, his choice in doing so must be a voluntary one. If the plaintiff's words or conduct make it clear that he refuses to accept the risk, he does not assume it. The plaintiff's mere protest against the risk and demand for its removal or for protection against it will not necessarily and conclusively prevent his subsequent acceptance of the risk, if he then proceeds voluntarily into a situation which exposes him to it. Such conduct normally indicates that he does not stand on his objection, and

has in fact consented, although reluctantly, to accept the danger and look for himself.

* * *

In this case, Home does not seriously dispute that he knew all the facts that a reasonable person would have wanted to know and consider when deciding whether to position himself or herself as Home did. He does contend, however, that a rational trier of fact could find that once he actually and subjectively discovered the hazard that later cul-minated in the accident, he had no reasonable alternative but to stand in front of it and protect his students. Taking the evidence and inferences in the light most favorable to Home, we think that a rational trier could so find. Accordingly, we conclude that whether Home voluntarily assumed the risk is a question of fact for the jury, and that summary judgment should not have been granted.

Reversed and remanded for further proceedings.

CASES ON THE SUPPLEMENTAL CD

Cicconi v. Bedford Central School District, 2005 N.Y. App. Div. LEXIS 8484. Note the reasoning why the court ruled that the doctrine of assumption of risk protected the school district.

Knight v. Jewett, (3 Cal.4th 296 [1992]). This is the seminal case concerning the doctrine of assumption of risk, in which the California Supreme Court considered the application of assumption of risk in light of the adoption of comparative fault principles.

Note the distinction made between "primary assumption of risk" and "secondary assumption of risk."

Ribaudo v. La Salle Institute, (2007 NY Slip Op 8431; 45 A.D.3d 556; 2007 N.Y. App. Div. LEXIS 11249). The court emphasized that the doctrine of primary assumption of the risk will not serve as a bar to liability if the risk is unassumed, concealed, or unreasonably increased.

QUESTIONS YOU SHOULD BE ABLE TO ANSWER

1. What is meant by an inherent risk? Give an example.

2. Explain the concept of primary assumption of risk.

3. What is secondary assumption of risk? Give an example.

4. What is meant by comparative fault?

5. Explain the role of an indemnification agreement in a facility lease agreement.

REFERENCES

Cases

Auburn School District No. 408 v. King County, 1999 Wash. App. LEXIS 1748.

Beaver v. Foamcraft, Inc., 2002 U.S. Dist. LEXIS 4651.

Bennett v. Hidden Valley Golf and Ski, Inc., 2003 U.S. App. LEXIS 1658.

Cooper v. The Aspen Skiing Company, 2002 Colo. LEXIS 528.

Daigle v. West Mountain, 2001 N.Y. App. Div. LEXIS 12326.

Eastman v. Yutzy, 2001 Mass. Super. LEXIS 157.

El-Halees v. Chauser, 2002 Cal. App. Unpub. LEXIS 8124.

Grace v. Kumalaa, 387 P.2d 872 (Hawaii 1963).

Hawkins v. Peart, 2001 Utah LEXIS 177.

Home v. North Kitsap School District, 965 P.2d 1112; 1998 Wash. App. LEXIS 1405.

Knight v. Jewett, 3 Cal.4th 296; 11 Cal. Rptr. 2d, 834 P.2d 696 (1992).

Leakas v. Columbia Country Club, 831 F. Supp. 1231 (Md. 1993).

Madsen v. Wyoming River Trips, Inc., 1999 U.S. Dist. LEXIS 77.

Pride Park Atlanta v. City of Atlanta, 2000 Ga. App. LEXIS 1330.

Riddle v. Universal Sport Camp, 786 P.2d 641 (Kan. 1990).

Robertson v. Travis, 393 So.2d 304 (La. 1980).

Saffro v. Elite Racing, Inc., 2002 Cal. App. LEXIS 2076 at 1.

Tremblay v. West Experience Inc., 2002 N.Y. App. Div. LEXIS 7591.

Truett v. Fell, 68 N.Y.2d 432.

Walsh v. Luedtke, 2005 Wisc. App. LEXIS 744.

Yang v. Voyagaire Houseboats, Inc., 2005 Minn. LEXIS 465.

Publications and Presentations

Gregg, C. R. (2000). "Inherent Risks," SSLASPA Conference, Albuquerque.

van der Smissen, B. (1990). *Legal liability and risk management for public and private entities.* Cincinnati: Anderson Publishing Co.

van der Smissen, B. (1997). How to Defend Yourself and Your Program. Unpublished handout at an SSLASPA Conference.

Volunteer Protection Act of 1997, PL 105-19 (S543) June 18, 1997.

—**Doyice J. Cotten**
SPORT RISK CONSULTING

A major category of defense for individuals and service providers in the fields of recreation and sport management is immunity from liability. Immunity is the state of being exempt from or protected against civil liability under certain circumstances. In this section, several types of immunity that apply to recreation and sport managers will be presented—ranging from sovereign immunity to sport-related statutes pertaining to the recreational user, sport volunteers, Good Samaritan acts, statutory assumption of risk, and shared responsibility. Since it is not possible to spell out the law in each state regarding each type of immunity, the reader is encouraged to use Table 2.22.1 to research the law in his or her state. Moreover, the reader should consult Table 2.21.1 in Section 2.21 *Defenses Against Negligence* for a summary of each of these defenses.

Many types of immunity are available to those in the fields of recreation and sport. Each has been designed to provide shelter from liability to one or more protected classes of people or entities. Statutes are aimed at providing protection for public entity service providers (tort claims acts, sovereign immunity, hazardous recreation statutes), private service providers (shared responsibility statutes, statutory assumption of risk statutes), nonprofit and charitable providers (charitable immunity), and property owners (recreational user statutes). Volunteer statutes are enacted to encourage volunteers (Volunteer Protection Act, state volunteer statutes), port volunteers (sport volunteer statutes), and medical emergency volunteers (Good Samaritan statutes, AED Good Samaritan statutes). There is also immunity designed to protect public employees (hazardous recreation statutes, tort claims acts, discretionary act immunity) and private employees (AED Good Samaritan statutes).

FUNDAMENTAL CONCEPTS

Sovereign/Governmental Immunity

Sovereign immunity refers to "the immunity of the state and its agencies, departments, boards, institutions, et al." (van der Smissen, 1990, p. 148). **Governmental immunity**, on the other hand, "is the protection afforded local governing entities, such as municipalities (cities, towns, villages) and schools" (van der Smissen, 1990, p. 148). It is important to understand that, while many states distinguish between the two concepts, the terms sovereign immunity and governmental immunity are often used interchangeably. In this section, the term "sovereign/governmental immunity" will be used to refer to both concepts.

There are two major limitations to sovereign/governmental immunity. First, *it applies only to governmental entities* and second, *it does not extend to the officers, agents, or employees of the governing entity* (except when the statute specifically provides for it). This doctrine of sovereign/governmental immunity was the commanding approach to immunity until the 1950s. However, the last half of the twentieth century has seen most states abolish or significantly weaken and restrict this immunity, so that it no longer has the dominant impact that it once did. The rationale for the change was that the immunity was unfair to the innocent victim of negligent actions by the governmental entity or its employees. Common law regarding immunity has been collected and arranged more systematically, or codified, in the tort claims acts. These acts, to be discussed below, extend immunity to government officers, agents, and employees in many states.

Tort Claims Acts

In 1946, Congress passed the **Federal Tort Claims Act** (28 U.S.C. 2671–2680 [1976]) with the intent of waiving sovereign/governmental immunity, thereby allowing liability exposure for the federal government comparable to that of the private sector. The statute removed the power of the federal government to claim immunity from a lawsuit for damages due to negligent or intentional injury by a federal employee in the scope of his/her work for the government. While the Act allows suit of the government in certain instances, unlike sovereign/governmental immunity, *it provides immunity for federal officials performing discretionary acts within the scope of their responsibilities*.

Individual states began to follow suit, passing their own **state tort claims acts** to enable individuals harmed by torts, including negligence, to file suit under certain conditions. *In essence, what these acts did was (1) to rescind sovereign/governmental immunity at the state level in those states and (2) to enumerate those areas or acts for which immunity was retained.*

Discretionary/Ministerial Function

One major change at this time was movement from that of governmental/proprietary function to the discretionary/ministerial doctrine. The **governmental/proprietary doctrine** classified the functions of public entities as either a fundamental **governmental function** (e.g., police, fire, and education), for which immunity was granted, or as a **proprietary function** (e.g., water works, electrical power, selling game refreshments, and other for-profit activities), for which no immunity was granted. The **discretionary/ministerial doctrine** grants immunity for discretionary acts, but, for the most part, not for ministerial acts.

Discretionary acts are those that involve deliberation, planning, decision-making, policy-making, and most often involve managerial level personnel such as the athletic director or head of the recreation department. **Ministerial acts** are more likely to involve operational acts, obedience of orders, performance of a duty, implementation of decisions or policies, and lower echelon employees such as assistant coaches and aerobics instructors. Under this doctrine, the classification is not based upon who performed the act, but upon the nature of the act. The rationale behind this immunity is to free the governing body charged with making policy decisions regarding public welfare from suits that might restrain them from performing their duties. Distinction between discretionary and ministerial acts, at best, is difficult, and has been growing increasingly so, as the courts in some states have persisted in blurring the lines of distinction, often interpreting even trivial decisions as discretionary. Classifying most acts as discretionary, in effect, strengthens the immunity of both the employee and the entity.

The governmental/proprietary doctrine provided immunity based upon the nature of the function provided by the governmental entity. Immunity was provided if the action was a "public good" function of the entity (an inspection of the recreation facility), but not for proprietary or money-making functions of the entity (operation of a soft-drink machine). The discretionary/ministerial doctrine provides immunity based on the act of the employee, not the function. Thus the same employee might be immune for actions deemed discretionary (policy-related planning for a 5K Run) and not immune for actions ruled ministerial (carrying out the policies for a 5K Run).

In *Feagins v. Waddy* (2007), a girl on the track team suffered injury when she was assigned to high jump in a meet without prior instruction. The court held that the coach had immunity as a state agent because the selection of participants for events involves an exercise of judgment and is, therefore, a discretionary duty.

Charitable Immunity

During the first half of the twentieth century, charitable immunity provided substantial liability protection to charitable, educational, and religious organizations. **Charitable immunity** is a doctrine that relieves or immunizes charitable organizations from liability for tort. The doctrine is based upon four premises: (1) public policy encourages charitable organizations since they benefit the public; (2) money possessed by such organizations was donated for other purposes and is held in trust; (3) since the recipient of the charity receives benefits, he or she, in turn, accepts the risks of negligence; and (4) there is no *respondeat superior* since the charity does not benefit from the actions of employees.

Charitable immunity, which focused on the protection of the agency or institution, has been repealed in most states. In some of the few states that retain some semblance of charitable immunity, the immunity has been emasculated to the point where its effectiveness is very limited. Volunteer immunity, however, is still important in a few states such as New Jersey (*Gilbert v. Seton Hall University*, 2003),Virginia (*Ola v. YMCA*, 2005), and Texas (*Chrismon v. Brown*, 2007).

Today, however, the volunteer protection acts do provide protection for the nonprofit or charitable institution volunteer. In addition, a few states still protect those gratuitously serving such institutions as a member, director, trustee, or board member.

Recreational User Statutes

In order to encourage private owners of natural, rural areas to allow others to use their property for recreational purposes, state legislatures began passing recreational use statutes in the 1960s. The **recreational user statute** is a law designed to provide protection for the private property-owner against lawsuits by parties injured while on the landowner's property for recreational purposes. Originally, the immunity laws applied when four conditions were met: (1) private landowners; (2) no fee charged; (3) unimproved, undeveloped land for recreational use; and (4) owner fulfilled his or her obligation to provide a warning for any known, concealed danger that would not be apparent to the recreational user.

Today, all states have enacted some type of recreational use statute. While differences exist among the statutes, they were enacted with comparable intent. Statutes generally (1) are intended to encourage landowners to make their property available to the public for recreational use; (2) stipulate that no fee is charged for the use of the land; (3) declare that the owner owes no duty of care to keep the land safe for use for recreational purpose nor to warn of a dangerous condition; (4) state that the landowner extends no assurance that the land is safe for any purpose and does not confer on the user the legal status of invitee or licensee; and (5) say that the landowner does not assume responsibility for or incur liability for any injury, death, or loss to any person or property caused by an act or omission of the landowner.

Resultant of the immunity provided by most such statutes, the provider's only duty is to warn of ultra hazardous situations and of known hidden hazards. In most states, the provider has no liability except for willful or malicious acts and for ultra-hazardous situations. The immunity generally applies to all activity risks and all open and obvious premise risks.

While enacted with the same purpose in mind, state recreational user statutes differ considerably due to judicial interpretations of the statutes. Courts in some states have broadened the scope of the statutes by interpreting them liberally (e.g., by applying the statute in cases where the injury occurred on a tennis court or when a fee was paid). The reader is encouraged to read an excellent presentation on the subject in Section 2.32 *Property Law*. The specific statutes for each state may be found in Table 2.22.1 of this section and a summary of recreational user immunity may be found in Table 2.22.1 in Section 2.21 *Defenses Against Negligence*.

Volunteer Immunity Statutes

Prior to the decade of the 1980s, lawsuits against volunteers in recreation and sport activities were rare. In that decade, insurance coverage became both expensive and difficult to obtain, some coverage was unavailable, more exclusions were included in policies, many agencies discontinued or reduced insurance coverage, volunteer lawsuits began to increase in frequency, and volunteer recruitment became more difficult. This predicament prompted a number of states to pass legislation aimed at protecting certain volunteers in recreational and sport activities (see Table 2.22.1).

State Volunteer Immunity Statutes

Additionally, in the late 1980s, state legislatures were encouraged to pass a model act designed to protect volunteers working with certain nonprofit organizations and governmental entities from liability for injuries resulting from the ordinary or gross negligence of the volunteers. The Model State Act called for immunity from civil liability for any act or omission of the volunteer that resulted in damage or injury if the volunteer was acting in good faith and within the scope of duty for a nonprofit organization or governmental entity—so long as the injury was not caused by wanton and willful misconduct and did not involve the operation of a motor

Table 2.22.1 State Recreation and Sport-Related Immunity Legislation

State	Recreational User Statutes	Rec/Sport Volunteer Statutes	Good Samaritan Statutes	AED Good Samaritan Statutes	Equestrian Immunity Statutes	Ski Operator Immunity Statutes	Skating Immunity Statutes	Other Sport & Recreation Statutes	General Sport & Recreation Statutes	Hazardous Recreational Activity Statutes
U.S.		P.L. 105-19 42 U.S.C.S. 14,501-14,505		P.L. 107-188 42 U.S.C.S. 238q						
AL	AC 35-15-(1-28)		AC 6-5-332	AC 6-5-332	AC 6-5-337		AC 6-5-342 Skateboard Parks			
AK	AS 09.65.200 AS 34.17.055		AS 09-65-090	AS 09.65.090	None	AS 05.45.010 to .210			AS 09.65.290	
AZ	ARS 33-1551		ARS 32-1471 ARS 32-1472 ARS 36.21.1	ARS 36-2261-2264	ARS 12-553	ARS 5-705 (1)		ARS 12-554 Baseball ARS 12-556 Motor Sports		
AR	ARS 18-11-301 to 307	ARS 16-120-102	ARS 17-95-101	ARS 20-13-1305 ARS 20-13-1306	ARS 16-120-201 to 202					
CA	CCC 846, 846.1		CCHSC 1799.102	ACC 1714.21 HSC 1797.190 SB 911 of 1999	None	5 county ordinances	See Hazardous Rec. Activity Statutes for Skateboard Parks			CGC 831.7
CO	CRS 33-41-101 to106	CRS 13-21-116	CRS 13-21-15.5	CRS 13-21-108.1	CRS 13-21-119	CRS 33-44-101 to 114		CRS 13-21-111.8(1) Sport Shooting CRS 13-21-120 Baseball		
CT	CGSA 52-557k		CGSA 52-557B	CGSA 52-557b	CGSA 52-557p	CGSA 29-201 to 214				
DE	7 DCA 5901-5907	16 DCA 6835 16 DCA 6836	16 DCA 6801	DCA 6801	10 DCA 8140					
FL	FS 375.251		FS 768.13	FS 768.1325	FS 773.01 to .05		FS 316.0085 Skateboard Parks			FS 316.0085
GA	OCGA 51-32.0 to 26; OCGA 27-3-1	OCGA 51-1-20.1	OCGA 51-1-230 OCGA 768.135	OCGA 31-11-53.1 OCGA 51-1-29.3	OCGA 4-12-1 to 5		OCGA51-1-43	OCGA 27-4-280 to 283 Fishing		
HI	HRS 520-1 to 8	HRS 662D- 4	HI 663-1.5	HRS 663-1.5	HRS 663B-1 to 2		HRS 662-19, HRS 46-72.5, HRS 662D-4		HRS 663-1.54	
ID	IC 36-1604		IC 5-330	IC 5-337	IC 6-1801 to 1802	IC 6-1101-1109		IC 6-1201 to 1206 Outfitters & Guides		
IL	745 ILCS 65/ 1 to 7	745 ILCS 80/1	745 ILCS 49/12	410 ILCS 4/30 745 ILCS 49/12	745 ILCS 47/1 to 47/999	745 ILCS 72/1 to 30	745 ILCS 72/1 to 30	745 ILCS 52/1 to /99 Hockey Facilities		745 ILCS 10/3-109
IN	ICA 14-22-10-2 to 2.5	ICA 34-30-4.2 ICA 34-30-19-3 to 4	ICA 34-30-12-1	ICA 16-31-6.2 ICA 34-30-12-1	ICA 34-6-240 to 43, 69, 95, 103; ICA 34-31-5-1 to5		ICA 34-31-6-1 to 4			
IA	ICA 461C.1 to 7		ICA 115.3 ICA 915.3	ICA 147A.10	ICA 673.1to 4		ICA 670.4 Skateboard Parks			
KS	KSA 58-3201 to 3207	KSA 60-3607	KSA 65-2891	KSA 65-6149a	KSA 60-4001 to 4004					

(continued)

State	Recreational User Statutes	Rec/Sport Volunteer Statutes	Good Samaritan Statutes	AED Good Samaritan Statutes	Equestrian Immunity Statutes	Ski Operator Immunity Statutes	Skating Immunity Statutes	Other Sport & Recreation Statutes	General Sport & Recreation Statutes	Hazardous Recreational Activity Statutes
KY	KRS 150.645 KRS 411.190		KRS 411.148 KRS 411.150	KRS 311.668	KRS 247.401 to 4029					
LA	LRS 9:2791, 2795	LRS 9:2798	LRS 9:2793	LRS 40:1236. 11 to .14 LRS 9:2793	LRS 9: 2795.1					
ME	14 MRSA 159- A		14 MRSA 164	22 MRSA 2150-C	7 MRSA 4101-4104A	26 MRSA 471-490G 32 MRSA 15201 to 15227	8 MRSA 601-608 8 MRSA 625	8 MRSA 801-806 Amuse Rides; 32 MRSA 15219 Hang Gliding		
MD	MCA 5-1101 to 1109	MCA 5-607 MCA 5-802	MCA 5-603	MCA 13-517	None					
MA	21 MGL 17C	231 MGL 85V	71 ALM 55A 111C ALM 20	112 ALM 12V1/2	128 MGL 2D	143 MGL 71H to 71S				
MI	MCLA 324.73301		MCLA 691.1501 MCLA 691.1507 MCLA 333.20965	MCLA 333.20965	MCLA 691.1661 to 1667	MCLA 408.321 to .344 or MSA 13A.82126	MCLA 445.1721 to .1726	MCLA 681. 1541 to .1544 MCLA 691.1544 Sport Shooting; MCLA 342.82126 Snow Mobiling		
MN	MSA 604A.20 to 27	MSA 604A.11	MSA 604A.01	MSA 604A.01	MSA 604A.12					
MS	MCA 89-2-1 to 27	MCA 95-9-3	MCA 63-3-405 MCA 73-25-37	MCA 41-60-33	MCA 95-11-1 to 7					
MO	MAS 537.345 to .348		RSM 537.037	RSM 190.092	MAS 537.325					
MT	MCA 70-16-301 to 302		MCA 27-1-714	MCA 50-6-505	MCA 27-1-725 to 728	MCA 23-2-732 to 736		MCA 23-2-651 to 656 Snowmobiling MCA 27-1-733 Rodeos		
NE	NRS 37-729 to 736		NRS 25-21, 186	NRS 71-51, 102	NRS 25-21.249 to .253					
NV	NRS 41.510	NRS 41.630	NRS 41.5000	NRS 41.500	None	NRS 455A.010 to .190	NRS 455B.200 to 300 Skateboard Parks	NRS 455B.010 to 455B.100 Amuse Rides		
NH	NHSA 212:34, NHSA 231A:1 to 8	NHSA 508.17	RSA 508:12	RSA 153-A:31	NHSA 508:19	NHSA 225A:1 to :26	NHSA 507 - B:11 Skateboard Parks			NHSA 507 B-11
NJ	NJS 13:1B-15. 134 to 142 NJS 2A:42A-2 to 10	NJS 2A:62A-6	NJS 2A:62A-1 NJS 26:2K-29	NJS 2A:62A-25	NJ S 5:15-1 to 12	NJS 34:4A-1; NJS 5:13-1 to 11	NJS 5:14-1 to 7	NJS 39:3C - 18 to 23		
NM	NMSA 17-4-7	NMSA 41-12-1 NMSA 41-12-2	NMSA 24-10-3	NMSA 34-10B-4	NMSA 42-13-2 to 5	NMSA 24-1-5 1-14				
NY	NY GOL 9:103		NYCLSPH 3000-a	NYCLSPH 3000-a NYCLSPH 3000-b	None	NY GOL 18-101 to -108 NYLL 865 to 868				
NC	NCGS 38A.1to 4		NCGS 20-166 NCGS 90-21.14	NCGS 90-21.15	NCGS 99E-1to 3	NCGS 99C-1 to 5	NCGS 99E-10 to 14			NCGS Art 99E – 21-25
ND	NDCC 53-08-01 to 06	NDCC 32-3-46	NDCC 32-03.1-02	NDCC 32-03.1-02.3	NDCC 53-10-01 to 02	NDCC 53-09-01 to 11				
OH	ORCA 1533.18 ORCA 1533.181		ORCA 2305.23	ORCA 2305.235	ORCA 2305.321	ORCA 4169.01 to 99	ORCA 4171.01 to .10			

(continued)

Table 2.22.1 State Recreation- and Sport-Related Immunity Legislation (continued)

State	Recreational User Statutes	Rec/Sport Volunteer Statutes	Good Samaritan Statutes	AED Good Samaritan Statutes	Equestrian Immunity Statutes	Ski Operator Immunity Statutes	Skating Immunity Statutes	Other Sport & Recreation Statutes	General Sport & Recreation Statutes	Hazardous Recreational Activity Statutes
OK	2 OS 1301-315 76 OS 5, 11 OS 76-10 to 15	76 OS 31	OS 76.5	76 OS 5A	OS 76 50.1 to -4					
OR	ORS 105.670 to .700		ORS 30.800 ORS 433.830	ORS 30.802	ORS 30.687 - .697	ORS 30.970 to .990				
PA	68 PCSA 477-1 to 7	42 PCSA 8332.1	42 PCSA 8332	42 PCSA 8331.2	None	42 PCSA 7102 or 40 PCSA 2051				
RI	RIGL 32-6-1 to 7	RIGL 9-1-48	RIGL 9-1-27.1 RIGL 9-1-34	RIGL 9-1-34	RIGL 4-21-1 to 4	RIGL 41-8-1 to 4		RIGL 9-20-5 Snow Mobiles & ATVs		
SC	SCCA 27-3-10 to 70		SCCA 15-1-310	SCCA 4-76-40	SCCA 47-9-710 to 730		SCCA 52-21-10 to 60			
SD	SDCLA 20-9-12 to 18		SDCLA 32034-3 SDCLA 20-9-3	SDCLA 20-9.4.1	SDCLA 42-11-1 to 5		SDCLA 32-20A-21 to 23	DCLA 32-20A-21 to S22 Snow Mobiling		
TN	TCA 11-10-101 to 105 TCA 70-7-101 to 105	TCA 62-50-201-203	TCA 63-6-218	TCA 63-6-218	TCA 44-20-101 to 105	TCA 68-114-102 to 107		TCA 70-7-201-204 Whitewater rafting		
TX	TCPRC 75.001 to .004	TCPRC 84.0001 to 008	VTCA 74.001-/003	TCPRC 74.001	TCPRC 87.001 to .005		THSCA 759.001 to .005 THSCA 760.001 to .006			
UT	UCA 57-14-1 to 7		UCA 78-11-22	UCA 28-8-7.5 or 75	UCA 78-27b-101 to 103	UCA 78-27-51 to 54	See Gen Rec & Sport Statutes for Skateboard Parks	UCA 47-3-1 to 3 Sport Shooting; UCA 78-27-61 Amuse Rides; UCA 78-27-62 Hockey Facil	UCA 78-27-63	
VT	12 VSA 5791-5795		12 VSA 519	18 VSA 907	12 VSA 1039	12 VSA 1036 to 1038	See Genl Rec & Sport Statutes for Skateboard Parks		12 VSA 1037	
VA	VCA 29.1-.509		VCA 8.00-225	VCA 8.01-225	VCA 3.1-796.130 to .133					
WA	RCW 4.24.200 to 210		RCW 4.24.300	RCW 70.54 310	RCW 4.24.530 to .540	RCW 70.117.010 to .040; RCW 79A.45.010 to .060				
WV	WVC 19-25-1 to 7		WVC 55-7-15	WVC 164D-3 to 4	WVC 20-4-1 to 7	WVC 20-3A-1 to 8		WVC 20-3B-1 to 5 Outfitters & Guides		
WI	WSA 895.52 to .525		WSA 895.48	WSA 895.48	WSA 895.481-895.481 3 (e)	WSA 895.525	See Gen Rec & Sport Statutes for Skateboard Parks		WSA 895.525	
WY	WYO STAT 34-19-101 to 106		WYO STAT 1-1-120	WYO STAT 35-26-102 to 103	WYO STAT 1-1-121 to 123	WYO.STAT. 1-1-121 to 123		WYO.STAT. 1-1-118 Rodeos	WYO.STAT. 1-1-121 to 123	

vehicle. The model act, however, intended no protection for the nonprofit or governmental agency for which the volunteer worked.

Subsequently, all states now have either (1) a general volunteer liability statute (often modeled after the Model State Act) designed to provide protection for volunteers, or (2) a statute intended to protect certain volunteers in recreation and sports activities (e.g., coaches, referees), or (3) both types of statutes. The general volunteer statutes vary greatly from state to state. Many of the states protect only directors or officers in the organization and all have exceptions to immunity. Common exceptions include the motor vehicle exception, action based on federal law, action that constitutes gross negligence, willful and wanton acts, and, in a few states, ordinary negligence. Many of these general state statutes are worded such that they should provide immunity for recreation and sport volunteers. Additionally, in 1997 the volunteer was provided with even more protection when Congress enacted the Volunteer Protection Act (discussed in detail below).

Recreation and Sport Volunteer Immunity Statutes

Nineteen states have passed some type of volunteer statute for volunteer sport coaches and officials.[1] In addition, a Hawaii statute protects volunteers at public skateboard parks and youth sport volunteers are specifically mentioned in the Oklahoma and Texas general volunteer immunity statutes.

There are ten points that are frequently addressed in recreation and sport volunteer immunity statutes.

1. The volunteer must be unpaid. Some statutes specify that officials (e.g., referees, umpires) may receive a small stipend and retain their immunity.

2. The volunteer must act in good faith.

3. The volunteer must act within the scope of his or her duties.

4. Protected parties are usually specified, and may include any or all of athletic coach, assistant coach, manager, assistant manager, instructor, official, referee, umpire, leader, league Kansas, and Mississippi restricts eligibility for immunity to sports officials who officiate at any level of competition.

5. Additionally, most statutes define the type organization (e.g., nonprofit, charitable, official, athletic trainer, and physician, or other healthcare provider. The law in Arkansas, educational) whose volunteers qualify.

6. Some states stipulate that protected parties must undergo an approved training program, usually relating to safety or first aid.

7. Some states specify that immunity does not protect when activities are unsupervised.

8. Most, but not all, exclude public and private school coaches from immunity.

9. It is the nature of the act that is protected. Most include immunity for ordinary negligence, but several include gross negligence, excluding only wanton and willful acts or intentional acts. Pennsylvania and New Mexico statutes specify immunity unless the conduct is substantially below the generally accepted level.

10. Almost all exclude negligence in the operation of a motor vehicle from immunity. Volunteer recreation and sport statutes may be found in Table 2.22.1.

Volunteer Protection Act (VPA)

The Volunteer Protection Act (VPA) was signed into law in 1997 (Public Law 105-19). This federal statute preempts state laws (except for those that provide for more volunteer protection than the VPA), and is intended to provide broad protection to volunteers nationwide under the following conditions:

---

[1]Arkansas, Colorado, Delaware, Georgia, Illinois, Indiana, Kansas, Louisiana, Maryland, Massachusetts, Minnesota, Mississippi, Nevada, New Hampshire, New Jersey, New Mexico, North Dakota, Pennsylvania, and Rhode Island.

- The volunteer was acting within the scope of the volunteer's responsibilities in the nonprofit organization or governmental entity at the time of the act or omission;

- If appropriate or required, the volunteer was properly licensed, certified or authorized by the appropriate authorities for the activities or practice in the state;

- The harm was not caused by willful or criminal misconduct, gross negligence, reckless harmed by the volunteer;

- The harm was not caused by the volunteer operating a motor vehicle . . . for which the State requires misconduct, or a conscious, flagrant indifference to the rights or safety of the individual. . . an operator's license; or . . . insurance.

Of particular interest is the second condition—that the immunity applies only if the volunteer is licensed, certified, or authorized when such empowerments are relevant. *It is important to note that the act does not affect the liability of any nonprofit or governmental entity—but rather protects only individuals from liability.* In *Avenoso v. Mangan* (2006), Mangan, a volunteer soccer coach, caused injury to Avenoso when he ran too close to him. The court granted summary judgment on the basis of the VPA, but ruled that the co-defendant soccer club did not qualify for immunity under the act.

Acts that are not encompassed by the statute include (1) crimes of violence or terrorism, (2) hate crimes, (3) sexual offense convictions, (4) violation of federal or state civil rights law, and (5) those committed while under the influence of drugs or alcohol. Punitive damages can be awarded only if the volunteer's actions constituted willful or criminal misconduct, or a conscious flagrant indifference to the rights and safety of the injured party. For losses due to physical or emotional pain, the volunteer will be liable only to the extent of his or her percentage of responsibility.

First Aid Statutes (Good Samaritan)

Every state has some form of Good Samaritan statute which is intended to provide immunity from liability for certain parties who voluntarily and gratuitously come to the aid of injured persons. Good Samaritan laws were developed to encourage both physicians and laymen to help others in emergency situations.

There is no general legal duty to assist or rescue injured parties in most states. An exception is Vermont, which requires a person who knows that another is exposed to grave physical harm shall give reasonable assistance to the exposed person if he can do so without danger or peril to himself. Penalty for violation, however, is only $100. Mississippi, North Carolina, and South Dakota require that the driver of a vehicle involved in an accident assist injured parties if needed if assisting presents no danger to the one assisting. Most then provide immunity for the driver. Georgia has a duty to assist and rescue in the event of watercraft accidents.

There are six elements that are common to most Good Samaritan statutes. The first is the stipulation of **who is protected** by the statute. The most common designation is any person who comes to the aid of another in an emergency situation. More than 40 states offer protection for any individual who assists in an emergency situation. Some states, however, restrict the immunity to healthcare personnel (physicians, surgeons, nurses, EMS personnel, physical therapists, and/or others) or those with first aid training. Many states exclude healthcare personnel from protection if the action is within the scope of the duty.

The second and third elements are that the parties must act in **good faith** and without expectation of **remuneration**. Almost every state specifies one or the other, and most list both. Fourth, almost all of the statutes specify that the action must occur in an **emergency situation** away from a medical facility. There are also many states that have statutes specific to assisting those choking on food in restaurants. A few statutes limit coverage to more specific situations (e.g., choking, crime victims, cardiopulmonary rescues, life-threatening situations, athletic events) and some apply to volunteer team physicians.

Fifth, the statutes almost always stipulate that the care must be done **at the scene** of the accident. A number also add protection during transport to the hospital.

Finally, virtually all of the statutes protect the "Good Samaritan" from liability for injury caused by acts or omissions or **ordinary negligence.** Some statutes specify that the individual must act as a reasonably prudent person would act and others specify "reasonable aid." Statutes in a few states specify that there is immunity unless there is reckless or willful and wanton conduct.

Another major difference among statutes is the **standard of care required.** Most states protect the volunteer from liability when the act is negligent, but not if it is grossly negligent, reckless, or willful and wanton. A few states, including Arkansas, Florida, and Mississippi require that the acts of the volunteer be those of a reasonable and prudent person. In these states, and possibly a few others, the "Good Samaritan" is *not* protected against liability for negligence. It is therefore prudent for one to know the law in one's own state. Good Samaritan legislation in each state may be found in Table 2.22.1.

While "Good Samaritan" laws differ considerably among states, the typical statute asserts that *any person who, in good faith, gratuitously renders emergency care at the scene of an accident cannot be held liable for injury resulting from acts and omissions unless the conduct constitutes gross negligence or willful/wanton conduct.* In addition, the concept is summarized in Table 2.21.1 in Section 2.21, *Defenses Against Negligence.*

In a recent California Supreme Court ruling (*Van Horn v. Watson*, 2008), the court held that the California Good Samaritan statute applied only to the rendering of care at the scene of a medical emergency and did not encompass rescue or extrication. Injuries incurred during a rescue or while transporting the injured party to medical aid (e.g., after an accident in a wilderness area) may subject the rescuer/transporter to civil liability. Californians are not the only ones who may be affected by this situation, since a number of other states have similar provisions in their statute.

AED Statutes

The development of the automated external defibrillator (AED) in the 1990s provided a major technological advance in the fight against sudden cardiac arrest deaths in the United States. The AED is a medical device which (1) recognizes the presence or absence of ventricular fibrillation; (2) is capable of determining if defibrillation should be performed; (3) can automatically charge and request delivery of an electrical impulse; and (4) can deliver an appropriate impulse upon action by the operator. While it has been estimated that more than half of the 250,000-plus deaths annually in the nation could be prevented by timely use of an AED, its widespread use has been hampered by the lack of laws enabling its use by non-medical personnel.

With the intent of encouraging the extensive use of the AED, some states began passing Good Samaritan legislation specifically aimed at AED usage, while others added the AED to existing Good Samaritan statutes. While all states have now passed some type of AED legislation, that legislation differs significantly from state to state in terms of (1) who is protected, (2) requirements for immunity, and (3) what acts are immunized. AED legislation in each state may be found in Table 2.22.1, and the immunity is summarized in Table 2.21.1 in Section 2.21 *Defenses Against Negligence.*

Parties protected may include any or all of the following: (1) trained users, (2) any user in a perceived emergency, (3) the entity that acquires the device, (4) the prescribing physician, (5) parties who train others to use the AED, or (6) certified healthcare professionals. A major difference involves the requirements for immunity. Many states offer immunity for **any user** who acts gratuitously and in good faith in a perceived medical emergency to render emergency care. Many other states provide the same immunity, but only to **trained users.** The definition of trained also differs considerably. Some states require that expected users (or employees) be trained, but that a "Good Samaritan" passerby is immune regardless of training. Legislation in a few states seems to legalize the use of the device, but provides no immunity.

There is also great variance in what acts are immunized by the law. At least one provides immunity only where the user acted as an ordinary reasonably prudent person would have acted—seemingly providing no immunity from negligence. Most specify no immunity protection for grossly negligent actions or willful or wanton misconduct, thereby providing immunity for negligence. Several exclude only willful and wanton actions from immunity, thus apparently creating immunity for grossly negligent acts. Several also seem to provide blanket immunity, specifying no restrictions on the immunity of an AED user.

A large number of states have enacted legislation to modify and/or improve their AED immunity statute. In addition, a number of states (Arkansas, California, Illinois, Indiana, Louisiana, Massachusetts, Michigan, New Jersey, New York, Oregon, Rhode Island, and Washington D.C.) have passed statutes requiring AED availability in health clubs. Some states have also enacted statutes regarding AEDs in schools. New York legislation requires devices in schools, Nevada requires them in some public schools and at some athletic events, and both Florida and Georgia require them in all public high schools offering athletics.

Cardiac Arrest Survival Act (CASA)

In an effort to further combat sudden cardiac arrest deaths, Congress passed the **Cardiac Arrest Survival Act** (2002) (42 *USCS* 238q[2002]). The legislation, like the state legislation preceding it, is designed to accelerate the widespread use of automated external defibrillators by providing Good Samaritan immunity in those states not having such protection. The legislation was intended to augment existing state "Good Samaritan" laws by providing federal liability protection for both users and purchasers of AEDs.

The law specifies that "**any person who uses** or attempts to use an AED device on a victim of a perceived medical emergency is immune from civil liability for any harm resulting from the use or attempted use of such device," including healthcare professionals outside the scope of their license or certification. This immunity to the Good Samaritan user applies regardless of training, and protects the user from liability for ordinary negligence. **Any person who acquires the device** is also immune from such liability, provided the harm was not due to failure of the acquirer to notify appropriate local entities of the placement of the device, to properly maintain and test the device, or to provide appropriate training to employees using the device.

CASA preempts state law only where state statute does not provide protection for a user or acquirer. Thus, CASA fills in the immunity gaps left by some state legislation since all users and acquirers are covered by state law (if state statute provides immunity) or by federal law (if immunity is not provided for by state law). When state law fails to protect either the user or the acquirer, CASA provides that protection.

Immunity is not provided by CASA: (1) for willful or criminal misconduct, gross negligence, reckless misconduct or a conscious, flagrant indifference to the rights or safety of the victim who was harmed; (2) for licensed health professionals operating within the scope of their employment; or (3) for certain healthcare providers or leasers of AEDs.

There are also some exclusions that would not normally be relevant to providers of health, fitness, recreation, and sport activities. These are (1) when the person using the device is a licensed or certified health professional acting within the scope of his or her duties; (2) a hospital, clinic or other entity with the purpose of providing health care; or (3) when the acquirer leased the AED to a healthcare entity and an employee caused harm while acting within the scope of the entity.

Shared Responsibility and Statutory Assumption of Risk Statutes

Legislation has been enacted in most states to help protect selected recreation and sport providers from liability for injuries resulting from the inherent risks of particular activities, or in many cases, from certain types of ordinary negligence by the provider. Some of these acts are in the form of shared responsibility statutes while others are more accurately designated as statutory assumption of risk statutes. These acts, originally called **sport safety acts**, usually seek to provide some liability protections for recreation and sport businesses that make certain activities available to the public.

Shared responsibility statutes generally have four distinguishing features. They enumerate the **duties of the recreation or sport provider**. Failure to satisfy these duties constitutes negligence and makes the statute inapplicable. Duties provided in such statutes have been deemed to establish a statutory standard of care. The second earmark of these statutes is that they specify **duties of the participant**. Common duties listed include the responsibility to read and obey signs and to stay within the limits of his or her ability. Failure to perform the required participant duties could constitute secondary assumption of risk. Secondary assumption of risk (formerly called contributory negligence) would serve to decrease situations in which recovery for participants is possible and may, at the same time, increase liability of the participant to other participants. Shared responsibility statutes usually contain certain **provisions that preclude recovery.** Most specify that recovery is not permitted when the injury resulted from inherent risks. Many statutes specifically define the inherent risks of the activity or sport, prompting many courts to grant summary judgment based upon the statute. The final feature of these statutes is that **some type of immunity is provided**—or perhaps, more accurately, they reassert that there is *no liability* for injuries resulting from the inherent risks. Some state that there is no liability for injuries resulting from the inherent risks of the activity while others provide that there is no liability unless the provider failed to comply with the specified duties. In some cases, they provide immunity from liability for certain types of negligence.

Some statutes are more accurately classified as **statutory assumption of risk statutes** since the major provision of the statute is to make clear that the participant is assuming the inherent risks of the activity. These statutes usually do not include duties of the participant. Notwithstanding the differences between these two types of statutes, the characteristic they have in common is that they usually are intended to protect the service provider from liability for injury resulting from the inherent risks of the activity, and in many cases, from liability for injuries resulting from ordinary negligence.

These two types of statutes have been grouped into six categories: (1) equine liability statutes; (2) skiing statutes; (3) skating statutes [i.e., roller-skating, ice-skating, skateboarding, in-line skating, skate parks]; (4) statutes pertaining to other activities; (5) general recreation and sport statutes; and (6) hazardous recreational activity statutes.

Equine Liability Statutes "Equestrian"

State legislatures have enacted equine liability statutes in 44 states over the past ten to fifteen years. Equine acts usually include horses, ponies, donkeys, mules, and hinnies. Statutes in some states also include llamas. The laws are designed to protect owners, sponsors, and organizers of named equine activities from liability for equine-related accidents resulting from the inherent risks of the activity, and in many cases from ordinary negligence. Most may be closer to statutory assumption of risk statutes than to shared responsibility statutes, since they generally do not specify responsibilities or duties of the participant. While the statutes differ somewhat from state to state, most equine statutes *immunize equine owners from liability for injuries resulting from the inherent risks of equine activities except when the provider*

1. Provided faulty equipment or tack that caused the injury;

2. Failed to make reasonable and prudent efforts to determine the ability of the participant to engage safely in the activity, or to determine the ability of the participant to safely manage the particular equine;

3. Failed to post warning of known dangerous latent conditions on the facilities; or

4. Commits an act or omission that is below the required level of care. The minimum level described varies by state, but includes ordinary negligence, gross negligence, reckless conduct, and willful and wanton conduct.

In general, these statutes do not provide the same protection as that provided by the immunity statutes in previous sections of this section since under most equine statutes, the provider remains liable for injuries resulting from some or all negligent acts.

Statutes generally define the equine activities covered by the law, the categories of providers protected, the immunity provided, the exceptions, signage requirements, and the inherent risks of equine activities. Usually included in the inherent risks are (1) equine behavior propensities, (2) unpredictability of animal reactions, (3) hazards such as surface and subsurface conditions, (4) collisions with other equines and objects, and (5) the potential of a participant to act in a negligent manner that may cause injury. Equine legislation in each state may be found in Table 2.22.1.

Ski Operator Immunity Statutes

Ski operator statutes were among the first shared-responsibility statutes—*intended to clarify the duties of the ski operator and the skier and to reduce litigation arising from injuries resulting from the inherent risks of skiing. At* least 27 state legislatures have enacted some type of shared responsibility ski statute. While these statutes differ considerably, they generally include duties of the ski operator, duties of the skier, a listing of the inherent risks of skiing, and the affirmation that the skier assumes the inherent risks of the activity and that the ski operator is not liable for injuries resulting from the inherent risks. Lists of operator and skier duties are generally extensive. These acts generally include no immunity for ordinary negligence; however, in some states, negligence is limited to the failure to perform specified duties.

States approach inherent risks in various ways. Some states (e.g., Tennessee, New Mexico, and Idaho) express that any injury not caused by a violation of the ski operator duties is an inherent risk of the activity and that subsequent legal action is barred. Colorado, North Carolina, and Alaska statutes specify that a violation of the statute by either operator or skier constitutes negligence. Other states require a jury to determine if the risk was inherent. Ski legislation in each state may be found in Table 2.22.1.

Skating Statutes

Eleven states have enacted either roller-skating or ice-skating shared-responsibility statutes. These statutes generally contain four critical sections: (1) duties of the operator—usually including posting of notices regarding duties of skaters and inherent risks of skating; (2) duties of the skater—usually including skating within the range of one's ability, maintaining control of the skater's speed and course at all times, and heeding safety warnings; (3) some of the inherent dangers of skating; and (4) a declaration that the skater assumes the inherent risks and a statement that a skater or operator who violates duties set forth is liable to an injured person in a civil action. Skating legislation in each state may be found in Table 2.22.1. Providers are generally liable only if they breach the operator duties listed in the statute.

Skateboard Parks.   Popular types of skating emerging in recent years have included skateboarding, roller-blading, roller skiing, and in-line skating. Several state legislatures have passed legislation protecting providers of facilities for such activities as well as for stunt or freestyle biking.

The Nevada legislature passed a shared-responsibility statute that provides limited protection for an agency or political subdivision of the state that provides skateboard parks for public use. Iowa passed an assumption of risk statute that immunizes municipalities and their employees from liability for injuries resulting from the inherent risks of skateboarding or in-line skating on public property. The injured person must have known or reasonably should have known that the activity created a substantial risk of injury. Likewise, the Utah and Vermont legislatures established statutory assumption of risk statutes providing protection from liability for inherent risks of skating and skateboard-type activities. The Vermont statute encompassed all providers of all sports and the Utah statute included county and municipalities providing facilities for bike riding, biking, skateboarding, roller-skating, and in-line skating (see *General Recreation and Sport Immunity Statutes* on the following page). *These statutes have granted protection to governmental providers (except Vermont which included all sport providers) and their employees from liability for injuries resulting from the* **inherent risks** *of the activities.*

California, Florida, and New Hampshire have enacted hazardous recreational activity legislation that includes skateboard parks (see *Hazardous Recreational Activity Immunity Statutes* below). *This legislation grants protection from liability for some types of* ordinary negligence *to governmental entities (and employees) that provide these activities.*

Statutes Pertaining to Other Activities

Immunity statutes affecting other recreation and sport activities have also been enacted. They include statutes dealing with amusement rides (3 states), baseball (2), fishing (1), hang gliding (1), hockey facilities (2), motor sports (1), outfitters and guides (3), rodeos (2), snowmobiling (5), and sport shooting (3). These statutes are as varied as the activities to which they relate. Some are true shared-responsibility statutes, while others are more accurately labeled statutory assumption of risk statutes as they simply declare that the participant assumes the inherent risks. However, regardless of the differences among these statutes, *the common link is that they are all intended to protect the provider from liability for injuries resulting from the inherent risks of the activity.* Legislation relating to these activities may be found in Table 2.22.1.

Snowmobile statutes usually announce that the operator is not liable for the inherent risks. In some states the immunity is extended to ordinary negligence. They, like the other statutes included in this paragraph, are shared-responsibility statutes, as they prescribe duties of participants and operators. Interestingly, in South Dakota, providers renting snowmobiles are liable only if they are grossly negligent. **Outfitter and Guide** statutes, usually true shared-responsibility statutes, designate duties of both operators and participants and limit the liability of the outfitter to those specified duties. They specify that operators are liable only in the event of negligence. **Amusement ride** statutes also fall into this category. They provide for rider and operator duties, and specify that the rider assumes the inherent risks. Also of interest, Nevada law states that riders *above age 13* assume the *open and obvious* inherent risks.

Acts relating to many activities are simply statutory assumption of risk statutes. For instance, **sport-shooting** statutes designate that the participant (and spectator in Colorado) assumes the inherent risks of the activity. In Utah, the statute names the risks and specifies that the risks that are obvious and inherent are assumed. Utah and Michigan statutes declare that operators are generally not civilly or criminally liable for noise, and limit claims of nuisance. **Rodeo** statutes immunize nonprofit Montana and Wyoming organizations sponsoring rodeos from liability for all actions except wanton and willful or intentional acts. The statute is applicable to volunteer participants (including minors with written parental permission) and only in amateur rodeos in Wyoming. New Jersey provides some immunity for persons in the business of **renting bicycles** providing the operator follows statutory requirements. The **hang gliding** statute merely proclaims that participants assume the inherent risks of the activity. The **fishing** statute in Georgia, the **baseball** statute in Colorado, and the **hockey facility** statutes in Utah and Illinois differ in that some spell out risks, some pertain to signage, and most specify duties of the property or facility owner or operator, but not of the participant (or spectator, in the baseball and hockey statutes). All, however, make it clear that the operator is not liable for injuries resulting from the inherent risks of the activities. Ironically, the baseball statute was named the Colorado Baseball Spectator Safety Act. Legislation relating to these activities may be found in Table 2.22.1.

General Recreation and Sport Immunity Statutes

Six states have enacted laws sometimes referred to as **omnibus legislation** (Spengler & Burket, 2001) that is intended to encompass a large number of activities and sports rather than one or two. These laws are designed to give the service provider immunity, in one law, from liability for injuries resulting from the inherent risks of a number of sports. These states are Alaska, Hawaii, Utah, Vermont, Wisconsin, and Wyoming. The Vermont statute is the most inclusive, including all sports and all providers and the Utah statute is the least inclusive—protecting only counties and municipalities from liability for rodeo, bike riding, biking, equestrian, skateboarding, roller skating, and in-line skating. Wisconsin and Wyoming protected all providers from more than 20 recreational and sport activities, while Alaska lists more than 30 activities. *In each of these states, providers are immune from liability for inherent risks, but retain liability for the negligence of the entity or its employees.* Some of these statutes prescribe duties of the participant and the provider, and thus, could be classified as shared responsibility statutes.

Hazardous Recreational Activity Immunity Statutes

Legislatures in two states, California and Illinois, have passed statutes similar to the omnibus legislation just mentioned—except for two main differences. First, *the laws protect only public entities and their employees.* Secondly, the statutes protect the service provider and its employees from liability *for at least some types of ordinary negligence.* Protection is not provided (1) for failure to guard or warn of a known dangerous condition, (2) when a fee is charged for participation in the activity (a fee may be charged for entrance into the park), (3) for failure to properly construct or maintain recreational equipment or machinery, (4) when the entity recklessly or with gross negligence promoted the participation, or (5) when the injury resulted from gross negligence or reckless conduct of the entity or its employees. Thus, the entity and its employees are not liable for ordinary negligence except for failure to guard or warn of a dangerous condition and for failure to properly construct or maintain recreational equipment and machinery. In each state, more than 30 sports and activities are included within the protection. California has passed subsequent legislation specifically listing skateboarding as a hazardous recreational activity.

Three other states—Florida, New Hampshire, and North Carolina—have passed similar legislation affecting fewer activities. The Florida and North Carolina statutes protect governmental entities and their employees from liability for ordinary negligence (except the failure to warn of dangerous conditions of which the participant cannot reasonably expect to have notice) for three hazardous activities—skateboarding, in-line skating, and freestyle bicycling. New Hampshire provides immunity from liability for ordinary negligence for municipalities and school districts that without charge provide facilities for skateboarding, rollerblading stunt biking, or roller skiing.

CASES ON THE SUPPLEMENTAL CD

Fowler v. Tyler Independent School District, (2007 Tex. App. LEXIS 6433,*;232 S.W.3d 335). Because it is a governmental unit, a school district is immune from suit under the doctrine of sovereign/governmental immunity. Here, the Fowlers claim that since TISD was renting its stadium to the two high schools, TISD was acting in a proprietary capacity at the time of Bridget Fowler's injury, and therefore was not protected by sovereign/governmental immunity from suit.

Mounts v. Van Beeste, (2004 Mich. App. LEXIS 2062). This is a case in which the court addresses the issue of whether the equine immunity statute applies.

Thompson v. Rochester Community Schools, (2006 Mich. App. LEXIS 3233). This is an interesting case involving sovereign/governmental immunity of a school, a number of employees, and the lack of emergency care administered to an unconscious student. There is a very informative discussion of gross negligence and proximate cause.

QUESTIONS YOU SHOULD BE ABLE TO ANSWER

1. Explain the intended function of the Federal Tort Claims Act and the state tort claims acts.

2. Give an example that illustrates how a school can lose immunity because of a proprietary act.

3. What are the restrictions placed on qualification for Good Samaritan immunity.

4. What are the main differences between the shared responsibility acts and the statutory assumption of risk laws?

5. Regarding the recreation and sport volunteer immunity statutes, describe the immunity granted to the volunteer and the immunity granted to the organization.

REFERENCES

Cases

Avenoso v. Mangan, 2006 Conn. Super. LEXIS 489.

Chrismon v. Brown, 2007 Tex. App. LEXIS 7745.

Feagins v. Waddy, 978 So.2d 712 (Ala. 2007).

Gilbert v. Seton Hall University, 2003 U.S. App. LEXIS 11722.

Ola v. YMCA, 2005 Va. LEXIS 93.

Van Horn v. Watson, 2008 Cal. LEXIS 14589.

Publications

Brown, J. (1997). Legislators strike out: Volunteer little league coaches should not be immune from tort liability. *Seton Hall J. Sports L., 7,* 559.

Carter-Yamauchi, C. A. (1996). Volunteerism—A risky business? Honolulu: Legislative Reference Bureau.

Centner, T. J. (2000). Tort liability for sports and recreational activities: Expanding statutory immunity for protected classes and activities. *J. Legis, 26,* 1.

Centner, T. J. (2001). Simplifying sports liability law through a shared responsibility chapter. 1 *Va. Sports & Ent. L. J., 1,* 54.

Chalat, J. H. (2000). Survey of ski law in the United States. Vail, CO: CLE International Ski Liability Conference.

Dawson, R. O. (1999). Equine activity statutes: Part I—IV. Online, Internet.www.law.utexas.edu/dawson/horselaw/update1.htm

Jordan, B. (2001). What is the Good Samaritan law? Online, Internet. http://pa.essortment.com/goodsamaritanl_redg.htm

Ridolfi, K. M. (2000). Law, ethics, and the Good Samaritan: Should there be a duty to rescue? *Santa Clara L. Rev., 40,* 957.

Runquist, L. A., & Zybach, J. F. (1997). Volunteer Protection Act of 1997—an imperfect solution. Online, Internet. www.runquist.com/article_vol_protect.htm

Slank, N. L. (1999). A symposium on tort and sport: Leveling the playing field. *Washburn L. J., 38,* 847.

Spengler, J. O., & Burket, B. P. (2001). Sport safety statutes and inherent risk: A comparison study of sport specific legislation. *Journal of Legal Aspects of Sport, 11*(2), 135.

van der Smissen, B. (1990). *Legal liability and risk management for public and private entities.* Cincinnati: Anderson Publishing Company.

—Doyice J. Cotten
SPORT RISK CONSULTING

While it is true, as we have seen, that California courts hold releases of liability to a high standard of clarity, it does not, in our view, require Olympian efforts to meet the standard. *An effective release is hard to draft only if the party for whom it is prepared desires to hide the ball, which is what the law is designed to prevent.* A release that forthrightly makes clear to a person untrained in the law that the releasor gives up any claim against the releasee for the latter's own negligence . . . or that the releasee cannot be held liable for *any and all risks* the releasor encounters while on the former's premises or using its facilities . . . , ordinarily passes muster. (*Cohen v. Five Brooks Stable*, 2008, pp. 27–28)

A **waiver** or **release of liability** in the recreation or sport setting is a contract in which the participant or user of a service agrees to relinquish the right to pursue legal action against the service provider in the event that the ordinary negligence of the provider results in an injury to the participant. Injuries in sport and recreation result from one of three causes: (1) inherent risks of the activity (common accidents), (2) negligence by the service provider or its employees, and (3) more extreme acts by the service provider or its employees (i.e., gross negligence, reckless conduct, or willful/wanton conduct). It is important to understand that *the waiver is usually meant to protect the service provider from liability for the ordinary negligence of the service provider or its employees.* It will not generally protect the service provider from liability for extreme forms of negligence.[1] Although providers are not generally liable for injuries resulting from the inherent risks of the activity, the document can include language that will help protect the provider from liability for injuries resulting from inherent risks (see Participant Agreements later in this section). The waiver is an important tool in the risk management arsenal of the service provider.

Although waivers are commonly used by more recreation- and sport-related businesses than ever before, many service providers are still under the erroneous impression that waivers are worthless and offer no protection to the service provider. The validity of a waiver, however, is determined by the law in each state and subsequently, the validity of a waiver will vary depending upon the state.

Cotten and Cotten (2009) have placed each state, territory, and Washington, D.C. into one of six categories, depending upon the degree of rigor required for a valid waiver by the courts in that state. Figure 2.23.1 presents an updated classification of each state, Washington, D.C., Virgin Islands, and Puerto Rico. The first category (Insufficient Information) includes jurisdictions in which little if any information exists regarding their waiver law. The second category (Lenient) includes the Virgin Islands and 10 states that not only allow waivers, but also have very lenient requirements for their validity. The third category (Moderate) includes 16 states and D.C. in which waivers are allowed and the requirements for validity are moderate in nature. The fourth category (Strict) includes 16 states that allow waivers, but maintain very rigorous requirements for a waiver to be upheld. The fifth category (Strict or Not Enforced) consists of four states in which the impact of the Constitution, legislation, or Supreme Court decisions is unclear. At the very least, waivers will have to pass rigorous standards for enforcement, and at the most, waivers will not protect the service provider from liability for negligence. The final category (Not Enforced) consists of three states in which waivers have been declared unenforceable either by statute or by the state Supreme Court. *Thus, in at least 43 states, D.C., and the Virgin Islands, a well-written, properly administered waiver, voluntarily signed by an adult, can be used to protect the recreation or sport business from liability for ordinary negligence by the business or its employees.*

---

[1]Waivers in four states (Florida, Illinois, Kentucky, and Pennsylvania) may be able to protect the service provider from liability for gross negligence. One West Virginia court (*Murphy v. North American River Runners, Inc.*, 1991) has stated that one may contract to accept a risk arising from negligence or reckless conduct.

Figure 2.23.1 Classification of States, Territories, and Washington, D.C. as to the Rigor Required for Enforceable Waivers

Insufficient Information	Lenient	Moderate	Strict	Strict or Not Enforced[2]	Not Enforced
Puerto Rico	Alabama	Colorado	Alaska	Arizona	Louisiana
Rhode Island	Georgia	D.C.	Arkansas	Connecticut	Montana
	Kansas	Florida	California	Hawaii	Virginia
	Maryland	Idaho	Delaware	Wisconsin	
	Massachusetts	Illinois	Indiana		
	Michigan	Iowa	Kentucky		
	Nebraska	Minnesota	Maine		
	North Dakota	New Mexico	Mississippi		
	Ohio	N. Carolina	Missouri		
	Tennessee	Oklahoma	Nevada		
	Virgin Islands	Oregon	New Hamp.		
		S. Carolina	New Jersey		
		South Dakota	New York		
		Texas	Pennsylvania		
		Washington	Utah		
		West Virginia	Vermont		
		Wyoming			

[2]The Supreme Court has interpreted the **Arizona** Constitution to mean that all assumption of risk questions are a matter for the jury and not to be decided by summary judgment. Recent Supreme Court rulings in **Connecticut** and **Wisconsin** seem to indicate that any sport- or recreation-related waivers are unenforceable in those states. The ultimate effect of **Hawaii** statute H.R.S. 663-1.54 is unclear, but it seems to prohibit waivers of liability for negligent acts.

Providers must understand, however, that not all waivers are upheld in lenient states and that many well-written waivers are upheld in strict states. The category simply indicates the degree of rigor or specific requirements that must be met in the state for a waiver to be enforceable. Providers should also understand that the law is in a constant state of change so requirements, and the categories into which states are placed, are always subject to change.

FUNDAMENTAL CONCEPTS

Requirements for a Valid Waiver

A waiver is a legal contract and, as such, must adhere to the basic requirements of contract law. Some contract requirements are presented here, but the reader should refer to Section 5.10, *Contract Essentials*, for more information regarding contracts.

Public Policy

A contract or waiver is not valid if it is against **public policy**—sometimes defined as that principle of law under which freedom of contract or private dealings is restricted for the good of the community. (*Merten v. Nathan*, quoting *Higgins v. McFarland*, 1955). A waiver is generally against public policy if (1) it pertains to a service important to the public, (2) if the parties are not of equal bargaining power (contracts of adhesion), (3) if there is an employer-employee relationship, or (4) it attempts to preclude liability for extreme forms of conduct such as gross negligence, reckless misconduct, or willful and wanton conduct. *The general rule in most states is that recreation- or sport-related waivers are not against public policy.*

Consideration

A valid contract requires that something of value be exchanged between parties. The courts have held that the opportunity to participate constitutes consideration on the part of the service provider. Waivers usually include language such as "In consideration for being allowed to participate, I hereby waive. . . ."

Parties to the Contract

Three important points relate to the parties involved in a waiver. They are parties barred from redress, parties protected by the contract, and capacity to contract (See also Section 5.10, *Contract Essentials*).

Parties Relinquishing Rights. When signing a waiver, the signer is obviously relinquishing the rights of the signer to hold the service provider liable in the event of injury. However, the spouse or heirs often file suit against the service provider when the signer is seriously injured or killed. A phrase in which the signer relinquishes (on behalf of self, spouse, heirs, estate, and assigns) the right to recover for injury or death is usually included in the waiver. Providers should be aware, however, that such a phrase is not enforceable in many states because those states hold that **loss of consortium**[3] and **wrongful death**[4] claims are independent causes of action and are not derivative upon whether the signer has or would have had a valid claim.

Parties Protected by the Waiver. The waiver must specify the parties protected by the agreement. Parties for which protection is often sought (e.g., corporation, management, employees, sponsors, volunteers) should be listed. An inclusive phrase such as ". . . and all others who are involved" may be included if desired.

Parties Who Do Not Have Capacity to Contract. The third point of importance regards the capacity of the individual to contract. Contract law specifies that certain classes of individuals do not have the capacity to contract. Among those classes are persons lacking mental capacity, those unduly influenced by drugs or alcohol, and persons who have not reached the age of majority (see the following section).

Waivers and Minors

It is well-established law that waivers signed only by the minor client are voidable (that is, the minor can void the contract at any time) and therefore unenforceable by the provider. No cases have been found in which a recreation- or sport-related waiver, signed only by the minor, was upheld when challenged in court. As a result, many providers require that a parent sign the waiver on behalf of the minor. Of concern to these service providers is the question of whether waivers are effective when signed by a parent or guardian on behalf of a minor client.

The general rule has long been that *a waiver is a contract and, in most states, a minor cannot be bound by a contract whether it is (1) signed by the minor or (2) signed by a parent or guardian on behalf of a minor.* So, while the service provider contracting with a minor is bound by the contract, the minor is not. Thus the waiver will not prevent the minor from taking legal action against a negligent service provider. This aspect of the general rule is well supported. In *Dilallo v. Riding Safely Inc.* (1997), a 14-year-old Florida girl signed a waiver absolving a stable of liability. The court held that "a minor child injured because of a defendant's negligence is not bound by her contractual waiver of her right to file a lawsuit." In a Pennsylvania case (*Emerick v. Fox Raceway*, 2004), the court did not enforce a waiver signed by a 16-year-old boy who misrepresented his age in order to enter a motocross race.

Since waivers signed solely by the minor are ineffective, providers have used three strategies in attempting to gain protection (see Figure 2.23.2). They have (1) required that the parent or guardian sign the waiver on behalf of the minor client (**parental waiver**); (2) required the parent to indemnify the provider (agree to repay

---

[3]**Loss of Consortium** is the loss of material services and intangibles such as companionship and sexual relations. The non-signing spouse of a participant suffering serious injury often seeks damages for loss of consortium.
[4]The non-signing spouse or others often seek damages through **wrongful death** actions when the cause of death was a negligent or willful act of another.

the provider for any loss suffered due to the participation of the minor, e.g., monetary award by the court) (**parental indemnity agreement**); and (3) most recently, by requiring the parent to sign a mediation/arbitration agreement by which the parent agrees to submit any claim to mediation and/or arbitration rather than filing a lawsuit (**parental arbitration agreement**). See Section 5.30, *Alternative Dispute Resolution*, for more information on mediation and arbitration.

In the past, parental waivers and parental indemnity agreements have not been effective. For example, a 10-year-old girl was injured when another child jumped into a swimming pool on top of her. The girl's mother signed a post-injury release in exchange for a $3275 settlement. Eight years after the accident, upon reaching the age of majority, the girl filed suit against the YMCA. The court stated that "It is well settled in Michigan that, as a general rule, a parent has no authority, merely by virtue of being a parent, to waive, release, or compromise claims by or against the parent's child" and ruled that the YMCA was not protected by the release signed by the mother (*Smith v. YMCA of Benton Harbor/St. Joseph*, 1996).

In recent years, however, courts in some states have begun to enforce waivers and indemnity agreements signed by parents on behalf of their minor children. California courts were the first to enforce parental waivers. In 1990, *Hohe v. San Diego Unified Sch. Dist.* made it clear that, while minors are free to disaffirm contracts signed by the minor, they cannot disaffirm contracts made by the parent or guardian of the minor. Since that time, numerous California courts have ruled similarly. The Supreme Court of Ohio also ruled waivers signed by parents in favor of non-profit, public service providers are enforceable against the minor child (*Zivich v. Mentor Soccer Club*, 1998). Courts in Connecticut, Florida, Georgia, Massachusetts, North Dakota, and Wisconsin have also enforced parental waivers. Trumping a Colorado Supreme Court ruling prohibiting parental waivers, the Colorado Legislature passed a statute allowing such waivers. The Alaska legislature has subsequently passed a statute allowing parental waivers. In 2009, a Minnesota appellate court enforced a waiver signed by the parent of a minor. In addition, courts in Connecticut and Massachusetts have upheld parental indemnity agreements, and courts in California, Hawaii, Ohio, Louisiana, New Jersey, and Florida have upheld agreements by which parents agreed to submit any claims of the minor to arbitration. Alternatively, courts in Idaho, Pennsylvania, and Texas have ruled that minors are not bound by parental arbitration agreements.

So parental waivers are now enforceable in at least six to ten states,[5] parental indemnity agreements are enforceable in at least two states, and parental arbitration agreements are enforceable in at least six states. It is also important to understand that parental waivers, indemnity agreements, and arbitration agreements have not been addressed by the courts in most states; hence, they may be enforced in a number of those states as well. Consequently, providers in all states might consider the use of such agreements when dealing with minor participants. However, in doing so, the provider should remember two things: (1) Always have the parents sign the document, and (2) Use liability protection in addition to the waiver and/or indemnity agreement.

Format of the Waiver

Waivers are generally found in one of four formats. The first is as a **stand-alone document**—one in which the only function of the document is to provide liability protection for the service provider (see Figure 2.23.3). The patron is asked to sign a sheet of paper containing only a waiver and related material. The second format is the **waiver within another document** such as a membership agreement, an entry form, or a rental agreement (see the example in the Significant Case). The third format is a **group waiver**—which generally includes a waiver at the top of a sheet on which several parties sign (e.g., a team roster, sign-in sheet at a health club). Both the waiver within another document and the group waiver can be effective when carefully worded and properly administered; however, many courts, and this author, have encouraged providers to use the stand-alone waiver since it can provide much more protection that the shorter agreements. The fourth format is the **disclaimer of liability**, often found on the back on tickets. A disclaimer is a statement asserting that the provider is not responsible for injuries. The disclaimer is not signed, provides no evidence that the participant agreed to it, and, with a few exceptions, is ineffective. There is no harm in including such disclaimers on the back of a ticket, but the service provider should operate on the assumption that the statement will not effectively protect the business.

---

[5]Refer to footnotes in Figure 2.23.2

Figure 2.23.2 States in Which Parental Waivers, Parental Indemnification Agreements, and Parental Arbitration Agreements May be Enforced

Parental Waivers		Parental Indemnity Agreements		Parental Arbitration Agreements	
State	Authority	State	Authority	State	Authority
Alaska	Statute	Connecticut	Appellate Court	California	Supreme Court
California	Many Appellate Decisions	Massachusetts	Appellate Court	Florida	Supreme Court
Colorado	Statute			Hawaii	Supreme Court
Connecticut[6]	Appellate Court ruling			Louisiana	U.S. District Ct.
Florida[7]	Two Appellate Courts			New Jersey	Supreme Court
Georgia	Two Appellate Courts[8]			Ohio	Appellate Court
Minnesota	Appellate Court ruling				
North Dakota	Supreme Court ruling				
Ohio	Supreme Court ruling				
Wisconsin[9]	Appellate Court ruling				

Participant Agreement

Since many courts recommend the use of a stand-alone document, that format will be emphasized in this section. In fact, the most comprehensive stand-alone document recommended is called a **participant agreement.** The participant agreement is a relatively new concept in liability protection and is much more than just a waiver. The agreement differs from the basic waiver in that it (1) is designed to improve the rapport and understanding between the provider and the participant; (2) increases the understanding of the rewards and activity risks of the participant, prepares them psychologically for any discomforts, making legal action less likely; (3) allows participants to make more informed decisions as to participation; and (4) provides a much broader range of protection. The mere existence of a waiver or participant agreement can often deter a party from filing a claim. If a claim is filed, either document provides the potential for early dismissal.

Content of the Participant Agreement. The participant agreement is much broader in scope than a simple waiver clause or even a broad stand-alone waiver. The contents of the document are meant to provide protections for the provider and to serve as an exchange of information (providing information about the activity to the participant and collecting information about the participant). Suggested content of the participant agreement is listed below and a sample agreement is shown in Figure 2.23.3.

1. Material meant to inform the participant of the **nature of the activity** and to help them understand and appreciate the risks involved;

2. An **assumption of inherent risk** to protect against liability for the inherent risks;

3. A **waiver** of liability as protection against ordinary negligence;

4. An **indemnification agreement** to provide further protection against both the risks of ordinary negligence and the inherent risks;

5. Five selected clauses calling for **severability** (provides that if any part of the document is void, the rest remains in effect), for **mediation and/or arbitration** (provides that any resultant claims will be submitted to mediation and binding arbitration rather than entering the court system) [see Section 5.30 *Alternative Dispute Resolution*], **venue and jurisdiction** (specifies where legal action must occur and which court has

---

[6]Refer to footnote 2 in this section.

[7]In *Kirton v. Fields* (2008), the Florida Supreme Court ruled that "a pre-injury release executed by a parent on behalf of a minor child is unenforceable against the minor or the minor's estate in a tort action arising from injuries resulting from participation in a commercial activity." p. 26 Note, however, that the ruling is specifically limited to commercial activities and does not necessarily apply to school or community sponsored activities.

[8]Neither case is completely applicable to sport and recreation waivers.

[9]Refer to footnote 2 in this section.

Lucky Horseshoe Trail Rides Participant Agreement
Assumption of Risk, Waiver of Liability, and Indemnification Agreement

Trail riding is a popular activity enjoyed by young and old alike. It combines wholesome physical activity, adventure, powerful animals, and the natural beauty of the out-of-doors. While the pleasure of such rides is unmistakable, Lucky Horseshoe Trail Rides (hereafter referred to as LHTR) wants to make certain that all riders are fully aware of the various inherent risks involved in such an activity. LHTR feels that it is important that riders know that certain risks cannot be eliminated without destroying the unique character of this activity; that some danger is involved in trail riding; and that on occasion, riders do suffer injury. LHTR does not want to frighten riders or reduce their enthusiasm for a trail ride, but we believe it is important that you be informed of the nature of the activity.

<u>Assumption of Inherent Risks.</u> It is impossible to list all of the inherent risks of horseback trail rides, but some are listed below to give the rider a better idea of the risks involved. Minor injuries such as being scratched by a bush or cactus, muscle soreness, bruises, sunburn, and sprains are frequent occurrences. More serious injuries such as exposure from extreme hot, cold, or wet conditions, altitude sickness, broken bones, concussions, cuts, and bites occasionally occur. Rare catastrophic events such as heart attack, stroke, paralysis, serious internal or head injuries, and death can occur. In addition, these injuries may occur in locations far from emergency medical care.

These injuries may be caused by falls from horses; unpredictable weather changes; the propensity of the horse to behave in ways that may result in injury, harm, or death to those around it; the unpredictability of the animal's reaction to sounds, sudden movement, unfamiliar objects, persons, or other animals; surface or subsurface conditions; collisions with other animals or objects; steep, uneven, or snow-covered terrain; actions of the rider or other riders; failure of tack or other equipment; and errors in judgment of the trail guide or other employees.

I understand that the inherent risks of horseback trail rides are serious and that horseback trail riding is a dangerous activity regardless of the care taken by LHTR and its employees. I have read the previous paragraphs and (1) I know the nature of the activity of horseback trail riding; (2) I understand the demands of this activity relative to my physical condition and riding skill level, and (3) I appreciate the potential impact of the types of injuries that may result from horseback trail riding. I hereby assert that my participation at the LHTR is voluntary and that I knowingly assume all of the inherent risks of the activity.

<u>Waiver of Liability.</u> **In consideration of permission to participate in a horseback trail ride, today and on all future dates, I, on behalf of myself, my spouse, my heirs, personal representatives, or assigns, do hereby release, waive, and discharge LHTR (including its officers, employees, volunteers, and agencies) from liability from any and all claims resulting from the inherent risks of the activity of trail riding or from the ordinary negligence of the LHTR.**

This agreement applies to (1) personal injury (including death) from incidents or illnesses arising from horseback trail ride participation at the LHTR (including, but not limited to, in and around the stable and corral, mounting and dismounting, riding, while dismounted during the ride, during any instruction by the staff, and all premises including bleachers, the associated sidewalks and parking lots); and to (2) any and all claims resulting from the damage to, loss of, or theft of property.

<u>Indemnification.</u> **I also agree to hold harmless, defend, and indemnify LHTR** (that is, defend and pay any judgment and costs, including investigation costs and attorney's fees) from any and all claims of mine, my spouse, family members, or others arising from my injury or loss due to my participation in horseback trail riding (including those arising from the inherent risks of trail riding or the ordinary negligence of LHTR).

I further agree to hold harmless, defend, and indemnify LHTR (that is, defend and pay any judgment and costs, including investigation costs and attorney's fees) against any and all claims of co-participants, rescuers, and others arising from my conduct in the course of my participation in horseback trail riding.

Relevant Binding Clauses.

<u>Covenant Not to Sue.</u> I covenant not to sue LHTR for any present or future claim arising directly or indirectly from my participation in horseback trail riding at LHTR. This includes claims resulting from the inherent risks of trail riding and the ordinary negligence of LHTR.

Figure 2.23.3 Illustrative Participant Agreement

Arbitration. I agree to engage in good faith efforts to mediate any dispute that might arise between me and LHTR. Any agreement reached will be formalized by a written contractual agreement at that time. Should the issue not be resolved by mediation, I agree that all disputes, controversies, or claims arising out of or relating to this contract shall be submitted to binding arbitration in accordance with the applicable rules of the *American Arbitration Association* then in effect. I further recognize that the issue must be submitted to binding arbitration in _____ County in the State of _____.

Venue and Jurisdiction. Likewise, I agree that if, in spite of this contract, legal action is brought against LHTR regarding a claim, the appropriate trial court for the county of _____ in the State of _____ has the sole and exclusive jurisdiction and that only the substantive laws of the State of _____ shall apply.

Severability. I further expressly agree that the foregoing Assumption of Risk, Waiver of Liability, and Indemnification Agreement is intended to be as broad and inclusive as is permitted by the laws of the State of _____ and that if any portion thereof is held invalid, it is agreed that the balance shall, notwithstanding, continue in full legal force and effect.

Integration Clause. I affirm that this agreement **supersedes any and all previous oral or written promises or agreements**. I understand that this is the entire agreement between me and LHTR and cannot be modified or changed in any way by representations or statements by any agent or employee of LHTR. This agreement may only be amended by a written document duly executed by all parties.

Acknowledgements, Assertions, and Agreements:
Health Status—I assert that I:
- Do not have asthma, diabetes, anaphylaxis, epilepsy, heart disease, or high blood pressure.
- Have no other medical problems that would contra-indicate participation in horseback trail riding.
- Possesses sufficient physical fitness and skill to enable safe participation in horseback trail riding.

Emergency Care—I authorize or agree:
- LHTR to administer emergency first aid, CPR, and use an AED when deemed necessary by LHTR.
- LHTR to secure emergency medical care or transportation (i.e., EMS) when deemed necessary by LHTR.
- LHTR to share my medical history with emergency medical personnel when deemed necessary by LHTR.
- To assume all costs of emergency medical care and transportation.

Rules and Safety Equipment—I agree:
- To abide by the rules established by LHTR.
- To inform LHTR immediately if I become aware of rider conduct or equipment condition that presents a danger to others or myself.
- That I understand the importance of and agree to wear any required equipment at all times while riding.
- That the LHTR will conduct the activity in good faith and may find it necessary to terminate my participation if the supervisor judges that I am incapable of safely meeting the rigors of the activity. I accept LHTR's right to take such actions for the safety of myself and/or other riders.

Acknowledgment of Understanding. I have read this 2-page <u>Participant Agreement–Assumption of Risk, Waiver of Liability, Indemnification Agreement, and Covenant not to Sue</u> and fully understand its terms. I understand that I am giving up substantial rights, including my right to sue LHTR for injuries resulting from the inherent risks of horseback trail riding or the ordinary negligence of LHTR. I further acknowledge that I am signing this agreement freely and voluntarily, and intend my signature to be a complete and unconditional release of all liability, including that resulting from the inherent risks of the activity or from the ordinary negligence of LHTR, to the greatest extent allowed by the laws of the State of _____.

_____   _____   _____
Printed Name of PARTICIPANT   Signature of PARTICIPANT   Date

Emergency Contact: _____   _____
                                   NAME/RELATION   TELEPHONE

Figure 2.23.3 Illustrative Participant Agreement (continued)

legal authority), **covenant not to sue** (a contract not to sue to enforce a right of action), and an **integration clause** which asserts that this is the entire agreement and supersedes any previous oral or written agreements;

6. Authorizations, assertions, and agreements regarding **health status, emergency care,** and **rules and safety** (information that allows the provider to better meet the needs of the participant and provide a safer activity environment); and

7. A **final acknowledgement of release and assumption of risk** prior to the signatures.

The scope of this book does not allow the presentation of further detail. For a complete discussion of waivers and participant agreements, including the waiver law in each state and more than 50 guidelines for writing and preparing waivers and participant agreements, the reader is referred to Cotten and Cotten, 2009.

SIGNIFICANT CASE

Stokes v. Bally's Pacwest, Inc. provides an excellent, straightforward example of the value of liability waivers in protecting against liability for negligence in the recreation or sport setting. The case illustrates very clearly the need to make sure the waiver is conspicuous and that the document plainly provides for protection against liability for negligence. When read carefully, one can see that Stokes specifically releases Bally's from liability for Bally's negligence. While the recommended waiver format is the stand-alone waiver, this waiver within another document is better than average and provided effective liability protection to Bally. Observe, also, that the fact the appellant did not read the waiver is irrelevant.

STOKES V. BALLY'S PACWEST, INC.

COURT OF APPEALS OF WASHINGTON, DIVISION ONE
113 Wn. App. 442; 54 P.3d 161; 2002 Wash. App. LEXIS 2233
September 16, 2002, Filed

[handwritten: Case Title & Citation]

OPINION: COX, A.C.J. —

* * *

[handwritten: Facts]

Persons may expressly agree in advance of an accident that one has no duty of care to the other, and shall not be liable for ordinary negligence (*Chauvlier v. Booth Creek Ski Holdings, Inc.*, 109 Wn. App. 334, 339, 35 P.3d 383 (2001)). Such exculpatory agreements are generally enforceable, subject to three exceptions. Because the "waiver and release" language at issue here was conspicuously stated in the agreement that Michael Stokes signed, we reverse both summary judgment orders and direct entry of summary judgment in favor of Bally's Pacwest Total Fitness Center on remand.

Stokes joined Bally's, a health club. He signed a retail installment contract that evidenced the terms and conditions of membership. The contract contained the waiver and release provisions at issue in this appeal. Several months after signing the agreement, Stokes slipped on a round metallic plate placed in a wooden floor at the club while playing basketball. He injured his knee and shoulder. Stokes sued Bally's, alleging that the health club's negligence caused him serious, painful, and permanent injuries. Bally's moved for summary judgment, which the trial court denied. According to the trial court, there were "material questions of fact whether the 'Waiver and Release' provisions set forth in the Retail Installment Contract [that Stokes signed], were sufficiently conspicuous or knowingly consented to by [him]."

[handwritten: Procedural History]

We granted discretionary review of that decision. Pursuant to RAP 7.2, we also granted Bally's permission to renew its summary judgment motion in the trial court in order to allow that court to consider this court's then recent decision in Chauvlier. Following Bally's renewed motion, the trial court again denied summary judgment for the same reason that it did before.

We now focus our attention on the two orders before us. To prevail on his ordinary negligence claim against Bally's, Stokes must establish that the health club owed him a duty. Whether such a duty exists is a question of law. As we recently noted in Chauvlier, our Supreme Court has recognized the right of parties, subject to certain exceptions, to expressly agree in advance that one party is under no obligation of care to the other, and shall not be held liable for ordinary negligence.

The general rule in Washington is that such exculpatory clauses are enforceable unless (1) they violate public policy; (2) the negligent act falls greatly below the standard established by law for protection of others; or (3) they are inconspicuous (*Scott v. Pacific West Mountain Resort*, 119 Wn.2d 484, 492, 834 P.2d 6 (1992). Neither of the first two of these exceptions is at issue here. The trial court expressly relied on only the third exception in making its rulings, denying summary judgment on the ground that a genuine issue of material fact existed whether the waiver and release clause was inconspicuous.

This court will not uphold an exculpatory agreement if "the releasing language is so inconspicuous that reasonable persons could reach different conclusions as to whether the document was unwittingly signed" (Chauvlier, at 341). Conversely, where reasonable persons could only reach the conclusion that the release language is conspicuous, there is no question of the document having been unwittingly signed. Whether Stokes subjectively unwittingly signed the form is not at issue. Rather, the question is whether, objectively, the waiver provision was so inconspicuous that it is unenforceable.

[handwritten: Issue]

As we stated in Chauvlier, a person who signs an agreement without reading it is generally bound by its terms as long as there was ample opportunity to examine the contract and the person failed to do so for personal reasons. Here, Stokes admitted that he did not remember reading the waiver and release provision of the contract. But this admission does not end our review. We must still determine whether the waiver and release language is inconspicuous so as to invalidate Stokes' release of Bally's from any duty to him for its alleged ordinary negligence.

We most recently considered whether a release was inconspicuous and unwittingly signed in Chauvlier. The release in that case was printed on a ski pass application. Comparing the release to those considered in *Baker and Hewitt v. Miller*, n16 we held that the release was sufficiently conspicuous to be enforceable. We noted that the release was not hidden within part of a larger agreement, and that it was clearly entitled "LIABILITY RELEASE & PROMISE NOT TO SUE. PLEASE READ CAREFULLY!." We also noted that the words "RELEASE" and "HOLD HARMLESS AND INDEMNIFY" were set off in capital letters throughout the agreement, and that the release contained the language, just above the signature line, "Please Read and Sign: I have read, understood, and accepted the conditions of the Liability Release printed above."

At the other end of the spectrum of reported cases is Baker (Baker, 79 Wn.2d at 202). There, our Supreme Court held that a disclaimer in a golf cart rental agreement, consisting of several lines of release language printed in the middle of a paragraph discussing other information, was so inconspicuous that enforcement of the release would be unconscionable

In McCorkle, another division of this court held that a trial court erred in granting summary judgment on McCorkle's negligence claims against a fitness club. The holding was that there were genuine issues of material fact whether a liability statement contained in a membership application McCorkle signed was sufficiently conspicuous.

The provision at issue in that case had as a heading "LIABILITY STATEMENT." In the first few sentences, the provision declared that the member accepted liability for damages that the member or the member's guests caused. The last sentence of the provision stated that the member waived any claim for damages as a result of any act of a Club employee or agent. And nothing in the document alerted the reader to the shift in the liability discussion from liability of the member to waiver of liability for claims against the Club.

The parties now before us cite to other cases, *Hewitt and Conradt v. Four Star Promotions* (Hewitt, 11 Wn. App. at 78-80; Conradt, 45 Wn. App. at 850). Both are factually distinguishable. In each of those cases, the waiver and release form was in a separate document, not a separate provision in one document.

Here, the release is more like that in Chauvlier and unlike that in Baker or McCorkle. In our view, reasonable minds could not differ regarding whether the waiver and release provisions in this retail installment sales contract were so inconspicuous that it was unwittingly signed. The language is conspicuous, as a matter of law, and it was not unwittingly signed.

The release provision in this retail installment contract, which Stokes signed, must be read in context. Several lines above Stokes signature is a section in bold type, which states:

NOTICE TO BUYER: (a) Do not sign this Contract before you read it or if any of the spaces intended for the agreed terms, except as to unavailable information, are blank. . . .

THIS IS A RETAIL INSTALLMENT CONTRACT, THE RECEIPT OF AN EXECUTED COPY OF WHICH, AS WELL AS A COPY OF THE CLUB RULES AND REGULATIONS AND A WRITTEN DESCRIPTION OF THE SERVICES AND EQUIPMENT TO BE PROVIDED, IS HEREBY ACKNOWLEDGED BY THE BUYER.

Immediately following Stokes' signature is a line, starting in bold and capital letters, stating: "WAIVER AND RELEASE: This contract contains a WAIVER AND RELEASE in Paragraph 10 to which you will be bound."

Paragraph 10, which is expressly referenced in the line directly below Stokes" signature, is entitled "WAIVER AND RELEASE." It states as follows:

You (Buyer, each Member and all guests) agree that if you engage in any physical exercise or activity or use any club facility on the premises, you do so at your own risk. This includes, without limitation, your use of the locker room, pool, whirlpool, sauna, steamroom, parking area, sidewalk or any equipment in the health club and your participation in any activity, class, program or instruction. You agree that you are voluntarily participating in these activities and using these facilities and premises and assume all risk of injury to you or the contraction of any illness or medical condition that might result, or any damage, loss or theft of any personal property. You agree on behalf of yourself (and your personal representatives, heirs, executors, administrators, agents and assigns) to release and discharge us (and our affiliates, employees, agents, representatives, successors and assigns) from any and all claims or causes of action (known or unknown) arising out of our negligence. This Waiver and Release of liability includes, without limitation, injuries which may occur as a result of (a) your use of any exercise equipment or facilities which may malfunction or break, (b) our improper maintenance of any exercise equipment or facili-

ties, (c) our negligent instruction or supervision, and (d) you slipping and falling while in the health club or on the premises. You acknowledge that you have carefully read this Waiver and Release and fully understand that it is a release of liability. You are waiving any right that you may have to bring a legal action to assert a claim against us for our negligence.

Unlike the waiver provisions in Baker and McCorkle, this paragraph discusses only Stokes' agreement to release Bally's from liability for its negligence. Stokes' argument that he believed that the paragraph somehow related to release from liability for his financial obligations under the retail installment sale agreement is wholly unpersuasive. As our Supreme Court stated in National Bank, it "would be impossible for a person of ordinary intelligence, much less a person of the intelligence and ability of appellant, to have misunderstood the contents of this instrument upon a casual reading thereof. . ." The same principle applies here. Reasonable persons could not disagree that the content of paragraph 10 is quite clearly a waiver and release of liability for negligence, not financial obligations. Likewise, reasonable persons could not disagree that the waiver and

release provisions of the paragraph are conspicuously displayed within the larger document.

Stokes also argues that an exculpatory provision may be placed in a document separate from the retail installment sales agreement, but concedes that this is not required. Bally's counters that RCW 63.14.020 and other laws require that the exculpatory clauses and financial terms and conditions between a health club and its members all must be within one document.

We need not decide in this case whether Bally's argument is correct. It is sufficient to state that no authority supports the proposition that an exculpatory clause must be contained in a separate document to be enforceable. Rather, what is required is that the release language in a document be conspicuous.

Rationale

The language at issue in this case is conspicuous and enforceable. Bally's owes no duty to Stokes for his injuries. Summary judgment in favor of Bally's is required.

We reverse both summary judgment orders, and direct entry of summary judgment in favor of Bally's on remand.

WE CONCUR.

Holding

CASES ON THE SUPPLEMENTAL CD

Kirton v. Fields, 2008 Fla. LEXIS 2378. This is the latest state supreme court ruling on the issue of parental waivers. Compare the two rationales. Also notice that this ruling applies only to waivers used by commercial businesses.

Moore v. Waller, (2007 D.C. App. LEXIS 476). Examine the discussion regarding unequal bargaining power and adhesion contracts. Also of interest is the section regarding the necessity of using the word "negligence." Finally, read and evaluate the waiver used in this case.

Cohen v. Five Brooks Stable, (2008 Cal. App. LEXIS 222). Study carefully the court's discussion regarding ambiguity and the use of the term "negligence."

QUESTIONS YOU SHOULD BE ABLE TO ANSWER

1. Explain what is meant by the term "public policy" and explain why recreation- and sport-related waivers are generally not against public policy.

2. Contrast the rationales for enforcing parental waivers with those against such enforcement.

3. Other than the waiver of negligence section of the participant agreement, what is the most important component? Defend your answer.

4. In *Stokes v. Bally's Pacwest*, how was the waiver made conspicuous? Why was it important that it be conspicuous?

5. Some people feel that a waiver is "bad" or unethical. Defend their use by a recreation- or sport-related business.

REFERENCES

Cases

Atkins v. Swimwest Family Fitness Center, 2005 Wisc. LEXIS 2.

Bothell v. Two Point Acres, Inc., 1998 Ariz. App. LEXIS 32.

Cohen v. Five Brooks Stable, 2008 Cal. App. LEXIS 222.

Coughlin v. T.M.H. International Attractions, Inc., 1995 U.S. Dist. LEXIS 12499 (Ky).

Craig v. Lakeshore Athletic Club, Inc., 1997 Wash. App. LEXIS 907.

Davis v. Sun Valley Ski Education Foundation, Inc., 1997 Ida. LEXIS 82.

Dilallo v. Riding Safely Inc., 687 So.2d 353 [Fla. 4th Dist. 1997].

Hanks v. Powder Ridge Restaurant Corporation, 2005 Conn. LEXIS 500.

Hohe v. San Diego Unified Sch. Dist., 274 Cal.Rptr. 647 (1990).

Huffman v. Monroe County Community School, 564 N.E.2d 961 (Ind., 1991).

Kirton v. Fields, 2008 Fla. LEXIS 2378.

Lantz v. Iron Horse Saloon, Inc., 717 So.2d 590 [Fla. 5th Dist. 1998].

Mahoney v. USA Hockey, Inc., 1999 U.S. Dist. LEXIS 19359.

Maurer v. Cerkvenik-Anderson Travel, Inc., 165 Ariz. Adv. Rep. 51 (1994).

Merten v. Nathan, 321 N.W.2d 173, quoting *Higgins v. McFarland*, 86 S.E.2d 168 at 172 (Va., 1955).

Moore v. Minnesota Baseball Instructional School, 2009 Minn. App. Unpub. LEXIS 299.

Murphy v. North American River Runners, Inc., 412 S.E.2d. 504 (1991).

Pena v. The Rolladium, 2002 Cal. App. Unpub. LEXIS 1466.

Phelps v. Firebird Raceway, Inc., 2005 Ariz. LEXIS 53.

Quinn v. Mississippi State University, 1998 Miss. LEXIS 328 59.

Reardon v. Windswept Farm LLC., 2006 Conn. LEXIS 330.

Smith v. YMCA of Benton Harbor/St. Joseph, 550 N.W.2d 262 [Mich. 1996].

Swierkosz v. Starved Rock Stables, 607 N.E.2d 280 (Ill., 1993).

Zivich v. Mentor Soccer Club, 1997 Ohio App. LEXIS 1577.

Publications

Cotten, D. J. and Cotten, M. B. (1997). *Legal aspects of waivers and releases in sport, recreation and fitness activities.* Canton, OH: PRC Publishing, Inc.

Cotten, D. J. and Cotten, M. B. (2009). *Waivers & Releases of Liability.* 7th ed. Sport Risk Consulting: www.lulu.com

van der Smissen, B. (1990). *Legal liability and risk management for public and private entities.* Cincinnati: Anderson Publishing Co.

2.24 Agreements Related to the Inherent Risks

—Doyice J. Cotten
SPORT RISK CONSULTING

This section presents three additional documents that can strengthen defenses for the service provider–the informed consent agreement, the agreement to participate, and the assumption of risk agreement. Each addresses the inherent risks of the activity, training program, or treatment and helps to produce a stronger assumption of risk defense.

INFORMED CONSENT AGREEMENTS

The **informed consent** agreement is a document used to protect the provider from liability for the informed, treatment risks of a treatment, program, or regimen to which the signer is subjected. The factor that makes the informed consent unique is that **something is done to the participant** by another party with the consent of the participant. It may be in the form of medical treatment, rehabilitation, therapy, fitness testing, or a training program (e.g., when one is to be treated for an injury by an athletic trainer, when a participant is to undergo a training program developed by a personal trainer). The document informs the signer of the risks, thereby enabling the signer to make an educated, informed decision. The informed consent is based in contract law; thus, the signing parties must be of age. The informed consent offers little or no protection against liability for injuries resulting from negligence.

The doctrine of informed consent derives from two principles: (1) a person's inherent right to control what happens to his or her body, and (2) the physician's fiduciary duty to the patient—to warn the patient of risks and make certain the patient knows enough to make an informed decision regarding his or her care. It is an ethical, moral, and legal concept that is ingrained in American culture.

There are two separate, but related, components of informed consent—**disclosure** and **consent** (Nolan-Haley, 1999). The doctrine requires that those who consent be competent (i.e., of legal age, intellectually capable of consent), sufficiently informed about the treatment to enable an educated decision, and consent voluntarily with no duress (Koeberle & Herbert, 1998).

Medicine

Informed consents originated with and have been primarily used in conjunction with the medical profession. The first cases defining informed consent appeared in the late 1950s and were based on the tort of **battery**—the intentional, unpermitted, unprivileged, and offensive touching (physical contact) of the person of one individual by another. Today most medical cases are based on **negligence** since consent is obtained and the issue is whether the consent was adequately "informed." Informed consent is more than simply getting a patient to sign a written consent form—it is a communication process by which the physician provides relevant information to enable the patient to make an educated, informed decision (American Medical Association, 1998). While state law regarding informed consent varies from state to state, generally physicians are required to inform regarding the nature of the proposed treatment, foreseeable risk and discomforts, anticipated benefits, alternative procedures, and instructions regarding food, drink, or lifestyles.

Human Subject Research

A major application of the informed consent has been in the area of human subject research. The American College of Sports Medicine (1999) stated that:

> By law, any experimental subject or clinical patient who is exposed to possible physical, psychological, or social injury must give informed consent prior to participating in a proposed project. (p. vi)

The Office of Human Subjects Research of the National Institutes of Health outlines requirements for such research. The consent should (1) be obtained in writing, (2) be understandable, (3) be obtained in non-coercive circumstances, and (4) contain no language suggesting a relinquishment of rights.

Some of the elements that should be included in the consent are: (1) purpose and duration of the research, (2) description of the procedures, risks, and discomforts involved, (3) benefits and compensation to the subject, (4) alternative procedures, (5) confidentiality policies, (6) compensation and treatment available in the event of injury, (7) whom to contact for questions, and (8) a statement of voluntary participation. They specify that the document should be written at a level below that of a high school graduate—making liberal use of subheads, avoiding multi-syllable words when possible, and keeping sentences short and understandable (Office of Human Subjects Research, 2000).

Sport and Fitness

In recent years, informed consents have been used more frequently in sport and fitness. Service providers are becoming more aware of the necessity of utilizing informed consents for participants in certain types of programs. Injury rehabilitation programs, fitness testing, and fitness regimens directed by personal trainers are three examples of situations in which the use of informed consents is standard practice.

Koeberle and Herbert (1998) describe the informed consent in the fitness setting as "a voluntary agreement from a client who has been informed of, appreciates, and understands the material and relevant risks associated with participation in the activity or range of activities involved in exercise testing and activity provided through prescription" (p. 52). Since having a client undergo an exercise prescription or fitness test can be construed as either actual or constructive contact, they stress that an informed consent is necessary to gain the client's permission for contact. Without the informed consent, the fitness professional is risking action for civil or criminal battery. Koeberle and Herbert suggest that informed consents in personal fitness settings do not require consent forms in the same detail as those required of physicians. The trainer is not held to a standard as high as that of the physician since activity programs contain a very low incidence of risk when compared to even the safest medical procedures.

The following guidelines for the content and administration of the informed consent for sport, recreation, and fitness activities are drawn from four sources (Herbert & Herbert, 2002;[1] Independent Review Consulting, Inc., 2000; Koeberle & Herbert, 1998; Oliver & Oliver, 2001).

Content

The content of the informed consent for the recreation, sport, and fitness setting should:

- Be in writing on a preprinted form;
- Be written in plain, understandable language;
- State the purpose of the exercise program, test, or prescribed action;
- Include a general description of the exercise program, test, or prescribed action;
- List any likely discomforts that might be associated with the program, test, or activity;
- List the potential risks and potential benefits of the exercise program, test, or activity;
- Be worded to allow all staff members to have physical contact or interact with the participant;
- Have participant acknowledge voluntary participation;
- Have participant acknowledge that consent was not signed under duress;

---

[1] Consult this publication for an in-depth look at the concept of the informed consent.

- Have participant acknowledge an opportunity to ask questions and have them answered to his or her satisfaction;
- Have participant acknowledge that the participant read and understood the informed consent document.

Administration

The administrative procedures relating to the obtaining and handling of the informed consent can make a difference in the effectiveness of the agreement.

- A separate form should be used for each type of activity (e.g., exercise program, test, rehabilitation, fitness activity).
- The professional should explain the content of the informed consent and give the participant an opportunity to ask and have his or her questions answered satisfactorily.
- The consent form should be signed by the participant and professional, and dated.
- A copy of the consent should be provided to the participant.
- The signed and dated consent should be placed in the participant's file.

If the participant is a **minor**,

- It is imperative that one or both parents sign the agreement;
- The provider should use an informed consent form written specifically for parents of minors;
- The consent should contain language directed to the parent by which the parent gives permission for the activity, acknowledges an understanding of the risks, and signs the agreement.

An illustrative informed consent for personal trainers is presented in Figure 2.24.1. This form is for illustrative purposes only and the reader is cautioned to consult a competent attorney for legal advice regarding such a form.

It is important that the recreation or sport manager understand that the informed consent is important in avoiding liability for injuries resulting from the inherent risks of the activity. It is equally important that the recreation or sport manager remember two things about the informed consent: (1) that the informed consent is contractual in nature, thus requiring the signature of a parent or guardian when the client is a minor, and (2) that the consent provides no protection against liability for injuries resulting from the negligence of the service provider, its employees, or its agents. For such protection, a waiver should be utilized (see Section 2.23 *Waivers and Releases*).

Documentation

Herbert and Herbert (2002) stress the importance of documentation and record-keeping when working with individuals who have consented to programs. Just as physicians now must keep detailed notes on patient visits (e.g., complaints, treatments, responses to treatment, instructions), personal trainers, therapists, and other providers utilizing informed consents should do the same. While the extent of documentation required might not be the same, all documentation and notes can serve as evidence and can help the provider recollect the facts if called upon to testify in the event of litigation—sometimes years later. Development and use of a standardized form that includes spaces for the date, signature, and notes is suggested.

Personal Fitness Training Program
Informed Consent

Program Objectives

I understand that my physical fitness program is individually tailored to meet the goals and objectives agreed upon by my personal trainer and myself.

Description of the Exercise Program

I understand that my exercise program can involve participation in a number of types of fitness activities. These activities will vary depending upon the objectives that my personal trainer and I establish, but can include: (1) aerobic activities including, but not limited to, the use of treadmills, stationary bicycles, step machines, rowing machines, and running track; (2) muscular endurance and strength building exercises including, but not limited to, the use of free weights, weight machines, calisthenics, and exercise apparatus; (3) nutrition and weight control activities; and (4) selected physical fitness and body composition tests, including but not limited to strength tests, cardiovascular fitness tests, and body composition tests.

Description of Potential Risks

I understand that my personal trainer cannot guarantee my personal safety because all exercise programs have inherent risks regardless of the care taken by a personal trainer. **I will initial the types of activities (including their risks) that my trainer and I have selected for my program to acknowledge that I understand the potential risks of my training program.**

_____ **Aerobic Activities.** I realize that participation in any cardiovascular activity may involve sustained, vigorous exertion which places stress on the muscles, joints, and cardiovascular system, sometimes resulting in injuries ranging from minor injuries (e.g., muscle soreness, pulled muscles, and musculo-skeletal strains and sprains) to the infrequent serious injury (e.g., torn ligaments, heart attack, and stroke) to the rare catastrophic incident (e.g., death, paralysis).

_____ **Muscular Endurance and Strength.** I realize that participation in muscular endurance and strength building activities involves repetitive exertions and maximal exertions which can result in stress-related injuries ranging from minor injuries (e.g., muscle soreness, muscle strains, and ligament injuries) to the infrequent serious injury (e.g., torn rotator cuffs, herniated disks or other back injuries, crushed fingers, and heart attack) to the rare catastrophic incident (e.g., death, paralysis).

_____ **Nutrition and Weight Control.** I realize that the nutrition and weight control program may involve a dietary change, selected nutritional supplements, and regular exercise. I also understand that no nutrition and weight control program is without risk and that some of the risks range from minor concerns (e.g., failure to achieve my goals, muscle soreness, and strains) to the infrequent serious injury (e.g., physical reaction to food supplements or nutrition products, adverse body reaction to weight loss, or heart attack) to the rare catastrophic incident (e.g., death, paralysis).

_____ **Fitness and Body Composition Tests.** I realize that participation in tests can result in injuries ranging from minor injuries (e.g., muscle soreness, pulled muscles, and sprains) to the infrequent serious injury (e.g., torn ligaments, back injuries, and heart attack) to the rare catastrophic incident (e.g., death, paralysis).

Description of Potential Benefits

I understand that a regular exercise program has been shown to have definite benefits to general health and well-being. **I will initial the types of activities (including their benefits) that my trainer and I have selected for my program to acknowledge that I understand the potential benefits of my training program.**

Figure 2.24.1 Illustrative Informed Consent for Personal Trainers

_____ **Aerobic Activities.** Loss of weight, reduction of body fat, improvement of blood lipids, lowering of blood pressure, improvement in cardiovascular function, reduction in risk of heart disease, increased muscular endurance, improved posture, and improved flexibility.

_____ **Muscular Endurance and Strength.** Loss of weight, reduction of body fat, increased muscle mass, improvement of blood lipids, lowering of blood pressure, improved strength and muscular endurance, improved posture.

_____ **Nutrition and Weight Control.** Loss of weight, reduction of body fat, improvement of blood lipids, lowering of blood pressure, improvement in cardiovascular function, reduction in risk of heart disease.

_____ **Fitness and Body Composition Tests.** Learn current status and gain information regarding areas needing improvement.

Participant Responsibilities

I understand that it is my responsibility to (1) fully disclose any health issues or medications that are relevant to participation in a strenuous exercise program; (2) cease exercise and report promptly any unusual feelings (e.g., chest discomfort, nausea, difficulty breathing, apparent injury) during the exercise program; and (3) clear my participation with my physician.

Participant Acknowledgments

In agreeing to this exercise program:

- I acknowledge that my participation is completely voluntary;
- I understand the potential physical risks and believe that the potential benefits outweigh those risks;
- I give consent to certain physical touching that may be necessary to ensure proper technique and body alignment;
- I understand that the achievement of health or fitness goals cannot be guaranteed;
- I have had a voice in planning and approving the activities selected for my exercise program;
- I have been able to ask questions regarding any concerns, and have had those questions answered to my satisfaction;
- I am in good physical condition, have no disability that might prevent my participation in such activities, and have been advised to consult a physician prior to beginning this program;
- I have been advised to cease exercise immediately if I experience unusual discomfort and feel the need to stop;
- I have read and understand the above agreement; I have been able to ask questions regarding any concerns I might have; I have had those questions answered to my satisfaction; and I am freely signing this agreement.

_____   _____   _____   _____   _____
Signature of Participant   Name of Participant (Print)   Date   Signature of Trainer   Date

_____   _____   _____
Signature of Parent/Guardian   Name of Parent/Guardian (Print)   Date
(If Participant Is a Minor)

_____   _____   _____
Signature of Parent/Guardian   Name of Parent/Guardian (Print)   Date
(If Participant Is a Minor)

Figure 2.24.1 Illustrative Informed Consent for Personal Trainers (continued)

AGREEMENTS TO PARTICIPATE

The **agreement to participate** (not to be confused with the participant agreement in Section 2.23) is a document intended to strengthen the defenses against liability for injuries resulting from the inherent risks of the activity. The agreement to participate is an agreement by which the signer is (1) made aware of and acknowledges knowledge of the inherent risks of the activity and (2) is informed of the rules of the activity and behavioral expectations and agrees to abide by them (van der Smissen, 1990). The agreement to participate is often used when persons are about to participate in an activity, sport, or class (e.g., extreme sport participants, physical education class members, participants in intramural or recreational programs). The agreement is based in tort law and does not constitute a formal contract; therefore it is an ideal instrument for dealing with minor participants. The agreement differs from the informed consent in that it is not a contract and nothing is *done to* the participant. Rather, the participant is **seeking to participate**.

The agreement to participate, unlike the informed consent, is not a contract. It is simply an agreement by which the participant is informed of the inherent risks and behavioral expectations of participants and affirms his or her assumption of the inherent risks of participation in the activity. However, like the informed consent, the signer (1) must have knowledge of the nature of the activity, (2) must understand the activity in terms of his or her own condition and skill, and (3) must appreciate the type of injuries that may occur. It is important to the provider that the participant understands these inherent risks and the provider should take steps (e.g., the agreement to participate) to insure this understanding. Since the agreement is merely informative in nature, it can be used when the participant or client is a minor. The signature of a parent is desirable from a public relations standpoint, but is not mandated.

The agreement provides protection in two ways. First, it helps to establish the primary assumption of risk defense by providing evidence that participation was voluntary and that the participant was aware of and assumed the inherent risks of the activity. Second, it strengthens the secondary assumption of risk defense (sometimes referred to as contributory fault) by showing that the participant knew the expected participant behaviors and agreed to adhere to them. By establishing that the participant was aware of the conduct expected, any conduct contrary to expected participant behaviors might be a factor in causing the injury to the participant. For instance, suppose a member of a racquetball class, after instruction prohibiting more than four players on a court at the same time, is injured while playing with five more players on the court. His negligent act could be considered a contributing factor to the injury, thereby preventing recovery in contributory negligence states, and reducing recovery in comparative negligence states. This, in effect, would either eliminate or reduce any liability by the teacher or provider.

Contents

There are no "magic phrases" that are either legally required or even universally useful in the construction of agreements to participate. There also is no ironclad format that is required. However, certain information should be in any agreement to participate and the following would serve as a logical order for inclusion (Cotten & Cotten, 2009).

Nature of the Activity

It is important that the activity be described in some detail. The description should be specific to the activity and not generic in nature. It should include a description of what the activity is like, remembering that the less familiar the participant is with the activity, the more detail required in the description. Include negative or unpleasant aspects that the participant should expect, how much physical stress is involved, and the intensity level of the activity. Each section of the agreement to participate is illustrated in Figure 2.24.2.

Possible Consequences of Injury

Two areas should be covered in this section. First, the participant should be made aware of the types of accidents that may occur in the specific sport involved. Here one should list some insignificant accidents that are common to the sport (being struck by the ball in racquetball), as well as some serious accidents that occur

Agreement to Participate and Liability Waiver
For Minors Participating in the *Annual 5K Fun Run*

All physical activities involve certain inherent risks. Regardless of the care taken, it is impossible to ensure the safety of all participants. The *5K Fun Run* is a vigorous, cardiovascular activity requiring *sustained running endurance, coordination, and running skill.* While the *Club* is using care in conducting the event, it is unable to eliminate all risk from the activity.

It is possible for *runners* to suffer common injuries such as *cramps, muscle strains, and sprains.* More serious, but less frequent, injuries such as *broken bones, cuts, concussions, heart attacks, strokes, paralysis, and death* may also occur. These injuries, and others, may result from such incidents as (but not limited to) *slips and falls, tripping, colliding with another runner, imperfections in the street surfaces, heat-related illnesses, and stress placed on the cardiovascular system.*

All *runners* are expected to follow these safety guidelines:

1. *Wear proper footwear.*
2. *Be alert for unanticipated hazards on the course.*
3. *Do not crowd other runners.*
4. *Consume adequate liquids during the run.*
5. *Follow all announced or posted rules.*

I agree to follow the preceding safety rules, all posted safety rules, and all rules common to *running.* Further, I agree to report any unsafe practices, conditions, or equipment to the *race* management.

I certify that (1) I possess a sufficient degree of physical fitness to safely participate in *the 5K Fun Run,* (2) I understand that I am to discontinue *running* at any time I feel undue discomfort or stress, and (3) I will indicate below any health-related conditions that might affect my ability to safely *complete the run* and I will verbally inform activity management immediately.

Circle: Diabetes Heart Problems Seizures Asthma Other _____

I have read the preceding information and my questions have been answered. **I know, understand, and appreciate the risks associated with *distance runs* and I am voluntarily participating in the activity. In doing so, I am assuming all of the inherent risks of the sport.** I further understand that in the event of a medical emergency, *management will call EMS to render assistance and that I will be financially responsible for any expenses involved.*

Signature of Participant	Date	Name of Participant (Please Print)
Signature of Parent	Date	Name of Parent (Please Print)
Signature of Parent	Date	Name of Parent (Please Print)

Waiver of Liability. In consideration of being permitted to run in the *5K Fun Run,* on behalf of myself, my family, my heirs, and my assigns, **the undersigned Participant and Parent or Guardian hereby release the *club* from liability for injury, loss, or death** to the minor, while *participating in the run or while in any way associated with participating in the event now or in the future,* **resulting from the ordinary negligence of the *club*, its agents, or employees.**

Signature of Participant	Date	Name of Participant (Please Print)
Signature of Parent	Date	Name of Parent (Please Print)
Signature of Parent	Date	Name of Parent (Please Print)

Figure 2.24.2 Illustrative Agreement to Participate for Minors

occasionally (falling and striking one's head on the floor in racquetball). Second, include some of the injuries that can occur in the sport. List some minor injuries that are common to the sport (e.g., bruises, strains, sprains in racquetball), some more serious injuries (e.g., loss of vision, broken bones, concussions), as well as catastrophic injuries (e.g., paralysis and death). Use phrases such as "some of the . . . ," "injuries such as . . . ," and "including, but not limited to . . ." in listing both accidents and injuries.

Behavioral Expectations of the Participant

The major purpose of this section is to transfer some of the responsibility for the participant's safety from the recreation or sport business to the participant. One might list several very important rules to which the participant is expected to adhere. An example in racquetball might be that participants are required to wear eye protection at all times. If there are few rules, they might be listed on the front of the agreement. If there are numerous rules, the participant might be referred to the back of the sheet where they are listed. In either case, giving the participant a copy of these rules would be desirable. Once again, one should not attempt to make the list all-inclusive.

Condition of the Participant

The participant should affirm that he or she possesses the physical condition and required competencies to participate in the activity safely. The required level, which will vary with the activity, should be described in Section I of the agreement. The participant will also affirm that the participant has no physical conditions that would preclude participation in the activity and will identify any conditions of which the recreation or sport business should be aware (e.g., heart problems, seizures, asthma). Particularly for vigorous activities, a statement that the participant should discontinue the activity if undue discomfort or stress occurs should be included. Participant affirmation of condition is generally adequate for activities such as 5K runs, health club memberships, and between-inning promotions at baseball games. Other situations might require more confirmation of condition. For example, residential camps usually require health histories and schools generally demand pre-participatory physical exams prior to varsity competition.

Concluding Statement

This concluding section should contain six items. They are: (1) a statement by which the participant affirms knowledge, understanding, and appreciation of the inherent risks of the activity; (2) affirmation that participation is voluntary, if that is the case; (3) an assumption of risk statement; (4) notice of the procedures to be followed in the event of an emergency and the financial responsibility of the participant for emergency actions; (5) insurance requirements; and (6) a space for the signature of the participant (and the parent if the participant is a minor) at the bottom of the agreement. The critical signature is that of the minor; however, the parent's signature is important for public relations purposes.

Optional Sections

Waiver. This is an optional section that may be used with agreements to participate (see Section 2.23, *Waivers and Releases*). This section should follow the signature section of the agreement to participate and provide space for a second signature by the participant (and parent, if the participant is a minor) relating specifically to the exculpatory clause (an illustrative agreement to participate including the critical information is given in Figure 2.24.2).

Parental Permission Form. This optional section merely gives permission for a minor to participate in the activity—strengthening neither the primary nor secondary assumption of risk defense. Contrary to widespread belief, neither the parent nor child is giving up the right to file suit in the event of injury due to negligence. The form has some public relations value in informing the parent of the activity in which the child will be participating and can be used to gain permission for emergency medical treatment, to assign financial responsibility for such treatment, and to obtain permission for the use of the participant's name and photograph. It may be convenient to include it as a component of the agreement to participate when the participant is a minor.

Using the Agreement to Participate

Some guidelines regarding the use of the agreement to participate can help to insure the effectiveness of the agreement in strengthening the assumption of risk and the contributory negligence defenses. First, presentation of the agreement should be accompanied by a verbal explanation of the risks participants will encounter through participation and of their responsibility for their own safety. Second, it is important to provide an opportunity for the signer to ask questions and gain clarification. Third, stress the participants' duty to inform you of any dangerous practices, hazardous conditions, or faulty equipment of which they may become aware while participating. This, however, in no way reduces or relieves the recreation or sport business of its duty to inspect the facility, examine the equipment, or supervise the activity. In addition, the language used in both the agreement and the verbal explanation should be appropriate to the age and maturity of the participant.

Finally, keep in mind that the agreement to participate can serve as important evidence in the event of a lawsuit. These records should be safely stored so that they may be retrieved when needed. The time during which a person may file a timely suit varies from one to four years after the injury, depending upon the state. However, keep in mind that a minor who is injured can generally file a suit until one to four years after reaching the age of majority. So in the event of an injury, it would be helpful to make and carefully store a file on that individual which would include the agreement to participate along with all other pertinent documentation (e.g., accident report, written statements by witnesses, parental permission slips).

ASSUMPTION OF RISK AGREEMENT

The **assumption of risk agreement** is quite similar to the agreement to participate. They both are intended to have the participant acknowledge the assumption of the inherent risks of the activity. Though they may differ in format and length, the assumption of risk agreement is a pact by which the participant or client is informed of the inherent risks of the activity and attests that he or she assumes the inherent risks of the activity. The participant or client further confirms that he or she (1) has been informed of the nature of the activity and its inherent risks, (2) understands the activity in terms of its demands on the participant's own physical condition and skill level, and (3) appreciates the type of injuries that may occur and the consequences of such injuries. Finally, the participant or client should verify that his or her participation is voluntary. The agreement can be used prior to participation in recreation and sport activities, prior to internships, or in almost any situation in which the service provider wants documentation that the participant understood and assumed the inherent risks of the activity. The assumption of risk agreement can be a stand-alone document, but is often (and should be) included as part of a liability waiver. *Regardless of its form, the assumption of risk agreement applies to assumption of the inherent risks and offers no protection against liability for provider negligence.*

As with the informed consent and the agreement to participate, the assumption of risk agreement may contain a written characterization of the nature of the activity and a listing of the inherent risks involved. The listing of the risks should not attempt to be all-inclusive, but should include the likely minor injuries, the unlikely major injuries, and the highly unlikely catastrophic injuries or death. One should not shy away from presenting the possibility of serious injuries.

The assumption of risk agreement used in conjunction with a liability waiver helps to provide more protection for the service provider. The waiver protects against liability for negligence while the assumption of risk statement helps to protect against liability for injuries resulting from the inherent risks of the activity. An assumption of risk agreement used with a waiver is presented in Figure 1, Section 2.23 *Waivers and Releases* and an agreement used without a waiver can be seen in the *Fairchild v. Amundson* Significant Case on page 117.

The importance of an up-to-date assumption of risk statement was made evident in a recent waiver case (*Niedbala v. SL–Your Partners in Health*, 2002). The Connecticut court failed to uphold a waiver when a health club client was injured while lifting weights since the club had no weight lifting equipment when Niedbala signed the waiver. Waiver language included:

> *"I understand and am aware that strength, flexibility and aerobic exercise, including the use of equipment, is a potentially hazardous activity. I also understand that fitness activities involve a risk of injury and even*

death and that I am voluntarily participating in these activities and using equipment and machinery with knowledge of the dangers involved. I hereby agree to expressly assume and accept all risks of injury or death."

The plaintiff argued that at the time he signed the waiver, he was not fully aware of the risks he was assuming because the facility did not contain the equipment he was using. The court stated that it was difficult to see how Niedbala could have foreseen the risk of using equipment that was not even on site at the time of signing and noted that he was inexperienced in the use of weights. The court asserted that the procurement of a new agreement when substantially different equipment is added does not create too great a burden for a sports facility.

King v. University of Indianapolis (2002), illustrates one of the limitations of an assumption of risk agreement. King signed an agreement prior to his death while practicing for varsity football. The agreement would have protected the university from liability had his death been due to the inherent risks, but offered no protection against the allegation of negligence. The case was remanded for trial. On the other hand, the court in *Stowers v. Clinton Central School Corporation* (2006), admitted an acknowledgement and release form into evidence that neither contained the word "negligence" nor relieved the defendant of liability for negligence. The court said the form was relevant to the defense of incurred risk since it provided evidence that the plaintiff knew and appreciated the risks involved and voluntarily accepted those risks.

Interestingly, some service providers use an assumption of risk clause while under the impression that it is a waiver of liability for negligence. In a health club case in California (*Zipusch v. LA Workout*, 2007), LA Workout included an assumption of risk agreement within its membership agreement. At the end of the assumption of risk, the club included the sentence "The member or guest will defend and indemnify LA Workout for any negligence EXCEPT the sole negligence of the club" (p. 3). The club learned that the agreement offered no protection against its negligence.

SIGNIFICANT CASE

This case illustrates perfectly the value of the assumption of risk agreement. Observe in reading the case four different facts that help to establish that Fairchild was aware of the inherent risks of whitewater rafting. It is also important to understand that the assumption of risk document protects Amundson from liability for an injury resulting from the inherent risks of the activity as contrasted with the waiver case in Section 2.23 in which the waiver protects the provider from liability for negligence. Note that in this case, negligence was not at issue before the trial court and was, therefore, not considered by the appellate court.

FAIRCHILD V. AMUNDSON

Court of Appeals of Washington, Division One
2001 Wash. App. LEXIS 149
January 29, 2001, Filed

Opinion By: Ronald E. Cox

At issue is whether Wild Water River Tours owed a duty to its customer, Thomas Fairchild, for injuries that he suffered during a rafting trip on the Toutle River. Because the doctrine of implied primary assumption of risk bars Fairchild's claim, we affirm the summary dismissal of this action.

In April 1995, Tom Fairchild participated in a whitewater rafting trip on the Toutle River. Rodney Amundson, d/b/a Wild Water River Tours (WWRT), guided the commercial rafting trip. Fairchild had been on whitewater rafting trips before, and knew that one of the dangers inherent in rafting was the possibility that rafters would fall out into the water. He also read brochures of WWRT that described certain dangers of river rafting.

On the day of the rafting trip, Fairchild and his church group assembled near the river under the supervision of WWRT. Fairchild donned a wetsuit, helmet, and life vest issued by WWRT. The rafters all signed an "Acknowledgement of Risk" form. WWRT guides then instructed them on paddling techniques and safety measures. The safety measures included instructions on maneuvering the raft near logs, rocks, and reversals. They also included instructions on swimming in the event rafters are in the water, pulling a swimmer back into the raft, and escaping from underneath a capsized raft.

River rapids are classified on a scale from class I (easiest) to class VI (most difficult). The Toutle River has two class IV rapids, one of which is known as Hollywood Gorge (Gorge). The Gorge also contains a "reversal," a point in the river subject to strong downward pressure that may cause a raft to overturn.

As they approached the Gorge, all the rafts stopped, and Amundson and other WWRT guides got out of the rafts and scouted the Gorge. After everyone returned to their rafts and re-entered the river, Amundson's raft successfully navigated through the Gorge to an eddy just beyond the reversal. Amundson then waited for the other rafts.

As Fairchild's raft entered the Gorge, it was sucked into a reversal, and all the occupants were thrown into the water. Amundson observed this from his raft and immediately paddled out of the eddy and into the river's current to retrieve Fairchild. Amundson and others administered CPR to Fairchild, who had been floating face down in the river, and resuscitated him. Thereafter, Fairchild went to a hospital, where he was treated and released the next day.

Fairchild sued. The trial court granted WWRT's motion for summary judgment.

Fairchild appeals.

Implied Assumption of Risk

Fairchild argues that material factual issues exist as to whether the doctrine of implied primary assumption of risk bars his recovery. We disagree.

We may affirm an order granting summary judgment if there are no genuine issues of material fact and the moving party is entitled to judgment as a matter of law. We consider all facts and reasonable inferences in the light most favorable to the nonmoving party. We review questions of law de novo.

The moving party bears the initial burden of showing the absence of a genuine issue of material fact. Once that burden is met, the burden shifts to the party with the burden of proof at trial to make a showing sufficient to establish the existence of an element essential to that party's case. If the claimant fails to meet that burden, the trial court should grant the motion because there can be no genuine issue of material fact given that a complete failure of proof concerning an essential element of the nonmoving party's case necessarily renders all other facts immaterial.

WWRT asserts that the doctrine of assumption of risk bars recovery. That doctrine has four facets: (1) express assumption of risk, (2) implied primary assumption of risk, (3) implied reasonable assumption of risk, and (4) implied unreasonable assumption of risk. Implied primary assumption of risk is at issue here. It occurs where the plaintiff impliedly has consented to relieve the defendant of an obligation or duty to act. With implied primary assumption of risk, the plaintiff engages in conduct from which consent is then implied. If implied primary assumption of risk is established, it bars any recovery.

At summary judgment, WWRT was required to show that (a) Fairchild had full subjective understanding of the nature and presence of a specific risk, and (b) he voluntarily chose to encounter the risk. Knowledge of and appreciation of the specific risk of danger, and voluntariness are questions of fact for the jury, except when reasonable minds could not differ.

Here, WWRT established both elements of implied primary assumption of risk. First, the evidence shows that Fairchild subjectively knew and understood the specific risk of falling into the water and drowning. Prior to the rafting trip, Fairchild read WWRT's brochures describing whitewater rafting on the Toutle River. The brochures listed the Toutle River as a class IV river and described rafting on that river as "fast & furious" and "[y]ou'll never know when you're going to hit crushing waves and bottomless holes." Fairchild testified in his deposition that he had been rafting on a slower river before and wanted a more exciting whitewater rafting trip when he signed up with WWRT. Prior to boarding the rafts, WWRT outfitted Fairchild with a wetsuit, helmet, and vest. It also instructed him on swimming techniques. Moreover, Fairchild admitted in his deposition that getting thrown from the raft into a rushing river was a danger inherent to whitewater rafting on the Toutle River. Reasonable minds could not differ in deciding that Fairchild knew of and appreciated the specific risk of falling into the water and possibly drowning. Likewise, reasonable minds could not differ that Fairchild was aware of the above specific risks when he signed the "acknowledgment of risk" form which states that:

> I am aware that participating in this raft trip arranged by Wildwater River Tours, its agents or associates, that I face certain risks, dangers, and personal property damage. This may include but not be limited to the hazards of traveling down rivers in inflatable rafts, accident or illness in remote places without medical facilities, forces of nature and travel by automobile or other conveyance. In consideration of, and as part payment for the right to participate in this trip and the services and food arranged for me by Wildwater River Tours, and its agents or associates, I do hereby acknowledge all of

> the above risks. The terms hereof shall serve as my acknowledgment of risk for my heirs, executors and administrators and for all members of my family . . . I have carefully read this agreement and fully understand its contents. (Italics ours)

The above facts all establish that Fairchild knew of the nature and presence of the specific risk of falling into the river and possibly drowning. It also shows that he voluntarily assumed those risks.

Fairchild attempts to establish that a genuine issue of material fact exists as to his subjective knowledge or understanding of the risk of being thrown into the water. We reject this argument.

"When a party has given clear answers to unambiguous [deposition] questions which negate the existence of any genuine issue of material fact, that party cannot thereafter create such an issue with an affidavit that merely contradicts, without explanation, previously given clear testimony." In his declaration, Fairchild stated that he was not aware of the risk of being thrown into the water at the time he signed the "acknowledgment of risk" form. But this contradicts, without explanation, Fairchild's prior deposition testimony in which he admitted that he knew of that specific risk. Thus, Fairchild has failed to establish a genuine issue of material fact on the issue of whether he subjectively knew the presence and nature of the risk of being thrown into the water.

Fairchild also attempts to show that a genuine issue of material fact exists as to whether he voluntarily chose to encounter the risk of being thrown into the water. He contends that because there were no reasonable alternatives available to him to assuming the inherent risks of river rafting, he did not voluntarily choose to assume those risks. We disagree.

Whether a plaintiff decides voluntarily to encounter a risk depends on whether he or she elects to encounter it despite knowing of a reasonable alternative course of action. In other words, the plaintiff must have had a reasonable opportunity to act differently or proceed on an alternate course that would have avoided the danger in order for assumption of risk to bar recovery.

Here, Fairchild chose to encounter the risk of being thrown into the water despite having numerous reasonable alternatives. He could have chosen to take a slower rafting trip. He could have elected to forego whitewater rafting altogether. He could have chosen not to continue with the trip once he reached the starting point or gotten out when his raft stopped and WWRT guides walked on the bank to scout the Gorge. In sum, Fairchild fails to establish a genuine issue of fact as to whether he voluntarily encountered the risk.

Fairchild also argues that he did not assume the risk of WWRT's alleged negligence in operating the raft because he knew that he might fall out of the raft and into the river. This was not an argument that Fairchild made below. Thus, we need not consider it for the first time on appeal. In any event, there is nothing in this record that establishes that any action or omission of WWRT was outside the scope of the risks that are inherent in the sport of river rafting.

We need not address Fairchild's contention that by signing the "acknowledgment of risk" form, he did not expressly assume the risk of falling into the water. WWRT does not argue that express assumption of risk applies to bar Fairchild's recovery. Rather, the issue is whether implied assumption of risk applies. We hold that it does.

Fairchild also asserts that the trial court improperly placed the burden of proof on him "to show that there was negligence rather than [placing] the burden on [WWRT] to show that no reasonable jury could find negligence from the material facts submitted in the record." There was no improper shifting of burden here. WWRT moved for summary judgment based on implied primary assumption of risk. It was then Fairchild's burden to show whether a genuine issue of material fact exists as to the doctrine. He simply failed to do so.

We affirm the order granting defendants' motion for summary judgment.

CASES ON THE SUPPLEMENTAL CD

McDermott v. Carie, (2005 MT 293; 329 Mont. 295; 124 P.3d 168; 2005 Mont. LEXIS 480). No cases involving agreements to participate have been found, however, this case illustrates the value of listing a selection of inherent risks on a waiver. In this Montana case (where waivers are not enforced) the document was admitted with the waiver language redacted to show the plaintiff understood the inherent *risks*.

Vaughan v. Nielson, (2008 Tex. App. LEXIS 6608). This case illustrates failure to obtain an informed consent in a medical situation. No sport, recreation, or fitness informed consent cases have been located.

King v. CJM Country Stables, (2004 U.S. Dist. LEXIS 7511). This case includes the Hawaii statute which says waivers are enforceable to protect against liability for inherent risks providing there is full disclosure of the inherent risks associated with the activity.

QUESTIONS YOU SHOULD BE ABLE TO ANSWER

1. What is the primary difference between an informed consent agreement and an agreement to participate?

2. Which of the three agreements in this section requires the signature of a parent? Why?

3. Explain what is meant by "disclosure" and "consent" when writing an informed consent agreement.

4. Explain how an agreement to participate might reduce or eliminate a service provider's liability for negligence.

5. What role did the Wild Water River Tours brochures and their "acknowledgement of risk" form play in the court's verdict in the Significant Case?

REFERENCES

Cases

Fairchild v. Amundson, 2001 Wash. App. LEXIS 149.

King v. University of Indianapolis, 2002 U.S. Dist. LEXIS 19070.

Niedbala v. SL—Your Partners in Health, 2002 Conn. Super. LEXIS 2835.

Stokes v. Bally's Pacwest, Inc., 54 P.3d 161 (2002).

Stowers v. Clinton Central School Corporation, 2006 Ind. App. LEXIS 2151.

Zipusch v. LA Workout, 2007 Cal. App. LEXIS 1652.

Publications

American College of Sports Medicine. (1999). Policy statement regarding the use of human subjects and informed consent. *Medicine and Science in Sports and Exercise, 31*(7), vi.

American Medical Association. (1998). *Informed consent.* Online, Internet. www.ama-assn.org/ama/pub/category/4608.html.

Cotten, Doyice J. and Cotten, Mary B. (2009). *Waivers & Releases of Liability.* 7th ed. Sport Risk Consulting: www.lulu.com

Herbert, D. L., & Herbert, W. G. (2002). *Legal aspects of preventive, rehabilitative and recreational exercise programs.* (4th ed.). Canton, OH: PRC Publishing, Inc.

Independent Review Consulting, Inc. (2000). *Post-approval requirements: informed consent.* Corte Madera, CA.

Koeberle, B. E., & Herbert, D. L. (1998). *Legal aspects of personal fitness training,* (2nd ed.). Canton, OH: PRC Publishing, Inc.

Nolan-Haley, J. M. (1999). Informed consent in mediation: A guiding principle for truly educated decision making. *Notre Dame L. Rev.,* 74, 775.

Office of Human Subjects Research (OHSR) National Institutes of Health. (2000). *Guidelines for writing informed-consent documents.* Online, Internet. http://ohsr.od.nih.gov/info_6.php3

Olivier, S. & Olivier, A. (2001). Informed consent in sport science. *Sportscience.* Online, Internet. www.sportsci.org/jour/0101/so.htm

van der Smissen, B. (1990). *Legal liability and risk management for public and private entities.* Cincinnati, OH: Anderson Publishing.

2.30 Recreation and Sport Management Applications

2.31 Premises Liability

—John Grady
UNIVERSITY OF SOUTH CAROLINA

"[T]he operator of a commercial recreational [or sport] facility, like the operator of any other business, has a general duty to exercise reasonable care for the safety of its patrons" (Schneider v. American Hockey and Ice Skating Center, Inc., 2001, p. 534).

Premises liability is the body of law which makes the person who is in possession of land or premises responsible for certain injuries suffered by persons who are present on the premises (American Lawyer Directory, n.d.). *Black's Law Dictionary* (2004) defines premises liability as "a landowner's or landholder's tort liability for conditions or activities on the premises" (p. 1219). The owner or operator of a sport or recreation business owes a duty to keep the premises safe for all who enter the facility or premises. A "safe" facility is not just safe for spectators; it is safe for participants, spectators, staff, and visitors (Seidler, 2005).

FUNDAMENTAL CONCEPTS

Duty of Care

A landowner "owes a duty of reasonable care to guard against any dangerous conditions on his or her property that the owner either knows about or should have discovered" [Restatement (Second) of Torts § 343 (1969)]. The specific legal duties owed by the sport or recreation business to its patrons arise not only because the patrons provide the business with an economic benefit and should, therefore, be entitled to protection from harm while on the premises but also because "the operator is in the best position to know of risks, or to discover risks, that threaten customers" (Maloy & Higgins, 2000, p. 35).

The legal duty that a landowner owes to individuals entering his or her premises depends upon the status of the entrant (62 AM. JUR. 2D Premises Liability § 68 (2005)). Persons entering the land are classified into three groups, each of which incur different levels of care depending on the entrant's relationship with the landowner. The landowner's duty to the entrant varies depending on whether the entrant was an invitee, licensee, or trespasser.

Invitee

"An invitee is a person who has an express or implied invitation to enter or use another's premise," such as a customer to a store (*Black's Law Dictionary*, 2004, p. 846). *Invitees are owed the greatest level of protection. The landowner is required to maintain his or her premises in a reasonably safe condition under the circumstances. The duty owed to an invitee also extends to warning about known dangers, inspecting the land for hidden dangers, and not exposing the invitee to an unreasonable risk.*

Patrons of sport and recreation businesses would typically be classified as **business invitees** because they are expressly invited onto the land and their presence also provides the business with some economic benefit. For example, spectators at a sporting event or participants in a commercial white water rafting trip would be classified as business invitees. Where the land is open to the public, such as a community park, the visitor would be classified as a **public invitee** since the visitor is invited to enter and remain on the property for a purpose for which the property is held open to the public (Black's Law Dictionary, 2004). A public invitee is owed the same legal obligations by the premise owner as a business invitee.

In *Creely v. Corpus Christi Football Team, Inc.* (2007), Creely was the owner of a cheerleading gym. Pursuant to a contract with the local football team, the Hammerheads, Creely became an official sponsor of the Hammerheads Cheerleaders and Shark Attack Rowdy Squad. In exchange for various types of advertising, she agreed to organize half-time performances by the cheerleading and tumbling camp participants. During a football game, Creely was getting ready for a half-time performance and was standing 25 to 30 feet into what she describes as a "tunnel," located at the end of the stadium next to the stage. A football from the field flew into the tunnel and hit her, injuring her left thumb. The injury required surgery.

Creely sued the Hammerheads for failing to exercise reasonable care in ensuring her safety during the football event. Creely attached a copy of the agreement she entered into with the Hammerheads. The court found that, by virtue of the agreement, Creely was an invitee on the premises. *The general rule is that an owner or occupier of land has a duty to use reasonable care to keep the premises under his control in a safe condition and to use reasonable care to protect an invitee from reasonably foreseeable injuries.* As the duty of reasonable care applies to stadium owners, the court found that the evidence was sufficient to establish that the Hammerheads owed her a duty of reasonable care.

Licensee

A **licensee** is "one who has permission to enter or use another's premises, but only for one's own purposes and not for the occupier's benefit" (*Black's Law Dictionary*, 2004, p. 939). *Social guests of the landowner are often classified as licensees.* For example, a landowner inviting neighbors over to swim in a private swimming pool in the landowner's backyard would be a licensee situation. Licensees are owed the same duties as invitees with one exception: *the licensee is to be warned or protected only from harms of which the possessor of the land is aware; there is no duty to inspect the land for hidden dangers.* When compared to the duty owed to invitees, the lower standard of care owed to licensees is justified if one compares the social guest to a member of the landowner's family. "The guest understands when he comes that he is to be placed on the same footing as one of the family, and must take the premises as the occupier himself uses them, without any preparations made for his safety . . . " (Prosser, 1942, p. 604).

Trespasser

A **trespasser** is one "one who intentionally and without consent or privilege enters another's property" (*Black's Law Dictionary*, 2004, p. 1543). *Trespassers are owed the least amount of protection, sometimes referred to as "zero duty."* In cases involving a trespasser, the landowner is only required to avoid **willful and wanton misconduct** (See Section 2.11, *Negligence*) and to refrain from making the premises more dangerous than the trespasser would ordinarily expect. For example, the landowner could not set a trap whereby the trespasser would be injured upon entering the land.

Attractive nuisance is an exception to the general liability standard for trespassers. Attractive nuisance is defined as "a dangerous condition that may attract children onto land, thereby causing a risk to their safety" (*Black's Law Dictionary*, 2004, p. 1097). The landowner can be held responsible for creating the dangerous condition because the landowner is obliged to realize that the condition is sufficient to lure persons, particularly children, onto the land. Attractive nuisance can also be applied where the person injured was a trespasser because the landowner should realize that the situation present on his/her land would be both attractive and dangerous. For example, an unguarded swimming pool with no safety fence would be considered an attractive nuisance. Most people would intuitively think to put a fence around a swimming pool (and likely must do so in order to comply with municipal codes for swimming pools). However, a frequently occurring risk that many landowners may not even think about, but which definitely could give rise to an attractive nuisance claim, is an unguarded trampoline in a homeowner's backyard. The probability of a trampoline luring neighborhood children onto the land is high and this type of recreational equipment can cause serious bodily injury if used improperly, particularly when used at night. Sport and recreation managers must also be vigilant about safeguarding active construction areas on their premises due to the potential for children to be lured into the construction area and become injured by climbing onto heavy-duty construction equipment or a pile of sand or gravel, for example. *Attractive nuisance may also apply to adults if the injury or death was the result of an attempt to rescue the child from danger on the land.* In the recreation context, it is important to recognize that a body of standing water, such as a lake or pond or flowing water, such as a creek, would not be considered an attractive nuisance in the absence of hidden inherent dangers because the danger of drowning in it is an apparent open danger (*City of Mangum v. Powell*, 1946).

Recreational User

A recreational user is someone who enters upon land for the purpose of engaging in a recreational activity covered under their state's recreational user statute and is recreating on land suitable for the activity and covered under the statute. For example, Arkansas's recreational user statute defines recreational purposes to include hunting, fishing, swimming, boating, camping, picknicking, and hiking, among others (A.C.A. § 18-11-302). "Most states hold that a person classified as a recreational user by statute is not given invitee or licensee status and is owed a duty comparable to a trespasser" (Carroll, Connaughton, & Spengler, 2007, p. 165). Recreational user statutes, in effect, serve as an affirmative defense to claims of negligence by those engaged in recreational activities on the landowner's property (Clark, 1998).

All fifty states have some form of landowner liability statutes. These statutes are "designed to encourage availability of private lands by limiting the liability of owners" (Lewis, 1991, p. 68). The public policy rationale behind recreational user statutes is rather straight-forward. The court in *Conant v. Stroup* (2002), interpreting Oregon's recreational user statute (Or. Rev. Stat. § 105.682), stated the statute's purpose as follows: If landowners "will make their lands available to the general public for recreational purposes, the state will 'trade' that public access for immunity from liability that might result from the use of the property" (pp. 275–276). (See Section 2.32, *Property law*).

Trend Toward the Reasonable Care Standard

The extent of the duty owed by landowners depends upon state law and varies from state to state. While the status of the visitor is still retained in most states, the legislatures or courts in many states have adopted a different standard of care for property owners. Eight states (Alaska, California, Hawaii, Louisiana, Montana, Nevada, New York, and Tennessee) have abolished the distinctions of invitee, licensee, and trespasser for purposes of premises liability (Daller, 2003). They now state that a *landowner owes a duty to act as a reasonable person in maintaining his property in a reasonably safe condition under the circumstances.*

Fifteen states (Delaware, Illinois, Iowa, Kansas, Maine, Massachusetts, Michigan, Nebraska, New Mexico, North Carolina, North Dakota, Rhode Island, West Virginia, Wisconsin, and Wyoming) and the District of Columbia have abolished the distinction between invitee and licensee and have determined that *owners and occupiers of land owe a duty to exercise reasonable care under the circumstances to any person that is lawfully on his or her property* (Daller, 2003). New Hampshire law is less clear. While in the past, the traditional three-pronged classification of entrants on land was in effect for determining the obligations of landowners, landowners now must use reasonable care in the maintenance or operation of their property. However, the court has ruled that the character of and circumstances surrounding the entry is relevant and important in determining the standard of care owed to the entrant (*Ouellette v. Blanchard*, 1976).

Given the variations in state law, it is important for landowners to recognize whether their state retains the legal distinctions for entrants of invitee, licensee, and trespasser. As a practical matter, however, a landowner who maintains a duty of reasonable care, the highest standard of care owed to invitees, should, in theory, always be protected from liability regardless of the status of the entrant.

Factors Affecting Liability

Foreseeability

Premises liability law imposes a duty upon landowners to only protect invitees from foreseeable dangers. In *McPherson v. Tennessee Football Incorporated* (2007), New Orleans Saints player Adrian McPherson participated in a preseason football game between the Saints and the Tennessee Titans in Nashville. Before the start of the second half, McPherson alleges that he was catching punts from the Saints' punter and that while doing so, T-Rac, the Titans' mascot, drove a golf cart in his area and struck and injured him. The court found that Tennessee law imposes a duty upon owners and operators of business premises to protect its customers from probable or foreseeable dangers and noted that this duty has been extended to supervision of athletic events. In another case, *Sall vs. Smiley's Golf Complex* (2006), a golf patron who was struck by lightning and suffered permanent injuries sued the golf course for failing to warn him about the risks of lightning while playing golf. The court found the golf course had no duty to protect or warn patrons of lightning because a lightning strike is not foreseeable.

Actual versus Constructive Notice

While the landowner has a duty to protect invitees from foreseeable dangers, the landowner (or invitor) is not the insurer of the invitee's safety (*Hammond v. Allegretti*, 1974). Before liability may be imposed, the premise owner must have actual or constructive notice of the danger. **Actual notice** refers to situations when the premise owner becomes aware of a problem or defect on the land. For example, an arena manager may discover that a pipe is leaking by discovering water on the floor during a periodic inspection of the restroom. There are a number of other ways for the premise owner to obtain actual notice of a danger. These include being told about it by an employee or patron or, in the worst case, discovering the problem when someone is injured as a result of it.

Constructive notice, on the other hand, arises in situations where the facility manager should have discovered the danger during the course of prudent facility management, including routine facility inspections. If the facility manager would have been aware of the condition by being reasonably attentive, the manager has constructive notice (*Sall vs. Smiley's Golf Complex*, 2006). Establishing that the facility manager had constructive notice may require the use of an expert witness to establish the legal standard of care and to detail what a reasonably prudent facility manager would have done under similar circumstances. For example, in evaluating what is a reasonable time for repair of a broken stadium seat, the expert witness's testimony could establish the reasonableness of the facility manager's actions and whether what was done complied with industry standards. "The determination of what constitutes a reasonable time period between inspections will necessarily vary according to the particular circumstances" (*Zipusch v. LA Workout*, 2007, p. 1293).

In *Stadt v. United Center Joint Venture* (2005), Gary Stadt was injured when he slipped and fell on a puddle of water in the "Standing Room Only" section of the United Center which was hosting a Chicago Black Hawks hockey game. Upon further inspection of the area where Stadt fell, a beer cup was discovered next to the puddle. Stadt sued for negligence, asserting that the defendants, including the facility, the team, and the facility maintenance company, were negligent for failing to maintain the premises in a reasonably safe condition. The defendants argued that they did not know of the spilled liquid on which the Stadt allegedly slipped and therefore could not be held liable for his injuries.

Stadt did not argue that the defendants actually knew about the liquid, so the issue before the court was whether the facility had constructive notice of liquid on the floor. "Constructive notice can be established under two alternative theories: (1) the dangerous condition existed for a sufficient amount of time so that it would have been discovered by the exercise of ordinary care, or (2) the dangerous condition was part of a pattern of conduct or a recurring incident" (*Culli v. Marathon Petroleum Co.*, 1988, p. 123). Because Stadt could not show when the spill occurred, he had to rely upon the **recurring incident theory.** Applying this theory, the court found that the spilling of liquids may be characterized as recurring incidents since patrons oftentimes spill drinks in the stadium, including the standing room only section where plaintiff fell. The court held that a dangerous condition that frequently occurs may establish constructive notice because the recurrence of the condition provides opportunities to take measures and rectify or prevent the condition.

"Open and Obvious" Dangers

A premises owner's duty to protect the invitee from an unreasonable risk of harm caused by a dangerous condition on the land generally does not encompass a duty to protect an invitee from **"open and obvious" dangers** (Marks, 2005). For example, a pothole in a stadium parking lot, snow and ice accumulating on an outdoor surface, or a puddle of water on a rainy day would all be considered "open and obvious" dangers because the conditions themselves serve as adequate notice of the danger.

However, if there are "special aspects" of a condition that make even an "open and obvious" danger "unreasonably dangerous," the landowner still is obligated to undertake reasonable precautions to protect invitees from the danger. In *Mann v. Shusteric Enterprises* (2004), a case involving an intoxicated bar patron who slipped and fell on ice and snow that had accumulated in the bar's parking lot during a blizzard, the court stated that "special aspects" are defined by whether an otherwise "open and obvious" danger is "effectively unavoidable" or "impose[s] an unreasonably high risk of severe harm" to the invitee (*Mann*, 2004, p. 579). Moreover, the court noted that the fact-finder must consider the condition of the premises, not the condition of the plaintiff, effectively minimizing the significance of the plaintiff's intoxication when he fell. A typical open and obvious danger, such as a pothole, would not give rise to these "special aspects" because the condition does not involve an especially high likelihood of injury, a reasonable person would typically be able to see the pothole and avoid it, and there is little risk of severe harm.

While premise owners have a duty to protect invitees from *unreasonable* risks of harm, *they are not absolute insurers of the safety of their invitees.* Therefore, *where a danger is "open and obvious," the premise owner cannot be held liable for a failure to warn the invitee of the danger.* However, practically speaking, this should not discourage premise owners from warning participants and patrons of any dangerous conditions, including dangers that might not presently exist but frequently occur (Carroll & Baker, 2006, p. 9).

There is one well-known exception to the duty to warn about "open and obvious" dangers. The **distraction exception** applies where the person would be distracted from noticing the "open and obvious" danger and, because of the distraction, fail take reasonable precautions to avoid the risk of danger. In *Menough v. Woodfield Gardens* (1998), a young man was injured while playing a pick-up game of basketball at the apartment complex owned by the defendant. The basketball court at the complex consisted of a single pole anchored inside a concrete-filled tire. During the course of play, the plaintiff made a "lay-up shot" at the net. When his foot came down, it landed on the tire, snapping plaintiff's ankle. The plaintiff testified that he had not played on the basketball court at the Woodfield Gardens apartment complex prior to the date he was injured. He stated that he first became aware of the tire under the basketball net when he fell on it.

The apartment complex argued that the risk of harm posed by a tire that anchored the pole holding a backboard and net was open and obvious and therefore it owed no duty to remedy that condition. The court found the distraction theory to be applicable in this case because it was reasonably foreseeable that he would have been distracted and fail to see the tire. Therefore, the apartment complex owed a duty of reasonable care to warn the ball player about the presence of the tire.

Limited Duty Rule

An exception to general negligence principles that applies to sport and recreation facilities, notably baseball stadiums and hockey arenas, is the **limited duty rule.** A sports facility operator's limited duty of care has two components: first, the operator must provide protected seating sufficient for those spectators who may be reasonably anticipated to desire protected seats on an ordinary occasion, and second, the operator must provide protection for spectators in the most dangerous section of the stands (*Akins v. Glens Falls City Sch. Dist.*, 1981). The second component of this limited duty ordinarily may be satisfied by the operator providing screened seats behind home plate in baseball and behind the goals in hockey (*Akins v. Glens Falls City Sch. Dist.*, 1981).

Hurst v. East Coast Hockey League (2006), explains how the courts have interpreted the limited duty rule. During the pre-game warm-ups at a minor league hockey game, Hurst entered the spectator area through a curtained concourse entrance behind one of the goals. While standing behind the goal, Hurst was struck in the face by a puck. At the time of the accident, the Civic Center ice rink was encircled with dasher boards and a protective Plexiglass wall. The court determined the risk of pucks leaving the ice rink and entering the spectator area is well-known, obvious, and inherent to the game of hockey. Therefore, the spectator assumed the risk of being hit by a fly puck.

Legal Obligations of Sport and Recreation Facility Managers

The sport or recreation manager's duty to use reasonable care to keep the premises under his/her control in a safe condition can be further delineated in terms of five obligations (Seidler, 2005).

Keep the Premises in Safe Repair

Routine maintenance by the facility management and staff is necessary to keep patrons safe while they are engaged in sport or recreation, either as a participant or spectator. For example, a fitness center would have an obligation to re-surface a swimming pool deck where the slip-resistant surface had worn off and an obligation to maintain exercise equipment used by patrons. In *Zipusch v. LA Workout* (2007), a health club member alleged that the club negligently maintained its exercise equipment. This resulted in a sticky substance remaining on a treadmill, causing Zipusch to lose her balance when her foot became stuck to it. In considering whether the health club kept the exercise equipment in working order, the court stated that, "unlike those who run outside on cracked sidewalks speckled with gum, [the plaintiff] and other health club members pay dues in exchange for access to a safe and well-maintained exercise environment" (p. 1292).

Inspect the Premises to Discover Obvious and Hidden Hazards

Periodic inspections are a necessary and expected obligation of facility managers. Through the use of inspection checklists, the facility is able to document that they have taken reasonable steps to discover hazards on the premises and remedy them. In addition to the claims for negligent maintenance, the court in *Zipusch v. LA Workout* (2007), discussed above, also considered whether LA Workout negligently failed to inspect the equipment. The court held that the health club had an obligation to inspect and maintain the equipment. Based on Zipusch's own observations, no staff member inspected or cleaned the equipment in the 85-minute time period prior to the accident. Because of the fact that numerous individuals are engaging in vigorous physical activity at the health club, a reasonable argument could be made that inspection of the premises was especially important, and that the time period between inspections was unreasonably long (*Zipusch*, 2007). Evidence that the facility manager failed to periodically inspect the premises before an accident is normally sufficient to infer that the risk existed long enough for the property owner, in the exercise of due care, to have discovered and removed it (*Ortega v. Kmart Corp.*, 2001).

Remove the Hazards or Warn Others of Their Presence

Once a dangerous condition is discovered on the premises, the facility manager has the obligation to either remove it or warn patrons of its presence. For example, consider college basketball patrons bringing wet umbrellas into an arena, which causing the floor to be slippery. This would be a typical situation where the facility manager has an obligation to try to keep the floor dry, likely by changing the arena's policy of allowing umbrellas to be brought into the arena in the first place. In addition, the facility manager would have an obligation to use "Wet Floor" signs near the entrance to warn patrons about the dangerous condition in the entry way. Other commonly occurring hazards in sport or recreation facilities include uneven surfaces or deteriorated materials or equipment.

For a hazard that cannot be removed, such as the threat of lightning on a golf course, the premise owner still has the obligation to warn participants about the danger that is present. While the golf course in the *Salls* (2006) case obviously could not remove the threat of lightning or other weather-related risks, the golf course's warning procedure was to blow an air horn as a signal to return to the clubhouse in the event of dangerous weather. The golf course's policies or procedures for inclement weather also called for the manager on duty to monitor the local television stations, radar images on the Internet, and visually inspect the weather by stepping outside and to monitor conditions using a weather radio.

Anticipate Foreseeable Uses and Take Reasonable Precautions to Protect

This obligation of the facility owner/operator to **anticipate foreseeable uses and activities by invitees and take reasonable precautions to protect the invitees from foreseeable dangers** takes into consideration the normal uses of the facility and frequently occurring incidents or activities by patrons (e.g., tailgating prior to a football game). In *Hayden v. University of Notre Dame* (1999), a season ticket holder at a Notre Dame football game was injured when, after the football was kicked into the stands, several people from the crowd lunged for the ball in an effort to retrieve it. Hayden claimed that Notre Dame was negligent in failing to protect her. Notre Dame argued that it owed no duty to protect her from a third party's criminal act (arguably a battery). Notre Dame contended that the third party's action was unforeseeable, and that it therefore owed no duty to anticipate it and protect her. Given evidence that there were many prior incidents of people being jostled or injured by efforts of fans to retrieve the ball, the court found that the totality of the circumstances established that Notre Dame should have foreseen that injury would likely result from the actions of a third party. As a result, it owed a duty to Hayden to protect her from such injury.

The **"totality of the circumstances" test** "requires landowners to take reasonable precautions to prevent foreseeable criminal actions against invitees" (*Delta Tau Delta v. Johnson*, 1999, p. 973). "Under the totality of the circumstances test, a court considers all of the circumstances surrounding an event, including the nature, condition, and location of the land, as well as prior similar incidents, to determine whether a criminal act was foreseeable" (p. 972). "A substantial factor in the determination is the number, nature, and location of prior similar incidents, but the lack of prior similar incidents will not preclude a claim where the landowner knew or should have known that the criminal act was foreseeable" (p. 973).

In *Maheshwari v. City of New York* (2004), a man was attacked by four concert-goers in a parking lot outside of a Lollapalooza concert while he was passing out religiously-based leaflets. (See the Supplemental CD) The court had to consider whether the City of New York, the owner of the stadium, owed Maheshwari a duty of care to be protected from the criminal acts of third parties. The third parties in this case were the young men who beat him up. The defendant claimed that it owed plaintiff no duty to prevent a random criminal act of this kind. In analyzing the issue of foreseeability, the court considered the predictability of criminal assaults at a concert of this type. The plaintiff maintained that the crime was foreseeable because defendants had notice of criminal activity at previous Lollapalooza festivals. Also, defendants knew of the tailgating that occurred in the parking areas before and during the concert, which increases the chances that criminal activity will occur, presumably because tailgaters may drink alcoholic beverages. The plaintiff further alleged that the defendants' negligence in providing security was a proximate cause of his injury. The defendants argued that any duty they owed to plaintiff did not include a guarantee of protection from a random act of violence. The court agreed with the defendants, finding that the brutal attack was not a foreseeable result of any security breach.

Conduct operations on the premises with reasonable care for the safety of all. No matter if the sport or recreation business consists of providing amusement at a water park or proving recreational opportunities on intramural fields, the facility manager must conduct operations on the premises in such a way that provides that anyone who comes onto the land will be safe. The golf lightning cases illustrate the point that when a golf course has taken steps to protect golfers from lightning strikes, it owes them a duty of reasonable care to implement its safety precautions properly (*Maussner v. Atlantic City Country Club, Inc.*, 1997). If a golf course builds shelters on the course for golfers who get stranded on the course during inclement weather, it must build lightning-proof shelters (*Maussner*, 1997). Similarly, if a golf course has an evacuation plan, the evacuation plan must be reasonable and must be posted (*Maussner*, 1997). Depending on the industry, there may be an industry standard or customary practice for how best to protect patrons from specific dangers common to that industry, such as lightning strikes on golf courses or how to protect skiers from colliding into snow making equipment on ski slopes.

SIGNIFICANT CASE

The case below illustrates several of the concepts in the section, including duty to provide a reasonably safe environment, foreseeability, and the duty to protect invitees from harm. Specifically, the case discusses negligence claims for failure to provide adequate security, failure to provide adequate staffing, failure to warn, and failure to train staff for the purpose of preventing some patrons from harming other patrons. The full case also contains alcohol liability issues which have been edited here for space reasons. All are commonly raised issues in sport and recreation premise liability actions.

HOPKINS V. CONNECTICUT SPORTS PLEX, LLC

SUPERIOR COURT OF CONNECTICUT, JUDICIAL DISTRICT OF NEW HAVEN, AT NEW HAVEN
2006 Conn. Super. LEXIS 1710 (2006)

OPINION

MEMORANDUM OF DECISION ON DEFENDANT'S MOTION FOR SUMMARY JUDGMENT

This case arises out of a claim for injuries as the result of an alleged assault by a Vincent Baker and a Reverend James Baker. The assault purportedly occurred at the defendant's premises which contains outdoor softball fields. The theory of liability lies in negligence and claims the defendant's employees were negligent in that

(a) They served liquor despite the fact that Vincent Baker and Rev. James Baker may have been intoxicated already;

(b) They failed to provide adequate security to prevent the violence which caused the plaintiff's injuries;

(c) They caused or allowed and permitted said premises to have noisy and unruly patrons, including but not limited to VINCENT BAKER, and REV. JAMES BAKER, when they had inadequate staff to control the same, creating a volatile situation;

(d) They failed to warn the plaintiff when under the circumstances [*2] it knew or should have known that the plaintiff could have been and was harmed by a patron, including, but not limited to VINCENT BAKER, and REV. JAMES BAKER, who was consuming alcohol on said premises;

(e) They served alcoholic beverages to VINCENT BAKER, and REV. JAMES BAKER, without having proper supervision of said premises and allowed VINCENT BAKER, and REV. JAMES BAKER, to consume an overabundance of alcoholic beverages:

(f) They maintained the aforesaid premises at said time and place in aforesaid conditions; and

(g) They failed to adequately train their agents, servants and/or employees to prevent patrons from harming other patrons and persons in attendance at said premises.

(First Revised Complaint)

Suit has also been filed against the Bakers; that case has been consolidated with the case now before the court. In this case the defendant Connecticut Sports Plex, LLC has filed a motion for summary judgment.

* * *

The negligence claim appears to fall into two categories. It is claimed that the defendant served alcohol to the Bakers when they "may have been intoxicated already"; they allowed them "to consume an overabundance of alcoholic beverages."

The plaintiff also makes another claim in negligence which generally [*4] speaking revolves around an alleged failure to exercise reasonable care for the safety of patrons of its facility. Thus it is said that the defendant failed to provide adequate security, failed to provide adequate staff to control noisy and unruly patrons, failed to warn the plaintiff of dangers presented by people like the Bakers who were consuming alcohol and failure to train staff for the purpose of preventing some patrons from harming other patrons.

(1) As noted this is a one-count complaint purporting to lie in common-law negligence and various allegations of negligence are asserted in the eight paragraph of the complaint which may be divided into two general aspects.

* * *

(a) The court will first discuss the general allegations regarding failure to provide adequate security, allowance of unruly and noisy patrons without the presence of adequate staff, failure to warn the plaintiff of possible harm from patrons including the Bakers who were consuming alcohol on the premises, failure to train employees to prevent patrons from harming other patrons. The plaintiff's deposition, which is attached to both briefs indicate that on the day in question he was a patron of the defendant's facility having played [*6] in a softball game which was part of a tournament. The defendant does not seem to dispute the fact that the plaintiff was a patron or business invitee of the defendant's premises at the time of this incident. There is no indication Hopkins had to pay to participate in the tournament but courts have held individuals can be invitees even where entry on the premises confers no pecuniary benefit, see Prosser & Keeton, Law of Torts § 61, pages 422–23, cf. *Guilford v. Yale University*, 128 Conn. 449, 23 A.2d 917 (1942) (person attending college reunion).

The question becomes what is the duty owed to persons such as the plaintiff by those who own or control premises such as the premises involved here which was used for conducting soft ball games. * * * Section 344 of the Restatement says:

*HN3*A possessor of land who holds it open to the public for entry for his business purposes is subject to liability to members of the public while they are upon the land for such a purpose, for physical harm caused by the accidental, negligent or intentionally harmful acts of third persons or animals, and by the failure of the possessor to exercise reasonable care to

(a) discover that such acts are being done or are likely to be done, or

(b) give a warning adequate to enable the visitors to avoid the harm, or otherwise protect against it.

Am. Jur.2d in somewhat more detail at § 57, page 411 makes the following comments which are more directly related to this case

HN4 The proprietor of a place of public amusement has a duty to maintain order on his or her premises and may be held liable for injuries resulting from the dangerous activities of a third person, whether such acts are accidental, negligent, or intentional, if he or she does nothing to restrain or control such conduct after he or she knows, or in the exercise of reasonable care could have [*8] known, of it. The proprietor must exercise due care to protect his or her patrons from assaults by other patrons, at least if the proprietor had knowledge of conduct which would naturally result in an injury, or if he or she might reasonably have anticipated an assault.

Where there has been a more or less sudden, direct attack, liability generally is not imposed, for the reason that the proprietor could not reasonably have anticipated the occurrence.

* * *

HN6(1) . . ." what constitutes reasonable care by the owner or operator of the amusement is partly dependent on the owner or operator's knowledge of the conditions threatening his patron's safety. Thus the owner or operator's duty

to [*10] protect his (her) patrons is often stated in terms of his (her) obligation to protect his (her) patrons not only against dangers of which he (she) has actual knowledge, but also against those which he (she) should reasonably anticipate."

Bearman v. University of Notre Dame, 453 N.E.2d 1196, 1198 (Ct. of App. Ind., 1983) patron at football game injured, university aware of alcohol consumption, tailgate parties); * * *

(2) Thus *HN7* courts look to the protective measures taken by the operator or owner "in view of the prior warning he (she) had that an assault might take place" . . . (where liability has been found) "courts have emphasized (things) such as prior trouble between the injured patron and his (her) assailant or general rowdiness among the patrons of the type that eventually lead to a patron's injury."

Bearman v. Univ. of Notre Dame, supra;* * *

(3) *HN8*In cases where liability has not been found the courts have pointed to circumstances showing that the owner or operator could not have reasonably anticipated an assault, such as the suddenness of the assault or the absence of assaults during prior events held on the premises.

* * *

The basic principles of the foregoing case law seem to be accepted by our Appellate Courts since they merely reflect basic common-law pronouncements of the duties owed by owners or controllers of premises. * * *

It should be noted that the plaintiff appears to take the position that the jury could very well find that the Bakers' [*13] assaults were not intentional but negligent or reckless. Given the allegations of the complaint and the deposition testimony this seems to be an unlikely supposition. * * *

*HN11*It is also true, for this court at least, that the technical rigors of a proximate cause analysis based on the supposition of an intentional intervening act can complicate an analysis and establish too sharp a dichotomy [*14] between the finding of a duty which is the basis of any negligence action and the question of imposition of liability. Thus Section 344 of the Restatement (2d) Torts says that

A possessor of land who holds it open to the public for entry for his (sic) business purposes is subject to liability to members of the public while they are upon the land for such a purpose, for physical harm caused by the accidental, negligent or intentionally harmful acts of third persons . . .

Comment f makes clear, however, that "since the possessor is not an insurer of the visitor's safety, he is ordinarily under no duty to exercise any care until he knows or has reason to know that the acts of the third person are occurring or are about to occur."

In other words the foreseeability of causing harm by a failure to act to prevent harm to a patron, for example, by another patron is a prerequisite to liability whether the tortfeasor acts or is about to act negligently, recklessly, or intentionally.

* * *

Based on the [*17] foregoing discussion the court will now try to discuss the facts of his case. [3]

* * *

[*18] (b) In support of its motion for summary judgment the defendant has offered the affidavit of Vincent Candelora who is now and was the manager of Sports Plex at the time of this incident on August 25, 2002. Mr. Candelora states that "the Sports Plex has no knowledge of any physical altercations between its patrons and guests prior to August 25, 2002 at (the premises in question). The affidavit is somewhat bareboned—it does not say when the Sports Plex began operating at the location, whether Candelora managed the premises from its inception, if not, how long before the August 25th date he began his duties. It only speaks apparently to physical altercations not the threat thereof which did not proceed to fisticuffs or actual physical contact. Issues such as general rowdiness or excessive drinking are not referred to in the affidavit. Also the general statement is made that "the Sports Plex" does not have knowledge of physical altercations—does this mean the management? Does it refer to all employees? Is there a reporting system to insure information about operations would be communicated to management by employees? Was Candelora always present when the premises were operating [*19] so he could himself make the observations which lead to his conclusion in the affidavit?

* * *

(c) The court has reviewed the general law in this area. Now the court will try to review the facts in light of the specifically relevant case law on the liability of owners or operators of places open to the public for entertainment or sports activities. There are not many Connecticut appellate or trial level on this issue; the court has looked at common-law cases from other jurisdictions.

_HN14_ The cases make clear that the operator of such a place of course has no duty to assign a guard [*26] or security person to every patron that enters its premises, _Warner v. Florida Jai Alai_, 221 So. 2d 777, 778 (Fla.App., 1969) * * *.

Whether or not security must be provided and the level of security depends in part on the forseeability that harm might be likely to occur. This can be found if there were past incidents of general fighting or rowdyism, _Napper v. Kenwood Drive In Theatre Co._, 310 S.W.2d 270 (Ky., 1958) * * *.

In this case the affidavit of the manager of the complex, Mr. Candelora, denies any knowledge of prior altercations on the premises. None of the deposition testimony of the plaintiff or Mr. Viora or the affidavit [*27] of Mr. Perry indicate that any of these individuals witnessed rowdy behavior or fighting in the past. And the plaintiff had been going to the complex since it opened, for years. The plaintiff, for example, had no problem with bringing his child to the facility to attend a baseball clinic and affirmatively said he never saw fights at the facility and never heard of any taking place.

On the day of the incident itself there was no fighting or rowdy behavior displayed by any patrons or by the Bakers and their friends prior to the actual incident. Hopkins said on that day he noticed no difference in the crowd on the day of the attack from other crowds he observed at other times he had been at the complex. Viora said before the actual incident he had no idea fighting would occur. Courts have attached importance to whether or not prior incidents have occurred and how much warning they would have given to owners of premises being sued. * * *

From the previous discussion of the facts presented to the court it is of course also true here that the Bakers in the past before this incident or before the attack [*29] on the day it occurred had not presented any problem or threat to Hopkins or other patrons, cf. _Nance v. Ball_, 134 So. 2d 35 (Fla.App., 1961) (assault on patron of bowling alley by person who previously threatened plaintiff), cf. _Dellinger v. Pierce_, supra.

* * *

Given the foregoing it cannot be said that the defendant violated any duty of care to the plaintiff based on a foreseeability test. What must be kept in mind is that this sports complex after all consisted of five softball fields frequented by adults apparently in organized leagues. We are not dealing with outbursts of violence or constant raucous behavior which might be likely to be a feature of rock-and-roll concerts and wrestling matches. The latter have been defined in one case as "not quiet and dignified affairs," _Whitfield v. Cox_, 189 Va. 219, 52 S.E.2d 72 (Va., 1949), also see on this point _Townsley v. Gardens_, supra, _Gold v. Heath_, 392 S.W.2d at page 306. [*32]

But the plaintiff could maintain that apart from matters such as the service of alcohol and absence of prior behavior that would serve to warn the defendant of danger to patrons, there was no security at all and this in itself could be a basis of liability. Mr. Viora testified that during the whole day he saw no security personnel at the sports complex to supervise the people using the softball field and their guests. But even if we assume there was a duty to supervise the patrons of the facility as said in _Gold v. Heath_, supra, 392 S.W.2d at page 306, quoting from a Florida case: _HN16_ "Usually, even where the duty to supervise may be found to exist, the supervision need be general only as distinguished from special or immediate. It would not be necessary to furnish every patron with an usher or attendant . . . In the case before us it is not fairly inferable from the complaint that general supervision would have prevented the injury caused by the impetuous or wayward boy who did the pushing," also see *Warner v. Florida Jai Alai*, 221 So. 2d 777, 779 (Fla.App. 1969).

* * *

Given the suddenness of the attack, general supervision could not have prevented the contact that occurred between Vin Baker and Hopkins. Even the presence of security [*34] personnel at some ideal number not otherwise defined would not have meant the incident as it involved Vin Baker would not have occurred, cf. *Whitfield v. Cox*, supra. The confrontation was sudden, occupied seconds of time and the operator of the complex had no warning or reason to suspect a confrontation like this would occur. *Corbitt v. Ringley-Crockett*, supra. * * *

* * *

It is true that reading comment f to § 344 of Restatement (2d) Torts it is clear that a defendant would have a duty of care if he knows acts of a patron such as an attack on another patron are about to occur or are occurring. The suddenness of the attack here make it impossible to say that that duty was violated.

* * *

The court concludes that the general negligence claims against the defendant based on a violation of a duty to ensure the safety of patrons on its premises should be dismissed.

* * *

In any [*44] event the motion for summary judgment is granted.

Corradino, J.

CASES ON THE SUPPLEMENTAL CD

Bearman v. Notre Dame, 453 N.E.2d 1196 (Ind. Ct. App. 1983). Pay particular attention to the discussion of duty owed and the foreseeability of harm given prior similar tailgating incidents.

Solis v. Kirkwood Resort Company, 94 Cal. App. 4th 354 (Cal. Ct. App. 1991). Focus on how the ski resort increased the inherent risks of skiing by creating the racing area which then triggered a duty to warn skiers about the enhanced risks.

Sciarrotta v. Global Spectrum, 944 A.2d 630 (N.J. 2008). Notice how the court's decision expands the limited duty rule to apply to all activities on the field of play, including pre-game warm-ups as well as clarifies the facility manager's duty to warn spectators in respect of objects leaving the field of play.

QUESTIONS YOU SHOULD BE ABLE TO ANSWER

1. From a policy perspective, why are business invitees owed the highest duty of care?

2. How and why does the court's willingness to expand the application of recreational user statutes provide additional protection from liability for sport and recreation businesses?

3. If a danger is "open and obvious," how does this fact alter the premise owner's duty to warn?

4. In applying the "totality of the circumstances" test to determine the foreseeability of criminal acts by third parties in a case for negligent security at a sport or recreation, what factors might be dispositive?

5. How does the limited duty rule differ from the business invitee rule in terms of the sport facility's duty to protect patrons?

REFERENCES

Cases

Akins v. Glens Falls City Sch. Dist, 424 N.E.2d 531 (Ct. App. N.Y. 1981).

City of Mangum v. Powell, 165 P.2d 136 (Okla. 1946).

Conant v. Stroup, 51 P.3d 1263 (Ct. App. OR 2002).

Creely v. Corpus Christ Football Team, Inc. d/b/a Corpus Christi Hammerheads, 2007 Tex. App. LEXIS 6769 (Ct. App. T.X., Thirteenth Dist. 2007).

Culli v. Marathon Petroleum Co., 862 F.2d 119 (7th Cir. 1988).

Delta Tau Delta v. Johnson, 712 N.E.2d 968 (Ind. 1999).

Hammond v. Allegretti, 311 N.E.2d 821 (Ind. 1974).

Hayden v. University of Notre Dame, 716 N.E.2d 603 (Ind. Ct. App. 1999).

Hurst v. East Coast Hockey League, Inc. et al., 637 S.E.2d 560 (S.C. 2006).

Maheshwari v. City of New York, 810 N.E.2d 894 (N.Y. App. 2004).

Mann v. Shusteric Enters., 683 N.W.2d 573 (Mich. 2004).

Maussner v. Atlantic City Country Club, Inc., 691 A.2d 826 (N.J. App.Div. 1997).

McPherson v. Tennessee Football Incorporated, 2007 U.S. Dist. LEXIS 39595 (M.D. Tenn. 2007).

Menough v. Woodfield Gardens, 694 N.E.2d 1038 (Ill. Ct. App. 1998).

Ortega v. Kmart Corp., 36 P.3d 11 (Cal. 2001).

Ouellette v. Blanchard, 364 A.2d 631 (N.H. 1976).

Saffro v. Elite Racing, Inc. 98 Cal.App.4th 173 (Cal. App. 4th Dist. 2002).

Sall v. Smiley's Golf Complex, (136 P.3d 471 (Kan. 2006).

Schneider v. American Hockey and Ice Skating Center, 777 A.2d 380 (N.J. App.Div. 2001).

Stadt v. United Center Joint Venture, 2005 U.S. Dist. LEXIS 9580 (N.D. Ill. 2005).

Zipusch v. LA Workout, Inc., 155 Cal.App.4th 1281 (Cal. Ct. App. 2007).

Publications

62 Am. Jur. 2d Premises Liability § 68 (2005).

American Lawyer Directory. (n.d.). Premise liability. Retrieved March 15, 2009 from http://www.statelawyers.com/Practice/Practice_Detail.cfm/PracticeTypeID:77

Carroll, M. S. & Baker, T. A. (2006). The use of constructive notice in slip and fall cases in sport facilities. *JOPERD*, *77*(8), 8–9.

Carroll, M., Connaughton, D., & Spengler, J. O. (2007). Recreational user statutes and landowner immunity: A comparison study of state legislation, *Journal of Legal Aspects of Sport*, *17*, 163–212.

Clark, P. F. (1998). Into the wild: A review of the recreational use statute. *New York State Bar Journal*, *70*(5), 22–26.

Daller, M. F. (2003). Tort Law Desk Reference. New York: Aspen Publishers.

Garner, B. A. (2004). *Black's law dictionary*, 8th ed. St. Paul, Minn: West Publ.

Lewis, J. (1991). Recreational use Statutes: Ambiguous laws yield conflicting results, 27 *Trial*, *27*, 68.

Maloy, C. R. & Higgins, B. P. (2000). *No Excuses Risk Management*. Carmel, IN: Cooper Publishing Group.

Marks, J. H. (2005). The limit to premises liability for harms caused by "known or obvious" dangers: Will it trip and fall over the duty-breach framework emerging in the Restatement (Third) of Torts? *Texas Tech Law Review*, *38*, 1–71.

Prosser, W. L. (1942). Business visitors and invitees, *Minnesota Law Review, 26,* 573.

Restatement (Second) of Torts (1969).

Seidler, T. (2005). Conducting a facility risk review. In H. Appenzeller, *Risk management in sport: Issues and Strategies* (2nd ed.), 317–328. Durham, NC: Carolina Academic Press.

Legislation

Ark. Code Ann.§ 18-11-302 (2008).

Or. Rev. Stat. Ann. § 105.682 (2007).

—Sarah J. Young

INDIANA UNIVERSITY

It is important that recreation and sport managers possess a basic understanding of property law because they are responsible for land areas containing sport facilities, parks, and natural attractions, such as lakes, rivers, cliffs, and hiking trails. This section will examine property law as it pertains to recreation and sport management with specific focus on real property, recreational use statutes, and nuisance actions.

FUNDAMENTAL CONCEPTS

Real Property

Real property is land and generally any structure that is affixed to, erected on, or growing on the land. Sport facilities are constructed and maintained on real property. It is essential that the recreation or sport manager possess a sound understanding of the legal aspects of acquisition and control of property.

Rights of Real Property

To gain a basic understanding of property law as it relates to recreation and sport, it is important to first identify the rights an organization has under different modes of acquisition. There are basically two types of rights in real property: fee simple absolute and less than fee simple. **Fee simple absolute** is the term used to describe a landowner who has complete control of the property. Swanson, Arnold and Rasmussen (2005) described fee simple absolute as a control that includes "the right to exclude others, to sell or contract away one or more rights, and to make any use of the property not restricted by law" (p. 207). A fee simple title means that the legal holder of the title has the authority to do whatever he desires to the property within the limits of the law.

Less than fee simple describes the use of property that is generally based on a contract. Examples of less than fee simple titles include easements, leases, use permits, and joint use or cooperative agreements (Swanson et al., 2005). The existence of less than fee simple titles is common in recreation, sport, and leisure services. For example, a community sports program conducted by a private association on a school-owned sports complex illustrates a joint use agreement. Additionally, pedestrian access strips across private oceanfront property enabling public access to the beach are easements and examples of less than fee simple rights in real property.

Modes of Acquisition

A number of modes of property acquisition are available to the recreation or sport manager. The most common one is **purchase** of a parcel of land or a facility. Acquisition of property through purchasing falls under the fee simple absolute category of rights. Typically, when one purchases a piece of property, total control of that land would be assumed. The purchase of property is usually based on a fair market value on which both the buyer and seller agree. However, there are a number of variations that both the buyer and seller may use to make the deal better from each of their perspectives. Buyers may choose to enter into an option to buy with the seller, thereby purchasing the right to buy the property with no other competition until a mutually agreed on date. Sellers may add restrictive covenants into the purchase that dictate how the property may be used. For example, a private off-road club may desire to purchase an open parcel of land from a municipality to be used for dirt bike and ATV trails. However, before purchasing, the buyer notices a noise restriction contained in the purchase agreement. This type of restrictive covenant would be detrimental to the purpose for which the land was to be used by the off-road club. As a result, buyers must be particularly aware of any restrictions in the title.

Gifts are another type of acquisition under the fee simple rights of real property that many recreation, sport, and leisure services agencies can use to their advantage. Property gifts can be made outright by the donor, as part of an annuity plan, or as the result of an individual's will. Although a gift of property is usually considered an asset to an organization, the manager should be aware of possible restrictions or requirements of the gift agreement. This is especially true if the title is not given in fee simple. For example, if a parcel of land is given to an entity, yet the gift is contingent on the performance of some function or service by the recipient, then the entity may want to carefully consider whether the gift is feasible to accept.

Dedication of land is yet another mode of acquisition in real property. This type of acquisition typically corresponds with the fee simple absolute rights. Mandatory or statutory, dedication of land requires land developers to set aside a portion of their development for public use purposes. Because development generally decreases open space, it increases the demand on remaining open spaces or existing park and recreation facilities. This provides the rationale for this type of acquisition (Swanson et al., 2005). Dedication of property can also be a voluntary act whereby a landowner dedicates land for public use. Typically two elements are necessary for a complete dedication: (1) the intention of the owner to dedicate, and (2) acceptance by the public. An example of a voluntary act of dedication is found in a Washington case where in 1899 a private landowner allowed the city to build a road across his property to the beach. The landowner dedicated the right-of-way to the city of Bainbridge Island. In the more than100 years since this transaction, the property had been subdivided and developed into lots, with several lot owners challenging the public's use of the right-of-way to gain access to the beach area. In an attempt to prevent public access, several lot owners erected a fence and a locked gate barring passage on the road. The court ruled that although the exact property boundary was not known, the intent of the original landowner had been to dedicate the road on his property to the city, the public had accepted the dedication, and the current lot owners were on notice as to the public nature of the area when they purchased their properties (*City of Bainbridge Island v. Brennan*, 2005).

When the owner of property is unwilling to sell his or her land, another mode of acquisition that can be implemented is known as **eminent domain** or **condemnation**. Under the U.S. Constitution, the taking of private property for public use cannot occur without just and fair compensation to the owner. Eminent domain is the power of the government to take private property, whereas condemnation is the vehicle through which this power is generally exercised. Condemnation of private property is appropriate only when the use of the property will be public, the public interests require it, and the property being condemned is necessary to accomplish a public purpose. In recent years a number of states have supported the use of eminent domain and condemnation for the construction of professional sport venues (Hubbard, 2008). This phenomenon is illustrated in *Goldstein v. Pataki* (2008), where a group of Brooklyn, New York property owners challenged an eminent domain taking for the purpose of building a new multi-use urban arena for the New Jersey Nets to be relocated and renamed the Brooklyn Nets. (See the Supplemental CD) Plaintiffs in the case argued that taking of their homes and businesses for a basketball arena did not meet the U.S. Constitution public use requirement. Further, plaintiffs claimed that behind the project's public benefits façade, the private developer of the project and owner of the Nets would stand to profit most from the project's completion. The court ruled in favor of defendant developers holding that the development of Atlantic Yards would not only provide a stadium for the Nets, but would also provide public open space, creation of affordable housing units and "redevelopment of an area in downtown Brooklyn afflicted for decades with substantial blight"(p. 52).

Related to the taking of property is **adverse possession**, or the transfer of property ownership over time in an actual, hostile, open, continuous, and exclusive manner. Dating back to ancient English common law, adverse possession has been used to clarify title to land as well as to discourage property owners from "sleeping on their rights" by neglecting to take the appropriate legal steps to maintain their property. One who claims title by adverse possession must provide clear evidence of actual, continuous, exclusive, visible, and distinct possession usually over a specified period of time. For example in the State of Pennsylvania, the time period for possession is 21 years (*Recreation Land Corp. v. Hartzfeld*, 2008). An example of adverse possession is found in *Hillsmere Shores Improvement Association v. Singleton* (2008), where several residents of a subdivision sought declaration for gaining title by adverse possession of a community beach situated between their lots and a river. For over 20 years, the residents maintained the property, built bulkheads along the waterfront, and were even assessed taxes on the property. The court ruled the residents had fully demonstrated that they had acquired title to the property through adverse possession.

Modes of acquisition falling under the less than fee simple rights of real property include easements, leases, and cooperative agreements. These modes of acquisition most often correspond with less than fee simple rights and refer to acquiring the use of property rather than ownership. An **easement** is defined as extending to certain individuals the right to use the land of another for a specific purpose. Affirmative and negative easements are most commonly recognized. An **affirmative easement** allows the right of use over the property of another such as allowing the public access to a road over the private property of a church camp to gain access to their own private lots (*Lyons v. Baptist School of Christian Training*, 2002). A **negative easement**, on the other hand, restricts use in a particular manner. For example, a scenic easement may restrict the construction of facilities to protect a beautiful vista (Swanson et al., 2005). **Leases** are used extensively in sport and recreation situations and are considered a common method of acquiring the use of land or buildings for a specified length of time. Finally, **cooperative agreements** are frequently used to allow two organizations to share the same facilities.

Land Use Controls

In addition to the acquisition of property, the recreation or sport manager must have a basic knowledge of the legal aspects of controlling the use of land under their supervision. A common law device of controlling land use is the public trust doctrine. **The public trust doctrine** provides that submerged and submersible lands are preserved for public use in navigation, fishing, and recreation. "Historically, the doctrine was applied primarily to water and submerged lands under navigable waters" (van der Smissen, 1990, p. 75); however, the doctrine has evolved to apply to dry lands as well. The main purpose of the public trust doctrine is the idea that certain natural resources belong to the public and should be preserved for the good of society. Management and control over the property held in trust cannot be relinquished by transfer of property (Garcia & Baltodano, 2005). Further, it is the responsibility of public agencies to control the use of these natural resources and areas so they can be enjoyed by current and future generations. A Michigan case concerning whether the public has a right to walk along the shores of the Great Lakes where a private landowner holds title to the water's edge illustrates the application of the public trust doctrine. Defendant landowners attempted to prevent plaintiff from walking along the shore of Lake Huron, which they maintained was trespassing on their private land. The Supreme Court of Michigan ruled the public trust doctrine preserves the rights of pedestrian use of the shores of the Great Lakes (*Glass v. Goeckel*, 2005).

Another type of land use control commonly implemented in recreation is **zoning**, defined as dividing "a municipality into geographical districts or zones and then regulating the nature and use of land in the various zones" (van der Smissen, 1990, p. 78). The regulation extends not only to the development of the land, but also to the structures on the land and the activities conducted thereon. Further, van der Smissen explained "zoning is primarily a legislative function of the municipality and represents judgment of the elected governing body as to how land should be utilized within its jurisdiction" (p. 79). In California, a private nonprofit water ski club purchased an island designated as open space and zoned as agricultural. The county's zoning ordinances allowed no more than one single-family residence per five-acre parcel of land. Over 35 years, however, the water ski club built 28 residential units and docks on the five-acre island. Because the water ski club had knowingly violated the county's zoning ordinance and land-use requirement, the court ruled in favor of the county demolishing all but one structure on the island (*Golden Gate Water Ski Club v. County of Contra Costa*, 2008).

The **control of activities** and the use of property are central to the issue of zoning. Zoning regulations generally correspond with a governmental agency's comprehensive plan to avoid claims of arbitrary or unreasonable zoning ordinances. This also ensures the proper use and development of property for current and future public needs. In Michigan, a township government was successful in permanently enjoining a private landowner from using his property as a hunting and gun club. The appellate court ruled the township was within its statutory authority to enact zoning ordinances and regulate the use of the land. In order to continue to engage in various shooting activities on his property, the landowner was required to seek special land use permits allowing for those activities (*Smolarz v. Colon Township*, 2005).

Recreational User Statutes ✳

Recreational user statutes are legislative acts that are established in all states for the purpose of protecting landowners from liability if they permit the public to use their property for recreation at no cost to the user (see Section 2.22, *Immunity*). In 1965, the Council of State Governments addressed a growing need in the United States for more recreational land by recommending that states pass an act known as the Model Act encouraging private landowners to open their property to the public for recreational enjoyment and use. Legislation of this type was eventually adopted by all 50 states but with a great deal of variation by state. As a result, one should be familiar with the aspects of the statute for a specific state. Yet, the overall essence of the statute is that landowners owe no duty to recreational users of their property (*Matheny v. United States*, 2006) creating a defense for negligence liability.

General Characteristics ▬

Although each state has its own variation of the recreational user statute and interpretations through case law, there are four general characteristics of the statute common to most states. These common denominators are discussed following.

The first of these characteristics involves the **type of property owners** to which the statute applies. In some states, the immunity protection provided by the statute is targeted toward private landowners, whereas in other states owners of public lands (i.e., local, state, and federal government agencies) are also afforded immunity. The original intent of the Model Act was to encourage private landowners to open their property to the public for recreational use. For example, a private landowner attempted to use the Illinois recreational use statute as a defense to a negligence claim of a woman injured on a luge-like sled run built in his backyard. The Illinois Supreme Court ruled that defendant was not shielded from liability by the state's recreational use statute because his sled run was not open to the public, but only to invited guests (*Hall v. Henn*, 2003). A number of states have broadened their interpretation from the private landowner to any property owner, lessees, tenants, occupants, or persons controlling the premises. As a result, many public agencies now look to recreational use statutes as an alternative source of immunity. For example, in Arizona a municipality successfully sought immunity under the state's recreational user statute from the negligence claim of a plaintiff who was injured while sledding down a hill in a city park (*Dickey v. City of Flagstaff*, 2003). In another case, a municipality in Montana was protected by the state's recreational use statute after plaintiff fell through a damaged plank on a city-owned dock where he was fishing (*Jobe v. City of Polson*, 2004). The broad interpretation of qualified property owners by many states has led to the practice of school districts also seeking protection under recreational user statutes. In *Auman v. School District of Stanley-Boyd* (2001), the Wisconsin court specifically addressed the issue of whether a school district could seek protection under the statute. Although the recreational user statute did not apply in the *Auman* case, a number of school districts have successfully defended themselves from liability for negligence using their state's statute (*Fritts v. Clover Park School District*, 2003; *Poston v. Unified School District No. 387*, 2008).

A second characteristic of the recreational user statute is that the landowner *cannot charge a fee* for individuals to use the premises. Although most state statutes have provided that immunity will not apply if a fee is charged, there is some variation among the states as to how "fee" is interpreted. Most courts have maintained immunity for landowners except where an actual fee has been charged for entry onto the land. This type of charge is a narrow interpretation of the law, which requires an explicit quid pro quo arrangement of payment in exchange for admission onto the premises. For example, in *Lee v. The Department of Natural Resources of the State of Georgia* (2003), plaintiff claimed his wife dislocated her elbow after tripping over a debris pile near the public restroom of a campground on Ossabaw Island. Although access to the island was free, plaintiff had been required to pay $29 for a wildlife management license to qualify for lottery-selected access to the island. The court ruled that the recreational property act did provide defendant immunity because the hunting license fees did not in any way constitute a fee for admission to the island. Illustrating another perspective of the quid pro quo arrangement, a Washington court ruled that the recreational use statute did not apply to a city owning a moorage dock within a municipal park. Plaintiff slipped and fell on a wet metal ramp leading to the dock. Although the city sought immunity under the recreational use statute and claimed they did not charge fees for use of the park's facilities, they did charge a boat moorage fee. The court ruled that because the city charged a fee of *any* kind, no immunity under the statute was available (*Plano v. City of Renton*, 2000).

Other states have interpreted the fee more broadly as any type of consideration. In states adhering to the idea that consideration constitutes a charge, almost any form of benefit to the landowner can trigger an exception to immunity. For example, in Nevada, the spouses of the plaintiffs in *Ducey v. United States* (1983), were killed in a flash flood in the Lake Mead National Recreational Area. The users had been boating and camping in the area and had paid rental fees and purchased various supplies from a concessionaire within the recreation area. The terms of the concession agreement obligated the concessionaire to remit less than 2 percent of its gross annual receipts from boat slip rentals and the general store to the owner of the recreation area. The receipt of this percentage was sufficient to be held as consideration under Nevada's recreational use statute. This was true even though the plaintiffs had not paid a fee to enter the recreational area. It is apparent that one should investigate a specific state's interpretation of charging fees.

A third characteristic of the recreational user statute is that immunity is provided for owners of *unimproved, or undeveloped, rural land retained in its natural condition.* Maloy (1997) defined unimproved lands as "real estate for which there has not been a labor cost or capital improvement intended to enhance its value for another purpose" (p. 59). The Pennsylvania Supreme Court emphasized this characteristic by stating the recreational user statute applied to large, undeveloped tracts of land suitable for outdoor recreation (*Stone v. York Haven Power Co.*, 2000). In another Pennsylvania case, plaintiff was injured while tobogganing in Valley Forge National Historical Park. The claim stated the toboggan hit a mound of snow that had allegedly built up around an old telephone junction box. The plaintiff claimed the junction box fell under the definition of developed or improved lands, but the court ruled the recreational user statute applied because Valley Forge was the type of unimproved property to which the statute was meant to apply (*Blake v. United States of America*, 1998).

The interpretation of this characteristic varies widely from state to state with a number of states applying the statute to developed recreational facilities such as ball fields, playgrounds, and swimming pools. For example, in Kansas, a court ruled that the statute provided defendant immunity after plaintiff slipped and fell in a wet hallway between a swimming pool and a locker room of a building owned by the state (*Robison v. State of Kansas*, 2002). In a Michigan case, the very issue of undeveloped lands was debated. Plaintiff in this case had injured her back while riding as a passenger on defendant's ATV and on defendant's 11-acre lot. Although portions of the lot were wooded and undeveloped, plaintiff was injured while riding on the mowed portion of defendant's backyard. The trial court ruled in defendant's favor based on the state's recreational user act. Yet upon appeal, the court reversed the trial court's ruling because the injury occurred while riding on the mowed portion of defendant's property. The appellate court interpreted the recreational user act as only pertaining to large tracts of undeveloped land. The Supreme Court of Michigan accepted the case and after review ruled in favor of defendants by stating there was no indication the legislature intended application of the statute be limited to undeveloped lands (*Neal v. Wilkes*, 2004).

A final general characteristic of the recreational user statute involves **obligations of the landowner**. The owner's only obligation under the statute is to provide a warning for any known concealed danger that would not be apparent to the recreational user. Owners have no duty to warn of open and obvious hazards, nor do they have a duty to warn of conditions that are unknown to them. A Kentucky case involving a skate park illustrates this characteristic. An 11-year-old boy was seriously injured when he inadvertently rode his bike from the beginner's section of a municipal skate park into the advanced section of the park, which contained an 11-foot bowl with nearly vertical walls. Because there had been two similar accidents a couple of months earlier, the city had consulted the park designer, who recommended a soft barrier be situated between the beginners' section and the 11-foot bowl. This barrier had not yet been installed when the accident leading to this case occurred. Although the trial court ruled defendants immune from liability under the recreational user statute, the appellate court was called on to determine whether the city had failed to guard or warn users of the risk. The court found there was evidence to raise a material fact that the city had failed to guard users from concealed hazards and failed to warn users of potential dangers (*Woods v. Louisville/Jefferson County Metro Government*, 2005).

A Two-Pronged Analysis of Applicability ✳

Many states use a two-pronged analysis to determine whether the recreational user statute applies and the defendant is entitled to immunity. The first analysis is whether the activity is a recreational activity. The determination of what constitutes a recreational activity has been the focus of a number of cases. In *Parent v. State of Tennessee* (1999), the Supreme Court of Tennessee ruled that an all-inclusive list explicitly enumerating every single activity that is recreational in nature would be extremely cumbersome. A majority of states use the phrase "included, but not limited to" (van der Smissen, 1990, p. 213) in providing a list of recreational activities. In an Ohio case, being a participant/spectator of the discus throw at a junior high school track meet was considered a recreational activity. The plaintiff who was hit in the face with a discus thrown by a teammate was not able to collect for damages because the school district was entitled to immunity under the recreational user statute (*Mason v. Bristol*, 2006). Conversely, a Texas court ruled that although a municipality provided recreation activities in an after-school program at a local community center, defendants failed to show that plaintiff had attended the program solely for recreational pursuits, meaning the statute did not apply (*Torres v. City of Waco*, 2001).

The second prong of the analysis is whether the plaintiff is recreating on land suitable for the activity. In *McCarthy v. New York State Canal Corp.* (1998), the court ruled that a concrete seawall on the Mohawk River was an area suitable for the recreational activity of fishing. Once again, there is some variation in the manner in which each state interprets the suitability of the land for recreational activity. In Hawaii, the proper focus is on the landowner's intent (*Howard v. United States of America*, 1999). In other words, if a landowner has opened up lands for recreational use without a fee, then it is not significant that a person coming onto the property may have a nonrecreational or commercial purpose in mind. In Wisconsin, the court must consider a number of different factors, including the nature of the property, the nature of the landowner's activity, and the reason the injured person is on the property (*Rintelman v. Boys and Girls Club of Greater Milwaukee*, 2005). Plaintiff fell while she was walking to move from one building to another at a residential camp. Although the nature of the property was recreational, the reason plaintiff was on the site was not for recreation or leisure purposes. Therefore, the court ruled that defendant was not immune to liability under Wisconsin's recreational use statute.

Nuisance Law ✳

Nuisance is an area of property law dealing with activity or use of one's property that produces material annoyance, inconvenience, and discomfort for those around the property. The law of nuisance is fairly comprehensive and includes that which endangers life and health, gives offense to the senses, violates laws of decency, or obstructs reasonable use of property. Nuisances are typically classified as public or private. **Public nuisances** are acts that obstruct the enjoyment or use of common property or cause inconvenience or damage to the public. For example, plaintiff homeowners around the New Britain, Connecticut minor league baseball stadium sued defendants, alleging the fireworks show coordinated with music constituted an offensive disruption to their lives on Friday nights throughout the Spring and Summer. The reverberations from the fireworks caused plaintiffs' houses to tremble and the smoke from the fireworks would linger for hours. The court acknowledged that while the fireworks generated revenue for the baseball team and the city, the burden of fireworks every Friday night home game was simply too much for residents to bear. The permanent injunctive relief reduced the number of fireworks shows to one time per month along with damages of $100 per plaintiff. (*Esposito v. New Britain Baseball Club, Inc.*, 2005).

Private nuisance is a nontrespassory invasion of another's interest in the use or enjoyment of his or her property. The primary factors to be considered in a private nuisance claim are the gravity of the harm to the plaintiff, the value of the defendant's activity to the community, the burden that will be placed on the defendant if a particular remedy is granted, and whether the defendant's activity was in progress when the plaintiff arrived at the locality. *Hot Rod Hill Motor Park v. Triolo* (2008), provides a good example of a private nuisance. Plaintiff claimed racing activities on defendant landowner's track was deafening, loud, excessive, and disturbing. The noise from race cars would cause neighbors' windows and light fixtures to shake, and prevent them from sleeping, watching television, or spending time outdoors during the evenings when the track was operating. The court ruled that while defendant had taken steps to reduce the noise, the track was a private nuisance that seriously interfered with his neighbors use and enjoyment of their property

Attractive nuisance is another dimension of nuisance law that is focused on children entering property because they are attracted by a unique, artificial condition such as a swimming pool (*Bennett v. Stanley*, 2001), paintball activity (*Goldhirsch v. Taylor*, 2000), or a trampoline (*Kopczynski v. Barger*, 2008). For the doctrine of attractive nuisance to apply, the landowner of the artificial condition should know or have reason to know that children are likely to trespass the premises. Additionally, the landowner should know or have reason to know that the condition will involve an unreasonable risk to trespassing children, and the children, because of their youth and inexperience, will not realize this danger. Finally, the burden of eliminating the condition is minimal to the landowner, yet, he or she fails to protect children from the condition. Attractive nuisance was the claim in *Butler v. Newark Country Club* (2005), when plaintiff's 8-year-old son fell through the ice and drowned in a pond located on a golf course while on his way to the local community center. The boy was accompanied by his 11-year-old sister and 13-year-old cousin, who had tested the ice by stomping on it prior to them playing on the pond. Although the pond was artificial in that it was man-made and contained a large spillway pipe, it was determined that was not the quality that had attracted the children to it. The court ruled that attractive nuisance doctrine did not apply because it was the natural properties (i.e., the frozen pond) that lured the children to venture onto the ice. Generally, park, recreation, and sport facilities are not nuisances, but may become such if not properly planned, located, or managed according to recognized standards.

SIGNIFICANT CASE

A landowner is not protected from liability for actions that are considered willful and wanton. This aspect of the statute is illustrated in the representative case of *Sulzen Ex Rel. Holton v. United States of America* (1999). Although the Hanging Rock Picnic Area, in this case, fits all the general characteristics needed for immunity under Utah's recreational use statute, the willful or malicious conduct exception was upheld by the court.

SULZEN EX. REL. HOLTON V. UNITED STATES OF AMERICA

U. S. District Court for the District of Utah
54 F. Supp.2d 1212; 1999 U.S. Dist. LEXIS 10283
June 29, 1999 Decided
June 30, 1999 Filed

Opinion By: Judge Tena Campbell

While visiting the Hanging Rock Picnic Area in American Fork Canyon, the plaintiff's daughter, Elizabeth Holton, was struck and killed by a rock which was dislodged by two teenagers climbing on a cliff above. Plaintiffs sued the United States as owner of the picnic area for failure to keep the area safe and for failure to warn Elizabeth Holton of the dangerous conditions in the area. The United States has moved for summary judgment based on the Utah Limitation of Landowner Liability Act. Plaintiffs argue that the Act does not apply to the Hanging Rock Picnic Area, or alternatively, that the United States is not entitled to the protection of the Act because the United States willfully disregarded a life threatening hazard.

* * *

A. Application of the Utah Limitation of Landowner Liability Act

The Federal Tort Claims Act (FTCA) waives the United States' sovereign immunity from tort actions arising from personal injury or death caused by the negligent or wrongful act or omission of any [Federal] employee. Under the FTCA, however, the United States is only liable in the same manner and to the same extent as a private individual under like circumstances. In other words, if a similarly situated private individual would not be liable under the appropriate jurisdiction's laws, then neither is the United States.

Because the accident in this case occurred on federal property in Utah, the tort law of the state of Utah applies. In Utah, the Utah Limitation of Landowner Liability Act (the Act) limits the liability of landowners who have opened their lands to the public free of charge for recreational use. Specifically, a landowner who falls within the scope of the Act owes no duty of care to keep the premises safe or to warn of dangerous conditions. Because the FTCA waives

sovereign immunity only to the extent that a private individual would be held liable under like circumstances, the Act applies to immunize the federal government from liability for injuries sustained by a plaintiff engaged in recreational use of federal property.

The United States maintains that the Hanging Rock Picnic Area falls within the protection of the Act and it is therefore entitled to summary judgment as a matter of law. Plaintiff argues that the Act does not apply because the picnic areas was the type of highly developed area that the Act intended to exclude.

* * *

After applying each of these factors to the undisputed facts in this case, the court finds that the Hanging Rock Picnic Area qualifies for limited immunity under the Act because it exhibits most, if not all, of these characteristics.

1. Rural

The Hanging Rock Picnic Area is the type of rural recreation area intended to be covered by the Act. In Utah and other jurisdictions, courts consider the rural nature of the land in determining whether the state's limitation on landowner liability act should apply. To decide if the land is rural, courts look to various characteristics including the remoteness, size and naturalness of the area. Each of these factors support the conclusion that the Hanging Rock Picnic Area is a rural area.

First, the Hanging Rock Picnic Area is a remote area, removed from urban or residential settings. Courts agree that the Act was intended to grant immunity from liability to owners of rural and semi-rural tracts of land, not to owners of land in residential and populated neighborhoods. However, the Hanging Rock Picnic Area is readily distinguishable from the urban or residential areas that other courts have excluded from the protection of the Act. The picnic area, which is located four miles from the mouth of American Fork Canyon in the Uintah National Forest, is certainly not a "stones throw" from a populated residential area. Instead, the Hanging Rock Picnic Area is the type of relatively remote area intended to be covered by the Act.

Second, the Hanging Rock Picnic Area is a part of the Uintah National Forest, a massive expanse of rugged land. Although the grassy picnic area itself is only approximately 200 feet wide by 300 feet long, the grassy area is not a separate and discrete area apart from the rest of the Uintah National Forest. The parties agree that there is not division between the picnic area and the American Fork River, the overhanging cliffs, or the other undeveloped areas of the Uintah National Forest. In fact, Ms. Holton was killed when two teenage boys, who had been visiting the picnic area, dislodged a rock while climbing on the nearby 200 foot cliff. Looking only to the grassy picnic area to determine the size of the land would be an artificial distinction, especially where the accident was caused by activity in an unaltered and natural area of the forest. When viewed in conjunction with the surrounding Uintah National Forest, the Hanging Rock Picnic Area is part of a large tract of open, vacant land in a relatively natural state within the scope of the Act.

Third, the Hanging Rock Picnic Area is a relatively natural setting in which visitors encounter elements found in the true outdoors, such as cliffs, heavily wooded areas, and rivers. In determining whether the property should be considered rural, some courts have considered whether the injury-causing element is normally found in the true outdoors. In this case, falling rock from an overhead cliff is unquestionably the type of danger only encountered in the true outdoors; such a danger would never be found in someone's backyard. The natural surroundings of the Hanging Rock Picnic Area support the conclusion that the area is the type of rural location intended to be covered by the Act.

2. Undeveloped

The Hanging Rock Picnic Area is relatively natural, undeveloped area of land within the protection of the Act. Plaintiff argues that the picnic area was a developed area because it had public restrooms, a paved parking area, and intentionally planted sod and because the course of the American Fork River had been altered to accommodate the picnic area. Other courts have held, however, that improvements such as shelters, toilet facilities, fireplaces, etc., are merely conveniences incidental to the use of the land for enumerated recreational activities and do not themselves take property out of a rural undeveloped classification. The improvements to the Hanging Rock Picnic Area merely made the area more accessible and enjoyable to the public and did not significantly alter the land's natural state.

The plain language of the Act evinces the legislature's intent to protect owners of relatively undeveloped land regardless of whether the land contains improvements, such as a parking lot or restrooms. The Act expressly includes roads, buildings, and structures within the definition of land covered by the Act. If the legislature intended to exclude all improved land from the scope of the Act, the Act would not expressly cover these artificial conditions.

Although human alterations or additions to the land may so change its character as to render the Act inapplicable, the focus should be on whether the land remains in a relatively natural state or has been developed and changed in a manner incompatible with the intention of the act. Here, the Hanging Rock Picnic Area contains some improvements, but is not developed to the point that it is removed from the type of land covered by the Act.

3. Appropriate for the Type of Activities Listed in the Statute

Application of the Act is limited to owners who have opened their property to the public for recreational purposes. The Act then provides:

> *Recreational purpose includes, but is not limited to, any of the following or any combination thereof: hunting, fishing, swimming, skiing, snowshoeing, camping, picnicking, hiking, studying nature, waterskiing, engaging in water sports, using boats, using off-highway vehicles or recreational vehicles, and viewing or enjoying historical archeological, scenic, or scientific sites. Utah Code Ann. @ 57-14-2(3) (Supp. 1998)*

The undisputed facts show that Hanging Rock Picnic Area is appropriate for many of the activities listed in the statute. The picnic area can be used for fishing, swimming (or at least wading), hiking, picnicking, studying nature or enjoying archeological or scenic sites, most of which cannot be conducted in a small city park like the park at issue in De Baritault. In addition, there is not requirement in the Act that the area be conducive to all of the enumerated activities. Therefore, this factor weighs in favor of finding Hanging Rock Picnic Area within the scope of the Act.

4. Open to the General Public Without Charge

It is undisputed that the picnic area was open to the public free of charge.

5. A Type of Land that Would Have Been Opened in Response to the Statute

The Act was intended to encourage landowners to permit gratuitous recreational use of their land. This policy of encouraging landowners to open land for recreational use applies equally to the federal government as to other landowners. Therefore, federal lands opened to the public are the types of land that would have been opened in response to the statute. It is immaterial that the Hanging Rock Picnic Area was open to the public ten years before the passage of the Act, because the land need not actually be opened in response to the Act, so long as it is the type of land that would have been opened in response to the statute.

Because the Hanging Rock Picnic Area exhibits at least some combination of the characteristics prerequisite to immunity under the recreational use statutes, the government is immune from liability for Ms. Holton's death unless plaintiffs can fall within one of the exceptions in the Utah Code Ann. @ 57-14-3.

B. Willful or Malicious Conduct Exception

The Act provides that an owner of land owes no duty of care to keep the premises safe for entry or use by any person entering or using the premises for any recreational purpose or to give any warning of a dangerous condition, use, structure, or activity on those premises to those persons. However, the Act does not limit liability where the owner charges for use of the land, where the injury is deliberate, willful or malicious, or where the injury results from willful or malicious failure to guard or warn against a dangerous condition, use, structure, or activity.

Plaintiffs argue that the willful or malicious failure to guard or warn exception applies in this case because the United States knew of the falling rock hazard at Hanging Rock Picnic Area and failed to take any action despite such knowledge.

* * *

As evidence that the United States had knowledge of a dangerous condition likely to result in serious injury, plaintiffs rely primarily on the deposition testimony of Robert Eastman, a park ranger. Mr. Eastman testified that before the accident he had observed shale rocks along the river, around the toilet area, and in the parking lot. He also testified that maintenance people had reported finding rocks in the grassy picnic area which would cause indentations in the grass. However, Mr. Eastman stated that he never believed that the rocks were falling from the cliff above. Although the willful and malicious exception re-

quires actual knowledge of a dangerous condition, the question of whether Mr. Eastman knew that the rocks were falling from the overhanging cliff requires a credibility determination not appropriate at the summary judgment stage. Mr. Eastman's knowledge before the accident that shale rocks had left indentations in the grass could support a conclusion that Mr. Eastman knew that rocks were falling from the cliff onto the picnic area and failed to act.

In addition to Mr. Eastman's testimony, plaintiffs point to a Forest Service memoranda and the deposition testimony of Forest Supervisor Peter Karp as evidence that the United States was aware that rocks had been falling from the cliff before the accident. The Forest Service memoranda dated September 7, 1995, indicates that the task force on the Hanging Rock Picnic Area, organized in response to Elizabeth Holton's accident, was concerned that unrecorded near misses had occurred at Hanging Rock. Mr. Karp also stated in his deposition that he was aware that rocks had fallen from the cliff from time to time before the accident. The ambiguity in the Forest Service memoranda and the Karp deposition regarding the time that Forest Service officials learned of the falling rocks raises a question for the trier of fact. Viewing the evidence in the light most favorable to the non-moving party, the fact finder could infer that the Forest Service knew of the falling rocks before Elizabeth Holton's accident.

Because plaintiffs have raised a question of fact as to whether the United States had knowledge of a dangerous condition that was likely to result in serious injury, defendants' motion for summary judgment must be denied. The question of whether the willful or malicious exception applies will be decided at trial.

For the foregoing reasons, defendants' motion for summary judgment is DENIED.

Another Related Significant Case

Section 2.21, *Defenses Against Negligence*

CASES ON THE SUPPLEMENTAL CD

Cudworth v. Midcontinent Communications, (380 F.3d 375, 2004). The reader should note the number of property law applications instituted by plaintiff to implicate liability upon the defendant.

Goldstein v. Pataki, (516 F.3d 50, 2008). The reader should note the court's opinion that once a valid public use has been discerned, it makes no

difference that the property will be transferred to private developers. Also of interest is to identify at what point is the public use requirement satisfied?

McAfee MX v. Foster, (2008 Tex. App. LEXIS 968). The reader should note the discussion of balancing the equities that courts must consider in determining an appropriate remedy for a nuisance claim.

QUESTIONS YOU SHOULD BE ABLE TO ANSWER

1. Explain the difference between fee simple absolute and less than fee simple absolute types of real property. What are examples of each?

2. What are the pros and cons of taking private property for professional sport venues?

3. What is the primary purpose of the recreational use statute? Identify the characteristics common to recreational use statutes.

4. Explain the two-prong analysis used by courts to determine whether the recreational use statute might apply to a situation.

5. What are the factors the court will consider in determining whether property contains an attractive nuisance?

REFERENCES

Cases

Auman v. School District of Stanley-Boyd, 635 N.W.2d 762 (2001).

Bennett v. Stanley, 748 N.E.2d 41 (2001).

Blake v. United States of America, 1998 U. S. Dist. LEXIS 1475 (1998).

Butler v. Newark Country Club, 2005 Del. Super. LEXIS 301 (2005).

City of Bainbridge Island v. Brennan, 2005 Wash. App. LEXIS 1744 (2005).

Cudworth v. Midcontinent Communications, 380 F.3d 375 (8th Cir. 2004).

Dickey v. City of Flagstaff, 66 P.3d 44 (2003).

Ducey v. United States, 713 F.2d 504 (1983).

Esposito v. New Britain Baseball Club, Inc., 895 A.2d 291 (2005).

Fritts v. Clover Park School District No. 400, 2003 Wash. App. LEXIS 2895 (2003).

Glass v. Goeckel, 703 N.W.2d 1 (2005).

Golden Gate Water Ski Club v. County of Contra Costa, 165 Cal. App. 4th 249 (2008).

Goldhirsch v. Taylor, 87 F. Supp.2d 272 (2000).

Goldstein v. Pataki, 516 F.3d 50 (2008).

Hall v. Henn, 802 N.E.2d 797, (2003).

Hillsmere Shores Improvement Association v. Singleton, 959 A.2d 130 (2008).

Hot Rod Hill Motor Park v. Triolo, 2008 Tex. App. LEXIS 9040 (2008).

Howard v. United States of America, 181 F.3d 1064 (1999).

Jobe v. City of Polson, 157 P.3d 743 (2004).

Kopczynski v. Barger, 887 N.E.2d 928 (2008).

Lee v. The Department of Natural Resources of the State of Georgia, 588 S.E.2d 260 (2003).

Lyons v. Baptist School of Christian Training, 804 A.2d 364 (2002).

Mason v. Bristol, 2006 Ohio App. LEXIS 5126 (2006).

Matheny v. United States of America, 469 F.3d 1093 (2006).

McAfee v. Foster, 2008 Tex. App. LEXIS 968 (2008).

McCarthy v. New York State Canal Corp., 244 A.D.2d 57 (1998).

Neal v. Wilkes, 685 N.W.2d 648 (2004).

Parent v. State of Tennessee, 991 S.W.2d 240 (1999).

Plano v. City of Renton, 14 P.3d 871 (2000).

Poston v. Unified School District No. 387, 189 P.3d 517 (2008).

Recreation Land Corporation v. Hartzfeld, 947 A.2d 771 (2008).

Rintelman v. Boys and Girls Club of Greater Milwaukee, 2005 Wisc. App. LEXIS 934 (2005).

Robison v. State of Kansas, 43 P.3d 821 (2002).

Smolarz v. Colon Township, 2005 Mich. App. LEXIS 997 (2005).

Stone v. York Haven Power Company, 749 A.2d 452 (2000).

Sulzen Ex Rel. Holton v. United States of America, 54 F. Supp.2d 1212 (D. Utah 1999).

Torres v. City of Waco, 51 S.W.3d 814 (2001).

Woods v. Louisville/Jefferson County Metro Government, 2005 Ky. App. LEXIS 106 (2005).

Publications

Garcia, R., & Baltodano, E. F. (2005). Free the beach! Public access, equal justice, and the California coast. *Stanford Journal of Civil Rights and Civil Liberties*, 2, 143–208.

Hubbard, T. E. (2008). For the public's use? Eminent domain in stadium construction. *Sports Lawyers Journal*, 15, 173–193.

Maloy, B. P. (1997). Immunity. In D. J. Cotten & T. J. Wilde (Eds.), *Sport law for sport managers* (pp. 54–62). Dubuque, IA: Kendall/Hunt Publishing Company.

Swanson, T., Arnold, R. C., Rasmussen, G. A. (2005). Physical resource planning. In B. van der Smissen, M. Moiseichik, & V. J. Hartenburg (Eds.), *Management of park and recreation agencies* (2nd ed., pp. 205–242). Ashburn, VA: National Recreation and Park Association.

van der Smissen, B. (1990). *Legal liability and risk management for public and private entities* (Vol. I & II). Cincinnati, OH: Anderson Publishing Company.

2.33 *Emergency Care*

—Kristi L. Schoepfer

WINTHROP UNIVERSITY

Approximately 7 million Americans receive medical attention for recreation and sport injuries each year; approximately one third of these injuries occur at a recreation or sport facility (Conn, Annest, & Gilchrist, 2003). Due to the heightened risk of injury in recreation and sport activities, ranging from minor to catastrophic harms, recreation and sport managers must understand the responsibility to plan for and provide emergency care. Emergency care can be defined as the provision of medical assistance to an injured person in an urgent, immediate, or unexpected circumstance. When injuries occur, recreation and sport managers (or staff) have a duty to provide competent medical assistance or summon such assistance in a timely manner. Also, emergency care includes planning for the various emergencies that are likely to occur in a recreation or sport setting.

FUNDAMENTAL CONCEPTS

Origins of the Duty

The responsibility to plan for and provide emergency care stems from a special relationship that exists between recreation and/or sport business and its participants/patrons. As defined in Section 2.11, *Negligence*, this special relationship creates a duty that gives rise to an obligation to protect the individual from an unreasonable risk of harm. Previous sections have outlined the various origins of this relationship, including inherent relationships, voluntary assumption of a relationship, and relationships created by statute (*see* Section 2.11, *Negligence*). Further, Section 2.31, *Premises Liability* outlined relationships that exist between premise owners/operators and visitors.

Inherent Relationship

An inherent relationship is one that is obvious or inseparable; it is essential to the activity. Such a relationship exists in many recreation and sport contexts, such as an activity director/participant or coach/player (see Section 2.11, *Negligence*). Regarding emergency care, an inherent relationship gives rise to the duty to plan for and provide emergency care. A participant or patron in the recreation or sport setting with an inherent relationship to the provider must be able to rely upon that provider for emergency care. For example, in the Significant Case (*Kleinknecht v. Gettysburg College*, 1993), the court provides a lengthy discussion of the relationship that existed between the college and the student athlete. This relationship, in addition to other considerations, resulted in a finding that the college had a duty to provide emergency care.

Voluntary Assumption

While the duty to provide emergency care is more often predicated on an inherent relationship, voluntary assumption must also be discussed. A duty is voluntarily assumed when an individual chooses to engage in an activity that creates a special relationship. For example, if an individual volunteers to coach a youth soccer team, he or she has voluntarily created a special relationship between him or herself and the players on the team. In this situation, the voluntary relationship results in a duty to provide emergency care (among others).

Individuals may assume a relationship by voluntarily rendering aid in an emergency circumstance. When volunteers provide emergency care, they have a duty to act as the reasonable person would in the same or similar circumstance; however, absent gross negligence or willful and wanton conduct, an individual who voluntarily renders aid will likely be covered by a Good Samaritan statute should a harm occur (see Section 2.22, *Immunity*).

Statute

A statute is a law passed by a legislative body that mandates or regulates conduct; thus, certain duties are mandated by statute. Regarding emergency care in the recreation and sport setting, many states have statutes requiring the provision of specific emergency services or equipment. For example, 12 states require health and fitness facilities to have automatic external defibrillators (AEDs) on site (this topic will be discussed more completely in a later part of the section). In these states, the duty to provide emergency care is mandated by statute.

In addition to creating a duty, statutes can also define certain specific emergency care responsibilities. For example, in Louisiana, a coach, manager, athletic trainer or official cannot be sued "for any loss or damage caused by any act or omission to act directly related to his responsibilities as a coach, manager, athletic trainer . . . or official, while actively conducting, directing, or participating in the sporting activities or in the practice thereof, unless the loss or damage was caused by the gross negligence of the coach, manager, athletic trainer . . . or official." [La. R.S. 9:2798 (2008)]. However, this limit on liability is *only* available if the benefiting party has participated in a safety orientation and training program established by the league or team of affiliation. The statute further directs that child CPR is a suggested component of the safety training. [La. R.S. 9:2798 (2008)]. Thus, by virtue of making limited liability contingent upon safety and child CPR training, the statute dictates that coaches, managers, athletic trainers and officials have the training required to provide emergency care.

Premises Liability

As discussed in Section 2.31, *Premises Liability*, premise owners and operators owe a duty to invitees to keep a facility reasonably safe. This includes an obligation to respond to medical emergencies in a prompt and competent manner. Regardless of whether an individual is an activity participant or a spectator, those patrons classified as invitees have a reasonable expectation of emergency care.

Elements of Emergency Care

Recreation and sport managers that have a duty to provide adequate emergency care must carefully consider four distinct elements. These include: (1) emergency planning; (2) appropriate personnel/injury assessment; (3) adequate equipment/certifications; and (4) implementation of emergency procedures. As will be discussed, all four elements are essential to adequately fulfilling the duty to provide emergency care.

Emergency Planning

Once a duty to provide emergency care is established, recreation and sport organizations must participate in emergency planning in order to adequately prepare for future emergencies. While no emergency can be anticipated with absolute certainty, many emergency circumstances in recreation and sport are reasonably foreseeable (see Section 2.11, *Negligence*). As such, all recreation and sport managers must engage in careful planning for all foreseeable emergencies.

Emergency planning includes reviewing each foreseeable emergency separately, and developing an **Emergency Response Plan** (ERP) according to the needs of individual emergency situations. According to the Risk Management Manual published by the National Intramural-Recreational Sports Association (NIRSA), an **ERP** is a "predetermined plan to deal with an emergency in an organized and efficient manner." It is important to note that general planning is not adequate; rather, specific emergencies must be planned for.[1] For example, Wake Forest University has carefully considered emergency care at each of its many athletic facilities. In addition, the Wake Forest Athletic Department communicates the plan by making the emergency plan for each area available online (see http://www.wfu.edu/sportsmedicine/eapinfo.html). While this cannot replace discussing and practicing the procedures, posting an ERP on an organization website results in increased access to the plan.

---

[1] Many organizations offer activity specific guides to emergency planning on their respective websites. See American College of Sports Medicine (www.acsm.org); U.S. Department of Education (www.ed.gov); American Heart Association (www.americanheart.org); American Red Cross (www.redcross.org); and National Athletic Trainers Association (www.nata.org).

While emergencies can include dangerous circumstances such as a fire or chemical spill, recreation and sport organizations more commonly deal with medical emergencies resulting from sport/activity participation, over-exertion, heat related illness, cardiac arrest, or other medical situations. According to the NIRSA Manual, the primary concern for medical emergencies is "dealing with the ill/injured person by ensuring that the plan covers immediate attention to the medical condition, coupled with an effective system to get professional assistance."

Appropriate Personnel/Injury Assessment

A well-written ERP will designate appropriate personnel to respond in a given emergency. These designations must be based on which staff members are best suited to respond quickly and competently in an emergency situation.

In determining staff roles and responsibilities, a recreation or sport manager must consider staff assignments; specifically, are there enough personnel available at any given time? Does each staff member know his or her role during a medical emergency? Is there a clear chain of command in place? According to the NIRSA Manual, there are three clear roles during an emergency: (1) the **charge person,** who assumes the overall responsibility and has specific training; (2) the **call person,** who calls and meets summoned emergency personnel; and (3) the **control person,** who is responsible for keeping people away from the scene. Recreation and sport managers must designate appropriate personnel to fill these roles.

In addition, when designating which staff members will respond in an emergency, and which roles they will play, a recreation or sport manager must consider each staff member's ability to assess injury. Injuries must be assessed immediately so that proper treatment can be administered. Minimally, key personnel in the recreation and sport industry should be certified in first aid and should be competent to assess various injury types. However, the staff member with highest level of certification, and most knowledge regarding injury assessment, should generally be designated in the charge role discussed earlier.

Adequate Certifications/Equipment

Recreation and sport managers must ensure that staff members have both the necessary certifications and medical equipment to respond in a medical emergency. While many emergencies require the prompt attention of professional emergency medical technicians, recreation and sport staff may need to care for the injured individual until professional care arrives. Requiring personnel to maintain appropriate certifications and having proper equipment in place will facilitate this interim care.

Mandatory certifications can vary depending on factors such as the specific activity involved, and the age of the participants. There are many professional organizations that provide published standards of practice to guide management decisions in recreation and sport. Examples of such organizations are listed in Section 4.21, *Standards of Practice.* While specific mandates vary depending on the activity, most published standards indicate that all personnel should maintain certifications in basic first aid, cardio- pulmonary resuscitation (CPR) and automated external defibrillation.

Regarding adequate medical equipment, all recreation and sport organizations should minimally be equipped with a first aid kit including items such as adhesive bandages, Save-A-Tooth, slings, finger splints, and ace wraps; these medical devices are often required to treat minor or moderate injuries. However, in a catastrophic situation such as sudden cardiac arrest, an **automated external defibrillator** (AED) is desirable. An **AED** is a portable electronic device that can be used by non-medical personnel to treat a person in cardiac arrest. Per the American Heart Association (AHA), more than 294,000 Americans experience sudden cardiac arrest (SCA) outside of a hospital each year. While only 7.9 percent of SCA victims survive, on average, CPR and early defibrillation with an AED more than double a victim's chance of survival.

There are two primary legal issues surrounding the use of AEDs. First, which facilities are required by law to have AEDs? Second, is immunity granted to those individuals using an AED in a medical emergency?

AED Required by Law. There is currently no legal mandate requiring AEDs in all facilities offering recreation and/or sport services. However, several states have adopted legislation that mandates AEDs in certain facilities, such as school buildings and health/fitness clubs.

In Colorado, Florida, Georgia, Illinois, Maryland, Nevada, New York, Ohio, Pennsylvania, and South Carolina, AEDs are required in some schools, although extent varies. For example, in Maryland, each school board is required to develop an AED program to ensure an AED is present at every school site; further, the statute requires that a person trained in the operation and use of an AED is present at every high-school sponsored athletic event [Md. Educ. Code Ann. § 7-425 (2008)]. Similarly, in Florida, "each public school that is a member of the Florida High School Athletic Association must have an operational automated external defibrillator on the school grounds." [Fla. Stat. § 1006.165 (2009)]. In Nevada, the Board of Regents of the University of Nevada must ensure that at least two automated external defibrillators are placed in central locations at each of: (1) The largest indoor sporting arena or events center controlled by the University in a county whose population is 100,000 or more but less than 400,000; and (2) The largest indoor sporting arena or events center controlled by the University in a county whose population is 400,000 or more. [Nev. Rev. Stat. Ann. § 450B.600 (2009)].

For health and fitness facilities, Arkansas, California, Illinois, Indiana, Louisiana, Massachusetts, Michigan, New York, New Jersey, Oregon, Rhode Island, and the District of Columbia require AEDs. In addition to requiring the presence of an AED, some statutes also dictate proper use requirements. For example, the Arkansas statute states specific requirements for the number, placement and use of AEDs in both staffed and unstaffed situations.

However, it is important to note that in states without statutory requirements, case law does not support a duty to maintain an AED. In *Rutnik v. Colonie Center Club, Inc.* (1998), *Atcovitz v. Gulph Mills Tennis Club, Inc.*, (2002) and *Salte v. YMCA* (2004), defendants were found not to have a duty to defibrillate patrons who suffered cardiac arrest. Further, even when facilities do have an AED on site, the duty to notify patrons of the AED's location may be questioned. In *Rotolo v. San Jose Sport and Entertainment, LLC* (2007), parents of the deceased alleged that the defendant owner/operator of an ice skating rink had a duty to notify users of the existence and location of an AED at the facility. In affirming the trial court's holding, the California Court of Appeals disagreed stating "the duty the parents sought to impose was not supported by the statutes or the principles developed in California common law."

Immunity for AED Use. All 50 states and the U.S. federal government have enacted legislation that provides some form of immunity to those non-medical persons who use an AED in a medical emergency. See Section 2.22, *Immunity*. Without these statutes, some recreation and sport managers might be hesitant to purchase and utilize AEDs due to the risk of alleged negligence for AED misuse. AED immunity statutes seemingly allow recreation and sport managers to create ERPs that include the use of AEDs in an emergency without fear of increased liability.

Most important to note is that the extent of the immunity provided, and to whom it applies, varies in each state. Prior to creating an ERP that includes an AED, a recreation or sport manager should thoroughly investigate the laws in the individual state, making certain to comply with any necessary training, maintenance, or supervisory provisions. Operating an AED outside of these legislative provisions may disqualify an individual from the immunity protection.

Implementation of Emergency Procedures

Even after the above considerations are made, recreation and sport managers must properly train staff and personnel regarding implementation of the ERP. A manager can never assume that personnel will be able to execute the plan in a given emergency situation.

Consider the facts in *Carter v. City of Cleveland*, (1998). Carter, a 12-year old boy, nearly drowned at the Alexander Hamilton indoor swimming pool. When Carter's body was discovered in the pool, emergency care was not summoned promptly. As a consequence of the near drowning, he developed acute bronchial pneumonia and was declared brain dead four days later. Lifeguards had not been instructed on the use of 911 nor told that it was necessary to first dial a nine to get an outside line. When asked about the lack of training, the pool manager testified that he just assumed that the guards had been briefed how to get an outside line to dial 911.

The court stated:

> The evidence overwhelmingly established that three city employees were unable to contact 911, despite several attempts to do so. It was further shown that these employees were never trained on the use of the phone system. As a result of their failure to contact 911, there was about a thirty-minute delay in Carter's treatment. The fact that the city had no policy in place or training regarding 911 is appalling. The seriousness of these omissions is highlighted by the fact that more than one hundred swimmers, mostly children unaccompanied by adults, frequented the city pool that day. However, something as basic and important as dialing 911 was not within the city employees' grasp. Not only did two of the senior lifeguards create a dangerous situation by leaving the pool area during an open swim session, but the city, in its admitted failure to train its employees on the use of 911, left them without the knowledge necessary to handle the emergency as it arose. We are unwilling to grant immunity to the city under this provision, and to find, as argued, that the city did nothing wrong on the day Carter suffered a near drowning.

This case clearly illustrates the need to train all recreation and sport staff on how to implement the Emergency Response Plan to ensure actual execution of proper emergency procedures.

Specific Sport and Recreation Applications

As noted, the duty to provide emergency care requires recreation and sport mangers to address the specific concerns present in varying participation and spectator opportunities. The following analysis is intended to identify some of the legal obligations that recreation and sport providers have in meeting the duty to provide emergency care to clients in various sport and recreation settings.

Sport Participation

School-based Sport. Emergency care for student athletes must be an important consideration in any school setting. Athletic administrators, coaches, and athletic trainers have a responsibility to ensure that student athletes with injuries or symptoms of medical distress (e.g., heat-related illness, diabetic coma, head trauma, etc.) receive prompt and competent emergency care.

There is ample case law to support this fact. First, in *Kleinknecht v. Gettysburg College* (1993), the U.S. Court of Appeals for the Third Circuit found that a college owes a duty of emergency care to student athletes that are recruited by the university (see the Significant Case). Also, In *Mogabgab v. Orleans Parish School Board* (1970), the Louisiana Court of Appeals found that sport coaches owe participants a legal duty to recognize when emergency care is needed and to promptly summon competent medical attention. Further, the court held that attempted first aid procedures should stabilize the situation until emergency medical personnel arrive; and, any attempted first aid should not take the place of prompt medical care (See the Supplemental CD for Section 4.23). Also, in *Pinson v. State*, (1995) and *Halper v. Vayo* (1991), the courts found that coaches or activity instructors must employ proper post-injury procedures so as to not aggravate the injury.

However, case law does not confirm a duty to provide emergency care in every situation. In *Kennedy v. Syracuse University* (1995), the court found that failure to have an athletic trainer present to render first aid was not the cause of an injured gymnast's injury, nor did it exacerbate the injury. In *Yatsko v. Berezwick* (2008), a female basketball player with a head injury was intentionally kept from trainers so she could remain in the game; she consequently suffered severe brain injuries. The court found that the coaches' actions did not "shock the conscience" and dismissed the claims. Lastly, in *Avila v. Citrus Cmty. Coll. Dist.* (2006), a baseball player was hit in the head with a pitch and suffered serious injuries. Avila claimed the college was negligent when it failed to provide medical care; however, the court found that the college was not liable because it was protected by the assumption of risk doctrine.

Youth Sport Programs. Similar to school-based programs, emergency care must be carefully considered in youth sport programs. This can be particularly challenging given the nature of youth sport and the prevalence of volunteer staff. While many programs are organized and offered through organizations such as the YMCA or community recreation centers, coaches and other supervisory staff are often volunteers. This poses a problem relative to the four considerations regarding emergency care. While organizations may be able to conduct emergency planning, it may not always be possible to identify adequate personnel with appropriate certifications. Depending on the local situation, volunteer coaches and others assisting may or may not be required to maintain certifications such as First Aid and CPR. Further, having appropriate emergency equipment available at all youth sport events is unlikely given the varied facilities in which youth sport take place. Lastly, properly communicating and actually implementing an ERP may be difficult for youth sport organizations who use volunteers. In spite of the logistical challenges regarding emergency care, youth sport organizations still must undertake emergency care planning.

Lasseigne v. American Legion, Nicholson Post #38 (1990), is an example of the logistical difficulties in communicating and implementing an ERP in youth sport. Jason Lasseigne was a member of an American Legion Little League team. After a regularly scheduled game was rained out, the team held a practice session on a wet, grassy playground instead of the regulation baseball field. Further, the practice was supervised by a team member's father, not the regular coach. During infield practice, Jason was hit on the head with a ball thrown by a team member. The fill-in coach examined Jason and ordered him to sit down; however, Jason resumed play shortly thereafter. Approximately 24 hours later, Jason underwent head surgery. The family filed a lawsuit against multiple parties, alleging that the parent supervising the practice "did not render such aid and assistance as would be expected from ordinary prudent persons in a like position." Further, the plaintiffs alleged that the practice was conducted without minimum safeguards for the safety of the participants. The appellate court held for the defendants because there was no issue of material fact regarding the reasonableness of coach's and supervisor's actions in the situation. Specifically, the court stated that both "acted reasonably under the circumstances . . . in light of the social utility of [their] conduct—namely the value of the services of volunteers in a youth sports program to the community in which they participate."

While the Court held in favor of the defendants in *Lasseigne*, the facts illustrate some of the potential concerns regarding emergency care in youth sport. Additional cases substantiate these concerns. In *Kelly, et al. vs. The Catholic Archdiocese of Washington D.C. et al.* (2004), a seventh grade CYO softball player severely injured her ankle (see the Supplemental CD). Her parents sued, alleging, among other claims, that the defendants failed to ensure coaches and volunteers were trained to handle emergencies involving injuries. Specifically, the parents contended that transporting the injured off the field and into her mother's care was improper. The parents stated she should have been left on the field until emergency technicians arrived. The court held that there was no delay in treatment attributable to the manner in which she left the field, nor was there a lack of emergency care training. Also, in *Myers v. Friends of Shenendehowa Crew, Inc.* (2006), a 14-year-old, who trained in rowing with defendant at a YMCA, fainted during practice. The supervisor took the child to the YMCA front desk and asked for a nurse; however, the child was left unattended after the request was made. The child subsequently fainted and hit her head, and had multiple seizures. In denying the defendants motion for summary judgment, the court held that a question of fact existed as to whether leaving the child unattended after an injury was negligent.

Recreation/Fitness Participants

Campus Recreation Centers. Participation rates in intramural and other recreational collegiate activities have increased significantly in recent decades. Along with this growth comes a rise in the number of accidents and injuries that occur in the campus recreational setting (Steir and Kampf, 2008).

With such a variety of intramural activities now offered, including non-traditional sports such as rock climbing, water polo, kayaking, skiing, and boxing, the emergency care planning process has become a more significant undertaking. Best practice requires campus recreation managers to create an ERP for each individual activity, carefully considering personnel, equipment and implementation. In *Spiegler v. State of Arizona* (1996), a female student working out in the campus weight room at the University of Arizona suffered a cardiac arrest. The ERP in place required the supervising student staff member to administer CPR as necessary; however, this was not done. The supervising student employee did call 911, but the impaired student suffered permanent brain damage. The jury found for the plaintiff stating that she had not been given the standard of care required by the campus policies for emergency care. Additional examples are found in *Lemoine v. Cornell University* (2003), where a student was injured when she fell from a rock-climbing wall during a rock-climbing class, and *Kyriazis v. University of West Virginia* (1994), where a male rugby participant was injured while playing intramural rugby.

Aquatics. Recreation and sport facilities with aquatic components such as swimming pools or lakes must carefully consider emergency care. Per published standards,[2] aquatic facility safeguards should include the following:

- Lifeguard personnel should be certified in Lifeguarding, First Aid, CPR, and AED;

- Appropriate rescue equipment should be available (backboard, neck brace, etc.);

- All personnel should be familiar with the location and proper use of rescue equipment;

- An effective emergency communication system must be in place and should be used during an incident to notify other personnel, as well as an emergency dispatcher, should Fire, Rescue, EMS or Law Enforcement personnel be required;

- Emergency response plans should be developed for all possible emergencies and implemented immediately when an emergency occurs.

While these safeguards are general in nature, more specific requirements exist. All states have specific regulatory codes that dictate what aquatic facilities must maintain regarding safety equipment, personnel, and certifications. However, even though many of the required elements of an ERP are mandated in an aquatics facility, managers of these areas still must carefully consider additional elements of emergency planning.

Cases that have considered emergency care in aquatics facilities also often consider whether supervision was adequate (see Section 2.34, *Supervision*) In *Robinson v. Chicago Park District* (2001), a swimmer at a county pool was spotted at the bottom of the deep end. Lifeguards on duty were alleged to have hesitated in retrieving the deceased, thus causing a delay in emergency care. Even though allegations existed that the deceased should have been resuscitated much sooner, the defendants were not liable pursuant to the Illinois Tort Immunity Act. Similarly, in *Trotter v. School District* (2000), a member of a freshman swim class died after struggling, and subsequently drowning, in the deep end of the school pool. The instructor hired to teach the freshman swimming class did not have water safety or lifeguarding certifications; also, there were problems accessing emergency lifesaving equipment. Although the Illinois Appellate court granted the school district's motion for summary judgment regarding immunity, the case was remanded to consider the question of whether the instructor was adequately skilled to provide supervision and/or first aid to a swim class. Lastly, in *Walker v. Daniels* (1991), a student at Fort Valley State College drowned during a recreational swim session that did not have the approval of campus administration. The lifeguards present were alleged to be inattentive; further, medical evidence demonstrated that the student had been underwater for at least four to six minutes before he was discovered, and additional time elapsed before emergency care was administered. The college was assessed damages of $1.5 million based on these breaches of duty.

Health Clubs and Spas. Fitness facilities and health clubs are highly susceptible to claims of negligence regarding inadequate emergency care. Failure to provide First Aid/CPR (*Lewin v. Fitworks of Cincinnati, LLC,* 2005); failure to summon emergency medical services (*Chai v. Sport and Fitness Clubs of America,* 2005); and, in some states failure to have and/or use an AED are all potential areas of risk for health/fitness facility operators (*Rotolo v. San Jose Sports and Entertainment, LLC,* 2007). In *L.A. Fitness International v. Mayer* (2008), the daughter of Alessio Tringali filed a wrongful death action against the club after her father died as a result of cardiac arrest suffered while using a step machine. Among other claims, Mayer asserted that L.A. Fitness failed to administer CPR; failed to have an AED on its premises; and failed to train its employees and agents to han-

---

[2]*The Standard of Care in Lifeguarding* (1993); see also, Lifeguarding and aquatic safety information, *available at* http://www.redcross.org/services/hss/aquatics.

dle medical emergencies. Noting that the issue of the duty owed by a health club owner to an injured patron was one of first impression in Florida, the Florida Court of Appeals held that L.A. Fitness satisfied its duty to render assistance when it summoned emergency medical assistance. Further, the court held that in Florida, there is no common law or statutory duty for a health club to have an AED on its premises (see the Supplemental CD).

Similarly, in *Brown v. Atlas-Kona Kai* (2009), a patron collapsed at defendant's facility while working out. The plaintiff (decedent's wife) alleged the fitness facility had a duty beyond summoning emergency assistance; she asserted the facility had a duty to have emergency equipment on hand, and to properly train employees to handle foreseeable medical emergencies. However, the California court held that the fitness facility's only duty was to promptly summon emergency services.

Many fitness and health clubs require patrons to sign a waiver and/or release of liability (see Section 2.23, *Waivers and Releases*). However, a valid waiver may not be enforceable regarding the failure to provide emergency care. In *Brown v. Bally Total Fitness Corporation* (2003), a patron experienced heart problems while on the treadmill. The plaintiff alleged "that defendant's employees failed to check decedent's pulse, failed to administer cardio-pulmonary resuscitation (CPR) and prevented a good Samaritan, off-duty police officer, from attempting life-saving procedures. In addition, plaintiffs alleged that defendant knew or should have known that its employees were not qualified, nor able, to provide emergency medical services, including CPR." After careful analysis of the waiver, the court reversed summary judgment for Bally's indicating that the waiver of liability did not apply to negligence in rendering emergency care.

Other Participant Activities. Court cases provide examples of other recreation and sport activities where emergency care was an issue.

- **Skating Rinks.** In *Spotlite Skating Rink Inc. v. Barnes* (2008), a 10 year-old died after falling and hitting her head on the ice rink operated by the defendant. The Supreme Court of Mississippi held that the skate rink had a duty to provide appropriate medical treatment to the patron, and that there was sufficient evidence to support a finding that the rink breached its duty of care to render aid (see the Supplemental Case CD).

- **Road Races/Fitness Challenges.** In *Gehling v. St. George's University School of Medicine* (1989), a medical student participated in a 2.5-mile road race sponsored by the University. After completing the race, Earl Gehling collapsed, suffering from heat stroke, and died a short time later. After reviewing the emergency care measures in place such as water on the course, trained medical staff, and a person trailing the race to aid injured runners, the Court found in favor of the defendant.

- **Adult Recreation/Sport Activities.** In *Colon v. Chelsea Piers Mgmt.* (2006), the decedent suffered cardiac arrest and died while playing in an adult basketball league at Chelsea Piers. The plaintiff alleged that the defendant had a duty to provide staff adequately trained in medical care, as well as maintain emergency equipment, such as a resuscitation device, on the premises. The court held that the operator of the basketball league did not have this duty and granted summary judgment for the defendant.

- **Golf.** Although no case law was found specifically addressing the duty to provide emergency care on a golf course, injuries in golf are common, and range from moderate, such as a ball strike (*Yoneda v. Tom*, 2006; *Sullivan-Coughlin v. Palos Country Club, Inc.*, 2004) to severe, such as a lightning strike (*Hames v. State*, 1991; *Maussner v. Atlantic City Country Club*, 1997). Further, according to the American Heart Association, golf courses rank in the top five most common public places for sudden cardiac arrest to occur. As such, golf course owner operators should have an ERP that adequately considers these common golf injuries, as well as the necessity and availability of an AED.

- **Professional Sport Teams.** All athletes risk injury, even professional ones. Take for example Korey Stringer of the Minnesota Vikings who died from heat stroke during football practice (*Stringer v. Minnesota Vikings Football Club, L.L.C.*, 2004) or Carl Phelps, a professional racecar driver who was injured at Firebird Raceway when his car erupt into flames, causing him severe burns (*Phelps v. Firebird Raceway, Inc.*, 2005). Allegations of inadequate medical care after the injury were made in both of these cases; however, the *Stringer* Court ruled that the plaintiff received emergency care. In Phelps, the primary issue was the validity of a waiver; the appellate court did not specifically address the issue of emergency care. However, both cases demonstrate that emergency care concerns must be present in professional sport.

Sport Spectators

Stadia. While the duty to provide emergency care is clearly a concern regarding participant injuries, sport spectators are also entitled to emergency care. Based on premises liability law, and the classification of sport patrons as invitees, stadium owners have a duty to provide a reasonably safe premise for spectators at sporting events. Sport and recreation facility managers must be concerned with the safety of attendees, spectators and patrons (Madden, 1998). Specific considerations regarding emergency care for spectators and patrons are discussed in Section 4.22, *Audits in Risk Management*; Section 4.23, *Crisis Management*; and Section 4.24, *Crowd Management*.

SIGNIFICANT CASE

The following case is one of the most significant regarding the duty to provide emergency care. The court provides a clear and thorough discussion of the origin of the duty; most notably, the court discusses the special relationship between the college and the athlete, as well as the foreseeability of the harm. When reading this case, take note of these two discussions, as well as the facts leading up to the allegation of negligence. This case clearly supports a need for emergency care planning, identification of appropriate personnel, equipment and certifications, as well as implementation of the ERP.

KLEINKNECHT V. GETTYSBURG COLLEGE

United States Court Of Appeals For The Third Circuit
989 F.2d 1360 (1993)

II. Factual History

In September 1988, Drew Kleinknecht was a sophomore student at the College, which had recruited him for its Division III intercollegiate lacrosse team. The College is a private, four-year liberal arts school. In 1988, it ****supported twenty-one intercollegiate sports teams involving approximately 525 male and female athletes. * * *

Lacrosse players can typically suffer a variety of injuries.**** Before Drew died, however, no athlete at the College had experienced cardiac arrest while playing lacrosse or any other sport.

In September 1988, the College employed two full-time athletic trainers, Joseph Donolli and Gareth Biser. Both men were certified by the National Athletic Trainers Association, which requires, *inter alia*, current certification in both cardio-pulmonary resuscitation ("CPR") and standard first aid. In addition, twelve student trainers participated in the College's sports program.* * *

Because lacrosse is a spring sport, daily practices were held during the spring semester in order to prepare for competition. Student trainers were assigned to cover both spring practices and games. Fall practice was held only for the players to learn "skills and drills," and to become acquainted with the other team members. No student trainers were assigned to the fall practices.

Drew participated in a fall lacrosse practice on the afternoon of September 16, 1988. Coaches Janczyk and Anderson attended and supervised this practice. It was held on the softball fields outside Musselman Stadium. No trainers or student trainers were present. Neither coach had certification in CPR. Neither coach had a radio on the practice field. The nearest telephone was inside the training room at Musselman Stadium, roughly 200-250 yards away. The shortest route to this telephone required scaling an eight-foot high cyclone fence surrounding the stadium. According to Coach Janczyk, he and Coach Anderson had

never discussed how they would handle an emergency during fall lacrosse practice.

[At] the September 16, 1988 practice ****Drew was a defenseman and was participating in one of the drills when he suffered a cardiac arrest. According to a teammate, Drew simply stepped away from the play and dropped to the ground. Another teammate stated that no person or object struck Drew prior to his collapse.

After Drew fell, his teammates and Coach Janczyk ran to his side. Coach Janczyk and some of the players noticed that Drew was lying so that his head appeared to be in an awkward position. No one knew precisely what had happened at that time, and at least some of those present suspected a spinal injury. Team captain Daniel Polizzotti testified that he heard a continuous "funny" "gurgling" noise coming from Drew, and knew from what he observed that something "major" was wrong. Other teammates testified that Drew's skin began quickly to change colors. One team member testified that by the time the coaches had arrived, "[Drew] was really blue."

According to the College, Coach Janczyk acted in accordance with the school's emergency plan by first assessing Drew's condition, then dispatching players to get a trainer and call for an ambulance. Coach Janczyk himself then began to run toward Musselman Stadium to summon help.

The Kleinknechts dispute the College's version of the facts. They note that although Coach Janczyk claims to have told two players to run to Apple Hall, a nearby dormitory, for help, Coach Anderson did not recall Coach Janczyk's sending anyone for help. Even if Coach Janczyk did send the two players to Apple Hall, the Kleinknechts maintain, his action was inappropriate because Apple Hall was not the location of the nearest telephone. It is undisputed that two other team members ran for help, but the Kleinknechts contend that the team members did this on their own accord, without instruction from either coach.

The parties do not dispute that Polizzotti, the team captain, ran toward the stadium, where he knew a training room was located and a student trainer could be found. In doing so, Polizzotti scaled a chain link fence that surrounded the stadium and ran across the field, encountering student trainer Traci Moore outside the door to the training room. He told her that a lacrosse player was down and needed help. She ran toward the football stadium's main gate, managed to squeeze through a gap between one side of the locked gate and the brick pillar forming its support, and continued on to the practice field by foot until flagging a ride from a passing car. In the meantime, Polizzotti continued into the training room where he told the student trainers there what had happened. One of them phoned Plank Gymnasium and told Head Trainer Donolli about the emergency.

Contemporaneously with Polizzotti's dash to the stadium, Dave Kerney, another team member, ran toward the stadium for assistance. Upon seeing that Polizzotti was going to beat him there, Kerney concluded that it was pointless for both of them to arrive at the same destination and changed his course toward the College Union Building. He told the student at the front desk of the emergency on the practice field. The student called his supervisor on duty in the building, and she immediately telephoned for an ambulance.

Student trainer Moore was first to reach Drew. She saw Drew's breathing was labored, and the color of his complexion changed as she watched. Because Drew was breathing, she did not attempt CPR or any other first aid technique, but only monitored his condition, observing no visible bruises or lacerations.

By this time, Coach Janczyk had entered the stadium training room and learned that Donolli had been notified and an ambulance called. Coach Janczyk returned to the practice field at the same time Donolli arrived in a golf cart. Donolli saw that Drew was not breathing, and turned him on his back to begin CPR with the help of a student band member who was certified as an emergency medical technician and had by chance arrived on the scene. The two of them performed CPR until two ambulances arrived at approximately 4:15 p.m. Drew was defibrillated and drugs were administered to strengthen his heart. He was placed in an ambulance and taken to the hospital, but despite repeated resuscitation efforts, Drew could not be revived. He was pronounced dead at 4:58 p.m.

As the district court observed, the parties vigorously dispute the amount of time that elapsed in connection with the events following Drew's collapse. The College maintains that "Coach Janczyk immediately ran to Drew's side, followed closely by assistant coach, Anderson. Team captain Polizzotti estimated that it took him no more than thirty seconds to get from the practice field to the training

room. The College contends that it took Moore no more than two minutes to get from the training room to Drew's side. In fact, the College maintains, the lacrosse team was practicing on this particular field because of its close proximity to the training room and the student trainers. The College estimates that an ambulance was present within eight to ten minutes after Drew's collapse.

The Kleinknechts, on the other hand, assert that as much as a minute to a minute and a half passed before Coach Janczyk arrived at Drew's side.**** They estimate that it took Polizzotti a minute and a half to arrive at the stadium training room from the practice field, advise someone on duty, and have that person notify Donolli. The Kleinknechts also estimate that it took Kerney two minutes and thirteen seconds to arrive at the College Union Building, speak to the student at the desk, and then have the secretary telephone for an ambulance. They point to Donolli's deposition testimony indicating that it took him approximately three minutes and fifteen seconds to arrive at the scene. The Kleinknechts further maintain, and the College does not dispute, that at least five minutes elapsed from the time that Drew was first observed on the ground until Head Trainer Donolli began administering CPR. Thus, the Kleinknechts contend that**** as long as twelve minutes elapsed before CPR was administered. They also estimate that roughly ten more minutes passed before the first ambulance arrived on the scene.

Prior to his collapse, Drew had no medical history of heart problems.****In January 1988, a College physician had examined Drew to determine his fitness to participate in sports and found him to be in excellent health. The Kleinknecht's family physician had also examined Drew in August 1987 and found him healthy and able to participate in physical activity.

Medical evidence indicated Drew died of cardiac arrest after a fatal attack of cardiac arrhythmia.

****

III. Issues on Appeal

The Kleinknechts present three general issues on appeal: (1) the district court erred in determining that the College had no legal duty to implement preventive measures assuring prompt assistance and treatment in the event one of its student athletes suffered cardiac arrest while engaged in school-supervised intercollegiate athletic activity; (2) the district court erred in determining that the actions of school employees following Drew's collapse were reasonable and that the College therefore did not breach any duty of care; and (3) the district court erred in determining that both Traci Moore and the College were entitled to immunity under the Pennsylvania Good Samaritan Act. [discussion omitted]

IV. Analysis

1. The Duty of Care Issue

Whether a defendant owes a duty of care to a plaintiff is a question of law ... In order to prevail on a cause of action in negligence under Pennsylvania law, a plaintiff must establish: (1) a duty or obligation recognized by the law, requiring the actor to conform to a certain standard of conduct; (2) a failure to conform to the standard required; (3) a causal connection between the conduct and the resulting injury; and (4) actual loss or damage resulting to the interests of another...

The Kleinknechts assert three different theories upon which they predicate the College's duty to establish preventive measures capable of providing treatment to student athletes in the event of a medical emergency such as Drew's cardiac arrest: (1) existence of a special relationship between the College and its student athletes; (2) foreseeability that a student athlete may suffer cardiac arrest while engaged in athletic activity; and (3) public policy [discussion omitted].

****

a. Special Relationship

The Kleinknechts argue that the College had a duty of care to Drew by virtue of his status as a member of an intercollegiate athletic team. The Supreme Court of Pennsylvania has stated that "duty, in any given situation, is predicated on the relationship existing between the parties at the relevant time. . . ." *Morena*, 462 A.2d at 684. The Kleinknechts argue that although the Supreme Court has not addressed this precise issue, it would conclude that a college or university owes a duty to its intercollegiate athletes to provide preventive measures in the event of a medical emergency.

In support of their argument, the Kleinknechts cite the case of *Hanson v. Kynast*, No. CA-828 (Ohio Ct. App. June 3, 1985), *rev'd on other grounds*, 494 N.E.2d. 1091 (Ohio 1986). In *Hanson* an intercollegiate, recruited lacrosse player was seriously injured while playing in a lacrosse game against another college. The plaintiff alleged that his university breached its legal duty to have an ambulance present during the lacrosse game. The trial court granted the defendant's motion for summary judgment based on its holding, *inter alia*, that

> *There is no duty as a matter of law for the Defendant College or other sponsor of athletic events to have ambulances, emergency vehicles, trained help or doctors present during the playing of a lacrosse game or other athletic events, and the failure to do so does not constitute negligence as a matter of law.*

The court of appeals reversed, concluding, "It is a question of fact for the jury to determine whether or not appellee University acted reasonably in failing to have an ambulance present at the field or to provide quick access to the field in the event of an emergency." *Id.* at 6. By directing the trial court to submit the case to a jury, the court of appeals implicitly held that the university owed a duty of care to the plaintiff.

Although the *Hanson* court did not specify the theory on which it predicated this duty, we think it reached the correct result, and we predict that the Supreme Court of Pennsylvania would conclude that a similar a duty exists on the facts of this case. Like the lacrosse student in *Hanson*, Drew chose to attend Gettysburg College because he was persuaded it had a good lacrosse program, a sport in which he wanted to participate at the intercollegiate level. Head Trainer Donolli actively recruited Drew to play lacrosse at the College. At the time he was stricken, Drew was not engaged in his own private affairs as a student at Gettysburg College. Instead, he was participating in a scheduled athletic practice for an intercollegiate team sponsored by the College under the supervision of College employees. On these facts we believe that the Supreme Court of Pennsylvania would hold that a special relationship existed between the College and Drew that was sufficient to impose a duty of reasonable care on the College.

****

Drew was not acting in his capacity as a private student when he collapsed. Indeed, the Kleinknechts concede that if he had been, they would have no recourse against the College. There is a distinction between a student injured while participating as an intercollegiate athlete in a sport for which he was recruited and a student injured at a college while pursuing his private interests, scholastic or otherwise. This distinction serves to limit the class of students to whom a college owes the duty of care that arises here. Had Drew been participating in a fraternity football game, for example, the College might not have owed him the same duty or perhaps any duty at all. There is, however, no need for us to reach or decide the duty question either in that context or in the context of whether a college would owe a duty towards students participating in intramural sports. On the other hand, the fact that Drew's cardiac arrest occurred during an athletic event involving an intercollegiate team of which he was a member does impose a duty of due care on a college that actively sought his participation in that sport. We cannot help but think that the College recruited Drew for its own benefit, probably thinking that his skill at lacrosse would bring favorable attention and so aid the College in attracting other students.

****

In conclusion, we predict that the Supreme Court of Pennsylvania would hold that the College owed Drew a duty of care in his capacity as an intercollegiate athlete engaged in school-sponsored intercollegiate athletic activity for which he had been recruited.

b. Foreseeability

This does not end our inquiry, however. The determination that the College owes a duty of care to its intercollegiate athletes could merely define the class of persons to whom the duty extends, without determining the nature of the duty or demands it makes on the College. Because it is foreseeable that student athletes may sustain severe and even life-threatening injuries while engaged in athletic activity, the Kleinknechts argue that the College's duty of care required it to be ready to respond swiftly and adequately to a medical emergency....

****

The type of foreseeability that determines a duty of care, as opposed to proximate cause, is not dependent on the foreseeability of a specific event ... Instead, in the context of duty, "the concept of foreseeability means the likelihood of the occurrence of a general type of risk rather than the likelihood of the occurrence of the precise chain of events leading to the injury." *Suchomajcz v. Hummel Chem. Co.*, 524 F.2d 19, 28 n.8 (3d Cir. 1975) (citing Harper & James, The Law of Torts § 18.2, at 1026, § 20.5, at 1147-49 (1956)).... Only when even the general likelihood of some broadly definable class of events, of which the particular event that caused the plaintiff's injury is a subclass, is unforeseeable can a court hold as a matter of law that the defendant did not have a duty to the plaintiff to guard against that broad general class of risks within which the particular harm the plaintiff suffered befell....

Even this determination that the harm suffered was foreseeable fails to end our analysis. If a duty is to be imposed, the foreseeable risk of harm must be unreasonable. *Griggs*, 981 F.2d at 1435. The classic risk-utility analysis used to determine whether a risk is unreasonable "balances 'the risk, in light of the social value of the interest threatened, and the probability and extent of the harm, against the value of the interest which the actor is seeking to protect, and the expedience of the course pursued.'" *Id.* at 1435-36 ...

Although the district court correctly determined that the Kleinknechts had presented evidence establishing that the occurrence of severe and life-threatening injuries is not out of the ordinary during contact sports, it held that the College had no duty because the cardiac arrest suffered by Drew, a twenty-year old athlete with no history of any severe medical problems, was not reasonably foreseeable. Its definition of foreseeability is too narrow. Although it is true that a defendant is not required to guard against every possible risk, he must take reasonable steps to guard against hazards which are generally foreseeable ... Though the specific risk that a person like Drew would suffer a cardiac arrest may be unforeseeable, the Kleinknechts produced ample evidence that a life-threatening injury occurring during participation in an athletic event like lacrosse was reasonably foreseeable. In addition to the testimony of numerous medical and athletic experts, Coach Janczyk, Head Trainer Donolli, and student trainer Moore all testified that they were aware of instances in which athletes had died during athletic competitions. The foreseeability of a life-threatening injury to Drew was not hidden from the College's view. Therefore, the College did owe Drew a duty to take reasonable precautions against the risk of death while Drew was taking part in the College's intercollegiate lacrosse program.

Having determined that it is foreseeable that a member of the College's interscholastic lacrosse team could suffer a serious injury during an athletic event, it becomes evident that the College's failure to protect against such a risk is not reasonable. The magnitude of the foreseeable harm—irreparable injury or death to one of its student athletes as a result of inadequate preventive emergency measures—is indisputable. With regard to the offsetting cost of protecting against such risk, the College prophesied that if this Court accepts that the College owed the asserted duty, then it will be required "to have a CPR certified trainer on site at each and every athletic practice whether in-season or off-season, formal or informal, strenuous or light," and to provide similar cardiac protection to "intramural, club sports and gym class." This "slippery slope" prediction reflects an unwarranted extension of the holding in this case. First, the recognition of a duty here is limited to intercollegiate athletes. No other scenario is presented, so the question whether any of the other broad classes of events and students posited by the College merit similar protection is not subject to resolution. Second, the determination whether the College has breached this duty at all is a question of fact for the jury ... This Court recognizes only that under the facts of this case, the College owed a duty to Drew to have measures in place at the lacrosse team's practice on the afternoon of September 16, 1988 in order to provide prompt treatment in the event that he or any other member of the lacrosse team suffered a life-threatening injury.

****

In reversing the district court's grant of summary judgment to the College, we predict that the Supreme Court of Pennsylvania would hold that a college also has a duty to be reasonably prepared for handling medical emergencies that foreseeably arise during a student's participation in an intercollegiate contact sport for which a college recruited him. It is clearly foreseeable that a person participating in such an activity will sustain serious injury requiring immediate medical attention.

* * *

Our holding is narrow. It predicts only that a court applying Pennsylvania law would conclude that the College had a duty to provide prompt and adequate emergency medical services to Drew, one of its intercollegiate athletes, while he was engaged in a school-sponsored athletic activity for which he had been recruited. Whether the College breached that duty is a question of fact. . . .

* * *

2. The Reasonableness of the College's Actions
On the duty question, it remains only for us to address the district court's second holding that the conduct of the College's agents in providing Drew with medical assistance and treatment following his cardiac arrest was reasonable. The court based this determination in part, if not in whole, on its conclusion that the College had no duty to consider what emergency assistance measures would be necessary were one of its student athletes to suffer a cardiac arrest during athletic activity. . . . Thus, its holding that the College did not breach any duty was dependent, at least in part, on its holding that the College had no duty to Drew to guard against emergencies occasioned by injuries the kind students participating in lacrosse might be ex-

pected to suffer. The question of breach must be reconsidered on remand in light of this Court's holding that the College did owe Drew a duty of care to provide prompt and adequate emergency medical assistance to Drew while participating as one of its intercollegiate athletes in a school-sponsored athletic activity.

* * *

V. CONCLUSION

The district court's holding that the College's duty of care to Drew as an intercollegiate athlete did not include, prior to his collapse, a duty to provide prompt emergency medical service while he was engaged in school-sponsored athletic activity will be reversed. The district court's holding that the College acted reasonably and therefore did not breach any duty owed to Drew following his collapse will likewise be reversed. We will remand this matter to the district court for further proceedings consistent with this opinion. . . .

CASES ON THE SUPPLEMENTAL CD

L.A. Fitness International v. Mayer, (2008 Fla. App. LEXIS 5893). The reader should note the court's holding that summoning professional emergency assistance satisfies the duty to provide emergency care.

Kelly v. McCarrick, (2004 Md. App. LEXIS 13). Note that an important issue was whether Tara's injuries were caused or exacerbated by care received, lack of care received, or by that Tara's in-

juries were either [**893] caused or exacerbated by any care that she received from these defendants, by any care that she did **not** receive, or by any lack of emergency care training of the coaches.

Spotlite Skating Rink, Inc. v. Barnes, (2008 Miss. LEXIS 322). The reader should note the court's interpretation of the duty to provide emergency care, and consider possible implications for service providers.

QUESTIONS YOU SHOULD BE ABLE TO ANSWER

1. Describe the four elements of emergency care.

2. As a manager of a health/fitness facility, should you advocate purchasing an AED? Why or why not?

3. What certifications should be held by all staff employed in recreation and sport?

4. How would you best communicate an ERP to your staff? How would you insure they read and understand the requirements?

5. Select a facility or activity at your school. What do you need to consider regarding the four elements of emergency care?

REFERENCES

Cases

Atcovitz v. Gulph Mills Tennis Club, Inc., 812 A.2d 1218 (2002).

Avila v. Citrus Cmty. Coll. Dist., 131 P.3d 383 (2006).

Brown v. Atlas-Kona Kai, 2009 Cal. App. Unpub. LEXIS 2108.

Brown v. Bally Total Fitness, 2003 Cal. App. Unpub. LEXIS 8245.

Carter v. City of Cleveland, 83 Ohio St. 3d (1998).

Chai v. Sport and Fitness Clubs of America, (2005).

Colon v. Chelsea Piers Mgmt., 2006 N.Y. Misc. LEXIS 2831.

Gehling v. St. George's University School of Medicine, Ltd., 705 F.Supp 761 (E.D.N.Y. 1989).

Halper v. Vayo, 568 N.E.2d 914 (1991).

Hames v. State, 1990 Tenn. App. LEXIS 53.

Kelly et al. v. Catholic Archdiocese of Washington D.C. et al., 841 A.2d 869 (2004).

Kennedy v. Syracuse University, 1995 U.S. Dist. LEXIS 13539.

Kleinknecht v. Gettysburg College, 989 F.2d 1360 (1993).

Kyriazis v. University of West Virginia, 450 S.E.2d 649 (1994).

L.A. Fitness International v. Mayer, 980 So.2d 550 (2008).

Lasseigne v. American Legion, 588 So.2d 614 (1990).

Lemoine v. Cornell University, 2003 N.Y. App. LEXIS 13209.

Lewin v. Fitworks of Cincinnati, (2005).

Maussner v. Atlantic City Country Club, Inc., 691 A.2d 826 (1997).

Mogabgab v. Orleans Parish School Board, 239 So.2d 456 (1970).

Myers v. Friends of Shenendehowa Crew, Inc., 31 A.D.3d 853 (2006).

Phelps v. Firebird Raceway, 83 P.3d 1090 (2004).

Pinson v. State, 1995 Tenn. App. LEXIS 807.

Robinson v. Chicago Park Dist., 757 N.E.2d 565 (2001).

Rotolo v. San Jose Sports and Entertainment, 2007 Cal. App. LEXIS 843.

Rutnik v. Colonie Center Club, Inc., 672 N.Y.S.2d 451 (1998).

Salte v. YMCA of Metroploitan Chicago Foundation, 814 N.E.2d 610 (2004).

Spiegler v. State of Arizona, Maricopa County Supreme Ct., Case No. CV92-13608.

Spotlite Skating Rink, Inc., v. Barnes, 988 So. 2d 364 (2008).

Stringer v. Minnesota Vikings Football Club, L.L.C., 686 N.W.2d 545 (2004).

Sullivan-Coughlin v. Palos Country Club, Inc., 812 N.E.2d 496 (2004).

Trotter v. School Dist., 733 N.E.2d 363 (2000).

Walker v. Daniels, Yatsko v. Berezwick, 2008 U.S. Dist. LEXIS 47280.

Yoneda v. Tom, 133 P.3d 796 (2006).

Publications

American Heart Association. *Heart Disease and Stroke Statistics–2009 Update. Circulation;* 2008. Available at: http://circ.ahajournals.org/cgi/reprint/CIRCULATIONAHA.108.191261

Conn, J., Annest, J., & Gilchrist, J. (2003). *Sports and recreation related industry episodes in the US population.* Injury Prevention, 177–123.

Connaughton, D. P., Spengler, J. O., & Zhang, J. J. (2007). *An analysis of automated defibrillator implementation and related risk management practices in health/fitness clubs.* 17 Legal Aspects of Sport, 81–106.

Dworkin, G. M. (1993). *The standard of care in lifeguarding,* in *American lifeguard magazine.* Available at http://www.lifesaving.com/issues/articles/standard_of_care.html

Eickhoff-Shemek, J. M., Herbert, D. L., & Connaughton, D. P. (2009). *Risk management for health/fitness professionals: Legal issues and strategies.* Baltimore, MD: Lippincott, Williams & Wilkins.

Madden, T. D. (1998). *Risk management and facility insurance.* In T. D. Madden (Ed.), Public assembly facility law (pp. 199–230). Irving, TX: International Association of Assembly Managers.

McGregor, I., MacDonald, J. (1990). *Risk management manual for sport and recreation organizations.* Corvallis, OR: NIRSA.

Prentice, W. E. (2006). *Athletic training: An introduction to professional practice.* New York, NY: McGraw Hill.

Spengler, J. O., Connaughton, D. P., & Pittman, A. T. (2006). *Risk management in sport and recreation.* Champaign, IL: Human Kinetics.

Steir, W. F., Schneider, R. C., Kampf, S. et. al. (2008). *Selected risk management policies, practices, and procedures for intramural activities at NIRSA institutions,* in Recreational Sport Journal, 32, 28–44.

Weisfeldt, M. L., Kerber, R. E., McGoldrick, R. P. et al. (1995). *A statement for healthcare professionals from the American Heart Association task force on automatic external defibrillation.*

Young, S. J., Fields, S. K., & Powell, G. M. (2007). *Risk perceptions versus legal realities in campus recreational sport programs,* in Recreational Sports Journal, 31, 131–145.

Legislation

A.C.A. § 20-13-1306 (2008).

A.C.A. § 20-13-1306 (b) (2008).

Cal. Health & Safety Code §104113(a)(1)(2006).

C.R.S. 22-1-125 (2008).

Fla. Stat. § 1006.165 (2009).

O.C.G.A. § 20-2-775 (2009).

105 ILCS 110/3 (2009).

210 ILCS 74/15 (2009).

Burns Ind. Code Ann. § 24-4-15-5 (2009).

La. Rev. Stat. Ann. 40:1236.11(2006).

La. R.S. 9:2798 (2008).

ALM GL ch. 93, § 78A (2009).

MCLS §333.26312 (2009).

Md. Educ.Code Ann. § 7-425 (2008).

Nev. Rev. Stat. Ann. § 450B.600 (2009).

NY CLS Gen Bus § 627-a (2009).

NY CLS Educ. § 917 (2009).

N.J. Stat. § 2A:62A-31 (2009).

ORS § 431.680 (2007).

ORC Ann. 3313.717 (2009).

R.I. Gen. Laws § 5-50-12 (2009).

S.C. Code Ann. § 59-17-155 (2008).

D.C. Code § 44-232 (2009).

2.34 Supervision

—**Lynne P. Gaskin**
UNIVERSITY OF WEST GEORGIA

—**Paul J. Batista**
TEXAS A & M UNIVERSITY

Most lawsuits filed against recreation and sport organizations for injuries sustained during activities allege not only negligence, but include the more specific complaint regarding inadequate supervision. In fact, van der Smissen (1990) estimated that approximately 80 percent of cases involving programmatic situations allege **lack of supervision** or **improper supervision**.

Supervision is a broad term denoting responsibility for an area and for the activities that take place in that area (Kaiser, 1986) and includes coordinating, directing, overseeing, implementing, managing, superintending, and regulating (*Longfellow v. Corey*, 1997). The courts have provided direction in defining non-negligent supervision.

For example, in *Toller v. Plainfield School District 202* (1991), the court determined that a teacher used reasonable care by teaching the rules of wrestling; demonstrating wrestling maneuvers; matching students according to height, weight, and size; and closely supervising them. Similarly, when learning an activity, students should receive proper instruction and preparation including basic rules and procedures, suggestions for proper performance, and identification of risks (*Scott v. Rapides Parish School Board*, 1999). In addition to an instructor's explaining how to use athletic equipment and demonstrating proper techniques, the importance of observing the participant's use of the equipment also has been emphasized (*David v. County of Suffolk*, 2003). *Kahn v. East Side Union High School District* (2003), emphasizes the importance of providing consistent, progressive instruction concerning safe performance of a skill and not coercing participants through threats.

FUNDAMENTAL CONCEPTS

Duty to Supervise

According to van der Smissen (1990), the **duty to supervise** arises from three sources: (1) a duty inherent in the situation, (2) a voluntary assumption of a duty, or (3) a duty mandated by law (see Section 2.11, *Elements of Negligence*). "The basis of the duty is whether or not there is a special relationship between plaintiff and defendant which requires that the defendant take affirmative action to provide a reasonably safe environment" (van der Smissen, 1990, p. 164).

When sponsoring an activity, certain organizational relationships such as school/students, fitness club/clients, and recreation department/participants, constitute **special relationships** and require the defendant organization to exercise reasonable care for the protection of participants under its supervision. Individual supervisors also have a duty to supervise that arises from the relationships inherent in the situation. These may include teacher/student, coach/player, recreation leader/participant, and supervisor/facility user. Negligence on the part of these individuals may result in both individual liability and liability for the organization (see Section 2.12, *Which Parties Are Liable?*).

In certain situations, there may be no duty to supervise, such as the immunity provided in numerous **recreational user statutes** (see Section 2.22, *Immunity*). Other examples include playgrounds at a recreation center, school grounds after hours, public beaches, and a nature trail in a public park (for a listing of individual state statutes, see Table 2.22.1 in Section 2.22, *Immunity*). However, the owner of the land, recreation department, school, or other sport or recreation organization can **voluntarily assume** a duty to supervise. If the decision is made to provide supervision (e.g., by having lifeguards supervise a beach and adjacent ocean at an unimproved city beach), such supervision must be non-negligent or the organization will be liable (*Fleuhr v. City of Cape May*, 1999).

In many cases, state legislatures impose a **statutory duty** to supervise various activities. For example, an Indiana statute requires roller-skating rink operators to have at least one floor supervisor for each 175 skaters, maintain the skating surface in proper and reasonably safe condition, clean and inspect the skating surface before each skating session, and maintain the rental skates in good mechanical conditions, among other duties. (Ind. Code § 34-31-6, *et seq.*, 2009). In *St. Margaret Mercy Healthcare Centers, Inc. v. Poland* (2005), the significant case at the end of this section, the plaintiff was injured while skating when she was knocked to the floor by a skater who was skating very fast and aggressively in violation of the statute. Although the defendant asserted that the plaintiff had assumed the inherent risks of skating (see Section 2.21, *Defenses Against Negligence*), including being knocked down by another skater, the court held the operator liable for not supervising properly according to the requirements imposed by the statute.

When a duty to supervise exists, the individual in the supervisory role also has a duty not to increase the risks inherent in learning, practicing, or participating in the activity or sport (*Rodrigo v. Koryo Martial Arts*, 2002; *West v. Sundown Little League of Stockton, Inc.*, 2002; *Lilley v. Elk Grove Unified School Dist.*, 1998; *Balthazor v. Little League Baseball, Inc.*, 1998; *Bushnell v. Japanese-American Religious & Cultural Center*, 1996).

Foreseeability and Causation Factors

When filing suit alleging improper supervision, plaintiffs must establish both that the injury was **reasonably foreseeable** under the circumstances, and that the defendant's negligent behavior was the **proximate cause** of the injury. Although supervisors are expected to be on site and in reasonable proximity to the activity they are supervising, failure to be present when an injury occurs does not necessarily mean that the supervisor is automatically liable. The plaintiff still must show that the failure to supervise was the proximate cause of the injury. In other words, no liability exists if the injury would have occurred notwithstanding the supervisor's absence (see Section 2.11, *Negligence*).

When the plaintiff alleges that the supervisor's absence was the proximate cause of the injury, the plaintiff must prove that the supervisor's presence would have prevented the injury. A number of cases, however, demonstrate that there are situations in which no amount of supervision would have prevented an injury. For example, a roller skater being struck by another skater (*Blashka v. South Shore Skating, Inc.*, 1993), basketball players bumping heads while jumping for the ball (*Kaufman v. City of New York*, 1961), a player running head first and colliding with a catcher who was blocking home plate (*Passantino v. Board of Educ.*, 1976), and a child falling down at a day care center while running in a grassy area of the playground (*Ward v. Mount Calvary Lutheran Church*, 1994).

Non-negligent supervision entails supervisors taking action to prevent reasonably foreseeable injuries to participants. For example, an injured plaintiff prevailed in a case in which he alleged negligent supervision since it was reasonably foreseeable that a catcher chasing a foul ball would trip over spectators who were allowed to congregate close to the base line. The supervisors had stopped the game twice prior to the injury to move the spectators back away from the third-base line and against the fence. The court found the defendants negligent for failing to control the crowd and found that the plaintiff was not guilty of contributory negligence (*Domino v. Mercurio*, 1963). In *Sheehan v. St. Peter's Catholic School* (1971), the court held that it was reasonably foreseeable that unattended students would throw rocks at each other, resulting in blindness in one of the children. Similarly, in *Dailey v. Los Angeles Unified School District* (1970), a boy died as a result of a head injury incurred during a slap-boxing incident. The person on duty at the time was in his office eating lunch rather than supervising the students. Because the injury to the boy was foreseeable and proper supervision would have prevented the injury, the court found that Dailey was liable for negligent supervision. Although *Ferguson v. DeSoto Parish School Board* (1985), involved an incident at a school, the principles established by the court should apply to all sport and recreation organizations:

> School teachers charged with the duty of superintending children in the school must exercise reasonable supervision over them, commensurate with the age of the children and the attendant circumstances. A

greater degree of care must be exercised if the student is required to use or to come in contact with an inherently dangerous object, or to engage in an activity where it is reasonably foreseeable that an accident or injury may occur. The teacher is not liable in damages unless it is shown that he or she, by exercising the degree of supervision required by the circumstances, might have prevented the act that caused the damage, and did not do so. It also is essential to recovery that there be proof of negligence in failing to provide the required supervision and proof of a causal connection between that lack of supervision and the accident.

In summary, if the potential for injury is foreseeable and the presence of the supervisor would have prevented the injury, there is a likelihood the defendant will be found liable. If, however, the injury was not reasonably foreseeable or would have occurred even if the supervisor had been there, there can be no liability. Supervisors cannot ensure the safety of participants and cannot be expected to prevent all injuries that might occur during the course of normal play or sporting activities.

Types of Supervision

Supervision, which may be general, specific, or transitional, should be predicated on the age, skill, experience, judgment, and physical condition of participants and the activity involved. **General supervision** is overseeing individuals or groups involved in an activity that does not require constant, unremitting scrutiny of the activity or facility. General supervision should be used to observe participants and activities on the playground, in the gymnasium, in the weight room, on a baseball field, or in the swimming pool, when the supervisor is not expected to have every individual under constant supervision (*Fagan v. Summers*, 1972; *Herring v. Bossier Parish School Board*, 1994; *Partin v. Vernon Parish School Board*, 1977; *Stevens v. Chesteen*, 1990). General supervision includes knowing what and how to observe, where to stand, how to move around the area, when to respond, and what action to take if a problem occurs.

Specific supervision is constant and continuous, the type of supervision that is more appropriate for individuals or small groups receiving instruction, involved in high-risk activities, or using areas that have the potential for serious injury. For example, participants who are learning an activity or skill need specific, direct supervision. Similarly, participants who are not able to perform a skill adequately need specific supervision. Specific supervision also is mandated when participants behave, or would be expected to behave, in ways that may injure themselves or others. Specific supervision also implies proximity; that is, how close the supervisor needs to be to the participants or activity to be effective. The more dangerous the activity, the more closely it should be supervised.

According to van der Smissen (1990), supervision cannot be categorized simply as general or specific, but is frequently **transitional** in nature. For example, supervision may change from specific, to general, then back to specific, depending on such factors as the participants' need for instruction, their ability to perform certain activities, their use of equipment, their involvement with others, and their use of the facility. As the potential for harm increases, the degree of supervision should increase proportionally. Specific supervision is appropriate when the supervisor perceives a situation as dangerous. Whether involved in general or specific supervision, or moving from one to the other, supervisors are expected to identify dangerous activities and intervene to stop the activity or facilitate its continuing safely.

Attributes of Proper Supervision

Qualifications of Supervisors

Organizations should hire only supervisors who have exhibited competence in properly supervising the participants involved, activities conducted, and facilities utilized. Whenever possible, supervisors should be regular, full-time employees who have appropriate qualifications and undergo regular staff development to improve their skill and knowledge. However, even a qualified supervisor could create liability for the organization if he/she fails to enforce the policies of the organization.

Individuals in supervisory positions should have the appropriate qualifications, certification, experience, and training necessary for the job. An example of standards regarding qualifications in the health and fitness industry is found in the benchmarks developed by the American College of Sports Medicine (ACSM). Notably, one of the six standards explicitly addresses supervision of youth services and programs, and another addresses competencies of those responsible for program supervision (American College of Sports Medicine, 1997). When supervisors in health and fitness facilities have appropriate **certification**, advanced training, and specialized qualifications, they will be held to the standard of a reasonably prudent person with the same certifications, training, and qualifications.

In a joint endeavor with the American Heart Association, ACSM advocated more stringent standards and guidelines for health and fitness facilities for cardiovascular screening, staffing (supervision), and emergency policies and procedures [ACSM & American Heart Association (AHA), 1998]. Both of these efforts have been recognized for their importance in assisting health and fitness facilities with standard of care issues (Herbert, 1997, 1998). Supervisors will be measured against these guidelines in determining whether they acted as reasonably prudent health and fitness practitioners.

Number of Supervisors

The number of persons required to provide reasonable supervision depends on the participants and the nature of the activity. Moreover, when plaintiffs allege negligence due to an insufficient number of supervisors, they must show that inadequate supervision was the proximate cause of the injury and that additional supervisors would have prevented the injury (*Kaczmarcsyk v. City & County of Honolulu*, 1982). Except for swimming pool and school playground cases, however, the courts generally have not imposed liability when there has been at least one supervisor present (Gaskin, 2003). Instead of focusing on the number of supervisors, the courts generally have examined whether the supervision was reasonable in light of the age, maturity, and experience of the participants and the circumstances that existed at the time of the accident. As the court said in *Glankler v. Rapides Parish School Board* (1993), "in considering a defendant's duty to a particular person, consideration should be given to the person's age, maturity, experience, familiarity with the premises and its dangers, and other factors which might increase or decrease the risk of harm to that person."

Not only must supervisors warn of dangers, they also must make sure the participants comply with the warnings and expected behavior. In *Rollins v. Concordia Parish School Board* (1985), a teacher warned very young students to slow down a merry-go-round because it was going too fast. When a dispute over a basketball arose between other students, her attention was drawn away from the children on the merry-go-round, and one of the children was hurt. The teacher and school were held liable for injuries to the student based on failure to supervise properly. Another teacher was available to be on the playground at the time, but instead she was allowed to take a break during the period rather than help supervise.

Established Standards of Conduct

To properly organize and manage an event, a supervisor must be familiar with any standards of conduct or practice that establish criteria for proper handling of the event. *Black's Law Dictionary* (Garner, 2004), defines a **standard** as "a model accepted as correct by custom, consent, or authority" and "a criterion for measuring acceptability, quality, or accuracy." Failure to adhere to recognized standards of practice can leave the supervisor subject to liability (see Section 4.21, *Standards of Practice*).

Primary Duties of Supervision

Although there are numerous legal duties associated with proper supervision of recreation and sporting activities, authors differ on the number and description of those duties (McCaskey & Biedzynski, 1996; Nygaard & Boone, 1985). These commonly recognized duties can be condensed to six primary general duties, each requiring that the prudent supervisor undertake various specific actions. The six duties are (1) effective planning, (2) proper instruction, (3) warning of risks, (4) providing a safe environment, (5) evaluating the physical and mental condition of participants, and (6) providing emergency care.

Effective Planning

Effective planning is the first, and most important, element of proper supervision. Just as successful coaches prepare game plans for upcoming games, the prudent recreation or sport manager will organize every activity or event in advance by taking into account all foreseeable dangers or risks of potential injury to the participants. Recreation and sport managers need to develop, implement, and evaluate a supervision plan for facilities, activities and individuals on the premises. Although many of the elements of proper supervision overlap, effective planning precedes all of them. Regardless of the situation, a systematic procedure should be developed to document specifically each component to be addressed in supervision: **who, what, when, where, how and why.** There should be both a master plan (including all the facilities, when they will be used, by whom, for what, and who will be supervising) and a detailed supervision plan for each area and activity. The prudent supervisor will ask, "What is the worst thing that could happen here, and how do we avoid it?"

Several cases support the necessity of having adequate supervision plans. In *Dailey v. Los Angeles Unified School Dist.* (1970), negligent supervision was at issue when the supervision plan did not provide for a formal supervision schedule, and allowed too much discretion on the part of subordinates. In *Broward County School Board v. Ruiz* (1986), the supervision plan failed to provide for supervision in an after-school waiting area. Due to inadequate supervision plans, negligence was found in each of these cases. In *Butler v. D.C.* (1969), no negligence was found because the school was using a supervision plan. Other cases where supervisors have created liability for themselves or their organizations include failure to prepare a plan (*Landers v. School District No. 203*, 1978), deviating from an approved plan (*Keesee v. Board of Education of the City of New York*, 1962), failing to follow an approved plan (*Brahatcek v. Millard School District No. 17*, 1979), and creating a hazardous plan (*DeGooyer v. Harkness*, 1944).

An effective supervision plan requires detailed planning, development, implementation, evaluation, and revision. Everyone involved in the activity should be involved in developing supervision plans, evaluating them, and revising them with primary emphasis on maintaining the safety of participants in a safe environment. Although the framework for a supervision plan may vary, the plan should be in writing, be specific, and be evaluated on a regular schedule to assess its effectiveness.

Proper Instruction

The standard of care imposed on supervisors is the degree of care that persons of ordinary prudence, charged with comparable duties, would exercise under the same circumstances (*Dailey v. Los Angeles Unified School District*, 1970). In *Green v. Orleans Parish School Board* (1978), a 16-year-old male was permanently paralyzed by injuries sustained while performing a wrestling drill in a required physical education class. While addressing the issue of whether the teacher's method of conducting the class was so substandard as to create an unreasonable risk of injury to students, the court described some of the attributes of **proper instruction**. The court included the following factors: an explanation of basic rules and procedures, suggestions for proper performance (of wrestling moves), identification of risks (including the extent of physical conditioning), the difficulty and inherent dangerousness of the activity, and the age and experience of the students. In *Scott v. Rapides Parish School Board* (1999), an 18-year-old student successfully sued for a knee injury sustained when the track coach gave him a tryout for the long jump without instructions on proper technique.

Proper instruction includes the requirement that participants be trained in the proper use of the premises and equipment involved in the activity. Supervisors and all staff members should make sure that all participants are instructed in the safe use of equipment and facilities; are observed to ensure that they are using the equipment and facility properly; and are informed of the risks and possible injuries associated with the equipment, facility, and activity (*Corrigan v. Musclemakers, Inc.*, 1999). In *Thomas v. Sport City, Inc.* (1999), a health club member was injured after he did not properly secure a squat machine that he had used. The court confirmed that the health and fitness facility has a duty to protect members from injury while they are on the premises, and that the duty includes insuring that the members know how to use the exercise equipment properly.

Proper instruction also should be clear, age appropriate, in logical sequence, and repeated as many times as necessary for the participants to understand the activity, and should include sufficient time for feedback (including questions and answers) for the instructor to be satisfied that the participants have grasped the directions.

Warnings of Risks

Supervisors of activities have a **duty to warn** of all inherent risks associated with the activity. **Inherent risks** are those that are foreseeable and customary risks of the sport or recreational activity (*Barakat v. Pordash*, 2005). Although most courts have concluded that participants assume the inherent risks of the activities in competitive sporting events, the rule may be different for other activities. When dangerous conditions exist or when there is an **elevated risk** of injury in conducting the activity, courts have found activity supervisors liable for failure to adequately warn of the risks or dangers involved. In *Corrigan v. Musclemakers, Inc.* (1999), despite the fact that the 49-year-old health club patron had never used a treadmill, her personal trainer placed her on the treadmill, left her unattended, and failed to instruct her how to adjust the speed, stop the belt, or operate the control panel. The court rejected the defendant's argument that plaintiff had assumed the risk, finding that the risks were not obvious to an untrained patron. The prudent supervisor will warn of all risks associated with any activity, assuming that the courts will scrutinize whether or not the participant was aware of all the risks, both inherent and otherwise.

Many states have passed various **immunity statutes** requiring that written warnings be posted for the proprietor or operator to benefit from limited liability. An example of such statutes is the equine statutes passed in virtually every state. These statutes generally require that the operator post a sign advising participants that taking part in the activity subjects them to assumption of all inherent risks of the activity, thereby relieving the operator from any liability for injury caused by such risks. The significant case in this section discusses a similar statute for roller-skating [see Section 2.22, *Immunity* (especially Table 2.22.1), Section 2.21, *Defenses Against Negligence*, and Section 3.10, *Property Law*].

Providing a Safe Environment

Courts often declare that supervisors are not **guarantors** that participants will not be hurt or injured. Stated another way, supervisors are not charged with a legal duty to protect participants from the inherent risks of the activity, or to eliminate all risks of taking part in the activity (*Kahn v. East Side Union High School District*, 2003; *Kelly v. McCarrick*, 2002). However, supervisors have a duty not to increase the risk of harm beyond that which is inherent in the activity (*Kahn*, 2003; *Kelly*, 2002), or to expose participants to risks that are concealed (*Benitez v. New York City Board of Education*, 1989).

Courts have established different standards for compulsory participation (such as required school physical education courses) and purely voluntary activities (such as extracurricular interscholastic school sports). In the latter, courts consistently hold that the participant assumes the inherent risks of the activity provided the participant is aware of the risks. Hurst and Knight (2003) summarized the difficulty in establishing liability against the coach and school in such cases by indicating that a successful plaintiff must prove "serious misconduct" amounting to "serious inattention, ignorance and indifference." In the compulsory participation circumstance, the defense of assumption of risk may not be a protection from liability when the injured party is compelled to participate by a superior (*Benitez v. New York City Board of Education*, 1989). The court's rationale is that participation and assumption of the risks are no longer voluntarily undertaken by the participant.

Providing a safe environment includes the obligation to provide **safe facilities** for participants by properly maintaining equipment, buildings, playgrounds, and other facilities. Although this duty is charged to the owner or operator, supervisors who work for the owners or operators continually must inspect the facility, repair or eliminate dangerous conditions, and warn users of concealed or hidden hazards (see Section 2.31, *Premises Liability*).

Another aspect of a safe environment is the proper use of equipment, particularly safety equipment. In *Leahy v. School Board of Hernando County* (1984), the court reversed and remanded a directed verdict for the school when a freshman football player was injured during an agility drill. The player was not provided a helmet because the school did not have a sufficient number of the correct sizes available. The coaches gave no special instructions to the players who did not have helmets or mouthpieces, but had them participate in drills with others who had been issued such equipment. Other cases involving equipment include liability for failing to require that a previously injured football player wear a neck roll according to doctor's instructions (*Harvey v. Ouachita Parish School Board*, 1996); reversal of a summary judgment for the school when a football player was injured after running into a blocking sled that was stored on the sidelines of the practice field (*Cruz v. City of New York*, 2001); reversal and remand of a case in which the school was held not liable for failing to furnish eye goggles that were necessary for the safety of the player (*Palmer v. Mount Vernon Township High School District 201*, 1995); and furnishing a football uniform, but not furnishing a knee brace to a recently injured player (*Lowe v. Texas Tech University*, 1975).

Evaluating the Physical and Mental Condition of Participants

The responsibility to supervise varies with the age and experience of participants, their mental condition, and the nature of the activity in which they are engaged.

Young Children. Supervisors observing young children have a heightened duty of care (*Ferguson v. DeSoto Parish School Bd.*, 1985). Ordinarily, it is necessary to exercise greater caution for the protection and safety of a young child than for an adult who possesses normal physical and mental faculties. A supervisor dealing with children must anticipate the ordinary behavior of children. Children usually do not use the same degree of caution for their own safety as adults do, and they often are thoughtless and impulsive. It is precisely this lack of mature judgment that necessitates a higher degree of supervision. (*Calandri v. Ione Unified School Dist.*, 1963).

Youth. Even older high school volleyball players who are left unsupervised may engage in horseplay and incur debilitating injuries (*Barretto v. City of New York*, 1997). However, at least one court rejected the theory that a lower standard of care is warranted when supervising high school (as opposed to elementary school) students (*Beckett v. Clinton Prairie School Corp.*, 1987).

Adults. In comparison with children, adults participating in activity generally require less supervision. Just as when dealing with children, however, supervisors must be alert to adults who may be involved in horseplay and be prepared to intervene as necessary.

Novices. The reasonableness of supervision is also related to the abilities of participants. It is foreseeable that novice participants (adult or children) may be injured primarily because they are unfamiliar with, and inexperienced in, the activity (*Brahatcek v. Millard School District*, 1979). Just as inexperienced children need closer supervision, when adults are novices, they also require close supervision because they are unfamiliar with the activity and its inherent risks.

Disabled Participants. Generally, greater caution is required for participants with disabling conditions, and the courts have provided sound direction for supervising children with disabling conditions. For example, in *Foster v. Houston General Insurance Co.* (1982), when a Special Olympics team was walking three blocks from campus to a gymnasium to practice basketball, a developmentally disabled child unexpectedly ran into the street and was run over, resulting in his death. The court noted that the teachers' duty was to protect the child from his own impulsive acts, and held that the teachers were negligent for failing to provide an adequate number of supervisory personnel, and for failing to select the safest route for the walk, particularly given the mental abilities of the students. Other cases have found liability for developmentally disabled children with poor hand-eye coordination running on the playground with other children (*Rodriguez v. Board of Education*, 1984), and an autistic child in a park district summer program walking to a water park (*Downey v. Wood Dale Park Dist.*, 1997).

Dangerous Activities. Participants involved in dangerous activities mandate a higher degree of supervision than others do. If an activity is dangerous or has the potential to be dangerous, it is essential that supervisors provide participants with detailed instructions, familiarize them with basic rules and procedures necessary for executing skills, and warn them of reasonably foreseeable dangers before they attempt the skill or engage in the activity. Both *Green v. Orleans Parish School Board* (1978), and *Carabba v. Anacortes School District No. 103* (1967), involved wrestling. Both courts held that continuous and constant supervision is required.

Mismatching. Mismatching is a situation in which a smaller, younger, less-skillful, and/or less-experienced participant is injured while participating with a larger, older, more skillful, and/or more experienced participant. Most mismatching cases involve a situation where one participant is an inexperienced, smaller member of a junior varsity team who is pitted against a larger, advanced skill-level player (*Tepper v. City of New Rochelle School District*, 1988). Allegations of mismatching also have been made where the defendant supervisor (teacher, coach, or leader) breached the standard of care by failing to fulfill his or her duties to provide non-negligent supervision by becoming a participant in the activity. Some courts have found the defendant supervisor at fault while others have ruled that participating while supervising did not constitute a breach of duty. Examples include a wrestling case in which the referee-instructor injured a high school wrestler while attempting to show him the fireman's carry (*Hearon v. May*, 1995), a tag game in an after-school child care program in which the adult-leader participated (*Longfellow v. Corey*, 1997), a touch football game in which the teacher participated during lunch recess (*Hamill v. Town of Southampton*, 1999), and an after-school Big Buddy Program in which a child was injured in a basketball game in which the coach participated (*Prejean v. East Baton Rouge Sch. Brd.*, 1999).

Although supervision often includes directing, teaching, and demonstrating techniques, it does not encompass prolonged, active participation that rises to the level of intense one-on-one competition that has a winner and a loser. Under such circumstances, the teacher, coach, or leader may be abandoning the role of supervisor and becoming an equal competitor with the participant(s).

Supervisors who use **coercion** or **threats** to induce participants to perform some activity raise the potential of liability in the event the participant is injured. It is not unusual for participants to make excuses why they should not perform the activity assigned by the supervisor. At that point, the supervisor is placed in the position of both doctor and psychiatrist, trying to determine whether the reluctance is legitimate or not. Caution should be used before coercing participants to continue with the activity. In *Kahn v. East Side Union High School District* (2003), the inexperienced swimmer had "a deep-seated fear that she would suffer a traumatic head injury from diving into shallow water" and had so informed her coaches. They ignored her fear and required her to dive, resulting in a broken neck. Although the court in this case did not find the coach responsible for negligent supervision, it did remand the case to the trial court for such a determination. In *Koch v. Billings School Dist. No. 2* (1992), a junior high student was encouraged by his teacher to squat-press 360 pounds against the plaintiff's protests. The plaintiff sustained significant injuries when he could not sustain the weight. Although the case was decided on sovereign immunity issues, the court remanded the case to determine whether the teacher was negligent in pushing the student to lift the weight. Supervisors must be very cautious to find the delicate balance between appropriately pushing participants to a higher level of performance, and coercing or threatening them unreasonably, thereby increasing the risk of injury.

Providing Emergency Care

In the event that a participant is injured during the conduct of the activity, a supervisor has a duty to provide proper emergency care (see Section 2.33, *Emergency Care*).

Adhering to Policies or Standards in Manuals

Knowledge of and adherence to policies in staff manuals have become increasingly important in helping supervisors demonstrate that they know what is expected of them and that they have followed these policies or standards in carrying out their responsibilities. In *Kahn v. East Side Union High School District* (2003), the Red Cross manual for swimming coaches, which the coach indicated that he followed, contained specific recommendations about the progression coaches should use in helping swimmers learn a racing dive. The coach failed to instruct the plaintiff how to perform a shallow-water racing dive before she was asked to do so in a competitive swim meet, resulting in her injury. Failure to follow the Red Cross standard was one of the pivotal factors in the court's decision to reverse and remand the case for further proceedings.

If the defendant fails to follow policies or standards in a manual that have been adopted, developed, and shared by the organization, association, or program, the individual may be accused of negligent supervision. Although having a policy manual demonstrates that there are standards employees are expected to follow, it is equally important that these policies are shared, discussed, and practiced. When policies are clear, well understood, and valued, employees have a sense of confidence in being up-to-date in adhering to standards of practice that reflect strong professional competency (see Section 5.21, *Standards of Practice*).

SIGNIFICANT CASE

In this case, an injured roller skater alleged that the roller rink operator was guilty of negligent supervision. Indiana has a statute placing a legal duty on rink operators to ". . . use reasonable care in supervising roller skaters." The court reviews the facts of the case to determine if the rink had discharged its obligations under the statute. Notice how the court analyzes the four elements of negligence to resolve the negligent supervision issue. The court also discusses the application of assumption of risk as a complete defense, and comparative fault in order to apportion damages.

ST. MARGARET MERCY HEALTHCARE CENTERS, INC. V. POLAND

Court Of Appeals of Indiana, Third District
828 N.E.2d 396; 2005 Ind. App. LEXIS 942 (2005)

OPINION

DARDEN, JUDGE

Statement of the Case

St. Margaret Mercy Healthcare Centers, Inc. (St. Margaret) appeals a jury verdict in which it was found partially at fault for a personal injury suffered by Barbara Poland (Poland) while she was roller skating at the Blade N Skate's rink, a facility owned and operated by St. Margaret. We affirm.

Facts

Poland and her husband went skating at St. Margaret's roller rink. It was "teen night," and according to the plaintiff, many skaters appeared to be skating "out of control and nobody seemed to be supervising them." Poland was skating during couples skating only, but was injured while trying to leave the skating floor as "all skate" began. She testified that she saw Brian Stewart skating very fast toward her while chasing another skater. Brian Stewart ran into Poland and knocked her to the floor, causing a shattered wrist, which required surgery.

Poland filed suit against St. Margaret, alleging that its negligent failure to supervise skaters was the proximate cause of her injury. St. Margaret asserted the affirmative defenses of assumption of risk, comparative fault, and fault of the non-party (i.e., Brian Stewart, who was not sued). The jury returned a verdict in favor of Poland, finding St. Margaret 50% at fault, and Stewart 50% at fault. St. Margaret appealed.

> [Note: The allegations in this case are based upon two sections of the Indiana "Limited Liability for Operators of Roller Skating Rinks" statute: Duties of Operator (Indiana Code § 34-31-6-1), and Assumption of Risks (Indiana Code § 34-31-6-3). The statutes are quoted in the opinion at various locations. For convenience, they have been quoted together here. The statutes read as follows:

> § 34-31-6-1. Duties of operator. An operator shall do all of the following with respect to a roller skating rink: * * * (3) When the roller skating rink is open for a session, have at least one (1) floor supervisor on duty for every one hundred seventy-five (175) roller skaters who: (A) has received appropriate training to carry out the floor supervisor's duties; and (B) uses reasonable care in carrying out the floor supervisor's duties. * * * (9) Use reasonable care in supervising roller skaters to comply with the requirements of section 2 [IC 34-31-6-2] of this chapter.

> § 34-31-6-3. Assumption of risks. (a) Roller skaters are considered to: (1) have knowledge of; and (2) assume; the risks of roller skating. (b) For purposes of this chapter, risks of roller skating include the following: (1) Injuries that result from collisions or incidental contact with other roller skaters or other individuals who are properly on the skating surface. * * *]

Decision

* * *

Due to the nature of roller skating, the Indiana Legislature imposed specific duties and responsibilities upon roller skating rink operators pursuant to Section 1. Correspondingly, as outlined in Section 2, the Indiana Legislature also imposed certain duties upon roller skaters. Furthermore, the Indiana Legislature has provided that, if a roller skating rink operator is in compliance with the specified duties and responsibilities outlined in Section 1, then * * * the operator is entitled to a complete defense against liability from roller skaters who experience falls due to collisions and incidental contact with other skaters while on the skating rink floor. However, if the evidence establishes that a roller skating rink operator is non-compliant with the statutorily imposed duties and responsibilities of an operator, as found in Section 1, the operator no longer is entitled to a complete defense * * * against a skater who sustains an injury related to its non-compliance; but, * * * the matter shifts to a comparative fault analysis.

Poland alleged in her complaint that St. Margaret's negligent failure to supervise skaters on the floor was the proximate cause of her injury. The tort claim of negligence has three elements: "(1) a duty owed by the defendant to the plaintiff; (2) a breach of that duty; and (3) injury to the plaintiff resulting from the defendant's breach." * * *

Breach of duty was highly contested in this case. Poland argued that St. Margaret breached a duty owed to her as a skater when it failed to use reasonable care in supervising skaters on the floor. Both sides agreed that it was teen night with a mixture of slow and fast pace skating. Poland testified that throughout the night she observed Brian Stewart skating very fast and aggressively; and, that some of the other skaters appeared to be out of control with no supervision. She and Mark testified that they saw a rink guard playing crack the whip with skaters. She testified that she witnessed four to five skaters holding hands while skating, which was a clear violation of St. Margaret's announced safety rule. Poland skated only during the couples' skating times when the pace was slower and fewer people were on the floor. She testified that there was no pause between the end of the slow skating and the beginning of the all skating. Poland testified that she was prevented from leaving the skating floor through one exit because it was jammed with skaters who were rushing onto the skating floor to participate in the all skating. As she attempted to leave through the next exit, she saw Brian Stewart chasing another boy, both of whom were skating very fast and aggressively toward her. She was unable to make the exit before being knocked to the skating floor by Brian Stewart and breaking her wrist.

St. Margaret countered with testimony from its employees and Brian Stewart. Charles Eyermann, a former floor supervisor, testified that though he worked the night of Poland's injury, he had no independent recollection of the night in question. However, he testified that in general and as a practice, neither he nor other roller skating rink guards would be involved in horseplay with skaters. He also testified that guards would never leave a skater's misbehavior unchecked. He further asserted that if skaters were as rowdy as Poland claims, he believes he would have recalled the evening, and he and the other guards would have instituted St. Margaret's discipline policy. He explained that St. Margaret's disciplinary policy used a three-tiered approach. First, a rule breaking skater would be warned to stop the behavior by a guard blowing a whistle. Second, if the conduct continued, the skater would be made to sit out for a time and then allowed to return. And, third, if the conduct continued, the skater would be made to leave the facility.

* * *

Brian Stewart testified that while skating someone bumped him, causing him to lose his balance and he accidentally kicked Poland's skates from under her. He also testified that he was skating at a normal rate of speed, although his speed was faster than Poland's speed. Further, he testified that he was skating alone and denied chasing or playing tag with any other skater when he knocked Poland down.

In summary, the jury heard evidence regarding St. Margaret's floor guards playing "crack the whip" with skaters; skaters violating St. Margaret's announced safety rules; how Brian Stewart and other skaters were permitted to skate aggressively and very fast; and, the overall lack of supervision of skaters by St. Margaret.

The evidence was conflicting; however, it was within the province of the jury to judge the credibility of witnesses and to weigh the evidence. * * * Whether St. Margaret breached a duty of care is a question of fact to be resolved by the jury. * * *

* * * As previously noted, Poland's claim for relief was founded in negligence and was based upon St. Margaret's breach of a duty owed to her as a roller skater. In its pleadings, and during its presentation of evidence and argument to the jury, St. Margaret denied that it was negligent in its supervision of skaters and asserted the affirmative defenses of: comparative fault, fault of the nonparty, and assumption of the risk by the plaintiff. * * *

Upon the jury reaching its verdict that St. Margaret failed to exercise reasonable care in supervising skaters on the floor, which was the proximate cause of Poland's injury, the jury was compelled to proceed to I.C. § 34-51-2-6 for a comparative fault analysis regarding damages, if any. * * * Indiana's Comparative Fault Statute requires that fault be apportioned among the parties; thus, the jury had the responsibility of apportioning fault between Poland, St. Margaret, and Brian Stewart, the nonparty. * * * We find the evidence sufficiently probative to support the reasonable finding by the jury that St. Margaret breached a duty to use reasonable care to properly supervise skaters on the floor. * * *

* * *

Upon reviewing the relevant statutes herein, we find that the Indiana Legislature has clearly spoken. Pursuant to Section 1, the legislature imposed specific duties and responsibilities upon roller skating rink operators. Further, pursuant to Section 1(3)(1)(B)(9), an operator is required to provide floor supervisors who are responsible to "use reasonable care in carrying out the floor supervisor's duties," including the "use of reasonable care in supervising roller skaters" to comply with Section 2. St. Margaret advances that if the jury should find that the operator has complied with the statutorily imposed duties, assumption of the risks by skaters is a complete defense in favor of operator against an action by a skater for injuries resulting from the assumed risks. On the other hand, St. Margaret concedes that pursuant to Section 4(b)(1)(2), the statute provides that if the jury should find that the operator did not comply with the statutorily imposed duties and responsibilities, the operator is no longer entitled to a complete defense, but that the parties proceed to comparative fault. St. Margaret argues, however, that even in a comparative fault analysis, assumption of risks by the skater is presumed as an element to be determined as a percentage of fault against the skater, and factored into the apportionment of fault among the parties and non-party. * * *

* * *

* * * Although the evidence was often conflicting and breach of duty was vigorously contested, it was within the province of the jury to assess the credibility of witnesses in weighing disputed evidentiary matters, resolving issues of conflict, and, ultimately, to determine fault among the parties. * * * We find that pursuant to Section 4(b)(1)(2), once the jury reached a verdict that St. Margaret had breached a statutorily imposed duty to use reasonable care, the jury was compelled to proceed apportionment of fault among the parties.

For purposes of comparative fault, the term fault "includes any act or omission that is negligent . . . toward the person.

* * * As noted, St. Margaret asserted the affirmative defense of assumption of risks by the skater. * * *

* * *

Generally, incurred risk is a question of fact for the jury. * * * Apportionment of fault is also a question of fact for the jury to determine. * * * "In determining whether a plaintiff incurred the risk of his or her injuries, a subjective analysis is required focusing on the plaintiff's actual knowledge and appreciation of the specific risk involved and voluntary acceptance of that risk." * * * It was therefore within the province of the jury to determine what percentage of fault, if any, should be apportioned among the parties. St. Margaret directs us to no authority which states a plaintiff must be apportioned some percentage of fault under comparative fault; neither have we found any such authority. Further, we do not find that the jury was somehow confused or misled by the language of the instruction into believing it was not to apportion any fault to Poland. The jury heard conflicting evidence regarding the behavior and conduct of the parties and nonparty, and apportioned fault as it believed the evidence dictated. We hold that the jury's verdict apportioning zero percentage of fault to Poland is supported by the evidence and the law.

We affirm.

CASES ON SUPPLEMENTAL CD

Brahatcek v. Millard School District, 202 Neb. 86, 273 N.W.2d 680 (Neb. 1979). Plaintiff alleged lack of supervision as the proximate cause of the 14-year-old student's death when he was struck by a golf club in a physical education class. The court discussed heightened supervision required for a young and inexperienced student.

Kahn v. East Side Union High School District, 75 P. 3d 30 (Cal. 2003). This case is a treasure trove of legal principles including proper supervision, proximate cause, primary assumption of risk, inherent

risks, duty not to increase the risks inherent of the activity, coercion to perform by an authority figure (coach), effect of applicable standards or guidelines established by professional associations, and use or nonuse of safety training manuals.

Zipusch v. LA Workout, Inc., 155 Cal. App. 4th 1281, 66 Cal. Rptr. 3d 704 (Cal. App. 2 Dist., 2007). Plaintiff alleged the health club was negligent for failing to inspect and maintain its exercise equipment when a sticky substance on a treadmill caused her fall, resulting in an injury.

QUESTIONS YOU SHOULD BE ABLE TO ANSWER

1. Identify the three sources from which the duty to supervise arises and briefly discuss the important aspects of each.

2. A participant is injured and alleges negligence on the part of the supervisor. Describe how the concepts of foreseeability and causation apply, specifically, concerning the presence or absence of the supervisor.

3. Identify and briefly describe the appropriateness of the three types of supervision as they relate to the age, skill, experience, judgment, and physical condition of participants and the activity involved.

4. When teaching or coaching, what are the most important concepts for one to consider in planning, instructing, and warning of risks involved in the activity?

5. What are the major concerns one should consider when supervising young children, high school students, adults, and individuals with varying abilities?

REFERENCES

Cases

Balthazor v. Little League Baseball, Inc., 62 Cal. App.4th 47, 72 Cal. Rptr.2d 337 (1998).

Barakat v. Pordash, 842 N.E.2d 120, 2005 WL 3074729 (Ohio App. 8 Dist., 2005).

Barretto v. City of New York, 229 A.D.2d 214; 655 N.Y.S.2d 484 (1997).

Beckett v. Clinton Prairie School. Corp., 504 N.E.2d 552 (Ind. 1987).

Benitez v. New York City Board of Education, 541 N.E.2d 29 (NY 1989).

Blashka v. South Shore Skating, Inc., 598 N.Y.S.2d 74 (App. Div. 2d Dept. 1993).

Brahatcek v. Millard School Dist., 202 Neb. 86, 273 N.W.2d 680 (Neb. 1979).

Broward County School Board v. Ruiz, 493 So.2d 474 (Fla. App. 1986).

Bushnell v. Japanese-American Religious & Cultural Center, 43 Cal. App.4th 525, 50 Cal. Rptr.2d 671 (1996).

Butler v. D.C., 417 F.2d 1150 (1969).

Calandri v. Ione Unified School Dist., 219 Cal. App.2d 542, 33 Cal.Rptr. 333 (1963).

Carabba v. Anacortes School District No. 103, 72 Wash.2d 939, 435 P.2d 936 (Wash. 1967).

Corrigan v. Musclemakers, Inc., 258 A.D.2d 861, 686 N.Y.S.2d 143 (1999).

Cruz v. City of New York, 288 A.D.2d 250 (N.Y. App. Div. 2001).

David v. County of Suffolk, 1 N.Y.3d 525 (2003).

Dailey v. Los Angeles Unified School District, 470 P.2d 360 (Cal. 1970).

DeGooyer v. Harkness, 13 N.W.2d 815 (SD, 1944).

Domino v. Mercurio, 17 A.D.2d 342, 234 N.Y.S.2d 1011 (1962), *aff'd*, 13 N.Y.S.2d 922, 193 N.E.2d 893, 244 N.Y.S.2d 69 (1963).

Downey v. Wood Dale Park Dist., 675 N.E.2d 973 (Ill. App. 1997).

Fagan v. Summers, 498 P.2d 1227 (Wyo. 1972).

Ferguson v. DeSoto Parish School Bd., 467 So.2d 1257 (La. 1985).

Fluehr v. City of Cape May, 732 A.2d 1035 (N.J. 1999).

Foster v. Houston General Insurance Co., 407 So.2d 759 (La. Ct. App. 1982).

Glankler v. Rapides Parish School Board, 610 So.2d 1020 (La. App. 1993).

Green v. Orleans Parish School Board, 365 So.2d 834 (La. Ct. App. 1978).

Hamill v. Town of Southampton, 261 A.D.2d 361, 689 N.Y.S.2d 196 (App. Div. 1999).

Harvey v. Ouachita Parish School Board, 674 So.2d 372 (La. App. 2 Cir. 1996).

Hearon v. May, 248 Neb. 887, 540 N.W.2d 124 (1995).

Herring v. Bossier Parish School Board, 632 So.2d 920 (La. Ct. App. 1994).

Kaczmarcsyk v. City & County of Honolulu, 63 Hawaii 612, 656 P.2d 89 (Hawaii 1982).

Kahn v. East Side Union High School District, 75 P.3d 30 (Cal. 2003).

Kaufman v. City of New York, 30 Misc.2d 285, 214 N.Y.S.2d 767 (1961).

Keesee v. Board of Education of the City of New York, 235 N.Y.S.2d 300 (N.Y. Sup. Ct. 1962).

Kelly v. McCarrick, 841 A.2d 869 (Md. Ct. Spec. App. 2002).

Koch v. Billings School Dist. No. 2, 833 P.2d 181 (Mt. 1992).

Landers v. School District No. 203, O'Fallon, 383 N.E.2d 645 (Ill. App. Ct.—5th Dist. 1978).

Leahy v. School Board of Hernando County, 450 So.2d 883 (Fla. Dist. Ct. App. 1984).

Lilley v. Elk Grove Unified School Dist., 68 Cal. App.4th 939, 80 Cal. Rptr.2d 638 (1998).

Longfellow v. Corey, 286 Ill. App.3d 366, 368, 675 N.E.2d 1386 (1997).

Lowe v. Texas Tech University, 540 S.W.2d 297 (Tex. 1976).

Palmer v. Mount Vernon Township High School District 201, 647 N.E.2d 1043 (Ill. App. Ct. 1995).

Partin v. Vernon Parish School Board, 343 So.2d 417 (La. App. 1977).

Passantino v. Board of Educ., 41 N.Y.S.2d 1022, 363 N.E.2d 1373, 395 N.Y.S.2d 628 (1977), *revg.* 52 A.D.2d 935, 383 N.Y.S.2d 639 (1976).

Prejean v. East Baton Rouge Sch. Brd., 729 So.2d 686 (La. 1999).

Rodrigo v. Koryo Martial Arts, 100 Cal. App.4th 946, 122 Cal. Rptr.2d 832 (2002).

Rodriguez v. Board of Educ., 104 A.D.2d 978, 480 N.Y.S.2d 901 (1984).

Rollins v. Concordia Parish School Board, 465 So.2d 213 (La. App. 1985).

Scott v. Rapides Parish School Board, 732 So.2d 749 (La. App. 1999).

Sheehan v. St. Peter's Catholic School, 29 Minn. 1, 188 N.W.2d 868 (1971).

Stevens v. Chesteen, 561 So.2d 1100 (Ala. 1990).

St. Margaret Mercy Healthcare Centers, Inc. v. Poland, 828 N.E.2d 396 (Ind. Ct. App. 2005).

Tepper v. City of New Rochelle School District, 531 N.Y.S.2d 367 (N. Y. Sup. Ct. 1988).

Thomas v. Sport City, Inc., 738 So.2d 1153 (La. App. 2nd Cir. 1999).

Toller v. Plainfield School District 202, 582 N.E.2d 237 (Ill. App. 1991).

Ward v. Mount Calvary Lutheran Church, 178 Ariz. 350, 873 P.2d 688 (Ariz. App. 1994).

West v. Sundown Little League of Stockton, Inc., 96 Cal. App.4th 351, 116 Cal. Rptr.2d 849 (2002).

Publications

American College of Sports Medicine. (1997). *ACSM's health/fitness facility standards & guidelines* (2nd ed.). Champaign, IL: Human Kinetics.

American College of Sports Medicine & American Heart Association. (1998). Recommendations for cardiovascular screening, staffing, and emergency policies at health/fitness facilities. *Medicine & Science in Sports & Exercise, 30*(6), 1009–1018.

Garner, B. A. (Ed.). (2004). *Black's law dictionary* (8th ed.). St. Paul, MN: Thomson/West.

Gaskin, L. P. (2003). Supervision of Participants. In D. J. Cotten & J. T. Wolohan (Eds.), *Law for recreation and sport managers* (pp. 138–148). Dubuque, IA: Kendall/Hunt.

Herbert, D. L. (1997). A review of ACSM's standards & guidelines for health & fitness facilities. *The Sports, Parks & Recreation Law Reporter, 11*(2), 23–24.

Herbert, D. L. (1998). New standards for health and fitness facilities from the American Heart Association (AHA) and the American College of Sports Medicine (ACSM). *The Sports, Parks & Recreation Law Reporter, 12*(2), 30–31.

Herbert, D. L. (2002). Enhanced qualifications of fitness personnel may result in increased liability. *Fitness Management, 18*(2), 36.

Hurst, T. R., & Knight, J. M. (2003). Coaches' liability for athletes' injuries and deaths. *Seton Hall Journal of Sport Law, 13*, 27–51.

Kaiser, R. A. (1986). *Liability and law in recreation, parks, and sports.* Englewood Cliffs, NJ: Prentice Hall.

McCaskey, A. S., & Biedzynski, K. W. (1996). A guide to the legal liability of coaches for a sports participant's injuries. *Seton Hall Journal of Sport Law, 6*, 7–125.

Nygaard, G., & Boone, T. H. (1985). *Coaches guide to sport law.* Champaign, IL: Human Kinetics.

van der Smissen, B. (1990). *Legal liability and risk management for public and private entities.* Cincinnati, OH: Anderson.

Zipusch v. LA Workout, Inc., 155 Cal. App. 4th 1281, 66 Cal. Rptr. 3d 704 (Cal. App. 2 Dist., 2007).

Legislation

Limited Liability for Operators of Roller Skating Rinks, Ind. Code Ann. § 34–31-6, et seq. (2009).

Volunteer Protection Act of 1997, 42 U. S. C. § 14501, et. seq. (2009).

2.35 Transportation

—Paul J. Batista
TEXAS A&M UNIVERSITY

Participants' safety and welfare should be the primary concern for those organizations that transport participants involved in recreation or sport activities. Both public and private entities, as well as individuals, must be aware of the duty of care required by law when providing transportation. The potential for liability extends not only to transporting them to and from events, but also to the use of vehicles in completing special tasks associated with the event (such as transporting injured persons to a hospital), and to supervisory concerns before, during, and after transport (see Section 2.34, *Supervision*).

FUNDAMENTAL CONCEPTS

Duty to Provide Transportation

Generally, when organizations sponsor recreation or sport activities, there may be a corresponding duty to provide transportation. If so, the transportation must be provided in a safe manner regardless of the mode of travel. The duty to provide transportation usually begins at the point of departure and continues until those using the transportation have been returned to the original departure point. Liability exists regardless whether the participants meet at the designated place and are then assigned a particular vehicle, or they are picked up by the driver at their homes or elsewhere. It may be possible to avoid liability by establishing a policy that no transportation will be provided for anyone for a particular event. In that case, participants are instructed to convene at the site of the event. However, this policy may not be practical if large numbers of people are involved, the distance to travel is far, or participants do not have access to an alternative form of transportation. The organization also needs to establish a policy governing the conditions under which a participant can leave an event by transportation other than that provided by the organization. For minors, parental permission should be required, with each child being "signed out" by the responsible parent or guardian. The supervisor should create a specific policy, and insure that everyone involved in transportation is aware of, and conforms to, the policy. Allowing a parent or participant to avoid the policy requirement by making exceptions will increase the potential for liability.

Duty of Care

When an organization provides transportation, it owes a duty of care with respect to such transportation. Generally, reasonable and ordinary care under the circumstances is the appropriate standard of care. However, there is authority that indicates that the operators of school buses are in the same general position as common carriers, requiring the highest degree of care consistent with the practical operation of the bus. The standard of care required of the drivers is determined by the particular circumstances. Some factors that may be considered in determining the standard of care include the age, knowledge, judgment, and experience of both the driver and passengers.

In a situation where a driver or organization has violated a specific statute enacted for the protection of the passengers, and that violation is the proximate cause of an injury, the standard of care is irrelevant. In that instance, the organization would be held absolutely liable.

Jurisdictions differ as to the duty required concerning supervision. In some jurisdictions the duty of care includes a duty to provide a location where participants can wait for the transportation with reasonable safety, and a duty to select a discharge point that does not needlessly expose them to any unreasonable or significant safety hazards. The duty to provide a reasonably safe location may also impose a duty upon the organization to provide proper supervision. In contrast, courts in other jurisdictions have ruled that the duty of an organization toward participants under its control applies only during the period they are transported to and from the event, beginning when the participant enters the vehicle and continuing until they have been safely discharged. Likewise, absent the existence of a special duty, this duty may not extend to situations where the participant is no longer under the organization's authority or is no longer under its physical custody. In order to decrease the potential of liability and insure the safety of participants, the best policy would include providing appropriate supervision from the time the participant arrives at the pick-up point at the beginning of the trip until the participant leaves the discharge point at the end of the excursion.

Transportation Options

The transportation of participants to and from recreation or sport events and activities can be accomplished in one of three ways: (1) through an independent contractor, (2) by using an organization-owned vehicle, or (3) by privately owned vehicles (owned either by the employee or by a non-employee third person, such as a participant's parent). The potential for liability varies from situation to situation with the least potential for liability existing where independent contractors are used, and the greatest potential where private vehicles are used. The risk of liability is not as high when an organization uses an independent contractor because most of the risk is transferred to the contractor. The risk of liability is greatest when non-employee vehicles are used because the organization has the least control. The keys to the determination of liability are the ownership of the vehicle and the relationship of the driver to the entity responsible for the participants.

Independent Contractor

If an organization can afford it, using an independent contractor for transportation is the best legal option, since the contract for service shifts liability to the contractor. The independent contractor may be of two types: common or private carrier. A **common carrier** is one that is in the business of transporting goods or persons for hire. A **private carrier**, on the other hand, only hires out to deliver goods or persons in particular cases. With regard to the qualifications of the driver and the condition of the vehicle, a common carrier is typically held to a higher standard of care than a private carrier or a noncommercial driver.

An organization may delegate its duty of safe transportation to third party independent contractors, but the organization must use due diligence to select a contractor with a proven safety record. In most cases, the primary issue for the court is whether the third party is truly an **independent contractor**. This determination is made based on several factors, including who has the right to control the manner in which the work (in this case, the transportation) is conducted, the method of payment, the right to discharge employees, the skill required, and who furnishes the tools, equipment, or materials needed to accomplish the work. With respect to transportation, if factors such as the use of specific vehicles, the driver, the route, the intermediate stops, and the manner of driving are all within the control of the transportation company and its employees, then it is likely the relationship is that of an independent contractor (see Section 2.12, *Which Parties Are Liable?* and Section 2.21, *Defenses Against Negligence*). This is an area fraught with danger, so consultation with an attorney prior to hiring an independent contractor is essential.

Be aware that an organization may not be able to avoid liability if the organization is negligent in its selection of an independent contractor. Therefore, it is always good administrative practice to investigate independent contractors carefully prior to entering into a contract with them. A recent analysis of Division 1 schools revealed that at least 85 used charter bus companies that had one or more deficiencies on federal government safety scores (Lavigne, 2009). The article highlights numerous actual and potential hazards when hiring charter bus companies, and includes suggested questions as well as links to government records to verify company safety records. Additionally, the Federal Motor Carrier Safety Administration (FMCSA) has issued a guide to hiring charter transportation that contains questions to ask and links to other safety information (FMCSA, n.d.). When researching a company for potential hire, secure a **certificate of insurance** verifying the company has sufficient liability insurance for the company and each vehicle, and the company's U.S. Department of Transportation number, which can be used to access the company's latest safety report at www.safer.fmcsa.dot.gov.

Transportation policy became a central theme in the National Transportation Safety Board (NTSB) report regarding the crash of an aircraft transporting members of the Oklahoma State University (OSU) basketball team and other team personnel (NTSB, 2003). Although it was determined that the pilot's spatial disorientations and failure to maintain positive manual control was the major cause of the accident, the NTSB concluded, "OSU did not provide any significant oversight for the accident flight."

OSU policy required charter flights and university airplane flights to be coordinated through the OSU flight department. However, since this specific flight was a donated flight, it was not coordinated through the flight department. Therefore, OSU had no records on file regarding the pilots or the plane as required by its flight department. OSU has since adopted a comprehensive transportation management system in an attempt to ensure necessary oversight. This comprehensive policy provides an outstanding model for transportation issues facing all organizations, and may be accessed at: http://www.okstate.com/SportSelect .dbml?DB_OEM_ID=200&SPID=162&SPSID=2438.

As a result of the OSU accident, the NTSB recommended that collegiate athletic associations review athletic team travel policies and develop a model transportation policy that could be implemented by member schools (NTSB, 2007). In response, the NCAA and the American Council on Education (ACE) produced a transportation manual titled Safety in Student Transportation: A Resource Guide for Colleges and Universities, which contains comprehensive information and recommendations. It is available on the Internet at: http://www.ue.org/documents/Safety%20in%20Student%20Transportation.pdf.

Organization-Owned Vehicles

For some organizations or entities, the use of an independent contractor is not a viable option due to the cost involved. Organization-owned vehicles are the most common means of transporting participants, and provide the next best transportation option. Since the organization owns the vehicles, it has the legal responsibility for the safe transportation of the participants. The organization has a duty to see that the vehicles are in safe operating condition and to see that the drivers are properly qualified. In the event of legal action, written policies, checklists, and maintenance records provide documentation that these duties have been fulfilled (see Section 4.11, *Risk Management Process* and Section 4.22, *Audits in Risk Management*).

Driver. Both the driver and the organization could be liable for the driver's negligence. In order to protect itself, the organization should require that the driver meet established qualifications that may include age, experience, special licenses, training, and verification of driving record. The organization should also use due diligence to determine that the driver complies with its transportation policies.

If an employee is acting in the course and scope of his/her employment when the accident occurs, both the driver and organization will be held liable for the driver's negligence. In *Foster v. Board of Trustees* (1991) (the significant case in this section), the Kansas court defined **course and scope of employment** as the employee "performing services for which he has been employed, or when he is doing anything which is reasonably incidental to his employment." However, when the driver commits an ***ultra vires* act** (i.e., an act that is outside the course and scope of employment), the negligence of the driver is not imputed to the organization. Examples of *ultra vires* acts include exceeding the speed limit, running a red light or stop sign, and deviating from the designated route. In *Smith v. Gardner* (1998), the court held that a baseball coach who, after an away game, drove the school van to purchase some tobacco products and decided to sightsee rather than returning to the hotel, was not acting within the course and scope of his employment. It is important to emphasize to drivers that they should not deviate from the scheduled route and itinerary without approval. In *Myricks v. Lynwood Unified School District* (1999), neither the school nor the city (which paid some of the expenses of the traveling summer basketball team) was liable for a driver's negligence because the driver was not acting within the scope of employment, since this was a summer team not affiliated with the school.

Vehicle. Being able to establish the roadworthiness of the vehicle is of utmost importance to the organization. With all organization-owned vehicles, the organization is responsible for maintenance, and failure to maintain the vehicle in a safe condition leaves the organization liable. All vehicles need to be maintained by competent maintenance personnel in accordance with the owner's manual and vehicle specifications. Any vehicle with maintenance problems (e.g., defective lights, worn tires) should not be used until the condition is corrected and documented. Complete documentation of all maintenance should be stored in a safe, accessible manner.

Prior to each trip, each vehicle needs to be inspected by a competent authorized maintenance person. After each trip, a similar inspection should be performed and the driver should report any problems encountered on the trip. Pre-trip and post-trip vehicle inspection forms and checklists need to be developed for this purpose. Emergency equipment (e.g., first aid kit, flares, flashers, spare tires, and jack) should also be included on these forms and in these inspections.

Policies. Prior to the trip, an administrator or another authorized individual must be informed of and authorize travel plans. A trip request form should be utilized which includes the purpose of the trip, the destination, lodging arrangements, route, contact phone numbers, a list of those traveling, the person in charge, and the driver. Irrespective of the mode of travel (e.g., car, van, bus, plane), policies need to be established that address who can travel, maximum distances, traveling at night, disciplinary action, emergency procedures, driver qualifications, maximum driving hours in a 24-hour period, and oversight of the drivers.

Schools. State laws control the right to use a vehicle owned by a school to transport students to activities other than classes. Some states have no restrictions while others limit the use of school buses to providing transportation to and from classes. Other states restrict use depending upon the source of operating funds, which may be a critical factor in the application of governmental immunity.

In the past, state sovereign immunity statues provided liability protection for cities or schools when their employees were negligent. **Sovereign immunity** is the legal theory that a person cannot sue a governmental body without its permission. It derives from the ancient theory that "the king can do no wrong." Now, however, most states have enacted **tort claims acts** that waive sovereign immunity and create liability for governmental entities under certain circumstances. Typically, these statutes make the governmental body liable for injuries caused by the operation of motor vehicles, but limit the amount of financial liability of the governmental institutions. The potential of liability for public colleges and universities, public secondary schools, school boards and districts, and other public agencies such as recreation departments, must be considered in light of these statutes (see Section 2.22, *Immunity*).

Privately Owned Vehicles

In some cases, organizations may find it convenient or necessary to use privately owned vehicles for transportation. The vehicles could be owned either by employees or by non-employees (e.g., parents, volunteers, and participants). In either case, liability for negligence is generally retained by the organization.

Before authorizing and approving use of private vehicles, risk management policies should be established to verify that both vehicles and drivers conform to adequate safety standards. These policies should require a physical inspection of the vehicle, review of maintenance records, and current insurance and registration on the vehicle. Policies should also ensure that the driver is properly licensed, has a good driving reputation, has a violation-free driving record, and has no impairments that would preclude driving.

Employee Vehicles. When an employee, as a part of his/her employment, uses a personal vehicle for transporting students or patrons, a **principal-agent relationship** is established. An organization is **vicariously liable** for employee negligence committed within the course and scope of employment. This will hold true even in the situation of an employee driving another employee's vehicle as in the case of *Murray v. Zarger*, (1994). Richard Zarger was a volunteer diving coach for Cory Area (Pennsylvania) High School and was compensated a small salary by the school district. While driving Cherese Murray, a member of the diving team, and three others in the head coach's car, Zarger was involved in an accident that resulted in Murray's death. Murray's estate filed suit for damages allegedly caused by the negligence of the school district, the car owner, and Zarger. The school district argued that Zarger was not an employee of the district on the following grounds: they had no control over the manner in which he performed; Zarger was not responsible for the swim team's performance; there was no agreement between Zarger and the school district; Zarger was used for his special diving skills only; and Zarger was an employee of two other companies. In holding that Zarger was an employee of the school district, the court stated that the definition of "employee" in the applicable state statute did not require that an employee be compensated or possess a formal employment contract with the government unit, but only that the person act in the government's interests (see Section 2.12, *Which Parties are Liable?*).

In this section's significant case, *Foster v. Board of Trustees* (1991), Christopher Foster was a basketball player making a recruiting visit to Butler County Community College. At the request of the head basketball coach, volunteer driver George Johnson picked Foster up at the airport, after which Foster was injured in a collision on the way to the campus. The issue in the case was Johnson's status as either an employee or a volunteer. The court examined the requirements for Johnson to be an employee (even though he was unpaid), found that he was an employee, and that his actions were negligent, thereby making the College vicariously liable for Johnson's negligence.

Use of privately owned vehicles increases the risks to the organization; therefore, the establishment and enforcement of **risk management policies** regarding the driver and the vehicle are essential (see Section 4.22, *Audits in Risk Management*). If the employee uses his or her privately owned vehicle as a service to the organization and in accordance with organization policy, most jurisdictions require that the driver exercise reasonable and ordinary care. The employee will be personally liable for negligent operation of the vehicle, in addition to the vicarious liability of the organization.

Non-employee Vehicles. When an organization has a duty to provide transportation and uses a private vehicle provided by someone who is not an employee, a principal-agent relationship is created just as it is when a privately owned employee vehicle is used. The organization is liable for the negligence of the driver. Because an organization has the least control when non-employee vehicles are used, this category creates the greatest risk of liability to the organization. It is imperative that the organization institute and enforce the risk management policies suggested at the beginning of the section, *Privately Owned Vehicles*.

Other Transportation Issues

State Codes. State legislatures enact laws that are related to transportation. However, sometimes it is not clear which part of the Code may apply. At issue in *Barnhart v. Cabrillo Community College* (1999), was whether or not an intercollegiate match was a field trip as defined under Title 5, California Code of Regulations, Section 5545. The court of appeals ruled that since school-related athletic activities necessarily include extracurricular sport programs, the trip was a field trip and would fall under the immunity granted in the Code.

Although most states, and the U.S. Congress, have passed volunteer protection statutes providing **immunity** or **limited liability** for volunteers under certain circumstances, virtually all of those statutes contain exceptions for operation of motor vehicles. For example, the federal Volunteer Protection Act (42 U. S. C. §14501, et. seq.) provides a defense for volunteers meeting the statutory criteria, but excepts from immunity a "volunteer operating a motor vehicle, vessel, aircraft, or other vehicle for which the State requires the operator or the owner of the vehicle, craft, or vessel to (A) possess an operator's license; or (B) maintain insurance." A typical state statute, the Texas Charitable Immunity and Liability Act of 1987 (Texas Civil Practice and Remedies Code § 84.001 et. seq.), creates volunteer liability for "the operation or use of any motor-driven equipment," but limits damages to the extent to which insurance coverage is required and exists, thereby protecting the volunteer who has secured the required insurance. Additional information on state volunteer driver laws may be found on the National Conference of State Legislatures website located at http://www.ncsl.org/programs/transportation/SVDLLaws.htm (see Section 2.22, *Immunity*). The sport or recreation manager should have the organization's attorney review the state Codes that are applicable to transportation. Knowledge of the Codes is a valuable tool in the policy-making process and can serve to minimize litigation.

Many states are considering banning driving while using electronic communications devices such as cell phones, text messaging, etc. Clearly, a reasonably prudent person would not be doing those things while driving students or participants. The organization should adopt a strict policy that requires leaving the roadway and stopping the vehicle in order to use a cell phone or similar device, except in cases of emergency.

Workers' Compensation. If an individual is injured in an automobile accident while within his/her scope of employment and the business required the employee to be at the place of the accident, workers' compensation may be applicable. In *Bolton v. Tulane University* (1997), Bolton was an assistant basketball coach returning from a recruiting trip, and was a passenger in an automobile driven by another assistant coach. She was injured when the driver fell asleep and the car ended up in a ravine. Tulane provided workers' compensation benefits and paid most of her medical bills, but Bolton sued the University for negligence, seeking additional damages. In deciding the workers' compensation claim, the Court of Appeals held that Bolton was in the course and scope of her employment, and workers' compensation was her exclusive remedy.

Van Accidents. According to the National Highway Traffic Safety Administration (NHTSA), between 1997 and 2006 there were 1,374 15-passenger vans involved in fatal crashes that resulted in 1,090 fatalities to occupants of such vans. Eighty-three percent of people who died in single vehicle rollovers of these vehicles were not wearing safety belts. (NHTSA, 2008a).

Van vs. School Buses. While most states require the use of school buses to transport children to and from school and school-related events, some states do not. According to the NHTSA (2008b):

- 29 states have laws or regulations that prohibit the use of vans for transporting public school students to and from school and school-related activities;

- 12 states have laws and regulations that prohibit the use of vans for transporting public school students to and from school, but allow the use of vans for school activity trips;

- 9 states allow the use of vans for transporting public school students to and from school and school-related activities. In many states, the laws and regulations do not apply to private and church-sponsored schools.

15-Passenger Vans. Recent research conducted by the NHTSA found that the risk of a rollover crash is greatly increased when ten or more individuals ride in a 15-passenger van. The risk of a rollover is increased because the center of gravity of the vehicle is raised when more passengers are transported. Placing any load on the roof also raises the center of gravity and increases the likelihood of a rollover. The result is less resistance to rollover and increased difficulty in steering. The NHTSA identified three major situations that can lead to a rollover in the 15-passenger vans: (1) The van goes off a rural road, striking a ditch, or soft shoulder; (2) the driver is fatigued or driving too fast, and; (3) the driver overcorrects. Further, 80 percent of people killed in 15-passenger vans were not wearing seat belts, and NHTSA estimates that people wearing seat belts are 75 percent less likely to be killed in a rollover crash. Organizations should create a policy requiring each person to wear a seat belt, and carefully adhere to the policy. Drivers should check compliance before beginning the trip. Other problems noted were the vans being driven by individuals under 22 years of age (lack of experience) and excessive speed. (NHTSA, n.d.)

On August 10, 2005, Congress passed the Safe, Accountable, Flexible, Efficient Transportation Equity Act: A Legacy for Users (23 U.S.C. § 101). Section 10309, 15-Passenger Van Safety, addresses new safety standards related to the use of 15-passenger vans. The Act defines a 15-passenger van as a vehicle that seats 10 to 14 passengers, not including the driver. The Act prohibits a school or school system from purchasing or leasing a new 15-pasenger van if it will be used significantly by, or on behalf of, the school or school system to transport preprimary, primary, or secondary school students to or from school or an event related to school, unless the 15-passenger van complies with the motor vehicle standards prescribed for school buses and multi-function school activity buses under this title. This prohibition does not apply to the purchase or lease of a 15-passenger van under a contract executed before the date of enactment of this legislation. (NHTSA, 2008b)

High profile accidents involving 15-passenger vans have led to litigation, usually against the van manufacturer. As a result, vehicle manufacturers have made some modifications to help the stability of the vehicle, and have made recommendations for the driver of the vehicle. These adjustments may decrease litigation against the manufacturer, but may result in more legal action against the organization and driver. Sport and recreation managers should know the facts before purchasing or using a 15-passenger van. If the entity already owns a van, the manager should contact the manufacturer and the NHTSA to find out how to make the van safer.

Team travel by van has created a problem that does not have an easy solution. Budget restrictions and squad size are major considerations when choosing to use vans or other modes of transportation. If the organization chooses to use a 15-passenger van, Hawes (2000), LaVetter (2005) and McGregor (2000) have made the following policy recommendations that parallel the identified causes of van accidents:

- Eliminate 15-passenger vans, if possible, and travel more frequently by bus;

- Eliminate coaches driving any vehicles, and enforce stricter driver qualifications;

- Limit the number of passengers in vans to fewer than 10, remove the rear seats from 15-passenger vans, and place passengers and equipment forward of the van's rear axle;

- Limit to 300 miles or five hours the number of hours or mileage driven by each driver per day, and avoid travel between midnight and 6 a.m.;

- Check the van's tire pressure frequently–and before and after every trip;

- Confer with your organization's insurance company or risk-management consultants;.

- Schedule competition to permit travel by different teams sharing the same bus;

- Set age limits for the driver, hire outside drivers, and give extensive driver training;

- Require seat belts to be worn at all times;

- Stress the importance of adhering to speed limits and the possible need to adjust speed due to weather conditions;

- Monitor weather conditions, and establish policies that permit the person in charge to decide when to spend the night in a hotel rather than continuing driving in hazardous conditions;

- Review vehicle maintenance policies.

Policy Recommendations

Every organization should have written travel policies, and should ensure that everyone adheres to them. Prudent administrators should ask and answer the following questions before approving any travel: (1) What is the purpose of the trip, (2) who is travelling, (3) who is in charge, (4) who is allowed to drive, and (5) are emergency procedures in place? The links earlier in this section would be a good starting point for developing such a policy. The policy should also require the following documentation: (1) a passenger checklist, (2) a key contact checklist provided to everyone involved in the travel decision, (3) emergency procedures for breakdowns and accidents, (4) accident report forms, if needed, and (5) pre- and post-trip vehicle inspection checklists. (McGregor, 2000).

SIGNIFICANT CASE

Christopher Foster was a high school senior basketball player making a recruiting visit to Butler County Community College (BCCC). George Johnson, a volunteer driver acting on behalf of the BCCC coach, picked Foster up at the airport. Returning to the school, Johnson was involved in an accident that killed him, and severely injured Foster. Foster filed suit for injuries claiming negligence on behalf of both Johnson and BCCC. The primary issue in the case was whether Johnson was an "employee" of BCCC, thereby creating vicarious liability for the College. Among other legal issues involved in the case are negligence, damages, sufficiency of the evidence, vicarious liability through respondeat superior, comparative negligence, and course and scope of employment.

FOSTER & CLARK V. BOARD OF TRUSTEES OF BUTLER COUNTY COMMUNITY COLLEGE, ET AL.

United States District Court For The District Of Kansas
771 F. Supp. 1122, 1991 U.S. Dist. LEXIS 11003

FRANK G. THEIS, UNITED STATES DISTRICT JUDGE

This matter is before the court on the motions for new trial filed by defendant Douglas S. Pringle, Special Administrator for the Estate of George D. Johnson ("Pringle") (Doc. 152) and defendants Board of Trustees of Butler County Community College, Butler County Community College, and Randy Smithson (collectively, "the BCCC defendants") (Doc. 153). * * *

This case arose out of a motor vehicle collision occurring at the intersection of Airport/Yoder Road and U.S. Highway 50 in Reno County, Kansas on March 22, 1987. Plaintiff Christopher Foster was a passenger in a car driven by George Johnson. Johnson was travelling south on Airport Road. Plaintiff Gregory Clark was travelling east on Highway 50. Johnson failed to stop at the stop sign on Airport Road and collided with the tractor-trailer rig driven by plaintiff Clark. Johnson died as a result of the injuries he received in the accident. Foster and Clark were injured.

Foster, a native of Ohio, was a high school senior at the time of the accident. He was visiting Kansas on a recruiting visit at the request of defendant Randy Smithson, the head coach of the BCCC basketball team. Johnson picked Foster up at the Wichita airport at Smithson's request. Smithson had previously taken several other recruits to Hutchinson for the National Junior College Basketball Tournament. Contrary to the instructions given by Smithson, Johnson took Foster to Hutchinson to watch the game. Johnson telephoned Smithson from Hutchinson just prior to the collision. Smithson told Johnson to bring Foster to El Dorado. Johnson was en route to El Dorado when the collision occurred. * * *

At the close of the evidence, the court directed a verdict in favor of the plaintiffs on the issue of respondeat superior,

ruling that Johnson was the servant or employee of the BCCC defendants and was acting within the scope of his authority at the time of the accident. On February 27, 1991 the jury returned a verdict finding plaintiff Clark 10% at fault and defendants 90% at fault. Damages in the amount of $2,257,000 were awarded to plaintiff Foster and in the amount of $302,000 to plaintiff Clark. After reducing the judgment by Clark's 10% fault, the court entered judgment in the amount of $2,031,300 in favor of Foster and $271,800 in favor of Clark. These motions for new trial followed.

* * *

The BCCC defendants raise the following issues: (1) the verdict is contrary to the evidence; (2) the amount of damages awarded is so excessive as to appear to have been based on passion and prejudice; (3) the court improperly allowed the jury to consider testimony regarding Johnson's lack of liability insurance coverage and evidence regarding the proof of insurance that must be provided by a student who is operating his own automobile in connection with a school function; (4) the court improperly refused to submit to the jury the questions of whether Johnson was the employee of BCCC and whether Johnson was operating within the scope of his employment at the time of the accident; (5) the court improperly refused to submit the issue of plaintiff Foster's comparative negligence to the jury; (6) the court improperly refused to allow testimony concerning plaintiff Clark's opinion that he considered the intersection where the accident occurred to be a dangerous one. * * *

* * *

* * * It was stipulated that Johnson ran the stop sign at the intersection of Airport Road and Highway 50. This fact alone would have been sufficient to support a finding that

Johnson was 100% at fault, notwithstanding the defendants' accident reconstructionist who opined that Clark committed several driving errors. The evidence certainly was sufficient to support a finding that defendants were 90% at fault for the accident. * * * [T]he evidence was sufficient to support the damages awarded. The verdict was not clearly against the weight of the evidence.

* * *

B. Excessiveness of Verdict

* * *

As with all of its functions as trier of fact, the jury has wide discretion in determining the amount of damages that will fairly compensate the aggrieved party. * * *

> *Absent an award so excessive as to shock the judicial conscience and to raise an irresistible inference that passion, prejudice, corruption or other improper cause invaded the trial, the jury's determination of the damages is considered inviolate. Such bias, prejudice or passion can be inferred from excessiveness. However, a verdict will not be set aside on this basis unless it is so plainly excessive as to suggest that it was the product of such passion or prejudice on the part of the jury.*

* * *

The damage award to Clark is not so excessive as to shock the judicial conscience. The damages in this case included the normal personal injury damage components of past and future medical expenses, lost past and future income, pain and suffering and aggravation of pre-existing condition. The court also instructed the jury on loss of enjoyment of life as a component of the award for pain, suffering, disabilities, and disfigurement. * * *

* * *

C. Evidentiary Rulings

* * *

At trial, plaintiffs introduced evidence that the BCCC defendants were negligent in selecting Johnson as a gratuitous employee. An employer may be liable for injuries to a third person which are a direct result of the incompetence or unfitness of his employee when the employer was negligent in employing the employee or in retaining him in employment when the employer knew or should have known of such incompetence or unfitness. *Plains Resources, Inc. v. Gable*, 235 Kan. 580, 591, 682 P.2d 653 (1984). Johnson was unfit to drive a basketball recruit since he lacked a driver's license and liability insurance and his vehicle was not registered. The BCCC defendants could have discovered Johnson's unfitness for the task had any investigation been conducted. The evidence introduced by the plaintiffs was relevant to show the BCCC defendants' negligence. The evidence of Johnson's lack of liability insurance was relevant to show that the BCCC defendants failed to use due care in selecting Johnson to perform the task of transporting Foster.

* * *

2. BCCC transportation and vehicle policies

In connection with the direct negligence claim and the evidence of Johnson's lack of insurance, the plaintiffs offered evidence of BCCC policies regarding use of college and personal vehicles. The BCCC Policies and Procedures Manual provides in pertinent part:

> ### College Vehicle Policy
>
> **College Vehicles.** *All persons, included students, employees, and noncollege personnel, must have a driving record review and clearance. Requests for students and noncollege employees to drive college vehicles must be approved by the Director of Buildings and Grounds. These requests must be in writing and forwarded through the Business Office.*
>
> **Personal vehicles.** *In cases when a college vehicle has been officially requested and is not available, the person making the request may be reimbursed for mileage if using a personal vehicle. In cases when an instructor or sponsor is not able to drive a college vehicle, a student with proof of current liability insurance may be permitted to use his/her car and be reimbursed for mileage with prior approval from the Director of Buildings and Grounds.*

* * * The BCCC Athletic Policies and Procedures Manual provides that "School transportation must be used whenever possible. Private cars should be used only with permission of the athletic director." * * *

While these policies were not directly applicable since Johnson was not officially a coach, they indicated a general school policy of requiring an inquiry before allowing a teacher or coach to drive a BCCC vehicle and proof of liability insurance before allowing a student to use a personal vehicle for BCCC business. It was undisputed that Smithson did not obtain the permission of the athletic director before arranging for Johnson to transport Foster. This evidence was relevant to plaintiffs' claim that the BCCC defendants were directly negligent in appointing Johnson as a gratuitous employee charged with the duty of transporting Foster.

* * *

D. Directed Verdict on Respondeat Superior

At the close of the evidence, the court directed a verdict on two issues: that Johnson was the servant or employee of BCCC and that Johnson was acting within the scope of his authority at the time of the accident. The BCCC defendants challenge this ruling.

* * *

* * * Under Kansas law, the controlling test in determining the existence of agency, so that the doctrine of respondeat superior would apply, is the right to control the purported employee. *Hendrix*, 203 Kan. at 155; *see also Hughes v. Jones*, 206 Kan. 82, 88, 476 P.2d 588 (1970). When agency relationship is in issue, the party relying on the existence of an agency relationship to establish his claim has the burden of establishing the existence of the relationship by clear and satisfactory evidence. *Highland Lumber Co.*, 219 Kan. at 370.

An employer is not liable for a tortious act committed by his employee, unless the act is done by authority of the employer, either express or implied, or unless the act is done by the employee in the course or within the scope of his employment. *Beggerly v. Walker*, 194 Kan. 61, 64, 397 P.2d 395 (1964). Under Kansas law,

> An employee is acting within the scope of his authority when he is performing services for which he has been employed, or when he is doing anything which is reasonably incidental to his employment. The test is not necessarily whether the specific conduct was expressly authorized or forbidden by the employer, but whether such conduct should have been fairly foreseen from the nature of the employment and the duties relating to it.

Williams v. Community Drive-in Theater, Inc., 214 Kan. 359, 364, 520 P.2d 1296 (1974) (quoting PIK 7.04); *Hollinger v. Jane C. Stormont Hospital and Training School for Nurses*, 2 Kan. App. 2d 302, 311, 578 P.2d 1121 (1978). Whether an act is within the employee's scope of employment ordinarily presents a question to be determined by the jury. *Williams*, 214 Kan. at 365 (quoting 53 Am. Jur. 2d, *Master and Servant* § 427). The liability of the employer for the acts of the employee depends upon whether the employee, when he did the wrong, was acting in the prosecution of the employer's business and within the scope of his authority or whether he had stepped aside from the business and had done an individual wrong. *Hollinger*, 2 Kan. App. 2d at 311.

The determination of whether an employee was acting within the scope of his employment involves a consideration of the individual factual setting of each case, including objective as well as subjective considerations. *Focke v. United States*, 597 F. Supp. 1325, 1339 (D. Kan. 1982). Several factors are relevant to the determination of scope of employment. First, the key consideration in determining whether an employee is acting within the scope of employment is the purpose of the employee's act rather than the method of performance. This calls for consideration of the objective circumstances of the incident as well as the subjective thoughts of the employee. *Id.* at 1340-41. Second, the court must examine whether the employee has express or implied authority to do the acts in question, although in certain situations, an employer may be liable for the acts of the employee, even if the acts are done in ex-

cess of the authority conferred. *Id.* at 1341. Third, the determination of whether an employee's acts are incidental to his employment involves a consideration of whether the employee's acts were reasonably foreseeable by the employer. Finally, the time at which the agent commits the alleged wrongful act is a factor to be considered, although it is not accorded great weight. *Id.*

Defendants have not argued that Smithson lacked the authority to hire Johnson to assist in Smithson's recruiting duties. Johnson could be an employee or servant even though no compensation was paid or expected. Whether compensation was paid or not paid is not determinative. *See Williams v. Community Drive-in Theater, Inc.*, 214 Kan. 359, 367, 520 P.2d 1296 (1974) (despite the fact that the employee was not paid by her employer for her services, she was the employer's employee at the crucial time). Additionally, it is not necessary that there be a formal employment contract.

The evidence that Johnson was acting as the employee of Smithson and was acting within the scope of his authority came from the testimony of defendant Smithson. Smithson had the right to control and indeed exercised significant control over Johnson. Smithson testified that he instructed Johnson on what to do that evening. Smithson testified that he instructed Johnson to pick up Foster from the airport, get him something to eat, take him to the motel in El Dorado and await Smithson's return from Hutchinson. Smithson gave Johnson twenty dollars to pay for dinner. Smithson further testified that when Johnson called late that evening from Hutchinson, Smithson told Johnson to bring Foster back to El Dorado as quickly and as safely as possible. Smithson gave Johnson directions on the two routes available from Hutchinson to El Dorado, via Highway 96 or via Airport Road/Highway 50. Smithson indicated that he used the Airport Road/ Highway 50 route. Smithson told Johnson to ask for directions to Airport Road from where Johnson was located.

Plaintiff's Exhibit 25 (Smithson's statement) indicates that Smithson initially intended Johnson to bring Foster to the basketball game in Hutchinson. Later, Smithson decided to have Johnson instead take Foster directly to the motel in El Dorado. Given this background, it would be foreseeable that Johnson might take Foster to Hutchinson instead of El Dorado. Driving to Hutchinson would therefore be within the scope of the employment.

Assuming that Johnson had deviated from the scope of his employment by going to Hutchinson, Johnson re-entered the scope of his employment after he talked to Smithson. Smithson specifically directed Johnson to return to El Dorado. Johnson was performing the service for which he had been employed, in the manner in which he had been instructed, when the accident occurred. The purpose of Johnson's acts was to return Foster to El Dorado. Johnson had express authority to drive Foster back to El Dorado. It was (or should have been) reasonably foreseeable to

Smithson that Johnson could become involved in an automobile accident on the way to El Dorado. Johnson committed the negligent act while he was performing the task which was appointed to him—taking Foster to El Dorado.

Defendants argued at trial that Johnson was only doing a favor for Smithson. Viewing the facts most favorably to the BCCC defendants, Johnson was a volunteer. He was doing a favor for Smithson. However, the fact that this undertaking was gratuitous is not fatal to the existence of an employer/employee relationship.

* * *

Construing the evidence in the light most favorable to the BCCC defendants, the evidence points only one way. There were no conflicts in the evidence. There was no evidence from which a reasonable mind could conclude that Johnson either was not the employee of BCCC or was not acting within the scope of his authority at the time of the collision. There was no evidence upon which the jury could properly find for the BCCC defendants on the issue

of employment and scope. Defendants have pointed to no such evidence in the record.

* * *

Having reviewed the evidence presented at trial, the court finds that the amount of the award to plaintiff Clark was not excessive. The amount was supported by the evidence. The court shall not grant a remittitur.

IT IS BY THE COURT THEREFORE ORDERED that defendant Pringle's motion for a new trial (Doc. 152) is hereby denied as to plaintiff Clark and is moot as to plaintiff Foster.

IT IS FURTHER ORDERED that defendants Board of Trustees of Butler County Community College, Butler County Community College, and Randy Smithson's motion for a new trial (Doc. 153) is hereby denied as to plaintiff Clark and is moot as to plaintiff Foster.

At Wichita, Kansas, this 12th day of July, 1991.

CASES ON THE SUPPLEMENTAL CD

Clement v. Griffin, (634 So. 2d 412, La.App. 4 Cir. 1994). This court discusses the duty owed by the defendant Community College to (1) maintain the vehicle, (2) select a qualified driver, and (3) properly train the driver. The court also discussed the defendant's vicarious duty to insure the driver properly operated the vehicle. In terms of transportation risk management, this case serves as a model course in "how *not* to do it."

Dixon v. Whitfield, 654 So. 2d 1230 (Fla. Dist. Ct. App., 1st Dist.). This Florida case affirms that schools have "a duty of reasonable care in providing (students) with safe transportation," but also verifies that schools have authority to hire independent contractors to operate the school buses. The defendants

were found to be independent contractors rather than employees. By hiring independent contractors, the school avoided liability for the student's death.

Myricks v. Lynwood Unified School District, 87 Cal. Rptr. 2d 734 (Cal. App. 2 Dist. 1999). A girls' summer basketball team made up of players from their high school team, and coached by their high school coach, took an out-of-state trip to play in summer basketball tournaments. After suffering injuries in an accident, team members sued the school as well as the city (which provided some financial support). The court held this was not a school-sponsored activity, so the school was not liable. The court also found that the city was not liable for providing only financial support.

QUESTIONS YOU SHOULD BE ABLE TO ANSWER

1. Name numerous specific duties related to providing safe transportation.

2. What are the benefits of using an independent contractor as opposed to other means of transportation?

3. What are the criteria courts use to determine whether a company is an independent contractor?

4. Discuss the relative merits of travelling in organization-owned, employee-owned, or non-employed owned vehicles, buses or 15-passenger vans.

5. Prepare a basic transportation policy for your organization, including specific rules and regulations relating to transporting participants to an activity 200 miles from your normal meeting place.

REFERENCES

Cases

Barnhart v. Cabrillo Community College, 90 Cal. Rptr. 2d 709 (Cal. App. 6 Dist. 1999).

Bolton v. Tulane University of Louisiana, 692 So.2d 1113 (La. App. 4 Cir. 1997).

Clement v. Griffin (634 So.2d 412, La.App. 4 Cir. 1994).

Foster v. Board of Trustees of Butler County Community College, 771 F. Supp. 1122 (D. Kan. 1991).

Murray v. Zarger, 642 A.2d 575 (Pa. Cmwlth. 1994).

Myricks v. Lynwood Unified School District, 87 Cal. Rptr. 2d 734 (Cal. App. 2 Dist. 1999).

Smith v. Gardner, 998 F. Supp. 708 (S.D. Miss. 1998).

Publications

Federal Motor Carrier Safety Administration (n.d.). *Moving Kids Safely—A guide to hiring charter transportation*. Retrieved April 20, 2009 from: http://www.fmcsa.dot.gov/safety-security/safety-initiatives/kids/brochure/textonly.html

Hawes, K. (2000, August 28). Warning: Road Risks Ahead. Precautions Reduce Dangers of Van-related Travel. *National Collegiate Athletic Association*, retrieved March 26, 2009, from: http://www.ncaa.org/wps/ncaa?ContentID=26469

LaVetter, D. (2005, December 5). Safety Must Drive Decisions in Van Use. *National Collegiate Athletic Association*, retrieved March 26, 2009, from: http://www.ncaa.org/wps/ncaa?ContentID=5329

Lavigne, P. (2009, March 31). Bus Safety an Issue for Colleges. *ESPN*, retrieved April 1, 2009, from: http://sports.espn.go.com/espn/otl/news/story?id=3997988&userid=63b283733d372ce0b01b1146c9fca4d4&messageid=308

McGregor, I. (2000, March 1). Travel Trouble: Developing Transportation Policies and Procedures. *Athletic Business*, Retrieved March 13, 2009, from: http://athleticbusiness.com/articles/article.aspx?articleid=162&zoneid=59

National Conference of State Legislatures (2009). Information for State Volunteer Driver Liability Laws. Retrieved from: http://www.ncsl.org/programs/transportation/SVDLLaws.htm

National Highway Traffic Safety Administration (NHTSA) (2008a). *Fatalities to Occupants of 15-Passenger Vans, 1997-2006*. Retrieved from: http://www-nrd.nhtsa.dot.gov/Pubs/810947.pdf

National Highway Traffic Safety Administration (NHTSA) (2008b). *15-Passenger Van Safety Actions Update*. Retrieved from: http://www.nhtsa.dot.gov/cars/problems/studies/15PassVans/VAP_rev1_2008.pdf

National Highway Traffic Safety Administration (NHTSA) (n.d.) *Reducing the Risk of Rollover Crashes in 15-Passenger Vans*. Retrieved from: http://nhtsa.gov/cars/problems/studies/15PassVans/

National Transportation Safety Board (NTSB) (2003). *Spatial Disorientation Cited in Crash of Airplane Carrying Oklahoma State University Athletes*. Retrieved from: http://www.ntsb.gov/pressrel/2003/030123a.htm

National Transportation Safety Board (NTSB) (2007). *NTSB Welcomes Move to Make Collegiate Team Travel Safer*. Retrieved from: http://www.ntsb.gov/pressrel/2007/070124.htm

Legislation

Safe, Accountable, Flexible, Efficient Transportation Equity Act: A Legacy For Users, 23 U.S.C. § 101 (2008).

Texas Charitable Immunity and Liability Act of 1987, Texas Civil Practice and Remedies Code § 84.001, et. seq. (2007).

Volunteer Protection Act of 1997, 42 U. S. C. § 14501, et. seq. (2009).

2.36   Products Liability

—Rebecca J. Mowrey
MILLERSVILLE UNIVERSITY OF PENNSYLVANIA

Imagine for a moment a local fitness center without equipment; an indoor climbing facility minus a climbing wall or safety harnesses; a track and field team without starting blocks, hurdles, or any jumping or throwing apparatus. Without their equipment, the first two businesses would merely be empty buildings, and the track and field team would not be very competitive. These examples make us acutely aware of how dependent the sport and recreation industries are upon specialized products. As recreation and sport professionals, we make countless decisions with regard to product selection, purchase, installation, use, and maintenance. Using these products permits our constituents to engage in thrilling recreational, competitive, or sport adventures such as skimming along ocean waves via a sailboard, negotiating challenging descents and turns on a mountain bike, or pursuing personal bests as an amateur or professional athlete.

When no one is injured as a result of product use, there is a tendency to throw caution to the wind and just have fun. However, as soon as injuries or property damages occur and lawsuits are filed, people across the sport and recreation product-chain may be surprised to realize their potential involvement. **Products liability** relates primarily to the negligent action of a manufacturer or seller who produces a defective product; hence the product is unreasonably dangerous to the user. While it is true that most professionals working in sport and recreation are not manufacturing or selling products, claims of products liability may provide recourse against liable parties involved *throughout* the chain of production and distribution of products. Therefore, sport and recreation professionals may be deemed as suppliers, included among those who loan, rent, or assign equipment to others, and can be liable if defective equipment is issued and the supplier should have known about the defect.

A case example that illustrates this point is found in *Everett v. Bucky Warren*, (1978). The court held that the coach, acting as a supplier, negligently selected for and supplied to his team defective and dangerous hockey helmets. Therefore, a sport or recreation management professional may be involved in products liability cases as one who selects, purchases, receives, installs, maintains, and uses products.

CATEGORIES OF PRODUCT DEFECTS

In this section we will examine the three categories of product defects commonly recognized by the courts and classified by the Restatement (third) of Torts (1997); namely, **design defects, manufacturing defects, and marketing defects**. Manufacturers make many decisions regarding products, including design, material selection, and construction. At each stage of a product's life, the product may fail or be defective, thereby rendering the product to be unreasonably dangerous. We will first examine how things might go wrong with a product from its very inception, the design stage.

Design defects occur in products that cause harm as a result of issues related to the faulty design of a product. Lots of good ideas do not hold up well to the requirements or demands of actual usage. We have an example of a design defect in *Brett v. Hillerich & Bradsby Co.*, (2001). The Hillerich and Bradsby Company manufactured baseball bats. Designers working with Hillerich and Bradsby discovered ways to make use of new aluminum materials resulting in improved performance by batters. High school pitcher and plaintiff Jeremy Brett, was seriously injured when hit by a ball coming off of one of these newly designed bats. He alleged that the Air Attack 2, an aluminum composite bat designed by Hillerich & Bradsby Co., had a design defect because it allowed batted balls to reach dangerous speeds, exceeding the reaction time needed for pitchers to protect themselves. The decision in this case was in favor of Brett, resulting in several states banning the use of Air Attack 2 and other similarly designed aluminum bats.

Manufacturing defects refer to production errors that result in flaws to an otherwise defect—free product, design, and manufacturing process. In *Diversified Products Corp. v. Faxon* (1987), Faxon purchased a weight machine manufactured by Diversified Products Corporation. He assembled the machine according to the manufacturer's instructions. While he was performing a standing curl, an eyebolt on the curl bar broke, causing him to fall backward. The eyebolt was a factory-assembled piece of the machine and Faxon had not altered this bar nor tampered with the eyebolt. Faxon's fall resulted in serious injuries to his spine. The court decided in favor of Faxon, finding sufficient evidence to support the plaintiff's claim that the eyebolt was defective while it was still in the possession of Diversified Products Corporation, and that this was a manufacturing defect that the Corporation should have detected prior to selling the machine to Faxon.

Marketing defects occur when the warnings or instructions accompanying a product are inadequate, rendering the product not reasonably safe. Warnings must address both foreseeable misuses of a product (van der Smissen, 1990; *Whitacre v. Halo Optical Products, Inc.*, 1987) as well as dangers inherent in the normal use of the product. In some jurisdictions, even if there is an absence of design and manufacturing defect, failure to warn may stand alone as a cause of action (*Garrett v. Nissen*, 1972; *Pavlides v. Galveston Yacht Basin*, 1984). We see an example of marketing defect in *Sullivan v. Nissen Trampoline Company*, (1967). *Sullivan* was using a mini–trampoline called an Aqua Diver. This product consisted of a mini–trampoline that people could bounce on and then dive into a pool or lake. As Sullivan bounced on the Aqua Diver, her foot became caught in the webbing that connected the trampoline to the base. The Nissen Trampoline Company did not provide any warning labels alerting users to this potential risk even though their own pre-market testing had shown this to be a risk.

We see another example of marketing defect in *Dudley Sports Co. v. Schmitt*, (1972). Schmitt, a high school student, was simply sweeping the storage room floor where a baseball-pitching machine was located. As he was sweeping the floor, the throwing arm of the unplugged and inactive pitching machine suddenly and unexpectedly snapped forward causing severe facial injuries to Schmitt. The court ruled that the manufacturer was negligent in designing the machine without a protective guard around the throwing arm mechanism. The court also concluded that Dudley Sports Co. failed to provide an adequate warning about the specific risks associated with their pitching machines, namely that the machine's throwing arm could be triggered when unplugged. According to the court, the warning label only implied that the machine could be dangerous when in use.

Now that we are familiar with the three categories of defects that might make one liable for harm associated with products, we will examine the three legal causes of action associated with products liability as well as the defenses for each.

CAUSES OF ACTION AND DEFENSES

Negligence, strict liability, and breach of warranty are the primary legal theories or causes of action under which recovery for products liability may be sought. In Section 2.10 you read about negligence and strict liability. To review, **negligence** is an unintentional tort that injures an individual in person, property, or reputation. **Strict liability** means that a defendant can be held liable without fault. In the context of product liability, strict liability would apply when there is nothing wrong with the design, manufacturing, or warning. You might be wondering how that is possible. Courts have held that some products are just too dangerous to exist. Therefore, if a manufacturer decided to design, manufacture and market such a product, an injured party could claim, under strict liability, that the product could not possibly be made safe and should not have been produced in the first place. **Breach of warranty** occurs when a product fails to fulfill either the expressed or implied warranty.

In Table 2.36.1 we will now examine the three causes of action under which recovery for products liability may be sought and the defenses to each cause of action.

Table 2.36.1 Common Causes of Action and Defenses Under Products Liability Law

Negligence	Strict Liability	Breach of Warranty
A manufacturer, supplier, or seller may be sued for negligence in design, testing, manufacturing, inspecting, packaging, labeling or distribution of a defective product), or for failure to warn (failure to warn users of the non-obvious risks presented by the product, including the dangers of misusing the product).	This cause of action may prevail when a product is deemed to be so inherently, and therefore unreasonably, dangerous that it cannot truly be made safe; regardless of the amount of care given to the design, construction, labeling, and inspection. For example, a jury may conclude that street luge is inherently dangerous and should not occur, thus finding those who manufacture street luge equipment liable using the theory of strict liability. No defense to strict liability is available if (1) the product is determined to be unreasonably dangerous, (2) a defect existed at the time of the sale, and (3) the product was used properly and was the cause of harm.	When a product fails to perform in a way that is promised (warranted), whether this warranty is expressed or implied, a breach of warranty has occurred. (See remainder of section for discussion of expressed and implied warranty).
Defenses to a Negligence Claim Include:	**Defenses to a Strict Liability Claim Include:**	**Defenses to a Breach of Warranty Claim Include:**
No evidence of duty, breach, proximate cause or harm.	1. Product was altered following purchase or misused in an unforeseeable manner by the plaintiff.	1. The product was altered.
Specifically:	2. An adequate warning was provided and/or secondary assumption of risk applied to the plaintiff.	2. The product was misused.
1. Product defect is unproven.	3. Wear and tear of the product, due to use and age of the product, was appropriate and predictable.	3. The product was not properly installed.
2. Product defect is not the cause of the harm.	4. The actions of the plaintiff contributed to the harm.	4. The user failed to properly maintain the product.
3. Evidence that an adequate warning of non-obvious risk was provided and assumed.	5. See discussion of the risk–utility balancing test.	5. The actions of the plaintiff contributed to the harm.
4. The danger/risk was open and obvious.		6. An adequate warning was provided and/or secondary assumption of risk applied to the plaintiff.
5. The failure to warn was not the cause of the harm.		
6. The actions of the plaintiff contributed to the harm.		
7. Reasonable care was used by the manufacturer, supplier, or seller; however, the defect was not detectable via reasonable care.		

Strict Liability Considerations

Now that we have the basics of product liability covered, we will examine some issues related to strict liability a bit further. Typically only manufacturers and sellers are subject to strict liability for defective products. In *Escola v. Coca-Cola Bottling Co. of Fresno* (1944), Justice Traynor summarizes the burden strict liability places upon manufacturers to resist bringing to market products that are hazardous to life and health.

> *Even if there is no negligence, however, public policy demands that responsibility be fixed wherever it will most effectively reduce the hazards to life and health inherent in defective products that reach the market. It is evident that the manufacturer can anticipate some hazards and guard against the recurrence of others, as the public cannot.*

So how does one determine if a product is unreasonably dangerous? Think of the manufacturers of modern roller-coasters and other adventure products. Furthermore, what one person thinks is unreasonable might be considered tame to another individual. Without a consistent gauge for measuring or determining what is "reasonable" and "unreasonable," product manufacturers may place themselves in jeopardy of strict liability. One solution might be the use of a **risk-utility balancing test** (Restatement (third) of Torts (1997)) to determine whether or not a product design is unreasonably dangerous. Under this test, a product is considered unreasonably dangerous if the dangers outweigh the social utility of the product. The factors commonly considered in risk-utility balancing are as follows:

1. The gravity of the danger,

2. The likelihood of injury,

3. The obviousness of the danger,

4. The feasibility and expense of an alternate design,

5. The common knowledge of consumers,

6. The adequacy of warnings,

7. The usefulness and desirability of the product as designed.

By examining a product against these seven factors of the risk-utility balancing test, those associated with product design and development are better situated to defend against strict liability. We will now turn our attention toward special considerations associated with breach of warranty as a cause of action in product liability cases.

Breach of Warranty Considerations

The traditional common law rule regarding warranties is that the plaintiff must have entered into a contractual relationship, or privity of contract,[1] with the defendant to claim breach of warranty as a cause of action. Many states no longer require privity of contract, as claims of breach of warranty are now primarily governed by the **Uniform Commercial Code (UCC)**. This Code provides for assumption of risk, misuse of the product, and failure to follow stated directions as potential defenses to a breach of warranty claim. Of further import, in the three alternative versions of the UCC, the classes of people to whom the warranty extends are defined. For example, in Alternative A, the version adopted by the most jurisdictions, the seller is liable for the personal injuries to the "buyer, members of the buyer's family, and guests in the buyer's home." Under the Alternative A version of the UCC, a seller sending athletic equipment home with a purchaser would need to provide guidance regarding where and how it should be stored and secured so siblings or other family members or house guests would not be injured by the equipment.

Under the UCC, implied warranties must accompany products. These warranties include the **implied warranty of merchantability**, promising that a product is "of fair average quality," and the **implied warranty of fitness**, promising that a product is "fit for the ordinary purposes for which such goods are used." (UCC 2-314). More specifically, the implied warranty of fitness addresses the product warranty promise extended to the buyer/user who is relying on the seller's expertise to provide an appropriate product fit for his/her particular purpose. In *Filler v. Rayex Corp.* (1970), a high school baseball coach had purchased sunglasses from the defendant based upon the marketing guarantees featuring "instant eye protection." The Rayex advertisements and product packaging specifically identified baseball players as an ideal user group for the Rayex product, as the players would benefit by using these "scientific lenses." Filler lost his right eye when a baseball hit the Rayex lens and it shattered. As explained by the court of appeals "Since they lacked the safety features of plastic or shatterproof glass, the sunglasses were in truth not fit for baseball playing, the particular purpose for which they were sold" (*Filler v. Rayex Corp.*, 1970, p. 338).

Another consideration related to breach of warranty is **misrepresentation of warranty**. This occurs when claims are made, primarily in the marketing or selling phase of a product's life, which are untrue or misleading. When the user's actions are based upon the misrepresentation of warranty and he/she is harmed or property is harmed, the claim to products liability may be misrepresentation of warranty. As an example of misrepresentation of warranty, we will examine *Hauter v. Zogarts*, (1975). Louise Hauter purchased a "Golfing Gizmo" for Fred, her 13-year-old son. The Gizmo consisted of a golf ball attached to an elasticized cord that was secured to the ground with metal pegs. Zogarts, the defendant and manufacturer of the Golfing Gizmo,

---

[1]"Privity of contract is one of the most basic rules of the common law of contract and one of the defining tests for the validity of any contract. This doctrine essentially determines who is a party to contract and who may rely upon the rights granted under the contract to sue another" (Lim, 2008).

marketed the product as a device that would improve one's swing with this claim: "COMPLETELY SAFE BALL WILL NOT HIT PLAYER." Fred Hauter suffered permanent brain damage after the cord wrapped around his golf club and the ball hit his head with great force. The Hauter's successfully sued, alleging misrepresentation of warranty and breach of expressed and implied liability.

They also successfully sued under strict liability as the court found that the Golfing Gizmo was too dangerous to exist. Although the Hauter case was decided before the Risk-Utility Balancing Test was established, it is easy to see that the Golfing Gizmo would likely fail on all seven factors of the Risk-Utility Balancing Test. In Hauter, the court ruled in favor of the plaintiff on all four causes of action. Regarding the charge of misinformation, the court found that the defendant breached the implied warranty of merchantability as the golf training device, intended for use by novices, would likely injure novice users.

Please note that the marketing on the package encouraged the user to "drive the ball with full power." The combination of this encouragement and the "COMPLETELY SAFE" promotion, according to the court, served to significantly misrepresent the risk to the user. It is virtually impossible to ever claim that a product is "100 percent" anything; "completely safe"; or even "safe" or "foolproof." It is best not to make such claims as part of programs or activities associated with sport or recreation.

In summary, design defects, manufacturing defects, or marketing defects resulting in property damage or personal injury to a user or bystander may lead to products liability for a manufacturer, seller, distributer, or supervisor. The causes of action used by plaintiffs in products liability cases will be negligence, strict liability, and/or breach of warranty.

Although some products are simply too dangerous to exist, other useful and quality products also disappear as a result or products liability claims. Sport and recreation professionals are wise to protect against these products liability cases as cost containment and free enterprise issues, in addition to and secondary to the desire to keep constituents as safe as possible. What is our connection to cost containment and free enterprise? When a manufacturer is successfully sued for design, manufacturing, or marketing defects; in many cases that corporation is hampered financially to the point of bankruptcy, or the corporation elects to no longer participate in the segment of the industry in which it has been sued. The result of these corporate decisions has a palpable impact upon sport and recreation professionals, resulting in less choice for consumers seeking products, and less competitive pricing. Alternatively, in many cases design improvements are the outcome of products liability cases. As you read the following case, consider all that you have learned from reading this section. The introduction to the Significant Case provides questions for you to respond to as you read through this design defect case.

SIGNIFICANT CASE

This is an ideal sample case for a products liability section as this design defect case involves all three products liability causes of action. This case will provide you with the opportunity to do some critical thinking, problem—solving, and apply some of your knowledge regarding products liability while you read. The questions and suggestions in the remainder of this case introduction will guide you. As you read, make note of the potential liability of different types of defendants, including the manufacturer, retail distributor, and general contractor for the basketball court. What defenses are argued by Cornell University regarding the Institution's duty of care to plaintiff Traub? What issues must the jury consider with regard to what an ordinary person would assume as inherent risks of playing basketball? What is the relevance of Traub's secondary assumption of risk to the case? The court endorsed the use of a risk-utility balancing test, but for what purpose? Lastly, why does the court mention whether or not dunking is a foreseeable use of a basketball hoop?

TRAUB V. CORNELL UNIVERSITY

United States District Court for the Northern District of New York
1998 U.S. Dist. LEXIS 5530

I. Factual Background
A. The Incident
On the date of his accident, Darren—who had been a student at Cornell for approximately ten months—played "pick-up" basketball on the Cornell basketball court. * * * After one or two games, Darren and several other players took turns attempting to dunk a basketball through one of the goals. As Darren descended from his second try, the heel and first joints below the fingertips of his right hand made contact with the rigid rim of the hoop. Darren fell to the macadam surface of the court to the right of the goal. * * * His body landed on top of his wrists. At this point, he was on his right side with his feet angled to the left.

B. Darren's Prior Basketball Experience
Darren began playing basketball approximately ten years prior to his accident. He received training in basketball from camp counselors and basketball coaches and himself coached five to twelve-year-olds. Darren played at the Cornell court approximately fifteen to twenty times prior to his accident. He had tried to dunk a basketball many times but never succeeded. Darren also never jumped high enough to make contact with the rim and never saw anyone else fall backward after making contact with a rigid rim. He claims that he was unaware of the danger posed by dunking a basketball into a goal with a rigid rim.

C. The Basketball Court and the Goals
In the mid-1980s Cornell began plans for a construction project that included the basketball court where Darren fell. Cornell's landscape architect specified a particular Burke model as the basketball equipment for the court. Although Burke's model package included backboard, uprights, supports, and fittings, Gared Sports, Inc. ("Gared"), a third-party defendant, actually manufactured the hoops,

rims, and goals. The rims of the goals were rigid, that is, they did not give way on contact.

M & B, the general contractor for Cornell's project, acquired the specified goals from Cushman, a sports equipment retailer. M & B constructed the court as specified in Cornell's specifications and installed the goals in accordance with the instructions accompanying them.

After completing the project in fall 1988, Cornell opened the basketball court for recreational use by "members of the Cornell community." Cornell provided no supervision and imposed no policies or guidelines for use of the court. Cornell also did not post any warnings on the court.

* * *

III. Overview of the Parties' Claims
Central to each of plaintiffs' claims is their contention that rigid rims unreasonably increase the risk to a player of attempting to dunk a basketball. According to plaintiffs' experts, when a player's hands come into contact with a rigid rim, the forward momentum of the player's upper body halts while the player's legs continue to swing under the basket. This pendulum-like effect increases the likelihood of an awkward fall. Plaintiffs' experts suggest that a breakaway hoop, which gives way on contact, is less likely to cause a player to have an awkward fall.

Defendants claim that they are entitled to summary judgment for several reasons. First, defendant Cornell argues that the Traubs' negligence claim fails because Darren assumed all risks inherent in playing basketball with a rigid hoop. The remaining defendants—Burke, M & B, and Cushman—argue that the Traubs' strict products liability claims should be dismissed because rigid rims are not unreasonably dangerous or defective. These defendants also argue that the negligence counts should be dismissed because (1) any risks presented by a rigid rim to a player attempting to dunk a ball are obvious; (2) Darren Traub assumed the risk of playing basketball with a rigid rim; and (3) the alleged defect was not the proximate cause of Darren's accident. Burke, M & B, and Cushman also contend that I should (1) dismiss the Traubs' express warranty claims because the defendants made no affirmation on which a purchaser relied and (2) dismiss the Traubs' implied warranty claims because there is no proof that the hoop and backboard were unsafe for the ordinary purpose for which they were intended. M & B also separately argues that it cannot be held liable because (1) it completed the court project in accordance with specifications given to it in Cornell and there were no obvious defects in those specifications and (2) it is not a seller within the meaning of the Uniform Commercial Code or the case law defining strict products liability and negligence.

* * *

DISCUSSION

II. Cornell

The Traubs sued Cornell only on a negligence theory. Cornell urges that it had no duty to Darren because he assumed all ordinary and perceivable risks of playing basketball on a court using a hoop with a rigid rim.

Although assumption of the risk generally is no longer an absolute defense in a negligence action, it sometimes functions like an absolute defense because it eliminates the duty that might otherwise be owed to a plaintiff who assumes the risk of engaging in a particular activity. Participants in an athletic activity consent "to those injury-causing events which are known, apparent or reasonably foreseeable consequences of their participation."

* * *

Cornell contends that Darren clearly assumed the risk of jumping high to dunk a ball because "what goes up must come down." The school argues that in light of Darren's years of basketball experience, his prior experience on the Cornell court, and the clear view he had of the hoop, he cannot credibly argue that he was unaware of the risks of dunking or of the fact that the hoop had a rigid rim. However, Darren does not claim he was unaware of the risk of falling when he attempted to dunk or of the fact that the hoop had a rigid rim, but rather that he was unaware of the enhanced risk presented by a rigid rim. See Traub Aff. pp 2-3. According to Dr. Marc A. Rabinoff, a professor of human performance, sport, and leisure studies and one of plaintiffs' experts, the enhanced risk of which Darren complains results from a phenomenon known as "hanging up," which occurs when a player's fingers, hands, and wrists come into contact with a rigid basketball hoop and "'hang up' momentarily on the rim." As the forward motion of the player's hands stops briefly, the legs and body continue in motion and swing under the basketball goal. Consequently, the player has no effective way to get his legs back under his torso, falls with his back angled toward the ground, and has an increased likelihood of serious injury.

* * *

Rabinoff also states that the danger of hanging-up "is not well known to amateur basketball players" * * * The question, then, is whether Darren's testimony that he lacked an appreciation of the danger presented by dunking with a solid rim is adequate to create an issue of fact on assumption of risk. Darren stated that he had never before jumped high enough to "hang up" on the rim and that he had never seen anyone else fall backward or be injured from "hanging up." Defendants argue that this testimony fails to create an issue of fact because "any person beyond the age of majority who moves in a forward direction and leaps into the air toward a stationary object must be deemed to be aware of the risk that his/her body may make contact with the stationary object which may result in halting the forward momentum of the body." Defendants rely on Section 496D, comment d, of the Restatement (Second) of Torts which indicates that "there are some risks as to which no adult will be believed if he says that he did not know or understand them." This comment does not apply to the phenomenon of hanging up. The examples cited in the comment—the risk of being burned by fire, drowning in water, or falling from a height—are all risks that every adult would indeed understand. In contrast, the risk of having one's fall distorted by hanging up on a rigid object is not necessarily one that would be perceived by every adult.

* * *

Therefore, I must deny Cornell's summary judgment motion on Count I.

III. M & B

Plaintiffs allege claims in negligence, express and implied warranty, and strict products liability against M & B. For varying reasons, each claim fails. M & B offers uncontroverted proof that it followed Cornell's specifications in procuring and installing the hoop and rims. Therefore, in order to hold M & B liable in negligence, the Traubs must show that "the defects [in the design were] so glaring and out of the ordinary as to bring home to the contractor that it was doing something which would be likely to cause injury." * * * Plaintiffs do not identify any defect in the specifications that was so glaring that M & B should have refused to construct the court in accordance with the specifications. Therefore, I grant M & B's motion insofar as it requests dismissal of Count X.

M & B also argues that it is entitled to dismissal of the Traubs' express and implied warranty claims because the transfer of the basketball hoops from M & B to Cornell was not a sale within the meaning of the Uniform Commercial Code warranty provisions.

* * *

The Cornell contract provided for the construction of a recreational area and primarily involved excavation, grading, masonry, paving, concrete, installation, and landscaping. The contract also specified, however, that M & B procure and install a specific model Burke basketball goal. The price of the goal was less than one half of one percent of the total contract price. Long estimates that since M & B's incorporation in 1975, the company has installed no more than twelve to twenty-four basketball goals of any type. M & B has never entered into a contract, the sole or primary purpose of which was to furnish a basketball goal.

* * *

In a "mixed" contract involving both goods and services, the Uniform Commercial Code's warranties do not apply if the service-oriented portions of the transaction predominate over the sales transactions. The uncontroverted facts described above establish that the service aspects of M & B's contract with Cornell predominated over the sales aspects. Therefore, Counts XII and XIII of the complaint must be dismissed.

M & B also argues that the Traubs' strict products liability counts must be dismissed because M & B is no more than a casual or occasional seller of basketball goals. * * * a plaintiff cannot hold a seller liable on a strict products liability theory if the seller "is not engaged in the sale of the product in issue as a regular part of its business." (citing Restatement [Second] of Torts § 402 A, comment f). The policy reasons for the distinction between regular and casual sellers are that (1) regular sellers—unlike casual sellers—can exert pressure on manufacturers for improved safety because of their ongoing relationship with the manufacturer; (2) regular sellers "can recover increased costs within their commercial dealings, or through contribution and or indemnification in litigation; "and (3) by marketing certain products as a regular part of their business, regular sellers assume[] a special responsibility to the public, which has come to expect them to stand behind their goods."

* * *

A contractor who buys only twelve to twenty-four basketball goals in a twenty year period is not in a good position to exert pressure on manufacturers to increase safety standards. This is especially true where the contractor is bound to buy the goal stated in the specifications. In addition, a contractor who buys equipment mandated by the owner cannot be said to be putting its reputation behind the product purchased. Therefore, the Traubs' strict products liability claims against M & B also must be dismissed.

IV. Cushman and Burke

Plaintiffs seek to hold Burke and Cushman liable on theories of express warranty, implied warranty, negligence and strict products liability.

A. Strict Products Liability

The Traubs' strict products liability claims against Burke and Cushman rest on allegations of defective design, defective manufacture, failure to warn, and failure to recall. Because plaintiffs submitted no evidence the rims were improperly manufactured, that claim must be dismissed. Both the failure to warn and the failure to recall claims assume that the design of the rim presented unreasonable dangers. Defendants thus urge that all three claims should be dismissed because plaintiffs can offer no evidence of defective design.

A plaintiff can hold a manufacturer liable in strict products liability for a design defect regardless of the manufacturer's knowledge of the defect. Strict liability may also be imposed on retailers and distributors. To hold a seller or manufacturer liable for a design defect, the plaintiff must establish that the product was "designed so that it was not reasonably safe and . . . the defective design was a substantial factor in causing plaintiff's injury." The plaintiff has the initial burden of showing that the product "was not reasonably safe because there was a substantial likelihood of harm and it was feasible to design the product in a safer manner." "[A] defectively designed product is one which, at the time it leaves the seller's hands, is in a condition not reasonably contemplated by the ultimate consumer and is unreasonably dangerous for its intended use." The product must be safe for its intended use "as well as an unintended yet reasonably foreseeable use." .2d 115, 348 N.E.2d 571 (1976). Plaintiffs urge that a rigid hoop is not reasonably safe because it is more likely to cause injury in the course of dunking than a break-away hoop. Defendants first contend that plaintiffs have not offered any competent proof that the rigid hoop is more likely to cause injury than a break-away hoop.

Plaintiffs' proof on the issue of design defect is contained in the affidavits of their experts. As noted previously, plaintiffs' experts claim that contact with a rigid rim distorts a player's descent from the basket and makes injury more likely. They also claim that break-away hoops are safer because they soften the direct impact to a player's fingers, hands, and wrists and lessen the possibility of "hanging up" on the rim. * * *

Plaintiffs have also offered competent proof that a safer design existed in the 1980's in the form of a break-away hoop. According to Dr. Roberts, patents on file in the United States Patent and Trademark Office from many years prior to Darren's accident cite improved player safety as a benefit of break-away hoop design. Plaintiffs also offer proof that break-away hoops have been used in indoor competition since the 1960's. Therefore, plaintiffs created issues of fact on both safety and the feasibility of an alternative design that are sufficient to defeat summary judgment on the existence of a defect.

Next, defendants argue that the hoop was in exactly the condition Darren would have anticipated and thus was not defective within the meaning of Robinson, which held that a defective product is one "in a condition not reasonably contemplated by the ultimate consumer." Defendants urge that because Darren was fully aware that the hoop had a rigid rim, he cannot recover in strict products liability. This argument fails because consumer's awareness of the danger of a product is only one factor the jury should consider in determining whether the product is reasonably safe.

Finally, defendants argue—but not with any great spirit—that plaintiffs have not established that dunking is a reasonably foreseeable use of a basketball hoop. Defendants concede "that dunking is a voluntary option attempted by many players of the game.'" Therefore, I must deny the motion for summary judgment on Counts III and XV.

B. Negligence

Counts II and XIV of the complaint are negligence counts against Burke and Cushman. As to Burke, the Traubs allege (1) failure to exercise reasonable care in designing and constructing the hoop and backboard; (2) failure to keep abreast of developments in the field of recreational equipment and to upgrade its design; (3) failure to warn of the dangers of rigid rims and/or to warn against attempting to dunk a basketball into a basketball goal with a rigid rim; (4) failure to advise of the availability of an alternative safer design; and (5) failure to make reasonable efforts to recall, modify, or replace the hoop. Plaintiffs charge that Cushman was negligent in (1) failing to keep abreast of developments in the field of recreational equipment; (2) selling the backboard and hoop to M & B; (3) failing to advise that a safer hoop design was available; (4) failing to warn; and (5) failing to recall, modify, or replace the hoop after the sale. Defendants seek dismissal of the negligence counts arguing that (1) Darren assumed the risk of using the hoops; (2) they had no duty to warn because any risk the hoops presented was obvious; and (3) plaintiffs presented no proof that any alleged defect was a proximate cause of Darren's injuries. For the reasons discussed under Point II, there are issues of fact concerning assumption of the risk. Similar reasons compel the conclusion that there are issues of fact as to whether the dangers of a rigid hoop are so obvious that defendants had no duty to warn. As previously noted, Darren contends that he did not understand that his fall would be distorted by contact with the rigid rim. The issue of whether an injured party knew of the danger presented by the product that injured him generally is for the jury. Defendants' final argument is that plaintiffs have not offered competent proof that any defect in the product caused Darren's injuries. However, plaintiffs' experts supplied competent proof that the rigid rim design contributed to Darren's injuries. Therefore, I must deny defendants' request for dismissal of Counts II and XIV of the complaint.

C. Express Warranties and Implied Warranties

Counts IV and XVI of the second amended complaint allege that Burke and Cushman breached express warranties. N.Y. U.C.C. § 2-313 provides:

(1) Express warranties by the seller are created as follows:

(a) Any affirmation of fact or promise made by the seller to the buyer which relates to the goods and becomes part of the basis of the bargain creates an express warranty that the goods shall conform to the affirmation or promise.

(b) Any description of the goods which is made part of the basis of the bargain creates an express warranty that the goods shall conform to the description.

(c) Any sample or model which is made part of the basis of the bargain creates an express warranty that the whole of the goods shall conform to the sample or model.

Plaintiffs contend that the 1988 Burke Catalog, which represents that its goal is of "slam dunk strength," operated as an express warranty that the goal was safe for dunking. Plaintiffs do not allege that they or any of the defendants read or relied on this catalog's representations. In order to show that a seller made an express warranty through a description in an advertisement, plaintiffs must show that a purchaser relied on that representation and that the representation thus became "part of the basis of the bargain." As plaintiffs conceded at oral argument, their express warranty claims must be dismissed because they cannot show that any purchaser relied on the statement in the Burke catalog.

Plaintiffs also claim that Burke and Cushman breached the implied warranty of merchantability. Section 2-314(c) states that in order to be merchantable, goods must be "fit for the ordinary purposes for which such goods are used. . . ." Although a claim for breach of the implied warranty of merchantability is quite similar to a claim of strict product liability/design defect, there are differences. Most importantly, the plaintiff in an implied warranty case need not establish that the social desirability of a safer design outweighs its cost or that an alternative design is feasible. Instead, the plaintiff can prevail by showing that the "product was not minimally safe for its expected purpose." *Id*. As noted above, plaintiffs created an issue of fact as to whether dunking is part of the expected purpose of a basketball hoop and as to whether the defendants' design was minimally safe for this purpose. Therefore, I must deny summary judgment on the implied warranty claims against Burke and Cushman.

* * *

It is so ordered.

CASES ON THE SUPPLEMENTAL CD

Bouillon v. Harry Gill Company (1973 Ill. App. LEXIS 1604). From Bouillon we learn about a plaintiff severely injured while pole vaulting. As you read the case, note the cause of action brought against Gill, the athletic equipment manufacturing giant.

Pell v. Victor J. Andrew High School (1984 Ill. App. LEXIS 1712). As you read Pell, identify which of the categories of products defects are relevant in this case.

Wissell v. Ohio High School Athletic Association, (1992 Ohio App. LEXIS 904). In Wissell we learn about a football player who was rendered a quadriplegic during a high school game. As you read this case, identify the grounds on which the plaintiffs appealed as well as the original products liability causes of action.

QUESTIONS YOU SHOULD BE ABLE TO ANSWER

1. Compare and contrast the three common causes of action in products liability cases.

2. Discuss how manufacturers might use the risk-utility balancing test.

3. Research the Hillerich & Bradsby Company online and discover what changes they have made to their product line as a result of being named as a defendant in multiple products liability cases.

4. What are the three categories of product defects identified in the Restatement (third) Tort law?

5. What is meant by the Implied Warranty of Fitness?

REFERENCES

Cases

Anthony Pools, Inc. v. Sheehan, 455 A.2d 434 (Md. 1983).

Arnold v. Riddell, Inc., 882 F. Supp. 979 (D. Kan. 1995).

Back v. Wickes Corp., 378 N.E.2d 964 (Mass. 1978).

Bhardwaj v. 24 Hour Fitness, Inc., 2002 Cal. App. Unpub. LEXIS 3288 (Cal. App. 2002).

Brett v. Hillerich & Bradsby Co., 2001 U.S. Dist. LEXIS 26319.

Byrns v. Riddell, Inc., 550 P.2d 1065 (Ariz. 1976).

Curtis v. Hoosier Racing Tire Corp., 299 F. Supp. 2d 777 (N.D. Ohio 2004).

Diversified Products Corp. v. Faxon, 514 So.2d 1161 (Fla. App. 1987).

Dudley Sports Co. v. Schmitt, 279 N.E.2d 266 (Ind. App. 1972).

Escola v. Coca-Cola Bottling Co. of Fresno, 150 P.2d 436 (1944).

Everett v. Bucky Warren, Inc., 376 Mass. 280, 380 N.E.2d 653 (1978).

Filler v. Rayex Corp., 435 F.2d 336 (1970).

Garrett v. Nissen, 498 P.2d 1359 (N. Mex. 1972).

Gentile v. MacGregor Mfg. Co., 493 A.2d 647 (N.J. Super. L. 1985).

Green v. BDI Pharmaceuticals, 2001 La. App. LEXIS 2390 (La. App. 2001).

Hauter v. Zogarts, 120 Cal. Rptr. 681, 534 P.2d 377 (1975).

Hurley v. Larry's Water Ski School, 762 F.2d 925 (11th Cir. 1985).

Levey v. Yamaha Motor Corp., 825 A.2d 554 (N.J. Super. 2003).

Mohney v. USA Hockey, Inc., 2001 U.S. App. LEXIS 3584 (6th Cir. 2001).

Mohney v. USA Hockey, Inc., 2005 U.S. App. LEXIS 14373 (6th Cir. 2005).

Pavlides v. Galveston Yacht Basin, 727 F.2d 330 (5th Cir. 1984).

Perton v. Motel Properties, Inc., 497 S.E.2d 29 (Ga. App. 1998).

Rodriguez v. Riddell Sports, Inc., 242 F.3d 567 (5th Cir. 2001).

Traub v. Cornell University, 1998 U.S. Dist. LEXIS 5530 (N.D.N.Y. 1998).

Sullivan v. Nissen Trampoline Company, 1967 Ill. App. LEXIS 938, (1967).

Whitacre v. Halo Optical Products, Inc., 501 So.2d 994 (La. App. 2 Cir. 1987).

Publications

Garrett, M. C. (1972). Allowance of punitive damages in products liability claims. *Georgia Law Review*, 6(3), 613–630.

Lim, R. (2008). The Doctrine of Privity of Contract. http://www.articlealley.com/article_655389_18.html

Nader, R. (1972). *Unsafe at any speed: The designed-in dangers of the American automobile.* New York: Grossman.

Plant, M. L. (1957). Strict liability of manufacturers for injuries caused by defects in products: An opposing view. *Tennessee Law Review*, 24(7), 938–951.

van der Smissen, B. (1990). *Legal liability and risk management for public and private entities.* Cincinnati, OH: Anderson Publishing Company.

Legislation

Restatement (Second) of Torts § 402A (1965).

Restatement (Third) of Torts § 2 and related comments (1997).

—Sarah J. Young

INDIANA UNIVERSITY

Imagine for a moment that you are traveling to an exotic island beach resort in the Caribbean where your travel agent booked reservations for you at a four-star hotel right on the beach. Your departure day finds you waiting for a flight delay that extends into hours causing you to miss your connecting flight and arrive one day late for your vacation. Upon check-in at the hotel, you discover they have overbooked and, because you are a day late, have switched your reservation to a three-star hotel two miles inland. The hotel shuttle is involved in a minor traffic accident en route to your new accommodations, causing you to crack your head on the window. Woozy, you finally get to your hotel, only to find that a family of mice has already taken up residence in your room. You inform the front desk that you must have another room (a clean one!) and go to the restaurant for a bite to eat while the hotel straightens out the room situation. At the restaurant, you eat some bad seafood, which resurrects itself at 3 o'clock in the morning. While you lay curled up on your bed watching the television because your stomach hurts, you learn there is a category-four hurricane headed straight for your location, and authorities are mandating evacuation of the island immediately.

Sound like a tourist's worst nightmare? This might lead one to think about the legal duties and responsibilities of travel agents, airlines, hotels, and restaurants to tourists. Although many of the legal concepts and principles discussed in other sections of this text apply to tourism settings, there are unique legal aspects that arise because of the very nature of tourism. Barth (2009) recognized the interconnectivity of travel and hospitality as one phenomenon that makes legal issues in tourism unique. For example, vacation packages often include transportation, lodging, meals, and recreation activities. When something goes wrong, and the tourist does not receive what was promised, which service provider should be held liable? It is the reliance of one or more service providers on others for quality performance that makes the area of tourism law more complex. Jurisdiction issues, differences in how travel terms are perceived, identity of the actual service provider, weather, civil unrest, and disease are all factors that can create problems for travelers, tourists, and hotel guests, as well as result in litigation. These factors are phenomena over which hotel and restaurant managers, travel agents, and tour operators may or may not have control. Yet, no one in the travel supply chain is immune from legal action. Therefore, what follows is an overview of legal issues unique to managers in the hospitality and travel industries.

FUNDAMENTAL CONCEPTS

Hotels

Dating back to English common law, innkeepers and hotel operators had a duty to receive travelers who registered as guests. Today, common law and statutory law identify hotels, motels, and other establishments providing lodging as places of public accommodation and continue to obligate hotel operators to receive all guests. There are circumstances, however, under which the hotel manager may refuse to register an individual as a guest. Typically, if a person is intoxicated, drunk or disorderly, suffers from an obvious contagious disease, brings property into the hotel that could pose a hazard to other guests (e.g., firearms, explosives, animals), or cannot pay for the price of the room, the manager has the right to refuse accommodation (Jeffries, 1995).

For a person visiting a hotel's property to qualify as a guest, the visit must be for the primary purpose for which the hotel operates—the rental of rooms suitable for overnight stay. The duty owed a guest by a hotel is the same as that owed to an invitee. In other words, the hotel owes a guest a reasonably clean and safe accommodation. An example of this duty is provided in *Copeland v. The Lodge Enterprises* (2000), where plaintiff was allegedly bitten by a brown recluse spider while staying at defendant's motel. Plaintiff claimed defendant was grossly negligent in failing to provide a safe premise, free of harmful insects, or failing to warn of their presence. In upholding its duty to provide a reasonably safe accommodation, defendant was able to provide monthly invoices from a pest control service showing they had taken reasonable measures to eliminate such pests.

In another example of the hotel's duty to its guests, plaintiff claimed defendant hotel failed to provide adequate security and fire protection after a fire at a Comfort Inn and Suites resulted in the deaths of six guests and severe injuries to 12 additional guests (*Allen v. Greenville Hotel Partners, Inc.,* 2006). The cause of the fire was arson, leading to plaintiff's negligence claim for the hotel installing inadequate sprinklers, leaving the back door to the hotel unlocked, and failing to install surveillance cameras. Additionally, plaintiff claimed the hotel had negligently trained their employees to disengage an active fire alarm until confirming the presence of an actual fire. Not only was this alleged training an obvious violation of fire safety codes, but it created an unnecessary delay in warning guests of the fire danger.

Overbooking

General contract law is enacted every time a potential guest inquires with the hotel as to the availability of a room for a definite period of time at a specified price. Once agreed upon, either verbally or in writing, a breach of this agreement by either the prospective guest or the hotel can result in liability for damages. The hotel reservation, once made and confirmed, constitutes a contract and binds the hotel to provide accommodations as well as the guest to stay there. Yet, many hotels overbook their rooms because of the persistent problem of no-show guests. History and experience prove that a certain percentage of guests will not use their reservations. As a result, some hotels overbook by the expected attrition rate, and then are not able to accommodate all their reservations when the expected no-show guests do actually appear. *Rainbow Travel Services v. Hilton Hotels, Corp.* (1990), showcases a classic example of the liability that can occur from intentional overbooking. Plaintiff was a tour operator who contracted a block of rooms with the Fontainebleau Hilton in Miami, Florida, for University of Oklahoma football fans. When the fans arrived, there were no rooms available at the Hilton because the hotel overbooked their capacity by 15 percent. Upon further investigation, it was discovered that Hilton had a policy regarding overbooking, stating that employees should never admit overbooking, but instead refer to factors beyond the hotel's control. The court ruled in favor of plaintiffs because defendants recklessly accepted more reservations than they were able to accommodate.

Protecting Guest Property

Guests bring a variety of personal property with them during their stays on hotel premises. Typically guests bring money, clothing, jewelry, computers, sports equipment, and perhaps, a vehicle. What is the legal responsibility of the hotel to their guests for this personal property? Historically, this responsibility is based on a rule of absolute liability holding the innkeeper liable for any loss of guest property that was "infra hospitium, or within the inn" (Garner, 2004, p. 796). This doctrine emanated from the time when not every innkeeper was honest and often was the culprit of missing guest property. There were exceptions, however, to the absolute liability rule. Loss of property because of an act of God (e.g., tornadoes, floods, earthquakes) and loss of property by a public enemy (e.g., terrorists or acts of war) were two exceptions for which the innkeeper was not held liable. A third exception was the negligence of the guest, such as leaving bags unattended in a hotel lobby, sidewalk, hallway, or public area.

Today most states have enacted statutes limiting liability for guest property loss. If a hotel adheres to the statutes it will be liable for the loss only up to an established maximum amount (e.g., $1,000). This is the case even if a guest's property is worth far more than the maximum amount. Although each state's statutes vary in the details, there are common provisions that hotels must generally follow:

1. The hotel must provide a safe available for guest property;
2. The hotel must post notices communicating the availability of safes;
3. The hotel must communicate to guests that their liability for lost or stolen property is limited;
4. The hotel must communicate the maximum recovery amount allowed.

The availability of limited liability provides an incentive for hotel managers to comply with the strict interpretation of these statutes. Without evidence of compliance, the hotel becomes liable under common law for the full amount of the lost or stolen property.

Within the hospitality industry there are times when a hotel or restaurant manager may be entrusted with a guest's property that is covered under a type of contract law other than the limited liability statute. The theory of bailment is often used by hotels and restaurants for valet parking, coat checks, laundry services, and luggage storage. A **bailment** is defined as the delivery of goods or personal property by one to another with the expectation the property will be returned in the same condition it was received (Garner, 2004). When one hands over possession of his/her personal property for safekeeping by another and the party knowingly has exclusive control over the property, a bailment is established. The individual who gives his/her property to another is known as the **bailor**, whereas the individual who accepts responsibility for the property is known as the **bailee**. Morris, Marshall, and Cournoyer (2008) identified the essential elements of a bailment as personal property, delivery of possession, acceptance of possession by bailee, and a bailment agreement, either implicit or express. Bailments only involve tangible, personal property like cars, clothing, and sports equipment. Such was the case of *Waterton v. Linden Motor, Inc.* (2006), when plaintiff parked her car in the garage of the hotel where she and her husband had reservations for the night. During the night their car was broken into and several items were stolen. Suing under the theory of bailment, plaintiff claimed the hotel had a duty to replace the lost property and fix the couple's damaged car. The court ruled that even though the car was parked on defendant's premises no bailment agreement had been established because plaintiff had not given possession of her car to the hotel (i.e., handed over the keys) nor had the hotel specifically accepted responsibility for possession of the car. Furthermore, because there was a sign posted in defendant's parking garage that purported to limit the inn's responsibility for any loss of or damage to guests' vehicles, the court ruled defendant was not liable for the damages.

Guest Privacy

A registered hotel guest has the right to privacy and peaceful possession of his/her room without disruption from hotel personnel. Morris et al. (2008) identified five exceptions to this right of hotel guests. An innkeeper is authorized to enter a guest's room for normal maintenance, to warn of imminent danger, for nonpayment of the room, when requested to enter by the guest, and upon expiration of the rental period. Unless there is a legal basis for entry, hotel staff and nonguests are not permitted to enter a guest's room at will. However, sometimes guests engage in illegal activity in their hotel rooms. If evidence of illegal activity is discovered by a hotel employee who is legally in the guest's room, the hotel has an obligation to report their findings to the police. This was the case in *United States v. Coles* (2006), when the hotel manager entered a guest's room to see if it was still occupied as well as to discuss with the guest his payment for the room. Upon entering, the manager observed a plastic bag and small vials containing a white substance. Believing he had seen illegal drugs, he contacted the police, which he was obligated to do.

Recreational Facilities

Often hotels will provide additional services and facilities such as spas, swimming pools, workout rooms, trails, putting greens, and other specialized facilities for their guests' enjoyment. In most states, the general standard for hotels is to exercise reasonable care in preventing injury to a guest who uses these activity areas. Whether reasonable care is exercised depends on the facts and circumstances in each case. In *Bradshaw v. ITT Sheraton Corporation* (2005), plaintiff sued after she fell off a carpeted transition incline leading to the dance floor. Summary judgment for the hotel was denied because there were factual questions as to whether defendant failed to exercise reasonable care to protect its guests from harm.

Because they are attractive to guests, especially children, most hotels and motels have aquatics facilities on their property, yet aquatics facilities represent a potential liability to the hotel operator. Attention to detail in maintaining a reasonably safe pool area is emphasized in *Uddin v. Embassy Suites Hotel* (2005), where the hotel was found negligent for a 10-year old girl's drowning because the water was so murky and cloudy that one witness stated she could not see her feet while standing in the pool. The court held that defendant had a duty to provide a reasonably safe swimming facility for guests who were classified as business invitees.

Because hotels have access to recreational activity areas does not always mean the area is within their **sphere of control**. *Fabend v. Rosewood Hotels and Resorts* (2004), illustrates this concept. Plaintiff sued the Rosewood Hotel and the National Park Service (NPS) after he was injured bodysurfing in the Virgin Islands. He claimed the hotel failed to warn him of a dangerous shorebreak condition on the beach, which created a forceful wave driving him into the sand and leaving him a quadriplegic. Although the hotel advertised the white, sandy beaches in their promotional materials, the NPS maintained physical control over all the beaches. Additionally, NPS provided signs and brochures warning visitors of the dangerous conditions of the park. The court ruled that because the beach was not in the hotel's sphere of control, it did not have a legal duty to warn swimmers of the shorebreak danger.

Travel and Tourism

Jurisdiction

A resident of New York City was injured while on vacation at a hotel casino in Las Vegas. The injured party sued the hotel for negligence, claiming the hotel's employees left a chair in a common pedestrian area, causing her to fall (*Smith v. Circus Circus Casinos, Inc.,* 2003). In which state, Nevada or New York, should the plaintiff make her claim? Most people expect to file a claim or commence a lawsuit in their local courts, yet when travel is involved, the plaintiff's local court must have jurisdiction (see Section 1.10, *The Legal System*). **Jurisdiction** is defined as the authority of the court to "decide a matter of controversy" (Garner, 2004, p. 867) as well as maintain control over the subject matter and parties to the dispute. In most states, jurisdiction over corporate defendants is determined by the amount and frequency of business defendants conduct in a given state. Generally, "doing business" depends on factors such as the existence of an office in the state, the solicitation of business, the presence of bank accounts or property in the state, and the presence of employees. The importance of establishing jurisdiction is illustrated in *Heidle v. Prospect Reef Resort* (2005), where plaintiff and her boyfriend vacationed in the British Virgin Islands. Plaintiff was injured when she fell into a cistern after the cover upon which she was standing caved in. As a resident of New York, and because she had purchased her vacation package through a travel wholesaler located in her home state, plaintiff brought forth her claim in a New York court. Yet, because defendant did not meet the criteria of doing business in the state of New York, plaintiff was unable to prove that a New York court would have jurisdiction.

Internet Sales. The sale of travel and vacation packages via the Internet has not only increased astronomically over the past decade, but also affects the jurisdiction of legal claims. A number of courts have adopted a sliding scale analysis categorizing websites as passive, active, or interactive for the purpose of determining whether specific jurisdiction exists (*Zippo Manufacturing, Co. v. Zippo Dot Com*, 1997). A passive website containing information about the hotel or travel destination available to the general public, but not providing a way to take reservations, is viewed as an insufficient basis for establishing jurisdiction. In *Cervantes v. Ramparts, Inc.* (2003), a California plaintiff filed suit against the Luxor Hotel located in Las Vegas, Nevada, after he slipped and fell in the hotel's restroom. Plaintiff tried to establish that California courts would have jurisdiction over the defendant because defendant maintained a Website accessible in California. The court disagreed, noting the hotel's website was passive and only provided information about the Luxor. On the other end of the scale, an interactive Website is generally characterized by information, e-mail communication, detailed descriptions of goods and services, and online sales. *Kaloyeva v. Apple Vacations* (2008), illustrates this type of web site. Plaintiffs, New York residents, sought relief for fraud, negligence, and breach of contract, *inter alia*, from defendant, a representative of Santana Beach Resort and Casino located in the Dominican Republic. Defendant provided to the general public a website on which customers could make reservations. The court ruled that jurisdiction over a defendant could be exercised under two conditions: (1) where the website is used to actively transact business, and (2) where a consumer can exchange information with the host computer. In *Kaloyeva*, Apple Vacations actively solicited business on its website and allowed consumers to enter into legal contracts based upon services advertised, resulting in defendants effectively placing their business and its services into the stream of commerce of the state of New York.

Forum Non Conveniens. Related to issues of jurisdiction is **forum non conveniens**, which refers to the discretionary power of the court to decline jurisdiction when "convenience of the parties and justice would be better served if the case was brought forth in another forum" (Garner, 2004, p. 680). In determining whether a different venue would be more convenient for the parties involved in a case, the court typically considers three factors provided by an analysis from a 1947 U.S. Supreme Court case (*Gulf Oil Corp. v. Gilbert*).

First, the court must determine whether an alternative forum exists. For example, an Illinois couple was the guest of the Atlantis Hotel in the Bahamas when the husband was injured in a jet ski accident. Plaintiff alleged negligence against the hotel since the jet ski business was on the beach owned and solely controlled by the hotel. The Bahamas was deemed an adequate alternative forum because Bahamian law follows the same basic principles of tort law as does an Illinois court (*Horberg v. Kerzner International Hotels Limited*, 2007).

Secondly, the court must determine the private interest of the litigant including the relative ease of access to sources of proof, availability of compulsory processes to obtain unwilling witnesses' attendance in court, cost of obtaining attendance of witnesses, the possibility of viewing the premises, and any other practical considerations that make the hearing of a case more expedient and less expensive.

The third and final consideration balances public interest factors such as court congestion, the burden of jury duty on the people of the community who have no relation to the litigation, and the appropriateness of trying a case in a forum familiar with the governing law of the case. A good illustration of how forum non conveniens works is found in *Campbell v. Starwood Hotels and Resorts*, (2008). A resident of Florida vacationing in the Bahamas was swimming in an area designated as safe by the hotel where he was a registered guest. While swimming, plaintiff was struck by a motorboat operated by a vendor who was contracted by the defendant hotel to provide water sports to hotel guests. Plaintiff sued defendant for a variety of negligence claims in federal district court while defendant moved to dismiss the case on the basis of forum non conveniens. After determining that the Bahamas was an adequate alternative forum because their laws recognized negligence as a cause of action, the court concluded that private and public interest factors favored the trial taking place in Florida. This decision was supported by the fact that the majority of witnesses were located in the United States and "the hardships associated with obtaining evidence while litigating in the Bahamas forum would be greater" (p. 13) than litigating the case in a Florida district court.

Often tourist destinations and common carriers will include a **forum selection clause** in the agreement between agency and tourist citing any litigation must be brought forth in the court where the agency is headquartered. Dickerson (2004) explained that hospitality and travel providers institute forum selection clauses as a way to discourage guests or travelers from prosecuting their legal claims. Historically and traditionally the courts have held firm in the enforcement of forum selection clauses once the terms and conditions of a contract have been reasonably communicated (*Morales v. Royal Caribbean Cruises*, 2006). For example in *Vega v. Norwegian Cruise Lines* (2007), the ticket for plaintiff's (residing in New York) cruise to the Bahamas contained a forum selection clause clearly stating that any legal disputes had to be litigated in the courts of Miami-Dade County, Florida. In another case, *Decker v. Circus Circus Hotel* (1999), although the web site placed the hotel into the stream of commerce in New Jersey, the defendant's web site contained a forum selection clause requiring all guests who made their reservations on-line to agree to have their disputes settled in Nevada courts. In each case the courts upheld the forum selection clauses.

The U. S. Supreme Court in *Carnival Cruise Lines, Inc. v. Shute* (1991), also noted the forum selection clause must be deemed fundamentally fair. Similarly, in *Lischinskaya v. Carnival Corporation* (2008), the court ruled the forum selection clause was fair and enforceable, primarily because plaintiff had plenty of time to review her ticket, and the explicitly stated terms contained within.

Although the majority of forum selection clause cases favor defendants, this is not always the case. *Stobaugh v. Norwegian Cruise Line* (1999), provides a good example of when a travel service provider's forum selection clause was deemed fundamentally unfair. Plaintiffs, residents of Texas, had contracted with the cruise line to take a seven-day cruise to Bermuda departing August 31. They received their passenger tickets with all the terms of the agreement, including the forum selection clause, on August 8. A few days before their departure, plaintiffs learned of several tropical storm systems in the Atlantic Ocean. On inquiring with Norwegian about refunds if they decided to cancel on account of the weather, they were told they should proceed with the trip and trust the judgment of the ship's captain. Plaintiffs did as was suggested, and defendant's ship sailed into Hurricane Eduardo, which allegedly resulted in physical and emotional injuries to many passengers on board. Plaintiffs filed a class action lawsuit in Texas court against Norwegian Cruise Lines, who asserted their forum selection clause (based in Florida) as a basis to dismiss the case. The court ruled against the cruise line stating that because their forum selection clause was not clearly communicated to passengers until after they paid in full for the cruise, the clause was not fair nor enforceable.

Transportation

Transportation is another major dimension of the travel and tourism industry with airplanes, cruise ships, buses, tour buses, trains, and taxis serving as common carriers. A **common carrier** is one who takes on the responsibility to transport from place to place any person who chooses to employ it for hire (Garner, 2004). A common carrier owes its passengers the highest degree of care with the passenger–carrier relationship continuing until the passenger has had a reasonable opportunity to reach a place of safety. Furthermore, common carriers are vicariously liable for their employees' intentional and negligent torts, even when they are committed outside the scope of employment (*Twardy v. Northwest Airlines, Inc.*, 2001).

Air travel is the method of choice for long-distance travel for many tourists. The contract between an airline and its passengers is known as a **tariff** and outlines the terms to which the passenger agrees when purchasing a ticket. The terms of the tariff affect how passengers are treated and vary among the major carriers. For example, not all airlines have the same policy regarding flight delays and how passengers whose flights are delayed are handled. The terms of handling flight delays are contained in the tariff, or ticket information. On the other hand, federal regulations require all airlines to provide a standard compensation to passengers who are bumped from their flights due to overbooking. Although most passengers accept the airlines' compensation, there are some who choose to claim damages for breach of contract of the tariff. A bumped passenger claiming contract damages may sue for costs of alternate transportation, meals, and compensation for inconvenience caused by the bump. Illustrated in *Stone v. Continental Airlines* (2005), plaintiff and his thirteen-year-old daughter on Christmas day were bumped from their flight from New York City to Telluride, Colorado, for a ski trip. Plaintiff was awarded damages totaling $3,110 for unrecoverable lodging accommodations, lost baggage, and inconvenience of missing the scheduled holiday vacation trip.

For airlines operating international flights, liability for personal injury, damaged or lost baggage, and damages caused by delays is limited by the Warsaw Convention. The Warsaw Convention is an international treaty, to which the United States is a party, governing and limiting the liability of air carriers transporting passengers and cargo on international flights. For example, in *Bernardi v. Apple Vacations* (2002), plaintiff originally filed her claim in a Pennsylvania state court for extreme and inhumane conditions suffered by passengers during an international flight. Yet, because the U.S. is a signatory to the convention, not only was defendant's liability limited, but plaintiff's state law claims were preempted by the Warsaw Convention. Applicable only to the actual flight, the Warsaw Convention does not limit the liability of airport security checkpoints for stolen bags, as shown by *Dazo v. Globe Airport Security Services*, (2002). The passenger's carry-on bag containing over $100,000 worth of jewelry was stolen as she passed through the metal detector on an international flight connecting in St. Louis, Missouri. The security company attempted to seek shelter from liability through the Warsaw Convention, but the court ruled the limitation on liability did not apply.

Vacations aboard luxury cruise ships have increased in popularity with more than 13 million people participating in cruises in 2008 (The State of the Cruise Industry, 2009). Modern-day cruise ships are essentially floating hotels (Barth, 2009; Dickerson, 2004) with amenities including ice-skating rinks, rock-climbing walls, golf simulators, water slides, private pools, spas, and planetariums. As a result, many of the legal issues of guest safety, security, and liability are similar to those faced by land-based hospitality managers. Furthermore, like all common carriers, those operating cruise ships are subject to a wide array of local, state, federal, and international laws. Yet, in addition to these legal principles, cruise ships and their passengers are subject to **maritime laws**, a system of law relating to navigable waters. In *Bird v. Celebrity Cruise Line, Inc.* (2005), plaintiff alleged that she became ill and was diagnosed with bacterial enteritis from food ingested on board the cruise. The district court found in favor of defendant because maritime law governed the case and plaintiff's allegations of implied warranty of merchantability and strict product liability are not recognized causes of action under maritime law. Furthermore, liability waivers used to protect cruise lines from liability for injuries aboard ship are not enforceable. Federal statute 46 App. U.S.C. Appendix §183c states:

> It shall be unlawful for . . . owner of any vessel transporting passengers . . . to insert any . . . provision or limitation purporting, in the event of loss of life or bodily injury arising from the negligence or fault, . . . to relieve such owner . . . from liability. . . . All such provisions or limitations . . . are declared to be against public policy and shall be null and void and of no effect.

Similar to the limits on liability provided for international air travel, the Athens Convention limits liability of cruise ships to passengers aboard cruises not touching a U.S. port. Although the United States is not a signatory to the Athens Convention, many of the cruise lines serving U.S. passengers are owned by companies located in countries that do abide by the terms of the convention. For example, in *Henson v. Seabourn Cruise Line Limited, Inc.* (2005), defendant sought limits on liability from negligence claims by the plaintiff. Defendant cruise line was flagged as a vessel of the Bahamas, which is party to the treaty, and the Athens Convention was included as a term in the ticket contract with the plaintiff. The court ruled, however, that because the cruise was scheduled to make several stops at U.S. ports, U.S. federal law prevailed over the liability limitations of the Athens Convention.

Agency Law

Inherent to understanding legal liability in the travel and tourism industry is agency law, an area of law governed by a combination of contract law and tort law (Cheeseman, 2004). At the heart of agency law is the principal-agent relationship. A party employing another to act on its behalf is known as the **principal**, whereas the **agent** becomes the party agreeing to act on another's behalf. The **principal-agent relationship** is created when both parties agree that the agent has the authority to represent the principal and can enter into contracts on the principal's behalf. This principal–agent relationship is illustrated in *Black v. Delta Airlines, Inc.* (2002), where the defendant airline denied that the travel agency from which plaintiff had purchased tickets was an agent of their company. Plaintiff had purchased two first-class tickets from a travel agency for a trip from Dallas, Texas, to Las Vegas, Nevada. Plaintiff was told by the travel agent that both he and his wife were confirmed for round-trip first-class travel. Yet, on arrival at the terminal gate, only plaintiff's ticket was confirmed for first-class and his wife's ticket was confirmed for coach with a priority wait list for first-class. On further investigation, it was discovered that the travel agency's computer showed confirmed first-class travel for both travelers, but Delta's computer showed confirmed first-class travel for only one ticket. Defendant moved for summary judgment by stating the travel agency was not acting as an agent for their airline. The court denied the motion and ruled that when a travel agent issues a ticket, the travel agent acts on behalf of the carrier.

Formation of the agency relationship can occur through an express agreement, an implied agreement, or an apparent agency. The express agreement involves either an oral or written contract, whereas the implied agreement is inferred by the conduct of both parties. An **apparent agent** is one whom the principal allows others to believe is acting as its agent, regardless of whether or not the principal has actually conferred that authority (Garner, 2004, p. 69). This concept is illustrated in *Cash v. Six Continents Hotels* (2004), where a tour operator, Harmony Tours, maintained a desk in the lobby of the Holiday Inn Sunspree Hotel in Montego Bay, Jamaica. Plaintiffs booked a tour with Harmony to Dunn's River Falls, where they were dropped off and left for a long period of time without guidance or assistance. It was during this time that plaintiffs were injured while trying to climb the waterfall. Plaintiffs sued the hotel for negligence, assuming that Harmony was an agent of the hotel. Evidence revealed that Harmony Tours was an independent contractor and that nowhere in the promotional literature of either the hotel or Harmony was it represented that Harmony was an agent of the hotel. Although the hotel allowed Harmony to promote its tours in their lobby, there was no agency relationship between the two service providers.

Travel Agents. Many people making travel plans use the services of a travel agent whose job is to provide customers travel information, organize travel packages, and sell travel services such as airline tickets, cruise vacations, hotel rooms, and excursion trips. Travel agents work on commission from airlines, hotels, tour operators, and other types of travel services, making them legal representatives (agents) of the service provider (principal). Although travel agents are viewed as legal representatives of different travel services, they also have a duty to their customers to act with skill, care, and diligence in rendering the kind of services that can reasonably be expected. Travel agents owe a fiduciary duty to their clients. For example, if an agent had a conflict of interest that would be adverse to the client, the agent must disclose that fact to the client. This was the case in *Krautsack v. Anderson* (2006), where plaintiff booked an African safari with his travel agent. The trip was booked for the dry season, but the trip was marred by extremely heavy rainfall due to El Nino. Plaintiff had checked with his travel agent prior to the trip about the unusual weather conditions, but was advised that the weather information plaintiff had received was incorrect and he should proceed with the trip. What defendant also failed to share with his client was that he had already paid his African suppliers and to cancel the trip at that point would have resulted in him losing any profits from plaintiff's booking.

Travel agents are not insurers or guarantors of customers' travel safety including quality issues of lodging accommodations. When a travel agent has knowledge of safety factors or quality issues, he/she has a duty to inform the customer of those facts. For example, in *Shlivko v. Good Luck Travel, Inc.* (2003), plaintiff sought a refund for the price of a vacation trip to London because she was dissatisfied with the unsanitary quality of the hotel accommodations. The court ruled that had defendant known about the quality of the accommodations and withheld that information from the plaintiff, then defendant would be held liable. As it turned out, the court found no evidence that defendant knew or had reason to know of the unsanitary hotel conditions, nor did they have a duty to investigate those conditions without a specific request.

Likewise, websites providing online users with travel related products and services are viewed as 21st-century travel agents. In *Hofer v. Expedia, Inc.* (2007), plaintiff booked her travel and accommodations to Jamaica via the Expedia.com website. Upon arrival at the resort hotel, plaintiff discovered the stairs leading up to the lobby of the hotel were dimly lit and did not have a handrail. During her stay plaintiff lost her balance at the top of those stairs and fell into an adjacent turtle pond, severely cutting her leg on sharp rocks in the pond. Plaintiff alleged Expedia breached its duty to warn her that the resort hotel's stairway was dimly lit and lacked a handrail. The court held that a travel agent cannot be held responsible for conditions at a hotel if the agent exercises no control over the facilities. Although the Expedia.com Website contained a promise that their "travel specialists visit thousands of hotels across the globe to ensure our descriptions are accurate and up-to-date" (p. 168), there was no evidence that Expedia exercised any control over the resort property where plaintiff was injured.

When customers rely on the expertise of travel agents for information about third-party suppliers (such as tour operators), the travel agent has a duty to provide accurate information and take reasonable care in investigating these travel suppliers. The role of the travel agent in terms of third-party suppliers is illustrated in *Adames v. Trans National Travel*, (1998). Plaintiff won a trip through a radio station contest that was chartered through defendant, a travel agency that in turn booked the transportation to Cancun, Mexico, and hotel accommodations for seven nights. While on the free trip, plaintiff purchased an excursion tour from an independent tour operator for an island adventure cruise on which plaintiff was injured. Plaintiff sued the travel agency claiming it had a duty to warn of dangers involved with all the activities of the travel package. The court granted summary judgment to the travel agency stating that to find such a duty would necessitate the travel agent to inform travelers of all possible dangers of each third-party excursion and that this would be too large of a burden on the travel industry.

Tour Operators. Tour operators are distinguished from travel agents in that operators are usually in a position to actually provide a travel service, such as excursions, guided tours, and trips. Tour operators are often considered the primary provider of the service, whereas the travel agent is a representative of their services. Tour operators can be held liable for their own negligent actions that result in injuries to tourists. A bicycle tour company could be held liable for selection of a dangerous road for the tour (*Coles v. Jenkins*, 1998). Likewise, a Peruvian tour operator involved in a traffic accident while transporting passengers from the airport could be liable for injuries to the passengers (*Vermeulen v. Worldwide Holidays, Inc.*, 2006). However, like the travel agent, if a tour operator is contracting with another third-party travel supplier, then they are not liable for the negligence of that third-party supplier provided they exercised care in the selection of the supplier. For example, a Missouri-based tour operator was not held liable for a client's negligence claim because they had contracted with a third-party to handle the ground transportation for an Egyptian tour on which plaintiff was a party (*Sachs v. TWA Getaway Vacations, Inc.*, 2000).

When a travel agent accepts the additional role of tour operator, the agent assumes the duties and responsibilities of the principal, or the actual service provider. An Arizona travel agency organized, promoted, sold, and operated student vacation tours to Mazatlan, Mexico, which plaintiff's eighteen-year old-daughter, Molly, had purchased. Part of the tour was a train ride called the party train, from which Molly fell when walking from one train car to another (*Maurer v. Cerkvenik-Anderson Travel*, 1994). The travel agency, relying on its role of agent, claimed it had no duty to control the train to make it safe, nor did it have knowledge of the specific condition causing Molly's death. The court disagreed and ruled that because of defendant's dual role as both agent and principal, the travel agency had a duty to warn of dangers of which they were aware, or should have been aware. In another illustration of a travel agent taking on the role of tour operator, a Chicago independent travel agent made arrangements for a private school's eighth-grade graduation trip to Six Flags near St. Louis, Missouri (*Lewis v. Elsin*, 2002). Additionally, the travel agent agreed to serve as the group's tour guide and accompanied them on the trip. Upon check-in at the hotel where the group was staying overnight, defendant left the group and went out for the evening. While absent from the group, one of the students drowned in the hotel's swimming pool. The travel agent/tour guide was sued because he had neglected his role as tour guide and failed to provide for appropriate supervision of the pool area for the group.

Tour operators can gain some protection by using liability waivers and disclaimers as illustrated in *Brocker v. Norwegian Cruise Line Limited*, (2007). Plaintiff, a cruise ship passenger, purchased a ticket for a shore-based deep-sea fishing excursion provided by a third party tour operator. While on the deep-sea fishing boat, plaintiff was injured when he fell through rotten boards on the deck into the boat's engine room. The guest ticket contract entered into by the parties precluded liability for conduct of the third-party tour operator, but was not successful in protecting the cruise line from plaintiff's negligence claim.

SIGNIFICANT CASE

Any entity within the travel supply chain can be sued for a variety of claims. This case illustrates the interconnectivity of the travel industry and how the dependence of one business on another does not necessarily mean liability for damages is shared by all travel service providers.

COLLETTE V. UNIQUE VACATIONS, INC.

State of Massachusetts, Appellate Division, Northern District
2004 Mass. App. Div. 59
2004 Mass. App. Div. LEXIS 19
March 30, 2004, Decided

Opinion By: Judge Greco

The evidence introduced during the trial of this case would have warranted a finding that the plaintiffs' honeymoon at Sandals Resort was ruined by a hurricane. What made this loss the subject of litigation as opposed to merely bad luck was Sandals' Blue Chip Hurricane Guarantee by which Sandals promised a free replacement vacation with round trip airfare if a hurricane interrupted a customer's stay. * * *

After a jury-waived trial, the plaintiffs recovered $3,922.00 on their breach of contract claim against Unique. The trial judge also found that Unique had violated the Consumer Protection Act, G.L.c. 93A, and awarded triple damages to the plaintiffs plus costs and attorney's fees. Unique filed this appeal on the ground *inter alia*, that the evidence was insufficient as a matter of law to warrant the court's findings against it on either the plaintiff's contract claim or their G.L.c. 93A claim.* * *

Viewed in the light most favorable to the plaintiffs, the evidence indicated the following: Plaintiffs Heather and Kevin Collette booked their honeymoon trip through the Vacation Outlet at Filene's Basement Store. The accommodation component of that trip was a stay of seven nights to be split between two Sandals resorts in Jamaica at Negril Beach and Montego Bay. One of the main reasons the Collettes picked Sandals was the hurricane guarantee mentioned above, which was set forth in writing in a Sandals' brochure and which they specifically discussed with the Vacation Outlet employee with whom they dealt. The Collettes paid for the accommodations by a check made out to the Vacation Outlet. The Vacation Outlet then, in turn booked the hotel reservations with defendant Unique Vacations, Inc. In so doing, the Vacation Outlet generated a written "Passenger Invoice and Confirmation," which listed Sunburst Holidays as the airline vendor and Unique as the hotel vendor. The Vacation Outlet also forwarded payment to Unique in the amount of the money paid by the Collettes, less Vacation Outlet's com-

mission. The Collettes had no personal dealing with any employee of Unique in planning their honeymoon.

Because of Hurricane Mitch, the Collettes were unable to use many of the facilities at Negril Beach. Three of the four restaurants there were closed, and many resort activities were not available. Moreover, the Collettes were not able to go to the second resort at Montego Bay. During their stay at Sandals, the Collettes had no contact with any employee of Unique to complain about the accommodations or for any other purpose. In fact, the Collettes' only interaction with Unique involved complaints which they made after the trip. After the Vacation Outlet contacted Unique to learn who would be the appropriate person at Sandals to address the Collettes' concerns, the Collettes sent G.L.c. 93A demand letters to Sandals, the Vacation Outlet, and Unique. Sandals and the Vacation Outlet responded, but Unique did not. Sandals' response, however, offered a complimentary stay at its resort but instructed the Collettes to contact Unique to select a date in order to accept its offer.

The Sandals brochure stated that "Sandals Resorts and beaches are represented worldwide by Unique Vacations." Unique is a Florida corporation with its principal place of business in Miami. Its Miami address was listed on the Sandals' brochure. If one were to call the toll free number given in the brochure, one would reach the offices of Unique and would be able to make reservations for any Sandals resort without going through a travel agent such as the Vacation Outlet. There was testimony at trial that Unique provided marketing and reservation services to Sandals and had the exclusive right to use the Sandals name and logo for purposes of taking reservations. No evidence was presented, however, as to who owned the two Sandals Resorts in Jamaica, who owned Unique, who held management positions in the corporations, or who held stock.

In essence, the evidence at trial indicated only that Unique was held out to be the worldwide representative of Sandals and had the exclusive right to use the Sandals name in the booking of reservations. Unique's only connection to the travel arrangements for the Collettes was its acceptance of payment from the Vacation Outlet. There was no evidence of what Unique did with this money. Such evidence would have warranted a finding that Unique was Sandals' agent and, perhaps, that the Collettes knew Unique was Sandals' representative, assuming they read every word in the brochure. However, Unique would not have become a party to any contract made with the Collettes because its principal, Sandals, was disclosed. Moreover, there was no evidence that Unique played any role in formulating or offering the Blue Chip Hurricane Guarantee, that the Collettes dealt directly with Unique in making their decision to go to Sandals, or that they even discussed the Hurricane Guarantee with anyone from Unique.

In these circumstances, the Collettes could have recovered on their breach of contract claim against Unique only if there had been some evidence which indicated that Sandals and Unique were engaged in a joint venture. * * * As noted, there was no evidence in this case that Unique had any role in the control or management of the Sandals resorts, other than to accept bookings. The Collettes' attempt to portray Unique as a Sandals principal is not advanced by their characterization of Unique as a tour operator. First, it is far from clear whether Unique was, in fact, a tour operator, which is defined as a seller of travel services that creates and sells travel packages. In any event, a tour operator is not liable for the negligence of a third part supplier of services which the tour operator does not operate, manage, or control.

* * *

Applying these factors, the evidence in the record before us was insufficient to permit the trial judge to disregard the separate corporate identities of Sandals and Unique. There was no evidence of who owned Sandals and who owned Unique, who ran the two companies, whether Unique did anything other than to take reservations, whether employees of Unique wrote the Sandals brochure or had any say in how the Sandals resorts were run or conversely, whether Sandals actively participated in the day to day operations of Unique. The Collettes could never have been deceived by Unique, never discussed the Guarantee with anyone from Unique, and had no reason to be aware of the mechanics of the reservation process or to be concerned about it. * * *

As the evidence was insufficient to permit a finding of a breach of contract or a G.L.c. 93A violation by Unique, the judgment against the defendant cannot stand. The judgment for the plaintiffs is reversed and vacated. A judgment for the defendant, Unique Vacations, Inc., is to be entered.

CASES ON THE SUPPLEMENTAL CD

Campbell v. Starwood Hotels and Resorts Worldwide, Inc., (2008 U.S. Dist. LEXIS 75883). The reader should note the consideration of all factors in determining the best court venue for this case (i.e., forum non conveniens).

Kaloyeva v. Apple Vacations, (866 N.Y.S.2d 488, 2008). The reader should identify how the court applied the test for defendant "doing business" in a State.

Sachs v. TWA Getaway Vacations, Inc., (125 F.Supp.2d 1368, 2000). Readers should note the role of each of the following this case: (1) open and obvious hazards, (2) defendant's control over services provided, and (3) defendant's notice of problems with third party suppliers.

QUESTIONS YOU SHOULD BE ABLE TO ANSWER

1. What is a hotel's legal responsibility to their guests for guest's personal property?

2. Explain the essential elements that must occur for the theory of bailment to apply.

3. How is jurisdiction determined when one uses the Internet to transact travel arrangements?

4. Explain the factors to consider when a claim of forum non conveniens is made.

5. What is the legal duty of travel agents to their clients?

REFERENCES

Cases

Adames v. Trans National Travel, 1998 Mass. Super. LEXIS 108 (1998).

Allen v. Greenville Hotel Partners, Inc., 2006 U.S. Dist. LEXIS 1855 (2006).

Bernardi v. Apple Vacations, 236 F. Supp. 2d 465 (2002).

Bird v. Celebrity Cruise Line, Inc., 428 F.Supp.2d 1275 (2005).

Black v. Delta Airlines, Inc., 160 S.W.3d 68 (2002).

Bradshaw v. ITT Sheraton Corporation, 2005 Mass. Super. LEXIS 331 (2005).

Brocker v. Norwegian Cruise Line Limited, 2007 U.S. Dist. LEXIS 54096 (2007).

Campbell v. Starwood Hotels & Resorts Worldwide, Inc., 2008 U.S. Dist. LEXIS 75883 (2008).

Carnival Cruise Lines, Inc. v. Shute, 111 S. Cr. 1522 (1991).

Cash v. Six Continents Hotels, 2004 U.S. Dist. LEXIS 2901 (2004).

Cervantes v. Ramparts, Inc., 2003 Cal. App. Unpub. LEXIS 1283 (2003).

Coles v. Jenkins, 34 F.Supp.2d 381 (1998).

Collette v. Unique Vacations, Inc., 2004 Mass. App. Div. LEXIS 19 (2004).

Copeland v. The Lodge Enterprises, Inc., 4 P.3d 695 (2000).

Dazo v. Globe Airport Security Services, 295 F.3d 934 (2002).

Decker v. Circus Circus Hotel, 49 F.Supp.2d 743 (1999).

Fabend v. Rosewood Hotels and Resorts, L.L.C., 381 F.3d 152 (2004).

Gulf Oil Co. v. Gilbert, 67 S. Ct. 839 (1947).

Heidle v. The Prospect Reef Resort, Ltd., 364 F.Supp.2d 312 (2005).

Henson v. Seabourn Cruise Line Limited, Inc., 2005 U.S. Dist. LEXIS 26221 (2005).

Hofer v. Expedia, Inc., 516 F.Supp.2d 161 (2007).

Horberg v. Kerzner International Hotels Limited, 2007 U.S. Dist. LEXIS 97693 (2007).

Kaloyeva v. Apple Vacations, 866 N.Y.S.2d 488 (2008).

Krautsack v. Anderson, 861 N.E.2d 633 (2006).

Lewis v. Elsin, 2002 Mo. App. LEXIS 435 (2002).

Lischinskaya v. Carnival Corporation, 865 N.Y.S.2d 334 (2008).

Maurer v. Cerkvenik-Anderson Travel, Inc., 890 P.2d 69 (1994).

Morales v. Royal Caribbean Cruises, Ltd., 419 F.Supp. 2d 97 (2006).

Rainbow Travel Services v. Hilton Hotels, Corp., 896 F.2d 1233 (10th Cir. 1990).

Sachs v. TWA Getaway Vacations, Inc., 125 F.Supp.2d 1368 (2000).

Shlivko v. Good Luck Travel, Inc., 763 N.Y.S.2d 906 (2003).

Smith v. Circus Circus Casinos, Inc., 304 F.Supp.2d 463 (2003).

Stobaugh v. Norwegian Cruise Line Limited, 5 S.W.3d 232 (1999).

Stone v. Continental Airlines, 804 N.Y.S.2d 652 (2005).

Twardy v. Northwest Airlines, Inc., 2001 U.S. Dist. LEXIS 2112 (2001).

Uddin v. Embassy Suites Hotel, 848 N.E.2d 519 (2005).

United States of America v. Coles, 2006 U.S. App. LEXIS 3122 (2006).

Vega v. Norwegian Cruise Lines, 2007 U.S. Dist. LEXIS 44642 (2007).

Vermeulen v. Worldwide Holidays, Inc., 2006 Fla. App. LEXIS 1551 (2006).

Waterton v. Linden Motor, Inc., 2006 N.Y. Misc. LEXIS 261 (2006).

Zippo Manufacturing Co. v. Zippo Dot Com, 952 F. Supp. 1119 (1997).

Publications

Barth, S. (2009). *Hospitality law* (3rd ed.). Hoboken, NJ: John Wiley & Sons.

Cheeseman, H. R. (2004). *Business law* (5th ed.). Upper Saddle River, NJ: Pearson Education.

Dickerson, T. A. (2004). Recent development: The cruise passenger's dilemma: Twenty-first-century ships, nineteenth-century rights. *Tulane Maritime Law Journal, 28*, 447–465.

Garner, B. A. (Ed.) (2004). *Black's law dictionary* (8th ed.). St. Paul, MN: Thomson/West Group.

Jeffries, J. P. (1995). *Understanding hospitality law* (3rd ed.). East Lansing, MI: Educational Institute of the American Hotel and Motel Association.

Morris, K. L., Marshall, A. G., & Cournoyer, N. G. (2008). *Hotel, restaurant, and travel law: A preventive approach* (7th ed.). Clifton Park, NY: Thomson Delmar Learning.

The state of the cruise industry in 2009: Well-positioned for challenging times. (2009, January 16). *Daily Travel & Tourism Newsletter*. Retrieved March 19, 2009 from http://www.traveldailynews.com

Legislation

46 App. U.S.C. Appendix § 183c (2006).

3.00

INTENTIONAL TORTS AND CRIMINAL ACTS

Some actions go beyond the level of the unintentional tort—negligence. Two such actions included in this section are intentional torts and criminal acts. An **intentional tort** is a tort, or wrong, in which the actor possessed intent or purpose to injure. An intentional tort contains three elements: (1) there must be an injury, (2) the act is the proximate cause of an injury, and (3) there must be intent to bring about the injury. Legal action must be instituted by the victim or plaintiff and in civil suits punishment generally takes the form of a monetary award to the victim.

Several intentional torts that are of particular interest to the recreation or sport manager are examined in this section. They are assault and battery, defamation, invasion of privacy, breach of fiduciary duty, tortious interference with contract, and intentional infliction of emotional distress.

Recreation and sport managers are becoming more concerned with the effects of crimes on their programs. **Criminal law is that body of law made up of state and federal statutes that define certain offenses of a public nature or wrongs committed against the state and specify corresponding punishment.** The punishment for crimes can range from fines to long-term prison sentences, depending upon the nature of the crime. The state must institute the action and there is generally no remuneration to the victim.

Sport-related crimes addressed in the section include criminal violence in sport, gambling, wire and mail fraud, and ticket scalping. Hazing is also addressed under criminal law, but it should be noted that hazing can be considered a crime or an intentional tort.

3.10 Intentional Tort Applications

3.11 Assault and Battery

—**Curt Hamakawa**

WESTERN NEW ENGLAND COLLEGE

Suppose that you, as a sport or recreation manager, just heard from one of your employees that "There's a fight out front and a guy is bleeding all over the place!" Your first reaction might be to respond quickly to the scene to try to break up the scuffle and render first aid. But after stabilizing the situation and returning to your office, you realize that the physical altercation resulting in injuries might lead to legal liability. Questions swirl through your head: What would be the **cause of action**? Who would be liable; just the aggressor or both combatants? Could you, as the manager, and the organization you work for, be liable as well? Might criminal charges be filed in addition to a civil lawsuit, as a result of the fight? And most importantly, what can you do to minimize risks of harm and legal liability to you and your organization?

Sport and recreation managers must be familiar with actions in **tort that constitute intentional harms**,[1] because as the manager in the above example may discover, liability for assault and battery could extend to management as well. **Assault** and **battery** generally involve either the threat of bodily harm or an unlawful touching of another person without justification or excuse. Both are torts as well as crimes (Black's Law Dictionary, 2004) and will be defined in more detail later in this section. You may be aware that it is not uncommon in the sport or recreation environment for a person to be harmed as a result of another's intentional conduct, both on and off the "field of play." One need only tune in to the news to learn about the latest and most sensational assault and battery cases involving professional athletes or other celebrity figures. One of the most highly publicized incidents was the "Malice at the Palace" or "Basketbrawl" that took place on November 19, 2004, at the Palace of Auburn between the NBA Detroit Pistons and Indiana Pacers. Near the end of the highly charged game, Piston forward/center Ben Wallace was fouled by Pacer forward Ron Artest, and after a shove back by Wallace, several players from both teams joined in the fray. After a spectator threw a cup at Artest near the scorer's table, Artest charged the stands and a melee broke out between several spectators and Pacers. In addition to NBA suspensions handed down to players on both teams, five Pacers and seven Pistons fans were criminally charged with assault and battery.

Aside from some well-publicized allegations of criminal and/or civil assault and battery involving high-profile athletes (e.g., Vancouver Canuck Todd Bertuzzi's career-ending sucker punch on Colorado Avalanche player Steve Moore in a game during the NHL's 2004 season; NBA's Kobe Bryant's 2003 sexual assault of a 19-year-old woman at a Vail, Colorado, resort; Los Angeles Laker Kermit Washington's infamous punch out of the Houston Rockets' Rudy Tomjanovich in 1977; and Golden State Warrior Latrell Spreewell's choking takedown of coach P.J. Carlesimo at a practice in 1997), local media are replete with reports that can and do give rise to liability for assault and battery. Thus, recreation and sport managers should be aware that their organizations are not immune from incidents involving participants, parents and other spectators, coaches and officials, security personnel, and anyone else who might find occasion to become engaged in behavior that meets the threshold requirements for assault and battery.

---

[1]Note that while intentional torts and negligence fall within the same family and classification as "civil wrongs," intentional torts are separate and distinct from negligence, which is addressed in Section 2.11, *Negligence*.

Although the conduct giving rise to assault and battery can result both in civil lawsuits and criminal charges, this section addresses only *civil* assault and battery. It is worth reiterating that in the sport and recreation context, parties to assault and battery could involve athletes, coaches, officials, spectators (including parents), club patrons, and any variety of "innocent" bystanders. Furthermore, while most sport- and recreation-related assaults and batteries never make the national headlines, it should not escape anyone's notice that such incidents occur with regularity. Consequently, sport and recreation managers must be educated about the potential risks to stakeholders posed by the intentional torts of assault and battery, and remain vigilant to these threats by devising measures to prevent or mitigate their occurrence.

FUNDAMENTAL CONCEPTS

While most people know—from their television and movie viewing habits, as well as from media reports—that assault and battery are types of crimes, probably fewer are aware that they also constitute **torts, which are** *civil* wrongs (Black's Law Dictionary, 2004). Thus, a person's conduct constituting assault and battery is actionable in both criminal and civil law. In other words, an individual who is accused of assault and battery can be charged by the police and prosecuted by the public prosecutor (referred to in the states variously as the district attorney, state's attorney, or prosecuting attorney, and in the federal system as the U.S. attorney) in criminal court, and be subject to criminal punishment (e.g., incarceration, probation, and/or fines), and/or be sued by the injured party for **damages** (i.e., monetary award to the plaintiff) in civil court. The reason that a person can be subjected to *both* civil and criminal prosecutions and not run afoul of **constitutional** provisions, is because the **Fifth Amendment** prohibition against **double jeopardy**[2] applies only to crimes, and not civil actions. You may recall that O.J. Simpson, who was found **not guilty** by the jury in his criminal trial for the murders of his ex-wife Nicole Brown Simpson and her friend, Ronald Goldman, subsequently was held **liable** for their **wrongful deaths** in the civil trial. In the sport and recreation environment, criminal prosecutions for assault and battery occur far less frequently than civil suits for several reasons.

First, the culture of sport is averse to the idea that someone should be held criminally responsible for causing harm to another person in an organized sporting or recreational activity, where harsh and even violent physical contacts are deemed "part of the game." Second, the **standard of proof** in a criminal case is a much higher burden than in a civil case,[3] thus making criminal prosecutions more difficult to win (which in part explains the differing **verdicts** in the O.J. Simpson cases mentioned above). And third, there is a societal reluctance to prosecute—never mind convict—a class of people who pursue the ideal of an active and healthy lifestyle and who are often venerated for their on-field achievements. Assault and battery cases that involve non-competitors (e.g., parents or spectators) or that involve athletes and occur off the field of competition (e.g., domestic abuse, bar fights) are entirely situation-dependent. Perhaps as many people believe that athletes-as-celebrities receive favorable treatment when it comes to criminal prosecution, as defendant-athletes believe they are unfairly singled out for prosecution *because* they are famous.

Thus, a district attorney's decision to prosecute a criminal defendant on behalf of the public and an aggrieved private party's decision to sue the same person for civil remedies arising out of the same set of facts are based on independent variables. Without a doubt, decisions *not* to prosecute or sue for assault and battery far outnumber decisions to bring legal action. Two prominent examples of havoc in the field of battle that did *not* result in either criminal charges or lawsuits include heavyweight boxer Mike Tyson's biting off part of Evander Holyfield's ear in a 1997 bout, and France's Zinedine Zidane's horrific head butt of Italy's Marco Materazzi near the end of the 2006 World Cup Final. The remainder of this section focuses on *civil* assault and battery, while *criminal* assault and battery are addressed elsewhere (see Section 3.21, *Sport Related Crimes*).

---

[2]Legal concept that protects an individual from being subjected to prosecution more than once for the same alleged crime.
[3]In a criminal case, the government must prove all the elements of a crime **beyond a reasonable doubt**, while in a civil case, a plaintiff need only prove his/her case by a **preponderance of the evidence**.

Torts of Assault and Battery

While the terms "assault and battery" commonly are used in concert, they are actually separate and distinct torts. Thus, in seeking redress for harms caused by any intentional tort, a **plaintiff's** lawsuit against a **defendant** for assault, battery, or both, will be dictated by the facts and circumstances of the case. By definition, assault and battery are intentional torts, meaning that the **tortfeasor** desired "to bring about [a] result that will invade [the] interests of another" (*Wager v. Pro*, 1979), as distinguished from **negligence**, which is characterized by "inadvertence, thoughtlessness, inattention, and the like" (Black's Law Dictionary, 2004).

Assault

Assault is the *attempt* to inflict physical harm on another individual, whether successful or not, of which the intended victim is aware (Legal Information Institute). In fact, the Louisiana Criminal Code defines assault as "an attempt to commit a battery, or the intentional placing of another in reasonable apprehension of receiving a battery" (LA-R.S. 14:36). Put another way, assault is an attempt or threat to cause offensive contact with another person, coupled with the victim's reasonable apprehension of immediate bodily harm. Even more succinctly, it is putting someone in fear of receiving a battery (Kinsella, 1996). Thus, the tort of assault can be committed without actually touching, striking, or doing bodily harm to the victim (*State v. Murphy*, 1972). Still, words alone—regardless how insulting, provocative, or threatening—without the requisite elements, do not constitute assault.

Elements of Assault. In order for an assault to occur, the following elements must be present:

- An intentional act by the defendant;
- That causes reasonable apprehension on the part of the plaintiff;
- Of imminent harmful or offensive contact.

For example, a coach's statement to a player that he will "ring his bell" if the player messes up the play again would not constitute assault, because mere words unaccompanied by any act to cause apprehension of imminent injury do not satisfy the elemental requirements. However, an ominous approach by a just-fouled pickup basketball player with a clenched fist and cocked arm, accompanied by some unflattering name-calling and his threat to "get even" would likely constitute assault if the second player feared that he was about to be struck by the fouled player. Importantly, the tortfeasor must have intended to cause a harmful or offensive contact with the plaintiff (American Law Institute, 2009), and the plaintiff's apprehension of fear cannot be derived from the defendant's **negligent** or **reckless** conduct.

Because assault requires apprehension of harm on the part of the victim, no assault can occur where the victim is not aware that he or she is about to be struck. Thus, for example, a field hockey player who is blindsided and intentionally taken down by an opposing player cannot sue for assault (although she could sue for battery!). Finally, the harmful or offensive contact must be imminent and likely to occur momentarily, as opposed to the more distant threat of a sports bookie to "break your legs" if he does not receive the amount owed him on losing bets within 24 hours of the event's outcome.

Battery

If assault can be characterized in a loose and general way as attempted battery, then the completion of the threat or act culminating in actual physical contact, without consent, is battery. Put another way, battery is the consummation of an assault (*People v. Solak*, 1985). The classic definition of **battery** is the "intentional and wrongful physical contact with a person without his or her consent that entails some injury or offensive touching" (*Mason v. Cohn*, 1981). Prosser and Keeton (1984) stated that the freedom from intentional and unpermitted contacts with an individual's person "extends to any part of the body, or to anything which is attached to it and practically identified with it." Thus, an untoward and unwelcomed contact with a person's clothing, handbag, backpack, or even a held object could be grounds for a suit in battery. Also, a baseball pitcher who intentionally throws a fastball at a heckling fan in the stands and injures him would be liable for battery even though the pitcher was not in the immediate physical presence of the fan.

Elements of Battery. In order for there to be a battery, the following elements must be present:

- Intentional conduct by defendant;
- Causing harmful or offensive contact to plaintiff;
- Without consent.

As with assault, battery is an intentional tort that requires a willful act on the part of the perpetrator. Unlike assault, however—which has no necessity of physical contact—battery (as the term implies) requires a "battering" or otherwise unwelcome or unpermitted touching. To be sure, there need not be any grievous injury; all that is required is a physical touching, however slight, as the law does not discriminate between degrees of force (*Steele v. State*, 1989). Thus, a jubilant fan who gets caught up in the excitement of his team's victory and spontaneously turns to kiss an unknowing spectator might be liable for battery (provided the gesture was unwelcomed and nonconsensual). The requirement of the tortfeasor's intent for battery applies to the resulting harmful or offensive contact to the victim, and not to the willful commitment to do the act. For example, in a case for battery against a golfer whose tee shot struck a resident who was standing outside her condominium bordering the fairway, the court said that the mere fact that the golfer *intended to hit the ball* was insufficient. What was required for battery was the golfer's intent to cause "an offensive contact with or unconsented touching of, or trauma upon [the plaintiff]" (*Hennessey v. Pyne, 1979*). An important distinction from assault is that battery does not require that the victim be aware of the harmful or offensive contact. There is no requirement that the plaintiff have an apprehension of the impending physical contact for battery to occur.

Consent

Consent, or rather the absence thereof, is an essential element in proving battery, and many cases will hinge on whether the plaintiff could be construed to have given his or her consent to participate in the activity that resulted in the allegation of battery. In a suit for battery brought by a high school basketball player against his coach, a question arose whether the physical contact at a pre-practice altercation involving wrestling techniques was consensual, since the coach disputed the player's assertions that he twice told the coach to release his arm. The coach characterized the incident instead as "playfully antagonistic" (*Goff v. Clarke*, 2003). This, of course, is a question of fact for the jury to determine, but it also raises the issue of consent in the realm of horseplay. One person might be enjoying the jovial, good-natured roughhousing activity, while another person is feeling abused and victimized. In *Clayton v. New Dreamland Roller Skating Rink* (1951), a woman who was skating at a roller skating rink injured her arm in a fall and was taken to the rink's first-aid room, where a rink employee proceeded to manipulate the woman's arm. The employee was not a medical doctor and not authorized to perform physical manipulation treatments. Yet in the face of protestations by the woman, he continued to work on the woman's arm by applying traction. Subsequently, the woman was taken to a hospital, where x-rays revealed a fracture. This case reaffirms the rule that, absent consent, even a do-gooder's unwanted physical intervention on the person of another would subject him to liability for assault and battery, regardless of noble intentions.

In a classic case of an injury sustained in the course of a game (*Cunico v. Miller*, 2002), a high school soccer goalie sued an opposing player, her parents, and the opposing player's coach after being kicked by the opposing player. In rejecting the battery claim, the court said that as a matter of law, plaintiff "consented to the inherent risks of soccer from the undisputed fact of her voluntary participation in the soccer game." Such consent negates one of the elements of a battery claim because "the act of stepping onto the field of play may be described as 'consent to the inherent risks of the activity'" (*Ritchie-Gamester v. City of Berkley*, 1999). In another case involving a game-related injury (*Overall v. Kadella*, 1984), the court held that while consent (to bodily contacts that are permitted by the rules of the game) is manifested by a player' participation in a hockey game, an intentional act causing injury that goes beyond what is ordinarily permissible is actionable in tort (see the Supplemental CD).

Defenses to Assault and Battery

Since winning a case of assault or battery requires the plaintiff to prove the elements of the tort by a preponderance of the evidence, any defense would be predicated on the **absence of one or more of the requisite elements.** A defendant could also claim self-defense or defense of another, in which the alleged assault and/or battery was justifiable in order to protect oneself or a third party from harm. Thus, in a heated exchange between a baseball manager and umpire who are nose-to-nose with one another, if the manager was readying to spew a wad of spit at the umpire's face, the umpire could raise his arms to protect himself, even if he brushes the manager's face or pushes him away in the process.

Express or Implied Consent. In the sport and recreation context, however, perhaps the most common defense against assault and battery is that the alleged victim either expressly or impliedly consented to the harms visited upon him or her. The reason is that where no public interest is implicated, the law does not seek to intervene by protecting against one's own folly (Prosser and Keeton, 1984). In other words, if in undertaking to enter a martial arts competition an athlete consents to any and all physical harms caused by an opponent in the ordinary course of the competition, the consent negates not only the opponent's otherwise wrongful conduct, but also the very existence of the tort. The concept of a person's consent to participate in sport applies whether the activity is ultimate fighting or table tennis.

For example, in the combative sports of boxing, ultimate fighting, wrestling, karate, judo, taekwondo and the like, the object of the game is to physically beat or subdue the opposing player/athlete, just as the rules of certain team sports condone blocking, tackling, and body checking, and otherwise encourage harsh physical play. As noted previously, conduct that would readily result in criminal action or civil lawsuits off the field of play is given closer scrutiny within the confines of organized sport, under the guise that injured participant is deemed to have consented to the contact and attendant risk of harm. Although in the right circumstances, an aggrieved party might still press for criminal prosecution and/or civil remedies.

Privilege. Another defense to intentional torts is that of privilege, which is in the realm of excuse or justification. An action that might otherwise result in liability is **privileged** if the defendant acted in furtherance of an interest of such social importance that it is entitled to legal protection, even though the plaintiff suffered harm (Prosser and Keeton, 1984). In essence, the tortfeasor is shielded from liability because circumstances and social policy permit or require it, as in the case of self-defense. In the sport and recreation context, a coach or trainer might be entitled to such privilege in demonstrating a skill or technique to a participant.

Immunity. Related, but different, is the concept of **immunity**, which prevents even the initiation of a lawsuit or prosecution. An example of immunity would be the acts of law enforcement personnel acting in their official capacities as peace officers. Thus, police officers who physically accost a criminal suspect in the performance of their duties would be immune from suit or criminal prosecution for assault and battery.

Tort Remedies

Typically, the remedies available to plaintiffs who prevail in suits in tort (including assault and battery) are **damages,** or the award of a sum of money to the plaintiff. **Compensatory damages** (also referred to as **actual damages**) are those which compensate the plaintiff for the injury sustained; the rationale being that such damages would restore the injured party to the position he or she would be in but for the injury (*Northwestern Nat. Cas. Co. v. McNulty*, 1962). In general, if the injury is slight or there is no substantial loss, the damages will be nominal, since the purpose of compensatory damages is not to provide the prevailing party with a windfall. On the other hand, **punitive damages** (also referred to as **exemplary damages**), may be awarded in cases of particularly grievous circumstances where the plaintiff suffered extreme anguish, or to punish the perpetrator for horrific or heinous behavior and to make an example of him (Black's Law Dictionary, 2004), as well as to deter others from engaging in similar conduct in the future. Punitive damages can amount to large sums of money, and are often criticized as a financial windfall by defendants because they reward the plaintiff above and beyond the extent of his or her injuries (see discussion of damages in Section 2.11, *Negligence*). It should be noted, however, that punitive damages are less commonly awarded, because courts must first be persuaded that the requisite extenuating circumstances exist to merit this extraordinary remedy.

Plaintiffs can also seek **equitable** relief, which takes the form of an **injunction** or **specific performance**. These are essentially court orders that command or prohibit an act. For example, in the wake of the infamous spectator-infused donnybrook at the Detroit Pistons-Indiana Pacers NBA game in 2004, Pacer Ron Artest obtained a **restraining order** against John Green, the Pistons fan who threw a cup at Artest that fueled the melee in the stands. The restraining order prohibits Green from coming within 60 feet of Artest.

Vicarious Liability

Recreation and sport managers should be aware that, although quite rare, supervisors and organizations have been held liable for the intentional torts committed by their employees under the employer-employee doctrine of *respondeat superior.* A significant, and practical, reason for naming parties in addition to the actual tortfeasor as defendants in a suit is that oftentimes the perpetrator is **judgment proof,** meaning that he or she does not have the assets with which to satisfy the plaintiff's award for damages. In order to attach liability to the employer, the tort must have been committed by an employee within the course and scope of employment. For example, under this theory, if security personnel at an event or a bouncer at a club wrongfully manhandles a patron resulting in injury, the patron could bring suit against the assailant's employer. On the other hand, if the employee committed an assault and/or battery in a capacity that was unrelated to the performance of his job (e.g., carrying out a personal grudge), then the employer would not be liable to the injured party. Thus, sport organization managers should be aware of this potential liability and take steps to ensure that their employees—particularly those employees whose duties contemplate the likelihood of physical contact with others—are properly trained in the appropriate use of force.

Toone v. Adams (1964), involved a suit by a minor league umpire against a baseball manager and his club for injuries sustained in a punch from a fan after a particularly contentious game. The umpire alleged that the manager's on-field protests of the umpire's calls incited the fan to commit the assault. The court, however, concluded that the manager and club were not liable because the manager's conduct was not directly related to the ensuing assault. In this case, the nexus between the manager's antics and fan's violent act was not sufficiently drawn for one to be a natural and proximate result of the other.

In *Godfrey v. Iverson* (2009), nightclub patron Marlin Godfrey was beaten up by NBA player Allen Iverson's bodyguard and suffered injuries that required hospital emergency room attention. Even though Iverson was not personally involved in the scuffle, he was present and watched the fight from the VIP section of the nightclub, standing on a couch and observing the action. The appellate court said that "negligent supervision arises when an employer knew or should have known that its employee behaved in a dangerous or otherwise incompetent manner, and that the employer, armed with that knowledge, failed to adequately supervise its employee," and upheld the trial court's verdict against Iverson and award of $260,000 for Godfrey. For other cases involving assault and battery and naming the assailants' employer as an additional defendant under the doctrine of vicarious liability, see *Hackbart v. Cincinnati Bengals*, (1979) and *Manning v. Grimsley*, (1981). (See the Supplemental CD.)

For an excellent discussion and to obtain a better understanding of an employer's liability for intentional torts committed by an employee, see *Baumeister v. Plunkett* (1996), where the court held that defendant Humana Hospital was not liable for the assault committed by a nursing supervisor on a nurse technician, because even though the assault occurred during the supervisor's course of employment (i.e., during working hours and at the hospital's premises), the act of violence was neither primarily employment-rooted nor reasonably incidental to the performance of the supervisor's duties.

SIGNIFICANT CASE

The following case involves an injury sustained by an age-group football player in practice as a result of his being the subject in a tackling demonstration conducted by a coach, and raises the issue of consent and whether the scope of this consent extends to his participation in direct physical contact with participants beyond his age and experience. Note the court's analysis of assault and battery, and its conclusion that that the plaintiff's apprehension of imminent harm—a requisite element of assault—was wanting in this case. Note also the court's admonishment on remand that the plaintiff could pursue its claim for punitive damages. The dissenting opinion that immediately follows the court's opinion is provided to illustrate the nuanced views of the law.

KOFFMAN V. GARNETT

Supreme Court of Virginia
265 Va. 12, 574 S.E.2d 258
Jan. 10, 2003

Present: All the Justices

Opinion by Justice Elizabeth B. Lacy

In this case we consider whether the trial court properly dismissed the plaintiffs' second amended motion for judgment for failure to state causes of action for gross negligence, assault, and battery.

* * *

In the fall of 2000, Andrew W. Koffman, a 13-year old middle school student at a public school in Botetourt County, began participating on the school's football team. It was Andy's first season playing organized football, and he was positioned as a third-string defensive player. James Garnett was employed by the Botetourt County School Board as an assistant coach for the football team and was responsible for the supervision, training, and instruction of the team's defensive players.

The team lost its first game of the season. Garnett was upset by the defensive players' inadequate tackling in that game and became further displeased by what he perceived as inadequate tackling during the first practice following the loss.

Garnett ordered Andy to hold a football and "stand upright and motionless" so that Garnett could explain the proper tackling technique to the defensive players. Then Garnett, without further warning, thrust his arms around Andy's body, lifted him "off his feet by two feet or more," and "slamm[ed]" him to the ground. Andy weighed 144 pounds, while Garnett weighed approximately 260 pounds. The force of the tackle broke the humerus bone in Andy's left arm. During prior practices, no coach had used physical force to instruct players on rules or techniques of playing football.

In his second amended motion for judgment, Andy, by his father and next friend, Richard Koffman, and Andy's parents, Richard and Rebecca Koffman, individually, (collec-

tively "the Koffmans") alleged that Andy was injured as a result of Garnett's simple and gross negligence and intentional acts of assault and battery. Garnett filed a demurrer and plea of sovereign immunity, asserting that the second amended motion for judgment did not allege sufficient facts to support a lack of consent to the tackling demonstration and, therefore, did not plead causes of action for either gross negligence, assault, or battery. The trial court dismissed the action, finding that Garnett, as a school board employee, was entitled to sovereign immunity for acts of simple negligence and that the facts alleged were insufficient to state causes of action for gross negligence, assault, or battery because the instruction and playing of football are "inherently dangerous and always potentially violent." In this appeal, the Koffmans do not challenge the trial court's ruling on Garnett's plea of sovereign immunity but do assert that they pled sufficient facts in their second amended motion for judgment to sustain their claims of gross negligence, assault, and battery.

* * *

The disparity in size between Garnett and Andy was obvious to Garnett. Because of his authority as a coach, Garnett must have anticipated that Andy would comply with his instructions to stand in a non-defensive, upright, and motionless position. Under these circumstances, Garnett proceeded to aggressively tackle the much smaller, inexperienced student football player, by lifting him more than two feet from the ground and slamming him into the turf. According to the Koffmans' allegations, no coach had tackled any player previously, so there was no reason for Andy to expect to be tackled by Garnett, nor was Andy warned of the impending tackle or of the force Garnett would use.

As the trial court observed, receiving an injury while participating in a tackling demonstration may be part of the sport. The facts alleged in this case, however, go beyond the circumstances of simply being tackled in the course of participating in organized football. Here Garnett's knowledge of his greater size and experience, his instruction implying that Andy was not to take any action to defend himself from the force of a tackle, the force he used during the tackle, and Garnett's previous practice of not personally using force to demonstrate or teach football technique could lead a reasonable person to conclude that, in this instance, Garnett's actions were imprudent and were taken in utter disregard for the safety of the player involved. Because reasonable persons could disagree on this issue, a jury issue was presented, and the trial court erred in holding that, as a matter of law, the second amended motion for judgment was inadequate to state a claim for gross negligence.

* * *

The trial court held that the second amended motion for judgment was insufficient as a matter of law to establish causes of action for the torts of assault and battery. We begin by identifying the elements of these two independent torts. See Charles E. Friend, Personal Injury Law in Virginia 6.2.1 (2d ed. 1998).

The tort of assault consists of an act intended to cause either harmful or offensive contact with another person or apprehension of such contact, and that creates in that other person's mind a reasonable apprehension of an imminent battery. Restatement (Second) of Torts 21 (1965); Friend 6.3.1 at 226; *Fowler v. Harper, et al.*, The Law of Torts 3.5 at 3:18-:19 (3d ed. Cum. Supp. 2003).

The tort of battery is an unwanted touching which is neither consented to, excused, nor justified. See *Washburn v. Klara*, 263 Va. 586, 561 S.E.2d 682 (2002); *Woodbury v. Courtney*, 239 Va. 651, 391 S.E.2d 293 (1990). Although these two torts "go together like ham and eggs," the difference between them is "that between physical contact and the mere apprehension of it. One may exist without the other." W. Page Keeton, Prosser and Keeton on Torts 10 at 46; see also Friend 6.3.

The Koffmans' second amended motion for judgment does not include an allegation that Andy had any apprehension of an immediate battery. This allegation cannot be supplied by inference because any inference of Andy's apprehension is discredited by the affirmative allegations that Andy had no warning of an imminent forceful tackle by Garnett. The Koffmans argue that a reasonable inference of apprehension can be found "in the very short period of time that it took the coach to lift Andy into the air and throw him violently to the ground." At this point, however, the battery alleged by the Koffmans was in progress. Accordingly, we find that the pleadings were insufficient as a matter of law to establish a cause of action for civil assault.

The second amended motion for judgment is sufficient, however, to establish a cause of action for the tort of battery. The Koffmans pled that Andy consented to physical contact with players "of like age and experience" and that neither Andy nor his parents expected or consented to his "participation in aggressive contact tackling by the adult coaches." Further, the Koffmans pled that, in the past, coaches had not tackled players as a method of instruction. Garnett asserts that, by consenting to play football, Andy consented to be tackled, by either other football players or by the coaches. Whether Andy consented to be tackled by Garnett in the manner alleged was a matter of fact. Based on the allegations in the Koffmans' second amended motion for judgment, reasonable persons could disagree on whether Andy gave such consent. Thus, we find that the trial court erred in holding that the Koffmans' second amended motion for judgment was insufficient as a matter of law to establish a claim for battery.

For the above reasons, we will reverse the trial court's judgment that the Koffmans' second amended motion for judgment was insufficient as a matter of law to establish the causes of actions for gross negligence and battery and remand the case for further proceedings consistent with this opinion.*

Reversed and remanded.

JUSTICE KINSER, concurring in part and dissenting in part.

I agree with the majority opinion except with regard to the issue of consent as it pertains to the intentional tort of battery. In my view, the second amended motion for judgment filed by the plaintiffs, Andrew W. Koffman, by his father and next friend, and Richard Koffman and Rebecca Koffman, individually, was insufficient as a matter of law to state a claim for battery.**

Absent fraud, consent is generally a defense to an alleged battery. See *Banovitch v. Commonwealth*, 196 Va. 210, 219, 83 S.E.2d 369, 375 (1954); *Perkins v. Commonwealth*, 31 Va. App. 326, 330, 523 S.E.2d 512, 513 (2000); *People ex rel. Arvada v. Nissen*, 650 P.2d 547, 551 (Colo. 1982); *Bergman v. Anderson*, 411 N.W.2d 336, 339 (Neb. 1987); *Willey v. Carpenter*, 23 A. 630, 631 (Vt. 1891); Restatement (Second) of Torts 13, cmt. d (1965). In the context of this case, "[t]aking part in a game manifests a willingness to submit to such bodily contacts or restrictions of liberty as are permitted by its rules or usages." Restatement (Second) of Torts 50, cmt. b (1965), quoted in *Thompson v. McNeill*, 559 N.E.2d 705, 708 (Ohio 1990); see also *Kabella v. Bouschelle*, 672 P.2d 290, 292 (N.M. Ct. App. 1983). However, participating in a particular sport "does not manifest consent to contacts which are prohibited by rules or usages of the game if such rules or usages are designed to protect the participants and not merely to secure the better playing of the game as a test of skill." Restatement (Second) of Torts 50, cmt. b (1965) quoted in Thompson, 559 N.E.2d at 708; see also Kabella, 672 P.2d at 292.

The thrust of the plaintiffs' allegations is that they did not consent to "Andy's participation in aggressive contact tackling by the adult coaches" but that they consented only to Andy's engaging "in a contact sport with other children of like age and experience." They further alleged that the coaches had not previously tackled the players when instructing them about the rules and techniques of football.

It is notable, in my opinion, that the plaintiffs admitted in their pleading that Andy's coach was "responsible . . . for the supervision, training and instruction of the defensive players." It cannot be disputed that one responsibility of a football coach is to minimize the possibility that players will sustain "something more than slight injury" while playing the sport. *Vendrell v. School District No. 26C*, Malheur County, 376 P.2d 406, 413 (Ore. 1962). A football coach cannot be expected "to extract from the game the body clashes that cause bruises, jolts and hard falls." *Id*. Instead, a coach should ensure that players are able to "withstand the shocks, blows and other rough treatment with which they would meet in actual play" by making certain that players are in "sound physical condition," are issued proper protective equipment, and are "taught and shown how to handle [themselves] while in play." *Id*. The instruction on how to handle themselves during a game should include demonstrations of proper tackling techniques. *Id*. By voluntarily participating in football, Andy and his parents necessarily consented to instruction by the coach on such techniques. The alleged battery occurred during that instruction.

The plaintiffs alleged that they were not aware that Andy's coach would use physical force to instruct on the rules and techniques of football since neither he nor the other coaches had done so in the past. Surely, the plaintiffs are not claiming that the scope of their consent changed from day to day depending on the coaches' instruction methods during prior practices. Moreover, they did not allege that

they were told that the coaches would not use physical demonstrations to instruct the players.

Additionally, the plaintiffs did not allege that the tackle itself violated any rule or usage of the sport of football. Nor did they plead that Andy could not have been tackled by a larger, physically stronger, and more experienced player either during a game or practice. Tackling and instruction on proper tackling techniques are aspects of the sport of football to which a player consents when making a decision to participate in the sport.

In sum, I conclude that the plaintiffs did not sufficiently plead a claim for battery. We must remember that acts that might give rise to a battery on a city street will not do so in the context of the sport of football. See Thompson, 559 N.E.2d at 707. We must also not blur the lines between gross negligence and battery because the latter is an intentional tort. I agree fully that the plaintiffs alleged sufficient facts to proceed with their claim for gross negligence.

For these reasons, I respectfully concur, in part, and dissent, in part, and would affirm the judgment of the circuit court sustaining the demurrer with regard to the claim for battery.

* Because we have concluded that a cause of action for an intentional tort was sufficiently pled, on remand, the Koffmans may pursue their claim for punitive damages.

** Although the circuit court sustained the demurrer with regard to the alleged battery on the basis that an intention to batter and inflict injury on Andy could not be inferred from the alleged facts, the majority does not address that holding. Since the majority discusses only the issue of consent, I confine my dissent to that question.

CASES ON THE SUPPLEMENTAL CD

Brokaw v. Winfield-Mt. Union Community School District, 2008 WL 4724739 (Iowa App.). Note the court's discussion and rationale for denying plaintiff's claim for punitive damages, on successful suit for battery.

Overall v. Kadella, 361 N.W.2d 352, 138 Mich.App. 351 (1985). Pay heed to the proposition that while a hockey player's participation in a game manifests his consent to bodily contacts that are permitted by the rules of the game, a player is liable for intentional acts resulting in injury that go beyond what is ordinarily permissible.

Manning v. Grimsley, 643 F.2d 20 (First Cir. 1981). Examines the issue of vicarious liability, and how an employer can be held liable for damages for injuries attributable to an employee's assault of a patron.

QUESTIONS YOU SHOULD BE ABLE TO ANSWER

1. What are the elements necessary to prove a case for assault? Battery?

2. Since assault and battery are crimes as well as torts, is it possible for a person to be prosecuted in criminal court and sued in civil court for committing the same acts? Why or why not?

3. How is negligence distinguishable from assault and battery?

4. What are the legal remedies available to a victim of civil assault and battery?

5. In the sport and recreation environment, how can managers insulate themselves and their organizations from liability for assault and battery?

REFERENCES

Cases

Baumeister v. Plunkett, 673 S.2d 994 (La. 1996).

Clayton v. New Dreamland Roller Skating Rink, 82 A.2d 458 (N.J. Super. 1951).

Cunico v. Miller, 2002 WL 339385 (Cal.App. 2 Dist.).

Godfrey v. Iverson, No. 07-7151 (D.C. Cir. 2009).

Goff v. Clarke, 302 A.D.2d 725, 755 N.Y.S.2d 493 (NY App.Div. 2003).

Hennessey v. Pyne, 694 A.2d 691 (R.I. 1979).

Mason v. Cohn, 438 N.Y.S.2d 462 (Sup. Ct. 1981).

Northwestern Nat. Cas. Co. v. McNulty, 307 F.2d 432 (5th Cir. 1962).

People v. Solak, 382 NW2d 495 (Mich.App. 1985).

Ritchie-Gamester v. City of Berkeley, 461 Mich. 73, 597 N.W.2d 517 (1999).

State v. Murphy, 500 P.2d 1276 (Wash.App. 1972).

Steele v. State, 778 P.2d 929 (Ok.Cr.App. 1989).

Toone v. Adams, 262 N.C. 403, 137 S.E.2d 132 (1964).

Wager v. Pro, 603 F.2d 1005 (D.C. Cir. 1979).

Publications

American Law Institute, (2009), Restatement (Second) of Torts.

FindLaw, http://injury.findlaw.com/assault-and-battery/elements-of-assault.html, accessed March 16, 2009.

Garner, B.A., ed. (2004), *Black's Law Dictionary*, 8th edition, Thomson West.

http://hoopedia.nba.com/index.php?title=Pacers-Pistons_Brawl, accessed March 15, 2009.

Keeton, W.P., Dobbs, D.B., Keeton, R.E., Owen, D.G. (1984), *Prosser and Keeton on Torts*, 5th ed., West Publishing Co., St. Paul, MN.

Kinsella, N.S. (1996), "Punishment and Proportionality: The Estoppel Approach," *Journal of Libertarian Studies*, 12:1.

Legal Information Institute, http://topics.law.cornell.edu/wex/asault, accessed December 17, 2008.

McCarthy, M., "Fan Who Ignited Brawl Forever Banned from Pistons' Homes Games," *USA Today*, November 17, 2006.

Legislation

LA-R.S. 14:36 (Louisiana Criminal Code), definition of assault.

3.12 Defamation

—John D. McMillen
CALIFORNIA STATE UNIVERSITY, FRESNO

Defamation is the communication of false statements that injures a person's reputation. Until recently, defamation law received little attention from the sport and recreation media. Today, due in part to advances in technology, defamation lawsuits commonly are a featured topic in the sport pages and sport talk shows, as mainstream media discusses steroid scandals, point shaving accusations, and other alleged defamatory comments.

FUNDAMENTAL CONCEPTS

The primary purpose of defamation law is to protect a person's personal, professional, and private reputation. Understanding defamation law is important because, as technology has advanced, so too has the opportunity for defamation lawsuits. Facebook, Twitter, and other popular social media outlets serve as breeding grounds for defamation lawsuits. This section, therefore, is designed to provide a general overview of the primary issues with which sport and recreation managers should be familiar in defamation law and how to protect themselves and their organization from such lawsuits.

Elements of Defamation

Defamation laws vary from state to state, but the underlying elements generally remain the same. To establish a valid claim for defamation, a plaintiff generally must prove four elements:

1. A false and defamatory statement of fact;

2. An unprivileged publication to a third party;

3. Fault or negligence of the publisher:

4. Damage or actual injury.

According to the Restatement (Second) of Torts § 558, a false and **defamatory statement** is one that "harms the reputation of another as to lower him [or her] in the estimation of the community or to deter third persons from associating or dealing with him." A false statement may purport to be factual, or if it is stated as one's opinion, it must imply the allegation of undisclosed defamatory facts as the basis for the opinion. For example, if a person states, "She's a great soccer player, but she's a steroid user," this qualifies as a statement of fact and is defamatory if false.

The **unprivileged publication** to a third party element requires communication either purposely or negligently to someone other than the person being defamed. No statement, no matter how false and degrading, can constitute defamation if it is made only to the person that is the basis of the statement. Defamation arises from a loss of reputation and a person cannot lose or have their reputation harmed if the statement is made only to that person. In other words, sending a sport celebrity an email stating that you believe he or she is a steroid user, even if you know this is untrue, is not defamation if it is not published to a third party.

The third element, fault, is the focal point of a defamation lawsuit. The degree of **fault** will depend on whether the plaintiff is a public official, a public person, or a private person (see below). "Private" plaintiffs must prove the defendant's fault amounts to negligence, whereas if the plaintiff is a "public person or a public official," the plaintiff has to prove "actual malice." The method of applying fault standards has been left open for states to interpret, but it is generally understood that defendants are given the most protection when plaintiffs are public officials or public persons.

The final element requires the plaintiff to demonstrate that he or she was **harmed** by the alleged defamation. Damages in defamation law fall under two categories: special and general damages (discussed below).

Slander versus Libel

Defamation is divided into two categories: libel and slander. **Libel** is defamation communicated through written or printed words, whereas **slander** is defamation communication through speaking. For example, defamatory materials posted to a fixed online location, such as Facebook, fall under libel, while using Youtube.com to broadcast a defamatory video falls under slander.

In defamation law, a written or verbal false comment is libel or slander **per se** when the allegation falls into one of the following categories:

1. It accuses the plaintiff of a crime involving moral turpitude;
2. It adversely affects the plaintiff's abilities in his or her profession, business, or trade,
3. It accuses the plaintiff of having a loathsome disease;
4. It accuses the plaintiff of sexual misconduct.

In other words, if statement falls into one of these four categories it is presumed that the reputation of the individual about whom the false statement was made will be injured. For example, falsely accusing a person of having sex with the entire soccer team in an Internet chat room would constitute libel per se (Carpenter, 1995). The same false accusation broadcast via Skype would fall under slander.

First Amendment Protections

The law of defamation has evolved as a tug-of-war between a plaintiff's right to enjoy his or her reputation and a defendant's right to freedom of speech under the First Amendment. For example, the media exist in large part to report on issues of public concern such as sporting events. However, individuals, including athletes and coaches, possess a right not to be subjected to falsehoods that impugn their character. The clash between these two rights can lead to expensive litigation and costly jury verdicts. Courts must balance the First Amendment and freedom of the press with individual rights and protection of one's reputation.

Modern defamation law evolved from the 1964 landmark case of *New York Times v. Sullivan* where the U.S. Supreme Court held that some defamatory statements were protected by the First Amendment. *New York Times* involved a newspaper article that made unflattering remarks about a public official, a politician. The Court maintained that "debate on public issues should be uninhibited, robust, and wide-open" (p. 270). The Court acknowledged that in public discussions about public officials mistakes can be made, and ruled that public officials could sue for false statements made about their public conduct only if the statements were made with "actual malice."

Actual malice means that the person who made the statement knew it was not true, or did not care whether it was true or not and therefore was reckless with the truth. An example would be when someone has doubts about the truth of a statement, but does not bother to check the facts before publishing the false statement.

Public Figures

In 1967, the Supreme Court extended the rule for public official defamation in the consolidated cases of *Curtis Publishing Co. v. Butts* and *The Associated Press v. Walker*. The cases featured plaintiffs Wally Butts, former athletic director of the University of Georgia, and Edwin Walker, a former general who had been in command of the federal troops during school desegregation in the 1950s.

Because the Georgia State Athletic Association, a private corporation, employed Butts, and Walker had retired from the Armed Forces at the time of their lawsuits, they were not considered public officials. The question before the Supreme Court then was whether to extend the rule in *New York Times v. Sullivan* to public figures. The Court agreed that both Butts and Walker were public figures. A **public figure** is an individual who has "commanded sufficient continuing public interest" (p. 155). Whether a person is classified as a public figure is a matter of law and does not depend on the desires of the individual.

Limited-Purpose Public Figures

Over the years, the Supreme Court has clarified the limits of the "actual malice" standard and the difference between public and private figures in defamation cases. In *Gertz v. Robert Welch, Inc.* (1974) the Court added another layer to defamation classifications. Gertz was a well-known Chicago lawyer who represented the family of a young man killed by police officer Richard Nuccio. Robert Welch Inc. published a monthly magazine article stating that Gertz had helped frame Nuccio and claimed Gertz was a communist. Both of these statements were false.

The Supreme Court had to determine whether Gertz was a private person or some sort of public figure. The Supreme Court distinguished between public figures and private persons, noting two differences: (1) Public officials and public figures have greater access to the media in order to counter defamatory statements; and (2) public officials and public figures, to a certain extent, seek out public acclaim and assume the risk of greater public scrutiny.

Gertz determined that certain persons could be classified as **limited-purpose public figures**. The Supreme Court noted that full-fledged public figures achieve "pervasive fame or notoriety." However, the court noted that sometimes an individual "injects himself or is drawn into a particular public controversy and thereby becomes a public figure for a limited range of issues" (418 U.S. 351). These limited-purpose public figures also have to meet the actual-malice standard.

Daubenmire v. Sommers (2004) set forth a three-part test to determine whether a person is a limited-purpose public figure: (1) there is a public controversy, (2) the plaintiff played a central role in the controversy, and (3) the alleged defamation was germane to the plaintiff's involvement in the controversy. For example, a concerned citizen who speaks up and draws media attention about the city's plan to build a new sport or recreation center downtown may qualify as a limited-purpose public figure.

Private Figures

Gertz v. Robert Welch, Inc., eventually concluded that Gertz was a private person, not a limited-purpose public figure, and established a different standard for private persons. The Court concluded that **private figures** refer to those persons who are not involved in public issues or employed as a public official. A private person does not have to show that a defendant acted with actual malice in order to prevail in a defamation suit. The private plaintiff usually must show that the defendant was negligent, or at fault. *Gertz* also ruled that private defamation plaintiffs could not recover punitive damages unless they showed evidence of actual malice.

Status of the Plaintiff

The above cases demonstrate that perhaps the most important legal issue in a defamation case is determining the status of the plaintiff. If the plaintiff is a public official, public figure, or limited-purpose public figure, the plaintiff must establish that the defendant acted with actual malice with clear and convincing evidence. Alternatively, private figures do not need to prove the defamatory statement was made with actual malice. Instead, a private plaintiff only has to prove his or her case by a preponderance of the evidence, a much lower burden of proof.

Most recreation and sport figures, such as coaches and athletes, are classified as limited-purpose public figures while participating in sport or recreation events, but outside of their sport careers they are considered a private person for purposes of defamation. Furthermore, while most public athletic directors, coaches, and other athletic and recreation administrators who receive compensation would appear to qualify as public officials under defamation law, at least one court has held that an assistant baseball recruiting coach at the University of Pittsburg was not classified as either a public official, public figure, or limited-purpose public figure (*Warford v. Lexington Herald*, 1990). In defamation law, therefore, classifying the plaintiff must be determined on a case-by-case basis.

Defenses

The three most common defenses to defamation are: (1) truth or opinion, (2) absolute privilege, and (3) qualified or conditional privilege.

Truth is an absolute defense to all defamation claims. A person cannot be prevented from telling the truth, even if that truth harms someone else. Further, one's **opinion** generally cannot constitute defamation since it is not offered as a statement of fact. For example, if a fan calls a radio show and says the food at the local stadium is as bad as the sports team, the fan's statement is not defamatory since taste will always be an opinion. Even if the team brought 100 witnesses to court to attest that the food is wonderful, the fan is still entitled to his or her opinion.

On the other hand, a person cannot say whatever they like and escape liability by casting a fact as an opinion. In other words, adding the word "opinion" to a defamatory statement does not necessarily shield the speaker from liability. The determining factor is whether the "opinion" is about a verifiable fact. For example, the same food critic fan would not be protected if he or she said, "in my opinion the food was horrible and the sports bar has rats." The statement about rats is defamatory (assuming it is false) because it is a verifiable fact.

Absolute privilege is a defense that applies to persons in legislative, judicial, administrative or executive branches of governments. In other words, for persons in these positions there is no liability for defamatory statements, regardless of their falsity or disregard for the truth, in order to avoid censorship that could otherwise benefit society.

Qualified or conditional privilege is similar to absolute privilege in that it applies in some situations that require the protection of communication in order to benefit society as a whole. Carpenter (1995) explained that for a statement to qualify under this privilege, it must be made (1) without knowledge of falsity, (2) by a person with reason to communicate the statement, and (3) communicated only to a person with a "justifiable interest in knowing." This privilege primarily applies to administrators when discussing employee behavior with managers or while offering employee references. This privilege would not, however, protect a recreation manager who knowingly made a false reference about an employee to a prospective employer.

Damages

In defamation proceedings, an injured plaintiff seeks redress for statements that are false and harmful to his reputation, against a defendant's assertion that his or her statements are truthful. Damages in defamation law fall under two categories: special and general damages. **Special damages** result from the actual loss the plaintiff can prove he or she sustained, such as lost wages or the loss of identified business customers. **General damages** are those damages that are nonquantifiable, such as personal humiliation, and mental anguish and suffering. In some egregious instances, **punitive or exemplary damages** are also granted for willful offenses where a defendant is treated as an example to prevent future similar behavior. Unless a plaintiff's lawsuit is for slander or libel per se, he or she must prove special damages.

Not only is the original author liable for the defamatory statements, but liability can attach depending on whether another party has distributed or published the defamatory statements. For example, "common carriers" (such as telephone companies) are not liable for defamation. "Distributors" of published material, such as bookstore owners, are liable only when they have actual knowledge of the defaming nature of the publication. "Publishers," by contrast, will be held liable for defamation regardless of their state of mind. See, e.g., Waldman, supra note 26, P 33 (Waldman, 1999).

CONCLUSION

The right to express oneself without restraint is fundamental to our individual freedoms. However, it is equally clear that this right should not be exercised in a way that would jeopardize another individual's interest in his reputation and good name. Courts have recognized the importance of these competing interests to prevent the uncurbed assault of one's character, while not allowing commentary and the exchange of ideas to be stifled unnecessarily. The need for balancing these two interests can be seen in the area of sports. Today's professional athlete, coach, and those associated with professional sports, as well as others who are involved with sport such as high school and college coaches and recreation managers, are continually under intense scrutiny from both the media and their peers. This pressure, or in some instances resentment, can cause individuals to make false statements, intended or not, which may give rise to litigation.

Sport and recreation managers must also remember that there are no gatekeepers in cyberspace and anyone with a computer is capable of targeting anyone else. Defamatory information is very difficult to remove once emailed, texted, or posted on the Internet. It is there for everyone to see and can cause untold damage from both the posting and the repeated access to the defamatory information. Sport and recreation managers should therefore educate themselves and their employees on the dangers of publishing false statements about other persons.

SIGNIFICANT CASE

Sport agent, Lamont Smith, filed a multi-million dollar defamation lawsuit against IMG and Tom Condon claiming that the sharp decline in his representation of high-end players is directly attributable to Condon's repeated defamatory comments to prospective professional players. This case illustrates how quickly conflicts can arise in the workplace and why sport and recreation managers must be fully aware of the potential legal consequences of their actions.

C. LAMONT SMITH V. IMG WORLDWIDE, INC. AND THOMAS J. CONDON

United States District Court for the Eastern District of Pennsylvania
437 F. Supp. 2d 297; 2006 U.S. Dist. LEXIS 37173 (2006)

BACKGROUND

On June 24, 2003, plaintiff, C. Lamont Smith, filed this action against Thomas J. Condon ("Condon") and Condon's employer, IMG Worldwide, Inc. ("IMG") in the Court of Common Pleas of Philadelphia. Plaintiff asserts claims of defamation and interference with prospective contractual relations that allegedly arose out of competition between plaintiff and Condon to represent highly-touted college football players prior to their entry into the National Football League ("NFL") draft. * * *

FACTS

The facts of this case are set forth in a previous opinion, *Smith v. IMG Worldwide, Inc.*, 360 F. Supp. 2d 681 (E.D. Pa. 2005). Therefore, only the facts necessary to the summary judgment decision are included in this memorandum.

Plaintiff and Condon are professional sports agents. Plaintiff, who is African-American, founded All Pro Sports and Entertainment, Inc. ("All Pro") in 1987. Smith Dep. at 11-12, Pl. Ex. 1. Since starting his own business, plaintiff has represented top-flight football players such as Eddie George, Jerome Bettis, and Barry Sanders. Presentation to Kenyatta Walker (hereinafter "Walker Presentation") at 5-10, Pl. Ex. 2. Between 1991 and 2000, plaintiff represented eleven (11) players selected in the first round of the NFL draft. Expert Report of Timothy K. Bradley, CPA (hereinafter "Bradley Report") at 3, Pl. Ex. 14. Between 2001 and 2004, plaintiff represented only one first-round draft pick. *Id*. Plaintiff alleges that this sharp decline in his representation of high-end players is directly attributable to Condon's repeated defamations to prospective professional players that plaintiff uses the "race card" in contract negotiations with NFL clubs. Compl. pp 13, 16, 19. Plaintiff specifically points to the recruitment of three players—Kenyatta Walker, Antonio Bryant, and Larry Johnson, Jr.—during which Condon allegedly made his "race card" remarks. *Id*.

Condon, who is white, is the President of IMG Football, which is a division of IMG. Condon Biography, Pl. Ex. 15. Under Condon, IMG Football has represented such football stars as Peyton Manning, Eli Manning, LaDainian Tomlinson, and Marvin Harrison in signing some of the most lucrative contracts in the NFL. *Id*. The Sporting News has named Condon the "most powerful agent in any sport." *Id*. Between 1997 and 2004, Condon negotiated contracts for twenty-nine (29) first-round draft picks. *Id*. Condon has denied having any conversations with prospective professional football players about plaintiff or plaintiff's relationships with NFL general managers. Condon Dep. at 72-73, Pl. Ex. 7.

A. Recruiting Kenyatta Walker

In November and December 2000, plaintiff and Condon were competing for a contract to represent Kenyatta Walker ("Walker"), an offensive lineman at the University of Florida and prospective professional football player. Anderson Dep. at 21-22, Pl. Ex. 5; Walker Dep. at 32-33, Def. Ex. 4. Plaintiff alleges that, in the course of the competition to sign Walker, Condon told Walker that plaintiff alienated general managers of NFL clubs because he "plays the race card in negotiating contracts." Compl. p 13.

Plaintiff testified that the alleged defamation involving Walker was communicated to him in a telephone conversation with Walker one day after Condon spoke with Walker. Smith Dep. at 25-26. According to plaintiff, Walker said that: he had been advised that general managers did not like dealing with me because I played the race card in negotiations. . . . [Walker said] that Tom Condon had advised him . . . that [he] better be careful with dealing with me because I play the race card. *Id*. at 26:2-4, 8-10. Plaintiff could not recall the exact date of this telephone conversation. *Id*. at 25. One of plaintiff's associates, Kent Anderson, testified that the telephone conversation occurred before the Southeastern

Conference championship game in 2000.[1] Anderson Dep. at 25:9-10.

Plaintiff testified that, prior to the alleged defamation, the recruitment of Walker was going "extremely well." Smith Dep. at 26:1-2. On the day after the alleged defamation, Walker uncharacteristically failed to return calls from Anderson. Anderson Dep. at 25. When Walker was finally reached later that day, Anderson testified that Walker "just sounded different." Id. at 25:25. Anderson asked Walker what had happened, and Walker responded that "he had met with IMG the night before." Id. at 26:5-6. Shortly thereafter, according to both Anderson and plaintiff, Anderson connected his call with Walker to the All Pro office in Denver and plaintiff joined the telephone conversation. It was in that [**6] telephone conversation that plaintiff said Walker told him about Condon's alleged defamatory remark. Smith Dep. at 25; Anderson Dep. at 28.

Walker has denied that the events took place in the manner described by plaintiff. Walker Dep. at 33, 41. Walker has no memory of anyone at IMG, including Condon, making anything more than general comments about plaintiff. Id. at 32-33. Condon generally denies all of plaintiff's allegations. Condon Dep. at 45. Walker signed with IMG after participating in the Sugar Bowl on January 2, 2001. Walker Dep. at 45. Walker testified that he chose IMG over plaintiff "strictly on who I was comfortable with." Id. at 46:24. When asked about plaintiff's supposed use of the "race card," Walker replied: "No. It was no race card on the decision with IMG or Lamont. If it was black or white or purple, [race] had nothing to do with it. It was what I felt was better for me." Id. at 49: 6-9. Walker was selected in the first round of the 2001 NFL draft by the Tampa Bay Buccaneers. Bradley Report at 7.

B. Recruiting Antonio Bryant

In January 2002, plaintiff and Condon were competing for a contract to represent Antonio Bryant ("Bryant"), a highly-skilled wide receiver from the University of Pittsburgh and prospective professional football player. Smith Dep at 37; Sanders Dep. at 47, Def. Ex. 5. Plaintiff alleges that, during a meeting with Bryant and Charles Sanders ("Sanders") in January 2002, Condon said that "Bryant needed to be careful about retaining [plaintiff] as his agent because plaintiff . . . 'plays the race card' in his negotiations with NFL clubs." Compl. p 16. While recruiting Bryant, Condon visited Sanders's home in Pittsburgh in January 2002. Sanders Dep. at 35-36; Singletary Dep. at 27, Pl. Ex. 11. Sanders, who advised Bryant in choosing an agent, testified that Condon commented on plaintiff's use

of race in contract negotiations during that meeting. Sanders Dep. at 45. According to Sanders, Condon said: 'Hey, you know something else you got to be careful of with Lamont is he plays the race card and a lot of the general manager[s] are getting tired of that. I know the [general manager] at Tennessee is tired of it, and, you know, that's not a good thing.' Id. at 45: 11-16. Although plaintiff alleges that the comments were made to Bryant and Sanders, Sanders testified that Bryant [**8] did not hear Condon make these remarks. Sanders Dep. at 47. Sanders testified that he mentioned the substance of Condon's statements to Bryant but that he did not attribute the information to Condon.[2] Id. at 48-49. Sanders also testified that questions about race were central to his conversations with Bryant regarding the selection of an NFL agent. [3] Id. at 48. Eventually, Bryant signed with plaintiff and was selected in the second round of the 2002 NFL Draft by the Dallas Cowboys. Schaffer Dep. at 14; Bradley Report at 6.

According to plaintiff, Sanders did not tell him about Condon's comments until Bryant signed a contract with the Dallas Cowboys. Smith Dep. at 38. Sanders corroborated plaintiff's recollection and testified that he did not repeat Condon's remarks to anyone until he met with plaintiff at the Cowboys' training facility in July 2002. Sanders Dep. at 47.

C. Recruiting Larry Johnson, Jr.

In December 2002 and January 2003, plaintiff was competing with other agents for the representation of Larry Johnson, Jr. ("Johnson, Jr."), a highly-touted running back from Pennsylvania State University and prospective professional football player. Compl. P 19. Plaintiff alleges that, in the course of the competition to sign Johnson, Jr., Condon told Larry Johnson, Sr. ("Johnson, Sr.") that plaintiff "played the 'race card' in contract negotiations." Id. At that time, Johnson, Sr. was assisting his son in selecting an NFL agent. Johnson Dep. at 63, Pl. Ex. 12.

Plaintiff testified that, at one point in their negotiations, Johnson, Sr. had expressed significant interest in obtaining plaintiff as his son's agent and that Johnson, Jr. "more than likely was going to sign with [plaintiff]." Smith Dep. at 51:17-18. According to plaintiff, that changed after he received a telephone call from Johnson, Sr. in which Johnson, Sr. said he had heard plaintiff used the "race card" in negotiations. Id. at 52. Johnson, Sr. refused to re-

---

[1]The Court takes judicial notice of the fact that, on December 2, 2000, the University of Florida football team played in the SEC Championship game. Available at, http://sportsillustrated.cnn.com/football/college/schedules/2000/team/ffa/ (last visited May 31, 2006).

[2]Sanders testified: "I wasn't like, 'Hey, Tom Condon said this.' . . . One thing we looked at was, 'Hey, how about relationships with these general managers? What if they don't like Lamont because he is black. . . ?" Sanders Dep. at 48:13, 16-18.

[3]Regarding the issue of race, Sanders testified: "[W]e felt race played a part in all of these decisions . . . most of the general managers are white guys and maybe they don't like Lamont because of that. . . . I know in my mind the comment that Condon made . . . fed into how I presented it to [Bryant]." Id. at 48:22-49:3.

veal the source of the comment to plaintiff. *Id.* at 52-53. However, he testified at his deposition that he heard from someone that plaintiff used the "race card" in negotiations, but "it wasn't [from] Tom Condon. . . ." Johnson Dep. at 34:24.

Johnson, Jr. selected Marvin Demhoff ("Demhoff"), who is not affiliated with plaintiff or defendants, to be his NFL agent. Johnson Dep. at 39. Johnson, Sr. explained that the "race card" comment had little or no effect on his son's decision to choose Demhoff rather than plaintiff. "[Lamont] never sold the idea that Larry [was] important to him . . . . That's what I was looking for. . . . And that never happened." *Id.* at 39: 7-15. Johnson, Jr. was selected in the first round of the 2003 NFL Draft by the Kansas City Chiefs. Bradley Report at 7.

Plaintiff's Claims
Plaintiff's asserts three counts against defendants in his Complaint. Count I alleges defamation by Condon in incidents involving Bryant, Johnson, Sr., Sanders, and Walker. Compl. pp 24–28. Count II alleges defamation against IMG under the doctrine of respondeat superior. *Id.* pp 29–33. Count III alleges two instances (Walker and Johnson, Jr.) of interference with prospective contractual relations against both defendants Condon and IMG. *Id.* pp 34–39. * * *

Plaintiff's Prima Facie Showing: Elements of a Defamation Claim

Defendants argue that plaintiff has failed to make a prima facie showing of the claim of defamation to Sanders. Def. Mot. at 6-9. That argument is based on the fact that Sanders served as an advisor to Bryant and that any repetition of Condon's statements to Bryant was of no legal consequence because Bryant selected plaintiff to serve as his NFL agent. *Id.* at 7. Also, defendants contend that the alleged remarks cannot be defamatory, as a matter of law, because Sanders understood Condon's remarks to be statements of opinion rather than fact. *Id.* at 7-8. Plaintiff responds that Condon's remarks constitute slander per se and that he has suffered general damages due to harm to his business reputation. Pl. Opp. at 19. Plaintiff also argues that Sanders understood Condon's remarks to be statements of fact and not opinion. *Id.*

A cause of action for most defamations exists only where a plaintiff successfully establishes: (1) the defamatory character of the communication, (2) its publication by the defendant, (3) its application to the plaintiff, (4) the understanding by the recipient of its defamatory meaning, (5) the understanding by the recipient of it as intended to be applied to the plaintiff, (6) special harm resulting to the plaintiff from its publication, and (7) abuse of a conditionally privileged occasion. 42 Pa. C.S.A. § 8343(a) (1998). Pennsylvania recognizes an exception to the requirement of showing special harm where the words spo-

ken constitute slander per se. *Clemente v. Espinosa*, 749 F. Supp. 672, 677 (E.D. Pa. 1990). Slander per se can be "words imputing (1) criminal offense, (2) loathsome disease, (3) business misconduct, or (4) serious sexual misconduct." *Id.* (citing Restatement (Second) of Torts § 570 (1977)).

While a plaintiff in a slander per se action need not make a showing of special damages, he or she must demonstrate general damages caused by the statement. *Synygy, Inc. v. Scott-Levin, Inc.*, 51 F. Supp. 2d 570, 581 (E.D. Pa. 1999); see also *Pennoyer v. Marriott Hotel Services, Inc.*, 324 F. Supp. 2d 614, 619 (E.D. Pa. 2004) ("The Restatement (Second) of Torts requires a victim of slander per se to make some showing of general damages. . . ."); *Pyle v. Meritor Sav. Bank*, 1996 U.S. Dist. LEXIS 3042, 1996 WL 115048, at *3 (E.D. Pa. Mar. 13, 1996) ("In a defamation per se case . . . a plaintiff must prove general damages from a defamatory publication and cannot rely upon presumed damages); *ProtoComm Corp. v. Fluent, Inc.*, 1994 U.S. Dist. LEXIS 18461, 1994 WL 719674, at *11 (E.D. Pa. Dec. 27, 1994).[8]

(1) Defamatory Meaning

It is the role of the Court to determine whether the statements at issue are capable of a defamatory meaning. *Corabi v. Curtis Publ'g Co.*, 441 Pa. 432, 273 A.2d 899 (Pa. 1971). Under Pennsylvania law, a statement is defamatory "if it tends so to harm the reputation of another as to lower him in the estimation of the community or to deter [**29] third persons from associating or dealing with him." *Cosgrove Studio & Camera Shop, Inc. v. Pane*, 408 Pa. 314, 182 A.2d 751, 753 (Pa. 1962). To make this determination, the Court "must consider not only the language of the statements, but also the context in which they were published." *Clemente*, 749 F. Supp. at 676 (citing *Pierce v. Capital Cities Communications, Inc.*, 576 F.2d 495, 502 (3d Cir.), cert. denied, 439 U.S. 861, 99 S. Ct. 181, 58 L. Ed. 2d 170 (1978)). The Court must also "evaluate 'the effect [the statement] is fairly calculated to produce, the impression it would naturally engender, in the minds of the average persons among whom it is intended to circulate.'" *Tucker v. Fischbein*, 237 F.3d 275, 282 (3d Cir.), cert. denied, 534 U.S. 815, 122 S. Ct. 42, 151 L. Ed. 2d 15 (2001) (quoting *Corabi*, 273 A.2d at 907).

---

[8]The Eastern District of Pennsylvania decisions cited above have followed the rule established in *Walker v. Grand Central Sanitation, Inc.*, 430 Pa. Super. 236, 634 A.2d 237 (Pa. Super. Ct. 1993). In Walker, the Pennsylvania Superior Court concluded that Pennsylvania law follows § 621 of the Restatement (Second) of Torts in requiring plaintiffs, when asserting slander per se claims, to produce evidence of general damages. Walker, 634 A.2d at 244. The Court will analyze the evidence presented to support each element in turn.

The Court concludes that Condon's alleged statements accusing plaintiff, another NFL agent, of injecting race into contract negotiations with NFL clubs are capable of defamatory meaning. Plaintiff states the "race card" comments were made at a time when several agents were competing to provide services to [*308] Bryant. These remarks were made (if at all) for the purpose of dissuading Bryant (by influencing Sanders's opinion of plaintiff) from signing with plaintiff and raised concerns about plaintiff's ability to negotiate with NFL general managers. As plaintiff's expert reports explain, accusations of the inappropriate use of race in conjunction with contract negotiations are devastating to an agent's reputation. One report states:

It would be a crippling impediment for any agent to be seen as generally disfavored by the management of NFL clubs and if that disfavor is premised on the belief that a black agent is antagonizing management by improperly interjecting race into negotiations, it is my opinion that player/clients will seek representation elsewhere.

Expert Report of William L. Strickland at 2, Pl. Ex. 4; see also Expert Report of Rick E. Smith, Pl. Ex. 3. Thus, the Court concludes that Condon's alleged remarks would cause others to question plaintiff's integrity in his business dealings with NFL clubs and would deter prospective professional football players from associating with plaintiff.

In making this determinating, the Court also rejects defendants' argument that Condon's alleged remarks "were pure expressions of opinion" and, therefore, incapable of a defamatory meaning. Def. Mot. at 8. It is true that expressions of opinion are not actionable unless they imply undisclosed, false and defamatory facts. *Bealer v. Mut. Fire, Marine and Inland Ins. Co.*, 2005 U.S. Dist. LEXIS 15755, 2005 WL 1819971, at *6 (E.D. Pa. Aug. 1, 2005) (citing *Parano v. O'Connor*, 433 Pa. Super. 570, 641 A.2d 607, 609 (Pa. Super. Ct. 1994)); see also Restatement (Second) of Torts § 566 (1977). But the evidence presented does not support defendants' contention that Condon was expressing an opinion. According to Sanders's testimony, Condon told him that: "[plaintiff] plays the race card and a lot of the general managers are getting tired of that. I know the guy at Tennessee is tired of it, and, you know, that's not a good thing." Sanders Dep. at 45:13-15. While Condon may have added his opinion by noting "that's not a good thing," Condon's alleged remarks to Sanders are statements of fact that plaintiff plays the "race card" in negotiating with NFL clubs and that many general managers disapprove of that tactic; they do more than imply defamatory facts, they expressly state such facts.

(2) Slander Per Se

Next, the Court must determine whether Condon's alleged remarks fall within the business misconduct category of slander per se. A statement is slanderous per se as an accu-

sation of business misconduct if it "'ascribes to another conduct, characteristics or a condition that would adversely affect his fitness for the proper conduct of lawful business.'" Clemente, 749 F. Supp. at 677-678 (quoting Restatement (Second) of Torts § 573 (1977)). The statement must be "peculiarly harmful to one engaged in [that] business or profession. Disparagement of a general character, equally discreditable to all persons, is not enough...." *Id*. at 678 (quoting Restatement (Second) of Torts § 573, Comment e). Comment e continues by stating that a conclusion of slander per se is appropriate if "the particular quality disparaged . . . is peculiarly valuable in plaintiff's business or profession." Restatement (Second) of Torts § 573, Comment e.

The Court concludes that Condon's alleged remarks to Sanders constitute slander per se. These comments are "peculiarly harmful" to plaintiff because his ability to represent professional football players is directly tied to his relationships with the general managers of NFL clubs. Since Condon's alleged remarks ascribe to plaintiff conduct that would adversely affect his fitness to conduct properly his duties as an agent, they constitute slander per se.

(3) Evidence of General Damages

Based on the foregoing conclusion that Condon's alleged remarks to Sanders constitute slander per se, the Court must determine whether plaintiff has produced evidence of general damages. General damages can derive from "impairment of reputation and standing in the community, personal humiliation, [or] mental anguish and suffering." *Sprague v. Am. Bar Ass'n*, 276 F. Supp. 2d 365, 368 (E.D. Pa. 2003) (quoting *Marcone v. Penthouse International Magazine*, 754 F.2d 1072, 1079 (3d Cir. 1985)).

Defendants contend that plaintiff has failed to demonstrate any general damages, because the remark had no affect on plaintiff's business relationship with Bryant. Def. Mot. at 9. But defendants' argument is misplaced. Plaintiff is not required to demonstrate special damages or pecuniary harm (i.e., that Bryant signed with another agent) due to Condon's alleged remarks to Sanders, because they amount to slander per se. Moreover, the Court finds evidence of general damages based on the harm caused to plaintiff's reputation and personal anguish allegedly suffered by plaintiff.

The evidence of harm to plaintiff's reputation is found in Sanders's deposition. Sanders testified that he considered Condon's statements to be "derogatory" but was not surprised to hear such comments uttered by another agent. Sanders Dep. at 45-46. "[Condon] is trying to say what he can do better and how he can help, he got a better relationship with general managers." *Id*. at 46:3-6. Sanders also testified that he mentioned the substance of Condon's statements to Bryant but did not attribute the information to

Condon. *Id.* at 48-49. He added that "I know in my mind the comment that Condon made . . . fed into how I presented it to [Bryant]." *Id.* at 49:1-3. When asked how important it is that an agent have a good relationship with general managers, Sanders responded, "It's important, very important." *Id.* at 111:22. Then, in a follow-up question, Sanders was asked whether the revelation that an agent had problems with a general manager would be cause for concern in selecting that agent. Sanders responded, "Yeah, absolutely. Yes." *Id.* at 112: 4. Based on this testimony, the Court finds that plaintiff has provided evidence of reputational harm, because Condon's alleged remarks affected Sanders's opinion of plaintiff, namely plaintiff's ability to effectively represent Bryant in contract negotiations with NFL clubs.[9]

Plaintiff has also presented evidence of personal anguish based on the concern that Condon's remarks caused him. Plaintiff testified that, upon learning of Condon's statements to Sanders, he called Tennessee Titans general manager Floyd Reece to determine whether Condon's remarks were an accurate depiction of plaintiff's reputation throughout the NFL. Smith Dep. at 37-38. Plaintiff stated:

I then, after being advised of that, called Floyd Reece and asked him, said, listen, there's something that's floating around here and I want to clarify something. I said, do you have any recollection of our discussions surrounding race, has race ever been an issue in any of our discussions that you can recall? And he laughed and said, well, we've talked about a lot of things and had a lot of battles, but race sure isn't one of them. *Id.* at 38: 5-13.

Plaintiff added that he "revisited the issue" with Reece in the spring of 2004 "just to make sure." *Id.* at 41. Plaintiff also testified that he mentioned Condon's comments to David Ware, an agent based in Atlanta. *Id.* In sum, plaintiff's testimony provides evidence of personal anguish caused by the revelation of Condon's comments because plaintiff responded by trying to allay his concerns by speaking with Reece, the Titans' general manager, at least twice.

---

[9]The Court need not rule on whether Sanders's repetition of the substance of Condon's alleged remarks to Bryant, even if never attributed to Condon, caused any damage to plaintiff.

(4) Evidence of All Other Elements of Defamation

The Court also concludes that plaintiff has produced sufficient evidence to demonstrate all of the other elements of the claim of defamation to Sanders. With respect to the second element, plaintiff has offered sufficient evidence to demonstrate publication based on Sanders's testimony that Condon made the alleged remarks to him. Sanders Dep. at 45-46. Third, the alleged statements made by Condon clearly applied to plaintiff, because Condon mentioned plaintiff in the statements. *Id.* With respect to the fourth element, defendants argue that Sanders understood the comments to be "mere 'puffing' by an agent to increase his chances of being selected by the player." Def. Mot. at 7. However, Sanders stated that he understood the defamatory nature of Condon's remarks. "I looked at it as a negative. . . . I thought it was a derogatory statement to make about [plaintiff]. . . ." Sanders Dep. at 45: 21, 24-25. Thus, there is evidence to support a finding that Sanders understood the defamatory meaning of Condon's alleged remarks. Fifth, the evidence presented supports a finding that Sanders understood that Condon's alleged remarks applied to plaintiff, because Sanders later repeated the comments to plaintiff. *Id.* at 47. Finally, the seventh element is not at issue because defendants have not asserted any privileges in defense of this claim. Therefore, plaintiff has produced evidence to support all elements of this claim.

Based on the foregoing analysis, the Court concludes that plaintiff has provided sufficient evidence to support each element of the claim of defamation to Sanders. Because there are genuine issues of material fact, the Court denies defendants' motion for summary judgment with respect to this claim.

CONCLUSION

The Court grants Defendants' Motion for Summary Judgment with respect to all of plaintiff's claims excepting plaintiff's claim of defamation to Sanders. As to that claim, the parties have presented genuine issues of material fact.

IT IS ORDERED that Defendants' Motion for Summary Judgment is **GRANTED IN PART** and **DENIED IN PART**.
* * *

CASES ON THE SUPPLEMENTAL CD

Don King Productions, Inc., v. James "Buster" Douglas, 742 F. Supp. 778 (S.D.N.Y., 1990). This case illustrates the application of defamation to sport figures.

Gertz v. Robert Welch, Inc., 418 U.S. 323 (1974). This case provides an example of defamation involving a limited-public person.

New York Times Co., v. Sullivan, 376 U.S. 254 (1964). Look for the requirement that public figures must prove actual malice.

QUESTIONS YOU SHOULD BE ABLE TO ANSWER

1. Why has defamation become more common in sport in recent years?

2. Explain the fundamental elements of a defamation claim.

3. What is the difference between a public official and private figure in a defamation lawsuit?

4. Compare and contrast a statement of fact versus an expression of opinion.

5. What are the common defenses to a defamation claim?

REFERENCES

Cases

Brooks v. Paige, 773 P.2d 1098 (Colo. App. 1988).

Don King Productions, Inc., v. James "Buster" Douglas, 742 F. Supp. 778 (S.D.N.Y., 1990)

Curtis Publishing Co., v. Butts, 388 U.S. 130 (1967).

Daubenmire v. Sommers, 805 N.E.2d 571 (Ohio App. 2004).

DiBella v. Hopkins, 187 F. Supp.2d 192 (S.D.N.Y. 2002).

Gertz v. Robert Welch, Inc., 418 U.S. 323 (1974).

Masson v. New Yorker Magazine, Inc., 960 F.2d 896 (9th Cir. 1991).

Milkovich v. Lorain Journal Co., 497 U.S. 1 (1990).

Montefusco v. ESPN, Inc., 2002 U.S. App. LEXIS 19740; 30 Media L. Rep. 2311 (3rd Cir. 2002).

New York Times Co. v. Sullivan, 376 U.S. 254 (1964).

Waldbaum v. Fairchild Publications, Inc., 637 F.2d 1287 (D.C. Cir.) *cert. denied,* 449 U.S. 898 (1980).

Warford v. Lexington Herald, 170 Cal. Rptr 411 (1990).

Washington v. Smith, 893 F. Supp. 60 (D.D.C. 1995).

PUBLICATIONS

Anderson, D. A. (1991). Is libel law worth reforming? *University of Pennsylvania Law Review, 140*(2), 487–554.

Anderson Publications, Inc. (2002, August). Focus on: Pending litigation. *Legal Issues in Collegiate Athletics, 3*(10), 4.

Anderson Publications, Inc. (2002, October). Court dismisses Evel Knievel's defamation suit against espn.com. *Computer & Online Industry Litigation Reporter, 20*(8), 5.

Carpenter, L. J. (1995). *Legal concepts in sports: A primer.* Reston, VA: AAHPERD.

Restatement (Second) of Torts § 555.

Waldman, B. (Fall 1999). A Unified Approach to Cyber-Libel: Defamation on the Internet, A Suggested Approach, *6 Rich. J.L. & Tech.* 9, P 33, at http://www.richmond.edu/JOLT/v6i2/note1.html

3.13   Other Intentional Torts

Invasion of Privacy
Breach of Fiduciary Duty
Tortious Interference with Contract
Intentional Infliction of Emotional Distress

—Gary Rushing

MINNESOTA STATE UNIVERSITY, MANKATO

Intentional torts are deliberate wrongs done to others that cause harm. This type of tort differs from negligence torts in that lack of due care or engaging in abnormally dangerous activity is immaterial. Liability for intentional torts is predicated on the tortfeasor purposely causing harm to another person or engaging in an activity that is substantially certain to harm another (Restatement of Torts, 1965). Recreation or sport-related intentional torts can occur on or off the playing field. This section discusses four "off field" intentional torts that occasionally occur in sport and recreation settings. They are invasion of privacy, breach of fiduciary duty, tortious interference with contract, and intentional infliction of emotional distress.

INVASION OF PRIVACY

Privacy, as defined by the courts, is "the right to be left alone; to live one's life as one chooses free from assault, intrusion, or invasion except as they can be justified by the clear needs of the community under a government of law" (*Rosenbloom v. Metromedia, Inc.*, 1971). The legal principles that serve as the bases for privacy protection are found primarily in three sources of the law—the Fourteenth Amendment, the Constitution, and tort law. The Fourteenth Amendment and the Constitution are concerned with the rights claims against any of the various governmental entities. Tort law is devoted to rights claims against a person or persons (Samar, 1991). Further, most states recognize the right of privacy either by means of common law case decisions or by applicable statutes (Carper & Mietus, 1995).

Right of privacy, as found in tort law, involves four distinct theories or ways in which one's privacy can be invaded. Keeton, Dobbs, Keeton, Prosser, and Owen (1984) explained that these theories do not concern one tort, but a complex of four kinds of invasion. They have little in common except that each represents an interference with the right "to be left alone," which is at the center of all wrongful invasion suits. The four types of invasion are (1) unreasonable intrusion on the seclusion of another, (2) appropriation of another's name or likeness, (3) unreasonable disclosure of private facts, and (4) publicity that unreasonably places the other in a false light before the public. Only one of the torts, not all four, must be proven for a successful claim of invasion of privacy.

Unreasonable Intrusion on Seclusion

The first form or theory is straightforward and concerned with the invasion of one's home or illegally searching someone's personal belongings or documents. Usually, the intrusion takes the form of window-peeking, eavesdropping, excessive surveillance, or constant annoyance (Yasser, McCurdy, Goplerud, & Weston, 2006). However, the courts have extended this tort to include eavesdropping by wiretap, unauthorized examining of a bank account, and compulsory blood-testing (Cross & Miller, 1995). Although untested in court, it would seem logical to assume that this notion would also include scanning of cellular phones and computer hacking. In addition to the actual intrusion, any information obtained in these or similar ways that is made public is also invasion of privacy. This is true even if the information obtained is truthful and it serves the public's right to know (Schubert, Smith, & Trentadue, 1986). The requisite question is: Was the intrusion offensive or objectionable to a reasonable person? (Keeton, Dobbs, Keeton, Prosser, and Owen, 1984). If so, then it is an illegal invasion of one's privacy.

A court case that illustrates this point is *Bilney v. Evening Star Newspaper Co.* (1979). In this dispute, six members of the University of Maryland basketball team brought action against reporters and newspaper publishers for articles detailing their poor academic standing, thus putting them in danger of being declared ineligible to play. The question was addressed as to how the reporters obtained the academic information they had published. The court determined that they had obtained the information from an anonymous source and that there was no evidence that the defendant news reporters had learned of the players' academic problems from confidential records or by any acts of invasion or intrusion. However, had the information been obtained through wiretaps, computer-hacking, or some other offensive manner, the court may have considered this to be invasion of privacy.

Appropriation

The second form of invasion of privacy involves the **unauthorized use of a person's name or likeness** for commercial purposes such as advertising or trade. The protection provided by this law is especially important to sport figures because it gives them some control over the extent to which their name and likeness can be commercially exploited. Without this control, an athlete would lose a significant source of income from commercial endorsements, trading cards, and other enterprises. It is the most common "privacy" complaint of athletes (Byrd, 1988).

Although sport figures can prohibit most unauthorized use of their names and likenesses, courts have upheld unauthorized uses for editorial purposes as well as when reused by publishers or broadcasters for campaigns to increase circulation or broadcasting audiences. When used in this manner, it is considered to be protected incidental use (Dill, 1986).

In a classic case that illustrates the salient issues in this area, Joe Namath sued *Sports Illustrated* (*Namath v. Sports Illustrated*, 1975) for the unauthorized use of his photo to promote subscription sales. He contended that this use was commercial and violated his **right to privacy**. Further, because he was in the business of endorsing products and selling the use of his name and likeness, it interfered with his right to profit from such sale. The photograph had originally been used without objection from Namath, in conjunction with a 1969 Super Bowl article. However, because it was reprinted to promote subscription sales, he felt he should be compensated for its use. In siding with *Sports Illustrated*, the court noted that the use of the photo was merely "incidental" advertising because it was used to illustrate the quality and content of the periodical in which it originally appeared.

In a similar invasion of privacy case (*Montana v. San Jose Mercury News, Inc.*, 1995), Joe Montana brought action against the *San Jose Mercury News* for misappropriation of his name, photograph, and likeness. At issue was the reproduction of Montana's photograph that originally appeared in conjunction with a 1990 Super Bowl victory for the San Francisco 49ers. His photo had been reproduced in poster form. Some of the posters were sold for five dollars each, and the rest were donated to charity organizations. The court reached a decision similar to that of the *Namath* case and found in favor of *San Jose Mercury News* for two reasons. First, the original newspaper account and the subsequent photograph constituted matters in the public interest. Second, the posters were sold to advertise the quality and content of its newspaper. They contained no additional information and they did not convey Montana's endorsement.

In another case, *Palmer v. Schonhorn Enterprises, Inc.* (1967), a toy manufacturing company appropriated the names and career profiles of golfers Arnold Palmer, Gary Player, Doug Sanders, and Jack Nicklaus for use in a game. In this situation, the court sided with the plaintiffs because the commercial use of their names and profiles was done without their permission and without compensation.

The appropriation theory of invasion of privacy generated the **right of publicity** cause of legal action (Breaux, 2005). The major difference between the two concepts is that redress in a right of privacy dispute is based on the mental duress resulting from "not being left alone," whereas the focus of redress in a right of publicity case is the compensation for the use of one's name and likeness for commercial reasons. Celebrities, including athletes, have had a difficult task in demonstrating to the courts that public exposure caused them mental duress in that "they sought such attention and profited from it" (Stapleton & McMurphy, 1999). For this reason, more and more states are adopting the right of publicity (Stapleton & McMurphy). (For more information on Right of Publicity, see Section 8.23, *Image Rights.*)

Unreasonable Disclosure of Private Facts

A third type of invasion of privacy involves public disclosure of private facts about an individual that an ordinary person would find objectionable. Public disclosure suits are sometimes referred to as embarrassment suits because they arise from objections to publicity of embarrassing private information (Dill, 1992). At the center of this type of suit is the balance between the public's right to know and the extent of the intrusion into one's private life. Although secondary issues must be satisfied to prevail in an embarrassment suit (see Keeton et al., 1984, pp. 856–857), where public figures such as sport personalities are concerned, there are two major issues that the courts will address. They are (1) whether the disclosed information was **truly private** or public, and (2) if the disclosed information was **highly offensive** to an ordinary person.

Private v. Public Facts

For a plaintiff to succeed in a public disclosure suit, it must be shown that the disclosed publicity was in an area where there was a legitimate expectancy of privacy. In other words, the disclosure must have involved truly private matters. What constitutes truly private for the average citizen, in terms of publicity, is different from that of a sport figure. Sports personalities, especially the highly paid athletes, have little privacy protection due to their public figure status. A **public figure** is someone who by "his [or her] accomplishments, fame, or mode of living, or by adopting a profession or calling which gives the public a legitimate interest in his doings, his affairs, and his character, has become a public personage" (Keeton et al., 1984, p. 859). (For an in-depth discussion of public figure status, see Section 3.12, *Defamation.*) By way of this notion, the Constitution allows the press to report matters that have become public interest.

The justification for this loss of privacy protection is the result of three considerations about public figures. First, public figures have, to a certain extent, sought publicity and have consented to it. Second, their personalities and affairs have become public and are no longer private business. Third, the press has a right to inform the public about those who have become matters of public interest (Prosser, 1960).

Are college athletes considered public figures? In the previously mentioned case of *Bilney v. Evening Star Newspaper Co.* (1979), because there was no evidence that the defendant news reporters had learned of the players' academic problems through improper methods, the court examined the issue of "public figure" status of the six players. The court reasoned that college basketball is a "big-time" sport and generates a great deal of public interest and excitement throughout the country. The court further stated that the players had "achieved the status of public figures . . . by virtue of their membership on the basketball team (and) . . . having sought . . . the limelight. . . . It's clear at least in this court that college athletes in big time sports are 'public figures'" (p. 574).

As for high school athletes, it remains unclear as to whether or not they would be considered public figures; however, a leading case on the subject suggests that most high school athletes will not be considered public figures regardless of their notoriety or the public interest (see *Wilson v. Daily Gazette Co.*, 2003). Deem (2006), however, suggested that courts prefer to find "much publicized" high school athletes to be limited-purpose public figures as opposed to all purpose public figures (see Section 3.12, *Defamation*).

In addition to the preceding issues dealing with private information, it should be noted that information that has been previously reported, or that has already been made accessible to the public through public records or other documentation, or that is newsworthy is not considered to be purely private in nature and therefore is discloseable (Berry & Wong, 1993).

Highly Offensive

Even though some facts may be newsworthy and therefore non-private, they may not be publishable if they can be viewed as highly offensive to the average person. Because community norms vary from jurisdiction to jurisdiction, courts may have mixed decisions regarding what is permissible disclosure. However, where public figures are concerned, even conservative courts will allow most private truthful facts, although embarrassing, to be disclosed unless they are "unredeemably offensive and not even remotely in the 'public interest'" (Dill, 1992, p. 137).

False Light Intrusion

Under this theory, an invasion of privacy occurs when publicity places the plaintiff in a **false light** in the public eye. For example, in a sport setting, this could occur if someone in the media uses a photograph or makes a statement about a sport figure that gives a false impression to the public. This false impression could emanate from "made-up" details, omitted facts, or misleading context (Dill, 1992).

However, for sport figures to prevail in a false-light suit, they must not only show that the published information was false, but also that the disclosure was done by one knowing it was false or who had reckless disregard for the truth. This standard was established in *Time, Inc. v. Hill* (1967), which held that the First Amendment protects reports of newsworthy matters.

False-light action is different from libel in that the publicity does not have to be defamatory. The depiction in question could be either complimentary or defamatory. Although most false-light cases involve unflattering portrayals, the central issue is "being left alone" from the effects of a false reputation or false publicity (Samar, 1991). Both false-light and libel complaints are permitted in some states; however, other states do not recognize false-light claims and permit only libel suits.

An example of false-light invasion occurred in the case of *Spahn v. Messner, Inc.*, (1967). This case centered on an unauthorized biography written about Warren Spahn, a celebrated pitcher for the Milwaukee Braves. The author used "invented dialogue, and imaginary incidents" which he knew to be false and knew to present an untruthful depiction of Spahn. Spahn objected to this portrayal even though parts of the story were complimentary. The court awarded Spahn $10,000 in damages and enjoined further publication of the book.

BREACH OF FIDUCIARY DUTY

Another intentional tort is breach of fiduciary duty or responsibility. *Black's Law Dictionary* (Black, 1979) defines a **fiduciary** as "[a] person having duty, created by his undertaking, to act primarily for another's benefit in matters connected with this undertaking." As an adjective, it means ". . . relating to or founded upon a trust or confidence" (p. 563). Carper and Mietus (1995) clarified this by adding that a fiduciary relationship is one involving a person in a position of trust who undertakes to act for the benefit of another. Examples of fiduciary relationships include lawyer-client, parent-child, and coach-athlete.

In the sport setting, the fiduciary relationship that is most troublesome is the association between a professional athlete and his or her agent (Ehrhardt & Rodgers, 1988; Powers, 1994). An agent can be responsible for managing many of the athlete's financial concerns. These may include "negotiating the athlete's employment agreement; securing, bartering and reviewing commercial opportunities; providing financial advice and income management; and counseling on legal and tax matters" (Sobel, 1987, p. 705). Because many of these dealings are legally binding to the represented athlete, the law imposes a high obligation of trustworthiness on the agent. If an agent violates this trust and the athlete is harmed as a result, the agent is guilty of tortious conduct and may have to make restitution [Restatement (Second) of Torts #874, 1984, p. 300].

A fiduciary duty requires that the sport agent act with complete honesty in all dealings with athlete-clients. In addition, the agent must avoid any personal **conflicts of interest**. In other words, the interests of the athlete must come before those of the agent. Also, an agent must not represent two adverse parties in the same transaction. For example, an agent cannot represent two or more athletes vying for the same endorsement contract nor represent both an athlete and the company with which he is negotiating for a contract. Finally, an agent must not receive hidden compensation or profits from third parties for transacting the player's business and must not take advantage of any business opportunity that rightfully belongs to the athlete (Schubert et al., 1986). An agent can avoid liability in this area by fully disclosing any possible conflicts of interest or other potentially improper conduct and obtaining the athlete's prior consent to the action.

Detroit Lions, Inc. v. Jerry Argovitz (1984), offers an instructional example of breach of fiduciary duty. In this case, Billy Sims' agent, Jerry Argovitz, engaged in a series of unethical practices with the intent of inducing Sims to sign a contract with the Houston Gamblers of the United States Football League. After the Gamblers made an offer to Sims, Argovitz failed to give the Detroit Lions an opportunity to match the bid. Sims signed with the Gamblers believing theirs to be the best offer. After it was revealed Argovitz was a substantial owner in the Gamblers' franchise and that he had withheld information that might have swayed Sims' decision, the court allowed Sims to rescind his contract and sign with the Detroit Lions. Sims was unaware of the extent of Argovitz's association with the Gamblers (See the Supplemental CD).

Dominion Sports Services, Inc. v. Bredehoft (2006), illustrates the necessity of having a valid fiduciary relationship established in order to have a successful claim of breach of fiduciary duty. Hockey North America (HNA) started an adult men's novice hockey league in Minnesota. Bradford Bredehof, an independent contractor, was hired as the local administrator of the league. His contract had a restrictive covenant that prohibited him from starting a competing league in the area. After HNA encountered financial difficulties and owed money to many creditors, Dominion Sports Services purchased its assets but retained the HNA league name. As the purchase was being negotiated, Bredehoft met with the players and informed them of HNA's financial problems. This discussion ultimately prompted them to organize their own competing league. Dominion filed suit against Bredehoft and others for breach of contract, breach of fiduciary duty, and tortious interference with contractual relations. The court ruled against HNA on all claims. HNA did not have a valid breach of contract or tortious interference claim against Bredehoft, because he did not have a contract with the new management. Dominion's purchase agreement explicitly stated that it would not assume the employment contracts of the former management employees. Without a valid contract, Bredehoft was never an agent of the new HNA; therefore, a breach of fiduciary duty claim could not be upheld.

TORTIOUS INTERFERENCE WITH CONTRACT

This tort involves the intentional inducement of another to breach one's contractual obligations (Schubert et al., 1986). Tampering is an alternate term sometimes used to describe when one team attempts to lure a player who is clearly under contract to another team. It is the equivalent of tortious interference with contract (Epstein, 2002). Because contracts play a vital role in sport, this is a significant area of concern. Inducement to break contracts has been alleged in situations that involve teams competing for talented players (*Cincinnati Bengals v. William Bergey, et al.*, 1974), boxing promoters arguing over promotion rights (*Don King Productions v. James "Buster" Douglas, et al.*, 1990), and agents interfering with a college player's eligibility (Gray, 2006; Woods & Mills, 1988).

There are three elements necessary to prove the existence of a wrongful interference tort:

1. A valid, enforceable contract must exist between two parties;

2. The defendant must have known of the contract's existence;

3. The defendant must have, without justification, knowingly induced either of the two parties from full performance of the contract. This interference must have been done for the purpose of advancing the economic interest of the inducer. It does not matter if the action was done in bad faith or with malice (the intention to harm another); however, bad faith or malice is usually a factor (Cross & Miller, 1985).

Plaintiff has the burden to prove that the defendant knew of the contract's existence and knowingly induced the breach of the contractual relationship. The defendant can refute the charge if it can be shown that the interference was justified or permissible. For example, aggressive marketing and advertising strategies may entice customers to break contracts with competitors but are not unlawful.

In a significant case involving a tortious interference complaint, the Cincinnati Bengals sued Bill Bergey (*Cincinnati Bengals v. William Bergey, et al.*, 1974), their premier linebacker, the Virginia Ambassadors, and the other 11 teams of the newly formed World Football League (WFL). At the heart of this complaint was the claim that the WFL defendants were inducing a breach of contract by Bergey and, unless enjoined, would do the same with other key players of the Bengals. While under contract with the Bengals, Bergey had negotiated and signed a contract with the Virginia team for his future services. His new contract was to begin when his existing Bengals contract expired. The Bengals felt that his signing of a contract with a different team while under contract with the Bengals would cause him not to perform his current contractual duties with them. The court denied an injunction, primarily because the Bengals failed to show how the negotiations and the subsequent contract signing interfered with the performance of his existing contract.

The case of *Central Sports Army Club v. Arena Association, Inc.* (1997), serves to illustrate another tortious interference cause of action and is instructive in the pertinent elements of a tortious interference situation. (See the Supplemental CD). The central issue in this case was a contract dispute between the Central Sports Army Club (CSKA), a Russian hockey club, and the Detroit Vipers of the International Hockey League (IHL). A 17-year-old Russian hockey player named Sergei Samsonov had originally entered into a one-year contract for the 1996–97 season with CSKA. For several reasons, including not being paid the promised compensation, he decided before the season began to play elsewhere. He retained an agent of Arena Associates, who began to make arrangements for him to play in the United States. This sport agent was working under the assumption that Samsonov did not have a valid contract with CSKA because he was only 17 when he signed the contract, his father had not signed the contract, and CSKA had failed to fulfill the terms of the contract.

Through his agency (Arena Associates), Samsonov's agent was able to obtain a visa and a 1996–97 player contract with the Detroit Vipers hockey team of the IHL. At the time of his signing the new 1996–97 season contract, the owner of the Vipers believed that Samsonov was under no obligation to play for the CSKA. When Samsonov began playing, CSKA filed a lawsuit in the United States, claiming among other things that the Detroit Vipers and Samsonov's agents tortiously interfered with their contract with Samsonov.

The first and the most pivotal issue in this tortious interference with contract case was whether or not a valid contract existed. Both Russian Civil Code as well as New York and Michigan laws allow a minor to void a contract unless he obtained express written consent of parents. Because Samsonov had signed his first contract when he was a minor and had not obtained his parents' permission, the court ruled that the CSKA contract was not valid. Additionally, even if a valid contract had existed, the plaintiffs failed to show the three necessary elements for tortious interference with contract: (1) that the defendants were aware of the contract between the CSKA and Samsonov, (2) that there had been inducement by the defendants, and (3) that the defendants had improper motive (*Central Sports Army Club v. Arena Association, Inc.*, 1997, p. 190).

INTENTIONAL INFLICTION OF EMOTIONAL DISTRESS

Intentional infliction of emotional distress (IIED) is a relatively recent tort claim for intentional conduct that results in extreme emotional distress (also called mental distress) (Clarkson, Miller, Jentz, & Cross, 2004) and is meant to protect a person's emotional tranquility (Wong, 2002). Although seldom successful due to its rigorous criteria, it has become a fairly common complaint in sport and recreation tort related lawsuits. In some jurisdictions it is referred to as the tort of "outrage" due to its standard that requires the conduct in question be such that it would cause a reasonable person to respond with outrage (Huffaker, 2001).

Elements of Intentional Infliction of Emotional Distress

In order to prove a claim of IIED, the plaintiff must demonstrate that: (1) the defendant acted *intentionally* or with *reckless* disregard of the probability of causing emotional distress, (2) the defendant's action must have been *extreme* and *outrageous*, and (3) the action must have caused *severe* emotional distress. It should be noted that mere insults, indignities, threats, annoyances, petty oppressions, or other trivialities would not sustain an IIED claim. The conduct in question has to be so *extreme* and *outrageous* "as to go beyond all possible bonds of decency, and to be regarded as atrocious, and utterly intolerable in a civilized community" (Prosser, 1964, pp. 46–47; Rest. 2d Torts, 46). Whether or not the conduct is illegal does not determine whether it meets this standard. Additionally, "The emotional distress must in fact exist, and it must be severe" (Prosser, p. 51; Rest. 2d Torts, 46).

Measuring severe distress poses a problem. Many jurisdictions require that the emotional distress manifest itself in some physical symptom or illness or some documented emotional disturbance. (See this section's significant case to examine exactly how the courts apply these criteria.)

Claims of IIED have arisen in a wide variety of situations in sport and recreation. These claims have included circumstances such as forcing an athlete to do "bear crawls" on hot asphalt for being late to practice (*Gorthy v. Clovis Unified Sch. Dist.,* 2006); a swimmer being forced to sit on a hot deck chair *(Kelly v. N. Highlands Recreation & Park Dist.,* 2006); failure of an official to inform players in a timely manner of their next game, thus causing them to be eliminated from a tournament (*Warren v. United States Specialty Sports Ass'n,* 2006); and a high school athlete who was distressed because he failed to make the varsity baseball team *(Cronk v. Suffern Senior High School,* 2006).

For various reasons, none of the above-mentioned cases was successful. However, one of the most common reasons for the lack of success is the inability to prove the stringent requirements of being *extreme* or *outrageous* conduct and causing *severe* emotional stress. *Chuy v. Philadelphia Eagles Football Club* (1979), is an oft-cited case that is exemplary in how to satisfy the high standards needed to succeed in an IIED claim. Don Chuy, an Eagles lineman, was subjected to severe emotional distress by a team doctor erroneously reporting to the news media that he had a life-threatening disease. When Chuy, who had no previous knowledge of the existence of the condition, heard of the statement he reportedly "panicked and his mind just snapped." In court, he was able to show that during a six-month period in which he had anticipated his death, he suffered extreme emotional anguish and torment, he became a mental wreck, lost his marriage, and suffered serious emotional stress. The court held that the doctor's conduct was sufficiently outrageous and stated:

> If you intentionally make a statement the material and probable consequences of which it will be known to the person and cause him or her emotional distress and if the making of that statement is shocking and outrageous and exceeds the bounds of decency with respect to its natural and probable impact, then a case of intentional infliction of emotional distress is made out (*Chuy v. Philadelphia Eagles Football Club*, 1979, p. 10).

Wong (2002), in referring to the above case, recommended that sport and recreation personnel be very cautious when they are making statements to the media about a participant's playing ability, a coach's employment tenure, or an athlete's injury status.

Negligent Infliction of Emotional Distress

Although not an intentional tort, a cause of action that is closely aligned with *IIED* is *negligent infliction of emotional distress.* The obvious difference between the two is that IIED is caused by an intentional act in which the defendant knew or should have known would cause severe emotional distress; whereas, NIED is the result of an act that negligently (unintentionally) causes severe emotional distress and resultant damage. In NIED, the plaintiff is relieved of the burden of proving that the defendant intended to cause severe emotional distress.

The requirements for proving NIED vary significantly from state to state; the requirements typically parallel the four elements necessary to prove negligence (see Section 2.11, *Negligence*). To establish a claim for NIED in most states, the plaintiff must demonstrate that: (1) the defendant owed a duty to the plaintiff not to create a foreseeable risk of inflicting emotional distress; it may be a general duty or one created by statute; (2) the defendant breached that duty by engaging in behavior that the defendant should have realized involved an unreasonable risk of causing emotional distress that might result in illness or bodily injury; (3) the plaintiff suffered injury in the form of extreme emotional distress; and (4) the breach of the duty was the proximate cause of the injury (Clinton & McKain, 2005). If these elements can be sustained then NIED has been proven.

In *Turner v. Manadalay Sports Entm't,* LLC, (2008), a fan was struck in the face by a foul ball while sitting in an unprotected area near a concession stand. She sued the team for negligence and NIED. The plaintiff was aware of stadium warnings regarding foul balls, and knew that the team was not responsible for resultant injuries. The Supreme Court of Nevada determined that the woman's negligence claim failed to survive summary judgment under the limited duty rule (see Section 2.31, *Premises Liability* for a description of the limited duty rule). Because she could not establish that there was breached duty of care owed to her, she was not able to establish her NIED claim either.

SIGNIFICANT CASE

Although the plaintiff was unsuccessful with his claims of *Intentional Infliction of Emotional Distress* and *Public Disclosure of Embarrassing Private Facts: Invasion of Privacy,* this case provides instructive examples of how the courts examine the above claims. Careful reading of the application of the criteria provides bountiful insight into how the courts evaluate both of these intentional torts. The reader should examine the closely the stringent criteria necessary to sustain an IIED claim.

CASSIE V. WALLED LAKE CONSOLIDATED SCHOOLS

COURT OF APPEALS OF MICHIGAN
2006 Mich. App. LEXIS 497
February 23, 2006, Decided

SUBSEQUENT HISTORY: Appeal denied by *Cassie v. Walled Lake Consol. Sch.,* 2006 Mich. LEXIS 1659 (Mich., Aug. 29, 2006)

PRIOR HISTORY: Oakland Circuit Court. LC No. 2003-052129-NZ.

DISPOSITION: Affirmed.

JUDGES: Before: Hoekstra, PJ, and Neff and Owens, JJ.

OPINION

PER CURIAM.

Plaintiff appeals as of right from the trial court's order granting defendants' motion for summary disposition and dismissing each of plaintiff's claims. We affirm.

At the start of the second semester of his junior year of high school, plaintiff transferred from Walled Lake Central High School (Central) to St. Mary Preparatory High School in Orchard Lake, Michigan (St. Mary). Plaintiff's transfer was the subject of rumor and gossip at Central because plaintiff was the quarterback of Central's football team, and a member of the basketball team. Before his transfer, he told Central's football coach, defendant Chuck Apap, that he believed Central's basketball program was in disarray and he was considering a transfer for that reason. Plaintiff made similar statements to others. When plaintiff's mother approached Central's principal, defendant David Barry, to sign transfer papers, she [*2] indicated that the transfer was academically motivated. Barry had received contrary information from Apap, the parents of other Central students, and an office secretary, whose children saw instant messages from plaintiff regarding his dissatisfaction with the basketball program. Barry also knew that plaintiff had a high grade point average at the time of his transfer.

Barry filed a complaint with the Michigan High School Athletic Association (MHSAA), asserting that plaintiff's transfer was athletically motivated. MHSAA rules require a transfer student to refrain from playing interscholastic sports for one semester following a transfer, but if a transfer is athletically motivated, the student is disqualified for two semesters following the transfer. After receiving St. Mary's response, the MHSAA concluded there was insufficient evidence that plaintiff's transfer was athletically motivated. After the MHSAA's decision, a reporter for the *Oakland Press* contacted Barry and Apap for comment, and published an article criticizing the MHSAA decision. Several weeks later, a *Detroit Free Press* reporter also contacted Apap and Barry and published an article that was critical of the [*3] MHSAA. Both Apap and Barry denied that they provided specific information to the reporters. Rather, they disclosed or affirmed general information, specifically that plaintiff was a good student, he had no discipline problems, and his parents had never complained about his academic progress, Central's programs, or Central's teachers. Both articles indicated Barry thought plaintiff's transfer was athletically motivated.

Barry appealed the MHSAA decision to the MHSAA executive board, which denied the appeal. Plaintiff commenced this action against Walled Lake Consolidated Schools, Barry, Apap, and Central's athletic director Nick Conti, who had told the Detroit Catholic League athletic director, Vic Michael, that plaintiff was a good student and athlete with no disciplinary problems. Plaintiff alleged a violation of MCL 600.2165, intentional infliction of emotional distress, defamation, abuse of process, and invasion of privacy. The trial court granted defendants summary disposition on all claims.

I   * * *

II   * * *

Plaintiff next argues his intentional infliction of emotional distress claim was improperly dismissed. A trial court's grant of summary disposition is reviewed de novo. *Ormbsy v. Capital Welding, Inc*, 471 Mich. 45, 52; 684 N.W.2d 320 (2004). In reviewing a motion under MCR 2.116(C)(10), we consider submitted admissible evidence in a light most favorable to the nonmoving party to determine whether a genuine issue of material fact exists. *Lockridge v. State Farm Mut Automobile Ins Co*, 240 Mich. App. 507, 511; [*5] 618 N.W.2d 49 (2000).

> *"To establish intentional or reckless infliction of emotional distress, a plaintiff must show (1) extreme and outrageous conduct, (2) intent or recklessness, (3) causation, and (4) severe emotional distress. Liability attaches only when a plaintiff can demonstrate that the defendant's conduct is so outrageous in character, and so extreme in degree, as to go beyond all possible bounds of decency, and to be regarded as atrocious and utterly intolerable in a civilized community. A defendant is not liable for mere insults, indignities, threats, annoyances, petty oppressions, or other trivialities."* [*Heckmann v. Detroit Police Chief*, 267 Mich. App. 480, 498; 705 N.W.2d 689 (2005), quoting *Lewis v. LeGrow*, 258 Mich. App. 175, 196; 670 N.W.2d 675 (2003).]

When considering whether conduct is so extreme and outrageous that it triggers liability, the court asks whether an average person would have his resentment aroused and exclaim, "outrageous!" when given the facts of the case. *Id.* at 498. Summary disposition may be granted if reasonable minds would agree that the conduct was not [*6] outrageous. *Id.* at 499. Even if the defendant acted tortiously or criminally, a claim will not arise without the requisite showing of outrageous conduct. *VanVorous v. Burmeister*, 262 Mich App 467, 481-482; 687 N.W.2d 132 (2004). In this case, defendants were entitled by MHSAA rules to challenge plaintiff's eligibility to play sports for a two-semester period. While some defendants later spoke to reporters, the reporters were already aware of the story, and talking to them did not rise to the outrageous level of behavior required to sustain a claim for intentional infliction of emotional distress. *Vanvorous, supra* at 481-482; cf. *Haverbush v. Powelson*, 217 Mich. App. 228, 230-233; 551 NW.2d 206 (1996).

Furthermore, to satisfy the element of severe emotional distress, the distress must be so severe that no reasonable person could be expected to endure it. *Haverbush, supra* at 235. In determining its severity, the intensity and duration of the distress should be considered. *Id.* In this case, plaintiff testified that he was "offended" and "annoyed." He thought people changed their attitude [*7] about him, and some people called him a traitor or a "sell out." Plaintiff discussed the issue with school counselors on approximately five occasions. This was insufficient to establish that plaintiff suffered distress of the intensity and dura-

tion necessary to sustain a claim for intentional infliction of emotional distress.

III

Regarding the invasion of privacy claim, the only communications at issue are those between defendants and the reporters. The common-law tort of invasion of privacy may be based on four distinct theories: (1) intrusion upon another's seclusion [*13] or solitude, or into another's private affairs; (2) a public disclosure of embarrassing private facts about the individual; (3) publicity, which places the plaintiff in a false light in the public eye; and (4) the appropriation of the plaintiff's likeness for the defendant's advantage. *Lewis, supra* at 193; *Doe v. Mills*, 212 Mich. App. 73, 80; 536 N.W.2d 824 (1995). Plaintiff appears to argue his claim was based on "public disclosure of private facts" about himself.

> *A cause of action for public disclosure of embarrassing private facts requires (1) the disclosure of information (2) that is highly offensive to a reasonable person and (3) that is of no legitimate concern to the public.* [*Doe, supra* at 80.]

In this case, Apap and Barry admitted talking to reporters. They disclosed or affirmed that plaintiff was a good student who did not have disciplinary problems and that they believed his transfer was athletically motivated. Clearly, there was a disclosure of information. However,

> *to satisfy the final element of an action for public disclosure of embarrassing private facts, the information disclosed [*14] must concern the individual's private life. Liability will not be imposed for giving publicity to matters that are already of public record or otherwise open to the public.* [*Doe, supra* at 82 (citation omitted).]

In *Swickard v. Wayne Co Medical Examiner*, 438 Mich. 536, 550-551, 554; 475 N.W.2d 304 (1991), the Court acknowledged that, to have a successful claim of public disclosure of embarrassing private facts, the matter at issue must not be of public concern. It gave examples of issues of public concern, which included publications concerning crimes, arrests, suicides, marriage, divorces, fires, catastrophes of nature, deaths from narcotics use, the birth of a child to a twelve-year-old girl, "and many other similar matters of genuine, even if more or less deplorable, popular appeal." *Id.*, quoting 3 Restatement of Torts, 2d, ß 652D, comment g, pp. 90–391. In this case, the subject matter that sparked the disclosures was already a matter of public interest. Plaintiff was a popular star athlete by all accounts. His potential transfer, which he discussed at school, resulted in gossip among [*15] students, parents, and staff. A complaint related to the transfer was made to the MHSAA, to which Central belonged. The rejection of that complaint became known to the reporters, and they explored the issue. The record does not divulge how the reporters came into possession of the story. Nevertheless, the subject matter, plaintiff's reason for transferring from Central High School was a matter of "genuine, even if more or less deplorable, popular appeal" and was not private. *Id.*

IV

* * *

Affirmed.

/s/ Joel P. Hoekstra

/s/ Janet T. Neff

/s/ Donald S. Owens

CASES ON THE SUPPLEMENTAL CD

Montana v. San Jose Mercury News, (1995 Cal. App. LEXIS 411). Examine the section dealing with *The Posters Reported on Newsworthy Events* and *A Newspaper Has a Constitutional Right to Promote Itself by Reproducing Its News Stories* they are the central reasons used to justify appropriation of Montana's image.

Detroit Lions v. Argovitz, (1985 U.S. App. LEXIS 14360). Please note that at the core of this Breach of Fiduciary case is the defendant's personal interest in Sims contracting with the Gamblers;conflicting with his fiduciary duty to advance Sims' best interests.

Central Army Sports Club v. Detroit Vipers, (1997 U.S. Dist. LEXIS 615). Please note the *No Inducement* and *No awareness of contractual obligations* explanations of the case.

These are key to a "contractual" interference case.

Cases from Other Sections

See cases related to Right to Publicity in Image Rights Section 7.4

QUESTIONS YOU SHOULD BE ABLE TO ANSWER

1. Compare and contrast defamation with false light invasion of privacy.

2. The four theories of invasion of privacy have one common theme. Name and briefly explain this theme.

3. List and briefly explain the elements necessary to support a claim of *Breach of Fiduciary Duty*.

4. List and briefly explain the necessary elements required to sustain a claim of *Tortious Interference with Contract*.

5. What is the "tort of outrage" and what is the reason for this designation?

REFERENCES

Cases

Bilney v. Evening Star Newspaper Co., 43 Md. App. 560; 406 A.2d. 652 (Md. App. 1979).

Central Sports Army Club v. Arena Association, Inc., 952 F. Supp. 181 (S.D.N.Y. 1997).

Chuy v. Philadelphia Eagles Football Club, U.S. App. LEXIS 16338 (1979).

Cincinnati Bengals v. William Bergey, et al., 453 F. Supp. 129 (1974).

Cronk v. Suffern Senior High School, 2005 N.Y. Misc. LEXIS 2820 (2005).

Davis v. Baylor University, 976 S.W.2d 5 (Mo. App. 1998).

Detroit Lions, Inc. v. Jerry Argovitz, 580 F. Supp. 542 (1984).

Dominion Sports Servs. Inc. v. Bredehoft, 2006 Minn. LEXIS 132 (Minn., Mar. 14, 2006).

Don King Productions v. James "Buster" Douglas, et al., 735 F. Supp. 522 (1990).

Gorthy v. Clovis Unified Sch. District, 2006 WL 236939 (E.D. Cal. 2006).

Holt v. Cox Enterprises, 590 F. Supp. 408 (N.D. Ga. 1984).

Kelly v. N. Highlands Recreation & Park Dist., 2006 U.S. Dist. LEXIS 39785 (E.D. Cal. 2006).

Montana v. San Jose Mercury News, Inc., 34 Cal. App.4th 790 (1995).

Namath v. Sports Illustrated, 48 A.D.2d 487; 371 N.Y.S.2d 10 (1975).

Palmer v. Schonhorn Enterprises, Inc., 323 A.2d 458 (1967).

Rosenbloom v. Metromedia, Inc., 403 U.S. 29; 29 L.Ed.2d 296 (1971).

Spahn v. Messner, Inc., 18 N.Y.2d 324; 274 N.Y.S.2d 877; 221 N.E.2d 543; *vacated* 387 U.S. 239; 18 L.Ed.2d 744 (1967).

St. Louis Convention & Visitors Commission v. National Football League, 154 F.3d 851 (8th Cir. 1998).

Time, Inc. v. Hill, 385 U.S. 374 (1967).

Turner v. Mandalay Sports Entm't, LLC, 180 P.3d 1172 (Nevada 2008).

Warren v. United States Specialty Sports Ass'n., Ok Civ. App 78 (Okla. Civ. App. 2006).

Wilson v. Daily Gazette Co., 588 S.E.2d 200 (2003).

Publications

Berry, R. C., & Wong, G. M. (1993). *Law and business of the sports industries* (2nd ed.). Westport, CT: Praeger Publishers.

Black, H. C. (1979). *Black's law dictionary* (5th ed.). St. Paul, MN: West Publishing Co.

Breaux, P. (2005). *Introduction to sports law and business.* Reno, NV: Bent Tree Press.

Byrd, L. L. (1988). Privacy rights of entertainers and other celebrities: A need for change. *Entertainment and Sports Law Reporter, 5*(95), 95–116.

Carper, D. L., & Mietus, N. J. (1995). *Understanding the law* (2nd ed.). St. Paul, MN: West Publishing Co.

Champion, W. T. (1991). *Fundamentals of sport law.* New York: CBC Publishing.

Clarkson, K. W., Miller, R. L., Jentz, G. A., & Cross, F. B. (2004). *West's business law* (9th ed.). Mason, OH: West Legal Studies in Business. Thompson Learning.

Clinton, M. & McKain, B. (2005). *Intentional infliction of emotional distress. Retrimeved* March 23, 2009. http://www.lawguys.com/Negligent_Infliction_of_Emotional_Distress.htm

Couch, B. (2000). How agent competition and corruption affects sports and the athlete-agent relationship and what can be done to control it. *Seton Hall Journal of Sports, 10,* L 111.

Cross, F. B., & Miller, R. L. (1995). *West's legal environment of business.* St. Paul, MN: West Publishing Co.

Deem, J. (2006). Student work: Freedom of the press: Classifying school athletes under the Gertz Public Figure Doctrine. *West Virginia Law Review, 108,* 799–839.

Dill, B. (1986). The journalist's handbook on libel and privacy. New York: The Free Press.

Ehrhardt, C. W., & Rodgers, J. M. (1988). Tightening the defense against offensive sports agents. *Florida State University Law Review, 16,* 634–674.

Epstein, A. (2002). Sports Law. Clifton Park, NY: Delmar Learning: West Legal Studies.

Gray, J. (2006). Sports agent's liability after Sparta. *Va. Sports & Ent. L. J.* 6, 141–162.

Huffaker, M. L. (2001). Recovery for infliction of emotional distress: A comment on the mental anguish accompanying such a claim in Alabama. *Alabama Law Review, 52* ,1003–1043.

Keeton, W. P., Dobbs, D. B., Keeton, R. E., Prosser, W. L., & Owen, D. G. (1984). *Prosser and Keeton on torts* (5th ed.). St. Paul, MN: West Publishing Co.

Powers, A. (1994). The need to regulate sports agents. *Seton Hall Journal of Sport Law, 4*, 253–274.

Prosser, W. L. (1960). Privacy. *Cal. L. Rev., 48*, 383–398.

Prosser, W. L. (1964). *Handbook of the law of torts.*(3d ed.). St. Paul, MN: West Publishing Co.

Ramsey, K. (2002, September 4). *Student records open to government.* University Daily Kansan.

Ruxin, R. (1993). *An athlete's guide to agents.* Boston: Jones and Bartlett Publishers.

Samar, V. J. (1991). *The right to privacy.* Philadelphia: Temple University Press.

Schubert, G., Smith, R. K., & Trentadue, J. C. (1986). *Sports law.* St. Paul, MN: West Publishing Co.

Smolla, R. A. (1999). Symposium on: Privacy and the law: The media's intrusion on privacy: Privacy and the first amendment right to gather news. *Geo. Wash. L. Rev., 67*, 1097.

Sobel, S. (1987). The regulation of sports agents: An analytical primer. *Baylor Law Review, 39*, 705–709.

Stapleton, L. L., & McMurphy, M. (1999). The professional athlete's right of publicity. *Marquette Sports Law Journal, 10*, 23–68.

Warren, S., & Brandeis, L. (1890). The right to privacy. *Harvard Law Review, 4*, 193.

Weistart, J. C., & Lowell, C. H. (1979). *Law and sports.* Charlottesville, VA: Michie/Bobbs Co.

Wong, G. (2002). *SPARTA Essentials of sports law.* Westport, CT: Praeger Publishers.

Woods, R. P., & Mills, M. R. (1988). Tortious interference with an athletic scholarship: A university remedy for the unscrupulous sports agent. *Alabama Law Review, 40*, 141–180.

Yasser, R., McCurdy, J. R., Goplerud, C. P., & Weston, M. A. (2006). *Sport law*: Cases and materials. Cincinnati, OH: Anderson Publishing Co.

Legislation

Restatement (Third) of the Law of Unfair Competition (1995).

Restatement of Torts, Second, Torts 8A (1965).

Restatement of Torts, Second § 46, com. d

Restatement (Second) of Torts #874, 1984

3.21 Sport-Related Crimes: Criminal Violence in Sport Gambling, Ticket Scalping, and Wire and Mail Fraud

—Barbara Osborne

UNIVERSITY OF NORTH CAROLINA

Criminal law is based on society's need to be free from harmful conduct. Unlike civil law where the goal is to compensate the wronged party, the broad aim of criminal law is to prevent injury to the health, safety, morals, and welfare of society. There is no plaintiff in a criminal case; the Prosecutor, representing the People, bears the burden of proving the defendant guilty "beyond a reasonable doubt"—a higher burden than the "preponderance of the evidence" standard used in civil actions.

Crimes may be divided into four categories: crimes against the person (such as assault, hazing, and homicide); crimes against property (such as vandalism and theft); crimes against public health, safety, and welfare (such as gambling and ticket scalping); and crimes against the government (such as RICO violations and terrorism) (Epstein, 2003). Crimes may also be divided into misdemeanors and felonies, based on the seriousness of the action against society. A **misdemeanor** is usually activity that results in fines or incarceration of less than one year. A **felony** generally results in sentences of a year or more in state or federal prison. This section examines criminal law in a sport and recreation context, looking at violent crimes such as assault and homicide as well as criminal activities such as gambling, ticket scalping, and wire and mail fraud.

FUNDAMENTAL CONCEPTS

The essential elements of all crime are an unlawful action and an evil intention. The prosecutor bears the burden of proving that the defendant both committed a voluntary, conscious act, legally known as **actus reus**, as well as that the defendant also possessed **mens rea**—a "guilty mind." The four criminal states of mind are: intentionally, knowingly, recklessly, and grossly. The criminal code of each state will indicate what actions and corresponding state of mind must be present to constitute the crime. A person acts **intentionally** if there is an act of the will. This mental state is required for specific intent crimes, meaning that the conscious objective of the actor is to cause the specific harm that resulted. A person acts **knowingly** when he or she has conscious understanding that harm is likely to occur as a result of the action. This mental state is one of general intent; it is assumed that a person intends the natural and ordinary consequences of his actions (*People v. Fitzsimmons*, 1895). The **recklessly** mental state is expressed when a person consciously disregards a substantial and unjustified risk that harm will result from one's actions. The mental state for acting **grossly** is carelessness or negligence resulting in bodily harm, thoughtless disregard for the consequences of one's actions, or heedless indifference to the rights and safety of others.

CRIMINAL VIOLENCE IN SPORT

Sport violence is not a new phenomenon. As early as 1895, a boxer was acquitted of manslaughter charges in New York for the death of his sparring partner during an exhibition match. In 1906, President Theodore Roosevelt was so distraught after watching the University of Pennsylvania football team attempt to reduce a Swarthmore star lineman to a bloody pulp that he threatened to outlaw football by Executive Order. In 1920, a pitch by New York Yankee Carl Mays killed Cleveland Indian Ray Chapman. Complaints that a participant intentionally injured another are most often addressed in the civil court system (see Section 3.11, *Assault and Battery*). However, some sport and recreation participants have been charged with and convicted of crimes for injuring fellow participants.

Prosecutors struggle to prove the necessary criminal intent of the defendant in sports violence cases—that the player consciously intended to cause bodily injury to the other player. It is assumed that a player operating in a setting in which violence is customary and approved is not acting with criminal intent, but merely following established practices of the sport. In 1978, Oakland Raiders safety Jack Tatum legally tackled New England Patriots wide receiver Darryl Stingley, leaving him paralyzed below the waist. In his book, *They Call Me Assassin*, Tatum bragged: "I never make a tackle just to bring someone down. I want to punish the man I'm going after. I like to believe my best hits border on felonious assault." These words would seemingly satisfy the requirement of evil intention. However, the words also illustrate standard, acceptable motivation on the playing field.

It is equally difficult to prove that an athlete engaged in unlawful action. A significant number of injuries occur from aggressive acts that are within the rules of the game. Other violent acts, which may border on the illegitimate, are still considered part of the game—baseball pitchers routinely throw warning and revenge pitches, and batters commonly retaliate by charging the mound and starting bench-clearing brawls. Similarly, fighting and use of a stick are customary activities in ice hockey.

There are many other reasons that prosecutors hesitate to file charges against athletes for acts of violence during the course of play. Prosecutors don't view athletes as "real criminals." Similarly, the victim of the athlete's violent actions usually does not want to file criminal charges against a fellow athlete, leaving the prosecution without a complainant. It is difficult to prove the actual elements of criminal conduct and obtain a guilty verdict. Even when prosecutors are successful, the sentences rarely amount to more than a slap on the wrist.

The first criminal case of a professional athlete charged for an act committed during the course of play in the United States, *State v. Forbes* (1975), illustrates the difficulty prosecutors have in convicting athletes. In 1975, Dave Forbes of the Boston Bruins checked Henry Boucha of the Minnesota North Stars against the boards with his elbows up and Boucha retaliated by punching Forbes. Both players exchanged words from their adjacent penalty boxes. When they returned to the ice, Boucha skated ahead of Forbes and struck Boucha in the face with the butt end of his stick. Forbes then jumped on Boucha and continued punching him until a third player separated them. Boucha required 25 stitches to close the cut near his right eye, and subsequent surgeries to repair a small fracture at the base of the eye socket and to correct a double vision problem. Forbes was indicted for aggravated assault with a dangerous weapon. After a highly publicized trial, the jury was split 9-3 in favor of conviction, but was unable to reach a unanimous verdict. The court declared a mistrial and the prosecutors declined to retry the case.

Criminal Assault

The intentional torts of assault and battery (see Section 3.11, *Assault and Battery*) should not be confused with **criminal assault,** although a civil lawsuit to recover damages and a criminal lawsuit to protect society from the defendant's acts may both be brought from a single incident. Unlike civil law, where the torts of assault and battery are universally defined, each state drafts its own criminal statutes. Although not a source of law, the **Model Penal Code** is a scholarly attempt to compile a comprehensive and coherent body of criminal law. In a majority of jurisdictions, an **assault** is either an attempt to commit a battery or the intentional creation of a reasonable apprehension in the victim's mind of imminent bodily harm. The Model Penal Code divides criminal assault into two categories: simple or aggravated. A person is guilty of **simple assault** if he attempts to cause or purposely, knowingly, or recklessly causes bodily injury to another; or negligently causes bodily injury to another with a deadly weapon; or attempts by physical menace to put another in fear of imminent serious bodily injury. In 2000, a 24-year-old girlfriend of a recreational hockey player was found guilty of assault of a sports official following a game between two men's "B" teams in Reston, Virginia. She received a 30-day suspended jail sentence for kicking the official in the groin. A person is guilty of **aggravated assault** if he attempts to cause serious bodily injury to another, or causes such injury purposely, knowingly, or recklessly under circumstances manifesting extreme indifference to the value of human life; or attempts to cause or purposely or knowingly causes bodily injury to another with a deadly weapon [Model Penal Code § 2.11.1 (2008)]. In 2006, the father of a freshman on the high school football team in Canton, Texas, was convicted of aggravated assault with a deadly weapon for shooting the coach just outside of the locker room. The coach was critically injured and the parent was sentenced to ten years in prison.

Homicide

If a participant's actions cause the death of an opponent or fellow participant, he or she may be charged with **homicide**. Nathan Hall worked as a ski lift operator on Vail Mountain. After his shift ended and the lifts were closed, he skied down to the base of the mountain. Hall sped straight down the mountain; arms out for balance, bouncing off the moguls, completely out of control. He flew off a knoll and collided with Allen Cobb, crushing Cobb's skull and killing him. The court convicted him of **reckless manslaughter** (*People v. Hall*, 2000) (see the Supplemental CD).

Involuntary manslaughter is the conscious disregard of a substantial and unjustifiable risk that would cause the death of another (Model Penal Code § 210.3). Whether a risk is substantial is determined by assessing both the likelihood that harm will occur and the magnitude of the harm should it occur. Whether a risk is justifiable is determined by weighing the nature and purpose of the conduct against the risk created by that conduct. Involuntary manslaughter may also be identified as **criminal negligence**. Criminal negligence is categorized by a greater deviation from the *reasonable person* standard than is required for civil liability (Model Penal Code § 210.4). The terms reckless manslaughter, involuntary manslaughter, and reckless homicide, may be used by different states for the same or very similar acts, as each crime is defined in the state criminal code. The differentiation may be only in the mens rea (the criminal intent) specified in the code.

Reckless homicide charges have been brought against owners and operators of amusement parks when safety violations result in death. In March 2004, the Rockin' Raceway amusement park manager was found guilty of reckless homicide when a woman riding the Hawk, a pendulum-like ride, fell 60 feet to her death when her safety harness came loose. Similarly, two state inspectors and a fair worker were charged with reckless homicide when an eight-year old boy died from electrical shock while he was standing in line for a bumper car ride.

In what is thought to be the first criminal indictment of a coach for reckless homicide for the heat-related death of an athlete, high school football coach Jason Stinson was indicted by grand jury for the death of 15-year-old Max Gilpin. The football player collapsed during a practice in late August (2008); his core body temperature reached 107 degrees. Witnesses testified that Stinson denied the player water. Gilpin was rushed to the hospital and died three days later. A civil complaint has also been filed by the family against six school coaches and administrators; however, Stinson was the only one criminally charged (*Crockett v. Stinson*, 2009).

Defenses

Consent. A criminal offense is a wrong against society; therefore consent has not historically been recognized as a defense. In general, it is against public policy for an individual to consent to be the victim of a crime. However, the Model Penal Code states that consent may be a defense to criminal charges *arising from conduct in a sports event*:

> *When conduct is charged to constitute an offense because it causes or threatens bodily injury, consent to such conduct or to the infliction of such injury is a defense if . . . the conduct and the injury are reasonably foreseeable hazards of joint participation in a lawful athletic contest or competitive sport. (Model Penal Code § 2.11.2(b) [2001]).*

Some courts have used the **reasonable foreseeability test,** similar to the test commonly used in tort actions (see Section 3.11, *Assault and Battery*), to measure consent (often referred to as "implied consent"). It is accepted that players consent to conduct that is within the bounds of the reasonably foreseeable hazards of the game. Conversely, players do not consent to injuries caused by intentional acts that are not part of the game. The complicated issue is determining which acts of violence are reasonably foreseeable. One method is to determine whether the conduct is a customary aspect of the game. In boxing, for example, it is reasonably foreseeable that an opponent would be knocked unconscious, as the objective of boxing is to render an opponent unconscious. Similar conduct, swinging a fist at an opponent's face or head, would not be reasonably foreseeable within the context of the game in sports such as basketball or soccer. The significant case in this section, *State v. Guidugli* (2004), provides an excellent history of this doctrine.

A few courts have applied a **rules of the game test,** where a participant would not consent to acts that were illegal under the rules of the sport. Although this is an easy test to apply, it is an extremely narrow approach to the consent issue. Every foul would be a potential crime—games as we know them would cease to exist as referees would blow the whistle and the law enforcement officials would rush in to take statements!

William Floyd argued the consent defense unsuccessfully in *State v. Floyd*, (1990). Floyd was convicted of two counts of assault without intent to inflict serious injury but causing bodily injury, a serious misdemeanor, for his part in a particularly violent brawl in a four-on-four YMCA recreational basketball game. The championship game was physical—fouls were hard, including considerable hacking and a lot of shoving under the boards. The referee called a foul, words were exchanged, there was some shoving and one of the players on the court threw a punch. A brawl ensued. The complainant, McHale, was standing on the sidelines when William Floyd, who was also on the sidelines, struck him in the face, knocking him to the floor. McHale suffered a concussion, severe hemorrhaging, and loss of brain tissue. He spent two days in intensive care and permanently lost the sense of smell. William Floyd left McHale unconscious on the floor and proceeded to attack Gregg Barrier and Duane Barrier—Gregg Barrier was also on the sidelines, while Duane Barrier had been in the game when play was halted. Duane Barrier suffered a severely deviated septum requiring reconstructive surgery. The defense argued consent, but the court found that there was no nexus between the defendant's actions and playing the game of basketball—particularly when play had ceased and the defendant was not on the court engaged in play at the time of the acts.

Self-defense. Within criminal law, a person who is not the aggressor in an encounter is justified in using a reasonable amount of force against his adversary when he reasonably believes that he is in immediate danger of unlawful bodily harm from his adversary and that the use of such force is necessary to avoid this danger (Model Penal Code § 3.04(1)). Applying self-defense is generally problematic for participants in sport for several reasons. First, the **amount of force** used is limited to that which is reasonably necessary. Most unlawful behavior in sports contexts involves contact and then escalating levels of retaliation. Another problem is timing: the participant/defendant must have had an honest belief that the danger of immediate, serious bodily harm was *imminent*. Athletes often retaliate after the danger has passed. The baseball player who charges the mound after being brushed back from the plate is no longer in danger from the pitch. Self-defense is also not a viable defense if the defendant was the initial aggressor in the incident. Additionally, some states allow self-defense only if the defendant **had no reasonable means of retreat.** In most situations, a player can stop the confrontation by retreating.

GAMBLING

Gambling in some form is now legal in 48 of the 50 states. Only Hawaii and Utah do not have some form of legalized gambling. State-sponsored gambling exists in the form of lotteries, pari-mutuel betting, bingo, and casinos. Although a majority of Americans view sports gambling as harmless fun, gambling on collegiate and professional sports is a crime in all states but Nevada.

Gambling on sports poses special concerns that are uniquely different from legally placing bets on games of chance in casinos or purchasing lottery tickets. The popularity of sports rests on the integrity of sports contests—the honest struggle within the framework of the game to determine the superior competitor. Sports gambling leads to **game fixing, point shaving**, and **bribery** of athletes and officials. Since the Black Sox scandal of 1919, professional sports figures have been implicated in gambling, point shaving, and game fixing. Baseball players Pete Rose and Denny McLain have been jailed and suspended, and Len Dykstra was placed on probation. Paul Hornung, Alex Karras, and Art Schlicter were suspended from the NFL. Veteran NBA referee

Tim Donaghy pled guilty to charges of wire fraud and transmitting gambling tips for his involvement in a gambling scandal that included games that he officiated.

There have also been problems in college sports—Arizona State University, Boston College, University of Kentucky, New York City College, Northwestern University, University of Rhode Island, Seton Hall, and Tulane University basketball teams have been implicated in point-shaving scandals. University of Nevada, Las Vegas basketball players have been charged with associating with known gamblers. Football players at Boston College and Northwestern have been implicated for placing bets on sporting events including several who bet against their own team. In 2004, the University of Michigan was involved in a major infractions investigation involving payments to men's basketball players by a booster from funds generated by an illegal gambling operation.

The ability to regulate gambling was traditionally held by the state under the **police power** to protect the health, safety, and welfare of the public. Sports gambling, unlike casinos and lotteries that are *regulated and taxed* by the state, siphons away revenue, tax dollars, and jobs. Gambling addiction costs the individual, the family, and the community.

The federal government has generally deferred to the states in the regulation of gambling. However, Congress demonstrated the power to regulate sports gambling under the **Commerce Clause** after Congressional investigations in the 1950s uncovered the activities of organized crime in the gambling industry. Evidence indicated that profits from illegal sports wagering helped finance other activities of organized crime, such as funding drug sales and loan sharking. Federal laws related to sports gambling include:

- The **Wire Communications Act of 1961** (Wire Act) prohibits the use of wire communications by persons or organizations engaged in the business of wagering, to transmit bets or wagers or information that assists in the placing of bets or wagers. It is important to note that a significant limitation of this legislation is that it does not penalize the individual bettor (18 U.S.C. § 1084). The government has used this legislation to prosecute Internet gambling operators;

- The **Interstate and Foreign Travel or Transportation in Aid of Racketeering Enterprising Act of 1961** (Travel Act) prosecutes those who travel in interstate commerce to distribute the proceeds of unlawful activity, commit a crime of violence to further unlawful activity or otherwise promote, manage, establish, or facilitate any unlawful activity (18 U.S.C. § 1952);

- **Racketeer-Influenced and Corrupt Organizations Act of 1970** (RICO) prohibits conspiring to engage in criminal enterprise. Although RICO includes sports gambling rings, it is difficult to prove conspiracy and racketeering activity at the level necessary to satisfy the elements of a RICO violation (18 U.S.C. § 1955);

- The **Bribery in Sporting Contests Act of 1979** made it a crime to bribe or attempt to bribe an individual in order to influence the outcome of a sporting contest (18 U.S.C. § 224);

- The **Professional and Amateur Sports Protection Act of 1992** (Bradley Bill) prohibits the expansion of state-sanctioned, authorized, or licensed gambling on amateur and professional sporting events in the United States (28 U.S.C. § 3702).

Internet Gambling

Internet gambling is defined as the placing of real money bets using one's personal computer via the Internet. Internet gambling has exploded to the point that it is probably the most important issue in sports gambling. In 1996, there were only two Internet sites with sports betting. By 2005, the number of Internet gambling sites was estimated at 1,800. From 2002–2003, revenue from legal Nevada sports betting grew by 11.98 percent, while Internet gambling increased 42 percent. Conservative estimates place the amount of money gambled annually over the Internet at $10 billion. Criminals use online gambling sites for **laundering** money, credit card **fraud**, fraudulent promises to pay bettors, and **tax avoidance**. Public Policy concerns also include prevention of underage gambling, consumer vulnerability, increased bankruptcies, and maintaining the ability of states to decide their own criminal regulatory schemes.

The biggest problem with restricting Internet gambling is the issue of **jurisdiction.** First, there are considerable differences in state laws and international laws. The problem then becomes which state law do you enforce, the state in which the gambling site is located or the state in which the bet is placed? What if the Internet site or the bet originates from another country? Australia, Belize, Lichtenstein, Austria, Belgium, Finland, Germany, Honduras, South Africa, Venezuela, Curaçao, Costa Rica, Grenada, Antigua, and the Dominican Republic all have taken steps to legalize Internet gambling to capitalize on the United States' prohibitive legal environment. Some of these countries will refuse to cooperate with those countries that attempt to control or restrict Internet gambling.

State v. Granite Gate Resorts, Inc. (1998), illustrates the jurisdiction problem. Granite Gate was a Nevada corporation that did business as On Ramp, a provider of Internet advertising. One of the sites advertised was WagerNet, an online wagering service that was to be available internationally in the fall of 1995. In the summer of 1995, Jeff Janacek, a consumer investigator for the Minnesota Attorney General's office, contacted WagerNet and was told that the betting service was legal. Subsequently, the state brought action against the nonresident corporation for deceptive trade practices, false advertising, and consumer fraud. The District Court of Ramsey County denied the defendants' motion to dismiss for lack of personal jurisdiction and the defendants appealed. The Court of Appeals held that the defendants were subject to personal jurisdiction in the state based on their actions of advertising on the Internet a forthcoming online gambling service and developing from the Internet a mailing list that included one or more Minnesota residents.

Minnesota's long-arm statute permits courts to assert jurisdiction over defendants to the extent that federal constitutional requirements of **due process** will allow. To satisfy the Due Process Clause of the Fourteenth Amendment, the state must show that the defendant has minimum contacts with the forum state such that the maintenance of the suit does not offend traditional notions of fair play and substantial justice. There must be some act by which the defendant purposefully avails itself of the privilege of conducting activities within the forum state, thus invoking the benefits and protections of its laws. A court must consider five factors in determining whether a defendant has established **minimum contacts** with the forum state: (1) the quantity of the defendant's contacts, (2) the nature and quality of the defendant's contacts, (3) the connection between the cause of action and the defendant's contacts, (4) the state's interest in providing a forum, and (5) the convenience of the parties. In close cases, doubts should be resolved in favor of retention of jurisdiction.

Federal legislation that was passed to address terrorism has bypassed the jurisdiction issues and provided another avenue for enforcement of gambling laws. The **PATRIOT Act** (2001) permits law enforcement officials to gather electronic evidence pertaining to illegal activities, including offshore money laundering regulations. The law does not contain any specific anti-gambling provisions, but it does regulate banking services and allows the government to seize accounts in offshore banks where there is evidence of illegal activity, which would include gambling. In March 2003, the U.S. Attorney accused PayPal, a subsidiary of EBay, of violating the PATRIOT Act. The lawsuit was settled with PayPal paying $10 million of gambling profits from illegal offshore gambling operations.

The **Unlawful Internet Gambling Enforcement Act (2006)** prohibits credit card companies and banks that do business in the United States from processing transfers, checks, credit cards, and other forms of payment for Internet gambling. The primary criticism against the legislation is that it expects banks and credit card companies to be self-regulating. Legislation has been proposed in 2009 that would effectively end the UIGEA and instead establish a licensing and regulatory framework for Internet gambling operations.

TICKET SCALPING

Ticket scalping is commonly defined as the reselling of tickets at a price higher than the established value. Historically, ticket scalping began in the late 19th century when people sold unused railroad tickets without authorization. This practice expanded into entertainment for theater productions, and eventually to sporting events. **Ticket brokers** emerged in the 20th century as remote outlets for the sale of theater and baseball tickets. A ticket broker, also known as a ticket speculator, is one who buys tickets and then resells them for more than their face value. Brokers generally worked with the authorized box office to sell tickets and retained a small service fee. With the emergence of computer technology, ticket brokers such as Ticketmaster have emerged as primary sellers (Benitah, 2005).

Beginning in 1905, states began to enact anti-scalping legislation. Public policy dictated that everyone should have equal and fair access to tickets to attend sport and entertainment events. Similarly, sport and entertainment promoters have a legitimate interest in regulating ticket sales and controlling business activity on their property. Venue owners and operators were also concerned for the safety and welfare of spectators who might be harassed on the street by scalpers. Generally, state statutes and municipal ordinances were enacted to prohibit the resale of tickets entirely, or to limit the amount above face value that tickets could be resold, or to limit the location of ticket scalpers relative to the venue. At its zenith, 45 of the 50 states had enacted some sort of legislation in order to curb the nuisances associated with ticket scalping. The legal authority to regulate ticket scalping falls within the police power of the state to regulate for the health, safety and welfare of the community.

With the explosion of personal communications technology, ticket scalping has moved off the street corners and into people's computers. Language has also changed from *ticket scalping to ticket resale* on the *secondary ticket market*. On-line ticket resale marketplaces such as StubHub, TicketsNow and RazorGator provide forums for consumers to buy and sell tickets. This practice often violated state and local laws; however the secondary ticket resellers limited their liability by posting links to the laws of each state on their websites and warning consumers not to break the law. Enforcement of ticket scalping laws in cyberspace was virtually nonexistent, and states began to repeal or amend ticket scalping laws to reflect current market practices. As of 2007, 42 states had repealed anti-scalping legislation (Jacoby, 2007).

Acceptance of the secondary ticket market has spawned new legal issues relating to consumer protection and ticket resale. In an effort to protect their rights in granting season ticket licenses, the New England Patriots sued StubHub to gain access to the names of season ticket holders who resold their tickets on that Website. The court ordered StubHub to release the names of their customers to the New England Patriots (*NPS, LLC v. StubHub, Inc.*, 2007). In another interesting case, the Chicago Cubs were sued by fans for creating their own secondary ticket provider (*Cavoto v. Chicago Naational League Ball Club, Inc.*, 2006). In 2002, the ownership of the Chicago Cubs created Wrigley Field Premium Ticket Services, a company that sold tickets to events at Wrigley Field. The Cubs ownership purchased blocks of tickets for Cubs baseball games and then resold them through Wrigley Field Premium Ticket Services at market prices rather than the face value of the ticket. This practice allowed the Cubs to maximize profit, as well as to protect profits from the league's revenue sharing agreement, since the earnings were credited to the ticket brokerage and not the baseball franchise. Cubs fans sued as a class action claiming that the team was scalping its own tickets, in violation of the state ticket scalping act. The trial court judge ruled that the Cubs were not in violation of the statute because the ticket brokerage was a separate corporation.

WIRE AND MAIL FRAUD

Unlike gambling and ticket scalping, which have traditionally been regulated by the states, wire and mail fraud is a federal crime. In 1865, Congress granted the Post Office Department the authority to regulate obscene materials. Additional legislation was passed in 1868 to limit illegal lotteries and monetary schemes. This early legislation met with little success. The first federal mail fraud statute emanates from an 1872 recodification of one of the sections of the Postal Act, making it a federal crime to use the mail system fraudulently.

The most notorious sports-related wire and mail fraud case is *U.S. v. Walters*, (1989). Norby Walters and his business partner Lloyd Bloom had signed 58 college football players to professional football contracts while they were still playing college ball. At the end of their collegiate careers, only two of the original 58 players decided to let Walters represent them. Walters and Bloom resorted to threats against the other 56. These threats led to a federal investigation and the agents were indicted on charges of conspiracy, RICO violations, and mail fraud. After a month-long trial and a week of deliberations, the jury convicted Walters and Bloom. However, the conviction was overturned by the United States Court of Appeals for the Seventh Circuit in 1993, which held that the forms mailed by the colleges to the NCAA verifying the players' eligibility were not sufficiently integral to the defendant's scheme of signing players to contracts prior to the expiration of their eligibility to support a mail fraud conviction. Even if the mailings were sufficient, the defendant did not cause the universities to use the mails. Finally, the conviction could not be sustained on the basis that the defendant deprived the universities of scholarship funds paid to the athletes who were no longer eligible because the defendant did not obtain any property from the universities by fraud.

A successful wire and mail fraud prosecution involved using a federal work-study program to circumvent NCAA rules. In *U.S. v. Brauman* (2006), Barton County Community College track coach Lance Brauman was convicted of mail fraud for falsifying student employment records. His action resulted in federal work-study funds being paid to student-athletes for work they did not perform. Wire and mail fraud charges did not stick in a bribery case involving the bid and selection process for the Winter Olympics. In *U.S. v. Welch* (2003), two members of the Salt Lake City Bid Committee (SLBC) for the 2002 Olympic Winter Games were indicted by a federal grand jury on 15 bribery-related counts of criminal misconduct in connection with the SLBC's activities in procuring the 2002 Games. A major international scandal, the defendants were accused of making direct or indirect illegal payments or benefits to International Olympic Committee members totaling approximately $1 million in value. Although the 10th Circuit Court of Appeals ruled that all the required elements to prove wire and mail fraud were present in the case, on remand the District Court acquitted the defendants on 15 felony counts of conspiracy, Travel Act violations, and wire and mail fraud relating to the bribery issues.

According to Title 18 U.S.C. §§ 1341-1346 (2002), it is illegal to use the mails or electronic communications for the purpose of executing a scheme to defraud. There are two basic elements to the crime of wire and mail fraud: (1) a scheme and intent to defraud, and (2) use of the mails or wire communications to execute the scheme. The use of the Postal Service, and all wired communications such as telephone and telegraph lines, the Internet, as well as the wireless communications devices that connect with wired communications methods are included. Some courts have ruled that the government must also prove a culpable participation in that use by defendant, either by making the use himself or by knowingly causing someone else to make the use.

A **scheme to defraud** is behavior calculated to deceive persons of ordinary prudence and comprehension. This element has two components: fraudulent intent and contemplation to harm or injure. To prove fraudulent intent, the government must prove that the defendant actually devised or intended to devise such a scheme. The focus is not upon conduct but on the state of mind or scheme. A contemplation of harm or injury may be inferred when a scheme has an injurious effect as a necessary result of its execution. It is also necessary that there must be a deprivation of money or property. In *U.S. v. Gray* (1996), assistant men's basketball coaches Kevin Gray, Gary Thomas, and Troy Drummond were convicted of conspiracy to commit mail and wire fraud, and various counts of mail and wire fraud in violation of 18 U.S.C. §§ 2, 371, 1343 and 1346. The three defendants were assistant men's basketball coaches who executed a fraudulent scheme to establish academic eligibility for five transfer students who were recruited from two-year colleges to play basketball at Baylor University. The coaches provided the recruits with written course work or answers to correspondence exams that were then represented to the various schools as the students' work. The court found that they committed fraud by depriving the recruits of scholarships, and depriving the University of the right to honest services.

The second element, causing **use of the mails or wire communications to execute the scheme**, has been interpreted to mean that the person acts with the knowledge that use of the mails will follow in the ordinary course of business, or where use of the mails can reasonably be foreseen even though not actually intended. A defendant need not make the mailing himself. It is sufficient that the mailing was a consequence known or reasonably foreseeable to him. There are limitations on the mailing element of the statute: letters mailed before the scheme is conceived or after it is completed are not subject to the mail fraud statute because mailing either before a scheme is conceived or after it has reached fruition does not further the scheme and cannot support a mail fraud conviction. The government must prove that the mailings were related to the alleged fraud. In *U.S. v. Walters* (1989), deceit was an ingredient of Walters' plan, but no evidence existed that he conceived a scheme in which mailings played a role. Conversely, in *U.S. v. Gray* (1996), the assistant coaches deliberately used the mails to transmit the fraudulent coursework.

It is not necessary for the government to show that the plan to defraud was complete in all its aspects from its inception in order to support a conviction for a conspiracy to defraud by the use of the mails. Thus, it is not necessary that any one particular overt act be proven in order to obtain a conviction for conspiracy to commit mail fraud, and there is no requirement of showing the actual use of the mails.

Mail Fraud Defenses. There are two primary defenses to a mail fraud prosecution: good faith and the statute of limitations. **Good faith** is a complete defense to a mail fraud prosecution. The good faith defense seeks to demonstrate that there was no intent. The **statute of limitations** for mail and wire fraud schemes is five years, except those that affect a financial institution, in which case the statute is 10 years. The statute runs from the last overt act in furtherance of the scheme.

The following case provides an excellent history of the difficult issues related to criminal prosecution for actions within the context of a recreational intramural basketball game.

STATE V. GUIDUGLI

Court of Appeals of Ohio, First Appellate District, Hamilton County
157 Ohio App. 3d 383; 2004 Ohio 2871; 811 N.E.2d 567; 2004 Ohio App. LEXIS 2529
June 4, 2004

GORMAN, JUDGE.

Viewed narrowly, this appeal presents a simple question: whether the trial court erred by convicting the defendant-appellant, Gino Guidugli, of misdemeanor assault, in violation of *R.C. 2903.13(A)*, for his role in a scuffle that broke out between members of opposing teams after a hard foul in a closely contested intramural basketball game at the University of Cincinnati. Viewed broadly, this appeal presents a far more complex social issue involving the wisdom of strictly applying the criminal law to physical altercations that arise within the context of sports contests, especially those contests that are already subject to league regulation and internal discipline—and particularly where the bodily injury to the alleged victim is not serious.

Unfortunately, the larger social question is not directly addressed by the legal issues presented on appeal, which concern only the sufficiency of the evidence and the competency of counsel in presenting Guidugli's unsuccessful claim of self-defense. Although questioning the necessity of prosecuting as a criminal offense what may have been dealt with internally by the University, and the harshness of the sentence imposed by the trial court, we are unable to find any reversible legal error. As a court of law, not of social policy, we affirm.

A HARD FOUL IGNITES A FIGHT

On March 9, 2003, Guidugli, the starting quarterback for the University of Cincinnati football team, was playing in an organized student intramural basketball game at the Armory Field House on the University of Cincinnati campus. When Guidugli's teammate protested a foul called by the referee, his teammate and an opposing player exchanged heated words, and the opposing player grabbed his teammate by the shirt. Both benches emptied as players took to the floor.

There was conflicting testimony regarding the nature of the ensuing scuffle. Keith Steineman, the intramural supervisor, described it as a "fracas" involving "pushing and shoving." He stated that supervisors were trained to "let players like work it out themselves so we don't get involved and get hit." Steineman testified, though, that the only punch he saw thrown was that by Guidugli. But one of

Guidugli's teammates, Doug Monaghan, testified that the pushing and shoving quickly escalated into a donnybrook. In his words, "fists were flying."

According to Steinman, he witnessed Guidugli enter the fracas, and it was his opinion that Guidugli was, initially at least, "trying to break up [the] scuffle." But he then saw Guidugli knock over one of the opposing players, Levi Harris, and "punch him with a full swing" around the eye. Chris Brunswick, who was acting as scorekeeper, testified that he thought Harris was already on the ground when Guidugli ran onto the court and punched him. Guidugli, however, testified that he was one of the players on the floor and had taken a position along the foul lane, getting ready for the foul shots, when the fight broke out. He stated that he saw another teammate of his, Kevin Hazel, punch Harris, and that he was pulling someone off Monaghan when he saw a punch coming in his direction out of the corner of his eye. He stated that when he turned around, he recognized the person attempting to throw the punch as Harris and he "just defended himself."

Whatever the degree of the fight, Steineman testified that afterward the teams "worked it out" and order was restored. Guidugli's team was told, apparently by Steineman, that they had forfeited the game and should leave the gym, which they did.

The university police were called after Steineman reported the "group fight" by radio to the main office. Officer Kevin Manz arrived two minutes after being dispatched, but some thirty to forty-five minutes after the incident. Although Guidugli and his team had left, Harris and his team had remained because they had another game. Officer Manz spoke to Harris, who was holding a wet cloth to the area around his left eye. Officer Mainz took photographs of Harris's face. Harris then signed a complaint charging Guidugli with criminal assault. Harris's affidavit accompanying the complaint stated, "As I was walking away I was hit with two punches, one from the side and one from the back. I was unaware who hit me." . . .

The trial court, upon hearing all the various versions of the fight and punch, rejected Guidugli's claim of self-defense, stating that the evidence showed that he had punched Harris in retaliation rather than to protect himself. The court thus convicted Guidugli of misdemeanor assault. After listening to arguments in favor of mitigation made by Guidugli's trial counsel, the court imposed a 180-day jail sentence, which it then suspended in favor of one year's probation with the conditions that Guidugli undergo 60 days of home incarceration using an electronic monitoring unit, and that he participate in any treatment or counseling, including anger management, recommended by the probation department. Further, Guidugli was required to pay a $100 fine and court costs.

On July 3, 2003, Guidugli, represented by new counsel, filed a written motion to mitigate, requesting the court to reconsider its sentence. In his motion, Guidugli asked the court to sentence him to community service only, asserting that the incident that had led to his conviction was an isolated event in which he had allowed his competitive nature to interfere with his better judgment. He claimed that he deeply regretted his behavior and had learned a valuable lesson that would preclude him from ever committing a similar offense. In support of his character, he pointed out that he had been a law-abiding citizen for the first twenty years of his young life and had maintained a grade point average of 3.27 as a business-management major at the University of Cincinnati while maintaining the rigorous schedule of a college athlete. He also pointed out that he had been an active member of CPAWS, a student-athlete group that took part in service projects throughout the greater Cincinnati area, and that he had voluntarily spoken at numerous fundraisers and had traveled to Mississippi Gulf Coast Community College to work as a camp counselor for disadvantaged children. He also observed that the sentence as imposed by the trial court had forced him to cancel plans to attend the Peyton Manning Sports Camp, and that it threatened his participation in certain media events important in garnering awards during the college football season, as well as his presence at a team training camp considered integral in preparation for the first game of the season. On July 7, 2003, the trial court denied the motion. On August 14, 2003, the trial court granted Guidugli's motion to stay further execution of the sentence pending this appeal.

* * *

Other Available Defenses—Sports Violence and the Criminal Law

In mitigation, in other words after the trial court's finding of guilt, defense counsel raised the argument for the first time that such fights were typical of hard fought athletic contests, particularly among young college-aged men eager to test their manhood. As defense counsel pointed out, "You don't have to go any further than Riverfront Stadium to see athletes in altercations." Defense counsel asked that the trial court take into consideration that "this young man [Guidugli], like all the other guys who are out there that night, were competitors and in a game. And the game got a little out of control at a point. And it escalated into this. . . . "

This argument brings into focus the larger question alluded to at the outset of this opinion: whether physical altercations arising in sports contests that are already subject to some form of internal regulation and discipline should necessarily result in criminal charges, at least where there are no serious physical injuries as a result. Legal scholars have questioned the strict application of the criminal law to sports contests in which, contrary to real-world norms that generally condemn such behavior, a premium is placed upon physical aggression, intimidation, and enforcement. See, e.g., Clarke, Law and Order on the Courts: The Application of Criminal Liability for Intentional Fouls During Sporting Events (2000), *32 Ariz.St.L.J. 1149*; Harary, Aggressive Play or Criminal Assault? An In Depth Look at Sports Violence and Criminal Liability (2002), *25 Colum. J.L. & Arts 197.*

"From an early age, athletes are taught to intimidate opponents and to precipitate physical altercations rather than to avoid them. Athletes learn that they need to be tough to get noticed and to excel in higher levels of competition." *Clarke, supra, at 1157-1158.* "Violence in sports can be attributed to many factors, including: the interplay between competition, frustration, and aggression; the "'game reasoning'" or "'port reasoning'" that supplements—or, at times, replaces—ordinary moral reasoning during sporting events; the degree of "'sport socialization'" that leads players to perceive sports violence as legitimate; *the sports norm of reciprocity for acts of aggression by opposing players;* and the significance placed upon winning at all costs. It is the confluence of these factors that create the curious world which is sports—a world in which real world behavioral models have no place." *Id. at 1155-1156* (emphasis supplied).

Given the unique social dynamic involved in sports, "criminal prosecution of sports participants for conduct that occurs with the playing of the game is rare." *Id. at 1168*, citing Yasser, McCurdy, and Gopelrud, Sports Law (1990) 378. Most prosecutions, not surprisingly, have involved hockey games. See Calvert-Hanson and Dernis, Revisiting Excessive Violence in the Professional Sports Arena: Changes in the Past Twenty Years? (1996), 6 Seton Hall L.Rev. 127, 138. Perhaps saying something about the American competitive nature, prosecutors in the United States have shown far less zeal in punishing sports violence than their Canadian counterparts, who have been observed to use the criminal law much more frequently. See White, Sports Violence as Criminal Assault: Development of the Doctrine by Canadian Courts (1986), *1986 Duke L.J. 1030, 1034.*

One stated rational for prosecutorial restraint is the inherent safeguards of league play, with its system of in-game punishment and suspension. As one commentator has written, "It is inevitable that players' passions will at times be aroused, but game officials and coaches are vested with the authority to impose sanctions for misconduct during the game. The penalties imposed by referees or umpires may seem minor when compared to those imposed on perpetrators of the same conduct outside the sport context, but those punishments are quick and certain, and are thought by some criminologists to be more effective in deterring undesirable behavior than the imposition of more severe penalties." *Clarke, supra, at 1192.*

* * *

Canadian courts were among the first to establish the implied-consent doctrine of sports in criminal cases, see *Regina v. Green* (Ont. Provincial Ct. 1970), 2 C.C.C.2d 442, and *Regina v. Maki* (Ont. Provincial Ct. 1970), 1 C.C.C.2d 333, but, interestingly, the American Law Institute had earlier adopted the doctrine in its 1962 Official Draft of the Model Penal Code. Section 2.11(2) of the code provides that consent can be an absolute defense to bodily harm if "the conduct and the harm are a reasonably foreseeable hazard of joint participation in a lawful athletic competition or competitive sport * * *."

The Model Penal Code section has no analog in the Ohio Revised Code. As a matter of decisional law, the doctrine, although acknowledged, has found limited application in American courts. See *State v. Floyd* (Iowa App.1990), 466 N.W.2d 919, 922; *People v. Freer* (1976), 86 Misc. 2d 280, 381 N.Y.S.2d 976, 979; and *State v. Shelley* (Wash. App. 1997), 85 Wn. App. 24, 929 P.2d 489, 493. Courts have appeared to draw the line between physical aggression that can be reasonably foreseen within the context of game play, and thus, by inference, consented to by the player, and violence that takes place after play has stopped, or is purely retaliatory, or exceeds in brutality or degree of injury anything that the player might have otherwise agreed to. For example, in *Floyd* the court refused to apply the doctrine to a recreational basketball game in which the defendant assaulted players resting on the sideline during a timeout. In *Freer*, the court held the doctrine inapplicable to a punch thrown by a football player in retaliation for a punch thrown by the complainant in the midst of a game tackle. And in *Shelley* the court refused to allow the doctrine to justify a punch thrown by another recreational basketball player who felt the blow justified after the complainant had scratched him across the face during play.

Our research has not disclosed any Ohio cases involving application of the implied-consent doctrine in a criminal prosecution for sports violence. In *State v. Dunham* (1997), 118 Ohio App. 3d 724, 693 N.E.2d 1175, this court rejected application of the doctrine of mutual consent to a prosecution for felonious assault arising out a street fight. In *Dunham*, we noted that the doctrine of mutual consent arose out of the ancient maxim *volenti non fit injuria* (no legal wrong is done to him who consents) that forms the basis in civil law of the doctrine of assumption of the risk. Notwithstanding the survival of the Roman principle in the area of torts, we nonetheless concluded that, except for professional or amateur boxing exhibitions held pursuant to *R.C. 3773.31*, "fighting must be held to be illegal in this state because each combatant may be guilty of an assault in law as well as the battery which might follow as a consequence of the exchange of blows or, at least, by the demonstration of the ability to do harm. The fact that street fighters agree to engage in a public brawl to settle old or current differences cannot and does not negate the penal consequences." *Id. at 729, 693 N.E.2d 1175.*

Given its limited application, and our holding in *Dunham*, we cannot say that Guidugli's trial counsel was ineffective for not advancing the doctrine of implied consent as another affirmative defense. As noted, trial counsel appears to have argued the doctrine, in principle at least, during mitigation following the verdict, but not before. Even if we were to assume that the doctrine exists in Ohio, it is unlikely that the trial court would have found the doctrine applicable in this case. To have successfully argued the doctrine, Guidugli would have had to have persuaded the trial court that the punch he threw was a foreseeable part of the game and one to which Harris impliedly consented. Although it is specious to suggest that basketball remains today a non-contact sport, it is quite a stretch to argue that retaliatory punches during a pause in play are to be accepted as the unavoidable cost of playing the sport at the intramural level. It bears emphasis in this regard that the punch, as described by the state's witnesses, was entirely outside the scope of play and did not arise, for example, as a result of a scuffle under the basket or in a fight for a rebound.

* * *

OFFICIAL'S TIME OUT

Finally, we observed earlier that the trial court imposed a 180-day suspended jail sentence, 60 days of home incarceration/electronic monitoring in lieu of the suspended sentence, one year of probation, anger management counseling as recommended by the probation department, a $100 fine, and court costs—all for a minor welt in a basketball game suffered by a complainant who could not leave work to attend the trial. Later, the trial court denied a motion to reconsider its sentence despite several cogent arguments advanced by new counsel. Although the sentence may appear harsh, it has not been challenged on appeal and is not in any case subject to review. Guidugli, as the starting quarterback on the University of Cincinnati football team, can now serve the balance of his sentence before fall practice and the upcoming season begins.[1] As Clarke notes, "Accountability among athletes is avoided by

---

[1] We note parenthetically that anger management counseling may be counterproductive for a starting quarterback having to compete at the NCAA Division I-A level.

the simple expedient of ignoring anything but the on-court consequences of behavior." *Clarke, supra, at 1156.* At the very least, it seems, among the lessons learned from this case is that while sports norms may be very different from real-world norms, conduct on the court may still have very serious real-world consequences off the court.

The judgment of the trial court is affirmed.

CASES ON THE SUPPLEMENTAL CD

In Re: MasterCard International, Inc., 313 F.3d 257 (5th Cir. 2002): Plaintiffs try to avoid on-line gambling debts by claiming credit card companies violated federal criminal laws.

People of the State of Colorado v. Hall, 999 P.2d 207 (Colo. Ct. App. 2000): Discussion of standard of care owed to another for the crime of reckless manslaughter involving a skiing incident between two skiers in Colorado.

State of Washington v. Shelley, 929 P.2d 489 (Wash. App. 1997): Discussion of upholding conviction of defendant convicted of assault in the second degree for a punch in the jaw during a pick-up basketball game.

Case from Section 7.40

U.S. v. Walters, 704 F. Supp. 844 (N.D. Ill. 1989). Sports agents accused of wire and mail fraud.

QUESTIONS YOU SHOULD BE ABLE TO ANSWER

1. What are the major similarities and differences between the criminal law and tort law in the context of sport and recreation law?

2. What are the elements of criminal assault?

3. What are the primary defenses used by defendants accused of assault in a sport context?

4. Why is Internet sports gambling a threat to the health, safety and welfare of the public, and what regulation exists to try to curb these threats?

5. What are the elements of mail fraud, and what are the primary defenses?

REFERENCES

Cases

Carroll v. State, 1980 OK CR 89.

Cavoto v. Chicago National League Ball Club, Inc., 222 Ill.2d 569 (2006).

Crockett v. Stinson, No. 08Cl10031 Jefferson Circuit Court for Kentucky. Reported in D.L. Herbert, "High School Football Coach Faces Wrongful Death Lawsuit and Criminal Prosecution," The Sports, Parks & Recreation Law Reporter, Vol.22, No. 4 (March, 2009) pp. 60-63.

In re MasterCard International, Inc., 313 F.3d 257 (5th Cir. 2002).

NPS, LLC v. StubHub, Inc., 22 Mass. L. Rep. 717 (2007).

People v. Fitzsimmons, 34 N.Y.S. 1102 (N.Y. Sup. Ct. 1895).

People v. Freer, 86 Misc. 2d 280 (1976).

People v. Hall, 999 P.2d 207 (2000).

Regina v. Green, 16 D.L.R.3d 137 (Ont. Prov. Civ. 1971).

Regina v. Maki, 14 D.L.R.3d 164 (Ont. Prov. Civ. 1970).

State v. Floyd, 466 N.W.2d 919 (1990).

State v. Forbes, No. 63280 (Hennepin Co. Minn. Dist Ct. *dismissed* Aug. 12, 1975).

State v. Granite Gate Resorts, Inc., 568 N.W.2d 715 (1997), *aff'd* 576 N.W.2d 747 (1998).

State v. Limon, No. 1999-CR-2892 (144th Jud. Dist. Ct. Bexar Co. Tex. 2000).

State of Washington v. Shelley, 85 Wn. App. 24, 929 P.2d 489 (1997).

U.S. v. Brauman, 2006 U.S. Dist. LEXIS 10914 (D. Kan. 2006).

U. S. v. Cohen, 260 F.3d 68 (2nd Cir. 2001).

U S. v. Gray, 96 F.3d 769 (5th Cir. 1996).

U.S. v. Walters, 704 F. Supp. 844 (N.D. Ill. 1989) *motion to dismiss denied*, 711 F. Supp. 1435 (N.D. Ill. 1989), *rev'd on other grounds*, 913 F.2d 388 (7th Cir. 1990), 775 F. Supp. 1173 (N.D. Ill. 1991), 997 F.2d 1219 (7th Cir. 1993).

U.S. v. Welch, 327 F.3d 1081 (10th Cir. 2003).

Publications

Barry, M. P., Fox, R. L., & Jones, C. (2005). Judicial Opinion on the Criminality of Sports Violence in the United States. *Seton Hall J. Sports L.,* 15, 1–34.

Benetah, J. (2005). Anti-scalping laws: Should they be forgotten? *Texas Review of Entertainment and Sports Law.*

Berry, R. C., & Wong, G. M. (1993). *Law and business of the sports industries.* (Vol. II, 2nd ed.) Westport, CT: Praeger.

Clarke, C. A. (2000). Law and order on the courts: The application of criminal liability for intentional fouls during sporting events. *Ariz. St. L.J.,* 32, 1149.

Claussen, C. L., & Miller, L. K. (2001). The gambling industry and sports gambling: A stake in the game? *Journal of Sport Management,* 15, 350–363.

CNN.com (2009, January 26). High school football coach charged in players death. Retrieved on June 1, 2009 from http://www.cnn.com/2009/CRIME/01/26/football.coach.indicted/index.html

Cook, K., & Mravic, M. (1999, May 17). Scorecard: college beanball shocker: A purpose Pitch. *Sports Illustrated*, p. 24.

Epstein, A. (2003). *Sports Law.* Clifton Park, NY: Thomson Delmar Learning.

Harary, C. (2002). Aggressive Play or Criminal Assault? An In Depth Look at sports Violence and Criminal Liability. *Colum. J. L. & Arts,* 25, 197–217.

Jacoby, J. (2007, August 8). Scrap Scalping Laws, *The Boston Globe* retrieved on June 1, 2008, from http://www.boston.com/news/globe/editorial_opinion/oped/articles/2007/08/08/scrap_scalping_laws/

Liddell, P., et. al. (2004). Internet Gambling: On a Roll? *Seton Hall Legislative Journal,* 28, 315–353.

Masoud, S. (2004, Summer). The offshore quandary: The impact of domestic regulation on licensed off-shore gambling companies. *Whittier Law Review, 25, 989-1009.*

Milloy, R. E. (2000). Basketball player's foul draws a jail term. *N.Y. Times on the Web*, March 9, 2000. Online Internet. www.nytimes.com

Model Penal Code § 2.11.1—2.11.2 (2001).

Model Penal Code § 210.3 (2001).

Model Penal Code § 210.4 (2001).

Model Penal Code § 3.04(1) (2001).

Restatement (2nd) of Torts § 50 cmt. b (1963).

Legislation

Bribery in Sporting Contests Act. 18 U.S.C. § 224 (2008).

Interstate and Foreign Travel and Transportation in Aird of Racketeering Enterprising Act, 18 U.S.C. § 1952 (2008).

Mail Fraud, 18 U.S.C. §§ 1341–1346 (2008).

Professional and Amateur Sports Protection, Chapter 178, 28 U.S.C. §§ 3701–3704 (2008).

Prohibition of Illegal Gambling Businesses, 18 U.S.C. § 1955 (2008).

Racketeer Influenced and Corrupt Organizations Act, 18 U.S.C. § 1961, et seq. (2008).

The PATRIOT Act, Pub. L No. 107-56 (Oct. 26, 2001).

Unlawful Internet Gambling Enforcement Act, 31 U.S.C. §§ 5361-5367 (2008).

Wire Communications Act of 1961, 18 U.S.C. § 1084 (2008).

3.22 Hazing

—Ellen J. Staurowsky
ITHACA COLLEGE

On an October day in 1881, seven upperclass students assaulted a Bowdoin College freshman in his dorm room as part of a hazing ritual (*Strout v. Packard*, 1884). The case offers a vivid description of escalating events not unfamiliar to us today. There was an invasion of an unsuspecting student's room, a beating, and general mayhem as more than one assailant threw "missiles" at the student. The issue raised in this case was whether a conspiracy existed among Strout's seven attackers and subsequently, who was liable for the harm done to Strout, who suffered, among other things, a serious eye injury after being hit with a thrown object. In ruling that there was not sufficient evidence to determine that a conspiracy existed, and culpability for the injury could be assigned only to the person from whose hand the object had been thrown, the judges of the Supreme Judicial Court of Maine raised considerations that resonate today about what constitutes hazing and who is responsible. Although the rights of the defendants were upheld in this case, there is a palpable sense in reading the opinion that the judges were aware that justice had not been served by so narrow a reading of the defendants' collective contribution to the events that occurred.

Over 120 years later, there remains much that is not known about the magnitude and degree of hazing as it occurs in school or professional sport and recreational settings, nor is it clear that existing hazing laws address the issues raised by these cases. Attributed in part to the codes of silence that surround hazing, and the power of peer pressure that discourages disclosure of incidents, the looming uncertainty of whether hazing can be effectively addressed is also connected to the expansiveness of the term itself and its multiple meanings. For example, in January of 2006, the University of Memphis campus newspaper reported an incident involving female members of the cross-country team, who were allegedly taken out for a night of partying by their teammates, appearing in sexually suggestive attire with the words "fresh meat" and "frosh" written on their foreheads. Although editors of *The Daily Helmsman* considered the incident potentially violative of Tennessee antihazing law, team members expressed a belief that the incident was an opportunity to bond (Laurie, 2006).

Recent instances illustrate the range of behaviors that may be identified as hazing. In November of 2008, seven members of the Morton Ranch cheerleading squad, aged 17 and 18, were indicted and charged as adults with a Class B misdemeanor for violating Texas's hazing statute. The indictment alleged that junior cheerleaders, having been picked up at their homes by teammates under the pretense of going to the local restaurant to participate in a traditional pre-dawn breakfast, were taken instead to a private home. Once there, the juniors were bound, blindfolded, and pushed into a swimming pool (Eriksen, Rogers, and Turner, 2008). Numerous collegiate teams have had a part or all of their seasons suspended during the past two years as a result of violating campus and athletic department hazing policies. While the hosting of team parties involving excessive drinking led to game and/or season cancellations for the Arizona State men's lacrosse team (Coyne, 2009), Curry College men's lacrosse team (Grautski, 2009), and Millersville women's lacrosse team (Associated Press, 2007), the Chapman University men's soccer team received a two-game regular season suspension along with a ban on post-season play after shaving first-year players and pouring hot sauce on them (Marty, 2006).

The University of Wisconsin band was also threatened with suspension in the fall of 2008 after allegations of hazing, alcohol abuse, and sexual misconduct were brought to the attention of band director Mike Leckrone. Following an investigation, university officials expressed a determination to change what they considered a "culture of hazing" where upperclass students bullied first year students ("UW lifts...", 2008). In December of 2008, Southern University band members were arrested and charged with aggravated second-degree battery and ritualistic acts for beatings believed to have resulted in two initiates being hospitalized in intensive care (Associated Press, 2008).

Whereas individual instances provide rich examples of behavior that falls within the scope of hazing definitions, research findings provide some measures of magnitude. Studies reveal that hazing occurs among students in grades 6 through college at rates ranging from just over 17 percent to 79 percent (Allan & Madden, 2008; Campo, Poulos, & Sipple, 2005; Crandall, 2003; Gershel, Katz-Sidlow, Small, & Zandieh, 2003; Hoover, 1999, 2000). Consistent across these studies is a finding that females are more likely to participate exclusively in acceptable forms of hazing while males are more likely to participate exclusively in unacceptable forms of hazing. Despite this apparent polar finding, there is a tremendous gray area where female athletes and students exhibit tendencies to engage in high-risk behaviors with frequencies that are very close to those of their male counterparts. At the high school level, Hoover (2000) reports that girls were consistently involved in all forms of hazing at very high levels: humiliating hazing, 39 percent; substance abuse, 18 percent; and dangerous hazing, 17 percent. According to Allan and Madden (2008), nine out of ten students who have experienced hazing behavior in college do not consider themselves to have been hazed.

Physical hazing coupled with excessive drinking is not exclusively a male preserve, as seen in the widely publicized Glenbrook North High School case, where a dozen girls and three boys were charged with misdemeanor battery charges. Under the guise of a powder puff football game, girls from the junior class were beaten and covered in mud, paint, feces, and garbage. Five of the victims were hospitalized, with one requiring stitches in her head. In total, the school board suspended 31 students for taking part in the incident, and several students were expelled (Fuller, 2003).

The general trends as documented in the research as well as individual instances show that recreation and sport managers must be proactive in their response to hazing by (1) anticipating that hazing will occur on teams and within student organizations; (2) questioning and monitoring the initiation activities of athletes, students, and employees; (3) working within existing organizational structures to formulate antihazing policies; and (4) developing antihazing education programs. They must also be informed about policies that exist within their organizations, and be knowledgeable about the local, state, and national laws that apply to hazing.

FUNDAMENTAL CONCEPTS

Definition and Scope

Definitions of hazing range from the succinct to the comprehensive. For example, in the state of Ohio, **hazing** "means doing an act or coercing another, including the victim, to do any act of initiation into any student or other organization that causes or creates a substantial risk of causing mental or physical harm to any person" (Ohio Revised Code 2903.31). In contrast, Florida law defines hazing to mean

> *any action or situation which recklessly or intentionally endangers the mental or physical health or safety of a student for the purpose of initiation or admission into or affiliation with any organization operating under the sanction of a postsecondary institution. Such term includes, but is not limited to, any brutality of a physical nature, such as whipping, beating, branding, forced calisthenics, exposure to the elements, forced consumption of any food, liquor, drug, or other substance, or other forced physical activity which could adversely affect the physical health or safety of the student, and also includes any activity which would subject the student to extreme mental stress, such as sleep deprivation, forced exclusion from social contact, forced conduct which could result in extreme embarrassment, or other forced activity which could adversely affect the mental health or dignity of the student (Florida State Code 240.1325).*

Whereas the statutory definition of hazing is important, so too is the interpretation of the meaning of the term "student organization." In *Duitch v. Canton City Schools* (2004), a freshmen high school student alleged that on "Freshman Friday," he was beaten in a restroom by eight to ten juniors and seniors. Both the trial and appellate courts found that "the actions of the students did not constitute initiation into any student or other organization" and that "the attack was merely due to the appellant's status as a freshman." Initiation into the entire student body rather than into a specific student organization prevented the appellant from finding relief under the existing hazing law in the state of Ohio (See Cases on the Supplemental CD).

The vast majority of hazing laws create a link between hazing and student welfare, thus limiting the applicability of the law to manifestations of hazing that may occur in other groups, like professional sport teams or athletic teams sponsored by national sport governing bodies (e.g., U.S. Olympic team). The New York statute reflects consideration for this possibility as seen in the language of the statute, which reads in part, "A person is guilty of hazing in the first degree when, in the course of another person's initiation into or affiliation with any organization . . . " (New York 120.16).

Civil Litigation

This section explores the legal basis on which a hazing victim may establish a cause of action in a civil suit. The question here is whether the offender and/or third party is liable for the injuries sustained by the plaintiff. In a civil case, a hazing victim may be awarded monetary damages.

Negligence. Within the past twenty years, as the number of hazing cases has risen, victims have increasingly sought redress in the courts, alleging negligence on the part of athletes who haze, as well as coaches, school administrators, and the institutions they represent.

At one time, college officials under the doctrine of *in loco parentis* could be held liable for hazing because administrators had a duty to care for their students much the same as parents had a duty to care for their children. Changing societal views of college students as young adults rather than dependent children shifted the burden of responsibility for student misbehavior from college officials to students. This does not mean, however, that there is no basis for an institutional or professional duty of care. Under the **landowner-invitee theory**, landlords owe a duty of reasonable care to those who are invited onto their property. Through offers of admission and assessment of fees, a similar relationship exists between institutions of higher education and their students (Crow & Rosner, 2002).

In *Knoll v. Board of Regents of the University of Nebraska* (1999), the Nebraska Supreme Court used this theory to reason that the university had an obligation to take steps to protect a student against reasonably foreseeable acts of hazing, which included abduction from his dorm room on campus, transport to a fraternity house off campus, and harm that accrued as a result of his attempt to escape. The implications of this case point to the necessity for school administrators and employers to acknowledge the history of hazing in athletics and to take proactive measures in the form of antihazing policies and education or risk failing in their duty to protect students and other persons associated with their organization (Crow & Rosner, 2002).

In *Siesto v. Bethpage Union Free School District* (1999), the Nassau County Supreme Court (NY) awarded summary judgment to the plaintiff, a member of the football team, who sustained a serious head wound as a result of a hazing incident that occurred in the locker room just a short distance from the coach's office. In dismissing the affirmative defenses of comparative negligence and assumption of risk asserted by the school district, the trial court determined that athletes who voluntarily participate in athletics do not assume the risk of injury resulting from being hazed.

Another common defense in hazing cases is the *doctrine of immunity*, which frees educational institutions and their employees from liability for negligence (Crow & Rosner, 2002). In *Caldwell v. Griffin Spalding County Board of Education, et al.* (1998), a first-year football player was attacked, beaten, and knocked unconscious in his dorm room during preseason. In a civil suit brought by the player against school officials, the Georgia Court of Appeals upheld a lower court ruling granting summary dismissal on the grounds that the principal, coach, and school board members were immune from civil liability.

In *Elbaz v. Beverly Hills Unified School District* (2007), a member of the BHUSD soccer team was severely beaten by several teammates while on a trip to play in a summer tournament in 2005. Attempting to assert three causes of action for negligence, the Court of Appeals of California upheld a lower court ruling granting a demurrer on the grounds that the school district was immune from liability because the trip to the tournament constituted a "field trip" or "excursion" rather than a "school sponsored activity." Whereas a "school sponsored activity" would have provided a basis for the complaint to proceed, under California law, students participating in "excursions" waive all claims against a school district for injury that occurs during such a trip.

Further, according to California law, the beating itself did not fall under the definition of hazing in the California Penal Code because the student was already a member of the team.

However, in *Meeker v. Edmunson* (2005), the U.S. Court of Appeals for the Fourth Circuit determined that a wrestling coach who had authorized physical attacks on rookies by other members of his team was not protected by qualified immunity. The court determined that the action of a school official to cause a student to be beaten is contrary to the constitutional rights of a student under the Fourteenth Amendment.

Coach accountability and culpability are receiving increased scrutiny as well. In August of 2008, two baseball coaches from Wilson High School in Western New York were charged with endangering the welfare of a child and failure to prevent alleged sex-related attacks on players during a team bus ride the previous Spring (Besecker, 2008). In the Spring of 2009, an Anderson County High School softball coach resigned her position after authorizing an event in which upper class players arranged for first-year teammates to stand in a hotel swimming pool wearing only one article of clothing, an event that violated the school's rules as well as Florida state law (Fowler, 2009). Also in the spring of 2009, five officials of the Las Vegas City Schools (the superintendent, athletic director, and three coaches) were accused of failing to report sexual assaults that younger players were subjected to during a pre-season football camp prior to the start of the academic year (Medina, 2009).

Following the worldwide distribution of videotaped evidence documenting the violent hazing of girls from Glenbrook (IL) North High School, questions were raised regarding the culpability of adults who had supplied alcohol to the underage participants in the event. Although existing Illinois law does not provide for social host liability, in the wake of this incident Illinois lawmakers are considering the adoption of legislation that would allow victims and their families to recover damages from the adults who willfully give, sell, or deliver alcohol to minors (Vock, 2003).

Signaling what may be increasing attempts to hold parents accountable for the behavior of their children, four former coaches at Mepham High School, who lost their sport-related job assignments following a well-publicized football hazing scandal, sued the parents of three of the students involved in the physical and sexual assaults of younger players, seeking $20 million in damages. The attorney for the coaches reasoned that the parents knew or had reason to know that their sons were prone to violence, and did not use care to restrain them ("Ex-coaches sue," 2004).

This section highlights several challenges that exist in establishing who is accountable and can be held liable in hazing cases. First, at the college and university level, negligence hinges on the ability to argue that a special relationship exists between the victim and the institution. In the absence of a **special relationship**, there is no **duty of care**. Second, in determining whether both parties (perpetrator and victim) may bear responsibility for hazing, the mere fact that an athlete agreed to participate on a team, by itself, does not provide a supportable rationale to establish **comparative negligence**. Third, coaches and school administrators may be **immune** from civil liability if their actions fall within the realm of professional discretion. Fourth, parents may be held negligent for not exercising appropriate supervision of their children.

Constitutional Rights—Students. In 1993, a high school football player was accosted by teammates while leaving the showers, forcibly restrained, and bound to a towel rack with athletic tape. His former girlfriend was then led into the locker room to see him hanging there (*Seamons v. Snow*, 2000). Upon Seamon's release from the team because of his refusal to apologize for reporting the incident, he filed suit claiming that his First Amendment rights to free speech had been violated by the coach and the school district (*Seamons v. Snow*, 1994). After the district court granted summary judgment in favor of the defendants in 1998, the appellate court reversed that decision, sending the case to trial—asserting for a second time that the coach was not entitled to qualified immunity for suspending Seamons from the team (*Seamons v. Snow*, 2000; see *Significant Case* later in this section).

In 2000, the Centennial Area School District (PA) settled a lawsuit brought forward by a former high school wrestler so as to avert a court decision regarding its liability. The wrestler alleged his Fourteenth Amendment right to protection of his own bodily integrity had been violated after the school failed to prevent his hazing, despite knowledge of the activity (*Nice v. Centennial Area School District*, 2000).

In *Perkins, et al. v. Alamo Heights Independent School District* (2002), two high school cheerleaders were stripped of their eligibility to try out for future teams by school authorities because of their involvement in a party where underage drinking and hazing occurred. They sought an injunction claiming their rights under Title IX and the equal protection clause of the U.S. Constitution had been violated because school officials had not provided an adequate hearing prior to taking action, and had engaged in disparate treatment of female students. In rejecting their request, the court determined that the "lengthy history of problematic behavior" exhibited by the team and advance warnings about inappropriate behavior served as adequate notice, and concluded that the evidence to show disparate treatment was unpersuasive (See Cases on the Supplemental CD).

These cases highlight two issues pertaining to the protection of student rights for coaches and administrators. In the *Seamons v. Snow* case, Coach Snow potentially violated Brian's First Amendment right to free speech by punishing him for breaking the silence that surrounds hazing. In contrast, the Alamo Heights school officials were successful in defending against allegations of failure to provide due process because they had given appropriate notice and acted preemptively to reduce liability prior to the hazing event occurring.

Constitutional Rights—School Officials. In *Cioffi v. Averill Park Central School District* (2006), a high school athletic director appealed the ruling from the U.S. District Court for the Northern District of New York granting summary judgment to the defendants. It was the assertion of the athletic director that the school district's decision to reorganize administrative staffing leading to the abolishment of his position as athletic director was the result of retaliation for complaints he made about the football coach's approach to student health and welfare. In the aftermath of a student filing a criminal charge for sexual assault which allegedly occurred during a football team hazing incident, the athletic director made public comments regarding threats to student safety and potential district liability. In taking issue with the lower court's findings, the U.S. Court of Appeals for the Second Circuit found that statements made by the athletic director about the assault were of public concern and that as an employee, the athletic director's comments should not be deprived of First Amendment protection. Further, the short time between the public statements made by the athletic director and the school district's decision to abolish his position was sufficient to raise a triable issue on causation (See Cases on the Supplemental CD).

In contrast to this case, a softball coach at Brewer School Department, challenged the non-renewal of her contract in violation of the Maine Human Rights Act. According to the plaintiff, the superintendent did not rehire her because of her sexual orientation. The school district, in turn, took the position that the plaintiff should not be rehired because of a history of hazing that had developed during the time that she was coaching the team. In the final analysis, the court granted summary judgment in favor of the defendant (*Cookson v. Brewer School Department*, 2007).

Other Civil Charges. As a result of *Davis v. Monroe County Board of Education* (1999), school administrators who show deliberate indifference in cases of peer-to-peer harassment may be subject to liability for the resulting damages. According to attorney David Doty, school administrators should be aware of the implications this holds for their handling of hazing cases ("Hazing is no joke," 2002). The pending case of *Snelling & Snelling v. Fall Mountain Regional School District, et al.* (2001), may well test this theory. Derek and Joel Snelling, members of the basketball team, claimed they were targets of persistent verbal and physical abuse by teammates, and, on occasion, by the coach. Although the district court granted summary judgment to Fall Mountain, dismissing Section 1983 claims made by the plaintiffs that the harassment violated their Fourteenth Amendment rights to substantive due process and equal protection, District Judge Joseph DiClerico also found a pattern of harassment that presented a trialworthy issue for action under Title IX and raised an issue as to whether the defendants were deliberately indifferent to the treatment of the brothers (*Snelling & Snelling v. Fall Mountain Regional School District, et al.*, 2001).

Hazing and Sex Crimes

In September of 2003, at a camp in the Pocono Mountains of Pennsylvania, Mepham High School varsity football players lured younger players into a cabin under the pretense that they would be subjected to some form of mild initiation. From that day forward until the end of camp, the new members of the team were sodomized, beaten, subjected to painful and humiliating treatment, and required to haze other players (Wencelblat,

2004). According to accounts, by the end of camp, the entire team knew what had happened but they all remained silent (Wayne County Grand Jury, 2004). There is strong evidence to suggest that, if not for the fact that two of the victims required medical treatment for their injuries, the incidents would not have been reported. Ultimately, four identified perpetrators were tried as juveniles rather than adult offenders and charged with involuntary deviate sexual intercourse, aggravated assault, and kidnapping (Wencelblat, 2004). Two pleaded guilty to felony charges and began serving time in a juvenile facility, a third pled guilty to felony charges and received a sentence of probation, and a fourth pled guilty to a misdemeanor charge.

Once notified that hazing had occurred at the camp, Mepham school officials cancelled the 2003 football season, reassigned the head football coach and one of the assistants who were tenured teachers to another school in the district, and elected not to reappoint them to their coaching positions the next year. The former coaches alleged they were improperly reassigned without explanation and denied due process to discuss the reasons for their reassignment (*McElroy & Canestero v. Bellmore-Merrick School District*, 2004). Although McElroy and Canestero were unsuccessful in their suit, this case illustrates the difficulties faced in balancing the interests and rights of students and teachers/coaches. The behavior of the coaches had been the subject of a Wayne County (PA) Grand Jury, who considered whether their conduct during the camp constituted crimes of endangering the welfare of children and recklessly endangering another person. The Grand Jury determined that by legal definition the coaches had not acted criminally, although there was "clear evidence that the coaches displayed a lack of common sense accountability." Given a history of previous hazing incidents in the program and in light of this finding, school administrators would have risked allegations of deliberate indifference if they had not acted in the manner they did. At the same time, Mr. McElroy has asserted that the burden of responsibility should have fallen on the players who committed the crimes, because they were bound by Mepham High School's student code of conduct (Jones, 2003).

Questions of accountability arise in the case of two Jupiter High School athletes charged as adults with aggravated stalking of a person under 16 (a third-degree felony that carries a sentence of up to five years in prison) and battery. According to the freshman who was pinned down by the athletes after gym class while they pushed themselves on him sexually, he had been bullied repeatedly, sometimes in the presence of coaches who did nothing about it (Abramson, 2009).

Criminal Hazing

In contrast to the civil justice system, where hazing victims personally seek relief for the harms done to them, in the criminal justice system, a state entity, such as a county prosecutor, will bring charges against alleged perpetrators for the purpose of determining whether they are guilty or innocent of a criminal act.

Antihazing Statutes. The number of states that have adopted antihazing statutes has increased dramatically from 25 in 1990 to 44 in 2009. While the number of athletes charged criminally for their participation in hazing activities has increased as well during that span of time, substantial barriers to the enforcement and prosecution of antihazing laws remain due to the lack of uniformity in the laws from state to state and the modest penalties that go along with them (Crow & Rosner, 2002; Sussberg, 2003). An analysis of current state statutes, which appears in Table 3.22.1, reveals the following information:

- Thirty-five of the 44 state codes (80%) classify hazing as a misdemeanor, whereas eight states expressly provide that hazing resulting in serious bodily harm and/or death is classified as a felony. The classification of hazing as a crime does not supersede or change penalties covered by other criminal statutes (see Classification of Crime column). Legislators in Wyoming, one of the states that does not have an antihazing law, are currently considering a bill that would make hazing a misdemeanor or felony (Barron, 2006).

- Nine antihazing statutes (20%) specify that it is a crime to fail to report an incident to authorities (see *Is Failure to Notify a Crime?* column).

- Of the existing antihazing statutes, nearly 35 percent (15 of 44) require schools to either develop antihazing policies and penalties, or devise specific means to educate students, teachers/faculty, and other employees about the state's antihazing laws (see *Is Antihazing Policy Required in School?* column).

Table 3.22.1 State Antihazing Laws

State	State Hazing Statute	Classification of Crime	Is Failure To Notify a Crime?	Is Antihazing Policy Required in Schools?	Is Victim's Willingness a Defense?	Public/Private Status of School; Educational Level
Alabama	16-1-23	Class C misdemeanor	Yes	No	No	Any school
Alaska	None					
Arizona	15-2301		No	Yes	No	Public
Arkansas	6-5-201	Class B misdemeanor	Yes	No	Yes	Any school
California	32050-1	Misdemeanor	No	No	Yes	Any school
Colorado	18-9-124	Class 3 misdemeanor	No	No	Yes	Any school
Connecticut	53-23(a)		No	No	No	Higher education
Delaware	9301-04	Class B misdemeanor	No	Yes	No	Each institution
Florida	240.326	1st degree misdemeanor, 3rd degree felony	No	Yes	No	College/university where students receive state financial assistance
Georgia	16-5-61	High and aggravated misdemeanor	No	No	No	Any school
Hawaii	None					
Idaho	18-917	Misdemeanor	No	No	Yes	College or university
Illinois	720 ILCS 120	Class A misdemeanor, Class 4 felony	No	No	Yes	Any school
Indiana	IC 35-4-2-2	Class A or B misdemeanor, Class C or D felony	No	No	No	Not restricted to school settings; any person
Iowa	708.10	Serious or simple misdemeanor	No	No	No	Any school
Kansas	21-3434	Class B misdemeanor	No	No	Yes	Any social or fraternal organization not limited to schools
Kentucky	164.375		No	Yes	Yes	State colleges & universities
Louisiana	17:1801		No	Yes	No	Only fraternities in any educational institution receiving state funds
Maine	6653		Yes	Yes	Yes	Public school; post-secondary institution incorporated or chartered by the state
Maryland	27-268H	Misdemeanor	No	No	No	Any school, college, or university
Massachusetts	269-17		Yes	Yes	No	Any student or other person on public or private property
Michigan	7504411	Misdemeanor, Felony	No		No	Educational Institution
Minnesota	127.465		No	Yes	Yes	Each school board; student or staff hazing
Mississippi	97-3-105	Misdemeanor	No	No	Yes	Not specific to schools; any organization

Table 3.22.1 State Antihazing Laws (continued)

State	State Hazing Statute	Classification of Crime	Is Failure To Notify a Crime?	Is Antihazing Policy Required in Schools?	Is Victim's Willingness a Defense?	Public/Private Status of School; Educational Level
Missouri	578.365	Class A misdemeanor, Class C felony	No	Yes	No	Public or private college or university
Montana	None					
Nebraska	28-311.06	Class II misdemeanor	No	No	No	Postsecondary educational institution
Nevada	200.605	Misdemeanor, Gross misdemeanor	No	No	No	High school, college, or university in the state
New Hampshire	631.7	Class B misdemeanor	Yes	No	No	Any school
New Jersey	2c:40-3	4th Degree crime	No	No	No	
New Mexico	None					
New York	120.16	Class A misdemeanor	No	No	Yes	Not specific to schools or students
North Carolina	9:14:35-38	Class 2 misdemeanor	Yes	No	Yes	Any school or college
North Dakota	12.1-17-08	Class A Misdemeanor Class B Misdemeanor	No	No	No	Not limited to schools
Ohio	2307.44; 2903.31	Misdemeanor	No	No	No	Any school
Oklahoma	21-1190	Misdemeanor	No	Yes	No	Any school
Oregon	163.197	Misdemeanor	No	No	Yes	College or university
Pennsylvania	5352	3rd Degree misdemeanor	No	Yes	No	Institution of higher education— associate degree or higher
Rhode Island	11-21-1	Misdemeanor	No	No	Yes	Any school
South Carolina	59-101-200	Misdemeanor	Yes	No	No	Institution of higher learning
South Dakota	None					
Tennessee	49-7-123		No	Yes	Yes institution	Higher education
Texas	37.152	Misdemeanor	Yes	Yes	No	Any school
Utah	76-5-107.5	Misdemeanor or felony	No	Yes	No (under 21)	High school level
Vermont	76		No	Yes	No	All educational institutions
Virginia	18.2056	Class I misdemeanor	No	No	Yes	Any school
Washington	28B.10.901	Misdemeanor	Yes	No	No	Any school
West Virginia	18-2.33	Misdemeanor	No	Yes	No	Public Schools
Wisconsin	948.51	Class A misdemeanor, Class E felony	No	No	Yes	
Wyoming	None					

Source: www.stophazing.org/law

However, there is considerable variability with regard to the level and type of school to which statutes apply. For example, 55 percent (24 of 43) include any school or other institution, whether private or public, while three are restricted solely to public schools. Additionally, 21 percent of the codes (9 of 43) pertain solely to higher education institutions (see *Public/Private Status of School; Educational Level* column).

- Fifty-nine percent (26 of 44) of the codes provide that implied or express consent on the part of the victim, or a willingness on the part of the person hazed to participate in their own hazing, is not an available defense (see *Is Victim's Willingness a Defense?* column).

- A further limitation is the lack of conformity across hazing laws regarding the mental harm associated with hazing (Sussberg, 2003). This has implications at several levels. First, there is evidence in existing literature on athlete hazing to show that female athletes are more likely to haze by subjecting victims to circumstances and situations designed to humiliate rather than physically harm. As a consequence, in those instances, an injury perpetrated against a female athlete may not be recognized as hazing. Second, although hazing laws limit the scope to physical harm, the full weight of the harm done to the victim is overlooked because physical attacks have physical and psychological repercussions.

As more states require schools to develop and implement anti-hazing policies, other considerations arise. At the University of Maine, for example, individual player and team penalties were assessed after incriminating photos of a rookie party posted on MySpace came to light. Fact-finding efforts revealed that the rookie party had been going on for several years and was considered a "tradition" by the players. In point of fact, the specific party which resulted in the sanctions had happened several years before the photos surfaced, resulting in two captains being relieved of their formal leadership roles for failure to report hazing that had been done to them. In effect, in this case, failure to report on the part of athletes who were hazed resulted in their being punished. According to University of Maine's dean of students, Robert Dana, "If a person is at the event, and they are not stopping it or facilitating exposure (of the event) to the athletic director or our office, they're complicit in hazing" (Atkinson, 2007).

Numerous improvements to existing antihazing laws have been proposed, including the adoption of a federal antihazing statute, and the imposition of a duty for school personnel to act on these issues (Edelman, 2004; Sussberg, 2003). Additionally, as Ball (2004) pointed out, the Federal Educational Rights and Privacy Act (FERPA), which prohibits the disclosure of student records, may be in conflict with the Campus Security Act (CSA), which requires colleges and universities to make full reports of crimes committed on their campuses. Given the secretiveness surrounding hazing, the protections afforded students may be contributing to schools maintaining silence around these incidents when they occur. Some argue that rather than more legislation at the state or federal level, another way to bring uniformity to the system would be for the NCAA to adopt a uniform policy regarding athlete misconduct, with hazing being one of the behaviors included in the policy (Gutshall, 2008).

According to the Texas statute, "Any other offense under this section which causes the death of another is a misdemeanor punishable by a fine of not less than $5,000 nor more than $10,000, confinement in county jail for not less than one year nor more than two years, or both such fine and confinement." In convictions where the violation did not result in death, the judge may substitute community service for imprisonment. In Michigan, a $10,000 penalty in cases where hazing results in death. In Rhode Island, penalty for school official allowing hazing to go on can receive a monetary penalty between $10 to $100 per year.

Whereas the evolution of antihazing law reflects a growing awareness that behavior assumed to be harmless may, in fact, be criminal, the definitional issues that remain to be resolved along with the meager penalties associated with hazing deserve consideration. As Table 3.22.2 shows, those convicted of hazing crimes are subject to modest fines that range between $10 and $10,000, imprisonment for as little as ten days to a maximum not to exceed one year, or a combination of both. As the Texas statute reveals, even when death results from hazing, the perpetrator may receive no more than two years in prison.

Increasingly, school hazing is being discussed in relationship to and in connection with other forms of violent behavior (Carr, 2005), including bullying. According to Stuart Green of the New Jersey Coalition for Bullying

Table 3.22.2 Penalties for Hazing

State	Minimum School Penalty	Minimum Fine	Maximum Fine	Sentence	Maximum Sentence	Both Fine & Sentence
Arkansas	Expulsion					
California		$100	$5,000		Not more than one year	Possible
Connecticut	Appropriate penalty					
Florida			$5,000			
Louisiana	Expulsion	$10	$100	10 days	30 days	Possible
Maryland			$500		6 months	Possible
Massachusetts			$3,000		12 months	Possible
Mississippi			$1000– 2,000		6 months	Possible
Michigan		$1000	$10,000[1]			
Nebraska			$10,000			
North Carolina	Expulsion		$500		6 months	Possible
Oklahoma			$500	$1500	3 months	Possible
Oregon			$1,000			
Pennsylvania	Withhold diploma, other punishment					
Rhode Island			$500[2]	30 days	12 months	Possible
South Carolina	Dismissal, Expulsion					
Texas		$500	$5,000	180 days	12 months	Possible[3]
Vermont			$5,000			
Washington	forfeit state-funded grants, scholarships, or awards					
West Virginia		$100	$1,000	9 months	Possible	

[1] In Michigan, a $10,000 penalty in cases where hazing results in death.

[2] In Rhode Island, penalty for school official allowing hazing to go on can receive a monetary penalty between $10 to $100 per year.

[3] According to the Texas statute, "Any other offense under this section which causes the death of another is a misdemeanor punishable by a fine of not less than $5,000 nor more than $10,000, confinement in county jail for not less than one year nor more than two years, or both such fine and confinement." In convictions where the violation did not result in death, the judge may substitute community service for imprisonment.

Awareness and Prevention, hazing is a more severe form of bullying where physical injury is more likely to occur (Cunningham, 2006). As momentum builds for more states to adopt anti-bullying legislation, there may be an increasing number of hazing victims who seek relief under anti-bullying laws. According to watchdog group, The Bully Police, 21 states currently have anti-bullying legislation ("The Bully Police," 2006). Federal legislation was also proposed by U.S. Representative John Shimkus (R-IL) in January of 2005 to amend the Safe and Drug-Free Schools and Community Act to include bullying and harassment (H.R. 284).

In this case, the court considered whether a high school football coach was liable for violating a player's free speech rights after dismissing the player from the team for refusing to apologize for reporting to authorities that he had been hazed by his teammates. The court also addressed whether the coach was entitled to qualified immunity.

SEAMONS V. SNOW

206 F.3d 1021 (2000)

High school football player who was assaulted by his teammates brought §1983 action against school district, football coach, and school's principal, alleging that player's free speech rights under First Amendment were violated when he was suspended and later dismissed from football team because he refused to apologize for reporting assault to police and school authorities. After summary judgment was granted for all defendants, 864 F.Supp. 1111, that judgment was reversed and remanded, 84 F.3d 1226. Upon remand, the United States District Court for the District of Utah, Dee v. Benson, J., again granted summary judgment for all defendants, 15 F.Supp.2d 1150. Player appealed. The Court of Appeals, Seymour, Chief Judge, held that: (1) if proven, coach's alleged actions could subject him to liability; (2) school district could be liable for coach's alleged conduct; (3) principal's lack of prior knowledge of or involvement in relevant events precluded his liability; and (4) coach was not entitled to qualified immunity.

Affirmed in part, reversed in part, and remanded.

* * *

SEYMOUR, CHIEF JUDGE.

This case arises out of the locker-room assault of a high school football player, Brian Seamons, by several of his teammates. Brian filed this action under 42 U.S.C. § 1983 against the school's football coach and principal, as well as the school district. * * *

In the fall of 1993, Brian Seamons was a student at Sky View High School in Smithfield, Utah, and a member of the school's football team. On Monday, October 11 of that year, Brian was assaulted in the locker room by a group of his teammates. As Brian emerged from the showers, four teammates grabbed him, forcibly restrained him, and then bound him to a towel rack with highly adhesive athletic tape. Another teammate brought a girl Brian had dated into the locker room so that she could see what had been done to him.

Brian and his parents reported this incident to the police and to school authorities, including Myron Benson, Sky

View's principal, and Doug Snow, the football coach. Two days after the assault, Brian and his parents met with Principal Benson and Coach Snow to discuss whether Brian would press criminal charges against the team members who assaulted him and whether Coach Snow would take any disciplinary action against them. Coach Snow stated he did not plan to remove any of the assailants from the team. Brian indicated that, in light of this, he would need to think about whether he wanted to remain on the team.

On Friday, October 15, the football team was scheduled to play an away game at Logan High School. That afternoon Brian informed Coach Snow that he wanted to remain on the team, and the two attended the traditional pre-game team-only spaghetti dinner in the school cafeteria. Coach Snow told Principal Benson that Brian was back on the team and everything had been worked out. In the meantime, Brian went home to get his uniform so he could dress for the game. When he returned to the school, Coach Snow asked Brian to meet with the four team captains, two of whom had participated in the assault. The purpose of this meeting, at which the Coach was present, was to allow the boys to clear up any residual hard feelings prior to the game.

During this meeting, a confrontation occurred between Brian and Dan Ward, a captain who had also been one of the assailants, over whether Brian should have to apologize to the team for reporting the assault to the police and school authorities. Specifically, Dan stated that he thought Brian had "betrayed the team" by reporting the assault and that Brian should not be allowed to play with the team until he apologized. Aplt.App., tab 14 at 376, 379. At this point, Coach Snow intervened and told Brian he needed to "forgive and forget and apologize" to the team captains. Id. at 359. When Brian refused, Coach Snow told him to "take the weekend and think about this," because without an apology he couldn't play with the team. Id. at 326. This ended the meeting.

Brian did not play in the game that night. He went home and told his parents he wasn't allowed to play because he had refused to apologize to the team. Brian's father,

Sherwin Seamons, called the principal and angrily told him what had transpired at the meeting. Principal Benson, surprised to hear that Brian wasn't going to attend the game, drove to Logan High School and discussed the matter with Coach Snow.

The following Tuesday, Brian confronted Coach Snow in school, telling him he wasn't going to apologize to the team and he still wanted to play football. At this point, Coach Snow told Brian that he was "sick of [his] attitude, sick of [his] father's attitude," and that he was off of the team. Aplt.App., tab 15 at 432–33. The following day the remainder of Sky View's football season was canceled.

* * *

A. FIRST AMENDMENT CLAIM

In ruling on the motion for summary judgment, the district court determined that Coach Snow did not ask Brian to apologize for reporting the assault, and that Brian's ultimate failure to be involved with the football team was unrelated to his speech or refusal to speak. *See Seamons III,* 15 F.Supp.2d at 1155, 1157. Given the conflicting testimony presented at the evidentiary hearing and contained in the depositions, we fail to see how the district court could reach these conclusions without resolving factual disputes—something it cannot do at this stage of the proceedings. *See,* e.g., *MacLean,* 247 F.Supp. at 190 ("The Court's role in summary judgment proceedings is not to resolve issues of fact, but merely to pinpoint those facts which are not at issue."). We note in particular that the district court devoted a large portion of its opinion to a discussion of the differing accounts of the captains' meeting offered by Brian, Coach Snow, and Dan Ward during the evidentiary hearing. *See Seamons III,* 15 F.Supp.2d at 1156–57.

* * * *1. Whether Coach Snow asked Brian to apologize to the team captains.*

The district court found that Brian was not asked to apologize for reporting the hazing incident. In his deposition and at the evidentiary hearing, Brian testified to the following: during the captains' meeting Dan Ward told him he had betrayed the team by reporting the assault and demanded an apology; when Brian refused, Coach Snow said he would need to "forgive and forget and apologize" in order to remain playing on the team; Coach Snow further stated, "we would need an apology before we let you back on the team." Coach Snow admits to making statements of this nature, although he denies ever directly telling Brian to apologize. If we credit Brian's version, and we must at this stage, there is clearly a disputed issue of fact as to whether Coach Snow asked Brian to apologize to the team captains.

2. The intended scope of this apology.

The district court found that, even if Coach Snow used the word "apologize," he was not asking Brian to apologize for

reporting the assault. Instead, the court concluded that "[t]he request for an 'apology' was not a demand, or a request, for Brian to say he was wrong for reporting the hazing incident; it was rather a request for a mutual reconciliation among Brian and his teammates to allow the boys to function together as friends and teammates." *Seamons III,* 15 F.Supp.2d at 1157. Brian testified that Coach Snow's statements regarding the apology came in response to a heated discussion between Brian and Dan Ward, wherein Dan insisted that Brian not be allowed to play unless he apologized for reporting the assault. Coach Snow interrupted the exchange and expressed his desire that Brian apologize in order to remain on the team. Coach Snow further stated that the team would need an apology before Brian could return. When these remarks are taken in context, it is reasonable to infer that Coach Snow was telling Brian he could not return to the team unless he apologized for reporting the assault. In any event, that is how Brian interpreted the statement, and a jury could properly do the same. Thus, the intended scope of the apology is also a matter of dispute.

One difficulty presented here is the fact that the scope of the requested apology is dependent in part on Coach Snow's intent in asking for it. The Coach's purpose in making these statements to Brian is not easily ascertained and requires inferences drawn from the Coach's behavior throughout the meeting and the broader controversy. This is precisely why summary judgment is not appropriate at this stage. * * *

3. Whether Brian's failure to apologize was a significant factor in his dismissal from the team.

The district court found that Brian had failed to produce facts showing a "legal causal connection between his speech and his ultimate failure to be involved with the football team." *Seamons III,* 15 F.Supp.2d at 1155. We disagree. There are ample facts in the record to indicate that Brian's suspension and dismissal from the football team were directly related to his failure to apologize for reporting the assault.

Brian testified that when Coach Snow told him to "take the weekend and think about it," he understood he was being told not to participate in that night's game. Aplt.App., tab 14 at 337, 350–52. Coach Snow testified that by making this statement he was telling Brian he couldn't participate in that night's game. *Id.* at 402, 405. Presumably, had Brian offered the apology at the captains' meeting he would have been allowed to suit up for the game. He was at school and ready to play on Friday. There was no indication that he didn't want to play or would be prevented from playing in the Logan game. The only thing that happened to alter this situation was the captains' meeting at which Brian was asked, and refused, to apologize. Thus, there is evidence that Brian's refusal to apologize was directly related to the fact that he couldn't play in the Friday game, which was, in effect, a temporary suspension from the team.

A few days later when Brian told Coach Snow he was not going to apologize, he did not think he needed to apologize, and he still wanted to play football, Coach Snow stated that he was "sick of [his] attitude" and took him off the team for good. Aplt.App., tab 15 at 472. It can clearly be inferred that this final confrontation, which resulted in Brian's dismissal from the team, was a product of Brian's refusal to apologize. * * *

In this case, the record indicates that Coach Snow, and only Coach Snow, was vested by the school district with the authority to make final decisions regarding membership on the Sky View football team. Aplt.App., tab 18 at 434, 436, 492. Because of this delegation of authority, the school district can be held liable for Coach Snow's actions on team membership. *See Pembaur*, 475 U.S. at 483, 106 S.Ct. 1292 ("Authority to make municipal policy . . . may be delegated by an official who possesses such authority . . .") * * *

B. QUALIFIED IMMUNITY

The district court alternatively found that even if the evidence supported a First Amendment claim, defendant officials were entitled to qualified immunity because "Brian has failed to show *any law* sufficiently well established in 1993 to support the proposition" that under the circumstances of the case he is entitled to relief. *Seamons III*, 15 F.Supp.2d at 1159 (emphasis added). "We review the district court's grant of summary judgment based on qualified immunity de novo, applying the same standard used by the district court." *Roberts v. Kling*, 144 F.3d 710, 711 (10th Cir.1998) (per curiam) (citation omitted).

When the case was last before us, we held that Brian's complaint stated a claim that defendants violated clearly established law and that they therefore were not entitled to qualified immunity. *See Seamons II*, 84 F.3d at 1238–39. We went on to note that defendants could reassert their entitlement to qualified immunity at summary judgment, but only if "Brian's allegations in the complaint prove to be unfounded." *Id.* at 1238. The district court's conclusion that the law was not clear in 1993 is inconsistent with our mandate and relevant case law.

* * *

Coach Snow was the person most directly involved with Brian's suspension and dismissal from the football team. It was his responsibility to determine who played on the team and to make disciplinary decisions. He orchestrated the captains' meeting, instructed Brian not to attend the Logan game when Brian refused to apologize, and arguably dismissed Brian from the team when Brian again expressed an unwillingness to apologize. "[A] reasonably competent public official should know the law governing his conduct." *Chapman v. Nichols*, 989 F.2d 393, 397 (10th Cir. 1993) (quotation omitted). A "precise factual correlation between the then-existing law and the case at-hand is not required." *Patrick v. Miller*, 953 F.2d 1240, 1249 (10th Cir. 1992) (quotation omitted). Coach Snow is not entitled to qualified immunity for his actions with respect to Brian's suspension and removal from the Sky View football team.

In the proceedings below, the district court expressed a belief that this case had gone on for too long, spawned an inordinate amount of controversy, and was not significant enough to warrant time in the federal courts. While this sentiment by a busy judge may be understandable, it cannot justify summary disposition in the face of genuine issues of material fact . . . Brian has asked for his day in court. Because he meets the requirements for stating a claim and alleging material facts in dispute, he is entitled to a trial.

CASES ON THE SUPPLEMENTAL CD

Cioffi v. Averill Park Central School District Board of Education, (2006 U.S. App. LEXIS 814). As you read this case, consider whether a school employee loses a right to publicly express concern about the health and safety of students in their programs.

Duitch v. Canton City Schools, (2004 Ohio App. LEXIS 1878). As you read this case, note the court's ruling regarding the term "hazing" as defined by Ohio state law.

Perkins & Phillips v. Alamo Heights Independent School District, (204 F. Supp.2d 991). (2002). In this case, were female cheerleaders treated differently than male athletes by being disciplined differently for their involvement in hazing? Was their treatment a violation of Title IX?

QUESTIONS YOU SHOULD BE ABLE TO ANSWER

1. Identify the range of behaviors that may constitute hazing.

2. What does it mean that consent is not a defense in a hazing case?

3. How might an athlete who has been hazed make a negligence claim against a school district or college? What grounds might they seek to establish in order for a negligence claim to be argued?

4. In *Cioffi v. Averill Park School District*, what was the issue related to the athletic director's right to express his concerns regarding the health and safety of athletes?

5. Under what circumstances may parents be held accountable for the actions of their children in hazing cases?

REFERENCES

Cases

Caldwell v. Griffin Spalding County Board of Education et al., 22 Ga. App. 892 (1998).

Cookson v. Brewer School Department et al., 2007 Me. Super. LEXIS 232.

Davis v. Monroe County Board of Education, 526 U.S. 629; 119 S. Ct. 1661; 143 L. Ed.2d 839 (1999).

Duitch v. Canton City Schools, et al., 157 Ohio App. 3d 80; 2004 Ohio 2173; 809 N.E. 2d 62 (2004)

Elbaz v. Beverly Hills Unified School District, 2007 Cal. App. Unpub. LEXIS 4318

Knoll v. Board of Regents of the University of Nebraska, 601 N.W.2d 757 (1999).

McElroy and Canestro v. Board of Education of the Bellmore-Merrick Central High School District, 5 Misc. 3d 321; 783 N.S.S.2d 781 (2004).

Meeker v. Edmunson et al., 415 F. 3d 317 (2005).

Nice v. Centennial Area School District, 98 F. Supp.2d 665 (2000).

Perkins & Phillips v. Alamo Heights Independent School District et al., 204 F. Supp.2d 991 (2002).

Seamons v. Snow, 864 F. Supp. 1111 (D. Utah 1994).

Seamons v. Snow, 206 F.3d 1021 (2000).

Siesto v. Bethpage Union Free School District, QDS: 72701944 (New York Law Journal, December 30, 1999).

Snelling & Snelling v. Fall Mountain Regional School District et al., 2001 DNH 57 (2001).

Strout v. Packard, 76 Me. 148 (1884)

Publications

Abromson, A. (2009, February 28). High school bullying or criminal stalking? Judge to decide. *Palm Beach Post*. Online. Internet. http://www.palmbeach post.com/

Allen, E. J., & Madden, M. (2008). Hazing in view: College students at risk. Initial findings from the national study of student hazing. Orono, ME: University of Orono. Online. Internet. http://www.umaine.edu/hazingstudy/hazinginview1.htm

Anderson, C. (2009, February 4). Fairhaven parents anquished over decision to file hazing lawsuit. *Southcoast Today*. Online. Internet. http://www.southcoasttoday.com/

Associated Press. (2005, September 12). Freshman made to sit in own vomit, urine. Online. Internet. http://www.espn.go.com/

Associated Press. (2005, October 18). Ex-NHL player Mantha suspended in hazing incident. Online. Internet. http://www.espn.go.com/

Associated Press. (2007, October 5). Millersville suspends three lacrosse players, cancels season after hazing probe. Online. Internet. http://www.sports.espn.go.com/espn/print?id=3050193&type=story

Associated Press. (2008, December 3). Six arrested in Southern University band hazing. *The Natchez Democrat.* Online. Internet. http://www.natchezdemocrat.com/

Atkinson, D. (2007, August 17). Hazing penalties off base says softball star's family. *The Daily News.* Online. Internet. http://www.newburyportnews.com/punews/local_story_229094006

Besecker, A. (2008, August 9). New allegations made in Wilson hazing case. *The Buffalo News.*

Campo, S., Poulos, G., & Sipple, J. W. (2005). Prevalence and profiling: Hazing among college students and points of intervention. *American Journal of Health Behavior, 29*(2), p. 37–149.

Carr, J. L. (2005). *American College Health Association campus violence white paper.* Baltimore, MD: American College Health Association.

Coyne, J. (2009, April). Arizona State program suspended. *Lacrosse Magazine 33*(4), p. 52.

Crow, B., & Rosner, S. R. (2002, Winter). Institutional and organizational liability for hazing in intercollegiate and professional team sports. *St. John's Law Review, 76.*

Cunningham, J. H. (2006, January 21). Coaches tackle hazing, bullying. Online. Internet. http://www.northjersey.com/

Eriksen, H., Rogers, B., & Turner, A. (2008, November 20). Morton Ranch cheerleaders indicted in hazing. Online. Internet. http://www.chron.com/disp/story.mpl/moms/6120825.html.

"Ex-coaches sue over students' behavior." (2004, August 4). *New York Law Journal, 24*, p. 2.

Fowler, B. (2009, April 14). Anderson County coach resigns after alleged hazing incident. *Knoxville News Sentinel.* Online. Internet. http://www.knoxnews.com/

Fuller, J. (2003, May 21). Judge upholds suspension of 2 Glenbrook North seniors. *Chicago Sun-Times,* p. 12.

Gershel, J. C., Katz-Sidlow, R. J., Small, E., & Zandieh, S. (2003). Hazing of suburban middle school and high school athletes. *Society for Adolescent Medicine, 32*(5), p. 333–335.

Grautski, A. (2009, April 2). Alleged hazing KO's Curry lacrosse. *The Boston Globe.* Online. Internet. http://www.boston.com/

Gutshall, B. (2008, Spring). A new uniform: NCAA policy and student-athlete misconduct. *University of Missouri-Kansas City Law Review, 76.*

Hazing defined. *Stophazing.org: Educating to eliminate hazing.* Online, Internet.

Hazing is no joke. (2002, January 16). *Your School and the Law, 32.* www.stophazing.org. (accessed January 17, 2002).

Hoover, N. O. (principal investigator). National survey: Initiation rites and athletes for NCAA sports teams. Alfred University (August 30, 1999). Online. Internet. www.alfred.edu/news/html/hazing_study.html

Hoover, N. O., & Pollard, N. J. Initiation rites in American high schools: A national survey. Alfred University (2000). Online, Internet. www.alfred.edu/news/html/hazing_study.html

Jones, L. (2003, October 14). Hazing in schools: Allegations highlight the challenge of ensuring safety. *New York Law Journal*, p. 16.

Laurie, M. (2006, January 19). Hazing or harmless fun? *The Daily Helmsman*. Online. Internt. http://www.dailyhelmsman.com/

Marty, E. (2006, September). Men's soccer receives punishment for hazing. *The Panther*, p. 1.

Medina, M. (2009, April 7). Adults charged in Robertson High hazing. KRQU.com. Online. Internet. http://www.krqu.com/

Phillips, K. (2005, December 5). High school wrestler accused of playing sexual prank on teammates. *Chicago Sun Times*, p. 20.

Report of the Wayne County Investigative Grand Jury pursuant to 42 Pa. C.S. Section 4552 Investigation #4. No. 26-2003-Crminal Misc. (2004, February 24). Published by *Newsday* on March 10, 2004. Online. Internet. http://www.newsday.com/

Rothstein, K. (2004, February 6). Holy Cross suspends rugby team 5 years for hazing. *The Boston Herald*, p. 5.

Sussberg, J. (2003). Shattered dreams: Hazing in college athletes. *Cordozo Law Review 24*.

"The Bully Police: A watch-dog organization—Advocating for bullied children." Online. Internet. http://bullypolice.org/national_law.html

"UW lifts marching band's suspension." (2008, October 10). *Channel3000.com* Online. Internet. http://www.channel3000.com/print/17673409/detail.html

Vock, D. (2003, May 20). Lawmakers try again on social host liability measures. *Chicago Daily Law Bulletin*, p. 1.

Legislation

Florida State Code 240.1325

Minnesota State Code 127.465

New York State Code 120.16

Note: These and other state hazing laws may be found at www.stophazing.org

Ohio Revised Code 2903.31

Other Reading

Ball, J. (2004). This will go down on your permanent record (but we'll never tell): How the Federal Education Rights and Privacy Act may help colleges and universities keep hazing a secret. *Southwestern University Law Review*, 477–511.

Edelman, M. (2004, Fall). Addressing the high school hazing problem: Why lawmakers need to impose a duty to act on school personnel. *Pace Law Review*, 15–50.

Wencelblat, P. (2004, Fall). Boys will be boys? An analysis of male-on-male heterosexual sexual violence. *Columbia Journal of Law and Social Problems*, 38–69.

4.00

RISK MANAGEMENT

The primary purpose of a risk management plan is not the avoidance of legal liability. Rather, it is the maintenance of a quality program; that is, one which deals reasonably and fairly with its clients or students and their families. A program that delivers what it says it will deliver, and does so in the context of reasonable management of the risks, is not assured of "safety" or freedom from lawsuits. But generally, if such a level of performance is achieved, legal liability issues are minimized and take care of themselves (Charles R. Gregg, *Staying in the Field and Out of the Courthouse*, 2002).

Many recreation and sport managers erroneously look upon risk management as safety or accident prevention. **Risk management** is much more than just safety or preventing accidents—it is an organized plan by which a recreation or sport business can manage or control both the programmatic risks and the financial risks facing the organization. Risk management involves not only *what to do* to control risks, but also involves *why to do it*—thus a sound risk management program is based upon the fundamental legal concepts discussed in Sections 2.10, *Negligence Theory*, 2.20, *Defenses*, and 2.30, *Recreation and Sport Management Applications*.

Section 4.00 is divided into two major parts. They are Section 4.10, *Risk Management Theory* and 4.20, *Recreation and Sport Management Applications*. *Risk Management Theory* discusses the fundamental concepts comprising risk management.

In Section 4.20, *Recreation and Sport Management Applications*, several crucial aspects of risk management are addressed. The recreation or sport manager is introduced to the role and importance of standards of practice in the risk management program and to the function of various audits in risk management. Two major problems that must be faced by the recreation or sport manager—crisis management and crowd management—are presented in newly revised chapters. Finally, *Managing Risks through Insurance* examines a crucial tool for transferring risks, and *Workers' Compensation* looks at the statute-mandated form of insurance required of recreation and sport businesses.

4.10 Risk Management Theory

4.11 Risk Management Process

—Robin Ammon, Jr.
SLIPPERY ROCK UNIVERSITY

Plunkett Research Ltd (2009) stated that the estimated size of the sport industry in the United States in 2008 was around $444.1 billion. Sport is not just a national phenomenon. When considered on an international basis, sport has reached epic proportions. Recreation constitutes what might be called a growth industry as well. In addition to the parks and recreation field, which is immense, there is the growth in the fitness industry, in traditional participant sports, in adventure sports, in extreme sports, and much more. This surge of recreation and sport activity has created a tremendous potential for injuries and financial losses.

Concern regarding the systematic management of risk in recreation and sport did not begin until the early 1970s. Even though the concept of risk management had been extensively used by private business for some time, the recreation and sport industries' interest in managing risks only came after sovereign governmental immunity began to erode and litigation related to sport and recreation began to rise (van der Smissen, 1990). The focus of risk management in the business industry was financial. When risk management concepts were first applied to the recreation and sport industries, a much broader focus was needed. Sharp, Moorman, and Claussen (2007) indicated that while risk management literature suggested the concept was necessary to limit legal liability, risk management for many years was perceived as a hindrance. Obviously, in light of the litigious nature of our society, risk management becomes a necessary encumbrance. Therefore, recreation and sport managers must be aware of the potential for injury and loss and must learn to effectively manage the immense risk that exists in their professions. The process of managing and controlling these risks has, over the last two or three decades, resulted in the field of risk management. The purpose of this section is to introduce the recreation or sport manager to the basics of the risk management process.

FUNDAMENTAL CONCEPTS

Risk management has been defined as controlling the financial and personal injury losses from sudden, unforeseen, unusual accidents and intentional torts (Ammon, 1993). Wong & Masteralexis (1998) termed it as "a management strategy to maintain greater control over the legal uncertainty that may wreak havoc on a sport business" (p. 90). In 2002, Corbett described risk management as "managing financial and human resources wisely, governing effectively, making decisions soundly and projecting a positive image towards sponsors, government funders and the community" (¶. 4). Spengler, Anderson, Connaughton & Baker (2009) defined it as a "course of action designed to reduce the risk (probability or likelihood) and loss to sport participants, spectators, employees, management and organizations" (p. 46).

The "loss" resulting from the risk can be physical or financial in nature. For example, risk managers must continually attempt to reduce the risks that injure patrons, thus decreasing the potential for lawsuits. In addition, financial losses may occur due to incidents such as vandalism, poorly written contracts, stolen equipment, and accidents in the facility's parking lot due to poor lighting. Risk management, however, doesn't seek to eliminate *all* risks, but rather creates an environment where the inherent and negligence risks within activities and services provided by an organization are minimized without producing a change in the activity itself.

Function of Risk Management

Recreation and sport managers have been exposed to a new society during the past 20 years—a society that has become enchanted with litigation, and a trend to which many professionals in the recreation and sport environment have fallen victim. Society will not tolerate inappropriate behavior or unsafe conditions, and recreation and sport managers must develop an awareness of the hazards for which they will be held accountable. An effective risk management plan will help to control and diminish the risks that confront today's recreation or sport managers.

In recreation and sport, risk management has been used to combine the traditional corporate interest of limiting financial risk with the interest of the recreation or sport industry—providing for increased patron safety. Additionally, many recreation and sport organizations are interested in showing a profit. Thus it becomes a fine balance between the businesses being profitable while providing as safe an environment as possible. By reducing the injuries to the participants or guests, the business at the same time reduces its financial exposure. When a good risk management plan is implemented, the potential for litigation diminishes. In *Telega v. Security Bureau, Inc.* (1998), the football missed the net on an extra point attempt and landed near Mr. Telega's seat. The ensuing scramble for the ball enveloped the plaintiffs and Mr. Telega sustained numerous injuries. Security and crowd management (a topic discussed in 4.24) are two key components of a risk management plan and, had they been in place, Mr. Telega's injuries could possibly have been avoided all together. In a similar case, *Hayden v. Notre Dame* (1999), the net employed by Notre Dame in the endzone at football games was not large enough to catch all kicked balls and no security staff members or student managers were stationed in the crowd to retrieve the balls. If the university had implemented a risk management plan, the court might have ruled that Notre Dame made a reasonable effort to prevent injury from occurring.

The death of 13-year-old Brittanie Cecil is a more recent illustration of unfortunate risk. In 2002 while attending her first hockey game at Nationwide Arena in Columbus, Ohio, Cecil was hit in the left temple by the deflected puck. As a result of the blow, she suffered a fatal blood clot. In response to this incident, the NHL ordered all of its venues to install protective netting prior to the start of the 2002–2003 season (Steinbach, 2003).

Beyond examining risks associated with a specific activity or event, recreation and sport managers must also examine risks related to public liability, excluding negligence, and risks related to their business operations (van der Smissen, 1990). Risks such as violation of employee rights, real and personal property owned by the organization (van der Smissen, 1990) and negligent hiring practices are of concern to those in the recreation and sport industry. In addition, the threat of terrorism (both domestic and foreign) and alcohol abuse at major sporting events have become major factors to be considered. A comprehensive risk management plan should address these and many other relevant issues.

The D.I.M. Process

The **D.I.M. process** was developed as a tool to establish an effective risk management program. When used as an anticipatory technique rather than as a reactionary procedure, the D.I.M. process will assist organizations in decreasing the chance of litigation. This simple process involves three basic components: (1) *Developing* the risk management plan; (2) *Implementing* the risk management plan; and (3) *Managing* the risk management plan. Every organization, no matter the size, should have a current risk management plan. Each plan, however, should be specifically developed for that provider. Every organization will have risks specific to that business. For example, due to the specific risks, a risk management plan that works for a football facility will not be the same as one used at a baseball venue (Ammon, Southall & Blair, 2004). However, components used in creating this plan will be similar no matter what type of organization. Thus, managers at golf courses, aquatic centers, ski areas, skateboard parks, or park and recreation departments will utilize the same basic principles.

Developing the Risk Management Plan

Developing a risk management plan consists of three separate stages: (1) identifying the risks, (2) classifying the risks, and (3) selecting methods of treatment for the risks.

Identification Stage. The **identification stage** is one of the key aspects of developing a successful risk management program. If the recreation or sport manager wants to control risks in the program, he or she must first identify those risks. Risks are present in all sport and entertainment facilities and events including privately or municipally owned buildings, professional or intercollegiate entertainment facilities, and outdoor or indoor recreational settings. Each event or activity is different and has its own unique risks or areas of potential loss. Identifying these risks, therefore, needs to be specific, constant, and ongoing.

An effective step to identify risk is to create categories of risk and then to list risks within each category. There are several approaches that can be used to **categorize risk**.

van der Smissen (1990) has categorized risks as (1) public liability caused by negligence in program services, (2) public liability (excluding negligence), (3) business operations, and (4) property exposures. Table 4.25.1 in Section 4.25, *Managing Risk Through Insurance* was developed using this categorization method. By studying the table, one can see the typical risks included in each category.

Often recreation and sport managers focus on bodily injuries resulting from **public liability caused by negligence.** Injuries may include death, quadriplegia or other paralysis, brain damage, loss of limbs, loss of senses, injury to internal organs, strains, sprains, fractures, ligament damage, cuts, punctures, and abrasions. This type of risk typically relates to the activities or a service offered by an organization and often occurs when a member of the organization is negligent in performing his or her duties. However, if risk identification is limited to only those bodily injuries that may occur in the services an organization provides, many financial risks to an organization will be overlooked.

Risks grouped under **public liability** (excluding **negligence**) include such areas as malpractice by personnel, product liability, intentional torts, employment practices, sexual harassment, and civil liberty violations. Recreation and sport managers should note that the management of risk relating to employment law issues is becoming a great concern to many in the recreation and sport industries (Curtis, 2002). A recent study indicated that human resource management was one of the main topics of study that current sport administrators felt should be taught to students earning a master's degree in sports administration (Kreutzer & Brown, 2000). Miller (1998) stated that while 55 percent of sport-related cases in 1995 were negligence cases, 11 percent were employment law cases. These cases involved sexual harassment, discrimination, equal pay disputes, and wrongful termination claims. Curtis (2002) added that the number of discrimination lawsuits in sport and recreation is increasing rapidly. Combining this information with the fact that the number of sexual harassment lawsuits is on the rise in the United States (Equal Employment Opportunity Commission, n.d.), recreation and sport managers need to pay particular attention to the identification of risk in the management of human resources while devising strategies to control this risk.

Property exposures are financial risks related to the ownership of real and personal property. Loss may occur as a result of fire, natural elements like lightning and floods, vandalism, and theft.

Recreation and sport managers can also be exposed to risks via their organization's **business operations.** These risks are financial risks that result from business interruption, embezzlement and theft, the medical condition of employees, the health of key personnel, and employee accidents and injuries. To identify risks associated with business operations, the recreation or sport manager should examine the organization's operational **policies and procedures** to determine if the policies and procedures expose the organization to loss. Also, the manager can **observe** his or her employees at work to identify any activities that may lead to sickness, accidents, or disability.

The methods used to look for potential risks will vary according to the nature of your organization and the extent of your organization's operation. Every organization, however, must establish a systematic procedure to assure that a complete risk assessment occurs (van der Smissen, 1990). Tools that can be used to identify risks include **questionnaires** and **discussions with employees** relating to employment practices. Recreation and sport managers must interact with their employees to determine if current employment practices may lead to loss. Also, it is helpful to **read the literature** published by professional organizations (e.g., The United States Professional Tennis Association) to learn about risks relating to employment practices of which the manager might not be aware. Finally, the recreation or sport manager can **consult with colleagues** to determine if he or she has overlooked a potential risk in this area. Recreation and sport managers should rely on the help of various **professionals** in identifying potential risks related to property exposures. For example, an insurance agent should be contacted to insure that the organization has adequate protection if the property is damaged due to fire or flood. Many agents, based on their experience with previous claims and injury reports, can also help in identifying various risks. For all risks, regular contact with employees and inspections of operations can enhance the previously mentioned methods of risk identification.

Classification Stage. Once the potential risks have been identified, the second stage in developing the plan is to **classify the risk**. The purpose of the classification stage is to determine how often (**frequency**) the risk may occur and the degree (**severity**) of the potential loss arising from the risk. Once the various risks have been identified, the risk manager takes each of the identified risks and evaluates them in terms of frequency and severity. The *frequency* of the risk is dependent on the number of times the risk or loss is likely to occur. The risk manager will view each identified risk and assign a frequency of "high," "medium," or "low." The *severity* of the risk is determined by the intensity of the potential injury and/or the degree of the threat to the financial stability of the organization. It is classified as "catastrophic," "critical," "moderate," or "low." The level of severity and the frequency are determined by the risk manager, based on his/her expertise derived from experience and training.

Prairie and Garfield (2004) (as cited in Sharp, Moorman & Claussen, 2007) and Spengler et al. (2009) have developed similar approaches to categorize the risks. Prairie and Garfield call the process "risk assessment" and look not only at the type of risks that occur at a specific organization but also at previous litigation that has ensued. The two authors discuss various "hot topics" including newly found risks that could turn into costly lawsuits. Once these risks have been identified they are categorized by their frequency and impact. Spengler et al. (2009) have the categorization process as the second step of what they call an Analysis. "Risk Evaluation" is the step where the identified risks are evaluated by their frequency and severity.

Regardless of the terminology, once the risks have been classified, a matrix can be created that allows a consistent approach to the classification process. A matrix gives the risk manager a method by which to classify all identified risks on the basis of frequency and extent of potential loss. Table 4.11.1 is such a matrix with

Table 4.11.1 Risk Category Matrix

	Severity of Injury or Financial Impact			
	Catastrophic Loss	**Critical Loss**	**Moderate Loss**	**Low Loss**
High Frequency	None	None	• Fan suffers hip injury when she trips in poorly lighted area in or about premises • Player injures knee due to uneven playing surface or wet spot on court	• Spectators evade admission fee • Spectator in bleachers suffers gouge from protruding screw
Medium Frequency	None	None	• Vandalism of arena • Player twists ankle on piece of ice thrown from the bleachers	• Incorrect change given to spectators • Fans suffer nausea from poorly prepared food at concession stands
Low Frequency	• Player breaks neck running into unpadded wall • Armed terrorist group takes hostages during tournament	• Spectator suffers facial laceration during altercation in bleachers • Poor crowd management leads to fight between players and fans	• Youth sustains eye injury during on-the-court promotion • Spectator suffers concussion from player diving into crowd after loose ball due to inadequate buffer zone	• Program seller gives away programs • Players' wallets are stolen from the locker room

some of the risks from a municipal basketball tournament placed into their proper categories. *All identified risks should be appropriately placed in the matrix, making clear the classification of each risk.* By placing the identified risks in the matrix, the risk manager will have successfully completed the classification stage. However, it should be noted that risk assessment and classification is an ongoing process, always subject to change.

Treatment of Risk. The final stage in developing the risk management plan is to determine a **treatment** for each identified and classified risk. A treatment is a method used to reduce, control, manage, or eliminate financial risks and bodily injuries. There are four basic treatments available to the risk manager. They are avoidance of the risk, transfer of the risk to another party, retention of the risk by the recreation or sport organization, and reduction treatment (Spengler, 2009) or control (Prairie & Garfield as cited in Sharp et al., 2007) of the risk through efforts to reduce the various types of hazards.

The type of treatment a risk manager uses for the identified and classified risks depends on the nature of the risk and the likelihood of the risk occurring. Although it is sometimes difficult to determine the appropriate treatment, a risk treatment matrix can assist in this process. This risk treatment matrix gives the recreation or sport manager guidance regarding the treatment needed for any given risk. The manager, having identified and categorized each risk in Table 4.11.1, should then refer to Table 4.11.2 for the appropriate treatment. *Note: While the contents of Table 4.11.1 vary from activity to activity, the contents of Table 4.11.2, once established by the philosophy and the finances of the organization, remain the same for all activities.*

Avoidance/Elimination. This treatment requires that these activities should not be included within the content of a program (avoidance) or they should be discontinued if they are presently being offered (elimination). Risks should be avoided when they could cause a catastrophic or critical loss with medium or high frequency. In other words, the severity of the incident would be great and risk management could not control the frequency. Ideally, a risk manager should identify these risks before the accidents occur and avoid them completely. For example, if a high-risk activity (such as "cheerleading") has the reputation for causing moderate to severe injuries, the school or athletic program may wish to avoid scheduling the activity if the risks cannot be controlled (*Noffke v. Bakke,* 2008). Decreasing or eliminating the number of activities that recreation and sport organizations offer is not an attractive option. Therefore, avoidance should not be the first choice for a risk manager. It should only be implemented as a last resort when risk is substantial and likelihood of injury is significant. For example, 40 years ago, the use of trampolines was a standard fixture in most physical education programs. Due to the large number (frequency) of students who were injured while jumping on the trampolines, as well as the severity of the injuries, the use of trampolines has been eliminated in almost every school district in the United Sates.

Transfer. Transfer is the shifting of the liability or responsibility for loss from the service provider to another party. This type of risk treatment occurs when two conditions exist: (1) the risk of loss is not so substantial as to warrant the avoidance of the activity, and (2) the risk is greater than the organization can assume on its own.

Table 4.11.2 Risk Treatment Matrix

	Severity of Injury or Financial Impact			
	Catastrophic Loss	**Critical Loss**	**Moderate Loss**	**Low Loss**
High Frequency	Avoidance	Avoidance	Transfer & Reduction	Transfer/Retain & Reduction
Medium Frequency	Transfer/Avoidance & Reduction	Transfer/Avoidance & Reduction	Transfer & Reduction	Retain & Reduction
Low Frequency	Transfer & Reduction	Transfer & Reduction	Transfer/Retain & Reduction	Retain & Reduction

An important means of transfer is through the purchase of appropriate **insurance** coverage[1] (see also Section 4.25, *Managing Risk Through Insurance* and Section 4.26, *Workers' Compensation*). There are many types of insurance policies in existence, and not all apply to the needs of every organization. Property insurance and personal injury liability insurance are often selected to provide protection from potential risks. It is important to understand that the insurance company will only cover the policyholder up to the limits of the coverage. For example, if a defendant has a $1 million liability policy and loses a $3 million judgment, the insurance company will *only* cover the first $1 million (Kaiser & Robinson, 1999).

Another important means of transfer is by **contract**. Examples of these contracts include liability waivers, indemnification clauses and the use of independent contractors. A **waiver** is a contract by which a person voluntarily gives up the right to sue another party (e.g., the service provider) for its negligence. The signer of the waiver (normally the participant) agrees to accept the risks of harm caused by the negligent actions of the other party. However, a waiver generally does not protect a service provider from liability for gross negligence or reckless misconduct. Also, in most states a waiver signed by, or on behalf of, a minor is unenforceable (see also Section 2.23, *Waivers and Releases*).

Indemnification clauses are clauses in a contract that provide for one party to indemnify or reimburse the other for loss. Such clauses are generally included in equipment and facility rental contracts. For instance, an organization leasing a facility generally agrees contractually to indemnify the facility owners against any loss or litigation resulting from the event. These clauses, sometimes called **hold harmless agreements,** require the organization to be compensated by the individuals renting the facility if any damage occurs during the event or if someone is injured and files suit against the facility owner. Thus the risks during the event are *transferred* to the outside organization (see also Section 2.12, *Which Parties Are Liable?* and Section 2.21, *Defenses Against Negligence*).

An **independent contractor** is a person or business that contracts to perform a specific task for a service provider. Independent contractors provide expertise and are generally free to perform tasks as they see fit. The independent contractor is not an ordinary employee of the organization. Some personnel (e.g., team doctors, referees, personal trainers, and aerobic instructors) may function as independent contractors. These individuals are personally responsible for their unemployment and liability insurance, and are generally solely responsible for their negligent actions. Many organizations use independent contractors to provide adventure activities (such as whitewater rafting, scuba, ropes courses, and rock climbing). A landowner is often immune from the contractor's negligence when they hire an independent contractor. The risk is transferred from the landowner to the independent party. However, a landowner is not always shielded from liability. If a landowner hires a contractor to perform an inherently dangerous activity, he or she then is responsible for supervising the actions of the contractor. A landowner must ensure the activity is being performed as safely as possible and that the contractor is taking the appropriate safety measures. This is known as the **inherently dangerous activity exception**. It should be noted that a landowner is not liable if a contractor's negligence is unusual in nature. However, a landowner *is* liable when the negligence of the contractor should have been initially considered by the landowner. The inherent dangerous activity exception is illustrated in *Hatch v. V.P. Fair Foundation and Northstar Entertainment*, (1999). The plaintiff was injured at a bungee jump operated by the Fair Foundation. Northstar Entertainment, the independent contractor, violated several of its own safety policies including: number of staff present, age of the controller, and failure to conduct a daily safety inspection. The operator failed to attach the bungee cord to the crane, resulting in a 170-foot fall and serious injuries to the back, legs,

---

[1]In order to reduce expenses, insurance companies often find that it is less expensive to settle lawsuits than litigate the claims. Settlements are often made in cases where the insurance company would have won in court. Rather than litigating the case, being found innocent and then paying a colossal legal bill, many insurance companies decide to settle out of court (Ammon et al., 2004). This strategy may actually backfire by increasing the number of lawsuits, since plaintiffs feel that, even with a weak case, they can settle for a substantial sum. As insurance companies gain the reputation of paying off claims, the number of suits will continue to grow. An additional problem that occurs when settling lawsuits involves individual employees defended by the organization. If the insurance company settles the claim, the employee has no opportunity to prove his or her innocence. This stigma can be quite traumatic and remain with the employee for many years.

and shoulders of the plaintiff. Due to the inherent dangerous activity exception the jury found that both the Fair Foundation and the contractor were liable, and awarded the plaintiff $5 million (see Section 2.12, *Which Parties Are Liable?* and Section 2.21, *Defenses Against Negligence*).

A combination of these methods of transfer is usually preferable. For example, if the service provider wishes to offer rock-climbing and realizes that the risk involved is too great for the organization, the provider may seek to transfer the risk. In this situation, the risk manager would pay an insurance company a premium to cover any physical or financial damages that may occur (Ammon et al., 2004). In addition, the manager can require that participants sign a liability waiver by which the participant releases the provider from liability for negligence. In doing so the provider has endeavored to transfer the risk to the insurance company and the participant. If the risk is substantial, as in rock-climbing, and cannot be adequately transferred, the activity should be avoided.

Retention. A third treatment of risks, retention, means that the organization keeps the risk and assumes financial responsibility for certain injuries or financial losses that may occur. Retention is often preferred for minor or insignificant risks. Retaining these risks is often less expensive than buying insurance to cover them.

Sometimes retention is termed **self-insurance**. In essence, the sport or recreation organization is simply paying a premium to itself. But this is not as easy as it sounds. If utilized, the organization must include retention as a line item in the budget and accumulate a reserve or "pool" of revenue to pay for such injuries (Ammon et al., 2004). This strategy requires a strong commitment from the organization's upper management not to use the unallocated capital for other purposes (Kaiser & Robinson, 1999).

Looking at the risk treatment matrix (Table 4.11.2), the risks to be retained are those that have a low potential for loss and occur with low to medium frequency. An organization can accept these risks due to the fact that there is very little chance of incurring substantial financial losses. This, of course, is assuming that once the risk manager decides to keep the risk, proper precautions are taken to decrease the occurrence and/or monetary losses associated with the risk.

Reduction. The fourth treatment, and arguably the most important, is the reduction of risks. Risk reduction is a proactive approach to the management of risks. The objective of reduction is to reduce the chance for injury as well as the chance of litigation. The reduction section of the risk management plan establishes a variety of operational practices for reducing the likelihood of loss related to the identified risk. All risks cannot be eliminated from an activity, but often the frequency and severity can be minimized by the proper maintenance of property and equipment, establishing emergency procedures, providing better training for personnel, and other risk reduction techniques. This should be the focus of any risk management program. For example, when efforts are made to reduce the frequency and severity of losses in a youth soccer league, there is less likelihood that losses will occur over a planned retention level. Requiring shin guards, anchoring the soccer goals, and inspecting the soccer field for obstructions or holes are all specific risk reduction techniques.

The primary objective of reduction is to be aware of potential losses (from the identification of risk) and to do something to reduce the potential loss. There are four major tools that the recreation or sport manager can use to reduce risk. The first is to **design a regular systematic inspection program**. A system of inspection must be established, a written record of that inspection must be kept, and a system of follow-up on hazards must be implemented. Inspection of facilities and equipment is a key to reducing loss. An organization is liable for the dangerous maintenance situations about which it knows and for those that it should have known if a proper professional job had been done on inspection (*Felipe v. Sluggers of Miami, Inc. and Sluggers, Inc.*, 2008).

Planned inspection should include machines that have critical parts such as pitching machines, and maintenance items like chlorine storage for a swimming pool. Individuals knowledgeable about the items they are inspecting must complete these inspections. Also, this type of inspection helps locate newly created risks caused by vandalism, abuse or misuse, and theft. If a hazard is found during inspection, a system for addressing the hazard must be implemented. The system should include the following steps: (1) the hazard must be reported to maintenance personnel; (2) the individual overseeing the area where the hazard is located must be notified; (3) the equipment or area must be taken out of service until the repair is made; (4) once the identified hazard is eliminated, maintenance personnel must inform the manager; and (5) there should be established steps to follow in the event the repair has not been made in a reasonable period of time. (See also Section 2.31, *Premises Liability* and Section 4.22, *Audits in Risk Management.*)

The second major tool involves **establishing a maintenance program for facilities and equipment**. The maintenance program must be described in an organization's risk management plan and include both preventative and remedial maintenance that occurs on a regular basis. With the exception of slips and falls, the failure to provide proper maintenance is the leading cause of litigation against most sport/entertainment facilities (Ammon et al., 2004).

A third tool involves **training the staff**. Staff should be trained to identify normal wear and tear and general deterioration of equipment, facilities, and other athletic areas that may lead to loss. Employees also need to understand how to conduct activities so that proper care is afforded program participants. The recreation or sport manager should see that his or her staff knows how to make sure participants have the proper skill level and conditioning for activities, understands proper supervision, and understands how to enact the organization's emergency procedures (see also Section 2.34, *Supervision*). For most situations, it is important that the staff know certain information about the participant that relates to the individual's ability to participate in the activity safely (van der Smissen, 1990). For example, in a swimming program, the skill level and developmental stage of participants must be known to place them in the proper class. An organization must determine what skill and conditioning level is required for participation in the program for each activity or service.

Finally, the fourth tool recreation and sport managers must utilize is **a system under which documents related to program participation may be filed**. They also must be able to retrieve these documents when necessary. Forms that should be filed include parental permission forms, agreements to participate, waivers, membership applications, contracts, inspection checklists, accident report forms, health records, records containing operations information, rules and regulations, copies of employee credentials, and any other program-related document. With the growing threat of litigation, the need to document and to preserve documentation takes on added importance. In 2008, a 19-year-old plaintiff suffered a damaged testicle when a pitching machine delivered a 60 mph baseball when the machine's light indicated it was off. The plaintiff's attorney argued that the defendant did not have a maintenance log, checklist or manuals or any safety policies. The defendants also had prior knowledge that the machine was operable even when the light was off. The jury returned a $1.16 million award to the plaintiff (*Felipe v. Sluggers of Miami, Inc. and Sluggers, Inc.*, 2008).

When a risk manager develops a risk management plan, the most efficient and effective way to decrease the occurrence of various risks is to use reduction techniques such as the above. When a risk manager decides to retain or transfer the risks, he or she must be ready to also incorporate these reduction techniques to insure that each situation is handled in a manner that will reduce the chance of liability. *A crucial concept to remember is that risk reduction should be a risk management treatment any time an activity is offered—in conjunction with transfer or retention.* If the risks are not managed with the use of reduction techniques, more claims will occur and greater costs will be incurred. This will create a drain on funds allotted for retained risks and will eventually cause the insurer to raise the organization's premiums to cover the risks in question. By utilizing reduction techniques to reduce the occurrence of risks, the service provider should be able to keep insurance premiums and budgeted expenses at a minimum. In fact, by managing the risks, it is probable that the number of claims will decrease, which may cause the insurance rates to diminish as well (Ammon et al., 2004).

Implementing the Risk Management Plan

The second component in the D.I.M. process consists of implementing the risk management plan. For this, **effective communication** is a key factor. Effective communication is more than telling personnel what to do. It involves listening as well. When management is seen to encourage suggestions and consider and act on employee concerns, the employees are more likely to bring their perspectives to management. It is of primary importance to *involve all employees in the risk management process.*

Each individual in an organization must understand the overall risk management plan and risk reduction strategies and know what his or her role is in implementing the plan. Therefore, it can be said that the effectiveness of the overall plan is in direct proportion to the effectiveness of the communication regarding the plan. If communication about the plan is nonexistent, incomplete, or inadequate, the program will become inoperable and the risks will not be reduced as they should be. Direct interpersonal communication is required to insure the plan functions properly.

A risk manager can supplement oral communication with printed guidelines outlining risk reduction techniques. These guidelines can be inserted in the employee manual during the first orientation. Examples of the items covered in the guidelines include: the organizational layout and operation, personnel and organizational management, rules and regulations of the business, responsibilities of various employees, correct methods of documenting records and reports, and emergency procedures. The manual is sometimes erroneously termed a "safety manual," but it is really the operating procedures for carrying out the risk management plan (Kaiser & Robinson, 1999).

Some organizations make the mistake of placing the entire risk management plan into every employee manual. The sheer comprehensiveness of the plan will cause many new hires to avoid reading the manual. Only place the pertinent portions of the overall plan into the specific employee's manual. Employee dedication to the process is a key component for a successful risk management plan. It must be clear to each employee that the practices and recommendations mentioned in the manual not only provide a safe environment for the program's participants, but will also protect the employee (Kaiser & Robinson, 1999).

The utilization of a **sound training program** is another way to ensure communication and the implementation of the risk management plan. An in-service education program can be used to communicate the responsibilities of the staff in relation to the plan and provide an opportunity for individuals to improve their ability to identify various types of risks so that they can fulfill the requirements of the plan more effectively. In-service educational opportunities allow the risk manager to explain the risk management plan to the organization's employees while stressing the importance of implementing the reduction strategies set forth in it. For risk reduction to be effective, three in-service areas need to be addressed on a regular basis: (1) communication of responsibilities—what is each individual's role in implementing the plan; (2) development of professional judgment and decision making—what standard of care is required of each employee; and (3) credential education/training—the provision of expertise or an increased knowledge base that will lead to an increased ability to make sound judgments. The risk manager must verify that personnel are qualified for their positions and hold the necessary certifications.

Managing the Plan

The final component of the D.I.M. process is to **manage the plan.** The first step in managing the plan is to **designate a risk manager** and the selection of a risk management committee. Sport and recreation organizations may hire a risk manager or assign one person the role of risk manager as part of his or her other duties. Effective risk managers and risk management committee members share many of the same traits. The risk manager must be a highly motivated individual, must be committed to risk management, and must be able to motivate others to believe in the risk management plan. Whichever system is chosen, the responsible party should monitor the risk management plan, implement changes, assist in fostering a genuine risk management attitude among other employees, conduct inspections, review accidents, and supervise in-service training (van der Smissen, 1990).

The second step in managing the plan is to provide the risk manager and committee with the **authority to lead.** This authority should be described in the policy statement of the organization because it provides a foundation for the plan. The policy statement should clearly delineate the responsibilities of the risk manager. The statement should outline and define the authority of the person responsible for administering the plan.

The management staff and ownership of the organization must also endorse and support the idea of risk management. They must be willing to assist the risk manager or risk management committee with verbal and financial support. Various costs are associated with any effective risk management plan–with insurance comprising perhaps the greatest outlay. Due to the society we live in and the potential for terrorism, the cost of some types of insurance have increased ten-fold. Therefore, the organization's budget should include a line item devoted specifically for the implementation continual assessment of the risk management plan. Without upper management's support a risk management plan will not succeed. The risk manager and the risk management committee must be given the freedom to act independently, but within the philosophy of the sport or recreation organization (Ammon et al., 2004).

Just as employee input is vital for the initial risk management policy, the third step in managing the plan is to **provide employees with the opportunity for continual input** into the risk management plan. Including employees, particularly some who have contact with clients; on the risk management committee is a possible source for this input. The continual success of a risk management plan mandates that employees, supervisors, and managers on all levels have the ability to interact with each other. Additionally, anyone else whose expertise may improve the quality of the risk management plan should be included in the overall risk management process. The size of the committee depends on the overall goals and size of the organization.

As previously mentioned, risks are constantly changing and shifting due to the variety of activities and programs employed by an organization. The size of the organization, the type of activity being conducted, the age of the participants, the skill level of the participants and the age of any associated venue will cause the risks to vary. The risks will never remain the same, so the assessment of these risks needs to not only remain flexible but constant. As soon as an organization ceases assessing the risks they open themselves up to potential litigation.

Risk management is a necessity for sport and recreation managers today. Even though many risks can be identified, classified, and treated, some hazards will still exist and accidents will occur. It is impossible and unrealistic to expect a risk manager to eliminate all injuries and financial losses. However, by developing an extensive risk management plan, implementing the plan, and bestowing the authority to manage the plan upon a concerned risk manager, recreation and sport managers can diminish a number of dangerous risks.

SIGNIFICANT CASE

The case illustrates the concept of foreseeability. The plaintiff argued the facility sold alcohol to intoxicated individuals and this fact along with the lack of sufficient security led to his injuries. However, the defendant maintained there had been no previous incidents of a similar nature. Therefore the defendant claimed they could not have foreseen that the incident could have occurred. Several key concepts such as the presence of a proper alcohol management plan, proper numbers of security staff and documentation of prior incidents are important to keep in mind while reading the case.

JOHNS HOPKINS V. CONNECTICUT SPORTS PLEX, L.L.C.

2006 Conn. Super. LEXIS 1710
June 9, 2006, Decided

This case arises out of a claim for injuries as the result of an alleged assault by a Vincent Baker and a Reverend James Baker. The assault purportedly occurred at the defendant's premises which contains outdoor softball fields. The theory of liability lies in negligence and claims the defendant's employees were negligent in that

(a) They served liquor despite the fact that Vincent Baker and Rev. James Baker may have been intoxicated already;

(b) They failed to provide adequate security to prevent the violence which caused the plaintiff's injuries;

(c) They caused or allowed and permitted said premises to have noisy and unruly patrons, including but not limited to Vincent Baker, and Rev. James Baker, when they had inadequate staff to control the same, creating a volatile situation.

* * *

Suit has also been filed against the Bakers; that case has been consolidated with the case now before the court. In this case the defendant Connecticut Sports Plex, LLC has filed a motion for summary judgment.

The rules to be applied in deciding such motions are well-known. The courts should not grant such a motion if there is a genuine issue of material fact. However, if there is no such issue they should be granted so that parties should not have to endure the expense and aggravation of litigation. On such a motion a court must view the evidence in the light most favorable to the non-moving party* * *. Courts should also be cautious about granting a motion for summary judgment when the allegations lie in negligence; "it must be quite clear what the truth is" any real doubt must be excluded, "a conclusion of negligence . . . is ordinarily one of fact," *Amendola v. Geremia*, 21 Conn.App. 35, 37, 571 A.2d 131 (1990); *Fogarty v. Rashaw*, 193 Conn. 442, 445, 476 A.2d 582 (1984). Also see *Maffucci v. Royal Park Ltd.*, 42 Conn.App. 563, 680 A.2d

333 (1996). "Ordinarily," however, does not cover the entire universe and even in a negligence case such a motion should be granted where it is appropriate to do so.

The negligence claim appears to fall into two categories. It is claimed that the defendant served alcohol to the Bakers when they "may have been intoxicated already"; they allowed them "to consume an overabundance of alcoholic beverages."

The plaintiff also makes another claim in negligence which generally speaking revolves around an alleged failure to exercise reasonable care for the safety of patrons of its facility. Thus it is said that the defendant failed to provide adequate security, failed to provide adequate staff to control noisy and unruly patrons, failed to warn the plaintiff of dangers presented by people like the Bakers who were consuming alcohol and failure to train staff for the purpose of preventing some patrons from harming other patrons.

* * *

The court will first discuss the general allegations regarding failure to provide adequate security, allowance of unruly and noisy patrons without the presence of adequate staff, failure to warn the plaintiff of possible harm from patrons including the Bakers who were consuming alcohol on the premises, failure to train employees to prevent patrons from harming other patrons. The plaintiff's deposition, which is attached to both briefs indicate that on the day in question he was a patron of the defendant's facility having played in a softball game which was part of a tournament. The defendant does not seem to dispute the fact that the plaintiff was a patron or business invitee of the defendant's premises at the time of this incident. There is no indication Hopkins had to pay to participate in the tournament but courts have held individuals can be invitees even where entry on the premises confers no pecuniary benefit, * * *The question becomes what is the duty owed to persons such as the plaintiff by those who own or control premises such as the premises involved here which was used for conducting soft ball games.

A possessor of land who holds it open to the public for entry for his business purposes is subject to liability to members of the public while they are upon the land for such a purpose, for physical harm caused by the accidental, negligent or intentionally harmful acts of third persons or animals, and by the failure of the possessor to exercise reasonable care to

(a) discover that such acts are being done or are likely to be done, or

(b) give a warning adequate to enable the visitors to avoid the harm, or otherwise protect against it.

* * * The proprietor of a place of public amusement has a duty to maintain order on his or her premises and may be held liable for injuries resulting from the dangerous activities of a third person, whether such acts are accidental, negligent, or intentional, if he or she does nothing to restrain or control such conduct after he or she knows, or in the exercise of reasonable care could have known, of it. The proprietor must exercise due care to protect his or her patrons from assaults by other patrons, at least if the proprietor had knowledge of conduct which would naturally result in an injury, or if he or she might reasonably have anticipated an assault.

Where there has been a more or less sudden, direct attack, liability generally is not imposed, for the reason that the proprietor could not reasonably have anticipated the occurrence.

* * *

The defendant Local 1010, as the possessor of the premises on that day, had the duty of exercising reasonable care and control to protect its invitees from dangers which might reasonably be anticipated to arise from the conditions of the premises or the activities taking place there "In particular, the possessor must exercise the power of control or expulsion which his occupation of the premises gives him over the conduct of a third person who may be present, to prevent injury to the visitor at his hands. He must act as a reasonable man to avoid harm . . . even from intentional attacks on the part of such third persons." Prosser, *Law of Torts* (4th Ed.) 61, p. 395. On the evidence, the jury could properly find that the defendant Local 1010 had failed to perform its duty to provide adequate police protection or otherwise to control the activities of its beer drinking guests, especially after the earlier outbreak of fisticuffs.

* * *

On the other hand, the insufficiency of the number of security personnel, their improper conduct under the circumstances, and other failures to adequately warn and protect patrons have been emphasized in cases where the owner or operator was held liable.

The basic principles of the foregoing case law seem to be accepted by our Appellate Courts since they merely reflect basic common-law pronouncements of the duties owed by owners or controllers of premises.

It should be noted that the plaintiff appears to take the position that the jury could very well find that the Bakers' assaults were not intentional but negligent or reckless. Given the allegations of the complaint and the deposition testimony this seems to be an unlikely supposition. Furthermore, in perhaps a departure from the Restatement (2d) Torts view, in our state . . . an actionable assault and battery may be one committed wilfully or voluntarily, and therefore intentionally; one done under circumstances showing a reckless disregard of consequences; or one committed negligently, * * *The observations and cases cited in the 75 A.L.R.3d article dealing with assaults in places of public amusement involve assaultive behavior by allegedly intoxicated parties and circumstances which indicate the assaulting party may not have acted with the requisite intentionality for Restatement purposes or the requirements of criminal law.

It is also true, for this court at least, that the technical rigors of a proximate cause analysis based on the supposition of an intentional intervening act can complicate an analysis and establish too sharp a dichotomy between the finding of a duty which is the basis of any negligence action and the question of imposition of liability. Thus Section 344 of the Restatement (2d) Torts says that

> A possessor of land who holds it open to the public for entry for his (sic) business purposes is subject to liability to members of the public while they are upon the land for such a purpose, for physical harm caused by the accidental, negligent or intentionally harmful acts of third persons . . .

Comment f makes clear, however, that "since the possessor is not an insurer of the visitor's safety, he is ordinarily under no duty to exercise any care until he knows or has reason to know that the acts of the third person are occurring or are about to occur."

In other words the foreseeability of causing harm by a failure to act to prevent harm to a patron, for example, by another patron is a prerequisite to liability whether the tortfeasor acts or is about to act negligently, recklessly, or intentionally.

And this fits in with the prescription of § 442B of the Restatement.

§ 442B. Intervening Force Causing Same Harm as That Risked by Actor's Conduct.

Where he negligent conduct of the actor creates or increases the risk of a particular harm and is a substantial factor in causing that harm, the fact that the harm is brought about through the intervention of another force does not relieve the actor of liability, except where the harm is intentionally caused by a third person and is not within the scope of the risk created by the actor's conduct.

Under § 442B the "intervention of another force: could be a negligent or reckless force (see § 344) but a category of force further separated out by § 442B is harm which is caused "intentionally." And comment c says the rule in § 442B "does not apply where the harm of which the risk has been created or increased by the actor's conduct is brought about by the intervening act of a third person which is intentionally tortious or criminal, and is not within the scope of the risk created by the original negligence." But then the comment goes on to say "Such tortious or criminal acts may in themselves be foreseeable, and so within the scope of the created risk, in which case the actor may still be liable for the harm . . ." (emphasis by this court). In other words foreseeability of harm is the prerequisite for finding negligence liability in the type of case now before the court whether the third party causing harm acted intentionally or negligently. The foreseeability requirements to impose liability on the premises operator may be stricter where intentional assaults are involved just because intentional assaults are more difficult to predict or foresee in the ordinary course of life but foreseeability has the same operative definition whether the third party is accused of being negligent or of acting intentionally. Foreseeability is the test.

* * *

In support of its motion for summary judgment the defendant has offered the affidavit of Vincent Candelora who is now and was the manager of Sports Plex at the time of this incident on August 25, 2002. Mr. Candelora states that "the Sports Plex has no knowledge of any physical altercations between its patrons and guests prior to August 25, 2002 at (the premises in question). The affidavit is somewhat bareboned—it does not say when the Sports Plex began operating at the location, whether Candelora managed the premises from its inception, if not, how long before the August 25th date he began his duties. It only speaks apparently to physical altercations not the threat thereof which did not proceed to fisticuffs or actual physical contact. Issues such as general rowdiness or excessive drinking are not referred to in the affidavit. Also the general statement is made that "the Sports Plex" does not have knowledge of physical altercations—does this mean the management? Does it refer to all employees? Is there a reporting system to insure information about operations would be communicated to management by employees? Was Candelora always present when the premises were operating so he could himself make the observations which lead to his conclusion in the affidavit?

But the defendant adds certain portions of the deposition of the plaintiff and others to support its position. The following relevant facts were testified to by the plaintiff,

Hopkins, in the portion of his deposition testimony attached to the defendant's motion.

(1) During softball season Hopkins was at the premises two or three times a week. He also played indoor football and his child attended a baseball clinic at the facility.

(2) On the day of the incident he was in a tournament and after the tournament had consumed six beers.

(3) He shook Vin Baker's hand and said play hard with the Celtics. Hopkins surmised Baker thought he said something worse and yelled he did not want to talk about baseball. Hopkins said Baker did not have to be so rude and Baker told him shut up and do not say another f_____ word.

(4) Hopkins said he walked to his vehicle and when asked what Baker's problem was said f___ him which Hopkins surmises Baker heard. Baker came over to him and yelled, Hopkins uttered another obscenity and was pushed down. "His guys" then dragged him thirty feet away and he was punched.

(5) The Reverend Baker then joined the fray saying he would take care of Hopkins and proceeded to pummel Hopkins. His friend Mike Viora tried to break the altercation up and it ended with some more words exchanged.

(6) The incident happened around 6 p.m. The deposition attached to the motion skips from page 50 to page 119 and at the top of the page it says

Q. Do you know whether they are or not?

A. No I don't.

Q. Okay. But no other employees or staff that you know of.

A. No.

Hopkins then said the incident happened very fast, ten seconds from the exchange of words to the time Baker came up to him. Hopkins apparently was not asked how long the actual physical alteration took, that is from the time Baker pushed him, including the time he said he was pummeled by Baker's entourage and the time the Reverend joined in and stopped hitting Hopkins.

Hopkins said he never saw the defendants consume alcohol or drugs. He said he never saw any physical fights while he was at the Sports Plex and never heard of any taking place at the premises. He also did not see the Bakers purchase alcohol and he could not tell if they were intoxicated.

The defendant also attached the deposition testimony of Mike Viora, a friend of Hopkins. He said the following:

(1) He had no idea a fight was gong to occur; if he did he would have tried to brace himself for it. The peo-

ple with Baker were not people that are at the complex all the time.

(2) Viora described the altercation, it was "bad" his shirt was ripped! No one helped him and Hopkins out—no one from their team or the complex. "Chick" an 85 year old who runs a hot dog stand apparently observed the fighting—Chick told someone on their team not to jump in to help Viora and Hopkins or they'd never play at the complex again.

(3) Beer was sold from a concession stand; it was sold to his teammates. He has no memory of beer being sold to anyone that was intoxicated.

The plaintiff attached portions of the Hopkins and Viora depositions to his objection which were not attached to the defendant's motion. The following additional facts were brought out in the Hopkins deposition:

(1) Hopkins in some detail describes being dragged from the original point of altercation and the attack he underwent by the Baker entourage and Reverend Baker. Viora tried to pull people off. Rev. Baker then said Hopkins had had enough and even tried to protect him from further assault.

(2) Viora had the same amount to drink as Hopkins that day—about six beers.

(3) Candelora told him not to come back to the complex after this incident, "they thought that I started the whole thing." ("they" refers to Candelora and a man who "was in charge of certain things" according to Hopkins.)

(4) As to the beer he consumed, Hopkins said he bought the beer at the complex, "you can't bring alcohol into the complex").

(5) He had been going to the complex from the time it opened—it had been opened for a period of years.

The deposition then skips a few pages and the following then occurred.

(6) He could not say if certain people (not identified) were wearing a uniform. He seemed to say he did not notice Sports Plex staff present (at the scene of the altercation presumably) other than "Chick Furino" and the other two who apparently were in the concession stand.

(7) Umpires were present but he does not know if they are hired by the complex—but no other staff was present that he knew of.

(8) On the day of the attack he only saw the Bakers sporadically [*23] at the complex. He did not observe the Bakers purchase beer from the concession stand.

(9) He noticed no difference in the crowd on the day of the incident from crowds there at other times. He saw no security guards on the day of the incident.

(10) Between games Baker and others would go inside Baker's vehicle.

(11) Hopkins brought a round of beers for the group he was with. They don't ask for an I.D. As to Chick Furino Hopkins does not know his position. He apparently was near the spot where the altercation began; Hopkins did not see him during the altercation but he did come up with his golf cart "towards the end" but "didn't do anything." Hopkins was not on the ground at that point. He also said he saw Furino try to break up the fight.

The plaintiff also attached portions of the deposition transcript of Mike Viora some of which were not included in the defendant's attachments. The court will reference factual assertions not included in the earlier discussion of the Viora deposition or not made clear.

(1) Viora said that at the time of the events in question neither he nor Hopkins were intoxicated. He said he saw Vin Baker during the day.

(2) Vioradescribes the beginning of events much as did Hopkins. He says in a private conversation between him and Hopkins the latter said F___ that or him. Vin Baker was thirty-four feet away—"nobody knew anything was going to happen until he (Baker) came over . . . pointing at (Hopkin's chest)."

(3) After the foregoing a crowd of people who were with Vin Baker grabbed Hopkins.

(4) Hopkins was pushed down a hill and Viora was being hit in the back—it was chaotic. A "little pull" then occurred and the Reverend Baker joins in saying "I'll take care of this myself" and Hopkins was on the ground. Viora pulled the Reverend off who said he in fact had stopped the fighting. Someone then called the police and everyone scattered. There had been about 40 people with Baker.

(5) Guys on the team were buying beer from the stand, putting it in baskets; he and Hopkins bought maybe one beer. He did not see people in the stand sell beer to anyone visibly intoxicated.

(6) Viora denied that he or Hopkins were intoxicated but "we were feeling good." No one in the stand selling the beer cut him or Hopkins off. In all the years he played there he never heard of anyone being cut off.

(7) During the altercation he saw "Chick" riding around and a "kid" named "Froggy" was talking to "Chick."

(8) During the entire day he was there Viora did not observe any security personnel on the premises nor was there a policeman on duty. No one came to the aid of Hopkins from the complex during the incident, he was the only one who did.

The plaintiff has also submitted an affidavit from a Michael Perry. He states that on the day of the incident he was a patron at the sports complex and played softball there from 10:00 a.m. to 2:00 p.m. He goes on to say that during two games on several occasions he observed Vin Baker and his friends consuming beer in the bleachers adjacent to the dug out.

The court has reviewed the general law in this area. Now the court will try to review the facts in light of the specifically relevant case law on the liability of owners or operators of places open to the public for entertainment or sports activities.

* * *

Whether or not security must be provided and the level of security depends in part on the forseeability that harm might be likely to occur. This can be found if there were past incidents of general fighting or rowdyism, * * *.

In this case the affidavit of the manager of the complex, Mr. Candelora, denies any knowledge of prior altercations on the premises. None of the deposition testimony of the plaintiff or Mr. Viora or the affidavit of Mr. Perry indicate that any of these individuals witnessed rowdy behavior or fighting in the past. And the plaintiff had been going to the complex since it opened, for years. The plaintiff, for example, had no problem with bringing his child to the facility to attend a baseball clinic and affirmatively said he never saw fights at the facility and never heard of any taking place.

On the day of the incident itself there was no fighting or rowdy behavior displayed by any patrons or by the Bakers and their friends prior to the actual incident. Hopkins said on that day he noticed no difference in the crowd on the day of the attack from other crowds he observed at other times he had been at the complex. Viora said before the actual incident he had no idea fighting would occur. * * *

From the previous discussion of the facts presented to the court it is of course also true here that the Bakers in the past before this incident or before the attack on the day it occurred had not presented any problem or threat to Hopkins or other patrons, cf. *Nance v. Ball*, 134 So. 2d 35 (Fla.App., 1961) (assault on patron of bowling alley by person who previously threatened plaintiff), cf. *Dellinger v. Pierce*, supra.

But the plaintiff does not rest his case on whether assaultive behavior had occurred prior to this incident. It could also be negligent to allow patrons who later attack others to bring and consume alcohol or to serve them alcohol with knowledge that they would become intoxicated or in fact did become intoxicated and liability can attach if such harm is thus foreseeable and steps such as added security and warnings of the danger presented thereby are not implemented. In *Bearman v. Univ. of Notre Dame*, 453 N.E.2d 1196 (Ind.App. 1983) a lady was injured while returning to her car after a football game by a drunk who knocked her down. The court said the university was aware that alcohol was consumed during and after games and tailgate parties were held in parking lots around the stadium. The court conceded that there was no showing the university had reason to know of the particular danger posed by the drunk who caused injury to Mrs. Bearman. But the court went on to say that the university "had reason to know that some people will become intoxicated and pose a general threat to the safety of other patrons. Therefore, Notre Dame is under a duty to take reasonable precautions to protect those who attend its football games from injury caused by the acts of third persons

In this case, however, there is not an iota of evidence presented to the effect that the Bakers were intoxicated or how their drinking in any way contributed to causing this altercation, or that any behavior induced by their drinking did or should have put the defendant and its employees on notice that their drinking and general behavior induced thereby posed a threat to anyone in general and Hopkins and Viora in particular, * * *

It is true that beer was sold to patrons at this facility and Viora said no one, to his knowledge, was ever cut off. From that one could surmise there would be a danger of people getting intoxicated and belligerent, But again there was no evidence that the Bakers were intoxicated or even appeared so to Hopkins and Viora who certainly had close contact with them and could have given a lay opinion to that effect.

Given the foregoing it cannot be said that the defendant violated any duty of care to the plaintiff based on a foreseeability test. What must be kept in mind is that this sports complex after all consisted of five softball fields frequented by adults apparently in organized leagues. We are not dealing with outbursts of violence or constant raucous behavior which might be likely to be a feature of rock-and-roll concerts and wrestling matches. The latter have been defined in one case as "not quiet and dignified affairs. But the plaintiff could maintain that apart from matters such as the service of alcohol and absence of prior behavior that would serve to warn the defendant of danger to patrons, there was no security at all and this in itself could be a basis of liability. Mr. Viora testified that during the whole day he saw no security personnel at the sports complex to supervise the people using the softball field and their guests* * * In the case before us it is not fairly inferable from the complaint that general supervision would have prevented the injury caused by the impetuous or wayward boy who did the pushing".

Also as to the confrontation with Vin Baker, Hopkin's deposition testimony indicates the incident developed quickly. He estimated the exchange of words he had with Vin Baker lasted thirty seconds. Seconds only passed until the time Baker actually approached Hopkins. The only time Vin Baker actually put his hands on Hopkins was when he first came up to Hopkins and pushed him. He did not fall. Vin Baker did not punch or kick Hopkins. People who had been with the Bakers then kept pushing him back but Hopkins cannot say what Vin Baker was doing at that point. At another point in his deposition Hopkins says "his guys" (meaning Vin Baker's friends) grabbed him and dragged him thirty feet. "They grabbed him, but they pulled him (apparently Baker) out of there." Then however he says "They took me into a corner 'him and his guys'" and proceeded to pummel him. Viora's deposition explicitly says that after Vin Baker pushed Hopkins, somebody grabbed Baker and he heard someone say "you got to get out of here." It was only then that "his crowd" grabbed Hopkins to begin striking him and ripping his shirt.

Given the suddenness of the attack, general supervision could not have prevented the contact that occurred between Vin Baker and Hopkins. Even the presence of security personnel at some ideal number not otherwise defined would not have meant the incident as it involved Vin Baker would not have occurred. The confrontation was sudden, occupied seconds of time and the operator of the complex had no warning or reason to suspect a confrontation like this would occur. Causation cannot be established—it cannot be said that failure to do or not to do anything by the defendant was a factor, let alone a substantial factor in the occurrence of this confrontation. And this is so whether Vin Baker's actions are characterized as negligent, reckless or intentional. To paraphrase *Noble v. Los Angeles Dodgers, Inc.*, 168 Cal. App. 3d 912, 214 Cal. Rptr. 395, 214 Cal. Rptr. 396 (Ct. of App., 1985) as to the Vin Baker confrontation, the "plaintiff's theory is purely and simply that the (defendant) (was) negligent in failing to effectively deter any and everyone from acting in such a manner."

As to the Reverend Baker, the relevant factual situation is much the same. After the initial Vin Baker-Hopkins confrontation, Hopkins was dragged some thirty feet according to deposition testimony by friends of Baker, the people who accompanied him to the premises. Reverend Baker's involvement appears to have come at the end of the ensuing melee when he pinned Hopkins down which allowed him to be pummeled. As Viora pulled Reverend Baker off Hopkins, Reverend Baker adopted the posture that he had helped Hopkins by breaking up the attack against him. Hopkins said Rev. Baker never kicked or punched him.

Again this whole second phase of the incident lasted an undefined but apparently brief amount of time. It was sudden and the defendant would have had no warning that an attack as ferocious as that described could have been expected by anything that occurred during the day the Bakers and their entourage were present.

It is true that reading comment f to § 344 of Restatement (2d) Torts it is clear that a defendant would have a duty of care if he knows acts of a patron such as an attack on another patron are about to occur or are occurring. The suddenness of the attack here make it impossible to say that that duty was violated.

A man named Chick Celentano or Furino who is described at various points as being 85 years old, the operator of the concession stand and riding around in a golf cart is said in deposition testimony to be at or near the scene of the altercation. Two other individuals were in the concession stand but from the depositions it is difficult to know how far they were from the second phase of the melee involving Rev. Baker and thus whether they could have done anything to break up the attack on Hopkins themselves or by helping Viora.

The exact location of Furino is not made clear. He is said to have driven up in his golf cart to the location of the Rev. Baker-Hopkins melee and he does not do anything but that was "toward the end." It is difficult to see what this one individual could have done to stop the attack or assist Mr. Viora and no where is this articulated except by generalized Viora statements that no one from the sports complex came to help.

Chick Furino also is alleged to have told one Froggy not to have the Hopkins-Viora teammates help Hopkins or they would not be allowed to play again at the sports complex. But this hearsay statement which could be objected to if sought to be introduced at trial could only have been made, if made at all, during the second phase of the melee involving Rev. Baker. Deposition testimony or affidavits from Furino (Celentano) or "Froggy" were not provided to the court so it can only speculate at what point in the altercation the statement was made which is critical for determining whether Furino, as an agent of the defendant, had a duty to assist Hopkins or Viora and whether such assistance would have prevented any injury or further injury to the plaintiff. Where in fact these "teammates" were located in relation to the altercation is not mentioned and Furino's statement may have merely reflected a general policy concerning anyone involved in altercations at the complex. As to whether Furino's statement prevented anyone besides defendant's employees from coming to Hopkins' or Viora's aid, the court cannot determine that question on what has been presented and no evidence by way of affidavit or deposition has been offered on this issue.

The court concludes that the general negligence claims against the defendant based on a violation of a duty to ensure the safety of patrons on its premises should be dismissed.

The claims of service of alcohol and failure to provide a safe environment for patrons of the sports facility cannot be divided into neat compartments at least in all respects. However, the court will now separately discuss the negligence claim of the plaintiff that the defendant served alcohol to the Bakers "without proper supervision and in overabundance" and when they "may" have been intoxicated. In one of the headings in its brief the plaintiff maintains that the "plaintiff's allegations of negligent service of alcohol survive" the defendant's motion. * * *

At common law it was the general rule that no tort cause of action lay against one who furnished, whether by sale or gift, intoxicating liquor to a person who thereby voluntarily became intoxicated and in consequence of his intoxication injured the person or property of either himself or of another. The reason generally given for the rule was that the proximate cause of the intoxication was not the furnishing of the liquor, but the consumption of it by the purchaser.

* * *

There is not any evidence that the altercation that occurred here was the result of serving alcohol to intoxicated patrons. The deposition testimony is to the contrary and has been previously discussed. Nor can the plaintiff persuade the court that there is an issue of fact as to whether the defendant served beer to Vin Baker knowing he was an alcoholic * * * The plaintiff asks the court to take judicial notice of the fact that Vin Baker is an alcoholic; this is said to be "known to the public and especially the sporting community." Websites, a newspaper article, and an "essay" are said to attest to this. This is not the type of matter of which the court could take judicial notice. Section 2-1 (c) of the Code of Evidence says a judicially noticed fact must not be subject to reasonable dispute in that it is either "(1) within the knowledge of people generally in the ordinary course of human experience or (2) generally accepted as true and capable of ready and unquestionable demonstration."

Both tests are not met here. That a particular N.B.A. player is an alcoholic or have alcohol problems may be known in the sporting community but it is hardly within the knowledge of people generally or certainly of this court. Neither can it be said that it is capable of "ready and unquestionable demonstration" when the source to verify that consists of website reference and article in newspapers. * * * A court may take judicial notice of all matters within the knowledge of people generally in the ordinary course of life's experience . . . The court sometime said that this type of information is in the mind of the trier and judicial notice serves to refresh that memory. This type of matter may be in the minds of basketball fans, and professional basketball fans in particular but the court cannot conclude it is in the mind of people generally. * * * There it was held notice could not be taken of the fact Barbieri, a well-known local and state politician, had been a Democratic town chairman and a powerful politician in our state, The knowledge the defendant, its owners, managers, and employees might have had about Baker's status or condition as an alcoholic could have been better explored through deposition testimony not by relying on the information referred to here to prove what is after all those individuals' personal knowledge.

The court concludes that the plaintiff has not offered anything to create a material issue of fact as to whether it should apply here. Also for the reasons discussed the court did not consider in the previous section any suggestion or claim that Vin Baker was an alcoholic in deciding whether the defendant violated its general duty to keep its premises reasonably safe for its patrons by serving alcohol to a person known by it to be an alcoholic.

In any event the motion for summary judgment is granted.

CASES ON THE SUPPLEMENTAL CD

Clahassey v. C Ami Inc., (2002 Mich. App. LEXIS 1352). The case illustrates the importance of a sound risk management plan. The reader needs to pay attention to how the location of the event and the failure to warn impacted the court's decision.

Maisonave v. Newark Bears, (2005 N.J. LEXIS 1108). Examine what the NJ Supreme Court decided about the limited duty rule. When did it apply? What was the standard of care in the other sections of the ballpark?

Sciarrotta v. Global Spectrum, (2008 N.J. LEXIS 314). The two aspects of the limited duty rule are discussed. Pay particular attention to the Supreme Courts conclusion pertaining to the pre-game warm-up.

QUESTIONS YOU SHOULD BE ABLE TO ANSWER

1. Describe the significance of risk management.

2. Explain the D.I.M. Process. What are the steps, and how do they relate to each other?

3. Discuss the various types of transfer. Which of them do you believe is used most often?

4. Analyze as many reduction treatments as you can think of. If you were a sport or recreation venue manager which ones would be of the highest priority?

5. Identify two to three risks that a sport or recreation manager would encounter. Classify the risks and then select a treatment for each risk.

REFERENCES

Cases

Felipe v. Sluggers of Miami, Inc. and Sluggers, Inc., No. 07-18180 CA 22, Miami-Dade County Circuit Court, 11th, FL 2008.

Hatch v. V.P. Fair Foundation and Northstar Entertainment, 990 S.W.2d 126; 1999 Mo. App. LEXIS 315.

Hayden v. Notre Dame, 716 N.E.2d 603; 1999 Ind. App. LEXIS 1697.

Noffke v. Bakke, 748 N.W.2d 195 (2008).

Telega v. Security Bureau, Inc., 719 A.2d 372 (Pa. Sup. Ct. 1998).

Publications

Ammon, R., Jr. (1993). Risk and game management practices in selected municipal football facilities. (Doctoral dissertation, University of Northern Colorado, 1993). *Dissertation Abstracts International, 54,* 3366A.

Ammon, R., Jr., Southall, R., & Blair, D. (2004). *Sport facility management: Organizing events and mitigating risks.* Morgantown, WV: Fitness Information Technology, Inc.

Corbett, R. (2002, August). *Risk management for sport organizations and sport facilities.* Presented at the Sports Management: Cutting Edge Strategies For Managing Sports as a Business Symposium, Toronto.

Curtis, T. (2002, Fall). Still the next big thing: Discrimination lawsuits keep coming in sports as the issue shows no sign of slowing. *SSLASPA Newsletter, 9*(3), 3.

Equal Employment Opportunity Commission. (n. d.). *Sexual harassment charges.* Retrieved January 13, 2003, from www.eeoc.gov/stats/harass.html

Kaiser, R., & Robinson, K. (1999). Risk management. In B. van der Smissen, M. Moiseichik, V. Hartenburg, & L. Twardzik (Eds.), *Management of park and recreation agencies* (pp. 713–741). Ashburn, VA: NRPA.

Kreutzer, A. L., & Brown, M. T. (2000, June). *Core business content: Is there a need for inclusion in sport management curriculum.* Paper presented at the meeting of the North American Society of Sport Management, Colorado Springs, CO.

Miller, L. K. (1998). Employment law issues. In H. Appenzeller (Ed.), *Risk Management in Sport* (pp. 403–416). Durham, NC: Carolina Academic Press.

Plunkett Sports Industry Almanac (2009). Retrieved March 7, 2009 from http://www.plunkettresearch.com/Industries/Sports/SportsStatistics/tabid/273/Default.aspx

Sharp, L. A., Moorman, A. M., & Claussen, C. L. (2007). *Sport law: A managerial approach*. Scottsdale, AZ: Holcomb Hathaway.

Spengler, J. O., Anderson, P. M., Connaughton, D. P., & Baker, T. A. (2009). *Introduction to sport law*. Champaign, IL: Human Kinetics.

Steinbach, P. (2003, January). Rethinking the rink. *Athletic Business,* pp. 43–48.

van der Smissen, B. (1990). *Legal liability and risk management for public and private entities*. Cincinnati, OH: Anderson Publishing Co.

Wong, G. M., & Masteralexis, L. P. (1998). Legal principles applied to sport management. In L. P. Masteralexis, C. A. Barr, & M. A. Hums (Eds.), *Principles and practice of sport management* (pp. 87–116). Gaithersburg, MD: Aspen Publishers.

4.20 Recreation and Sports Management Applications

4.21 Standards of Practice

—JoAnn M. Eickhoff-Shemek
UNIVERSITY OF SOUTH FLORIDA, TAMPA

In a negligence lawsuit, a **standard of care** will be applied to measure the competence of a professional. If the professional's conduct falls below such a standard, he/she may be liable for injuries or damages resulting from such conduct (Black, 1991). The standard of care can be determined in various ways, but one way is from **standards of practice** developed and published by **professional** and **independent** organizations. This section will focus on the legal implications associated with these types of standards, not those dealing with accreditation, licensure, certification, statutes, or those developed by risk management authorities (e.g., some states and municipalities) and insurance companies.

Standards of practice published by professional organizations are commonly referred to as standards, guidelines, recommendations, or position statements. Many professional organizations have published these documents to provide benchmarks of desirable practices for practitioners and managers. In addition to these types of standards, there are "technical physical specifications" (van der Smissen, 2000) published by independent organizations such as the American Society of Testing and Material (ASTM), the Consumer Product Safety Commission (CPSC), and equipment manufacturers. For example, ASTM has published standard specifications for safety signage for fitness equipment/facilities and standard specifications for playground equipment. CPSC has published standard specifications on equipment such as bicycle helmets and on facilities such as spas, hot tubs, and whirlpools. Equipment manufacturers also publish specifications regarding proper use, installation, maintenance, warnings, and so forth, with regard to the various types of equipment they sell.

Published standards of practice can be entered into evidence (via expert testimony) in a court of law to help determine the standard of care or **duty** that a defendant owes to a plaintiff. Therefore, it is critical for recreation and sport managers to apply these standards of practice into their risk management plans.

FUNDAMENTAL CONCEPTS

Potential Legal Impact of Published Standards of Practice

Published standards of practice can serve as a shield (minimize liability associated with negligence) for the defendant who adheres to them. However, they can also serve a sword (increase liability associated with negligence) for the defendant who does not adhere to them. As demonstrated in Figure 4.21.1, published standards of practice can be introduced as evidence via expert testimony to help determine duty. If the defendant's conduct is inconsistent with these standards of practice, it can result in a breach of duty that can then lead to negligence. However, if the defendant's conduct is consistent with the standards of practice, it will be difficult for the plaintiff to prove there was a breach of duty.

Generally, the failure to adhere to published standards of practice can lead to claims of "ordinary" negligence against the defendant(s) as demonstrated in the Significant Case (*Elledge v. Richland/Lexington School District Five*) presented in this section. However, "gross" negligence claims also can be made against the defendant, e.g., see *Xu v. Gay* (2003). (See the cases on the Supplemental CD.) In addition to ordinary and gross negligence claims, plaintiffs also might file a "breach of express warranty" claim against the defendant.

For example, the complaint filed in *Gloria Hicks v. Bally Total Fitness Corp.* not only included a wrongful death action for both ordinary and gross negligence, but also for breach of express warranty (Herbert, 2009). The wrongful death actions in this 2008 case involved the failure of Bally Total Fitness Corp. to provide appropriate emergency care (*e.g.,* administer CPR and use an AED) to Malcolm Hicks when he suffered a sudden cardiac arrest while exercising at the fitness club. Mr. Hicks died several days later in the hospital. In the breach of express warranty claim, the plaintiff claimed that ". . . Bally pledged, agreed and warranted to it members that it would . . . conform to all relevant laws, regulations and published standards . . ." and ". . . would support and abide by guidelines and recommendations of the American College of Sports Medicine . . ." (Herbert, 2009, pp. 4–5).

Standards of Practice Published by Professional Organizations

Following is a list of some of the professional organizations that have published standards of practice for various types of recreation and sport practitioners/managers. By no means is this a comprehensive list.

Exercise/Fitness Professionals

1. **American College of Sports Medicine.** ACSM's Health/Fitness Facility Standards and Guidelines

2. **American College of Sports Medicine and American Heart Association Joint Position Statement.** Recommendations for Cardiovascular Screening, Staffing, and Emergency Policies at Health/Fitness Facilities and Automated External Defibrillators in Health/Fitness Facilities

3. **International Health, Racquet & Sportsclub Association.** IHRSA Club Membership Standards

Strength and Conditioning Professionals

National Strength & Conditioning Association. *Strength & Conditioning Professional Standards & Guidelines*

Recreation Professionals

1. **National Therapeutic Recreation Society and National Recreation and Park Association.** *NTRS Code of Ethics and Interpretive Guidelines*

2. **American Therapeutic Recreation Association.** *ATRA Standards of Practice*

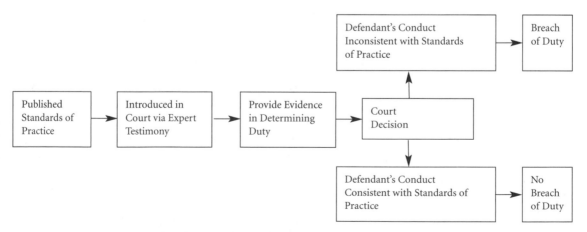

Figure 4.21.1. Example of the Potential Legal Impact of Published Standards of Practice

Physical Educators

American Alliance for Health, Physical Education, Recreation and Dance–National Association for Sport and Physical Education. *Moving into the Future: National Physical Education Standards*

Coaches

American Alliance of Health, Physical Education, Recreation and Dance–National Association for Sport and Physical Education. *National Standards for Sport Coaches*

Athletic Trainers

Board of Certification (BOC). Standards of Professional Practice

The Proliferation of and Inconsistency Among Published Standards of Practice

One of the major purposes for developing and publishing standards of practice is to help standardize the delivery of services. Published standards of practice serve as "benchmarks" of practices that reflect the minimal acceptable level of service owed to participants and that should be universally applied by properly trained and educated professionals (Eickhoff-Shemek, Herbert, & Connaughton, 2009). Most often, these are developed by leaders within a given organization using a consensus and peer-review approach. However, a major challenge for some recreation and sport managers is that there has been a proliferation of such published statements, not to mention the many inconsistencies that exist among them.

This is especially true in the exercise/fitness field. In addition to the three published documents listed above under "exercise/fitness," several other organizations (e.g., Medical Fitness Association, YMCA, Aerobics and Fitness Association of America) have also published standards of practice in recent years. Unfortunately, these professional organizations have not worked together to adopt one uniform set of published standards of practice for all exercise/fitness professionals to follow, which has resulted in many inconsistencies among the published standards of practice. Not only do these inconsistencies make it difficult for exercise/fitness professionals to know which standards of practice they should follow, but these inconsistencies also allow expert witnesses to select—among the various standards of practice—those that best support their individual opinions. This can lead to differences in court rulings with regard to the establishment of the standard of care owed to participants in exercise and fitness programs. Therefore, given the inconsistencies that exist (discussed next), it is recommended that professionals *"follow those [published standards of practice] that are the most authoritative or safety oriented in their approach, regardless of how they are defined and/or stated . . ."* (Eickhoff-Shemek, Herbert, & Connaughton, 2009, p. 53).

Inconsistencies in Terminology

Certain professional organizations (e.g., ACSM and NSCA) have distinguished, by definition, a standard from a guideline (Tharrett, McInnis, & Peterson, 2007; NSCA, 2001). Both ACSM and NSCA have defined **standards** as requirements and **guidelines** as recommendations. Standards are written as "must" statements and guidelines are written as "should" statements. Other published standards of practice, e.g., *Standards of Professional Practice* (published by the BOC for athletic trainers) use the term "standards" in the title of their publication, but all the standards are written as "should" or "shall" statements, not "must" statements. Another inconsistency in the use of terminology is demonstrated in the ACSM and American Heart Association (AHA) joint position paper titled *Recommendations for Cardiovascular Screening, Staffing, and Emergency Policies at Health/Fitness Facilities* which includes requirements (must statements) and recommendations (should statements), though the title specifically states "recommendations" (see the cases on the Supplemental CD).

Although differences clearly exist on how professional organizations define and use the terms standards and guidelines, does it make a difference to the courts when establishing the standard of care? In *Xu*, Ning Yan died from a severe head injury resulting from a fall off a treadmill that had only ½ feet clearance behind it at the defendant's fitness facility. The expert witness for the plaintiff, Dr. Marc Rabinoff, stated that the industry's standard of care for the safety distance behind treadmills should be a minimum of five feet. Though he did not specify the industry standards he was referring to, he did state that they were voluntary, not mandatory. Interestingly, the court made no distinction with regard to voluntary or mandatory stating that the "defendant's ignorance of and failure to implement these standards . . . establishes a case of ordinary negligence . . . " (p. 171). It appears from this case that even though the expert witness stated in his testimony that the industry standards were voluntary, the court still considered them as evidence of the standard of care that the defendant owed to Yan. Therefore, to minimize liability associated with published standards of practice, it is important for recreation and sport managers to implement all of them regardless of how they are defined and/or stated by the professional organizations that publish them.

Inconsistencies in Practice Behaviors or Actions

The specific required and/or recommended behaviors or actions that should be adopted also can vary among the various standards of practice published by professional organizations. For example, IHRSA's published standards of practice (IHRSA Club Membership Standards, 2005) do not require their clubs to have an Automated External Defibrillator (AED). However, ACSM does require health/fitness facilities to have an AED. ACSM Standard #7 states that "Facilities must have as part of their written emergency response system a public access defibrillation (PAD) program" (Tharrett, McInnis & Peterson, 2007, p. 2).

Inconsistencies also exist among standards of practice published by independent organizations. In the *Standard Specification for Motorized Treadmills* (2001), published by ASTM, the minimum clearance dimensions that are "required around each treadmill for access to, passage, around, and emergency dismount . . . " are "0.5 m (19.7 in.) on each side of the treadmill and 1 m (39 in.) behind the treadmill" (p. 5). However, these dimensions may differ as stated by equipment manufacturers in their published owners' manuals. For example, in the Owner's Manual of the Cybex 750T Treadmill (2007), it specifies 79 inches clearance behind the treadmill, almost double the ASTM standard. The clearance dimension on each side is the same as the ASTM standard.

The Law and Standards of Practice Continually Change

New issues can arise which can potentially change the law as well as published standards of practice. It is important for recreation and sport managers to stay abreast of these changes. For example, in recent years several states have passed legislation that mandate fitness facilities to have an AED (Eickhoff-Shemek, Herbert, & Connaughton, 2009). In addition, several professional organizations have recently revised their published standards of practice to "require" fitness facilities to have an AED versus recommending an AED. Recreation and sport managers also need to stay abreast of new standards that are under development. For example, the ASTM has launched a new initiative to develop inclusive fitness equipment standards (NCPAD, 2008). These standards are being designed to help facilities comply with Title III of the Americans with Disabilities Act (ADA). Finally, it is important for recreation and sport managers to carefully consider both applicable laws and published standards of practice when developing their risk management plans.

Standards of Practice as They Apply to Risk Management

It is essential for recreation and sport managers to incorporate applicable standards of practice into their risk management plan. Managers are ultimately responsible for the development and implementation of the risk management plan. However, all professionals responsible for the program must be involved in various aspects of the risk management process.

Head and Horn (1997) developed a five-step risk management decision-making process: (1) identifying and analyzing exposure to loss, (2) examining alternative risk management techniques, (3) selecting risk management techniques, (4) implementing techniques, and (5) monitoring results. This five-step approach can be adapted into the following four steps with regard to the application of standards of practice (see also Section 4.11, *Risk Management Process*).

Step 1. Identifying and Selecting Applicable Standards of Practice

Because there are so many published standards of practice from a variety of organizations, it is challenging for the recreation and sport manager to be aware of all applicable standards and to determine which ones should be selected and incorporated into the risk management plan. A risk management advisory committee (e.g., experts in the field, a knowledgeable lawyer, and an insurance expert) can provide excellent assistance in this step as well as the remaining steps. Because it is almost impossible to know which standards of practice will be introduced into a court of law, it is best to select those that are the most authoritative or safety oriented in their approach.

Step 2. Developing Risk Management Strategies That Reflect Standards of Practice

This step involves writing procedures that would describe specific responsibilities or duties that staff members would carry out given a particular situation. For example, all programs should have written emergency procedures that not only reflect published standards of practice, but also describe specific tasks that staff members must follow when someone is hurt.

Once the written procedures are finalized, they should be included in the facility's policy and procedures manual. Policies and procedures from this manual can also be introduced as evidence in determining duty (see *Darling v. Charleston Community Hospital* (1964), where the defendant's own by-laws along with published standards were entered into evidence to determine duty). It is best for the procedures be written clearly and succinctly without too much detail. Too much detail in the written procedures will not allow for a certain amount of flexibility the staff members may need in a particular situation and may make it difficult for the staff to remember everything they are to do.

Step 3. Implementing the Risk Management Plan

Implementation of the risk management plan primarily involves staff training. Staff training will help ensure that staff members carry out the written policies and procedures properly. The policy and procedures manual should be used with initial training for new employees as well as with regular in-service training throughout the year for all employees. In regular in-service trainings, actual practice of a particular procedure (e.g., emergency procedures) should take place. It is also important to explain to staff members why it is essential that they carry out their duties appropriately from a legal perspective.

Step 4. Evaluating the Risk Management Plan

Evaluation of the risk management plan should be done throughout the year. For example, the recreation and sport manager should regularly supervise staff to be sure they are carrying out their duties appropriately and if they are not, corrective action should take place, which may involve re-training. Evaluation should also occur after each injury to determine if the staff carried out the emergency procedures correctly and to determine if anything could be done to prevent a similar incident in the future. A formal evaluation of the entire risk management plan should be done at least annually. Like the law, standards of practice are not static and can change and evolve over time. Therefore, written procedures will need to be updated periodically to reflect these changes.

SIGNIFICANT CASE

The following case demonstrates that courts do allow expert witnesses to introduce published standards of practice as admissible evidence in determining duty in negligence cases. The trial court in this case excluded evidence provided by expert witnesses involving standards of practice published by ASTM and CPSC. The plaintiffs claimed that the trial court erred in excluding this evidence and appealed. The Court of Appeals of South Carolina (*Elledge v. Richland/Lexington School District Five*, 2000) found that the trial court did error in refusing to admit relevant evidence of the ASTM and CPCS industry standards. Citing a variety of cases to support its decision, the Court of Appeals stated: *"Safety standards promulgated by government or industry organizations in particular are relevant to the standard of care for negligence. . . . Courts have become increasingly appreciative of the value of national safety codes and other guidelines issued by governmental and voluntary associations to assist in applying the standard of care in negligence cases. . . . A safety code ordinarily represents a consensus of opinion carrying the approval of a significant segment of an industry, and it is not introduced as substantive law but most often as illustrative evidence of safety practices or rules generally prevailing in the industry that provides support for expert testimony concerning the proper standard of care"* (pp. 477–478). (Emphasis added). The Court of Appeals reversed the trial court's decision and the Supreme Court of South Carolina affirmed the Court of Appeals decision. This is an excellent case to illustrate that not adhering to published standards of practice can lead to charges of negligence.

ELLEDGE V. RICHLAND/LEXINGTON SCHOOL DISTRICT FIVE

Supreme Court of South Carolina
2002 S.C. LEXIS 235
November 25, 2002, Filed

Opinion: Justice Waller

We granted a petition for a writ of certiorari to review the Court of Appeals' decision in *Elledge v. Richland/Lexington Sch. Dist. Five*, 341 S.C. 473, 534 S.E.2d 289 (Ct. App. 2000). We affirm.

Facts

On December 9, 1994, nine-year-old Ginger Sierra (Ginger) slipped and fell on a piece of playground equipment at Irmo Elementary School where she attended fourth grade. The playground equipment was a metal monkey bar device which the children walked upon; it extended above the ground approximately two feet. As a result of the fall, Ginger broke her right leg. The growth plate in that leg was significantly damaged, and Ginger eventually underwent surgery in both legs to remove the growth plates. * * *

Ginger and her mother, Christine Elledge (collectively respondents), sued petitioner Richland/Lexington School District Five (the District) for negligence. A jury returned a verdict for the District. On appeal, the Court of Appeals reversed and remanded for a new trial. * * *

At trial, James Shirley, the principal at Irmo Elementary since 1990, testified that shortly after he arrived at the school, he had concerns about the school's playground. He

was especially concerned by the lack of a fall surface and by the height of some of the playground equipment. As to the monkey bar which Ginger fell on, Shirley stated that children had been walking on it and this was also a concern. In 1991, Shirley contacted Jim Mosteller who redesigned the playground. As part of the playground renovations, the monkey bar which Ginger fell on was modified by Mosteller. Originally, the monkey bar was higher and had a bench underneath it. As part of the modifications performed in 1991, the height was lowered from about four feet to two feet, and the bench was removed. On the modified monkey bar, students would walk or crawl across it, although there were no hand-held supports on the side. Shirley testified that he knew the children were walking across the apparatus after the modification.

Both of respondents' playground safety experts testified that the monkey bar was, in its original form, designed to develop children's upper body strength. Archibald Hardy stated that this piece of equipment was known as a "pull and slide" and the children were supposed to lie back on the bench underneath the bars and pull themselves along the apparatus. According to Hardy, the original design "definitely wasn't for walking" because the metal rungs were small enough for children's hands and were "fairly slick." The modification to the equipment encouraged children to "run up and jump on top of it;" however,

Hardy stated that children "shouldn't have been playing on top of it at all." Hardy, who sold to and installed playground equipment for Irmo Elementary, had visited the playground on several occasions since 1992, and had recommended to Shirley that all the older equipment on the playground be "bulldozed."

Steven Bernheim, respondents' other expert, similarly testified about the equipment and stated that it "was not meant as a climber." According to Bernheim, the equipment was safe as originally designed, but in its modified form, it was unsafe because the narrow bars were originally designed for hands, not feet, and no grit had been placed on the metal bars to prevent slipping.

Bernheim stated generally that the playground at Irmo Elementary did not meet the proper safety standards in the industry. Respondents sought, however, to introduce specific evidence regarding the Consumer Product Safety Commission (CPSC) guidelines for playground safety and the American Society for Testing and Materials (ASTM) standards for playground equipment. The trial court granted the District's motion in limine to exclude this evidence. At trial, respondents argued that this evidence was relevant to establishing the District's common law duty of care. The trial court found the evidence inadmissible because the guidelines were not "binding" on the District and the District had not "adopted" them in any way.

Respondents proffered the following evidence. Bernheim would have testified that in 1994, when Ginger fell, the CPSC guidelines and ASTM standards were in effect and would have applied to "any group . . . utilizing the playground equipment for public use," including a school district. He stated that these guidelines are industry standards and are distributed to schools via superintendents' or principals' meetings. Significantly, Bernheim opined that the District should have had policies and procedures in place for retrofitting existing equipment so that it complied with the guidelines. Furthermore, Bernheim believed the modified monkey bar did not comply with the national guidelines because there were no handrails and no grit on the walking surface. According to Bernheim, because Ginger's injury involved getting caught in an entrapment between the ladder areas, it was the type of injury the guidelines are designed to prevent. While Bernheim acknowledged that the industry standards were guidelines only, he stated they are what the playground equipment industry "stands by."

Respondents also proffered testimony from the District's purchasing coordinator, Joe Tommie. According to Tommie, the District would specify in its bids for purchasing new playground equipment that the equipment must meet the CPSC guidelines and ASTM standards. He stated: "That's normally the standard we use to ensure that we purchase safe equipment."

* * *

On appeal, respondents argued the exclusion of this evidence was prejudicial error. The Court of Appeals agreed. Stating that "evidence of industry standards, customs, and practices is 'often highly probative when defining a standard of care,'" the Court of Appeals held the trial court erred by excluding evidence of the CPSC guidelines and ASTM standards. *Elledge*, 341 S.C. at 477, 534 S.E.2d at 290–91.

* * *

The Court of Appeals found the trial court was under "the mistaken belief that the District must have adopted these national protocols before such evidence was admissible. . . . While such proof might be necessary in attempting to establish negligence *per se*, it is not required when the evidence is offered to demonstrate an applicable standard of care." *Id.* at 478, 534 S.E.2d at 291. As to the District's argument there was no prejudice from any error, the Court of Appeals stated that the "exclusion of this testimony was clearly prejudicial since such evidence would tend to show the District's compliance with industry standards, which directly conflicts with the District's assertion that such standards were never recognized." *Id.* at 480, 534 S.E.2d at 292.

Issue

Did the Court of Appeals correctly decide that the trial court's exclusion of the CPSC guidelines and ASTM standards evidence was reversible error?

Discussion

The District argues that the trial court correctly excluded the CPSC guidelines and ASTM standards evidence. Specifically, the District maintains respondents failed to establish that these guidelines were accepted and used by school districts in South Carolina to determine the safety of existing playground equipment. In addition, the District contends that even if the trial court erred, the error was not prejudicial. We disagree.

To establish a cause of action in negligence, a plaintiff must prove the following three elements: (1) a duty of care owed by defendant to plaintiff; (2) breach of that duty by a negligent act or omission; and (3) damage proximately resulting from the breach of duty. * * * In our opinion, respondents' proffered evidence was relevant to, and admissible on, the first required element of negligence—the District's duty of care to respondents. * * * We agree with Chief Judge Hearn's observation that the trial court was under "the mistaken belief that the District must have adopted these national protocols before such evidence was admissible." *Elledge*, 341 S.C. at 478, 534 S.E.2d at 291.

As recognized by the Court of Appeals, the general rule is that evidence of industry safety standards is relevant to establishing the standard of care in a negligence case. See, e.g., *McComish v. DeSoi*, 42 N.J. 274, 200 A.2d 116, 120–21 (N.J. 1964) (holding that construction safety manuals and codes were properly admitted as objective standards of safe construction); *Walheim v. Kirkpatrick*, 305 Pa. Super. 590, 451 A.2d 1033, 1034–35 (Pa. Super. 1982) (holding that safety standards regarding the safe design and use of trampolines, including ASTM standards, were admissible on the issue of the defendants' negligence, even though the defendants were unaware of the standards); *Stone v. United Eng'g*, 197 W. Va. 347, 475 S.E.2d 439, 453–55 (W.Va. 1996) (no error to admit evidence of safety standards for the design and guarding of conveyors even though the standards had not been imposed by statute and did not have "the force of law"); see generally Daniel E. Feld, Annotation, *Admissibility in Evidence, on Issue of Negligence, of Codes or Standards of Safety Issued or Sponsored by Governmental Body or by Voluntary Association*, 58 A.L.R.3d 148, 154 (1974) (modern trend is to admit safety codes on the issue of negligence). This kind of evidence is admitted not because it has "the force of law," but rather as "illustrative evidence of safety practices or rules generally prevailing in the industry." *McComish v. DeSoi*, 200 A.2d at 121.

Indeed, the District even acknowledges this is the general rule. Respondents' expert, Bernheim, laid an adequate foundation for the admission of these safety standards when he stated they: (1) were in effect at the time of Ginger's accident, * * * and (2) would have applied to any group using playground equipment for public use, including a school district. Thus, the Court of Appeals correctly held that the trial court erred by excluding evidence of the CPSC guidelines and ASTM standards.

The District, however, argues this evidence was inadmissible because respondents did not show that school districts generally accepted or followed the guidelines with regard to existing playground equipment. * * * We find this argument completely unavailing. Since the evidence showed the District followed the CPSC guidelines when purchasing new playground equipment, and the guidelines are intended for general playground safety which logically includes the maintenance of existing playground equipment, the District's contention that the safety standards somehow did not apply to it on existing equipment is simply untenable. It is clear to us that a public school is exactly the type of entity to which the public playground safety guidelines should, and do, apply. Simply because the District did not utilize the guidelines in 1994 with regard to existing equipment does not mean that it should not have. * * *

We find this evidence is highly probative on the issue of defining the District's duty of care. Rules 401, 402, SCRE (evidence is relevant and admissible if it has any tendency to make the existence of any fact of consequence to the action more or less probable than it would be without the evidence); see also *Elledge*, 341 S.C. at 477, 534 S.E.2d at 290 ("Evidence of industry standards, customs, and practices is 'often highly probative when defining a standard of care.'") (quoting 57A Am.Jur.2d Negligence § 185 (1999)). Consequently, we hold the trial court abused its discretion by excluding this evidence. * * *

The District further argues that any error made by the trial court did not result in prejudice to respondents. The District contends that the evidence was cumulative to the admitted testimony of respondents' experts and the expert testimony was limited only by excluding specific references to the safety standards. We disagree.

Evidence of objective safety standards is generally offered "in connection with expert testimony which identifies it as illustrative evidence of safety practices or rules generally prevailing in the industry, and as such it provides support for the opinion of the expert concerning the proper standard of care." *McComish v. DeSoi*, 200 A.2d at 121 (emphasis added); see also *Brown v. Clark Equip. Co.*, 62 Haw. 530, 618 P.2d 267, 276 (Haw. 1980) (evidence of safety codes is "admissible as an alternative to or utilized to buttress expert testimony") (emphasis added).

Respondents sought to introduce evidence of industry standards to identify and establish the duty of care owed by the District to respondents. According to respondents' expert, the modified monkey bar did not comply with the guidelines. According to the District's purchasing coordinator, the District utilized the guidelines to ensure the safety of new equipment purchases. The import of the expert's evidence is clear. Respondents sought to show that the same standards that were used to purchase safe new equipment, should have been used to safely modify and/or maintain the existing equipment.

Furthermore, this type of evidence constitutes an objective standard and as such would have greatly enhanced the opinions offered by respondents' experts. We therefore disagree with the District's argument that the evidence would have been cumulative to the experts' testimony. One of the main purposes of industry standard evidence is to provide support for an expert's opinion on what the applicable standard of care is, and thus, the evidence is not merely cumulative to the expert's testimony. * * *

In addition, we note that the bulk of the experts' testimony went to the element of breach of duty whereas the specific evidence of industry standards was intended to establish the applicable duty of care. In other words, while respondents' experts were allowed to offer their opinions that the equipment did not conform with the industry's guidelines and was not meant to be walked upon, this testimony primarily relates to breach of a duty, not to demonstrating precisely what the objective duty of care was. Since the evidence at issue went to a different element on the negligence cause of action—duty versus breach—clearly the evidence cannot be considered cumulative.

Accordingly, we hold the trial court's error in excluding this evidence prejudiced respondents' case.

Conclusion

The general rule is that evidence of industry safety standards is admissible to establish the standard of care in a negligence case. The evidence of CPSC guidelines and ASTM standards which respondents sought to have admitted in the instant case is exactly the type of evidence contemplated by this general rule. The Court of Appeals correctly held the trial court committed reversible error in excluding the evidence. Therefore, the Court of Appeals' opinion is AFFIRMED. * * *

CASES ON THE SUPPLEMENTAL CD

Darling v. Fairfield Medical Center, 142 Ohio App. 3d 682 (2001 Ohio App. LEXIS 3268). This case involved specifications published in the manufacturer's Owner's Manual regarding proper set up of a treadmill and provision of cautions and warnings. Note the court's rationale for not applying the assumption of risk defense.

L.A. Fitness International v. Mayer, 980 So. 2d 550 (2008 Fla. App. LEXIS 5893). This case involved IHRSA and ACSM standards regarding emergency procedures. Describe why most recreation and sport managers would not agree with the appellate court's ruling in this case.

Xu v. Gay, 257 Mich. App. 263 (2003 Mich. App. LEXIS 1505). This case involved industry standards regarding the distance (clearance) behind treadmills. Explain why the court ruled that the failure to implement the standards did not establish a case of gross negligence.

QUESTIONS YOU SHOULD BE ABLE TO ANSWER

1. Describe the potential legal impact of published standards of practice.

2. Investigate and then develop a list of the standards of practice published by both professional and independent organizations that apply to your specific practice as a recreation and sport manager.

3. Explain what recreation and sport managers should do if they find inconsistencies among the published standards of practice.

4. Describe how published standards of practice can be applied to the four risk management steps. Include the specific actions that recreation and sport managers should take within each step.

5. Using the court's reasoning in the Significant Case (*Elledge*), explain how and why published standards of practice can be relevant to the standard of care.

REFERENCES

Cases

Darling v. Charleston Community Hospital, 200 N.E.2d 149 (Ill. App. Ct. 1964).

Elledge v. Richland/Lexington School District Five, 341 S.C. 473 (S.C. Ct. App. 2000).

Elledge v. Richland/Lexington School District Five, LEXIS 235 (S.C. 2002).

Xu v. Gay, 668 N.W.2d 166 (Mich. App. 2003).

Publications

Black, H. (1991). *Black's law dictionary* (6th ed.). St Paul, MN: West Publishing Company.

Eickhoff-Shemek, J., Herbert, D., & Connaughton, P. (2009). *Risk management for health/fitness professionals: Legal issues and strategies.* Baltimore, MD: Lippincott Williams & Wilkins.

Head, G., & Head, S. (1997). *Essentials of risk management* (Vol. I, 3rd ed.). Malvern, PA: Insurance Institute of America.

Herbert, D. (2009). New AED case filed. *The Exercise Standards and Malpractice Reporter, 23*(1), 1, 4–7.

IHRSA Club Membership Standards (2005). In *IHRSA's guide to club membership & conduct.* (3rd. ed.). Boston, MA: International Health, Racquet & Sportsclub Association (IHRSA).

NCPAD (2008). *New ASTM initiative: Inclusive fitness equipment standards.* NCPAD F.I.T.T. Column, available at: http://www.ncpad.org/fitt/fact_sheet.php?sheet=658, Chicago, IL: The National Center on Physical Activity and Disability (NCPAD).

NSCA (2001). *Strength & conditioning professional standards & guidelines,* available at: http://www.nsca-lift.org/Publications/SCStandards.pdf, Colorado Springs, CO: National Strength and Conditioning Association (NSCA).

Owner's manual of the Cybex 750T treadmill (2007). Medway, MA: Cybex International Inc.

Standard specification for motorized treadmills. (2001). F 2115. West Conshohocken, PA: American Society of Testing and Materials International (ASTM).

Tharret, S., McInnis, K., & Peterson, J. (Eds.) (2007). *ACSM's health/fitness facility standards and guidelines* (3rd ed.). Champaign, IL: Human Kinetics.

van der Smissen, B. (2000). *Standards and how they relate to duty and liability.* Paper presented at the 13th Annual Sport, Physical Education, Recreation and Law Conference, Sponsored by the Society for the Study of the Legal Aspects of Sport and Physical Activity, Albuquerque, NM.

4.22 Audits in Risk Management: Risk Management Plan, Legal Audit, and Facility Audit

—Todd L. Seidler
UNIVERSITY OF NEW MEXICO

College Student Rendered Quadriplegic Receives $9,000,000
Coach Sues for Breach of Contract
Pool Drain Cover Case Settled for $30.9 Million
Programs Eliminated: Title IX Lawsuit Follows
Coach Charged With Sexual Harassment
Soccer Net Cross-bar Crushes Boy to Death
University Loses Age-Discrimination Suit
High School Tennis Player Electrocuted
Overloaded Bleachers Collapse Killing One and Injuring Over 200

These are real headlines of actual incidents. Thousands of people are injured each year as a result of watching, volunteering, working, or participating in sport and physical activities. As a result of those injuries, litigation against the sponsoring organization or recreation or sport business often occurs. Due in part to the expansion of programs, an increase in the number of participants, and the proliferation of personal injury lawsuits, risk management has become one of the most important concerns for today's sport or recreation manager. As covered throughout this text, managers of recreation and sport programs have a number of legal duties they are obligated to perform. Management in a well-run recreation or sport organization will take all reasonable precautions to ensure the provision of safe programs, facilities and equipment for all participants, spectators, and staff. As discussed in previous chapters, the establishment of a good, effective, formal risk management program has become the expected standard of practice for all sport and recreation programs.

In addition to litigation resulting from physical injury, recreation and sport managers are often faced with a wide variety of other legal actions such as contract disputes, employment issues, Title IX claims, compliance with Occupational Safety and Health Administration (OSHA) and Americans with Disabilities Act (ADA) regulations, and allegations of Constitutional rights violations. As a result of the increase in litigation against recreation and sport agencies, managers of these agencies are increasingly called upon to defend themselves and their organizations from legal challenges. The purpose of this section is to present three risk management tools for recreation and sport managers—the **risk management plan**, the **legal audit**, and the **facility audit**. Each of these can be of immense value in protecting against harm to individuals and defending an organization from litigation. Other sections throughout the text have focused on the risk management process and on many of the legal issues facing today's sport and recreation managers. Throughout this section, the reader will be directed to other sections of the text that will expand on the specific topic being discussed.

RISK MANAGEMENT PLAN

According to van der Smissen (1996), "There are two types of risks: the risk of financial loss and the risk of personal injury" (p. 173). She goes on to say, "A **risk management plan** is more than safety checklists! It is the systematic analysis of one's operations for potential risks or risk exposures and then setting forth a plan to reduce such exposures" (p. 173). A good risk management plan analyzes all potential risks that an organization faces and selects the optimal method to treat each.

As described in previous chapters, there are four methods of treating risks once they have been identified. They are (1) risk avoidance or elimination, (2) risk reduction, (3) risk retention, and (4) risk transfer (see also Section 4.11, *Risk Management Process*).

It is important to recognize that every risk management plan should be unique and be developed specifically for each particular organization. A youth baseball league will be faced with different risks and have different requirements than will a high school athletic department, a college recreation program or a nonprofit organization sponsoring a large event. All components that are appropriate for a given situation should be included in the risk management plan.

In developing a risk management plan, it is important to understand the concept of developing **layers of protection**. This means that whenever an identified risk cannot be completely eliminated, several strategies should be used to treat the risk. For instance, instead of relying on just a waiver to protect against a successful lawsuit, the waiver should be used in conjunction with other methods of treating the risk. In this way, if the waiver is successfully challenged in court, there are several other protections still in place. Examples may include developing an informed consent, special releases from a physician for a pre-existing condition, extra insurance, regular inspections, or special training for personnel. The more layers of protection that are in place, the more likely the organization will be able to successfully defend itself in court.

The following are the major components of a risk management plan for a typical recreation or sport organization. This is only an outline as many of these concerns are discussed in depth in chapters throughout this text. References to the appropriate chapters will be provided when appropriate. It is also important to note that this is a generic outline and that each organization must develop a plan that is customized for its particular situation. Finally, the reader should realize there is no one best format or outline for a risk management plan. Most formats are acceptable as long as each of the sources of risks is addressed.

Organization Description

It is not always necessary but is usually advantageous to begin with an overview and description of the organization along with its purpose and function. The following information may be useful:

- Organization mission statement—statement of philosophy;
- A description of the services or programs provided;
- An overview of the clientele served;
- A description of the facilities and spaces that will be utilized;
- The organizational structure of the organization—organizational chart;
- Financial resources.

Personnel

As part of an overall risk management plan, it may be desirable to review or develop policies and procedures for personnel as might be found in the organization's personnel manual (see also Section 4.11, *Risk Management Process*). When discussing ways to avoid employment litigation, Schuler and Jackson (1996, p. 608) state "One excellent avoidance technique is to undertake a comprehensive audit of all employment procedures, policies, and practices to ensure that all are in accord with the rapidly changing state and federal employment laws." A review of personnel-related policies and procedures should include the following:

- Develop thorough hiring procedures to ensure that employees are qualified to perform the job they are hired to do. This may include required initial and ongoing training for each position. Background checks, both in-state and out-of-state, should be required for all positions that work with children or other susceptible populations. This is a minimum requirement—it is advisable that they be conducted for all employees since responsibilities may change after one is employed;

- Develop complete and accurate job descriptions for all personnel, and describe the essential tasks necessary to do each job including individual responsibilities for safety and risk management. (This is also helpful in fully complying with the ADA);

- Provide an evaluation and discipline process that allows for accurate and thoroughly written documentation of employee performance and discipline. This may include termination procedures;

- Develop and implement a policy of nondiscrimination in the workplace. Comply with the requirements of federal and state laws that prohibit discrimination on the basis of race, religion, national origin, age, sex, pregnancy, and disability;

- Develop a procedure to field complaints of sexual harassment in the workplace. Be sure it effectively protects the rights of the accused and the accuser. Ensure compliance with government-mandated training requirements regarding the illegality of sexual harassment;

- Review all policies and procedures for possible due process considerations;

- Provide a location for conducting employment interviews that is fully accessible to those with disabilities, pursuant to the ADA;

- Ensure the hiring process is not subject to claims of discrimination because of a narrow applicant pool;

- Update the employee handbook, manual, or policy to ensure compliance with recent changes to state and federal employment laws. Check your employment manual for any provisions that are contrary to state or federal law;

- Post all required notices in the workplace (e.g., "Sexual Harassment is Illegal," state and federal wage and hour laws, state and federal OSHA guidelines, state and federal fair employment laws, privacy laws and the Family and Medical Leave Act);

- Consider if a policy regarding violence in the workplace is appropriate for your situation;

- Ensure compliance with the Immigration and Naturalization Service requirement to complete work authorization (I-9) forms for all employees.

Conduct of Activities

This section of the risk management plan is a description of the programs being offered and the necessary standards for conduct (see also Section 2.34, *Supervision*). Issues to consider include:

- **Proper Instruction.** Policies ensuring adequate instruction and providing for proper methodology and progression;

- **Warnings and Participation Forms.** Review or develop all appropriate pre-participation forms; physical exam, waiver, warning, assumption of risk, parental consent, consent for emergency treatment, as well as any other appropriate forms necessary for the activities sponsored by the organization (see also Section 2.23, *Waivers and Releases* and Section 2.24, *Agreements Related to Inherent Risks*);

- **Mismatch Situations.** Review or develop policies to avoid mismatches. [Should prevent mismatches between participants and also between children and staff or other adults] (see also Section 2.34, *Supervision*);

- **Transportation Policy.** If transportation is provided for participants, a thorough policy regarding vehicles, inspections, driver qualifications and training, insurance, maintenance and record keeping is necessary (see also Section 2.35, *Transportation*);

- **Hazing Policy.** if applicable, a hazing policy should be developed, communicated and enforced (see also Section 3.22, *Hazing*);

- **Rules.** Develop, communicate, and enforce rules that govern behavior of all participants, spectators, staff, and visitors.

General Supervisory Practices

Supervision is almost always an issue when injuries occur in recreation and sport programs (see also Section 2.34, *Supervision*). Some aspects of supervision that need to be addressed are:

- A supervisory plan that outlines duties, responsibilities, qualifications, and schedules of supervisors;

- Management of behavior of participants, spectators, staff, and visitors. Crowd control can be considered an aspect of behavior management (see also Section 4.24, *Crowd Management*);

- Rules and regulations for supervisors as well as participants, spectators, staff, and visitors;

- Security and access control;

- Emergency care of the injured and accident reporting (see also Section 2.33, *Emergency Care*);

- Protection of participants, spectators, staff, and visitors from foreseeable criminal acts;

- A plan for supervision if the regular supervisor must leave participants for a period of time.

Facilities

Recreation and sport managers should attempt to reduce or eliminate the foreseeable hazards related to environmental conditions. A **facility audit** is a systematic method of identifying such hazards and risks related to a sport or recreation facility and determining the optimal method of treating each. The audit should cover all facilities, equipment, and both indoor and outdoor spaces. A detailed description of the facility risk audit is provided later in this section (see also Section 2.31, *Premises Liability*). The audit should address:

- Hazardous conditions
- Equipment
- Facility layout
- Maintenance
- OSHA

- Security
- Health hazards
- Access control
- ADA
- Signage

Crisis Management and Emergency Response Plans

Identify the crisis and emergency situations that are likely to occur and develop response plans and procedures for each. This should include all documentation and forms that are to be used. Once developed, regular training of appropriate personnel is necessary to ensure that the plans are carried out as anticipated. The **emergency response plan** should include first-aid plans, reporting procedures (911) and medical services policies (see also Section 2.33, *Emergency Care* and Section 4.23, *Crisis Management*). Types of emergencies and crisis situations that may be planned for include:

- Personal injuries of participants, spectators, staff, visitors
- Earthquake
- Fire
- Bomb or terrorism threat
- Medical emergencies—care for the injured

- Civil disturbance
- Weather related emergencies— tornado, hurricane, lightning, flood
- Hazardous material spill
- Dealing with participants, family members of victims, lawyers, and the media

Insurance Coverage

Make certain the necessary insurance is in place and that it is adequate for foreseeable events (see also Section 4.25, *Managing Risk Through Insurance* and Section 4.26, *Workers' Compensation*). Every possible situation that can be envisioned should be considered to determine whether all staff, participants, volunteers, administrators and visitors will be adequately protected. Without such coverage, an injured party may sue in order to pay medical bills and other costs. When evaluating insurance plan coverages, consider:

Organization or Business

- General liability
- Umbrella liability
- Employment practices liability
- Property
- Event
- Motor vehicle

Participant

- Basic medical (often required of participant)
- Catastrophic injury

Employee

- Workers' compensation
- Liability protecting employees

As mentioned previously, this is a generic risk management outline. The needs of each business or organization differ depending upon its goal, the activities offered, its size, whether it's public or private, and many other factors. In some organizations other areas should be included in the risk management plan. Some possible topics to add may be identified during a legal audit.

THE LEGAL AUDIT

A **legal audit** is a formal review of policies that attempt to address all pertinent legal aspects of the organization. A legal audit involves a complete legal checkup of the organization in which all aspects of the operation are examined in order to discover and minimize potential financial threats. Although the line between a risk management plan and a legal audit is often blurred, a legal audit includes more than what is typically thought of as a risk management plan. The legal audit helps ensure the *legal health* of a recreation or sport program and should be done in conjunction with the risk management plan of the organization. The legal audit is typically broken down into a four-step process.

Content of the Legal Audit

A list of the areas that are appropriate to address for the particular organization must be identified. Such a list can sometimes be obtained through legal counsel or from an insurer, but will most likely have to be developed within the organization. The structure of the legal audit covers a number of different categories and will vary somewhat from one organization to another. The legal requirements of a private sport organization may be very different from those of a nonprofit entity. Since some of the categories may not be applicable in certain situations and the number will vary somewhat, it is necessary for the sport or recreation manager to select those that are appropriate for a given situation. Such a comprehensive list of pertinent information helps to create a profile from which one can determine the current and potential *legal health* problems of the entity and to address these problems before they reach crisis proportions. If produced internally, it can be very helpful to develop the audit with the help of legal counsel, financial advisors, insurance specialists, and/or a risk management consultant.

According to Grange and Oliver (1985), some categories that may be included in a legal audit are:

- General information regarding the entity
- Governance/authority of the entity
- Function and purposes of the entity
- Policies related to contracts
- Financial information
- Books and records
- Information regarding property/facilities
- Employee and labor relations
- Personnel policies and records
- Operational licenses
- Records supporting tax-exempt status
- Copyright and/or patent records
- Regulatory requirements
- Compliance with government regulations (e.g., Title IX, ADA)

Fried (1999) also provides a list of issues that should be considered for inclusion:

- Partnership agreements
- Corporate formation procedures
- Tax issues
- Advertising liability
- Contract negotiations and compliance
- First aid and OSHA regulations
- Selling food and licensing/permits
- Government relations
- Zoning issues
- Nuisance from noise
- Insurance
- Facility rental agreements
- Sponsorship contracts
- Employment issues
- Employer liability
- Dangerous facilities
- Liability for the acts of volunteers
- Product liability
- Criminal law
- Real estate issues
- Alcohol-related concerns
- Crowd management
- Copyright, trademark, and patent issues
- Property rights
- Spectator violence
- Drug testing

Selecting the Manager and Committee

Once the list has been established, a qualified staff person must be selected and assigned to manage the legal audit process. It is crucial that a person be selected who is sensitive to detail, who has the ability, and has the perceived authority to secure cooperation of other employees. The logical person may be the business manager if one exists in the organization. With smaller organizations, the athletic director or program administrator may be the best one to manage the process. Proper selection is key to a successful audit.

Once the manager has been chosen, a committee can then be selected to help carry out the audit. The members of the committee should represent the various major areas of the business operation. It is important to note that those selected for a legal audit committee are often different from those selected for a risk management committee.

It is also essential to obtain expert evaluation of the audit by legal, financial, and managerial counsel. For example, an attorney can examine the audit from a legal standpoint, a CPA can inspect it from a financial standpoint, and a manager or someone from upper administration can study it from an operational point of view. Large organizations may have the necessary experts available to help, but others may have to hire outside consultants at this point. Specific examples include bringing in a specialist to study an athletic department's compliance with Title IX, hiring an insurance expert to evaluate the organization's current insurance package, or having an attorney review hiring policies and contracts.

Conducting the Audit

When an appropriate committee has been selected, it is time to conduct the audit. Each committee member is selected to study the policies and procedures specific to his or her area of expertise. Often, two or more will share interest areas and should collaborate on their evaluation. The committee should then come together and discuss each part individually with input from all members. As agreement on one area is achieved, the committee addresses the next item in the audit. Eventually, the committee should come to agreement on all aspects of the audit and prepare recommendations to the upper administration.

Implementing the Audit

For the final step, upper administration should receive copies of the completed legal audit. Typically, those overseeing the organization must then decide whether to act on each recommendation. A careful review of the document will help to sensitize them to areas that require immediate attention as well as those requiring long-range consideration. The more support garnered from these administrators, the stronger and more effective the entire process will be. It is important to note that this is an ongoing process. The audit should be reviewed on a regular basis and it should never be assumed that, because it was done before, it is still adequate.

The legal audit is becoming an essential task of sport and recreation managers and has a direct impact on the legal and financial health of their organizations. Sport and recreation managers must become familiar with the details of legal audits and be able to develop and refine them in order to improve the organization's protection from litigation.

THE FACILITY AUDIT

A **facility audit** is a systematic method of identifying the hazards and risks related to a sport or recreation facility and determining the optimal method of treating each. A claim of unsafe facilities is one of the most common allegations made in lawsuits alleging negligence in recreation or sport programs. Addressing facility liability, Page (1988) called it one of the largest subcategories within the broad spectrum of tort law. When determining the conduct expected of a facility manager, courts have ruled that they be held to a standard of that of a reasonably prudent and careful facility manager. As specified in Section 2.31, *Premises Liability*, a facility operator has a general duty to exercise reasonable care for the safety of its patrons. That duty for ordinary care includes the obligation to:

- Inspect regularly for hazards or dangers;
- Properly maintain the premises and correct defects;
- Warn users, participants, and spectators about hazards or dangers that are not readily apparent;
- Warn users, participants, and spectators about the inherent risks of the sport or activity.

A facility audit helps to ensure that the above obligations are carried out. If someone is injured in a facility and initiates a lawsuit claiming that the injury was caused by a situation the facility manager should not have allowed to exist, the court will partially base its findings of liability on the concept of foreseeability. Was it foreseeable that the situation in question was likely to cause an injury? If the court determines that a reasonable, prudent facility manager would have recognized a potential danger and acted to reduce or eliminate the hazard and the defendant did not, the chances of being found liable for the injury are greatly enhanced. However, if it is determined that a reasonable, prudent facility manager probably would not have identified the situation as likely to cause an injury, the potential for liability is greatly reduced.

It is the legal obligation of facility managers and program directors to address or treat all foreseeable risks in one way or another in order to reduce each unreasonable risk as much as possible. According to Eickhoff-Shemek, Herbert, and Connaughton (2009, p. 289), "In general, facilities should be properly designed, equipped, and maintained in all program areas if liability is to be controlled at manageable levels. All areas should be regularly checked and kept free of defects and nuisances to minimize the chances of participant injury, illness, or death". Additionally, Wolohan states, (2006, p.116) "Establishing a system of inspection, including documenting the dates of inspection, any potential problem areas and all necessary corrective measures, also can help dramatically cut down on a facility's potential liability". The best method of performing the above obligations and ensuring facility safety is through the development of a facility risk audit. This audit consists of a systematic inspection for potential hazards and developing a procedure for dealing with the hazards identified. The facility risk audit is broken down into two major parts: (1) the inspection (comprehensive, periodic, or daily), and (2) risk treatment.

Inspections

Comprehensive Inspections

The **comprehensive inspection** is conducted by one or more staff members who walk throughout the facility trying to identify as many potential risks or hazards as possible. Typically, the larger the organization or facility, the more people will make up an inspection team. It is often advantageous to include inspectors who have different backgrounds or specialties. A maintenance person will look at the facility from a different point of view than will a coach or a security officer. Each will look at the facility from his/her own unique perspective and possibly identify different hazards. It is usually desirable and beneficial to have someone from outside the organization come in and inspect. Often, those who work in a facility become used to the environmental conditions they see every day and may not notice a hazard, whereas someone looking at it from a fresh point of view may spot it easily. It is often beneficial for two sport or recreation managers to trade off and inspect each other's facility. The more people that are designated to inspect for hazards, the less likely it is that significant hazards will be overlooked. Also, it can be beneficial to hire a professional risk management consultant to come in and assist in conducting the initial inspection and with the development of checklists for daily, periodic, and comprehensive inspections.

In addition to identifying hazardous conditions, other facility issues must be addressed as part of the facility audit. Issues that may expose the organization to legal threats other than lawsuits from injury should be identified and dealt with. Among these are access control, security, compliance with ADA, Title IX and OSHA regulations and proper signage regarding warnings and rules for facility usage.

The comprehensive inspection should include all areas inside (e.g., gyms, locker rooms, pools, hallways, lobbies, restrooms) and outside (e.g., playgrounds, fields, sidewalks, parking lots, fences) of the building(s) as well as other associated areas. Each inspector should independently tour the entire facility and make a list of potential hazards. The individual lists should then be compiled into one comprehensive list of potential hazards. This comprehensive list must then be prioritized. The priority list will establish the order in which the hazards will be treated. The more likely a hazard is to cause an injury and the more serious the potential injury, the higher the priority assigned to that hazard. Following completion of the priority list, each hazard must be considered and the best method of treating each determined (see Risk Treatment, below). It is important to understand that a thorough comprehensive inspection should occur on a regular basis (annually or more often if needed). In between these major inspections, periodic inspections should take place.

Periodic Inspections

After the comprehensive inspection is complete, an ongoing program of inspections should be implemented. In most facilities, it is appropriate to conduct **periodic inspections** on a daily, weekly, biweekly, and/or monthly basis, whatever is called for by the activities and usage of that particular facility. It is common practice to develop several different types of inspection checklists. It is often a good idea to develop checklists that can be used for **daily inspections**. Such an inspection should cover safety items that are likely to occur or change quickly such as checking for standing water or trash on a court, making sure doors are secure or looking for holes on a softball field. An example of the need for frequent inspections is illustrated in *Zipusch v. LA Workout, Inc.*, 2007 Cal. App. LEXIS 1652. Zipusch filed suit for personal injuries sustained when she was injured on a treadmill. She claimed her foot became stuck to a sticky substance on the treadmill, causing her to fall. As part of her claim, she alleged the club's failure to inspect and maintain the exercise equipment resulted in the sticky substance remaining on the treadmill. The Court of Appeal felt that a reasonable argument could be made that inspecting the premises was especially important and the case was remanded to the trial court for further proceedings.

Performing inspections on a less frequent basis, such as weekly or monthly, might include looking for hazards that are less likely to occur or that take time to develop. Examples may include inspections of bleachers for loose bolts, bent or broken supports, damaged footboards, or loose railings. Also, checking for frayed cables or worn pulleys on weight machines, proper functioning of treadmills and other cardio equipment, and inspecting basketball backboards and rims for loose bolts and padding are examples of hazards that may occur over time. When determining how often a particular inspection should occur, the courts will apply the reasonable and prudent standard. Inspections should occur as often as a reasonable and prudent professional would do in the same or similar circumstances. Facility managers should use their best professional judgment to determine the frequency of the periodic inspections. The more quickly a problem may occur or the greater the usage of the facility, the more often an inspection should be conducted.

In a spectator facility, however, it is often more appropriate to perform an inspection immediately **prior to each event**. The inspection in such a facility may focus on issues of spectator safety such as hazards that may cause a slip or trip and fall, the condition of seats and bleachers and emergency response equipment (e.g., fire extinguishers, alarms, and emergency lighting).

Developing the Checklists

Once the hazards identified through the comprehensive and periodic inspections have been identified, a checklist with which to perform periodic facility inspections on a regular, ongoing basis should be developed. This checklist should be designed for each facility and customized for that particular situation. It is all too common that sport and recreation managers will borrow a checklist from another facility, put their name and logo on it, and use it for their facility. This is not a safe or effective practice. Every facility and situation is unique. Therefore, every checklist should be customized for a given situation. It can be very helpful to study checklists from other facilities and borrow ideas from them, but it is essential that each item be suitable for the situation. It is also important to keep the checklist relatively straightforward and simple. If it is so long and complex that it becomes a major operation to perform, it probably won't be performed correctly, if at all. On the other hand, all items of importance must be included. All checklists should be modified as facility conditions and equipment change. It is important to ensure that checklists are appropriate, complete and up to date.

When developing a facility checklist, the following items should be included in order for it to be as effective as possible:

- Name of the organization
- Inspector's name (printed)
- Date of inspection
- Location of inspection (if needed)
- Inspector's signature
- Problems discovered

Figure 4.22.1 is an example of a daily checklist, while Figure 4.22.2 represents how a monthly checklist may appear. When writing the questions for the checklist, it can be very helpful to write them so that if each item is satisfactory, the *Yes* column will be checked (see Figures 4.22.1 and 4.22.2). This way it will be easy to look at each page of the list and see if any checks appear in the *No* column. If none exist, no problems were identified.

Risk Treatment

Once the potential hazards in the facility have been identified and prioritized, one or more **risk treatment** methods are utilized in order to eliminate each risk or at least make it as safe as possible. Section 4.11, *Risk Management Process*, provides a good description of treating risks after they have been identified. When treating physical hazards related to facilities or equipment, two methods are typically used:

1. **Risk Elimination.** Fix it so that it is no longer a problem.

2. **Risk Reduction.** If it cannot be eliminated, make it as safe as possible and identify other methods of treating the remaining hazard.

Deciding on the optimal method(s) of risk treatment will rely on the best professional judgment of the facility and risk managers and staff involved. As each hazard is dealt with, the next one on the list can then be addressed. This does not mean that items with a lower priority on the list must wait until the ones before have been treated. If an item cannot be treated immediately, it is important to not wait to go to the next hazard on the list and deal with it. Many situations can be quickly and easily treated and removed from the priority list while others may take some time.

With some hazards it will be obvious how to best remedy the situation. For example, if there is a hole in a soccer field, repair it and determine its source. If it was a one-time incident, the hazard has been eliminated and no more concern is necessary. If, however, the problem is likely to recur, as when the holes are caused by gophers, the cause should be remedied as soon as possible. If it will take some time before it can be fixed permanently, it may be necessary to compensate for it by warning participants of the hazard, using cones to block off the area, posting warning signs, or closing the area until repair is completed.

Daily Inspection Checklist

Inspector's Name _____ Kevin Finn _____ Date ___ 9/17/09 ___

Location of Inspection _____ Main Gym _____

Inspector's Signature _____

Instructions for Inspector:

1. Inspect and complete all items.

2. Include comments on all "NO" responses.

3. Fill-out and report problems on completion of inspection.

# Potential Hazard	YES	NO	COMMENTS
1. Floor clear of obstacles and debris	✓		
2. Floor clear of standing water	✓		
3. Floor swept, good traction	✓		
4. All standards, mats & goals properly stored	✓		
5. All other equipment properly stored	✓		
6. Gym rules clearly posted	✓		
7. Bleachers secure and in good repair	✓		
8. Warning sign on bleachers clearly visible	✓		
9. All lights undamaged and working		✓	Light over center court is out
10. Emergency procedures clearly posted	✓		
11. Emergency telephone accessible	✓		
12. Emergency phone numbers and directions to facility are posted by the phone	✓		
13. Rims unbroken, straight & in good shape	✓		
14. Backboards unbroken & in proper position	✓		
15. Wall pads in place	✓		
16. Access—Ingress and egress points opened or locked as appropriate		✓	N.E. outside door open
17. Supervisor present	✓		
18. No unsupervised children present	✓		
19. All of participants' equipment properly stored in hallway	✓		
20. Other	✓		

Figure 4.22.1. Joe Dailey Recreation Center

Monthly Inspection Checklist

Inspector's Name _____ Paul Edwards _____ Date ___ 9/3/09 ___

Location of Inspection _____ Weight Room _____

Inspector's Signature _____

Instructions for Inspector:

1. Inspect and complete all items.

2. Include comments on all "NO" responses.

3. Fill-out and report problems on completion of inspection.

# Potential Hazard	YES	NO	COMMENTS
1. Weight machines clean & lubricated	✓		
2. Cables, belts and pulleys undamaged	✓	✓	Belt on leg curl frayed
3. Benches, seats and back rests secure	✓		
4. Proper storage available for weights, bars	✓		
5. All other equipment properly stored	✓		
6. Weight room rules clearly posted	✓		
7. Instruction signs clearly visible		✓	Missing on overhead press
8. Warning signs clearly visible	✓		
9. Flooring flat and level			
10. Emergency procedures clearly posted	✓		
11. Emergency telephone accessible	✓		
12. Emergency phone numbers and directions to facility are posted by the phone	✓		
13. Emergency exits clearly marked	✓		
14. Electrical cords out of traffic flow	✓		
15. Cardio machines in good working order	✓		
16. Proper spacing between machines	✓		
17. Other	✓		

Figure 4.22.2. Joe Dailey Recreation Center

Another example of risk reduction is illustrated when the sideline of a basketball court is two feet from a concrete block wall, an obvious hazard that must be dealt with. It is probably not possible to completely eliminate the hazard by moving the wall out several more feet. One method to reduce the hazardous situation might be to use floor tape and create a new sideline a few feet inside the current one. It may also be appropriate to warn the participants of the situation and to pad the wall. For a permanent fix, the boundary lines may be moved away from the wall, thereby increasing the buffer zone. The baskets may also have to be moved to match the new lines. Making the basketball court smaller may seem like an extreme measure, but it is a totally appropriate way to reduce such a dangerous condition.

Again, for most facility hazards, completely eliminating the dangerous condition is the ideal method of risk treatment. However, when a hazard cannot be completely eliminated, sport and recreation managers must be creative and determine the optimal way to protect everyone involved.

Documentation

Documenting and saving everything that relates to organizational legal issues, safety, and risk management is essential to protecting the assets of the organization and is good management practice. If litigation occurs, the court will want to see evidence of what the organization or business has done to protect others from harm. An organized, thorough, consistent method of documenting all efforts to make a program safe and legally sound is an integral part of any risk management program, legal audit, or facility audit. In each of these, documenting all efforts provides good protection for the organization. Keeping good records is essential if one has to demonstrate in court that everything that could be reasonably expected had been done. The old adage, "If it wasn't written down, it didn't happen" is a great one to apply to such programs. It is important to keep copies of all aspects of the risk management plan as well as the factors addressed in the legal audit. Finally, all records should be stored in such a way that they are safe, secure, and easily retrievable. Digitally saving documents on CDs or DVDs is an excellent way to store large amounts of information. Multiple copies can then be stored in different locations to ensure availability in future years.

CONCLUSION

In order for a risk management program to be most effective, it must be valued by the organization. If the employees believe that the upper administration feels that the safety of all participants, spectators and staff is an important aspect of the culture of the organization, they are more likely to take their risk management responsibilities seriously. Administrators should communicate the need for and reward efforts toward making the facility as safe as it can be.

The need for recreation and sport managers to do risk management becomes increasingly clear every day. We have both a moral and legal obligation to do our best to both provide safe programs and to protect the assets of the organization. Along with the increased awareness of the necessity to provide risk management programs and legal audits has come a need for help in developing them. Sport and recreation managers often do not have the background and expertise required to develop a risk management plan that will keep injuries to a minimum and provide maximum protection against litigation. This has created an opportunity for those with such expertise to sell their services and help administrators devise appropriate plans, policies, and procedures. There are a number of risk management consultants that provide such a service in the recreation and sport fields and the number is increasing. Many risk management consultants have specialized knowledge in certain areas and have developed great expertise in their area. Examples of such areas include playgrounds, aquatics, strength and conditioning programs, crowd control, the use of waivers and outdoor adventure programs. Along with specialized knowledge in managing risk for recreation and sport businesses, opportunities are appearing for positions as professional risk managers. More and more, large organizations are recognizing the need to have a person who is knowledgeable in risk management on the staff. Large arenas and stadiums, school districts and city park and recreation departments are examples of entities that are now hiring professionals with these unique skills. Good risk management is now expected of all recreation and sport organizations.

QUESTIONS YOU SHOULD BE ABLE TO ANSWER

1. When discussing a risk management plan, what is meant by "layers of protection?"

2. What is the difference between a legal audit and a facility audit?

3. What duty and obligations do facility managers owe to patrons using their facilities?

4. Why is it important to document the things that are done for safety and risk management?

5. How do you determine how often a facility inspection should be performed?

REFERENCES

Cases

Burkart v. Health & Tennis Corporation of America, Inc., 1987 Tex. App. LEXIS 7544.

Flores v. 24 Hour Fitness, 2005 Cal. App. Unpub. LEXIS 207.

Range v. Abbott Sports Complex, 2005 Neb. LEXIS 36.

Zipusch v. LA Workout, Inc., 2007 Cal. App. LEXIS 1652.

Publications

Appenzeller, H. (1993). *Managing sports and risk management strategies.* Durham, NC: Carolina Academic Press.

Appenzeller, H. (2006). *Successful sport management.* Durham, NC: Carolina Academic Press.

Appenzeller, T. (2000) *Youth sport and the law.* Durham, NC: Carolina Academic Press.

Berg, R. (1994). Unsafe. *Athletic Business, 18(4),* 43–46.

Borkowski, R. P. (1997). Checking out checklists. *Athletic Management,* IX(1), 18.

Coalition of Americans to Protect Sports. (1998). *Sports injury risk management & the keys to safety.* North Palm Beach, FL: CAPS.

Cotten, D. J., & Wolohan, J. T. (2003). *Sport law for sport managers.* Dubuque, IA: Kendall/Hunt Publishing Co.

Dougherty, N. J. (1993). *Principles of safety in physical education and sport.* Reston, VA: National Assn. for Sport and Physical Education.

Dougherty, N., & Seidler, T. (2007). Viewpoints: Injuries in the buffer zone: A serious risk management problem. *Journal of Physical Education Recreation and Dance, 78(2),* 4–7.

Eickhoff-Shemek, J., Herbert, D., & Connaughton, D. (2009). Risk Management for Health/Fitness Professionals. Philadelphia, PA: Lippincott, Williams & Wilkins.

Fried, G. B. (1999). *Safe at first.* Durham, NC: Carolina Academic Press.

Grange, G. R., & Oliver, N. S. (1985). Head off trouble with a legal audit. *Association Management.* Nov. 103 B 104.

Hart, J. E., & Ritson, R. J. (2003). *Liability and safety in physical education and sport.* Reston, VA: National Assn. for Sport and Physical Education.

Jewell, D. (1992). *Public assembly facilities* (2nd ed.). Malabar, FL: Krieger Publishing Co.

Kaiser, R., & Robinson, K. (1999). Risk management. In B. van der Smissen, M. Moiseichik, V. Hartenburg, and L. Twardgik (Eds.), *Management of park and recreation agencies* (pp. 713–741). Ashuba, VA: NRPA.

Maloy, B. P. (1993). Legal obligations related to facilities. *Journal of Physical Education, Recreation, and Dance, 64*(2), 28–30, 68.

Page, J. A. (1988). *The law of premises liability*. Cincinnati: Anderson Publishing Co.

Schuler, R. S., & Jackson, S. E. (1996). *Human resource management: Positioning for 21st century*. Minneaplois/St. Paul: West Publishing Co.

Seidler, T. (2006). Planning and designing safe facilities. *Journal of Physical Education Recreation and Dance, 77*(5), 32–37, 44.

Seidler, T. L. (2005). Conducting a facility risk review. In H. Appenzeller (Ed.), *Risk management in sport: Issues and strategies*. Durham, NC: Carolina Academic Press.

Seidler, T. L. (2005). Planning facilities for safety and risk management. In Sawyer, T. (Ed.), *Facility design and management for health, fitness, physical activity, recreation and sports facility development.* (pp. 129–136). AAHPERD. Dubuque, IA: Kendall/Hunt.

van der Smissen, B. (1990). *Liability and risk management for public and private enterprises*. Cincinnati, OH: Anderson Publishing Co.

van der Smissen, B. (1996). Tort liability and risk management. In B. L. Parkhouse (Ed.), *The management of sport: Its foundations and applications* (pp. 164–183). St. Louis, MO: Mosby.

Wolohan, J. (2006). Tour of duties. *Athletic Business, 30*(11), 110–116.

4.23 Crisis Management

—Daniel Connaughton
UNIVERSITY OF FLORIDA

—Thomas A. Baker, III
UNIVERSITY OF GEORGIA

How important is crisis management to the recreation or sport manager? Contrast two situations in which a crisis was reasonably foreseeable—the 1993 University of Wisconsin/Michigan football game, where it was announced in the school paper that the students would charge the field after a Wisconsin victory, and the June, 2000, Atlanta Braves/New York Mets baseball game that was John Rocker's first trip to New York after controversial remarks in a *Sports Illustrated* article. In each situation, there was the potential for a crisis and the likelihood of serious injury. In the University of Wisconsin situation, newspapers reported that University management increased uniformed security from about 55 to about 65 officers. The increase proved inadequate, resulting in more than 60 injuries. In contrast, the Mets and New York City increased the number of assigned officers from 60 to 560 (plus an unnamed number of plainclothes officers in the stands), the Mets placed a limit of two on the number of beers that could be purchased at one time, and the Mets constructed a chain-link fence to protect Rocker in the bullpen. As a result of the crisis management measures taken, there were no serious incidents, and consequently, the crisis was averted.

The potential for many crisis situations regularly confronts the recreation or sport manager. The athletic director learns that one of his athletes just committed suicide. A fire breaks out in the gymnasium. A set of bleachers collapses injuring dozens of spectators. An employee or athlete is arrested and charged with a crime. Each of these situations constitutes a crisis situation. What should staff members do in a crisis situation? A common mistake that many sport or recreation managers make is thinking that they and their staff will automatically know what to do in the event of a crisis. However, in many crisis situations, there is no plan, and the staff does not know how to properly, quickly, and calmly react. According to a survey of intercollegiate athletic administrators, 93 percent of National Collegiate Athletic Association (NCAA) athletic departments experienced a crisis within the period studied (1999–2000), yet fewer than half of the respondents had written plans in place to deal with the crisis. Furthermore, only 22 percent of the athletic directors reported that they provided any crisis management training to their staffs (Syme, 2005). Having an established crisis philosophy and **Crisis Management Plan (CMP)** will prepare an organization in the event of an actual crisis. A comprehensive CMP will address major crisis risks, ranging from fires, bleacher collapses, bomb threats, criminal activity, violent acts, litigation against the organization, and major power outages to environmental emergencies such as hurricanes and floods.

On a daily basis, numerous problems, incidents, and issues confront the recreation or sport manager. A serious medical emergency arises when a serious illness or injury occurs involving a participant, spectator, or staff member. Although such situations are important and may involve the utilization of an emergency medical plan, they typically do not constitute a crisis—unless they are improperly handled. Regular incidents require organizational resources to respond, but they are usually readily manageable, and normal business can still take place while the incident is dealt with. Nevertheless, these types of incidents can quickly escalate into crises if they are not brought under control, if there is significant media coverage, and/or if several resources are required from within, or from outside, the organization. Herman and Oliver (2001) defined a crisis as a sudden situation that threatens an organization's ability to survive: an emergency, a disaster, a catastrophe. A crisis may involve a death or injury, lost access to the use of facilities and/or equipment, disrupted or significantly diminished operations, unprecedented information demands, intense media scrutiny, and irreparable damage to an agency's reputation (p. 6). A crisis situation is generally an unforeseen situation that can be extensive in its scope of disruption and damages to the organization. Although a crisis may strike without warning, others may build over time. For example, the sudden accidental death of an athlete or employee may catch everyone in the organization by surprise. In other cases, the actions, or inactions, of key personnel may cause a crisis to come about slowly. In both examples, staff may claim they "never saw it coming." A crisis may result in extensive organizational damage that typically cannot be corrected very easily or quickly. Crises often threaten the organization's mission and reputation and can have an adverse effect on business, fund-raising, and overall public relations. Outside assistance is often necessary. The organization may even need to be closed for a period of time to reestablish services and repair damage.

In summary, crises have common characteristics. First, they are negative. Second, a crisis can create improper or distorted perceptions. Third, crises are almost always disruptive to the organization. Finally, a crisis typically takes the organization by surprise, and the organization is placed in a reactive mode. Therefore, having a crisis management plan is particularly important for smaller organizations because they often have fewer resources to draw from when a crisis erupts. The purpose of this section is to assist the recreation or sport manager in becoming more informed about crisis planning and management.

FUNDAMENTAL CONCEPTS

Crisis management, a subset of risk management, focuses on allowing the organization to achieve its mission under extraordinary circumstances. The primary goal of managing a crisis is public safety. Not addressing public safety can intensify the damage from a crisis (Coombs, 2007). Secondary goals are to prevent the crisis from damaging the organization's (1) ability to achieve its mission and goals, (2) reputation, and/or (3) finances. **Crisis management** is a process intended to prevent or reduce the damage a crisis can cause to an organization and its stakeholders (Coombs, 2007). Having a crisis management plan in place is critical because it facilitates the establishment of a unified organizational philosophy, thereby eliminating the need to decide how to respond and what to do during a crisis situation (Ajango, 2003).

CRISIS MANAGEMENT PLAN

Every organization is at risk of facing a crisis. How and where a crisis occurs can seldom be controlled. What can be controlled is how an organization prepares, reacts, and responds. A key determinant of how well an organization will cope in the midst of a crisis is how well it addressed its crisis management plan (CMP) before the actual crisis occurs. The steps an organization takes months, or even years, prior to a crisis occurring may be as important as its immediate response to a crisis.

The primary goal of planning for crises is to develop comprehensive, written contingency plans based on currently existing resources and operational capabilities that will enable the organization to effectively deal with crises. CMPs cannot be copied from a book or from plans developed by other organizations, but rather must be specifically developed for each and every program. Every program has unique factors that must be considered. However, several basic components should form the foundation of CMPs.

A piece that is commonly missing or overlooked when developing CMPs lies in the relationship between the overall CMP and the organization's core values. Whether an organization wants to set, and present, a tone of open communication, care, and concern or one of quiet toughness, the long-term strategy will be a reflection of the organization's values. If employees at all levels do not agree with, or are not aware of, the philosophy behind the CMP, there is a high probability that the plan will not proceed smoothly once it is put into action. Perhaps one of the worst possible things that can happen to an organization undergoing a crisis is for an unexpected lack of agreement on core philosophies to surface. To avoid this pitfall, an organization should prioritize its intent and objectives regarding its CMP. There should be a stated purpose behind the plan, specifically as it relates to the organization's mission and philosophy. Well before crisis occurs, CMP decision makers should freely discuss how a post accident investigation would be conducted. Various opinions should be carefully considered. Several other questions should also be carefully considered prior to developing a CMP. Are the needs of a victim(s) a priority? Are employees' opinions secondary? Will legal ramifications drive the plan, or is public reputation more of a concern? It is important to discuss these issues and identify the organization's philosophy and goals prior to the onset of a crisis (Ajango, 2003).

Developing the Plan

The initial step in developing and writing a CMP is to **formulate a planning committee** who will begin the process. Awareness is the initial step to preparedness, and a crucial step in crisis planning is identification. Once the organization's philosophy and goals as they relate to managing a crisis are identified, the committee's primary task is to **identify the significant possible risks and crises** that may arise in their organization. The committee should scrutinize the core functions of the organization to identify and, in many cases, reduce or eliminate risks that could cast the organization into crisis mode. Examples of such crises may include an incident or event that would potentially result in serious injury or death, result in litigation, deter customers or otherwise impair income, impair the organization's ability to meet its core operating expenses, render the organization unable to deliver core services, or garner negative publicity and/or media attention resulting in the death of the organization.

Crisis risks can be categorized into avoidable (preventable) and unavoidable (unpreventable). Avoidable crisis risks may include actual or alleged client/participant maltreatment, service or product failure, severe injuries or death, transportation-related mishaps, and criminal conduct. Unavoidable crisis risks may include natural disasters (hurricanes, tornadoes, floods, wildfires, etc.), bomb threats, hazardous material incidents, terrorist attacks, and utility failures (Herman & Oliver, 2001). Although an organization may not be able to prevent these events from occurring, they can identify which ones are inherent to their area and are more likely to strike and then take steps to be as prepared as practically and reasonably possible to cope with the events if they occur.

Once crisis risks are identified, similar to a risk assessment, a crisis assessment is performed. However, instead of broadly focusing on any potential risk, a crisis assessment highlights the risks that would put the organization into crisis mode. Therefore, situations that could severely jeopardize the organization's credibility and/or resources should be the focus. Similar to classifying risks (see Section 4.11, *Risk Management Process*), potential crises should be individually assigned frequency and severity ratings. A frequency rating estimates how often this crisis may occur. A severity rating is based on how damaging to the organization the crisis would be if it does occur. Looking at the two ratings, an organization can determine its greatest risks (see Table 4.11.1, *Risk Category Matrix*, in Section 4.11, *Risk Management Process*).

The next step is to develop an action plan for crisis response for each major crisis risk that may confront the organization. An action plan is a document that details carefully considered courses of action. These alternatives can be selected when a crisis occurs.

When developing such plans, identify all resources that may be needed in each crisis situation. Consider resources in the immediate area. Contact the local/state offices of the Federal Emergency Management Agency (FEMA), U.S. Department of Education, American Red Cross, local hospital, police and fire departments, and emergency medical services. Determine how they respond to crisis and how they may be able to assist your organization (Schirick, 2002).

Developing an action plan answers the crucial question: "What will we do if a crisis occurs?" In some cases, aspects of an organization's action plans may be identical, regardless of the cause, or source, of the crisis. For instance, a uniform step in an action plan may be contacting an insurance broker. In other cases, specific crises may require unique, specific responses. A beginning point for formulating action plans is to revisit the major crisis risks initially identified. The following sections present several components that should be considered as general guidelines when developing action plans.

Personnel Issues. There are two phases to personnel preparation. The first involves actions to be taken by the frontline leader (the person(s) in charge of the activity when the crisis occurs). Personnel should be educated on what immediate steps to follow (e.g., calling 911, activating the CMP). The second phase of personnel preparation involves subsequent actions to take in the crisis situation. The action plan should identify, by job title, those employees who will handle, or actively assist with, the crisis. Specific duties and responsibilities of each responder should be outlined in a simple and very clear format. The action plan should account for personnel trained to render emergency care, communication procedures, an incident reporting system, and a follow-up approach. In addition, personnel should know how to address the ongoing cause of the crisis (e.g., a gunman, terrorist, fire). They should know whom to contact for assistance (see Section 2.33, *Emergency Care*).

When developing the action plan and addressing the preceding components, input from various organizational levels and other affected agencies should be solicited. Both managerial and frontline staff should be consulted as well as athletes/participants and outside agencies, including groups such as local EMS, fire and police departments, legal counsel, crisis planning and management consultants, and the organization's insurance company.

Facility Issues. The location of emergency exits and shelters; gas, power, and water shutoff valves; alarm systems; backup power systems; main electrical panels; and fire hoses/extinguishers should be clearly identified. Location(s) for meeting EMS and other authorities (e.g., police, fire, and utility personnel) should be identified. Evacuation procedures should also be developed.

Emergency Equipment Issues. Identify the type of equipment available (e.g., public address and communication equipment, firefighting equipment, first aid kits, automated external defibrillators). Identify where each is stored and who will access it.

Communication Issues. Two major aspects of effective communication are necessary. The first involves the immediate notification of the proper authorities (e.g., police, medical personnel, mental health personnel). Designate who makes such calls and in what order. It is important to identify and get to know outside experts who will work side by side with your organization in a crisis. During a crisis is not the time to meet these key people. Train staff as to where and how to make emergency communications. The location of telephones and other communication devices should be specified, and emergency phone numbers should be identified.

The second aspect of effective communications involves the need to quickly communicate with constituencies. For example, an athletic director may need to communicate with EMS, law enforcement, victims and their families, parents of athletes, school officials and other employees, professionals who can provide crisis counseling and other support, news media, and possibly others following a riot incident at a sporting event. Before the crisis occurs the following should be considered.

- Who will need to be contacted in the event of a crisis?

- What is the best method to communicate? (Consider telephone, broadcast fax, news conference, public address system, intercom, pagers, etc.)

- What backup system is available if the primary means of communication is compromised?

- Is the list of personnel that would need to be contacted readily available to more than one staff member?

- Who is responsible for making the communication—one person or a group of people? (Herman & Oliver, 2001)?

A crucial factor is communication with the **news media**. It is often the adverse publicity, rather than the actual damage from the crisis itself, that severely damages the organization. Therefore, a preassigned, trained spokesperson should contact the media at the earliest possible time. When speaking to these parties, the spokesperson should stick to the basic facts (e.g., type of crisis, which medical facility the victim was transported to, number of victims) and never assign or admit fault. The medical staff that provide care should only furnish medical or fatality information. Questions regarding insurance should be answered by the insurance agent/company. Finally, questions regarding liability should be addressed by the organization's risk management department or legal counsel. The staff should also be instructed not to speak to anyone regarding the incident unless approval has been obtained from the designated spokesperson. All requests for information should be immediately directed to the designated spokesperson. (For more on dealing with the media, see the following section.)

Documentation. Determine when and who completes what reports. Assigned personnel should know how to complete them and to whom they should be sent. Establish policies for filing and retaining reports.

Follow-up Procedures. There are several aspects to the follow-up procedures. First, it is necessary for the media spokesperson to follow up with the media. Depending on the crisis and its impact, there may need to be a follow-up with the victims, their families, classmates, colleagues, teammates, and/or friends, as well as with employees. Finally, it is important that the CMP be evaluated and modified where necessary.

DEVELOPING A CRISIS MANAGEMENT MANUAL

An organization's **crisis management manual** should address the most likely crises it may face and suggest methods for handling those crises. The manual serves as a checklist of what to do when and whom to contact. Herman and Oliver (2001) suggest keeping the format simple and easy to read, using short sentences and bulleted phrases, using flowcharts to indicate responsibilities and actions, including boxes that can be checked when the task is completed, and using tabs for quick access.

Forming a Crisis Response Team

A small team should be formed to coordinate an organization's response to a crisis. This team needs to be formed and trained *before* a crisis occurs. Proper training will allow the team to react more calmly, effectively, and efficiently. The makeup of the crisis response team will vary depending on a number of factors, including the size of the organization, the nature of the services provided by the organization, the likely sources of crisis in the organization, and the organization's prior experience responding to a crisis. The makeup of the team may include the executive director, department heads, senior staff members, physical plant/building superintendent, board members, legal counsel, and outside advisors.

Practicing the Plan

Although responses to certain crises cannot be easily rehearsed, others can be simulated, practiced, or simply discussed to enhance readiness for an actual crisis and to identify any flaws in the action plans. When feasible, the plan should be tested in conditions as close to real life as possible. When flaws are noticed, the plans should be modified accordingly. Every time an organization conducts a CMP drill, key personnel involved should do a brief review of the exercise. Documentation of the review should be maintained by the organization. In between major drills, in-service training and tabletop exercises keep the strategies and process fresh in the minds of staff (Herman & Oliver, 2001; James, 2008).

Surviving a Crisis

The first step in addressing a crisis is to recognize and acknowledge it may be occurring. Oftentimes, individuals in organizations have different perceptions of when a crisis is at hand. It is important to recognize the signs of a crisis so the CMP has the best chance of working effectively.

Activating the Plan

Once a crisis has been recognized, the plan should be followed. According to Herman and Oliver (2001), the team leader should contact the crisis response team and attempt to answer the following questions.

- What has occurred?

- Who has been affected by the events thus far? Who are the known victims?

- What steps have been taken to control the crisis? Who has done what?

- Is the media aware of the crisis? Are we prepared to give a statement?

The crisis response team should discuss and carefully decide what steps need to be taken to:

- Provide and/or arrange care or support for the victims;

- Notify key personnel;

- Respond to media inquiries;
- Brief the staff and key constituents of the organization;
- Ensure continued service delivery or coordinate transfer to another provider;
- Secure important documents, files, computer backups, etc.;
- Ensure that the communication systems are up and operating.

Proper Crisis Communication

One of the most important aspects of handling a crisis is communication. How an organization communicates with key constituents, responds to inquiries and criticisms, handles the media, and tells its story may very well determine its survival. A failed communications strategy can be disastrous for any organization. All communication during a crisis should be carefully considered and orchestrated. Whether it is directed to an internal or external audience and whether it is written, visual, or verbal, extra care should be taken when crafting messages. Seymour and Moore (2000) recommended applying the "Five Cs" to crisis communication.

1. **Care.** The public is often very reluctant to forgive a lack of compassion from an organization whose programs or services caused harm. An effective spokesperson is one who can express empathy and care with conviction and sincerity.

2. **Commitment.** The organization's message should clearly indicate that it is committed to investigating the incident and preventing future occurrences.

3. **Consistency.** A clear plan of how the organization will respond and what its spokesperson will say ensures a consistent message.

4. **Coherence.** It is important to be clear, be concise, and stick to the facts.

5. **Clarity.** Because the opportunity to convey a message may be slim and come without warning, it is vital to avoid jargon, technical terms, and other language that may confuse the listener.

Dealing with the News Media

Organizations should educate designated spokespersons who will work with the news media during a crisis situation. This aspect of the CMP should address the following details.

- Who decides what information is released?
- Who speaks for the organization/releases materials to media? Typically one spokesperson should be designated. A central spokesperson provides a singular face for the media that the public begins to become familiar with. Centralized information also minimizes miscommunication. Backup spokespeople should be designated in the event that the central spokesperson is unavailable or is the subject of the crisis.
- Which members of the news media should be notified in a crisis?
- What are the phone numbers of key media people?
- What are the logistical details including locations where press conferences can be held; phone lines that media can use to call in; backup power supplies; parking area for the media; and what support staff is available to assist.

At the first sign of a potential crisis involving an organization, whether before or after exposure in the news media, preparations for a timely, accurate, and appropriate response must begin. News media will expect and demand an immediate response. If the organization does not provide an immediate response, others will. Others may provide inaccurate information, or may try to use the opportunity to attack the organization. Therefore, crisis managers must have a timely response (Coombs, 2007). A decision on whether a news conference and/or release would be an appropriate means of conveying information to the news media and public must be made. What means of internal communication will be used if the crisis affects employees and participants should also be determined. At the earliest possible stage, advise staff members of the situation. Give clear instructions regarding handling the media and telephone calls and alert them that they may be called to perform special duties related to the incident. Discuss alternative or additional means of conveying information. This might include such items as letters to parents, clients, or fans, letters to newspaper editors, or consultation with boards. Use of the Internet and websites can also help to provide a quick response.

Information files should be set up to contain all materials related to the incident. Internet, newspapers and television reports should be scanned daily for related stories. If necessary, arrange for videotaping of any TV coverage. Related material, including clippings, statements, memos, and any other documents should be filed in chronological order. Plan to frequently update employees and administrators on the status of the incident. Conduct a follow-up assessment to determine what did and did not work, and what changes might be made in the future for improved media relations during a crisis.

Guidelines for the Media Contact Person

Several strategies exist that will make dealing with the media as positive as possible. In any crisis, try to find out as much information as possible. That way, you avoid inadvertently saying the wrong thing or sending unintended messages.

The following are seventeen guidelines for dealing with the media:

- Always return media calls, even if they call repeatedly and/or are hostile. Ignoring them will not make the problem disappear. The more cooperative you appear, the better;

- Occasionally, a media representative will make a special request. If possible and if it does not violate the CMP, an effort should be made to accommodate reasonable requests;

- Avoid antagonizing media representatives. A sharp tone at a press conference, during a telephone call, or elsewhere may affect your relationship with that individual and with others who may hear the conversation;

- Try to remain levelheaded at all times when speaking to the media. Some of their questions may seem hostile or may seem like a personal attack. It must be remembered that they are trying to get as much information as possible on a crisis-oriented story that may have widespread impact to their audiences;

- Refrain from getting mad or taking it personally when asked tough questions;

- Always try to have an answer for reporters' questions and always tell the truth. However, never be afraid to say, "I don't know, but I'll find out";

- Avoid using "no comment." Doing so often makes it appear that you have something to hide;

- Additionally, stay "on the record" in all interviews. Any comment worth stating should be said "on the record." If you go "off the record," be prepared to hear or read it. Although it is unethical for reporters to report "off the record" comments, anything can, may, and will be done to advance a story;

- Consider how information you release may affect others. If things you say will result in the media calling other organizations or individuals, call those individuals first to alert them to the information;

- When speaking to the media, be sure to credit other agencies or individuals assisting with the crisis, including your staff. This enhances relationships and reflects well on you;

- Try to be proactive with new information. If you acquire new information regarding the crisis advise the media;

- When communicating with the media and/or the public, accurate information is important. People desire correct information about what occurred and how it may affect them. Due to the time pressure associated with a crisis response, there is a risk of providing inaccurate information. Incorrect statements can make an organization appear incompetent and/or inconsistent (Coombs, 2007). Admit when a mistake has been made and correct it as soon as possible. This is often the first step to reestablishing confidence and credibility with the public and key constituencies;

- Maintaining a sense of humor is important, but inappropriate humor will work against you;

- Professional dignity is very important, particularly in unpleasant times;

- As the crisis progresses, take notes. They can help you remember things and may be useful for later review;

- If you are on camera, always dress professionally. Casual or mussed clothing may send a signal to viewers that things are out of control;

- Try to give yourself some downtime and stress reduction. Overwork and little sleep can lead to misstatements and irritability.

Debrief Employees and Others Affected

When a crisis results in serious injuries or death(s), stress and trauma counseling for employees and other victims must be made available (Coombs, 2007). Even when victims survive, there may still be emotions to deal with, particularly for first responders. There may be feelings of guilt; others may recall their initial reaction, panic, or response. Some may wonder if they could have done more (James, 2008).

Critical Incident Stress Management (CISM) is a specific seven-stage group crisis intervention technique that has been adapted and used by rescue, disaster, and health-care groups in different settings, programs, and industries (Everly & Mitchell, 1999). This technique is designed to bring "psychological closure" to groups of victims or witnesses after a traumatic event and ideally is implemented 24 hours after the end of someone's involvement with the event. A professional needs to facilitate the process where each participant describes the event that occurred, their reaction to the event and its psychological impact, and then learns how to manage the related stress (Herman & Oliver, 2001).

Have plans for dealing with emotional and mental health needs of staff, classmates, teammates, or friends and family of the victim(s) (Bacon & Anderson, 2003). Have procedures for communicating with the immediate families of all victims. Some organizations may have psychologists or mental health professionals available for the victims and/or their families, whereas others may refer affected individuals to available, trained professionals. Prior relationships with such trained professionals can be very helpful in these situations.

Evaluate the Response

Once the crisis is over, an evaluation should occur in a timely fashion.

- First, consider and review why the crisis occurred. What, if anything, could have been done to prevent or limit the crisis?

- Next, *how soon was the crisis noticed and how was it handled* should be evaluated. What was done appropriately or inappropriately should be addressed.

- Were others who were involved or affected timely informed?

- How effective was the crisis response team? Were certain skills or talents missing in the makeup of the team?

- How was the action plan followed? Was it effective and useful? What could have been done better?

- Also, *similar scenarios* should be examined. For example, what would you do in a similar situation in the future?

- Does the plan need to be changed? If so, how? Revising CMPs is an ongoing process.

- Finally, *send notes of appreciation* to those who have been of service, outside and inside the organization, including your own staff.

USEFUL WEBSITES FOR CRISIS MANAGEMENT INFORMATION AND MATERIALS

The *Nonprofit Risk Management Center* has a significant number of references (resources, articles, tutorials, tests, fact sheets, links, etc.) available regarding risk and crisis management. Their website is located at: www.nonprofitrisk.org/

The *U.S. Department of Education* provides many crisis management-related educational materials including but not limited to: Crisis Planning Guide, Practical Information on Crisis Planning, Action Guide for Emergency Management at Institutions of Higher Education, and Tips for Helping Students Recovering from Traumatic Events. Their website is located at: http://www.ed.gov/admins/lead/safety/emergencyplan/index .html

The *International Association of Assembly Managers* (IAAM) provides information, training, and certification on several crisis management issues including but not limited to: crowd management, and venue safety and security. Their website is located at: http://iaam.org/

The *Federal Emergency Management Agency* (FEMA) provides information and training on disasters, planning for emergencies, and risk management. Their website is located at: http://www.fema.gov/

In the Significant Case that follows, the defendants had a CMP that proved to be inadequate. Despite knowing in advance that the students planned to charge the field following a victory, insufficient precautions were taken to prevent the students from charging the field. More than 60 injuries resulted. Newspaper reports revealed that many University officials made potentially damaging statements to the press following the crisis. One official, in an attempt to make the necessary corrections to avoid a duplicate disaster, stated, "We can't ignore any possibility about what could be done to prevent this. We have to sit down and find some answers." Problems that were investigated included overcrowding in the student section, duplicate tickets, students moving from their seats in other sections of the stadium to the student section, use of alcohol inside the stadium, whether students should be assigned to seats instead of general admission, and whether the entire student section should be moved or dispersed (Schultz, 1993). *Despite the failure of the crisis management plan to prevent the disaster, no defendant was found liable for his or her actions or inactions due to governmental immunity.*

ENEMAN V. RICHTER

COURT OF APPEALS OF WISCONSIN, DISTRICT FOUR
217 Wis. 2d 288; 577 N.W.2d 386
February 5, 1998, Released

Opinion: Roggensack, J.

The appellants alleged they suffered personal injuries after a University of Wisconsin football game at Camp Randall Stadium, which injuries they claim resulted from the negligence of David Ward, Patrick Richter, Susan Riseling, Michael Green and David Williams, while the respondents were employed by the State on behalf of the University of Wisconsin. Respondents moved for summary judgment, based on the common law doctrine of public officer immunity. The circuit court concluded there were no material factual disputes and dismissed the appellants' claims. Because we agree that the material facts are not in dispute and that the respondents are entitled to immunity, we affirm.

* * *

BACKGROUND

This is a consolidated appeal of summary judgments dismissing the claims of the appellants, all of whom are alleged to have suffered personal injuries when they were crushed by persons attempting to come onto the playing field at Camp Randall Stadium after the 1993 Wisconsin/ Michigan football game. They assert their injuries would not have occurred if certain gates had not been closed by security personnel at the conclusion of the game and that the closing of the gates constituted negligence. David Ward, Chancellor for the University of Wisconsin-Madison; Patrick Richter, Athletic Director for the University of Wisconsin-Madison; Susan Riseling, Chief of Police and Security for the University of Wisconsin-Madison; Michael Green, Camp

Randall Facilities and Events Coordinator; and David Williams, a University police officer in Riseling's department, were state governmental employees on the date of the appellants' alleged injuries. They filed an answer denying negligence, and based on their status as state governmental employees, they asserted the affirmative defense of discretionary immunity, on which they moved for summary judgment.

Camp Randall Stadium is the site used for football games and other outdoor events at the University of Wisconsin-Madison. The football field is encircled by a chain link fence with a walkway between the fence and the bottom row of bleachers. Ingress and egress of the bleachers varies, depending on the section of the stadium. Sections O and P are at issue in this lawsuit. The lower rows of sections O and P exit to the walkway and then through the home team tunnel. It was also possible for those rows to exit to the field itself, even though security personnel directed spectators not to do so.

Prior to the 1993 football season, access to the field was limited by hand held ropes, which provided no real barrier to a spectator determined to enter the field. In anticipation of the 1993 football season, the University installed metal gates that could be positioned to close off the walkway at the bottom of the bleachers in order to permit the team to exit the field into the tunnel without interference from the spectators. When the walkway was closed off by the gates, sections O and P spectators' means of egress was restricted, until the team had made its way through the tunnel and the gates were opened again.

On October 30, 1993, after the University of Wisconsin's football team defeated the University of Michigan's team at Camp Randall, many of the students in sections O and P attempted to come onto the playing field. However, a few minutes before the game's end, the gates had been closed and latched by security personal. This provided a significant barrier to the spectators' egress onto the field, and it also created a dead end for tunnel egress from sections O and P, at a time when spectators were moving down the bleachers to exit the stadium or to push onto the field. The appellants were crushed against a metal railing and the gates when security personnel were unable to quickly unlatch the gates to open them.

Ward and Richter had no personal responsibility to manage the crowd at the Camp Randall games. On the other hand, Riseling's, Green's and Williams's activities at Camp Randall were arguably within the scope of the Standard Operating Procedures for Camp Randall relating to crowd control. Additionally, prior to the Michigan game, and subsequent to the installation of the gates, Riseling knew that it was possible that the students might try to rush onto the field at the game's end. In response to this potential for congestion in the student sections, she formulated and issued a directive entitled, "POST GAME CROWD TACTICS," whose goal was "to prevent injury to people—officers, band members and fans." The plan outlined a general strategy to follow which, in her judgment, would have prevented injury. Although her plan was implemented by security personnel, it was not successful.

DISCUSSION

* * *It is well established that this court applies the same summary judgment methodology as the circuit court. *Smith v. Dodgeville Mut. Ins. Co.*, 212 Wis. 2d 226, 232, 568 N.W.2d 31, 34 (Ct. App. 1997). We first examine the complaint to determine whether it states a claim, and then we review the answer to determine whether it presents a material issue of fact or law. *Id.* If we conclude that the complaint and the answer are sufficient to join issue, we examine the moving party's affidavits to determine whether they establish a prima facie case for summary judgment. *Id.* If they do, we look to the opposing party's affidavits to determine whether there are any material facts in dispute which entitle the opposing party to a trial. *Id.* at 233, 568 N.W.2d at 34.

Whether immunity lies because of the common law doctrine of public officer immunity is a question of law which we review de novo. *Kimps v. Hill*, 200 Wis. 2d 1, 8, 546 N.W.2d 151, 155 (1996) (citing *K.L. v. Hinickle*, 144 Wis. 2d 102, 109, 423 N.W.2d 528, 531 (1988)). A question of law is also presented when we decide whether the safe place statute applies to this case. *Ruppa v. American States Ins. Co.*, 91 Wis. 2d 628, 639, 284 N.W.2d 318, 322 (1979).

Public Officer Immunity.

* * *

Based on the information before us, we assume, without deciding, that there was a compelling and known danger of injury of sufficient magnitude to create a ministerial duty to act for Riseling, as Chief of Police and Security, due to her knowledge of the possibility of a crowd surge onto the field. However, Riseling did not ignore the potential danger. She, with the assistance of others, formulated a plan, the "POST GAME CROWD TACTICS," the goal of which was "to prevent injury to people—officers, band members and fans."

The plan established no specific tasks that were to be performed at a time certain; rather, it made general statements and set general guidelines such as,

We expect that if Wisconsin wins today, especially if it is a close game, there will be an attempt by fans to come onto the field.

> If there is a crowd surge, officers at that point will make the initial decision to move aside and begin pulling back to the goalpost assignment. Lt. Johnson will be observing from the press box and will make decisions on giving the command for all officers to pull back.

There may be times during and after the game when people crowd the fence and put pressure against it. Actively encourage them to move back. If it seems there is danger of the fence breaking (it has in the past) move back to a safe position. * * * Here, the formation of the post-game crowd control plan represented Riseling's judgment about how best to reduce the potential for injury to persons at the game. "A discretionary act is one that involves choice or judgment." *Kimps*, 200 Wis. 2d at 23, 546 N.W.2d at 161 (citation omitted). Additionally, the implementation of the plan required Riseling, Green and Williams to respond to their assessment of what the crowd's actions required. By its very nature, the way the plan was effected had to change from moment to moment because the plan was responsive to the crowd. Reacting to the crowd also constituted the exercise of discretion. Furthermore, neither the documents nor the testimony contained in any of the portions of the depositions submitted in opposition to respondents' motion for summary judgment established a factual dispute about whether any specific acts were required of any of the respondents. Therefore, we conclude that the decision about what type of a plan to formulate to safely manage the crowd, as well as the implementation of the chosen plan, were discretionary, not ministerial, acts.

4. Non-governmental acts.

* * *

Here, documents provided in support of, and in opposition to, the respondents' motion for summary judgment establish no inconsistency between the actions of those respondents whose job duties took them personally into crowd control management activities, and the University's policy of safe management of the crowd at football games. Rather, they acted in accord with the General Operating Procedures for Camp Randall Stadium. Neither the formulation of the plan nor the implementation of it required highly technical, professional skills, such as a physician's. Therefore, we conclude that the respondents' activities were governmental in nature and we decline to extend the exception to immunity found in Gordon in this context.

* * *

CONCLUSION

Because the appellants have submitted no evidentiary facts from which we could conclude that the respondents had ministerial duties which they failed to perform and because neither the safe place statute nor any other theory of liability put forth by the appellants applies to the respondents, we affirm the summary judgment dismissing appellants' claims against the respondents.

By the Court.—Judgment affirmed.

CASES ON THE SUPPLEMENTAL CD

Cater et al. v. City of Cleveland, (1998 Ohio LEXIS 2212). Pay special attention to the defendant's lack of proper training and practice in how to call the emergency medical services. How did this affect the outcome of the crisis and lawsuit?

Kleinknecht v. Gettysburg College, (1993 U.S. App. LEXIS 6609). The reader should pay particular attention to the defendant's response to Kleinknecht's collapse on the field. How could they have been better prepared for such a crisis?

Mogabgab v. Orleans Parish School Board, (1970 La. App. LEXIS 5219). Carefully review the coaches' response to this medical emergency. What should they have done differently?

QUESTIONS YOU SHOULD BE ABLE TO ANSWER

1. Explain what is meant by the term "crisis."

2. Identify several possible crises that could affect a specific, local recreation or sport business.

3. Identify and explain the main components of a Crisis Management Plan (CMP).

4. Search for examples of CMPs for recreation or sport management-related organizations/facilities on the Internet. Review them and identify their strengths and weaknesses.

5. Explain several ways you would go about rehearsing (practicing) different aspects of a CMP.

REFERENCES

Case

Eneman v. Richter, 577 N.W.2d 386; 1998 Wisc. App.

Publications

Ajango, D. (2003). The ultimate goal in crisis response. In *Recreation & Adventure Program Law Conference Proceedings*. Vail, CO, p. C1–6.

Bacon, V. L., & Anderson, M. K. (2003). Crisis interventions for sport related incidents. *The Sport Journal*, 6(4). Retrieved December 15, 2005, from http://www.thesportjournal.org/2003Journal/Vol6-No4/crisis.asp

Cheley, D. (1997, Spring). *Crisis at camp . . . What do we do now?* Paper presented at American Camping Association Mid-States Conference.

CNN/Sports Illustrated. (2002, November 24). *That kind of Fiesta. . . . Postgame fires, car damage leads to 45 arrests of OSU fans*. Associated Press. Retrieved March 25, 2009, from http://sportsillustrated.cnn.com/football/college/news/2002/11/23/rowdy_fans_ap

Coombs, W. T. (2007). *Ongoing crisis communication: Planning, managing, and responding* (2nd ed.). Los Angeles: Sage.

Coombs, W. T. (2007, October 30). *Crisis management and communications*. Gainesville, FL: Institute for Public Relations. Retrieved March 20, 2009, from http://www.instituteforpr.org/essential_knowledge/detail/crisis_management_and_communications

Everly, G. S., & Mitchell, J. T. (1999). *Critical incident stress management: CISM, a new era and standard of care in crisis intervention* (2nd ed.). Elliot City, MD: Chevron Publishing.

Herman, M. L., & Oliver, B. B. (2001). *Vital signs: Anticipating, preventing and surviving a crisis in a non-profit*. Washington, DC: Nonprofit Risk Management Center.

James, M. (2008, October). Sudden death at a fitness center. *Fitness Management*. Retrieved March 20, 2009, from http://fitnessmanagement.com/articles/article.aspx?articleid=2505&zoneid=28

Seymour, M., & Moore, S. (2000). *Effective crisis management: Worldwide principles and practice*. New York: Cassell.

Schirick, E. (2002, March). Risk management and crisis response are you prepared? *Camping Magazine*. Retrieved March 20, 2009, from http://www.acacamps.org/campmag/rm023risk.php

Schultz, R. (1993, November 1). Richter looks for solutions. *The Capital Times*, p. B1.

Stoldt, G. C., Miller, L. K., Ayres, T. D., & Comfort, P. G. (2000). Crisis management planning: A necessity for sport managers. *International Journal of Sport Management, 4*, 253–266.

Syme, C. (2005, January 17). Writing about a crisis is the best way to avert one. *The NCAA News Online*. Retrieved March 20, 2009, from http://www.ncaa.org/wps/ncaa?ContentID=5760

USA Today. (2003, January 3). *Hello, Columbus*, p. C13. AP Wire.

U.S. Department of Education. (2009). *Emergency Planning*. Retrieved March 21, 2009, from http://www.ed.gov/admins/lead/safety/emergencyplan/index.html

4.24 Crowd Management

—Robin Ammon, Jr.
SLIPPERY ROCK UNIVERSITY

—Nita Unruh
UNIVERSITY OF NEBRASKA/KEARNEY

Recreation, sport, and entertainment events have a variety of commonalities. Each involves some type of activity. The activity may vary greatly, ranging from a church-league basketball game or an intercollegiate field hockey match to the Coachella Valley Music and Arts Festival. All of these events are held in or at some type of venue. The venues take on numerous forms such as stadiums, arenas, swimming pools, theaters, parks, and ski areas. Each of these events will entail numerous risks that could result in personal and/or financial loss. A sampling of these risks includes a simple slip and fall, vandalism, fights among spectators, or a terrorist attack. One of the final similarities between these events is that, in most cases, they involve a crowd. A **crowd** is a group of individuals who gather to involve themselves in some specific event. A major element in providing a safe, entertaining, and valuable experience for the consumer is effective crowd management This section will discuss the development of crowd management and modern techniques of effective crowd management.

FUNDAMENTAL CONCEPTS

A facility or event manager has a duty to provide as safe and secure an environment as possible. van der Smissen (1990) classified **crowd management** as part of the duty facility managers owe to their patrons to protect them from unreasonable risk of harm from themselves or other individuals. The International Association of Assembly Managers (1997) defined crowd management as a tool to assist facility or event managers in providing a safe and enjoyable environment for their guests by implementing the facility/event policies and procedures. A crowd manager's responsibilities include managing the movement and activities of the crowd/guests, assisting in emergencies, and assisting guests with specific concerns related to their enjoyment and/or involvement with the event.

Why Is Crowd Management Important?

The facility manager has a legal duty to provide a reasonably safe environment. Failure to meet this duty can result in legal liability for both the entity and the manager. There are certain situations in which there is no duty to protect the user of the facility. If there is no foreseeable risk of an injury occurring, there can be no liability.

Foreseeability as defined by Black (1990) is the "reasonable anticipation that harm or injury is a likely result from certain acts or omissions" (p. 649). If the facility manager fails to foresee a crowd-related incident that would have been foreseen by a reasonable, prudent facility manager, injuries resulting from the incident leave the organization and manager vulnerable to a lawsuit. **Therefore a** prudent facility manager will *need to* anticipate rather than react (see also Section 2.11, *Negligence*).

Foreseeability, however, is not as clear as it once was. Due to the litigious nature of our society, individuals at various events *expect* to be kept safe no matter the risk. The plaintiff in *Cohen v. Sterling Mets* (2007), was a vendor in the stands at Shea Stadium who was injured by a spectator scrambling for a t-shirt that had been launched into the stands during a between-the-innings promotional give-away. A public address announcement had been made prior to the promotion and security was present, but the vendor felt he should be compensated for his injuries.

Fans rushing onto the athletic field at the end of a game have become a common sight–making such incidents foreseeable. Some universities such as Southern Methodist University have purchased collapsible goal posts, while others, like the University of Florida, employ both uniformed law enforcement officers and additional outsourced security staff and dogs to keep the fans from rushing the field. A third group, as evidenced by The Ohio State University, recognizes the difficulty of trying to prevent tens of thousands of fans from going where they want. The fans are allowed on the field to celebrate if they are so inclined—regardless of the possible consequences.

These crowd situations are by no means unique to the United States. In March, 2009, a wall collapsed from the pressure of fans pushing each other while attempting to gain entry to a qualifying match for the 2010 World Cup in Abidjan, Ivory Coast. During the ensuing stampede 19 spectators died and 132 were injured. Police firing tear gas to disperse the crowd were blamed for the disaster (Associated Press, 2009).

Sport and recreation managers need to be aware of the impact of trends in society relating to foreseeability and crowd management problems. For example, in 2008 a large crowd of frenzied shoppers at a New York Wal-Mart trampled a security employee to death during the early stages of Black Friday. Wal-Mart executives stated they could not have anticipated such a tragic incident. However, they had expected a large number of early shoppers and employed additional outsourced crowd management staff, scheduled extra internal security, and store associates, as well as using barricades to control the early morning shoppers (Neff, 2008).

Evolution of Crowd Management

An examination of the history of crowd management reveals some type of security measures have always been used at major sport/entertainment events. In the early Roman days, lions and other wild animals took care of anyone attempting to "rush the field." Since those early days, providing the appropriate number of trained crowd management personnel has become a more structured endeavor.

Two of the early rock and roll band promoters, Bill Graham on the west coast and Barry Fey in the mid-west, are often credited with recognizing the need for adequately trained crowd management staff. They, along with a few other promoters, realized that uniformed law officers were not the best individuals to protect the bands and their fans during the late 1960s and early 1970s. Graham and Fey introduced the concept of using "peer group" security personnel recruited from the same demographics as the concert fans. Not only were the early "peer group" security better able to relate to the crowds, but the T-shirt security (as they were called) also received specific training in how to deal with rock and roll fans.

Many sport and recreation managers contract with outside companies to provide the crowd management service for their venues. This practice of contracting outside agencies is known as **outsourcing**. At every major sporting event a shirt or jacket emblazed with "Event Staff" helps the spectator know that some measure of security is being provided. Some events still use **uniformed** or **off-duty law enforcement** officers, but due to high salaries, improper training, and promoter concerns, using uniformed security for crowd management duties is no longer the industry standard. However, uniformed security is still used to provide security services and to arrest intoxicated or unruly individuals at many events. In addition, because of the heightened concerns since September 11, 2001, more facilities are turning to armed law enforcement officers in addition to the outsourced crowd management staff.

Contracting or outsourcing crowd management services eliminates the headaches associated with the hiring, firing, training, and scheduling of the crowd management staff. In 1967, Contemporary Services Corporation (CSC) became the pioneer in peer-group security. CSC has expanded to provide service to various political, sport and entertainment venues and events, including the 2004 Summer Olympics and Paralympics in Athens, Greece. Landmark Event Staffing Services is one of the newer crowd management companies whose management brings over 50 years of experience to the industry. Located in six states across the U.S., Landmark employees are trained in the latest techniques pertaining to crowd and risk management as well as guest services. The reputation of Landmark has already made its mark by securing clients in the entertainment industry, intercollegiate football and basketball venues, NFL stadiums, and MLB baseball parks across the country. Another company that provides security, primarily on the West Coast, is StaffPro. It services over 3,000 concerts, sporting events, conventions, and special events every year (Contemporary Services, n.d.; Landmark, n.d.; Staff Pro, n.d.).

Crowd Management Since September 11, 2001

The terrorist actions of September 11 have forever affected the way facilities and events are managed. An international survey found that 94 percent of the respondents identified security as the most important component for a stadium event (Geigle, 2002). Since then a multitude of events have been classified as "National Special Security Events". This classification allows the federal government to take over the control of the security of the event. The Secret Service takes charge and, along with the Federal Emergency Management Agency (FEMA) and the FBI, devises a comprehensive security plan.

Operational costs for sport/entertainment events have increased exponentially because insurers now view these types of events as attractive targets for terrorists. Insurance claims from the attacks on September 11 have been estimated to be around $40 billion (Baugus, 2003). The availability of terrorist insurance will remain limited and the premiums astronomical for an indefinite period. It has been estimated that an attack on a major sport/entertainment venue could result in 15 times the deaths that occurred on 9/11/01 (Abernethy, 2004). Thus it is paramount for sport/recreation/entertainment facility operators to recognize their venue's vulnerability and take corrective measures. Guidelines developed and security measures implemented to combat terrorism are effective crowd management techniques under any circumstances.

Changes in Operational Procedures

Working along with the International Association of Assembly Managers (IAAM) the U. S. Department of Homeland Security has developed a tool that allows venue security managers the opportunity to assess the vulnerabilities of their public assembly facilities. The Vulnerability Self-Assessment Tool (VSAT) is an online program designed for stadium and other venue managers to integrate along with their "*standard operating procedures*". The VSAT is modeled after programs successfully used by the Transportation Security Administration to identify vulnerability at airports and other transportation facilities. The VSAT was "adapted to incorporate industry safety and security best practices for critical infrastructure to assist in establishing a security baseline for each facility" (Launch, 2005, p. 1).

Tools such as the VSAT can be implemented and utilized by any type of venue no matter its size or degree of importance. In addition, the vulnerabilities identified by such tools are not only for threats posed by potential "terrorists". Emotional and violent fans, mentally ill criminals, disgruntled employees and local community members who object to the traffic congestion or noise generated from various events can all pose a threat to the effective operations of a sport/recreation/entertainment facility (Abernethy, 2004). Such a tool should examine such topics as the following.

Physical Security Measures. A small vehicle loaded with explosives parked near a facility can cause tremendous damage and multiple deaths (e.g., the Oklahoma City bombing). Thus the parking and delivery policies of the facility should be examined. Security checks along with biometric verification can be utilized. Large concrete planters can be situated to keep trucks (or cars) from parking too close to the venue's walls. Filled with flowers and plants, these barriers need not appear ominous. Sensors can be installed to quickly detect the release of chemical and biological agents.

Technological communication networks, such as **closed circuit television** (CCTV) should be installed around venue access points (e.g., doors, gates, windows). In addition, sensors should also closely monitor access points for the air conditioning, ventilation and water systems.

Central Monitoring. A control room or command post should be established for the management of facility security, and should be located in a position that can survey the overall event. This is crucial for effective communication. Having the command post in a central location will allow the staff to view the entire venue, and enable them to utilize binoculars to identify disruptive or intoxicated individuals. In the UK, the command post or control room by law must have a view of the stadium interior. The trend in the United States has been to establish a centralized location that contains a variety of CCTV monitors. This control room is usually situated in a secure location inside the stadium, and is manned 24 hours a day, 365 days a year. In addition a game-day command post is located higher up in the venue that provides good lines of sight for representatives of the various command agencies such as law enforcement, emergency medical, facility maintenance, and crowd management. A specific number of staff members should be equipped with multi-channel radios, with each channel designated for specific groups (e.g., channel 1—peer group; channel 2—housekeeping; channel 3—law enforcement; channel 4—medical services). Staff members from each group may then be contacted by the command post, via radio, to handle various situations quickly and safely.

Evacuation. Response time to a terrorist attack becomes critical especially depending on the type of weapon used. Each facility should have a specific evacuation plan in place for a variety of attack scenarios. Electronic signs and emergency lighting are extremely important. Panic can increase the number of deaths as well as spread any contamination resulting from the attack. Most facilities today have devised an evacuation plan but often leave out important components, such as the evacuation of their disabled guests.

Security Systems. Terrorists conduct a significant amount of surveillance before carrying out an attack. Once they have identified a "soft" target they begin their plans. An effective security system can discourage them from attempting an attack as well as "harden" the facility. The current system must be examined, threat assessment carried out, and associated probabilities identified. Cost should not be the deciding factor but obviously needs to be taken into consideration. Based on the information collected, a plan can be properly developed to reduce vulnerability to acceptable risk levels (Abernethy, 2004). However, no matter the level of preparedness, the facility manager needs to be able to adapt. For example, Hurricane Katrina taught facility managers that telephone service, water, heating/air conditioning, electricity and other essential services may be disrupted for extended periods of time. In addition, if the towers used by cell phones are damaged, a sport/recreation/entertainment facility (e.g., Louisiana Superdome) can have its communication system rendered totally inoperative. The purchase and use of satellite phones may need to be investigated.

New NFL Policies

Prior to the 2008 season, the NFL and its 32 teams agreed upon a Fan Code of Conduct. The Code states:

> When attending a game, you are required to refrain from the following behaviors: behavior that is unruly, disruptive, or illegal in nature, intoxication or other signs of alcohol impairment that results in irresponsible behavior, foul or abusive language or obscene gestures, interference with the progress of the game (including throwing objects onto the field), failing to follow instructions of stadium personnel, and verbal or physical harassment of opposing team fans (McCarthy, 2008, ¶ 1–3).

Violators of the Code face various penalties that may include ejection and revocation of season tickets if the behavior is judged to be detrimental enough. The league has sent a firm message that they intend to hold season ticket owners responsible for the conduct of anyone using their tickets and occupying their seats (McCarthy, 2008).

The Code requires fans to abstain from behaviors that hamper the enjoyment of other fans or interfere with the product on the field of play ("NFL teams", 2008). With the increased scrutiny on potential alcohol problems inside the facility, some fans try to circumvent the policies by engaging in outlandish behavior outside the stadium while tailgating before the game begins (Muret, 2008). Decreasing the number of intoxicated fans entering the stadiums was one of the main focal points for the Code.

Additional initiatives have been put in place at numerous stadiums to stop intoxicated spectators from entering the stadium or from driving home drunk after the event. Several stadiums have employed separate groups of crowd management staff to walk among the spectators entering the stadium, in the hopes of preventing these individuals from gaining access to the stadium. Other teams, such as the Pittsburgh Steelers, provide fans with a designated phone number where the fans can text message the control room if they observe an obnoxious or intoxicated third party. They also provide a 1-800 number for similar fan usage. An alcohol management team will then be dispatched to the location to assess the situation and eject the transgressors if deemed necessary. Other facilities offer "designated driver" programs where individuals sign a pledge card not to drink and oftentimes are rewarded by being provided with free soft drinks during the game. Each of these initiatives demonstrates the intent of the NFL to curtail alcohol transgressions and to enforce the Code of Conduct.

Crowd Management Legislation

During the summer of 2002 a father and son breached U.S. Cellular Field security, came onto the field and proceeded to attack the Kansas City Royals first base coach during a baseball game. This confrontation, along with four incidents of field intrusion during the 2004 baseball season at the Great American Ball Park, has prompted state legislators from Ohio to propose legislation pertaining to persons who enter any restricted area at a place of public amusement. Major League Baseball witnessed 39 field intrusions during the 2004 season, which resulted in 38 arrests. The penalties for this type of action are very light in many states. Ohio state legislators hope that stricter penalties will not only deter these altercations, but also serve as motivation to prosecute the offenders. The proposed new law would "allow an owner or lessee of a place of public amusement, an agent of the owner or lessee, or a performer or participant at a place of public amusement to use reasonable force to restrain and remove a trespasser from a restricted portion of the place of public amusement" (p. 5). The types of restricted areas covered by the legislation would include playing fields, athletic surfaces, stages, and locker and dressing rooms (Sherborne, 2005).

Searches and Resulting Litigation

Outsourced crowd management and security companies play a large role in managing and controlling the public in office buildings, schools, parks, recreation and sport facilities, and concert venues. The courts have placed various limitations on the authority of private crowd management companies. Often, any violation of state law will cause a crowd manager to be held to the same civil and criminal liability as any private individual. In addition, the courts have ruled that a search of a person's belongings without their consent will generally be viewed as trespass. Many of the claims of illegal searches allege a violation of privacy rights and rely on the Fourth Amendment's guarantee of freedom from unreasonable searches. In determining if a search is legal, the courts look at three issues: (1) if the conduct was considered to be state action, (2) if the conduct could be considered a search, and finally (3) if the search was reasonable. Most legal experts agree that all three criteria are met when photos are taken or a search is required to gain entrance to a recreation or sport facility (Miller, Stoldt, & Ayres, 2002).(See Section 6.15, *Search and Seizure / Right to Privacy*).

Most fans willingly put up with the increased security after the terrorist attacks on 9/11/01. However as the years have gone by with no further incidents, many individuals have become less tolerant of the increased security measures, especially those pertaining to searches. From a legal perspective, recent cases address the legal questions regarding pat-down searches and their impact on crowd management policies.

In 2005, the Supreme Court of North Dakota held that a mass pat-down search of spectators at college ice hockey games was unconstitutional (*State of North Dakota v. Seglen*, 2005). Seglen, a minor, was searched by a campus police officer upon entering the ice arena on the campus of the University of North Dakota. A can of beer was found in his possession and he was cited for it. The court found signage in the arena warning of the search did not mean the plaintiff consented to the search and that a physical "pat-down" search was more intrusive than a limited visual search. Even though the facility was privately owned, the officer conducting the search was found to be acting in an official capacity as a police officer for the University of North Dakota, so the Fourth Amendment applied. The state Supreme Court ruled that the search was intrusive and violated Seglen's Fourth Amendment rights.

The next two cases were a result of the NFL's "limited" pat-down search policy that was put into practice before the 2005 season at every NFL stadium. This directive was implemented as a result of a potential threat by terrorists. Raymond James Stadium halted their searches after Gordon Johnston, a Tampa Bay Buccaneer season ticket holder, sued the Tampa Bay Sports Authority, the government agency that runs Raymond James Stadium. Similar to Seglen, Johnston claimed that the pat-downs were a violation of his Fourth Amendment rights. Johnston successfully challenged the NFL policy in two state courts and one Federal court; however, in June, 2007, a three-judge panel of the United States Court of Appeals, Eleventh Circuit ruled that Johnston gave up his right to challenge the searches when he consented to them. The judges held that since the fans knew about the search before entering and submitted to it they voluntarily consented to the search. The court stated, "considering Johnston's ticket was only a revocable license to attend games, there is in the court's opinion at least a question concerning whether Johnston had a constitutional right to pass voluntarily through the stadium gates without being subjected to a pat-down search, even if he had not consented to one" (*Johnston v. Tampa Sports Authority*, 2007).

As per the new NFL directive the San Francisco 49ers began searching all fans entering Monster Park during the 2005 football season. Mr. and Mrs. Sheehan purchased season tickets and were subjected to pat-down searches during each home game during that season. In December, 2005, after the season was completed, the Sheehan's filed suit against the team, claiming the 49ers violated their privacy rights. The trial court dismissed the action. The court stated the Sheehans did not have a reasonable expectation of privacy since they were subjected to the pat-down searches every game during the 2005 season. Therefore, they had full notice of the pat-down policy, consented to the pat-down prior to admittance to the game and never complained. Therefore, the Sheehans had no reasonable expectation of privacy. The Sheehans appealed the decision and the state Court of Appeals dismissed the case (153 Cal. App. 4th 396, 2007 Cal.) In March 2009, the state Supreme Court restored the case. The court stated they believed the case warranted further review and instructed the 49ers to justify the search policy. The Supreme Court reversed the Court of Appeals decision and remanded the case. It will be interesting to see how the decision of this case impacts the NFL's search policy.

Crowd Management Plan

A crowd management plan is an important component of the overall risk management plan of any organization whose activities or events are attended by large numbers of people. The facility manager is either directly or indirectly responsible for both risk management and crowd management. In order for the facility manager to effectively carry out these responsibilities, an effective crowd management plan addressing such issues as capacity of the venue, geographic location, demographics of guests, and type of event must be designed and implemented. In the event of litigation alleging failure to control crowds, courts will look to see if such a plan existed, if it was in writing, how it was implemented, and how it was disseminated to the involved employees. Each employee needs to be aware of his or her role in the plan, even if it is only a small part (see also Section 4.11, *Risk Management Process*).

Trained and Competent Staff

The first component of a good plan is to have properly trained and competent staff to carry out the policies. **Screeners/searchers** are employed as the first group of trained staff to identify and turn away prohibited items. Such items could be bottles, cans, coolers, cameras, weapons, fireworks, umbrellas, or alcoholic beverages. This "search," depending on the event and local statutes, may be a visual screening or a physical "pat-down." In light of the terrorist threat emanating from the tragedies on September 11, 2001, this search has become a much more critical element of the crowd management plan. Before September 11, 2001, the biggest concern for event managers stemmed from alcohol problems. Now, crowd managers must make their spectators feel safe while at sport facilities.

The second group of crowd management personnel is the **ticket takers** who collect tickets from those entering the facility. The main role of the ticket-taker is to ensure that everyone entering the event has a valid ticket for that day's event.

Ushers comprise the third wave of crowd management personnel. They should be well versed in facility layout, knowing directions to and locations of first aid stations, pay phones, restrooms, concession stands, authorized smoking areas, and exits. Ushers should also assist the guests in finding their seats. The usher should observe the patrons and call for assistance when necessary to assist injured patrons, remove food and beverage spills, and defuse potential crowd altercations.

The last wave in crowd management is perhaps the most visible—the **peer-group** or **T-shirt** security. Peer group security is trained to handle crowd disturbances such as unruly, disruptive, or intoxicated patrons. These individuals will also assist in protecting the athletes or performers on the floor or field of the facility.

Most recreation, sport, and entertainment facilities also require additional peer-group security personnel to fill various crowd management roles backstage and/or in the press box.

To reduce the risk of a lawsuit due to personnel errors, whether outsourced personnel are used or the facility hires its own security personnel, it is paramount for all staff—ticket-takers, screeners, ushers, or T-shirt security—to go through an **orientation program**. This orientation should include an understanding of the facility layout, location of first-aid stations, restrooms, telephones, lost and found, emergency exits, and perhaps most important, a clear understanding of their duties and authority (including the legal ramifications of their actions).

Crisis Management and Emergency Action Plan

The second major component in a crowd management plan is to prepare for crises or emergencies. Being prepared for crises and emergencies includes the capacity to respond to two types of situations—a crisis or an individual injury or illness. **Crises** include events such as fire, bleacher collapses, bomb threats, power loss, tornados, and, in today's society, terrorist activities. **Emergencies** generally take the form of medical problems (e.g., heart attacks, injuries from falls, heat-related illnesses).

Crisis management plans and emergency action plans are necessary so minor problems don't become serious ones and serious ones don't become a disaster. Such plans must be designed and implemented by crowd managers, practiced, and documented (see also Section 2.33, *Emergency Care* and Section 4.23, *Crisis Management*).

Procedure for Handling Disruptive, Unruly, or Intoxicated Patrons

The third component of an effective crowd management plan pertains to dealing with **fan ejections.** Examples of behaviors that could result in an ejection include disruptive or unruly behavior, intoxication, possession of prohibited items that screeners should have removed but overlooked, evasion of admission fees, or field intrusion. Another problem that may necessitate an ejection is third-party assaults. Third-party assaults occur for various reasons, some foreseeable and some not. Foreseeability does not depend on whether the exact incident was foreseeable. The question is whether an incident of that general nature was reasonably foreseeable. However, if there has been a history of violence or disruptive behavior, the courts have held that actions should be taken to prevent such occurrences (*Bishop v. Fair Lanes Georgia Bowling, Inc.*, 1986; *Cassanello v. Luddy*, 1997; *Leger v. Stockton*, 1988).

Well-written policies should be established that address ways to handle disruptive behavior. The language should be clear and concise, stating what actions will not be tolerated and what measures will result. Ejection policies should be printed on tickets and posted for patrons. Policies may differ among athletic event, recreational activity, or concert depending upon the request of the event manager. It is crucial for personnel with ejection authority to be well trained regarding the legal ramifications of their role (e.g., individual liability, understanding of human rights, protection of evidence, excessive force, rules of detention and arrest, and crimes against persons and property). It is also very important that ushers and other staff members who do not have ejection authority receive in-service training regarding their role.

Usually it is best to include a warning before an actual ejection takes place. If an ejection is necessary, it should be carried out swiftly. Handling patrons in this way sends a quick, but firm message to others in the crowd as to what will and will not be tolerated.

Every ejection must be properly documented. This is an extremely crucial step in the ejection process, as it serves to produce a valuable defense for the crowd management employee and facility administration if subsequent litigation ensues. In addition, photographs or video should be utilized as an additional step in the ejection process. This measure accurately portrays the ejected fan's condition and further protects the employees from unnecessary legal harassment. As previously mentioned, closed-circuit televisions (CCTV's) are prevalent in every type of sport and recreation venue and they can assist in documenting fights as well as ejections.

Effective Communication Network

An effective communication network is the fourth component of an effective crowd management plan. The network allows the crowd management staff to work efficiently and cooperatively to handle situations as they occur. Representatives from each group (facility management, medical, security, and law enforcement) should have input in the organization of the communication network. Familiarity with the communication network should be a part of the employee orientation and training for each event. Crowd management needs more than a risk avoidance emphasis. The decisions made in the first two minutes after an incident will save lives.

Effective Signage

The fifth component of a crowd management plan is **signage**. Signage is an underutilized tool in risk and crowd management. Signage may be directional or informational in nature and each has its own specific function. **Directional signs** have a number of important uses. Directional signs provide patrons with directions to important locations such as interstate highway entrances and exits, main roadways, and parking areas. Other directional signs serve to indicate the correct entrance gate or portal, as well as directing the patrons to the ticket office.

Informational signs are signs that inform the public. Prohibited items (e.g., cans, bottles, backpacks, weapons, food, recording devices, and cameras) and rules (including ejection policies) are often communicated through such signs. Spectators appreciate being treated fairly and will normally abide by directives if previously informed. In addition, directional signage helps to provide answers to spectator questions by identifying the location of concession stands, first-aid rooms, telephones, restrooms, smoking areas, and exits.

Implementation and Evaluation of the Plan

As with the risk management plan, the last step in a crowd management plan is the **implementation and evaluation** of the plan. A recreation or sport facility will not benefit from a well-written crowd management plan unless it is effectively implemented during an event. Implementation should start with a review of both the risk and crowd management policies before the event. Event-specific activities, such as half-time promotions, VIP guests on the sideline, or band members coming out into the crowd should be discussed. Each staff member should understand how the activity might affect his or her event responsibilities. After an event, all of the personnel should come together for a debriefing. They should also look into ways to improve the plan. As stated earlier, a crowd management plan should be flexible and allow for change as needed. Without implementation and evaluation, a well-organized crowd management plan becomes ineffective.

SIGNIFICANT CASE

This case is an excellent example of what can happen if a facility doesn't plan properly or utilize an effective crowd management plan. The evidence in the case showed the facility operators breached their duty to the plaintiff. The operators were aware that the concert would likely be canceled, but they failed to make a timely announcement of the cancellation. In addition, they failed to formulate a plan for dealing with the patrons once the announcement was made. Finally there was no plan in place to properly execute a safe and organized exit from the arena.

HEENAN V. COMCAST SPECTACOR

Common Pleas Court of Philadelphia County, Pennsylvania
2006 Phila. Ct. Com. Pl. LEXIS 138

Plaintiff instituted this civil action against Defendants Comcast Spectacor and Spectrum Arena L.P., claiming Defendants were negligent, providing inadequate security and failing to take proper security measures to ensure the safety of patrons. Plaintiff alleged riotous behavior erupted after the announcement that the hard rock band Guns 'N Roses would not play and that she was injured when she fell as she and other concert-goers hurried out of the facility.

* * *

The jury returned a verdict in favor of Plaintiff, against Defendants/Appellants, in the amount of $ 140,000, finding that Defendant's negligence was a factual cause of Plaintiff's injury.

Defendants filed a Post-Trial Motion claiming that the evidence failed to provide a sufficient legal or factual basis for the verdict rendered. Defendants also claimed that the Court erred and such errors required the entry of j.n.o.v. or a new trial. Defendants asserted in the very least that remittitur was required to adjust Plaintiff's large and unsupported award.

This Court denied Defendants' Motion for Post-Trial Relief and this appeal followed.

FACTS AND EVIDENCE PRESENTED AT TRIAL:

On December 6, 2002, Plaintiff had gone to the First Union Center to attend a concert by Guns 'N Roses. She testified that she wasn't a Guns 'N Roses fan, but went along with friends who had arranged tickets and a limousine to transport them. Plaintiff arrived at about 7:30 pm. She testified that some of the pre-concert performances had already taken place at that point. Pre-concert bands and a DJ played until approximately 9:30 PM. Nothing happened from that time until about 11:10, when the lights went on and a pre-recorded announcement was played indicating that Guns 'N Roses would not perform.

Plaintiff testified that the crowd became unruly and angry when the announcement was made. She testified there was commotion, things such as food and drinks being thrown from the upper levels and that people began to run to the exits, some of them carrying chairs from the facility. She testified that she feared for her safety and felt she needed to leave quickly. The only security she saw at this point were two employees wearing yellow jackets standing just outside the concrete barriers beyond the exits.

At that point, Plaintiff along with a large and growing crowd attempted to leave the building as quickly as possible. Once outside, the crowd grew dense around her. Plaintiff moved with the crowd, unable to see past five or six feet to the front of her. She lost sight of her friends, and in the confusion she fell, sustaining the injuries which are the subject of this suit.

After falling, she could not get up or put weight onto her foot. Strangers she described as Good Samaritans picked her up and carried her outside of the complex where she saw her friends who then carried her to the limousine. They rode back to New Jersey where they originally started and her friend drove her home where she needed help getting into the house. Plaintiff testified she was in pain the next morning, thinking she sprained her ankle badly. Her friend helped her to the emergency room at Jeanes Hospital, where she was admitted for surgery to be performed the following day. She testified that a plate and three screws were inserted into her ankle and a ligament needed repair.

Plaintiff testified that she was unable to walk for six weeks without crutches and that she needed pain medication for approximately five weeks. * * * She testified she missed two months of work and that she has permanently lost the ability to do many things she enjoyed such as snow skiing, roller blading and walking for exercise. She testified that she has a permanent scar on her foot and ankle which makes her self-conscious and prevents her from wearing certain styled shoes. Finally, she testified that depending on the weather, the area of injury feels tight and that at times her leg muscles cramp on the injured leg. * * *

The Vice-President of Security and Services for Comcast Spectacor, Michael Hasson, testified regarding the events of December 6, 2002. Mr. Hasson testified concerning security issues, the notice of the concert's cancellation, the actions he took after he learned of the cancellation and the significant damage to the facility resulting from the crowd's reaction to the concert's cancellation.

* * *

Mr. Hasson testified that at 7:45 PM he received notice from the Risk Manager and the Facilities Manager, Peter Lukko and John Page, that they learned the concert might be cancelled. He testified that they put together a plan at that point in case the concert was indeed cancelled.

He testified that at 9:00 PM he ordered that all trashcans in the facility and the barricades outside the facility be removed for fear that they might be thrown in protest or anger by the crowd after the cancellation. He testified that at that point, he was planning on evacuating the crowd. At that point he asked the security personnel at the nearby Phantom's game to come to the First Union Center when the Phantom's game let out. Beer had been served throughout the night until just before the cancellation announcement was made although he ordered concession stands to be closed piecemeal.

Mr. Hasson testified that he knew that the same band had recently cancelled a show in Vancouver on November 7, 2002 and that a riot ensued, causing significant damage. He acknowledged that the dynamics of this crowd may require additional precautions.

* * *

Plaintiff's expert, security consultant Terence Gibbs, testified that in his opinion Comcast failed to properly train its security staff assigned to the Guns 'N Roses concert. He cited the deficiencies in training on evacuation procedures and crowd management. He also testified that there was a failure to properly and adequately supervise security personnel assigned to this concert. Specifically he explained how the loss of crowd control by security enabled the crowd to develop into an escape or mob crowd. He testified that the security supervisors should have been trained, should have sent in teams of officers and should have been in position when the announcement was made. He explained how a spectator crowd can grow and ferment into a riotous crowd as the tenor of the crowd grows more frustrated and the level of anger rises. He explained how announcements should be made in stages to offset anger and enable willing patrons to leave earlier.

* * *

Defendants did not present their own security expert to the jury to present a contrary opinion.

DISCUSSION:

This Court Was Satisfied That Plaintiff Met Her Burden of Proof in This Negligence Claim.

Plaintiff claimed that Appellant was negligent for failing to provide adequate security at this event, including failing to plan exit and crowd management strategies in the event of a concert cancellation and that this failure caused her to fall and sustain injuries. Plaintiff claimed that Appellants knew or should have known of the risk to patrons like Plaintiff, to whom they owed a duty, in the event of a cancellation the night of the concert by Guns 'N Roses. Plaintiff claimed the last-minute cancellation was foreseeable considering Defendants' knowledge of the Band's recent cancellation under similar circumstances and the resulting damage.

The Restatement of Torts § 344 provides:

"A possessor of land who holds it open to the public for entry for his business purposes is subject to liability to members of the public while they are upon the land for such a purpose, for physical harm caused by the accidental, negligent, or intentionally harmful acts of third persons or animals, and by the failure of the possessor to exercise reasonable care to (a) discover that such acts are being done or are likely to be done, or (b) give a warning adequate to enable the visitors to avoid the harm, or otherwise to protect them against it."

* * *

". . . the possessor . . . is then required to exercise reasonable care to use such means of protection as are available, or to provide such means in advance because [*14] of the likelihood that third persons . . . may conduct themselves in a manner which will endanger the safety of the visitor."

* * *

". . . the possessor . . . may . . . know or have reason to know, from past experience, that there is a likelihood of conduct on the part of third persons in general which is likely to endanger the safety of the visitor, even though he has no reason to expect it on the part of any particular individual. If the place or character of his business, or his past experience, is such that he should reasonably anticipate careless or criminal conduct on the part of third persons, either generally or at some particular time, he may be under a duty to take precautions against it, and to provide a reasonably sufficient number of servants to afford a reasonable protection."

Under Section 344, therefore, Defendants owed a duty to Plaintiff to anticipate possible dangers and to take reasonable precautions against such. The hasty exit by nearly

14,000 Guns 'N Roses fans, all disappointed, some angry and some violent, can be considered harmful third party conduct referred to in § 344 which Defendants should have anticipated and formulated a plan to protect visitors such as Plaintiff.

It is necessary under § 344 that reasonable measures be taken to control the conduct of third persons, or to give adequate warning to enable patrons to avoid possible harm. Section 344 imposes liability where the occupant fails in one of two duties—either to take reasonable care to discover dangerous conduct of third persons is likely to occur, or to take reasonable care to provide appropriate precautions.

* * * Defendants argue that their actions in this case were reasonable under § 343 and Plaintiff failed to prove otherwise. To the contrary, the hazard to be anticipated and protected against was the chaotic rush to leave by roughly 14,000 Guns 'N Roses fans, all disappointed, some angry and some violent, all of whom waited hours for a performance for which they paid and which, before the cancellation announcement, had no indication that the Band would not play. Plaintiff questioned the Defendants' reasonableness in waiting until 11:10 PM to make the first announcement of any kind regarding the cancellation despite having information early in the evening that the concert was in doubt.

* * *

Defendants argued that Plaintiff failed to meet her burden of proving causation. We disagreed and found to the contrary that she offered sufficient evidence that Defendants' security failures resulted in the chaos and rush to leave the facility and that caused her to fall and sustain injuries.

Defendants rely on the fact that Plaintiff could not state with certainty what precisely caused her to fall and that she was unaware of the danger and all of the incidents occurring at the First Union Center when she left the building. Defendants argue that if Plaintiff was unaware of the acts of destruction and violence occurring that these could not have been related to her fall and could not have caused her injury. To the contrary, whether Plaintiff was aware of all of these occurrences or not, much of the crowd was and she testified that she was aware to some degree of what was happening. Many of the roughly 14,000 people witnessed what was happening and many were aware of danger. Plaintiff presented evidence that because Defendants failed to update the audience throughout the night and because there was no plan in place, roughly 14,000 disappointed, frustrated and angry patrons were attempting to leave the building at once. Many in this crowd had been drinking alcohol based on Mr. Hasson's testimony, many were disappointed and many were angry. Whether Plaintiff was aware of all of this or not, the crowd around her was attempting to flee quickly, and this very easily could have caused her to fall. She testified that she was frightened and that the crowd was growing dense around her as everyone tried to leave the facility. A jury could find, and presumably did find, that such an exit by this large crowd could have caused her fall and resulting injury.

* * *

Through Plaintiff's cross-examination of Michael Hasson, Plaintiff established enough evidence with which a jury could find that Defendants' were aware that a danger might arise if the show were cancelled and that Defendants' failed to plan and provide adequate security in such an event. * * *

Mr. Hasson's responses further support Plaintiff's theory that Defendants knew that this particular crowd could be problematic and that accordingly, he failed to take reasonable steps to plan and protect patrons. His responses and testimony may have been seriously questioned by the jury. For example, Mr. Hasson refused to say that behavior by fans was violent. This behavior, described above, resulted in the substantial physical damage to the facility. The jury heard of the property damage detailed above as well as injuries to people including the six people getting hit with chairs, a fifteen year old being trampled upon and other injuries occurring within the moments following the cancellation announcement. Yet Mr. Hasson insisted on calling these acts "crowd dynamics in a very agitated sense" rather than violence and he refused to characterize this crowd as an angry mob. He testified that no patrons were running but then conceded when questioned further that possibly a few patrons were running to the exits.

He refused to call this scene a riot when questioned on cross but on direct he specifically used the term riot when he stated that the police were justified in protecting their own property by keeping their vehicles away from the facility because "when you see riots and such like that, you usually notice from the TV, you will see police cars overturned." While he refused to call this crowd "an angry mob" he testified that two hours before the cancellation announcement he removed all trash cans, outside barriers and anything the crowd could get their hands on. These statements further supported Plaintiff's claim that Defendants' were negligent as they foresaw the reaction of the crowd which would likely prove dangerous but they did not take reasonable steps to prepare and to protect patrons such as Plaintiff to ensure an orderly and safe exit.

* * *

This Court found that Plaintiff met her burden of proof concerning negligence: she offered the required proof of duty, breach, causation and injury. Accordingly, Defendants' Motions were properly denied.

CONCLUSION

The Court's Orders were proper and should be affirmed.

Bearman v. University of Notre Dame (1983 Ind. App. LEXIS 3387). Analyze the court's reasoning about foreseeability. Even though the university may not know the particular danger posed by an intoxicated third party they should have foreseen that some people would become intoxicated and pose a general threat to the safety of other patrons.

Cohen v. Sterling Mets (2007 N.Y. Misc. LEXIS 5270). This case provides an excellent example of how the assumption of risk defense is viewed in comparison to the duty a sport venue has to protect employees and spectators. The concept of between-the-innings promotions and the risks they entail is also touched upon.

Moening v. University of Toledo (2006 Ohio Misc. LEXIS 174). Consider the court's analysis about primary assumption of risk. The plaintiff was an invited guest to the game, but as soon as he set foot onto the playing surface that status changed. The change in status resulted in no duty being owed by the university.

Cases from Other Chapters

Section 2.31 *Johns Hopkins v. Connecticut Sports Plex, L.L.C.* (2006 Conn. Super. LEXIS 1710). The case illustrates the concept of foreseeability. Several key concepts such as the presence of a proper alcohol management plan, proper numbers of security staff and documentation of prior incidents are important to keep in mind while reading the case.

QUESTIONS YOU SHOULD BE ABLE TO ANSWER

1. Describe three reasons why crowd management is a necessary component of an effective risk management plan.

2. Do an Internet search on Bill Graham and Barry Fey. What were some of the major concerns for the early promoters?

3. Research the NFL's Fan Code of Conduct. Do you believe it will be effective?

4. Analyze the *Seglen*, *Johnston*, and *Sheehan* cases. What are two similarities between the three cases?

5. Identify the components necessary for an effective crowd management plan. How would you implement a crowd management plan?

REFERENCES

Cases

Bishop v. Fair Lanes Georgia Bowling, Inc., 803 F.2d 1548 (11th Cir. 1986).

Cassanello v. Luddy, 302 N.J. Super. 267; 695 A.2d 325; 1997 N.J. Super. LEXIS 286.

Johnston v. Tampa Sports Authority, 490 F.3d 820; 2007 U.S. App. Lexis 15190.

Leger v. Stockton, 249 Cal. Rptr. 688 (July 25, 1988).

Stark v. The Seattle Seahawks, et al., CASE NO. C06-1719JLR, 2007 U.S. Dist. LEXIS 45510.

State of North Dakota v. Seglen, 700 N.W.2d 702; 2005 N.D. LEXIS 160.

Publications

Abernethy, B. (2004, November). Worst-case scenarios. *Stadia*. Retrieved November 27, 2004, from http:www.stadia.tv/archive/user/archive_article.tpl?id=20041124173315

Associated Press. (2009, March 30). Ivory Coast soccer fans blame police for deadly stampede that killed 19. *FoxNews.com*. Retrieved April 1, 2009, from http://www.foxnews.com/story/0,2933,511555,00.html

Baugus, R. V. (2003, January/February). Insurance escalates in wake of attacks. *Facility Manager, 19*(1), 28–30.

Black, H. C. (1990). *Black's Law Dictionary* (6th ed.). St. Paul: West Publishing Co.

Contemporary Services Corporation (n. d). About us. Retrieved January 11, 2006, from http://www.contemporaryservices.com/pages/about.html.

Demick, B. (2009, February 22). Beijing's Olympic building boom becomes a bust. *Los Angeles Times*, retrieved March 16, 2009, from http://www.latimes.com/news/nationworld/world/la-fg-beijing-bust22-2009feb22,0,5564951.story

Geigle, M. (2002, Showcase special). Safe is sound. *Stadia, (19)*, 130–133.

Highs and lows from 2008. (2008, December 22). *Street & Smith's SportsBusiness Journal.* Retrieved March 13, 2009, from http://sportsbusinessjournal.com/article/61028

International Association of Assembly Managers. (1997, February 15–16). *Duties of a crowd assembly facilitator.* Paper presented at the Crowd Management Curriculum Workshop. Irving, TX.

Landmark Event Staffing Services (n.d.). Home page. Retrieved March 30, 2009, from https://www.landmarkeventstaff.com/Home_Page.html

McCarthy, M. (2008, Aug. 6). NFL unveils new code of conduct for its fans. *USA Today.* Retrieved March 25, 2009, from http://www.usatoday.com/sports/football/nfl/2008-08-05-fan-code-of-conduct_N.htm

Miller, L. K., Stoldt, G. C., & Ayres, T. D. (2002, January). Search me: Recent events make surveillance efforts even more likely to pass judicial muster. *Athletic Business, 26*(1), 18, 20–21.

Muret, D. (2006, Feb. 11) NFL, stadiums rethinking alcohol policies. *Street & Smith's SportsBusiness Journal.* Retrieved March 25, 2009, from http://www.sportsbusinessjournal.com/article/58026

Neff, J. (2008, December 8). Marketing blamed in Wal-Mart death; Lawsuit says advertising 'specifically' designed to attract large crowds. *Advertising Age.* 23

NFL teams implement fan code of conduct (2008). NFL.com. Retrieved March 25, 2009, from http://www.nfl.com/news/story?id=09000d5d809c28f9&template=without-video&confirm=true

Sherborne, P. (2005, April). Crowd control legislation considered in Ohio. *VENUEStoday, 4*(14), 4–5

Staff Pro (n. d.). History. Retrieved January 20, 2006 from http://www.staffpro.com/aboutus/history.asp

van der Smissen, B. (1990). *Legal liability and risk management for public and private entities.* Cincinnati, OH: Anderson Publishing Co.

4.25 Managing Risk Through Insurance

—Doyice J. Cotten
SPORT RISK CONSULTING[1]

Insurance is a method by which an individual or business pays a defined expenditure (premium) to protect against the possibility of a large, undetermined future loss or expense. Conducting business without insurance is like rock climbing without a safety line—very risky. Insurance spreads the financial risks and costs of an individual or business among a large group of persons or businesses so that the losses of those few who experience them are shared with the many who do not. In so doing, insurance provides protection against financial catastrophe and is an indispensable risk management technique.

Many persons look at the purchase of insurance and risk management as one and the same. This, however, is not true. Risk management involves the identification of risks, determination of the extent of the risks, and the implementation of one or more control approaches. Control approaches include: (1) elimination of the activity; (2) reduction of risks through operational control; (3) retention (through such techniques as self-insurance, current expensing, and deductibles); (4) transfer by contract (through indemnity agreements, exculpatory clauses, and by requiring insurance by the other party); and (5) purchasing insurance from an insurance company.

Obviously, insurance is but one of many techniques available to help manage risks in a recreation or sport business. The recreation or sport manager should purchase insurance to protect against all risks that could have a significant impact upon the financial integrity of the business, but should not try to insure against every possible risk and potential loss. In addition to protection against property loss, loss of business income, and monetary judgments in lawsuits, insurance also protects the recreation or sport business from legal expenses resulting from litigation.[2] It is usually less expensive to simply pay for minor losses when they occur. A major danger, however, is that failure to meet claim reporting requirements can jeopardize coverage when a seemingly minor injury (a strained knee) eventually reveals itself as a major injury (an ACL tear). It is obviously important that the recreation or sport manager be knowledgeable enough to determine which risks are of such a magnitude as to allow retention by the business, which can be transferred by contract, and which require protection through insurance coverage. The purpose of this section is to help the recreation or sport manager become more informed about this aspect of risk management and, subsequently, be able to better protect the business from financial risks.

FUNDAMENTAL CONCEPTS

Understanding the Policy

To become more knowledgeable about insurance and to be better able to protect the recreation or sport business from financial risks, the recreation or sport manager must learn to read and understand an insurance policy. Most can be long and confusing, particularly if one does not know exactly what to look for and does not know the contextual meaning of the terms used. Novick (2000) suggested that the policy should **not** be read like a book or article—from beginning to end. He suggests that the policy be read in the following order for maximum understanding.

---

[1]Special thanks to Denise Brown, Claims Coordinator for **Fitness Pak**, Chico, CA, for making sure this section is up-to-date and accurate.

[2]It is estimated that the average legal expense incurred by an insurance company in taking a suit to trial is approximately $35,000. When the business is insured (and the loss is covered), the insurance company absorbs this cost. When there is no insurance, the business incurs this expense (usually, even if the business wins the lawsuit).

Declarations

This is the section that includes the facts and figures regarding your particular policy. This section includes such items as the name of the insured, address, policy period, coverages, amounts of insurance, the applicable deductibles, and the cost of the policy. If parties other than the corporate entity are covered (e.g., employees, directors), those parties should be named in the declarations section. Careful study of this section can help one to better understand the coverage of the policy.

Endorsements

Look for the endorsements at the end of the policy. **Endorsements** are coverage provisions, added by the carrier, which change the terms of coverage in the main body of the policy. These may broaden or extend coverage in certain instances and may limit or reduce coverage in others. This final section of the policy is an identification of the specific endorsements included with your policy.

The reader should turn to the referenced portion in the main body of the policy and note the endorsement number in the margin beside the coverage language the endorsement is to replace. Do this for each endorsement. Then, when the reader begins to read the main body of the policy, the reader can flip to each endorsement at the appropriate time.

Endorsements may be added when the policy is purchased or at a later date as the needs of the recreation or sport business change. Examples of endorsements might include adding insured persons, coverage of fine art, and peak-season coverage (which increases inventory coverage by 25 percent during the peak season when inventory is higher than usual). A separate Difference in Conditions policy or endorsement might be purchased to protect against earthquake and flood.

Definitions

The key terms of the policy are defined in this section. The reader must understand the terms in this section in order to understand the coverage that is being purchased. Many key words or phrases used in the document are carefully defined. Examine these carefully because many terms have specific meanings in insurance that may differ from the recreation or sport manager's concept of the term. For instance, one might assume that "personal injury" refers to physical injuries of an individual. However, personal injury refers to injuries caused by such acts as slander, libel, false arrest, false imprisonment, humiliation, and invasion of privacy. The reader should refer back to this section when encountering an unfamiliar term.

Contractual Agreement

This part is the actual contractual agreement between the insurance company and the recreation or sport business. The statement of agreement may be quite short. The section simply states that the insurance company agrees to insure the business to the extent indicated in the declarations in exchange for the agreed-upon premium.

The **coverages section** includes a listing of what is being insured in the policy. Following each coverage is a detailed explanation of what is included in the coverage. For example, the building might be listed including any attached structures. The section might state that rental structures away from the main building are not included. This section will also include the perils that the insurance covers (e.g., fire, theft). Additional benefits coverage includes coverage of newly acquired property.

The **exclusions section** of the policy describes what is not covered by the policy. Items that are often excluded from a standard commercial policy include landscaping, buildings under construction, and cash. Some perils that are usually excluded from the standard policy are earthquake; volcanic eruption; water damage from floods, sewers, or surface ground water; power interruption; war; and nuclear hazard. When a coverage is needed by the business that is not listed in the inclusions and is excluded by the exclusions, riders or endorsements adding the coverage to the policy may be purchased.

The **conditions section** sets forth the various things the recreation or sport business must do to meet the obligations of the insured. Some of these conditions might include prompt reporting obligations following a loss, giving sworn affirmation of loss, providing an inventory, or provision of receipts.

This section also includes the responsibilities of the insurance company in the event of a claim. Specified here are such things as when cash replacement is mandated, when replacement items may be utilized, procedures to be followed if the insurer and insured fail to agree on the loss, and whether repair is the option of the insurance company.

Determining Necessary Coverage[3]

In reviewing a current insurance policy or when considering the initial purchase of insurance coverage, the recreation or sport business must take four steps to make a wise insurance purchase. First, examine the risks and potential losses that the organization might encounter. Then, establish an effective risk reduction program to reduce the likelihood of the risks occurring. Third, identify the remaining risks and determine which are of a magnitude that can be safely retained by the business and which might be handled by transfer by contract. Finally, the remaining risks that can significantly impact the business should then be covered by an insurance policy that will protect the business from financial loss.

Table 4.25.1 provides a list of financial risks faced by recreation or sport businesses. Of course, the risks faced vary from one type of business to another, so many of the risks listed in the table will not apply to a particular business and some businesses may encounter risks that are not listed. Nevertheless, the table can serve as a guide or checklist in helping the recreation or sport manager make certain the business is properly covered.

Types of Insurance Coverage

There are several types of insurance coverage. Each is designed to offer protection from loss for certain risks. The two types that are most indispensable for a recreation or sport business are property insurance and general liability insurance. Other types of insurance include umbrella liability, liability protection for employees, employment practices liability, motor vehicle, workers' compensation, and event insurance. Each type will be explained below.

Property Insurance

Property insurance is the primary means of protecting the recreation or sport business from loss due to damage or destruction of its facility, the facility contents, and accompanying properties. There are three levels of property coverage offered: basic, broad (or extended coverage), and special form (sometimes referred to as open perils). The **basic coverage** includes protection against a limited number of hazards (e.g., fire, malicious mischief, lightning, explosion, windstorm, aircraft or vehicles, sprinkler leakage, sinkhole collapse, volcanic action, and vandalism). **Broad coverage** includes protection against the exposures listed in basic coverage plus several other exposures (e.g., falling objects, weight of ice, water damage, and smoke). **Special form** coverage includes all losses except those that are specifically excluded (e.g., collapse, burglary, and theft). The recreation or sport manager should examine the policy carefully to determine what risks are included under each type of coverage, and should realize that even with special form coverage, some property risks are not covered. If the recreation or sport manager feels more coverage is needed, additional endorsements must be purchased. Some exposures that might not be included and might require additional endorsements include theft by employees, vehicles such as golf carts, and boilers. Property insurance also does not include normal wear and tear, cracking, settling, vermin, earthquakes, or floods.

---

[3]Independent contractors in recreation and sport activities (e.g., aerobics instructors, personal trainers, massage therapists) should remember that their operation constitutes a business entity and needs insurance just as larger recreation and sport businesses do. Independent contractors are not generally covered by the insurance of the club at which they work. By way of example, **Fitness Pak** offers liability plans for ACE-certified professionals with coverage ranging from $1 million to $6 million. The policy covers legal expenses and any financial judgments for covered losses (up to the limits of the policy) against the insured. The policy cost ranges from $155 to $288 annually.

Table 4.25.1 Typical Financial Risks Faced by Recreation & Sport Businesses

Property Exposures	Public Liability (Excluding Negligence)	Public Liability (Neligence)
Fire	Malpractice by Personnel	Death
Smoke	Products Liability	Paralysis
Natural Elements	Contractual Liability (Including	Brain Damage
Wind & Tornado Damage	Indemnification)	Loss of Limbs
Flood	Advertisers Liability	Loss of Senses
Lightning	Dram Shop/Host Liquor Liability	Internal Organ Injuries
Rain		Infliction of Emotional Stress
Hail	Intentional Torts (Personal Injury)	Broken Bones
Earthquake	Defamation	Damaged Ligaments & Tendons
Debris Removal	False Arrest or Imprisonment	Sprains and Strains
Vandalism & Malicious Mischief	Malicious Prosecution	Cuts, Punctures, Abrasions, & Bruises
Riot	Invasion of Privacy	
Explosion	Wrongful Entry or Eviction	Vehicles:
Boiler & Machinery	Assault and Battery	Injury to Other Persons
Damage to Signs		Damage to Property of Others
Glass Coverage	Employment Practices	Damage to non-owned or Leased
Damage to Parking Lots & Fences	Sexual Discrimination	Vehicles
Damage by Aircraft	Racial Discrimination	
	Handicap Discrimination	Directors & Officers Liability
Valuable Papers	Age Discrimination	Professional Liability
Electronic Data Processing	Sexual Harassment	Independent Contractors Liability
Computer Systems	Civil Liberty Violations	Adventure & Tripping Liability
Money & Property		Sponsor Liability
Theft, Burglary, Disappearance	**Business Operations**	Trip Liability
Embezzlement & Employee Dishonesty	Business Interruption	Event Liability
Off Premises Coverage	Loss of Income	
Counterfeit Losses	Extra Expenses	Watercraft
	Sickness/Accidents/Disability of	Injury to Other Persons
Moveable Equipment (golf carts,	Employees	Damage to Property of Others
mowers, etc.)	Health of Key Personnel	
Golf Green Coverage	Workers' Compensation	Injury to Participant
Damage to Property of Others (on your		Catastrophic Injury to Participant
premises)		Pollution Liability
		Suits by Employees (For Wrongful
Company Vehicles		Termination, Breach of Employment
Damage to Vehicle (collision)		Contract)
Damage to Vehicle (non-collision: theft,		
vandalism, tree limb)		
Damage to Vehicle (uninsured motorist)		
Damage to other Vehicles or Property		

Adapted from van der Smissen, B. (1990). *Legal Liability and Risk Management for Public and Private Entities.* Cincinnati: Anderson Publishing Company.

Two endorsements of special importance to many recreation or sport businesses are **extra expense insurance** and **business income insurance**. Extra expense insurance protects the business against certain indirect losses that may occur. For instance, if a health spa is destroyed by fire, some expenses that may be encountered are rental of another building during rebuilding, leasing equipment, and advertising expense. Business income coverage includes loss of income due to the insured peril and continuing expenses such as the salaries of key personnel while the business is closed.

The recreation or sport manager has other choices when purchasing property insurance. One is whether to purchase **actual cash value** or **replacement cost** insurance. Replacement cost is usually preferred because it pays the entire cost to replace the property rather than an estimate of the actual current value of the property (which might fall far short of what is needed to replace the item). Most policies have a **coinsurance** clause that requires the recreation or sport business to insure the property to at least 80 percent of the replacement cost or actual cash value, depending upon the form chosen. Failure to coinsure for the amount specified in the policy will result in a significant decrease in benefits in the event of a loss. The amount of the **deductible** is another decision that must be made. The business pays the deductible when a claim is made. For instance, if a storm does $3,000 damage to the building and the business carries a $500 deductible, the business pays the first $500 and the insurance covers the remaining $2,500. The higher the deductible, the lower the cost of the insurance, so a business can save money by carrying a high deductible and retaining that degree of risk.

The recreation or sport manager should determine what exposures are covered by the property insurance, determine from Table 4.25.1 and a knowledge of the risks of the particular recreation or sport business what property exposures are uncovered, and with the help of the insurance agent, determine the best way to provide the protection needed. Most companies offer packages combining several endorsements at a cost less than purchasing the endorsements individually.

A popular property protection enhancement is **building ordinance coverage**. This coverage protects the entity in the event fire or some other catastrophe destroys all or part of the building and ordinances require additions that were not in the damaged building. For instance, the addition of an elevator to meet ADA requirements might be mandated. With this enhancement, the cost to add an elevator would be covered by the policy.

General Liability Insurance

The purchase of **general liability insurance** protects the recreation or sport business from financial loss in the event a person suffers injury or property loss as a result of the negligence of the business or its employees. The policy is called commercial general liability (CGL). If the business is sued and the loss is covered, CGL will cover the legal costs and any award for damages up to the limit of the policy. The insurance company also has the option of paying a settlement to the plaintiff in order to avoid court expenses and risk of a larger award.

Recreation or sport businesses should and usually do carry general liability insurance with coverage of one million dollars or more. Like property insurance, endorsements may be added to supplement the basic coverage. Some of the common endorsements by businesses include the following. **Errors and omissions** coverage (professional liability or malpractice liability) can protect the business from liability for errors by medical personnel, or, in sport settings, by trainers, therapists, or exercise physiologists. **Cross liability** coverage broadens the policy to protect the business from suits from within the organization. For example, CGL would not protect if an injured volunteer worker sued an employee or if an injured employee sued a director. Cross liability would expand the coverage to include suits other than third-party suits. **Pollution liability** is a coverage often purchased by some recreation or sport businesses (e.g., golf courses). This coverage protects the business if acts by the business result in pollution and damage to neighboring property. For instance, a chemical spill in a stream on a golf course could result in damage to the property of others and subsequent legal action against the business.

There are numerous other exclusions from a CGL policy for which endorsements are available. Some of these are damage to the property of others which is stored on your property (saddle animals, watercraft, golf clubs, etc.), fire damage to adjacent property, advertising, adventure and tripping programs, wrongful dismissal, pollution or contamination of the environment, owned saddle animals, owned watercraft, and human rights violations such as sexual harassment.

Employment Practices Liability

Employment practices liability provides protection for such claims as (1) wrongful termination, (2) sexual harassment, (3) equal pay violations, and (4) discrimination (racial, sex, age, and disability). Some policies cover any violation of certain state and federal statutes, including antidiscrimination laws, Americans with Disabilities Act (ADA), Age Discrimination in Employment Act (ADEA), and the Equal Pay Act.

When this type of policy first emerged a few years ago, the costs were prohibitive for most small recreation or sport businesses. The policies also required a very large deductible. As this policy became more popular, both premiums and deductibles decreased, but both are currently increasing.[4]

---

[4]**Fitness Pak** (club insurance specialists located in Chico, CA) offers a $1 million policy with a **$10,000** deductible suitable for a large, high-end, single-location club for about **$4,500** per year.

Umbrella Liability

Umbrella liability is a policy that greatly increases the liability protection at a reasonable cost. The policy might increase liability coverage from $1 million to $5 million or more and would come into effect only after the limit of the CGL has been surpassed. This extension of coverage generally applies to the CGL policy, the vehicle coverage, and the workers' compensation insurance.

Liability Protecting Employees

Some recreation or sport businesses not only purchase liability insurance to protect the business, but also purchase insurance to protect employees in the event of legal action. The most common of these is **directors and officers liability** that usually provides general liability protection of $1 million or more for their "wrongful acts." Wrongful acts include error, misstatement, misleading statement, act, omission, and neglect of duty in the person's insured capacity. Coverage generally excludes: actions not within the scope of their duties; breach of contract; fines and penalties; dishonesty, infidelity, or criminal activities; human rights or sexual harassment violations; and failure to maintain adequate insurance.

Employee benefits liability is a type of coverage that is currently very popular, inexpensive, and easy to find. To illustrate the coverage, suppose a club pays for health insurance for its employees, but forgets to add a new employee to the policy. Some time later the person is sick, has a claim, and finds no coverage. Employee benefits liability would cover this oversight. Coverage now is usually on a claims-made basis—meaning claims must be promptly and properly made within the term of the policy. Failure to do so would invalidate coverage.

Some recreation or sport businesses provide **professional** or **malpractice insurance** for some or all employees. The professional insurance is designed to protect the employee from liability for negligence in acts related to giving professional advice or counsel. Suits often name the employee personally because the practice today is to sue all who may be potentially at fault; because the act may be an *ultra vires* act leaving only the employee as vulnerable; and because with governmental entities, the entity may be immune, leaving only the employee. Malpractice insurance applies primarily to persons in legal or health-related areas. Malpractice insurance protects both the individual and the business.

Professional and malpractice insurance can also be purchased by the individual employee. Policies are often available through a professional organization at very reasonable rates. They may also be purchased from one's insurance company, but the charge will be significantly higher. One should be aware that many exclusions exist on the policies.

Motor Vehicle Insurance

The recreation or sport manager must be certain that all business vehicles are adequately covered. Maintain coverage for damage to the business vehicles (collision, comprehensive, and uninsured motorist); damage to other vehicles, property, or persons (liability); and medical coverage for injured parties. Business vehicles should be covered with a commercial automobile policy. One's personal automobile policy generally is inadequate for use with business vehicles.

In automobile insurance, as in property insurance, the amount of the deductible must be decided for both collision (damages to your automobile from the collision with another object) and comprehensive (damage to your automobile other than from collisions, e.g., vandalism to your auto, tree limb falling on your auto). Once again, the higher the deductible, the smaller the premium.

In some recreation or sport businesses, employees occasionally must drive personal automobiles for business purposes. A **non-owned automobile** endorsement may be purchased to insure the business in such cases. Coverage may also be extended to include volunteers who use their own vehicles. If the organization cannot insure the business use of personal vehicles for employees or volunteers, procedures should be instituted to ensure that the owners of all such vehicles have adequate coverage. (Both non-owned automobile and hired vehicle endorsements can be added to the CGL when there is no need for owned auto coverage.)

Many recreation or sport businesses have occasion to rent or lease vehicles for varying periods of time. The business may purchase a stand-alone policy or an endorsement on the firm's automobile policy that covers **hired vehicles**. This policy can provide both liability protection and coverage for the rental vehicle. Be aware, however, that neither the stand-alone policy nor the endorsement (nor for that matter, insurance purchased from the rental company) will cover the loss or theft of personal property or equipment stored in the vehicle.

Other desirable endorsements are **uninsured/underinsured motorist coverage**, **bodily injury coverage**, and **property damage**. This coverage applies in the event that the other party has no insurance or the limits of that party's insurance have been reached. Typically this policy carries a $250 property damage deductible.

Workers' Compensation

Workers' compensation is a no-fault, statutory-based insurance that provides for compensation to employees who suffer injury in the course of their employment. It is mandated in most states (see Section 4.26, *Workers' Compensation*). The worker receives compensation for lost income, both temporary and long term, and medical expenses incurred. The law in each state limits the amount of compensatory income allowed. In most states, all recreation or sport businesses with three or more full-time employees are required to carry workers' compensation insurance coverage.[5] The cost of this insurance varies with the amount of risk involved in that type of business and with the claims record of each individual sport business. The premium is based on a certain number of dollars per hundred of payroll for the business. Representative costs per $100 dollars of payroll might range from $15 for a riding club, $6 for a country club, $2 for a health spa, to less than $1 for a business involving all clerical or desk work.

Injured workers simply file a claim in order to receive compensation for work-related injuries. They neither have to file suit against the employer nor prove negligence or fault on the part of the employer. The employee, however, generally cannot receive compensation for pain and suffering through workers' compensation (see also Section 4.26, *Workers' Compensation*).

Event Insurance

Many recreation or sport businesses sponsor or conduct events either on an occasional or a regular basis. For any event, the business should purchase additional liability insurance if the event is not included in the CGL policy of the business. The amount of additional insurance coverage depends upon the event and how much investment is involved and/or whether the business is dependent upon a profit from the event. Also, many parties (e.g., venue, merchandisers, media, sponsors, concessionaires, and competing teams) may need to be named as additional insureds on your policy.

A common event liability policy would include bodily injury, personal injury, and property damage; an incident policy which would cover payment for medical expense for minor injuries (injured files a claim; no suit necessary); and settlement for uncontested claims in exchange for a release.

An important coverage for many events is that for **nonappearance/cancellation of event**. Bases for cancellation are specified and the policy generally includes costs, anticipated revenues, and anticipated profits. For some events, **life or accident coverage of participants** is purchased. Other typical endorsements include **automobiles, crime, prize indemnity, fire** (for damages that may not fall under the CGL), and **media coverage** (e.g., loss of signal, failure of transmission, breach of contract by media).

Requiring Insurance of Other Parties

There are situations when it is important that a recreation or sport business require that other parties have insurance coverage. Some of these situations include (1) when another party or organization rents your facility for some type of event, (2) when a contractor or his workers are on the premises for remodeling, repair, or other work, and (3) when independent contractors make use of your facility.

---

[5]In California, the law requires that a business provide workers' compensation coverage even if there is only one employee.

Certificate of Insurance. It is good policy to require that such groups provide the recreation or sport business with a certificate of insurance. This proof of insurance is a form (called an ACORD form certificate) from the insurance company verifying that the party is covered by liability insurance. If the presence of the party covers a period of time, it may be necessary to require a certificate of insurance again at a later date to insure that coverage is still in force.

Additional Insured Endorsement. Many businesses require that the other party (e.g., building contractor doing renovations on the premises) name the recreation or sport business as an additional insured party on their insurance coverage. Additional insured status clearly provides coverage when the additional insured has a claim made against it because of the activities of the named insured. The Additional Insured Endorsement is attached with the ACORD form. The form provides details about the coverage, including the insurance company name, the policy number, the dates and limits of coverage, and the name of the agent.

Event Policy. Recreation and sport businesses that make their facilities available to other groups generally require that the organization or group purchase and show proof of a specified amount of event insurance (see previous section). Health clubs, for instance, often make their club available to groups for a dance, party, or even sleepovers. These provide additional revenue and, at the same time, familiarize a number of potential clients with the club. The club generally requires that the group purchase a 24-hour event policy that can be obtained from a specialty insurance provider. Another example of when a user might be required to purchase event insurance would be when a rock group promoter rents a gymnasium for a rock concert.

Independent Contractors. Most recreation and sport businesses do not provide liability insurance coverage for independent contractors (e.g., physical therapists, massage therapists, and personal trainers in health clubs). It is important that the independent contractor be required to carry liability insurance coverage.

Selecting the Agent and Carrier

Few administrators in recreation or sport management are insurance experts. This fact magnifies the importance of selecting both a good agent and a good carrier.

In selecting the carrier, it is important to select a carrier who specializes in recreation or sport entities similar to yours. Such companies often offer enhancements and riders that non-specialists cannot provide. They know the unique types of problems faced by your type of business. Also, it is important to make certain the company has an A rating and has been in business for a number of years.

When selecting an agent, try to find one who has at least a few recreation or sport clients similar to your entity. The better the agent understands the recreation or sport business, the more helpful the agent can be in recommending important coverages that might be critical to the business and in eliminating, or reducing, unnecessary coverages. Also, make certain the agent works for a company that specializes in recreation or sport entity protection. Select an agent from your region. The agent should walk through your facility and discuss your exposures with you. Finally, do not select an agent who is inexperienced or will not take the time to explain coverages and help you evaluate your needs.

SIGNIFICANT CASE

The *York Insurance Company v. Houston Wellness Center, Inc.* is a simple case that illustrates one of the most common mistakes made by the purchasers of insurance—failure to examine closely the exclusions in the coverage.

YORK INSURANCE COMPANY V. HOUSTON WELLNESS CENTER, INC.

Court of Appeals of Georgia, Third Division
261 Ga. App. 854; 583 S.E.2d 903; 2003 Ga. App. LEXIS 794
June 20, 2003, Decided

Opinion Blackburn, Presiding Judge.

York Insurance Company ("York") appeals the trial court's denial of its motion for summary judgment, arguing that under the plain language of the policy it issued to Houston Wellness Center, Inc. ("Houston"), it had no duty to indemnify and defend Houston in a bodily injury suit filed against it. Finding that coverage was clearly and unambiguously excluded under the terms of the policy, we reverse the trial court's denial of York's motion.

The standard of review of the trial court's denial of [York's] motion for summary judgment is a de novo review of the evidence to determine whether there is any genuine issue of material fact as to the elements required to establish the causes of action stated in the complaint. To obtain summary judgment, [York] as the moving party must demonstrate that there is no genuine issue of material fact, and that the material evidence, viewed in the light most favorable to the nonmoving party, warrants judgment as a matter of law.

In a single enumeration of error, York contends that the trial court erred in denying its motion for summary judgment, arguing that under the unambiguous terms of the insurance policy which it issued to Houston, it was not required to defend and indemnify Houston in a bodily injury suit filed against it by Anne Vandalinda. Specifically, York argues that Vandalinda's allegations against Houston fit squarely within an exclusion in the policy.

An insurance policy is governed by the ordinary rules of contract construction. The hallmark of contract construction is to ascertain the intention of the parties. O.C.G.A. § 3-2-3. However, when the terms of a written contract are clear and unambiguous, the court is to look to the contract alone to find the parties' intent. Under Georgia law, an insurance company is free to fix the terms of its policies as it sees fit, so long as such terms are not contrary to law, and it is equally free to insure against certain risks while excluding others. An insurer's duty to defend is determined by comparing the allegations of the complaint with the provisions of the policy. (Citations and punctuation omitted.) *Capitol Indem. Corp. v. L. Carter Post 4472 Veterans of Foreign Wars.* n2

Vandalinda signed up for a three-month membership with Houston, a health and fitness club, in order to get physically fit. In her complaint, Vandalinda alleged that she was given instructions by one of Houston's employees on the use of various exercise machines. At the time of her injury, Vandalinda was using an exercise machine which develops the triceps. Vandalinda tried to release the machine using her arms as she had been instructed to do by Houston's employee. However, the complaint alleges the [*4] machine improperly released from Vandalinda's control "due to improper instructions" given by the employee, and, as a result, Vandalinda experienced pain in her left arm for which surgery was later required.

York issued to Houston a commercial general liability policy which contained the following exclusion:

> *This insurance does not apply to "bodily injury," "property damage" or "personal and advertising injury" arising out of the rendering of or failure to render any service, treatment, advice or instruction relating to physical fitness, including services or advice in connection with diet, cardio-vascular fitness, body building or physical training programs.* [Italics added]

It is apparent from the allegations of the complaint that Vandalinda's claim against Houston falls within the policy exclusion. Her "bodily injury arose out of the . . . failure" of Houston's employee "to render . . . advice or instruction relating to physical fitness, including . . . advice in connection with . . . body building or physical training programs." Accordingly, coverage for Vandalinda's bodily injury was excluded by the unambiguous language of the policy endorsement.

Where the language of the contract fixing [*5] the extent of coverage is unambiguous, as here, and but one reasonable construction is possible, this court must enforce the contract as written. A term in an insurance policy that unambiguously and lawfully limits the insurer's liability may not be extended beyond what is fairly within its plain terms. [York] was entitled to judgment as a matter of law because coverage was excluded for this loss. (Citation omitted.) *Bold Corp. v. Nat. Union Fire Ins. Co. &c.* n3

Judgment reversed. Ellington and Phipps, JJ., concur.

Regan v. Mutual of Omaha Insurance Company, (2007 Ill. App. LEXIS 894). This case involves a swimming injury incurred by a baseball player on a team trip. Examine the wording of the policy restrictions and their interpretation by the court.

Maciasz v. Fireman's Fund Insurance Company and Chicago Insurance Company, (988 So. 2d 991; 2008 Ala. LEXIS 11). This case involves a client who was injured in an automobile accident on the way to camp. The primary issue examined by the court is whether the insurance policy is ambiguous.

Bedford Central School District v. Commercial Union Insurance Company, (295 A.D.2d 295; 742 N.Y.S.2d 671; 2002 N.Y. App. Div. LEXIS 5737). A student lost an eye while participating on a challenge course owned by another school. The issue was whether the student was covered as an additional insured. Note the reasons given for the judgment.

QUESTIONS YOU SHOULD BE ABLE TO ANSWER

1. When a recreation or sport manager purchases insurance for a business or entity, what are the steps to take in determining the amount of coverage needed?

2. An independent contractor also needs insurance. Generally, what type of insurance is of most importance to the contractor? Explain why?

3. Explain what is meant by (1) exclusions and (2) conditions.

4. Distinguish between liability insurance and umbrella liability coverage.

5. What should be the major factors in selecting an agent and a carrier?

REFERENCES

Cases

York Insurance Company v. Houston Wellness Center, Inc., 2003 Ga. App. LEXIS 794.

Publications

Brooks, D. (1985). Property Insurance. *Risk management today.* Washington: ICMA.

Castle, G., Cushman, R., & Kensicki, P. (1981). *The business insurance handbook.* Homewood, Ill.: Dow Jones-Irwin.

Corbett, R. (1995). *Insurance in sport and recreation.* Edmonton, Alberta: Centre for Sport and Law.

Dahlgren, S. (2000, April). Covering your assets. *Athletic Business.* p. 59.

Kufahl, S. (2002, August). Business without a safety line? *Club Industry,* p. 18.

Mehr, R., Cammack, E., & Rose, T. (1985). *Principles of insurance.* Homewood, Ill.: Richard D. Irwin, Inc.

Novick, L. B. Murky waters: Insurance basics for nonprofits. Washington, D.C.: *Nonprofit Risk Management Institutes.*

Sundheim, F. (1983). *How to insure a business.* Santa Barbara, Calif: Venture Publications.

van der Smissen, B. (1990). *Legal liability and risk management for public and private entities.* Cincinnati: Anderson Publishing Co.

Wilkinson, D. G., (Ed.). (1988). *The event planning process.* Levine, M. A., Kirke, G., Zitterman, D. B., and Kert, E. Insurance. Willowdale, Ontario, Can.: The Event Management & Marketing Institute.

4.26 Workers' Compensation

—John T. Wolohan
ITHACA COLLEGE

Under common law, when an employee was injured on the job, there was a good chance the injuries would go uncompensated due to the doctrines of assumption of risk, contributory negligence, and the fellow servant rule (Larson, 1992). Those injured workers who could overcome the preceding defenses usually faced a series of other problems before they received any compensation for their injuries. First, the injured workers, faced with little or no income, were under enormous financial pressure to settle their claims. The injured worker therefore usually received much less than the true value of his or her claim to support themselves and their families. Second, even if the injured employee was able to withstand the financial pressure and could afford to litigate the claim, the employer was often able to use the court system to his or her advantage and delay paying the employee any compensation. Finally, if the injured worker was lucky enough to recover his or her damages, the award was usually reduced by hefty attorney fees (Prosser & Keeton, 1984).

In an effort to protect injured workers and alleviate the injustice of the common law system, states began to enact workers' compensation legislation, modeled after the German and English systems. The first state to enact workers' compensation legislation was New York in 1910. By 1949, every state in the country had enacted some form of workers' compensation law. The workers' compensation legislation, which is different in every state, provides benefits, including lost wages, usually around one-half to two-thirds of the employee's weekly wages, and medical care to an employee who is injured or killed in the course of employment, regardless of fault. The right to compensation benefits is based on one simple test: Was there a work-connected injury? In exchange for this protection, the injured worker agrees to forego any tort claim he or she might have against the employer (Larson, 1992). The workers' compensation system, therefore, acts like a "bargain" between the employer and employee. The employer, in exchange for immunity from lawsuits, provides employees with swift, though limited, compensation for work-related injuries. In return, injured workers are guaranteed compensation for their injuries (Ashbrook, 2008).

Workers' compensation is, therefore, a form of strict liability. It does not matter whether the injury was caused by the employee's negligence or pure accident; *all the employee has to show is that he or she was injured in the course of employment* (Larson, 1992). As a result, the injured worker receives quick financial assistance with minimal interruption in his or her life.

FUNDAMENTAL CONCEPTS

The basic policy behind the workers' compensation system is that the cost of the product should bear the blood of the worker (Prosser & Keeton, 1984). In other words, the employer is required by the state to compensate the employee through private insurance, state-funded insurance, or self-insurance for any damages suffered by the employee. The employer should treat the cost of workers' compensation insurance as part of the cost of production. These extra costs are then added to the cost of production and passed on to the consumer.

Eligibility Requirement

Although every state has its own workers' compensation laws, there are two requirements that every injured employee must satisfy before he or she can recover workers' compensation benefits. The first requirement is that the person must show that he or she was an employee of the organization. An **employee** is defined as any person in the service of another under any contract of hire. In reviewing the relationship between an individual and a recreation or sport organization to determine if he or she was in fact an employee, the courts use an "economic reality test" (*Coleman v. Western Michigan University*, 1983). Under the economic reality test, the court examines the following factors to determine whether there existed an expressed or implied contract for hire.

1. Does the employer have the right to control or dictate the activities of the proposed employee?

2. Does the employer have the right to discipline or fire the proposed employee?

3. The payment of "wages" and, particularly, the extent to which the proposed employee is dependent upon the payment of wages or other benefits for his daily living expenses; and

4. Whether the task performed by the proposed employee was "an integral part" of the proposed employer's business (*Coleman v. Western Michigan University*, 1983 at 225).

In *Coleman v. Western Michigan University* (1983), the Michigan Court of Appeals, citing the *Rensing v. Indiana State University Board of Trustees* (1983) decision, concluded that scholarship athletes are not employees within the meaning of the workers' compensation statute. In particular, the court found that Coleman could only satisfy the third factor of the "economic reality test," that his scholarship did constitute wages. As far as the other factors, the court found that the university's right to control and discipline Coleman required by the first two factors was substantially limited. In considering the fourth factor, the court held "that the primary function of the defendant university was to provide academic education rather than conduct a football program." The term *integral*, the court held, suggests that the task performed by the employee is essential for the employer to conduct his business. The "integral part" of the university is not football, the court said, but education and research.

The second requirement every employee must meet before he or she can collect workers' compensation is that *the injury suffered by the employee must have occurred in the course of his or her employment.*

Recreation or sport managers need to be conscious of workers' compensation in the following areas: staff employees, volunteers, and scholarship athletes. With staff employees, it is clear that the recreation or sport manager should follow the local laws governing workers' compensation insurance. How volunteers and scholarship athletes are classified is much more difficult. For example, a number of states, including California, Oregon, Minnesota, and Tennessee, allow "volunteers" to be covered under the employer's workers' compensation plan (Wong & Wolohan, 1996).

Workers Compensation and Small Businesses

As mentioned earlier, workers' compensation is primarily regulated by the individual states, and therefore there is no single cohesive set of rules governing benefits, coverage, or premium computation. There are, however, some things that every business, no matter how big or small, must know. First, no matter how small your business, if you have employees, you need workers' compensation insurance. As a result, workers' compensation insurance can be a significant expense for any small business.

Second, to satisfy the workers' compensation obligations, all an employer has to do is simply purchase an insurance policy. In most states, these policies can be purchased from an insurance company. There are, however, five states and two U.S. territories (North Dakota, Ohio, Puerto Rico, the U.S. Virgin Islands, Washington, West Virginia, and Wyoming), that require employers to get coverage exclusively through state-operated funds (Priz, 2005). Thirteen states also allow employers the option of purchasing their insurance either with the state fund or private insurance. Those states that offer employers this option are Arizona, California, Colorado, Idaho, Maryland, Michigan, Minnesota, Montana, New York, Oklahoma, Oregon, Pennsylvania, and Utah (Priz, 2005).

Third, it is important to remember that if a business fails to carry workers' compensation insurance and an employee is injured, the employer can be required to not only pay the employee's medical expenses, death benefits, lost wages, and vocational rehabilitation out of pocket, but also be liable for any penalties levied by the states (Priz, 2005).

Independent Contractors

Whether an individual is hired as an independent contractor or an employee may impact the obligation an employer has under each state's workers' compensation law. For example, some states require all workers to be covered under its workers' compensation programs, regardless of whether or not they are employees or independent contractors. Some states, on the other hand, only require employees to be covered. As a result, it is important that employers know their state's laws to determine who in fact is covered and what must be required of them to comply (Priz, 2005).

Volunteers

Although covering "volunteers" under your workers' compensation plan may seem like a less-attractive option considering the up-front expense for the organization of paying for workers' compensation insurance, there are a number of important benefits from this option. First, by covering "volunteers" under your workers' compensation plan, if a volunteer is injured, you can save your organization both time and money by avoiding a negligence lawsuit. Second, by covering "volunteers" under your workers' compensation plan, you save your organization from any bad publicity that a lawsuit would generate. Finally, you also protect your volunteers from financial hardship by providing them benefits under workers' compensation (Wong & Wolohan, 1996).

For example, in 1999, a girls' softball umpire in Montana was stepping away from the plate when a player accidentally hit him. When a workers' compensation claim was filed on behalf of the umpire, the investigation revealed that local recreation league umpires and referees had no workers' compensation insurance and possibly no medical coverage at all. Without workers' compensation, recreational league umpires have to rely on their own personal medical insurance. The cost for the league to cover the referees under workers' compensation would have been about $3.08 per referee (Hull, 2000). It is important to note that the decision did not affect officials of school games because they were specifically exempted from the law.

State Legislation Covering Athletes

In affirming the decision of the California Workers' Compensation Appeals Board, the California Court of Appeals in *Graczyk v. Workers' Compensation Appeals Board* (1986), denied workers' compensation benefits to Ricky Graczyk after he sustained head, neck, and spine injuries while playing football for California State University, Fullerton. The Court of Appeals ruled that it was the intent of the state legislature to exclude Graczyk, and all scholarship athletes, from receiving workers' compensation benefits for injuries received on the playing field. The court pointed out that the California State Legislature specifically amended the state's workers' compensation statute to exclude "any person, other than a regular employee, participating in sports or athletics who receives no compensation for such participation other than the use of athletic equipment, uniforms, transportation, travel, meals, lodging, or other expenses incidental thereto" from the definition of employee.

The California State Legislature amended the statute further in 1981 when it specifically excluded "[a]ny student participating as an athlete in amateur sporting events sponsored by any public agency, public or private nonprofit college, university or school, who receives no remuneration for such participation other than the use of athletic equipment, uniforms, transportation, travel, meals, lodging, scholarships, grants in aid, and other expenses" from the definition of employee [*Graczyk v. Workers' Compensation Appeals Board*, 1986; West's Ann. Cal. Labor Code § 3353 (k)]. Hawaii, New York, and other states have followed California's example of expressly excluding scholarship athletes from workers' compensation benefits.

Another area where states have amended their workers' compensation statutes is the exclusion of professional athletes. In *Tookes v. Florida State University* (Claim No. 266-39-0855), a basketball player at Florida State University suffered a knee injury during the 1981–82 season, which required him to sit out most of the season. As a result of his injury, Tookes filed a workers' compensation claim for lost wages and medical expenses. Tookes argued that he was an employee of the university, due to his athletic scholarship, and therefore entitled to workers' compensation benefits (Wong, 1994).

The Florida Department of Labor and Employment Security and Industrial Claims judge, however, disagreed. The judge determined that there was no employer-employee relationship between Tookes and the university. Even if there was an employer-employee relationship between Tookes and the university, the judge held that Tookes would still be ineligible for benefits. If Tookes was employed by the university to play basketball, under Florida law he would be considered a professional athlete and therefore a member of a class specifically excluded under the Florida Workers' Compensation Statute (Wong, 1994). Besides Florida, at least five other states—Massachusetts, Missouri, Pennsylvania, Texas and Washington—exclude or limit workers' compensation benefits to professional athletes or have considered amending their state workers' compensation statutes to exclude professional athletes (Wolohan, 1994).

Consequences of Additional Coverage

As illustrated by *Rensing v. Indiana State University Board of Trustees* (1983), the issue of whether or not a scholarship athlete is an employee is a difficult one. For example, in most states, workers' compensation insurance rates are determined by actuarial tables that take into account the number of accidents and claims for that particular group of employees. If athletes were suddenly added into the group of school employees, the number of injuries and claims of the group would rise substantially. This would make it difficult, if not impossible, for colleges and universities to find an insurance company willing to insure them. Even if the school could find an insurance company, the increased exposure would require the insurance company to raise rates. Faced with higher insurance rates and/or the potential liability of self-insuring, many schools would be forced to reevaluate whether the increased cost and exposure is worth having an athletic program.

Other Possible Consequences

Additional Workers' Compensation Claims. If scholarship athletes are considered employees of their school, there could be an increase in the number of workers' compensation claims filed and benefits paid (Wolohan, 1994).

Tax Effect on School. If scholarship athletes were considered employees of their school, there would be some interesting tax questions for both the colleges or universities and the scholarship athletes. For example, does the scholarship athlete now have to pay taxes on the value of the scholarship? Also, will schools now be required to pay FICA and Medicare tax on the student's income? If so, how are the taxes to be paid (Wolohan, 1994)?

Employee Benefits. If scholarship athletes are considered employees of the school, are scholarship athletes eligible for employee benefits? Besides tuition, room, board, and books, are scholarship athletes now going to be eligible for life, medical, and dental insurance? How about the school's employee retirement plan, would scholarship athletes be eligible (Wolohan, 1994)?

Nonscholarship Athletes. Even if scholarship athletes are considered employees of the school, what about athletes who do not receive athletic scholarships? Because these athletes receive no compensation, they have no contractual relationship with the university to compete in athletics. Therefore, the nonscholarship athlete could never be deemed an employee and would never be covered by workers' compensation (Wolohan, 1994).

NCAA Catastrophic Injury Insurance Program. One of the reasons scholarship athletes have sought workers' compensation benefits in the past is to recover out-of-pocket medical expenses. Although most schools will pay the medical expenses of injured athletes, there usually is a limit to their generosity. In fact, it is not uncommon for a school to stop paying an injured athlete's medical and other bills. This is especially true when the injury is permanently disabling, and the injured athlete requires prolonged medical care.

In an effort to alleviate such hardships, and perhaps to prevent future court challenges on the status of scholarship athletes, the NCAA in August 1991 implemented a Catastrophic Injury Insurance Program covering every student who participates in college athletics. The NCAA's Catastrophic Insurance Plan covers student-athletes, student coaches, student managers, student trainers, and cheerleaders who have been catastrophically injured while participating in a covered intercollegiate athletic activity. The policy has a $75,000 deductible and provides benefits in excess of any other valid and collectible insurance up to $20,000,000.

The NCAA's Catastrophic Injury Insurance Program automatically insures every college athlete, student coach, student manager, student trainer, and student cheerleader who participates in NCAA sports against catastrophic injuries. The NCAA's plan is similar to workers' compensation in that it provides medical, dental, and rehabilitation expenses plus lifetime disability payments to students who are catastrophically injured, regardless of fault. The plan also includes $25,000 if the individual dies within 12 months of the accident.

The NCAA plan is more attractive than workers' compensation in a number of ways. First, scholarship athletes can collect benefits without litigating the issue of whether or not the athlete is an employee of the college or university. Second, the NCAA's plan provides the athlete with benefits immediately, without time delays, litigation costs, and the uncertainties involved in litigation. Finally, another benefit of the NCAA's plan is that it guarantees that catastrophically injured athletes will receive up to $120,000 toward the cost of completing their undergraduate degree. (For more information on the NCAA's Catastrophic Injury Insurance Program go to the NCAA Website: http://www.ncaa.org/insurance/catastrophic.html.)

Although maybe not the most recent case, the following case is significant in that it provides the reader with a thorough review of the issues surrounding scholarship athletes who suffer career-ending or life-threatening injuries. In particular, the case analyzes the definitions of "employee" for purposes of the workers' compensation laws.

RENSING V. INDIANA STATE UNIVERSITY BOARD OF TRUSTEES

Supreme Court of Indiana
444 N.E.2d 1170 (1983)

The facts established before the Industrial Board were summarized by the Court of Appeals:

"The undisputed testimony reveals that [Indiana State University Board of Trustees] the Trustees, through their agent Thomas Harp (the University's Head Football Coach), on February 4, 1974 offered Fred W. Rensing a scholarship or 'educational grant' to play football at the University. In essence, the financial aid agreement, which was renewable each year for a total of four years provided that in return for Rensing's active participation in football competition he would receive free tuition, room, board, laboratory fees, a book allowance, tutoring and a limited number of football tickets per game for family and friends. The 'agreement' provided, inter alia, the aid would continue even if Rensing suffered an injury during supervised play which would make it inadvisable, in the opinion of the doctor-director of the student health service, 'to continue to participate,' although in that event the University would require other assistance to the extent of his ability.

The trustees extended this scholarship to Rensing for the 1974–75 academic year in the form of a 'Tender of Financial Assistance.' Rensing accepted the Trustees' first tender and signed it (as did his parents) on April 29, 1974. At the end of Rensing's first academic year the Trustees extended a second 'Tender of Financial Assistance' for the 1975–76 academic year, which tender was substantially the same as the first and provided the same financial assistance to Rensing for his continued participation in the University's football program. Rensing and his father signed this second tender on June 24, 1975. It is not contested the monetary value of this assistance to Rensing for the 1975–76 academic year was $2,374, and that the 'scholarship' was in effect when Rensing's injuries occurred.

* * *

Rensing testified he suffered a knee injury during his first year (1974–75) of competition which prevented him from actively participating in the football program, during which time he continued to receive his scholarship as well as free treatment for his knee injury. The only requirement imposed by the Trustees (through Coach Harp) upon Rensing was attendance at his classes and reporting daily to the football stadium for free whirlpool and ultrasonic treatments for his injured knee.

* * *

As noted above, the financial aid agreement provided that in the event of an injury of such severity that it prevented continued athletic participation, 'Indiana State University will ask you to assist in the conduct of the athletic program within the limits of your physical capabilities' in order to continue receiving aid. The sole assistance actually asked of Rensing was to entertain prospective football recruits when they visited the University's Terre Haute campus.

During the 1975 football season, Rensing participated on the University's football team. In the spring of 1976 he partook in the team's annual three week spring practice when, on April 24, he was injured while he tackled a teammate during a punting drill.

* * *

The specific injury suffered by Rensing was a fractured dislocation of the cervical spine at the level of 4–5 vertebrae. Rensing's initial treatment consisted of traction and eventually a spinal fusion. During this period he developed pneumonia for which he had to have a tracheostomy. Eventually, Rensing was transferred to the Rehabilitation Department of the Barnes Hospital complex in St. Louis. According to Rensing's doctor at Barnes Hospital, one Franz Steinberg, Rensing's paralysis was caused by the April 24, 1976 football injury leaving him 95–100% disabled." *Rensing v. Indiana State University Board of Trustees*, supra, at pp. 80–82 (footnotes omitted).

Rensing's appeal to the Industrial Board was originally heard by a Hearing Member who found that Rensing had "failed to sustain his burden in establishing the necessary relationship of employer and employee within the meaning of the Indiana Workmen's Compensation Act," and rejected his claim. *Id.* at p. 83. The Full Industrial Board adopted the Hearing Member's findings and decision; then this decision was reversed by the Court of Appeals.

In this petition to transfer, the Trustees argue that there was no contract of hire in this case and that a student who accepts an athletic "grant-in-aid" from the University does not become an "employee" of the University within the definition of "employee" under the Workmen's Compensation Act, Ind. Code § 22-3-6-1(b), (Burns Supp., 1982). On the other hand, Rensing maintains that his agreement to play football in return for financial assistance did amount to a contract of employment.

Here, the facts concerning the injury are undisputed. The contested issue is whether the requisite employer-employee relationship existed between Rensing and the Trustees so as to bring him under the coverage of our Workmen's Compensation Act. Both the Industrial Board and the Court of Appeals correctly noted that the workmen's compensation laws are to be liberally construed. *Prater v. Indiana Briquetting Corp.*, (1969) 253 Ind. 83, 251 N.E. 2d 810. With this proposition as a starting point, the specific facts of this case must be analyzed to determine whether Rensing and the Trustees come within the definitions of "employee" and "employer" found in the statute, and specifically whether there did exist a contract of employment. Ind. Code § 22-3-6-1, supra, defines the terms "employee" and "employer" as follows:

"(a) 'Employer' includes the state and any political subdivision, any municipal corporation within the state, any individual, firm, association or corporation or the receiver or trustee of the same, or the legal representatives of a deceased person, using the services of another for pay."

"(b) The term 'employee' means every person, including a minor, in the service of another, under any contract of hire or apprenticeship, written or implied, except one whose employment is both casual and not in the usual course of the trade, business, occupation or profession of the employer."

The Court of Appeals found that there was enough evidence in the instant case to support a finding that a contract of employment did exist here. We disagree.

It is clear that while a determination of the existence of an employee-employer relationship is a complex matter involving many factors, the primary consideration is that there was an intent that a contract of employment, either express or implied, did exist. In other words, there must be a mutual belief that an employer-employee relationship did exist. *Fox v. Contract Beverage Packers, Inc.*, (1980) Ind. App., 398 N.E. 2d 709, *Gibbs v. Miller*, (1972) 152 Ind. App. 326, 283 N.E. 2d 592. It is evident from the documents which formed the agreement in this case that there was no intent to enter into an employee-employer relationship at the time the parties entered into the agreement.

In this case, the National Collegiate Athletic Association's (NCAA) constitution and bylaws were incorporated by reference into the agreements. A fundamental policy of the NCAA, which is stated in its constitution, is that intercollegiate sports are viewed as part of the educational system and are clearly distinguished from the professional sports business. The NCAA has strict rules against "taking pay" for sports or sporting activities. Any student who does accept pay is ineligible for further play at an NCAA member school in the sport for which he takes pay. Furthermore, an institution cannot, in any way, condition financial aid on a student's ability as an athlete. NCAA Constitution, Sec. 3-1-(a)-(1); Sec. 3-1-(g)-(2). The fundamental concerns behind the policies of the NCAA are that intercollegiate athletics must be maintained as a part of the educational program and student-athletes are integral parts of the institution's student body. An athlete receiving financial aid is still first and foremost a student. All of these NCAA requirements designed to prohibit student-athletes from receiving pay for participation in their sport were incorporated into the financial aid agreements Rensing and his parents signed.

Furthermore, there is evidence that the financial aid which Rensing received was not considered by the parties involved to be pay or income. Rensing was given free tuition, room, board, laboratory fees, and a book allowance. These benefits were not considered to be "pay" by the University or by the NCAA since they did not affect Rensing's or the University's eligibility status under NCAA rules. Rensing did not consider the benefits as income as he did not report them for income tax purposes. The Internal Revenue Service has ruled that scholarship recipients are not taxed on their scholarship proceeds and there is no distinction made between athletic and academic scholarships. Rev. Rul. 77-263, 1977-31 I.R.B. 8.

As far as scholarships are concerned, we find that our Indiana General Assembly clearly has recognized a distinction between the power to award financial aid to students and the power to hire employees since the former power was specifically granted to the Boards of Trustees of state educational institutions with the specific limitation that the award be reasonably related to the educational purposes and objectives of the institution and in the best interests of the institution and the state. Ind. Code § 20-12-1-2(h) (Burns 1975).

Furthermore, we find that Ind. Code § 22-4-6-2 (Burns 1974) is not applicable to scholarship benefits. In that statute, which deals with contributions by employers to unemployment insurance, employers are directed to include "all individuals attending an established school . . . who, in lieu of remuneration for such services, receive either meals, lodging, books, tuition or other education facilities." Here, Rensing was not working at a regular job for the University. The scholarship benefits he received were not given him in lieu of pay for remuneration for his services in playing football any more than academic scholarship benefits were given to other students for their high scores on tests or class assignments. Rather, in both cases, the students received benefits based upon their past demonstrated ability in various areas to enable them to pursue opportunities for higher education as well as to further progress in their own fields of endeavor.

Scholarships are given to students in a wide range of artistic, academic and athletic areas. None of these recipients is covered under Ind. Code § 22-4-6-2, supra, unless the student holds a regular job for the institution in addition to the scholarship. The statute would apply to students who work for the University and perform services not integrally connected with the institution's educational program and for which, if the student were not available, the University would have to hire outsiders, e.g., workers in the laundry, bookstore, etc. Scholarship recipients are considered to be students seeking advanced educational opportunities and are not considered to be professional athletes, musicians or artists employed by the University for their skills in their respective areas.

In addition to finding that the University, the NCAA, the IRS and Rensing, himself, did not consider the scholarship benefits to be income, we also agree with Judge Young's conclusion that Rensing was not "in the service of" the University. As Judge Young stated:

> *"Furthermore, I do not believe that Rensing was 'in the service of' the Trustees. Rensing's participation in football may well have benefited the university in a very general way. That does not mean that Rensing was in the service of the Trustees. If a student wins a Rhodes scholarship or if the debate team wins a national award that undoubtedly benefits the school, but does not mean that the student and the team are in the service of the school. Rensing performed no duties that would place him in the service of the university." Rensing v. Indiana State University, at 90.*

Courts in other jurisdictions have generally found that such individuals as student athletes, student leaders in student government associations and student resident-hall assistants are not "employees" for purposes of workmen's compensation laws unless they are also employed in a university job in addition to receiving scholarship benefits.

All of the above facts show that in this case, Rensing did not receive "pay" for playing football at the University within the meaning of the Workmen's Compensation Act; therefore, an essential element of the employer-employee relationship was missing in addition to the lack of intent. Furthermore, under the applicable rules of the NCAA, Rensing's benefits could not be reduced or withdrawn because of his athletic ability or his contribution to the team's success. Thus, the ordinary employer's right to discharge on the basis of performance was also missing. While there was an agreement between Rensing and the Trustees which established certain obligations for both parties, the agreement was not a contract of employment. Since at least three important factors indicative of an employee-employer relationship are absent in this case, we find it is not necessary to consider other factors which may or may not be present.

We find that the evidence here shows that Rensing enrolled at Indiana State University as a full-time student seeking advanced educational opportunities. He was not considered to be a professional athlete who was being paid for his athletic ability. In fact, the benefits Rensing received were subject to strict regulations by the NCAA which were designed to protect his amateur status. Rensing held no other job with the University and therefore cannot be considered an "employee" of the University within the meaning of the Workmen's Compensation Act.

It is our conclusion of law, under the facts here, including all rules and regulations of the University and the NCAA governing student athletes, that the appellant shall be considered only as a student athlete and not as an employee within the meaning of the Workmen's Compensation Act. Accordingly, we find that there is substantial evidence to support the finding of the Industrial Board that there was no employee-employer relationship between Rensing and the Trustees, and their finding must be upheld.

For all of the foregoing reasons, transfer is granted; the opinion of the Court of Appeals is vacated and the Industrial Board is in all things affirmed.

CASES ON THE SUPPLEMENTAL CD

Coleman v. Western Michigan University, 125 Mich. App. 35; 336 N.W.2d 224; (1983). This case examines whether fighting, when following his coach's instructions, is part of a professional hockey players job and therefore covered by workers' compensation.

Norfolk Admirals and Federal Insurance Company v. Ty A. Jones, 2005 Va. App. LEXIS 443. This case examines whether fighting, when following his coach's instructions, is part of a professional hockey players job and therefore covered by workers' compensation.

Rudolph v. Miami Dolphins, 447 So. 2d 284 (Fla. App., 1983). This case examines the impact the Florida Workers' Compensation Act on professional athletes.

Waldrep v. Texas Employers Insurance Association, 21 S.W.3d 692 (Tex. App, 2000). This case reexamines the issue of college athletes and whether they are employees of the schools.

QUESTIONS YOU SHOULD BE ABLE TO ANSWER

1. Are college athletes covered under workers' compensation?

2. How do you determine if an individual is an employee of an organization?

3. What are some of the benefits of the NCAA's Catastrophic Injury Insurance Program?

4. What are the benefits and disadvantages to workers of state enacted workers' compensation programs?

5. What are the benefits and disadvantages to employers of state enacted workers' compensation programs?

REFERENCES

Cases

Coleman v. Western Michigan Univ., 125 Mich. App. 35, 336 N.W.2d 224 (1983).

Graczyk v. Workers' Compensation Appeals Board, 184 Cal. App.3d 997, 229 Cal. Rptr. 494, 58 A.L.R. 4th 1245, 34 Ed. Law Rep. 523 (Cal. App. 2 Dist., Aug 8, 1986).

Rensing v. Indiana State University Board of Trustees, 437 N.E.2d 78 (1982).

Rensing v. Indiana State University Board of Trustees, 444 N.E.2d 1170 (1983).

State Compensation Fund v. Industrial Commission, 135 Colo. 570, 314 P.2d 288 (1957).

Tookes v. Florida State University, 203.436.0785.

University of Denver v. Nemeth, 257 P.2d 423 (1953).

Van Horn v. Industrial Accident Commission, 219 Cal. App. 2d 457, 33 Cal. Rptr. 169 (1963).

Publications

Ashbrook, W. J. (Summer, 2008). Defining "Employee" Within Arizona's Workers' Compensation Statute: An Argument for Inclusion. *Arizona State Law Journal*, 40, 69–712.

Bacon, J. (1997, Oct. 21). Jury: Injured college athlete ineligible for workers' comp. *USA Today*.

Hull, R. (2000, April 26). Referees and umpires cry foul in workers' comp decision. *The Daily Inter Lake*.

Larson, A. (1992). *The law of workers' compensation*. New York: Matthew Bender & Co.

NCAA Catastrophic Injury Insurance Policy. http://www.ncaa.org/insurance/catastrophic.html

Priz, E. (2005). *Ultimate guide to workers' compensation insurance*. Irvine, CA: Entrepreneur Press.

Prosser, W. L., & Keeton, W. P. (1984). *The law of torts* (5th ed.). St. Paul, MN: West Publishing Co.

Stumes, L. (2002a, Feb. 28). Rising premiums create unstable racing industry. *San Francisco Chronicle,* p. C7.

Stumes, L. (2002b, Dec. 22). Trainers, owners get some relief. *San Francisco Chronicle,* p. B15.

Wolohan, J. T. (1993, June). Ruling may have Texas-size impact. *Athletic Business, 17,* 22–23.

Wolohan, J. T. (1994). Scholarship athletes: Are they employees or students of the university? The debate continues. *Journal of Legal Aspects of Sport, 4,* 46–58.

Wong, G. M. (1994). *Essentials of amateur sports law* (2nd ed.). Westport, CT: Praeger Publishing.

Wong, G. M., & Wolohan, J. T. (1996, March). Pitching in. Schools have alternatives in determining volunteers' legal status. *Athletic Business, 20,* 10–14.

5.00

CONTRACT LAW

Contract law is one of the most fundamental duties performed by sport and recreation administrators. Therefore, it is important for all persons involved in the sport and recreation business to understand the basics of contract law. Further, once a contract is drafted, the recreation or sport manager must implement the terms of the contract and must understand the ramifications of failing to meet the contractual obligations. The following section examines the essentials of contract formation and the elements necessary for a legally valid contract.

The *Contract Law* section is divided into three parts. The first part reviews the fundamental aspects of all contracts, presents some principles of interpretation used by the courts in deciding contract disputes, discusses the concept of breach of contract and the remedies for breach, refers to provisions that are typically found in all contracts, and familiarizes you with the principles relating to signature authority. The first part is also meant as an introduction to subsequent sections that deal with sport-specific contract law topics in more detail. The second part applies the essential contract elements to employment contracts, and game, event, and sponsorship contracts. The third section looks at alternative dispute resolution methods and their growing role in sport and employment contracts.

5.10   Contract Essentials

—**Bridget Niland**

DAEMEN COLLEGE

Since before medieval times, contracts have served as the cornerstone of any business relationship (Simpson, 1986). Although contract law has greatly evolved since then, its principle function has remained the same: to provide a framework for the enforcement of promises (Davis, 1997; Hanson, 2006).

In the sport and recreation industry, managers encounter contracts on an almost daily basis (Miller, Comfort & Stoldt, 2001). For example, two contractual agreements govern the day-to-day operations of the National Football League (NFL): the collective bargaining agreement between the players and the league and the standard player contract between a player and team. Other examples of contracts in the sport and recreation industry include: membership agreements at health and fitness facilities; liability waivers between participants and athletic event operators; scholarship agreements between student-athletes and colleges; vendor contracts between concessions and professional teams or college athletic departments; and facility lease agreements between club sport teams and school districts.

Contract law is complex. As such, sport and recreation managers should consult an attorney before entering into an agreement (Sharp, 2007). Nonetheless, because of the important and pervasive role contracts play in the sport and recreation industry, it is important for managers to understand the basic principles of contract law. The purpose of this section therefore is to familiarize sport and recreation managers with the fundamental concepts of contract law and explore how those concepts apply within the industry.

FUNDAMENTAL CONCEPTS

"Contract" is a formal term to describe a voluntary agreement that imposes duties and benefits upon the parties. A contract is a promise or a set of promises for which, if breached, the law will provide a remedy [Restatement (Second) Contracts § 1]. If properly formed, a contract creates a private law between the parties. If a dispute should arise between the parties, the contract is the first resource a court will consider in resolving the matter.

There are three sources of contract law in the United States: common law principles, the Restatement of Contracts and the Uniform Commercial Code. As mentioned in Section 1.10, *The Legal System*, common law is created by previous court decisions involving similar issues. The bulk of the common law of contracts evolved through state, rather than federal court systems. The Restatement of Contracts is a compilation of contract law principles drafted by legal scholars from throughout the United States. Although it lacks the authority of common law, courts often look to the Restatement for guidance in deciding contractual disputes. The Uniform Commercial Code (U.C.C.) is a set of laws that all states but Louisiana have adopted in whole or in part. Article 2 and of the U.C.C applies to contracts for the sale of goods, which includes items such as sporting equipment and game tickets (Wong, 2002).

Common law, the Restatement and the U.C.C. all recognize different types of contractual agreements. The most basic distinction is between express or implied contracts. In an **express contract,** the parties clearly state the terms of their agreement, verbally or in writing. The standard player contract common in professional sports is one example of an express contract. **Implied contracts** occur when the conduct indicates that an agreement exists, yet there is no proof of a formal exchange of promises. For example, an implied contract exists when the parties continue to perform duties of an expired contract (*Athletes Foot Brands, LLC v. Whoohah, Inc.*, 2007). There is little legal consequence between the two types of contracts; however, it is easier to prove the existence of a contract that is expressed and in writing (Shubert, Smith & Trentadue, 1986). As such, it is best to formalize all agreements in a written document.

Contract law classifies contracts by whether they are valid, void or voidable. If a court determines that a contract is **valid**, then it will enforce the contract or grant some other relief to the non-breaching party. A court will not enforce a contract that fails to meet the legal requirements or is contrary to some other rule of law. In such cases, the contract is rendered either **void**, meaning neither party is obligated to perform, or **voidable**, which provides one party the option of canceling the agreement.

Contract Formation

The goal of sport and recreation managers should be to structure all contracts so that they are valid and enforceable should a dispute arise. The essential terms to a valid and enforceable contract are agreement; offer; acceptance; consideration; capacity; and legality.

Agreement (Mutual Assent)

The first step in creating a valid and enforceable contract is to confirm that the parties mutually assent to the fundamental terms of the agreement. Mutual assent is simply evidence that the parties had a "meeting of the minds" as to the agreement. Courts will determine mutual assent by considering whether the parties had the same understanding as to the material terms of the agreement starting with the offer and acceptance (Miller, Comfort & Stoldt, 2001).

Offer

An offer is a conditional promise from the offeror (the party who makes the offer) to the offeree (the party to whom the offer was made). An offer occurs when one party demonstrates a willingness to enter into an agreement with definite terms that leaves another party in a position to respond [Restatement (Second) Contracts § 24]. In order for there to be a valid offer, the following terms usually need to be include: (1) the parties; (2) the subject matter; (3) the time and place for the subject matter to be performed; and (4) the consideration or price to be paid (Wong, 2002). For example, Sport Agent offers to represent Superstar in endorsement negotiations with a major sneaker company in exchange for Superstar agreeing to pay Sport Agent five percent of the endorsement earnings.

Most offers involve an exchange of promises that create a **bilateral contract**. An example of a bilateral contract within the sport and recreation industry is a scheduling agreement between college football teams, wherein the offeror, Private U, promises to pay the offeree, State U, $10,000 in exchange for State U's promise to play an "away" contest on Private U's campus. A **unilateral contract**, by contrast, involves the offeror making a promise to the offeree if the offeree takes some specified action. An example of a unilateral contract in recreational sports would be a 5-kilometer road race that offers prize money to the first finisher. The only method of accepting the offer is to win the race. Promising to win the race or even running in the race does not respond to offer.

Acceptance

In addition to demonstrating a unilateral contract, the 5k road-race also highlights the importance of acceptance in contract formation. The offeror is not bound and an agreement is not formed until the offeree accepts the offer. Only the offeree can accept the offer from the offeror. An offeree can accept an offer by signature, verbally, through performance (in the case of a unilateral contract) or any other mode permitted by the offeror [Restatement (Second) Contracts § 30]. Unless the parties agree otherwise, an offer is accepted when it is sent (i.e., mailed, faxed or by email), even if the acceptance is lost in delivery or transmission. This is known as the mailbox rule.

In limited circumstances, silence by the offeree can be construed as acceptance of the offer. To avoid confusion as to acceptance, sport and recreation managers should formally respond to each offer (Wong, 2002). If the acceptance does not mirror the offer, it is a counteroffer [Restatement (Second) Contracts § 58]. A **counteroffer** alters the terms of the offer, and is not acceptance. Rather, it terminates the offeror's offer and creates a new offer. *Brooks v. Paige* demonstrates the affect of a counteroffer. During contract negotiations, Brooks, a star soccer player, responded to the Colorado Avalanche's salary offer by asking for a larger amount. The team declined and Brooks later filed a law suit related to the contract negotiations. In reviewing Brook's claims, the Colorado state court held that Brooks' response to the Avalanche's initial offer was a counteroffer that terminated the Avalanche's offer and created a new offer, which the team rejected.

Consideration

In addition to offer and acceptance, an enforceable contract must also include consideration. Consideration is the exchange of something of value between the parties. It involves each party giving up something to gain the benefit of the contract. If an agreement lacks this exchange, the contract is unenforceable (Berry & Wong, 1994). Agreements that are based on **gifts** are typically dismissed for lack of consideration because there is no mutual exchange of detriment and benefit. One party is merely benefiting from another's generosity.

Past actions, those actions occurring prior to the making of the contract and not intended to induce a promise, are also insufficient consideration. In such instances, the offeror is making a promise because the event occurred; he is not making the promise in order to get the event to happen. For example, in *Blackmon v. Iverson* (2003), plaintiff sued basketball star Allen Iverson, alleging that he was the first to suggest that Iverson use "The Answer" as a nickname for product merchandising. Iverson later decided to use the term for a line of apparel with Reebok. Iverson then promised to pay the plaintiff twenty-five percent of those earnings. Iverson recanted this promise and plaintiff sued to enforce what he argued was a valid oral contract. In dismissing the claim, the court held that the agreement lacked consideration for two reasons. First, plaintiff's suggestion of the nickname constituted a gift as there was no evidence he sought to be compensated at that time. Second, Iverson's after-the-fact offer to pay the plaintiff a portion of the earnings amounted to **past consideration** between the two parties.

Capacity

Contracts are voluntary agreements. As such, parties to a contract must possess the capacity to comprehend its terms and how those terms affect the party's legal interests. Courts will not enforce agreements in which one of the parties is shown to have lacked the capacity to represent his or her interests effectively (Wong, 2002). To void the contract, the party must show that they either lacked sufficient mental capacity, due to age or a medical condition, or were so intoxicated that the party could not understand the nature of the agreement. In either instance, contract law renders the agreement voidable by the impaired party.

For example, as a matter of public policy, "courts have protected minors from improvident and imprudent contractual commitments by declaring that the contract of a minor is voidable at the election of the minor after he attains his majority" [*Jones v. Dressel*, 623 P.2d 370 at 373(1981)]. Accordingly, with the exception of the necessaries of life (e.g., food, clothes), contracts are unenforceable against the minor, but enforceable against the other party (Sharp, 2007). The process of a minor rescinding a contract to which he or she is a party is known as **disaffirmance**. For example, in *Milicic v. Basketball Marketing Co., Inc.* (2004), the court upheld a professional basketball player's right to rescind an agency agreement he entered into as a minor.

A party can also affirm a contract entered into as a minor by simply continuing to perform his or her contractual duties as an adult. For example, the plaintiff in *Jones v. Dressel* was seventeen when he signed a contract with a recreation company that ferried skydivers to a parachute jumping site. The contract included an exculpatory agreement protecting the company from liability for accidents during or leading up to sky diving activities. The plaintiff continued to use the company's services in the several months after he turned eighteen. Just before his nineteenth birthday, plaintiff was injured when the company's plane crashed en-route to the jumping site. As a result, the plaintiff filed a negligence lawsuit against the sky-diving company and its owner. In dismissing the suit, the court held that although a minor at the time he signed the exculpatory agreement, the contract was nonetheless enforceable because plaintiff continued to use the services of the company to sky dive in the months after his eighteenth birthday.

Legality

Courts will not enforce a contract involving illegal action or subject matter or that violates public policy. For example, a court will not enforce an agreement between an athletic trainer and a professional athlete under which the trainer agreed to inject the athlete with illegal performance enhancing drugs. Courts also will refuse to enforce employment contracts that include overly broad **covenants not to compete**. Also known as non-compete clauses, these provisions attempt to limit the ability of an employee to compete against the employer in the event that the employment is terminated or the employee resigns. Most coaching contracts include some type of non-compete clause. For example, it is common for a team to prohibit a head coach from accepting another head coaching position within the same league, conference, or state. (See: Section 5.21, *Employment Contracts*)

Sport managers, however, must take care in drafting non-compete clauses because courts will not enforce clauses that are geographically broad or extend for an unduly long period of time. Such agreements, courts have reasoned, constitute an unfair restraint of trade. If properly drafted, covenants not to compete can be an effective tool in limiting the coaching carousel described in *Northeastern University v. Brown*, (2004). In that case, Northeastern University (NU) attempted to enforce a non-compete clause against Donald Brown, its head football coach. The coach's contract contained a provision that prohibited him from discussing coaching opportunities at other institutions without first gaining permission from NU's president, a provision included in almost all coaching contracts. When the University of Massachusetts attempted to hire Brown without NU's permission, NU filed a breach of contract lawsuit and sought an injunction to bar the coach from leaving. The court upheld the NU's claims citing that the close proximity of the two institutions greatly increased the likelihood that NU would suffer irreparable harm if the contract were not enforced.

Special Doctrines of Contract Law

In addition to establishing the essential terms necessary to form a valid contract, sport and recreation managers should also be aware of the following special doctrines of contract law.

Promissory Estoppel

Promissory estoppel is a remedy courts will apply when an agreement lacks the requirements of a contract (i.e., consideration), but nonetheless creates some form of detrimental reliance by one or more of the parties. Courts may apply promissory estoppel when plaintiff has shown that the agreement included (1) a promise that reasonably expected reliance, (2) there was reliance on the promise, and (3) an injustice to the party who relied on the promise.

Promissory estoppel is a common claim in breach of contract lawsuits filed by disgruntled student-athlete against college athletic programs. For example, in *Fortay v. University of Miami* (1994), the plaintiff, a highly recruited football student-athlete, sued the university after he failed to secure the starting quarterback position. Fortay claimed that during the recruiting process and again while an enrolled student, two of the university's football coaches promised him the position. After he was passed over for the spot, he filed the suit hoping to recover $10 million in damages (compensatory and punitive) for the broken promise. The case ultimately settled and the terms were not disclosed, but it opened the door to similar lawsuits against college coaches who make unreasonable promises during the recruiting process (*New York Times*, 1996).

Statute of Frauds

The Statue of Frauds is a legal doctrine dating back to common law in England. Under the doctrine, certain transactions must be in writing to be enforced. Transactions common to the sport and recreation industry and subject to the statute of fraud includes: (1) contracts that cannot be performed within a year; (2) agreements to guarantee another party's debt; (3) agreements for the sale or lease of land and; (4) contracts in which an executor or administrator promises to be personally liable for the debt of an estate. For example, courts have dismissed attempts by student-athletes to enforce a coach's verbal offer of a four-year athletic scholarship because such an agreement could not be performed within a year and thus must be in writing under the statute of frauds (*Shepard v. Loyola Marymount University*, 2002).

Parol Evidence Rule

Under the parol evidence rule, a written contract is a complete final statement of the parties agreement (i.e., fully integrated), any prior or contemporaneous oral or written statements that alter, contradict or add new information regarding the agreement are inadmissible in any court proceeding concerning the contract

[Restatement (Second) Contracts § 213]. The rule is intended to address breach of contract disputes in which one or more of the parties' referenced drafts of the contract or statements made in the negotiations process.

The rule also covers contracts where it is unclear whether all relevant terms were included. For example, in *Chuy v. Philadelphia Eagles Football Club* (1977), the plaintiff, Donald Chuy, a lineman for the Philadelphia Eagles, filed a breach of contract claim against the Eagles after the team released him under a provision in the standard player contract. Chuy argued that his contract with the team was actually a compilation of three separate contracts, one of which would have prevented his dismissal. The court waivered on considering the other contracts noting that the contracts constituted parol evidence. Another case involving the parol evidence rule and comments made between a head football coach and an athletic director during contract negotiation is *Vanderbilt University v. DiNardo*, which is examined in more detail in Section 5.21, *Employment Contracts*.

Breach of Contract

A breach of contract occurs when a party to the agreement fails to perform the duties imposed under the contract. The degree of non-performance dictates the remedy sought by the non-breaching party. A minor breach exists when one party substantially performs most of its duties under the agreement. In such circumstances, the non-breaching party may negotiate with the breaching party as to the remaining duties owed under the contract, or seek damages that resulted from the minor breach. A minor breach does not automatically relieve the non-breaching party from fulfilling its obligations under the contract. A material breach occurs when one party either fails to perform its duties under the contract or its performance was so inferior that it destroys the original intent of the agreement. Under those circumstances, the non-breaching party may immediately rescind the contract and file a lawsuit to recover damages (Wong, 2002). To succeed on a breach of contract claim, the non-breaching party will have to show: (1) there was a valid contract; (2) plaintiff performed as specified by the contract; (3) defendant failed to perform as specified by the contract; and (4) plaintiff suffered an economic loss as a result of the defendant's breach of contract.

Duty to Mitigate

Prior to issuing legal remedies, a court will consider whether the non-breaching party attempted to mitigate its damages. This duty to mitigate requires the non-breaching party to take actions that will reduce the loss incurred by the breach if possible. Basketball legend Michael Jordan's contract with now defunct communication company MCI provides an example of a plaintiff's duty to mitigate. In that case, Jordan attempted to collect compensation for an endorsement contract with MCI despite the company's bankruptcy. The company objected citing that upon learning of MCI's collapse Jordan made no attempts to mitigate his loss of the MCI compensation. The court agreed that Jordan did have an obligation to mitigate damages and required Jordan to submit additional evidence as to why his failure to mitigate should not bar recovery of his lost compensation (*In re Worldcom, Inc.*, 2007).

Defenses to a Breach of Contract Claim

To defeat a breach of contract claim, the breaching party often argues that the agreement lacked one or more elements of an enforceable contract. A defendant also may argue that one or more of the parties was mistaken as to the subject matter of the contract and thus there was no agreement. Mistake defenses are only successful if the breaching party can show that the mistake was mutual and involved the subject matter of the agreement. Generally, courts do not rescind contracts based on a unilateral mistake of the breaching party or contracts involving mutual mistakes over the value of the exchange. However, courts may rescind contracts involving fraud in either the inception of the contract or in the inducement to sign the contract. For example, football coach Rick Rodriguez sought such relief in *West Virginia University v. Rodriguez*. Rodriguez was under contract as the school's head football coach when he accepted the same position at the University of Michigan. WVU sued for breach of contract. In an attempt to defeat WVU's claim, Rodriguez argued that the employment contract was unenforceable because he had been fraudulently induced to sign the agreement by WVU's president. The case settled before the court could rule on the merits. Under the terms of the settlement, however, WVU received $4 million dollars in damages from Rodriguez and the University of Michigan.

A defendant also may contend that the contract is void because one or more of the parties lacked the authority to bind the organization or athlete to the contract. Employees act as agents of the employer and subject to agency law have actual authority, apparent authority or no authority to bind the organization to a contract. To avoid legal disputes and the associated costs, it is in the best interest of sport and recreation organizations to clearly communicate the authority and limits to authority of its employees in contractual settings (Sharp, 2007).

Remedies for a Breach of Contract

If a court finds that a party has breached a contract, it will grant relief that attempts to place the non-breaching party in the same position as if the contract had been performed [Restatement (Second) Contracts, 1981, § 347]. There are several types of remedies available to the non-breaching party: legal remedies, equitable remedies, and restitution.

Legal Remedies

Legal remedies are most prevalent and result in the court awarding the non-breaching party a monetary award for the damage incurred due to the breach. Monetary damages are distinguished as compensatory, consequential, nominal, punitive, or liquidated.

Compensatory Damages. Compensatory damages are awarded to compensate the non-breaching party for the loss of the bargain. Compensatory damages are calculated according to one of three theories. Under an **expectation interest** theory, compensatory damages will reflect the benefit the non-breaching party expected to receive from the contract. An award based on **reliance expectation** reflects the losses suffered in the non-breaching party's belief that the breaching party would perform. A damage award under this theory could include expenses and investments made by the non-breaching party in anticipation that the breaching party would perform its duties under the contract. The **restitution interest** focuses on placing the non-breaching party in the condition it was in prior to the formation of the breached contract (Wong, 2002).

Consequential Damages. Consequential damages are awarded where there are foreseeable damages that result from circumstances out of the contract. To recover consequential damages, the non-breaching party must show that the breaching party knew or had reason to know that a breach will cause special damages to the other party. For example, a professional sports team buys computer software that will allow automated ticket purchases. The computer software fails and the team spends $15,000 on temporary employees who process orders over the phone. In this situation, the team may seek to recover the $15,000 paid to the temporary employees.

Nominal Damages. Courts will award nominal damages in situations when a breach of contract occurred, but did not result in any significant economic loss. Cases resulting in nominal damages are usually motivated by principle, not money. Nominal damage awards amount to a few dollars. Nominal damages would be an appropriate remedy to a breach of contract claim involving a scheduling dispute in which the non-breaching party was able to secure another opponent and did not suffer any loss in revenue.

Punitive Damages. Punitive damages are awarded to punish a defendant's reprehensible behavior and discourage others from doing the same in the future. Punitive damages are more common in tort lawsuits. Nonetheless, a small number of jurisdictions in the United States allow punitive damages in breach of contract claims involving malicious or oppressive behavior.

Liquidated Damages. Liquidated damages are the only legal remedies not determined by a court or jury. These damages arise from a clause in the contract that specifies the damage award should either party fail to perform its duties under the agreement (Wong, 2002). In order for the clause to be enforced, it must be consistent with the actual harm suffered. Clauses that include a damage amount that far exceeds the actual harm constitute an unenforceable penalty. Liquidated damage provisions are common in professional and college sport employment contracts, as well as contest scheduling agreements. An example of such a clause is the 2006 football scheduling agreement between the University of Buffalo (UB) and West Virginia University. Initially, WVU had agreed to pay UB $150,000 to play a home football contest on WVU's campus. The contract between the two schools contained a liquidated damages clause that required the breaching party to pay the non-breaching party $200,000. After the contract was signed, UB was contacted by Auburn University and offered $450,000 to play a game on their campus on the same day as the WVU game. UB accepted Auburn's offer and breached the contract with WVU. As a result, UB was obligated to pay WVU $200,000 (Thamel, 2006).

Equitable Remedies

There are certain contractual disputes that cannot be adequately remedied by a monetary award. In such cases, court will look to non-monetary judgments referred to as equitable remedies. The most common forms of equitable remedies are specific performance and injunctions.

Specific Performance. Specific performance requires the breaching party to perform its duties under the contract. Courts will award specific performance in cases that are unique, such as the purchase of an autographed jersey or tickets to a particular sporting event. Specific performance may be impossible depending on the terms of the contract. For example, courts rarely order specific performance for a breach of a personal service contracts such as a player's or coach's contract. In addition, plaintiffs seeking specific performance must show that there is no other appropriate legal remedy that will make them whole. A claim for specific performance will fail if requested to merely place a burden or penalty on the breaching party (*Brotherson v. The Professional Basketball Club, LLC,* 2008). In *Brotherson,* the plaintiffs, season ticket holders of the Seattle SuperSonics, sought to punish the defendant for moving the team to Oklahoma City by requesting that the court enforce all the agreements with ticketholders residing in Seattle. Because the plaintiffs did not truly seek to retain the benefit of specific courts, the court rejected their claims for relief. For an additional example of season ticket holders seeking specific performance in a breach of contract case see *Yocca v. Pittsburgh Steelers, Inc.,* 2004.

Injunction. An injunction is a court order either preventing a party from doing some action, or requiring the party to do a certain act. Courts will usually only issue an injunction when there is evidence that a party will be irreparably harmed if relief is not granted (Wong, 2002). There have been numerous injunction cases against the NCAA in which a student-athlete seeks to enjoin, or prevent, the NCAA from applying a particular eligibility rule. In the context of a contract dispute involving a player or coach, this type of equitable relief is often referred to as a negative injunction because it is commonly used to block the player or coach from breaching a contract and going to play or work for another sport organization (Johnson, 1989).

Rescission and Restitution

Contracts that are unconscionable or involve illegal or fraudulent conduct, mistake or duress are often rescinded or voided by courts. The act of rescission undoes the contract. It is most often accomplished by ordering restitution, which requires all parties to return the consideration provided and any benefits reaped from the agreement (Sharp, 2007).

For example, rescission and restitution are often at issue in disputes involving health and fitness club memberships (*Robinson v. Lynmar Racquet Club, Inc.,* 1993). In *Robinson,* the plaintiff terminated her fitness club membership still owing two months of dues. The club filed a suit to collect the dues. Arguing that the contract violated the Colorado Consumer Protection Act, plaintiff also filed a lawsuit seeking rescission and restitution. In deciding the dispute, the court noted that the party seeking restitution must be capable of returning the opposite party to the position it occupied prior to entering into the contract. The court ultimately rejected Robinson's claim noting that she was unable to do this. More specifically, plaintiff could not restore defendant with her use of its facilities and services that she had received over the course of the contract. As such, rescission was not a remedy available to resolve the dispute.

Another example is *Taylor v. Wake Forest University* (1972), which involved a scholarship student-athlete who became academically ineligible to play football for the institution. As a result, the institution cancelled his athletic scholarship. In response, the student-athlete filed a breach of contract suit. In dismissing the student's case, the court noted that Taylor had failed to comply with his contractual obligation to the school and, as such, the school was entitled to rescind his athletic scholarship.

SIGNIFICANT CASE

The following case examines the issues involved in forming a valid and enforceable contract. It also discusses the choice of remedies a court has in resolving a breach of contract dispute. Finally, the case provides an example of the legal affect of a college athletic scholarship.

R. J. HENDRICKS V. CLEMSON UNIVERSITY

Supreme Court of South Carolina
578 S.E.2d 711(2003)

Opinion

Respondent, R. J. Hendricks, II ("Hendricks") was recruited out of high school by several colleges to play baseball. He received a scholarship from St. Leo College, a Division II school in Florida, and chose to attend St. Leo because it was closest to home. In his junior year at St. Leo, Hendricks received permission to talk with Division I schools about transferring in order to play baseball for a Division I team in his final year of eligibility. Hendricks's father contacted Tim Corbin ("Corbin"), assistant coach at Clemson, to inquire about a transfer for his son. Clemson pursued a one-time transfer exception for Hendricks from the NCAA, and Hendricks applied for admission and was accepted by Clemson. Hendricks received a book scholarship for approximately $ 200 to $ 250, but no other scholarship, athletic or otherwise, from Clemson.

At the time of his transfer, Hendricks had earned 80 of the 130 credit hours required for the degree he was pursuing at St. Leo in Business Administration, with a cluster in Restaurant and Hotel Management. Clemson did not offer the same major. When Hendricks decided to transfer to Clemson, he knew he would have to return to St. Leo for a final semester (in essence, for an extra semester) in order to graduate from St. Leo with his original major.

Sometime in August, prior to registration, Hendricks met with the athletic academic advisor assigned to him by Clemson's Student-Athlete Enrichment Program, Barbara Kennedy-Dixon ("Kennedy-Dixon"). As Clemson did not offer Hendricks's major, Kennedy-Dixon advised Hendricks to declare himself a Speech and Communications major. Pursuant to her advice, Hendricks enrolled in fifteen hours for the fall semester. A week and a half into the semester, however, Kennedy-Dixon realized she had not evaluated whether Hendricks was in compliance with the NCAA's fifty-percent rule, which required a student athlete to complete at least fifty percent of the course requirements toward his major to be eligible to compete during his fourth year of college enrollment. Recognizing her mistake, Kennedy-Dixon advised Hendricks to drop one class and add two speech classes, increasing his credit hours from fifteen to eighteen. Hendricks changed his

classes as advised. Kennedy-Dixon discussed the mistake with her graduate assistant, but did not report it to the director of the program. A few days before the end of the semester, Kennedy-Dixon realized that she had miscalculated the total number of electives Hendricks could take and, consequently, that he would not comply with the NCAA's fifty percent rule.

Upon discovering her mistake, Kennedy-Dixon filed a waiver application with the NCAA in which she claimed responsibility for Hendricks's failure to satisfy the rule, and requested that the NCAA waive the rule to allow Hendricks to play baseball. The NCAA denied the appeal. Hendricks passed all of his fall course hours and remained at Clemson for the spring semester, but was not allowed to play baseball. He returned to St. Leo the next fall without a scholarship as planned. Hendricks graduated on schedule in December, but stayed on at St. Leo for the spring semester to play baseball because he had not used his final year of eligibility.

Clemson won the NCAA regional title that spring and went to the College World Series. In his deposition, Clemson's head coach, Coach Leggett, stated there was no limit on the number of players allowed on the non-traveling team, but that the traveling team was limited to 25 players. Based on Hendricks's performance in fall practice, Coach Leggett testified it would have been very hard for Hendricks to make the traveling team. Coach Leggett met with Hendricks at the end of the fall semester (before he was aware Hendricks was ineligible) and explained to him that there were 3 players ahead of him in the line-up for both of the positions Hendricks played, catcher and first base.

In her deposition, Kennedy-Dixon admitted her mistakes were likely caused by personal stress she was experiencing at the time. She gave birth to a premature baby in June (before advising Hendricks in August), and was traveling to Greenville daily to visit her baby who remained in neonatal intensive care until October of Hendricks's first semester at Clemson. Kennedy-Dixon described the purpose of her job as follows: "We have a two-fold purpose . . . . We try to help our students maintain academic excellence and certainly to make sure that they remain academically eligible according to the NCAA and graduate."

Hendricks sued Clemson for negligence, breach of fiduciary duty, and breach of contract for Kennedy-Dixon's mistakes that made him ineligible to play baseball at Clemson. The trial court granted Clemson's motion for summary judgment on all causes of action. The Court of Appeals reversed summary judgment, finding that genuine issues of material fact existed regarding the viability of each of Hendricks's causes of action.

LAW/ANALYSIS

Summary judgment is appropriate where there is no genuine issue of material fact, and the moving party is entitled to judgment as a matter of law. *Hamiter v. Retirement Div. of South Carolina Budget and Control Bd.*, 484 S.E.2d 586 (1997). In determining whether any triable issues of fact exist, the evidence and all reasonable inferences must be viewed in the light most favorable to the nonmoving party.

* * *

III. Breach of Contract
Hendricks argues there is at least a genuine issue of material fact regarding the existence of a contract between him and Clemson. We disagree.

A contract is formed between two people when one gives the other sufficient consideration either to perform or refrain from performing a particular act. *Benya v. Gamble*, 321 S.E.2d 57 (Ct. App. 1984). Offer and acceptance are essential to the formation of a contract. If the evidence is conflicting or raises more than one reasonable inference, the issue should be submitted to the jury.

For support, Hendricks and the Court of Appeals cite cases from several jurisdictions that have acknowledged the possibility that "the relationship between a student and a university is at least in part contractual." *Carr v. St. John's University*, 17 A.D.2d 632 (1962). Many of these cases involve disputes between student athletes and their schools. *Ross v. Creighton Univ.*, 957 F.2d 410 (7th Cir. 1992); *Taylor v. Wake Forest Univ.*, 191 S.E.2d 379 (1972). Other cases involve claims related to the quality of the education received by the student. *Cencor, Inc. v. Tolman*, 868 P.2d 396 (Colo. 1994); *Wickstrom v. North Idaho College*, 725 P.2d 155 (Idaho 1986).

All of these cases, however, recognize that not all aspects of the student/university relationship are subject to a contract remedy. *Cencor*, 868 P.2d 396; *Ross*, 957 F.2d 410. Just as courts have prohibited recovery in tort for educational malpractice claims, courts have been equally reluctant to permit claims relating to academic qualifications of students or to the quality of education received when they are brought in contract. In barring contract actions for educational malpractice claims, courts have noted that the policy concerns that preclude those claims in tort apply with equal force when the claim is brought in contract. In *Ross*,

a student athlete sued the university alleging that the accepted him knowing he was not qualified academically to participate in its curriculum, and made a specific promise to provide certain services to him to enable him to participate meaningfully in the academic curriculum. The court allowed the claim to proceed as a breach of contract action, but made clear that the lower court would not reach the question of whether the university had provided *deficient* academic services. The court limited the inquiry to a determination of whether the university had provided *any* real access to its academic curriculum at all.

In *Cencor*, the court adhered to the same distinction, delineating between subjective and objective claims. In that case, the plaintiffs asserted that certain provisions of their enrollment agreements and the school's catalog constituted express contract terms. The court allowed plaintiffs' breach of contract claims to go forward to the extent it referenced "specific services for which the [plaintiffs] allegedly paid and which Cencor allegedly failed to provide." The court placed no value on the plaintiffs' general allegations that they had not received the education they had been promised, and instead made clear that the claim was proceeding based on the plaintiffs' allegations that Cencor had obligated itself to provide such tangible things as modern equipment and computer training for all students.

Clemson admits that some aspects of the student/university relationship are indeed contractual, but argues Hendricks has not pointed to an identifiable contractual promise that Clemson failed to honor in this case. We agree. Hendricks fails to point to any written promise from Clemson to ensure his athletic eligibility, and submits no real evidence to support his claim that such a promise was implied. He did not discuss NCAA academic eligibility until he was already enrolled at Clemson. His conversations with Kennedy-Dixon in June, according to both his deposition and Kennedy-Dixon's deposition, were limited to what major would most easily transfer back to St. Leo.

Hendricks's claim calls for an adjudication of the *deficiency* of Clemson's services. As such, allowing Hendricks's claim to proceed would invite courts to engage in just the type of subjective analysis that courts prohibiting educational malpractice claims in tort and contract have avoided.

IV. Damages
As discussed, we find no actionable duty or contract existed under the circumstances presented. Accordingly, it is unnecessary to address Hendricks' claim for damages.

CONCLUSION

For the foregoing reasons, we **REVERSE** the Court of Appeals and reinstate the trial court's grant of summary judgment in favor of Clemson on all causes of action.

CASES ON THE SUPPLEMENTAL CD

Blackmon v. Iverson, 324 F.Supp.2d 602 (E.D. Pa. 2003). This case looks the issue of past consideration and whether an individual's promise created a valid contract.

Brotherson v. The Professional Basketball Club, LLC, 2009 U.S. Dist. LEXIS 13912 (W.D. Wash. 2009).

This case examines whether a brochure soliciting season tickets created a contract between the team and the buyers.

Ross v. Creighton University, 957 F.2d 410 (7th Cir. 1992). This cases examines what legal duty colleges have to educate scholarship athletes.

QUESTIONS YOU SHOULD BE ABLE TO ANSWER

1. What are some examples of contracts in the sport and recreation industry?

2. What are the three sources of contract law in the United States?

3. What are the four elements of an enforceable contract?

4. What will the non-breaching party have to show to succeed on a breach of contract claim?

5. What are the different remedies to a successful breach of contract claim?

REFERENCES

Cases

Athletes Foot Brands, LLC v. Whoohah, Inc., 2007 U.S. Dist. LEXIS 74778 (D. Idaho 2007).

Blackmon v. Iverson, 324 F.Supp.2d 602 (E.D. Pa. 2003).

Brooks v. Paige, 773 P.2d 1098 (Colo. Ct. App. 1988).

Brotherson v. The Professional Basketball Club, LLC, 2009 U.S. Dist. LEXIS 13912 (W.D. Wash. 2009).

Chuy v. Phiadelphia Eagles Football Club, 431 F.Supp. 254 (E.D. Pa. 1977).

Fortay v. University of Miami, 1994 U.S. Dist. LEXIS 1865 (D.N.J. 1994).

Hanlon v. Providence College, 615 F.2d 535 (1st Cir. 1980).

Hendricks v. Clemson, S.E.2d 711 (S.C. 2003).

In re Worldcom, Inc., 2007 WL 446735 (Bkrtcy. S.D.N.Y. 2007).

Jones v. Dressel, 623 P.2d 370 (Colo. 1981).

Milicic v. Basketball Marketing Co., Inc., 857 A.2d 689 (Pa. Super. Ct. 2004).

Northeastern University v. Brown, 2004 Mass. Super LEXIS 64 (2004).

Robinson v. Lymar Racquet Club, 851 P.2d 274 (Colo. App. 1993).

Shepard v. Loyola Marymount Univ., 2002 Daily Journal DAR 11545 (Cal. App.2d Dist. 2002).

Taylor v. Wake Forest Univ., 191 S.E.2d 379 (1972).

Vanderbilt University v. DiNardo, 174 F.3d 751 (6th Cir. 1999).

West Virginia University v. Rodriguez, 2008 WL 1739259 (Trial Pleading) (N.D.W.Va. Feb. 1, 2008).

Yocca v. Pittsburgh Steelers Sports, Inc., 854 A.2d 425 (Pa. 2004).

Publications

American Law Institute. (1981). *Restatement (second) of the law of contracts*. St. Paul, MN: American Law Institute.

Berry, R., & Wong, G. (1994). *The Law and Business of the Sports Industries* (3rd. ed.). Westport, CT: Prager Publishing.

Davis, T. (1997). Balancing Freedom of Contract and Competing Values in Sports. *South Texas Law Review 38*, 1115.

Hanson, S. (2006). Athletic Scholarships as Unconscionable Contracts of Adhesion: Has the NCAA Fouled Out? *Sports Law Journal 13*, 41–77.

Johnson, A. (1989). The Argument for Self-Help Specific Performance: Opportunistic Renegotiation of Player Contracts. *Connecticut Law Review 22*, 61.

Miller, L., Comfort, P., & Stoldt, G. (2001). Teaching Perspective: Contracts 101: Basics and Applications, *Journal of Legal Aspects of Sport 11*, 79.

Sharp, L. (2007). Contract essentials. In Cotton, D. & Wolohan, J. *Law for recreation and sport managers* (4th ed.). pp. 364–374. Dubuque, IA: Kendall/Hunt Publishing.

Shubert, G., Smith J., & Trentadue, R. (1986). *Sport law* (1st ed.). St. Paul, MN: West Publishing.

Simpson, A. (1987). *A History of the Common Law of Contract: The Rise of the Action of Assumpsit* (2d ed.), Oxford: Oxford Publishing.

Sports People: Football: Fortay and Miami Settle. (1996, June 25). *New York Times*, p. B6.

Thamel, P. (2006, August 23). *In College Football, Big Paydays for Humiliation. New York Times*, p. A1.

Wong, G. (2002). *Essentials of Sports Law* (3rd ed.). Westport, CT: Prager Publishing.

5.21 Employment Contracts

—**Rodney L. Caughron**
NORTHERN ILLINOIS UNIVERSITY

Historically, employment contracts in sport and recreation were a matter of a handshake or a simple letter of agreement. With the increased level of compensation—both in contractual salary and outside income—and the tenuous nature of a coach or administrator's position, employment contracts have evolved into complex legal documents, often involving complicated negotiations. However, no matter how complicated the contracts have become, employment contracts are essentially the same as other contracts in the "real" world. The only difference is that they have the propensity to be broken on a much more frequent basis—often with the assent of both parties. That is why the more complicated and specific a contract can be crafted, the more both parties will benefit because the contracts reduce ambiguity and specifically define the terms of the contractual association (Yasser, McCurdy, Goplerud, & Weston, 2000).

FUNDAMENTAL CONCEPTS

As competition and winning have become more vital to the economic interests of the sport organization, both intercollegiate and professional, the tenure of coaches and administrators at a particular institution have become more tenuous (Greenberg & Thomas, 2005, p. 9). If the coach doesn't win, the organization will try to "unload" them (as demonstrated in *Cole v. Valley Ice Garden*, 2005), in many cases by buying the coach or administrator's contract out to secure a new person for the position. It is necessary, therefore, that both parties be protected by an employment contract that is meticulously drafted to satisfy the needs of both the coach/administrator and the institution (Greenberg, 2001). Greenberg gives some very good advice to anyone creating a contract when he stated, "If words are not subject to clear and simple, Webster-style definitions, they should not be in the contract" (Greenberg, 2006).

Elements of a Common Contract

Although it is important to note that no two contracts will be alike, there are a number of elements that are commonly found in every intercollegiate coaching contract. These elements can also serve as a model for other employment contracts. These contracts often involve special perks and other common employment benefits as well as salary. For example, in John Calipari's $31.65 million deal with the University of Kentucky, his base pay is listed at just $400,000 per year. The contract, however, is packed with perks beyond his annual salary, including membership to the country club of his choice, two cars, 20 prime "lower-level" season tickets to UK home games, eight tickets for each UK home football game, and incentives for reaching the NCAA Sweet Sixteen and Final Four and winning a national title. It is important to note that although all contracts have most of the same elements, each contact should be tailored for the particular job. Following are some of the most common elements of a sport-related contract.

Duties and Responsibilities

- The contract should state that the employee agrees to devote his/her best effort to full-time performance as the position requires.

- There should be a specific list of responsibilities required to be performed by the employee.

- The contract should also include a general phrase that the employee agrees to perform other duties assigned to him or her, and mutually agreed upon.

Term of Employment

- The length of the contract should be explicit. For example in *Lindsey v. University of Arizona* (1987), the terms of employment were unclear. Due to breach of an oral commitment by the university to extend his contract for three additional years, Lindsey won a substantial judgment. In another case, *Small v. Juniata College* (1997), the court found that Small's employment contract was for a one-year term and that the college personnel manual termination procedures did not affect the status of these one-year appointments.

Rollover Provisions

- Rollover provisions allow the organization to extend an employee's contract for an extra year, with the mutual agreement of the employee and organization. Even NCAA President Myles Brand was able to exercise a two-year rollover extension to his current contract, renewing the contract through 2009 ("NCAA president," 2005).

- Rollover provisions tend to be one-sided in favor of the employee, exemplified in the statement by *Atlanta Journal-Constitution* reporter Jeff Schultz, who stated, "Now a coach can have an iron-clad, no-escape contract signed in vampire blood . . . then weasel out of rollover contracts and jump across the street for a raise" (Schultz, 2006). This is especially true when the contract's rollover agreement requires specific terms of notice for terminating the employee, allowing the employee to collect more monetary damages if the contract is terminated by the organization. For example, in *Cherry v. A-P-A Sports, Inc.* (1983), Cherry's contract provided that if his contract was not renewed for an additional two years, he would automatically receive $35,000 in compensation.

Reassignment Clause

- A reassignment clause allows for the removal of the employee from the originally contracted position and reassignment to another position that is consistent with the employee's education and experience. For example, in *Monson v. State of Oregon* (1995), the University of Oregon had included a provision for reassignment, which they exercised, changing his assignment from men's basketball coach to golf coach. The court upheld the reassignment because it was part of the contractual language.

- The issue of reassignment and "future" loss of income due to the reassignment was addressed in *Smith v. Alanis & Zapata County Independent School District*, (2002). Smith was hired as the head high school football coach and athletic coordinator, but was reassigned midyear in accordance with his contract. Smith claimed that his removal as head coach, although not reducing his current salary per the contract, would have an effect on future income as a head coach. The court concluded that contract law in Texas did not allow compensation for future earning capacity, and therefore, the actions of the school district were within the scope of the employment contract.

- A reassignment clause should be coupled with the avoidance of any language in the contract that gives the employee the right to be in any specific titled position (e.g., head coach).

- A reassignment clause places the burden of terminating the contract on the employee if he/she chooses not to take the reassignment.

Compensation Clause

- A compensation clause should include the guaranteed base salary, terms of pay increases over the time of the contract, fringe benefits, moving and relocation expenses, bonuses, additional retirement benefits, and other compensation that the organization itself provides the employee.

- All compensations should be specifically delineated and agreed upon.

Fringe Benefits

- This area can include myriad benefits that organizations are offering employees and administrators. They may include complementary cars, travel, loans, moving and housing expenses, and tickets. Many of the benefits are offered to the normal employee, but in many situations the benefits for the coach or administrator are inflated or outside the normal employees benefits.

- The type, amount, date the benefit is available, and penalties for termination of contract should be explicitly written out within the contract.

Bonuses and Incentives

- Bonuses and incentives are becoming more important to all employees. They may include signing bonuses, incentives based on team success, and in the case of college and university coaches and administrators, graduation rates of student–athletes.

- In *White v. National Football League* (2007), a player (Ashley Lelie) that did not report to training camp was fined by his team (Denver Broncos) $220,000 of the player's option bonus according to the team's interpretation of the NFL CBA. The court saw it differently and ruled that the option was earned as soon as it had been awarded and could not be recovered by the team.

Provisions for Outside and/or Supplemental Income

- These sources of income may include radio and television contracts; endorsements; shoe, apparel and equipment contracts; income from speeches and written materials, as well as camps and other various sources of supplemental income.

- The organization should include in the contract that it is not legally liable for claims arising from these outside income sources.

- A provision in the contract should stipulate that the organization retains the right of final approval for all agreements for outside income sources made by the employee.

- Greenberg and Smith (2007) delineate the non-base income earned by Bruce Pearl, University of Tennessee Head Men's Basketball coach in the 2006–2007 season. Pearl's base salary was $300,000, but with his additional income sources, Pearl's reported income was approximately $1.5 million that season.

Termination Clause

- A termination clause should state that termination may be caused by the death or criminal conduct. For example, in *Maddox v. University of Tennessee* (1995), the court upheld the dismissal of Maddox, an alcoholic, due to his arrest for drunk driving. Maddox contended that his dismissal was due to his alcoholism, which violated the Americans with Disabilities Act of 1990 (ADA) and the Rehabilitation Act of 1973. The court did not agree, commenting that the termination was for his criminal act and the subsequent negative publicity. In a similar case, ABC TV terminated an employee after he was arrested for selling cocaine. The plaintiff claimed he was covered under ADA, but the court ruled that his termination was based on the plaintiff's breach of the morals clause in his contract because he lied about the situation (*Nader v. ABC Television*, 2005).

- The contract should also contain a termination for "just cause" clause, so that if the employee violates either the organization's rules, its affiliation rules, civil or criminal laws, moral turpitude, refusal to perform duties, and so forth, the employee can be fired. These may be explicitly expressed or implied in the contract or in the "customs and mores" of the organization or society. For example, in *Deli v. University of Minnesota* (1994), the head women's gymnastics coach and her husband, the assistant coach, were terminated when the gymnasts viewed a videotape of the coach and her husband having sex. The court upheld the dismissal of both of the coaches, based on the indiscretions with the videotape and for other "just cause" reasons. Other examples are *McKenzie v. Wright State University* (1996), and *Farner v. Idaho Falls School District*, (2000). In *McKenzie v. Wright State University* (1996); the court upheld the dismissal of McKenzie for NCAA rules violations, which were specifically mentioned in her employment contract as cause for termination. The *Farner* case demonstrated how the master contract for high school teachers, when incorporating coaching and extra duties, requires the same "just cause" for termination as does the teaching aspect of the contract. To terminate without just cause violates the individual's due process rights.

- The termination should also spell out the due process rights employees have to challenge their termination. This could include a formal hearing within the organization or the use of an arbitrator. For example, in *Stamps Public Schools v. Colvert* (1996), Colvert was able to prove that the school district had violated its own procedures and had not given him his contractually guaranteed due process. This was also the case with Rick Neuheisel, former head football coach at the University of Washington. Neuheisel was fired six months before the end of his original contract with Washington, based on a questionable investigation by the NCAA concerning Neuheisel's involvement in an NCAA men's basketball betting pool. Washington fired Neuheisel because he originally denied involvement and then admitted to it. Neuheisel filed a lawsuit against Washington based in part on the university's denial of contractually guaranteed due process and the subsequent hearing. Neuheisel and Washington later settled for a cash payment of $2.5 million (from the NCAA for defamation) and $500,000 in cash and $1.5 million in a forgiven loan from the university (Greenberg & Thomas, 2005).

- Termination without cause allows the organization to fire the employee for any reason. This will usually come with a price, in that the organization will usually have to negotiate a settlement with the employee if a termination occurs. This was not the case in *Frazier v. University of the District of Columbia* (1990), however, where the court found that Frazier was an at-will employee and could be terminated at any time.

- In a very interesting case (*O'Brien v. The Ohio State University*, 2007), James O'Brien, Head Basketball Coach at The Ohio State University (OSU), was terminated by the athletic director for a "material breach" of his coaching contract. O'Brien gave a $6,000 loan to a recruited basketball player's mother in Yugoslavia in early 1999 (although the athlete was ruled a professional and was not able to play for OSU), based on humanitarian reasons and his belief that the athlete was not eligible anyway. O'Brien disclosed the loan to Geiger the Athletic Director in 2004, and OSU self-reported the loan as a NCAA violation. OSU fired O'Brien on June 8, 2004 for a "material breach" of his contract (pp. 41–42). OSU referred to the loan issues as a "for cause" violation of Section 5.1(a) of the contract (p. 42). The court, in what could only be termed an indictment of Geiger, OSU counsel and the NCAA, sided with O'Brien in the application of the contract and the proper authority to fire the coach. Specifically, the court stated that OSU fired O'Brien for a major NCAA violation, prior to an NCAA determination, and did not follow the letter of the contract, and that even after the NCAA did investigate and make a determination, "the trial court found the NCAA report and its related testimony and evidence to be unreliable . . . (p. 22). The appellate court sustained the trial courts award to O'Brien of $2,494,972.83 for his firing without cause (p. 3).

- Greenberg (2006) suggests that termination should be characterized not as for cause or not for cause, but as an agreed upon liquidated damages amount, paid to the coach when he or she is fired.

Buyout Provisions

- A buyout provision allows the employee or institution to terminate the contract on the payment of a specified amount of money. For example, in *Tolis v. Board of Supervisors of Louisiana State University*

(1992), the court upheld an oral agreement to buy out Tolis's contract, which the defendants later violated. The court held that the Board of Supervisors must abide by their oral buyout agreement.

- A buyout provision may include a liquidated damages clause (see *Vanderbilt University v. DiNardo*, 1999).

- An interesting situation that put both the coach and owner in a tight predicament was the $7 million buyout provision that was not exercised against George Karl, former head coach with the Milwaukee Bucks. Karl's contract was not extended by the team, yet the owner at the time, Herb Kohl—who was trying to sell the team—refused to exercise the buyout to save money and make the team more marketable. This essentially left Karl a lame duck coach, but without any remedy except to quit and forfeit his contract (Hunt, 2003).

Arbitration Agreement

- An arbitration agreement is a clause in the contract that stipulates that if any dispute arises from the interpretation of the contract or other factors concerning the contract, the issues will be dealt with through arbitration (see *Miami Dolphins Ltd. v. Williams*, 2005).

- The areas to be arbitrated should be specifically delineated within this section of the contract.

- The benefit of arbitration is that it reduces the cost of litigation for both parties. A good example of this is when Bill Parcells broke his contract with the New England Patriots and signed a contract to coach with the New York Jets. Instead of taking the issue to court, both sides allowed National Football League Commissioner Paul Tagliabue to arbitrate the dispute.

- An interesting case challenging the ability of NFL Commissioner Tagliabue to serve as the arbitrator in contract disputes within the NFL involved coaches with the Minnesota Vikings, who after they were fired claimed they were entitled to incentive pay under their contract. The appellants filed suit to remove Tagliabue as the arbitrator in their dispute, but the court stated that nowhere in the Federal Arbitration Act is there an allowance to challenge an arbitrator—biased or not—prior to a decision by the arbitrator (*Alexander, et al. v. Minnesota Vikings Football Club LLC & National Football League*, 2002).

Covenant Not to Compete

Covenants not to compete are also commonly used in coaching contracts. For example, in the new football coach's contract, the school could include a clause prohibiting the coach from accepting another head coaching position at any school in the same conference for five years after leaving his current school. The purpose of the clause is to protect the competitive advantage of the school, while at the same time not overly restricting the coach's future earning possibilities. If the clause is too restrictive in scope or time (*MacGinnitie v. Hobbs Group*, 2005), courts will refuse to enforce it against the coach.

An interesting case dealing with sports agencies and non-compete clauses in employment contracts was addressed in *Steinberg Moorad & Dunn, Inc. v. Dunn*, (2005). The court reversed a lower court decision when it ruled that, under California law, non-compete clauses are invalid in contracts. Steinberg, Moorad & Dunn (SMD) had accused Dunn of breach of contract after he left the firm and started his own sports agency firm, taking several of SMD's professional athlete clients with him.

Although these elements may not be exhaustive, they set a framework from which sport and recreation managers involved in contract development can operate.

Discussion of Contract Issues

Typically in sports the employee has the advantage in any contractual situation in which the employee unilaterally decides to terminate the contract. If an employee unilaterally terminates his or her contract, thus breaching the conditions of the contract, the sport organization has essentially no remedy to "force" the employee to perform their duties. The reason the courts are unwilling to enforce such contracts is that to compel performance of a contractual duty would constitute a violation of the Thirteenth Amendment's prohibition against involuntary servitude. In addition, the court has stated that it would be unable to monitor the level of coaching performance and enforce proper coaching skills in a coaching contract (Cozzillio & Levinstein, 1997).

Although unable to compel the employee to perform his or her duties, the sport organization may acquire injunctive relief, which prohibits the employee from acquiring similar employment at another sport organization. This was evident in the case of Chuck Fairbanks and the New England Patriots. Fairbanks, who was head coach of the New England Patriots, breached his contract with New England to take the head coaching position with the University of Colorado. To prevent Fairbanks from leaving, the Patriots obtained injunctive relief, prohibiting the University of Colorado from entering into a coaching contract with Fairbanks (*New England Patriots Football Club Inc. v. University of Colorado*, 1979).

In some instances, problems arise between parties of an employment contract based on their personal relationships and friendship. One typical situation is when there is a verbal understanding that in the future a specific employment relationship will be consummated contractually by the two parties, and the agent of the organization does not have the authority to make such an agreement, or due to the fact that it is only an agreement and not yet a contract, the relationship does not transpire. This was the case in *Barnett v. Board of Trustees for State Colleges and Universities A/K/A University of Louisiana System*, (2001). Barnett was originally hired as basketball coach at Northwestern State University in 1994. A plan was formulated by Barnett and the then-university president, which would elevate Barnett to athletic director in 1996. A letter from the president was sent to Barnett confirming this agreement in 1995, pending approval by the university Board of Trustees. Louisiana state law required personnel appointments at the university to be approved by the Board of Trustees. Before Barnett could be appointed to the athletic director's position, a new president took office at the institution, and someone else was hired as athletic director. Barnett filed suit against the university for breach of contract. The court ruled that no contract existed because all contracts had to be submitted to the board, and Barnett was aware of this prerequisite from the beginning of the agreement. This case demonstrates the importance of employees knowing the exact procedural requirements for contracts with a particular institution or organization to become valid and actionable. *Meinders v. Dunkerton Community School District* (2002), is an example of a similar situation at the high school level.

It is interesting to note that even when an employee breaches his or her contract and jumps from one organization to another, in most cases the parties involved eventually agree on a settlement, either financial or, in the case of professional teams, financial and possible trade of draft picks. For example, the New York Jets settled with the New England Patriots to obtain Bill Parcells for a reported $300,000 charitable donation and the Jets' third- and fourth-round draft picks in 1997, their second-round choice in 1998, and their first-round pick in 1999 (Rosenthal, 1997).

In addition, the contract will often also specifically list other perquisites that the coach or administrator may be entitled to, although not always explicitly delineating each item. For example, in *Rodgers v. Georgia Tech Athletic Association*, (1983) (see the supplemental CD), Rodgers, the head football coach at Georgia Tech, asked the court to award him the value of the perquisites for the remainder of his terminated contract. In reaching its decision, the court eliminated those perquisites directly related to the function of Rodgers' job as head coach (i.e., a secretary), but awarded Rodgers the value of those items that were regularly provided to him either through the Association or from outside sources (i.e., television and radio revenues). The court also eliminated items that were gifts, and those items that the Association did not have knowledge of or contemplate as part of the contract. Therefore, the *Rodgers* case set a precedent that allows coaches or administrators to recover items that are specifically or tacitly provided for by the sport organization and those items that the coach or administrator and the organization would normally expect to be perquisites under the contract (*Rodgers v. Georgia Tech Athletic Association*, 1983).

Independent Contractors vs. Employee

A growing issue in the sport, fitness, and recreational industries is the hiring of independent contractors to perform duties that were typically performed by employees. Although the use of independent contractors is a good way to reduce costs and an organization's legal liability, not every individual will actually meet the standards of an "independent contractor." The classification of workers has significant implications for the employer in terms of taxes, tort liability, and other forms of employee compensation (Caughron & Fargher, 2004).

Darryll Halcomb Lewis brought to light the importance of this issue when dealing with sports officials. Halcomb Lewis states that if a sports official hurt on the job is considered an independent contractor, two consequences result: (1) the referee is barred from filing a worker's compensation claim, and (2) that absent legislated immunity, the organization hiring the official may be held liable for those injuries (Halcomb Lewis, 1998). This was echoed in *Wadler v. Eastern College Athletic Conference* (2003), in which a claim of Title VII discrimination based on race was dismissed against an athletic conference due to a lack of an employer–employee relationship—essentially recognizing a college baseball umpire as an independent contractor due to the employment relationship he had with the defendants in the case.

Although no specific test has been adopted universally by all jurisdictions, the Internal Revenue Service has developed a checklist that includes twenty criteria for determining whether someone is an independent contractor or an employee. The status of the individual is dependent on the following (the more reliant the individual is on the employer, the greater likelihood they are an employee):

1. **Instructions.** Level of instruction to accomplish the work, and the level of supervision;
2. **Training.** Initial and ongoing training;
3. **Integration.** Independence of individual within the workplace;
4. **Services rendered personally.** Ability of individual to subcontract;
5. **Hiring, supervising, and paying assistants.** Ability to hire and treat others as employees by the worker;
6. **Continuing relationship.** The relationship is based on a specific period of time or completion of a specific task;
7. **Set hours of work.** Role of the employer in setting the schedule of the individual;
8. **Full-time required.** Role of the employer in setting minimum or full-time work requirement;
9. **Doing work on employer's premises.** The level of on-site supervision and reliance on employer's facilities and equipment;
10. **Order or sequence set.** Level the employer sets the pattern of work by individual;
11. **Oral or written reports.** The amount of paperwork the individual must file with the employer;
12. **Payment by the hour, week, or month.** Method of payment and the inclusion of sick and vacation days;
13. **Payment of business and/or traveling expenses.** Level of compensation employer provides individual to perform work;
14. **Furnishing of tools and materials.** Level of use by individual of employer's equipment;
15. **Significant investment.** Records are kept to identify individual's contribution (e.g., purchase of equipment) to the employer's facilities;
16. **Realization of profit or loss.** The individual is responsible for their own business accounting and insurance;
17. **Working for more than one firm.** Do the customers pay the individual directly, and can the individual contract with other employers in the same business?
18. **Making services available to the public.** Level of independence the individual has in marketing, advertising, and working independent of employer;
19. **Right to discharge.** Level of ability of employer to discipline and fire individual;
20. **Right to terminate.** Can the individual end relationship with employer or are they bound contractually (Internal Revenue Service, pp. 298–299) (see Caughron & Fargher, 2004, for a full explanation of the classification process).

This case covers a multitude of contractual issues that are important to individuals involved in contract development and negotiations. The most important issue this case brings forward is that when developing a contract, each side must specifically state their expectations concerning elements of the agreement and write them out explicitly. This is illustrated in the reasons given in the contract for a lengthy contract, program stability, as well as the acceptance of liquidated damages, and the inclusion of the extension into the entire scope of the original contract. Lastly, this case shows that the court will recognize conditional acceptance of contracts, even verbal, which determine the enforcement of the contract.(See the supplemental CD.)

VANDERBILT UNIVERSITY V. DINARDO

United States Court of Appeals for the Sixth Circuit
174 F.3d 751 (6th Cir. 1999)

Opinion: J. Gibson

On December 3, 1990, Vanderbilt University and Gerry DiNardo executed an employment contract hiring DiNardo to be Vanderbilt's head football coach. Section one of the contract provided:

The University hereby agrees to hire Mr. DiNardo for a period of five (5) years from the date hereof with Mr. DiNardo's assurance that he will serve the entire term of this Contract, a long-term commitment by Mr. DiNardo being important to the University's desire for a stable intercollegiate football program. . . .

The contract also contained reciprocal liquidated damage provisions. Vanderbilt agreed to pay DiNardo his remaining salary should Vanderbilt replace him as football coach, and DiNardo agreed to reimburse Vanderbilt should he leave before his contract expired. Section eight of the contract stated:

Mr. DiNardo recognizes that his promise to work for the University for the entire term of this 5-year Contract is of the essence of this Contract to the University. Mr. DiNardo also recognizes that the University is making a highly valuable investment in his continued employment by entering into this Contract and its investment would be lost were he to resign or otherwise terminate his employment. . . . Accordingly, Mr. DiNardo agrees that in the event he resigns or otherwise terminates his employment as Head Football Coach, prior to the expiration of this Contract, and is employed or performing services for a person or institution other than the University, he will pay to the University as liquidated damages an amount equal to his Base Salary (later negotiated as his net salary), . . . multiplied by the number of years (or portion(s) thereof) remaining on the Contract.

* * *

Vanderbilt initially set DiNardo's salary at $100,000 per year. DiNardo received salary increases in 1992, 1993, and 1994.

On August 14, 1994, Paul Hoolahan, Vanderbilt's Athletic Director . . . talk(ed) to DiNardo about a contract extension. (DiNardo's original contract would expire on January 5, 1996). Hoolahan offered DiNardo a two-year contract extension. DiNardo told Hoolahan that he wanted to extend his contract, but that he also wanted to discuss the extension with Larry DiNardo, his brother and attorney.

Hoolahan telephoned John Callison, Deputy General Counsel for Vanderbilt, and asked him to prepare a contract extension. Callison drafted an addendum to the original employment contract which provided for a two-year extension of the original contract, specifying a termination date of January 5, 1998. Vanderbilt's Chancellor, Joe B. Wyatt, and Hoolahan signed the Addendum.

On August 17, Hoolahan returned to Bell Buckle with the Addendum. He took it to DiNardo at the practice field where they met in Hoolahan's car. DiNardo stated that Hoolahan did not present him with the complete two-page addendum, but only the second page, which was the signature page. DiNardo asked, "what am I signing?" Hoolahan explained to DiNardo, "it means that your contract as it presently exists will be extended for two years with everything else remaining exactly the same as it existed in the present contract." Before DiNardo signed the Addendum, he told Hoolahan, "Larry needs to see a copy before this thing is finalized." Hoolahan agreed, and DiNardo signed the document. . . .

On August 16, Larry DiNardo had a telephone conversation with Callison. They briefly talked about the contract extension, discussing a salary increase. Larry DiNardo testified that as of that date he did not know that Gerry DiNardo had signed the Addendum, or even that one yet existed.

DiNardo stated publicly that he was "excited" about the extension of his contract. . . .

On August 25, Callison faxed Larry DiNardo "a copy of the draft Addendum to Gerry's contract." Callison wrote on the fax: "let me know if you have any questions." The copy sent was unsigned. Callison and Larry DiNardo had several telephone conversations in late August and September, primarily discussing the television and radio contract. . . .

In November 1994, Louisiana State University contacted Vanderbilt in hopes of speaking with DiNardo about becoming the head football coach for L.S.U. Hoolahan gave DiNardo permission to speak to L.S.U. On December 12, 1994, DiNardo announced that he was accepting the L.S.U. position.

Vanderbilt sent a demand letter to DiNardo seeking payment of liquidated damages under section eight of the contract. Vanderbilt believed that DiNardo was liable for three years of his net salary: one year under the original contract and two years under the Addendum. DiNardo did not respond to Vanderbilt's demand for payment.

Vanderbilt brought this action against DiNardo for breach of contract. DiNardo removed the action to federal court, and both parties filed motions for summary judgement. The district court held that section eight was an enforceable liquidated damages provision, not an unlawful penalty, and that the damages provided under section eight were reasonable. *Vanderbilt University v. DiNardo*, 974 F. Supp. 638, 643 (M.D. Tenn. 1997). The court held that Vanderbilt did not waive its contractual rights under section eight when it granted DiNardo permission to talk to L.S.U. and that the Addendum was enforceable and extended the contract for two years. *Id.* at 643-45. The court entered judgement against DiNardo for $281,886.43. *Id.* at 645. DiNardo appeals.

I.

DiNardo first claims that section eight of the contract is an unenforceable penalty under Tennessee law. DiNardo argues that the provision is not a liquidated damage provision but a "thinly disguised, overly broad non-compete provision," unenforceable under Tennessee law.

* * *

Contracting parties may agree to the payment of liquidated damages in the event of a breach. *See Beasley v. Horrel*, 864 S.W.2d 45, 48 (Tenn. Ct. App. 1993). The term "liquidated damages" refers to an amount by the parties to be just compensation for damages should a breach occur. *See Id.* Court will not enforce such a provision, however, if the stipulated amount constitutes a penalty. *See Id.* A penalty is designed to coerce performance by punishing default. *See Id.* In Tennessee, a provision will be considered one for liquidated damages, rather than a penalty, if it is reasonable in relation to the anticipated damages for breach, measured prospectively at the time the contract was entered into, and not grossly disproportionate to the

actual damages. *See Beasley*, 864 S.W.2d at 48; *Kimbrough & Co. v. Schmitt*, 939 S.W.2d 105, 108 (Tenn. Ct. App. 1996). When these conditions are met, particularly the first, the parties probably intended the provision to be for liquidated damages. However, any doubt as to the character of the contract provision will be resolved in favor of finding it a penalty.

* * *

DiNardo contends that there is no evidence that the parties contemplated that the potential damage from DiNardo's resignation would go beyond the cost of hiring a replacement coach. . . .

DiNardo's theory of the parties' intent, however, does not square with the record. The contract language establishes that Vanderbilt wanted the five-year contract because "a long-term commitment" by DiNardo was "important to the University's desire for a stable intercollegiate football program," and that this commitment was of "essence" to the contract. Vanderbilt offered the two-year contract extension to DiNardo well over a year before his original contract expired. Both parties understood that the extension was to provide stability to the program, which helped in recruiting players and retaining assistant coaches. Thus, undisputed evidence, and reasonable inferences therefrom, establish that both parties understood and agreed that DiNardo's resignation would result in Vanderbilt suffering damage beyond the cost of hiring a replacement coach.

* * *

The stipulated damages clause is reasonable under the circumstances, and we affirm the district court's conclusion that the liquidated damages clause is enforceable under Tennessee law.

* * *

II.

DiNardo next argues that Vanderbilt waived its right to liquidated damages when it granted DiNardo permission to discuss the coaching position with L.S.U. Under Tennessee law, a party may not recover liquidated damages when it is responsible for or has contributed to the delay or nonperformance alleged as the breach. *See V.L. Nicholson Co. v. Transcom Inv. And Fin. Ltd., Inc.*, 595 S.W.2d 474, 484 (Tenn. 1980).

Vanderbilt did not waive its rights under section eight of the contract by giving DiNardo permission to pursue the L.S.U. position. *See Chattem, Inc. v. Provident Life & Accident Ins. Co.*, 676 S.W.2d 953, 955 (Tenn. 1984) (waiver is the intentional, voluntary relinquishment of a known right). First, Hoolahan's permission was quite circumscribed. Hoolahan gave DiNardo permission to talk to L.S.U. about their coaching position; he did not authorize DiNardo to terminate his contract with Vanderbilt. Second, the employment contract required DiNardo to ask Vanderbilt's athletic director for permission to speak with another school about a coaching position, and Hoolahan testified that granting a coach permission to talk to another school about a position was a "professional courtesy." Thus, the parties certainly contemplated that DiNardo could explore other coaching positions, and indeed even leave Vanderbilt, subject to the terms of the liquidated damages provision. *See Park Place Ctr. Enterprises, Inc. v. Park Place Mall Assoc.*, 836 S.W.2d 113, 116 (Tenn. Ct. App. 1992) ("all provisions of a contract should be construed as in harmony with each other, if such construction can be reasonably made . . ."). Allowing DiNardo to talk to another school did not relinquish Vanderbilt's right to liquidated damages.

* * *

III.

DiNardo claims that the Addendum did not become a binding contract, and therefore, he is only liable for the one year remaining on the original contract, not the three years held by the district court.

A.

DiNardo argues that the Addendum did not extend section eight, or that there is at least a question of fact as to whether the Addendum extended section eight.

. . . When the agreement is unambiguous, the meaning is a question of law, and we should enforce the agreement according to its plain terms. *Richland Country Club, Inc. v. CRC Equities, Inc.*, 832 S.W.2d 554, 557 (Tenn. Ct. App. 1991).

DiNardo argues that the original employment contract explicitly provides that section eight is limited to "the entire term of this five-year contract," and the plain, unambiguous language of the Addendum did not extend section eight. He points out that the Addendum did not change the effective date in section eight, unlike other sections in the contract.

The plain and unambiguous language of the Addendum read in its entirety, however, provides for the wholesale extension of the entire contract. Certain sections were expressly amended to change the original contract expiration date of January 5, 1996, to January 5, 1998, because those sections of the original contract contained the precise expiration date of January 5, 1996. The district court did not err in concluding that the contract language extended all terms of the original contract.

B.

DiNardo also claims that the Addendum never became a binding contract because Larry DiNardo never expressly approved its terms. DiNardo contends that, at the very least, a question of fact exists as to whether the two-year Addendum is an enforceable contract.

* * *

Under Tennessee law, parties may accept terms of a contract and make the contract conditional upon some other event or occurrence. *See Disney v. Henry*, 656 S.W.2d 859, 861 (Tenn. Ct. App. 1983). DiNardo argues that the Addendum is not enforceable because it was contingent on Larry DiNardo's approval.

There is evidence from which a jury could find that Larry DiNardo's failure to object did not amount to acceptance of the Addendum. The parties were primarily negotiating the radio and television contract during the fall of 1994. We cannot say that Larry DiNardo's failure to object by December 12, 1994, constituted an acceptance of the Addendum as a matter of law.

* * *

Accordingly, we affirm the district court's judgement that the contract contained an enforceable liquidated damage provision, and we affirm the portion of the judgement reflecting damages calculated under the original five-year contract. We reverse the district court's judgement concluding that the Addendum was enforceable as a matter of law. We remand for a resolution of the factual issues as to whether Larry DiNardo's approval was a condition precedent to the enforceability of the Addendum and, if so, whether the condition was satisfied by Larry DiNardo's failure to object.

We affirm in part, reverse in part, and remand the case to the district court for further proceedings consistent with this opinion.

CASES ON THE SUPPLEMENTAL CD

Mullen v. Parchment School District, 2007 Mich. App. LEXIS 1704 (Mich. Ct. App. 2007). This case examines the impact of Collective Bargaining Agreement on extra duty coaching contracts.

Rodgers v. Georgia Tech Athletic Association, 303 S.E.2d 467 (Ga. Ct. App. 1983). This case examines the true value of college coaching contracts.

Vanderbilt University v. DiNardo, 174 F.3d 751 (6th Cir. 1999). This case examines prole evidence, liquid damages and when contracts are formed.

QUESTIONS YOU SHOULD BE ABLE TO ANSWER

1. Why is it important to distinguish between an employee and an independent contractor? And what process is used to make that distinction?

2. Why is it important to include language in a contract that defines the terms of termination of that contract?

3. Why is it important to be very specific in an employment contract when defining the terms of reassignment of the signee?

4. Are verbal employment contracts able to survive judicial scrutiny?

5. Despite the existence of a legally binding contract, why are employers unable to force the contracted employee or independent contractor to complete the agreed upon work required in the contract?

REFERENCES

Cases

Alexander, et al. v. Minnesota Vikings Football Club LLC & National Football League, 649 N.W.2d 464 (2002).

Barnett v. Board of Trustees for State Colleges and Universities A/K/A University of Louisiana System, 806 So. 2d 184; 2001 La. App. LEXIS 1676 (La.App. 1 Cir, 2001).

Cherry v. A-P-A Sports, Inc., 662 P.2d 200 (Colo. App. 1983).

Cole v. Valley Ice Garden, 113 P. 3d 275 (Mont. 2005).

Deli v. University of Minnesota, 511 N.W.2d 46 (Minn. Ct. App. 1994).

Farner v. Idaho Falls School District, 135 Idaho 337; 17 P.3d 281 (2000).

Frazier v. University of the District of Columbia, 742 F. Supp. 28 (D.D.C. 1990).

Lindsey v. University of Arizona, 157 Ariz. 48, 754 P.2d 1152 (Ariz. Ct. App. 1987).

MacGinnitie v. Hobbs Group, LLC, 2005 U.S. App. LEXIS 16853; 18 Fla. L. Weekly Fed. C 832 (11th Cir. 2005).

Maddox v. University of Tennessee, 62 F.3d 843 (6th Cir. 1995).

McKenzie v. Wright State University, 683 N.E.2d 381 (Ohio App. 1996).

Meinders v. Dunkerton Community School District, 645 N.W.2d 632 (IA Sup. 2002).

Miami Dolphins Ltd. v. Williams, 356 F. Supp. 2d 1301 (S.D. Fla. 2005).

Monson v. State of Oregon, 901 P.2d 904 (Or. App. 1995).

Nader v. ABC Television, 2005 U.S. App. LEXIS 19536 (2nd Cir. 2005).

New England Patriots Football Club Inc. v. University of Colorado, 592 F.2d 1196 (1st Cir. 1979).

O'Brien v. The Ohio State University, 2007 Ohio 4833 (Ohio App. 10th, 2007).

Rodgers v. Georgia Tech Athletic Association, 303 S.E.2d 467 (Ga. Ct. App. 1983).

Small v. Juniata College, 547 Pa. 731; 689 A.2d 235 (1997).

Smith v. Alanis & Zapata Independent School District, 2002 Tex. App. Lexis 5437 (TX App, 3rd 2002).

Stamps Public Schools v. Colvert, No. CA95-318 (Ark. Ct. App. 1996).

Steinberg Moorad & Dunn, Inc. v. Dunn, 2005 U.S. App. LEXIS 5162 (9th Cir. 2005).

Tolis v. Board of Supervisors of Louisiana State University, 602 S.2d 99 (La. App. 1992).

Vanderbilt University v. DiNardo, 174 F.3d 751 (6th Cir. 1999).

Wadler v. Eastern College Athletic Conference, 2003 U.S. Dist. LEXIS 14212 (S. Dist, N.Y. 2003).

White v. National Football League, 183 L.R.R.M. (BNA) 2796 (D. Minn. 2007).

Publications

Caughron, R., & Fargher, J. (2004). Independent contractor and employee status: What every employer in sport and recreation should know. *Journal of Legal Aspects of Sport, 14*(1), 47–61.

Cozzillio, M., & Levinstein, M. (1997). *Sport law: Cases and materials*. Durham, NC: Carolina Academic Press.

Greenberg, M. (2001, Fall). College coaching contracts revisited: A practical perspective. *Marq. Sports L.Rev., 12,* 153–226.

Greenberg, M. (2006, Fall). Symposium: National Sports Law Institute Board of Advisors: Termination of college coaching contracts: When does Adequate cause to terminate exist and who determines its existence? *Marquette Sports Law Review, 17,* 197–257.

Greenberg, M., & Smith, J. (2007, Fall). A study of Division I assistant football and men's basketball coaches' contracts. *Marquette Sport Law Review, 18,* 25–72.

Greenberg, M., & Thomas, R. (2005, April–June). The Rick Neuheisel case—lessons learned from the "washout" in Washington. *For the Record: The Official Newsletter of the National Sports Law Institute, 16*(2), 6–11.

Halcomb Lewis, D. (1998, Winter). After further review, are sports officials independent contractors? *American Business Law Journal, 35,* 249.

Hunt, M. (2003, June 3). Limbo tune doesn't get coaches dancing. *Milwaukee Journal Sentinel*, p. 01C.

Internal Revenue Service. (n.d.). *Internal Revenue Manual, 4600 Employment tax procedures*, Exhibit 4640-1. Washington, DC: Department of the Treasury, Internal Revenue Service.

NCAA president receives 2-year extension. (2005, August 5). *The Associated Press*, Sports News.

Rosenthal, J. (1997, March 7). Parcells case a journey through contract law precedent. *New York Law Journal.*

Schultz, J. (2006, January 13). AD exit strips Hewitt of ally. *The Atlanta Journal-Constitution*, p. 1H.

Yasser, R., McCurdy, J., Goplerud, C., & Weston, M. (2000). *Sports law: Cases and materials* (4th ed). Cincinnati, OH: Anderson Publishing Co.

5.22 Game, Event, and Sponsorship Contracts

—**John D. McMillen**
CALIFORNIA STATE UNIVERSITY, FRESNO

Planning, implementing, and managing a sport or recreation game/event is a complex task. Today's sport and recreation manager may be required to arrange everything from hiring an event management firm, to leasing the facility, to securing corporate sponsorships. The instruments that bind all these arrangements together are game, event, and sponsorship contracts.

Understanding the essential components of game, event, and sponsorship contracts is important because these agreements often involve large sums of money as well as legally obligate the sport and recreation manager and host organization to the terms of the agreement. This section, therefore, is designed to provide a general overview of the primary contractual issues sport and recreation managers should be familiar with when working with these kinds of agreements. With foresight and planning, game, event, and sponsorship agreements can help ensure that the game/event runs as planned.

FUNDAMENTAL CONCEPTS

Depending on the game/event, a variety of parties will enter into contracts with the host organization. These include corporate sponsors, vendors, concessionaires, officials, insurance brokers, mascots, personnel, and television or radio networks, just to name a few. The legal principles associated with these agreements parallel the requirements of performance or service contracts discussed in Section 5.10, *Contract Essentials*. These contracts, for example, identify the parties; specify the time, place, and manner of performance; list the obligations of the parties; and set forth provisions in case one party cannot carry out its obligation. The primary difference between game, event, and sponsorship contracts and other types of contracts is the bargained-for subject matter. The type of arrangement desired, therefore, will dictate the specific terms and content of the agreement.

Sponsorship Contracts

Sport sponsorship is a multibillion-dollar business and has been a prominent marketing tool at least since the 1984 Olympic Games (IEG, 2006). Sport sponsorship can be found at virtually all levels of sport, from Pop Warner to Professional Sports to the Olympic Games. Sponsorships come in various forms, such as, stadium naming rights which first appeared in 1987 when the Los Angeles Forum was renamed "the Great Western Forum" (Mayer, 2005). Since then, naming rights have become a lucrative revenue generating tool (Mayer, 2005). The New York Mets currently have the largest naming deal of $400 million with Citgroup (Business of Sports Network, 2009).

Modern naming right agreements go beyond the name of the stadium and include the naming rights to entryways, the field, or even breezeways (Mayer, 2005). These agreements may be a separate agreement or part of a larger corporate sponsorship agreement (Mayer, 2005).

A sponsorship contract, whether it is between a company and an athlete or a company and a sport or recreation event, is a legal document that binds two or more parties to agreed-upon obligations. Sponsorship deals have grown dramatically in the past decade, from $11.1 billion in 1997 to an estimated $26.5 billion in 2005 (SponsorClick, 2002).

On the surface, sport sponsorship appear like a win-win proposition for both the sport organization and the corporate sponsor. By attaching their names to sports teams, companies reap publicity at relatively low cost. But, as several companies have discovered recently, there's also an element of risk. For example, the BMW sponsored team sailboat was eliminated from the America's Cup qualifying competition in Valencia, Spain, before the main event even started. The cost of the failed Cup bid was reported at nearly $200 million (Ewing, 2007). Unexpected losses such as this have drawn more focus on the sponsorship agreement and the specific language of the contract.

Logistically, sponsorship contracts are an agreement whereby corporate sponsors provide financial packages or some in-kind product (e.g., uniforms, equipment, soft drinks) to the game/event in exchange for advertising space or a promise to use the product by the host organization in a manner that is beneficial to the sponsor. The exact terms of these agreements are then drafted into a **sponsorship contract**. These contracts vary in their construction from a relatively simple $1,500 signage arrangement found in many minor league baseball leagues and some college football bowl games (Heller & Hechtman, 2000) to a sophisticated Olympic sponsorship agreement valued well into the millions of dollars.

Fundamental clauses of a sponsorship agreement include the length of the agreement, the rights granted to the host organization and sponsor, form of payment, use of any marks or products, and termination of the agreement. Although sport and recreation managers likely will not draft sponsorship contracts, it often is the manager's duty to secure whatever agreements are necessary to make the game/event run as planned. The following are additional clauses that sport and recreation managers should be familiar with when working with sponsorship contracts.

Exclusive and Nonexclusive Rights

One of the most important components of sponsorship agreements is the "exclusivity" clause. Many sponsors demand exclusive sponsorship rights within their product or service category. Nike, for example, would not likely sponsor a sport or recreation event if the event already has a sponsorship agreement with Adidas or Reebok. An exclusive sponsorship contract does not mean, however, that competitors will not attempt to advertise their product at or near the event. *Ambush marketing,* sometimes referred to as *parasite marketing,* is a marketing strategy that attempts to dilute an official sponsor's association with a game/event. In other words, a nonpaying sponsor attempts to affiliate its organization with the event even though it has not paid for the rights to do so.

Ambush marketing occurs in a variety of ways. One common instance is when a nonsponsory company purchases advertising time before or during an official event, allowing the company to associate itself with a sport or recreation event without having to pay any sponsorship fees. In other instances, a nonsponsory company might use a logo, symbol, or words that are similar to the logo of the official game/event sponsor (e.g., Buy our pizza while you are watching the "Big Game"). If these images create a "likelihood of confusion," this could violate the Lanham Act (see Section 7.22, *Principles of Trademark Law*). There have also been instances where companies bought advertising rights directly outside the venue sponsored by a competitor company (e.g., if Northwest Airlines advertised on a billboard just outside the United Center in Chicago).

Many nonsponsory companies are creative in their ambush marketing strategies and technically may not violate the law. For example, in *National Hockey League, et al. v. Pepsi-Cola Canada Ltd.*, the National Hockey League alleged that although Pepsi did not have any rights to NHL trademarks, it used "confusingly similar" marks in a contest called the "Diet Pepsi $4,000,000 Pro Hockey Playoff Pool," whereby fans matched information under bottle caps with actual NHL playoff results to become eligible for prizes. The Supreme Court of British Columbia ruled that Pepsi used a sufficient disclaimer stating that it was not an official sponsor of the NHL. In essence, the judge stated that because Pepsi sells soft drinks and the NHL's product is hockey, there can be no confusion in the consumers' minds as to which product belongs to which company (Wong, 2002). Cases such as this stress the importance of an airtight sponsorship agreement.

Legal issues may also arise between two official sponsors of the same event. During the 1994 World Cup, for example, both Sprint and MasterCard were official corporate sponsors. MasterCard secured exclusive rights to all debit and credit cards, whereas Sprint negotiated exclusive local and long-distance telephone rights. As a promotion, however, Sprint created phone cards, and MasterCard sued, alleging that Sprint's cards infringed on its exclusive debit card rights. This case was arbitrated and settled by allowing Sprint to give away, not sell, its existing phone cards (see *MasterCard International v. Sprint Communications Co.*, 1994).

Another aspect to consider in sponsorship agreements is what efforts the host organization will take to preserve and protect the sponsor's rights should ambush marketing occur. No sponsorship agreement can prevent ambush marketing from occurring, but the contract can help the host organization and its official sponsors to better understand what steps are going to be taken to minimize its affects (Moorman & Greenwell, 2005).

In addition, if an athlete endorses a sport or recreation event, the contract should incorporate many of the clauses discussed within this section. For example, the contract should take into consideration any possible league rules and policies surrounding the marketing of its athletes. The NHL, for example, does not permit its players to be involved in any endorsement of alcoholic or tobacco products.

Venue Concerns

Security, concessions, personnel, and facility leases are the primary provisions covered in the venue portion of the sponsorship agreement. If the venue already has permanent corporate signage, this may pose special legal concerns. For example, it is not unusual for a new event to be sponsored by a competitor of the venue's current sponsor (e.g., Visa versus MasterCard). Some organizations, therefore, may even request that no signs be present at or around the local vicinity of the venue, a common requirement of the NCAA at its Final Four basketball tournament. In these instances, the signage must either be covered up or the existing sponsorship contracts renegotiated. It also may be helpful for the host organization to seek a "variance of contract," meaning the original agreement is amended to temporarily suspend the agreement for a specific period of time while the new sport or recreation tenant occupies the venue. Managers, therefore, will need to examine all current venue agreements to determine whether there are a certain number of days or events before a competing company legally can have a presence in the venue. Otherwise, the new venue agreement could violate an existing contract. In other words, venue rights could greatly impact which corporations can solicit to sponsor an upcoming sport or recreation game/event.

The Olympic Games are considered the pinnacle venue of sport sponsorship. Few events enable companies to reach so many people around the world—even though sponsors are not allowed to put their names on advertisements at Olympic venues. Visa, for example, was one of 12 leading sponsors which paid $866m for a four-year association covering the Turin winter games in 2006 and the 2008 Summer Game in Beijing (Economist.com, 2008).

Option to Renew and Right of First Refusal

Options to renew and the right of first refusal are also important clauses in a sponsorship agreement. The **option to extend or renew** gives sponsors the choice to lengthen the current agreement when the contract expires. The **right of first refusal** allows sponsors to make an offer to retain sponsorship rights for future games/events. In practical terms, the right of refusal also allows sponsors to walk away from negotiations with the option to match any competitor's offer. Depending on the length of the original contract, sport and recreation managers can protect themselves from these clauses by a provision that mandates that a specific time frame be designated by which the sponsor must declare its intention to either continue or dissolve the relationship. Eight months to a year should be sufficient time for sport and recreation managers to secure another sponsor should the corporate sponsor discontinue its involvement.

Intellectual Property Rights

Many athletic associations and professional sport leagues, such as the NFL and NBA, have a small number of "primary" sponsors that guarantee the association or league a set amount of money or product and services in exchange for certain sponsorship rights (Wong, 2002). In other words, the company has the right to use the association's or league's logo while promoting its product. These rights are often seen on television commercials with a phrase similar to, "Southwest Airlines, the official airline of the NFL."

In addition, consumers spend millions of dollars on licensed sport and recreation products each year. From these sales corporations generate a portion of their revenue from the use of team/corporate sponsor logos, known as trademarks (see Section 7.22, *Principles of Trademark Law*). Sport and recreation managers, therefore, must be careful to properly secure and protect the trademarks associated with the game/event (see *Marvel Entertainment Group, Inc. v. The Hawaiian Triathlon Corp.*, 1990).

The agreements that legally allow managers to use corporate logos during the game/event are referred to as **licenses,** or a clause might be written directly into the sponsorship agreement: "Sponsor grants a non-exclusive license to use any trademark or other intellectual property rights in connection with providing the management provisions stated herein" (Heller & Hechtman, 2000). All "works for hire" (see Section 7.22, *Principles of Trademark Law*) also should be included into the agreement: "As part of the services provided, all original logos, concepts, designs, mechanicals, and layouts for the event shall be deemed 'works made for hire' and the Sponsor shall be considered the 'author' of such works" (Heller & Hechtman, 2000).

Sport and recreation managers should also recognize that all promotional materials must be examined to determine whether it abides by the appropriate intellectually property laws. Signage, T-shirts, pamphlets, logos, Websites, and other game/event promotional materials cannot infringe on the rights of the trademark, copyright, or patent owner. To avoid excessive delays in the approval process, sport and recreation managers should specify an appropriate turnaround time to view these materials. It is also important to negotiate how long the materials or logos can be used after the game/event has concluded. It may be both a contract and trademark violation to display logos after the time period specified in the contract. For example, if the Orange Bowl requires that FedEx terminate all uses of its Orange Bowl logos on its trucks within 30 days after the bowl game, failure to do so would not only breach the contract but would also violate the Orange Bowl's intellectual property rights.

Finally, managers must be cognizant of potential geographic rights. International sponsors, for example, may seek authority to use trademarks in some or all countries participating in the event, whereas national sponsors in all likelihood will only be interested in using the marks in the host country. These kinds of clauses are popular in larger venues like World Cup Soccer and the Olympic Games. However, the Internet has added a new twist on geographic rights. Because the Internet has no boundaries, all games or events potentially could have national or international appeal. Therefore, the host organization may want to incorporate specific language to protect these territorial rights. One possible solution is to limit the trademark's use to a certain language on the Web page (e.g., English or Spanish) or per event/sport.

Fees and Expenses

Equally important as the actual services to be performed in the sponsorship agreement is the payment of fees and expenses. Management fees for sport and recreation events can run into the hundreds of thousands of dollars, depending on the nature and length of the event. Understandably, event management firms seek fair compensation and timely reimbursement for expenses in the agreement, whereas the corporate sponsor is most concerned that the fees correspond to the nature of the services provided. In general, sponsorship agreements must state the specific amount of money or in-kind goods or services and reimbursement of expenses that are to be performed by all parties. Payment schedules and delivery of services should also be expressly defined to avoid any confusion.

In addition, many events now require sponsors to guarantee a certain amount of services and money to market the event. Other possible areas to negotiate include privileges associated with the sponsorship of the game/event, such as tickets, signage, hospitality, and travel. For smaller events, these items often are included as a benefit, but any of these stipulations should be incorporated into the sponsorship agreement to avoid any future misunderstandings.

Media Issues

Depending on the size and commercial draw of the game/event, sport and recreation managers may have to deal with a variety of media contracts, such as cable, satellite, television, radio, and the Internet. Most television contracts include exclusivity and territorial stipulations that then can be licensed to smaller markets or different stations. NBC, for example, obtained the exclusive rights for the 2002 Winter Olympic Games, but then licensed these rights for limited use to the cable network TNT, allowing it to broadcast Olympic coverage that was limited to specific days and certain hours. Whatever the median of technology used, these types of clauses are certain to become even more common with the increasing international demand for U.S. sporting events.

Other Considerations

It is important that host organization clarify in the agreement all the services it will perform. At the same time, managers should seek an agreement whereby the sponsor acknowledges that the nature of the event may make it impossible to list all the services to be rendered. In other words, managers need authority to go beyond the scope of services outlined within the agreement when necessary to successfully perform the duties associated with the event. To protect managers who are required to perform duties or services outside the written agreement, a provision should be included that allows an adjustment in management fees.

Managers also should keep in mind that some sponsors may demand an **approval clause** for other cosponsors. For example, Pepsi may not want to sponsor an event with McDonald's because of its affiliation with Coca-Cola.

Term and **cancellation** clauses are important in case the game/event is cancelled. These clauses not only allow corporate sponsors and sport and recreation managers the ability to commit to the event, but also ensure flexibility if the event is cancelled. The recent assault of hurricanes along the Gulf and Florida coasts are prime examples of why these clauses are necessary. Overall terms of the agreement can be as short as a few weeks or as long as several years, and cancellation provision may be "at-will," which requires no prior notice, or it can require that certain conditions be met before cancellation.

State law governs the **jurisdiction** of the sponsorship contract. Consequently, a contract's effect may vary depending on the laws of a particular state. Therefore, to avoid possible jurisdiction problems, the agreement should specify the state law to be applied should a dispute arise. For example, if the host organization is in Ohio and the corporate sponsor principally is located in California, the contract might state that "Ohio law will govern this agreement."

Confidentiality may be an important component of sponsorship agreements, particularly if one party provides the other with access to proprietary information such as marketing plans, financial information, client lists, and sales information (Heller & Hechtman, 2000). Also, like all other contracts, sponsorship contracts should define any specific conditions that will be considered a breach of contract as well as specify the amount of **damages**, known as "liquidated damages," should a breach occur. All liquidated damages, however, must be reasonable and based on the actual damage or loss incurred by the nonbreaching party. Otherwise, a court may refuse to enforce excessive liquidated damages. Finally, parties may wish to consider **indemnification** provisions. For example, "Sponsor will indemnify and hold harmless Event Management Firm and its shareholders, affiliates, officers, directors, and employees from and against all claims, expenses, suits, and judgments arising from or connected with a breach of this agreement by the Sponsor, any negligent or intentional acts of the Sponsor in connection with the event, or any violation of the intellectual property rights of a third party associated with the use of the Sponsor's trademarks" (Heller & Hechtman, 2000).

Due to increased work stoppages in professional sports, a growing trend is to include a "force majeure" or **work stoppage provision** into the sponsorship contract (Wong, 2002). Although typically associated with facility or event contracts, these clauses are becoming more common in sponsorship agreements and protect against unforeseeable natural or human events that are beyond the control of the parties of the contract and render the contract impossible (Wong, 2002). This provision may protect one or both parties in the event of a work stoppage from things such as a strike or a lockout, such as the 2004–05 National Hockey League work stoppage.

Another trend is to designate **alternative dispute resolution** provisions within contracts to protect the organization in case of a disagreement regarding the terms of the agreement. Because litigation is expensive, arbitration is the preferred method of resolution, as it provides a speedy and relatively inexpensive means to resolve disputes. If possible, the chosen law should be that of the organization's home state because of convenience and knowledge of the applicable law (see Section 5.30, *Alternative Dispute Resolution*).

Game and Event Contracts

Game contracts are agreements designed to facilitate a game/contest between two organizations. Because of these agreements' potential impact on present and future game schedules, these contracts should be prepared with care and under the advisement of legal counsel. In general, both game and event contracts will contain many of the same provisions as sponsorship agreements. For example, sport and recreation managers will need to consider intellectual property rights, as well as the location, date, and time of the game, provisions for officials, governing rules, potential television and radio rights, lease agreements, complimentary or paid tickets, travel expenses and other related costs, and any potential termination and breach procedures.

Event contracts are similar to game contracts in design and concept. The term *event*, however, has a dual meaning. It can signify a single sport/recreation event (e.g., the Super Bowl) or a combination of events (e.g., the NCAA basketball tournament). Event contracts are also synonymous with pre- and post-event activities. In other words, event contracts may not only refer to a game contract, but also to individual or combined agreements for the entire operation of an event from the facility lease, concessions, marketing, and corporate sponsorships, to potential radio or television rights. Like game contracts, event contracts should be prepared with care and should include the essential components of game contracts, as well as any other clauses specific to the event's operations.

Lease Agreements

To increase revenues, many organizations now lease facilities to third parties for rental fees. The facility lease may directly influence the success and ease in which a game/event operates (see *Houston Oilers v. Harris County Texas, et al.*, 1997). Whereas a facility lease agreement may be as simple or complex as the parties desire, under the Statute of Frauds (see Section 5.10, *Contract Essentials*), all leases must be in writing. In addition to routine elements of time, keys, and opening and closing schedules (Clement, 1998), sport and recreation managers should consider using escape clauses, options to renew, assignment rights, maintenance, restrictive covenants, exit clauses, parking, concessions, merchandise revenue, insurance, and indemnification clauses, as well as sponsorship and signage stipulations in the lease portion of the agreement (Miller, 1997).

Personnel

A variety of employees are needed to run a sport or recreation game/event. Hiring and retaining quality professional employees, therefore, is central to all sport and recreation venues. Sport and recreation managers must be cognizant of how to limit liability regarding personnel issues. Managers, for example, often hire officials, police and/or crowd-control personnel, concessionaires, and emergency personnel. Each of these arrangements can be negotiated for a single game/event or an entire season. Because of the potential liability associated with the type of employment relationship between the host organization and the event personnel (e.g., volunteers, interns, at-will employees, and independent contractors), sport and recreation managers should carefully construct the written agreement to clarify the employment relationship (see Section 5.21, *Employment Contracts*). For example, an at-will employment relationship easily can be defined by the event contract: "The parties shall be and act as independent contractors and under no circumstances will this agreement or the relationship between the parties be construed to be an agency, partnership, joint venture, or employment agreement" (Heller & Hechtman, 2000). Furthermore, managers should be aware that some personnel may ask to be a "secured" party, meaning that they will be paid first should the event become bankrupt. Typically, secured employees seek 25 percent up front, 50 percent with satisfactory progress, and the remaining 25 percent on the completion of the work (Irwin, Sutton, & McCarthy, 2002).

SIGNIFICANT CASE

NASCAR filed a $100 million lawsuit against AT&T, accusing the wireless provider of interfering with its exclusive sponsorship agreement with rival wireless company Nextel. NASCAR's lawsuit asks to be granted the right to kick AT&T—and all telecommunications companies other than Nextel—out of its top racing series. This case illustrates how even the smallest conflict quickly can turn into a lawsuit and is an example of why a qualified attorney should draft contracts to ensure that all parties and their rights are protected.

AT&T V. NASCAR

United States Court of Appeals for the Eleventh Circuit
494 F.3d 1356; 2007 U.S. App. LEXIS 19182 (2007)

Background

Appellant NASCAR is the sanctioning body of stock car racing. Each year, NASCAR holds 17 of the top 20 attended sporting events in the United States. NASCAR races are broadcast in over 150 countries to approximately 75 million fans. NASCAR consists of three major national series as well as eight regional series and one local grassroots series. One of NASCAR's highest profile and most visible racing series is known as the "Cup Series." From 1972–2003, the series was known as the "Winston Cup Series" and was sponsored by R.J. Reynolds Tobacco Company.

On June 17, 2003, NASCAR and Appellant Sprint Nextel, which is engaged in the business of providing telecommunications services, entered into the "Nextel **Sponsorship Agreement**," providing that beginning with the 2004 Season, Sprint Nextel would become the Official Series Sponsor of the NASCAR NEXTEL Cup Series. The Nextel **Sponsorship Agreement** was originally executed between NASCAR and Nextel Communications, which has since merged with Sprint Corporation and changes its name to Sprint Nextel Corporation.

The Nextel **Sponsorship Agreement** granted exclusivity to Sprint Nextel as the sole telecommunications company sponsoring NASCAR Cup Series races. Sprint Nextel agreed to pay a publicly reported price of $700 million for its exclusive sponsorship rights over a 10-year period. To implement Sprint Nextel's exclusivity, the Nextel **Sponsorship Agreement** contained, *inter alia*, a "Category" definition and a list of "Competitors." The parties agreed that Sprint Nextel would receive exclusive sponsorship rights in its Category, which includes wireline and wireless communications services, including local and long distance services, wireless services, two-way radio services and associated equipment such as wireless phones and PDAs (e.g., Palm Pilots).

Sprint Nextel insisted upon exclusivity in its Category of telecommunications services because it believed that without such rights, a Competitor might attempt to enter the sport as a sponsor. The Nextel **Sponsorship Agreement** defines "Competitor" to include certain designated companies, including Alltel, AT&T, AT&T Corp., AT&T Wireless, SBC Communications, BellSouth and Cingular. Under the Nextel **Sponsorship Agreement,** Competitors of Sprint Nextel are barred from advertising and sponsorships in connection with NASCAR Nextel Cup Series events.

During the negotiation of the Nextel **Sponsorship Agreement,** Sprint Nextel became aware that certain Sprint Nextel Competitors already sponsored two racing teams, including the # 31 Car, which since 2001 had been sponsored by Cingular Wireless LLC. The # 31 Car, which races in NASCAR's Cup Series, is owned by RCR and driven by Jeff Burton. As an accommodation to the racing teams already sponsored by Sprint Nextel Competitors, NASCAR and Sprint Nextel incorporated into the Nextel **Sponsorship Agreement** narrow exceptions to Sprint Nextel's exclusivity. The Nextel **Sponsorship Agreement** identified the racing teams, including RCR's # 31 Car, that under certain terms and conditions would be permitted by NASCAR to continue their pre-existing **sponsorship agreements** with Sprint Nextel Competitors. Pursuant to the provisions of the Nextel **Sponsorship Agreement** providing narrow exceptions to Sprint Nextel's exclusivity, NASCAR agreed to take all legally permissible steps to protect Sprint Nextel's exclusivity.

NASCAR regulates stock car racing through annual contracts between itself and drivers and car owners, known as "Driver and Car Owner Agreements." NASCAR, RCR and Jeff Burton are parties to a 2007 Driver and Car Owner Agreement (the "RCR Agreement").[4] The RCR Agreement implements the exclusivity NASCAR granted Sprint Nextel, *inter alia*, placing Sprint Nextel Competitors' product or service identifications on the # 31 Car.

[4]Since at least 2004, NASCAR and RCR have executed materially indistinguishable annual agreements.

However, an Addendum to the RCR Agreement designed to give effect to the narrow exceptions envisioned by the Nextel **Sponsorship Agreement** includes a grandfather clause that permits RCR to renew its non-complying sponsorship so long as the sponsor's brand position is not increased on the # 31 Car. In addition, the grandfather clause provides that in the event the sponsorship relationship with the Sprint Nextel

Competitor is not renewed, RCR will not be permitted to enter into a subsequent **sponsorship agreement** with a different Sprint Nextel Competitor. [5]

Appellee AT&T Mobility is a limited liability company formerly known as Cingular Wireless LLC ("Cingular") whose members are subsidiaries of AT&T Inc. and BellSouth Corporation. Since 2001, when it entered into its first **sponsorship agreement** with RCR (the "Cingular **Sponsorship Agreement**"), Cingular has been the primary sponsor of the # 31 Car.[6] Pursuant to the Cingular **Sponsorship Agreement,** the # 31 Car originally featured the Cingular brand and logo as part of its paint scheme. However, on December 29, 2006, AT&T Inc. merged with BellSouth Corporation. In connection with the merger, Cingular changed its name to AT&T Mobility LLC and is currently transitioning its trade name, brand, and logos from "Cingular Wireless" to "AT&T."

On January 4, 2007, after the merger of AT&T Inc. and BellSouth Corporation, RCR submitted for NASCAR's approval a paint scheme for the # 31 Car that, while maintaining the Cingular Wireless logo on the hood of the car, introduced the AT&T logo on the rear quarter panel. On January 16, 2007, NASCAR rejected RCR's proposed change to the paint scheme basing its decision on its belief that the Sprint Nextel **Sprint Nextel Sponsorship Agreement** prohibited the display of the AT&T logo and that RCR's grandfather right pursuant to the Addendum in the RCR Agreement applied only to the Cingular logo.

On March 26, 2007, AT&T Mobility filed an amended complaint against NASCAR setting forth claims for, *inter alia*, breach of the RCR Agreement and breach of the implied covenant of good faith and fair dealing. AT&T Mobility also sought a declaratory judgment from the district court that it could place the name, brand, logos, and marks of its choosing on the # 31 Car, driver uniforms, helmets, and in all merchandising and licensing rights, in-

cluding a change of its name, brand, logos, and marks to "AT&T." In addition, AT&T Mobility requested a preliminary injunction enjoining NASCAR from interfering with its right to place its name, brand, logos, and marks on the # 31 Car. On May 18, 2007, the district court concluded that AT&T Mobility had standing as a third party beneficiary of the RCR Agreement to sue NASCAR and granted the requested preliminary injunction.

II. DISCUSSION

We generally review a district court's order of a preliminary injunction with deference, reversing only in the event of an abuse of discretion. *See Delta Air Lines, Inc. v. Air Line Pilots Ass'n, Intern.*, 238 F.3d 1300 (11th Cir. 2001) ("[T]he grant of permanent injunctive relief is generally reviewed for an abuse of discretion."); *Cumulus Media, Inc. v. Clear Channel Communications, Inc.*, 304 F.3d 1167 (11th Cir. 2002) (noting the "trial court is in a far better position . . . to evaluate that evidence, and we will not disturb its factual findings unless they are clearly erroneous."); *but see Solantic, LLC v. City of Neptune Beach*, 410 F.3d 1250, 1253 (11th Cir. 2005) ("We review the district court's . . . application of the law *de novo*, premised on the understanding that application of an improper legal standard is never within a district court's discretion.").

Standing, however, "is a threshold jurisdictional question which must be addressed prior to and independent of the merits of a party's claims." *Dillard v. Baldwin County Comm'rs*, 225 F.3d 1271, 1275 (11th Cir. 2000); *EF Hutton & Co., Inc. v. Hadley*, 901 F.2d 979, 983 (11th Cir. 1990). In fact, we are obliged to consider standing *sua sponte* even if the parties have not raised the issue because an appellate court "must satisfy itself not only of its own jurisdiction, but also of that of the lower courts in a cause under review." *Bochese v. Town of Ponce Inlet*, 405 F.3d 964, 975 (11th Cir. 2005); *see also Florida Ass'n of Med. Equip. Dealers v. Apfel*, 194 F.3d 1227, 1230 (11th Cir. 1999) (stating that "every court has an independent duty to review standing as a basis for jurisdiction at any time, for every case it adjudicates."). As with all jurisdictional issues, this Court reviews standing *de novo. See, e.g., McKusick v. City of Melbourne, Fla.*, 96 F.3d 478, 482 (11th Cir. 1996); *Univ. of S. Ala. v. Am. Tobacco Co.*, 168 F.3d 405, 408 (11th Cir. 1999).

For AT&T Mobility to have standing to challenge NASCAR's decision under the RCR Agreement to prohibit the display of the AT&T logo on the # 31 Car, it must establish that it has suffered an injury in fact. *See Lujan v. Defenders of Wildlife*, 504 U.S. 555, 560, 112 S. Ct. 2130, 2136, 119 L. Ed. 2d 351 (1992). To establish injury in fact, AT&T Mobility must first demonstrate that NASCAR has invaded a "legally protected interest" derived by AT&T Mobility from the RCR Agreement between NASCAR and RCR. *See Dillard*, 225 F.3d at 1275 (11th Cir. 2000).

---

[5]On April 4, 2005, in response to marketplace rumors concerning mergers in the telecommunications industry, NASCAR sent a letter to RCR clarifying that in the event Cingular Wireless LLC's name changed, NASCAR interpreted the grandfather clause as prohibiting any paint scheme or branding on the # 31 Car that promoted this new name or a new third party.

[6]The original Cingular **Sponsorship Agreement** expired in 2004, but was renewed by the parties and is set to expire in December 2010.

The question of whether, for standing purposes, a non-party to a contract has a legally enforceable right is a matter of state law. *See, e.g., Miree v. DeKalb County*, 433 U.S. 25, 29-33, 97 S. Ct. 2490, 53 L. Ed. 2d 557 (1977) (holding that, even when the United States was a party to the contracts at issue, "whether petitioners as third-party beneficiaries of the contracts have standing to sue" was a question of state law, not of federal common law); *see also Osman v. Hialeah Hous. Auth.*, 785 F.2d 1550, 1550 (11th Cir. 1986) (observing that whether a plaintiff has a constitutionally protected property interest in an employment contract is a question of state law).

Notwithstanding AT&T Mobility's status as a non-party to the RCR Agreement, Georgia law permits a "beneficiary of a contract made between other parties for his benefit [to] maintain an action against the promisor on the contract." GA. CODE ANN. § 9-2-20(b) (West 2007). However, in order for a third party to have standing to enforce a contract under section 9-2-20(b) of the Georgia Code, it must clearly appear from the contract that it was intended for his benefit. *Danjor v. Corporate Constr., Inc.*, 272 Ga. App. 695, 613 S.E.2d 218, 220 (Ga. Ct. App. 2005); *Rowe v. Akin & Flanders, Inc.*, 240 Ga. App. 766, 525 S.E.2d 123, 125 (Ga. Ct. App. 1999); *Backus v. Chilivis*, 236 Ga. 500, 224 S.E.2d 370, 372 (Ga. 1976). We disagree with the district court's conclusion that the RCR Agreement on its face illustrates an intention by NASCAR and RCR to benefit Cingular (now AT&T Mobility). A third party beneficiary need not be specifically named in the contract, but the parties' intention to benefit the third party must be evident from the face of the contract. *See Northen v. Tobin*, 262 Ga. App. 339, 585 S.E.2d 681 (Ga. Ct. App. 2003); *Plantation Pipe Line Co. v. 3-D Excavators, Inc.*, 160 Ga. App. 756, 287 S.E.2d 102 (Ga. Ct. App. 1981). The RCR Agreement clearly did not require RCR to renew its sponsorship with Cingular. In fact, under the RCR Agreement, RCR was free to seek the sponsorship of any company not included within the narrow universe of Sprint Nextel Competitors as defined by the Sprint Nextel **Sponsorship Agreement.** The Addendum to the RCR Agreement was intended to protect RCR from the potential harm caused by a sudden loss of sponsorship due to Sprint Nextel's exclusivity. Any benefit to Cingular (now AT&T Mobility) resulting from NASCAR's commitment to grant RCR the option to continue and renew its **sponsorship agreement** was merely incidental to NASCAR's intended purpose of preserving RCR's choice of sponsorship. The mere fact that Cingular (now AT&T Mobility) would "benefit incidentally from performance of the agreement is not alone sufficient." *Danjor*, 613 S.E.2d at 220.

That the RCR Agreement limited RCR's options with respect to seeking a new sponsor in the telecommunications industry is insufficient evidence of an intention to make Cingular (now AT&T Mobility) an intended beneficiary of the RCR Agreement. The Addendum to the RCR Agreement prevented RCR from allowing Cingular to increase its brand position on the #31 car or executing a new **sponsorship agreement** with another Sprint Nextel Competitor. Any effect these limitations had in persuading RCR to keep Cingular (now AT&T Mobility) as its sponsor was incidental to the intended purpose of providing RCR the option to renew its current sponsorship if, and only if, it elected to do so, and freezing the status quo with respect to the sponsorship of racing teams by Sprint Nextel Competitors. Consequently, we are unable to see how the parties could have intended these sponsorship guidelines to produce anything more than an incidental benefit to Cingular (now AT&T Mobility). Further, we are unable to conclude that in executing the RCR Agreement NASCAR promised to render any performance to Cingular. Georgia law is clear that there must be "a promise by the promisor to the promisee to render some performance to [the] third person and it must appear that both the promisor and the promisee intended that the third person should be the beneficiary." *Danjor*, 613 S.E.2d at 220. The promisor NASCAR made a promise only to the promisee RCR to preserve and protect RCR's **sponsorship agreement** with Cingular notwithstanding the exclusivity granted to Sprint Nextel.

RCR was the intended beneficiary of that promise, not Cingular. Nothing in the RCR Agreement required NASCAR to ensure that RCR continued with Cingular as its sponsor. RCR had the option to discontinue or elect not to renew its **sponsorship agreement** with Cingular, and NASCAR assumed no duty to preserve or protect Cingular's (or any of its successor's) rights in the event RCR exercised that option. NASCAR's admission that RCR may continue to display the branding of "Cingular" despite its status as a Sprint Nextel

Competitor is inapposite to the question of whether Cingular (now AT&T Mobility) is an intended third party beneficiary of the RCR Agreement. NASCAR's admission is simply evidence of its recognition of RCR's right pursuant to the RCR Agreement to continue its current sponsorship, combined with a statement of which logos NASCAR believes RCR is permitted to display pursuant to the RCR Agreement.

The mere fact that RCR has opted to exercise its right to retain Cingular as its sponsor does not convert that option into a "legally protected right" for Cingular or AT&T Mobility under NASCAR's agreement with RCR. RCR's absolute discretion under the RCR Agreement to retain Cingular as its sponsor, and NASCAR's lack of a role in RCR's decision, foreclose the possibility that Cingular or AT&T Mobility is a third party beneficiary of such agreement. It is well settled that a "plaintiff generally must assert his own legal rights and interests, and cannot rest his claim to relief on the legal rights or interests of third parties." *Warth v. Seldin*, 422 U.S. 490, 499, 95 S. Ct. 2197, 45

L. Ed. 2d 343 (1975); *see also Miccosukee Tribe of Indians of Florida v. Florida State Athletic Com'n*, 226 F.3d 1226, 1230 (11th Cir. 2000) ("Absent exceptional circumstances, a third party does not have standing to challenge injury to another party.").

Because Cingular (now AT&T Mobility) was neither a party to nor an intended beneficiary of the RCR Agreement, it has not itself suffered a legally cognizable injury as a result of NASCAR's interpretation of the Addendum to the RCR Agreement. Thus, even though it might benefit collaterally from an interpretation of the RCR Agreement that is inconsistent with NASCAR's posi-tion, AT&T Mobility lacks standing to enforce its interpretation of the RCR Agreement.

III. CONCLUSION

We conclude that under Georgia law AT&T Mobility was not a third party beneficiary of the RCR Agreement executed between NASCAR and RCR and, as a result, AT&T Mobility lacks standing to challenge NASCAR's interpretation of that agreement. Therefore, the district court's preliminary injunction is VACATED and the matter is REMANDED for dismissal.

CASES ON THE SUPPLEMENTAL CD

Baden Sports, Inc. v. Kabushiki Kaisha Molten, 541 F. Supp. 2d 1151 (2008). This case examines issues concerning patents and false advertising.

Ford Motor Company v. Kahne, 379 F. Supp. 2d 857 (ED Mich., 2005). This case examines whether a professional stock car driver breached his contract with the car company.

United States Olympic Committee v. Xclusive Leisure & Hospitalityltd.; Beijingticketing.com, 2008 U.S. Dist. LEXIS 78640 (2008). This case examines who has the right to sell various event tickets.

QUESTIONS YOU SHOULD BE ABLE TO ANSWER

1. What is the primary difference between game, event, and sponsorship contracts?

2. Explain the fundamental clauses of a typical sponsorship agreement.

3. What is the name of the agreements that legally allow managers to use corporate logos during a sport or recreation game or event?

4. What clause allows sponsors the choice to lengthen the current agreement when the contract expires?

5. What clause do sponsors often demand to prevent competitors from sponsoring the same event?

REFERENCES

Cases

Houston Oilers v. Harris County Texas, et al., 960 F. Supp 1202 (S.D. Texas 1997).

Marvel Entertainment Group, Inc. v. The Hawaiian Triathlon Corp., 132 F.R.D. 143 (S.D. N.Y 1990).

MasterCard International v. Sprint Communications Co., 23 F.3d 397 (2d. Cir. 1994).

National Hockey League, et al. v. Pepsi-Cola Canada Ltd., 42 C.P.R.3d 390 (B.C. 1992).

Publications

Business of Sports Network (2009), *Sports sponsorship meets the recession*, available at: http://www .businessofsportsnetwork.com/index.php?option=com_content&view=article&id=14:hot-button-sports -banking-and-sponsorships-meet-the-recession

Clement, A. (1998). *Law in sport and physical activity* (2nd ed.). Aurora, OH: Sport and Law Press, Inc.

Economist.com (2008). *Sponsorship form: The value of sport to other businesses,* available at: http://www.economist.com/specialreports/displaystory.cfm?story_id=11825607

Ewing, J. (2007). *Sports Sponsorship: A risky game companies love lending their names to winning teams. But what if a team loses, or worse, finds itself embroiled in scandal?* Business Week, available at: http://www.businessweek.com/globalbiz/content/jun2007/gb20070607_140258.htm

Heller, J. G., & Hechtman, J. A. (2000). Corporate sponsorships of sports and entertainment events: Considerations in drafting a sponsorship management agreement. *Marq. Sports L. Rev., 11,* 23.

IEG (2006, December 26). IEG sponsorship report. Retrieved March 31, 2007, from http://www .sponsorship.com/iegsr

Irwin, R. L., Sutton W. A., & McCarthy, L. M. (2002). *Sport promotion and sales management.* Champaign, IL: Human Kinetics.

Mayer, F. A. (2005). Stadium financing: Where we are, how we got here, and where we are going. *Vill. Sports & Ent. L. Forum, 12,* 195.

Miller, L. K. (1997). *Sport business management.* Gaithersburg, MD: Aspen Publishing.

Moorman, A. M., & Greenwell, T. C. (2005). Consumer attitudes of deception and the legality of ambush marketing practices. *J. Legal Aspects of Sport, 15,* 183.

Sponsorship Marketing Global 2004. Retrived June 3, 2009, from http://www.sponsorclick .com/docs/en/smg04_highlights.pdf

Wong, G. M. (2002). *Essentials of amateur sports law* (3rd. ed.). Westport, CT: Greenwood Publishing Group.

5.30 Alternative Dispute Resolution: Arbitration, Negotiation, and Mediation

—Rebecca J. Mowrey
MILLERSVILLE UNIVERSITY OF PENNSYLVANIA

Imagine: you are competing for a position on the USA Track & Field Olympic Team. This is your dream, your goal, your obsession. For over ten years you and your family and friends have made significant sacrifices and commitments enabling you to get to this elite level of athletic preparation and competition. Then, following a preliminary heat of your event you are notified that due to an eligibility rule violation you have been disqualified from further participation in the meet. With this one statement from a United States Olympic Committee (USOC) official, your dream, and all that you have worked so hard and so long to accomplish, has been crushed.

When you learn more about the alleged violation, you are absolutely certain that there has been a mistake. During the past twelve hours you and your coaches have already appealed the decision through all the USA Track & Field Association options available to you, and in each decision your appeal has been denied by Association officials. With your next preliminary heat scheduled to begin in less than six hours, you now turn your appeal efforts toward a group (**panel**) of neutral decision-makers (**arbitrators**) who are knowledgeable about track & field, as well as the USOC and USA Track & Field Association rules and procedures. This is the last level of appeal available to you. The panel has the full authority to listen to all parties, evaluate all evidence presented, and then make a final and, in most cases, **binding** (not open to further appeal or reversal) decision regarding your eligibility to continue to participate in the USA Olympic Trials. You may write the outcome of this imaginary story for yourself; however, it illustrates several of the unique elements of **arbitration**, and why the International Olympic Committee (IOC), and many International Sports Federations and National Governing Bodies representing a myriad of sport and recreation industries, support the use of arbitrators to address the complex disputes that arise during domestic and international events.

With the popularity of televised courtroom dramas such as *Law and Order*, you might think of litigation as the only road to resolving legal disputes. In reality, litigation is just one, albeit the most popular, of several avenues that individuals or groups may pursue for legal remedy. However, litigation is not always an appropriate means for resolving a dispute. **Alternative dispute resolution** (ADR) is a blanket term that includes negotiation, mediation, and arbitration, among other options, as alternatives to adjudication of disputes, with mediation and arbitration being the most commonly used of the three (www.law.cornell.edu/adr.html). The use of ADR can be voluntarily pursued by the disputing parties or mandated by a contract or waiver (see also Section 2.23, *Waivers and Releases*). Recreation and sport managers interested in personnel-related cases and disputes would be well served to develop a working knowledge of all ADR procedures, language, and the benefits of each specific process.

FUNDAMENTAL CONCEPTS

Going to court can be a costly and lengthy process; in recognition of this fact, the federal government established the **Administrative Dispute Resolution Act of 1990**, 5 U.S.C.A. 581, which requires all federal agencies to establish policies for the voluntary use of ADR as a "prompt, expert and inexpensive means of resolving disputes as an alternative to litigation in federal courts."

ADR Basics

Generally Assumed ADR Benefits v. Litigation:

- Reduced costs (i.e., no attorney fees, limited discovery);

- Usually significantly faster/less time in dispute (i.e., limited pretrial discovery, overscheduled courts);

- "Expert's" decision can be rendered instead of a non-expert jury or judge. ADR panelists frequently specialize in the types of disputes they hear / decide;

- Greater flexibility and creative solutions instead of win/lose;

- Proceedings and outcome can be kept confidential;

- ADR is considered to be the best option when there is a desire to maintain or reestablish the relationships in conflict. This could be critical to schools, offices, teams, or organizations.

- Increased satisfaction with the outcome and process.

Generally Assumed ADR Limitations v. Litigation:

- Legal precedent, if desired, is not established through ADR;

- Absence of procedural safeguards if an arbitrator makes an error of law or fact;

- Limited opportunity for appeal (in most cases appeals are only granted for arbitrator bias, fraud, or decisions rendered which exceed the arbitrator's authority);

- Enforcement of decisions is voluntary unless bound by contract (i.e., CBA).

Arbitration

Arbitration is the most formal of the ADR approaches discussed in this section, yet it is much less rigid than traditional litigation. Arbitration differs from negotiation and mediation significantly, as the arbitrator is not concerned with reaching a decision that is agreeable to the disputing parties. In this process a dispute is submitted to a neutral third party or arbitrator who listens to the disputants and considers the submitted evidence and then makes a decision or award.

The **Federal Arbitration Act of 1925**, 9 U.S.C. Section 1 (FAA) established federal law supporting arbitration as an alternative to litigation. The American Bar Association (ABA), the Uniform Law Commissioners (ULC), and the American Arbitration Association (AAA) approved the **Uniform Arbitration Act of 1955** (UAA) to establish procedure and policy standards for arbitration.

Since Congress's passage of the FAA and approval of the UAA, the number and complexity of arbitration cases has grown dramatically. In many of these cases, the FAA and the UAA failed to provide direction regarding substantive issues, and the need to update and modernize these Acts was evident. Specifically, consensus was reached by active arbitrators that revisions were needed to address the following points: (1) the need to modernize outdated provisions, clarify ambiguities under the Act, and codify important case-law developments; (2) the need to give primary consideration to the autonomy of contracting parties, provided their arbitration agreement conforms to basic notions of fundamental fairness because arbitration is a consensual process; (3) the need to maintain the essential character of arbitration as a means of dispute resolution distinct from litigation, particularly in regard to efficiency, timeliness and cost; and (4) because most parties intend arbitral decisions to be final and binding, the need to limit court involvement in the arbitration process unless unfairness or denial of justice produces clear need for such involvement." (www.nccusl.org). To address these concerns, the Revised Uniform Arbitration Act (RUAA) was approved in 2000. The RUAA added significant procedural provisions absent from the UAA, including the use of electronic records and documents which was not a consideration in 1955 (www.aaa.org).

It might help you to think of the arbitration process as a simplified trial with limited discovery and relaxed rules regarding evidence (www.adr.org). Although organizations may attach unique elements to their **arbitration clause**, most proceedings contain the following five elements:

1. **Demand for Arbitration.** A written demand for arbitration identifying the parties, the dispute, and the relief or remedy sought must be submitted to the opposing party. The arbitration request is less formal than writing a complaint in a civil action, but the issues to be arbitrated must be clear;

2. **Response.** The opposing party typically responds in writing, stating whether they agree that the issue is subject to arbitration under the existing contract or other relevant documents;

3. **Selection of Arbitration Panel.** A single arbitrator or panel with sufficient knowledge of the subject matter is selected. This process might be described in the arbitration clause of a contract or a permanent arbitrator might be designated;

4. **Arbitration Hearing.** Although similar to a trial in some respects, namely, the presentation of witnesses, documents, briefs, memoranda, and closing arguments, the process differs from a trial in that written transcripts are only provided if the parties order them, the evidentiary rules are relaxed, and the extent of discovery and cross-examination are often limited (UAA of 1955);

5. **Decision.** After hearing from all parties the arbitrator renders a decision (www.adr.org).

The decision of an arbitrator may be disputed and, under the RUAA, be vacated if: (1) the award was procured by corruption, fraud, or undue means; (2) there was evidence of partiality or corruption in the arbitrators; (3) the arbitrators were guilty of misconduct in refusing to postpone the hearing, on sufficient cause shown, or in refusing to hear evidence pertinent and material to the controversy; or of any other misbehavior by which the rights of any party have been prejudiced; or (4) the arbitrators exceeded their powers, or so imperfectly executed them that a mutual, final, and definite award on the subject matter submitted was not made (9 U.S.C. § 11).

The use of arbitration may be mandated in some contracts but be completely voluntary in others. In **voluntary arbitration** situations, the arbitration is mutually agreeable to both parties and may be **binding** or **nonbinding**, as determined in advance by the involved parties or the arbitration agreement. In **mandatory arbitration** situations, the disputing parties are often required to utilize arbitration as their sole method of addressing unresolved grievances according to the arbitration clause of their employment contracts (see Section 5.21, *Employment Contracts*), and in these cases the decision is typically binding (www.adr.org). Arbitration decisions are not typically subject to any further judicial review or appeal unless there is evidence that the arbitrator committed fraud or some other form of professional misconduct during the proceeding. If this is the case, the Federal Arbitration Act of 1925 provides for an appeal, and for review of the decision by a judge or court.

There are two common approaches to determining the number of arbitrators; either the disputing parties agree on one arbitrator or they are each represented by their own arbitrators and a third impartial arbitrator joins them to form an **arbitration panel**. Disputing parties can seek assignment of an arbitrator from several nongovernment organizations, such as the **American Arbitration Association** (AAA), which maintains a registry of qualified arbitrators or "neutrals."

Arbitration agreements now commonly appear in waivers and service contracts, requiring signers to pursue arbitration, not litigation. In *Cronin v. California Fitness* (2005), it was revealed that the two-page contract gym members sign includes an arbitration agreement capping damages for either party at an amount equal to the annual membership fee. Furthermore, the party making the claim must pay the arbitration cost, discovery is restricted, and the arbitration results must be kept confidential.

Negotiation

Negotiation refers to a consensual bargaining process used primarily to resolve disputes and complete transactions such as labor contracts (also see Sections 5.10, *Contract Essentials*; 5.21, *Employment Contracts*; and 5.22, *Game, Event, and Sponsorship Contracts*). The intent of the negotiation process is to arrive at an agreement that is acceptable to all involved parties. The negotiators in these situations are attempting to obtain their client's goals and directives, so some concessions or compromises might be made to obtain the client's desired outcomes. You have likely engaged in hundreds of informal negotiations in your lifetime as you agree to trade resources with your friends, such as the use of your car, computer, phone, video games, or your proofreading skills, for something of theirs that you value. There are four basic steps to negotiation: (1) planning how you will approach the other parties, (2) exchanging information and requests, (3) offering and counter-offering concessions and compromises, and (4) reaching an agreement that is mutually acceptable to all parties (www.adr.org). Negotiations are typically confidential, so you will rarely have the opportunity to follow the progress of a negotiation unless you are one of the principal parties involved.

Mediation

Mediation is a process in which a **neutral mediator** works collaboratively with the opposing parties to identify the areas of conflict and to assist them in reaching a settlement or agreement that is mutually satisfactory (www.mediate.com). Mediation is a consensual, nonbinding process, as the **mediators** have no power to impose or force a solution on the parties. The neutrality of the mediator is critical to ensure a sense of fairness while maintaining the integrity of the process. In some cases, the ability of the mediator to offer a different perspective will help resolve the conflict (www.campus-adr.org). You may have served unofficially as a mediator while keeping the peace between friends or classmates. If so, you have discovered one of the unique aspects of mediation versus negotiation or arbitration—the goal is to preserve the relationships and to reach an amicable resolution. As a result, mediation is a good choice for disputants who have strategic alliances or common interests that need to be maintained, such as teammates and coworkers (www.mediate.com). Another distinction of mediation is the potential to invoke the use of this process as a conflict intervention or conciliation as part of a larger conflict management program. In other words, as a conflict is developing and escalating, disputants might seek the involvement of a mediator before their conflict reaches a point of stalemate. The role of mediation in this manner is particularly effective when dealing with repetitive conflicts between individuals who need or wish to continue their working relationship (www.adr.org).

A less common approach for dispute management, but particularly useful when seeking to rebuild community or relationships i.e., team, staff, or inter-agency disputes; the **restorative justice (RJ)** process is focused on addressing the harm and restoring or rebuilding the prior relationship. Although RJ is actually a theory of criminal justice, often times the RJ results outperform the desired effect of traditional mediation approaches. The RJ process, among other restorative outcomes, provides the opportunity for victims and offenders to meet face-to-face in a mediated forum, and for each party to fully express the impact the event(s) or harm has had upon him /her. Offenders may reflect upon the impact of their decisions and be held accountable for their actions while victims may seek answers and meaningful restitution (www.restorativejustice.org).

Collective Bargaining, Labor Disputes, and ADR

Many employee groups, including professional athletic players associations, have a **collective bargaining agreement** (CBA) with their employers. A CBA refers to an agreement between the employer and the labor union or organization that regulates the terms and conditions of employment for all the employees of a single employer. In some labor matters, the CBA may mandate that certain disputes (e.g., differences in interpretation of the CBA, grievances, salary disputes) must be resolved through mandatory arbitration or that mediation may be sought by either party (www.campus-adr.com). The collective bargaining agreements of the professional sport leagues in the United States provide for grievances to be addressed through an arbitration process. However, every CBA contains specific clauses and procedures regarding how and when arbitration will be used that are unique to that CBA and sport. Since 1974, the CBA for Major League Baseball (MLB) has permitted eligible players to file for salary arbitration. From 1974-2009, a total of 487 MLB salary cases have been decided through arbitration (mlb.mlb.org).

When the parties of a CBA agree to enter into arbitration, the issues the arbitrator(s) is to address are clearly communicated. For example, in the *Matter of the Arbitration Between Terrell Owens and the National Football League (NFL) Players Association v. The Philadelphia Eagles and the NFL Management Council* (2005), an arbitrator was asked by the parties, Terrell Owens and the NFL Players Association, to examine the decision of the Philadelphia Eagles' management to suspend Owens. Specifically, the arbitrator was asked to reach a decision on the following two issues: (1) was the four-week disciplinary suspension for just cause; if not, what should the remedy be; and (2) was it a violation of the CBA for the Club to exclude the Player from games and practices, following the four-week suspension? The arbitrator's conclusions and decision follow:

> *In summary, there is ample room to find that the Club could respond to this Player's actions, suspending him without pay to the limits permitted by the collective bargaining agreement for his behavior in this matter. Thereafter, the Coach properly exercised his inherent discretion to conclude that, on balance, the team would be better protected and better off by practicing and fielding a team that did not include Mr. Owens. The problem—a continuing one—was almost entirely off-field, and the response properly dealt with that reality. Both responses, the disciplinary and the discretionary, were specifically understood by these parties and fully countenanced as part of this collective bargaining relationship. The disciplinary side of the equation is expressly established in Article VIII. The non-disciplinary response is part of the core and character of a coaches discretion; significantly, but predictably, it is nowhere constrained by the CBA. The finding, therefore, is that the Club has shouldered its burden of providing clear and convincing evidence of the Player's misconduct and, moreover, that the four-week suspension was for just cause. Additionally, there was no violation of the labor agreement inherent in the Club's decision to pay Mr. Owens, but not to permit him to play or practice, due to the nature of his conduct and its destructive and continuing threat to the team.*

> *AWARD*

> *The grievance is denied.*

> *Richard I. Bloch, Esq.*

> *November 23, 2005*

ADR Applications in Sport and Recreation

In professional sports almost all contract disputes between the players and/or coaches and teams are resolved through an arbitration process. For example, in 2008 an arbitrator ruled that former Dallas Mavericks coach Don Nelson was entitled to nearly 6.3 million dollars in deferred salary and compensation payments. Mavericks' owner Mark Cuban alleged that Nelson had violated a noncompete clause in his contract when he became head coach of the Golden State Warriors in 2006.

In the context of intercollegiate sports, the NCAA has utilized ADR approaches to resolve disputes in limited cases. In 1991, the NCAA enacted a legislative policy that capped or restricted the earnings or salaries of some coaching staff personnel at NCAA universities and colleges. These restricted-earnings coaches could not be compensated more than $12,000 during the traditional academic year and no more than $4,000 for summer employment (*Law v. NCAA*, 1998). The NCAA's restricted-earnings policy was found to be in violation of federal antitrust law (see Section 7.32, *Antitrust Law: Amateur Sport Applications*). The NCAA appealed the decision of the district court and also entered into mediation with the plaintiffs. As a result of the mediation process, a $54.5 million settlement was announced in 1999 (www.ncaa.org).

ADR and International Sport Disputes

Disputes in international sport settings raise several unique dilemmas, such as when to follow the legal system of the host country versus that of the athlete's country of residence. Also, most legal systems do not accommodate the need for nearly immediate decisions to remove athletes from further competition or to approve them for continued competition. The arbitration format is ideal for addressing international disputes that are bound by different judicial systems.

The IOC realizing the need for effective and efficient conflict resolution, established the Court of Arbitration for Sport (CAS) (www.tas-cas.org). Since establishing the CAS, arbitration has been used to bridge the gap between differing legal systems and to reach a speedy decision that is imperative during multiday events such as the Olympics and world championships. The CAS consists of three divisions: the Appeals Arbitration Division, the Ad Hoc Division, and the Ordinary Arbitration Division. Athletes who disagree with the decisions of their sport federation or sport regulation body during non-Olympic times would seek arbitration through the CAS Appeals Arbitration Division. The Ad Hoc Division is charged with resolving disputes that occur during the Olympic Games, whereas the CAS Ordinary Arbitration Division addresses commercial contract disputes (i.e., official vendors and media). The CAS has courts in Lausanne, Switzerland; New York City, New York, USA; and Sydney, Australia. Unless all parties agree to follow another country's form of law, the CAS court will use Swiss law or the law of the country where the involved sport federation is located (www.tas -cas.org). The International Council of Arbitration for Sport (ICAS) was established in 1994 to administer the CAS and to provide a process for arbitration that is neutral and independent of the IOC. The primary responsibilities of the ICAS are to select neutral arbitrators and to protect the rights of all parties (Oschutz, 2002).

Since establishment, the CAS has seen a dramatic increase in appeals filed for arbitration, with many cases tied to drug testing issues. In 2006, the Federation Internationale de Football Association (FIFA) requested that the CAS provide a legal opinion regarding the World Anti–Doping Agency's (WADA) Anti–Doping Code (CODE). FIFA specifically wished to know if the CODE complied with Swiss law, and if FIFA's sanctions related to doping offences was in compliance with the CODE. The CAS determined that the FIFA policies were in compliance with the CODE. This complex case required arbitrators with knowledge of FIFA, Swiss law, WADA, and the CODE.

In *United States Anti-Doping Agency v. Floyd Landis*, the CAS Panel upheld the 2007 American Arbitration Association Panel decision, resulting in Landis's disqualification from the 2006 Tour De France and suspending him from competition from January 30, 2007-January 30 2009. Furthermore, the CAS Panel ordered Landis to pay $100,000 towards the United States Anti–Doping Agency's (USADA) CAS Arbitration costs. At the request of Landis, all court records were made public, and this was the first public anti–doping hearing ever conducted. The Supplemental CD includes the American Arbitration Association (AAA) Panel decision, the dissenting opinion of Christopher L. Campbell, a member of the AAA Arbitration Panel, and the CAS Panel decision. You may also find video of the testimony given in these two arbitration cases (AAA and CAS) testimony on the Internet.

Understandably, the number of CAS appeals usually increases during the years in which the Summer or Winter Olympic Games are held. In February 2009, the CAS dismissed the appeal of Swedish wrestler Ara Abrahamian regarding the IOC decision to strip the bronze medal from him during the 2008 Summer Olympic Games. The IOC made their decision after Abrahamian dropped his medal on the floor in protest of a penalty call. In their ruling, the CAS stated that "the decision of the IOC Executive Board was not disproportionate in the circumstances." Additional CAS decisions can be found at their Website www.tas-cas.org.

ADR, Sport Specialists, and Violence

The ICAS, AAA, and the professional player associations have already increased the demand for arbitration and negotiation specialists who are knowledgeable about sport. It is likely that the value of mediation will continue to be appreciated in these situations as well (Galton, 1998). Historically, it is common for the professional sport model to influence the intercollegiate, interscholastic, and club sport programs. Jeffrey Schalley (2001) argued that arbitration can be used to eliminate violence in sports. He proposed that language could be added to the CBA arbitration clauses to address "injury compensation resulting from reckless or intentional torts." Would this work as a deterrent? Without a CBA available in amateur sport settings, perhaps an arbitration clause regarding violence will begin to appear in athlete codes of conduct and/or in waivers and in participation agreements. As schools, universities, and communities address the growing concerns regarding "bullying," hazing, and conflict among their student athlete populations, the position of ADR sport specialist might become as commonplace as that of team physician.

SIGNIFICANT CASE

The following case illustrates the ways by which an Arbitrator reaches a decision. This case was selected because it is *NOT* a WADA case. So many of the CAS and AAA sport—related cases are doping—related; however, other sensitive and critical matters are also decided through arbitration such as team selection. You will note that although this is an appeal of a prior decision, the case is much different from Court of Appeal decisions. Note also the timeliness and costs issues addressed by the Arbitrator that are unique to Arbitration cases. Lastly, if you were Mr. Nieto in this AAA case, would you be satisfied that justice had been served?

IN THE MATTER OF THE ARBITRATION BETWEEN
RE: 77 190 00275 08 JENF

Jamie Nieto
and
USA Track & Field
and
Dustin Jonas Affected Athlete

AWARD OF ARBITRATOR

I, THE UNDERSIGNED ARBITRATOR, having been designated by the American Arbitration Association and in accordance with the United States Olympic Committee Bylaws, having been duly sworn, and having duly heard the proofs and allegations of the Parties, and the Affected Athlete do hereby, AWARD, as follows:

1. This is a difficult case involving two outstanding athletes, only one of whom can go to the Olympics. The decision by USA Track and & Field ("USATF"), the national governing body, to select Dustin Jonas over Jamie Nieto has been challenged by Mr. Nieto as being in violation of Section 220522(a)(14) of the Ted Stevens Olympic and Amateur Sports Act (the "Stevens Act") and Section 9.1 of the United States Olympic Committee ("USOC") Bylaws.

2. The issue to be determined is whether, by requiring athletes to achieve the international qualifying standard by the end of the U.S. Olympic Team Trials for Track & Field (the "Olympic Trials") on July 6, 2008, the USATF has impermissibly denied Mr. Nieto the opportunity to participate in the Olympic Games.

3. In light of all the evidence, the Arbitrator determines that USATF's July 6 deadline neither violates the Stevens Act nor otherwise denies Mr. Nieto the opportunity to participate. The arbitrator therefore denies Mr. Nieto's appeal.

Background

4. Under the rules of the International Association of Athletics Federations ("IAAF") for the 2008 Beijing Olympics, a country may send up to three qualified athletes for each individual event, provided that all athletes achieve the "A" qualifying standard set by the IAAF. The 2008 "A" standard for men's high jump is 2.30 meters. For the high jump event and other events, the IAAF rules require that athletes achieve the "A" standard between January 1, 2007, and July 23, 2008.

5. For the high jump event and other events, the USATF athlete selection procedures for the 2008 Olympics (the "USATF Selection Procedures") provided that, if at least three athletes achieved the "A" standard between January 1, 2007 and the end of U.S. Olympic Team Trials for Track & Field (the "Olympic Trials") on July 6, 2008, then the top three such finishers at the Trials would be nominated to the 2008 U.S. Olympic Team. This represented a departure from the USATF's practice in previous years of letting top finishers at the Trials "chase the standard" following the Olympic Trials until the IAAF deadline.

6. Prior to the Olympic Trials, Mr. Jonas had achieved the "A" standard; Mr. Nieto had not yet achieved the "A" standard.

7. At the Trials, Mr. Nieto tied for second place but failed to achieve the "A" standard of 2.30 meters. Mr. Jonas tied for sixth place.

8. In accordance with its Selection Procedures, USATF nominated to the Team the top three finishers at the Trials who had by the end of the Trials achieved the "A" standard. Mr. Jonas was nominated to the Olympic Team; Mr. Nieto was not.

9. Six days after the Trials, on June 12, 2008, Mr. Nieto achieved the "A" standard in competition at Cork, Ireland, with a jump of 2.30 meters.

10. On July 15, 2008, Mr. Nieto filed a Demand for Arbitration with American Arbitration Association, along with a Statement of Dispute and various exhibits. The Arbitrator's jurisdiction arises from the USOC Olympic Games Code of Conduct and Grievance Procedures.

11. Also on July 15, 2008, David W. Rivkin was selected by the American Arbitration Association to serve as the sole Arbitrator in this case. After receiving certain disclosures from the Arbitrator, the parties agreed to the selection of Mr. Rivkin. On the morning of July 16, 2008, the Arbitrator held a one-hour preliminary hearing by telephone. On July 17, 2008, USATF and Mr. Jonas made submissions to the Arbitrator.

12. On July 18, 2008, the Arbitrator held a seven-hour hearing at the offices of Debevoise & Plimpton LLP in New York, NY. The hearing included Mr. Nieto, Mr. Jonas, USATF, and the parties' legal representatives. Rana Dershowitz and John Ruger of the USOC participated as observers. During the hearing, each of the parties, including Mr. Jonas, was able to present evidence, question witnesses, and make arguments. Each of the athletes made certain statements and was subject to questioning by counsel for all sides.

Decision

13. Mr. Nieto claims that by requiring athletes to achieve the "A" qualifying standard by July 6, 2008, instead of by the IAAF deadline of July 23, 2008, USATF has impermissibility denied him the opportunity to participate in the Olympic Games as provided in Section 9 of the USOC Bylaws. He argues that the USATF Selection Procedures (*i*) lack a rational basis and (*ii*) violate Section 220522(a)(14) of the Stevens Act, which prohibits USATF as a National Governing Body ("NGB") from having "eligibility criteria related to amateur status or participation in the Olympic Games . . . more restrictive than those of the appropriate international sports federation." He seeks an order to USATF to select him for the Olympic Team.

14. Mr. Jonas and USATF have made a motion to dismiss this case. They assert that Mr. Nieto's claim is more properly a facial challenge to the USATF Selection Procedures, and that it therefore must be brought only under Section 220527 of the Stevens Act and Section 10 of the USOC Bylaws. The provisions require a complainant to exhaust remedies within the NGB and within the USOC before demanding arbitration. They also assert that the relief that Mr. Nieto seeks—an order placing him on the Olympics team—is unavailable under these provisions.

15. The issues raised by the motion to dismiss focus on the complicated interplay among the provisions of the Stevens Act and the USOC Bylaws. USATF and Mr. Jonas make compelling arguments that if an athlete believes that procedures adopted by an NGB violate the mandates of the Stevens Act, then they must be challenged, as they can be under Section 220527 of the Stevens Act and Section 10 of the USOC Bylaws, before athletes and others operate under and rely upon them, and that the remedies provided in those documents do not extend to an order changing an NGB's team selection. On the other hand, the Stevens Act and the USOC Bylaws, especially their Section 9, provide

important rights to athletes to protect their opportunity to participate.

16. In *Mary C. McConneloug v. USA Cycling*, AAA Case No. 30 190 00750 04 (July 20, 2004), another Olympics eligibility case, I ruled that the NGB could not change the rules on the athletes after the time period for Olympics qualifying had elapsed. Similarly, after athletes had relied upon the USATF Selection Procedures through the Olympics Trials, an athlete has a heavy burden to convince an arbitrator to adopt different rules after the fact. That is particularly so where, as here, the alleged violation of the rule is clear on its face—the "A" standard deadline of July 6, 2008 instead of July 23, 2008—and was known to the athletes well in advance of the final selections, as compared to a situation where the rules may create ambiguities that are not clear until they are finally applied.

17. Nevertheless, I would not want to fashion a rule that all such challenges must be brought under Section 220527 of the Stevens Act or Section 10 of the USOC Bylaws, because that could impose a serious limitation on the rights of athletes to have the opportunity to participate, as provided in Section 9 of the USOC Bylaws. Because I hold below that the USATF Selection Procedures do not violate either the Stevens Act or the USOC Bylaws, I do need to determine in this case where that line should be drawn or finally to decide the motion to dismiss.

18. *First*, Mr. Nieto has not carried his burden of persuasion to show that the USATF rule barring athletes from chasing the "A" qualifying standard after the end of the Trials on July 6, 2008, lacks a rational basis. USATF has submitted evidence of several rationales for the July 6 deadline that Mr. Nieto cannot prove are irrational by a preponderance of evidence.

19. USATF reasonably believed that the practice of chasing the standard after the Olympics Trials had a negative effect on the physical preparedness of athletes chasing the standard, who were forced to peak twice before the Olympic Games, and on the mental and emotional preparedness of athletes who believed that they had made the team but were in danger of being bumped from it by a competitor chasing the standard. It is reasonable for USATF to give athletes a year and a half to meet an international qualifying standard and then to say that all final selections will be made at the end of the Olympics Trials. Such a rule provides an element of certainty to the athletes that is clearly beneficial. It is a cruel irony that part of the reason for the USATF's current, earlier deadline is the disappointment that Mr. Nieto suffered in 2005 when he was bumped off the World Championships team by another athlete who met the international standard only after the national trials. The rationale for the new rule, however, is not diminished by the misfortune of this reversal.

20. Mr. Nieto argued that USATF had not presented evidence that these performance issues affected high jump

athletes in particular. However, it is rational for USATF to want to apply a single qualification deadline to athletes in all of its events, except where an event, like the marathon, has clearly different performance issues.

21. USATF also submitted evidence of a logistical rationale for the July 6 deadline. Although it is doubtful that USATF needed to know the composition of its 2008 Olympic Team on July 6 in order to submit names of the athletes to the USOC and to the Beijing Olympics Organizing Committee or to arrange the logistics of getting the athletes, coaches, and medical professionals to Beijing, it is certain that these logistical preparations take some amount of time. In light of those logistical considerations, it is rational for USATF to chose a deadline some time in advance of the final deadline for submitting names to the Olympics organizers and to choose as that deadline, for the reasons mentioned above, an event like the Olympics Trials.

22. In arguing against the rationale of the USATF Selection Procedures, Mr. Nieto presented powerful evidence that the means by which USATF adopted these procedures were seriously flawed. It appears that members of the Athletes Advisory Committee, like Mr. Nieto, were not properly consulted, and notice of meetings and of the adoption of the procedures was not properly given before their adoption. Evidence of such procedural violations is more important in a case challenging the validity of the procedures before they have been finally implemented, such as in an action under Section 220527 of the Stevens Act or Section 10 of the USOC Bylaws, than in a claim to change the procedures after the fact. However, USATF should be on notice that if it acts in such a manner in the future in adopting, it may face a serious facial challenge under those provisions.

23. *Second*, USATF's July 6 deadline for achieving the "A" qualifying standard does not violate Section 220522(a)(14) of the Stevens Act. The prohibition on NGB eligibility criteria more restrictive than those of the appropriate international sports federation must be understood in context. Violations of Section 220522 result in the suspension of the NGB or even in the revocation of its recognition. Thus, in determining whether a certain requirement, like a time deadline, is an eligibility criterion that is more restrictive than an international standard, one must take into account the seriousness of the sanction. In this context, it seems clear that the drafters of Section 220522(a)(14) intended to cover serious aberrations from the international standard and not aberrations that may be immaterial. For example, USATF could not permissibly have set its "A" qualifying standard for the high jump at more than 2.30 meters, as that is a critical eligibility criterion.

24. An aberration in the time deadline for achieving that standard, however, must be very material in order to fall within that proscription. A literal reading of this Section would lead to the absurd result that USATF must wait until the end of the day on July 23, the IAAF qualification deadline, to select its team. Because the IAAF qualification deadline is also the deadline for submitting the names of participating athletes, USATF could be unable in this circumstance to submit its names for the Olympic Team on time. On the other hand, it is clear that USATF could not permissibility have set a qualification deadline in, for example, July of 2007, thereby depriving athletes of over half the time allotted by the IAAF to achieve the "A" standard. In this case, limiting athletes' opportunity to meet the "A" standard by about two weeks—or about 3% of the total qualifying window—is not a material aberration that could violate the Stevens Act. This conclusion is reinforced by the rationale reasons for doing so that are described above.

25. Because the USATF Selection Procedures did not materially or unreasonably restrict athletes' opportunities to achieve the "A" qualification standard, they do not violate Section 220522(a)(14) of the Stevens Act.

26. Because the USATF Selection Procedures neither lack a rational basis nor violate the Stevens Act, they do not deny Mr. Nieto an opportunity to participate in the Olympic Games under Section 9 of the USOC Bylaws.

Therefore, I AWARD as follows:

Mr. Nieto's claim is hereby denied.

The administrative fees of the American Arbitration Association totaling $750.00 shall be borne by Mr. Nieto.

This Award is in full settlement of all claims submitted to this Arbitration. All claims not expressly granted herein are hereby, denied.

CASES ON THE SUPPLEMENTAL CD

Landis v. United States Anti–Doping Agency, Arbitral Award, CAS 2007/A/1394	United States Anti–Doping Agency v. Landis, Campbell Dissenting Opinion, United States–20 September 2007 Arbitration Case 30 190 00847 06
United States Anti–Doping Agency v. Landis, Arbitration Award, United States–20 September 2007 Arbitration Case 30 190 00847 06	

QUESTIONS YOU SHOULD BE ABLE TO ANSWER

1. Compare and contrast the common procedures of negotiation, mediation and arbitration.

2. Identify a recently tried sport or recreation case. Identify both the positive and negative arguments for using ADR vs. adjudication procedures to resolve this dispute.

3. Review the three related Section 5.13 cases on the Supplemental CD. Determine if you agree with the Majority or Dissenting Arbitrators and indicate why.

4. In the Significant Case included in this section, point #16 references *Mary C. McConneloug v. USA Cycling*, AAA Case No. 30 190 00750 04 (July 20, 2004), Locate this arbitration case and compare the reasoning in the appeal and decision in McConneloug v. USA Cycling to the reasoning the Arbitrator uses in the Significant Case.

5. Arbitration experts have stated that the MLB Salary Arbitration agreement has resulted in significantly higher salaries for players. Is this a direct result of the use of arbitration versus negotiation or other practices? Be prepared to debate the truth of these statements and support your position with facts.

REFERENCES

Cases

Cronin v. California Fitness, 2005 Ohio App.LEXIS 3056.

Law v. NCAA, 134 F.3d 1010 (10th Cir. 1998).

Sprewell v. Golden State Warriors, 266 F.3d 979 (9th Cir. 2001).

Arbitration Proceedings

Administrative Panel Decision Adidas AG v. Zhifang Wu Case No. D2007-0032

CAS 2007/A/1394 Floyd Landis v. United States Anti–Doping Agency

Mr. Ross Rebagliati and International Olympic Committee (IOC). (CAS, Ad Hoc Div., Ref: Arb., NAG 2, Final Award; www.tas-cas.org.

United States–20 September 2007 Arbitration Case 30 190 00847 06 United States Anti–Doping Agency v. Floyd Landis, Majority Opinion

Publications

Cozzillio, M., & Levinstein, M. S. (1997). *Sports law cases and materials*. Durham, NC: Carolina Academic Press.

Donegan, F. (1994). Examining the role of arbitration in professional baseball. *Sports Lawyer Journal, 1*, 183.

Galton, E. (1998). Mediation programs for collegiate sports teams. *Dispute Resolution Journal, 53*, 37–39.

Haslip, S. (2001). A consideration of the need for a national dispute resolution system for national sports organizations in Canada. *Marquette Sports Law Review, 11*(2), 245–270.

Katsh, E., & Rifkin, J. (2001). *Online dispute resolution: Resolving conflicts in cyberspace.* San Francisco: Jossey-Bass.

Oschutz, F. (2002). Harmonization of anti-doping code through arbitration: The case law of the court of arbitration for sport. *Marquette Sports Law Review, 12*(2), 675–702.

Schalley, J. (2001). Eliminate violence from sports through arbitration, not the civil courts. *The Sports Lawyers Journal, 8*(1), 181–206.

Legislation

Administrative Dispute Resolution Act of 1990, 5 U.S.C.A. 581.

Federal Arbitration Act of 1925, 9 U.S.C.

Revised Uniform Arbitration Act of 2000

Uniform Arbitration Act of 1955.

Websites

www.aaa.org

www.adr.org

www.law.cornell.edu/adr.html

www.campus-adr.org

www.mediate.com

www.ncaa.org

www.sportslaw.org

www.restorativejustice.org

www.tas-cas.org

www.mediate.com

www.wipo.org

6.00

CONSTITUTIONAL LAW

The United States Constitution provides everyone certain rights and protections. Before the courts can apply constitutional protections, however, certain threshold questions must be asked. The following section examines the constitutional safeguards of the First, Fourth, Fifth, and Fourteenth Amendments as they apply to due process, equal protection, and the right to privacy and how they relate to the sport and recreation industries.

The *Constitutional Law* section is divided into two parts. The first part examines some of the fundamental principles of Constitutional law, including state action, due process, equal protection, and search and seizure. This part also serves as an introduction to the principles of Constitutional law. The second part examines how the issues of due process, equal protection, and search and seizure apply specifically to the sport, health and fitness, and recreation industries.

6.10 Concepts

6.11 Judicial Review, Standing, and Injunctions

—Jim Masteralexis
WESTERN NEW ENGLAND COLLEGE

—Lisa Pike Masteralexis
UNIVERSITY OF MASSACHUSETTS

Sport and recreation managers make decisions regarding athletic rules and regulations on a daily basis. Although the courts generally take a "hands-off" approach to reviewing decisions by private athletic organizations, in a limited number of situations courts will review the actions of private athletic organizations to ensure that they have applied the rules and regulations properly. The following section examines when a court will review an athletic organization's action, when a plaintiff has standing to challenge a decision by private athletic organizations, and what types of injunctive relief the courts can order to bar the athletic organization from going forward with its decision.

FUNDAMENTAL CONCEPTS

Judicial Review

Scope of Review

As a general rule, courts decline to intervene in the internal affairs of private, voluntary organizations that govern professional and amateur sports. The reasoning behind this policy is that membership in the organizations is voluntary and the organizations are self-regulating. The court will, however, review the decisions where one of the following conditions is met:

1. The rule or regulation challenged by the plaintiff exceeds the scope of the athletic association's authority;

2. The rule or regulation challenged by the plaintiff violates an individual's constitutional rights;

3. The rule or regulation challenged by the plaintiff violates an existing law, such as the Sherman Antitrust Act or the Americans with Disabilities Act.;

4. The rule or regulation challenged by the plaintiff is applied in an arbitrary and/or capricious manner;

5. The rule or regulation challenged by the plaintiff violates public policy because it is considered fraudulent or unreasonable;

6. The athletic association breaks one of its own rules.

The harshness of a rule is not by itself grounds for judicial review. Relief is granted only where the plaintiff can prove to the court that one of the preceding conditions has been met. Even where a rule is subject to review, the court's role is limited. A court will not review the merits of the rule, but simply decide whether the application of the rule is invalid on the basis of meeting one of the five conditions listed.

Application. Despite the standards listed earlier, decisions to grant injunctions in cases that appear factually similar may vary. This is due to variations in precedent across jurisdictions or differences in regional standards, such as when a community is given the right to determine standards. An example would be in the distinction between free speech and obscenity. The U.S. Supreme Court has deferred to communities to define obscenity, so what may be considered obscene in Dallas might not be considered obscene in New York City. It may also be due to the application of state laws or state constitutional rights that grant greater protections than federal laws. One area in which this is common is where states have stronger privacy protections than the Fourth Amendment.

Married Students. One area where there has been some variation is when an amateur athletic association has imposed rules barring married students from participation in high school athletics. In one case, *Estay v. La Fourche Parish School Board* (1969), a married high school student challenged his exclusion from all extracurricular activities. The Louisiana Court of Appeals held that the school board had the authority to adopt the regulation. The regulation survived equal protection scrutiny because the court found there was a rational relationship between the rule and its stated objective of promoting completion of high school before marriage. Finally, the court held that the rule was not arbitrary and capricious, for it was applied uniformly and impartially against anyone who sought to participate in extracurricular activities, not simply athletics. Eight years later and in another jurisdiction, the Colorado Court of Appeals ruled for the student-athlete, stating that he possessed a fundamental right to marry and the reasons proffered by the school board did not establish a compelling state interest to justify the violation of the plaintiff's equal protection rights (*Beeson v. Kiowa County School District*, 1977).

Alcohol and Drugs. Similarly, jurisdictions vary when enforcing rules that prohibit the use of alcohol and drugs, often called good conduct rules. If the rules address a legitimate sport-related purpose, courts will often find that they are within the scope of the association's authority. But where the rule is intrusive and broadly attempts to regulate the conduct of a student-athlete during the off-season or conduct unrelated to athletic participation, a court will likely strike it down. In *Braesch v. De Pasquale* (1978), the Supreme Court of Nebraska ruled that a rule prohibiting drinking served a legitimate rational interest by directly affecting the discipline of a student-athlete. The court also ruled that the rule was not arbitrary nor an unreasonable means to attain the legitimate end of deterring alcohol use among student-athletes. On the other hand, in *Bunger v. Iowa High School Athletic Association* (1972), another court struck down a good conduct rule prohibiting the use of alcoholic beverages. During the summer, the plaintiff was riding in a car containing a case of beer. The car was pulled over by the police, and the four minors in the car were issued citations. The plaintiff reported the incident to his athletic program and was suspended in accordance with the state athletic association rule. The Iowa Supreme Court held the rule was invalid on the grounds that it exceeded the scope of the athletic association's authority. The Court based its decision on the fact that the incident was outside the football season, beyond the school year, and did not involve the illegal use of alcohol.

Athletic Associations. Cases involving athletic association rules that infringe on the constitutional right to freedom of expression have also exhibited variation. In *Williams v. Eaton* (1972), a group of fourteen African-American football players for the University of Wyoming sought permission from their coach to wear black armbands in their game against Brigham Young University to protest the beliefs of the Mormon Church. The coach dismissed them from the team for violating team rules prohibiting protests. In a court action challenging the rule, the court held that the First Amendment rights of the players to freedom of speech could not be paramount to the rights of others to practice their religion free from a state-supported (University of Wyoming) protest. On the other hand, *Tinker v. Des Moines Independent School District* (1969), held that student-athletes wearing politically motivated black armbands protesting the Vietnam War in a public high school were found to have a constitutionally protected right to freedom of expression.

Standing

Standing is a plaintiff's right to bring a complaint in court. To establish standing the plaintiff must meet three criteria:

1. The plaintiff bringing the action must have sustained an injury in fact;
2. The interest that the plaintiff seeks to be protected is one for which the court possesses the power to grant a remedy;
3. The plaintiff must have an interest in the outcome of the case.

The question of standing is generally raised by the defense seeking to dismiss a case and not one the court will raise on its own. In other words, as an initial matter, the plaintiff does not possess a burden of proof with regard to standing, but may be forced to show standing if the defendant raises the issue.

Application

The issue of standing was a determinative factor for the Federal Court when they ruled on a **motion to intervene** in the case of *ProBatter Sports, LLC v. Joyner Technologies*. A motion to intervene can be brought by anyone who is not involved in a court case if they have an interest in the case and it would be difficult for that person, or company, to protect their interest unless they were a party in the case. ProBatter was the owner of all the rights to a "unique" baseball video pitching simulator. In May 2005, ProBatter filed suit against Joyner in the Federal District Court for the Northern District of Iowa alleging patent infringement of their "134 Patent" and "154 Patent". In December 2005, ProBatter filed another lawsuit in the Federal District Court for the District of Connecticut against another company, Sports Tutor, alleging patent infringement of two different patents, the "649 Patent" and the "924 Patent". Sports Tutor was the owner of the "Home Plate non-video pitching system". In February 2006, Sports Tutor filed a motion to intervene in the case in Iowa arguing that it had an interest in the subject mater of the case between ProBatter and Joyner and that their ability to protect their business interest would be impeded if they were not represented in the case. ProBatter opposed Sports Tutor's motion to intervene. The Federal Court for the Northern District of Iowa denied Sports Tutor's motion to intervene because the "649 Patent" and the "924 Patent" were not an issue in the Iowa case. In addition, Pro Batter did not make any claims in Iowa concerning Sports Tutor's Home Plate non-video pitching machine. The Iowa Federal Court held that Sports Tutor did not have standing to intervene because they did not sustain an injury in fact and they could adequately protect their interest in the Connecticut case.

Injunctive Relief

Types of Injunctive Relief

There are four types of injunctive relief available: the temporary restraining order, the preliminary injunction, the permanent injunction, and specific performance.

The **temporary restraining order** is generally issued to a plaintiff in an emergency situation, without notice (appearance at hearing) to the defendant, and is usually effective for a maximum of ten days. Before a court will grant the temporary restraining order, a plaintiff must prove that he/she will face irreparable harm and that money damages would be an inadequate remedy.

The **preliminary injunction** is granted to a plaintiff prior to a trial on the merits of a legal action and lasts throughout the trial process of the case. The defendant is given notice to appear at the hearing for the injunction and may argue against the granting of the preliminary injunction. To be awarded a preliminary injunction, the plaintiff must prove:

1. The plaintiff will face a substantial threat of irreparable harm without the preliminary injunction. (Often where money damages would be an inadequate remedy, granting the injunction would provide the only remedy):

2. The balance of the hardships favors the plaintiff;

3. The plaintiff possesses a likelihood of success on the merits of the pending case;

4. Granting the injunction will serve the public interest.

A **permanent injunction** requires the plaintiff to prove the same four elements but is awarded as a remedy following a full hearing on the merits of the case. Finally, **specific performance** is a court order that may be available to the victim of a breach of contract. Specific performance requires that a defendant comply with (honor) the contract. Because money is generally an adequate remedy for a contract breach, specific performance is rarely used. The court will grant this remedy in situations where the subject matter is extremely rare. An example in sport where a court may be willing to grant specific performance is with a breach of a contract for the sale of sports memorabilia. There may be only one Honus Wagner baseball card in the world, and money may be an inadequate remedy to replace the card if the seller were to break the contract. In such a case the non-breaching party might seek an injunction for specific performance because the card is priceless and rare.

Specific performance will not be granted to enforce a contract of a professional athlete. Although there may be only one LeBron James, if he were to break his contract with the Cleveland Cavaliers, the court would not grant the Cavaliers a specific performance injunction to force James to honor his contract with the club. The reason is that by granting such an injunction, the court would be forcing James to work and would find its order in conflict with the U.S. Constitutional prohibition against slavery. In such cases, however, there is a remedy for professional teams. Courts are willing to grant negative injunctions against athletes who breach their contracts. A negative injunction is actually a preliminary or permanent injunction (depending on the time it is sought by the team—prior to trial or as part of a breach of contract award at the end of trial). The effect of the negative injunction is to prohibit the player from playing his or her sport for any other team or event than the plaintiff's. In this way the court is not ordering the athlete to work, but simply prohibiting him/her from playing his/her sport anywhere except for the team possessing the valid and enforceable contract.

Scope. When a plaintiff seeks judicial review of a decision, the plaintiff will also request a temporary restraining order and/or a preliminary injunction to bar the rule from being applied. Injunctive relief is designed to prevent future wrongs, rather than to punish past actions. It is only used to prevent an irreparable injury that is suffered when monetary damages will be inadequate to compensate the injured party. An injury is considered irreparable when it involves the risk of physical harm or death; the loss of a special opportunity; or the deprivation of unique, irreplaceable property. For example, a high school senior student-athlete may be granted an injunction to compete in a championship game because he/she may never again have that opportunity.

Application. A recent significant Ohio state trial court case, *Oliver v. National Collegiate Athletic Association* ("NCAA"), applied both judicial review and injunctions in reversing a ruling of the NCAA. Andrew Oliver was a star high school pitcher in Ohio and in June 2006 the Minnesota Twins ("Twins") drafted him in the seventeenth (17th) round of the amateur baseball draft. Oliver retained the services of attorneys Robert Baratta, and Tim Baratta ("Baratta") to be his sports advisors and attorneys. Oliver had also been offered a full baseball scholarship at Oklahoma State University ("OSU"). At the end of the summer of 2006, Oliver, his father and Baratta met with representatives of the Twins at the Oliver home and the Twins offered Oliver $390,000 to sign with their team. Oliver rejected the offer and decided to attend OSU. In March of 2008 Oliver decided to terminate Baratta and hired the Boras Corporation to be his advisors and attorneys. Baratta sent an invoice for $113,750 to Oliver for legal services. Oliver brought the invoice to the OSU compliance office and to the Boras Corporation and refused to pay the bill.

In May 2008 Baratta mailed and faxed a letter to the NCAA alleging that Oliver violated NCAA rules by virtue of Baratta attending the meeting with the Twins in 2006. As a result of this complaints, OSU investigated Oliver's amateur status and indefinitely suspended him from playing baseball for violating NCAA Bylaw 12.3.1 by allowing Baratta to previously telephone the Twins on his behalf and attending the meeting at the Oliver home.

On August 18, 2008, Oliver was reinstated to play baseball at OSU when he was granted a temporary restraining Order by the Ohio Court of Common Pleas. However, in October 2008 OSU filed for reinstatement by the NCAA for Oliver, even thought the Court had already granted him the reinstatement. The NCAA, in December 2008, suspended Oliver for one (1) year and charged him with a year of eligibility. The NCAA later reduced the penalty to a suspension from 70 percent of the baseball season and with no loss of eligibility. Oliver filed suit in Ohio court requesting that the court review the NCAA decision, declare that it was legally incorrect and requested injunctive relief to order the NCAA to allow him to play.

The relevant NCAA Bylaw, section 12.3.1, states:

> *A lawyer may not be present during discussions of a contract offer with a professional organization or have any direct contact (in person, by telephone or by mail) with a professional sports organization on behalf of the individual. A lawyer's presence during such discussions is considered representation by an agent.*

The Ohio court ruled that the NCAA's decision was arbitrary and capricious because it allows an athlete to retain an attorney but impermissibly limits what the attorney can do by prohibiting him from attending meetings with the professional organization. In addition, the court held that only the Ohio Supreme Court has the authority to regulate the conduct of Ohio attorneys, not the NCAA. The Court ruled that Oliver, a citizen of Ohio, had the right to have an attorney present when he met with the Twins to help him make an important decision. The Court granted Oliver a permanent injunction ordering the NCAA to reinstate his eligibility to play baseball.

SIGNIFICANT CASE

The Indiana High School Athletic Association case that follows provides an excellent example of an appellate court's review of the grounds for granting a preliminary injunction against conduct that is arbitrary and capricious and conduct that violates an organization's own rules. The case also discusses in detail the concept of public interest in the granting of injunctive relief. The case involves an appeal by Indiana High School Athletic Association (IHSAA) of the trial court's issuance of a permanent injunction against the IHSAA's denial of full eligibility and a hardship exception for a student–athlete. The trial court found that the IHSAA's decision was arbitrary and capricious. Upon appeal, the IHSAA asserts that the trial court's findings are clearly erroneous, given the broad discretion afforded to its eligibility decisions.

THE INDIANA HIGH SCHOOL ATHLETIC ASSOCIATION, INC. V. DURHAM

Court of Appeals of Indiana, Fifth District
748 N.E.2d 404 (2001)

FACTS

In the summer of 1999, Bernard Durham (B.J.) transferred from Park Tudor High School (Park) to North Central High School (North Central). B.J. participated in varsity cross-country and track during his freshman and sophomore years at Park. B.J. had attended private school, either at Park or at St. Richard's School since second grade. B.J. has three brothers who also attended private schools.

During 1998, B.J.'s mother, Joan Durham, and her husband, Tim Durham, separated and initiated divorce proceedings. Tim is not B.J.'s biological father. B.J.'s biological father lives in France and does not contribute to B.J.'s support. * * * [T]he time came to sign 1999-2000 re-enrollment contracts for B.J. and his three brothers in their private schools. At that time, Joan and Tim's divorce was not yet final. Joan decided not to sign the contracts because she could no longer afford the tuition to send her children to private schools. She instead enrolled her sons in the public school system where they resided. B.J. enrolled in North Central. In the fall of 1999, an IHSAA transfer form was completed on behalf of B.J. so that he could continue participating in sports at North Central. Joan indicated on the form that the recent divorce created such a financial burden on her that she could not afford to keep B.J. enrolled at a private school. Joan also provided the IHSAA with financial information and court filings to support the listed reason for B.J.'s transfer. * * *

Park, as the sending school, also had to offer the reason for B.J.'s transfer. Initially, Park had included in the transfer form that B.J. told coaches, administrators, and other students that "he wanted to go to a better track/c.c. [cross-country] program and that is why he is leaving." B.J. denied making such statements. However, Park changed its position after speaking with its athletic director who had subsequently learned that B.J.'s family situation prompted the transfer. Park recommended that B.J. be awarded full

eligibility to compete in sports at North Central. On August 25, 1999, IHSAA Assistant Commissioner Sandy Searcy granted B.J. only limited eligibility, which prohibited B.J. from competing at the varsity level, and denied B.J. a hardship exception.

The Durhams, through North Central's athletic director, appealed that decision to the IHSAA Executive Committee. The Durhams were led to believe that the question of whether B.J. transferred for athletically motivated reasons would not be an issue discussed at the hearing scheduled before the Executive Committee. A hearing was held, at which B.J., Joan, and the athletic directors from both schools testified. Evidence was presented that B.J. had been running with the junior varsity cross-country team at North Central, and that if he enjoyed full eligibility, B.J. would be one of the school's top runners. Joan testified that B.J. had suffered a great deal as a result of the IHSAA's decision. She relayed that he had problems with anxiety in the past, and that his running had helped him through this difficult time for his family. B.J. testified that he did not want to leave Park, and that he refused to explain why he was leaving when asked about the move at Park. Assistant Commissioner Searcy also testified that she was convinced that the change in the Durham's financial circumstances was permanent and substantial although not beyond their control. Park's athletic director, referring to Park's initial comment on B.J.'s transfer form, stated that the reference was the result of bantering between athletes and coaches due to the rivalry with North Central.

The Executive Committee agreed with Assistant Commissioner Searcy's decision, denying B.J. full eligibility and issuing findings. The Executive Committee concluded that B.J. transferred schools without a change in residence and failed to fit within any of the criteria of the Transfer Rule to gain full eligibility. Further, the Committee determined that B.J. did not meet the necessary conditions to gain full eligibility through the hardship exception to the Transfer Rule. Even though Searcy had testified that there had been a permanent and substantial change in financial circumstances, the IHSAA Executive Committee reasoned that B.J. failed to produce sufficient proof that the reason for transfer was beyond the control of him and his family. The IHSAA also noted that some evidence existed that the transfer may have been motivated by athletic reasons, even though the Durhams did not know that this was an issue before the Executive Committee.

DISTRICT COURT'S ORDER

The Durhams sought a temporary restraining order in court. On September 17, 1999, the trial court granted the temporary restraining order. On September 20, 1999, B.J. filed the complaint asking that the IHSAA's decision be overturned and that a permanent injunction be issued. * * * On October 22, 1999, the court granted the permanent injunction and found that the IHSAA's findings were arbitrary and capricious. * * * The IHSAA appealed.

DISCUSSION

Upon appeal, the IHSAA asserts that the trial court applied the standard of review over its decisions improperly. The IHSAA contends that its rulings are entitled to great deference and should be reversed only if they are willful and unreasonable without consideration of the facts and circumstances in the case. In this case, the IHSAA argues that the trial court merely reweighed the evidence and substituted its own decision. The Durhams insist that this case is moot because the time for the injunction has expired * * *. Alternatively, the Durhams counter that the IHSAA's conduct is not free from judicial review, and the IHSAA violated its own rules in denying B.J. a hardship exception.

I. IHSAA—Background And Rules

The IHSAA is a voluntary association designed to regulate interschool athletic competition. It establishes standards for eligibility, competition, and sportsmanship. For each school year, the IHSAA publishes a manual containing * * * specific rules regarding eligibility. The rule in question in this case is Rule 19, known as the Transfer Rule. The Transfer Rule guides athletic eligibility when a student moves to a new school district. Rule 19-4 provides that a student will be ineligible for 365 days if he or she transfers schools for "primarily athletic reasons." Further, Rule 19-6.2 gives the IHSAA the authority to grant limited eligibility to a student who transfers to another school without a corresponding change of residence by his or her parent(s)/guardian(s). However, if one or more of the criteria under Rule 19-6.1 are met, then a student may enjoy full and immediate eligibility, even without a change of residence by his or her parent(s)/guardian(s).

If none of the criteria in Rule 19-6.1 are met, then a student must fall within the hardship exception to the Transfer Rule to gain full and immediate eligibility. Rule 17.8, entitled "Hardship" grants the authority to set aside any rule, including the Transfer Rule, if certain conditions are met. In particular, Rule 17-8.1 lists these three conditions:

a. Strict enforcement of the Rule in the particular case will not serve to accomplish the purpose of the Rule;

c. The spirit of the Rule has not been violated; and

d. There exists in the particular case circumstances showing an undue hardship that would result from enforcement of the Rule.

Further, among those situations to receive general consideration for a hardship exception is: "a change in financial condition of the student's family may be considered a hardship, however, such conditions or changes in conditions must be permanent, substantial and significantly beyond the control of the student or the student's family." IHSAA Manual, Rule 17-8.4.

When a student moves to a new school district, an investigation and a transfer report must be completed if athletic eligibility at the new school is desired. Included in this report are forms filled out by the sending school, the receiving school, and the student and/or the student's parent(s)/guardian(s). The report must include the relevant circumstances and documents and recommendations regarding immediate eligibility from both schools.

II. Mootness

Initially, the Durhams assert that the IHSAA's appeal should be denied because the case is moot. The Durhams contend that there are no outstanding issues between the parties because the injunction has been lifted, the issue of attorney fees has been decided, and North Central did not win any State titles with B.J.'s participation. However, the IHSAA replies that the problem with the majority of litigation surrounding eligibility decisions is that the injunction granted by the trial court expires before the matter has been fully litigated and appealed. The IHSAA also contends that the case is not moot because its Restitution Rule, below, allows the IHSAA to make the school forfeit victories, team awards, and funds received from a tournament if it has been determined that an ineligible student athlete has competed for that school.

The Restitution Rule, Rule 17-6 of the IHSAA Bylaws, reads:

If a student is ineligible according to Association Rules but is permitted to participate in interschool competition contrary to Association Rules but in accordance with the terms of a court restraining order or injunction against the student's school and/or the Association and the injunction is subsequently voluntarily vacated, stayed, or reversed or it is finally determined by the court that injunctive relief is not or was not justified, any one or more of the following action(s) against such school in the interest of restitution and fairness to competing schools shall be taken:

  a. *Require individual or team records and performances achieved during participation by such ineligible student be vacated or stricken;*

  b. *Require team victories be forfeited to opponents;*

  c. *Require team or individual awards earned be returned to the Association; and/or*

  d. *If the school has received or would receive any funds from an Association tournament series in which the ineligible individual has participated, require that the school forfeit its share of net receipts from such competition, and if said receipts have not been distributed, authorize the withholding of such receipts by the Association.*

Alternatively, the IHSAA argues that even if the issues have been decided in this case, this court should hear the case because it involves questions of public interest.

An issue becomes moot when it is no longer live and the parties lack a legally cognizable interest in the outcome or when no effective relief can be rendered to the parties. * * * When the principal questions in issue have ceased to be matters of real controversy between the parties, the errors assigned become moot questions and the court will not retain jurisdiction to decide them. * * * An actual controversy must exist at all stages of the appellate review, and if a case becomes moot at any stage, then the case is remanded with instructions to dismiss. The Durhams insist that the IHSAA failed to assert evidence that there is a live controversy. The evidence about how the Restitution Rule may create a live controversy was introduced only through the Appendix to the IHSAA's Reply Brief.

* * *

Regardless of whether we consider the affidavit, an exception to the mootness doctrine applies. The IHSAA relies upon the exception that an otherwise moot case may be decided on the merits if the case involves a question of great public interest. Indiana courts recognize that a moot case can be reviewed under a public interest exception when it involves questions of great public importance. * * * The IHSAA argues that this exception applies to the instant case because the issue involves children and education, matters that are considered of great public concern, and our court has previously held that a challenge to an IHSAA eligibility rule is an issue of substantial public interest. * * * We agree.

While at first glance high school athletics may not seem to be of great public importance, according to the IHSAA, over 160,000 students statewide participate in sports under the IHSAA eligibility rules. Thus, this issue touches many in our state. Further, the issue of eligibility when a student transfers schools has arisen several times and has been the subject of much litigation* * * Also, the specific issue of a student transferring schools after his or her parents' divorce is likely to recur. * * * The public interest exception to the mootness doctrine applies to this case, allowing us to decide the merits.

III. Were the Trial Court's Findings Clearly Erroneous?

A. Our Standard of Review
The IHSAA asserts that the trial court's findings were clearly erroneous. In this case, the trial court issued an injunction to prevent the IHSAA from enforcing its ruling against B.J. When we review an injunction, we apply a deferential standard of review. * * * The grant or denial of an injunction is discretionary, and we will not reverse unless the trial court's action was arbitrary or constituted a clear abuse of discretion.* * *An abuse of discretion occurs when the trial court's decision is clearly against the logic and effect of the facts and circumstances or if the trial court misinterprets the law. *Id.*

* * *

B. Did the Trial Court Fail to Apply the Correct Standard of Review Governing IHSAA Decisions?
The IHSAA argues that the trial court failed to apply the deferential standard of review afforded to its administrative rulings in granting the Durham's request for a permanent injunction. In *Carlberg*, 694 N.E.2d 222, our supreme court delineated how a trial court should review an administrative ruling made by the IHSAA. Although the IHSAA is a voluntary association, the court held that student challenges to IHSAA decisions are subject to judicial review. *Id.* at 230. The court reasoned that student athletes in public schools do not voluntarily subject themselves to IHSAA rules, and students have no voice in rules and leadership of the IHSAA. *Id.* The court then determined that IHSAA decisions are analogous to government agency decisions and, hence, adopted the "arbitrary and capricious" standard of review used when courts review government agency action. *Id.* at 231. The arbitrary and capricious standard of review is narrow, and a court may not substitute its judgment for the judgment of the IHSAA. *Carlberg*, 694 N.E.2d at 233. "The rule or decision will be found to be arbitrary and capricious 'only where it is willful and unreasonable, without consideration and in disregard of the facts or circumstances in the case, or without some basis which would lead a reasonable and honest person to the same conclusion.'" *Id.* (quoting *Dep't of Natural Res. v. Ind. Coal Council, Inc.*, 542 N.E.2d 1000, 1007 (Ind. 1989), *cert. denied*, 493 U.S. 1078 (1990)).

In particular, the IHSAA takes issue with the trial court's holding that because B.J. met all of the criteria for the hardship exception, the IHSAA erred in denying him one. The

IHSAA contends that even if B.J. would have met all of the criteria listed in the Hardship Rule, Rule 17-8.1, he is not entitled to mandatory relief. Rather, the IHSAA maintains that relief under the Hardship Rule is a matter of grace. In other words, the IHSAA has the discretion of whether to grant a hardship exception even if the Durhams proved that (1) strict enforcement of the Transfer Rule will not serve to accomplish the purpose of the Rule, (2) the spirit of the Transfer Rule has not been violated, and (3) an undue hardship would result if the Transfer Rule was enforced

* * *

However, the IHSAA's position leaves its administrative decisions denying a hardship exception free from judicial review of any sort. While the text of the Hardship Rule states that the IHSAA "shall have the authority to set aside the effect of any Rule," the IHSAA's stance that it can deny a hardship exception even when the student meets the listed criteria implies both that it may have no ascertainable standards for granting or denying a hardship and that its hardship determinations are free from judicial review. IHSAA Manual, Rule 17-8.1. If the IHSAA is truly analogous to a governmental agency, then it must also establish standards on which to base its decisions.

Our supreme court in *Carlberg*, established the appropriate standard of review for IHSAA decisions in no uncertain terms. To reiterate, the *Carlberg* court stated that an IHSAA decision is arbitrary and capricious if it is "willful and unreasonable, without consideration and in disregard of the facts or circumstances in the case, or without some basis which would lead a reasonable and honest person to the same conclusion." 694 N.E.2d at 233 (citation omitted). The IHSAA's suggestion that the Hardship Rule is entitled to an increasingly narrow standard of judicial review flies in the face of the *Carlberg* decision. In *Carlberg*, the supreme court upheld the IHSAA's Transfer Rule in part because there are provisions in place to lessen the severity of the rule. *Carlberg*, 694 N.E.2d at 233. The court reasoned that granting immediate and full eligibility either under the listed exceptions to the Transfer Rule or under the Hardship Rule and granting limited eligibility at the junior varsity or freshman level serves to balance the possible harsh effects of the Transfer Rule. *Id.* If we accepted the IHSAA's assertion that its decisions to deny a hardship exception fall under a more stringent standard of review than the arbitrary and capricious standard enunciated in *Carlberg*, then we would be taking away one of the underpinnings of that case.

Thus, we hold that trial courts may determine whether the denial of a hardship exception in a particular case was the result of arbitrary and capricious action by the IHSAA. In this case, the trial court did not fail to give weight to the IHSAA's broad discretion, as the IHSAA alleges. Rather, in rendering its decision that the IHSAA acted arbitrarily and capriciously, the trial court looked at the IHSAA's particular decision with respect to B.J., applied the appropriate standard, and concluded that the IHSAA's conduct rose to the level of willful and unreasonable decision making that was in disregard of the facts and circumstances before it. For this, the trial court was well within its discretion.

C. Were the IHSAA's Findings Clearly Erroneous?
Finally, the IHSAA asserts that even if the trial court used the appropriate standard of review governing its decisions, the trial court's findings were clearly erroneous. The IHSAA asserts that the evidence, as adduced in its written findings, supports its denial of full eligibility and a hardship exception. In particular, the IHSAA asserts that some evidence existed that B.J. transferred for athletically motivated reasons. It points to the bantering about North Central having a better cross-country and track program. The trial court concluded that this was "hearsay within hearsay" and was not substantial evidence. The IHSAA counters that hearsay is admissible during administrative proceedings, and can be found to be substantial evidence of probative value. * * * The IHSAA also contends that the Durhams failed to establish that the purpose of the Transfer Rule would not be served by denying B.J. a hardship exception due to this evidence of "school jumping."

Here, the trial court did not abuse its discretion in holding that the IHSAA's conclusion that there was some evidence supporting that B.J. transferred for athletic reasons was arbitrary and capricious. Although hearsay may be admissible in administrative proceedings, this evidence of bantering was based upon Park Tudor's mistaken assumption that B.J. was transferring for athletic reasons. As soon as Park Tudor officials learned of the Durhams' circumstances, the transfer report was corrected to reflect that they recommended that B.J. be given full eligibility under a hardship exception. Thus, any evidence of athletic motivation was recanted by Park Tudor. Further, Park Tudor's retraction is against their own interest, as it would seem that Park Tudor would be interested in not having B.J. compete against it due to its rivalry with North Central. Despite this, Park Tudor supported B.J.'s pursuit of a hardship exception.

Additionally, the Durhams were led to believe that athletic motivation would not be an issue in B.J.'s case. It is unfortunate that the IHSAA listed athletic motivation as a reason for transfer even though little or no evidence supports it. This practice was denounced in *Martin*, 731 N.E.2d at 11, which noted that the IHSAA uses the possibility of an athletically-motivated transfer, although admittedly not primarily athletically motivated, as a "poison pill" to keep students from receiving a hardship exception even if there is no substantial evidence to that effect. In the instant case, the trial court recognized this practice and found no evidence in the record to support the IHSAA's conclusion that athletic motivation played a role in B.J.'s transfer. Thus, the trial court's findings with respect to athletic motivation were not clearly erroneous.

Further, the IHSAA argues that B.J. did not establish undue hardship because he failed to show that his family's circumstances were beyond his or his family's control and that he could not afford to attend private school. The IHSAA contends that the trial court merely reweighed the evidence of the family's finances, and that the Durhams still enjoyed a high standard of living. The IHSAA concluded that the decision to send B.J. to North Central was a choice.

Rule 17-8.1, the general section of the Hardship Rule, states that the IHSAA may grant a hardship exception if (1) strict enforcement of the rule in the particular case will not serve to accomplish the purpose of the rule; (2) the spirit of the rule has not been violated; and (3) there exists in the particular case circumstances showing an undue hardship that would result from enforcement of the rule. Thereafter, specific circumstances are listed as candidates for hardship exceptions. One such circumstance that may be considered a hardship is a change in financial condition of the student or a student's family if the change is permanent, substantial, and significantly beyond the control of the athlete or the athlete's family.

The Seventh Circuit Court of Appeals considered this issue in *Crane*, 975 F.2d 1315, and held that the IHSAA's denial of full eligibility was arbitrary and capricious where a student whose parents were divorced had transferred schools after a change in custody. *Crane*, 975 F.2d at 1322. The IHSAA has concluded that the student failed to prove that the move was beyond his control, as the change in custody occurred after Crane had some discipline problems and trouble with his grades in school. The Seventh Circuit, finding that this decision was arbitrary and capricious, reasoned that the IHSAA had ignored the plain language of its rules and instead used "rambling rationalizations" to come to a "pre-ordained result." *Id.* at 1323, 1325. The court noted that the IHSAA changes its interpretation of its rules depending upon the situation before it. *Id.* at 1325. We also addressed this issue in *Avant*, 650 N.E.2d 1164 (Ind. Ct. App. 1995). In *Avant*, we held that the IHSAA's denial of a hardship exception was supported by the evidence. *Id.* at 1169. Avant transferred from a private to a public school, and Avant's enrollment at a private school created a financial hardship on the family. However, the family's financial situation had not changed, and there was also evidence that Avant had disagreements with his basketball coach. Further, the family's financial situation was never listed on the transfer report. Thus, we concluded that the IHSAA's decision to deny Avant a hardship exception was not arbitrary and capricious. *Id.*

Unlike *Avant*, in this case there was a change in the Durhams' family finances due to the divorce, and this change was documented in the transfer report submitted to the IHSAA. This change was caused by something beyond their control, Joan's recent divorce. Included in the specific list of situations receiving consideration for a hardship exception is a substantial and permanent change in financial condition of the student or the student's family significantly beyond the control of the student or the student's family.

With the evidence submitted by Joan in the IHSAA administrative proceedings regarding her recent divorce and family's change in finances, no reasonable and honest person could conclude that the Durhams have not met this specific consideration listed within the Hardship Rule.

The trial court in the case before us found that the IHSAA ignored its own rules and instead interjected a condition of undue hardship not found in its rules that the Durhams prove their poverty before B.J. be given a hardship exception. We agree.

Contrary to IHSAA's assertion, the Hardship Rule does not read that an athlete's family must prove that it is a hardship case. In fact, financial hardship or poverty is not contained within the change in financial condition provision or the Hardship Rule generally. Instead, the "hardship" referred to in the Hardship Rule focuses on the hardship faced by the student athlete if the rule is strictly enforced. In this case, B.J. would face a hardship if he had to run at the junior varsity level because through no fault of his own and without any athletic motivation, B.J. was forced to transfer schools because of a substantial and permanent change in his family's financial condition. Just as in *Crane*, the IHSAA is attempting to adjust its interpretation of the Hardship Rule to meet the particulars of this case.

Even if we were to read a financial hardship requirement into the Hardship Rule, the Durhams would meet such a condition. The evidence in the record is undisputed that Joan had a significant amount of debt and her income had decreased by sixty-seven percent as a result of the divorce. At first glance, Joan's taxable income of $134,620 may not appear to suggest a family in financial hardship. However, a closer look reveals that Joan's monthly expenses are about equal to her monthly income. Joan's mortgage and utilities total $ 96,000 yearly, and she has many other regular expenses including health care, insurance, and various household expenses. Joan also has no assets that she could access to alleviate her financial burdens. Although Joan may be able to sell her house, she would net very little in proceeds after her mortgage debt was satisfied. Further, Joan would like to keep her children in the family home to avoid more disruption in their lives, in light of the divorce. The IHSAA should not be in the business of second-guessing personal financial decisions, but should accept the circumstances as they are.

Given the evidence in this case, the trial court did not abuse its discretion in overturning the IHSAA's denial of full eligibility and refusal to grant a hardship exception. While it may be true that in other cases, *see IHSAA v. Vasario*, 726 N.E.2d 325, 333 (Ind. Ct. App. 2000) and *Avant*, 650 N.E.2d at 1169, we have recognized the IHSAA's broad discretion in refusing to grant a student a hardship exception, this discretion is not unreviewable and is subject to the arbitrary and capricious standard upon review. The evidence in this case overwhelmingly leads to the conclusion that the reasons the IHSAA created the Transfer Rule, deterrence of athletic recruiting and equality in competition, would not be served by denying B.J. a hardship exception. The trial court did not simply reweigh the evidence and substitute its opinion, but instead found that the IHSAA ignored the facts and circumstances before it in rendering its decision. No reasonable and honest person would have concluded that B.J. should be denied a hardship exception in this case. This case embodies the reason the Hardship Rule was created. Although the IHSAA contends that its decisions are virtually unreviewable, a court does have the discretion to identify arbitrary and capricious conduct. The trial court in this case properly identified arbitrary and capricious action by the IHSAA.

Judgment affirmed.

CASES ON SUPPLEMENTAL CD

ProBatter Sports, LLC. v. Joyner Technologies, 2006 WL 625874 (N.D. Iowa 2006). The courts description of the lack of standing because the cases in Iowa and Connecticut concerned different patents illustrates problems in standing

Oliver v. National Collegiate Athletic Association, Court of Common Pleas, Erie County Ohio, Docket 2008-CV-0762 (February 9, 2009). The courts description and analysis of the rule prohibiting lawyers from being present to negotiate professional contracts for amateur athletes and the unfairness that is creates is instructive.

NFL v. Coors Brewing and NFL Players Incorporated, 1999 U.S. Lexis 32547. The court gives a clear review of the preliminary injunction elements concerning a trademark infringement case concerning the phrase "the official beer of the NFL players".

QUESTIONS YOU SHOULD BE ABLE TO ANSWER

1. What standard will a court use to review a decision of a private voluntary organization such as the NCAA?

2. What standards will the court use to determine if a person has standing to bring an action in court?

3. What are the four types of injunctive relief?

4. When and under what circumstances will a court issue a permanent injunction?

5. What is specific performance?

REFERENCES

Cases

Beeson v. Kiowa County School District, 567 P.2d 801 (Colo. Ct. App. 1977).

Braesch v. De Pasquale, 265 N.W.2d 842 (Neb. Sup. Ct. 1978).

Bunger v. Iowa High School Athletic Association, 197 N.W.2d 555 (Sup. Ct. 1972).

Estay v. La Fourche Parish School Board, 230 So.2d 443 (La. Ct. App. 1969).

Indiana High School Athletic Association, Inc. v. Durham, 748 N.E.2d 404 (2001).

Oliver v. National Collegiate Athletic Association, Court of Common Pleas, Erie County Ohio, Docket 2008-CV-0762 (February 9, 2009).

ProBatter Sports, LLC. v. Joyner Technologies, 2006 WL 625874 (N.D. Iowa 2006).

Tinker v. Des Moines Independent School District, 383 F.2d 988, rev'd 393 U.S. 503 (1969).

Williams v. Eaton, 468 F.2d 1079 (10th Cir. 1972).

6.12 State Action

—**Stacey Altman**
EAST CAROLINA UNIVERSITY

In litigation in which an individual claims that s/he has been deprived of rights guaranteed by the United States Constitution, courts will first consider whether the deprivation was caused by conduct "fairly attributable" to a governmental entity (*Lugar v. Edmondson Oil*, 1982). The only exceptions to this general rule of requiring a finding of state action before applying the analysis appropriate to constitutional claim involved have been made in situations involving the Thirteenth Amendment. The Thirteenth Amendment protects individual rights against interference from public and private action. All other provisions of the Constitution that protect individual rights apply, either by their express language or implicit meaning, only to the conduct of state (governmental) actors (Emanuel, 1998).

In some cases, determining whether conduct is attributable to a governmental entity, and thus subject to constitutional challenge, is fairly easy. For instance, if the claim is that a federal statute itself violates the Constitution (e.g. by inappropriately categorizing based on gender or race), the existence of state action is apparent because the statute had to have been enacted by a legislative unit of government. However, if the claim is that an eligibility rule enforced by a state high school athletic association or college conference violates a constitutionally protected right, determining the existence of the requisite state action to sustain the claim is more complex.

FUNDAMENTAL CONCEPTS

State Action Analysis

The Supreme Court's first articulation of the state action requirement occurred in the *Civil Rights Cases* (1883). The Court held that the guarantees of equal protection and due process, given by the Fourteenth Amendment, apply by their own terms exclusively to state action (Emanuel, 1998). Historically, courts used two theories to determine whether seemingly private conduct is fairly attributable to the state for the purpose constitutional analysis: (1) the **public function theory** and (2) the **nexus or entanglement theory**. More recently, courts have utilized three other theories: (1) the symbiotic relationship theory; (2) the joint activity theory; and (3) the state compulsion test (*Gallagher v. Neil Young Freedom Concert*, 1995).

Although courts have been deciding cases requiring a determination regarding state action for a very long time, "state action is a variable concept that vexes the interests of bright line-drawing," (Lively, et. al, 1996). As the Court put it, "the doctrines are too generally phrased to be self-executing; the cases are sensitive to fact situations and lack neat consistency, thus the analysis should include attention to the "ad-hoc cases that have not yet congealed into formal categories," (*Logiodice v. Trustees of Maine Central Institute*, 2002). A general explanation of these theories and their application to state action determinations in sport and recreation management contexts is included below.

Public Function Theory

When using the **public function theory**, courts consider whether a private actor is performing functions that have been traditionally reserved to government or that are governmental in nature (Rotunda & Nowak, 1999). This theory emerged in what have been called the "*White Primary Cases*". In *Smith v. Allwright* (1944), the Court held that because the election process is a public function, private political parties are agents of the state when controlling the nominating process. In *Terry v. Adams* (1953), the rationale in *Smith* was extended to "pre-primaries" (Emanuel, 1998). The public function theory has also been used to ascribe state actor status to a private company when it owns and operates a town that provides the services and contains the residential and commercial areas that any other municipality would (*Marsh v. Alabama*, 1946). In another case involving First Amendment guarantees, the Court held that the operation of shopping centers could also be considered a public function, thus making certain activities occurring at the center constitutionally protected (*Amalgamated Food Employees v. Logan Valley Plaza*, 1968). However, in *Hudgens v. NLRB* (1976), the Court rejected the *Logan Valley* holding and denied relief to picketers who claimed a right to advertise their strike in a shopping center. Hudgens marked the beginning of the Court's unwillingness to continue to broadly construe what activity is considered a public function. This was evident in *UAW v. Gaston Festivals, Inc.*, (1995). In *UAW*, the Court made it clear that the functions of the festival organizer were not those that were exclusively traditionally reserved to the City of Gastonia and thus determined that state action was not present when the festival organizers rejected the union's application for a booth at the festival. Emanuel (1998) suggested that it is likely that public function theory will be applied only if two conditions are met: (1) the function is one that is traditionally the exclusive domain of the state; and (2) a statute or constitutional provision actually requires the state to perform the function (see also, *Jackson v. Metropolitan Edison Co.*, 1974 and *Flagg Bros. v. Brooks*, 1978).

Involvement Theories. The nexus/entanglement, symbiotic relationship, and joint activity theories involve a determination regarding the extent of government's involvement with private activity. When applying the nexus theory, courts have held that private activity may be deemed state action when government is heavily involved in it, commands or encourages it, or is benefited by it (Emanuel, 1998). *Shelley v. Kraemer* (1948), illustrated how government might command private activity (Drew, 2001). In *Shelley*, the Court held that judicial enforcement of covenants that restricted property from being owned by anyone other than Caucasians would be, in essence, actively commanding private actors to engage in conduct subject to challenge under the Constitution (Drew, 2001). At issue in *Burton v. Wilmington Parking Authority* (1961), was whether a relationship between a public parking facility and a private restaurant (located within the public parking facility) could lead to a finding of state action that would, in turn, enable the restaurant's discriminatory policies to be disputed. The Court, found that because the public parking facility's financial success was so heavily dependent on the lease with the restaurant, the state's involvement was sufficient to attribute the restaurant's actions to the state. By contrast, in *Blum v. Yaresky*, the Court refused to find such a symbiotic relationship between government and a nursing home despite the fact that the state heavily subsidized the operation of nursing home and paid for 90 percent of the patient's medical expenses. *Blum* and the two state action cases that immediately followed, *Rendell-Baker v. Kohn* and *Lugar v. Edmondson Oil Co.* limit the scope of the nexus theory such that state regulation or subsidization alone will not be enough to warrant a finding of state action. It is the *Blum* trilogy that appears to be most relevant for understanding subsequent state action cases (Pierguidi, 2000).

Application to Sport and Recreation Organizations

Traditionally, the courts have held that the action of any public school, state college, or any of their officials is state action. However, when private organizations govern or administer sport and recreation state action is not so readily apparent.

Recreational Clubs and Facilities. In *Evans v. Newton* (1966), the Supreme Court held that the operation of a park owned by private trustees constituted state action. Justice Douglas, writing for the Court, seemed to be invoking the public function theory when he stated that, "the service rendered even by a private park of this character is municipal in nature," (Evans, 1966). Yet, he also noted that the city's entwinement in the management and control of the park (cleaning, watering, and patrolling) and the park's tax-exempt status had a significant impact on the decision to subject the policy of allowing only whites to use the park to judicial review. Operation of other recreational facilities, such as country clubs or amusement parks, have not been nor are they likely to be construed as governmental in nature because subsequent cases have held that only those functions traditionally exclusively carried out by government will be deemed public functions (*UAW* and *City of N.Y. Dep't of Parks & Rec*). A notable exception is the interesting case of *Pitt v. Pine Valley Golf Club* (1988), where the plaintiff claimed that a membership rule, that restricted homeownership in the Borough of Pine Valley to members of the Pine Valley Golf Club, violated the 5th and 14th Amendments of the Constitution. When making the requisite state action inquiry, the court noted that the club was in essence issuing a zoning ordinance. Because the power to make zoning ordinances is traditionally reserved to the state, the court found state action to be involved.

In *Perkins v. Londonderry Basketball Club* (1999), the court held that a voluntary, non-profit organization that enjoyed tax-exempt status was not a state actor even though it availed itself of public facilities free of charge and its board members were also members of the town's Recreation Commission. In *Hippopress v. SMG* (2003), the plaintiff was unable to demonstrate that there was a sufficiently close relationship between SMG, a facility management group and the City of Manchester which had contracted with SMG to manage its multi-purpose sports and entertainment venue to establish SMG's conduct as state action. Without meeting this threshold, Hippopress was unable to proceed with its state and federal constitutional claims.

Cases where state action was found to exist in circumstances similar to those describe above include: *Fortin v. Darlington Little League* (1975), where the extent of public facility use has been important and *Stevens v. New York Racing Association* (1987), where the plaintiff was able to show the existence of state action under the "symbiotic relationship" theory. The court noted that state action existed because of the extent state funding. (See also Section 6.26, *Private Clubs in Sport and Recreation*).

High School Athletic Associations. Historically, most courts have found state high school interscholastic athletic associations to be state actors. (See, e.g., *Oklahoma High School Ass'n v. Bray*, 1963; *Louisiana High School Athletic Ass'n v. St. Augustine High School*, 1968; *Moreland v. West Pennsylvania Interscholastic Athletic League*, 1978; *Griffin High School v. Illinois High School Ass'n*, 1987; and *Indiana High School Ass'n v. Carlberg*, 1997.) In *Barnhorst v. Missouri State High School Ass'n* (1980), the court found that the functions served by the state high school athletic association were similar enough to the functions of the state in providing education to find state action under the public function theory.

When using the nexus theory courts typically note the following factors in support of finding a nexus between the association and the state: (1) public (tax-supported) schools make up the majority of the association's membership, (2) the association's officials are public school employees (3) the association and its members use public facilities that have been built and are maintained by public funds, (4) association members are eligible for state retirement programs (5) the association is subsidized by the state by either direct funding or tax concessions (Lehr and Altman, 2001).

The issue seems to have been settled when the United States Supreme Court reversed the Sixth Circuit in *Brentwood v. Tennessee Secondary School Athletic Association* and held that the association's regulatory activity should be treated as state action owing to the pervasive entwinement of state school officials in the structure of the association. Since *Brentwood*, the courts have consistently found high school athletic associations to be state actors (See e.g. *Cmtys. for Equity v. Mich. High School Athletic Ass'n*, 2006; *Rottman v. Pennsylvania Athletic Ass'n*, 2004; *Jones v. W. Va. State Bd. of Educ.*, 2005; *Christian Heritage Academy v. Oklahoma Secondary School Activities Ass'n*, 2007; and *Mancuso v. Massachusetts Interscholastic Athletic Ass'n*, 2009).

However, that is not always the case. [See e.g. *Bukowski v. Wisconsin Interscholastic Athletic Ass'n* (2006), distinguishing the facts from those in *Brentwood* and *Leffel v. Wisconsin Interscholastic Athletic Ass'n* and holding that a superintendent's affidavit indicating an Association program received federal funding was not enough evidence to show "that the State is so pervasively entwined with the management and control of the WIAA to the point of largely overlapping identity (p. 11)"].

Some courts are asked to analyze whether state high school athletic associations are state/public actors for the purpose of applying particular **state laws**. In *Hood v. Ill. High Sch. Ass'n* (2005), the Association was not considered to be a "local public entity" for the purpose of applying the tort immunity act at issue. In *Breighner v. Mich. High Sch. Ath. Ass'n.*, the Association was determined not to be a "public body" within the meaning of the Michigan Freedom of Information Act.

National Organizations Governing College Athletics. Over 1,050 public and private institutions of higher education are *active* members of the National Collegiate Athletic Association (NCAA). Membership is available to any accredited four-year school that meets its standards. Junior and community colleges are not eligible for NCAA membership, but are often members of the National Junior College Athletic Association

(NJCAA). Some schools, despite being eligible for NCAA membership, have chosen to join the National Association of Intercollegiate Athletics (NAIA) (Jones, 1999). All of these associations are private organizations and membership is voluntary.

Prior to the mid-1980s, courts slightly constrained the autonomy of these organizations by concluding that the associations' conduct amounted to state action and thus were subject to the requirements of the Constitution. The most widely discussed cases addressing this issue involve the NCAA. In *Regents of the University of Minnesota v. NCAA* (1976), the court acknowledged that the action taken by the NCAA had generally been accepted as the equivalent of state action. For other examples, see *Buckton v. NCAA* (1973), (holding that in supervising and policing most intercollegiate athletics nationally, the NCAA performed a public function, sovereign in nature, which subjected it to constitutional scrutiny) and *Howard University v. NCAA* (1975), (holding that pervasive influence of state-supported universities in the NCAA required a finding of state action).

The tendency of courts to find that the NCAA was a state actor came to a halt in the mid-1980s. In 1984, the Fourth Circuit ruled, in *Arlosoroff v. NCAA*, that the NCAA's regulation of intercollegiate athletics was not a function traditionally reserved to the state and that even if the NCAA's regulatory function may be of some public service it is not enough to convert it to state action. Moreover, unless the eligibility rule was adopted as a result of governmental compulsion, there could be no state action (*Arlosoroff*, 1984). In *NCAA v. Tarkanian* (1988), the U.S. Supreme Court, in reaching the conclusion that NCAA's involvement in the events that led to the suspension of Coach Tarkanian did not constitute state action, relied on the following factors: (1) the NCAA was not a joint participant with UNLV when the NCAA represented the interests of its entire membership in the investigation of a member institution, (2) the NCAA never had power to directly discipline university employees, (3) UNLV voluntarily complied with NCAA rules, and (4) neither the university, nor any arm of the state had delegated to the NCAA any governmental powers for the purposes of its investigation (e.g. to subpoena witnesses). Since Tarkanian, courts have been reluctant to deem the NCAA a state actor (*NCAA v. Smith*, 1999). Recently however, there has been a resurgence of commentators arguing that the NCAA should be considered a state actor (See *Cohane v. NCAA*, 2007).

College Conferences. In those cases that have determined intercollegiate athletic conferences to be state actors, the following factors were important: (1) the public nature of the of the members of the college athletic conference, (2) that the conference received direct funds or tax breaks from the state, and (3) that the contests sponsored by the conference were held in public facilities (Wilde, 2000). In *Stanley v. Big Eight Conference* (1978), the fact that the conference was composed solely of state supported public universities that delegated supervision over intercollegiate athletics to the Big Eight, was enough to establish the requisite state action to proceed with the procedural due process claim involved. However, judicial dicta in *Weiss v. Eastern College Athletic Conference* (1983), and the holding *Hairston v. Pac-10 Conference* (1994), suggest that conferring state actor status on college conferences, at least for the purpose of constitutional claims, is more difficult now.

Organizations Created by Governments. Like the American Legion, Big Brothers/Big Sisters of America and the National Ski Patrol System, Inc., the United States Olympic Committee (USOC) is a federally created private organization. In a close decision in *San Francisco Arts & Athletics, Inc. v. USOC* (1987), the Court, concluded that the USOC's federal charter and the rights granted to it by the Amateur Sports Act of 1978 (e.g. exclusive control over the word "Olympic" and certain symbols) did not entwine the USOC and federal government to the extent that would warrant a finding of state action.

When presented with the issue of determining whether the U.S.O.C.'s action amounted to state action, Judge Pratt, writing for the court in *DeFrantz v. USOC*, (1980), stated:

> *The USOC is an independent body, and nothing in its chartering statute gives the federal government the right to control that body or its officers. Furthermore, the facts here do not indicate that the federal government was able to exercise any type of 'de facto' control over the USOC. . . . All it had was the power of persuasion. We cannot equate this with control. To do so in cases of this type would be to open the door and usher the courts into what we believe is a largely nonjusticiable realm, where they would find themselves in the untenable position of determining whether a certain level, intensity, or type of 'Presidential' or 'Administrative' or 'political' pressure amounts to sufficient control over a private entity so as to invoke federal jurisdiction.*

In *Johnston v. Tampa Sports Authority* (2006), the court noted that the TSA was a public entity created by the Florida Legislature and that it could not simply "contract away" its public status. Rather, TSA, the court held, has an obligation to maintain the stadium it manages in a manner that protects the constitutional rights of its patrons. In subsequent litigation, the TSA continued to be deemed a state actor (*Johntson v. TSA*, 2008). (See Supplemental CD.) In *Sheehan v. San Francisco 49er* (2009), the court analyzed a similar pat-down policy and came to the conclusion that only private action was involved in the searches at issue there.

Koller (2008) argues that the United States Anti-Doping Agency (USADA) should be considered a state actor despite the fact that the Agency purports to have been created by the USOC. Among the reasons she gives in support of her argument are the following: (1) Congress designated the USADA as the United States' "official" anti-doping agency, (2) the USADA was created as a private, not-for-profit corporation, which undertakes its duties pursuant to a contract with the USOC to administer the United States' drug testing programs, and (3) The USADA receives the majority of its funding from the United States Government through the Office of National Drug Control Policy (ONDCP).

Professional Sports Leagues. Rarely have the activities of professional sport leagues or teams been deemed state action. Professional sport leagues, whether described as joint ventures of independent clubs or as a single entity, are most often characterized as private businesses (Wilde, 2000). They do not perform a function that has been traditionally reserved to the state, and historically, entwinement with government has been limited. In *Ludtke v. Kuhn* (1978), the court did recognize that the New York Yankees entwinement with government was sufficient to consider the team's enforcement of Commissioner Kuhn's policy of excluding female reporters from the clubhouse state action. The aspects of the situation that court noted as important included: (1) the city had exercised its power of eminent domain to acquire Yankee Stadium, (2) the city was authorized by statute to lease the stadium to the Yankees (not the highest bidder), (3) the stadium was renovated at a cost of $50 million to the city. Conversely, in *Long v. NFL* (1994), the fact that a city collected an amusement tax on tickets or that it constructed a stadium for a team were not enough to find the state involvement necessary to sustain a constitutional challenge to the NFL's drug testing policy.

Legal commentators have increasingly addressed the notion that the activities of professional sport franchises could be deemed state action. For example, Guggenheim (1998) argued that a challenge to the Cleveland Indians "Chief Wahoo" mark might viably claim that the Indian's use of the mark constitutes discriminatory state action based on the team's relationship with the city and Jacob's Field. Fielder (2002), in arguing that the Pickens clause unconstitutionally restrained the free speech rights of NFL players, reasoned that the relationship between Cincinnati Bengals, Inc. and Hamilton County could serve as state involvement required to subject the clause to review. In a time when professional sport franchises usually receive, among other things, the use of modern public facilities (including stadiums and parking areas) without the burden of maintenance, tax incentives, and the use of the city's name that arguably enhances the team's ability to attract fans and sponsors entwinement may be more readily apparent (Guggenheim, 1998).

SIGNIFICANT CASE

There have been a number of recent cases challenging the "pat-down policies" at various professional sport venues. The following case illustrates some of the issues raised and the nature of the relationship between teams, leagues, and stadium managers.

STARK V. THE SEATTLE SEAHAWKS

United States District Court for the District of Washington

2007 U.S. Dist. LEXIS 45510

---

* * *

Plaintiffs Fred and Kathleen Stark challenge the pat-down searches that are a condition of a ticket-holder's entry to National Football League ("NFL") games held at Qwest Field & Event Center ("Qwest Field"). The Starks, who are season ticket-holders, contend that the pat-downs constitute unreasonable searches in violation of the Fourth Amendment, pursuant to 42 U.S.C. § 1983 ("Section 1983"), and Art. I, § 7 of the Washington State Constitution. For purposes of these motions, Defendants' sole contention is that the pat-down searches, which are authorized by private entities and conducted by private security personnel, do not constitute "state action," as required to state a claim for a constitutional violation. The facts pertinent to these motions are not in dispute.

In their Complaint, the Starks name the private entities responsible for conducting the pat-down searches: the Seahawks team (a member of the NFL), its owner, Football Northwest, and First & Goal (a Washington corporation that leases Qwest Field for the benefit of the Seahawks). They also name the public entity that owns Qwest Field, the Stadium Authority, and its Board of Director's Chair, Lorraine Hine. The Starks contend that the private entities and the Stadium Authority are so closely entwined in the operation of Qwest Field that the searches conducted by the private entities constitute state action.

Relationship Between the Stadium Authority and the Seahawks

In 1997, the Washington Legislature enacted the Stadium and Exhibition Centers Financing Act ("Stadium Act") setting forth a comprehensive financing plan for a new stadium and exhibition hall. The legislature passed the Stadium Act in response to concerns that the then owner of the Seahawks, Ken Behring, planned to move the Seahawks to California. In an attempt to keep the team in the greater Seattle area, Football Northwest negotiated and eventually acquired an option to purchase the Seahawks from Mr. Behring. Football Northwest announced that it would not exercise its option to purchase the team unless

there was a public commitment "to enable and partially fund construction of a new football stadium for the Seahawks." The passage of the Stadium Act followed. The Stadium Act created the Stadium Authority entity, granting it authority to "construct, own, remodel and operate" an event center. See RCW § 36.102.050. Shortly after the Stadium Act went into effect, the Stadium Authority, in consultation with First & Goal, began construction on what is now called Qwest Field. The parties do not dispute that Qwest Field, which cost approximately $430 million to build, is a public facility owned by the Stadium Authority. The majority of funding, approximately $300 million, for the development and construction of Qwest Field came from public funds, with First & Goal financing the remaining $130 million.

In November 1998, upon completion of construction of Qwest Field, the Stadium Authority and First & Goal entered into a Master Lease agreement making First & Goal "the sole master tenant." The Master Lease vests First & Goal with "exclusive power and authority to possess, operate, use, sublease, and enter into . . . agreements" involving Qwest Field. In return, First & Goal pays an annual rent to the Stadium Authority of $850,000, plus any reasonable operating expenses that exceed the annual rent. With some exceptions set forth below, First & Goal retains all revenues derived from its operation of Qwest Field.

Both the Stadium Act and the Master Lease require First & Goal to pay the Stadium Authority 20% of the net profits from the Exhibition Hall (a building next to the stadium) into a common schools fund. First & Goal also collects and remits to the Stadium Authority a 1.2% ticket surcharge that the Stadium Authority uses to pay down its tax obligation—$37 million in deferred sales tax on construction costs. The Stadium Authority also receives fixed payments from the sale of the naming rights for Qwest Field, which go toward major maintenance and modernization improvements of Qwest Field. Finally, if the Seahawks are sold within 25 years of the issuance of the bonds used to finance construction, the state will receive 10% of the gross selling price. RCW § 43.99N.020(2)(b)(vi).

NFL Pat-Down Policy

In August 2005, the NFL adopted a policy mandating "limited pat-down inspections" of everyone entering NFL stadiums on the day of an NFL event. First & Goal, at the Seahawks' behest, implemented the pat-downs at the start of the 2005 season, and in accordance with NFL guidelines. First & Goal hired a third-party security vendor, Staff Pro, which provides about 180 licensed private security guards to visually inspect bags and conduct the pat-downs of ticket-holders on a same-gender basis. The Starks do not offer any evidence to suggest that the Stadium Authority had any role in planning or implementing the pat-down searches, or that it approved, encouraged, or was even consulted about these procedures. Defendants, on the other hand, provide evidence that the Stadium Authority had no role in the implementation or execution of the pat-down searches.

* * *

State Action

To prevail on their federal and state constitutional claims, the Starks must show that the pat-down searches at Qwest Field are fairly attributable to state action. The Fourth Amendment prohibits only unreasonable searches conducted by the government or its agents. *United States v. Jacobsen*, 466 U.S. 109, 113, 104 S. Ct. 1652, 80 L. Ed. 2d 85 (1984). Private conduct may be considered government action if the deprivation of a federal right is fairly attributable to the state. *Lugar v. Edmondson Oil Co. Inc.*, 457 U.S. 922, 937, 102 S. Ct. 2744, 73 L. Ed. 2d 482 (1982) (noting that the Fourteenth Amendment sets forth an "essential dichotomy" between government action subject to scrutiny and private conduct, "however discriminatory [*9] or wrongful," for which it offers no shield). Conduct that constitutes state action also satisfies Section 1983's "under color of law" requirement; *Brentwood Acad. v. Tennessee Secondary Sch. Athletic Ass'n*, 531 U.S. 288, 295, 121 S. Ct. 924, 148 L. Ed. 2d 807 (2001). Similarly, Washington's constitutional protections against unreasonable searches cannot be invoked absent state action. *State v. Carter*, 151 Wn.2d 118, 85 P.3d 887, 890 (Wash. 2004).

The Starks do not contend that the Stadium Authority conducted or authorized the pat-down searches. Instead, they argue that the Stadium Authority and First & Goal are so closely entwined that First & Goal's actions can fairly be attributed to the Stadium Authority. In furtherance of their theory, the Starks argue that there is a symbiotic relationship between the Stadium Authority and First & Goal, or alternatively, that First & Goal is performing an act that is "governmental in nature." The courts recognize the former theory as the "joint activity" test for state action, and the latter as the "public function" test. Although the Ninth Circuit recognizes at least four different criteria, or tests, to identify state action, see *Kirtley v. Rainey*, 326 F.3d 1088, 1092 (9th Cir. 2003), the court limits its analysis to these

two test, as there is no evidence or argument in support of the application of the remaining two tests for state action. Notwithstanding, the court conducts its analysis mindful of the Supreme Court's direction in Brentwood:

> *What [constitutes state action] is a matter of normative judgment, and the criteria lack rigid simplicity. . . . No one fact can function as a necessary condition across the board . . . nor is any set of circumstances absolutely sufficient, for there may be some countervailing reason against attributing activity to the government. (531 U.S. at 295).*

Joint Activity

Courts have found joint activity sufficient to impute state action in two general patterns: concerted or conspiratorial activity between state and private actors and the existence of a symbiotic relationship. The Starks argue the latter, that the Stadium Authority is in a symbiotic relationship with First & Goal. A symbiotic relationship occurs when the government has "so far insinuated itself into a position of interdependence with [a private entity] that it must be recognized as a joint participant in the challenged activity." *Burton v. Wilmington Parking Auth.*, 365 U.S. 715, 725, 81 S. Ct. 856, 6 L. Ed. 2d 45 (1961). As evidence of the alleged symbiotic relationship between the Stadium Authority and First & Goal, the Starks point to the following: (1) First & Goal leases Qwest Field, a publicly-owned facility, from the Stadium Authority; (2) the Stadium Authority shares revenue with First & Goal in the form of a ticket surcharge, naming rights payments, and profits from the Exhibition Hall; and (3) Washington state owns an equity stake in the Seahawks if the team is sold within 25 years from the issuance of the construction bonds. The Starks also point to various provisions in the Master Lease requiring First & Goal to provide benefits to the public not normally associated with commercial leases. For example, the Master Lease requires that the Seahawks offer a certain number of affordable tickets, that First & Goal comply with minority and woman-owned hiring goals, and that First & Goal make payments into a fund for the development of youth athletic facilities. While these facts establish an on-going relationship between the public and private entities, they do not, without more, show that the Stadium Authority "has so far insinuated itself into a position of interdependence" with First & Goal, or the other Seahawks Defendants, such that there is a symbiotic relationship between the two. See Burton, 365 U.S. at 725.

The Starks rely on *Burton and Halet v. Wend Inv. Co.*, 672 F.2d 1305 (9th Cir. 1982), to argue that state action is satisfied by showing the integration and alignment of financial interests between the public and private entities. In Burton, the Supreme Court considered whether a restaurant's refusal to serve plaintiff because of his race could fairly be attributed to the public entity that owned the building that housed the restaurant. 365 U.S. at 723. In finding state action, the Court stressed that the restaurant was located on public property and that the rent from the restaurant contributed to the support of the public building. The Court was further convinced of state action by the argument that the restaurant's profits, and hence the state's financial position, would suffer if it did not discriminate based on race. Similarly, in Halet, the Ninth Circuit found sufficient evidence of state action where the county leased land to a private entity who owned and operated an apartment complex on the land. 672 F.2d at 1310. The Ninth Circuit found a symbiotic relationship between the county and the owner based on the fact that the county owned the land and had developed it using public funds, the county leased the land to the owner for the benefit of providing housing to the public, and the county controlled the use and purpose of the apartment, as well as the rent the owner could charge, a percentage of which was paid to the county. *Id.*

In Burton and Halet, the Supreme Court and Ninth Circuit found symbiotic relationships between the public and private entities based primarily on the presence of a mutually beneficial relationship. Subsequent courts that have considered the definition of a symbiotic relationship, however, have narrowed the scope and application of Burton. In *Rendell-Baker v. Kohn*, 457 U.S. 830, 842, 102 S. Ct. 2764, 73 L. Ed. 2d 418 (1982), for example, decided shortly after the Ninth Circuit decision in Halet, the Supreme Court rejected a symbiotic relationship argument because, although the state and private school were in a mutually beneficial relationship, there was no showing that the state derived any benefit from the challenged activity—i.e., the termination of school personnel. 457 U.S. at 842-43. In distinguishing Burton, the Court emphasized that there was evidence that the state in Burton actually "profited from the restaurant's discriminatory conduct." The Rendell-Baker Court found no such connection between the benefit conferred to the state by the school and the challenged activity, and thus no symbiotic relationship. In *Morse v. N. Coast Opportunities, Inc.*, the Ninth Circuit later expounded on the Supreme Court's decision in Rendell-Baker, finding "that governmental funding and extensive regulation without more will not suffice to establish governmental involvement in the actions of a private entity." 118 F.3d 1338, 1341 (9th Cir. 1997) (citing Rendell-Baker in overruling *Ginn v. Mathews*, 533 F.2d 477 (9th Cir. 1976), a decision relying on Burton). The Morse court noted that Burton's symbiotic relationship test requires additional evidence of interdependence, such as "the physical location of the private entity in a building owned and operated by the State, and a showing that the State profited from the private entity's discriminatory conduct." Morse, 118 F.3d at 1341. Thus, the Starks must tie the Stadium Authority's profits to the pat-down searches conducted by the private entities.

* * *

In light of Rendell-Baker and Morse, the court therefore considers additional factors for determining whether a symbiotic relationship exists in this case. While the Starks point to several ways in which the Stadium Authority and First & Goal benefit from their relationship, they do not offer sufficient evidence that the Stadium Authority operates Qwest Field, or that it profits from the allegedly unconstitutional pat-down searches. There is no dispute regarding the Stadium Authority's grant to First & Goal of the exclusive right to operate Qwest Field. See Master Lease § 2.1 ("[First & Goal] has the exclusive power and authority to . . . operate . . . [Qwest Field]"). The parties do dispute, however, whether the evidence supports a finding that the Stadium Authority profits from the pat-down searches.

The Starks contend that the Stadium Authority indirectly benefits from the searches because the Seahawks want to make fans feel more secure, and more likely to purchase tickets. These hypothetical increased ticket sales, according to the Starks, correlate to greater profit for the Stadium Authority based on the 1.2% ticket surcharge it receives from First & Goal. As explained by the Stadium Authority, and not refuted by the Starks, however, the ticket surcharge paid to the Stadium Authority is not profit, but is used to pay a tax obligation the Stadium Authority owes on the construction of the stadium. The tax obligation is a set amount, $37 million that First & Goal owes to the Stadium Authority. Sec. Am. to Master Lease § 18.2.4. If the surcharge is not sufficient to retire the debt at the time specified in the Master Lease, First & Goal must make up the difference. First & Goal's obligation to collect the surcharge and pay it to the Stadium Authority ceases once it reaches the set amount. *Id.* Thus, the only effect the supposed increased ticket sales has on the surcharge is potentially to retire the debt sooner; an increase in ticket sales does not therefore directly profit the Stadium Authority.

The Starks' remaining arguments regarding the Stadium Authority's ability to profit from the pat-down searches are unavailing. The Starks point to rental and naming rights payments that the Stadium Authority receives from First & Goal, yet there is no dispute that these are fixed amounts that do not depend on ticket sales. The Starks also contend that the Stadium Authority profits from the revenues received from the Exhibition Hall, a separate building next to the stadium. Again, the uncontroverted evidence before the court is that there is no pat-down search prior to entering this building and, on days when the Seahawks are playing at 'Qwest Field, the revenue from the Exhibition Hall does not go to the Stadium Authority. Finally, the Starks point to the State's 10% interest in the Seahawks if they are sold within 25 years after issuance of the construction bonds. The court fails to see how this interest, which is pure speculation at this time, supports a finding that the Stadium Authority profits from the current pat-down search policy at Qwest Field.

Although the court acknowledges the existence of a beneficial relationship between the private entities and the Stadium Authority in this case, and that they may even publicly proclaim themselves a "model for public-private partnerships," this does not rise to the level of a symbiotic relationship. The Stadium Authority did not participate in the original decision to conduct pat-down searches of ticket-holders, nor did it control, profit, or directly benefit from the pat-down searches conducted by the private entities at Qwest Field. Accordingly, the court concludes that the Starks have failed to come forth with sufficient evidence to meet the symbiotic relationship test for demonstrating state action.

PUBLIC FUNCTION

In the alternative, the Starks contend that the pat-downs constitute state action because the Stadium Authority "delegated nearly its entire public function to First & Goal" and conferred the "governmental" responsibility of managing a publicly owned stadium required to yield numerous public benefits. One way to find state action is by showing that the private entity exercises powers "traditionally exclusively reserved to the State." *Jackson v. Metro. Edison Co.*, 419 U.S. 345, 352, 95 S. Ct. 449, 42 L. Ed. 2d 477 (1974). In support of this theory, the Starks offer testimony by the Executive Director of the Stadium Authority, that the Master Lease requires First & Goal to provide certain public benefits to the community, that are not typical to a commercial lease. Similarly, the Starks offer evidence that the Stadium Authority's mission is to provide "economic and entertainment benefits to residence across the State of Washington." Essentially, the Starks contend that because the Stadium Authority was created to provide a public benefit, i.e., an event center, its delegation of this duty to First & Goal does not relieve it of liability for First & Goal's actions. The Starks' reliance on the public function test is misplaced. The public function test is not satisfied simply because a private entity performs a public function; rather, it requires that the public function be one that is traditionally reserved to the government. While providing an event center may be considered a public function in light of the directives in the Stadium Act, the court is not persuaded that operating an event center is a function that has traditionally and exclusively been reserved to the state. Indeed, there are very few functions considered "exclusively reserved to the state" when determining state action. See *Flagg Bros. v. Brooks*, 436 U.S. 149, 158, 98 S. Ct. 1729, 56 L. Ed. 2d 185 (1978) ("While many functions have been traditionally performed by governments, very few have been 'exclusively reserved to the State.'"). The context in which courts have recognized traditional state functions include administering elections, *Terry v. Adams*, 345 U.S. 461, 73 S. Ct. 809, 97 L. Ed. 1152 (1953); and running a company-owned town, *Marsh v. Alabama*, 326 U.S. 501, 66 S. Ct. 276, 90 L. Ed. 265 (1946). The court concludes that operating an event center, on the other hand, does not rise to the level of a traditional state function. See, e.g. *Jackson v. Metro. Edison Co.*, 419 U.S. 345, 352, 95 S. Ct. 449, 42 L. Ed. 2d 477 (1974) (holding that utility services, though marked with a strong public interest, were not the exclusive prerogative of the state, but associated with both the public and private spheres); *** Indeed, the Ninth Circuit's Lee decision, which the Starks rely on, "turn[ed] on what is quintessentially an exclusive and traditional public function—the regulation of free speech within a public forum." 276 F.3d at 556-57 (holding that regulating speech within the Rose Quarter Commons was state action, but emphasizing "we do not hold that everyone who leases . . . a state-owned public forum will necessarily become a State actor") (citing *Lansing v. City of Memphis*, 202 F.3d 821, 828-29 (6th Cir. 2000)).

The expenditure of public funds for the construction of Qwest Field does not alter the court's analysis. In Rendell-Baker, the Supreme Court held that a privately owned school that received up to 99% of its funding from public sources and was subject to significant public regulation did not perform a traditionally exclusive public function. 457 U.S. at 842; see also *Blum v. Yaretsky*, 457 U.S. 991, 1011-12, 102 S. Ct. 2777, 73 L. Ed. 2d 534 (1982) (finding no public function where state subsidized operating and capital costs of nursing homes and paid 90% of patients' medical expenses). The relevant question is not whether a private group served a public function, or served one funded by the public, but rather whether the function was one "traditionally the *exclusive* prerogative of the State." Rendell-Baker, 457 U.S. at 842 (emphasis in original) (citations omitted).

Finally, to the extent the Starks argue that providing security is a public function, for the same reasons as stated above, the court concludes that it is not. In so concluding, the court finds the Tenth Circuit's decision in Gallagher persuasive. 49 F.3d at 1457. Under analogous facts to those before the court in this case, the Tenth Circuit held that providing security for a company that leased a government-owned facility did not constitute a public function. (concluding that where two private firms planned and conducted pat-down searches independently of university officials, the public function test was not satisfied). Because neither operating a stadium nor providing security is a function traditionally and exclusively reserved to the state, the court concludes that the pat-down searches conducted by private actors at Qwest Field do not constitute state action.

CONCLUSION

For the reasons stated above, the court grants Defendants' motions for summary judgment. The court directs the clerk to enter judgment consistent with this order.

Brentwood Academy v. Tennessee Secondary Sch. Ath. Ass'n., 531 U.S. 288 (2001). Be sure to note what facts about the structure of the Association were important to the Court.

Johnston v. Tampa Sports Authority, 442 F. Supp. 2d 1257 (M.D. Fla., 2006). After reading this case and the Section 7.12 Significant Case, try to determine what teams have relationships with their sta-

dium/host city that might subject their practices to constitutional analysis.

NCAA v. Tarkarnian, 488 U.S. 179 (1988). Most courts and commentators maintain that this case removed any question of whether the NCAA could be considered a state actor. Can you find any support in the opinion or elsewhere for an alternate view?

QUESTIONS YOU SHOULD BE ABLE TO ANSWER

1. Why is it important to understand what organizations could be deemed state actors?

2. Summarize the state action analysis in a paragraph or less.

3. Has there ever been a case in which a sport or recreation organization has been considered to be performing a "public function"?

4. What makes in the outcome in *Johnston* different than the outcome in *Sheehan*?

5. Draft a fact pattern that you think would present a challenging state action analysis.

REFERENCES

Cases

Amalgamated Food Employees v. Logan Valley Plaza, 391 U.S. 308 (1968).

Arlosoroff v. NCAA, 746 F.2d 1019 (4th Cir. 1984).

Blum v. Yaresky, 457 U.S. 991 (1982).

Breighner v. Mich. High Sch. Ath. Ass'n, 683 N.W.2d 639 (Mich. 2004).

Brentwood v. Tennessee Secondary Sch. Ath. Ass'n, 531 U.S. 288 (2001).

Buckton v. NCAA, 366 F.Supp. 1152 (D. Mass. 1973).

Bukowski v. Wisconsin Intercollegiate Ath. Ass'n, 726 N.W.2d 356 (Ct. App. Wisc. 2006).

Burton v. Wilmington Parking Authority, 365 U.S. 715 (1961).

Civil Rights Cases 109 U.S. 3 (1883).

Cohane v. NCAA, 2007 U.S. App. LEXIS 1841 (2nd Cir. 2007).

Cmtys. for Equity v. Mich. High Sch. Ath. Ass'n, (6th Cir. 2004).

DeFrantz v. USOC, 492 F.Supp. 1181 (D.D.C. 1980).

Evans v. Newton, 382 U.S. 296 (1966).

Flagg Bros. v. Brooks, 436 U.S. 149 (1978).

Fortin v. Darlington Little League, 514 F.2d 344 (1st Cir. 1975).

Gallagher v. Neil Young Freedom Concert, 49 F.3d 1442 (10th Cir. 1995).

Griffin High Sch. v. Illinois High Sch. Ass'n (7th Cir. 1987).

Hairston v. PAC-10 Conference, 893 F.Supp 1485 (W.D. Wash. 1994) *aff'd*, 101 F.3d 1315 (9th Cir. 1996).

Hippopress, LLC v. SMG, 837 A.2d 347 (N.H. 2003).

Hood v. Illinois High Sch. Ass'n, 835 N.E.2d 938 (Ill. App. Ct. 2005).

Howard Univ. v. NCAA, 510 F.2d 21 (D.C. Cir. 1975).

Hudgens v. NLRB, 424 U.S. 507 (1976).

Jackson v. Metropolitan Edison, Co., 419 U.S. 345 (1974).

Jones v. West Virginia State Bd. Of Educ., 622 S.E.2d 289 (W.Va. 2005).

Johnston v. Tampa Sports Authority, 442 F.Supp. 2d 1257 (M.D. Fla 2006).

Johnston v. Tampa Sports Authoirty, 490 F.3d 820 (11th Cir. 2007).

Logiodice v. Trustees of Central Maine Institute, 296 F.3d 22 (1st Cir. 2002).

Long v. NFL, 870 F.Supp 101 (N.D. Pa. 1994).

Louisiana High Sch. Ath. Ass'n v. St. Augustine High School, 396 F.2d 224 (5th Cir. 1968).

Ludtke v. Kuhn, 461 F.Supp. 86 (S.D. N.Y. 1978).

Lugar v. Edmondson Oil Co., 457 U.S. 922 (1982).

Mancuso v. Massachusetts Interscholastic Ath. Ass'n. Inc., 900 N.E.2d 518 (Mass. 2009).

Marsh v. Alabama, 326 U.S. 501 (1946).

Moreland v. West Pennsylvania Interscholastic Ath. League, 572 F.2d 121 (3rd Cir. 1978).

NCAA v. Smith, 525 U.S. 459 (1999).

NCAA v. Tarkanian, 488 U.S. 179 (1988).

Oklahoma High Sch. Ass'n v. Bray, 321 F.2d 269 (10th Cir. 1963).

Perkins v. Londonderry Basketball Club, 196 F.3d 13 (1st Cir. 1999).

Pitt v. Pine Valley Golf Club, 695 F.Supp.778 (D. NJ, 1988).

Regents of the Univ. of Minnesota v. NCAA, 560 F.2d 352 (8th Cir. 1976).

Rendell-Baker v. Kohn, 457 U.S. 830 (1982).

Rottman v. Pennsylvania Ath. Ass'n, 349 F.Supp.2d 922 (W.D. Pa 2004).

San Francisco Arts & Athletics, Inc. v. USOC, 483 U.S. 522 (1987).

Sheehan v. San Francisco 49ers, Ltd., 2009 Cal. LEXIS 1638 (Ca. 2009).

Shelley v. Kraemer, 334 U.S. 1 (1948).

Smith v. Allwright, 321 U.S. 649 (1944).

Stanley v. Big Eight Conference, 463 F.Supp. 920 (W.D. Mo. 1978).

Stark v. The Seattle Seahawks, 2007 U.S. Dist. LEXIS 45510 (W.D.Wash 2007).

Stevens v. New York Racing Ass'n, 665 F.Supp 164 (E.D.N.Y. 1987).

Terry v. Adams, 344 U.S. 883 (1952).

UAW, Local 5285 v. Gaston Festivals, Inc., 43 F.3d 902, 906 (4th Cir. 1995).

Weiss v. Eastern College Ath. Conference, 563 F.Supp. 192 (E.D. Pa. 1983).

Publications

Drew, J. (2001). The Sixth Circuit dropped the ball: An analysis of *Brentwood Academy v. Tennessee Secondary School Athletic Association* in light of the Supreme Court's recent trends in state action jurisprudence. *Brigham Young University Law Review*, 1313–1347.

Emanuel, S. (1998). Constitutional law (17th ed.). Fredrick, MD: Aspen Publishers, Inc.

Fielder, T. (2002, Spring/Summer). Keep your mouth shut and listen: The NFL player's right to free expression. University of Miami Business Law Review, *10*, 548–583.

Guggenheim, J. (1998). The Indian's chief problem: Chief Wahoo as state sponsored discrimination and disparaging mark. Cleveland State University Law Review, *46*, 217–237.

Koller, D. (Winter, 2008). Frozen in time: The state action doctrine's application to amateur sports. *St. John's Law Review, 83*, 183–233.

Lehr, C. and Altman, S. (2001, July). Finally a resolution: High school athletic associations are state actors! *The Sports Medicine Standards and Malpractice Reporter, 13*, 39–41.

Lively, D., Haddon, P., Roberts, D., & Weaver, R. (1996). *Constitutional law: Cases, history and dialogues.* Cincinnati, OH: Anderson Publishing Co.

Pierguidi, D. (2000). Absent strong connections to a state government, a high school athletic association cannot be construed as a state actor: *Brentwood Academy v. Tennessee Secondary School Athletic Ass'n*. Seton Hall Journal of Sport Law, *10*, 435–493.

Wilde, T. J. (2000). State action. In D. J. Cotten, J. T. Wolohan & T. J. Wilde (Eds.), Law for recreation and sport managers (2nd Ed.) pp. 415–426. Dubuque, IA: Kendall/Hunt Publishing Co.

—**Linda L. Schoonmaker**
THE CITADEL

—**John T. Wolohan**
ITHACA COLLEGE

Although the framers of the U.S. Constitution did not have sport and recreation in mind when they drafted it, the guarantees and rights granted to citizens that are contained in the document have had, and will continue to have, an impact on the sport and recreation industries. As a result, sport and recreation managers must have an understanding of our constitutionally protected rights and how they impact sport and recreation programs.

FUNDAMENTAL CONCEPTS

One of the rights contained in the United States Constitution is that of due process. Due process, which is defined as "a course of legal proceedings according to those rules and principles which have been established by our jurisprudence for the protection and enforcement of private rights" (*Pennoyer v. Neff*, 1877), is protected by the constitutional guarantees found in both the Fifth and Fourteenth Amendments. Enacted in 1791, the Fifth Amendment applies to the federal government and states, "No person shall . . . be deprived of life, liberty, or property without due process of law." The Fourteenth Amendment, enacted in 1868, extends the applicability of the due process guarantee to the states. The Fourteenth Amendment reads " . . . nor shall any state deprive any person of life, liberty, or property without due process of law."

Many state constitutions also prohibit the denial of due process. Since the due process protections apply to governmental action, not to those of private entities, before an individual may proceed with a due process claim, he or she must first clear two hurdles. First, the plaintiff must establish that there is state action. If able to show state action, the second test he or she must establish is that deprivation must infringe on a life, liberty, or property interest.

State Action

Before a court can conclude that an individual's due process rights have been violated, the court must first determine if the defendant is a *state actor*. As a general rule, public schools and universities as well as state high school athletic associations are considered state actors for constitutional purposes. However, for a more detailed discussion of state action, see Section 6.12, *State Action*.

Life, Liberty, or Property Interest

Since there would never be a case involving the taking away of an individual's life interest in the sport industry, the rest of this section examines liberty and property interests. The U.S. Supreme Court has defined **liberty interest** as follows: "without doubt, it denotes not merely freedom from bodily restraint but also . . . generally to enjoy those privileges long recognized . . . as essential to the orderly pursuit of happiness by free men" (*Meyer v. Nebraska*, 1923). With regard to due process and deprivation of a liberty interest, the Court in *Wisconsin v. Constantineau* (1971), stated, "where a person's good name, reputation, honor, or integrity is at stake because of what the government is doing to him, notice and an opportunity to be heard are essential." In a later case, the Court extended the requirements that are necessary to invoke a liberty interest. In that case, the Court concluded that: ". . . this line of cases does not establish the proposition that reputation alone, apart from some more tangible interests such as employment, is either 'liberty' or 'property' by itself sufficient to invoke the . . . protections of the Due Process Clause" (*Paul v. Davis*, 1976). This "more tangible interests" requirement has become known as the "**stigma plus**" test.

An example of the application of this "stigma plus" test in the sport industry is found in *Stanley v. Big Eight Conference* (1978). (One of the cases on the Supplemental CD). In this case, Stanley was relieved as head football coach at Oklahoma State University because of an NCAA investigation that implicated him in NCAA rules violations. Stanley brought a due process suit claiming that the action taken would have a stigmatizing effect on his ability to pursue his livelihood as a coach. The court ruled that: ". . . the 'more tangible interest' is Stanley's employment with OSU which has recently been terminated due at least in part to the allegations contained in the report, and his professional reputation which will determine his future employment opportunities" (*Stanley v. Big Eight Conference*, 1978).

The U.S. Supreme Court has defined a **property interest** as follows: "To have a property interest in a benefit, a person clearly must have more than an abstract need or desire for it. He must have more than a unilateral expectation of it. He must, instead, have a legitimate claim of entitlement" (*Board of Regents v. Roth*, 1972).

In the collegiate setting, plaintiffs have asserted that they either have a property right because he or she has a property interest in their scholarship or has a property right in a future professional career. In *Hall v. University of Minnesota* (1982), the court ruled that Hall did have a protected property right based on his future opportunity to play professional basketball. In another example, *Gulf South Conference v. Boyd* (1979), the court found that there was a property right of present economic value in a college athletic scholarship. It is important to note that since both of these cases were heard, the NCAA has reduced the length of athletic scholarships from a four year scholarship to one year renewable scholarships. As a result, as long as schools follow certain procedures, scholarships athletes only have a property interest in the current one year scholarship.

It should also be noted that must courts are unwilling to find that an athlete has a property interest in participating in athletic simply passed on his or her professional career opportunity. As a general rule, the courts have held that such a property interest was to speculative to be protected. In addition, the courts generally have not recognized a right of non-scholarship athletes to participate in intercollegiate athletics (*Colorado Seminary v. NCAA*, 1978).

At the high school level, the "entitlement" most often asserted in the sport setting is that of the right to participate in athletics. In particular, students argue that they have a property interest in participating in sports arising out of their right to an education. The Supreme Court, however, has specifically stated that education is not among the rights afforded explicit or implicit protection in the Constitution (*San Antonio Independent School District v. Rodriguez*, 1972). Even though the right to an education is not grounded in the United States Constitution, a state may grant a right to an education either explicitly and implicitly by requiring school attendance (*Goss v. Lopez*, 1975). However, even if a student has a constitutionally protected right to an education based on mandatory attendance or mandatory physical education requirement, the courts must still determine whether or not that right includes the right to participate in interscholastic athletics.

As a general rule, the courts have ruled that participate in interscholastic athletics a privilege, not a right. Over time, the courts, both at the federal and state levels, have generally been consistent in this view (*Morrison, et al. v. Roberts*, 1938; *State of Indiana v. Lawrence Circuit Court*, 1959; *Taylor v. Alabama High School Athletic Ass'n*, 1972; *Niles v. University Interscholastic League*, 1983; *Zehner v. Central Berkshire Regional School District*, 1996; *Wooten v. Pleasant Hope R-VI School District and Stout*, 2000).

Although the overwhelming majority of courts have found that there is no right to participate in interscholastic athletics, it should be noted that there are a couple of jurisdiction that have found a right to participate in interscholastic athletics (*Moran v. School District #7, Yellowstone County*, 1972; *Duffley v. New Hampshire Interscholastic Athletic Association*, 1982). There is also one jurisdiction that has ruled that although there is no right to participate in interscholastic athletics, a student's interest in participating is not entirely unprotected (*Stone v. Kansas State High School Activities Association*, 1988). In addition, although finding no constitutionally protected right in participation, other courts have ruled the state may enact rules that create one: *Arkansas Activities Association v. Meyer*, (1991) (although "there is clearly no constitutional right to play sports or engage in other school activities," rules may create one, but no violation of equal protection or due process in any event); *French v. Cornwell*, (1979) (assuming, without deciding, due process protection applies, but ultimately holding due process not violated); *Butler v. Oak Creek Franklin Sch. Dist.*, (2001) (assumed due process applied because defendant did not argue lack of property entitlement as basis for summary judgment).

Due Process Analysis

After a plaintiff has established that he or she has been deprived of a life, liberty or property interest, he or she can then proceed with demonstrating to the court how their due process rights have been violated. Due process of law is composed of two areas of inquiry. The first is **substantive due process**, which requires the regulation or rule to be fair and reasonable in content as well as application. The essence of substantive due process is protection from arbitrary and capricious actions. The inquiry into substantive due process asks two questions. First, does the regulation or rule have a proper purpose? Second, if so, does the regulation or rule clearly relate to the accomplishment of that purpose?

Over time, the courts have adopted general principles that serve to guide them in their decisions regarding rules and regulations of voluntary associations. First, as a general rule, in the absence of mistake, fraud, collusion, or arbitrariness, the decisions of the governing body of an association will be accepted as conclusive and the courts will not interfere with the internal affairs of voluntary associations. As a result, voluntary associations may adopt any bylaws and rules that is reasonable and it will be deemed valid and binding on the members of the association unless the bylaw or rule violates some law or public policy. It is not the responsibility of the courts to inquire into the expediency, practicability, or wisdom of the bylaws and regulations of voluntary associations. These general principles are equally applicable to cases involving athletic governing bodies (*Kentucky High School Athletic Association v. Hopkins County Board of Education*, 1977).

The rationale that athletic governing bodies have given for their rules and regulations is that it is their responsibility to create and administer rules and regulations that maintain a level playing field for all participants. Examples of courts upholding the rules and regulations of athletic governing bodies include *Berschback v. Grosse Pointe Public School District* and *Ternan v. Michigan High School Athletic Association, Inc.*, 1986; *Palmer v. Merluzzi*, 1989; and *Spring Branch Independent School District, et al. v. Stamos*, 1985. In each of these cases, the court deemed the rule or regulation that was at issue to be rationally related to its stated purpose. In the following cases, the courts found that the actions of the athletic governing body were unreasonable, capricious, and arbitrary: *Diaz v. Board of Education of the City of New York*, 1994; *Manico v. South Colonie Central School District*, 1992; and *Tiffany v. Arizona Interscholastic Association, Inc.*, 1986.

The second area in the due process inquiry involves **procedural due process**, which addresses the methods used to enforce the regulation or rule. Procedural due process examines the decision-making process that is followed to determine whether the regulation or rule has been violated and what sanction, if any, will be imposed. The goal of procedural due process is to ensure fair treatment.

After it has been determined that procedural due process is due to the plaintiff, the question becomes, what procedures should be followed to ensure fair treatment? Over time, the U.S. Supreme Court has provided guidance in answering that question. "Due process is flexible and calls for such procedural protections as the particular situation demands" (*Morrissey v. Brewer*, 1972). "Parties whose rights are to be affected are entitled to be heard; and in order that they may enjoy that right they must be notified" (*Baldwin v. Hale*, 1863). The greater the right or interest that is going to be deprived, the greater procedural due process owed to the plaintiff (*Goldberg v. Kelly*, 1970). Finally, the Court developed a balancing test to be used to determine the extent to procedural due process (*Mathews v. Eldridge*, 1976). In that case the Court stated that it must, first, examine "the private interest that will be affected by the official action; second, the risk of an erroneous deprivation of such interest through the procedures used, and the probable value, if any, of additional or substitute procedural safeguards; and finally, the Government's interest, including the function involved and the fiscal and administrative burdens that the additional or substitute procedural requirement would entail" (*Mathews v. Eldridge*, 1976, p. 335).

To understand how these procedural due process requirements apply to an educational setting, we look to the opinion of the U.S. Supreme Court in *Goss v. Lopez*, (1975). In *Goss*, a number of students in schools in the

Columbus, Ohio, school district were suspended from school for ten days for disruptive behavior. The students brought suit claiming their due process rights had been violated. The Court ruled that for suspensions of ten days or less the students "must be given *some* kind of notice and afforded *some* kind of hearing" (*Goss v. Lopez*, 1975). The Court further outlined the procedures that needed to be followed to meet the standard they had established. Specifically, the student must be given oral and written notice of the charges against him and, if he or she denies them, an explanation of the evidence the authorities have and an opportunity to present his side of the story. The court also held that there need be no delay between the time of the notice and the time of the hearing (*Goss v. Lopez*, 1975).

We can see the application of the standards established in *Goss* in two sport cases, *Pegram v. Nelson* (1979), and *Palmer v. Merluzzi*, (1989). In both the cases, student–athletes were suspended from school for ten days and from athletics for four months and sixty days, respectively. In both cases, the student-athletes were given notice and a hearing that afforded them the opportunity to refute the allegations against them. The courts in both cases ruled that the procedures that were followed afforded the student–athletes all the procedural due process they were owed (*Pegram v. Nelson*, 1979; *Palmer v. Merluzzi*, 1989).

Four other sport cases provide the sport and recreation manager with further guidance in the development of due process procedures. In the first case, *Kelley v. Metropolitan County Board of Education of Nashville* (1968), the plaintiff high school student-athlete was suspended from athletic competition by the Board of Education without being formally charged with a rule violation. The court held that due process requires published standards, formal charges, notice, and a hearing and granted an injunction that prevented the enforcement of the suspension (*Kelley v. Metropolitan County Board of Education of Nashville*, 1968).

In the second case, *Behagen v. Intercollegiate Conference of Faculty Representatives* (1972), two student–athletes were suspended for fighting with their opponents during a collegiate basketball game. The students brought suit claiming they were denied due process. The court held that their due process rights had been violated. In its opinion, the court outlined the procedures that needed to be followed to meet rudimentary requirements of due process. The procedures are as follows: (1) written notice of the time and place of the hearing at least two days in advance; (2) notice of the specific charges; (3) a hearing in which the athletic director hears both sides of the story; the hearing should include the presentation of direct testimony in the form of statements by each of those directly involved in relating their versions of the incident; (4) a list of witnesses to the plaintiff prior to the hearing; (5) a written report of the findings of fact and the basis for punishment; (6) tape recordings of the proceedings; and (7) an appeals procedure (*Behagen v. Intercollegiate Conference of Faculty Representatives*, 1972).

The third case is *Butler v. Oak Creek-Franklin School District*, (2001). In this case, the plaintiff was given a twelve-month suspension for violation of the Athletic Code. The court detailed the due process that was owed to the plaintiff, specifically, (1) predeprivation process, (2) notice, (3) need for a hearing, and (4) the right to an impartial decision maker (*Butler v. Oak Creek-Franklin School District*, 2001).

The fourth case, *Stanley*, was discussed earlier. Stanley was relieved as head football coach at Oklahoma State University because of an NCAA investigation that implicated him in NCAA rules violation, and Stanley filed suit claiming his due process rights had been violated. In its opinion, the Court provided guidance as to steps that could be followed to meet the demands of due process. Those steps are (1) notice of the infractions with which plaintiff is charged; (2) a list of witnesses the defendants will utilize to support each charge could be provided to the plaintiff; (3) plaintiff could report in writing each charge he specifically denies; (4) a list of witnesses the plaintiff wishes to have produced for confrontation and cross-examination could be provided to the defendant; and (5) the plaintiff could furnish the names of the witnesses he will rely on in his defense of each charge (*Stanley v. Big Eight Conference*, 1978).

International Sports

The guarantee of due process protections for athletes who participate in international competitions are contained in the constitutions and bylaws of the International Olympic Committee (IOC), its member National Olympic Committees (NOCs), International Sport Federations (IFs), and National Sport Federations (NFs).

In 1983, the IOC established the Court of Sport Arbitration (CAS). The CAS operated as an arm of the IOC until 1994, when it was restructured as an independent agency and renamed the International Court for the Arbitration of Sport (ICAS). The restructuring was deemed necessary following criticism that the CAS was too closely tied to the IOC. Beginning with the 1996 Summer Olympics in Atlanta, the IOC and its member NOCs, IFs, and NFs all agreed to submit disputes to mandatory and binding arbitration conducted by the ICAS. In addition, there is a mandatory and binding arbitration clause in the Olympic entry form that all athletes, coaches, and officials must sign as a condition of their Olympic participation (Bitting, 1998). The number of cases brought before the ICAS has increased since the Atlanta Games as athletes and sport governing bodies become more aware of the process of arbitration (Nafziger, 2001). For more information on ICAS, see Section 5.30, *Alternative Dispute Resolution* and http://www.tas-cas.org/news.

SIGNIFICANT CASE

In this case, the plaintiff tried to demonstrate to the court that her reputation as an athlete was a constitutionally protected right and that as a result she should be accorded due process rights. In addressing this question, the court examined the plaintiff's potential financial opportunities and the due process she might be owed.

NATIONAL COLLEGIATE ATHLETIC ASSOCIATION V. YEO

Supreme Court of Texas
171 S.W.3d 863 (2005)

When Coach Michael Walker recruited Joscelin Yeo, a high school student in the Republic of Singapore, to enroll at the University of California at Berkeley, she had already achieved fame in her country as a swimmer. At Berkeley, she won numerous All-American awards and was a member of a world-record-setting relay team in 1999.

Before the 2000–2001 school year, Walker left Berkeley for the University of Texas at Austin. He was helping coach the Singapore Olympic team, of which Yeo was a member, and she went with him to UT-Austin. Berkeley and UT-Austin are both members of the National Collegiate Athletic Association ("NCAA"), which prescribes rules for determining the eligibility of student athletes to engage in competition. A member that violates these rules is subject to sanctions. NCAA rules generally prohibit a student who transfer from one four-year member institution to another from participating in intercollegiate athletic competitions for one full academic year, but this restriction may be waived under certain circumstances if the former institution does not object. Berkeley refused to waive the restriction, and thus Yeo was ineligible to compete at UT-Austin for an academic year.

As permitted by NCAA rules, Yeo did not enroll in classes for the fall semester of 2000 in order to compete in the Olympics. In compliance with the one-year restriction, she did not participate in intercollegiate events during the semester or the spring semester, when she was enrolled in classes. UT-Austin mistakenly believed that Yeo's first semester had counted toward satisfying the restriction and that she was free to engage in competition beginning the fall semester of 2001. After Yeo competed in four events, Berkeley complained to the NCAA, UT-Austin confessed its error and agreed that Yeo would sit out the reminder of the semester, but the NCAA required that she not participate in the first four events the following spring, to match the four events in which she had been disqualified. Yeo did not know of UT-Austin's discussions with the NCAA and simply did as UT-Austin told her.

UT-Austin then added three swimming events at the beginning of its spring semester schedule. After Yeo had sat out those events and a fourth one, UT-Austin allowed her to rejoin the swim team, but Berkeley again complained, arguing that the added events could not be used to satisfy the one-year restriction. NCAA staff agreed and on March 6 issued a decision that Yeo not participate in the next three regularly scheduled events, including the 2002 NCAA women's swimming and diving championship on March 22. UT-Austin immediately appealed the staff decision to the NCAA Student-Athlete Reinstatement Committee ("the SARC"), and a telephonic hearing was scheduled for the next day. For the first time, UT-Austin told Yeo of the problem and advised her simply to plea for sympathy. She did, but at the conclusion of the hearing, the SARC upheld the staff decision.

At UT-Austin's suggestion, Yeo then obtained legal counsel, who persuaded Berkeley on March 15 to waive Yeo's one-year restriction, something it had refused to do before. Counsel mover SARC to reconsider, especially in light of this development, but it refused.

On March 20, Yeo sued UT-Austin and its vice president for institutional relations and legal affairs, Patricia Ohlendorf, to enjoin them from disqualifying her from competing in the championship meet two days later and for a declaration that UT-Austin had denied her procedural due process as guaranteed by the Texas Constitution. That same day, the trial court issued a temporary restraining order granting Yeo the injunctive relief requested. On March 21, the NCAA intervened in the action, but Yeo moved to strike the intervention, and after a hearing later that day, the trial court granted Yeo's motion. The next morning, the NCAA sought mandamus relief from the court of appeals, and UT-Austin appealed from the temporary restraining order. That afternoon, the court of appeals denied the petition for mandamus and dismissed the interlocutory appeal for want of jurisdiction. Yeo competed in the championship meet.

In November 2002, after a trial to the bench, the trial court rendered judgment for Yeo, declaring that UT-Austin had denied Yeo procedural due process guaranteed by the Texas Constitution, thereby depriving her of protected liberty and property interests. The court permanently enjoined UT-Austin from declaring Yeo ineligible in the future without affording her due process and from punishing her for participating in past competitions, including the 2002 women's championship. The trial court also awarded Yeo $164,755.50 in attorney fees through an appeal to this Court.

The NCAA appealed from the order striking its intervention, and UT-Austin appealed from the judgment. The court of appeals affirmed. We granted the NCAA's and UT-Austin's petition's for review.

Since the championship meet in March, 2002, Yeo has, of course, moved on. When the briefs were filed in this case, we were told that Yeo had graduated from UT-Austin, received a Rhodes Scholarship, and ended her college swimming career. But none of the parties argues that the case has become moot, because the injunction prevents the NCAA from imposing retroactive sanctions under its "Restitution Rule". We agree that the case is not moot.

We first consider whether Yeo has an interest protected by due process of law under article I, section 19 of the Texas Constitution. In doing so, we look as usual to cases construing the federal constitutional guarantee of due process as persuasive authority. The parties have not identified any difference between the state and federal guarantees material to the issues in this case.

Yeo does not challenge our holding in *Stamos* that a student has no interest in participating in extracurricular activities that is protected by the Texas Constitution's guarantee of due process of law. Nor does she dispute that under NCAA rules, she was ineligible to participate in the 2002 women's swimming and diving championship. Yeo argues that she was entitled to notice and a meaningful hearing before NCAA rules were applied to her because of her unique reputation and earning potential. Had she been disqualified from competing in the championship meet, she contends, people would have suspected that it was her own misconduct and not for UT-Austin's mistakes in attempting to comply with NCAA rules. Yeo acknowledges that the United States Supreme Court has held that reputation alone is not a protected liberty or property interest. But it is the degree of her interests, Yeo contends, and not merely their character, that bring them within constitutional protection. A student-athlete with a lesser reputation or less certain of her earning potential, she contends, would not have the same rights. The court of appeals agreed:

> In connection with the permanent injunction, the trial court made several material findings of material fact that are essentially unchallenged: (1) Yeo had already established a world-class reputation and her "good name, outstanding reputation, high standing in her community, her unblemished integrity and honor are particularly important in the Republic of Singapore and in light of her cultural background";

> (2) if NCAA rules did not prohibit athletes from accepting professional compensation while competing in NCAA sanctioned events, Yeo "would be immediately eligible to capitalize on her public persona by entering into lucrative endorsement and marketing opportunities as well as being eligible for prize winnings due to her performance as a member of Singapore's national team"; and (3) "UT-Austin represented to [Yeo] at the time she transferred from [Cal-Berkeley] to become a student-athlete at UT-Austin that UT-Austin would not jeopardize or compromise [Yeo's] eligibility to compete on behalf of UT-Austin in NCAA competition."

These findings of fact support Yeo's theory that her athletic reputation, which was established even *before* she began attending Cal-Berkley and competing under NCAA regulations, constitutes a protected interest for purposes of due course of law. Yeo had competed in two Olympic games before attending college and had been named sportswoman of the year and Olympic flag-bearer for her native country, Singapore. At both the temporary restraining order and permanent injunction hearings, Yeo represented that it was this continuing interest in her athletic and professional reputation that UT-Austin had damaged by its actions.

Here, Yeo presented testimony from multiple witnesses indicating that she had established a reputation as a world-class athlete in her home country of Singapore *separate and apart from her intercollegiate swimming career.* As a result, much of her reputation had been build outside of the United States and the structure of NCAA intercollegiate athletics. We cannot say that the trial court erred in holding that Yeo had a protected interest under these facts.

UT-Austin, joined by various *amici curiae*, contends that an affirmance in this case will create a protected interest in every intercollegiate student-athlete to participate in athletic events. We reject this argument and note that we reach this decision because of the unique fact pattern with which we are presented. Based upon the largely undisputed findings of fact, Yeo had already established a protected interest in her reputation as an athlete long before she came to this country to swim competitively as a student-athlete under NCAA rules. Our holding that Yeo, under these facts, has a protected interest should not be read as extending that same protection to every other intercollegiate athlete. The determination of whether a student-athlete has a protected interest is necessarily fact-specific, depending on that athlete's specific situation and reputation. Each such case must be decided on its own merits, in light of the financial realities of contemporary athletic competition. We hold that Yeo's established liberty interest in her reputation as an athlete is entitled to due course of law protection and we affirm the trial court's decision in that regard.

We reject Yeo's argument and the court of appeals' holding. The United States Supreme Court has stated, and we agree, that whether an interest is protected by due process depends on its *weight* but on its *nature*. Yeo does not take issue with this principle but argues in effect that the weight of an interest can determine its nature. A stellar reputation like hers, Yeo contends and the court of appeals concluded, is categorically different from a more modest reputation. We disagree. The loss of either may be, to its owner, substantial. The court of appeals held that whether a reputation is constitutionally protected must be decided case by case, but it did not suggest a measure for distinguishing one case from another, and neither does Yeo. We see none, which convinces us that the *nature* of one's interest in a good reputation is the same no matter how good the reputation is.

Yeo's claimed interest in future financial opportunities is too speculative for due process protection. There must be an actual legal entitlement. While student-athletes remain amateurs, their future financial opportunities remain expectations.

Yeo argues that her reputation and future financial interests are entitled to constitutional protection under our decision in *University of Texas Medical School v. Than*. There we held that a medical student charged with academic dishonesty had a protected liberty interest in a graduate edu-

cation. But since *Than* we have refused to accord a student's interest in athletics in the same protection. We decline to equate an interest in intercollegiate athletics with an interest in graduate education.

Accordingly, we hold that Yeo has asserted no interests protected by article I, section 19 of the Texas Constitution. The case must therefore be dismissed. While we need not reach the NCAA's arguments that it should have been permitted to intervene, we expressly disapprove the court of appeals' conclusions that the NCAA's interests were not sufficiently implicated to warrant intervention, and that intervention would have unduly complicated the case.

We have twice reminded the lower courts that "judicial intervention in [student athletic disputes] often does more harm than good." As the Fifth Circuit has said, judges are not "super referees". Along the same vein, the United States Supreme Court has observed: "Courts do not and cannot intervene in the resolution of conflicts which arise in the daily operation of school systems and which do not directly and sharply implicate basic constitutional values." We reiterate this counsel to the trial courts and courts of appeals.

The judgment of the court of appeals is reversed, and judgment is rendered that Yeo take nothing.

CASES ON THE SUPPLEMENTAL CD

Stanley v. Big Eight Conference, 463 F. Supp. 920 (W.D. MO. 1978). The case examines what due process an athletic conference that is investigating a coach must supply to satisfy the coach's due process rights.

Stone v. Kansas State High School Activities Association, 761 P.2d 1255 (Kan. App. 1988). In this case the court holds that high school students do have a constitutionally protected interest in participating in extracurricular activities.

Palmer v. Merluzzi, 868 F.2d 90 (3rd Cir. 1989). This case examines whether a student was ade-

quately notified of the accusation against him and was provided a meaningful opportunity to argue against his scholastic and athletic suspensions.

Mancuso vs. Massachusetts Interscholastic Athletic Association, 453 Mass. 116; 900 N.E.2d 518 (2009). This case examines whether students have a "legitimate claim of entitlement," to her participation in interscholastic athletics under State law, if the law recognizes a right to an education, which includes physical education.

QUESTIONS YOU SHOULD BE ABLE TO ANSWER

1. Due process protections are found in what Amendments?

2. The three rights protected by the Due Process clause are: "life, . . . , or. . . ."

3. In determining whether your **substantive due process** has been violated, the courts will review whether the regulation or rule is . . . ?

4. In determining whether your **procedural due process** has been violated, the courts will review what?

5. Is participation in high school sports a privilege or a protected right?

REFERENCES

Cases

Arkansas Activities Association v. Meyer, 805 S.W.2d 58 (1991).

Baldwin v. Hale, 68 U.S. 223 (1863).

Behagen v. Intercollegiate Conference of Faculty Representatives, 346 F. Supp. 602 (D. Minn. 1972).

Berschback v. Grosse Pointe Public School District and *Ternan v. Michigan High School Athletic Association, Inc.*, 397 N.W.2d 234 (Mich. App. 1986).

Board of Regents v. Roth, 408 U.S. 564 (1972).

Butler v. Oak Creek-Franklin School District, 172 F. Supp. 2d 1102 (E.D. Wis. 2001).

Colorado Seminary v. NCAA, 417 F. Supp. 885 (D. Colo. 1976), *aff'd*, 570 F.2d 320 (10th Cir. 1978).

Diaz v. Board of Education of the City of New York, 618 N.Y.S.2d 984 (Sup. 1994).

Duffley v. New Hampshire Interscholastic Athletic Association, 446 A.2d 462 (Sup. Ct. N.H. 1982).

French v. Cornwell, 276 N.W.2d 216 (1979).

Goldberg v. Kelly, 397 U.S. 266 (1970).

Goss v. Lopez, 419 U.S. 565 (1975).

Gulf South Conference v. Boyd, 369 So. 553 (Sup. Ct. Ala. 1979).

Hall v. University of Minnesota, 530 F. Supp. 104 (D. Minn. 1982).

Kelley v. Metropolitan County Board of Education of Nashville, 293 F. Supp. 485 (M.D. Tenn. 1968).

Kentucky High School Athletic Association v. Hopkins County Board of Education, 552 S.W.2d 685 (Ky. App. 1977).

Manico v. South Colonie Central School District, 584 N.Y.S.2d 519 (Sup. 1992).

Mathews v. Eldridge, 424 U.S. 319 (1976).

Meyer v. Nebraska, 262 U.S. 390 (1923).

Moran v. School District #7, Yellowstone County, 350 F. Supp. 1180 (D. Mont. 1972).

Morrison, et al. v. Roberts, 183 Okl. 359, 82 P.2d 1023 (Sup. Ct. Okl. 1938).

Morrissey v. Brewer, 408 U.S. 471 (1972).

National Collegiate Athletic Association v. Yeo, 114 S.W. 3d 584, rev'd 171 S.W. 3d 863 (Tex. 2003).

Niles v. University Interscholastic League, 715 F.2d 1027 (5th Cir. 1983).

Palmer v. Merluzzi, 868 F.2d 90 (3rd Cir. 1989).

Paul v. Davis, 424 U.S. 693 (1976).

Pegram v. Nelson, 469 F. Supp. 1134 (M.D. N.C. 1979).

Pennoyer v. Neff, 95 U.S. 714 (1877).

San Antonio Independent School District v. Rodriguez, 411 U.S. 1 (1972).

Spring Branch Independent School District, et al. v. Stamos, 695 S.W.2d 556 (Tex. 1985).

Stanley v. Big Eight Conference, 463 F. Supp. 920 (W.D. MO. 1978).

State of Indiana v. Lawrence Circuit Court, 162 N.E.2d 250 (Sup.Ct. Ind. 1959).

Stone v. Kansas State High School Activities Association, 761 P.2d 1255 (Kan. App. 1988).

Taylor v. Alabama High School Athletic Association, 336 F. Supp. 54 (M.D. Ala. 1972).

Tiffany v. Arizona Interscholastic Association, Inc., 726 P.2d 231 (Ariz. App. 1986).

Wisconsin v. Constantineau, 400 U.S. 433 (1971).

Wooten v. Pleasant Hope R-VI School District and Stout, 139 F.Supp. 835 (W.D. Mo. 2000).

Zehner v. Central Berkshire Regional School District, 921 F. Supp. 850 (D. Mass. 1996).

Publications

Bitting, M. R. (1998). Comments: Mandatory, binding arbitration for Olympics athletes: Is the process better or worse for "job security?" *Florida State University Law Review, 25,* 655.

Due process law in Florida struck down. (1994, November 21). *NCAA News,* pp. 1, 20.

Nafziger, J. A. R. (2001). Article and Speech: Arbitration of rights and obligations in the international sports arena. *Valparaiso University Law Review, 35,* 357.

Netzle, S. (1992). The Court of Arbitration for Sport: An alternative for dispute resolution in U.S. sports. *The Entertainment and Sports Lawyer, 10,* 1–4, 25–28.

Websites

http://www.tas-cas.org/news

—Sarah K. Fields
THE OHIO STATE UNIVERSITY

In 1868, just after the Civil War, Congress enacted the Fourteenth Amendment to the United States Constitution. The Equal Protection Clause of that amendment decreed that "no state shall . . . deny to any person within its jurisdiction the equal protection of the laws." According to contemporary debates on the floor of the House of Representatives and the Senate, the Equal Protection Clause was not intended to be applied literally to all people: it was meant to provide some rights to African-American men; those rights were not intended to include the right to vote, to serve on a jury, or to marry white women. The framers of the Fourteenth Amendment clearly never intended that the clause be applied to women of any race. Thus from the first day, the Equal Protection Clause's literal universal inclusion has been limited, and the challenge for the courts over the past century and a half has been to determine what those limitations are and how to apply the Equal Protection Clause both practically and fairly.

Society and the laws constantly distinguish or discriminate between different groups of individuals. Not everyone is treated equally; for example, eight year olds are not allowed legally to drink alcohol, to join the military, or to drive cars. The Equal Protection Clause simply requires that similarly situated people be treated similarly and that the states be able to articulate and justify why they treat one group differently than another group. Over time, the courts have concluded that to determine if the government's classification is legal under the Equal Protection Clause, the test, or standard of review, will vary according to what category of people the classification describes. Today, courts usually use one of three different standards of review: (1) the easiest test to survive is **mere rationality** and most classifications are tested under this standard; (2) a more difficult middle tier, sometimes called **intermediate scrutiny**, applies to gender classifications; and (3), a very difficult to pass test of **strict scrutiny** applies to deprivations of fundamental rights and to classifications which are suspect—race, **alienage** (status of a foreigner legally within the country) , and national origin.

The legal reach of equal protection derives from several sources. Although originally the Fourteenth Amendment only applied to the actions of the states, subsequent Supreme Court interpretation has concluded that the federal government must also comply with equal protection, both because it would be irrational to assume that the state governments must provide equal protection but the federal government would not and because the Fifth Amendment includes a "due process" clause. The Supreme Court ruled in *Bolling v. Sharpe* (1954), that the Fifth Amendment's due process clause inferred an equal protection component for the federal government. Equal protection also derives from the Civil Rights Act of 1871 (42 USC § 1983) which prohibits persons acting under color of law from depriving people of "rights, privileges, or immunities secured by the Constitution." This law protects individuals from having a governmental actor infringe upon their constitutional rights, including their right of equal protection. Additionally every state constitution has some parallel language to the Equal Protection Clause of the Fourteenth Amendment to the U.S. Constitution, and individuals may file suit in state courts under their state Equal Protection Clause.

FUNDAMENTAL CONCEPTS

State Actor

Before a court can conclude that one's equal protection rights have been violated, the court must find that the defendant is a **state actor**. For an extended discussion of state action, what this means, and how to determine who a state actor is, see Section 6.12, *State Action*. In general, however, public schools and universities are considered state actors, as are community parks and recreation organizations. These means that they must comply with equal protection. Although in general, purely private organizations have greater freedom to discriminate between groups and are not usually limited by equal protection, occasionally courts have concluded that some private organizations have been so intertwined with governmental powers (such as using public facilities or acting in lieu of a governmental agency) that they too can be deemed state actors.

Standing

In order for a plaintiff to file a constitutional claim, the plaintiff must have a direct stake in the outcome of the case in order to have *standing*, see Section 6.11, *Judicial Review, Standing, and Injunctions*. Simply having an interest in the outcome of a case or the topic in general does not satisfy the standing requirement.

Purposeful Discrimination

Courts have determined that the Equal Protection Clause only protects individuals from intentional or **purposeful discrimination**. Unintentional discrimination or a **disparate impact**—when one group is more greatly burdened by a classification than another—on one group does not necessarily mean that equal protection has been violated. For example, on average men are taller than women, so if a fire department has a height minimum taller than the average height of women, more women may be excluded than men. This would be a disparate impact, but by itself, it would not be purposeful discrimination; to prove the regulation violated the Equal Protection Clause, a plaintiff would need evidence to indicate the height minimum was intended to exclude women.

Standards of Review

Lowest Tier Rational Basis Review

The rational basis review or "**mere rationality**" test is the easiest standard of review and many classifications have survived legal challenges because the state actor has been able to establish that *the classification is rationally related to a legitimate governmental interest*. As mentioned in the example in the introductory section to this section, eight year old children cannot legally drink alcohol, join the military, or drive because the vast majority of eight year olds are too young to make safe, informed decisions about their choices and drinking, joining the military, or driving could be dangerous to them and to others. The government has a legitimate interest in the safety of its children and its citizens, and the legal limitations placed on children are rationally related to that legitimate interest. This test applies when the classification the state uses is not subject to one of the more difficult standards of review as described later in this section.

Residency Classifications. Sport and recreation have provided a variety of examples of classifications that have been challenged on equal protection grounds. In *Baldwin v. Fish & Game Commission of Montana* (1978), when the Supreme Court concluded that the different classification of residents and non-residents of a state, and charging them different fees for hunting licenses, was rationally related to the legitimate state purpose of preserving a finite resource. (This case is available on the accompanying computer disc.)

Classifications of Athletes Compared to Non-athletes. In *Schaill by Kross v. Tippecanoe County School Corp.* (1988), a student challenged the school district's drug-testing policy, which tested only athletes. The court concluded that the district had a legitimate interest in keeping the athletic arena free from drugs, and that testing was rationally related to interest (for more information on this topic see Section 6.23, *Drug Testing*).

Eligibility Rules. A number of eligibility rules have survived equal protection challenges in which mere rationality was the test. In *Spring Branch Independent School District v. Stamos* (1985), a high school athlete challenged the state's "no pass no play" rule which required athletes to maintain a minimum grade point average in order to be eligible to play high school sports. The Texas Supreme Court concluded that the state had a legitimate interest in promoting a strong educational environment and that the minimum grade standard was rationally related to that interest. In a different Texas case, the court upheld the state athletic association rule banning high school players aged nineteen years and older from high school competition. The court concluded that the rule was rationally related to the legitimate state interests of keeping a "level playing field" and protecting younger players from competition with much older and more experienced athletes (*Blue v. University Interscholastic League*, 1980).

More recently, courts in two different states let eligibility rules stand despite equal protection challenges. In 2007, a federal district court in New York upheld a school district rule that athletes have tetanus shots prior to participation in outdoor sports. A young man whose family's religious beliefs precluded vaccinations had argued that the rule violated his equal protection rights. The court concluded that the classification was rationally related to the state's legitimate interest in the safety of its students (*Hadley v. Rush Henrietta Center School District*, 2007). In Washington, the father of a middle school football player was himself a high school football coach and volunteer coach for his son's middle school team. The WIIA had a rule that prohibited high school coaches from working for more than twelve weeks each season with middle school players who would later be attending their school. The plaintiff's son's team had a season just over thirteen weeks long. The father challenged the rule on equal protection grounds, but the court concluded that the legitimate state interest in promoting a "level playing field," minimizing recruiting, and minimizing pressure on young athletes was rationally related to the twelve-week rule (*Jones v. Washington Interscholastic Activities Association*, 2007).

Intermediate Scrutiny

Quasi-suspect classifications are subject to intermediate scrutiny. Thus far the Supreme Court has consistently found *gender and illegitimacy to be quasi-suspect categories*, but gender is the most relevant quasi-suspect classification for the sport and recreation manager. The Supreme Court created this middle tier of testing in a series of gender discrimination lawsuits in the 1970s. Prior to legal decisions, gender discrimination had been traditionally examined under the mere rationality test and government discrimination against women frequently survived this test. For example, in *State v. Hunter* (1956), a woman convicted of wrestling without a state license appealed her conviction on the grounds that the state law violated her equal protection rights: the state at that time only issued wrestling licenses to men. She lost her case because the Oregon Supreme Court concluded that the classification was rationally related to the state's legitimate interest in protecting public health, morals, and participants' safety.

As the Women's Rights movement of the twentieth century progressed, however, the Supreme Court made it more difficult for local, state and Federal governments to utilize gender classifications. In *Craig v. Boren* (1976), the majority of the Court held that to survive equal protection scrutiny, *a gender classification must be substantially related to an important governmental objective.*

Gender Classifications and Contact Sport. Female athletes have used the Equal Protection Clause to gain the right to try out of contact sports teams such as football in *Force by Force v. Pierce City R-VI School District* (1983), and wrestling *Adams v. Baker*, (1996). (The *Adams* case is available on the accompanying computer disc.) In each case the courts recognized that other gender discrimination legislation like Title IX would not help the athlete. The enforcement regulations for Title IX, for example, exempt contact sport from the law, and the Equal Protection Clause can be used to close that exemption. For more information see Section 7.11, *Gender Equity: Opportunities to Participate.* In *Force* and *Adams*, the defendant school districts had argued primarily that the state had an important interest in protecting the female athletes from the dangers of co-educational contact sport, in protecting the psyche of the boys' they would compete against, and in maintaining a smoothly run sports program. First the courts rejected the arguments that the state had an important interest in the psyche of only the male athletes and in logistical ease (like needing a separate changing space for the female athlete). Although the courts agreed that the safety of all students was an important state interest, they did not agree that a gender classification was substantially related to that important interest because that classification erroneously presumed that all boys were bigger and stronger than all girls and thus a gender classification failed to have a substantial relationship with the important governmental interest in children's safety.

In the converse, schoolboys who have filed equal protection lawsuits to gain access to traditionally female sports like field hockey have been much less successful. For example in 1987, a New Jersey state court concluded that the school district's rule barring boys from playing on girls' sports teams did not violate the state version of the Equal Protection Clause. The school had argued that the classification was substantially related to the important governmental interest in redressing past gender discrimination in high school sport. The court agreed, noting that if boys were to play on girls' teams it might result in fewer girls participating (because boys would take their spots on the team) and that some girls might quit sport altogether when faced with a male competitor (*B.C. v. Cumberland Regional School District*).

Gender Discrimination and Scheduling Seasons. In 2006, the Sixth Circuit Court of Appeals ended a long-running battle between a group called Communities for Equity and the Michigan High School Athletic Association. The MHSAA had, for years, scheduled many girls' sports in so-called off- or non-traditional seasons. For example, although the game of basketball has traditionally been a winter sport, in Michigan high school girls played in the fall season. Communities for Equity believed this distinction to be a violation of equal protection and filed suit on those grounds. The MHSAA argued that scheduling girls' sport in non-traditional seasons allowed more girls and boys to play sports and also allowed both boys and girls access to the best facilities and practice and competition times without having an internal fights for court or game times. The Sixth Court of Appeals affirmed a lower court decision that the distinction was indeed a violation of the Equal Protection Clause because the state failed to establish that the gender classification was substantially related to that important interest. The court particularly condemned the MHSAA for only scheduling girls' teams in the off-seasons, noting that if scheduling was really so challenging and if non-traditional scheduling was really so helpful, the burden could have been borne equally by boys' and girls' teams (2006).

Workplace Discrimination. The Equal Protection Clause has also been used as a cause of action in response to gender discrimination in the sporting workplace. A female reporter was barred from the New York Yankees' locker room in the city, owned and maintained Yankee Stadium. The Yankees and Major League Baseball argued that the state had an important governmental interest in protecting the privacy of its players, in promoting a family atmosphere in the sport, and in complying with traditional standards of decency. Although the court agreed that protecting the players' privacy was an important governmental interest, they did not agree that barring women from the locker room was substantially related to that interest, given that the privacy could be accorded with the use of towels, robes, or other clothing (*Ludtke v. Kuhn* 1978). For more information on this topic see Section 7.12, *Gender Equity: Coaching and Administration.*

Strict Scrutiny

Fundamental Rights Deprivation. Strict scrutiny is triggered when a state deprives a person of his or her fundamental rights. These fundamental rights include those articulated in the Constitution—freedom of speech and the right to assemble peaceably for example—and also some rights not articulated. The right to vote, to travel and to privacy have been established as fundamental rights. Education has been deemed a non-fundamental right and participating in sport has simply been deemed a privilege; therefore, for sport and recreation managers, fundamental rights deprivations are relatively uncommon.

Fundamental rights deprivations, however, can occur. For example, a Texas school district had a rule prohibiting married students from participating in extracurricular activities including sport. The district seems to have argued that the rule was intended to help the married student succeed in his or her education and marriage as well as to discourage early marriage between students. The court concluded that because the right to marry is fundamental, the district needed to prove that the *classification was necessary to achieve a compelling governmental interest.* The court found the district failed to do this because the district had no evidence that banning married students from extracurricular activities helped married students in any aspect of their lives (*Bell v. Lone Oak Independent School District*, 1974).

Suspect Classifications. Suspect classifications can also trigger strict scrutiny. The Supreme Court has concluded that race, national origin, and alienage are suspect classifications. To survive an equal protection challenge, the state must prove that *the suspect classification is necessary to achieve a compelling governmental interest, and the classification must be the least restrictive means of achieving that interest.* This test is very stringent and very few laws involving suspect classifications have survived the test and been deemed constitutional.

That said, one recreation case did involve what seemed to be racial discrimination. After long operating racially segregated city pools, the city of Jackson, Mississippi, was ordered to desegregate its pools towards the end of the 1960s because segregation violated the Equal Protection Clause. The city, arguing that they could not afford to operate its pools anymore, closed four of the pools and leased the fifth pool to a private organization that limited access to whites only. Several African-American residents sued, arguing that the city had violated their equal protection rights by closing the pools to African-Americans only, as white citizens had the option of joining the private organization. A closely divided Supreme Court concluded that city could close its pools to avoid racial integration because all citizens, not just African-American ones, were denied access (*Palmer v. Thompson*, 1971) and the city had no obligation to operate pools.

A more typical strict scrutiny case, however, is that of *St. Augustine High School v. Louisiana High School Athletic Association* (1967). The LHSAA had traditionally banned non-white students from participating in the organizations' interscholastic sports program. After the schools themselves were integrated by court order, the LHSAA dropped ban of non-white participants. The member schools themselves, however, remained overwhelmingly white. In 1965 St. Augustine High, a predominantly African-American school, planned to apply for membership. Before the LHSAA voted, however, they changed their rules and announced that any potential member schools would be required to bring a petition with the support of two-thirds of the representatives of the schools in their district, and then would need a two-thirds vote of support from those member schools present at the LHSAA meeting. In 1966 when St. Augustine appeared with their petition, the member schools voted to deny the school membership even though it met all other criteria. In response to the school's equal protection lawsuit, the Fifth Circuit Court of Appeals concluded that the LHSAA had no compelling interest in excluding potential member schools simply because their students were not white.

Sliding Scale Approach

The three-tier level of testing as described above evolved from the traditional two-tier level of testing (mere rationality and strict scrutiny). Some scholars argue that the courts have on occasion engaged in something known as the sliding-scale approach. This approach, championed by the late Supreme Court Justice Thurgood Marshall, maintained that the courts should dispense with the rigid tier system and balance the rights and interests of the individuals and the state in determining the appropriate level of scrutiny.

As a practical matter, courts, including the U.S. Supreme Court, have seemed to tinker with the levels of tests in their analyses. For example, in 1996 in *U.S. v. Virginia*, the Virginia Military Academy attempted to justify its male-only admission policy against the federal government's claims that the policy violated the Equal Protection Clause. Writing for a six-person majority, Justice Ruth Bader Ginsberg seemed to rely on the intermediate level of scrutiny, but added that a state actor must have an "exceedingly persuasive" justification for gender segregation, adding that gender classifications would trigger "skeptical scrutiny." The majority found that VMI's male-only admission policy was a violation of the Equal Protection Clause, because the state had failed to provide that exceedingly persuasive justification. In his concurrence Chief Justice William Rehnquist supported in the decision of the majority but did so while clearly articulating the traditional intermediate scrutiny test. Justice Anton Scalia, in his dissent, argued adamantly against Justice Ginsberg's ratcheted-up test for gender classifications.

The sport and recreation manager should be aware that the tests surrounding equal protection have evolved over time and are likely to continue to do so.

Over- and Under-Inclusive

Perhaps the most common reason that courts reject classifications as violating equal protection is because the classification includes more people than it should or, both alternatively and sometimes simultaneously, the classification does not include all the people it should in order to meet the objective of the law. For example in *Sullivan v. University Interscholastic League* (1981), the state athletic association argued that their rule making transfer students ineligible to compete in varsity basketball and football was rationally related to their legitimate interest in discouraging the recruiting of athletes, a practice which undermined the educational experience of a student. The Texas Supreme Court agreed that the state did have a legitimate interest in promoting a "level playing field," in emphasizing education over athletics, and in discouraging the recruitment of athletes. The court, however, thought the rule was not rationally related to the interest because it was over-inclusive; the rule applied to all transfer students, even those who transferred for reasons completely unrelated to sport. For example, if a student transferred because a parent got a better job and the family moved, the student was ineligible. (This case is included on the accompanying computer disc.)

For an example of a classification being struck down because it was both over- and under-inclusive, consider the case of a student athlete who challenged a rule preventing married students from participating in high school sports. The state argued that the rule existed to promote a wholesome high school atmosphere, to discourage married students from discussing sex in the locker room, to reduce drop-out rates, and to encourage married students to focus on their education and marriage. He won because the court concluded that the rule was over-inclusive: some married students of good character would do nothing to detract from a wholesome atmosphere and this student in particular had been allowed to play while the case was pending, and his grades improved, he held a part-time job, and he remained married. The court concluded the rule was also under-inclusive because it did not bar the participation of students who engaged in pre-marital sex nor those students who were of poor character (*Indiana High School Athletics Ass'n v. Raike*, 1975).

SIGNIFICANT CASE

Fusato v. Washington Interscholastic Activities Association is an example of one of the most recent cases involving discrimination against someone because of their national origins in sport. Note how the court applied the strict scrutiny test and dismissed the state's arguments justifying their classification.

FUSATO V. WASHINGTON INTERSCHOLASTIC ACTIVITIES ASSOCIATION

Court of Appeals of Washington, Division Three
970 P.2d 774 (Wash. App. 1999)

Tomoe Fusato challenges the Washington Interscholastic Activities Association's (WIAA) residence and transfer rules, which, with few exceptions, forbid students from playing varsity athletics if they did not relocate to a school district with their parents. The superior court reversed the administrative decision against Ms. Fusato and found the WIAA's rules violated the Fourteenth Amendment's Equal Protection Clause. Although the matter is moot, we proceed and decide the trial court did not err taking judicial notice of certain facts. We conclude that although no fundamental right is threatened, the rule of strict scrutiny applies. This is so because the challenged rules discriminatorily impact Ms. Fusato as a member of a suspect class based upon national origin and there is no showing of a compelling state interest being served by these rules. Additionally, the WIAA did not demonstrate that the least restrictive means were used to accomplish the regulatory purposes of their rules. Accordingly, we affirm.

FACTS

Ms. Fusato, a Japanese National, moved from Okinawa to live with her aunt and uncle in Kettle Falls. The purpose of the move was to experience American culture and help ease the biases prevalent against Americans arising from recent criminal conduct on the part of American servicemen. She was told she was ineligible for varsity sports at Kettle Falls High School under WIAA rules.

The WIAA, a nonprofit organization, regulates interscholastic athletics at 385 secondary schools under RCW 28A.600.200. WIAA Rule 18.10.1(A) does not allow transferring students to be immediately eligible for varsity competition unless they transfer with their "entire family unit." Since Ms. Fusato moved without her parents a "hardship" was required for eligibility. Because neither the District 7 Eligibility Committee nor the Executive Board of the WIAA found her case to be a hardship under WIAA Rule 18.22.1, her eligibility was denied.

The Stevens County Superior Court, Judge Stewart, on appeal from the WIAA regulatory process, initially entered a temporary restraining order, permitting Ms. Fusato to play varsity sports pending final hearing. Judge Schroeder re-

viewed and maintained the temporary order at a continuation hearing. Finally, Judge Baker at the hearing on the merits, held the rules excluded a class of students based on national origin. The court further found the rules have a disparate impact based on this suspect class. The court took judicial notice that "almost every foreign exchange students and/or I-20 VISA students—it's almost unheard of in a high school setting—that such foreign students are here with their parents." The court also took judicial notice that "a typical foreign exchange or I-20 VISA student is unable to ever establish a hardship under the transfer rules."

The trial court concluded there was no compelling state interest in the WIAA residence and transfer rules and, accordingly, found them to be in violation of the Equal Protection Clause in the Fourteenth Amendment of the United States Constitution.

* * *

ANALYSIS: Equal Protection

1. Issue. The issue is whether the trial court erred by using strict scrutiny and deciding the WIAA residence and transfer rules violated the Equal Protection Clause of the Fourteenth Amendment.

2. Standard of Review. Constitutional challenges are reviewed de novo. *See Washam v. Sonntag*, 74 Wn.App. 504, 507, 874 P.2d 188 (1994) (addressing whether statute violates state constitution as issue of law subject to de novo review).

3. Discussion. The challenger of a rule, regulation or statute claiming an equal protection violation may have to meet one of three different legal standards for judging whether a violation exists. *City of Richland v. Michel*, 89 Wn.App. 764, 768-70, 950 P.2d 10 (1998). The choice is based upon the factual context, giving rise to different degrees of scrutiny in ascending order of difficulty of proof: strict, intermediate, or minimum.

One of three standards of review has been employed when analyzing equal protection claims. Strict scrutiny applies when a classification affects a suspect class or threatens a fundamental right. Intermediate or heightened scrutiny, used by this court in limited circumstances, applies when important rights or semisuspect classifications are affected. The most relaxed (minimum) level of scrutiny, commonly referred to as the rational basis or rational relationship test, *applies when a statutory classification does not involve a suspect or semisuspect class and does not threaten a fundamental right.*

State v. Manussier, 129 Wn.2d 652, 672-73, 921 P.2d 473 (1996), *cert. denied*, 520 U.S. 1201, 117 S. Ct. 1563, 137 L. Ed. 2d 709 (1997) (citations omitted). It normally follows that the party seeking to uphold the rule, regulation, or statute generally prefers the minimum scrutiny standard, using the rational relationship test.

Deciding the degree or standard of scrutiny is our first task. *Harris v. Department of Labor & Indus.*, 120 Wn.2d 461, 476-77, 843 P.2d 1056 (1993). Here, Ms. Fusato argues for strict scrutiny and defends the trial court's decision while the WIAA argues for the lesser minimum scrutiny standard and use of the rational relationship test. When strict scrutiny is involved, the classification will be upheld if it is shown to be necessary to accomplish a compelling state interest. *Westerman v. Cary*, 125 Wn.2d 277, 294, 892 P.2d 1067 (1994). If the complaining party demonstrates strict scrutiny is the proper test under the facts, then the burden shifts to the party seeking to uphold the rule, regulation, or statute "to show the restrictions serve a compelling state interest and are the least restrictive means for achieving the government objective. If no compelling state interest exists, the restrictions are unconstitutional." *First United Methodist Church v. Hearing Examiner*, 129 Wn.2d 238, 246, 916 P.2d 374 (1996).

If neither a suspect class is involved nor a fundamental right is threatened, the appropriate standard of review is the rational basis test. *Manussier*, 129 Wn.2d at 673. We answer three questions when deciding if the rational relationship test applies.

1. Does the classification apply alike to all members within the designated class?

2. Do reasonable grounds exist to support a distinction between those within and without each class? and

3. Does the class have a "rational relationship" to the purpose of the legislation?

Harris, 120 Wn.2d at 477. Because the trial court agreed with Ms. Fusato that the strict scrutiny test applies here, we examine it first.

Washington courts have recognized there is no fundamental right to engage in interscholastic sports. *Darrin v. Gould*, 85 Wn.2d 859, 873, 540 P.2d 882 (1975). It follows that for Ms. Fusato to prevail, the WIAA residence and transfer rules must discriminate against a suspect class to warrant strict scrutiny review. Suspect classifications include those based on race, national origin, or alienage. U.S. CONST. amend. XIV; *State v. Wallace*, 86 Wn.App. 546, 552, 937 P.2d 200, *review denied*, 133 Wn.2d 1028, 950 P.2d 478 (1997). Ms. Fusato alleges discrimination and disparate impact based on her national origin.

Under the WIAA residence and transfer rules, foreign exchange and I-20 VISA students, persons of identifiable foreign national origins, cannot compete at the varsity level because their parents usually do not accompany them to the United States. Thus, disparate impact based on alienage is present. Therefore, for persons of foreign national origin the sole recourse is to apply for hardship exception under the WIAA rules. WIAA rule 18.22.1 provides:

A. A hardship exists only when some unique circumstances concerning the student's educational, physical or emotional status exist and only when such circumstances are beyond the student's or, where applicable, their family unit' or legal guardian's control.

B. The circumstances must be totally different from those which exist for the majority or even a small minority of students (e.g., usual maturation problems or family situations which do not cause severe and abnormal emotional problems, and academic or athletic deficiencies in a school's curriculum or extracurricular activities do not constitute a hardship).

C. There must be no reason to believe that the decision and/or the execution of the decision concerning the student's academic status was for athletic purposes.

D. The burden of providing evidence that a hardship exists shall be borne by the student.

E. There shall be a direct, causal relationship between the alleged hardship and the student's inability to meet the specific eligibility rule(s).

The trial court found, and we agree, a typical foreign exchange or I-20 VISA student cannot meet the hardship criteria. While the alleged purpose of the rules is to prevent school "jumping" for athletic purposes and to ensure equal treatment, the practical effect is that some students are severely limited in eligibility based solely on their national origin. Concerning similar residence and transfer rules, the Indiana Supreme Court points out:

The rules as presently constituted penalize a student-athlete who wishes to transfer for academic or religious reasons or for any number of other legitimate reasons. Surely, denying eligibility to such transferees in no way furthers IHSAA objectives.

Indiana High Sch. Athletic Ass'n v. Carlberg, 694 N.E.2d 222, 238 (Ind. 1997). Similarly, the application of the rules to Ms. Fusato does not further their stated purposes.

However, the United States Supreme Court has repeatedly held that disparate impact, alone, does not violate the Fourteenth Amendment. *See Harris v. McRae*, 448 U.S. 297, 324 n.26, 100 S. Ct. 2671, 65 L. Ed. 2d 784 (1980) (disparate impact based on financial circumstance); *Personnel Admin. v. Feeney*, 442 U.S. 256, 273, 99 S. Ct. 2282, 2293, 60 L. Ed. 2d 870 (1979) (disparate impact based on gender); *Washington v. Davis*, 426 U.S. 229, 96 S. Ct. 2040, 48 L. Ed. 2d 597 (1976) (disparate impact based on race). Specifically, disparate impact of a suspect class does not trigger strict scrutiny unless the party challenging the government action demonstrates an element of purposeful discrimination or intent. *Macias v. Department of Labor & Indus.*, 100 Wn.2d 263, 269-70, 668 P.2d 1278 (1983).

The burden is on the party alleging discrimination to prove the existence of purposeful discrimination. *Batson v. Kentucky*, 476 U.S. 79, 93, 106 S. Ct. 1712, 90 L. Ed. 2d 69 (1986). The court must undertake "a sensitive inquiry into such circumstantial and direct evidence of intent as may be available." *Id.* (citing *Village of Arlington Heights v. Metropolitan Hous. Dev. Corp.*, 429 U.S. 252, 266, 97 S. Ct. 555, 50 L. Ed. 2d 450 (1977)). Circumstantial evidence may suffice to establish purposeful discrimination. *Batson*, 476 U.S. at 93.

During Ms. Fusato's first administrative hearing, one of the committee members stated in response to an allegation that schools were abusing foreign exchange students:

I don't really think that was the reason. The abusing of the foreign exchange program was not the problem. The problem was that people were bitching and complaining about the fact that we[']re giving them [foreign students] special privileges and these other people are getting turned down[.] [Our] own people within the country, and that's why they changed the rule. I'm sure that's the reason.

For the WIAA to modify its rules to specifically discriminate against foreign exchange or I-20 VISA students in an attempt to make participation fairer for "our students" establishes discriminatory purpose or intent. Thus, strict scrutiny is warranted because we have both discriminatory impact based upon national origin or alienage and discriminatory purpose.

The WIAA now has the heavy burden of proving that it is necessary to discriminate based on national origin to further a compelling interest. It does not seek to meet this burden but argues solely that the rational relationship applies. In view of our rejection of that proposition, our analysis is complete. We decide the strict scrutiny test applies to these facts shifting the burden to the WIAA to show a compelling state interest. We conclude the WIAA has not met its burden to show a compelling state interest was served by the challenged rules. Further, the WIAA has made no effort to demonstrate that the least restrictive regulatory means have been employed to accomplish the stated purposes. Therefore, we hold the challenged residence and transfer rules are invalid under the equal protection clause of the federal constitution and affirm the trial court.

CASES ON THE SUPPLEMENTAL CD

Adams v. Baker, 919 F. Supp. 1496 (D. Kan. 1996). The reader should note the state's justifications for gender discrimination and how the court characterized them.

Baldwin v. Fish and Game Commission of Montana, 436 U.S. 371 (1978). Examine Montana's arguments for treating resident and non-resident hunters differently.

Sullivan v. University Interscholastic League, 616 S.W.2d 170 (Tex. 1981). Texas recognized the dangers of high schools recruiting strong athletes, but the state's answer is an example of how a statute can be overbroad.

QUESTIONS YOU SHOULD BE ABLE TO ANSWER

1. Why doesn't equal protection require that the Augusta National Golf Club (home of the Masters Tournament) allow women to join the club?

2. What are the three different standards of review for classifications under the Equal Protection Clause? Explain which standard should be used for which classification.

3. What does it mean for a statute to be void for being over- or under-inclusive? How can a statue be both over- and under-inclusive simultaneously?

4. In *Fusato v. Washington Interscholastic Activities Association* what evidence did the court have that suggested the discrimination was intentional or purposeful and not simply a matter of disparate impact?

5. Some scholars argue that the middle level of scrutiny for gender classifications should be collapsed into the strict scrutiny category. Explain why you think this is a logical or illogical argument.

REFERENCES

Cases

Adams v. Baker, 919 F. Supp. 1496 (D. Kan. 1996).

Baldwin v. Fish & Game Commission of Montana, 436 U.S. 371 (1978).

Bell v. Lone Oak Independent School District, 507 S.W.2d 636 (Tex. Civ. App. 1974).

B.C. v. Cumberland Regional School District, 531 A.2d 1059 (N.J. Super. 1987).

Blue v. University Interscholastic League, 503 F. Supp. 1030 (N.D. Tex. 1980).

Bolling v. Sharpe 347 U.S. 497 (1954).

Communities for Equity v. Michigan High School Athletic Ass'n, 178 F. Supp. 2d 805 (W.D. Mich. 2001), *aff'd*, 459 F. 3d 676 (6th Cir. 2006).

Craig v. Boren, 429 U.S. 190 (1976).

Force by Force v. Pierce City R-VI School District, 570 F. Supp. 2010 (S.W. Mo. 1983).

Hadley v. Rush Henrietta Center School District, No. 05-CV-6331T, 2007 U.S. Dist LEXIS 30586 (W.D. N.Y., April 25, 2007).

Indiana High School Athletics Ass'n v. Raike, 329 N.E.2d 66 (Ind. Ct. App. 1975).

Jones v. Washington Interscholastic Activities Ass'n, No. C07-711RSL, 2007 U.S. Dist. LEXIS 54711 (W.D. Wash., July 26, 2007).

Ludtke v. Kuhn, 461 F. Supp. 86 (S.D. N.Y. 1978).

Palmer v. Thompson, 403 U.S. 217 (1971).

Schaill by Kross v. Tippecanoe County School Corp., 679 F. Supp. 833 (N.D. Ind. 1988).

Spring Branch Independent School District v. Stamos, 695 S.W.2d 556 (Tex. 1985).

State v. Hunter, 300 P.2d 455 (Ore. 1956).

St. Augustine High School v. Louisiana High School Athletic Ass'n., 270 F. Supp. 767 (E.D. La. 1967), *aff'd.*, 396 F.2d 224 (Fifth Cir. 1968).

Sullivan v. University Interscholastic League, 616 S.W.2d 170 (Tex. 1981).

United States v. Virginia, 518 U.S. 515 (1996).

Publications

Fields, Sarah K. (2005). *Female Gladiators: Gender, Law, and Contact Sport in America*. Champaign, IL: University of Illinois Press.

Karst, Kenneth (1977). Equal Citizenship under the Fourteenth Amendment. *Harvard Law Review 91*, 1–69.

Sullivan, K. M. and Gunther, G. (2007). *Constitutional Law*, 16th ed. Minneapolis: West Publishing.

Legislation

U.S. Constitution, Amend. 5.

U.S. Constitution, Amend. 14 § 1.

42 U.S.C. § 1983.

6.15   Search and Seizure / Right to Privacy

—Margaret E. Ciccolella
UNIVERSITY OF THE PACIFIC

The right of privacy is fundamental to American heritage and to rights guaranteed by the United States Constitution. While the word "privacy" is not found in the United States Constitution, privacy interests are found in "penumbra" of rights guaranteed through the Constitution; e.g., the First, Fourth, Fifth, and Fourteenth Amendments safeguard privacy interests relevant to freedom of expression, substantive due process, equal protection, and search and seizure of one's person and/or personal effects.

The interpretation of the nature and extent of privacy protections have been contested within the context of education and its athletic programs. First Amendment protections dealing with personal conduct and expression have been challenged by considering the authority of the schools to regulate hair length (*Menora v. Illinois High School Assn.*, 1982;), dress (*Dunham v. Pulsifer*, 1970; *Zeller v. Donegal School District*, 1975), on-and-off-court field behavior (*Bunger v. Iowa H.S. Athletic Assn.*, 1972) and marriage/parenthood of student-athletes (*Davis v. Meek*, 1972; *Estay v. LaFourche Parish School Board*, 1969; *Indiana High School Athletic Assn. v. Raike*, 1975; *Perry v. Granada Municipal School District*, 1969). Confidentiality of educational records protected by the Family Educational Rights and Privacy Act, also known as the Buckley Amendment, has been challenged (*Marmo v. NYC Board of Education*, 1968). The Freedom of Information Act, often used as a basis on which to challenge confidentiality has been challenged itself (*Arkansas Gazette Co. v. Southern State College*, 1981). Clearly, privacy exceeds Fourth Amendment protections and is addressed through the Constitution and in federal statutory law.

However, it is the Fourth Amendment of the United States Constitution that is considered the "heart" of privacy protection and is therefore central to any discussion of the issue. It is the primary purpose of this section to focus upon privacy interests of student-athletes as they relate specifically to the Fourth Amendment of the United State Constitution. Perhaps no issue illustrates this better than case law on urinalysis-drug-testing of high school and intercollegiate athletes. The significant case for this section, *University of Colorado v. Derdeyn* (1993), considered random, suspicionless drug testing of college athletes by using a Fourth Amendment analysis. It may be helpful for the reader to refer to Section 6.23, *Drug Testing*, for a review of its significant case, *Vernonia v. Acton*, (1995). These two cases came to different conclusions regarding the constitutionality of drug testing of athletes and offer an opportunity for legal and factual comparisons.

FUNDAMENTAL CONCEPTS

The Fourth Amendment

The Fourth Amendment to the United States Constitution states:

> *The right of the people to be secure in their persons, houses, papers, and effects against unreasonable searches and seizures, shall not be violated, and no Warrant shall issue, but upon probable cause, supported by Oath or affirmation, and particularly describing the place to be searched, and the persons or things to be seized.*

> *(United States Constitution, Amendment IV)*

The Fourth Amendment, made applicable to the states by virtue of the Fourteenth Amendment, guarantees that individuals are protected against *"arbitrary invasions by governmental officials"* (*O'Connor v. Ortega*, 1987). Note that only unreasonable searches and seizures are prohibited. Also, in the context of conduct by law enforcement, warrants based upon probable cause are required.

Once a search or seizure is characterized as "unreasonable," it is unconstitutional and therefore is prohibited. In the context of athletics, searches of lockers, personal items, or a person become potentially serious invasions of privacy by the language of the Fourth Amendment. Valid warrants based upon probable cause are rarely the situation in athletics because school searches are not typically under the authority of law enforcement. More commonly, in the context of public school-aged and college-aged athletes, searches and seizures occur under the authority of school officials.

It is important to distinguish constitutionally permissible from constitutionally prohibited conduct as determined by the Fourth Amendment. Fourth Amendment analysis of search and seizure privacy interests must consider three basic issues. First, does the conduct represent state (governmental) action? Second, is the conduct a search? Third, is the search reasonable?

Is There State Action?

The Fourth Amendment protects individuals from invasions of privacy by the government. It does not protect against the conduct of private individuals or organizations. The NCAA is not subject to Fourth Amendment scrutiny because the regulatory functions of the NCAA are considered to represent private and not state action (*Arlosoroff v. NCAA*, 1984). Action or conduct by state, local, or federal officials is state or governmental action for purposes of the Fourth Amendment. For example, public, not private, schools are subject to Fourth Amendment standards of review.

Is the Conduct a Search?

Under Fourth Amendment analysis, a search occurs when an expectation of privacy which society is prepared to consider reasonable is infringed (*Schaill v. Tippecanoe County School Corp.*, 1989). The United States Supreme Court has held that the collection and testing of urine constitute a search under the Fourth Amendment (*Skinner v. Railway Labor Executives' Assn.*, 1989). This is especially relevant to athletes subject to mandatory urine testing. In *Skinner*, the Court stated:

> It is not disputed, however, that chemical analysis of urine, like that of blood, can reveal a host of private medical facts about an employee, including whether he or she is epileptic, pregnant, or diabetic. Nor can it be disputed that the process of collecting the sample to be tested, which may in some cases involve visual or aural monitoring of the act of urination, itself implicates privacy interests. (pp. 1413–14)

There remains a legitimate expectation of privacy for both the college and public school student that a student's urine is not subject to public scrutiny. The courts continue to hold that the mandatory urine testing of student-athletes constitutes a search and seizure (*University of Colorado v. Derdeyn*, 1993; *O'Halloran v. University of Washington*, 1988; *Vernonia v. Acton*, 1995).

This does not mean that mandatory urine testing of students will result in a violation of the Fourth Amendment. In *O'Halloran v. University of Washington* (1988), the constitutionality of drug testing college athletes was upheld even though it was concluded that, "the NCAA's urine testing program is a search for Fourth Amendment analysis." In 1995, the Supreme Court held that mandatory, random urinalysis testing of public school athletes represented a reasonable search under a Fourth Amendment analysis (*Vernonia v. Acton*, 1995). Most recently, the Supreme Court extended this holding to public school students who participate in competitive extramural activities (*Board of Education v. Earls*, 2002).

It is clear that urine testing of student-athletes represents a search. The more crucial question is whether the search is reasonable. Reasonableness, by considering all of the events or the "totality of the circumstances" surrounding a search, will ultimately determine whether a Fourth Amendment violation has occurred.

Is the Conduct a Reasonable Search?

The Fourth Amendment prohibits only unreasonable searches. However, the test of reasonableness under the Fourth Amendment is not capable of precise definition or mechanical application. The Supreme Court consistently asserts what is "reasonable" depends on the context within which a search takes place (*National Treasury*

Employees Union v. Von Raab, 1989; *Skinner v. Railway Labor Executives' Assn.*, 1989). In *New Jersey v. T.L.O.* (1985), the proper standard for assessing the legality of a school search by school officials was determined. In this case, school officials searched a student's purse for drugs. *The Supreme Court held that reasonableness of a search involved a two-fold inquiry.* First, *was the search justified at its inception*, e.g., was there reasonable suspicion for the search? Second, *was the search reasonable in its scope*, e.g., were the measures adopted reasonably related to the objectives of the search and not excessively intrusive in light of the age and sex of the student and the nature of the infraction?

In light of the *T.L.O.* holding and in the context of warrantless school searches, it is common for a court to determine reasonableness by (1) considering the existence of reasonable suspicion for the search, and (2) balancing the degree of intrusion on individual privacy interests against governmental interests in conducting the search.

Reasonable Suspicion. Reasonable suspicion has been defined as "the existence of reasonable circumstances, reports, information, or reasonable direct observation" leading to the belief that illegal drugs have been used (*Horsemen's Benevolent & Protective Assn. v. State Racing Commission*, 1989). The University of Colorado (CU) amended its suspicionless urine testing program by including a rapid eye examination (REE). REE became the basis for a subsequent mandatory urinalysis on the basis that a positive REE test provided reasonable suspicion of drug use. Other physical and behavioral characteristics were also used as a basis for reasonable suspicion including excessive aggressiveness and poor health habits (*University of Colorado v. Derdeyn*, 1993).

Vernonia v. Acton (1995), which held that random, suspicionless urinalysis testing of public school athletes met the requirements of the Fourth Amendment, had dissents from Justices O'Connor, Stevens, and Souter, who spoke strongly to the historical requirement of suspicion in safeguarding Fourth Amendment privacy interests:

> *For most of our constitutional history, mass, suspicionless searches have been generally considered per se unreasonable within the meaning of the Fourth Amendment. . . . [W]hat the Framers of the Fourth Amendment most strongly opposed, with limited exceptions wholly inapplicable here, were general searches—that is, searches by general warrant, by writ of assistance, by broad statute, or by any other similar authority. Protection of privacy, not evenhandedness, was then and is now the touchstone of the Fourth Amendment. (pp. 2398–2399) [T]here is a substantial basis for concluding that a vigorous regime of suspicion-based testing . . . would have gone a long way toward solving Vernonia's school drug problem while preserving the Fourth Amendment rights of James Acton. (pp. 2403–2404)*

New Jersey v. T.L.O. (1985) required individualized suspicion, but because of the facts of that case, the Court was not required to consider whether circumstances could ever exist that could negate the need for individualized suspicion. *Vernonia v. Acton* (1995) may well have provided the circumstances missing in *New Jersey*. It is interesting to consider the possible role of sport as a factual circumstance leading to this diversion from *New Jersey*. Given the dissent noted above, it will be equally interesting to consider factual distinctions made by the Supreme Court in the future and the role of sport in providing those distinctions.

Balancing Test. In addition to considering the existence of reasonable suspicion, the courts typically balance the degree of the intrusion on an individual's privacy interests against the government's interests in testing.

Privacy Interests of the Student-Athlete

Privacy interests of athletes have included the following arguments (*Hill v. NCAA*, 1994):

1. There are few activities in our society more personal or private than the passing of urine. Therefore, the visual or aural monitoring of urination implicates privacy interests;

2. Monitored urine collection is embarrassing and degrading thereby violating privacy and dignitary interests protected by the Fourth Amendment;

3. Chemical analysis of urine violates medical confidentiality because it can reveal a host of private medical facts, e.g., epilepsy, pregnancy, diabetes;

4. Urinalysis testing interferes with privacy rights associated with the right to control one's own medical treatment, including the right to choose among legal medications;

5. Urinalysis testing attempts to regulate "off-the-field" personal conduct thereby violating the right to engage in constitutional protections for enormously diverse personal action and belief.

Alternatively, it has been argued that athletes subject to drug testing have diminished expectations of privacy rendering a Fourth Amendment analysis an insufficient basis on which to declare a Constitutional violation. For example, "communal undress" inherent in athletic participation suggests a reduced expectation of privacy. Also, health examinations are fairly routine to participants in vigorous activities. In the context of such examinations, viewing and touching is tolerated among relative strangers that would be firmly rejected in other contexts (*O'Halloran v. University of Washington*, 1988). More recently the Supreme Court of the United States in *Vernonia v. Acton* (1995) has stated: "Legitimate privacy expectations are even less with regard to student-athletes. School sports are not for the bashful. They require 'suiting up' before each practice or event, and showering and changing afterwards. Public school locker rooms, the usual sites for these activities, are not notable for the privacy they afford." (pp. 2392–2393).

Governmental Interests Served by Urine Testing

The other side of the balancing test considers the governmental interests served by urine testing. In the context of urine testing of student-athletes, the government must show a special need because the testing exceeds the normal need for law enforcement and occurs in the absence of a warrant or probable cause. A search unsupported by probable cause can be constitutional, we have said, "when special needs, beyond the normal need for law enforcement, make the warrant and probable-cause requirement impracticable" (*Vernonia v. Acton*, 1995, p. 2391).

Examples of special needs that have been successfully asserted to justify warrantless, mandatory urine testing of the intercollegiate athlete include: (1) providing fair and equitable competition, (2) guarding the health and safety of student-athletes, and (3) deterring drug use by testing (*Hill v. NCAA*, 1994; *O'Halloran v. University of Washington*, 1988). With regard to public school athletes, these needs as well as the role of the school standing *in loco parentis* to the children entrusted to it has recently and successfully been argued to support mandatory, random urinalysis testing of public school athletes (*Vernonia v. Acton*, 1995). The doctrine of *in loco parentis* has no role in higher education.

SIGNIFICANT CASE

This case is unique because it holds that a policy of random, suspicionless urine testing of college athletes violates the Fourth Amendment to the United States Constitution. Specifically, this case illustrates the competing privacy interests of the students balanced against the government's interests in testing. The trial court's concluding remarks offer a perspective that may represent a minority view in current cases on this issue but one ultimately supported by Colorado's Supreme Court in this particular case: "We must remember that, after all, it is only athletic games we are concerned with here . . . The integrity of athletic contests cannot be purchased at the costs of privacy interests protected by the Fourth Amendment. . . . A government that invades the privacy of its citizens without compelling reason, no longer abides by the constitutional provisions essential to a free society (*University of Colorado v. Derdeyn*, [1993])."

UNIVERSITY OF COLORADO V. DERDEYN

Supreme Court of Colorado
863 P.2d 929 (1993)

We granted certiorari in order to determine whether random, suspicionless urinalysis-drug-testing of intercollegiate student-athletes by the University of Colorado, Boulder (CU), violates the Fourth Amendment to the United States Constitution or Article II, Section 7, of the Colorado Constitution. Following a bench trial conducted in August of 1989 in which a class of current and prospective CU athletes challenged the constitutionality of CU's drug-testing program, the Boulder County District Court permanently enjoined CU from continuing its program. The trial court found that CU had not obtained voluntary consent from its athletes for such testing, and it declared such testing unconstitutional under both the federal and state constitutions. The Colorado Court of Appeals generally affirmed. See *Derdeyn v. University of Colorado*, 832 P.2d 1031 (Colo. App. 1991). We agree with the court of appeals, that in the absence of voluntary consents, CU's random, suspicionless urinalysis-drug-testing of student athletes violates the Fourth Amendment to the United States Constitution and Article II, Section 7, of the Colorado Constitution. We further agree, that the record supports the finding of the trial court that CU failed to show that consents to such testing given by CU's athletes are voluntary for the purposes of those same constitutional provisions. Accordingly, we affirm the judgment of the court of appeals.

I.

CU began a drug-testing program in the fall of 1984 for its intercollegiate student athletes. CU has since amended its program in various ways, but throughout the existence of the program participation was mandatory in the sense that if an athlete did not sign a form consenting to random testing pursuant to the program, the student was prohibited from participating in intercollegiate athletics at CU.

CU's third amended program, which became effective August 14, 1988, contained numerous changes. First, it added alcohol, "over-the-counter drugs," and "performance-enhancing substances such as anabolic steroids" to the list of drugs for which students could be tested. Second, the term "athlete" was defined to include "all student participants in recognized intercollegiate sports, including but not limited to student athletes, cheerleaders, student trainers and student managers." Third, random "rapid eye examination (REE)" testing was substituted for random urinalysis, and a urinalysis was performed only after a "finding of reasonable suspicion that an athlete has used drugs," and at the athlete's annual physical examination. Failure to perform adequately on an REE was considered "prima facie reasonable suspicion of drug use [except with regard to steroids]," and the student was required to provide a urine specimen for testing purposes if the student did not perform adequately on the REE. In addition, if a student exhibited "physical or behavioral characteristics indicating drug use including, but not limited to: tardiness, absenteeism, poor heath [sic] habits, emotional swings, unexplained performance changes, and/or excessive aggressiveness," this was also considered reasonable suspicion of drug use, and the student was required to take a urine test. Fourth, urine samples were to be collected "within the Athletic Department facilities," and athletes were "directed to provide a urine specimen in a private and enclosed area" while a monitor remained outside. The monitor would then receive "the sample from the athlete and check the sample for appropriate color, temperature, specific gravity and other properties to determine that no substitution or tampering has occurred." Fifth, the athletes were required to give their consent to releasing test results to the Head Athletic Trainer at [CU]; my parent(s) or legal guardian(s), if I am under the age of 21; the head coach of any intercollegiate sport in which I am a team member;

the Athletic Director of [CU]; my work supervisor (if applicable) and the Drug Counseling Program at the Wardenburg Student Health Center.

Following a bench trial conducted in August of 1989, the trial court entered its written findings of fact, conclusions of law, and order and judgment. The trial court found that "obtaining a monitored urine sample is a substantial invasion of privacy." It found that the REE does not function, in any sense, as "reasonable suspicion" of drug use. Because of its disastrous ability to predict drug use, it functions more as an avenue to inject arbitrary judgments into an otherwise random selection of students for testing. Similarly, it found that "like the REE, the [other] reasonable suspicion criteria [as set forth by CU] are incapable of indicating drug use to any degree" (emphasis in original). The trial court also found that while the University labels the program as a "Drug Education Program", there is little education. . . . There is no ongoing educational component of the program. Testing is clearly its major focus. Finally, the trial court found that there is no evidence that the University instituted its program in response to any actual drug abuse problem among its student athletes. There is no evidence that any person has ever been injured in any way because of the use of drugs by a student athlete while practicing or playing a sport.

The fact that CU's athletes signed forms consenting to random drug testing did not alter the trial court's conclusion. Rather, the trial court found that CU failed to demonstrate that the consents given by the athletes were voluntary, and also held that "no consent can be voluntary where the failure to consent results in a denial of the governmental benefit."

On these bases, the trial court declared that CU's drug-testing program was unconstitutional. It permanently enjoined CU from "requiring any urine samples from student athletes for the purposes of drug testing, whether those tests occur on a random basis or as a result of the 'reasonable suspicion' criteria stated," and it permanently enjoined CU from "requiring student athletes participation in the Rapid Eye Exam procedure." In addition, the trial court held that "reasonable suspicion" is not the appropriate standard to warrant urinalysis-drug-testing of athletes by CU, and that such testing is impermissible absent probable cause under either the Fourth Amendment or Article II, Section 7, of the Colorado Constitution.

The Colorado Court of Appeals generally affirmed.

We granted CU's petition for writ of certiorari on the following issues:

- In the context of the University's drug-testing program, is suspicionless drug testing constitutionally reasonable?

- Can student athletes give valid consent to the University's drug-testing program if their consent is

a condition of participation in intercollegiate athletics at the University?

II.

The Fourth Amendment to the United States Constitution protects individuals from unreasonable searches conducted by the government, *Von Raab*, 489 U.S. at 665, even when the government acts as the administrator of an athletic program in a state school or university. See *Schaill ex rel. Kross v. Tippecanoe County Sch. Corp.*, 864 F.2d 1309 (7th Cir. 1989); *Brooks v. East Chambers Consol. Indep. Sch. Dist.*, 730 F. Supp. 759 (S.D. Tex. 1989); cf. *New Jersey v. T.L.O.*, 469 U.S. 325, 333-37, 83 L. Ed. 2d 720, 105 S. Ct. 733 (1985) (holding that the Fourth Amendment prohibits unreasonable searches and seizures conducted by public school officials acting as civil authorities). Furthermore, because it is clear that the collection and testing of urine intrudes upon expectations of privacy that society has long recognized as reasonable, . . . these intrusions must be deemed searches under the Fourth Amendment *Skinner*, 489 U.S. at 617. It follows that CU's urinalysis-drug-testing program must meet the reasonableness requirement of the Fourth Amendment.

A search must usually be supported by a warrant issued upon probable cause. Von Raab, 489 U.S. at 665. However, neither a warrant, nor probable cause, nor any measure of individualized suspicion is an indispensable component of reasonableness in every circumstance. *Id.*; Skinner, 489 U.S. at 618-24. Rather, where a Fourth Amendment intrusion serves special governmental needs, beyond the normal need for law enforcement, it is necessary to balance the individual's privacy expectations against the Government's interests to determine whether it is impractical to require a warrant or some level of individualized suspicion in the particular context.

CU advances alternative theories to support its claim that its drug-testing program is reasonable under the Fourth Amendment. First, CU argues that its drug-testing program is reasonable under the Fourth Amendment because of the student athletes' diminished expectations of privacy and the compelling governmental interests served by the program. Second, CU argues that even if its drug-testing program is not otherwise constitutionally reasonable, there is no constitutional violation because its student athletes voluntarily consent to testing. We address these arguments in turn.

A.

CU argues that its drug-testing program is reasonable under the Fourth Amendment because of the student athletes' diminished expectations of privacy and the compelling governmental interests served by the program. We therefore consider in turn (1) the degree to which CU's drug-testing program intrudes on the reasonable expectations of privacy of student athletes and (2) the magnitude of the governmental interests served by the program. We then balance these factors in order to determine whether CU's drug-testing program is reasonable under the Fourth Amendment.

1.

[W]e now consider CU's arguments that the magnitude of the intrusion of its drug-testing program on the reasonable expectations of privacy of its student athletes was minimal.

(a) CU argues that collection of the urine sample in a closed stall with aural monitoring minimizes any intrusion. We agree that aural monitoring is less intrusive than visual monitoring, but as we have already noted, the trial court found that CU and the other defendants have refused to agree that they will not return to the policy which was initially challenged in this class action [i.e., the policy according to which students were visually monitored while providing a urine sample]. In fact, defendants have indicated that there are circumstances under which they would return to that policy.

(b) CU argues that student athletes' expectations of privacy with regard to urinalysis are diminished because they routinely give urine samples as part of an annual, general medical examination, and because they regularly undergo close physical contact with trainers. In this regard, it is true that the United States Supreme Court has recognized that urine tests are less intrusive when the "sample is . . . collected in a medical environment, by personnel unrelated to the [employee's] employer, and is thus not unlike similar procedures encountered often in the context of a regular physical examination." Skinner, 489 U.S. at 626-27. Similarly, the Seventh Circuit Court of Appeals has stated that if an individual is required by his job to undergo frequent medical examinations, then that individual will perceive random urinalysis for drug-testing purposes as being less intrusive. Dimeo, 943 F.2d at 682. In this case, however, the trial court heard testimony that samples for random urinalysis-drug-testing were not collected in a medical environment by persons unrelated to the athletic program.

(c) CU argues that student athletes' expectations of privacy with regard to urinalysis are diminished because they submit to extensive regulation of their on- and off-campus behavior, including maintenance of required levels of academic performance, monitoring of course selection, training rules, mandatory practice sessions, diet restrictions, attendance at study halls, curfews, and prohibitions on alcohol and drug use.

Although it is obviously not amenable to precise calculation, it is at least doubtful that the testimony relied upon by CU fully supports CU's assertion that its student athletes are "extensively regulated in their on and off-campus behavior," especially with regard to all of the particulars that CU asserts. More importantly, none of the types of regulation relied on by CU entails an intrusion on privacy interests of the nature or extent involved in monitored collection of urine samples.

(d) CU argues that student athletes' expectations of privacy with regard to urinalysis are diminished because they must submit to the NCAA's random urinalysis-drug-testing program as a condition of participating in NCAA competition. In this regard, CU's athletic director testified that at NCAA championship events, the NCAA conducts random drug testing of athletes as well as testing of the top three finishers and certain starting players, and evidence in the record suggests that NCAA athletes are required to sign consent forms to such testing.

Despite the fact that students might dislike the NCAA drug-testing program, it seems that they must consent to it in order to be NCAA athletes, and submission to one such program could reduce the intrusiveness of having to submit to another. On the other hand, the trial court heard testimony suggesting that part of what is intrusive about the CU program is that it transformed what might otherwise be friendly, trusting, and caring relations between trainers and athletes into untrusting and confrontational relations.

(e) CU argues that student athletes' expectations of privacy with regard to urinalysis are diminished because the consequences of refusing to provide a urine sample are not severe. We appreciate that in comparison to losing one's job, as would be the consequence in some government employee/drug-testing cases, e.g., Bostic, 650 F.Supp. at 249, not being able to participate in intercollegiate athletics can be regarded as less of a burden. It is, to be sure, only a very small percentage of college athletes whose college "careers" are essential as stepping stones to lucrative contracts—or to any contract—as professional athletes. On the other hand, however, we must also recognize that many intercollegiate athletes who otherwise could not afford a college education receive athletic scholarships that enable them to obtain a college degree and thereby increase their earning potential.

(f) Finally, CU argues that student athletes expectations of privacy with regard to urinalysis are diminished because positive test results are confidential and are not used for the purposes of criminal law enforcement. It is true that an intrusion by the government outside the context of criminal law enforcement is generally less of an intrusion than one for the purposes of law enforcement. However, as a matter of law, we already take this fact into account when we analyze this case according to the standards of cases like Skinner and Von Raab, rather than according to the standards of typical cases in the area of criminal procedure where there are very few and well defined exceptions to the requirement of a warrant based on probable cause. In other words, were we to attribute less weight to the students' privacy interests because this is not a criminal case, and also start with the premise that Skinner and Von Raab control, we would be, in effect, giving double weight in our analysis to the fact that we are not dealing with an issue in criminal procedure.

(g) Having reviewed the record in light of each of CU's assertions, it is clear that in some places CU seems to overstate its case, while in others, it has a valid point. On balance, however, we are in full agreement with the conclusion of the trial court that CU's random, suspicionless urinalysis-drug-testing of athletes is an "intrusion [that] is clearly significant."

2.

CU asserts several interests in maintaining its drug-testing program. These interests are preparing its athletes for drug testing in NCAA championship events, promoting the integrity of its athletic program, preventing drug use by other students who look to athletes as role models, ensuring fair competition, and protecting the health and safety of intercollegiate athletes.

We begin our consideration of these interests by observing that suspicionless urinalysis-drug-testing by the government has been upheld in numerous cases, and in many of those cases, courts have characterized the relevant government interests as "compelling." Skinner, 489 U.S. at 628 (government has "compelling" interest in testing railroad employees whose "duties [are] fraught with such risks of injury to others that even a momentary lapse of attention can have disastrous consequences"); Von Raab, 489 U.S. at 670 (government has "compelling interest in ensuring that front-line [drug] interdiction personnel [in the United States Customs Service] are physically fit, and have unimpeachable integrity and judgment"); Id. at 677 (government has a compelling interest in protecting truly sensitive information from those who might compromise such information); Id. at 679 (government has "compelling interests in preventing the promotion of drug users to positions where they might endanger the integrity of our Nation's borders or the life of the citizenry"); Cheney, 884 F.2d at 610 (government has a "compelling safety interest in ensuring that the approximately 2,800 civilians who fly and service its airplanes and helicopters are not impaired by drugs"). However, the Supreme Court has not held that only a "compelling" interest will suffice, see Skinner, 489 U.S. at 624; cf. Von Raab, 489 U.S. at 666, and some courts have upheld suspicionless urinalysis-drug-testing by the government without finding a compelling interest. Dimeo, 943 F.2d at 681, 683, 685 (explaining that decreasing levels of intrusiveness require decreasing levels of government justification, declining to characterize as compelling the government's interest in protecting professional jockeys, starters, and outriders from injuring one another at the race track, characterizing the state's financial interest as "substantial," and holding that these two interests outweigh "the very limited privacy interest[s]" of professional jock-

eys, starters, and outriders); International Bhd. of Elec. Workers, Local 1245 v. Skinner, 913 F.2d 1454, 1462, 1463, 1464 (9th Cir. 1990) (finding that the government has a "great" interest in the safety of the natural gas and hazardous liquid pipeline industry, and holding that this "strong" interest is sufficient to justify random urinalysis testing of pipeline workers). Hence, rather than trying to characterize CU's interests as "compelling," "strong," "substantial," or of some lesser degree of importance, we think it is more instructive simply to compare them with other types of commonly asserted interests that have been held sufficient or insufficient to justify similar intrusions.

CU asserts no significant public safety or national security interests. This is not by itself dispositive, but absent a showing by CU that its athletes have a greatly diminished expectation of privacy or that its program is not significantly intrusive, the great majority of cases following Skinner and Von Raab clearly militate against the conclusion that CU's program is a reasonable exercise of state power under the Fourth Amendment. This is so despite the fact that CU's interest in protecting the health and safety of its intercollegiate athletes, like its interest in protecting all of its students, is unquestionably significant.

We have not been persuaded that CU's athletes have a greatly diminished expectation of privacy, nor are we persuaded that CU's program is not significantly intrusive. In addition, we question whether some of the interests asserted by CU are even significant for Fourth Amendment purposes. For example, although the integrity of its athletic program is, like all the other interests asserted by CU, a valid and commendable one, it does not seem to be very significant for Fourth Amendment purposes. See Local 1245 v. NRC, 966 F.2d at 525 (In evaluating a program for random drug testing of employees absent individualized suspicion, the court said, "The NRC wisely decided to refrain from pursuing its integrity of the workforce rationale on appeal. This rationale has almost uniformly been rejected by the courts as insufficient to justify drug testing of employees."); O'Grady, 888 F.2d at 1196. Similarly, although the promotion of fair competition builds character in athletes and enhances the entertainment value of athletic events, CU does not explain why the promotion of fair competition is itself an important governmental interest, just as it does not explain why preventing the disqualification of its athletes at sporting events is an important governmental interest.

We therefore hold, based on a balancing of the privacy interests of the student athletes and the governmental interests of CU, that CU's drug-testing program is unconstitutional under the Fourth Amendment. More specifically, we hold that random, suspicionless urinalysis-drug-testing by CU of student athletes is unconstitutional under the Fourth Amendment if that testing is conducted according to the procedures utilized in any of CU's drug-testing programs to the date of trial, or if that testing is conducted in a manner substantially similar to any of the procedures utilized in any of CU's drug-testing programs to the date of trial. Furthermore, because the Colorado Constitution provides at least as much protection from unreasonable searches and seizures as does the Fourth Amendment, CU's drug-testing program is also unconstitutional under Article II, Section 7, of the Colorado Constitution.

B.

CU asserts, however, that even if its drug-testing program is not otherwise constitutionally reasonable, there is no constitutional violation because its student athletes voluntarily consent to testing. We next address that argument.

A warrantless search of an individual is generally reasonable under the Fourth Amendment if the individual has voluntarily consented to it. *Schneckloth v. Bustamonte*, 412 U.S. 218, 219, 222, 36 L. Ed. 2d 854, 93 S. Ct. 2041 (1973). A voluntary consent to a search is "a consent intelligently and freely given, without any duress, coercion or subtle promises or threats calculated to flaw the free and unconstrained nature of the decision." *People v. Carlson*, 677 P.2d 310, 318 (Colo. 1984) (citing Bustamonte, 412 U.S. 218, 36 L. Ed. 2d 854, 93 S. Ct. 2041, and *People v. Helm*, 633 P.2d 1071 (Colo. 1981)). Whether consent to a search was voluntary "is a question of fact to be determined from all the circumstances. . . ." Bustamonte, 412 U.S. at 248–49.

The trial court heard specific direct testimony from several intercollegiate student athletes who described how and when they were presented with consent forms to sign, and why they signed them. CU had the opportunity to cross-examine these students, and to present direct testimony of its own. The intercollegiate student athlete who testified on behalf of CU was not asked about how or when she was told of the drug-testing program, how or when she was presented with a consent form to sign, or why she signed the form. The Athletic Director for CU and CU's Head Athletic Trainer testified in general about how and when intercollegiate student athletes are notified about the drug-testing program, although neither testified about how and when the students are actually presented with consent forms to sign.

The evidence produced during this trial failed to establish that the consents given by the University's student-athletes are voluntary. It is quite clear that they are "coerced" for constitutional purposes by the fact that there can be no participation in athletics without a signed consent.

The trial court permanently enjoined CU "from requiring any urine samples from student athletes for the purposes of drug testing. . . ." In view of our conclusion that it was unnecessary to address the unconstitutional conditions issue, we recognize the possibility that in the future CU might be able to devise a program involving truly voluntary consents to drug testing. In such event, CU is free to apply for modification or dissolution of the injunction.

III.

For the foregoing reasons, we affirm the judgment of the court of appeals.

CASES ON THE SUPPLEMENTAL CD

Brannum v. Overton County School Board, (2008 Tennessee WESTLAW 06-5931). Middle-school students successfully sued alleging violations of their privacy rights under the Fourth Amendment when video-surveillance cameras were installed in locker rooms.

Hill v. NCAA, 7 Cal.4th 1 (1994). Stanford University student-athletes sued contending that the NCAA's drug testing program violated the right of privacy as explicitly guaranteed under the California Constitution. The Fourth Amendment was not used since a private actor's conduct was at issue. This case meticulously analyzes privacy rights, examines the competing arguments of the NCAA and students, and details the requirements for a privacy cause of action.

Wooten v. Pleasant Hope R-VI School District, 139 F.Supp.2d 835 (2000). High school student sued alleging common law violations of privacy when her coach publicly disclosed her dismissal from the softball team. Public disclosure of private facts and the distinction of false light and defamation are specifically addressed in this case.

QUESTIONS YOU SHOULD BE ABLE TO ANSWER

1. What language in the Fourth Amendment protects against privacy intrusions by government?

2. The Fourth Amendment protects against "unreasonable" searches. Define and give an example of a "search". Describe/explain the analysis used to determine a "reasonable search."

3. On what basis has it been concluded that student-athletes have "diminished expectations of privacy" with regard to a Fourth Amendment analysis?

4. In addition to drug testing, give examples of privacy interests of student-athletes that have been or could be the subject of litigation?

5. *University of Colorado v. Derdeyn* (1993) is a unique case in that it held that the drug-testing program of a public University violated the Fourth Amendment privacy interests of student-athletes. Distinguish this case from others reaching a different conclusion.

REFERENCES

Cases

Arkansas Gazette Co. v. Southern State College, 620 S.W.2d 258 (1981).

Arlosoroff v. NCAA, 746 F.2d 1019 (1984).

Board of Education v. Earls, 122 S.Ct. 2559.

Bunger v. Iowa H. S. Athletic Assn., 197 N.W.2d 555 (1972).

Davis v. Meek, 344 F. Supp. 298 (1972).

Dunham v. Pulsifer, 312 F. Supp. 41 (1970).

Estay v. LaFourche Parish School Board, 230 So.2d 443 (1969).

Hill v. National Collegiate Athletic Assn., 865 P.2d 633 (1994).

Horsemen's Benevolent & Protective Assn. v. State Racing Commission, 532 N.E.2d 644 (1989).

Indiana High School Athletic Assn. v. Raike, 329 N.E.2d 66 (1975).

Marmo v. NYC Board of Education, 289 N.Y.S.2d 51 (1968).

Menora v. Illinois High School Assn., 683 F.2d 1030 (1982).

National Treasury Employees Union v. Von Raab, 109 S.Ct. 1384 (1989).

New Jersey v. T.L.O., 105 S.Ct. 733 (1985).

O'Connor v. Ortega, 107 S.Ct. 1492 (1987).

O'Halloran v. University of Washington, 679 F. Supp. 997 (1988).

Perry v. Granada Municipal School District, 300 F. Supp. 748 (1969).

Schaill v. Tippecanoe County School Corporation, 864 F.2d. 1309 (1989).

Skinner v. Railway Labor Executives' Assn., 109 S.Ct. 1402 (1989).

University of Colorado v. Derdeyn, 863 P.2d 929 (1993).

Vernonia School District 47J v. Acton, 115 S.Ct. 2386 (1995).

Zeller v. Donegal School District, 517 F.2d 600 (1975).

Legislation

United States Constitution, Amend. 1.

United States Constitution, Amend. 4.

United States Constitution, Amend. 14.

6.20 Recreation and Sport Management Applications

6.21 Voluntary Associations and Eligibility Issues

—Colleen Colles
NICHOLS COLLEGE

—Jo Williams
UNIVERSITY OF SOUTHERN MAINE

By definition, a **voluntary association** is, "a group of individuals joined together on the basis of mutual interest or common objectives, especially a business group that is not organized or constituted as a legal entity" (*Random House,* 2009). Accordingly, state high school athletic associations, the National Federation of High Schools (NFHS), the National Collegiate Athletic Association (NCAA), the National Parks and Recreation Association (NPRA) and the Boy and Girl Scouts of America are all examples of voluntary sport and recreation associations (see also Section 6.26, *Private Clubs in Sport and Recreation*).

In reviewing the rules voluntary associations establish for eligibility or the right to participate in the organization, the courts have historically been reluctant to overturn the bylaws, rules, and regulations of these associations unless they violate constitutional law, public policy or were enforced in an **arbitrary or capricious** manner (see *Gorman v. St. Raphael Academy,* 2004). By joining voluntary associations, the courts have held that participants agree to follow the rules and regulations of such organizations (*Indiana High School Athletic Association v. Reyes,* 1997).

The following section examines the jurisdiction of courts with regard to voluntary associations and some of the specific eligibility requirements enacted by such organizations. In particular, the section will examine the eligibility requirements of both state high school athletic associations and the NCAA.

FUNDAMENTAL CONCEPTS

Voluntary associations get their authority to govern through a combination of federal, state, and local legislation, and in some cases, litigation (Conn, 2003). States often grant school boards the authority to join governing associations, thereby relieving themselves of the oversight, decision-making and enforcement. Local schools have significant independence in determining the rules and regulations regarding their participation in interscholastic sports; however, state athletic associations play a significant role by providing state-wide governance for interscholastic athletics (Mitten, Davis, Smith & Berry, 2005).

Judicial Review

Generally, the courts will not interfere with the internal affairs of a voluntary association. For example in *Rottmann v. Penn Interscholastic Athletics Association* (2004), the court held that:

> In the absence of mistake, fraud, collusion or arbitrariness, the decisions of such associations will be accepted by the courts as conclusive. Such associations may adopt reasonable rules which will be deemed

valid and binding upon the members of the association unless the rule violates some law or public policy. It is not the responsibility of the federal courts to inquire into the expediency, practicability, or wisdom of those regulations (page 933).

As noted in *NCAA v. Yeo* (2005), "judicial intervention in [student athletic disputes] often does more harm than good . . ." and "judges are not 'super referees.'" This notion of judicial deference to the associations was highlighted by the court in *NCAA v. Lasege* (2001), when it stated that members of voluntary associations should be free from unwarranted interference from the courts and members should be allowed to "paddle their own canoe."

However, there are limited exceptions to this non-interference tenet. For example, in *Florida High School Athletic Association v. Marazzito* (2005), the court affirmed that intervention in the internal affairs of a voluntary association may be appropriate under **exceptional circumstances**. Specifically, a court should only intervene under the following two conditions: (1) a substantial property, contract or economic rights will be adversely affected by the association's action and the internal procedures of the association were unfair or inadequate or (2) the association acted maliciously or in bad faith.

The courts have also consistently ruled that the regulations and/or decisions of associations cannot be unreasonable, arbitrary, or capricious (*Indiana High School Athletic Association v. Durham*, 2001; *Gorman v. St. Raphael Academy*, 2004). When allegations of "unreasonableness" arise, courts will decide if the rule has a rational relationship to a reasonable goal of the association (Mitten, et al, 2005).

It is important to note that the member schools are considered "voluntary" members of the governing associations, so judicial review is very limited; however, students are not deemed "voluntary" members and are therefore afforded the stricter arbitrary and capricious standard of review. The focus of many lawsuits involving voluntary sport and recreation associations is on the arbitrary and capricious standard and violations of constitutional rights.

Arbitrary and Capricious Standard

In *Indiana High School Athletic Association v. Carlberg* (1997), the Supreme Court of Indiana found that the transfer rule advanced a legitimate goal of the IHSAA, and as enforced against Carlberg was not arbitrary and capricious and therefore did not violate the student's federal right of equal protection. In reaching this decision, two important points were noted by the court. First, the arbitrary and capricious standard of review is narrow and the court cannot substitute its judgment for the judgment of the IHSAA. Second, the court stated "the rule or decision will be found to be arbitrary and capricious "only where it is willful and unreasonable, without consideration and in disregard of the facts or circumstances in the case, or without some basis which would lead a reasonable and honest person to the same conclusion."

In another case involving a transfer student's request for a hardship exception, the IHSAA's decision to deny the student-athlete eligibility was deemed arbitrary and capricious because the IHSAA did not take into account that a substantial change to the family's financial condition had occurred and that the change was out of the student's control. Thus, the court determined that the student should have met the requirements for a hardship waiver (*IHAA v. Durham*, 2001).

State or Federal Constitutional Rights

Since high school athletic associations are widely accepted as **state actors**, the decisions of these associations are subject to constitutional review. (*Brentwood Academy v. Tennessee Secondary School Athletic Association*, 2001; *Communities for Equity v. Michigan High School Athletic Association*, 2000) (see also Section 6.12, *State Action*). As state actors, these voluntary associations cannot deny citizens equal protection and/or due process guaranteed by the Federal Constitution. (see Section 6.14, *Equal Protection*). The **Equal Protection Clause of the Fourteenth Amendment** provides a constitutional method for checking the fairness of the application of the law. If an association cannot demonstrate a connection between the rule and its purpose, then an equal protection violation may have occurred. Thus, voluntary associations must practice due diligence by providing procedural due process whenever disciplinary action is taken.

It should be noted however that while high school athletic associations have been deemed state actors for constitutional purposes, thereby limiting their regulatory authority, the NCAA has not. Therefore, while the actions of state high school associations are subject to Constitutional review, the courts will not review those of the NCAA (see *NCAA v. Tarkanian,* 1988).

High School Privilege

High school eligibility rules are essentially the products of state high school activities/athletics associations. Typically, local school districts' representatives to the association decide in parliamentary fashion the rules for conducting the athletic events throughout the state. Such agreement is necessary to ensure that fairness reigns in athletics competition across the state. These associations are created to deal with the management of **extracurricular activities,** which by definition are all those activities for students that are sponsored or sanctioned by an educational institution that supplement or complement, but are not a part of, the institution's required academic program or regular curriculum. Participation is voluntary and, more important, a *privilege* in the reasoning of courts, which may be extended at the discretion of the school board. The board, therefore, may decide, usually through its participation in the state high school athletics association, the terms under which students may exercise the privilege. When eligibility standards are challenged in the courts, they must in most circumstances withstand only rational basis scrutiny (see Section 6.14, *Equal Protection*). This means that if the requirements are rationally related to the purpose of activity and not arbitrary, capricious, or unjustly discriminatory, they will be upheld by the courts (*Letendre v. Missouri State High School Activities Association,* 2002; see the Supplemental CD).

Academic Standards. Alternative means of demonstrating academic eligibility for athletic participation in high schools include grade point average (GPA), courses passed in previous and/or current semesters, courses passed in previous year, percent daily attendance, enrollment in minimum number of classes, enrollment in minimum full-credit courses, GPA or passing grades in current or previous grading periods, and maintaining a grade of 70 in each class during six-week grading period to stay eligible for the next six-week grading period (Texas). Thus, a variety of standards are used by different states to demonstrate academic qualification for athletic participation in high schools.

Transfer Rules. High school associations create transfer rules to preclude student-athletes from "**jumping**" (enrolling in different school) for reasons pertaining to athletics. There are many legitimate reasons for transfers involving such things as family relocations, employment, divorce, etc., and as such, constitute a basis for exceptions within the rules. Transfer rules appear to be popular targets for legal challenges based upon claims of violations of equal protection, freedom of religion, right to travel, and due process (see *Beck v. Missouri State High School Activities Association,* (1993). In 1997, the Texas University Interscholastic League faced nine (9) court cases in situations involving transferring for athletic purposes. Yet courts have generally upheld transfer rules under rational judicial scrutiny. Since no fundamental right is being violated, nor any suspect class being established, the transfer rule need only be rationally related to a legitimate state interest to be upheld by the court. If, however, the student-athlete can establish fraud, collusion, or arbitrariness, the possibility exists for a successful challenge.

Home-Schooled Student Eligibility

Should students schooled at home be permitted to participate for local school athletic teams? A number of states, including Arizona, Colorado, Florida, Idaho, Iowa, Maine, Michigan, Minnesota, New Hampshire, North Dakota, Oregon, Utah, Vermont and Washington, currently require public schools to allow homeschoolers access to sports. Potential student-athletes must meet specific eligibility requirements. Even though some state legislatures have supported homeschoolers in providing access to the privilege of public school activities, the courts in many states have taken a different position denying claims that statutory and constitutional rights have been violated.

In *Jones v. West Virginia State Board of Education* (2005), the state Supreme Court overturned a trial court ruling that the West Virginia Secondary School Activities Commission (WVSSAC) violated a home-schooled student's rights to equal protection and breached its duty to promulgate reasonable rules and regulations. In reversing the decision, the Supreme Court stated that the WVSSAC did not violate the student's rights because the challenged statute pertained to providing educational resources, not athletic resources, to home-schooled students. The court also stated that there is no fundamental right to participate in interscholastic sport and the school had a rational basis for excluding homeschooled children from participating in interscholastic sports. Similarly, in *Angstadt v. Midd-West School District* (2003), the parents of a home-schooled girl alleged violations of her First and Fourteenth Amendment rights when, as an enrolled ninth grade student at a local charter school, she was denied participation in the local public school district's athletic programs. She alleged she was deprived of a liberty or property interest without due process of law because of unreasonable, arbitrary, and capricious requirements. Again, the courts found no statutory right to participate in extracurricular activities.

In the meantime, athletic competitions and leagues for "homeschoolers" have become more commonplace at the local, regional and national levels. The Homeschool World Series Association in Baseball and the National Christian Homeschool Basketball Championship have seen significant growth.

Redshirting. The practice of delaying or postponing an athlete's competition in order to extend the athlete's career is known as "**redshirting.**" For purposes of maximizing athletic success, redshirting is an effective strategy to take advantage of an extra year's growth and maturity and, of course, skill development. Moreover, parents of team sport athletes have demonstrated a willingness to "hold back" students a year in school so as to create an aggregate of student-athletes more likely to win championships. High school athletics association rules do not permit the practice of redshirting because it is contrary to the educational mission. Furthermore, redshirting creates unfair competition advantages, possible dangerous mismatches, and unwarranted exclusion of peer student-athletes.

On the other hand, high school athletics associations recognize illness or injury and purely academic determinations of grade level as legitimate reasons for exceptions to rules precluding redshirting and make appropriate allowances. To handle the problem of redshirting, however, **rules of longevity** must be invoked. Longevity rules determine the limits for participation in terms of (1) semesters/years allowed to complete competition, and (2) a maximum age beyond which interscholastic competition may not continue. For example, most high school association rules limit a student athlete to eight consecutive semesters in which to complete interscholastic competition. Similarly, most associations do not permit competition among student-athletes who have reached their nineteenth birthday before beginning his/her senior year. In general, courts have agreed with the rational argument that longevity and redshirting regulations preserve the privilege of interscholastic sports competition, consistent with their educational mission.

Based on concerns in this area, the NCAA adopted new legislation in 2007 that focused on academic preparation and placed limitations on the amount of time needed to complete core curriculum requirements (Bylaw 14.3.1.2.1). Upon entering high school in ninth grade, students must meet academic eligibility standards in four years.

Separating Public and Private Schools

Proposals to separate private and public high schools for postseason competitions have been addressed by several state athletic associations. Proponents of the measures believe that separating the schools will address the competitive inequities created by the private schools' ability to "recruit" students regardless of geographic boundaries. Opponents argue that the separation will dilute the competition and cause major restructuring for the governing associations (Evans, 2005). Resistance from a state high school athletic association was highlighted in *Christian Heritage Academy v. Oklahoma Secondary School Activities Association*, (2007). This case was originally filed in 1998 as Christian Heritage Academy was denied the opportunity to participate in state athletic competition (see the Supplemental CD).

Intercollegiate Regulations

Individual eligibility rules for intercollegiate competition begin at the specific institution where the student is enrolled. Depending upon the institution's characteristics and mission, specific eligibility standards for representing that institution in intercollegiate athletic competition may be imposed. Such standards must reflect at a minimum the requirements of the conference in which it competes and, further, the association of conferences and institutions in which it holds membership. The largest such association of four-year institutions is the National Collegiate Athletic Association (NCAA). This discussion will focus on the eligibility rules and bylaws of the NCAA and various legal challenges of those rules (see www.NCAA.org).

Article 1.3.1 of the *NCAA Manual* (2008–09) declares its basic purpose:

> *The competitive athletics programs of member institutions are designed to be a vital part of the educational system. A basic purpose of this Association is to maintain intercollegiate athletics as an integral part of the educational program and the athlete as an integral part of the student body and, by so doing, retain a clear line of demarcation between intercollegiate athletics and professional sports (p. 1).*

Thus, the NCAA is a private, voluntary association of four-year institutions that share a common interest in preserving amateur intercollegiate athletics as part of the educational mission.

Academic Regulations. To maintain the educational mission, the NCAA has legislated at the annual conventions of its members explicit rules for qualifying individuals academically for competition on two dimensions: initial and continuing. To meet *initial* qualifications, that is, to be academically eligible to compete upon matriculation, the student-athlete must currently demonstrate the following (Bylaw 14.3.1.1):

1. Graduation from high school;

2. Successful completion of a required core curriculum of 16 approved academic courses in specified subjects;

3. Specified minimum GPA in the core curriculum; and

4. Specified minimum SAT or ACT score.

Determination of **initial eligibility** is conducted by the Eligibility Center and includes a review of academic and amateurism standards. If the student satisfactorily meets the standards, the student is deemed a "qualifier" and is academically eligible to participate and receive athletically related financial aid. If the standards are not met, the applicant is restricted from competing (but may practice), may not receive athletically related financial aid, and surrenders one of his or her four years of competition eligibility.

To satisfy **continuing eligibility** requirements, the student-athlete must demonstrate a consistent record of progress toward a degree. To register "satisfactory progress" the student-athlete's academic record at the beginning of the fall semester or quarter of each year in residence must indicate completion of a requisite percent of course requirements in the student-athlete's particular academic program at a requisite percent of the GPA required for graduation at the particular institution.

In addition, the student-athlete must be enrolled full-time (minimum 12 semester credit hours) in order to maintain current athletic eligibility. Dropping below full-time enrollment immediately disqualifies the student from athletic competition.

Amateurism. As stated previously, the NCAA's basic purpose highlights a focus on the amateur status of student athletes and the NCAA Manual (2008–09) consistently refers to the maintenance of a "clear line of demarcation between intercollegiate athletics and professional sports" (p. 1, p. 61). Bylaws applied to amateurism contain restrictions on activities that occur prior to and after enrollment. Initial amateur certification is managed by the Eligibility Center and must be retained throughout the student-athletes enrollment. Amateurism status is closely monitored in areas including involvement with professional teams, use of agents, employment, and promotional activities.

A significant case challenging the NCAA's authority to regulate eligibility is *Bloom v. NCAA*, (2004) (see the Supplemental CD). This case highlighted the application of the law with regard to voluntary associations and addressed Bloom's amateur status. The court held that the NCAA had not been arbitrary and capricious in enforcing its rules and denying a waiver for Bloom.

Transfer Rules. NCAA rules governing eligibility following transfer from one institution to another are rather complex because of the great mobility of the age group. The purposes of transfer rules is to preclude recruitment of athletes from one institution to another, and to discourage interruptions of academic progress due to transfers because of reasons pertaining to athletics. The general principle stated in Bylaw 14.5.1 requires a student who transfers to a member institution from any other collegiate institution to complete one full academic year of residence at the certifying institution before being eligible to compete. There are multiple exceptions to this requirement; the most notable being those involving transfers from two-year colleges.

Longevity. The NCAA, too, is concerned with the problems presented by interminable eligibility and older-than-expected participants. With regard to the former, the NCAA decided four years of intercollegiate competition is the maximum allowable, regardless of where or at how many institutions the competition takes place. Further, the individual student-athlete is permitted five consecutive calendar years from original matriculation to complete four years of eligibility. Thus, an accommodation is possible following a transfer, or even a redshirt year for maturation or injury, and so on. In addition, student-athletes may also seek waivers if they undertake military service, serve with religious organizations, or become pregnant.

With regard to age, the membership became alarmed at the infusion of older athletes, particularly foreign athletes with the advantage of seasoning and experience, supplanting the scholarships of younger athletes. So, in 1980 the membership passed "the age rule," Bylaw 14.2.4.5, which credits any organized sports competition in a particular sport in each 12-month period following the athlete's twentieth birthday as a year of NCAA competition eligibility.

SIGNIFICANT CASE

Readers should pay particular attention to the court's discussion of vague and overbroad regulations.

MOLLY ROTTMANN V. PENNSYLVANIA INTERSCHOLASTIC ATHLETIC ASSOCIATION

United States District for the Western District of Pennsylvania
349 F. Supp. 2d 922 (2004)

District Judge.

This is an action in civil rights under the Civil Rights Act of 1871, 42 U.S.C. § 1983. Plaintiff is the head varsity girls' basketball coach at North Catholic High School. The Pennsylvania Interscholastic Athletic Association (the "PIAA") suspended plaintiff for one year for violating its Anti-Recruiting Rule. Plaintiff claims that the Rule, which proscribes the recruiting of grade school and high school students for athletic purposes, violates, among other things, her right to freedom of speech.

Plaintiff has filed a motion for a preliminary injunction on the ground that the PIAA's Anti-Recruiting Rule is facially unconstitutional under the First Amendment because it is a content-based ban on protected speech and is vague and overbroad. She seeks orders lifting her suspension and declaring the Anti-Recruiting Rule unconstitutional. For the reasons set forth below, the motion will be DENIED.

I. BACKGROUND

A. The PIAA and its Anti-Recruiting Rule

* * *

The PIAA is a Pennsylvania non-profit corporation. Approximately 1,400 public and private high schools in Pennsylvania have voluntarily joined the PIAA. The PIAA develops and enforces rules regulating interscholastic athletic competition among its member schools. Allegheny County school districts are part of District VII of the PIAA, also known as the Western Pennsylvania Interscholastic Athletic League, or the "WPIAL." The parties do not dispute that the PIAA is a state actor for section 1983 purposes. *Brentwood Academy v. Tennessee Secondary School Athletic Association,* 531 U.S. 288, 298-305, 148 L. Ed. 2d 807, 121 S. Ct. 924 (2001).

* * *

Upon applying for membership in the PIAA, member schools agree to conduct their interscholastic athletic programs in accordance with the PIAA By-Laws and Board of Directors decisions. One such By-Law is the Anti-Recruiting Rule. The Anti-Recruiting Rule, found in Article VI of the PIAA By-Laws, forbids recruiting of students for the purpose, "in whole, or in part," of participating in athletics at a school.

The Anti-Recruiting Rule subjects schools, and their coaches, to sanctions:

> *if the District Committee finds that the school, a representative of the school's athletic personnel, or any other person affiliated with the school, approached a student, or a parent or guardian of that student, or an adult with whom that student resides, and attempted to influence and/or influenced that student to transfer to that school, either in whole or in part, for any athletic purpose, or otherwise engaged in recruiting students, either in whole or in part, for an athletic purpose . . .*

* * *

The PIAA has amended its Anti-Recruiting Rule several times in recent years. It amended the Rule in May of 2001 after the Pennsylvania General Assembly directed the PIAA to make the Rule more stringent. Under the 2001 amendment, a school found to have recruited students was given the option of either suspending the coach involved in the activity or suffering other sanctions. The PIAA again amended the Rule in December of 2002 to require disqualification, directly by the PIAA, of any coach determined to have engaged in recruiting. In May of 2003, the PIAA added explanatory language regarding the purposes of the Rule and illustrations of activities that would violate the Rule. The main difference between the Anti-Recruiting Rule that existed in December 2002 and the one that exists now is that the current rule explains the purposes of the Rule and includes illustrations of the type of conduct that violates the Rule. The general substance of the Rule has not significantly changed as a result of the recent amendments.

B. Plaintiff's Recruiting and Suspension

In March of 2004, the WPIAL Committee directed North Catholic to investigate information it had received that plaintiff may have engaged in recruiting. Plaintiff was accused of recruiting April Austin, then an eighth-grade student and standout basketball player at St. Bartholomew's grade school. North Catholic reported back to the Committee, which held a hearing on the matter on June 29, 2004. The WPIAL Committee determined that plaintiff had engaged in ". . . recruiting April Austin for an athletic purpose while April was in eighth grade at St. Bartholomew's Grade School . . ." during the 2002–2003 season. July 1, 2004 letter from L. Hanley to E. Scheid. The WPIAL Committee suspended plaintiff for one year for her post-December 2002 conduct. For her pre-December 2002 conduct, North Catholic was directed to either suspend plaintiff for that same year or be suspended from participation in the PIAA. North Catholic was also publicly censured.

* * *

Plaintiff appealed the WPIAL Committee decision to the PIAA Board of Appeal, which held a hearing on July 22, 2004. At the hearing, plaintiff was represented by counsel, presented witnesses and documents, and testified on her own behalf. After the hearing, the Board affirmed the WPIAL Committee's decision. The Board additionally made the following pertinent findings:

12. During the 2003–2003 girls' basketball season, Coach Rottmann attended approximately four to six of April's games at St. Bartholomew.

13. After each contest she attended, Coach Rottmann approached various members of both teams, usually at courtside or in locker rooms, to offer congratulations or to extend a greeting. April Austin was consistently among the players so congratulated or so greeted.

14. Coach Rottmann's interpretation of her behavior is that she was not alone in her course of conduct, and that she either inferred an obligation from the North Catholic administration or instituted her own requirement to "make a presence" at these contests.

21. Coach Rottmann spoke to eighth-grade girls' basketball players as a representative of the North Catholic girls' basketball program.

22. Coach Rottmann's purpose in speaking to eighth-grade girls' basketball players was to introduce herself to them as the head coach of North Catholic's varsity girls' basketball team.

23. The evidence presented to the Board of Appeal demonstrated that Coach Rottmann's course of conduct was intended to influence eighth-grade girls' basketball players, including April Austin, to attend North Catholic and to play girls' basketball for Coach Rottmann.

24. Coach Rottmann's conduct was clearly intended to recruit girls' basketball players to attend

North Catholic, was conducted in an interscholastic girls' basketball setting, was directed at girls' basketball players, and was further intended to recruit, either in whole or in part, for the girls' basketball program at North Catholic.

25. Coach Rottmann's consistent course of conduct toward April Austin and her family during the 2002–2003 girls' basketball season, while not heavy-handed and while not including any commitments or offers, was nonetheless intended to influence April that North Catholic was where she should attend and participate in interscholastic girls' basketball upon promotion from the eighth-grade.

August 3, 2004 letter from PIAA Board of Appeal to E. Scheid.

The Board of Appeal affirmed the WPIAL Committee's one year suspension of plaintiff. That suspension began on June 29, 2004 and will end on June 28, 2005. For the recruiting conduct that occurred prior to the December 2002 amendments, the Board of Appeal modified the punishment levied on North Catholic and directed North Catholic to either suspend plaintiff or forfeit championship rights for two years, rather than be suspended from the PIAA entirely.

Plaintiff filed this suit on October 12, 2004, and sought a temporary restraining order and preliminary injunction two weeks later. Plaintiff now seeks a preliminary injunction: (1) lifting her one year suspension because the December 2002 version of the Recruiting Rule under which she was punished was unconstitutional; and (2) declaring the current Recruiting Rule unconstitutional.

* * *

III. DISCUSSION

Plaintiff seeks two forms of preliminary injunctive relief: (1) an order vacating her one year suspension under the December 2002 Anti-Recruiting Rule; and (2) an order prospectively enjoining enforcement of the current version of the Anti-Recruiting Rule. Plaintiff claims that the Anti-Recruiting Rule is a content-based ban on protected speech that cannot survive under the strict scrutiny test. Plaintiff also contends that the Anti-Recruiting Rule is unconstitutional because it is vague and overbroad.

We find that plaintiff has not shown a likelihood that she will succeed on the merits of either of her constitutional challenges to the Rule. Without such a showing, the motion must be denied.

A. The Constitutional Tests—Burdens on Speech

***

When a regulation is aimed at suppressing the content of protected speech, the strict scrutiny test applies. *Turner*

Broadcasting System, Inc. v. FCC, 512 U.S. 622, 642, 129 L. Ed. 2d 497, 114 S. Ct. 2445 (1994). Under the strict scrutiny test, a restriction must serve a compelling state interest and be narrowly tailored to achieve that interest by the least restrictive means possible.

Where a regulation does not seek to regulate the content of speech itself, but instead seeks to curb the undesirable secondary effects of speech by proscribing the time, place, and manner of it, the intermediate scrutiny test applies. *Ben Rich Trading v. City of Vineland*, 126 F.3d 155, 160 (3d. Cir. 1997). Under the intermediate scrutiny test, a regulation is valid if it is content neutral, is narrowly tailored to serve a substantial interest, and leaves alternative avenues of speech open to the speaker.

1. Application of the Pickering-Connick Test

Plaintiff contends that the Anti-Recruiting Rule is subject to strict scrutiny because it is a "complete ban on coach/prospective student speech." Plaintiff argues that the Rule cannot survive a strict scrutiny level of constitutional analysis because it could be more narrowly drawn to allow recruiting if the student initiated the contact, or to provide for written disclosure of a school's recruiting interest in a student prior to contact.

We disagree and, as stated later herein, find that the Anti-Recruiting Rule does not place a total ban on speech between coaches and "prospective students." Rather, we find that the *Pickering-Connick* test is applicable in this case.

* * *

Under the *Pickering-Connick* test, we must first determine whether plaintiff's speech addressed a matter of public concern. Here the restriction on speech is a prohibition on high school coaches recruiting students to enroll in a particular school, in whole or in part, to play sports for that school. Plaintiff's efforts to influence Ms. Austin to attend North Catholic High School, in whole or in part, to play basketball for her at North Catholic is not speech on a matter of public concern. In fact, by definition, the concern was private and personal in nature: encouraging Ms. Austin to attend North Catholic instead of some other school, so that she could play on plaintiff's team, rather than someone else's team.

Which high school a teenager plays basketball for does not relate to any matter of political, social, or other concern to the community. In content, form, and context, plaintiff's recruiting of this girl for her basketball program by extolling the advantages of North Catholic High School does not qualify as speech addressing a matter of public concern.

Nor are we persuaded by plaintiff's testimony that she was not seeking to recruit Ms. Austin to attend North Catholic, in whole or in part, for athletic purposes, but was simply encouraging her and other girls to continue playing sports and to continue a Catholic school education. First, we did not find her testimony in this regard credible. Nor do we find credible her testimony that she did not realize that her conduct was prohibited recruiting.

Second, and of equal importance, her testimony is contrary to the findings of the PIAA. At the hearing before the PIAA, plaintiff was represented by counsel, presented evidence on her behalf, and cross examined the witness against her. The PIAA, after considering the evidence, made findings that were supported by the record. We will not reweigh the evidence, reevaluate the credibility of the witness, or otherwise provide plaintiff a *de novo* review on the merits of whether she, in fact, engaged in recruiting activity as found by the PIAA.

Moreover, she does not contend, and there is nothing in the record or the pleadings to establish, that the PIAA finding was fraudulent, arbitrary, capricious, or a result of discriminatory animus. Therefore, we will not interfere with the PIAA determination.

Finally, we note parenthetically that if it were determined that plaintiff's recruiting activities addressed a matter of public interest and we were to engage in the next step of analysis, the Anti-Recruiting Rule at issue would easily pass constitutional muster. The Rule's purpose in promoting academics over athletics, protecting students from exploitation, and maintaining competitive equity greatly outweigh any public interest in allowing plaintiff to recruit standout eighth grade athletes to play girls' basketball at North Catholic High School.

2. Application of the Intermediate Scrutiny Test

Again, we hold that the *Pickering-Connick* test applies to the case. We recognize, however, that reasonable minds could differ on the issue and therefore we now address the intermediate scrutiny test.

The Anti-Recruiting Rule passes constitutional muster under the intermediate scrutiny test. We find from the credible evidence that it serves the substantial government interests of prioritizing academics over athletics, protecting young student athletes from exploitation, and ensuring an even playing field among competing schools. The Rule is narrowly drawn to serve those interests: it proscribes only recruiting of students, in whole or in part, for athletic purposes.

Finally, the Rule allows alternative avenues of communication regarding the North Catholic athletic programs. The Rule does not prevent plaintiff from talking about her basketball program, rather it proscribes the manner and circumstances in which she may do so. The court found Mr. Cashman, the Executive Director of the PIAA, to be a credible witness and finds that the Rule does not prohibit plaintiff from speaking about her basketball program at open houses at the school and answering questions regarding the basketball program there; the Rule does not preclude North Catholic from putting information about the basketball program on the school's website along with information about all of its activities and programs; the Rule does not prohibit placing information about the basketball program in written literature about the school or discussing it at a general assembly of eighth graders; the Rule does not prohibit coaches from holding skills clinics and speaking at school dinners. Indeed, the record reflects that North Catholic and plaintiff have engaged in all of these exact informational activities without sanction from the PIAA.

What the Rule forbids, among other things, is plaintiff's repeated approaching of Ms. Austin, as a representative of North Catholic High School's basketball team, after her stellar on-court performances at St. Bartholomew's grade school, to talk with her about basketball and North Catholic. Plainly, the Rule is not a content ban on speech regarding a school's basketball program. Instead, the Rule seeks to curb the secondary effects of speech directed at students, and their parents, regarding athletic programs by proscribing the time, place, and manner of such speech and does so in a constitutionally permissible way.

B. Vague and Overbroad

1. Vagueness

A regulation is unconstitutionally vague when it either forbids or requires the doing of an act in terms so vague that men of common intelligence must necessarily guess as to its meaning and differ as to its application. In addition, a regulation may be vague where it impermissibly delegates broad discretion to decision makers to apply the rule in an arbitrary and discriminatory manner.

A plaintiff has standing to challenge a regulation on the basis of vagueness only if it is vague as applied to that person. The Court of Appeals for the Third Circuit has found that when a litigant's conduct clearly falls within the permissible purview of a regulation, such an individual lacks standing to challenge the regulation on the grounds of vagueness. *Aiello v. City of Wilmington,* 623 F.2d 845, 850 (3d Cir. 1980).

Plaintiff cannot succeed in her facial challenge to the Anti-Recruiting Rule on the ground that it is vague because she does not have standing to assert such a challenge. Plaintiff's conduct clearly falls within the reasonable purview of the Rule. As the PIAA Board of Appeals found, plaintiff, as a representative of North Catholic High School, repeatedly approached April Austin at her basketball games. Further, her contacts were intended to influence her to attend North Catholic. There is no real question that repeatedly approaching a standout student athlete and attempting to influence her enrollment decision constitutes recruiting. As such, plaintiff does not have standing to mount a facial attack to the Rule on the grounds of vagueness.

Apart from this defect in standing, there is no need to guess at to the Rule's meaning and there is no undue discretion delegated to the enforcement bodies. The terms

"recruiting", "athletic purpose" and "encourage" are not esoteric terms. They each have plain and common meanings. They are neither vague nor ambiguous. The Rule as a whole and the words used within are clear and definitively reflect the PIAA's intent that school personnel are not to influence, to any degree, a student's decision to attend a certain school based on athletics. There is no real confusion over the meaning of these words and the proscriptions of the Rule.

Furthermore, there is no undue discretion delegated to the decision makers under the Rule. Although plaintiff may not agree with the result, there is no real dispute that the WPIAL Committee and the PIAA Board of Appeals applied the proscriptions of the Anti-Recruiting Rule to plaintiff's conduct in an objective way to arrive at a determination that, under all the circumstances, she recruited Ms. Austin. The PIAA's findings are very clear in reciting what it was about plaintiff's conduct that they found to be in violation of the Rule. The Rule gives no more discretionary power to the PIAA than any regulation gives to the body charged with applying it to a specific set of facts.

We find that plaintiff has not shown a reasonable likelihood that she will succeed in proving that the Anti-Recruiting Rule are unconstitutionally vague.

2. Overbreadth

A regulation is overbroad if it punishes a substantial amount of protected speech, when judged in relation to the regulation's legitimate sweep. *Virginia v. Hicks,* 539 U.S. 113, 118-19, 156 L. Ed. 2d 148, 123 S. Ct. 2191 (2003). The overbreadth doctrine was established out of concern that the threat of enforcement of an overly broad regulation may deter or chill constitutionally protected speech, especially when the regulation imposes criminal sanctions. The Supreme Court has repeatedly cautioned, however, against striking down a statute on its face due to overbreadth where there are a substantial number of situations to which it might be validly applied. *Parker v. Levy,* 417 U.S. 733, 760, 41 L. Ed. 2d 439, 94 S. Ct. 2547 (1974).

Plaintiff cannot succeed in her facial challenge to the Anti-Recruiting Rule on the ground that it is overbroad. There are a substantial number of ways that the Rule can be validly applied. For instance, it prevents schools from providing financial incentives or promising positions to students who agree to attend a school. Therefore, under Supreme Court precedent, there is a reluctance to strike down the Rule on this basis.

Apart from this reluctance, we find that this is not a case in which to uphold such a constitutional challenge. The Rule does not punish a substantial amount of protected speech, when judged in relation to its legitimate sweep. The Rule punishes that speech, and conduct, that is aimed at influencing a student to attend a school for athletics. Substantial government interests are advanced by forbidding such activity.

Nor are we persuaded by plaintiff's claim that she is now afraid to talk with students, at all, about attending North Catholic High School for fear that she will be sanctioned for violations of the PIAA's Anti-Recruiting Rule. Plaintiff cannot make the Rule constitutionally overbroad by giving it an unreasonably overbroad reading. There is no legal or factual basis for a finding that the Rule is overbroad.

IV. CONCLUSION

As a general rule nationwide, courts will not interfere with the internal affairs of state scholastic athletic associations.

In the absence of mistake, fraud, collusion or arbitrariness, the decisions of such associations will be accepted by the courts as conclusive. Such associations may adopt reasonable rules which will be deemed valid and binding upon the members of the association unless the rule violates some law or public policy. It is not the responsibility of the federal courts to inquire into the expediency, practicability, or wisdom of those regulations.

We find that the Anti-Recruiting Rule is not unconstitutional. As such, it is not the place of this court to engage in any further inquiry into the facts and circumstances of plaintiff's case.

CASES ON THE SUPPLEMENTAL CD

Bloom v. National Collegiate Athletics Association, 93 P. 3d 621 (Colo. Ct. App. 2004). This case examines a student request of a waiver of NCAA rules restricting student athlete endorsement and media activities.

Christian Heritage Academy v. Oklahoma Secondary School Activities Association. 483 F.3d 1025 (U.S. App. 2007). This case examines whether there is a legitimate difference between a private religious school and public schools.

Letendre v. Missouri State High School Athletics Association, 86 S.W. 3d 63 (Mo. Ct. App. 2002). This case examines whether a state high school activities association bylaw prohibiting students from competing on both a school and a non-school team in the same sport during the school team's season violated constitutional law.

QUESTIONS YOU SHOULD BE ABLE TO ANSWER

1. What does it mean to enforce a rule or policy in an arbitrary and capricious manner? Give a specific sport- or recreation-related example.

2. High school athletic associations generally accepted as state actors. Why?

3. In general, how have the courts ruled with regard to challenges brought against high school transfer rules?

4. In order to be *initially* qualified as eligible to compete in NCAA athletics, what academic achievements must a student-athlete demonstrate?

5. What are rules of longevity and how do they apply to interscholastic and NCAA eligibility?

REFERENCES

Cases

Angstadt v. Midd-West School District, 377 F.3d 338 (U.S. App. 2004).

Beck v. Missouri State High School Activities Association, 837 F. Supp. 998 (E.D. Mo. 1993).

Bloom v. National Collegiate Athletics Association, 93 P. 3d 621 (Colo. Ct. App. 2004).

Brentwood Academy v. Tennessee Secondary School Athletic Association, 531 U.S. 288 (2001).

Christian Heritage Academy v. Oklahoma Secondary School Activities Association, 483 F.3d 1025 (U.S. App. 2007).

Communities for Equity v. Michigan High School Athletic Association, 80 F. Supp. 2d. 729 (W.D. Mich. 2000).

Florida High School Athletic Association v. Marazzito, 891 So. 2d 653 (Fl. App. 2005).

Gorman v. St. Raphael Academy, 853 A.2d 28, 37 (R.I. 2004).

Indiana High School Athletic Association v. Carlberg, 694 N.E.2d 222 (Supr. Ct. Ind. 1997).

Indiana High School Athletic Association v. Durham, 748 N.E.2d 404 (Ind. App. 2001).

Indiana High School Athletic Association v. Reyes, 694 N.E.2d 249 (Ind. App. 1997).

Jones v. West Virginia State Board of Education, 218 W. Va. 52, 622 S.E.2d 289 (Supr. Ct. W.V. 2005).

Letendre v. Missouri State High School Athletics Association, 86 S.W. 3d 63 (Mo. Ct. App. 2002).

National Collegiate Athletic Association v. Lasege, 53 S.W. 3d (Supr. Ct. KY, 2001).

National Collegiate Athletic Association v. Tarkanian, 488 U.S. 179 (1988).

National Collegiate Athletic Association v. Yeo, 171 S.W. 3d 863 (Supr. Ct. Texas 2005).

Rottmann v. Pennsylvania High School Athletic Association, 349 F. Supp.2d 922 (W.D. Penn. 2004).

Publications

Conn, J. (2003). Voluntary Sport and Recreation Associations. In D. J. Cotton & T. J. Wolohan (Eds.), *Law for Recreation and Sport Managers* (3rd Ed.) pp. 476–482. Dubuque, IA: Kendall/Hunt Publishing Co.

Evans, M. (2005). Thursday vote could separate state's public, private high schools. (2005, October 19). *The Associated Press State & Local Wire*. Retrieved November 16, 2005, from Lexis Nexis Academic database.

Mitten, M. J., Davis, T., Smith, R. K., & Berry, R. C. (2005). *Sport Law and Regulation: Cases, Materials, and Problems*. New York: Aspen Publishers.

NCAA Manual. (2008–09). Indianapolis: NCAA.

voluntary association. (n.d.). *Dictionary.com Unabridged (v 1.1)*. Retrieved January 14, 2009, from Dictionary.com website: http://dictionary.reference.com/browse/voluntary association

Legislation

United States Constitution, Amendment XIV.

—Michael Gibbons
ST. JOHN FISHER COLLEGE

Regulating athlete behavior is an issue for athletic administrators at all levels of sport participation. Those who seek to regulate athlete behavior use various forms, including team rules, codes of conduct, and league or association rules. While most of the legal challenges have addressed conduct issues in high school, recent instances of athlete misconduct at both collegiate and professional leagues have shed light on the broad complexity of this problem at all levels of sport. Athletes at all levels who violate team or league rules involving prohibited behavior do so at the risk of being suspended and losing the privilege to play for their respective teams.

When athletes are suspended from teams, the main legal challenges involve claims based on violations of constitutional law, contract law, employment and labor law. For example, suspending a public high school or collegiate athlete from a team raises constitutional questions involving due process; whereas the same sanction at the professional level might give rise to issues of employment and labor law. Regardless of the sport level, athletic administrators would be well advised to develop code of conduct policies that clearly identify the proscribed conduct and provide for due process, even when the law does not require it.

FUNDAMENTAL CONCEPTS

Generally, high school athletic associations, schools, and coaches have the right to make rules and regulations governing the conduct of its members. In most states, this authority comes from the state legislature and is delegated to athletic associations and school boards to create and enforce rules with respect to extracurricular activities, including athletics. These rules govern a wide range of issues, including athletic eligibility, sportsmanship, and the use of tobacco, alcohol and drugs. In addition to athletic association rules, high schools have athlete codes of conduct that work together with student codes of conduct to provide notice of prohibited behavior, sanctions, and process.

When rules are violated and penalties imposed, members may challenge the sanctions on the basis that the rules are arbitrary or that their application is somehow flawed. Rules are also challenged pursuant to the Due Process Clause and Equal Protection Clause of the Fifth and Fourteenth Amendments, as well as the First Amendment, to the United States Constitution. As you will see from the discussion below, the most common legal challenge is a claimed Procedural Due Process violation. See Section 6.13, *Due Process*, for a complete discussion of both Procedural Due Process and Substantive Due process.

Arbitrary or Unreasonable

In addition to the constitutional issues discussed below, dismissals from athletic participation are challenged pursuant to an arbitrary and capricious or reasonableness standard. Athletic Associations and school officials are granted broad discretion to make and enforce rules related to student discipline. This power to discipline applies to student conduct while in school, to extracurricular activities after school, and to conduct that occurs outside the control of school officials. Courts will generally not interfere with the enforcement of disciplinary rules, provided they are reasonably related to school officials' ability to maintain order and discipline within the institution.

A school's authority to punish for out-of-school conduct by student-athletes was addressed in *Bunger v. Iowa High School Athletic Association*, (1972). In this case, the high school athletic association promulgated good conduct rules in an effort to help high schools address a drinking problem involving athletes at member schools. Bunger, a football player and minor, challenged his six-week suspension from athletic participation after he was found to be a passenger, during the summer, in a car that had beer in it. The Iowa Supreme Court held the rule invalid because the IHSAA did not have statutory authority to make rules and also provided guidance on the merits of the rule itself. While the court recognized that school authorities have the power to regulate conduct "which directly relates to and affects management of the school and its efficiency," the court found the relationship too tenuous where the conduct occurred "outside the season, beyond the school year, [with] no illegal or even improper use of beer." Consequently, the court found the rule to be overbroad and unreasonable.

Suspensions may also be found to be arbitrary in instances where the school board has not adopted the good conduct rules or the person who disciplines does not have the authority to do so (*Manico v. South Colonie Central School District*, 1992). In *Manico*, a wrestler was suspended after he admitted to stealing eight packages of muffins from the school cafeteria. He then challenged the two-day academic and extracurricular suspension given by the associate principal, as well as an entire season suspension given by the athletic director. The court held that the athletic director's suspension was arbitrary because the source of the good conduct rule, the Interscholastic Athletic Guide, was not adopted by the school board. Even if adopted, the Guide did not provide the athletic director with the authority to punish. While courts generally find good conduct rules reasonable (Bartlett, 1993), athletic administrators should be mindful of what constitutes effective rules in terms of clarity, scope and authority to punish. We turn now to constitutional challenges to good conduct rules.

State Action

As noted in Section 6.12, *State Action*, Constitutional review is appropriate where a state actor infringes on a person's state or federal constitutional rights. Thus, a threshold issue in constitutional challenges to athletic association and school rules is state action. State and local departments of recreation, as well as public high schools and colleges, are state actors; while private clubs, high schools and colleges generally are not. High school athletic associations are widely considered to be state actors and therefore subject to constitutional review (*Brentwood Academy v. Tennessee Secondary Athletic Ass'n*, 2001). Unlike high school athletic associations, the NCAA is not a state actor for constitutional purposes (*NCAA v. Tarkanian*, 1988). A more thorough discussion of state action can be found in Section 6.12, *State Action*.

Procedural Due Process

When an athlete is suspended or removed from a team for misconduct, the most common legal challenge is based on a procedural due process violation. In other words, the suspended athlete challenges his dismissal claiming that he has a right to participate in athletics that cannot be taken away by the government unless he receives procedural due process (e.g., notice and a hearing). While the majority of courts have held that athletic participation is a privilege as opposed to a right, a minority of courts have held otherwise. This section addresses the constitutional basis for the "right to participate" in athletics and some of the relevant case law.

A Protectable Interest

To be successful in a due process claim, the suspended athlete must be able to connect his "right to participate" to a protectable interest conferred by law. This argument is based on the due process clause of the Fourteenth Amendment, which prohibits a state actor from depriving "any person of life, liberty or property without due process of law." Since a life interest is not at issue here, the athlete must demonstrate that he has been deprived of a "liberty or property" interest within the meaning of the Fourteenth Amendment. Liberty and property interests are not created by the Federal Constitution; rather, they are created by state laws or rules that entitle citizens to certain benefits. For example, states that require mandatory school attendance can create a property interest in education. Since state laws grant their citizens a right to a public education, students cannot be suspended without due process. A number of suspended high school athletes have argued that they have a property interest in athletics participation as an outgrowth of their right to an education. Others have claimed that their property interest stems from the prospect for athletic scholarships.

The majority of courts have rejected these arguments based on the standard articulated by the Supreme Court in *Board of Regents v. Roth*, (1972). The Roth court stated that, "to have a property interest in a benefit, a person clearly must have more than an abstract need or desire for it. He must have more than a unilateral expectation of it. He must, instead, have a legitimate claim of entitlement to it." While courts have found that high school students have legitimate claims to education based on state laws, most federal and state appellate courts have not found the same with respect to extracurricular activities, including athletics. In *A.C. v. Board of Education for Cambridge Community School District* (2005), the court could not find an Illinois statute or case law that created a protectable property interest in athletics participation. In *Thorns v. Madison District Public Schools* (2007), plaintiffs were unable to identify any Michigan law that establishes an entitlement to participate in extracurricular activities such as high school football (see the Supplemental CD). In *Taylor v. Enumclaw School District* (2006), a Washington court of appeals noted that participation in sports or any other extracurricular activity is not required for graduation or mandated by state law. Thus, most plaintiffs have not been successful convincing courts that they have a property interest in participating in athletics that stems from their right to an education.

Likewise, the potential of a college scholarship or professional playing career have not been held to be sufficient enough to trigger a procedural due process hearing. In *Jordan v. O'Fallon High School District* (1999), the plaintiff claimed he had a protected property interest in a future college scholarship that should have afforded him a procedural due process hearing prior to his suspension for consuming alcohol in violation of the school's zero tolerance conduct code. Applying the Roth standard, the Jordan court noted, "students can need, want, and expect to participate in interscholastic athletics, but students are not entitled to participate in them." After rejecting the college scholarship argument as too speculative, the Jordan court explained the administrative burden on schools as thus, "if the opportunity to earn college financial assistance were to elevate participation in interscholastic athletics into a protected property right, school districts would have to afford procedural due process in practically all disciplinary actions where student participation in outside activities was at stake." Similar reasoning was employed in an earlier decision, *Dallam v. Cumberland Valley School District* (1975), where the court held that the State creates a property interest in the entire process, and that "the myriad activities which combine to form that education process cannot be dissected to create hundreds of separate property rights . . . " To do so would require a due process hearing every time a student is removed from an extracurricular activity."

Similarly, the majority of courts have been reluctant to find a constitutionally protected property interest in intercollegiate athletics. While high school students may argue that a property interest in athletics participation derives from state laws establishing a right to an education, there are no such laws that require a college education. Consequently, courts have found that athletes do not have a constitutionally protected right to compete in intercollegiate athletics. As with challenges by high school athletes, courts have refused to find a protectable property interest based on arguments that sports participation is an integral part of the educational process or that participation will lead to a professional playing career (*Colorado Seminary v. NCAA*, 1976; *NCAA v. Yeo*, 2005). In *Yeo*, the Texas Supreme Court refused to accept a world-class swimmer's argument that her ineligibility would damage her reputation and result in lost revenue through potential sponsorships. Claims based on future earnings, even where the athlete is highly skilled in a particular sport, routinely fail because they are too speculative. While courts do not generally recognize a protected property interest in the renewal of an athletic scholarship (*Conard v. The University of Washington*, 1992), they do "recognize a student-athlete's property interest in the economic value of his or her athletic scholarship, which constitutes a one-year contract with his or her university" (Mitten & Davis, 2008).

There are, however, a minority of courts that have held that high school and college students have a property interest in extracurricular activities. In *Butler v. Oak Creek-Franklin School District* (2000), a Wisconsin Federal Court found a property interest in athletics participation was created by the high school's student/parent handbook, its Athletic Code, Wisconsin Interscholastic Association rules, a state attorney general's opinion requiring public schools to apply athletic disciplinary codes reasonably, and two state laws (see the Supplemental CD). Other courts, also in the minority, have found that due process was required because of both the importance of interscholastic athletics to the educational process and its impact on the student's ability to obtain a college scholarship and further his education (*Duffley v. N.H. Interscholastic Athletic Assoc.*, 1982; *Boyd v. Board of Directors*, 1985). The potential for economic rewards for college athletes was also substantial enough to require minimum due process prior to suspension (*Behagen v. Intercollegiate Conference of Faculty Representatives*, 1972). Despite these cases, the vast majority of courts have held that participation in athletics is a privilege and not a protectable interest, the deprivation of which requires due process.

What Process Is Due

In cases where courts have found that due process applies, the question becomes what process is due. In *Goss v. Lopez* (1975), the Supreme Court considered this issue with respect to a suspension from public school for disciplinary reasons and found that due process requires "that the student be given oral or written notice of the charges against him and, if he denies them, an explanation of the evidence the authorities have and an opportunity to present his side of the story." In *Smith v. Chippewa Falls* (2002), the plaintiff was suspended from athletics participation for attending a party where alcohol was served, in violation of the athletic code of conduct. After the court declined to find a property interest in athletic participation which would entitle plaintiff to a procedural due process hearing, the court concluded that plaintiff was nevertheless afforded due process under Goss when he participated in a "give and take" with school officials investigating his case and during the appeal process established by the athletic code.

There are many decided cases where courts, after finding that a suspended athlete does not have a protectable property interest in athletics, conclude that the school still provided at least minimal due process. While it may be that due process is provided in these instances because there is an accompanying school suspension, specific due process language is often included in both school and student athlete codes of conduct. Thus, it appears that most athletic associations and schools recognize the importance of extracurricular activities, including athletics, operate under notions of fairness, and provide at least minimal due process protections to students accused of violating association rules and codes of conduct.

Equal Protection

A student-athlete may also claim that a high school, college or athletic association's decision to suspend an athlete from extracurricular activities violates his right to equal protection. The Fourteenth Amendment to the United States Constitution provides that no State shall "deny to any person within its jurisdiction the equal protection of the laws." To establish a prima facie case for an equal protection violation, plaintiffs must demonstrate that they: (1) are members of a protected class (or a fundamental right has been affected), (2) who are similarly situated to members of another class, and (3) were treated differently from members of the other class (*Thorns v. Madison District Public Schools*, 2007). An equal protection violation also requires a finding of purposeful, as opposed to unintentional, discrimination.

As you will recall from the discussion of equal protection in Section 6.14, *Equal Protection*, a law or rule is given strict scrutiny where the state's classification or treatment infringes on a people in terms of their ability to exercise a fundamental right or where the people are members of a suspect class. Where the rule does not affect a suspect class or fundamental right, courts will uphold the rule upon a finding that it rationally relates to a legitimate government interest. While some plaintiffs have claimed membership in a suspect class or that a fundamental right has been infringed, courts have generally applied the rational basis test to challenges to athlete suspension for misconduct. Even though students do not have a constitutional right to participate in extracurricular activities, schools cannot discriminate in the selection or treatment of participants once the program is offered.

In *Thorns*, plaintiffs and two other black student football players were suspended from school for 180 days compared to a 10-day suspension for white students involved in the same fight. Plaintiffs were unable to demonstrate that they were similarly situated to the white students because of the difference in the amount and reliability of the evidence of their respective involvement in the fight. Since the groups were not similarly situated, they could not be treated differently. In *Hadley v. Rush Henrietta Central School District*, a lacrosse player challenged the school district's policy requiring a tetanus shot because his religion prohibited the administration of such immunizations. Because the rule was neutral on its face, the court applied the rational basis test and upheld the rule as a reasonable measure for ensuring student safety. A 60-day extracurricular suspension for drug and alcohol use was also found to be rationally related to enforcement of the school's drug policy (*Palmer v. Merluzzi*, 1988; see the Supplemental CD). Equal protection claims are generally unsuccessful because courts treat athletic suspensions using the rational basis test.

First Amendment

Student-athletes have also challenged their dismissal from teams under the First Amendment to the United States Constitution. In assessing the athlete's conduct and subsequent removal, courts balance the coach's need to maintain order and discipline against the athlete's First Amendment right to free speech and association. Courts analyze such cases pursuant to the test set forth by the U. S. Supreme Court in *Tinker v. Des Moines Independent Community School District*. In order to constitutionally restrain student speech under Tinker, school officials must show "facts which might reasonably have led [them] to forecast substantial disruption of or material interference with school activities." A few recent cases demonstrate the application of the Tinker standard to student conduct directed at coaches of high school team sports.

In *Pinard v. Clatskanie School District*, plaintiffs were members of the boys varsity basketball team who alleged physical and psychological abuse by their coach. They sought his resignation through a signed petition, refused to board the bus for their next game and were dismissed from the team. The Ninth Circuit held that the petition was constitutionally protected speech under Tinker because the conduct could not reasonably have led school officials to forecast substantial disruption of a school authority. However, the court also held that the players' refusal to board the bus was not protected because it "substantially disrupted the operation of the basketball program." The Sixth Circuit reached a different result regarding the use of a petition in *Lowery v. Euverard*. Plaintiffs were members of the football team who claimed that the coach engaged in inappropriate behavior, including humiliating players, using inappropriate language, and requiring a conditioning program in violation of high school rules. Plaintiffs and thirteen other players signed a petition stating, "I hate Coach Euvard [sic] and I don't want to play for him." Plaintiffs were dismissed from the team, and they sued the coach and other school officials in Federal district court claiming that the dismissal violated their First Amendment rights. The Sixth Circuit held that the students' were properly dismissed from the team because their conduct could reasonably have been forecasted as a disruption in the coach's authority and team unity.

Professional Sports

In professional sport leagues, the authority to discipline clubs, owners, employees, and athletes resides with the league commissioner. This authority to discipline stems from league constitutions, by-laws, player contracts, and collective bargaining agreements, and includes the right to suspend athletes for on-field and off-field misconduct. Players, through their bargaining unit, can negotiate some limits to this authority (Mitten & Davis, 2008). For example, the union can have input on the types of conduct that can be disciplined, the severity of sanctions, and the athlete's right to appeal. These limitations notwithstanding, the commissioner has broad authority to discipline athletes for conduct that threatens the integrity or "best interests" of the league. In addition to the authority to discipline found in league constitutions and collective bargaining agreements, there has been a growing trend for leagues and teams to develop personal conduct policies.

Leagues and teams have personal conduct policies that allow commissioners to discipline for a wide range of conduct that threatens the integrity and public confidence in the sport, including on-field violence, gambling, drug use, domestic abuse, and other criminal conduct (Mitten & Davis, 2008). A well-publicized example is the NFL's Personal Conduct Policy. The policy applies to all persons associated with the NFL. Thus, coaches and front-office personnel are held to the same standard of conduct. Conviction for alleged criminal conduct is not a prerequisite to league sanctions. The NFL policy states, "It is not enough simply to avoid being found guilty of a crime. Instead, as an employee of the NFL or a member club, you are held to a higher standard and expected to conduct yourself in a way that is responsible, promotes the values upon which the league is based, and is lawful." Indeed, league commissioners are not required to base their decisions on whether the conduct leads to an arrest, indictment or conviction.

This approach to player discipline is consistent with the way employees are treated in other occupations. If an employer can show that the employee's alleged misconduct harms the employer's business interests, it can impose reasonable sanctions, including dismissal. Moreover, principles of labor law and private association law allow commissioners to discipline athletes with minimal interference by the legal system. (Ambrose, 2008). While courts grant commissioners broad authority to discipline player misconduct, professional sport organizations are generally careful to ensure that their disciplinary proceedings satisfy minimum due process requirements by providing notice and a hearing to accused players. (Ambrose, 2008). Players, like employees in other contexts, who do not agree with league imposed discipline may have the penalty reviewed by an impartial arbitrator. The length of the penalty, as well as the severity of the misconduct, will influence whether union representatives will support the player's appeal. In Major League Baseball and the National Baseball Association, an arbitrator will review a player's grievance pursuant to a "just cause" standard.

SIGNIFICANT CASE

This case is a good example of a court's treatment of a plaintiff's claim that his due process rights were violated when he was suspended from school and participation in high school sports. Despite ruling that there is no protectable property interest in athletics, the court ruled that the parents and child received adequate due process.

A.C. V. BOARD OF EDUCATION FOR CAMBRIDGE COMMUNITY UNIT SCHOOL

United States District Court for the Central District of Illinois
2005 U.S. Dist. Lexis 38070

BACKGROUND

According to the Complaint in this matter, in April 2005, Plaintiff A.C. was a junior at Cambridge High School and was involved in three different school-sponsored athletic teams. On April 5, 2005, he discharged what he contends was a toy gun at one or more students in the parking lot of the High School after school had been dismissed for the day. Following an investigation, Principal Monte Munsinger ("Munsinger") determined that the gun was not a toy, but rather a look-alike weapon, which fired small plastic BBs, and gave A.C. a ten-day academic suspension. The Athletic Council subsequently made a similar finding and imposed a 365-day suspension from all extracurricular athletic activities. Both Munsinger and the Athletic Council found that A.C.'s possession and use of the look-alike weapon constituted Gross Misconduct under the Student Handbook.

Plaintiffs bring this litigation claiming that A.C.'s due process rights were violated by the actions of the Defendant. Plaintiffs have now filed a Motion for Preliminary Injunctive Relief, asking the Court to enjoin Defendant from enforcing A.C.'s 365-day athletic suspension withholding his right to participate in school athletics. On Monday, December 19, 2005, the Court held an evidentiary hearing on the Motion during which several witnesses testified and numerous exhibits were introduced. This Order follows.

DISCUSSION

In this circuit, injunctive relief is warranted if the movant can make a threshold showing: (1) that the movant has some likelihood of success on the merits of the underlying litigation; (2) that no adequate remedy at law exists; and (3) that the movant will suffer irreparable harm if the injunction is not granted. If these three conditions are met, then the Court must balance the harm to the movant if the injunction is not issued against the harm to the defendant if it is issued improvidently and consider the interest of the public in whether the injunction is to be granted or denied. The Court then sits as a court of equity, weighing all these factors and employing a sliding-scale approach. That is, the

more likely the plaintiff's chance of success on the merits, the less the balance of harms need weigh in its favor.

Here, the Court need look no further than the first element of the test, as the Court finds that the record presented in this case does not establish that Plaintiffs have some likelihood of success on the merits of the underlying litigation. The Due Process Clause of the Fourteenth Amendment provides that "no state shall . . . deprive any person of life, liberty, or property, without due process of law." U.S. Const. Amend. XIV § 1. A procedural due process claim against government officials requires proof of inadequate procedures and interference with a liberty or property interest. *Board of Curators of University of Missouri v. Horowitz*, 435 U.S. 78, 82, 98 S. Ct. 948, 55 L. Ed. 2d 124 (1978). Thus, in order to have any likelihood of success on a procedural due process claim, Plaintiffs must demonstrate that they have a protectable property or liberty interest at stake. Such interests are "are not created by the Constitution. Rather, they are created and their dimensions defined by an independent source such as state statutes or rules entitling the citizen to certain benefits." *Goss v. Lopez*, 419 U.S. 565, 572-73, 95 S. Ct. 729, 42 L. Ed. 2d 725 (1975), *citing Board of Regents v. Roth*, 408 U.S. 564, 577, 92 S. Ct. 2701, 33 L. Ed. 2d 548 (1972).

Plaintiffs contend that A.C. has a protectable property interest in continued participation in the athletic program and prospects for college scholarships attendant to such participation. In Roth, the Supreme Court clarified the parameters of a protectable property interest in the educational setting: To have a property interest in a benefit, a person clearly must have more than an abstract need or desire for it. He must have more than a unilateral expectation of it. He must, instead, have a legitimate claim of entitlement to it

408 U.S. at 577. Given this definition, courts in other jurisdictions have repeatedly held that there is no protectable property or liberty interest in participating in interscholastic athletics. *Hamilton v. Tennessee Secondary School Athletic Association*, 552 F.2d 681, 682 (6th Cir. 1976), *citing*

Mitchell v. Louisiana High School Athletic Association, 430 F.2d 1155, 1157-58 (5th Cir. 1970) (finding that the privilege of participating in interscholastic athletics falls outside the protection of due process); *Hebert v. Ventetuolo*, 638 F.2d 5, 6 (1st Cir. 1981) (finding that since there is no property right to play interscholastic sports, there is no constitutional entitlement to any process whatsoever); *Rutledge v. Arizona Board of Regents*, 660 F.2d 1345, (9th Cir. 1981); *Poling v. Murphy*, 872 F.2d 757, 764 (6th Cir. 1989); In re United States ex rel. Missouri State High School Activities Ass'n., 682 F.2d 147, 153 (8th Cir. 1982); *Burrows v. Ohio High School Athletic Ass'n.*, 891 F.2d 122 (6th Cir. 1989); *Smith v. Chippewa Falls Area Unified School District*, 302 F.Supp.2d 953, 957 (W.D. Wis. 2002) (noting that the preponderance of federal district courts considering the question have held that the opportunity to participate in extracurricular activities is not a protected property interest). Similarly, the Illinois courts have noted that "students can need, want, and expect to participate in interscholastic athletics, but students are not entitled to participate in them" in holding that participation in athletics does not rise to the level of a protected interest. *Jordan v. O'Fallon Township High School Dist. No. 203 Board of Education*, 302 Ill.App.3d 1070, 706 N.E.2d 137, 140, 235 Ill. Dec. 877 (1999); *Clements v. Board of Education of Decatur Public School Dist. No. 61*, 133 Ill. App. 3d 531, 478 N.E.2d 1209, 1210, 88 Ill. Dec. 601 (1985).

In support of their argument that they have a protectable property interest, Plaintiffs primarily rely on two related decisions in *Butler v. Oak Creek-Franklin School District*, 116 F.Supp.2d 1038 (E.D. Wis. 2000), and 172 F.Supp.2d 1102 (E.D.Wis. 2001). With all due respect, these decisions are non-binding precedent that the Court finds to be readily distinguishable. As previously noted, a property interest is derived from an independent source such as state statutes or rules granting an entitlement to benefits. Goss, 419 U.S. at 572-73. Such was the case in Butler, where the district court found that the school's student handbook, the school's Athletic Code, the rules of the Wisconsin Interscholastic Athletic Association, a state attorney general's opinion, and two state laws combined to provide the student's entitlement to continued athletic participation. 172 F.Supp.2d at 1110. Plaintiffs have not cited, and the Court is otherwise unaware of, any analogous laws, opinions, or rules existing in the state of Illinois that could serve as the source of an entitlement. To the contrary, it would appear that Illinois courts have taken the position that there is no such rule or regulation. *See* Jordan, 302 Ill.App.3d at 1076 (finding that "football is neither an integral part of a quality education nor a requirement under any rule or regulation governing education in this State.... Simply put, playing high school football is a privilege rather than a right." Thus, the Court must reject the suggestion that the decision in Butler properly supports Plaintiffs' position in this case.

While the Seventh Circuit has not expressly addressed this issue, two opinions involving related issues provide some indication of how the Court of Appeals might rule if it were to consider this question directly. In *Schaill v. Tippecanoe County School Corp.*, 864 F.2d 1309, 1323 (7th Cir. 1988), the Seventh Circuit relied on the First Circuit's decision in Hebert in noting "that there is room for doubt whether a student has a constitutionally protected liberty interest in being free of the potential stigma associated with removal from an athletic team." In *Todd v. Rush County Schools*, 133 F.3d 984, 986 (7th Cir. 1998), the Court of Appeals also suggested that extracurricular activities, such as athletics, are only a privilege rather than a right. Accordingly, the Court finds that the Court of Appeals would likely follow the existing persuasive precedent cited above and hold that participation in interscholastic sports does not implicate any protectable liberty or property interest.

The Court therefore concludes that Plaintiffs have failed to demonstrate that they have any protectable liberty or property interest in continued participation in school athletics. Having so found, the Court need not go on to consider to what process Plaintiffs would have been entitled or whether the process that was provided was sufficient.

Even assuming *arguendo* that continued participation in interscholastic sports could rise to the level of a protectable property interest in Illinois, on the record before the Court, it would appear that Plaintiffs received constitutionally adequate process with respect to the 365-day athletic suspension that was imposed. In Goss, the Supreme Court clarified that a student given a suspension for disciplinary infractions was entitled to "oral or written notice of the charges against him, and if he denies them, an explanation of the evidence the authorities have and an opportunity to present his side of the story." 419 U.S. at 581. These procedures need only be "rudimentary", amounting to "an informal give-and-take between student and disciplinarian." *Id.* at 584. A hearing is adequate even if it is conducted before a disciplinarian who "himself has witnessed the conduct forming the basis for the charge."

While the version of the April 5, 2005, incident testified to by A.C. during the hearing is somewhat inconsistent with the statement that he gave to Munsinger, as reflected in Munsinger's investigation summary, the material procedural details are essentially undisputed. The evidence produced during the evidentiary hearing indicated that A.C. and/or his mother had multiple oral conversations with school officials regarding the nature of the charges against him, as well as the possible penalties at stake. In a letter dated April 25, 2005, Plaintiffs received written notice that the Athletic Council would convene a meeting on April 29, 2005, to consider possible disciplinary action against A.C. During this meeting, the Plaintiffs requested a postponement of the hearing to allow the coach of A.C.'s current sport to be present, and the request was granted. On May 3, 2005, the Athletic Council convened. Munsinger made a presentation regarding the results of his investigation into the facts of the April 5, 2005, incident, including the basis for his conclusion that the gun was a look-alike weapon. Based on the information presented both to the Athletic Council and during the evidentiary hearing before this Court, it is clear that the gun possessed by A.C. was fairly characterized as a look-alike weapon. Plaintiffs were given the opportunity at the Athletic Council hearing to ask questions and present evidence on their own behalf and did in fact argue that the weapon was not a look-alike and that A.C.'s actions did not rise to the level of gross misconduct. The Athletic Council then deliberated and issued its decision to impose the 365-day athletic suspension. Such process clearly satisfies the requirements of Goss.

* * *

Parenthetically, the Court would note that the process, while constitutionally adequate, was not perfect. There is evidence in the record that on April 21, 2005, the Board of Education announced that A.C. would receive a 365-day athletic suspension after hearing testimony in executive session from only one side of the incident and without any opportunity to participate by Plaintiffs, who had been told that A.C.'s situation was not on the agenda for that meeting. Even though it is not outcome determinative, if true, this would seem to be a fundamental breach of fairness by the Board of Education. There was also evidence indicating that this was the first and only time that the Board of Education had ever made a recommendation to the Athletic Council as to what its decision should be and that Munsinger, who investigated and imposed the academic suspension, served as the "prosecutor" before the Academic Council and asked whether any Council member disagreed with the recommendation of the Board. While this may in part be explained by the fact that this was also the first time that the Board had encountered a perceived weapons violation and the coach who testified during our court hearing stated that he would have reached the same conclusion even without the recommendation from the Board, these facts are nevertheless suggestive of an unnecessarily aggressive involvement by the Board. That is especially true in view of the fact that the School District's Student Handbook appears to contemplate that the Athletic Council will act independently of any academic discipline imposed by the principal and the School Board.

Thus, the Court must conclude that Plaintiffs have not demonstrated a likelihood of success on the merits of their due process claim with respect to the 365-day athletic suspension. Accordingly, their request for preliminary injunctive relief must be denied.

* * *

CASES ON THE SUPPLEMENTAL CD

Butler v. Oak Creek-Franklin School District, 116 F. Supp. 2d 1038 (2000). The reader should pay particular attention to the context in which the court finds a protectable property interest in high school athletic participation.

Palmer v. Merluzzi, 689 F. Supp. 400 (1988). Often considered a leading case in this area of law, the decision provides an excellent discussion of how courts generally treat a plaintiff's challenge to an athletic suspension based on procedural due process and equal protection grounds.

Thorns v. Madison District Public Schools, 2007 U.S. Dist. LEXIS 40639 (E.D. Michigan, 2007). Plaintiffs make both due process and equal protection arguments in this case.

QUESTIONS YOU SHOULD BE ABLE TO ANSWER

1. Explain what is meant by procedural due process.

2. Why do courts find a property interest in education and not athletics participation?

3. Why have courts been reluctant to accept the argument that a college scholarship or professional contract is a protectable property interest?

4. Explain how an athletic suspension based on misconduct can be challenged under equal protection, what test courts generally apply, and whether these challenges are generally successful.

5. Are professional sport leagues and teams required to provide due process to athletes accused of misconduct in violation of a league or team conduct policy?

REFERENCES

Cases

A.C. v. Board of Education for Cambridge Community Unit School District, 2005 U.S. Dist. LEXIS 38070 (C.D. Ill. 2005).

Behagen v. Intercollegiate Conference of Faculty Representatives, 346 F. Supp. 602 (D. Minn. 1972).

Board of Regents v. Roth, 408 U.S. 564 (1972).

Boyd v. Board of Directors, 612 F. Supp. 86 (E. D. Ark. 1985).

Brentwood Academy v. Tennessee Secondary Athletic Association, 531 U.S. 288 (2001).

Bunger v. Iowa High School Athletic Association, 197 N.W.2d 555 (1972).

Butler v. Oak Creek-Franklin School District, 116 F. Supp.2d 1038 (2000).

Colorado Seminary v. NCAA, 417 F. Supp. 885 (1976); *aff'd* 570 F.2d 320 (1978).

Conard v. The University of Washington, 834 P.2d 17 (1992).

Dallam v. Cumberland Valley School District, 391 F. Supp. 358 (M. D. Pa. 1975).

Duffley v. N.H. Interscholastic Athletic Association, 122 N.H. 484 (1982).

Goss v. Lopez, 419 U.S. 565 (1975).

Hadley v. Rush Henrietta Central School District, 409 F. Supp.2d 164 (W.D.N.Y. 2006).

Jordan v. O'Fallon Township High School District, 302 Ill. App. 3d 1070 (1999).

Lowery v. Euverard, 497 F.3d 584 (2007).

Manico v. South Colonie Central School District, 584 N.Y.S.2d 519 (1992).

NCAA v. Tarkanian, 488 U.S. 179 (1988).

NCAA v. Yeo, 171 S.W.3d 863 (Tex. 2005).

Palmer v. Merluzzi, 689 F. Supp. 400 (1988); *aff'd* 868 F.2d 90 (1989).

Pinard v. Clatskanie School District, 467 F.3d 755 (2006).

Smith v. Chippewa Falls Area Unified School District, 302 F. Supp.2d 953 (W.D. Wis. 2002).

Taylor v. Enumclaw School District, 132 Wn. App. 688 (2006).

Thorns v. Madison District Public Schools, 2007 U.S. Dist. Lexis 40639 (E. D. Michigan 2007).

Tinker v. Des Moines Independent Community School District, 393 U.S. 503 (1969).

Publications

Ambrose, R. (2008). Note: The NFL makes it rain: Through strict enforcement of its conduct policy, the NFL protects its integrity, wealth, and popularity. 34, *William Mitchell Law Review*, 1069.

Bartlett, L. (1993). The court's view of good conduct rules for high school student athletes, 82 *Educational Law Reporter* 1087.

Mitten, M. J., & Davis, T. (2008). Athlete eligibility requirements and legal protection of sports participation opportunities, 8, *Virginia Sports and Entertainment Law Journal*, 71.

Legislation

United States Constitution, Amendment I.

United States Constitution, Amendment XIV.

Websites

National Football League Players Association. 2008 Personal Conduct Policy, available at:
http://www.nflplayers.com/images/fck/NFL%20Personal%20Conduct%20Policy%202008.pdf

—**John T. Wolohan**
—**Genevieve Gordon**
ITHACA COLLEGE

Perhaps the greatest threat facing the integrity of sports, as well as the health and safety of today's athletes, is the continued use of performance-enhancing drugs. In an attempt to protect their sports and athletes from this threat, athletic administrators and organizations from the interscholastic, intercollegiate, Olympic, and professional levels have implementing drug-testing programs. However, as the Bay Area Laboratory Co-Operative (BALCO) scandal, which erupted in June 2003, when a syringe containing the designer steroid THG (tetrahydrogestrinone) was sent to the United States Anti-Doping Agency (USADA) and eventually entangled some of the biggest names in professional sports and international track and field, including Berry Bonds, Jason Gambi, and Marion Jones, demonstrated, athletic administrators and organizations seem to be fighting a losing battle.

In their haste to rid sports of performance-enhancing drugs, however, some people have voiced concern that sports and recreational organizations may be violating the privacy rights of the very athletes they are trying to protect. This section examines the various legal principles raised when an institution or organization implements a drug-testing program for athletes.

FUNDAMENTAL CONCEPTS

The main legal areas governing drug testing of athletes are constitutional law and labor law. The law that will govern a particular complaint depends on the individual. For example, drug testing high school or college athletes raises a number of constitutional issues concerning the athlete's right to due process and privacy, as well as protection against illegal search and seizure and self-incrimination. The drug testing of professional athletes will usually be resolved through internal grievance and arbitration systems set up within the league's collective bargaining agreement (CBA).

Constitutional Law

The first question to ask whenever a constitutional law issue arises is, "Is there **state action**?" The safeguards of the U.S. Constitution apply only when state action is present. State action is defined as any action taken directly or indirectly by a state, municipal, or federal government. Therefore, before an athlete can claim that a drug-testing program violated his or her constitutional rights, the entity being challenged must be shown to be part of the federal, state, or municipal government. (For more information on state action, see Section 6.12, *State Action*).

As discussed in Section 6.12, *State Action*, public high schools and colleges are state actors, and students attending these institutions benefit from the protections afforded under the constitution. Private entities, such as the NCAA and professional sports teams, on the other hand, are not subject to constitutional challenges. For example, in *Long v. National Football League* (1994), a former football player sued the NFL after he tested positive for anabolic steroids and was suspended pursuant to the league's drug-testing policy. In dismissing his claim, the District Court held that Long failed to show a sufficiently close nexus between the actions of the city and city officials and the decision of the NFL to establish an actionable constitutional claim based on his suspension for anabolic steroids. The court concluded that Long was suspended based on independent medical conclusions and NFL policy objectives over which the state had no influence.

Even when the state is involved in the drug testing of professional athletes, the courts have afforded wide latitude to such programs. For example, in *Shoemaker v. Handell* (1986), five jockeys challenged the New Jersey

Racing Commission's regulations requiring drug testing of jockeys. The jockeys claimed that this constituted an illegal search and seizure and was a violation of their Fourth Amendment rights. The Court of Appeals, in upholding the regulations, held that the commission's concern for racing integrity warranted the tests and that as long as the commission kept the results confidential, there was no violation of the jockeys' rights.

The Fourth Amendment

Once state action has been established, an organization must meet the requirements of the Fourth Amendment to the U.S. Constitution before it can implement a drug-testing program. The Fourth Amendment provides that:

— *[T]he right of the people to be secure in their persons, houses, papers and effects, against unreasonable searches and seizures, shall not be violated, and no Warrants shall issue, but upon probable cause, supported by Oath or affirmation, and particularly describing the place to be searched and the persons or things to be seized.*

For any drug test to be constitutional under the Fourth Amendment, the "search" or test must be reasonable. To determine whether a drug test satisfies the reasonableness requirement, the court must balance the intrusion of the test on an individual's Fourth Amendment interests against its promotion of legitimate governmental interests. In conducting this balancing test, the court examines the following three factors.

— The first factor to be considered is whether the individual has a **legitimate privacy expectation** on which the search intrudes. The Fourth Amendment only protects those expectations of privacy that society recognizes as legitimate. What expectations are legitimate varies, of course, depending on whether the individual asserting the privacy interest is at home, at work, in a car, or in a public park. In addition, the legitimacy of certain privacy expectations may depend on the individual's legal relationship with the state. For example, the expectation of privacy by high school students would be less than individuals in college or members of the general population. The reason high school athletes have a lower privacy expectation to the fact that schools have a custodial and tutelary responsibility for the students. Also affecting the privacy expectations of athletes is the fact that athletes shower and change together before and after each practice or game; therefore, their expectation of privacy is small. As the Supreme Court noted in *Vernonia School District v. Acton* (1995), "high school sports are not for the bashful."

— The second factor to be considered is the **character of the intrusion.** In determining the character of the intrusion, the court examines both how the drug test collects samples and the type of information being collected. For example, is the individual required to give a blood test, which courts would find invasive, or a urine sample, which is far less invasive? As for the type of information that is obtained by the test, the test should only look for illegal drug and performance-enhancing drugs. Another issue that impacts the character of the intrusion is who receives the test results and how the information is used. The test information should only be disclosed to those limited individuals who have a need to know.

— The final factor to be considered is the *nature and immediacy of the governmental concern* and the efficacy of the drug test in meeting those concerns. In other words, the court must determine whether the state's interest in conducting the drug test is important enough to justify intruding on an individual's genuine expectation of privacy.

The Fourth Amendment also requires that before any search can be conducted there must be **probable cause.** The Supreme Court, however, has recognized that a search unsupported by probable cause can be constitutional when the state has special needs. As the Supreme Court noted in *Vernonia School District v. Acton* (1995), because of the student's age, the state has "special needs" in the public school context. Those same "special needs," however, do not exist at the college, Olympic, or professional levels.

Post–Vernonia Expansions

Since the United States Supreme Court's decision in *Vernonia*, high schools have sought to extend drug testing to more and more students. In 2002, the United States Supreme Court, in *Board of Education v. Earls* (2002), extended the scope of *Vernonia* to include all extracurricular activities. In Earls, the school district instituted a policy that required all students who participated in any competitive extracurricular activities, including band members, choir members, academic team members, and athletic team members, to submit to drug testing. In upholding the policy, the U.S. Supreme Court held that the drug-testing policy reasonably served the school district's important interest in detecting and preventing drug use, and the policy did not violate the Fourth Amendment's prohibition against unreasonable searches and seizures.

In *Safford Unified Sch. Dist. # 1 v. Redding* (2009), the United States Supreme Court was asked to determine whether 13-year-old Savana Redding's Fourth Amendment right was violated when she was subjected to a strip search of her bra and underpants by school officials acting on reasonable suspicion that she had brought forbidden prescription and over-the-counter drugs to school.

In holding that the strip search of Redding was unreasonable and a violation of the Fourth Amendment, the Supreme Court ruled that in order for a school search to be permissible in its scope, the measures adopted must be reasonably related to the objectives of the search and not excessively intrusive in light of the age and sex of the student and the nature of the infraction. In the Redding case, the court found that the content of the suspicion failed to match the degree of intrusion. In particular, the Supreme Court noted that the school official knew before the search that the pills were only prescription-strength ibuprofen and over-the-counter naproxen, common pain relievers equivalent to two Advil, or one Aleve. In addition, there was no reason to suspect that the drugs were concealed in her underwear.

In addition to individual high schools, state high school athletic associations have also started mandatory testing of athletes. In December 2005, New Jersey became the first state to require random steroid testing for athletes on high school teams that qualify for postseason play. The program only tests for performance-enhancing drugs in championship tournaments. Following New Jersey's example, Illinois, Texas and Florida also started anti-steroid testing programs. After two years and having spent close to $100,000, Florida discontinued its program in 2009. In justifying the decision, Florida officials pointed to the fact that out of the 600 tests it conducted, only one athlete had tested positive. Another state considering dropping its program is Texas. Having spent $6 million on its program, and testing 29,000 athletes, the program has only found 11 who have tested positive for steroids (Popke, 2009).

Consent Forms

An individual can voluntarily waive his or her Fourth Amendment rights and submit to a drug-testing program. However, even when an individual consents to a drug test, there can be constitutional problems. For example, in *University of Colorado v. Derdeyn* (1993), a group of student-athletes who had signed consent forms challenged the university's mandatory drug testing program. In upholding the student's challenge, the Colorado Supreme Court held that the university failed to show that the students' consent to such testing was voluntary. Absent such voluntary consent, the court concluded that the university's random, suspicionless urinalysis drug-testing program violated the students' constitutional rights.

State Constitutions

It is also important to note that individual state constitutions may afford more liberal protections to citizens with respect to search and seizure when compared to the U.S. Constitution. For example, in *Hill v. NCAA* (1994), Jennifer Hill, a member of the swimming team at Stanford University, challenged the NCAA's drug-testing program by arguing that it violated her privacy rights under the California State Constitution. In particular, Hill pointed to the NCAA's procedure for collecting urine samples and the consent form, which asked students to disclose medical and sexual information.

In ruling against Hill, the California Supreme Court held that the NCAA's drug-testing policy involving monitoring of urination, testing of urine samples, and inquiry concerning medication did not violate the students' constitutional right to privacy. In holding that the program was consistent with the privacy provisions of the state constitution, the California Supreme Court held that the NCAA's interest in protecting both the health and safety of the athletes and the integrity of the programs outweighed Hill's privacy interests *Hill v. NCAA*, (1994).

Another case involving a state constitutional challenge is *Bally v. Northeastern University*, (1989). David Bally alleged that Northeastern's policy requiring student–athletes to consent to drug testing as a condition of participating in intercollegiate sports violated his civil rights and right to privacy. The Massachusetts Supreme Judicial Court, however, rejected both of these arguments.

✳ Due Process

Another theory used by athletes to challenge the constitutionality of drug-testing programs is due process. As discussed in Section 6.13, *Due Process,* to establish a violation of due process, an individual must establish that he or she has some type of property or liberty interest that has been adversely affected. Unfortunately, for the student–athletes, it is clear from past court decisions that participation in athletics is not a property right, but is a privilege not protected by Constitutional due process safeguards. For example, in *Brennan v. Board of Trustees* (1997), John Brennan, a student-athlete at the University of Southwestern Louisiana, challenged a positive drug test for anabolic steroids on due process grounds. In the case, Brennan requested and received two administrative appeals in which he contended that the positive test results were "false" due to a combination of factors, including heavy drinking and sexual activity the night before the test and his use of nutritional supplements. Following the unsuccessful appeals, USL complied with the NCAA regulations and suspended Brennan from intercollegiate athletic competition for one year. In rejecting his claim, the court held that Brennan had no liberty or property interest in participating in intercollegiate athletics.

✳ Labor Law

Another legal area governing drug testing is labor law. In professional sports, the conduct of the players is governed by a contract that is negotiated between the league, representing the owners, and the players' association, representing the players. This contract or collective bargaining agreement addresses the conditions of the athletes' employment. Because drug-testing programs affect an athlete's condition of employment (if they test positive, they cannot play), it is a mandatory subject of bargaining and must be part of the CBA.

One problem with drug testing in professional sports, as demonstrated by the fight over drug testing in Major League Baseball, is the conflict of interest both the union and management have in having a strong testing program. Because the job of the MLBPA and its Executive Director Donald Fehr is to protect the players from anything that might impact their work, which the current drug testing program clearly does, it is in the union's best interest to fight to keep testing out of baseball. In addition, bigger and stronger players are able to hit more home runs, which is a big fan attraction.

As a result of this conflict, it is not surprising that the union only agreed to allow drug testing of Major League Baseball players under the threat of Congressional intervention and if baseball could demonstrate that there was a problem. As a result, in 2003, MLB conducted drug testing for the first time. Because more than 5 percent of the major league players tested, tested positive, the threshold established by the union, MLB was able to implement a drug testing for real in 2004. Even though the 2003 tests were intended to be confidential, with no penalties imposed on any players who tested positive, two of the 103 players to test positive in 2003, Alex Rodriguez and Sammy Sosa, have been identified.

The penalties under the current Major League Baseball Drug Testing Policy for a player who test positive for performance-enhancing substances are: a 50-game suspension for the first offense; 100-game suspension for a second offense; and a permanent suspension from the major or minor leagues for a third. As of 2009, the best know player to be penalized under the program is Manny Ramirez, a 12-time All-Star with 533 home runs, was suspended for 50 games. In addition MLB's drug policy requires drug suspensions to be unpaid. Therefore, Ramirez lost around $7.7 million, or nearly a third of his $25-million salary this year.

✳ World Anti-Doping Agency

In March 2003, the World Anti-Doping Agency announced a consolidated drug-control program for all international sports. In developing the World Anti-Doping Code (the Code), which was signed by sixty-five sports federations and over fifty nations, including the United States, United Kingdom, Russia, France, Germany, and

Australia, covers all Olympic sports, the federations that govern them, and all their athletes, WADA sought to create a single list of banned drugs, a uniform system for testing for them, and penalties for violators. Up until the Code was developed, each Olympic sport operated under its own drug program.

Since it entered into force on January 1 2004, the Code has led to several significant advances in the global fight against doping in sport, and has brought about harmonization to a system where previously rules had varied, and in some cases did not exist. Additionally, the Code allowed for sanctioning in cases where there was no positive doping test, but evidence that an anti-doping rule violation has occurred. For example, Marion Jones won five medals during the 200 Olympic Games, and even though she passed every drug test she took during the games, was stripped of her medals after she admitted taking performance-enhancing drugs.

One of the main complaints of the 2003 Code was the inflexibility surrounding violations. The Code held athletes responsible for all positive findings, no matter how the drug got into their bodies. For a first violation under the 2003 Code, an athlete received an automatic 2-year ban from competition. A second violation, and the athlete was banned for life.

In an effort to provide some flexibility, the Code was revised as of January 1, 2009. However, the revised 2009 Code also requires athletes to submit to no-notice, out-of-competition tests anytime, anywhere. To do this, every athlete on the national testing register, and any elite athlete in an Olympic or major team sport, must report his or her whereabouts to their national anti-doping organizations for at least one hour a day between the hours of 6 am and 11 pm, seven days a week, three months in advance. Failure of the athlete to be where he or she said they would be counts as a strike. Three strikes in an 18-month period and the athlete is automatically banned from competition. (For more information on the 2009 WADA Code, see: http://www.wada-ama .org/rtecontent/document/code_v2009_En.pdf)

Although there have been some calls in Congress and outside the United States to apply the Code to America's professional sports leagues, the leagues and players have resisted those calls. Therefore, the only professional American sports league athletes subject to the Code are those players from the NBA and the NHL who take part in the Olympics and certain other international competitions. As the Floyd Landis arbitration case illustrates, American individual sport athletes are subject to the WADA Code. During the 2006 Tour de France, Floyd Landis, who would eventually win the race, tested positive for the presence of exogenous testorterone. In his arbitration hearing, the arbitration panel ruled that Landis was stripped of his 2006 Tour de France win, and ineligibility for competition for two years. In 2008, Landis challenged the penalty imposed by the **United States Anti-Doping Association (USADA)**, the agency in United States responsible for managing the testing and adjudication process of the athletes in the US Olympic and Paralympic Movement. The Court of Arbitration for Sport (CAS), in *Landis v. USADA* (2007), upheld USADA penalty and also required Landis to pay the $100,000 in legal expenses USADA incurred in the arbitration.

The following case the U.S. Supreme Court was asked to examine the issue of high schools' drug tests of student-athletes. In particular, the court examined what type of rights and of privacy expectations high school students have when they attend public schools.

VERNONIA SCHOOL DISTRICT 47J V. ACTON

United States Supreme Court
515 U.S. 646 (1995)

According to the District Court: "[T]he administration was at its wits end and . . . a large segment of the student body, particularly those involved in interscholastic athletics, was in a state of rebellion. Disciplinary actions had reached 'epidemic proportions.' The coincidence of an almost three-fold increase in classroom disruptions and disciplinary reports along with the staff's direct observations of students using drugs or glamorizing drug and alcohol use led the administration to the inescapable conclusion that the rebellion was being fueled by alcohol and drug abuse as well as the student's misperceptions about the drug culture." At that point, District officials began considering a drug-testing program. They held a parent "input night" to discuss the proposed Student Athlete Drug Policy (Policy) and the parents in attendance gave their unanimous approval. The school board approved the Policy for implementation in the fall of 1989. Its expressed purpose is to prevent student athletes from using drugs, to protect their health and safety, and to provide drug users with assistance programs.

The Policy applies to all students participating in interscholastic athletics. Students wishing to play sports must sign a form consenting to the testing and must obtain the written consent of their parents. Athletes are tested at the beginning of the season for their sport. In addition, once each week of the season the names of the athletes are placed in a "pool" from which a student, with the supervision of two adults, blindly draws the names of 10% of the athletes for random testing. Those selected are notified and tested that same day, if possible. The student to be tested completes a specimen control form which bears an assigned number. Prescription medications that the student is taking must be identified by providing a copy of the prescription or a doctor's authorization. The student then enters an empty locker room accompanied by an adult monitor of the same sex. Each boy selected produces a sample at a urinal, remaining fully clothed with his back to the monitor, who stands approximately 12 to 15 feet behind the student. Monitors may (though do not always) watch the student while he produces the sample, and they listen for normal sounds of urination. Girls produce samples in an enclosed bathroom stall, so that they can be

heard but not observed. After the sample is produced, it is given to the monitor, who checks it for temperature and tampering and then transfers it to a vial. The samples are sent to an independent laboratory, which routinely tests them for amphetamines, cocaine, and marijuana. Other drugs, such as LSD, may be screened at the request of the District, but the identity of a particular student does not determine which drugs will be tested. The laboratory's procedures are 99.94% accurate. The District follows strict procedures regarding the chain of custody and access to test results. The laboratory does not know the identity of the students whose samples it tests. It is authorized to mail written test reports only to the superintendent and to provide test results to District personnel by telephone only after the requesting official recites a code confirming his authority. Only the superintendent, principals, vice-principals, and athletic directors have access to test results, and the results are not kept for more than one year. If a sample tests positive, a second test is administered as soon as possible to confirm the result. If the second test is negative, no further action is taken. If the second test is positive, the athlete's parents are notified, and the school principal convenes a meeting with the student and his parents, at which the student is given the option of (1) participating for six weeks in an assistance program that includes weekly urinalysis, or (2) suffering suspension from athletics for the remainder of the current season and the next athletic season. The student is then retested prior to the start of the next athletic season for which he or she is eligible. The Policy states that a second offense results in automatic imposition of option (3); a third offense in suspension for the remainder of the current season and the next two athletic seasons.

In the fall of 1991, James Acton, then a seventh grader, signed up to play football at one of the District's grade schools. He was denied participation, however, because he and his parents refused to sign the testing consent forms. The Actons filed suit, seeking declaratory and injunctive relief from enforcement of the Policy on the grounds that it violated the Fourth and Fourteenth Amendments to the United States Constitution and Article I, § 9, of the Oregon Constitution. After a bench trial, the District

Court entered an order denying the claims on the merits and dismissing the action. 796 F.Supp., at 1355. The United States Court of Appeals for the Ninth Circuit reversed, holding that the Policy violated both the Fourth and Fourteenth Amendments and Article I, § 9, of the Oregon Constitution. 23 F.3d 1514 (1994). We granted certiorari.

II.

The Fourth Amendment to the United States Constitution provides that the Federal Government shall not violate "[t]he right of the people to be secure in their persons, houses, papers, and effects, against unreasonable searches and seizures . . ." We have held that the Fourteenth Amendment extends this constitutional guarantee to searches and seizures by state officers, *Elkins v. United States*, 364 U.S. 206, 213 (1960), including public school officials, *New Jersey v. T.L.O.*, 469 U.S. 325, 336–337 (1985). In *Skinner v. Railway Labor Executives' Assn.*, 489 U.S. 602, 617 (1989), we held that state-compelled collection and testing of urine, such as that required by the Policy, constitutes a "search" subject to the demands of the Fourth Amendment.

As the text of the Fourth Amendment indicates, the ultimate measure of the constitutionality of a governmental search is "reasonableness." At least in a case such as this, where there was no clear practice, either approving or disapproving the type of search at issue, at the time the constitutional provision was enacted, whether a particular search meets the reasonableness standard "'is judged by balancing its intrusion on the individual's Fourth Amendment interests against its promotion of legitimate governmental interests.'" Skinner, supra, at 619. Where a search is undertaken by law enforcement officials to discover evidence of criminal wrongdoing, this Court has said that reasonableness generally requires the obtaining of a judicial warrant. . . . But a warrant is not required to establish the reasonableness of all government searches; and when a warrant is not required (and the Warrant Clause therefore not applicable), probable cause is not invariably required either. A search unsupported by probable cause can be constitutional, we have said, "when special needs, beyond the normal need for law enforcement, make the warrant and probable-cause requirement impracticable." *Griffin v. Wisconsin*, 483 U.S. 868, 873 (1987).

We have found such "special needs" to exist in the public school context. There, the warrant requirement "would unduly interfere with the maintenance of the swift and informal disciplinary procedures [that are] needed," and "strict adherence to the requirement that searches be based upon probable cause" would undercut "the substantial need of teachers and administrators for freedom to maintain order in the schools." T.L.O., 469 U.S., at 340, 341. The school search we approved in T.L.O., while not

based on probable cause, was based on individualized suspicion of wrongdoing. As we explicitly acknowledged, however, "'the Fourth Amendment imposes no irreducible requirement of such suspicion,'" *Id.*, at 342, n. 8. We have upheld suspicionless searches and seizures to conduct drug testing of railroad personnel involved in train accidents, see Skinner, supra; to conduct random drug testing of federal customs officers who carry arms or are involved in drug interdiction, and to maintain automobile checkpoints looking for illegal immigrants and contraband, . . . and drunk drivers. . . .

III.

The first factor to be considered is the nature of the privacy interest upon which the search here at issue intrudes. The Fourth Amendment does not protect all subjective expectations of privacy, but only those that society recognizes as "legitimate." What expectations are legitimate varies, of course, with context, depending, for example, upon whether the individual asserting the privacy interest is at home, at work, in a car, or in a public park. In addition, the legitimacy of certain privacy expectations vis-a-vis the State may depend upon the individual's legal relationship with the State. For example, in Griffin, we held that, although a "probationer's home, like anyone else's, is protected by the Fourth Amendmen[t]," the supervisory relationship between probationer and State justifies "a degree of impingement upon [a probationer's] privacy that would not be constitutional if applied to the public at large." 483 U.S., at 873, 875. Central, in our view, to the present case is the fact that the subjects of the Policy are (1) children, who (2) have been committed to the temporary custody of the State as schoolmaster. Traditionally at common law, and still today, unemancipated minors lack some of the most fundamental rights of self-determination—including even the right of liberty in its narrow sense, i.e., the right to come and go at will. They are subject, even as to their physical freedom, to the control of their parents or guardians. . . . When parents place minor children in private schools for their education, the teachers and administrators of those schools stand in loco parentis over the children entrusted to them. In fact, the tutor or schoolmaster is the very prototype of that status. . . . In T.L.O. we rejected the notion that public schools, like private schools, exercise only parental power over their students, which of course is not subject to constitutional constraints. 469 U.S., at 336. Such a view of things, we said, "is not entirely 'consonant with compulsory education laws,'" and is inconsistent with our prior decisions treating school officials as state actors for purposes of the Due Process and Free Speech Clauses, T.L.O., at 336. But while denying that the State's power over schoolchildren is formally no more than the delegated power of their parents, T.L.O. did not deny, but indeed emphasized, that the nature of that power is custodial and tutelary, permitting a degree of supervision and control that could not be exercised over free adults. "[A] proper educational environment requires close supervision of schoolchildren, as well as the enforcement of rules against conduct that would be perfectly permissible if undertaken by an adult." 469 U.S., at 339. While we do not, of course, suggest that public schools as a general matter have such a degree of control over children as to give rise to a constitutional "duty to protect" . . . we have acknowledged that for many purposes "school authorities ac[t] in loco parentis," . . . with the power and indeed the duty to "inculcate the habits and manners of civility." Id., at 681. Thus, while children assuredly do not "shed their constitutional rights . . . at the schoolhouse gate," Tinker v. Des Moines Independent Community School Dist., 393 U.S. 503, 506 (1969), the nature of those rights is what is appropriate for children in school. . . .

Fourth Amendment rights, no less than First and Fourteenth Amendment rights, are different in public schools than elsewhere; the "reasonableness" inquiry cannot disregard the schools' custodial and tutelary responsibility for children. For their own good and that of their classmates, public school children are routinely required to submit to various physical examinations, and to be vaccinated against various diseases. Particularly with regard to medical examinations and procedures, therefore, "students within the school environment have a lesser expectation of privacy than members of the population generally."

Legitimate privacy expectations are even less with regard to student athletes. School sports are not for the bashful. They require "suiting up" before each practice or event, and showering and changing afterwards. Public school locker rooms, the usual sites for these activities, are not notable for the privacy they afford. The locker rooms in Vernonia are typical: No individual dressing rooms are provided; shower heads are lined up along a wall, unseparated by any sort of partition or curtain; not even all the toilet stalls have doors. As the United States Court of Appeals for the Seventh Circuit has noted, there is "an element of 'communal undress' inherent in athletic participation," Schaill by Kross v. Tippecanoe County School Corp., 864 F.2d 1309, 1318 (1988). There is an additional respect in which school athletes have a reduced expectation of privacy. By choosing to "go out for the team," they voluntarily subject themselves to a degree of regulation even higher than that imposed on students generally. In Vernonia's public schools, they must submit to a preseason physical exam (James testified that his included the giving of a urine sample, App. 17), they must acquire adequate insurance coverage or sign an insurance waiver, maintain a minimum grade point average, and comply with any "rules of conduct, dress, training hours and related matters as may be established for each sport by the head coach and athletic director with the principal's approval."

Record, Exh. 2, p. 30, P 8. Somewhat like adults who choose to participate in a "closely regulated industry," students who voluntarily participate in school athletics have reason to expect intrusions upon normal rights and privileges, including privacy. See Skinner, 489 U.S., at 627.

IV.

Having considered the scope of the legitimate expectation of privacy at issue here, we turn next to the character of the intrusion that is complained of. We recognized in Skinner that collecting the samples for urinalysis intrudes upon "an excretory function traditionally shielded by great privacy." 489 U.S., at 626. We noted, however, that the degree of intrusion depends upon the manner in which production of the urine sample is monitored. Under the District's Policy, male students produce samples at a urinal along a wall. They remain fully clothed and are only observed from behind, if at all. Female students produce samples in an enclosed stall, with a female monitor standing outside listening only for sounds of tampering. These conditions are nearly identical to those typically encountered in public restrooms, which men, women, and especially schoolchildren use daily. Under such conditions, the privacy interests compromised by the process of obtaining the urine sample are in our view negligible. The other privacy-invasive aspect of urinalysis is, of course, the information it discloses concerning the state of the subject's body, and the materials he has ingested. In this regard it is significant that the tests at issue here look only for drugs, and not for whether the student is, for example, epileptic, pregnant, or diabetic. See Id., at 617. Moreover, the drugs for which the samples are screened are standard, and do not vary according to the identity of the student. And finally, the results of the tests are disclosed only to a limited class of school personnel who have a need to know; and they are not turned over to law enforcement authorities or used for any internal disciplinary function. . . .

Respondents argue, however, that the District's Policy is in fact more intrusive than this suggests, because it requires the students, if they are to avoid sanctions for a falsely positive test, to identify in advance prescription medications they are taking. We agree that this raises some cause for concern. In Von Raab, we flagged as one of the salutary features of the Customs Service drug-testing program the fact that employees were not required to disclose medical information unless they tested positive, and, even then, the information was supplied to a licensed physician rather than to the Government employer. See Von Raab, 489 U.S., at 672-673, n. 2. On the other hand, we have never indicated that requiring advance disclosure of medications is per se unreasonable. Indeed, in Skinner we held that it was not "a significant invasion of privacy." 489 U.S., at 626, n. 7. It can be argued that, in Skinner, the disclosure went only to the medical personnel taking the sample, and the Government personnel analyzing it, . . . and that disclosure to teachers and coaches—to persons who personally know the student—is a greater invasion of privacy. Assuming for the sake of argument that both those propositions are true, we do not believe they establish a difference that respondents are entitled to rely on here. The General Authorization Form that respondents refused to sign, which refusal was the basis for James's exclusion from the sports program, said only (in relevant part): "I . . . authorize the Vernonia School District to conduct a test on a urine specimen which I provide to test for drugs and/or alcohol use. I also authorize the release of information concerning the results of such a test to the Vernonia School District and to the parents and/or guardians of the student." App. 10-11. While the practice of the District seems to have been to have a school official take medication information from the student at the time of the test, that practice is not set forth in, or required by, the Policy, which says simply: "Student athletes who . . . are or have been taking prescription medication must provide verification (either by a copy of the prescription or by doctor's authorization) prior to being tested." *Id.*, at 8. It may well be that, if and when James was selected for random testing at a time that he was taking medication, the School District would have permitted him to provide the requested information in a confidential manner—for example, in a sealed envelope delivered to the testing lab. Nothing in the Policy contradicts that, and when respondents choose, in effect, to challenge the Policy on its face, we will not assume the worst. Accordingly, we reach the same conclusion as in Skinner: that the invasion of privacy was not significant.

V.

Finally, we turn to consider the nature and immediacy of the governmental concern at issue here, and the efficacy of this means for meeting it. In both Skinner and Von Raab, we characterized the government interest motivating the search as "compelling." Skinner, *supra*, 489 U.S., at 628, (interest in preventing railway accidents); Von Raab, *supra*, 489 U.S., at 670 (interest in insuring fitness of customs officials to interdict drugs and handle firearms). Relying on these cases, the District Court held that because the District's program also called for drug testing in the absence of individualized suspicion, the District "must demonstrate a 'compelling need' for the program." 796 F.Supp., at 1363. The Court of Appeals appears to have agreed with this view. See 23 F.3d, at 1526. It is a mistake, however, to think that the phrase "compelling state interest," in the Fourth Amendment context, describes a fixed, minimum quantum of governmental concern, so that one can dispose of a case by answering in isolation the question: Is there a compelling state interest here? Rather, the phrase describes an interest that appears important enough to justify the particular search at hand, in light of other factors that show the search to be relatively intrusive

upon a genuine expectation of privacy. Whether that relatively high degree of government concern is necessary in this case or not, we think it is met. That the nature of the concern is important—indeed, perhaps compelling—can hardly be doubted. Deterring drug use by our Nation's schoolchildren is at least as important as enhancing efficient enforcement of the Nation's laws against the importation of drugs, which was the governmental concern in Von Raab, or deterring drug use by engineers and trainmen, which was the governmental concern in Skinner. School years are the time when the physical, psychological, and addictive effects of drugs are most severe. "Maturing nervous systems are more critically impaired by intoxicants than mature ones are; childhood losses in learning are lifelong and profound"; "children grow chemically dependent more quickly than adults, and their record of recovery is depressingly poor." . . . And of course the effects of a drug-infested school are visited not just upon the users, but upon the entire student body and faculty, as the educational process is disrupted. In the present case, moreover, the necessity for the State to act is magnified by the fact that this evil is being visited not just upon individuals at large, but upon children for whom it has undertaken a special responsibility of care and direction. Finally, it must not be lost sight of that this program is directed more narrowly to drug use by school athletes, where the risk of immediate physical harm to the drug user or those with whom he is playing his sport is particularly high. Apart from psychological effects, which include impairment of judgment, slow reaction time, and a lessening of the perception of pain, the particular drugs screened by the District's Policy have been demonstrated to pose substantial physical risks to athletes. . . .

As for the immediacy of the District's concerns: We are not inclined to question—indeed, we could not possibly find clearly erroneous—the District Court's conclusion that "a large segment of the student body, particularly those involved in interscholastic athletics, was in a state of rebellion," that "[d]isciplinary actions had reached 'epidemic proportions,'" and that "the rebellion was being fueled by alcohol and drug abuse as well as by the student's misperceptions about the drug culture." 796 F.Supp., at 1357. That is an immediate crisis of greater proportions than existed in Skinner, where we upheld the Government's drug-testing program based on findings of drug use by railroad employees nationwide, without proof that a problem existed on the particular railroads whose employees were subject to the test. . . . As to the efficacy of this means for addressing the problem: It seems to us self-evident that a drug problem largely fueled by the "role model" effect of athletes' drug use, and of particular danger to athletes, is effectively addressed by making sure that athletes do not use drugs. Respondents argue that a "less intrusive means to the same end" was available, namely, "drug testing on suspicion of drug use." Brief for

Respondents 45-46. We have repeatedly refused to declare that only the "least intrusive" search practicable can be reasonable under the Fourth Amendment. Skinner, supra, at 629, n. 9 (collecting cases). Respondents' alternative entails substantial difficulties—if it is indeed practicable at all. It may be impracticable, for one thing, simply because the parents who are willing to accept random drug testing for athletes are not willing to accept accusatory drug testing for all students, which transforms the process into a badge of shame.

Respondents' proposal brings the risk that teachers will impose testing arbitrarily upon troublesome but not drug-likely students. It generates the expense of defending lawsuits that charge such arbitrary imposition, or that simply demand greater process before accusatory drug testing is imposed. And not least of all, it adds to the ever-expanding diversionary duties of schoolteachers the new function of spotting and bringing to account drug abuse, a task for which they are ill prepared, and which is not readily compatible with their vocation. . . . In many respects, we think, testing based on "suspicion" of drug use would not be better, but worse.

VI.

Taking into account all the factors we have considered above—the decreased expectation of privacy, the relative unobtrusiveness of the search, and the severity of the need met by the search—we conclude Vernonia's Policy is reasonable and hence constitutional. We caution against the assumption that suspicionless drug testing will readily pass constitutional muster in other contexts. The most significant element in this case is the first we discussed: that the Policy was undertaken in furtherance of the government's responsibilities, under a public school system, as guardian and tutor of children entrusted to its care. Just as when the government conducts a search in its capacity as employer (a warrantless search of an absent employee's desk to obtain an urgently needed file, for example), the relevant question is whether that intrusion upon privacy is one that a reasonable employer might engage in, see *O'Connor v. Ortega*, 480 U.S. 709; so also when the government acts as guardian and tutor the relevant question is whether the search is one that a reasonable guardian and tutor might undertake. Given the findings of need made by the District Court, we conclude that in the present case it is.

We may note that the primary guardians of Vernonia's schoolchildren appear to agree. The record shows no objection to this districtwide program by any parents other than the couple before us here—even though, as we have described, a public meeting was held to obtain parents' views. We find insufficient basis to contradict the judgment of Vernonia's parents, its school board, and the District Court, as to what was reasonably in the interest of these children under the circumstances. The Ninth Circuit held that Vernonia's Policy not only violated the Fourth Amendment, but also, by reason of that violation, contravened Article I, § 9, of the Oregon Constitution. Our conclusion that the former holding was in error means that the latter holding rested on a flawed premise. We therefore vacate the judgment, and remand the case to the Court of Appeals for further proceedings consistent with this opinion.

It is so ordered.

CASES ON THE SUPPLEMENTAL CD

Shoemaker v. Handell, 795 F.2d 1136 (1986). This case examines the state's interest in drug testing jockeys in the horse-racing industry.

Hill v. National Collegiate Athletic Association, 865 P.2d 633 (1994). This case examines whether the NCAA drug testing program violates state constitutional protections.

Board of Education of Independent School District No. 92 of Pottawatomie County v. Earls, 536 U.S. 822 (2002). This case examines whether the state can expand drug testing programs to include all middle and high school students who participate in any extracurricular activity, not just sport.

QUESTIONS YOU SHOULD BE ABLE TO ANSWER

1. What are some of the constitutional protections available to fight an unwanted drug test?

2. Why are NCAA athletes unable to challenge the NCAA drug testing program under the fourth Amendment of the United States Constitution?

3. How does the court determine if a drug test is reasonable under the Fourth Amendment of the United States Constitution?

4. Drug testing of professional team athletes in the Unites States are governed by what?

5. What is WADA? What role does it play in sports?

REFERENCES

Cases

Bally v. Northeastern University, 403 Mass. 713, 532 N.E.2d 49 (1989).

Board of Education of Independent School District No. 92 of Pottawatomie County v. Earls, 536 U.S. 822 (2002).

Brennan v. Board of Trustees, 691 So.2d 324 (1997).

Foschi v. United States Swimming, Inc., 916 F. Supp. 232 (1996).

Hill v. National Collegiate Athletic Association, 865 P.2d 633, 26 Cal. Rptr.2d 834 (1994).

Landis v. USADA, CAS 2007/A/1394.

Long v. National Football League, 870 F. Supp. 101 (1994).

Safford Unified Sch. Dist. # 1 v. Redding, 2009 U.S. LEXIS 4735.

Shoemaker v. Handell, 795 F.2d 1136 (1986).

Trinidad School District v. Lopez, 963 P.2d 1095 (1998).

University of Colorado v. Derdeyn, 863 P.2d 929 (Colo. 1993).

Vernonia School District 47J v. Acton, 515 U.S. 646 (1995).

Publications

Popke, M. (2009, April). Drug Wars. *Athletic Business,* p.12.

Legislation

United States Constitution, Fourth Amendment.

Websites

http://www.wada-ama.org/rtecontent/document/code_v2009_En.pdf

6.24 *Participants with Disabilities*

—John T. Wolohan
ITHACA COLLEGE

In 2006, Tatyana McFadden was a 16-year-old high school junior at Atholton High School. Although a world class athlete, McFadden, who has spina bifida and has been paralyzed from below her waist since early childhood, sued Howard County officials under § 504 of the Rehabilitation Act of 1973 and Title II of the Americans with Disabilities Act, seeking the right to participate in races alongside non-wheelchair racers, so-called "mixed races" because, although racing at the same time, athletes in wheelchairs do not compete directly against the able-bodied runners *McFadden v. Cousin*, (2006).

After a hearing on McFadden's motion for a preliminary injunction, the court granted the motion and she was permitted by local and state authorities in Maryland (including defendants here) to race alongside non-disabled racers. In addition, in negotiations with Howard County officials, McFadden reached agreement on how individual and team points would be awarded based on her participation in races sanctioned by the County.

While at first glance it is easy to dismiss the actions of the Howard County officials as discriminatory, the officials did have some legitimate concerns. First, does allowing McFadden to compete in a wheelchair against non-disabled racers fundamentally alter the race? Second, since individuals in wheelchairs have an advantage over longer distances, does awarding McFadden points unfairly change the outcome of meets? Also, while the track is eight lanes wide, does allowing a wheelchair on the track pose a danger to other runners who are not accustomed to having it on the track?

As the McFadden case illustrates, the line between lawful refusal to extend eligibility requirements and illegal discrimination against individuals with disabilities is getting cloudier all the time. This is especially true since 1990, when the Americans with Disabilities Act (ADA) was signed into law. Yet even with the enactment of the ADA, individuals with disabilities still face a number of obstacles in their struggle to participate in athletics. This section examines some of the many problems of individuals with disabilities in their fight to participate in sport and recreation activities.

⁂FUNDAMENTAL CONCEPTS

✗ As recently as 1970, children with learning disabilities were denied access into a number of state public school systems because it was thought that their presence would interfere with the learning environment of students without any disabilities (Clement, 1988). To remedy this situation, Congress, in the early 1970s, began enacting federal legislation designed to increase the opportunities available to individuals with disabilities (Clement, 1988). The first law passed by Congress was the Rehabilitation Act of 1973.

⁂The Rehabilitation Act of 1973

— Section 504 of the Rehabilitation Act states that:

> *"No otherwise qualified handicapped individual in the United States, . . . shall solely by reason of his handicap, be excluded from participation in, be denied the benefits of, or be subjected to discrimination under any program or activity receiving Federal financial assistance. . . ." [29 U.S.C. 794 (Supp. V 1993)]*

One of the stated intents of the Rehabilitation Act was to provide individuals with disabilities the opportunity to participate in physical education and athletic programs or activities without being discriminated against due to their disability. For an individual to successfully pursue a claim under § 504, he or she must establish four elements: (1) that he or she is an *individual with a disability*; (2) that he or she is *otherwise qualified* for the athletic activity; (3) that he or she is being excluded from athletic participation *solely by reason of* their disabilities; and (4) that the *school, or institution is receiving federal financial assistance* (29 U.S.C. 794).

Because most challenges under § 504 hinge on the determination of the "otherwise qualified" element or the "solely by reason of" element, an examination of the meaning of those two elements is important. The U.S. Supreme Court, in *Southeastern Community College v. Davis* (1979), interpreted the phrase "otherwise qualified" to mean someone who is able to meet all of a program's requirements in spite of his or her handicap (*Southeastern Community College v. Davis*, 422 U.S. 397, at 406, 1979). Davis, who suffered from a serious hearing disability, sought entry into Southeastern Community College's school of nursing. The Supreme Court, in finding that Davis's hearing disability made it impossible for her to safely complete the nursing program, stated that §504 of the Rehabilitation Act does not compel an institution to disregard an individual's disability or to make substantial modifications in their programs to accommodate individuals with disabilities.

In *Alexander v. Choate* (1985), the Supreme Court addressed what types of modifications would be required under §504 when it held that although an organization need not be required to make fundamental or substantial modifications to accommodate an individual's disability, *it may be required to make reasonable ones*. Reasonable accommodation may include (1) making facilities used by employees readily accessible to and usable by individuals with disabilities, and (2) job restructuring, part-time or modified work schedules, acquisition or modification of equipment or devices, the provision of readers or interpreters, and similar actions [34 C.F.R. § 104.12. (b)].

- The requirement that an individual be excluded *solely by reason of* the disability is met if the individual is being excluded due to their disability. For example, in *Poole v. South Plainfield Board of Education* (1980), the South Plainfield Board of Education denied Richard Poole the right to participate in South Plainfield's interscholastic wrestling program due to the fact that he was born with one kidney. Therefore, the court concluded that Poole was being excluded from participation in athletics "solely by reason of" the fact he had one kidney.

- The issue of whether someone is being excluded "solely by reason of" their disability is more difficult when an individual, due to an illness or learning disability, is over the athletic association's maximum age requirement by the time he or she reaches their senior year in high school. *University Interscholastic League (UIL) and Bailey Marshall v. Buchanan* (1993) is a perfect illustration of the problem presented in these cases. In *UIL v. Buchanan* two nineteen-year-old students who were diagnosed with learning disabilities sought a permanent injunction against the enforcement of UIL's rule requiring all athletes to be under nineteen years old. In support of the age requirement, the UIL argued that the age requirement was necessary to ensure the safety of the participating student-athletes and to ensure the equality of competitors. The UIL also argued that the age rule did not discriminate against the plaintiffs because of their handicaps, but was applied equally against all students. Therefore, the plaintiffs were ineligible due to their ages, not their handicaps.

The Court of Appeals in affirming the trial court's injunction, enjoined UIL from enforcing the age rule against the plaintiffs, held that except for their handicaps the students would have turned nineteen after September 1 of their senior year and would have been age-eligible to participate in interscholastic athletics. In determining whether UIL had made reasonable accommodations for the plaintiffs' disabilities, the Court of Appeals examined the waiver mechanism UIL had in place for other eligibility rules. The waiver of the age rule, the Court of Appeals found, would be a reasonable accommodation by UIL to ensure that individuals with disabilities achieve meaningful access. The UIL's "no exception" policy to the age requirement, therefore, had to yield to the reasonable accommodation requirement of § 504 of the Rehabilitation Act.

For other cases challenging high school athletic association eligibility rules, see: *Cruz v. Pennsylvania Interscholastic Athletic Association*, (2001); *Dennin v. Connecticut Interscholastic Athletic Conference*, (1996); *Johnson v. Florida High School Activities Association*, (1995); *Pottgen v. Missouri State High School Athletic Association*, (1994); and *Sandison v. Michigan High School Athletic Association*, (1995).

Individuals with Disabilities Education Act (IDEA)

On the heels of the Rehabilitation Act of 1973, Congress enacted the Education for All Handicapped Children Act of 1975. The purpose of the Education for All Handicapped Children Act was to increase the educational opportunity available to children with disabilities by providing the children a free appropriate public education that emphasizes special education and related services designed to meet their unique needs [20 U.S.C. 1400 (c)]. In 1990, the Education for All Handicapped Children Act was amended and renamed the **Individuals with Disabilities Education Act (IDEA).**

To satisfy the goal of the IDEA, local educational agencies, together with the student's teacher and parents, are required to develop a written statement or individualized education program (IEP) outlining achievable educational objectives for the student. Although less specific with regard to athletics than those pursuant to §504 of the Rehabilitation Act, the regulations adopted under the IDEA do require each public agency to ensure that a variety of educational programs and services, including physical education, available to children without disabilities are available to those covered under the act. Besides providing educational programs and services, each public agency is also required to provide nonacademic and extracurricular activities and services in such manner as is necessary to afford children with disabilities an equal opportunity for participation in those services and activities [34 C.F.R. § 300.306(a)]. For example, in *Lambert v. West Virginia State Board of Education* (1994), a high school basketball player, who has been deaf since birth, won the right to require her school to provide her with a sign language interpreter so that she could compete on the girl's basketball team. In holding that the Board of Education was required to provide a signer for the plaintiff, the court found that the assistance of a signer was a reasonable accommodation that provided the plaintiff with equal access to extracurricular activities.

Another example of a student-athlete successfully using the IDEA to gain participation rights is *Crocker v. Tennessee Secondary School Athletic Association*, (1992). In *Crocker* the plaintiff transferred from a private school into his local public high school so that he could receive the special education he needed, which was not available in the private school. When the plaintiff attempted to participate in interscholastic athletics at his new school, the TSSAA ruled that he was ineligible. According to TSSAA rules, any student who transfers from one TSSAA member school to another is ineligible to participate in interscholastic sports for 12 months. The plaintiff argued that the TSSAA, by enforcing its transfer rule, was depriving him of his rights guaranteed under the IDEA. In ruling for Crocker, the Court held that because the plaintiff's transfer was motivated by his handicap, TSSAA's refusal to waive its transfer rule violated the IDEA.

Another important issue under IDEA is whether the student's participation in interscholastic athletics is a related service that should have been incorporated into his or her individualized education program (IEP). The importance of including participation in interscholastic athletics in a student's IEP can be seen in *T.H. v. Montana High School Association*, (1992). In *T.H. v. MHSA*, the plaintiff, after being diagnosed as having a learning disability, was provided with an IEP in accordance with the IDEA. One component of the IEP was for the plaintiff to participate in interscholastic athletics as a motivational tool. Before his senior year, the Montana High School Association ruled T.H. ineligible to compete in interscholastic athletics due to his age. The court, in finding for the plaintiff, held that when participation in interscholastic sports is included as a component of the IEP, the privilege of competing in interscholastic sports is transformed into a federally protected right.

Ted Stevens Olympic and Amateur Sports Act

Another piece of legislation impacting the rights of individuals with disabilities is the **Ted Stevens Olympic and Amateur Sports Act** (36 U.S.C. § 220501). Originally passed in 1978 and called the Amateur Sports Act (36 U.S.C. § 371), the current version of the law was adopted in 1998 after the law's sponsor, Senator Ted Stevens of Alaska, and grants the U.S. Olympic Committee (USOC) exclusive jurisdiction over amateur athletics in the United States, including all matters pertaining to U.S. participation in the Olympic Games, the Paralympic Games, and the Pan-American Games.

In particular, the Amateur Sports Act required the USOC to "encourage and provide assistance to amateur athletic programs and competition for handicapped individuals, including, where feasible, the expansion of opportunities for meaningful participation by handicapped individuals in programs of athletic competition for able-bodied individuals" [36 U.S.C. § 374 (13)].

The USOC attempted to accomplish this goal by establishing the Committee on Sport for the Disabled and by financially supporting various other sports organizations, such as Disabled Sports USA and the Wheelchair Sports USA, to name a couple.

The Ted Stevens Olympic and Amateur Sports Act places a greater responsibility on the USOC and its constituent organizations to serve elite athletes with a disability, in particular Paralympic athletes. As a result of the 1998 amendments, the USOC has sought to expand the opportunities available to athletes with disabilities by establishing a Paralympic Division within the USOC, providing increased funding and logistical support for athletes and sporting bodies, and recognizing Paralympic athletes as members of the USOC Athletes Advisory Committee and providing other avenues for input from Paralympic athletes.

Not everyone, however, has been happy with the amount of money and other support the USOC provides to Paralympic athletes. For example, in *Hollonbeck v. USOC*, (2008), Scot Hollonbeck, Jose Antonio Iniguez, and Jacob Walter Jung Ho Heilveil challenged the USOC's policy of providing Athlete Support Programs only to Olympic team members, to the exclusion of Paralympic team members, as violating §504 of the Rehabilitation Act.

In rejecting Hollonbeck and the other athletes' claim, the Tenth Circuit Court ruled that the athletes were not "otherwise qualified" for the Athlete Support Programs *Hollonbeck v. USOC*, (2008). In addition, the court ruled that the USOC's policy of excluding paralympians was neither facially discriminatory nor discriminatory by proxy. The policy did not contain an explicit requirement of not being disabled; further, the designation of "Olympic athlete" was not a proxy for non-disabled athletes, as there was no fit between being an Olympic athlete and not being disabled. Finally, though Hollonbeck and the others argued that the policy effectively screened out disabled amateur athletes, the court ruled that disparate impact, by itself, did not create a prima facie case under § 504 *Hollonbeck v. USOC*, (2008).

✳ The Americans with Disabilities Act (ADA)

Perhaps the most powerful weapon individuals with disabilities have in their fight to participate in interscholastic athletics is **The Americans with Disabilities Act (ADA)**. Signed into law July 26, 1990, the purpose of the ADA is "to provide a clear and comprehensive national mandate for the elimination of discrimination against individuals with disabilities." The ADA focuses on eradicating barriers by requiring public entities to consider whether reasonable accommodations could be made to remove any barrier created by a person's disability (Wolohan, 1997). The ADA defines a "qualified individual with a disability" as any individual with a disability, either physically or mentally, "who, with or without reasonable modifications to rules, policies, or practices, the removal of architectural, communication . . . barriers, or the provision or auxiliary aids and services, meets the essential eligibility requirements for the receipt of services or the participation in programs or activities provided by a public entity" (42 U.S.C. 12115). The ADA is divided into five sections covering the rights of the disabled in the areas of employment, public services, transportation, and telecommunications. The three sections athletic administrators should be aware of are Title I, which covers employment; Title II, which covers public services; and Title III, which covers public accommodations and services operated by private entities.

Even if an individual is able to meet all the requirements of the ADA, the law does not require an organization to accommodate a person "*when that individual poses a direct threat to the health or safety of others*" (28 C.F.R. § 36.208). For example, in *Anderson v. Little League Baseball, Inc.* (1992), a youth baseball coach, who was confined to a wheelchair and had coached Little League Baseball for the previous three years as an on-field coach, sued the league after it adopted a policy prohibiting coaches in wheelchairs from on-field coaching. In support of the policy, the league claimed that the coach posed a direct threat to the health or safety of the athletes and that the policy was intended to protect the players from collisions with the wheelchair. In ruling for the coach, the Court said that the league's policy fell markedly short of the requirements of the ADA. The court found no evidence indicating that the plaintiff posed a direct threat to the health or safety of others.

Ever since the U.S. Supreme Court's ruling in Martin, sport and recreation administrators around the country have been forced to ask themselves what rules are essential to the nature of sport. In *Kuketz v. Petronelli*, 821 N.E.2d 473 (MA. 2005), Stephen Kuketz, a nationally ranked wheelchair racquetball player, wanted to join the

Brockton Athletic Club men's "A" league so that he could compete against the best able-bodied players available to help prepare for upcoming international wheelchair competitions. Because of his physical limitations, however, Kuketz requested that the club allow him the wheelchair-racquetball-standard two bounces during "A" league play, instead of the one bounce allowable under standard racquetball rules.

Citing safety reasons, the club rejected Kuketz's request. Disappointed with the decision, Kuketz sued the club, claiming the decision violated both federal and state antidiscrimination laws, and that the ADA required the club to conduct an individualized assessment both of his abilities and of the reasonableness of the requested modification.

In evaluating whether the club unlawfully discriminated against Kuketz when it refused to modify its policies and practices, the Supreme Judicial Court of Massachusetts held that, unlike the use of carts in golf, the allowance for more than one bounce in racquetball was inconsistent with the fundamental character of the game. As expressly articulated in the rules of racquetball, the court found that the essence of the game of racquetball is the hitting of a moving ball with a racquet before the second bounce. Giving a player in a wheelchair two bounces and a player on foot one bounce in head-to-head competition would alter such an essential aspect of the game that it would be unacceptable, even if it affected all competitors equally. In addition, the court found that, unlike golf, the speed at which racquetball is played is important and is one of the factors distinguishing players in different levels. Therefore, if one player were allowed to play the game with two bounces, it would require a change in the strategy, positioning, and movement of the players during the game, and would essentially create a new game, with new strategies and new rules.

As for Kuketz's argument that the club should do an individual assessment of his particular circumstances before rejecting his specific modification requests, the court found that this argument was based on a misreading of the ADA and *Martin*. In particular, the court held that although an individualized inquiry was required by the ADA, no assessment was necessary if waiving the one-bounce rule would cause a fundamental alteration to the nature of the event. Therefore, because Kuketz's requested modification would in fact require the waiver of an essential rule of competition, the club did not need to make an individualized inquiry to determine the reasonableness of those modifications (Wolohan, 2005).

Another interesting ADA case involving high school athletes is *Badgett v. Alabama High School Athletic Association*, (2007). Like the McFadden case in the introduction, Mallerie Badgett, who has cerebral palsy and uses a wheelchair, sued the Alabama High School Athletic Association (AHSAA) under Section 504 of the Rehabilitation Act, and Title II of the Americans with Disabilities Act in an attempt to force them to allow her to compete against able-bodied athletes.

The AHSAA had a separate wheelchair division. All the athletes competing in the division and their times in each event would be recorded at each meet. The wheelchair athletes with the eight fastest times in each event throughout the entire track and field season would automatically advance to the state championship without having to compete in the section qualifying meet. Once in the state meet, the wheelchair athletes representing their respective school teams would compete for the state championship in the wheelchair division. Badgett, however, was the only competitor in the Alabama wheelchair division. As such, she did not want to compete in a separate wheelchair division because, among other reasons, she believes that competing alone makes her an "exhibition" rather than a part of her team.

The district court, however, after reviewing the evidence and arguments presented, rejected Badgett's claims. In support of its' findings, the court ruled that the modifications requested by Badgett: (1) allowing her to race alongside able-bodied athletes, and (2) allowing her individual points earned to count toward her team's point total in the able-bodied track and field division were unreasonable. In particular, the court noted that neither the ADA nor the Rehabilitation Act requires a public entity to adopt the "best" modification or the modification requested by a person with a disability; rather, these statutes require only a *reasonable* modification *Badgett v. Alabama High School Athletic Association*, (2007). The separate division implemented by the AHSAA, the court ruled, was reasonable.

In addition, the court also deferred to AHSAA's findings that adopting Badgett's request would raise legitimate safety concerns that are inherent in having able-bodied athletes and wheelchair athletes compete in mixed heats. The AHSAA's conclusions regarding these legitimate safety issues, the court held, should be respected if reasonable and supported by the available evidence *Badgett v. Alabama High School Athletic Association*, (2007). As for Badgett claim that she could participate safely alongside able-bodied athletes, the court ruled that the AHSAA must be allowed to adopt a longer-term view. Adopting Badgett's proposed modification, the court found, would in future competitions require the AHSAA to conduct a detailed, individualized evaluation of every wheelchair athlete's skill and ability to race safely with able-bodied runners. Such evaluations make this approach administratively unworkable and unreasonable (*Badgett v. Alabama High School Athletic Association*, 2007). Of particular importance to the court was the AHSAA's evidence that separate wheelchair divisions and/or staggered starting times are the norm in road races and national or international track and field competitions. This evidence, the court ruled, bolsters a finding that the separate division appropriately addresses the concerns of wheelchair athletes.

Finally, the court ruled that allowing Bedgett's individual points to count toward her team's total in the able-bodied track and field division, especially when no other school in the entire state has a wheelchair athlete, would be unfair and therefore unreasonable. Such a modification, the court ruled, would fundamentally alter the nature of the track and field events in the able-bodied divisions.

- **Title I—Employment.** Title I provides that "no covered entity shall discriminate against a qualified individual with a disability because of the disability of such individual in regard to job application procedures, the hiring, advancement, or discharge of employees, employee compensation, job training, and other terms, conditions, and privileges of employment" (42 U.S.C. § 12112). Title I of the ADA is covered in more detail in Section 7.16, *Title I of the Americans with Disabilities Act*.

Following in his father's footsteps on disability legislation, on September of 2008, President George W. Bush signed the **Americans with Disabilities Act Amendments Act of 2008**. The ADA Amendments Act of 2008, which went into effect on January 1, 2009, is intended to restore some of the ADA's original intent and restore coverage to some employees who have been cut out of the law's protections. For more information on Title I of the ADA and the ADA Amendments Act of 2008, see Section 7.16, *Title I of the Americans with Disabilities Act*.

- **Title II—Public Services.** The section that covers the activities of high school athletic associations is Title II—Public Services. Title II, which is based on §504 of the Rehabilitation Act, provides that "no qualified individual with a disability shall, by reason of such disability, be excluded from participation in or be denied the benefits of the services, programs, or activities of a public entity, or be subjected to discrimination by any such entity" (42 U.S.C. § 12132).

In interpreting the meaning of Title II, the Courts used the case history of §504 of the Rehabilitation Act. To establish a violation of Title II of the ADA, therefore, an individual must establish the following elements: (1) that he or she is a "qualified individual with a disability"; (2) that he or she is "otherwise qualified" for the activity; (3) that he or she is being excluded from athletic participation "solely by reason of" their disabilities; and (4) that he or she is being discriminated against by a public entity.

- **Title III—Public Accommodations and Services Operated by Private Entities.** The provisions of Title III provide that "no individual shall be discriminated against on the basis of disability in the full and equal enjoyment of the goods, services, facilities, privileges, advantages, or accommodations of any place of public accommodation by any person who owns, leases, or operates a place of public accommodation" (42 U.S.C. § 12182).

SIGNIFICANT CASE

The following case raises two interesting questions concerning the application of the Americans with Disabilities Act: first, whether the Act protects access to professional golf tournaments by a qualified entrant with a disability; and second, whether a disabled contestant may be denied the use of a golf cart because it would "fundamentally alter the nature" of the tournaments to allow him to ride when all other contestants must walk.

PGA TOUR, INC. V. CASEY MARTIN

United States Supreme Court
532 U.S. 661 (2001)

JUSTICE STEVENS delivered the opinion of the Court.

This case raises two questions concerning the application of the Americans with Disabilities Act . . . to a gifted athlete: first, whether the Act protects access to professional golf tournaments by a qualified entrant with a disability; and second, whether a disabled contestant may be denied the use of a golf cart because it would "fundamentally alter the nature" of the tournament, to allow him to ride when all other contestants must walk.

I.

Petitioner PGA TOUR, Inc., a nonprofit entity formed in 1968, sponsors and cosponsors professional golf tournaments conducted on three annual tours. About 200 golfers participate in the PGA TOUR; about 170 in the NIKE TOUR; and about 100 in the SENIOR PGA TOUR. PGA TOUR and NIKE TOUR tournaments typically are 4-day events, played on courses leased and operated by petitioner. The entire field usually competes in two 18-hole rounds played on Thursday and Friday; those who survive the "cut" play on Saturday and Sunday and receive prize money in amounts determined by their aggregate scores for all four rounds. The revenues generated by television, admissions, concessions, and contributions from cosponsors amount to about $300 million a year, much of which is distributed in prize money.

There are various ways of gaining entry into particular tours. For example, a player who wins three NIKE TOUR events in the same year, or is among the top-15 money winners on that tour, earns the right to play in the PGA TOUR. Additionally, a golfer may obtain a spot in an official tournament through successfully competing in "open" qualifying rounds, which are conducted the week before each tournament. Most participants, however, earn playing privileges in the PGA TOUR or NIKE TOUR by way of a three-stage qualifying tournament known as the "Q-School."

Any member of the public may enter the Q-School by paying a $3,000 entry fee and submitting two letters of reference from, among others, PGA TOUR or NIKE TOUR members. The $3,000 entry fee covers the players' greens fees and the cost of golf carts, which are permitted during the first two stages, but which have been prohibited during the third stage since 1997. Each year, over a thousand contestants compete in the first stage, which consists of four 18-hole rounds at different locations. Approximately half of them make it to the second stage, which also includes 72 holes. Around 168 players survive the second stage and advance to the final one, where they compete over 108 holes. Of those finalists, about a fourth qualify for membership in the PGA TOUR, and the rest gain membership in the NIKE TOUR.

Three sets of rules govern competition in tour events. First, the "Rules of Golf," jointly written by the United States Golf Association (USGA) and the Royal and Ancient Golf Club of Scotland, apply to the game as it is played, not only by millions of amateurs on public courses and in private country clubs throughout the United States and worldwide, but also by the professionals in the tournaments conducted by petitioner, the USGA, the Ladies' Professional Golf Association, and the Senior Women's Golf Association. Those rules do not prohibit the use of golf carts at any time.

Second, the "Conditions of Competition and Local Rules," often described as the "hard card," apply specifically to petitioner's professional tours. The hard cards for the PGA TOUR and NIKE TOUR require players to walk the golf course during tournaments, but not during open qualifying rounds. On the SENIOR PGA TOUR, which is limited to golfers age 50 and older, the contestants may use golf carts. Most seniors, however, prefer to walk.

Third, "Notices to Competitors" are issued for particular tournaments and cover conditions for that specific event. Such a notice may, for example, explain how the Rules of Golf should be applied to a particular water hazard or man-made obstruction. It might also authorize the use of carts to speed up play when there is an unusual distance between one green and the next tee.

The basic Rules of Golf, the hard cards, and the weekly notices apply equally to all players in tour competitions. As one of petitioner's witnesses explained with reference to "the Masters Tournament, which is golf at its very highest level . . . the key is to have everyone tee off on the first hole under exactly the same conditions and all of them be tested over that 72-hole event under the conditions that exist during those four days of the event."

II.

Casey Martin is a talented golfer. As an amateur, he won 17 Oregon Golf Association junior events before he was 15, and won the state championship as a high school senior. He played on the Stanford University golf team that won the 1994 National Collegiate Athletic Association (NCAA) championship. As a professional, Martin qualified for the NIKE TOUR in 1998 and 1999, and based on his 1999 performance, qualified for the PGA TOUR in 2000. In the 1999 season, he entered 24 events, made the cut 13 times, and had 6 top-10 finishes, coming in second twice and third once.

Martin is also an individual with a disability as defined in the Americans with Disabilities Act. Since birth he has been afflicted with Klippel-Trenaunay-Weber Syndrome, a degenerative circulatory disorder that obstructs the flow of blood from his right leg back to his heart. The disease is progressive; it causes severe pain and has atrophied his right leg. During the latter part of his college career, because of the progress of the disease, Martin could no longer walk an 18-hole golf course. Walking not only caused him pain, fatigue, and anxiety, but also created a significant risk of hemorrhaging, developing blood clots, and fracturing his tibia so badly that an amputation might be required. For these reasons, Stanford made written requests to the Pacific 10 Conference and the NCAA to waive for Martin their rules requiring players to walk and carry their own clubs. The requests were granted.

When Martin turned pro and entered petitioner's Q-School, the hard card permitted him to use a cart during his successful progress through the first two stages. He made request, supported by detailed medical records, for permission to use a golf cart during the third stage. Petitioner refused to review those records or to waive its walking rule for the third stage. Martin therefore filed this action. A preliminary injunction entered by the District Court made it possible for him to use a cart in the final stage of the Q-School and as a competitor in the NIKE TOUR and PGA TOUR. Although not bound by the injunction, and despite its support for petitioner's position in this litigation, the USGA voluntarily granted Martin a similar waiver in events that it sponsors, including the U.S. Open.

IV.

Congress enacted the ADA in 1990 to remedy widespread discrimination against disabled individuals. In studying the need for such legislation, Congress found that "historically, society has tended to isolate and segregate individuals with disabilities, and, despite some improvements, such forms of discrimination against individuals with disabilities continue to be a serious and pervasive social problem." . . .

To effectuate its sweeping purpose, the ADA forbids discrimination against disabled individuals in major areas of public life, among them employment (Title I of the Act), public services (Title II), and public accommodations (Title III). At issue now, as a threshold matter, is the applicability of Title III to petitioner's golf tours and qualifying rounds, in particular to petitioner's treatment of a qualified disabled golfer wishing to compete in those events.

Title III of the ADA prescribes, as a "general rule":

"No individual shall be discriminated against on the basis of disability in the full and equal enjoyment of the goods, services, facilities, privileges, advantages, or accommodations of any place of public accommodation by any person who owns, leases (or leases to), or operates a place of public accommodation." 42 U.S.C. § 12182(a).

The phrase "public accommodation" is defined in terms of 12 extensive categories, which the legislative history indicates "should be construed liberally" to afford people with disabilities "equal access" to the wide variety of establishments available to the nondisabled.

It seems apparent, from both the general rule and the comprehensive definition of "public accommodation," that petitioner's golf tours and their qualifying rounds fit comfortably within the coverage of Title III, and Martin within its protection. The events occur on "golf courses," a type of place specifically identified by the Act as a public accommodation. § 12181(7)(L). In addition, at all relevant times, petitioner "leases" and "operates" golf courses to conduct its Q-School and tours. § 12182(a). As a lessor and operator of golf courses, then, petitioner must not discriminate against any "individual" in the "full and equal enjoyment of the goods, services, facilities, privileges, advantages, or accommodations" of those courses. *Ibid.* Certainly, among the "privileges" offered by petitioner on the courses are those of competing in the Q-School and playing in the tours; indeed, the former is a privilege for which thousands of individuals from the general public pay, and the latter is one for which they vie. Martin, of course, is one of those individuals. It would therefore appear that Title III of the ADA, by its plain terms, prohibits petitioner from denying Martin equal access to its tours on the basis of his disability. . . .

Petitioner argues otherwise. To be clear about its position, it does not assert (as it did in the District Court) that it is a private club altogether exempt from Title III's coverage. In fact, petitioner admits that its tournaments are conducted at places of public accommodation. Nor does petitioner contend (as it did in both the District Court and the Court of Appeals) that the competitors' area "behind the ropes" is not a public accommodation, notwithstanding the status of the rest of the golf course. Rather, petitioner reframes the coverage issue by arguing that the competing golfers are not members of the class protected by Title III of the ADA.

According to petitioner, Title III is concerned with discrimination against "clients and customers" seeking to obtain "goods and services" at places of public accommodation, whereas it is Title I that protects persons who work at such places. As the argument goes, petitioner operates not a "golf course" during its tournaments but a "place of exhibition or entertainment," . . . and a professional golfer such as Martin, like an actor in a theater production, is a provider rather than a consumer of the entertainment that petitioner sells to the public. Martin therefore cannot bring a claim under Title III because he is not one of the "'*clients or customers* of the covered public accommodation.'" Rather, Martin's claim of discrimination is "job-related" and could only be brought under Title I—but that Title does not apply because he is an independent contractor (as the District Court found) rather than an employee.

* * *

We need not decide whether petitioner's construction of the statute is correct, because petitioner's argument falters even on its own terms. If Title III's protected class were limited to "clients or customers," it would be entirely appropriate to classify the golfers who pay petitioner $3,000 for the chance to compete in the Q-School and, if successful, in the subsequent tour events, as petitioner's clients or customers. In our view, petitioner's tournaments (whether situated at a "golf course" or at a "place of exhibition or entertainment") simultaneously offer at least two "privileges" to the public—that of watching the golf competition and that of competing in it. Although the latter is more difficult and more expensive to obtain than the former, it is nonetheless a privilege that petitioner makes available to members of the general public. In consideration of the entry fee, any golfer with the requisite letters of recommendation acquires the opportunity to qualify for and compete in petitioner's tours. Additionally, any golfer who succeeds in the open qualifying rounds for a tournament may play in the event. That petitioner identifies one set of clients or customers that it serves (spectators at tournaments) does not preclude it from having another set (players in tournaments) against whom it may not discriminate. It would be inconsistent with the literal text of the statute as well as its expansive purpose to read Title III's coverage, even given petitioner's suggested limitation, any less broadly.

* * *

V.

As we have noted, 42 U.S.C. § 12182(a) sets forth Title III's general rule prohibiting public accommodations from discriminating against individuals because of their disabilities. The question whether petitioner has violated that rule depends on a proper construction of the term "discrimination," which is defined by Title III to include:

"a failure to make reasonable modifications in policies, practices, or procedures, when such modifications are necessary to afford such goods, services, facilities, privileges, advantages, or accommodations to individuals with disabilities, *unless the entity can demonstrate that making such modifications would fundamentally alter the nature* of such goods, services, facilities, privileges, advantages, or accommodations." § 12182(b)(2)(A)(ii) (emphasis added).

Petitioner does not contest that a golf cart is a reasonable modification that is necessary if Martin is to play in its tournaments. Martin's claim thus differs from one that might be asserted by players with less serious afflictions that make walking the course uncomfortable or difficult, but not beyond their capacity. In such cases, an accommodation might be reasonable but not necessary. In this case, however, the narrow dispute is whether allowing Martin to use a golf cart, despite the walking requirement that applies to the PGA TOUR, the NIKE TOUR, and the third stage of the Q-School, is a modification that would "fundamentally alter the nature" of those events.

In theory, a modification of petitioner's golf tournaments might constitute a fundamental alteration in two different ways. It might alter such an essential aspect of the game of golf that it would be unacceptable even if it affected all competitors equally; changing the diameter of the hole from three to six inches might be such a modification. Alternatively, a less significant change that has only a peripheral impact on the game itself might nevertheless give a disabled player, in addition to access to the competition as required by Title III, an advantage over others and, for that reason, fundamentally alter the character of the competition. We are not persuaded that a waiver of the walking rule for Martin would work a fundamental alteration in either sense.

As an initial matter, we observe that the use of carts is not itself inconsistent with the fundamental character of the game of golf. From early on, the essence of the game has been shot-making—using clubs to cause a ball to progress from the teeing ground to a hole some distance away with as few strokes as possible. That essential aspect of the game is still reflected in the very first of the Rules of Golf, which declares: "The Game of Golf consists in playing a ball from the *teeing ground* into the hole by a *stroke* or successive strokes in accordance with the rules." . . . Over the years, there have been many changes in the players' equipment, in golf course design, in the Rules of Golf, and in the method of transporting clubs from hole to hole. Originally, so few clubs were used that each player could carry them without a bag. Then came golf bags, caddies, carts that were pulled by hand, and eventually motorized carts that carried players as well as clubs. "Golf carts started appearing with increasing regularity on American golf courses in the 1950's. Today they are everywhere. And they are encouraged. For one thing, they often speed up play, and for another, they are great revenue producers." There is nothing in the Rules of Golf that either forbids the use of carts, or penalizes a player for using a cart. That set of rules, as we have observed, is widely accepted in both the amateur and professional golf world as the rules of the game. The walking rule that is contained in petitioner's hard cards, based on an optional condition buried in an appendix to the Rules of Golf, is not an essential attribute of the game itself.

Indeed, the walking rule is not an indispensable feature of tournament golf either. As already mentioned, petitioner permits golf carts to be used in the SENIOR PGA TOUR, the open qualifying events for petitioner's tournaments, the first two stages of the Q-School, and, until 1997, the third stage of the Q-School as well. Moreover, petitioner allows the use of carts during certain tournament rounds in both the PGA TOUR and the NIKE TOUR....

Petitioner, however, distinguishes the game of golf as it is generally played from the game that it sponsors in the PGA TOUR, NIKE TOUR, and (at least recently) the last stage of the Q-School—golf at the "highest level." According to petitioner, "the goal of the highest-level competitive athletics is to assess and compare the performance of different competitors, a task that is meaningful only if the competitors are subject to identical substantive rules." The waiver of any possibly "outcome-affecting" rule for a contestant would violate this principle and therefore, in petitioner's view, fundamentally alter the nature of the highest level athletic event. The walking rule is one such rule, petitioner submits, because its purpose is "to inject the element of fatigue into the skill of shot-making," and thus its effect may be the critical loss of a stroke. As a consequence, the reasonable modification Martin seeks would fundamentally alter the nature of petitioner's highest level tournaments even if he were the only person in the world who has both the talent to compete in those elite events and a disability sufficiently serious that he cannot do so without using a cart.

The force of petitioner's argument is, first of all, mitigated by the fact that golf is a game in which it is impossible to guarantee that all competitors will play under exactly the same conditions or that an individual's ability will be the sole determinant of the outcome. For example, changes in the weather may produce harder greens and more head winds for the tournament leader than for his closest pursuers.... Whether such happenstance events are more or less probable than the likelihood that a golfer afflicted with Klippel-Trenaunay-Weber Syndrome would one day qualify for the NIKE TOUR and PGA TOUR, they at least demonstrate that pure chance may have a greater impact on the outcome of elite golf tournaments than the fatigue resulting from the enforcement of the walking rule.

Further, the factual basis of petitioner's argument is undermined by the District Court's finding that the fatigue from walking during one of petitioner's 4-day tournaments cannot be deemed significant. The District Court credited the testimony of a professor in physiology and expert on fatigue, who calculated the calories expended in walking a golf course (about five miles) to be approximately 500 calories—"nutritionally . . . less than a Big Mac." 994 F. Supp. at 1250. What is more, that energy is expended over a 5-hour period, during which golfers have numerous intervals for rest and refreshment. In fact, the expert concluded, because golf is a low intensity activity, fatigue from the game is primarily a psychological phenomenon in which stress and motivation are the key ingredients....

Moreover, when given the option of using a cart, the majority of golfers in petitioner's tournaments have chosen to walk, often to relieve stress or for other strategic reasons....

Even if we accept the factual predicate for petitioner's argument—that the walking rule is "outcome affecting" because fatigue may adversely affect performance—its legal position is fatally flawed. Petitioner's refusal to consider Martin's personal circumstances in deciding whether to accommodate his disability runs counter to the clear language and purpose of the ADA. As previously stated, the ADA was enacted to eliminate discrimination against "individuals" with disabilities, and to that end Title III of the Act requires without exception that any "policies, practices, or procedures" of a public accommodation be reasonably modified for disabled "individuals" as necessary to afford access unless doing so would fundamentally alter what is offered, § 12182(b)(2)(A)(ii). To comply with this command, an individualized inquiry must be made to determine whether a specific modification for a particular person's disability would be reasonable under the circumstances as well as necessary for that person, and yet at the same time not work a fundamental alteration....

To be sure, the waiver of an essential rule of competition for anyone would fundamentally alter the nature of petitioner's tournaments. As we have demonstrated, however, the walking rule is at best peripheral to the nature of petitioner's athletic events, and thus it might be waived in individual cases without working a fundamental alteration. Therefore, petitioner's claim that all the substantive rules for its "highest-level" competitions are sacrosanct and cannot be modified under any circumstances is effectively a contention that it is exempt from Title III's reasonable modification requirement. But that provision carves out no exemption for elite athletics, and given Title III's coverage not only of places of "exhibition or entertainment" but also of "golf courses," . . . its application to petitioner's tournaments cannot be said to be unintended or unexpected. . . .

Under the ADA's basic requirement that the need of a disabled person be evaluated on an individual basis, we have no doubt that allowing Martin to use a golf cart would not fundamentally alter the nature of petitioner's tournaments. As we have discussed, the purpose of the walking rule is to subject players to fatigue, which in turn may influence the outcome of tournaments. Even if the rule does serve that purpose, it is an uncontested finding of the District Court that Martin "easily endures greater fatigue even with a cart than his able-bodied competitors do by walking." The purpose of the walking rule is therefore not compromised in the slightest by allowing Martin to use a cart. . . . As a result, Martin's request for a waiver of the walking rule should have been granted.

* * *

The judgment of the Court of Appeals is affirmed.

CASES ON THE SUPPLEMENTAL CD

Dennin v. Connecticut Interscholastic Athletic Conference, 913 F. Supp. 663 (1996). In this case, the court ruled that waiving an eligibility requirement was a reasonable accommodation required under the ADA for high school athletic associations.

Poole v. South Plainfield Board of Education, 490 F. Supp. 948 (D. N.J. 1980). The case examines whether school officials have the right to prevent an student from participating in athletics due to a medical condition.

Sandison v. Michigan High School Athletic Association, 64 F.3d 1026 (6th Cir. 1995). In this case, the court ruled that waiving an eligibility requirement was not a reasonable accommodation required under the ADA for high school athletic associations.

QUESTIONS YOU SHOULD BE ABLE TO ANSWER

1. What are the 4 elements needed before establishing a claim under Section 504 of the Rehabilitation Act?

2. What is the importance of an individualized education program (IEP) for interscholastic athletes under IDEA?

3. How does the court determine reasonable accommodation under either the ADA or Rehabilitation Act?

4. How should the courts consider claims allowing the requested modification would poses a direct threat to the health or safety of others?

5. Can you compare the decisions in the McFadden and Badgett? Did one court correctly interpret the laws while the other misinterpreted it?

REFERENCES

Cases

Alexander v. Choate, 469 U.S. 287 (1985).

Anderson v. Little League Baseball, 794 F. Supp. 342 (1992).

Badgett v. Alabama High School Athletic Association, 2007 U.S. Dist. LEXIS 36014.

Booth v. El Paso Independent School District, Civil No. A-90-CA-764 (Tex. Dist. Ct. 1990).

Crocker v. Tennessee Secondary School Athletic Association, 980 F.2d 382 (6th Cir. 1992).

Cruz v. Pennsylvania Interscholastic Athletic Association, 175 F.Supp 2d 485, (E.D.Pa., 2001).

Dennin v. Connecticut Interscholastic Athletic Conference, 913 F. Supp. 663 (1996).

Hollonbeck v. USOC, 513 F.3d 1191, (10th. Cir. 2008).

Johnson v. Florida High School Activities Association Inc., 899 F. Supp. 579 (M.D. Fla. 1995).

Knapp v. Northwestern University, 101 F.3d 473 (7th Cir. 1996).

Kuketz v. Petronelli, 821 N.E.2d 473 (MA. 2005).

Lambert v. West Virginia State Board of Education and the West Virginia Secondary School Activities Commission, 447 S.E.2d 901 (W.Va. 1994).

McFadden v. Cousin, No: AMD 06-648 (D.Md. 2006).

McFadden v. Grasmick, 485 F. Supp. 2d 642 (2007).

PGA Tour, Inc. v. Casey Martin, 532 U.S. 661 (2001).

Poole v. South Plainfield Board of Education, 490 F. Supp. 948 (D. N.J. 1980).

Pottgen v. Missouri State High School Athletic Association, 40 F.3d 926 (8th Cir. 1994).

Sandison v. Michigan High School Athletic Association, 64 F.3d 1026 (6th Cir. 1995).

School Board of Nassau County, Fla. v. Arline, 480 U.S. 273 (1987).

Southeastern Community College v. Davis, 422 U.S. 397 (1979).

T.H. v. Montana High School Association, CV 92-150-BLG-JFB (1992).

University Interscholastic League and Bailey Marshall v. Buchanan, 848 S.W. 2d. 298 (1993).

Williams v. Wakefield Basketball Association, (CA-01-10434-DPW) (2003).

Publications

Clement, A. (1988). *Law in sport and physical activity*. Dubuque, IA: Brown & Benchmark.

Lakowski, T. (Summer, 2009). Athletes with Disabilities in School Sports: A Critical Assessment of the State of Sports Opportunities for Students With Disabilities. *Boston University International Law Journal*, 27, 283.

Wolohan, J. (1997a). An ethical and legal dilemma: Participation in sports by HIV infected athletes. *Marquette Sports Law Journal*, 7, 345.

Wolohan, J. (1997b). Are age restrictions a necessary requirement for participating in interscholastic athletic programs? *UMKC Law Review*, 66, 345.

Wolohan, J. (2003, March). The big dance: Administrators must tread carefully when deciding whether to accommodate individuals with disabilities. *Athletic Business*, pp. 20–24.

Wolohan, J. (2005, June). Bounce check: A club is not required to change its racquetball league rules for a wheelchair athlete. *Athletic Business*, pp. 18–22.

Legislation

The Rehabilitation Act of 1973, 29 U.S.C. § 701 *et seq.*

The Individuals with Disabilities Education Act, 20 U.S.C. § 1400 *et seq.*

The Americans with Disabilities Act, 42 U.S.C. § 12101 *et seq.*

The Amateur Sports Act, 36 U.S.C. § 371–396.

Ted Stevens Olympic and Amateur Sports Act, 36 U.S.C. § 220501-220529.

—Susan Brown Foster

SAINT LEO UNIVERSITY

Courts have been faced with a myriad of religious issue cases. One of the central themes running through the challenges is the inherent conflict between the Establishment Clause and Free Exercise Clause. Both clauses can be found in the First Amendment to the United States Constitution, which states: "Congress shall make no law respecting an establishment of religion, or prohibiting the free exercise thereof . . ."

The courts have interpreted these words under the **Establishment Clause** to mean the government or any of its entities may not promote a specific religion. At the same time, under the **Free Exercise Clause**, the courts have ruled that the government may not stand in the way of any individual who wishes to practice his/her religion. As a result, public institutions find it difficult to apply either of the two clauses too vigorously without violating the other clause.

FUNDAMENTAL CONCEPTS

The Dichotomies

There are several dichotomies that give rise to the rights of one party versus the rights of another involved in a given situation. The courts have had to resolve many of these conflicting arguments as discussed below.

The Establishment Clause v. Freedom of Speech

The trigger point for the numerous cases regarding the First Amendment is: What is middle ground between the establishment of religion and allowance for freedom of speech? As stated in *Board of Education of the Westside Community Schools v. Mergens* (1990), there is a "crucial difference between government speech endorsing religion which the Establishment Clause forbids, and private speech that may contain a prayerful message, which the Free Speech and Free Exercise Clauses protect." In attempting to assist governmental bodies in determining a safe haven approach for student prayer, the courts have established several general concepts.

Student-Initiated Prayer. In *Santa Fe High Independent School District v. Doe* (2000), students voted on whether or not to have an "invocation" and then voted on the person to deliver it. The U.S. Supreme Court ruled against the School District because it felt:

- There was substantial control over content by the principal;

- An invocation had historically been delivered before football games;

- The message was labeled an invocation;

- There was perceived intent to continue the practice of delivering a religious message.

In *Adler v. Duval County School Board* (2001), it was the students who decided whether or not to have an opening or closing message at graduation. If the students decided to have such a message, the senior class selected a student volunteer(s) to give the message. The content of the message was left up to the individual student. No one was allowed to review content. The Eleventh Circuit Court clearly felt this process exonerated the school board from establishing any religion while still allowing a prayer to be said if the volunteer so chose, thus supporting Freedom of Speech.

Administrative Control and Influence. In 1992, on remand from the Supreme Court following their *Lee v. Weisman* (1992), decision in which the court ruled that providing for nonsectarian prayer by a school-selected clergyman violated the Establishment Clause, the Fifth Circuit rendered its "Clear Creek Prayer Policy" in *Jones v. Clear Creek Independent School District*, (1992). This policy allowed a student-selected, student-given, non-sectarian, nonproselytizing invocation and benediction at high school graduation.

Similar to *Adler, Santa Fe*, and *Jones* is *Appenheimer v. School Board of Washington Community High School District 308* (2001), where the school indicated they allowed elected senior class officers to make a decision regarding the inclusion of an invocation at commencement. The officers solicited volunteers for all speeches, including the invocation. The U.S. Central District Court for Illinois disallowed the practice because the Chair of the English Department had the final say over content and prohibited a student from speaking if it was felt the prayer was inappropriate.

Although *Adler, Jones*, and *Appenheimer* are not Supreme Court decisions, these decisions enforce the common theme in *Santa Fe* that administrative control will render any prayer policy invalid. The Courts have indicated an invocation is possible if true student control can be proven. The Freedom of Speech and Free Exercise Clauses in the First Amendment do not permit suppression of student-initiated prayer. To do so would display hostility toward religion, a violation of the Free Exercise Clause. Some courts have implied and stated that teaching students that prayer itself is forbidden is a demonstration of hostility and leads into the next dichotomy.

Rights of the Employee in a Public School Setting

Public schools certainly have a difficult situation when a coach wishes to practice a personal religious way of life by, for example, staying in the locker room or bowing their head during even a student-initiated prayer. Is a public school prohibiting an employee from exercising their freedom of religion when complying with the Establishment Clause?

In *Borden v. School District of the Township of East Brunswick* (2009), Borden, a head football coach had been employed by the school district for 23 years. There had always been a prayer tradition since Borden became coach although it was not always led by him. Borden decided to change the tradition where he said prayer for the first pre-game dinner of each season. For every game thereafter, he asked everyone to stand and chose a senior to say a prayer. Additionally, Borden asked the players to take a knee in the locker room to discuss game strategy after which he led the team in prayer. In year three of this new tradition, a complaint was filed against the coach for his practices. Subsequently, the school district directed Borden to cease these traditions and provided guidelines that coincided with previous court rulings that any prayer had to be truly student-initiated. These guidelines also stipulated that any representative of the school district could not participate. Borden decided to comply with the guidelines but filed suit against the school district claiming violation of his First Amendment rights to freedom of speech and other Federal and New Jersey constitutional and statutory rights.

In his case, Borden was initially granted a summary judgment that stated the coach's desire to bow his head in silence or take a knee did not violate the Establishment Cause or his other rights as claimed. After this ruling, he asked the senior captains to take a vote among the players to see if they wished to continue the prayer tradition. The vote favored the tradition and Borden stood and bowed his head during the pre-meal prayer and took a knee for the pre-game prayer although students led both initiatives. On appeal by the school district, the Third Circuit reversed this decision stating that a school district violates the Establishment Clause if a reasonable observer would perceive the practice to be a government endorsement. Despite Coach Borden's original intent of creating team unity and instilling respect, his 23-year history of allowing prayer and subsequently leading prayer, even though he had ceased this practice, was a violation of the Establishment Clause. Using other previously determined balancing tests, the court declared that Borden's silent acts were not measures of public concern and that an employee's personal rights could not overshadow the fact that Borden was a state actor. Even his silent acts could be construed as an endorsement of religion. The Supreme Court denied a writ of certiorari in 2009. (See Section 6.12, *State Action*).

Religion v. Prayer

This second dichotomy is a little more subtle. The courts have stated that the offering of a prayer, especially when there is no reference to deity, is not necessarily religious entanglement. In *Chaudhuri v. State of Tennessee* (1997), the Tennessee State University administration, after repeated challenges to its prayer allowance at university functions, authorized a moment of silence. At the graduation ceremony following the initiation of this policy, a university-selected local pastor and prominent educator asked the audience to stand in a moment of silence. The audience proceeded to recite "The Lord's Prayer." The Sixth Circuit Court implied that many religions cite this prayer, and it was not an endorsement of any particular religion even if a local pastor was invited by the administration to ask the audience to stand.

Other courts have expressed the opinion that religion is not irrelevant to education. Religious thought is part of education and many curricula. However, teaching of a particular religion or advancing particular religious views by educators is forbidden under the entanglement theory.

Graduation Ceremonies v. Extracurricular Activities

Courts have ruled that graduation is, and has always been, a rather solemn occasion, which has historically been marked with prayer. However, as the Supreme Court noted in *Santa Fe*, "regardless of whether one considers a sporting event an appropriate occasion for solemnity, the use of an invocation to foster such solemnity is impermissible when it constitutes prayer sponsored by the school." Additionally, the court felt that because school officials were present and had authority to stop the prayer, it implied the school district's endorsement.

Another case dealing with prayer at a sporting event is *Doe v. Duncanville Independent School District*, (1995). The Fifth Circuit Court allowed the singing of a religious-themed song before each game for secular reasons, but disallowed prayer before a game due largely to entanglement, while still stating there was no solemnity in a basketball game.

Several parties have attempted to assert a **limited open forum theory** as a rationale for providing free speech. To establish a limited open forum, an individual must first show that there is governmental intent to open the event to the public. A graduation ceremony is generally not a public event. Individuals are invited to attend by virtue of their relationship with one of the graduates. Second, a public forum may be limited to specific speakers to discuss specific subjects, thus the term "limited open forum." The graduation ceremony itself is not open to general assembly or for debate of a number of different issues. If a public forum is to be created, the government must allow general access.

The limited public forum has been used extensively in cases for one main reason: if graduation is designated as a limited public forum, the government cannot discriminate against speech even if the message is religious. In general, a gathering is a public forum if general access or random use is allowed. The Eleventh Circuit Court in *Santa Fe*, citing *Perry Education Association v. Perry Local Educators' Association* (1983), discussed three classifications.

1. **Traditional public**. A venue that is generally acceptable of assembly and debate (e.g., parks and streets);

2. **Public created by government designation**. A place or channel of communication for use by the public at large for assembly and speech or for discussion;

3. **Nonpublic**. Government-owned property to which the First Amendment does not guarantee access.

In *American Civil Liberties Union of New Jersey v. Black Horse Pike Regional Board of Education* (1996), a principal denied an ACLU member the right to speak at graduation on the topic of safe sex and condom use after the senior class voted to have some form of prayer at graduation. The court highlighted this as an example of the control administrators have over the speech topics at graduation, thus establishing a nonpublic use of public property. In *Adler*, the plaintiffs claimed the school board provided a platform and opportunity for prayer, thus creating the situation where a student graduation speaker converted a private speech into a "public, state-sponsored speech." In rejecting this argument, the court held that by simply "providing the platform, the speech becomes public." The Eleventh Circuit Court, citing the 1984 Equal Access Act, stated that the northern Florida county school board policy of allowing student-elected speakers to deliver a message of any content did not violate the Establishment Clause. The graduation venue is equally available for religious or secular expression as would be allowed under the Equal Access Act, but support for designating graduation ceremonies as public forums, limited or otherwise, is not there.

The Maturity of the Audience. In several cases, the courts have indicated the age of an audience can be a determining factor. College graduation ceremonies, where religious exercise was permitted, is one example. *Chaudhuri* involved a college professor who practiced Hinduism and the college custom of allowing prayers or moments of silence at university-related events. *Tanford v. Brand* (1996), involved a law professor, two law students, and a senior who protested the practice of allowing a 150-year-old tradition of invocations and benedictions at Indiana University graduations. Both courts indicated that one purpose of higher education is to advance and foster appreciation of diverse viewpoints. Merely asking a mature adult audience to stand and listen to a nonsectarian, nonproselytizing message did not coerce individuals into endorsing or accepting another religion. In both cases, the university selected the clergyman to deliver the message. This practice was identical to the situation in *Lee v. Weisman* (1992), where a middle school administration selected a rabbi. However, the *Lee* court felt the age of the audience led to coercion because the students would not have as much freedom, nor feel as comfortable, to state an objection due to peer pressure.

Prayer in postsecondary education has largely gone untested by the Supreme Court, as acknowledged by the Fourth Circuit in *Mellen v. Bunting*, (2003). Even so, this Circuit went on to rule that a supper prayer at Virginia Military Institute (VMI) violated the Establishment Clause citing coercion as the main constitutional issue.

The Three Tests

The Supreme Court has established three complementary and occasionally overlapping tests to examine religious practices challenged under the First Amendment. These tests include the three-part Lemon Test, the Coercion Test, and the Endorsement Test.

The Lemon Test

The three-part **Lemon Test** is the one with the longest pedigree. Under the *Lemon* test, a government practice is unconstitutional if (1) it lacks a secular purpose, (2) its primary effect either advances or inhibits religion, or (3) it excessively entangles government with religion (*Lemon v. Kurtzman*, 1971).

The Coercion Test

In the **Coercion Test**, which the Court announced in *Lee v. Weisman* (1992), school-sponsored religious activity is analyzed to determine the extent, if any, to which it has a coercive effect on students. "Unconstitutional coercion [occurs] when: (1) the government directs (2) a formal religious exercise (3) in such a way as to oblige the participation of objectors" (*Jones v. Clear Creek Independent School District*, 1992). For example, in *Santa Fe*, the Supreme Court stated that band members and cheerleaders who are required to attend a football game because of their membership in those groups in effect are coerced into listening to any prayer or message delivered. This was part of their rationale in striking down prayer before football games.

The Endorsement Test

The **Endorsement Test**, created by Supreme Court Justice Sandra Day O'Connor in a concurring opinion in *Lynch v. Donnelly* (1984), seeks to determine whether the government endorses religion by means of the challenged action. In deciding that a city's inclusion of a nativity scene in its Christmas display was constitutional, Justice O'Connor felt the clarifying test for the Establishment Clause was that governmental intent or a governmental practice not convey or communicate a message of endorsement or disapproval of religion. For example, in *Ingebretsen on Behalf of Ingebretsen v. Jackson Public School District* (1996), Mississippi had passed a "School Prayer Statute" allowing students to initiate nonsectarian, nonproselytizing prayer at compulsory and noncompulsory events including sporting events. The Fifth Circuit Court, while ruling the practice constitutional for graduation, held the statute was unconstitutional under all the tests for other events. The Fifth Circuit Court stated that allowing school officials in their capacity to lead students in prayer when it does not set aside time for anything else not only constituted coercion but clearly endorsed religion.

The following case involves student-initiated prayer before a high school football game. Although it is clear that a public school cannot promote a specific religion, it is not clear what happens when the school allows student-initiated prayer. In examining the case, it is important to look at how much, if any, control school administrators have over the content or the student selected to give the prayer.

SANTA FE HIGH INDEPENDENT SCHOOL DISTRICT V. DOE

United States Supreme Court
530 U.S. 290 (2000)

Prior to 1995, the Santa Fe High School student who occupied the school's elective office of student council chaplain delivered a prayer over the public address system before each varsity football game for the entire season. This practice, along with others, was challenged in District Court as a violation of the Establishment Clause of the First Amendment. While these proceedings were pending in the District Court, the school district adopted a different policy that permits, but does not require, prayer initiated and led by a student at all home games. The District Court entered an order modifying that policy to permit only nonsectarian, nonproselytizing prayer. The Court of Appeals held that, even as modified by the District Court, the football prayer policy was invalid.

* * *

We granted the District's petition for certiorari, limited to the following question: "Whether petitioner's policy permitting student-led, student-initiated prayer at football games violates the Establishment Clause." We conclude, as did the Court of Appeals, that it does.

II

The first Clause in the First Amendment to the Federal Constitution provides that "Congress shall make no law respecting an establishment of religion, or prohibiting the free exercise thereof." The Fourteenth Amendment imposes those substantive limitations on the legislative power of the States and their political subdivisions. . . . In *Lee v. Weisman*, we held that a prayer delivered by a rabbi at a middle school graduation ceremony violated that Clause. Although this case involves student prayer at a different type of school function, our analysis is properly guided by the principles that we endorsed in Lee.

As we held in that case:

> "The principle that government may accommodate the free exercise of religion does not supersede the fundamental limitations imposed by the Establishment Clause. It is beyond dispute that, at a mini-

mum, the Constitution guarantees that government may not coerce anyone to support or participate in religion or its exercise, or otherwise act in a way which 'establishes a [state] religion or religious faith, or tends to do so.'" Id. at 587.

In this case the District first argues that this principle is inapplicable to its October policy because the messages are private student speech, not public speech. It reminds us that "there is a crucial difference between government speech endorsing religion, which the Establishment Clause forbids, and private speech endorsing religion, which the Free Speech and Free Exercise Clauses protect." . . . We certainly agree with that distinction, but we are not persuaded that the pre-game invocations should be regarded as "private speech."

These invocations are authorized by a government policy and take place on government property at government-sponsored school-related events. Not every message delivered under such circumstances is the government's own. We have held, for example, that an individual's contribution to a government-created forum was not government speech. . . . Although the District relies heavily on Rosenberger and similar cases involving such forums, it is clear that the pre-game ceremony is not the type of forum discussed in those cases. The Santa Fe school officials simply do not "evince either 'by policy or by practice,' any intent to open the [pre-game ceremony] to 'indiscriminate use,' . . . by the student body generally." . . . Rather, the school allows only one student, the same student for the entire season, to give the invocation. The statement or invocation is subject to particular regulations that confine the content and topic of the student's message. By comparison, in Perry we rejected a claim that the school had created a limited public forum in its school mail system despite the fact that it had allowed far more speakers to address a much broader range of topics than the policy at issue here. As we concluded in Perry, "selective access does not transform government property into a public forum." 460 U.S. at 47.

Granting only one student access to the stage at a time does not, of course, necessarily preclude a finding that a school has created a limited public forum. Here, however, Santa Fe's student election system ensures that only those messages deemed "appropriate" under the District's policy may be delivered. That is, the majoritarian process implemented by the District guarantees, by definition, that minority candidates will never prevail and that their views will be effectively silenced.

Recently, in *Board of Regents of Univ. of Wis. System v. Southworth*, 529 U.S. 217 (2000), we explained why student elections that determine, by majority vote, which expressive activities shall receive or not receive school benefits are constitutionally problematic:

"To the extent the referendum substitutes majority determinations for viewpoint neutrality it would undermine the constitutional protection the program requires. The whole theory of viewpoint neutrality is that minority views are treated with the same respect as are majority views. Access to a public forum, for instance, does not depend upon majoritarian consent. That principle is controlling here."

Like the student referendum for funding in Southworth, this student election does nothing to protect minority views but rather places the students who hold such views at the mercy of the majority. Because "fundamental rights may not be submitted to vote; they depend on the outcome of no elections," . . . the District's elections are insufficient safeguards of diverse student speech.

In Lee, the school district made the related argument that its policy of endorsing only "civic or nonsectarian" prayer was acceptable because it minimized the intrusion on the audience as a whole. We rejected that claim by explaining that such a majoritarian policy "does not lessen the offense or isolation to the objectors. At best it narrows their number, at worst increases their sense of isolation and affront." 505 U.S. at 594. Similarly, while Santa Fe's majoritarian election might ensure that most of the students are represented, it does nothing to protect the minority; indeed, it likely serves to intensify their offense.

Moreover, the District has failed to divorce itself from the religious content in the invocations. It has not succeeded in doing so, either by claiming that its policy is "'one of neutrality rather than endorsement'" or by characterizing the individual student as the "circuit-breaker" in the process. Contrary to the District's repeated assertions that it has adopted a "hands-off" approach to the pre-game invocation, the realities of the situation plainly reveal that its policy involves both perceived and actual endorsement of religion. In this case, as we found in Lee, the "degree of school involvement" makes it clear that the pre-game prayers bear "the imprint of the State and thus put school-age children who objected in an untenable position." 505 U.S. at 590.

The District has attempted to disentangle itself from the religious messages by developing the two-step student election process. The text of the October policy, however, exposes the extent of the school's entanglement. The elections take place at all only because the school "board has chosen to permit students to deliver a brief invocation and/or message." The elections thus "shall" be conducted "by the high school student council" and "upon advice and direction of the high school principal." The decision whether to deliver a message is first made by majority vote of the entire student body, followed by a choice of the speaker in a separate, similar majority election. Even though the particular words used by the speaker are not determined by those votes, the policy mandates that the "statement or invocation" be "consistent with the goals and purposes of this policy," which are "to solemnize the event, to promote good sportsmanship and student safety, and to establish the appropriate environment for the competition."

In addition to involving the school in the selection of the speaker, the policy, by its terms, invites and encourages religious messages. The policy itself states that the purpose of the message is "to solemnize the event." A religious message is the most obvious method of solemnizing an event. Moreover, the requirements that the message "promote good citizenship" and "establish the appropriate environment for competition" further narrow the types of message deemed appropriate, suggesting that a solemn, yet nonreligious, message, such as commentary on United States foreign policy, would be prohibited. Indeed, the only type of message that is expressly endorsed in the text is an "invocation"—a term that primarily describes an appeal for divine assistance. In fact, as used in the past at Santa Fe High School, an "invocation" has always entailed a focused religious message. Thus, the expressed purposes of the policy encourage the selection of a religious message, and that is precisely how the students understand the policy. . . . We recognize the important role that public worship plays in many communities, as well as the sincere desire to include public prayer as a part of various occasions so as to mark those occasions' significance. But such religious activity in public schools, as elsewhere, must comport with the First Amendment.

The actual or perceived endorsement of the message, moreover, is established by factors beyond just the text of the policy. Once the student speaker is selected and the message composed, the invocation is then delivered to a large audience assembled as part of a regularly scheduled, school-sponsored function conducted on school property. The message is broadcast over the school's public address system, which remains subject to the control of school officials. It is fair to assume that the pre-game ceremony is clothed in the traditional indicia of school sporting events, which generally include not just the team, but also cheerleaders and band members dressed in uniforms sporting the school name and mascot. The school's name is likely written in large print across the field and on banners and flags. The crowd will certainly include many who display the school colors and insignia on their school T-shirts, and jackets. It is in a setting such as this that "the board has chosen to permit" the elected student to rise and give the "statement or invocation."

In this context the members of the listening audience must perceive the pre-game message as a public expression of the views of the majority of the student body delivered with the approval of the school administration. In cases involving state participation in a religious activity, one of the relevant questions is "whether an objective observer, acquainted with the text, legislative history, and implementation of the statute, would perceive it as a state endorsement of prayer in public schools." . . . Regardless of the listener's support for, or objection to, the message, an objective Santa Fe High School student will unquestionably perceive the inevitable pre-game prayer as stamped with her school's seal of approval.

The text and history of this policy, moreover, reinforce our objective student's perception that the prayer is encouraged by the school. When a governmental entity professes a secular purpose for an arguably religious policy, the government's characterization is, of course, entitled to some deference. But it is nonetheless the duty of the courts to "distinguish a sham secular purpose from a sincere one." . . .

According to the District, the secular purposes of the policy are to "foster free expression of private persons . . . as well [as to] solemnize sporting events, promote good sportsmanship and student safety, and establish an appropriate environment for competition." We note that the District's approval of only one specific kind of message, an "invocation," is not necessary to further any of these purposes. Additionally, the fact that only one student is permitted to give a content-limited message suggests that this policy does little to "foster free expression." Furthermore, regardless of whether one considers a sporting event an appropriate occasion for solemnity, the use of an invocation to foster such solemnity is impermissible when, in actuality, it constitutes prayer sponsored by the school. And it is unclear what type of message would be both appropriately "solemnizing" under the District's policy and yet non-religious.

Most striking to us is the evolution of the current policy from the long-sanctioned office of "Student Chaplain" to the candidly titled "Prayer at Football Games" regulation. This history indicates that the District intended to preserve the practice of prayer before football games. The conclusion that the District viewed the October policy simply as a continuation of the previous policies is dramatically illustrated by the fact that the school did not conduct a new election, pursuant to the current policy, to replace the results of the previous election, which oc-

curred under the former policy. Given these observations, and in light of the school's history of regular delivery of a student-led prayer at athletic events, it is reasonable to infer that the specific purpose of the policy was to preserve a popular "state-sponsored religious practice."

School sponsorship of a religious message is impermissible because it sends the ancillary message to members of the audience who are non-adherents "that they are outsiders, not full members of the political community, and an accompanying message to adherents that they are insiders, favored members of the political community." . . . The delivery of such a message over the school's public address system, by a speaker representing the student body, under the supervision of school faculty, and pursuant to a school policy that explicitly and implicitly encourages public prayer is not properly characterized as "private" speech.

III

The District next argues that its football policy is distinguishable from the graduation prayer in Lee because it does not coerce students to participate in religious observances. Its argument has two parts: first, that there is no impermissible government coercion because the pre-game messages are the product of student choices; and second, that there is really no coercion at all because attendance at an extracurricular event, unlike a graduation ceremony, is voluntary.

The reasons just discussed explaining why the alleged "circuit-breaker" mechanism of the dual elections and student speaker do not turn public speech into private speech also demonstrate why these mechanisms do not insulate the school from the coercive element of the final message. In fact, this aspect of the District's argument exposes anew the concerns that are created by the majoritarian election system. The parties' stipulation clearly states that the issue resolved in the first election was "whether a student would deliver prayer at varsity football games," and the controversy in this case demonstrates that the views of the students are not unanimous on that issue.

One of the purposes served by the Establishment Clause is to remove debate over this kind of issue from governmental supervision or control. We explained in Lee that the "preservation and transmission of religious beliefs and worship is a responsibility and a choice committed to the private sphere." 505 U.S. at 589. The two student elections authorized by the policy, coupled with the debates that presumably must precede each, impermissibly invade that private sphere. The election mechanism, when considered in light of the history in which the policy in question evolved, reflects a device the District put in place that determines whether religious messages will be delivered at home football games. The mechanism encourages divisiveness along religious lines in a public school setting, a result at odds with the Establishment Clause. Although it is true that the ultimate choice of student speaker is "attributable to the students," the District's decision to hold the constitutionally problematic election is clearly "a choice attributable to the State."

The District further argues that attendance at the commencement ceremonies at issue in Lee "differs dramatically" from attendance at high school football games, which it contends "are of no more than passing interest to many students" and are "decidedly extracurricular," thus dissipating any coercion. Attendance at a high school football game, unlike showing up for class, is certainly not required in order to receive a diploma. Moreover, we may assume that the District is correct in arguing that the informal pressure to attend an athletic event is not as strong as a senior's desire to attend her own graduation ceremony.

There are some students, however, such as cheerleaders, members of the band, and, of course, the team members themselves, for whom seasonal commitments mandate their attendance, sometimes for class credit. The District also minimizes the importance to many students of attending and participating in extracurricular activities as part of a complete educational experience. As we noted in Lee, "law reaches past formalism." 505 U.S. at 595. To assert that high school students do not feel immense social pressure, or have a truly genuine desire, to be involved in the extracurricular event that is American high school football is "formalistic in the extreme." We stressed in Lee the obvious observation that "adolescents are often susceptible to pressure from their peers towards conformity, and that the influence is strongest in matters of social convention." *Id.* at 593. High school home football games are traditional gatherings of a school community; they bring together students and faculty as well as friends and family from years present and past to root for a common cause. Undoubtedly, the games are not important to some students, and they voluntarily choose not to attend. For many others, however, the choice between whether to attend these games or to risk facing a personally offensive religious ritual is in no practical sense an easy one. The Constitution, moreover, demands that the school may not force this difficult choice upon these students for "it is a tenet of the First Amendment that the State cannot require one of its citizens to forfeit his or her rights and benefits as the price of resisting conformance to state-sponsored religious practice."

Even if we regard every high school student's decision to attend a home football game as purely voluntary, we are nevertheless persuaded that the delivery of a pre-game prayer has the improper effect of coercing those present to participate in an act of religious worship. For "the government may no more use social pressure to enforce orthodoxy than it may use more direct means." As in Lee, "what to most believers may seem nothing more than a reasonable request that the nonbeliever respect their religious practices, in a school context may appear to the nonbeliever or dissenter to be an attempt to employ the machinery of the State to enforce a religious orthodoxy." The constitutional command will not permit the District "to exact religious conformity from a student as the price" of joining her classmates at a varsity football game.

The Religion Clauses of the First Amendment prevent the government from making any law respecting the establishment of religion or prohibiting the free exercise thereof. By no means do these commands impose a prohibition on all religious activity in our public schools. . . . Indeed, the common purpose of the Religion Clauses "is to secure religious liberty." . . . Thus, nothing in the Constitution as interpreted by this Court prohibits any public school student from voluntarily praying at any time before, during, or after the school day. But the religious liberty protected by the Constitution is abridged when the State affirmatively sponsors the particular religious practice of prayer.

IV

Finally, the District argues repeatedly that the Does have made a premature facial challenge to the October policy that necessarily must fail. The District emphasizes, quite correctly, that until a student actually delivers a solemnizing message under the latest version of the policy, there can be no certainty that any of the statements or invocations will be religious. Thus, it concludes, the October policy necessarily survives a facial challenge.

This argument, however, assumes that we are concerned only with the serious constitutional injury that occurs when a student is forced to participate in an act of religious worship because she chooses to attend a school event. But the Constitution also requires that we keep in mind "the myriad, subtle ways in which Establishment Clause values can be eroded," . . . and that we guard against other different, yet equally important, constitutional injuries. One is the mere passage by the District of a policy that has the purpose and perception of government establishment of religion. Another is the implementation of a governmental electoral process that subjects the issue of prayer to a majoritarian vote.

The District argues that the facial challenge must fail because "Santa Fe's Football Policy cannot be invalidated on the basis of some 'possibility or even likelihood' of an unconstitutional application." . . . Our Establishment Clause cases involving facial challenges, however, have not focused solely on the possible applications of the statute, but rather have considered whether the statute has an unconstitutional purpose. Writing for the Court in Bowen, THE CHIEF JUSTICE concluded that "as in previous cases involving facial challenges on Establishment Clause grounds, . . . we assess the constitutionality of an enactment by reference to the three factors first articulated in

Lemon v. Kurtzman, 403 U.S. 602, 612 (1971) . . . which guides 'the general nature of our inquiry in this area' . . . Under the Lemon standard, a court must invalidate a statute if it lacks "a secular legislative purpose." . . . It is therefore proper for us to examine the purpose of the October policy.

As discussed, the text of the October policy alone reveals that it has an unconstitutional purpose. The plain language of the policy clearly spells out the extent of school involvement in both the election of the speaker and the content of the message. Additionally, the text of the October policy specifies only one, clearly preferred message—that of Santa Fe's traditional religious "invocation." Finally, the extremely selective access of the policy and other content restrictions confirm that it is not a content-neutral regulation that creates a limited public forum for the expression of student speech. Our examination, however, need not stop at an analysis of the text of the policy.

This case comes to us as the latest step in developing litigation brought as a challenge to institutional practices that unquestionably violated the Establishment Clause. One of those practices was the District's long-established tradition of sanctioning student-led prayer at varsity football games. The narrow question before us is whether implementation of the October policy insulates the continuation of such prayers from constitutional scrutiny. It does not. Our inquiry into this question not only can, but must, include an examination of the circumstances surrounding its enactment. Whether a government activity violates the Establishment Clause is "in large part a legal question to be answered on the basis of judicial interpretation of social facts. . . . Every government practice must be judged in its unique circumstances. . . ." Our discussion in the previous sections demonstrates that in this case the District's direct involvement with school prayer exceeds constitutional limits.

The District, nevertheless, asks us to pretend that we do not recognize what every Santa Fe High School student understands clearly—that this policy is about prayer. The District further asks us to accept what is obviously untrue: that these messages are necessary to "solemnize" a football game and that this single-student, year-long position is es-

sential to the protection of student speech. We refuse to turn a blind eye to the context in which this policy arose, and that context quells any doubt that this policy was implemented with the purpose of endorsing school prayer.

Therefore, the simple enactment of this policy, with the purpose and perception of school endorsement of student prayer, was a constitutional violation. We need not wait for the inevitable to confirm and magnify the constitutional injury. . . . Therefore, even if no Santa Fe High School student ever offered a religious message, the October policy fails a facial challenge because the attempt by the District to encourage prayer is also at issue. Government efforts to endorse religion cannot evade constitutional reproach based solely on the remote possibility that those attempts may fail.

This policy likewise does not survive a facial challenge because it impermissibly imposes upon the student body a majoritarian election on the issue of prayer. Through its election scheme, the District has established a governmental electoral mechanism that turns the school into a forum for religious debate. It further empowers the student body majority with the authority to subject students of minority views to constitutionally improper messages. The award of that power alone, regardless of the students' ultimate use of it, is not acceptable. . . . Such a system encourages divisiveness along religious lines and threatens the imposition of coercion upon those students not desiring to participate in a religious exercise. Simply by establishing this school-related procedure, which entrusts the inherently nongovernmental subject of religion to a majoritarian vote, a constitutional violation has occurred.

Our examination of those circumstances above leads to the conclusion that this policy does not provide the District with the constitutional safe harbor it sought. The policy is invalid on its face because it establishes an improper majoritarian election on religion, and unquestionably has the purpose and creates the perception of encouraging the delivery of prayer at a series of important school events.

The judgment of the Court of Appeals is, accordingly, affirmed.

CASES ON THE SUPPLEMENTAL CD

Adler v. Duval County School Board, 250 F.3d 1330 (11th Cir. 2001), cert. denied, 534 U.S. 1065 (2001). The reader should compare this decision regarding use of public school facilities and equipment and administrative control with the Santa Fe case.	*Borden v. School District of the Township of East Brunswick*, 533 F. 3d. 153 (3rd Cir. 2008). This case closely examines personal rights of an employee serving as a state actor with the rights of a school district to enforce religious freedoms found in the First Amendment to the United States Constitution.

Chaudhuri v. State of Tennessee, 130 F.3d 232 (1997). This case provides guidelines regarding when a prayer may be allowed for activities such as a college graduation.

Lee v. Weisman, 505 U.S. 577 (1992). This case should be compared to the Chaudhuri case above because it explains why prayer should not be al-lowed at all graduations. It also is considered a landmark case because it is the case that established the Coercion Test.

Lynch v. Donnelly, 465 U.S. 668 (1984). The Endorsement Test discussed in this section was established in a concurring opinionin this case.

QUESTIONS YOU SHOULD BE ABLE TO ANSWER

1. Compare the roles of the administration in *Sante Fe* and *Adler*, and discuss why the courts came to differing conclusions.

2. Present situations that show how a coach can and cannot be involved in prayer before a sporting contest.

3. Discuss the different environments of college graduation and a K-12 graduation exercise and why the courts have differed in the allowance of prayer.

4. Discuss the difference between a graduation and a sporting event and the general position of the courts.

5. Discuss the three sporting event scenarios of prayer, a song such as *God Bless America*, and the Pledge of Allegiance and in what situations these three events may or may not be allowed.

REFERENCES

Cases

Adler v. Duval County School Board, 250 F.3d 1330 (11th Cir. 2001), *cert. denied*, 534 U.S. 1065 (2001).

American Civil Liberties Union of New Jersey v. Black Horse Pike Regional Board of Education, 84 F.3d 1471 (1996).

American Civil Liberties Union of Ohio Foundation, Inc. v. Ashbrook, 375 F. 3d 484 (6th Cir. 2004).

Appenheimer v. School Board of Washington Community High School District 308, 2001 WL 1885834 (C.D. Ill.).

Barnes-Wallace v. The Boy Scouts of America, 275 F. Supp. 2d. 1259 (S.D. Cal. 2003).

Board of Education of Westside Community Schools v. Mergens by and through Mergens, 496 U.S. 226 (1990).

Borden v. School District of the Township of East Brunswick, 533 F. 3d. 153 (3rd Cir. 2008).

Borden v. School District of the Township of East Brunswick, 129 S.Ct. 1524 (2009).

Brown v. Gilmore, 258 F.3d 265 (2001).

Chaudhuri v. State of Tenn., 130 F.3d 232 (1997).

Doe v. Duncanville Independent School Dist., 70 F.3d 405 (1995).

Freethought Soc. of Greater Philadelphia v. Chester County, 334 F. 3d 247 (3rd Cir. 2003).

Ingebretsen on Behalf of Ingebretsen v. Jackson Public School Dist., 88 F.3d 274 (C.A. 5, 1996).

Jones v. Clear Creek Independent School Dist., 977 F.2d 963 (C.A. 5, 1992).

Lee v. Weisman, 505 U.S. 577 (1992).

Lemon v. Kurtzman, 403 U.S. 602 (1971).

Lynch v. Donnelly, 465 U.S. 668 (1984).

Mellen v. Bunting, 327 F. 3d 355 (C.A. 4, 2003).

Newdow v. Eagen, 309 F. Supp. 2d 29 (D.C. 2004).

Perry Education Association v. Perry Local Educators' Association, 460 U.S. 37 (1983).

Santa Fe High Independent School District v. Doe, 530 U.S. 290 (2000).

Tanford v. Brand, 932 F. Supp. 1139 (S.D. Ind., 1996).

Zelman v. Simmons-Harris, 536 U.S. 639 (2002).

Publications

Mullin, S. A. (2003). The place for prayer in public policy: A reevaluation of the principles underlying the decision in *Santa Fe Independent School District v. Doe*. *S. Tex. L. Rev.*, *44*, 555–644.

Legislation

U.S.C.A. Const. Amend. I.

6.26 Private Clubs in Sport and Recreation

—Windy Dees
GEORGIA SOUTHERN UNIVERSITY

In addition to gender discrimination, numerous other forms of discrimination such as race, national origin, religion, and sexual orientation (among others) have existed within private sport and recreational organizations for decades. However, while discrimination at golf and country clubs seem to grab most of the headlines, they are not the only private institutions where discriminatory membership practices have been documented. Swimming, boating, hunting and fishing clubs (*U.S. v. Lansdowne Swim Club,* 1989; *Gibbs-Alfano v. Ossining Boat & Canoe Club,* 1999; *Durham v. Red Lake Fishing & Hunting Club, Inc.,* 1987), service groups (*Roberts v. U.S. Jaycees,* 1984), and even the Boy Scouts (*Boy Scouts of America v. Dale,* 2003) have faced litigation due to their strict exclusivity.

The purpose of this section is to identify and examine the legal aspects surrounding membership into private sport and recreation clubs. Some of these areas include: the First Amendment to the United States Constitution (Freedom of Association), the Fourteenth Amendment to the United States Constitution (Equal Protection), the Civil Rights Act of 1964, and the Americans with Disabilities Act (ADA). At the conclusion of this section, you should be able to: (a) define what it means to be a truly private club, (b) describe the legal rights of private organizations and how they qualify for private exemption status, (c) understand the legislation and key cases that have affected private clubs over the last several decades, and (d) be able to provide suggestions as to how private sport and recreation facilities could more effectively manage and/or eradicate discriminatory membership practices.

FUNDAMENTAL CONCEPTS

Private Clubs and Discrimination

According to the Merriam-Webster dictionary (2009) and the definitions provided for the terms "private" and "club", one could define a **private club** as "a group identified by some common characteristic that is intended for or restricted to the use of a particular person, group, or class" (*such as a private yacht club*). Using the example of a private yacht club, this type of organization may commence with a group of individuals who share the common characteristic of a passion for boating, and wish to create a club and restrict membership to those who enjoy the same leisure activity. In order to join this private club, members may be required to pay dues, attend meetings, provide service, or fulfill any number of prerequisites.

The Merriam-Webster dictionary (2009) defines the term **discrimination** as, "the act, practice, or an instance of discriminating categorically rather than individually; prejudiced or prejudicial outlook, action, or treatment" (*such as racial discrimination*). Using our previous example, if an individual was denied membership into the yacht club simply because he or she was black, this would be considered racial discrimination. Conversely, an individual may be granted membership into a private organization but still denied specific privileges based on a particular characteristic, such as gender; this practice is also considered to be discriminatory (*Wanders v. Bear Hill Golf Club, Inc.,* 1998). For example, in 2008, Arizona's attorney general filed suit against the Phoenix Country Club, alleging it discriminated against women by prohibiting them from enjoying the same amenities and networking opportunities as men. The prominent Arizona country club has separate dining facilities for its male and female members. There is a male-only grill as well as a female-only grill. However, it is well known within the club and community that the men's grill boasts superior amenities and is utilized for networking and other business purposes. Female members claimed they were denied access to these special privileges (*USA Today,* 2008).

Freedom of Association

The first ten Amendments to the United States Constitution are known collectively as the Bill of Rights, and these pieces of legislation are the foundation on which our country stands. The Bill of Rights ensures that citizens of the United States are afforded certain freedoms and civil liberties. The United States Supreme Court constitutionally protects the "Freedom of Association" under the First and Fourteenth Amendments to the United States Constitution in two distinct ways: (1) *intimate association* (an aspect of the Fourteenth Amendment's protection of privacy) and (2) *expressive association* (an aspect of the First Amendment's protection of free speech).

The Fourteenth Amendment

The Fourteenth Amendment to the United States Constitution does not explicitly state that citizens are guaranteed the right of privacy; however, through a series of decisions, the Court has acknowledged a certain level of privacy which is Constitutionally protected (*Loving v. Virginia,* 1967; *Pierce v. Society of Sisters,* 1925; *Prince v. Massachusetts,* 1944). "The Court has long recognized that, because the Bill of Rights is designed to secure individual liberty, it must afford the formation and preservation of certain kinds of highly personal relationships as a substantial measure of sanctuary from unjustified interference by the State" (*Roberts v. U.S. Jaycees,* 1984). **Intimate Association** is the term used to describe one's right to form extremely personal relationships with a small number of individuals, such as in marriage or relationships with parents, children, and relatives. However, these are not the only intimate relationships that are protected. According to *Roberts,* any relationship between a small group of people that carries "deep attachments and commitments" and forms because an individual shares "distinctly personal aspects of one's life" is protected by intimate association.

The First Amendment

The First Amendment states that, "Congress shall make no law respecting an establishment of religion, or prohibiting the free exercise thereof; or abridging the freedom of speech, or of the press; or the right of the people peaceably to assemble, and to petition the Government for a redress of grievances" (U.S. Const. Amend I). Although it does not directly state that individuals have the right to freely form their own associations, the Supreme Court has interpreted the First Amendment to allow for this based on the right to freedom of expression. In *Roberts v. U.S. Jaycees* (1984), the Supreme Court ruled that "an individual's freedom to speak, to worship, and to petition the government for the redress of grievances could not be vigorously protected by interference by the State unless a correlative freedom to engage in group effort toward those ends were not also guaranteed." Therefore, **Expressive Association** refers to one's right to join with others in the pursuit of political, social, economic, educational, religious, and cultural objectives.

The Civil Rights Act of 1964

The Civil Rights Act of 1964 (Civil Rights Act) was enacted to protect citizens' constitutional rights and prohibit various forms of discrimination. The act exists:

> *To enforce the constitutional right to vote, to confer jurisdiction upon the district courts of the United States to provide injunctive relief against discrimination in public accommodations, to authorize the attorney General to institute suits to protect constitutional rights in public facilities and public education, to extend the Commission on Civil Rights, to prevent discrimination in federally assisted programs, to establish a Commission on Equal Employment Opportunity, and for other purposes (42 U.S.C. § 2000).*

Title VII

Title VII of the Civil Rights Act prohibits discrimination in places of employment [42 U.S.C. § 2000e-2(a)] where the employer's business influences interstate commerce, meaning trade, traffic, commerce, transportation, transmission, or communication among the several States [42 U.S.C. § 2000e(g)]. Title VII states the following regarding employer practices:

It shall be an unlawful employment practice for an employer, a person engaged in an industry affecting commerce who has 15 or more employees for each working day in each of 20 or more calendar weeks in the current or preceding calendar year,

1. to fail or refuse to hire or to discharge any individual, or otherwise to discriminate against any individual with respect to his compensation, terms, conditions, or privileges of employment, because of such individual's race, color, religion, sex, or national origin; or

2. to limit, segregate, or classify his employees or applicants for employment in any way which would deprive or tend to deprive any individual of employment opportunities or otherwise adversely affect his status as an employee, because of such individual's race, color, religion, sex, or national origin.

The Civil Rights Act does, however, make an exception for private organizations. It states that "A bona fide private membership club (other than a labor organization) which is exempt from taxation under section 501(c) of Title 26 [the Internal Revenue Code of 1954]" is exempt from the provisions of the act. In order to qualify for this exemption, private clubs must meet certain criteria. The Equal Employment Opportunity Commission (EEOC), which was also established under the Civil Rights Act, is an organization whose mission is, among other things, to protect and assist various classes of individuals who have historically been victims of employment discrimination. The EEOC is also responsible for determining whether a private club or organization meets the proposed criteria and qualifies for the exemption under the Civil Rights Act. The EEOC evaluates the following three factors:

1. The extent to which the organization limits its facilities and services to club members and their guests;

2. The extent to which and/or the manner in which the organization is controlled or owned by its membership;

3. Whether and, if so, to what extent and in what manner, the organization publicly advertises to solicit members or to promote the use of its facilities or services by the general public.

Title II

Title II of the Civil Rights Act prohibits discrimination in places of public accommodation (42 U.S.C. § 2000a) which affect interstate commerce; meaning trade, traffic, commerce, transportation, transmission, or communication among the several States [42 U.S.C. § 2000e(g)]. The four categories of establishments that serve the public sector include:

1. Any inn, hotel, motel, or other establishment which provides lodging to transient guests, other than an establishment located within a building which contains not more than five rooms for rent or hire and which is actually occupied by the proprietor of such establishment as his residence;

2. Any restaurant, cafeteria, lunchroom, lunch counter, soda fountain, or other facility principally engaged in selling food for consumption on the premises, including, but not limited to, any such facility located on the premises of any retail establishment; or any gasoline station;

3. Any motion picture house, theater, concert hall, sports arena, stadium, or other place of exhibition or entertainment; and

4. Any establishment (A)(i) which is physically located within the premises of any establishment otherwise covered by this subsection, or (ii) within the premises of which is physically located any such covered establishment, and (B) which holds itself out as serving patrons of such covered establishment (Title II of ADA).

Like Title VII, Title II also states that the provisions established within the law do not apply to private clubs because these organizations are not open to the public. When addressing the issue of private club status under Section 2000a(e), rather than examining one particular issue, the court use a "factor analysis" approach to determine if a club is truly private and warrants exemption from Title II legislation. In particular, the courts examine the following relevant factors:

1. The genuine selectivity of the group in the admission of its members;

2. The membership's control over the operations of the establishment;

3. The history of the organization;

4. The use of the facilities by nonmembers;

5. The purpose of the club's existence;

6. Whether the club advertises for members;

7. Whether the club is profit or nonprofit;

8. The formalities observed by the club such as bylaws, meetings, etc. (*U.S. v. Lansdowne Swim Club*, 1989).

There have been many cases over the years where sport and recreational clubs' private status has been challenged on the basis of one or more of the previous eight factors (*Castle Hill Beach Club v. Arbury*, 1955; *Daniel v. Paul*, 1969; *Durham v. Red Lake Fishing & Hunting Club, Inc.*, 1987; *U.S. v. Richberg*, 1968; *Wright v. Cork Club*, 1970). Out of all eight factors, no one factor controls the determination of private status, but the two which have proven to be most significant are: (1) the club's selectivity with respect to membership, and (2) the use of the club's facilities by nonmembers (FindLaw, 2000). The courts have ruled in a series of decisions that a genuinely private club must demonstrate strict exclusivity in its selection processes or it may not be classified as private (*Nesmith v. YMCA*, 1968; *U.S. v. Lansdowne Swim Club*, 1989; *Wright v. Cork Club*, 1970). Moreover, the courts have historically ruled against private clubs which offer too many services to nonmembers or open areas of the club to the public for commercial purposes (*Cornelius v. BPOE*, 1974; *New York v. Ocean Club*, 1984; *U.S. v. Jack Sabin's Private Club*, 1967; *U.S. v. Lansdowne Swim Club*, 1989).

State Anti-Discrimination Statutes

In 1997, Robert and Wynn Harris filed a gender discrimination lawsuit against the Meadowlands Country Club under the Pennsylvania Human Relations Act (PHRA), which is the Pennsylvania equivalent to federal anti-discrimination statutes. The PHRA prohibits discrimination against individuals based race, color, religion, sex and other protected characteristics (P.S. §§ 951-963 Section 3 (1997). According to the plaintiffs, only men were equity holders in the county club, and only men could vote and hold office. Women were also restricted from teeing off before the men and using the men's grill. Lastly, the couple asserted the club was not private because it opened its facilities to non-members and corporations for golf and tennis tournaments, wedding receptions, bar mitzvahs and other outside events, and the pro shop was also open to the public (*The New York Times*, 1997). When factors such as these are considered together and reveal that a "private" club is actually a public facility, then anti-discrimination statutes like the PHRA will apply (*Borne v. The Haverhill Golf and Country Club*, 1999; *Wanders v. Bear Hill Golf Club, Inc.*, 1998).

Americans with Disabilities Act (Ada)

According to the United States Department of Justice, Civil Rights Division, the Americans with Disabilities Act (ADA) is intended to provide comprehensive civil rights protection for "individuals with disabilities" (ADA, 2009). Title III of the ADA exempts private clubs and religious organizations from the majority of its requirements. Title III of the ADA defines the term private club as:

> *A private club or establishment exempted from coverage under Title II of the Civil Rights Act of 1964 (which prohibits discrimination on the basis of race, color, national origin, etc.).*

The rule, therefore, is that any entity that would be exempt under Title II of the 1964 Civil Rights Act would also be exempt under Title III of the ADA. Likewise, an entity that would fail the test of a private club under Title II of the 1964 Civil Rights Act would also fail the test under Title III of the ADA. The EEOC and the Department of Justice employ the same factor analysis approach to determine if a private organization qualifies for an exemption under Title III of the ADA that they use when granting exceptions under Title II of the Civil Rights Act. All eight factors are scrutinized and a decision is made regarding the club's private status (ADA, 2009).

Suggestions for Eradicating Discrimination

The prevalence of discrimination lawsuits in private sport and recreation clubs is decreasing. This trend is seemingly due to the state and federal government's growing interest in the eradication of civil rights discrimination. According to Lasseter (2006), there are a variety of ways in which the government can enact legislation to prevent discriminatory behavior by private clubs and organizations. For example, some states have already begun to disallow certain tax deductions if a private club is found to discriminate (see *Commonwealth of Kentucky, Kentucky Commission on Human Rights v. Pendennis Club*, 2004). Although this has proven to be a successful method for decreasing discriminatory practices, if the private club is willing to forgo the revenue it will remain legally protected. A more effective means of preventing private club discrimination, therefore, might be through more legislation. For instance, the State of Connecticut in 1997 passed an unprecedented piece of legislation prohibiting discrimination at private clubs. The law states:

> *This law prevents a private country club that has at least twenty members and nine holes of golf and which either financially profits from nonmembers or holds a liquor license from discriminating in its membership or access policies. It also requires that private clubs allow all members equal access to the facilities.*

California, Michigan, and Louisiana have passed similar legislation, albeit not as comprehensive in their terminology. The laws are bold steps in the right direction to prevent private clubs from hiding behind the "private" label, when they are truly public facilities that cater to and profit from the local communities in which they operate.

SIGNIFICANT CASE

The following case illustrates the eight-factor test for determining if a club is "truly private." Examining the specific circumstances considered by the court of appeals and relied on by the district court helps to understand some of the protections granted to private organizations and clubs as well as the legal issues involved when an individual challenges the organization or club's rules and practices.

UNITED STATES OF AMERICA V. LANSDOWNE SWIM CLUB

United States Court of Appeals for the Third Circuit
894 F.2d 83 (1990)

This appeal is taken from the judgment of the district court, after a non-jury trial, that the Lansdowne Swim Club (LSC) discriminated against blacks on the basis of race or color in violation of Title II of the Civil Rights Act of 1964, 42 U.S.C. §§ 2000a-2000a-6 (1982). LSC challenges the findings of the district court on three grounds: that it is an exempted private club, that it is not a place of public accommodation, and that the United States failed to prove a pattern or practice of racial discrimination. We will affirm the judgment of the district court.

I. Because the district court opinion thoroughly sets forth the facts, *United States v. Lansdowne Swim Club*, 713 F. Supp. 785 (E.D. Pa. 1989), we shall only summarize them here. LSC, a nonprofit corporation organized under the laws of Pennsylvania, is the only group swimming facility in the Borough of the Lansdowne, Pennsylvania. Since its founding in 1957, LSC has granted 1400 full family memberships. Every white applicant has been admitted, although two as limited members only. In that time, however, LSC has had only one non-white member.

The uncontroverted experiences of the following Lansdowne residents are significant. In 1976, the Allisons wrote to LSC requesting an application but LSC did not respond. Dr. Allison is black; his three children are part-black. In 1977, the Allisons twice again wrote for an application but LSC did not respond. The following year, the Allisons repeated the procedure with similar results. In 1983, the Allisons filed a timely application and otherwise qualified for membership. Nonetheless, they were rejected. Two of the Ryans' adopted children are black. The Ryans then complained to the media and picketed LSC, joined by the Allisons. In 1986, the Iverys, who are black, filed a timely application and otherwise qualified for membership. Nonetheless, they were rejected (as were the Ryans and Allisons who had again applied). ***

II. LSC's first argument is that it is a private club. Under Title II, "a private club or other establishment not in fact open to the public" is exempt from the statute. 42 USC.

§ 2000a(e). LSC has the burden of proving it is a private club. *See Anderson v. Pass Christian Isles Golf Club, Inc.*, 488 F.2d 855, 857 (5th Cir. 1974). Although the statute does not define "private club", cases construing the provision do offer some guidance. The district court distilled eight factors from the case law as relevant to this determination. Three of which it found dispositive of LSC's public nature: the genuine selectivity of its membership process, e.g., *Tillman v. Wheaton-Haven Recreation Ass'n.*, 410 U.S. 431 (1973), its history, e.g., *Cornelius v. BPOE*, 382 F. Supp. 1182 (D. Conn. 1974), and use of its facilities by nonmembers, *Id.* Appellant disputes these findings.

First, the court concluded that LSC's membership process was not genuinely selective. Essential to this conclusion was the court's finding that "LSC possesses no objective criteria or standards for admission." The court identified four "criteria" for admission to LSC: being interviewed, completing an application, submitting two letters of recommendation and tendering payment of fees. We agree, and LSC apparently concedes, that these criteria were not genuinely selective. Nonetheless, LSC challenges the court's failure to consider membership approval a criterion for admission. We agree with the district court, however, that a formal procedure requiring nothing more than membership approval is insufficient to show genuine electivity. See *Tillman*, 410 U.S. at 438-39. In addition, LSC stipulated that the only information given to the members prior to the membership vote is the applicants' names, addresses their children's name s and ages, and the recommenders' identities. In such a situation, the court was correct to conclude that LSC "provides no information to voting members that is useful in making an informed decision as to whether the applicant and his or her family would be compatible with existing members." Therefore, even if membership approval were considered a fifth criterion, it would not make the process any more genuinely selective in this case.

The district court also found the yields of the membership process indicative of lack of selectivity. Since 1958,

LSC has granted full memberships to at least 1400 families while denying them to only two non–black families. LSC contends that emphasizing the few instances of non-black applicant rejection "misconstrues the significance of selectivity. The crucial question should be whether the members exercised their right to be selective rather than the statistical results of the exercise of that right." As the Court of Appeals for the Fourth Circuit noted a decade ago, formal membership requirements "have little meaning when in fact the club does not follow a selective membership policy." *Wright v. Salisbury Club,* Ltd., 632 F.2d 309, 312 (4th Cir. 1980) (citing Tillman, 410 U.S. at 438-39). We find the evidence of lack of selectivity convincing.

Second, the court concluded that "the origins of LSC suggest that it was intended to serve as a 'community pool' for families in the area and not as a private club." We believe there was ample evidence to support this finding. A founder of LSC testified that LSC was created as a community pool for the neighborhood children. LSC's stipulations confirm the public nature of the facility: organizers solicited Lansdowne-area residents, conducted public recruitment meetings an accepted every family that applied for membership before opening.

Third, the court concluded that use of the facility by nonmembers "undercut LSC's claim that it is a private club." Among other reasons, the court cited the following factors. LSC hosts several swim meets and diving meets each year but does not prohibit the general public form attending. LSC also sponsors two to four pool parties each year, for which members and association may sell an unlimited number of tickets to persons who are not members. In addition, LSC's basketball and volleyball courts, located on its parking lot, are open to the public. Finally, LSC permits the local Boys' Club to use its parking lot for an annual Christmas tree sale that is open to the public. Although LSD contends such use is de minimus, we are persuaded otherwise.

III. LSC also contends that it is not a "place of public accommodation" as defined in Title II. Under the statute, a place of public accommodation has two elements: first, it must be one of the statutorily enumerated categories of establishments that serve the public, 42 U.S.C. § 2000a(b); second, its operations must affect commerce, *Id.*

A. The district court concluded that the whole complex, both the recreational areas and the snack bar, was an establishment which served the public. The court began by identifying LSC as a "place of . . . entertainment", one of the categories of covered establishments. "LSC concedes that its swimming and other recreational areas make it an 'establishment'", but maintains that the snack bar is not a covered establishment. The district court held that "bifurcation has no support in the plain language of the Act of

the case law interpreting it." Under the facts in the case, we agree. Nonetheless, the court also found the snack bat to be a "facility principally engaged in selling food for consumption on the premises", another category of covered establishments. LSC stipulated that "food for consumption on the premises of the Club is sold" at the snack bar. We believe these findings were sufficient to render the entire facility a covered establishment which serves the public.

B. The district court also concluded that the "affecting commerce" requirement was met. Initially, the court discussed the recreational areas, which it correctly deemed a place of entertainment under § 2000a(b)(3). Under Title II, the operations of a place of entertainment affect commerce if "it customarily presents . . . sources of entertainment which move in commerce". *Id.* § 2000a(c)(3). The court found the slicing board, manufactured in Tesac, and guests from out of state to be sources of entertainment which moved in commerce. See *Scott v. Young,* 421 F.2d 143, 144-45 (4th Cir.) (both recreational apparatus originating out of state and patrons from out of state who entertain other patrons by their activity constitute "sources of entertainment which move in commerce") (relying on *Daniel v. Paul,* 395 U.S. 298, 307-08, 23 L. Ed. 2d 318, 89 S. Ct. 1697 (1969)), *cert. Denied,* 398 U.S. 929, 90 S. Ct. 1820, 26 L. Ed. 2d 91 (1970). Implicitly conceding this, LSC argues that they do not satisfy "the requisite degree of interstate involvement." Nonetheless, the court found both to be "customarily presented:, the sliding board because it is permanently installed, and the out of state guests because the attend regularly and constitute a significant percentage of the guests (13% in 1986, 8% in 1987). We believe these findings, and the court's consequent finding that operation of the recreational areas affects commerce, are supported by the evidence.

The court then considered the snack bar, which it correctly deemed a facility principally engaged in selling food for consumption on the premises under § 2000a(b)(2). Under Title II, the operations of this category covered establishments affect commerce if "it serves or offers to serves interstate travelers or a substantial portion of the food which it serves . . . has moved in commerce". *Id.* § 2000a(c)(2). The court found the "affecting commerce" requirement satisfied in three ways. First, it was stipulated that the snack bar serves interstate travelers. Although LSC contends that the statute is meant to cover tourists lured from other states by advertising, the plain language of the statute provides no support for this view. Second, the court found that the snack bar offers to serve all users of the facility, including guests. Third, the court found that a substantial portion of the food served by the snack bar has moved in interstate commerce. The parties stipulated that the syrup in the "Coca-Cola" beverages was produced in Maryland. The court found that many of the purchases at the snack bar were for cold drinks, of which "Coca-Cola" beverages were the most popular. Nonetheless, appellant claims the substantiality test has not been met, citing *Daniel v. Paul*, 395 U.S. 298, 23 L. Ed. 2d 318, 89 S. Ct. 1697 (1969), in which the Supreme Court found the test met when three of the four foods sold had moved in interstate commerce. *Id.* at 305. In light of the broad remedial purpose of Title II, we refuse to read the requirement or Daniel so narrowly. These findings are not clearly erroneous.

***

CASES ON THE SUPPLEMENTAL CD

Commonwealth of Kentucky, Kentucky Commission on Human Rights v. Pendennis Club, 153 S.W. 3d 784 (2004). This case examines whether the Kentucky Commission on Human Rights was authorized to investigate a private club to determine whether they engaged in discrimination.

Koebke v. Bernardo Heights Country Club, 115 P.3d 1212 (2005). This case examines the club violated whether club violated California Domestic Partner Rights and Responsibilities Act of 2003 when it refused to allowed a member domestic partner the same rights as a spouse.

Roberts v. United States Jaycees, 104 S. Ct. 3244 (1984). This case examines whether an organization can prohibit admitting women as a regular member.

QUESTIONS YOU SHOULD BE ABLE TO ANSWER

1. Explain in your own words what it means to be a "truly private club" and describe a sport or recreational organization which falls into this category.

2. Based on what you have learned about private clubs in this section, go online to that particular private sport or recreational organization's website and try to determine if it is truly private. Is it actually a place of public accommodation? Explain why or why not.

3. What is the purpose of the Civil Rights Act of 1964, and why is an understanding of this piece of legislation important to future recreation and sport managers?

4. Other than the suggestions listed in the section, what else would you recommend the government, public officials, or private organizations do to eliminate discrimination in private clubs?

5. If you were to establish your own sport club, would you establish it as a public or private organization? Explain your rationale.

REFERENCES

Cases

Borne v. The Haverhill Golf and Country Club, Lexis 523 (Mass. Super. 1999).

Boy Scouts of America v. Dale, 530 US 640 (2003).

Brown v. Loudoun Golf & Country Club, Inc., 573 F. Supp. 399 (E.D. Va. 1983).

Castle Hill Beach Club v. Arbury, 144 N.Y.S.2d 747 (Sup. Ct. 1955).

Commonwealth of Kentucky, Kentucky Commission on Human Rights v. Pendennis Club, 153 S.W. 3d 784 (2004).

Cornelius v. BPOE, 382 F. Supp. 1182 (D. Conn. 1974).

Crawford v. Willow Oaks Country Club, 66 F. Sup.2d 767 (E.D. Va. 1999).

Daniel v. Paul, 395 U.S. 298, 89 S. Ct. 1697 (1969).

Durham v. Red Lake Fishing & Hunting Club, Inc., 666 F. Supp. 954 (W.D. Tex. 1987).

Gibbs-Alfano v. The Ossinging Boat & Canoe Club, Inc., 47 F. Supp.2d 506 (S.D. N.Y. 1999).

Loving v. Virginia, 388 U.S. 1, 12 (1967).

Nesmith v. YMCA, 397 F.2d 96 (4th Cir. 1968).

New York v. Ocean Club, 602 F. Supp. 489 (E.D. N.Y. 1984).

Pierce v. Society of Sisters, 268 U.S. 510, 535 (1925).

Prince v. Massachusetts, 321 U.S. 158, 166 (1944).

Roberts v. United States Jaycees, 104 S. Ct. 3244 (1984).

United States v. Jack Sabin's Private Club, 265 F. Supp. 90 (E.D. La. 1967).

United States v. Lansdowne Swim Club, 713 F. Supp. 785 (E.D. Pa. 1989).

United States v. Richberg, 398 R.2d 523 (5th Cir. 1968).

Wanders v. Bear Hill Golf Club, Inc., Lexis 650 (Mass. Super. 1998).

Wright v. Cork Club, 315 F. Supp. 1143 (D.C. Tex. 1970).

Publications

Americans with Disabilities Act (ADA). (2009). Retrieved March 30, 2009 from http://www.ada.gov/t3hilght.htm

FindLaw. (2000). *Anti-discrimination laws applicable to private clubs or not?* Retrieved from http://library.findlaw.com/2000/Oct/1/130527.html

Lasseter, A. (2006). Country club discrimination after *Commonwealth v. Pendennis*. *Boston College Third World Law Journal, 36*, 11.

Merriam-Webster's Dictionary Online. (2009). Retrieved March 29, 2009 from http://www.merriam-webster.com/dictionary/private

Merriam-Webster's Dictionary Online. (2009). Retrieved March 29, 2009 from http://www.merriam-webster.com/dictionary/club

Merriam-Webster's Dictionary Online. (2009). Retrieved March 29, 2009 from http://www.merriam-webster.com/dictionary/discrimination

The New York Times. (1997). *THE GOLF REPORT: No room in the grill: Woman cites inequality*. Retrieved from http://www.nytimes.com/1997/10/09/sports/the-golf-report-no-room-in-the-grill-woman-cites-inequality.html?sec=&spon=&pagewanted=all

USA Today. (2008). *Arizona country club sued for alleged discrimination*. Retrieved from http://www.usatoday.com/news/nation/2008-09-17-2274072038_x.htm

Legislation

United States Constitution Amendment I.

United States Constitution Amendment XIV.

42 USC. § 2000a (2000).

42 USC. § 2000e (2000).

Ky. Rev. Stat. Ann §344.130.

P.S. §§ 951-963(3) (1997).

7.00

SPORT AND LEGISLATION

In addition to the federal Constitution, Congress has also enacted a number of laws that affect the sport and recreation industry. The *Sport and Legislation* section examines those laws and the impact they have on the industry. The section is divided into four parts. The first part reviews federal laws as they apply to discrimination in the sport and recreation industry. The section examines such areas as gender equity and race, age, sex, and disability discrimination. The second part examines intellectual property law. In particular, the sections review how important copyright, trademark, and patent law are to the sport and recreation industries. The third part examines federal antitrust and labor laws and how they are applied to professional and amateur sports. The final part of the *Sport and Legislation* section examines sport agent legislation. In particular, the section reviews sport agent legislation and the impact of the Uniform Athlete Agent Act of sport agents.

7.11 Gender Equity: Opportunities to Participate

—Linda Jean Carpenter, Emerita

BROOKLYN COLLEGE

Sport is the laboratory experience through which students gain skills such as decision-making, risk evaluation, teamwork, leadership, self-appraisal, and personal esteem. These skills are the same skills that allow graduates to successfully use their other academic skills in their adult lives and employment circumstances. As a result, sport's place on campus in the form of intramurals, recreation, athletics, and physical education is defensible, not because of any possible revenue generation or because of fan support, but because of the valuable skills it provides, which are not easily obtained elsewhere in the educational setting.

The skills obtainable through sport have value to both female and male participants. The legal imperatives for equity found in the Fourteenth Amendment of the United States Constitution and Title IX of the Education Amendments of 1972 (and a variety of similarly worded state legislation) are the two most frequently used tools to judicially increase gender equitable participation in sport.

Between the Fourteenth Amendment and Title IX, most circumstances within education are covered. The Fourteenth Amendment requires a state actor; Title IX does not. Title IX requires the presence of federal financial assistance, the Fourteenth Amendment does not. Both cover gender discrimination. Both cover employees and students.

FUNDAMENTAL CONCEPTS

Constitutional Issues

The Equal Protection Clause of the Fourteenth Amendment is the generic protector of equal rights. It guarantees that no **state actor** such as a federal, state, or local governmental agency, or, for example, public school and recreation program, can gratuitously classify people and treat them differently based on those classifications without having a defensible reason.

Levels of Scrutiny

Strict/High: Necessary to Accomplish a Compelling State Interest. The defensible reason required to constitutionally treat people differently varies depending on the classification scheme employed. If, for example, a public school (*state actor*) classified its students by race and then treated its African-American students differently, the reason used to defend the constitutionality of such an action would have to withstand the Court's highest level of scrutiny. The school would need to show that its racially based discrimination was *necessary to accomplish a compelling state interest*. It is difficult to imagine a reason for racial discrimination that would meet such a test.

Mild/Low: Rationally Related to a Legitimate State Interest. As an alternative example, consider the scenario where a public school's (*state actor*) physical education program classified its students by skill level and, as a result, restricted its beginning-level students to a beginning-level course while allowing the more highly skilled students to have access to a variety of advanced electives. The Court would use a lower level of scrutiny to determine if discrimination based on skill level was constitutional. The school would only have to show that its discrimination was *rationally related to a legitimate state interest.* Protecting beginners from the injuries likely to occur if they participated with highly skilled athletes or performed advanced movements for which they were either untrained or unconditioned would appear to be rationally related to the legitimate state interest of protecting the health and safety of the community's schoolchildren.

Intermediate/Midlevel: An Evolving Middle Ground. Most classification schemes are reviewed by the courts using either the strict/high or mild/low levels of scrutiny. Typically only those classifications based on race, alienage, or nationality face strict/high scrutiny. Almost all other classification schemes face only the mild/low level. In the last few decades, however, we have seen the judicial review of classification schemes based on age, gender, and disability elevated from the mild/low level of scrutiny to a reasonably amorphous midlevel of scrutiny.

In its June 1996 decision involving coeducation at Virginia Military Institute (116 S.Ct. 2264) (see the Supplemental CD) the Supreme Court elevated the scrutiny applied to *gender* discrimination even higher within this middle ground to a level requiring an exceedingly persuasive justification. Thus if a state actor discriminates on the basis of gender, it will need to show that doing so was considerably more than rationally related to a legitimate state interest, but it will not need to show that it was necessary to accomplish a compelling state interest.

Why is discrimination based on age, disability, and particularly gender becoming more difficult to justify constitutionally? The change probably reflects the changing attitudes of society to this type of discrimination as reflected in the various civil rights legislative Acts such as Titles VI, VII, and IX.

Cases involving gender discrimination in sport and recreation have used the Fourteenth Amendment, but the more prevalently used tool is Title IX. For this reason, and because of the presence of a fuller discussion of constitutional issues elsewhere in this text, the remaining portion of this section dealing with participation issues will focus on Title IX. However, before proceeding to a deeper discussion of Title IX, a brief mention of an issue involving the interrelationship of the Constitution's Fourteenth Amendment and Title IX is appropriate. May the victim of discrimination (in this particular case, discrimination was in the form of sexual harassment) sue using BOTH Title IX and the Fourteenth Amendment? The Supreme Court answered that question in *Fitzgerald v. Barnstable School Comm.* (see Supplemental CD), when it held that the plaintiff does NOT have to lose constitutional rights at the school-house door or playground gate. Neither did Congress intend for Title IX to be the solitary mechanism for combating gender-based discrimination in school settings.

Title IX

A Brief History

Title IX was enacted by Congress on June 23, 1972, to prohibit gender discrimination in the nation's education programs. Three basic elements must all exist for Title IX's jurisdiction to be triggered. The elements are:

- **Gender Discrimination.** Title IX does not protect against discrimination based on race or age; it protects solely against gender discrimination;

- **Federal Funding.** The receipt of federal funding is required so that the enforcement of Title IX has administrative teeth. If an institution is found to be violating Title IX, its federal funding may be terminated. However, it should be noted, no federal money has ever been removed from a campus due to a Title IX violation;

- **Education Program.** The definition of this element brought early controversy to the implementation of Title IX. The U.S. Supreme Court's 1984 *Grove City v. Bell* decision resulted in the word *program* being defined as a "subunit" of an institution. As a result of *Grove City*, any subunit that did not receive federal funding would not be obligated to refrain from gender discrimination. Thus college-level athletics and physical education programs, which typically receive no federal funding, were no longer obligated by Title IX to refrain from gender discrimination. In 1988, however, Congress passed the Civil Rights Restoration Act of 1987 over presidential veto saying, in effect, that the Court had misunderstood

Congress' intent to have Title IX apply on an institution-wide basis. So, as of 1988, Title IX once again applies to college-level athletics and physical education programs, as well as to all education programs in institutions that receive federal funding.

Title IX Enforcement

There are three main pathways to enforce Title IX. The complainant or plaintiff may select any of the three and need not exhaust in-house remedies first. The first method is internal. Each institution under the jurisdiction of Title IX must have a designated Title IX officer. The Title IX officer's job is to educate the faculty, staff, and students about the rights and responsibilities imposed by Title IX and to deal with any Title IX complaints filed in-house.

The second method of enforcement is through the Office for Civil Rights of the U.S. Department of Education. Once an administrative complaint is filed with the OCR (legal standing is NOT required in order to file), the OCR investigates and, if violations are found, negotiates a "letter of resolution" with the institution in which the institution agrees to a time frame and a list of changes to be made.

The third method involves the filing of a federal lawsuit by someone with legal standing. This method has found increasing favor among plaintiffs since the Supreme Court's unanimous 1992 *Franklin v. Gwinnett County Public Schools* (see the Supplemental CD) decision, which made it clear that compensatory and perhaps even punitive damages are available to victims of intentional gender discrimination under Title IX.

Title IX Requirements

When Title IX was enacted in 1972, there was only the one-sentence law saying:

> *"No person in the United States shall, on the basis of sex, be excluded from participation in, be denied the benefits of, or be subjected to discrimination under any education program or activity receiving Federal financial assistance."*

In addition to the one-sentence law, formal regulations were promulgated and ultimately gained the force of law. Even though most Title IX cases and controversies have related to its application to sport, Title IX applies to all of education. However, because of continuing controversy about the details of Title IX's implementation in the area of sport, policy interpretations were adopted in 1979. Policy interpretations do not have the force of law but courts are required to give them significant deference. Another, yet much weaker, source of information about the requirements of Title IX is found in the 1990 *OCR Investigator's Manual*, which provides insight into how the OCR views its own requirements. OCR also has the ability and, some would argue the obligation, to clarify areas of the law that are found to be confusing. Letters of clarification have been issued over the years to explain specific issues that have been the center of controversy such as the applicability of a three pronged test relating to the measurement of the adequacy of opportunities to participate. Letters of clarification do not have the force of law but theoretically simply restate the law. However, some OCR letters of clarification, such as the "Additional Clarification" issued in 2005 concerning the use of surveys to determine interest in participation, may exceed a restatement and attempt to alter the law.

Recreation Program Application

Recreation programs are also often under the jurisdiction of Title IX. As long as all three elements (federal money, allegations of sex discrimination, and education program) are met, recreation programs are included in the jurisdiction of Title IX. It would be difficult to conceive of a campus-based recreation program that would not be under Title IX jurisdiction.

Nonscholastic, community-based recreation programs need not be operated by the state or federal government to be under the jurisdiction of Title IX. The recreation program's primary activity need not be conducting educational programs; it only needs to include an educational component in its programs to be under the jurisdiction of Title IX. If a recreation program is found to be under the jurisdiction of Title IX, offering more activities or more participation opportunities for its male clients, offering those activities in better facilities, or providing a higher quality officiating staff for its male clients, would be examples of potential Title IX violations.

Athletics Application

There are many specific requirements of Title IX relating to coaching, facilities, equipment, travel, and so on. However, if a female is not provided an opportunity to participate, it matters very little if she would have had equal access to coaching, facilities, equipment, travel, and so on. However, since if you are not on the team, you don't need a uniform, coaching and the other items, this section will focus on the legal requirements for participation rather than on the treatment of athletes once they are participating.

Title IX's regulations require that "the selection of sports and levels of competition effectively accommodate the interests and abilities of members of both sexes." According to the policy interpretations (U.S. Department of Education Athletic Guidelines, 1979), an institution has effectively accommodated the interests of its students if it satisfies any ONE of the following three benchmarks:

1. Participation opportunities for male and female students are provided in numbers substantially proportionate to their respective enrollments;

2. The institution can show a history and continuing practice of program expansion demonstrably responsive to the developing interest and abilities of the members of the underrepresented sex;

3. The institution can show that it is fully and effectively meeting the interests and abilities of the underrepresented sex.

Institutions that have maintained their commitment to the legal requirements of gender equity over the years have had no difficulty in meeting either Benchmark 2 or 3 and thus don't even need to address the issue of proportionality found in Benchmark 1. However, institutions that have ignored the requirements of Title IX or that have failed to implement plans to provide equitable athletic participation opportunities for their female students, more than three decades after the passage of Title IX, are now facing a quandary. They have not satisfied Benchmark 2 because they have not expanded their program for their female students. Similarly, if a group of female athletes demonstrates interest and ability sufficient to support the creation of a team in a particular sport in which it would be reasonable to find suitable competition in the school's traditional competitive region, the institution cannot claim that it has satisfied Benchmark 3. That leaves Benchmark 1: proportionality.

For many reasons, including past discrimination and social influences, very few schools meet Benchmark 1. Typically, the courts have found such institutions to be violating Title IX's requirement to effectively accommodate the interests and abilities of its female (historically underrepresented sex) student-athletes. Such institutions are therefore at risk of losing their federal funding in addition to being liable for possible compensatory and punitive damages.

Consternation and controversy surrounding the measurement of equitable participation has been unabated by the fact that the status of the law and the application of the three-prong test (as found in the 1979 Policy Interpretations and as reiterated unchanged in the form of a 1996 clarification letter from the Office for Civil Rights) has been very straightforward.

One of the three tests of participation, the proportionality prong (Benchmark 1) was created to provide a "safe harbor." In this context "safe harbor" means that a school that can show it has met the proportionality prong will be exempt from creating additional participation opportunities for females, even if there are significant numbers of females who are denied participation. The school would be granted the "safe harbor" exemption because it is assumed that if its ratio of female athletes mirrors the ratio of females in the student body, gender equity in participation has been met.

Reality has demonstrated that schools that have not gradually moved toward compliance over the years or that have left favored teams' budgets and inflated participation numbers unrestrained find that they can meet none of the three prongs in any reasonable way. They cannot rewrite history to meet prong 2, and they cannot claim that they have met the interests and abilities of the underrepresented sex (prong 3) as long as there are sufficient able and interested females wanting to participate, unless they are attempting to take advantage of the 2005 Further Clarification regarding the use of electronic surveys, contrary to the recommendation of the NCAA. Therefore, the only prong over which such an institution has retained any degree of control is the proportionality prong.

Some institutions have manipulated compliance within the proportionality prong in ways that, in effect, reduce participation for males and sometimes even the historically underrepresented females. By canceling men's minor sport teams, the absolute number of male participants is reduced, and the male/female athlete ratio moves closer to the ratio in the student body without having to increase participation opportunities for women. This manipulation is contrary to the spirit of Title IX. Even so, administrators have often defended their decision to cut men's minor sport teams, rather than restrain favored teams, by placing the blame for the cancellation of men's teams on Title IX. The popularity of various sports waxes and wanes even in the absence of Title IX, but those whose sports are cut are understandably frustrated.

Frustration born of the manipulation of the proportionality prong resulted in the creation of the Commission on Opportunity in Sport during the summer of 2002 under the direction of the then-Secretary for the Department of Education. The Commission was created to "strengthen enforcement" and "expand . . . opportunities to ensure fairness for all athletes." The Commission members were asked to respond to eight questions, some of which might be reflective of preconceived notions of the answers and some of which seem far afield of the requirements of Title IX. The eight questions are:

1. Are Title IX standards for assessing equal opportunity in athletics working to promote opportunities for male and female athletes?

2. Is there adequate Title IX guidance that enables colleges and school districts to know what is expected of them and to plan for an athletic program that effectively meets the needs and interest of their students?"

3. Is further guidance or other steps needed at the junior- and senior-high-school levels, where the availability or absence of opportunities will critically affect the prospective interests and abilities of student athletes when they reach college age?

4. How should activities such as cheerleading or bowling factor into the analysis of equitable opportunities?

5. The [Education] Department has heard from some parties that, whereas some men athletes will "walk on" to intercollegiate teams—without athletic financial aid and without having been recruited—women rarely do this. Is this accurate and, if so, what are its implications for Title IX analysis?

6. How do revenue-producing and large-roster teams affect the provision of equal athletic opportunities?

7. In what ways do opportunities in other sports venues, such as the Olympic, professional leagues, and community recreation programs, interact with the obligations of colleges and school districts to provide equal athletic opportunity? What are the implications for Title IX?

8. Apart from Title IX enforcements, are there other efforts to promote athletic opportunities for male and female students that the department might support, such as public-private partnerships to support the efforts of schools and colleges in this area?

The Commission's hearings were robust with strong rhetoric on all sides. The Commission's report, which was vague in direction, did little to calm any partisan fears. A minority report was issued and all interested in the issue of Title IX awaited some further action from the OCR. When further action finally came, it came in the form of a "Letter of Further Guidance." The Letter of Further Guidance reaffirmed OCR's support of the existing requirements of Title IX and promised more diligent enforcement. The Letter also renewed the appropriateness of the three-part test, including the proportionality option.

How would you respond to each of the Commission's questions after seeking out data and a variety of points of view? For one organization's response, check the following Website:–http://www.aahperd.org/nagws/template.cfm?template=titleix_papers.html

For a time, it seemed that finally, Title IX and its requirements were settled in both practice and in the law. Then, on January 11, 2005, OCR issued another letter, this time known as the "Additional Clarification of Intercollegiate Athletics Policy: Three-Part Test—Part Three." (See the following Website for a copy of the letter and also for the accompanying technical manual: http://www.ed.gov/about/offices/list/ocr/docs/title9guidanceadditional.html.)

The 2005 Additional Clarification Letter was much more than a clarification. It provided for the use of an OCR-created survey instrument to assess interest and ability among students. The survey contains no standard for measuring sufficient interest, and thus regardless of the results, no finding of sufficient interest would be mandated. If a school elects to use the OCR survey instrument, even via an email survey sent to student accounts, the school gains a presumption of having met the interests and abilities of its historically underrepresented students, regardless of the results of the survey (due to the lack of standards to measure sufficient interest). To make it clear: the simple use of the survey, regardless of its outcome, conveys the presumption. According to the 2005 Additional Clarification of Letter, the presumption of compliance is only rebuttable "if the OCR finds direct and very persuasive evidence of unmet interest sufficient to sustain a varsity team, such as the recent elimination of a viable team for the underrepresented sex or a recent, broad-based petition from an existing club team for elevation to varsity status." The hurdle to be overcome to rebut the presumption is very high indeed.

In part because of the difficult-to-overcome presumption, the use of an email survey format, which is unlikely to produce high response rates (a nonresponse is interpreted as disinterest), and the format of the questions within the OCR survey instrument, the NCAA swiftly called on the OCR to withdraw the 2005 Additional Letter. Furthermore, the NCAA strongly urged its member institutions to refrain from using the OCR survey.

As of this writing OCR has not withdrawn its letter, and few, if any, NCAA members have elected to use the survey instrument offered in the letter.

Opportunities to Participate Free from Harassment

Having the opportunity to participate but facing sexual harassment while participating is not much of an opportunity at all. Sexual harassment invades many areas of human interaction, and the Fourteenth Amendment to a small degree and Titles VII and IX to a larger degree are useful tools with which to combat sexual harassment.

Title IX is specifically applicable to sexual harassment of students by both their teachers and coaches. Title VII, on the other hand, applies only in the workplace, and thus does not protect students. See Section 7.14, *Sexual Harassment* for a full discussion of harassment.

SIGNIFICANT CASE

Although a relatively old case, the following case is used to illustrate the Title IX guidelines published by the office for civil rights and those requirements needed to come into compliance with the law.

ROBERTS V. COLORADO STATE UNIVERSITY

United States Tenth Circuit Court of Appeals
998 F.2d 824 (10th Cir. 1993)

Current and former members of the Colorado State University's fast pitch softball team sued the university after it announced the discontinuation of the fast pitch softball program. The students, suing as individuals, claimed Title IX violations.

The district court found Title IX violations existed and issued a permanent injunction reinstating the softball program. When, somewhat later, the court held a status conference, the court found the institution had been apparently dragging its feet. Therefore, the court amplified its earlier orders to require defendant to hire a coach promptly, recruit new members for the team, and organize a fall season.

* * *

A.

This controversy concerns one subject of the regulations implementing Title IX.34C.F.R.§ 106.41(c) provides:

A recipient which operated or sponsors interscholastic, intercollegiate, club or intramural athletes shall provide equal athletic opportunity for members of both sexes. In determining whether equal opportunities are available the Director [of the Office for Civil Rights] will consider, among other factors:

(1) Whether the selection of sports and levels of competition effectively accommodate the interests and abilities of members of both sexes[.]

Although § 106.41(c) goes on to list nine other factors that enter into discrimination of equal opportunity in athletics, an institution may violate Title IX simply by failing to accommodate effectively the interests and abilities of student athletes of both sexes.

In 1979, the Department of Health, Education, and Welfare issued a policy interpretation explaining the ways in which institutions may effectively accommodate the interests and abilities of their student athletes.

The Policy Interpretation delineates three general areas in which the OCR will assess compliance with the effective accommodation section of the regulation, as follows:

1. The determination of athletic interests and abilities of students;

2. The selection of sports offered; and

3. The levels of competition available including the opportunity for team competition.

The OCR assesses effective accommodation with respect to opportunities for intercollegiate competition by determining:

1. Whether intercollegiate level participation opportunities for male and female students are provided in numbers substantially proportionate to their respective enrollments; or

2. Where the members of one sex have been and are under represented among intercollegiate athletes, whether the institution can show a history and continuing practice of program expansion which is demonstrably responsive to the developing interest and abilities of the members of that sex; or

3. Where the members of one sex are under represented among intercollegiate athletes, and the institution cannot show a continuing practice of program expansion such as that cited above, whether it can be demonstrated that the interests and abilities of the members of that sex have been fully and effectively accommodated by the present program.

In effect, "substantial proportionality" between athletic participation and undergraduate enrollment provides a safe harbor for recipients under Title IX. In the absence of such gender balance, the institution must show that it has expanded and is continuing to expand opportunities for athletic participation by the under represented gender, or else it must fully and effectively accommodate the interests and abilities among members of the under represented gender.

In addition to assessing whether individuals of both sexes have the opportunity to compete in intercollegiate athletics, the OCR also examines whether the quality of competition provided to male and female athletes equally reflects their abilities. This will depend on whether, program wide, the competitive schedules of men's and women's teams "afford proportionally similar numbers of male and female athletes equivalently advanced competitive opportunities," *Id.*, or "[w]hether the institution can demonstrate a history and continuing practice of upgrading the competitive opportunities available to the historically disadvantaged sex as warranted by developing abilities among the athletes of that sex." However, "[i]nstitutions are not required to upgrade teams to intercollegiate status or otherwise develop intercollegiate sports absent a reasonable expectation that intercollegiate competition in that sport will be available within the institution's normal competitive regions."

B.

The district court found that plaintiffs met their burden of showing that defendant could not take shelter in the safe harbor of substantial proportionality. The district court reviewed a substantial quantity of statistical data, and made the undisputed finding that following the termination of the varsity softball program, the disparity between enrollment and athletic participation for women at CSU is 10.5 percent. Defendant maintains that, as a matter of law, a 10.5 percent disparity is substantially proportionate.

The OCR has instructed its Title IX compliance investigators that "[t]here is no set ratio that constitutes 'substantially proportionate' or that, when not met, results in a disparity or a violation." Investigator's Manual at 24. However, in the example immediately preceding this statement, the Manual suggests that substantial proportionality entails a fairly close relationship between athletic participation and undergraduate enrollment. Furthermore, in a Title IX compliance review completed in 1983, the OCR found that CSU's athletic participation opportunities for men and women were not substantially proportionate to their respective enrollments. During the three years that were the subject of that review, the differences between women enrolled and women athletes were 7.5 percent, 12.5 percent, and 12.7 percent. The district court relied on these sources, as well as expert testimony that a 10.5 percent disparity is statistically significant, in concluding that CSU could not meet this first benchmark. *See also Cohen v. Brown University*, 809 F. Supp. 978,991 (D.R.I. 1992) (see Supplemental CD) (11.6 percent disparity not substantially proportionate) *aff'd*, 991 F.2d 888 (1st Cir. 1993). Without demarcating further the line between substantial proportionality and disproportionality, we agree with the district court that a 10.5 percent disparity between female athletic participation and female undergraduate enrollment is not substantially proportionate. The fact that many or even most other educational institutions have a greater imbalance than CSU does not require a different holding.

C.

The district court also found that defendant could not prove a history and continuing practice of expansion in women's athletics at CSU. Defendant argues that the district court should have given greater weight to its dramatic expansion of women's athletic opportunities during the 1970s. In essence, defendant suggests reading the words "continuing practice" out of this prong of the test. In support of this position, defendant offers anecdotal evidence of enforcement at other institutions, and the OCR's 1983 finding of compliance for CSU, which was contingent upon CSU's fulfilling the provisions of a plan that CSU never met.

Although CSU created a woman's sports program out of nothing in the 1970s, adding eleven sports for women during that decade, the district court found that women's participation opportunities declined steadily during the 1980s. Furthermore, although budget cuts in the last twelve years have affected both men and women athletes at CSU, the district court found that women's participation opportunities declined by 34 percent, whereas men's opportunities declined by only 20 percent. The facts as found by the district court (and largely undisputed by defendant) can logically support no other conclusion than that, since adding women's golf in 1977, CSU has not maintained a practice of program expansion in women's athletics, and indeed has since dropped three women's sports.

We recognize that in times of economic hardship, few schools will be able to satisfy Title IX's effective accommodation requirement by continuing to expand their women's athletics programs. Nonetheless, the ordinary meaning of the word "expansion" may not be twisted to find compliance under their prong when schools have increased the relative percentages of women participating in athletics by making cuts in both men's and women's sports programs. Financially strapped institutions may still comply with Title IX by cutting athletic programs such that men's and women's athletic participation rates become substantially proportionate to their representation in the undergraduate population.

The heart of the controversy is the meaning of the phrase "full and effective accommodation of interests and abilities." Defendant maintains that even if there is interest and ability on the part of women athletes at CSU, the university is obliged to accommodate them only to the extent it accommodates men. Thus, the argument goes, plaintiffs cannot be heard to complain because both women's softball and men's baseball were eliminated in the last round of cuts and there are more disappointed male than female athletes at CSU. The First Circuit rejected this position in *Cohen*, and so do we. "[T]his benchmark sets a high standard; it demands not merely some accommodation, but full and effective accommodation. If there is sufficient interest and ability among members of the statistically under represented gender, not slaked by existing programs, an institution necessarily fails this prong of the test." *Id.* at 898.

Based on the district court's subsidiary findings of fact, we conclude that plaintiffs met the burden of showing that CSU has not accommodated their interest and abilities fully and effectively. Questions of fact under this third prong will be less vexing when plaintiffs seek the reinstatement of an established team rather than the creation of a new one. Here, plaintiffs were members of a successful varsity softball team that played a competitive schedule as recently as the spring of 1992. Although apparently four plaintiffs have transferred and one has been dismissed, seven or eight plaintiffs remain at CSU for at least part of the 1993–94 school year and would be eligible to play on a reinstated team. We agree with the district court that CSU fails the third prong of effective accommodation test.

CASES ON THE SUPPLEMENTAL CD

Fitzgerald v. Barnstable School Committee, 129 S.Ct. 788 (2009). This case examines whether Title IX was the exclusive mechanism for addressing gender discrimination in schools or a substitute for § 1983 suits as a means of enforcing constitutional rights.

Franklin v. Gwinnett County Public Schools, 503 U.S. 60 (1992). This case examines whether Title IX provides a damages for individual students.

United States v. Virginia, 518 U.S. 515 (1996). This case examines Virginia's policy of denying women admission to the Virginia Military Institute, a publicly funded university.

QUESTIONS YOU SHOULD BE ABLE TO ANSWER

1. Does Title IX protect members of discontinued men's teams? Why or why not?

2. Is the lack of money a defense to Title IX?

3. Should failure of Benchmark 1 (proportionality) solely create an irrefutable presumption of either compliance with or violation of Title IX's accommodation/opportunity requirement? If yes, why? If no, why?

4. May a student who has been discriminated against sue using both Title IX and the 14th Amendment as legal theories or must the student select only one theory?

5. Evaluate the recreational sport program at your school or in your community and determine if you think the program is complying with the requirements of Title IX.

REFERENCES

Cases

Cohen v. Brown University, 991 F.2d 888 (1st Cir. 1993), 8879 F. Supp. 185 (D. R.I. 1995), *cert. denied.*

Cook v. Colgate University, 802 F. Supp. 737 (1992) vacated as moot 992 F.2d 17 (2nd Cir. 1993).

Davis v. Monroe County Board of Education, 526 U.S. 629 (1999).

Favia v. Indiana University of Pennsylvania, 7 F.3d 332 (3rd Cir. 1993).

Fitzgerald v. Barnstable, 555 US____ (2009).

Franklin v. Gwinnett County Public Schools, 503 U.S. 60 (1992).

Grove City v. Bell, 465 U.S. 555 (1984).

Kelley v. University of Illinois, 35 F.3d 265 (7th Cir. 1994).

Mercer v. Duke University, No. 01-1512, 4th Circuit, November 15, 2002.

Oncale v. Sundowner Offshore Services, 523 U.S. 75 (1998).

Pederson v. Louisiana State University, 912 F. Supp. 892 (La. 1996).

Roberts v. Colorado State University, 814 F. Supp. 1507 (D. Colo.) *aff'd in relevant part sub nom. Roberts v. Colorado State Bd. of Agric.,* 998 F.2d 824 (10th Cir.), *cert. denied,* 114 S. Ct. 580 (1993).

United States v. Virginia Military Institute, 116 S.Ct. 2264 (1996).

Publication

U.S. Department of Education. (1979). Athletic Guidelines.

Legislation

Title VII: 42 USC sections 2000e-17, plus additions made by the Civil Rights Act of 1991, Pub.L. No. 102–166, 105 Stat 1071 (1991).

Title IX: Education Amendments of 1972, §§ 901-909 as amended, 20 U.S.C.A. §§ 11681-11688. 40 Fed. Reg. 24, 128 (1975) currently appearing at 34 C.F.R. §§ 106 (1992).

U.S. Department of Education Athletic Guidelines; Title IX of the Education Amendments of 1972; A Policy Interpretation; Title IX and Intercollegiate Athletics, 44 Fed. Reg. 71, 413, 71, 423 (1979).

7.12 Gender Equity: Coaching and Administration

—Barbara Osborne
UNIVERSITY OF NORTH CAROLINA AT CHAPEL HILL

Although opportunities to participate for girls and women in sport in the United States have increased dramatically over the past 40 years, (see Section 7.11, *Gender Equity: Opportunities to Participate*) leadership and employment opportunities for women have not. In some cases, women's opportunities in sport and recreation administration have actually decreased.

Vivien Acosta and Linda Jean Carpenter have conducted a longitudinal study, "Women in Intercollegiate Sport" since 1977. Their research shows that although there are more women employed in administrative and coaching positions in intercollegiate athletics than ever before, the number of women as a percentage of total administrators and coaches is not close to the 90 percent representation in the 1970s when most colleges and universities had separate men's and women's athletics departments. As of 2008, only 21.3 percent of athletics directors at all NCAA institutions were women, with Division III having the highest percentage of female athletics directors at 33.7 percent. However, 11.6 percent of schools have no women employed in athletics administration. Less than half (42.8 percent) of women's athletics teams have a female head coach, a percentage that continues to decrease. There are more paid assistant coaches in women's college athletics than ever before, and 57.1 percent of those positions are held by women. Sports medicine and sports information lag woefully behind, with only 27.3 percent of women employed as head athletics trainers. Athletics communications appears to mirror the professional sports media, as only 11.3 percent of sports information directors are women (Acosta & Carpenter, 2009). In addition to barriers in employing women in college athletics programs, a gender gap also exists in salaries, with female coaches earning on average only 62 percent of what male coaches make (Osborne & Yarbrough, 2001).

There are many possible explanations for the decline in women's employment as athletics administrators and coaches. Combining men's and women's athletics programs in the 1970s and 1980s was less of a merger of two departments and more of take-over by the men's athletics department, resulting in elimination of female athletics administrators. This transition also resulted in paid positions and improved pay for coaches of women's teams, making positions coaching women more attractive to men. Research indicates the sex of the person making the employment decision matters, and male athletics directors are more likely to hire men (Acosta and Carpenter, 2002).

FUNDAMENTAL CONCEPTS

Employment discrimination laws prevent employers, including sport and recreation organizations, from discriminating on the basis of race, sex, religion, country of national origin, disability, and age. These laws seek to prevent bias in all aspects of employment including hiring, work assignment, compensation, promotion, and termination. The United States Equal Employment Opportunity Commission (EEOC) is the federal agency responsible for these laws. This section will examine constitutional and statutory protection against employment discrimination based on gender, including the issues of pay equity, pregnancy, and retaliation.

Constitutional Law and Civil Rights Acts

The United States Constitution prohibits discrimination based on gender under the Equal Protection clause of the Fourteenth Amendment. Because the proposed Equal Rights Amendment to the United States Constitution was never ratified, the federal courts apply an intermediate scrutiny standard, meaning that the government action must be substantially related to an important government interest (see Section 6.14, *Sexual Harassment*).

Additionally, 42 U.S.C. §1983 of the Civil Rights Act of 1871 provides for damages when federal constitutional rights are violated. Section 1983 claims may also be used to redress deprivation of a right guaranteed by a federal statute.

Besides Federal Constitution, state constitutions may also provide heightened protection from discrimination based on sex. For example, the State Constitution of Illinois states in its Bill of Rights that all persons have the right to be free from discrimination on the basis of race, color, creed, national ancestry, and sex. As a result, in Illinois, and other states that have included sex or gender as a protected category in their state constitution heighten the constitutional protection, requiring the courts to use a strict scrutiny review.

State civil rights legislation also provides additional protection from gender discrimination. For example, in Michigan, the Elliott-Larsen Civil Rights Act prohibits discriminatory practices on the basis of religion, race, color, national origin, sex, age, height, weight, familial status, and marital status in the exercise of civil rights. As a result, when Hazel Park refused to hire Geraldine Fuhr as the boys' varsity basketball coach, even though she had 10 years experience as the girls' varsity basketball coach, and eight years as the assistant boys varsity basketball coach.

Fuhr and John Barnett, who had been coaching the boys' freshman basketball team for the past two years, were the only two applicants for the position. When Barnett was hired, and Fuhr was told by the school principal that she did not get the job because of her gender, she sued the school district for sex discrimination under Title VII and the Elliot-Larsen Act. A jury held in Fuhr's favor, awarding her $245,000 in present damages and $210,000 in future damages. Subsequently, the district court ordered Hazel Park to hire Fuhr as the boys' varsity basketball coach, and struck the jury's award of future damages, but granted Fuhr attorney's fees. Hazel Park appealed, but the Sixth Circuit affirmed, finding that Hazel Park had intentionally discriminated against Fuhr on the basis of sex by not hiring her as the head boys' basketball coach.

However, as protection against discrimination varies from state to state, and federal Constitutional protection is only at an intermediate level, additional federal legislation has been needed to address gender inequity in the workforce.

Equal Pay Act of 1963

An amendment to the Fair Labor Standards Act of 1938 (29 U.S.C.A. § 201-219), the Equal Pay Act (EPA) prohibits employers from discriminating on the basis of sex by paying a higher wage to an employee based on their sex for equal work on a job that requires equal skill, effort and responsibility when the job is performed under similar working conditions. Skill is measured as equal based on experience, training, education and ability required in performing the job, effort is the amount or degree of physical or mental exertion required to perform the job successfully, and responsibility is measured by the degree of accountability required with emphasis on the importance of the job obligation.

Once the employee has proved differential pay for equal work, the burden then shifts to the employer to justify the wage difference through one of the defenses outlined in the Act: seniority, merit, quantity or quality of production, and any factor other than the sex of the employee. If the employer offers a justification, the employee has one final opportunity to provide evidence that the employer's defense is pretext and that the real reason for the pay inequity is gender discrimination. The burden of proof standard in an Equal Pay Act claim is very high, making it difficult for an employee to win a claim.

An example of how difficult it can be to establish a claim under the Equal Pay Act is *Stanley v. University of Southern California*, (1999). Marianne Stanley was the USC women's basketball program when she began negotiating a new contract with Michael Garrett, Athletics Director at USC. Stanley asked for a contract equal to that of the men's basketball coach at USC. The athletics director agreed that Stanley was worth more, but explained that the athletics department could not afford to pay that type of an increase. The negotiations continued, with the athletics department making offers and Stanley making counter offers. Stanley then retained an attorney to negotiate the terms of a new contract and the athletics director responded by withdrawing a multi-year offer, and instead offered a one-year contract. Stanley asked for additional time to consider the offer, and in the meantime, her current contract expired. On July 15, the AD sent a memo to Stanley withdrawing his offer and informing her that he would be seeking other candidates to fill her position.

Stanley filed a lawsuit claiming that the athletics director and USC had engaged in sex discrimination and retaliation. She argued that she was entitled to be paid a salary that was equal to the salary of the men's basketball coach as the positions required equal skill, effort and responsibility, and is performed under similar working conditions. USC refuted the claim, offering evidence that the men's basketball coach had substantially different qualifications and experience. USC argued that the men's coach had substantial public-relations and revenue-generating skills, including nine years of marketing experience. Additionally, he had authored two best-selling novels, performed as an actor in a movie, and had appeared on television. USC also argued that the men's and women's basketball coaching positions were not equivalent positions, as the men's coaching position required substantial public relations and promotional activities related to generating revenue. The university argued that the men's basketball team generated greater attendance, attracted more media interest, inspired larger donations, and produced substantially more revenue than the women's basketball team, which placed greater pressure on the men's basketball coach. The court agreed with the university and found that factors other than gender caused the difference in salary.

As illustrated by *Stanley*, the first hurdle a plaintiff must establish is that the positions are equal. This is difficult, since female athletic administrators are often in a unique position within the athletics department and usually have no male counterpart in job that is substantially equal. Coaches, however, may have less difficulty when there are both male and female versions of the same team, but as in the Stanley case, courts do not always find that the coach of the men's team and the coach of the women's team in the same sport have substantially equal positions. A coach may choose to compare her position with that of a male coach of another sport, but differences in the number of athletes coached, number of assistant coaches necessary, variety of player positions to train, number of games in a season, and other sport-related factors make it easy for the court to conclude that working conditions are not similar.

If the coach or administrator is able to establish an equal comparator, it is still extremely difficult to refute the employer's affirmative defense. Employers are quite successful at establishing that their pay decisions stem from any factor other than sex. Athletics programs have successfully asserted the following justifications for paying male coaches more than comparable female coaches: the men's team produces more revenue than the women's team; the coaching marketplace demands higher salaries for the best coaches; current salary was based on past salary; and the male coach has additional duties. Sex of the athletes coached should not be an acceptable defense, as the sex of the student-athlete is a factor based on sex and not a gender-neutral factor (EEOC Guidelines, 1997).

Title VII of Civil Rights Act of 1964

Title VII protects broadly against discrimination on the basis of race, color, religion, country of national origin and sex. Like the Equal Pay Act, Title VII protects against discrimination in compensation. However, the Equal Pay Act is limited to equal pay for equal work, while Title VII offers a victim significantly broader protection. Victims may make claims for failure to hire or promote, or for improper firing on the basis of sex. Additionally, employers may not discriminate on the basis of sex with respect to the terms, conditions, and privileges of employment beyond pay (See Ch. 7.13 for a thorough examination and analysis of Title VII).

An example of the broader protection provided by Title VII is the case of Kathryn Tomlinson who filed a complaint with the EEOC against the Phoenix Suns. Tomlinson was employed by the Suns as a member of the "Zoo Crew," an entertainment troupe that shoots T-shirts into the stands, assists with half-time promotions, performs with the team mascot, and participates in community events to promote the team. Although Tomlinson and two other female employees performed well as members of the Zoo Crew, the Suns adopted a new hiring policy for the following season, limiting the positions to talented males with athletic ability. Unable to reapply for their former jobs, the women filed a complaint against the Suns and the stadium management team. To resolve the case, the Suns paid over $100,000 to the plaintiffs, and were required to provide training to employees, supervisors, and management prohibiting sex discrimination as well as establishing policies to ensure that sex-restrictive job announcements would not be created in the future.

Title IX of Education Amendments of 1972

Although Title IX of the Education Amendments of 1972 is best known for providing opportunities for girls to participate in athletics (see Ch. 7.11), the statute also prohibit any educational institution that is a recipient of federal funding from discriminating against an applicant or employee on the basis of sex. It further prohibits discrimination on the basis of sex in hiring, promoting, awarding tenure, demoting, transferring, laying off or terminating an employee. Job classifications, assignments, and training may not be made on the basis of sex either. Rate of pay, or any other form of compensation or benefits may not be related to sex, and the language of the compensation section (§ 106.54) mirrors the requirements of the Equal Pay Act.

Although Title IX provides a cause of action for coaches who complain of employment discrimination on the basis of sex at federally funded schools, coaches still have difficulty winning these cases in court. Anderson & Osborne (2008) report that only half of Title IX claims of employment discrimination that were litigated and appealed were favorable to the plaintiff coach or administrator. It is also important to note that Title IX only provides protection against discrimination based on the gender of the coach, not the athletes.

Retaliation

Retaliation occurs when an employee suffers an adverse employment action in response to an action that the employer perceives negatively, such as complaining about unfair treatment to athletes, lack of comparable facilities for practice and/or competition, or other inequitable situations. Neither the plain language of Title IX nor the Regulations specifically allows for a claim of retaliation, however, the Supreme Court in *Jackson v. Birmingham Board of Education* (2005), concluding that teachers, coaches, and administrators who complain of sex discrimination on behalf of themselves or others have a right to sue if they are victims of retaliation. Since that decision, there have been a number of lawsuits against colleges and universities across the country, including several in California that have attracted attention because of the large jury awards and settlements.

For example, Fresno State University has been battling complaints about gender discrimination within the athletics program for several years. First, Diane Milutinovich, an athletic administrator, was dismissed from her position for "budget reasons" after she complained about inequities in the men's and women's athletics programs. Then the women's volleyball coach, Lindy Vivas, and women's basketball coach, Stacy Johnson-Klein were fired after questioning administrators and complaining about inequities in facilities, staffing, and employment demands between the men's and women's athletics programs. To settle the law suit with Milutinovich, Fresno State agreed to pay her $3.5 million. In addition, juries in two separate trials found that the university intentionally discriminated against the coaches and awarded $5.85 million to Vivas and $19.1 million to Johnson-Klein.

Pregnancy Discrimination Act of 1978

The fundamental physical difference between men and women is the ability to bear children, and childbearing as well as childrearing responsibilities have contributed to bias against women in hiring, promotion, and salaries. This physiological difference has historically been used to justify differential treatment between the sexes in a variety of situations. In *Bradwell v. Illinois* (1872), the Supreme Court justified a state's refusal to issue a law license on the basis of sex because "the natural and proper timidity and delicacy which belongs to the female sex evidently unfits it for many of the occupations of civil life." In *Muller v. Oregon* (1908), the Supreme Court upheld an Oregon law that prohibited women from working for more than 10 hours per day because "woman's physical structure and the performance of maternal functions place her at a disadvantage in the struggle for subsistence." Although medicine and science have refuted those old-fashioned opinions regarding the proper role of women in society, many people still believe that working mothers are less productive employees who should be paid less because they will have childcare responsibilities that may conflict with work priorities. The Pregnancy Discrimination Act combats that discriminatory reasoning by prohibiting employers from negatively impacting employment or benefits on the basis of pregnancy and childbirth.

Lilly Ledbetter Fair Pay Act of 2009

The gender wage gap in the United States in 2007 is about 22.2 percent, which translates to women earning about 78 cents for each dollar that a man would earn for the same job. The limitations of the Equal Pay Act, reluctance of women to file lawsuits against their employers, and the uncertainty involved in going to court have all contributed to the persistent gender wage gap in the United States. For example, Lilly Ledbetter worked as a supervisor at the Goodyear plant in Gadsden, Alabama for almost twenty years. Just as Ledbetter prepared to retire, she was informed through an anonymous note that she had been paid significantly less than her male peers who were doing the same job. Ledbetter filed suit under Title VII and the trial jury awarded Ledbetter back pay and damages worth more than $3 million. On appeal, the U.S. Supreme Court overturned the decision and held that employees must file wage discrimination complaints within 180 days of the original pay decision, no matter when they became aware of the disparity. As a result, Ledbetter was left with nothing (*Ledbetter v. Goodyear Tire & Rubber Co.*, 2007). This decision significantly restricted the time period in which victims may file claims, severely weakening the statutory protections provided under Title VII.

Unhappy with the Supreme Court's ruling in Ledbetter, Congress passed the Lilly Ledbetter Fair Pay Act of 2009. The Act allows victims of pay discrimination to assert their rights under the Equal Pay Act and Title VII for full compensatory and punitive damages. In addition, the Act establishes that an unlawful employment practice occurs each time an individual is paid if that compensation is affected by application of a discriminatory compensation practice or decision. The Act also requires the EEOC of the U.S. Department of Labor to issue regulations and survey pay data that will allow it to improve enforcement of the law.

SIGNIFICANT CASE

This recent Supreme Court decision has expanded the scope of Title IX protection for coaches and administrators who suffer retaliation for speaking out against gender inequity in their athletics programs.

RODERICK JACKSON V. BIRMINGHAM BOARD OF EDUCATION

Supreme Court of the United States
544 U.S. 167 (2005)

Justice O'Connor delivered the opinion of the Court.

Roderick Jackson, a teacher in the Birmingham, Alabama, public schools, brought suit against the Birmingham Board of Education (Board) alleging that the Board retaliated against him because he had complained about sex discrimination in the high school's athletic program. Jackson claimed that the Board's retaliation violated Title IX of the Education Amendments of 1972, Pub L 92-318, 86 Stat 373, as amended, *20 U.S.C. § 1681 et seq*. The District Court dismissed Jackson's complaint on the ground that Title IX does not prohibit retaliation, and the Court of Appeals for the Eleventh Circuit affirmed. *309 F.3d 1333 (2002)*. We consider here whether the private right of action implied by Title IX encompasses claims of retaliation. We hold that it does where the funding recipient retaliates against an individual because he has complained about sex discrimination.

I

Because Jackson's Title IX claim was dismissed under *Federal Rule of Civil Procedure 12(b)(6)* for failure to state a claim upon which relief can be granted, "we must assume the truth of the material facts as alleged in the complaint." *Summit Health, Ltd. v. Pinhas, 500 U.S. 322 (1991)*.

According to the complaint, Jackson has been an employee of the Birmingham school district for over 10 years. In 1993, the Board hired Jackson to serve as a physical education teacher and girls' basketball coach. Jackson was transferred to Ensley High School in August 1999. At Ensley, he discovered that the girls' team was not receiving equal funding and equal access to athletic equipment and facilities. The lack of adequate funding, equipment, and facilities made it difficult for Jackson to do his job as the team's coach.

In December 2000, Jackson began complaining to his supervisors about the unequal treatment of the girls' basketball team, but to no avail. Jackson's complaints went unanswered, and the school failed to remedy the situation. Instead, Jackson began to receive negative work evaluations and ultimately was removed as the girls' coach in May 2001. Jackson is still employed by the Board as a

teacher, but he no longer receives supplemental pay for coaching.

After the Board terminated Jackson's coaching duties, he filed suit in the United States District Court for the Northern District of Alabama. He alleged, among other things, that the Board violated Title IX by retaliating against him for protesting the discrimination against the girls' basketball team. Amended Complaint 2-3, App. 10-11. The Board moved to dismiss on the ground that Title IX's private cause of action does not include claims of retaliation. The District Court granted the motion to dismiss.

The Court of Appeals for the Eleventh Circuit affirmed. *309 F.3d 1333 (2002)*. It assumed, for purposes of the appeal, that the Board retaliated against Jackson for complaining about Title IX violations. It then held that Jackson's suit failed to state a claim because Title IX does not provide a private right of action for retaliation, reasoning that "[n]othing in the text indicates any congressional concern with retaliation that might be visited on those who complain of Title IX violations." *Id., at 1344*. Relying on our decision in *Alexander v. Sandoval, 532 U.S. 275, 149 L. Ed. 2d 517, 121 S. Ct. 1511 (2001)*, the Court of Appeals also concluded that a Department of Education regulation expressly prohibiting retaliation does not create a private cause of action for retaliation: "Because Congress has not created a right through Title IX to redress harms resulting from retaliation, [the regulation] may not be read to create one either." *309 F.3d, at 1346*. Finally, the court held that, even if Title IX prohibits retaliation, Jackson would not be entitled to relief because he is not within the class of persons protected by the statute.

We granted certiorari, *542 U.S. 903, 159 L. Ed. 2d 266, 124 S. Ct. 2834 (2004)*, to resolve a conflict in the Circuits over whether Title IX's private right of action encompasses claims of retaliation for complaints about sex discrimination. Compare *Lowrey v. Texas A & M Univ. System, 117 F.3d 242, 252 (CA5 1997)* ("[T]itle IX affords an implied cause of action for retaliation"); *Preston v. Virginia ex rel. New River Community College, 31 F.3d 203, 206 (CA4 1994)*.

II. A. Title IX prohibits sex discrimination by recipients of federal education funding. The statute provides that "[n]o person in the United States shall, on the basis of sex, be excluded from participation in, be denied the benefits of, or be subjected to discrimination under any education program or activity receiving Federal financial assistance." *20 U.S.C. § 1681(a)*. More than 25 years ago, in *Cannon v. University of Chicago, 441 U.S. 677, 690–693, 60 L. Ed. 2d 560, 99 S. Ct. 1946 (1979)*, we held that Title IX implies a private right of action to enforce its prohibition on intentional sex discrimination. In subsequent cases, we have defined the contours of that right of action. In *Franklin v. Gwinnett County Public Schools, 503 U.S. 60, 117 L. Ed. 2d 208, 112 S. Ct. 1028 (1992)*, we held that it authorizes private parties to seek monetary damages for intentional violations of Title IX. We have also held that the private right of action encompasses intentional sex discrimination in the form of a recipient's deliberate indifference to a teacher's sexual harassment of a student, *Gebser v. Lago Vista Independent School Dist., 524 U.S. 274, 290–291, 141 L. Ed. 2d 277, 118 S. Ct. 1989 (1998)*, or to sexual harassment of a student by another student, *Davis v. Monroe County Bd. of Ed., 526 U.S. 629, 642, 143 L. Ed. 2d 839, 119 S. Ct. 1661 (1999)*.

In all of these cases, we relied on the text of Title IX, which, subject to a list of narrow exceptions not at issue here, broadly prohibits a funding recipient from subjecting any person to "discrimination" "on the basis of sex." *20 U.S.C. § 1681*. Retaliation against a person because that person has complained of sex discrimination is another form of intentional sex discrimination encompassed by Title IX's private cause of action. Retaliation is, by definition, an intentional act. It is a form of "discrimination" because the complainant is being subjected to differential treatment. See generally *Olmstead v. L. C., 527 U.S. 581, 614, 144 L. Ed. 2d 540, 119 S. Ct. 2176 (1999)* (Kennedy, J., concurring in judgment) (the "normal definition of discrimination" is "differential treatment"); see also *Newport News Shipbuilding & Dry Dock Co. v. EEOC, 462 U.S. 669, 682, n. 22, 77 L. Ed. 2d 89, 103 S. Ct. 2622 (1983)* (discrimination means "less favorable" treatment). Moreover, retaliation is discrimination "on the basis of sex" because it is an intentional response to the nature of the complaint: an allegation of sex discrimination. We conclude that when a funding recipient retaliates against a person *because* he complains of sex discrimination, this constitutes intentional "discrimination" "on the basis of sex," in violation of Title IX.

The Court of Appeals' conclusion that Title IX does not prohibit retaliation because the "statute makes no mention of retaliation," *309 F.3d, at 1344*, ignores the import of our repeated holdings construing "discrimination" under Title IX broadly. Though the statute does not mention sexual harassment, we have held that sexual harassment is intentional discrimination encompassed by Title IX's private right of action. *Franklin, 503 U.S., at 74*. Thus, a recipient's deliberate indifference to a teacher's sexual harassment of a student also "violate[s] Title IX's plain terms." *Davis, supra, at 64...* Likewise, a recipient's deliberate indifference to sexual harassment of a student by another student also squarely constitutes "discrimination" "on the basis of sex." *Davis, 526 U.S., at 64*. "Discrimination" is a term that covers a wide range of intentional unequal treatment; by using such a broad term, Congress gave the statute a broad reach. See *North Haven Bd. of Ed. v. Bell, 456 U.S. 512, 521....*

Congress certainly could have mentioned retaliation in Title IX expressly, as it did in § 704 of Title VII of the Civil Rights Act of 1964, 78 Stat 257, as amended, 86 Stat 109, *42 U.S.C. § 2000e-3(a)* (providing that it is an "unlawful employment practice" for an employer to retaliate against an employee because he has "opposed any practice made an unlawful employment practice by [Title VII], or because he has made a charge, testified, assisted, or participated in any manner in an investigation, proceeding, or hearing under [Title VII]"). Title VII, however, is a vastly different statute from Title IX, see *Gebser, 524 U.S., at 283-284, 286-28 ...* and the comparison the Board urges us to draw is therefore of limited use. Title IX's cause of action is implied, while Title VII's is express. See *Id., at 283-284....* Title IX is a broadly written general prohibition on discrimination, followed by specific, narrow exceptions to that broad prohibition. See *20 U.S.C. § 1681*. By contrast, Title VII spells out in greater detail the conduct that constitutes discrimination in violation of that statute. See *42 U.S.C. §§ 2000e-2* (giving examples of unlawful employment practices), *2000e-3* (prohibiting "[o]ther unlawful employment practices," including (a) "[d]iscrimination" in the form of retaliation; and (b) the discriminatory practice of "[p]rinting or publication of notices or advertisements indicating prohibited preference . . ."). Because Congress did not list *any* specific discriminatory practices when it wrote Title IX, its failure to mention one such practice does not tell us anything about whether it intended that practice to be covered.

Title IX was enacted in 1972, three years after our decision in *Sullivan v. Little Hunting Park, Inc., 396 U.S. 229 (1969)*. In *Sullivan*, we held that Rev Stat § 1978, *42 U.S.C. § 1982*, which provides that "[a]ll citizens of the United States shall have the same right . . . as is enjoyed by white citizens . . . to inherit, purchase, lease, sell, hold, and convey real and personal property," protected a white man who spoke out against discrimination toward one of his tenants and who suffered retaliation as a result. Sullivan had rented a house to a black man and assigned him a membership share and use rights in a private park. The corporation that owned the park would not approve the assignment to the black lessee. Sullivan protested, and the corporation retaliated against him by expelling him and taking his shares. Sullivan sued the corporation, and we upheld Sullivan's cause of action under *42 U.S.C. § 1982* for "[retaliation] for the advocacy of [the black person's] cause." *396 U.S., at 237.* Thus, in *Sullivan* we interpreted a general prohibition on racial discrimination to cover retaliation against those who advocate the rights of groups protected by that prohibition.

Congress enacted Title IX just three years after *Sullivan* was decided, and accordingly that decision provides a valuable context for understanding the statute. As we recognized in *Cannon*, "it is not only appropriate but also realistic to presume that Congress was thoroughly familiar with *[Sullivan]* and that it expected its enactment [of Title IX] to be interpreted in conformity with [it]." *441 U.S., at 699....* Retaliation for Jackson's advocacy of the rights of the girls' basketball team in this case is "discrimination on the basis of sex," just as retaliation for advocacy on behalf of a black lessee in *Sullivan* was discrimination on the basis of race.

B. The Board contends that our decision in *Alexander v. Sandoval, 532 U.S. 275 (2001)*, compels a holding that Title IX's private right of action does not encompass retaliation. *Sandoval* involved an interpretation of Title VI of the Civil Rights Act of 1964, 78 Stat 252, as amended, *42 U.S.C. § 2000d et seq.*, which provides in *§ 601* that no person shall, "on the ground of race, color, or national origin, be excluded from participation in, be denied the benefits of, or be subjected to discrimination under any program or activity" covered by Title VI. *42 U.S.C. § 2000d. Section 602 of Title VI* authorizes federal agencies to effectuate the provisions in *§ 601* by enacting regulations. Pursuant to that authority, the Department of Justice promulgated regulations prohibiting funding recipients from adopting policies that had "the effect of subjecting individuals to discrimination because of their race, color, or national origin." *28 C.F.R. § 42.104(b)(2) (1999)*. The *Sandoval* petitioners brought suit to enjoin an English-only policy of the Alabama Department of Public Safety on grounds that it disparately impacted non-English speakers in violation of the regulations. Though we assumed that the regulations themselves were valid, see *532 U.S., at 281*, we rejected the contention that the private right of action to enforce intentional violations of Title VI encompassed suits to enforce the disparate-impact regulations. We did so because "[i]t is clear ... that the disparate-impact regulations do not simply apply *§ 601*—since they indeed forbid conduct that *§ 601* permits—and therefore clear that the private right of action to enforce *§ 601* does not include a private right to enforce these regulations." *Id., at 285....* Thus, *Sandoval* held that private parties may not invoke Title VI regulations to obtain redress for disparate-impact discrimination because Title VI itself prohibits only intentional discrimination.

The Board cites a Department of Education regulation prohibiting retaliation "against any individual for the purpose of interfering with any right or privilege secured by [Title IX]," *34 C.F.R. § 100.7(e) (2004)* (incorporated by reference by *§ 106.71*), and contends that Jackson, like the petitioners in *Sandoval*, seeks an "impermissible extension of the statute" when he argues that Title IX's private right of action encompasses retaliation. Brief for Respondent 45. This argument, however, entirely misses the point. We do not rely on regulations extending Title IX's protection beyond its statutory limits; indeed, we do not rely on the Department of Education's regulation at all, because the statute *itself* contains the necessary prohibition. As we explain above ... the text of Title IX prohibits a funding recipient from retaliating against a person who speaks out against sex discrimination, because such retaliation is intentional "discrimination" "on the basis of sex." We reach this result based on the statute's text. In step with *Sandoval*, we hold that Title IX's private right of action encompasses suits for retaliation, because retaliation falls within the statute's prohibition of intentional discrimination on the basis of sex.

C. Nor are we convinced by the Board's argument that, even if Title IX's private right of action encompasses discrimination, Jackson is not entitled to invoke it because he is an "indirect 15dvers[m]" of sex discrimination. Brief for Respondent 33. The statute is broadly worded; it does not require that the victim of the retaliation must also be the victim of the discrimination that is the subject of the original complaint. If the statute provided instead that "no person shall be subjected to discrimination on the basis of *such individual's* sex," then we would agree with the Board. Cf. *42 U.S.C. § 2000e-2(a)(1)* ("It shall be an unlawful employment practice for an employer ... to discriminate against any individual ... because of *such individual's* race, color, religion, sex, or national origin" (emphasis added)). However, Title IX contains no such limitation. Where the retaliation occurs because the complainant speaks out about sex discrimination, the "on the basis of sex" requirement is satisfied. The complainant is himself a victim of discriminatory retaliation, regardless of whether he was the subject of the original complaint. As we explain above ... this is consistent with *Sullivan*, which formed an important part of the backdrop against which Congress enacted Title IX. *Sullivan* made clear that retaliation claims extend to those who oppose discrimination against others. See *396 U.S., at 237,* (holding that a person may bring suit under *42 U.S.C. § 1982* if he can show that he was "punished for trying to vindicate the rights of minorities").

Congress enacted Title IX not only to prevent the use of federal dollars to support discriminatory practices, but also "to provide individual citizens effective protection against those practices." *Cannon, 441 U.S., at 704....* We agree with the United States that this objective "would be difficult, if not impossible, to achieve if persons who complain about sex discrimination did not have effective protection against retaliation." Brief for United States as *Amicus Curiae* 13. If recipients were permitted to retaliate freely, individuals who witness discrimination would be loathe to report it, and all manner of Title IX violations might go unremedied as a result. See *Sullivan, supra, at 237.*...

Reporting incidents of discrimination is integral to Title IX enforcement and would be discouraged if retaliation against those who report went unpunished. Indeed, if retaliation were not prohibited, Title IX's enforcement scheme would unravel. Recall that Congress intended Title IX's private right of action to encompass claims of a recipient's deliberate indifference to sexual harassment. See generally *Davis, 526 U.S. 629.* Accordingly, if a principal sexually harasses a student, and a teacher complains to the school board but the school board is indifferent, the board would likely be liable for a Title IX violation. See generally *Gebser, 524 U.S. 274.* But if Title IX's private right of action does not encompass retaliation claims, the teacher would have no recourse if he were subsequently fired for speaking out. Without protection from retaliation, individuals who witness discrimination would likely not report it, indifference claims would be short circuited, and the underlying discrimination would go unremedied.

Title IX's enforcement scheme also depends on individual reporting because individuals and agencies may not bring suit under the statute unless the recipient has received "actual notice" of the discrimination. *Id., at 288, 289-290.*... If recipients were able to avoid such notice by retaliating against all those who dare complain, the statute's enforcement scheme would be subverted. We should not assume that Congress left such a gap in its scheme.

Moreover, teachers and coaches such as Jackson are often in the best position to vindicate the rights of their students because they are better able to identify discrimination and bring it to the attention of administrators. Indeed, sometimes adult employees are "'the only effective 16dversary[ies]'" of discrimination in schools. See *Sullivan, supra, at 237.*...

D. The Board is correct in pointing out that, because Title IX was enacted as an exercise of Congress' powers under the Spending Clause, see, *e.g., Davis, supra, at 640,* . . . , "private damages actions are available only where recipients of federal funding had adequate notice that they could be liable for the conduct at issue," *Davis, supra, at 640.* When Congress enacts legislation under its spending power, that legislation is "in the nature of a contract: in return for federal funds, the States agree to comply with federally imposed conditions." *Pennhurst State School and Hospital v. Halderman, 451 U.S. 1, 17 (1981).* As we have recognized, "[t]here can . . . be no knowing acceptance [of the terms of the contract] if a State is unaware of the conditions [imposed by the legislation on its receipt of funds]." *Ibid.*

The Board insists that we should not interpret Title IX to prohibit retaliation because it was not on notice that it could be held liable for retaliating against those who complain of Title IX violations. We disagree. Funding recipients have been on notice that they could be subjected to private suits for intentional sex discrimination under Title IX since 1979, when we decided *Cannon. Pennhurst* does not preclude private suits for intentional acts that clearly violate Title IX. *Davis, supra, at 642.*

Indeed, in *Davis,* we held that *Pennhurst* did not pose an obstacle to private suits for damages in cases of a recipient's deliberate indifference to one student's sexual harassment of another, because the deliberate indifference constituted intentional discrimination on the basis of sex. *Davis, supra, at 650.* . . . Similarly, we held in *Gebser* that a recipient of federal funding could be held liable for damages under Title IX for deliberate indifference to a teacher's harassment of a student. *524 U.S., at 287-28.* In *Gebser,* as in *Davis,* we acknowledged that federal funding recipients must have notice that they will be held liable for damages. See *Davis, supra, at 642.* . . . But we emphasized that "this limitation on private damages actions is not a bar to liability where a funding recipient intentionally violates the statute." *Davis, supra, at 642.* . . . Simply put, "*Pennhurst* does not bar a private damages action under Title IX where the funding recipient engages in intentional conduct that violates the clear terms of the statute." *Davis, supra, at 642.*...

Thus, the Board should have been put on notice by the fact that our cases since *Cannon,* such as *Gebser* and *Davis,* have consistently interpreted Title IX's private cause of action broadly to encompass diverse forms of intentional sex discrimination. Indeed, retaliation presents an even easier case than deliberate indifference. It is easily attributable to the funding recipient, and it is always—by definition—intentional. We therefore conclude that retaliation against individuals because they complain of sex discrimination is "intentional conduct that violates the clear terms of the statute," *Davis, 526 U.S., at 642,* and that Title IX itself therefore supplied sufficient notice to the Board that it could not retaliate against Jackson after he complained of discrimination against the girls' basketball team.

The regulations implementing Title IX clearly prohibit retaliation and have been on the books for nearly 30 years. Cf., *e.g., Id., at 643* (holding that Title IX's regulatory scheme "has long provided funding recipients with notice that they may be liable for their failure to respond to the discriminatory acts of certain nonagents"). More importantly, the Courts of Appeals that had considered the question at the time of the conduct at issue in this case all had already interpreted Title IX to cover retaliation. See, *e.g., Lowrey, 117 F.3d, at 252; Preston, 31 F.3d, at 206.* The Board could not have realistically supposed that, given this context, it remained free to retaliate against those who reported sex discrimination. Cf. *Davis, supra, at 644* (stating that the common law of torts "has put schools on notice that they may be held responsible under state law for their failure to protect students from the tortious acts of third parties"). A reasonable school board would realize that institutions covered by Title IX cannot cover up violations of that law by means of discriminatory retaliation.

To prevail on the merits, Jackson will have to prove that the Board retaliated against him *because* he complained of sex discrimination. The amended complaint alleges that the Board retaliated against Jackson for complaining to his supervisor, Ms. Evelyn Baugh, about sex discrimination at Ensley High School. At this stage of the proceedings, "[t]he issue is not whether a plaintiff will ultimately prevail but whether the claimant is entitled to offer evidence to support the claims." *Scheuer v. Rhodes, 416 U.S. 232, 236 (1974).* Accordingly, the judgment of the Court of Appeals for the Eleventh Circuit is reversed, and the case is remanded for further proceedings consistent with this opinion.

It is so ordered. ***

CASES ON THE SUPPLEMENTAL CD

Fuhr v. School Disrict. of Hazel Park, 364 F.3d 753 (6th Cir. 2004). This case examines the claim by a high school coach, who was the head coach of the girl's varsity team and of a lower level boy's team, that she was passed over for the boy's head coaching position because of her gender.

Stanley v. University of Southern California, 13 F.3d 1313 (1994). This case examines whether there are legitimate differences between coaching a men's basketball teams and a women's team.

Weaver v. The Ohio State University, 71 F. Supp.2d 789 (S.D. Ohio 1998). This case examines whether the women's field hockey coach was terminated in retaliation for complaints that she made concerning the condition of the artificial turf at the athletic field or for legitimate reasons.

QUESTIONS YOU SHOULD BE ABLE TO ANSWER

1. What are the limitations of Constitutional protections against discrimination based on sex?

2. Explain the elements of an Equal Pay Act claim and how the burden of proof shifts from plaintiff to defendant and back to plaintiff as a case proceeds.

3. Explain the protection against employment discrimination under Title IX. What are the limitations of this legislation?

4. How does Title IX protect employees from employer retaliation for complaining about gender inequities within athletics programs?

5. How does the Lilly Ledbetter Fair Pay Act improve protection against pay discrimination compared to the Equal Pay Act?

REFERENCES

Cases

Bradwell v. Illinois, 83 U.S. 130 (1872).

Fuhr v. Sch. Dist. of Hazel Park, 364 F.3d 753 (6th Cir. 2004).

Jackson v. Birmingham Board of Education, 544 U.S. 167 (2005).

Ledbetter v. Goodyear Tire & Rubber Co., 550 U.S. 618 (2007).

Muller v. Oregon, 208 U.S. 412 (1908).

Stanley v. University of Southern California, 13 F.3d 1313 (9th Cir. 1994).

Stanley v. University of Southern California, 178 F.3d 1069 (9th Cir. 1999).

Weaver v. The Ohio State University, 71 F. Supp.2d 789 (S.D. Ohio 1998).

Publications

Acosta, V., & Carpenter, L. (2008). Women in intercollegiate sport—A longitudinal, National study—Thirty-one year update. Retrieved on May 1, 2009, at acostacarpenter.org/2008%20Summary%20Final.pdf

Anderson, P., & Osborne, B. (2008). A Historical Review of Title IX Litigation. *Journal of Legal Aspects of Sport*, 18(1), 127–168.

Osborne, B., & Yarbrough, M. V. (2001). Pay Equity for Coaches and Athletic Administrators: An Element of Title IX? *University of Michigan Journal of Law Reform*, *34*(1&2), 231–251.

Press Release (2003 October 9). EEOC Resolves Sex Discrimination Lawsuit Against NBA's Phoenix Suns and Sports Magic for $104,500. Retrieved from the U.S. Equal Employment Opportunity Commission website on April 7, 2009, at http://www.eeoc.gov/oress/10-9-03b.html

Women's Sports Foundation (n.d.). Coaching—Do Female Athletes Prefer Male Coaches?: The Foundation Position. Retrieved May 4, 2009, from http://www.womenssportsfoundation.org/Content/Articles/Issues/Coaching/C/Coaching—Do-Female-Athletes-Prefer-Male-Coaches-The-Foundation-Position.aspx

Legislation

Civil Rights Act of 1987 (Pub. L. No. 100–259, 102 Stat. 28).

EEOC Notice Number 915.002, *Enforcement Guidance on Sex Discrimination in the Compensation of Sports Coaches in Educational Institutions* (Oct. 29, 1997). Retrieved on May 1, 2009, from http://www.eeoc.gov/policy/docs/coaches.html

Elliott-Larsen Civil Rights Act, Mich. C. L. § 37.2101 (2009).

Equal Pay Act of 1963, 29 U.S.C. § 206(d).

Fair Labor Standards Act of 1938, 52 Stat. 1060.

Ill. Const. Art. 1, Sec. 17 (2009).

Lilly Ledbetter Fair Pay Act, 111 P.L. 2 (2009).

Pregnancy Discrimination Act of 1978 (42 U.S.C.A. § 2000e(k)).

Title VII of Civil Rights Act of 1964, 42 U.S.C. § 2000 2(a)(1)(2).

Title IX of the Educational Amendments of 1972, 20 U.S.C. § 1681–1688.

7.13   Title VII of the Civil Rights Act of 1964

—Lisa Pike Masteralexis
—Stephanie A. Tryce
UNIVERSITY OF MASSACHUSETTS-AMHERST

The Civil Rights Act of 1964 is a comprehensive federal law prohibiting discrimination in many settings, including elections, housing, federally funded programs, education, employment, and public facilities and accommodations. Title VII of the Civil Rights Act addresses employment discrimination and is the focal point of the act. It became the first comprehensive federal law prohibiting employment discrimination. An employer may distinguish between applicants or employees provided the employer's criteria are within Title VII's limits. Generally, a distinction that is made on the basis of an employee's characteristics (race, gender, religion, national origin); it will be discriminatory under Title VII.

FUNDAMENTAL CONCEPTS

Scope

Title VII broadly prohibits discrimination in employment. Section 703 (a) states:

> It shall be an unlawful employment practice for an employer—(1) to fail or refuse to hire or to discharge any individual, or otherwise discriminate against any individual with respect to his compensation, terms, conditions, or privileges of employment, because of such individual's race, color, religion, sex, or national origin; or (2) to limit, segregate, or classify his employees or applicants for employment in any way which would deprive or tend to deprive any individual of employment opportunities or otherwise adversely affect his status as an employee, because of such individual's race, color, religion, sex, or national origin [42 U.S.C. §§ 2000e-2(a)].

Title VII applies to employers with fifteen or more employees working at least twenty calendar weeks whose organizations affect interstate commerce. Employers can be individuals, partnerships, joint ventures, corporations, unincorporated associations, and government entities. The definition also includes employment agencies and labor organizations (unions or players associations). Title VII, however, excludes from its definition of employer the U.S. government and some departments of the District of Columbia, Native American tribes, and bona fide membership clubs, such as country clubs. To be considered a bona fide membership club under Title VII, the club must qualify for tax-exempt status under the charitable exemption provision of the Internal Revenue Code and must be established for defined social or recreational purposes or for a common literary, scientific, or political objective.

Graves v. Women's Professional Rodeo Association, Inc. ("WPRA") (1990), makes clear that professional associations, which sanction events will not be considered employers unless they clearly fit the definition of employer. In *Graves*, a male rodeo barrel racer charged that the defendant nonprofit association, which organized female rodeo contestants and sanctioned events, had discriminated against him on the basis of gender when it denied him membership. WPRA was not an "employer" under Title VII because its members were not employees. WPRA did not pay wages, withhold taxes, or pay insurance for members. Furthermore, rules only permitted an opportunity for members to compete for prize money raised by rodeo sponsors, not by the WPRA.

Administration of Title VII

A five-member, presidential-appointed administrative agency, the Equal Employment Opportunity Commission ("EEOC") is charged with the administration of Title VII. The EEOC carries out a number of functions, including investigating charges of employment discrimination. It attempts to conciliate alleged violations. Where the EEOC does not find reasonable cause to go forward with conciliation or where conciliation is not fruitful, the complaining party may proceed with a private Title VII lawsuit. The EEOC may also file suit in federal district court to enforce Title VII, or it may intervene in any private employment discrimination lawsuit. For example, in *EEOC v. National Broadcasting Co., Inc.*, the EEOC brought suit on behalf of a female applicant for the position of television sports director alleging sex discrimination in violation of Title VII. Further, the EEOC creates guidelines and regulations for the interpretation of Title VII. Although the guidelines and regulations do not possess the full force and effect of law, they are subject to great judicial deference. For example, in *Meritor Savings Bank, FSB v. Vinson* (1986), the U.S. Supreme Court relied on EEOC guidelines to define hostile environment sexual harassment.

Civil Rights Act of 1991

The Civil Rights Act of 1991 was introduced into Congress with the stated goal of negating five U.S. Supreme Court decisions that severely limited important protections granted by employment discrimination laws. The Act also established a Glass Ceiling Commission and a Glass Ceiling Initiative through the Department of Labor to examine whether a glass ceiling existed to keep women and minorities underrepresented in management and decision-making positions.

This Act amended the Civil Rights Act of 1964 to permit jury trials and compensatory and punitive damages in addition to back pay for *all* claims of intentional discrimination under Title VII, not just racial and ethnic discrimination. Thus, defendants are liable for declaratory or injunctive relief and attorney's fees where a plaintiff proves discrimination based on protected class status was a motivating factor for any employment practice, even if other factors also motivated the decision (called **mixed motive cases**). A plaintiff is not, however, entitled to back pay, reinstatement, or compensatory or punitive damages in mixed motive cases.

The Civil Rights Act of 1991 prohibits "race norming," a practice whereby test scores are adjusted on the basis of race or other Title VII classification. It also adopted the defenses of "business necessity" and "job-related" practices as bases for which an employer can justify an employment practice challenged as discriminatory. Finally, the 1991 Act eliminated challenges to affirmative action consent decrees from individuals who had notice and an opportunity to object when the decree was entered or whose interests were adequately represented by another individual or organization.

Classes Protected under Title VII

Title VII prohibits employment discrimination on the basis of race, color, religion, gender, or national origin in hiring, firing, training, compensating, designating work assignments, promoting, demoting, or any other employment activity. Thus, any employment decision, practice, or policy that segregates individuals and treats them differently on the basis of the preceding classifications violates Title VII.

Race

Although much of the U.S. Civil Rights Movement focused on the treatment of African Americans, Title VII's definition of race is much broader. It is not limited to ethnological races, but protects all classes of people from dissimilar treatment, including, but not limited to Hispanics, Native Americans, and Asian Americans.

Racial discrimination cases involving coaches and athletic directors arose from decisions made in the course of public school desegregation. For example, in *Cross v. Board of Education of Dollarway, Arkansas School District* (1975), the plaintiff, a black high school football coach at a black high school in a segregated school district, was demoted to assistant coach when his school integrated with a white high school. Cross was passed over for the position twice, when white coaches with fewer qualifications were hired. On the second instance, the school superintendent suggested the defendant school board deviate from its policy to promote within to search outside the district for a white coach. The superintendent was of the opinion that the white players would not play for a black coach and the community was not ready for a black head coach and athletic director. The school board never considered Cross's application for the position. The court found the school board's refusal to even consider Cross's application was clear evidence of individual disparate treatment on the basis of his race. As a result Cross was entitled to back pay equal to the difference in the amount he would have received as head coach and that which he did receive as assistant coach. Additionally, the defendant was ordered to promote Cross to the position of head football coach and athletic director or to compensate him at a salary comparable to the position.

In April 2005 a California jury awarded Mike Terpstra, former California State University Stanislaus men's basketball coach, $540,000 in damages in a reverse race discrimination case. Terpstra, a white male, claimed his race was a factor in the university's decision to allow his contract to expire after the 2002–2003 season, because they were interested in replacing him with a black coach. Although Terpstra was ultimately replaced with another white male coach, the jury found that race was a factor when the university allowed his contract to expire.

An expansion of racial discrimination has come in same-race cases. In *Ross v. Douglas County* (2001), the Eighth Circuit Court of Appeals held that an African-American employee could assert a claim of racial harassment directed toward him by his African-American supervisor. The court found that the African-American supervisor's behavior was discriminatory "whatever the motive." Furthermore, the Court determined that "the only reason Ross was called a 'nigger' was because he was black" and that the supervisor's race "did not alter this." The case, however, does not serve to make clear the distinction between the content of the improper behavior at issue and the motivation for the behavior in the first instance. Juries are likely to have difficulty separating the racially obvert nature of the conduct from whether racial bias was the reason for the harassment in the first place. We will have to wait to see if the U.S. Supreme Court will bring clarity to the issue in the future.

Color

An employer's distinction on the basis of skin pigment or the physical characteristics of an applicant or employee's race are discriminatory. For instance, if an employer favors light-skinned African Americans over dark-skinned African Americans, it is treating African Americans differently on the basis of color. Color discrimination often intersects with racial discrimination.

National Origin

In national origin discrimination cases, the focus is on one's ancestry. This does not include U.S. territories such as Puerto Rico or the Virgin Islands. Title VII does not prohibit employment discrimination solely on the basis of citizenship. For example, in *Dowling v. United States* (1979), the plaintiff argued that the National Hockey League and the World Hockey Association only hired Canadian referees, and thus, discriminated against him on the basis of his national origin. The court dismissed the claim as it stated that Title VII does not bar employment discrimination on the basis of alienage or citizenship. However, the lack of U.S. citizenship may not be used as a method of disguising discrimination that is actually based on race or national origin. An employer may follow a policy of employing only U.S. citizens, but may not give unequal treatment to different noncitizens based on their country of origin. Rules that require communication in "English only" are allowed only where the employer can prove that such a rule is a business necessity.

Sex

Title VII's sex discrimination cases have primarily involved women, but it also applies to men. For example, in *Medcalf v. University of Pennsylvania* (1998), an EEOC investigation found that University of Pennsylvania ("Penn") had discriminated against male applicants when hiring the new women's crew coach. The EEOC found that Penn took extraordinary measures to recruit only female candidates, and that the university failed to interview Andrew Medcalf, its assistant men's rowing coach, even though he was highly recommended by both his immediate supervisor and several current male and female rowers. More recently, in *Babyak v. Smith College* (2001), a jury awarded James Babyak $1.65 million in an age, gender bias, and retaliation case. Babyak, a former coach for the basketball and soccer teams at Smith, a women's college, was fired from his position in 1997 due to poor performance. Babyak, 56, however, maintained that the college wanted a younger woman for the position. He also established that his performance was satisfactory by pointing to the facts that, in the 1995–1996 season, the basketball team, under his direction, won more games than any other basketball team in the history of Smith College, and the soccer team had won six conference championships.

It is the gender of the employee discriminated against, not the gender of the athletes an employee coaches, which form the basis for Title VII discrimination. The plaintiffs in *Jackson v. Armstrong School District* (1977), lost their Title VII claim because they alleged they were paid less money because they were coaching girls' basketball, rather alleging that they were discriminated against because they were women. The defendant avoided liability by establishing that men coaching girls' basketball were paid the same amount as the women.

Title VII's protection against sex-based discrimination includes sexual harassment, but does not include discrimination on the basis of sexual orientation. In 1978 Congress amended Title VII's language "on the basis of sex" to include protection against discrimination on the basis of pregnancy, childbirth, or other related medical conditions (including abortion).

The theory of sexual harassment comes from this section of the Act. Liability for sexual harassment was introduced as a legal theory in the late 1970s and continues to evolve, with the most recent decisions focusing on same-sex harassment and employer liability (both are discussed in Section 7.14, *Sexual Harassment*).

Although Title VII does not protect against sexual orientation discrimination in the workplace, twenty-two states have added protection against discrimination on the basis of sexual orientation in their employment discrimination laws. At the same time, and possibly in response to this movement, a number of jurisdictions have sought to prohibit homosexuality in their state and/or local governments.

In *Price Waterhouse v. Hopkins* (1989), the U.S. Supreme Court stated that where the employer bases employment decisions on gender stereotyping, a Title VII claim may be sustained. The key in the determination is whether the harassment occurred because of the victim's sex. In *Bibby v. Philadelphia Coca Cola Bottling Co.*, (2001), the Third Circuit of Appeals rejected a plaintiff's claim of unlawful harassment and enumerated three ways to prove where same-sex harassment occurred on account of the victim's sex: "(1) proof that the harasser sexually desires the victim; (2) proof that the harasser displays hostility to the presence of a particular sex in the workplace; and (3) proof that the harasser's conduct was motivated by a belief that the victim failed to conform to the stereotypes of his or her gender."

The scope of Title VII sex discrimination claims now also includes transgender. In *Smith v. City of Salem* (2004), the U.S. Court of Appeals for the Sixth Circuit held that a transsexual has a viable cause of action under Title VII if he is discriminated against because of his failure to conform to sex stereotypes by exhibiting less masculine and more feminine mannerisms and appearance. The Sixth Circuit, relying on *Price Waterhouse*, found that "sex" encompasses both the biological differences between men and women, and gender discrimination, which is based on the failure to conform to stereotypical gender norms. Although Title VII does not protect against sexual orientation discrimination, per se, it is possible that the decision in *Salem* could be used by the Lesbian, Gay, Bisexual, Transgender and Questioning ("LBGTQ") community to bring claims under Title VII by asserting that they have been discriminated against for failure to conform to stereotypical gender norms. Also, see *Schroer v. Billington*, (2008).

Religion

All well-recognized faiths and even those considered unorthodox (provided the court is convinced that the purported belief is sincere and genuinely held, and not simply adopted for an ulterior motive) are protected under Title VII. An employer must make **a reasonable accommodation** to an employee's religious practices and observances, unless it would place an **undue hardship** on the employer. An employer's obligation is simply to make a reasonable accommodation to an employee.

Theories of Liability

Courts applying Title VII have established four theories of liability: individual disparate treatment, systemic disparate treatment, disparate impact, and retaliation.

Individual Disparate Treatment

There are two ways to prove intentional discrimination. The first is through direct evidence of intent from the defendant's statements. In *Morris v. Bianchini, et al.* (1987), the plaintiff and another woman were passed over for promotion to athletic director of the health and fitness club in favor of less qualified males. The reason they were given was that the club sought "a macho, male image" for its athletic director. This statement was used as evidence of intent by the club's management to discriminate against two qualified women in favor of a less qualified candidate on the basis of gender. Another example is *Biver v. Saginaw Township Community Schools, et al.* (1986), in which the plaintiff alleged discrimination in failing to hire her for a boys' or girls' basketball team coaching position. The court accepted as evidence of the superintendent's discriminatory intent his statement that "hell would freeze over before he would hire a woman for a boys' coaching position." The superintendent claimed it was not discriminatory, as his policy was to hire men to coach boys and women to coach girls. The plaintiff challenged his credibility by showing many instances in which he had hired men to coach girls.

A second method by which one can prove discrimination is through the use of an ***inference***. A plaintiff can establish an inference for the court by comparing how an employer treats similarly situated employees of different protected classes. The model for using an inference to prove discriminatory intent was established by *McDonnell Douglas Corp. v. Green*, (1973). According to *Texas Department of Community Affairs v. Burdine* (1981), the McDonnell Douglas model is as follows: "[f]irst, the plaintiff has the burden of proving by the preponderance of the evidence a prima facie case of discrimination. Second, if the plaintiff succeeds in proving the prima facie case the burden shifts to the defendant 'to articulate some legitimate nondiscriminatory reason for the employee's rejection.' Third, should the defendant carry this burden, the plaintiff must then have an opportunity to prove by a preponderance of the evidence that the legitimate reasons offered by the defendant were not its true reasons, but were a pretext for discrimination." Thus, "[t]he ultimate burden of persuading the trier of fact that the defendant intentionally discriminated against the plaintiff remains at all times with the plaintiff" (*Texas Department of Community Affairs v. Burdine*, 1981). Under this widely relied upon standard, a ***prima facie case*** is established by the plaintiff showing:

(If applicant)

1. Applicant is a member of a protected class.

2. Applicant applied for a job for which the employer was seeking applicants.

3. Applicant was qualified to perform the job.

4. Applicant was not hired.

5. Employer filled the position with a non-minority or continued to search.

(If employee)

1. Employee is within the protected class.

2. Employee was performing the task satisfactorily.

3. Employee was discharged or adversely affected by change in working conditions.

4. Employee's work was assigned to one in a nonminority category.

The burden then shifts to the defendant to rebut the plaintiff's presumption by producing evidence that the plaintiff was rejected and someone else preferred for a ***legitimate, nondiscriminatory reason*** (*Texas Department of Community Affairs v. Burdine*, 1981). The defendant's burden is one of production, not persuasion. For the reason to be legitimate it must be lawful, clear, and reasonably specific. In other words, when comparing the chosen applicant or employee with the plaintiff, the defendant should elaborate on the criteria necessary for hiring or promotion, the basis for the comparison of the candidates, and that the person hired or promoted, rather than the plaintiff, possessed the qualities the defendant was seeking (*Herman v. National Broadcasting Co., Inc.*, 1984). The defendant need not prove that the chosen employee was a superior candidate, but simply that there were legitimate, nondiscriminatory reasons to justify the employer's decision. It is difficult for a defendant to raise this defense without clear qualification criteria for hiring. For instance, in *Jackson v. World League of American Football* (1994), the court refused to grant summary judgment in a racial discrimination case where the World League of American Football had not set clear qualifications for the position of head football coach. Once the employer provides a legitimate, nondiscriminatory reason for the alleged discrimination, the burden then shifts back to the employee to prove that the legitimate reason is in fact a *pretext* for intentional discrimination. There are a number of ways a plaintiff may establish evidence of pretext, including:

1. providing direct evidence of prejudice toward the plaintiff or members of the protected class;

2. presenting statistical evidence of an unbalanced work force;

3. presenting evidence of a rejection of a high number of protected class members; and

4. proving that the articulated reason for rejection has not been consistently applied to members of the majority as it has to protected class members (Player, 1988).

An example of the last point occurred in *Davis v. McCormick* (1995), where the plaintiff, a female coach, was subject to a more stringent disciplinary policy and her discipline was arguably more severe than any male coach's discipline. The court found that this raised a reasonable inference that the plaintiff's discipline was a pretext for intentional discrimination.

A plaintiff may also present the fact that the legitimate, nondiscriminatory reason was not given to the plaintiff at the time the employment decision was made as evidence that it was an afterthought and, thus, a pretext. For example, in *Baylor v. Jefferson County Board of Education* (1984), a black teacher-coach proved the defendant school board's transfer of him to a teaching-only position was racially motivated. Baylor successfully proved that the defendant's legitimate, nondiscriminatory reason for the job transfer was developed after his hearing and decision to transfer him out of coaching were made.

Finally, failing to comply with the usual hiring procedures may indicate that discriminatory actions were involved. For instance, as noted earlier in *Cross* (1975), the school superintendent suggested that the school board deviate from its policy of promoting from within to search outside the district for a white coach. In *Peirick, v. Indiana University-Purdue* (2005), the Court refused to grant summary judgment in a sex discrimination case where the plaintiff offered sufficient evidence that demonstrated "either that a discriminatory reason more likely motivated the employer or that the employer's proffered explanation is unworthy of credence."

Harassment. The Supreme Court in *Meritor Savings Bank, FSB v. Vinson* (1986), stated that the EEOC "has held and continues to hold that an employer has a duty to maintain a working environment free of harassment based on race, color, religion, sex, [or] national origin . . . and that the duty requires positive action where necessary to eliminate such practices or remedy their effects." Courts have applied this theory to harassment on the basis of race (*Johnson v. NFL*), religion (*Compston v. Borden, Inc.*, 1976), national origin (*Cariddi v. Kansas City Chiefs Football Club*, 1977), and gender (*Meritor Savings Bank, FSB v. Vinson*, 1986). By far, the application of the harassment theory is most developed for discrimination on the basis of sex. Sexual harassment is a type of disparate treatment employment discrimination. A thorough discussion of sexual harassment is found in Section 7.14, *Sexual Harassment*. The hostile environment theory of liability can also be applied to harassment on the basis of race, color, religion, or national origin.

Systemic Disparate Treatment

Under the theory of systemic disparate treatment, plaintiffs challenge broad sweeping employment policies that are discriminatory, such as an employer's policy not to hire women or to segregate employees by race. A plaintiff's initial burden is to "establish by preponderance of the evidence that discrimination is an employer's standard operating procedure—the regular, rather than the unusual practice" (*Lowery v. Circuit City*, 1998, *quoting Teamsters v. United States*, 1977). This creates an inference that hiring or promotion practices were made in furtherance of this discriminatory policy.

When challenging system wide patterns or practices, plaintiffs often rely on statistical evidence bolstered with evidence of individual discriminatory treatment. The statistics will compare the racial, ethnic, or gender balance of the qualified labor population with the population of a workforce that draws employees from that population. In *Teamsters* (1977), the court stated that statistics showing an imbalance are probative because such imbalance is often a telltale sign of purposeful discrimination. Absent discrimination, it is assumed that over time nondiscriminatory workplace practices will result in a workforce that is representative of a region's general population.

Once a plaintiff establishes a presumption of a discriminatory pattern or practice, the burden then shifts to the employer to demonstrate why an inference of discrimination could not be drawn from the plaintiff's evidence. Here the defendant has two options. First, the defendant can attack the plaintiff's statistical evidence as inaccurate or insignificant. Second, the employer may seek to provide a nondiscriminatory explanation for the apparently discriminatory result. As with individual disparate treatment, once a defendant produces this explanation, the burden will shift to the plaintiff to persuade the court that the defendant's stated explanation is in fact a pretext for discrimination.

Disparate Impact

Disparate impact discrimination exists where a plaintiff is challenging a neutral employment practice, regardless of intent, that has a discriminatory effect on a protected group. This model only applies where the employer has instituted a specific procedure, usually a criterion for employment, which the plaintiff can show has a causal connection with a protected class's imbalance in the workforce (*Pouncy v. Prudential Insurance Co. of America*, 1982).

The prima facie case requires that the employee or the EEOC prove the employment practice or policy has an adverse impact on the protected group to which the employee belongs. This is usually established through statistical evidence documenting the impact of the practice on the protected class. The use of statistical evidence is difficult and the plaintiff's methodology may be attacked as flawed. For instance, in *Wynn v. Columbus Municipal Separate School District* (1988), a plaintiff female coach used the disparate impact model to challenge her employer's practice of having the head football coach also serve as the athletic director. She argued that the practice had a disparate impact on females, because it was extremely rare that a female would be qualified to be a head football coach. The plaintiff presented statistical evidence from her state, Mississippi. Of the 192 high school athletic directors in the state only 62 were not head football coaches, no women were head football coaches, and just two athletic directors were women. The court found her theory flawed on two grounds. First, the fact that very few women in Mississippi were selected to serve as athletic director had very little relationship to the issue of whether the defendant, Columbus School District, discriminates against women as athletic director. Second, the plaintiff's statistical evidence is drawn from a pool that includes not only females from the protected class, but a number of nonmembers of that class, namely males who are not qualified as football coach and thus, are denied the athletic director position as well. The court stated the better approach would be to consider the discriminatory treatment of qualified female coaches in the Columbus schools who had been denied the position of athletic director. Thus, the plaintiff lost on her disparate impact claim, but was successful under her disparate treatment theory.

Employers may also rebut the plaintiff's argument by attacking the statistical analysis or producing evidence that the practice is "job-related." This requires proof that the challenged employment practice is necessary to achieve some legitimate business objective, the practice actually achieves that objective, and there is no reasonable alternative for accomplishing the objective without a discriminatory effect. Once the employer establishes the barrier is "job-related", the burden shifts back to the plaintiff to prove that the barrier is a pretext for discrimination, by showing there are other adequate devices that do not discriminate against a protected class.

Retaliation

Title VII provides a cause of action for retaliation in response to a plaintiff's filing of a claim of employment discrimination. Section 704 (a) of Title VII provides that:

> it shall be an unlawful employment practice for an employer to discriminate against any of his employees . . . because [that employee] has opposed any practice made an unlawful employment practice by this subchapter, or because he has made charge, testified, assisted or participated in any manner in an investigation proceeding, or hearing under this title [42 U.S.C. $ 2000e-3(a)].

The plaintiff's burden of proof in retaliation claims mirrors that in other Title VII suits. The plaintiff bears the initial burden of establishing a prima facie case of retaliation. To establish the prima facie retaliation case, the plaintiff must show by a preponderance of the evidence that (1) the plaintiff engaged in a statutorily protected activity, (2) adverse action was taken against the plaintiff by the employer subsequent to and contemporaneously with such activity, and (3) a causal link exists between the protected activity and the adverse action (*Jalil v. Advel Corp.*, 1989). Once the plaintiff has established a prima facie case, the defendant may introduce evidence providing legitimate, non-retaliatory reasons for its conduct. If the defendant properly introduces such evidence, the burden shifts back to the plaintiff to show that the defendant's justification is merely pretext for unlawful retaliation. See *Lowery v. Texas A&M University d/b/a Tarleton State University* (1998), where a Lowery, former women's basketball coach, alleged that defendants were liable under Title VII, Title IX, and 42 U.S.C. §1983 and the Constitution's First and Fourteenth Amendments for retaliating against her by removing her as Women's Athletics Coordinator in response to comments she made criticizing the university and its officials on gender equity issues.

Additional Defenses

Bona Fide Occupational Qualification

It is not illegal to discriminate on the basis of religion, gender, or national origin if an employer can show the classification is a bona fide occupational qualification (BFOQ). Race and color are never BFOQs. The BFOQ defense requires the employer to prove that members of the excluded class could not safely and effectively perform essential job duties and the employer must have a factual basis for believing that persons in the excluded class could not perform the job. The BFOQ must also be reasonably necessary to the normal operation of the business. An example might be a situation where a boys' overnight recreational program hires only male floor counselors. If the counselors will live in dorms with the boys, the recreation program may prefer males for the comfort of the boy campers and for role modeling. Finally, customer preference cannot be the basis for a BFOQ.

Business Necessity

Business necessity serves as a defense to a disparate impact discrimination claim, where a particular practice causes a protected class to face discrimination. The employer may prove that a particular practice is "job related" and thus a business necessity despite the discriminatory impact of the practice (*Griggs v. Duke Power Co.*, 1971).

Affirmative Action

Affirmative action involves creating policies for giving preference to those underrepresented in the workplace. The policies often possess goals/timetables for increasing percentages of underrepresented workers to rectify past discrimination. The affirmative-action policy may be voluntary or court ordered as a result of a lawsuit. Affirmative action policies often result in discrimination against the overrepresented classes, termed reverse discrimination. It is legal provided:

- The discrimination results from a formal, systematic program;
- The program is temporary, operating only until its goals are reached;
- The program does not completely bar the hiring/promotion of non-minorities;
- The program does not result in the firing of non-minority workers;
- The program does not force the employer to hire/promote unqualified workers.

Where the program is court-ordered, it must be based on actual evidence of discrimination. Where the program is voluntary, it must be based actual evidence of discrimination or evidence that those in underrepresented groups had been underutilized in the past.

Remedies

Section 706(g) provides the following power to remedy employment discrimination under Title VII:

> *If the court finds that the respondent has intentionally engaged in or is intentionally engaging in an unlawful employment practice . . . the court may enjoin the respondent from engaging in such unlawful employment practice, and order such affirmative action as may be appropriate, which may include, but is not limited to, reinstatement or hiring of employees with or without back pay . . . or any other equitable relief as the court deems appropriate. . . .*

A successful plaintiff most often is awarded back pay. A back pay order requires the defendant to pay all lost wages and benefits that would have been earned were it not for the illegal discrimination. The trial court may grant interest on these wages.

The following case is an example of a Title VII lawsuit involving a retaliation claim. The employees argued that they were dismissed because of their opposition to the NFL's discriminatory employment practices.

THOMAS, ET. AL. V. NATIONAL FOOTBALL LEAGUE PLAYERS ASSOCIATION

U.S. Court of Appeals for the District of Columbia Circuit
131 F.3d 198 (1997)

EDWARDS, Chief Judge:

A principal claim in this case is that the defendant, acting pursuant to "mixed motives," unlawfully retaliated against the plaintiffs in violation of Title VII, 42 U.S.C. § 2000e *et seq.* (1994). The issues on appeal require us to delimit the requirements of *McDonnell Douglas Corp. v. Green,* 411 U.S. 792, (1973), *Texas Dep't of Community Affairs v. Burdine,* 450 U.S. 248 (1981), and *Price Waterhouse v. Hopkins,* 490 U.S. 228 (1989), with respect to a plaintiff's *prima facie* case, a defendant's burden of production, and the ultimate burdens of persuasion, in a retaliation/ mixed-motives case.

The actions giving rise to this lawsuit occurred when Eugene Upshaw, Executive Director of the National Football League Players Association ("NFLPA"), first laid off, then terminated employees Valerie Thomas and Rita Raymond on the stated grounds that they had been disloyal in criticizing NFLPA staff and policies in an anonymously distributed document and in several legally taped telephone calls. Julie Taylor-Bland (Bland at the time of the events) resigned in the aftermath of the firing of the other two. Before leaving the employ of the NFLPA, Thomas and Bland had suggested, in conversations with management that NFLPA promotion policy discriminated against African-American women. The three women subsequently sued the NFLPA, charging that the lay-off and discharge of Thomas and Raymond, and the alleged constructive discharge of Bland, came in retaliation to their opposition to discriminatory employment practices, and hence violated Title VII.

After trial, the District Court granted judgment as a matter of law to the NFLPA on the plaintiffs' claim that there existed a pattern and practice of discrimination at the NFLPA. * * * It then found that Thomas had been unlawfully fired, that Raymond had not made out a *prima facie* case of retaliation, and that Bland had not been fired at all. The trial court granted Thomas back pay and prejudgment interest, but declined to reinstate her. *Thomas, et al., v. National Football League Players Ass'n,* 941 F. Supp. 156 (D.D.C. 1996), *reprinted in* J.A. 279. * * * *Thomas, et al., v. National Football League Players Ass'n,* No. 91-3332 (D.D.C. Nov. 26, 1996). The NFLPA now appeals the deci-

sions adverse to it; Thomas, Raymond, and Bland cross-appeal the decisions adverse to them.

We affirm the District Court's judgment on the merits as to Thomas, Raymond, and Bland's claims.

* * *

I. BACKGROUND

In 1988, Thomas, Raymond, and Bland worked for the NFLPA and belonged to Office and Professional Employees International Union, Local 2 ("Local 2"). After the NFLPA's unsuccessful strike against the owners during the 1987 season, the NFLPA's finances suffered, and NFLPA Executive Director Upshaw devised a new budget for the NFLPA which sought to reduce personnel costs through attrition. The board of directors of the NFLPA met during the first week of March 1988, and elected George Martin president and Mike Davis vice president. The board declined to adopt Upshaw's proposed budget, instead demanding a ten percent reduction in personnel costs by lay-off.

After a banquet held in conjunction with the board meeting, Martin convened an informal gathering in his hotel room that included Thomas and Bland. Thomas and others complained about promotional opportunities for African-Americans and women in the Local 2 bargaining unit. Some time after March 10, 1988, Martin organized a second meeting, which Thomas and Bland also attended. Similar concerns were raised, and someone present accused Upshaw of racism.

In the weeks that followed, Martin and Davis conducted personal and telephone interviews with staff on a range of employment-related subjects. Interviewees were assured of confidentiality. In their interviews, Thomas and Bland expressed views on race and sex discrimination at the NFLPA. Davis also interviewed Raymond. Around the same time, Upshaw implemented the NFLPA board's directive to lay off some employees to cut costs. Prior to the lay-offs, Upshaw heard from Davis that Thomas and Raymond had criticized various employees in telephone conversations with Davis, and were suspected of producing and circulating a document harshly critical of the

NFLPA. The document was headed and referred to as "What every player should know about the NFLPA." It included, among other allegations, a variety of claims about unfair promotion practices at the NFLPA. It did not include allegations of racial discrimination.

On March 18, 1988, Upshaw laid off six employees, including Thomas and Raymond. When Thomas returned to her office after learning of the lay-offs, she discovered workers changing the locks on her door and shutting down her computer. At a time proximate to the lay-offs, Martin undertook to investigate the employees' allegations of misconduct at the NFLPA, and asked Upshaw about minority issues at the NFLPA. Martin told Upshaw that Thomas had called him a racist and had complained about promotion of African-Americans and women. Martin and Davis each gave copies of the "What every player should know" memorandum to Upshaw. Davis told Upshaw about his telephone conversations with Thomas and Raymond and that Raymond had mailed him a copy of the memorandum.

On March 23, 1988, Davis gave Upshaw tapes of his telephone conversations with Thomas and Raymond. According to Upshaw's un-contradicted testimony, the conversations included ad hominem attacks on various NFLPA employees, including Upshaw. On the tapes, Raymond promised to send a copy of the "What every player should know" memorandum to Davis. Upshaw concluded that Thomas and Raymond had written the memo.

On April 12, 1988, five of the six employees laid off on March 18 were fired for cause. Upshaw sent each employee an identical letter explaining the firing on the grounds that the employees had libeled and slandered NFLPA personnel; had violated confidentiality; and had shown disloyalty towards and intentionally embarrassed the NFLPA. Upshaw later testified that he fired Thomas and Raymond for what he believed they had said and written about the NFLPA employees. Some weeks later, Bland asked Upshaw about a newly open paralegal/secretary position, and Upshaw told her that he "did not see her in the job"; on May 20, 1988, Bland resigned.

Local 2 pursued grievances against the NFLPA on behalf of Thomas and Raymond. The grievances were appealed to arbitration and an arbitrator ruled that the two had been dismissed without just cause. The arbitrator's award ordered reinstatement, but the NFLPA failed to comply. Thomas, Raymond, and Bland also filed timely charges with the Equal Employment Opportunity Commission ("EEOC"), which, after some delay, issued "no cause" determinations on all their claims. At trial, the District Court dismissed as a matter of law plaintiffs' claim of a pattern and practice of discrimination. It found for Thomas and awarded her back pay, without reinstatement, with prejudgment interest for twenty-one months after her firing, based on expert testimony that estimated the time it should have taken Thomas to find new employment. The District Court found against Raymond, who did not appear at trial. Finally, the District Court found that Bland had not been constructively discharged.

II. ANALYSIS

Burdens of Pleading, Production, and Persuasion Under Title VII.

Title VII makes it unlawful to retaliate against an employee who "has opposed any practice made an unlawful practice" by the statute. 42 U.S.C. § 2000e-3(a). The legal framework for analyzing retaliation claims under Title VII is as follows.

As in all Title VII cases, the plaintiff must first make out a *prima facie* case of unlawful employment action. *McDonnell Douglas Corp. v. Green,* 411 U.S. 792 (1973). Where retaliation is alleged, a *prima facie* case requires a showing that (1) plaintiff engaged in protected activity, (2) plaintiff was subjected to adverse action by the employer, and (3) there existed a causal link between the adverse action and the protected activity. *Mitchell v. Baldrige,* 759 F.2d 80, 86 (D.C. Cir. 1985). A rebuttable presumption of unlawful discrimination arises when a plaintiff makes out a *prima facie* case. *Texas Dep't of Community Affairs v. Burdine,* 450 U.S. 248, 254 (1981). The defendant may rebut the presumption by asserting a legitimate, non-discriminatory reason for its actions. The defendant's responsibility at this stage has been characterized as a "burden of production," because the ultimate burden of persuasion remains with the plaintiff.

When a defendant satisfies the burden of production, the presumption of discrimination dissolves; however, the plaintiff still has the opportunity to persuade the trier of fact that the defendant's proffered reason was not the actual or sole basis for the disputed action. The plaintiff may aim to prove that a discriminatory motive was the only basis for the employer's action, or the plaintiff may seek to show that the employer was motivated by both permissible and impermissible motives. The plaintiff often will—quite reasonably—argue both alternatives. *See Price Waterhouse v. Hopkins,* 490 U.S. 228, 247 n.12 (Brennan, J.) * * * Where a plaintiff argues that discriminatory motvation constituted the only basis for the employer's action, the plaintiff may persuade the trier of fact of the pretextual nature of the defendant's asserted reason "either directly by persuading the court that a discriminatory reason more likely motivated the employer or indirectly by showing that the employer's proffered explanation is unworthy of credence." *Burdine,* 450 U.S. at 256.

Where, on the other hand, the plaintiff argues that the action resulted from mixed motives, a slightly different model operates. A plaintiff asserting mixed motives must persuade the trier of fact by a preponderance of the evidence that unlawful retaliation constituted a substantial factor in the defendant's action. *Price Waterhouse,* 490 U.S. at 276 (O'Connor, J., concurring); *Id.* at 259 (White, J., concurring). When the plaintiff successfully shows that an unlawful motive was a substantial factor in the employer's action, the defendant may seek to prove in response that it would have taken the contested action even absent the discriminatory motive. If the defendant fails to persuade the trier of fact by a preponderance of the evidence that it would have taken the action even absent the discriminatory motive, the plaintiff will prevail.

This burden on a defendant in a mixed-motives case has been characterized both as an affirmative defense, and as a shifting burden of persuasion. The question of characterization is "semantic," and need not be definitively resolved. What is noteworthy, however, is that under *Price Waterhouse* a defendant who is guilty of acting pursuant to an unlawful motive may nonetheless escape liability by proving that it would have made the same decision in the absence of the unlawful motivation. In short, the ultimate burden of persuasion as to the facts constituting the defense properly falls on the defendant in a mixed-motives case, because the plaintiff has proven that unlawful motivation constituted a substantial factor in the defendant's action. "Where a plaintiff has made this type of strong showing of illicit motivation, the fact finder is entitled to presume that the employer's discriminatory animus made a difference to the outcome, absent proof to the contrary from the employer." *Price Waterhouse*, 490 U.S. at 276 (O'Connor, J., concurring).

Appellant's Claims
Meaning and Requirement of Direct Evidence
Appellant NFLPA, the defendant below, argues that, under *Price Waterhouse*, the burden of persuasion shifts to the defendant only where the plaintiff has provided "direct" rather than "inferential" evidence of discriminatory animus. We reject this contention. Under *Price Waterhouse*, the burden of persuasion shifts to the defendant when the plaintiff has shown by a preponderance of "any sufficiently probative direct or indirect evidence" that unlawful discrimination was a substantial factor in the employment decision. *White v. Federal Express Corp.*, 939 F.2d 157, 160 (4th Cir. 1991).

* * *

As this court recently noted, "the distinction between direct and circumstantial evidence has no direct correlation with the strength of [a] plaintiff's case." *Crawford-El v. Britton*, 93 F.3d 813, 818 (D.C. Cir. 1996) (*en banc*), *cert. granted*, 117 S. Ct. 2451 (U.S. 1997). The purported distinction between "circumstantial" or "inferential" and "direct" evidence urged here does not make logical sense, because the decision to shift the burden of persuasion properly rests upon the strength of the plaintiff's evidence of discrimination, not the contingent methods by which that evidence is adduced.

* * *

District Court Decision on the Merits
The District Court * * * found that Thomas engaged in protected activity by participating in two conversations

with Martin in which she raised the issue of discrimination against women and African-Americans in promotion at the NFLPA, and by distributing the memo to Martin. The District Court found that the NFLPA fired Thomas "immediately following" the protected activity, and permissibly concluded that Thomas had made out a prima facie case. Because it did not find evidence that Raymond engaged in protected conduct, the District Court correctly found that Raymond had not made out a *prima facie* case. The District Court further found that Bland was not constructively discharged, because she had not presented evidence of aggravating factors making her work intolerable Neither of these conclusions was clearly erroneous; the legal framework for both was correct.

The District Court then assessed the evidence that served to refute the NFLPA's claim that it had non-discriminatory reasons sufficient to fire Thomas. It found that the way in which the firing followed Upshaw's learning of Thomas's taped comments; the unusual security measures surrounding the firing; and Upshaw's possession of the memorandum which he believed Thomas had co-authored sufficed to prove that Thomas's firing was motivated "in substantial measure" by her protected activity. This constituted an acceptable finding of mixed motives, and was not clearly erroneous. Although the District Court did not cite *Price Waterhouse*, it correctly concluded that the burden of persuasion had shifted, and that as a result "it was NFLPA's burden to demonstrate that Thomas would have been discharged regardless of her protected activity." In the District Court's view, "the NFLPA failed to sustain that burden" in that it did not successfully separate permissible from impermissible motives in its decision. This conclusion was not clearly erroneous, either, but reflected the fact finder's assessment of the evidence surrounding the firing.

Rejection of Statistical Evidence
The District Court correctly ruled as a matter of law that plaintiffs did not make out a prima facie statistical case of a pattern and practice of discrimination on the part of the NFLPA. The crucial basis for this ruling was that plaintiffs' expert did not consider the relevant qualifications of those passed over or approved for promotion. A *prima facie* case of statistical disparity must include the minimum objective qualifications of the applicants. Here, the expert did not account for minimum qualifications. Indeed, he could not have done so, because Appellees never specifically requested qualification standards from Appellant in discovery. We need not reach the District Court's other reasons for dismissal, because even if the trial court had found adequate sample size and statistical significance (which it did not), a non-discriminatory, qualifications-based reason for the disparate impact could have existed. * * *

The Relief
The District Court awarded Thomas back pay from the date of her firing to December 1989, by which time, it found, she should have secured employment. The District Court did

not abuse its discretion in weighing expert testimony regarding job availability to arrive at this time period.

* * *

The District Court did not abuse its discretion in declining to reinstate Thomas. Although the acrimony of litigation alone probably would not suffice to rule out reinstatement, *see Dickerson v. Deluxe Check Printers, Inc.*, 703 F.2d 276, 281 (8th Cir. 1983), the District Court's denial of reinstatement reflected its own observation that some of Thomas's actions "might well have warranted discharge [as it] reasonably concluded that reinstatement would not serve the interests of justice where the employee engaged in behavior that could conceivably have given rise to a legitimate discharge under other circumstances."

The District Court awarded Thomas prejudgment interest on the back pay. The presumption strongly favors prejudgment interest, but the trial court may disallow interest where attributable to substantial, unexplained delay by the plaintiff. Although Thomas reasonably awaited the EEOC's disposition of her request for a right to sue letter, which was delayed through no fault of her own, the same cannot be said of the three-year period during which Thomas and her co-plaintiffs repeatedly amended their complaint. The District Court must reconsider this issue on remand.

* * *

III. CONCLUSION

For the foregoing reasons, the judgment of the District Court is affirmed regarding Thomas, Raymond, and Bland.

So ordered.

CASES ON THE SUPPLEMENTAL CD

Lowrey v. Texas A&M University System, 11 F. Supp. 2d 895 (1998). This case examines whether the university and its' officials discriminated against the coach on the basis of her sex.

Peirick v. Indiana University-Purdue University Indianapolis, 2005 U.S. Dist. LEXIS 32479. This case examines whether the university had a legitimate reason for firing an employee.

Wynn v. Columbus Municipal Separate School District, 692 F. Supp. 672 (1988). This case examines whether an applicant was unlawfully discriminated against on the basis of her sex when she was denied the position of Athletic Director.

QUESTIONS YOU SHOULD BE ABLE TO ANSWER

1. What are the classes protected by Title VII?

2. How does a plaintiff put forth the evidence for a Title VII prima facie case, if the plaintiff is an applicant for a job? What if the plaintiff is an employee?

3. What aare the differences between cases based on disparate impact and disparate treatment discrimination under Title VII?

4. What defenses are available to a defendant accused of violating Title VII?

5. What is affirmative action and how does it sometimes lead to claims of reverse discrimination?

REFERENCES

Cases

Babyak v. Smith College, No. 99-204 (Hampden Co., Mass., Dist. Ct. 2001).

Baylor v. Jefferson County Board of Education, 733 F.2d 1527 (11th Cir. 1984).

Bianchi v. City of Philadelphia, No. 99-CV-2409, 2002 WL 23942 (E.D. Pa. Jan 2, 2002).

Bibby v. Philadelphia Coca Cola Bottling Co., No. 00-1261 (3d Cir. August 1, 2001).

Biver v. Saginaw Township Community Schools, et al., 805 F.2d 1033 (6th Cir. 1986).

Cariddi v. Kansas City Chiefs Football Club, 568 F. Supp. 87 (8th Cir. 1977).

Compston v. Borden, Inc., 424 F. Supp. 157 (S.D. Ohio 1976).

Cross v. Board of Education of Dollarway, Arkansas School District, 395 F. Supp. 531 (E.D. Ark. 1975).

Davis v. McCormick, 898 F. Supp. 1275 (C.D. Ill. 1995).

Dowling v. United States, 476 F. Supp. 1018 (D. Mass. 1979).

EEOC v. National Broadcasting Co., Inc., 753 F. Supp. 452 (S.D. N.Y. 1990).

Graves v. Women's Professional Rodeo Association, Inc., 907 F.2d 71 (8th Cir. 1990).

Griggs v. Duke Power Co., 401 U.S. 424 (1971).

Herman v. National Broadcasting Co., Inc., 774 F.2d 604 (7th Cir. 1984).

Jackson v. Armstrong School District, 430 F. Supp. 1050 (W.D. Penn. 1977).

Jackson v. World League of American Football, 65 Fair Emp. Prac. Cas. 358 (S.D. N.Y. 1994).

Jalil v. Advel Corp., 873 F. 2d 701 (3rd Cir. 1989).

Lowery v. Circuit City, 158 F.3d 742 (1998).

Lowery v. Texas A&M University d/b/a Tarleton State University, 11 F.Supp.2d 895 (1998).

McDonnell Douglas Corp. v. Green, 411 U.S. 792 (1973).

Medcalf v. University of Pennsylvania, 2001 U.S. Dist. Lexis 10155.

Meritor Savings Bank, FSB v. Vinson, 477 U.S. 57 (1986).

Morris v. Bianchini, et al., 43 Fair Emp. Prac. Cases 647 (E.D. Va. 1987).

Peirick v. Indiana University-Purdue, 2005 U.S. Dist. LEXIS 32479.

Pouncy v. Prudential Insurance Co. of America, 668 F.2d 795 (5th Cir. 1982).

Price Waterhouse v. Hopkins, 490 U.S. 228, 250-51 (1989).

Ross v. Douglas County, 244 F.3d 620 (2001).

Schroer v. Billington, 577 F.Supp. 2d 293 (D.D.C. 2008).

Simmons v. Sports Training Institute, 52 Fair Emp. Prac. Cas. 1322 (S.D. N.Y. 1990).

Smith v. City of Salem, 378 R.3d 566 (6th Cir. 2004).

Teamsters v. United States, 431 U.S. 324 (1977).

Texas Department of Community Affairs v. Burdine, 450 U.S. 248 (1981).

Wynn v. Columbus Municipal Separate School District, 692 F. Supp. 672 (N.D. Miss. 1988).

Publications

Player, M. A. (1988). *Employment discrimination law*. St. Paul, MN: West Publishing Co.

Zimmer, M. J., Sullivan, C. A., & Richards, R. F. (1988). *Cases and materials on employment discrimination*. Boston: Little, Brown, and Co.

Legislation

Title VII of the Civil Rights Act of 1964, 42 U.S.C. § 2000e et seq. (1990).

7.14 Sexual Harassment

—Barbara Osborne
UNIVERSITY OF NORTH CAROLINA AT CHAPEL HILL

With increasing numbers of girls and women participating and working in sports and recreation settings, managers today need to be aware of the problem of sexual harassment. Whether it is a health club owner promising to promote an aerobics instructor in exchange for sexual favors, a coach initiating inappropriate conversations, touching, or engaging in sexual relationships with athletes at the club, middle school, high school, or collegiate levels, a journalist who is propositioned by a team owner, or an athlete sexually teasing or taunting a peer, sexual harassment is a major problem in the sports and recreation industry and in society as a whole.

FUNDAMENTAL CONCEPTS

Sexual Harassment in the Workplace

Although the Civil Rights Act of 1964 was enacted to prevent discrimination on the basis of sex, as well as race, color, religion, and national origin, the courts did not recognize sexual harassment as sex discrimination until *Williams v. Saxbe*, (1976). In that case, Federal District Court Judge Charles Richey ruled that sexual harassment is a form of sex discrimination actionable under Title VII if the harassment places an artificial barrier on employment. Other early cases, *Barnes v. Costle*, (1977) and *Miller v. Bank of America* (1979), narrowly recognized sexual harassment only in situations when the subordinate's employment opportunities were conditioned on entering into a sexual relationship with a superior, commonly described as quid pro quo sexual harassment.

In 1980, the Equal Employment Opportunity Commission (EEOC), the administrative agency charged with enforcing Title VII, developed Guidelines acknowledging sexual harassment as "discrimination because of sex". The Guidelines took a broader approach than the courts and defined sexual harassment as:

Unwelcome sexual advances, requests for sexual favors, and other verbal or physical conduct of a sexual nature constitute sexual harassment when:

1. submission to such conduct is made either explicitly or implicitly a term or condition of an individual's employment;

2. submission to or rejection of such conduct by an individual is used as the basis for employment decisions affecting such individual; or

3. such conduct has the purpose or effect of unreasonably interfering with an individual's work performance or creating an intimidating, hostile or offensive working environment.

It is important to note "unwelcome" as a key to the definition of sexual harassment. Conduct is unwelcome if the employee did not solicit or incite it and when the employee regards the conducts as undesirable or offensive. A charging party's claim will fail if the allegedly offensive conduct was "welcome." Table 7.14.1 provides a list of behaviors or actions that may be considered harassment given the circumstances.

The EEOC's Guidelines define two types of sexual harassment: "quid pro quo" and "hostile environment." **Quid pro quo harassment** occurs when "submission to or rejection of such conduct by an individual is used as the basis for employment decisions affecting such individual" [29 C.F.R § 1604.11(a)(2)]. Quid pro quo harassment covers all **tangible employment actions**, defined as any significant change in employment status, such as hiring, firing, failing to promote, or reassignment. Submitting to sexual advances in order to retain

Table 7.14.1. Sexually Harassing Behaviors

Behavioral
Ogling, leering, staring, gestures, mooning, flashing

Verbal
Request for dates, asking personal questions, lewd comments, dirty or sexual jokes, whistling, catcalling, obscene calls, sexual comments or rumors

Written/Visual
Love letters, poems, obscene letters, cards, notes, posters, pictures, cartoons, graphics, sexual graffiti

Touching
Violation of personal space, patting, rubbing, pinching, bra-snapping, caressing, blocking movement, kissing, groping, grabbing, tackling, hazing

Power
Retaliation, using position to request dates or suggest sexual favors, gender-directed favoritism, disparate treatment, hazing rituals, bullying, intimidation, condescending or patronizing behavior

Threats
Quid pro quo demands, conditioning evaluations or references on sexual favors, retaliation for refusal to comply with requests

Force
Attempted rape or assault, rape, assault, pantsing, stripping, extreme forms of hazing, stalking, sexual abuse, physical abuse, vandalism

---

employment is also a tangible employment action, although there is no advancement or demotion in the employee's work status (*Jin v. Metropolitan Life Ins. Co*, 2002). The critical factor is the link between the sexual conduct and the benefit, even if the person demanding the sexual benefit is not the employer. In these cases, the courts uniformly apply strict liability in the same manner that they apply it in racial or religiously motivated cases under Title VII (see Section 7.13, *Title VII of the Civil Rights Act of 1964*).

The second type of sexual harassment, **hostile environment**, occurs when a hostile or offensive workplace environment is created for members of one sex. The first case recognizing hostile environment sexual harassment was *Meritor Savings Bank, FSB v. Vinson* (1986), where the Supreme Court recognized that the repeated actions of a supervisor could so contaminate the work environment that it altered the conditions of employment. The Court also expanded the scope of Title VII to include situations that did not result in direct or tangible economic loss. However, the Supreme Court did not define what behavior would constitute a hostile environment, only stating that the harassment must be so severe that it creates an abusive working environment.

In determining whether there is a hostile environment, the courts will use a three-step approach:

1. The totality of the circumstances;

2. Whether a reasonable person in the same or similar circumstance would find the conduct sufficiently severe or pervasive to create an intimidating, hostile or abusive work environment (objective test); and

3. Whether the plaintiff perceived the environment to be hostile or abusive (subjective test).

Totality of the Circumstances. Because sexual attraction may play a role in the day-to-day social exchange between employees, the distinction between invited, uninvited-but-welcome, offensive-but-tolerated, and flatly rejected sexual advances may be difficult to discern. An examination of the totality of the circumstances—the nature of the conduct, the context in which the incidents occurred, the frequency of the conduct, its severity and pervasiveness, whether it was physically threatening or humiliating, whether it was unwelcome, and whether it unreasonably interfered with an employee's work performance—is necessary. Whether there is a repeated pattern of relatively benign behavior or a single incident of gross behavior is not conclusive. The most important analysis is whether the conduct negatively altered the work environment.

Reviewing all the circumstances in determining whether an environment is hostile or abusive also requires both a subjective and an objective test. The **reasonable person (objective test)** requires the plaintiff to prove that the conduct is severe or pervasive enough that a reasonable person would objectively find it hostile or abusive. The **employee's perception (subjective test)** requires that the plaintiff subjectively perceive the environment to be so hostile and abusive that it altered the employment climate. However, in *Harris*, the Supreme Court established that the plaintiff does not have to prove psychological injury to prove that she was sexually harassed.

Under the EEOC guidelines issued in 1999, an employer is always liable for the actions of a supervisor that result in a tangible effect of employment status of the victim. The employer is liable for harassment by coworkers if the employer knew or should have known of the misconduct, unless it can show that it took immediate and appropriate corrective action. Harassment by non-employees—for example customers, vendors, or club members—are the employer's responsibility under a similar negligence standard, which also takes into account the extent of the employer's control over the harasser.

The Supreme Court and the 1999 Guidelines allow for an employer to avoid liability with a two-part **affirmative defense**. The employer bears the burden of proving by a preponderance of the evidence both of these elements:

1. The employer exercised reasonable care to prevent and promptly correct harassment.

2. The employee unreasonably failed to take advantage of any preventive or corrective opportunities provided by the employer or to avoid harm otherwise.

To show reasonable care to prevent and correct harassment, the employer must have established, publicized, and enforced anti-harassment policies and grievance procedures prior to the complaint of harassment. This includes handing out a copy of the policy and complaint procedure to every employee, posting them in central locations, and including them in employee handbooks. The policy and procedures should include a clear explanation of prohibited conduct, an assurance of protection from retaliation for the complainant, a clearly described complaint process, and a promise of confidentiality. The complaint procedure should also provide accessible contact people to receive complaints (although some courts have ruled that reporting to any employee in a supervisory role is sufficient). A prompt, thorough, and impartial investigation should be conducted as soon as the employer learns of a complaint. The employee should be assured that immediate and appropriate corrective measures will be taken, and the employer should initiate intermediate protective measures against further harassment. If it is determined that harassment has occurred, the employer must take immediate corrective/disciplinary action to effectively end the harassment.

The Guidelines also established that the employer must show that the employee did not exercise reasonable care by taking advantage of preventive opportunities, complaint procedures, or other ways to avoid harm. A failure to complain in a timely manner about persistent harassment could eliminate the employer's liability. If some, but not all, of the harm could have been avoided by an earlier compliant, damages awarded would likely be reduced.

Once the employer has established both parts of the affirmative defense, the employee has the opportunity to rebut the employer's assertion that the employee unreasonably failed to complain or otherwise avoid harm. The 1999 Guidelines lists three explanations that may be reasonable: (1) risk of retaliation, (2) employer-created obstacles in the complaint process or procedures, and (3) belief that the complaint mechanism is not effective.

Although it is illegal to retaliate against an individual for opposing employment practices that discriminate based on sex or for filing a discrimination charge, testifying, or participating in any way in an investigation, proceeding, or litigation under Title VII, research indicates that most employees who fail to report harassment fear retaliation. It is the employer's burden to prove that this fear is unwarranted. One of the easiest ways to satisfy this burden is to have and promote a complaint process that maintains confidentiality and does not punish employees who complain.

State Legislative Protection. State legislation can greatly enhance protection against sexual harassment in the workplace. In *Morehouse v. Berkshire Gas Co.*, obscenely defaced photos of plaintiff Sheryl Morehouse were posted at the Berkshire Gas Company Fall Classic Golf Tournament (one was hung at the first tee, another was affixed to a garbage barrel at the fifth tee and was urinated on, another was attached to the flag at the ninth hole, and at least five more defaced photos were recovered from various other spots). Under *Mass. Gen. Laws* *ch. 151B, s 4(5)* individuals may be held liable for aiding or abetting discriminatory conduct that is prohibited under state law. Under Title VII, only the employer is liable for the acts of employees under the guidelines previously discussed. Massachusetts legislation broadens the application of sexual harassment protection by holding individuals liable for their behavior, as well as others as aiders or abettors. This state legislation also extends the scope of responsibility of the employer, even when the supervisory employees are not acting within the scope of their employment (such as socially golfing at an outing).

Sexual Harassment in the Schools

The other major act of legislation related to sexual harassment is Title IX of the Education Act of 1972. Although it is most often referenced in relation to girls' participation in sport (see Section 7.11, *Gender Equity: Opportunities to Participate*), Title IX prohibits discrimination on the basis of sex by any educational institution receiving federal funds. Sexual harassment is discrimination based on sex that is prohibited by Title IX.

The Office of Civil Rights (OCR) in the U.S. Department of Education is responsible for enforcing Title IX. In the 2001 OCR guidance, sexual harassment is defined as it applies to educational institutions as unwelcome conduct of a sexual nature that rises to a level that denies or limits a student's ability to participate in or benefit from the school's programs.

Because the employment case law under Title VII is more developed, the courts have often referred to Title VII to guide them in Title IX cases. However, the Supreme Court takes a very different approach to institutional liability under Title IX compared to employer liability under Title VII. *Gebser v. Lago Vista Independent School District*, (1998)—decided just 4 days before the *Burlington* and *Faragher* cases—indicates that damages under Title IX are only available when the institution has actual knowledge of the offensive behavior. The Court explicitly rejected the application of agency principles that it applies in Title VII sexual harassment cases. Relying on the "contractual nature" of Title IX, the Court reasoned that Title IX as a Spending Clause statute requires that the institution have actual notice and be deliberately indifferent to the reported behavior before it would be held liable.

For example, in *Davis v. Monroe County Board of Education* (1999), a fifth grader suffered sexual harassment by one of her classmates over several months. Although the victim and her mother repeatedly informed her teachers of the harassment, no one at the school made any effort to separate the two students (who sat next to each other in class) or to discipline the harasser. The Supreme Court concluded that student–student sexual harassment claims under Title IX should be analyzed in the same way as teacher–student sexual harassment. The Court found that schools are responsible for both preventing peer sexual harassment and for handling claims of peer sexual harassment in a prompt and effective manner once an appropriate administrator has actual notice. (See the Supplemental CD for the complete case).

The OCR Revised Sexual Harassment Guidance explains the liability of the educational institution under Title IX. If the employee engages in sexual harassment while carrying out responsibilities to provide benefits and services to students, the institution is responsible for the discriminatory conduct, remedying its effects, and preventing future occurrences whether or not it has notice of the harassment. If the employee is acting outside the scope of his or her assigned duties (and sexually harassing behavior is almost always considered outside the scope of the employee's duties), the institution must take prompt and effective action to stop the harassment and prevent its recurrence on notice of the harassment. The institution is considered to have engaged in its own discrimination if it fails to act and allows the student to be subjected to a hostile environment that denies or limits the student's ability to participate in or benefit from the school's program. The institution is responsible for peer or third-party harassment if the institution knew or reasonably should have known of the harassment and failed to take prompt and effective action. This liability is based on the contractual nature of Title IX, which promises an educational environment free from discrimination.

Whether the harasser is an employee or a peer, the victim of sexual harassment bears the burden of proving the following elements:

1. That he/she is a member of a protected group based on his/her sex;
2. That he/she was subjected to unwelcome conduct of a sexual nature;

3. That the conduct was so severe, pervasive, and objectively offensive that it denied equal access to the school's educational opportunities or benefits;

4. That a school official with authority to take corrective action had actual knowledge or notice of the behavior;

5. That the school official was deliberately indifferent to the conduct and failed to reasonably respond.

The Supreme Court in *Gebser* and *Davis* did not address the issue of whether a school could raise an affirmative defense by having an effective sexual harassment policy. Schools are required by Title IX regulations to adopt and publish grievance procedures to address sexual discrimination. The procedures do not have to be specific to harassment, but should provide an effective manner for preventing and addressing sexual harassment. The OCR recently reissued the following criteria for evaluating a school's grievance procedure:

1. Notice of policies and procedures must be sent to students, parents (for elementary and secondary students), and employees, including where complaints may be filed.

2. The procedure must actually be applied to complaints alleging harassment.

3. An adequate, reliable, and impartial investigation of the complaints must be conducted, including the opportunities to present witnesses and other evidence.

4. A designated, prompt time frame should be established for the complaint and investigative process.

5. Notice of the outcome of the complaint must be given to the parties involved.

6. An assurance must be made that the school will take corrective measures to eliminate current harassment and similar instances of harassment in the future.

If an educational institution implements these guidelines when developing its sexual harassment policies and procedures, it should function to reduce instances of harassment and provide protection for its students. It may also mitigate liability if a complaint is made to the OCR or a civil suit is filed.

Coach/Athlete Sexual Harassment

Although the liability of the institution is the same when the harasser is a coach and the victim is an athlete as that for teacher/student harassment, there are unique circumstances in the athletics context that merit closer attention. Although the number of female athletes has increased dramatically over the past 40 years, the number of female coaches has decreased. This increases the number of men coaching female athletes and also increases the opportunity and possibility of sexual harassment. Male coach/female athlete is not the only context in which sexual harassment occurs, but it is significantly greater than any other combination.

Touching, keeping track of the athlete's life outside athletics, and nicknames are routinely accepted as part of a coach-athlete relationship and could be harmless. However, this conduct should be measured by the **unwelcomeness standard**: conduct is unwelcome if the athlete did not request or invite it and it is offensive to the victim. The power dynamic in coach–athlete relationships (factors such as power, trust, and control) may affect the ability of a female athlete to freely consent or decline sexual contact, so administrators and coaches must measure whether the conduct is harassing by its impact on the athlete, and not just by the intent of the coach.

Peer Sexual Harassment in Athletics

Complaints of peer harassment are increasing dramatically. A female swimmer from the University of Pittsburgh filed a civil suit seeking reinstatement to the university swim team claiming she was released as a result of her complaints of harassment against a swimmer on the men's team. A former placekicker on the University of Colorado football team publicly alleged that she was sexually harassed by her teammates, which led to her transfer to the University of New Mexico. She stated that she was "treated like a piece of meat" and constantly called "names that are unrepeatable." The student–athlete indicated she reported the incidents to the coach several times during the season, but the harassment persisted. An educational institution is liable for peer harassment when the harassing conduct is reported and the administration fails to reasonably respond.

Athletics departments may also be held liable under Title IX when a student-athlete (or even a recruit) sexually assaults a student, whether the assault occurred on or off campus. The first case to find that a school may be liable was *Williams v. Board of Regents of the University System of Georgia*, (2007). In this case, a female student was allegedly gang raped by three male athletes. The plaintiff claimed that the university was liable under Title IX because the coach, athletics director and university president were aware that the student–athlete who attacked the plaintiff had a history of sexual assaults before he was recruited and admitted to the university. The 11th Circuit held that given the past history of the recruited student-athlete, the institution had "before the fact notice" and should have made efforts to prevent future harassment from occurring. The 10th Circuit made a similar ruling regarding the alleged rape of female students by football players and recruits at the University of Colorado (see *Simpson v. University of Colorado* in the Supplemental CD).

This is the leading case of sexual harassment in the recreation industry. The Supreme Court addressed the conflict of opinions issued by the lower courts and thoroughly explains the new standards for establishing employer liability under Title VII.

BETH ANN FARAGHER V. CITY OF BOCA RATON

United States Supreme Court
524 U.S. 775 (1998)

Between 1985 and 1990, while attending college, petitioner Beth Ann Faragher worked part time and during the summers as an ocean lifeguard for the Marine Safety Section of the Parks and Recreation Department of respondent, the City of Boca Raton, Florida (City). During this period, Faragher's immediate supervisors were Bill Terry, David Silverman, and Robert Gordon. In June 1990, Faragher resigned.

In 1992, Faragher brought an action against Terry, Silverman, and the City, asserting claims under Title VII, *42 U.S.C. § 1983,* and Florida law. So far as it concerns the Title VII claim, the complaint alleged that Terry and Silverman created a "sexually hostile atmosphere" at the beach by repeatedly subjecting Faragher and other female lifeguards to "uninvited and offensive touching," by making lewd remarks, and by speaking of women in offensive terms. The complaint contained specific allegations that Terry once said that he would never promote a woman to the rank of lieutenant, and that Silverman had said to Faragher, "Date me or clean the toilets for a year." Asserting that Terry and Silverman were agents of the City, and that their conduct amounted to discrimination in the "terms, conditions, and privileges" of her employment, Faragher sought a judgment against the City for nominal damages, costs, and attorney's fees.

Following a bench trial, the United States District Court for the Southern District of Florida found that throughout Faragher's employment with the City, Terry served as Chief of the Marine Safety Division, with authority to hire new lifeguards (subject to the approval of higher management), to supervise all aspects of the lifeguards' work assignments, to engage in counseling, to deliver oral reprimands, and to make a record of any such discipline. Silverman was a Marine Safety lieutenant from 1985 until June 1989, when he became a captain. Gordon began the employment period as a lieutenant and at some point was promoted to the position of training captain. In these positions, Silverman and Gordon were responsible for making the lifeguards' daily assignments, and for supervising their work and fitness training.

The lifeguards and supervisors were stationed at the city beach and worked out of the Marine Safety Headquarters, a small one-story building containing an office, a meeting room, and a single, unisex locker room with a shower. Their work routine was structured in a "paramilitary configuration," with a clear chain of command. Lifeguards reported to lieutenants and captains, who reported to Terry. He was supervised by the Recreation Superintendent, who in turn reported to a Director of Parks and Recreation, answerable to the City Manager. The lifeguards had no significant contact with higher city officials like the Recreation Superintendent.

In February 1986, the City adopted a sexual harassment policy, which it stated in a memorandum from the City Manager addressed to all employees. In May 1990, the City revised the policy and reissued a statement of it. Although the City may actually have circulated the memos and statements to some employees, it completely failed to disseminate its policy among employees of the Marine Safety Section, with the result that Terry, Silverman, Gordon, and many lifeguards were unaware of it.

From time to time over the course of Faragher's tenure at the Marine Safety Section, between 4 and 6 of the 40 to 50 lifeguards were women. During that 5-year period, Terry repeatedly touched the bodies of female employees without invitation, would put his arm around Faragher, with his hand on her buttocks, and once made contact with another female lifeguard in a motion of sexual simulation. He made crudely demeaning references to women generally, and once commented disparagingly on Faragher's shape. During a job interview with a woman he hired as a lifeguard, Terry said that the female lifeguards had sex with their male counterparts and asked whether she would do the same.

Silverman behaved in similar ways. He once tackled Faragher and remarked that, but for a physical characteristic he found unattractive, he would readily have had sexual relations with her. Another time, he pantomimed an act of oral sex. Within earshot of the female lifeguards, Silverman made frequent, vulgar references to women and sexual matters, commented on the bodies of female lifeguards and beachgoers, and at least twice told female lifeguards that he would like to engage in sex with them. Faragher did not complain to higher management about Terry or Silverman. Although she spoke of their behavior to Gordon, she did not regard these discussions as formal complaints to a supervisor but as conversations with a person she held in high esteem. Other female lifeguards had similarly informal talks with Gordon, but because Gordon did not feel that it was his place to do so, he did not report these complaints to Terry, his own supervisor, or to any other city official. Gordon responded to the complaints of one lifeguard by saying that "the City just [doesn't] care."

In April 1990, however, two months before Faragher's resignation, Nancy Ewanchew, a former lifeguard, wrote to Richard Bender, the City's Personnel Director, complaining that Terry and Silverman had harassed her and other female lifeguards. Following investigation of this complaint, the City found that Terry and Silverman had behaved improperly, reprimanded them, and required them to choose between a suspension without pay or the forfeiture of annual leave.

On the basis of these findings, the District Court concluded that the conduct of Terry and Silverman was discriminatory harassment sufficiently serious to alter the conditions of Faragher's employment and constitute an abusive working environment. The District Court then ruled that there were three justifications for holding the City liable for the harassment of its supervisory employees. First, the court noted that the harassment was pervasive enough to support an inference that the City had "knowledge, or constructive knowledge" of it. Next, it ruled that the City was liable under traditional agency principles because Terry and Silverman were acting as its agents when they committed the harassing acts. Finally, the court observed that Gordon's knowledge of the harassment, combined with his inaction, "provides a further basis for imputing liability on [sic] the City." The District Court then awarded Faragher one dollar in nominal damages on her *Title VII claim.*

A panel of the Court of Appeals for the Eleventh Circuit reversed the judgment against the City. Although the panel had "no trouble concluding that Terry's and Silverman's conduct . . . was severe and pervasive enough to create an objectively abusive work environment," it overturned the District Court's conclusion that the City was liable. The panel ruled that Terry and Silverman were not acting within the scope of their employment when they engaged in the harassment, that they were not aided in their actions by the agency relationship, and that the City had no constructive knowledge of the harassment by virtue of its pervasiveness or Gordon's actual knowledge. * * *

Since our decision in *Meritor,* Courts of Appeals have struggled to derive manageable standards to govern employer liability for hostile environment harassment perpetrated by supervisory employees. While following our ad-

monition to find guidance in the common law of agency, as embodied in the Restatement, the Courts of Appeals have adopted different approaches. We granted certiorari to address the divergence, and now reverse the judgment of the Eleventh Circuit and remand for entry of judgment in Faragher's favor.

II.

A.

Under Title VII of the Civil Rights Act of 1964, "it shall be an unlawful employment practice for an employer to fail or refuse to hire or to discharge any individual, or otherwise to discriminate against any individual with respect to his compensation, terms, conditions, or privileges of employment, because of such individual's race, color, religion, sex, or national origin." *42 U.S.C. § 2000e-2*(a) (1). We have repeatedly made clear that although the statute mentions specific employment decisions with immediate consequences, the scope of the prohibition " 'is not limited to "economic" or "tangible" discrimination,' " and that it covers more than " 'terms' and 'conditions' in the narrow contractual sense." Thus, in *Meritor* we held that sexual harassment so "severe or pervasive" as to " 'alter the conditions of [the victim's] employment and create an abusive working environment' " violates *Title VII.*

So, in *Harris,* we explained that in order to be actionable under the statute, a sexually objectionable environment must be both objectively and subjectively offensive, one that a reasonable person would find hostile or abusive, and one that the victim in fact did perceive to be so. We directed courts to determine whether an environment is sufficiently hostile or abusive by "looking at all the circumstances," including the "frequency of the discriminatory conduct; its severity; whether it is physically threatening or humiliating, or a mere offensive utterance; and whether it unreasonably interferes with an employee's work performance." Most recently, we explained that Title VII does not prohibit "genuine but innocuous differences in the ways men and women routinely interact with members of the same sex and of the opposite sex." A recurring point in these opinions is that "simple teasing," offhand comments, and isolated incidents (unless extremely serious) will not amount to discriminatory changes in the "terms and conditions of employment."

These standards for judging hostility are sufficiently demanding to ensure that Title VII does not become a "general civility code." Properly applied, they will filter out complaints attacking "the ordinary tribulations of the workplace, such as the sporadic use of abusive language, gender-related jokes, and occasional teasing." We have made it clear that conduct must be extreme to amount to a change in the terms and conditions of employment, and the Courts of Appeals have heeded this view.

While indicating the substantive contours of the hostile environments forbidden by Title VII, our cases have established few definite rules for determining when an employer will be liable for a discriminatory environment that is otherwise actionably abusive. Given the circumstances of many of the litigated cases, including some that have come to us, it is not surprising that in many of them, the issue has been joined over the sufficiency of the abusive conditions, not the standards for determining an employer's liability for them. There have, for example, been myriad cases in which District Courts and Courts of Appeals have held employers liable on account of actual knowledge by the employer, or high-echelon officials of an employer organization, of sufficiently harassing action by subordinates, which the employer or its informed officers have done nothing to stop. In such instances, the combined knowledge and inaction may be seen as demonstrable negligence, or as the employer's adoption of the offending conduct and its results, quite as if they had been authorized affirmatively as the employer's policy. * * *

Finally, there is nothing remarkable in the fact that claims against employers for discriminatory employment actions with tangible results, like hiring, firing, promotion, compensation, and work assignment, have resulted in employer liability once the discrimination was shown.

A variety of reasons have been invoked for this apparently unanimous rule. Some courts explain . . . that when a supervisor makes such decisions, he "merges" with the employer, and his act becomes that of the employer. Other courts have suggested that vicarious liability is proper because the supervisor acts within the scope of his authority when he makes discriminatory decisions in hiring, firing, promotion, and the like. Others have suggested that vicarious liability is appropriate because the supervisor who discriminates in this manner is aided by the agency relation. Finally, still other courts have endorsed both of the latter two theories.

The soundness of the results in these cases (and their continuing vitality), in light of basic agency principles, was confirmed by this Court's only discussion to date of standards of employer liability, in *Meritor*, which involved a claim of discrimination by a supervisor's sexual harassment of a subordinate over an extended period. In affirming the Court of Appeals' holding that a hostile atmosphere resulting from sex discrimination is actionable under Title VII, we also anticipated proceedings on remand by holding agency principles relevant in assigning employer liability and by rejecting three *per se* rules of liability or immunity. We observed that the very definition of employer in Title VII, as including an "agent," expressed Congress's intent that courts look to traditional principles of the law of agency in devising standards of employer liability in those instances where liability for the actions of a supervisory employee was not otherwise obvious, and although we cautioned that "common-law principles may not be transferable in all their particulars to Title VII," we cited the Restatement § 219-237, with general approval.

We then proceeded to reject two limitations on employer liability, while establishing the rule that some limitation was intended. We held that neither the existence of a company grievance procedure nor the absence of actual notice of the harassment on the part of upper management would be dispositive of such a claim; while either might be relevant to the liability, neither would result automatically in employer immunity. Conversely, we held that Title VII placed some limit on employer responsibility for the creation of a discriminatory environment by a supervisor, and we held that Title VII does not make employers "always automatically liable for sexual harassment by their supervisors," contrary to the view of the Court of Appeals, which had held that "an employer is strictly liable for a hostile environment created by a supervisor's sexual advances, even though the employer neither knew nor reasonably could have known of the alleged misconduct," *477 U.S. at 69-70.*

Meritor's statement of the law is the foundation on which we build today. * * *

B.
The Court of Appeals identified, and rejected, three possible grounds drawn from agency law for holding the City vicariously liable for the hostile environment created by the supervisors. It considered whether the two supervisors were acting within the scope of their employment when they engaged in the harassing conduct. The court then enquired whether they were significantly aided by the agency relationship in committing the harassment, and also considered the possibility of imputing Gordon's knowledge of the harassment to the City. Finally, the Court of Appeals ruled out liability for negligence in failing to prevent the harassment. Faragher relies principally on the latter three theories of liability.

I.

A "master is subject to liability for the torts of his servants committed while acting in the scope of their employment." Restatement § 219(1). This doctrine has traditionally defined the "scope of employment" as including conduct "of the kind [a servant] is employed to perform," occurring "substantially within the authorized time and space limits," and "actuated, at least in part, by a purpose to serve the master," but as excluding an intentional use of force "unexpectable by the master."

Courts of Appeals have typically held, or assumed, that conduct similar to the subject of this complaint falls outside the scope of employment. In so doing, the courts have emphasized that harassment consisting of unwelcome remarks and touching is motivated solely by individual desires and serves no purpose of the employer. For this reason, courts have likened hostile environment sexual harassment to the classic "frolic and detour" for which an employer has no vicarious liability.

These cases ostensibly stand in some tension with others arising outside Title VII, where the scope of employment has been defined broadly enough to hold employers vicariously liable for intentional torts that were in no sense inspired by any purpose to serve the employer. . . .

The proper analysis here, then, calls not for a mechanical application of indefinite and malleable factors set forth in the Restatement, but rather an enquiry into the reasons that would support a conclusion that harassing behavior ought to be held within the scope of a supervisor's employment, and the reasons for the opposite view. The Restatement itself points to such an approach, as in the commentary that the "ultimate question" in determining the scope of employment is "whether or not it is just that the loss resulting from the servant's acts should be considered as one of the normal risks to be borne by the business in which the servant is employed."

In the case before us, a justification for holding the offensive behavior within the scope of Terry's and Silverman's employment was well put in Judge Barkett's dissent: "[A] pervasively hostile work environment of sexual harassment is never (one would hope) authorized, but the supervisor is clearly charged with maintaining a productive, safe work environment. The supervisor directs and controls the conduct of the employees, and the manner of doing so may inure to the employer's benefit or detriment, including subjecting the employer to Title VII liability." It is by now well recognized that hostile environment sexual harassment by supervisors (and, for that matter, co-employees) is a persistent problem in the workplace. An employer can, in a general sense, reasonably anticipate the possibility of such conduct occurring in its workplace, and one might justify the assignment of the burden of the untoward behavior to the employer as one of the costs of doing business, to be charged to the enterprise rather than the victim.

Two things counsel us to draw the contrary conclusion. First, there is no reason to suppose that Congress wished courts to ignore the traditional distinction between acts falling within the scope and acts amounting to what the older law called frolics or detours from the course of employment. Such a distinction can readily be applied to the spectrum of possible harassing conduct by supervisors, as the following examples show. First, a supervisor might discriminate racially in job assignments in order to placate the prejudice pervasive in the labor force. Instances of this variety of the heckler's veto would be consciously intended to further the employer's interests by preserving peace in the workplace. Next, supervisors might reprimand male employees for workplace failings with banter, but respond to women's shortcomings in harsh or vulgar terms. A third example might be the supervisor who, as here, expresses his sexual interests in ways having no apparent object whatever of serving an interest of the employer. If a line is to be drawn between scope and frolic, it would lie between the first two examples and the third,

and it thus makes sense in terms of traditional agency law to analyze the scope issue, in cases like the third example, just as most federal courts addressing that issue have done, classifying the harassment as beyond the scope of employment.

The second reason goes to an even broader unanimity of views among the holdings of District Courts and Courts of Appeals thus far. Those courts have held not only that the sort of harassment at issue here was outside the scope of supervisors' authority, but, by uniformly judging employer liability for co-worker harassment under a negligence standard, they have also implicitly treated such harassment as outside the scope of common employees' duties as well. If, indeed, the cases did not rest, at least implicitly, on the notion that such harassment falls outside the scope of employment, their liability issues would have turned simply on the application of the scope-of-employment rule.

It is quite unlikely that these cases would escape efforts to render them obsolete if we were to hold that supervisors who engage in discriminatory harassment are necessarily acting within the scope of their employment. The rationale for placing harassment within the scope of supervisory authority would be the fairness of requiring the employer to bear the burden of foreseeable social behavior, and the same rationale would apply when the behavior was that of co-employees. The employer generally benefits just as obviously from the work of common employees as from the work of supervisors; they simply have different jobs to do, all aimed at the success of the enterprise. As between an innocent employer and an innocent employee, if we use scope of employment reasoning to require the employer to bear the cost of an actionably hostile workplace created by one class of employees (i.e., supervisors), it could appear just as appropriate to do the same when the environment was created by another class (i.e., co-workers).

The answer to this argument might well be to point out that the scope of supervisory employment may be treated separately by recognizing that supervisors have special authority enhancing their capacity to harass, and that the employer can guard against their misbehavior more easily because their numbers are by definition fewer than the numbers of regular employees. But this answer happens to implicate an entirely separate category of agency law (to be considered in the next section), which imposes vicarious liability on employers for tortious acts committed by use of particular authority conferred as an element of an employee's agency relationship with the employer. Since the virtue of categorical clarity is obvious, it is better to reject reliance on misuse of supervisory authority (without more) as irrelevant to scope-of-employment analysis.

2.

The Court of Appeals also rejected vicarious liability on the part of the City insofar as it might rest on the concluding principle set forth in § 219(2)(d) of the Restatement, that an employer "is not subject to liability for the torts of his servants acting outside the scope of their employment unless . . . the servant purported to act or speak on behalf of the principal and there was reliance on apparent authority, or he was aided in accomplishing the tort by the existence of the agency relation." Faragher points to several ways in which the agency relationship aided Terry and Silverman in carrying out their harassment. She argues that in general offending supervisors can abuse their authority to keep subordinates in their presence while they make offensive statements, and that they implicitly threaten to misuse their supervisory powers to deter any resistance or complaint. Thus, she maintains that power conferred on Terry and Silverman by the City enabled them to act for so long without provoking defiance or complaint.

The City, however, contends that § 219(2)(d) has no application here. It argues that the second qualification of the subsection, referring to a servant "aided in accomplishing the tort by the existence of the agency relation," merely "refines" the one preceding it, which holds the employer vicariously liable for its servant's abuse of apparent authority. But this narrow reading is untenable; it would render the second qualification of § 219(2)(d) almost entirely superfluous (and would seem to ask us to shut our eyes to the potential effects of supervisory authority, even when not explicitly invoked). The illustrations accompanying this subsection make clear that it covers not only cases involving the abuse of apparent authority, but also to cases in which tortious conduct is made possible or facilitated by the existence of the actual agency relationship.

We therefore agree with Faragher that in implementing Title VII it makes sense to hold an employer vicariously liable for some tortious conduct of a supervisor made possible by abuse of his supervisory authority, and that the aided-by-agency-relation principle embodied in § 219 (2)(d) of the Restatement provides an appropriate starting point for determining liability for the kind of harassment presented here. Several courts, indeed, have noted what Faragher has argued, that there is a sense in which a harassing supervisor is always assisted in his misconduct by the supervisory relationship. The agency relationship affords contact with an employee subjected to a supervisor's sexual harassment, and the victim may well be reluctant to accept the risks of blowing the whistle on a superior. When a person with supervisory authority discriminates in the terms and conditions of subordinates' employment, his actions necessarily draw upon his superior position over the people who report to him, or those under them, whereas an employee generally cannot check a supervisor's abusive conduct the same way that she might deal with abuse from a co-worker. When a fellow employee harasses, the victim can walk away or tell the offender where to go, but it may be difficult to offer such responses to a supervisor, whose "power to supervise—[which may be] to hire and fire, and to set work schedules and pay rates—does not disappear . . . when he chooses to harass through insults and offensive gestures rather than directly with threats of firing or promises of promotion." Recognition of employer liability when discriminatory misuse of supervisory authority alters the terms and conditions of a victim's employment is underscored by the fact that the employer has a greater opportunity to guard against misconduct by supervisors than by common workers; employers have greater opportunity and incentive to screen them, train them, and monitor their performance.

In sum, there are good reasons for vicarious liability for misuse of supervisory authority. That rationale must, however, satisfy one more condition. We are not entitled to recognize this theory under Title VII unless we can square it with *Meritor's* holding that an employer is not "automatically" liable for harassment by a supervisor who creates the requisite degree of discrimination, and there is obviously some tension between that holding and the position that a supervisor's misconduct aided by supervisory authority subjects the employer to liability vicariously; if the "aid" may be the unspoken suggestion of retaliation by misuse of supervisory authority, the risk of automatic liability is high. To counter it, we think there are two basic alternatives, one being to require proof of some affirmative invocation of that authority by the harassing supervisor, the other to recognize an affirmative defense to liability in some circumstances, even when a supervisor has created the actionable environment.

There is certainly some authority for requiring active or affirmative, as distinct from passive or implicit, misuse of supervisory authority before liability may be imputed. That is the way some courts have viewed the familiar cases holding the employer liable for discriminatory employment action with tangible consequences, like firing and demotion. And we have already noted some examples of liability provided by the Restatement itself, which suggests that an affirmative misuse of power might be required.

But neat examples illustrating the line between the affirmative and merely implicit uses of power are not easy to come by in considering management behavior. Supervisors do not make speeches threatening sanctions whenever they make requests in the legitimate exercise of managerial authority, and yet every subordinate employee knows the sanctions exist; this is the reason that courts have consistently held that acts of supervisors have greater power to alter the environment than acts of co-employees generally. How far from the course of ostensible supervisory behavior would a company officer have to step before his orders would not reasonably be seen as actively using authority? Judgment calls would often be close, the results would often seem disparate even if not demonstrably contradictory, and the temptation to litigate would be hard to resist. We think plaintiffs and defendants alike would be poorly served by an active-use rule.

The other basic alternative to automatic liability would avoid this particular temptation to litigate, but allow an employer to show as an affirmative defense to liability that the employer had exercised reasonable care to avoid harassment and to eliminate it when it might occur, and that the complaining employee had failed to act with like reasonable care to take advantage of the employer's safeguards and otherwise to prevent harm that could have been avoided. This composite defense would, we think, implement the statute sensibly, for reasons that are not hard to fathom.

Although Title VII seeks "to make persons whole for injuries suffered on account of unlawful employment discrimination," its "primary objective," like that of any statute meant to influence primary conduct, is not to provide redress but to avoid harm. As long ago as 1980, the Equal Employment Opportunity Commission (EEOC), charged with the enforcement of Title VII, *42 U.S.C. § 2000e-4,* adopted regulations advising employers to "take all steps necessary to prevent sexual harassment from occurring, such as . . . informing employees of their right to raise and how to raise the issue of harassment." and in 1990 the Commission issued a policy statement enjoining employers to establish a complaint procedure "designed to encourage victims of harassment to come forward [without requiring] a victim to complain first to the offending supervisor." It would therefore implement clear statutory policy and complement the Government's Title VII enforcement efforts to recognize the employer's affirmative obligation to prevent violations and give credit here to employers who make reasonable efforts to discharge their duty. Indeed, a theory of vicarious liability for misuse of supervisory power would be at odds with the statutory policy if it failed to provide employers with some such incentive.

The requirement to show that the employee has failed in a coordinate duty to avoid or mitigate harm reflects an equally obvious policy imported from the general theory of damages, that a victim has a duty "to use such means as are reasonable under the circumstances to avoid or minimize the damages" that result from violations of the statute. An employer may, for example, have provided a proven, effective mechanism for reporting and resolving complaints of sexual harassment, available to the employee without undue risk or expense. If the plaintiff unreasonably failed to avail herself of the employer's preventive or remedial apparatus, she should not recover damages that could have been avoided if she had done so. If the victim could have avoided harm, no liability should be found against the employer who had taken reasonable care, and if damages could reasonably have been mitigated no award against a liable employer should reward a plaintiff for what her own efforts could have avoided.

In order to accommodate the principle of vicarious liability for harm caused by misuse of supervisory authority, as well as Title VII's equally basic policies of encouraging forethought by employers and saving action by objecting employees, we adopt the following holding in this case and in *Burlington Industries, Inc.* v. *Ellerth,* also decided today. An employer is subject to vicarious liability to a victimized employee for an actionable hostile environment created by a supervisor with immediate (or successively higher) authority over the employee. When no tangible employment action is taken, a defending employer may raise an affirmative defense to liability or damages, subject to proof by a preponderance of the evidence, see *Fed. Rule. Civ. Proc. 8(c).* The defense comprises two necessary elements: (a) that the employer exercised reasonable care to prevent and correct promptly any sexually harassing behavior, and (b) that the plaintiff employee unreasonably failed to take advantage of any preventive or corrective opportunities provided by the employer or to avoid harm otherwise. While proof that an employer had promulgated an antiharassment policy with complaint procedure is not necessary in every instance as a matter of law, the need for a stated policy suitable to the employment circumstances may appropriately be addressed in any case when litigating the first element of the defense. And while proof that an employee failed to fulfill the corresponding obligation of reasonable care to avoid harm is not limited to showing an unreasonable failure to use any complaint procedure provided by the employer, a demonstration of such failure will normally suffice to satisfy the employer's burden under the second element of the defense. No affirmative defense is available, however, when the supervisor's harassment culminates in a tangible employment action, such as discharge, demotion, or undesirable reassignment.

Applying these rules here, we believe that the judgment of the Court of Appeals must be reversed. The District Court found that the degree of hostility in the work environment rose to the actionable level and was attributable to Silverman and Terry. It is undisputed that these supervisors "were granted virtually unchecked authority" over their subordinates, "directly controlling and supervising all aspects of [Faragher's] day-to-day activities." It is also clear that Faragher and her colleagues were "completely isolated from the City's higher management." The City did not seek review of these findings.

While the City would have an opportunity to raise an affirmative defense if there were any serious prospect of its presenting one, it appears from the record that any such avenue is closed. The District Court found that the City had entirely failed to disseminate its policy against sexual harassment among the beach employees and that its officials made no attempt to keep track of the conduct of supervisors like Terry and Silverman. The record also makes clear that the City's policy did not include any assurance that the harassing supervisors could be bypassed in registering complaints. Under such circumstances, we hold as a matter of law that the City could not be found to have exercised reasonable care to prevent the supervisors' harassing conduct. Unlike the employer of a small workforce, who might expect that sufficient care to prevent tortious behavior could be exercised informally, those responsible for city operations could not reasonably have thought that precautions against hostile environments in any one of many departments in far-flung locations could be effective without communicating some formal policy against harassment, with a sensible complaint procedure. . . .

III.

The judgment of the Court of Appeals for the Eleventh Circuit is reversed, and the case is remanded for reinstatement of the judgment of the District Court.

It is so ordered.

CASES ON THE SUPPLEMENTAL CD

Davis v. Monroe County Board of Education, 526 U.S. 629 (1999). This case establishes the standards for institutional liability for peer sexual harassment.

Fitzgerald v. Barnstable School Committee, 129 S. Ct. 788 (2009). This case examines whether Title IX precludes a constitutional claim under § 1983.

Simpson v. University of Colorado, 500 F.3d 1170 (10 th Cir. 2007). This case examines the liability of an educational institution for the sexual assault of students at off campus party by recruits and student-athletes.

QUESTIONS YOU SHOULD BE ABLE TO ANSWER

1. Define sexual harassment under Title VII.

2. Define sexual harassment under Title IX.

3. Explain the similarities and differences between the elements of a plaintiff's complaint and employer or institutional liability under Title VII and Title IX.

4. Explain how the court determines whether or not the workplace is a hostile environment.

5. Explain what an employer must do in order to avoid liability with an affirmative defense.

REFERENCES

Cases

Barnes v. Costle, 561 F.2d 983 (D.C. 1977).

Burlington Industries, Inc. v. Ellerth, 524 U.S. 742 (1998).

Davis v. Monroe County Board of Education, 119 S.Ct. 1161 (1999).

Faragher v. City of Boca Raton, 524 U.S. 775 (1998).

Gebser v. Lago Vista Independent School District, 524 U.S. 274 (1998).

Harris v. Forklift Systems, Inc., 510 U.S. 17 (1993).

Jin v. Metropolitan Life Ins. Co., 295 F.3d 335 (2nd Cir. 2002).

Meritor Savings Bank, FSB v. Vinson, 477 U.S. 57 (1986).

Miller v. Bank of America, 600 F.2d 211 (9th Cir. 1979).

Morehouse v. Berkshire Gas Co., 989 F. Supp. 54, 61 (D. Mass. 1997).

Simpson v. University of Colorado, 500 F.3d 1170 (10th Cir. 2007).

Williams v. Board of Regents of University System of Georgia, 477 F.3d 1282 (11th Cir. 2007).

Williams v. Saxbe, 1976 413 F.Supp. 654 (D.D.C. 1976).

Publication

George, B. G. (1999). Employer liability for sexual harassment: The buck stops where? *Wake Forest Law Review, 34*(1), 1–25.

Legislation

EEOC Notice 915.002 (6/18/1999) Enforcement Guidance: Vicarious Employer Liability for Unlawful Harassment by Supervisors.

OCR Notice: Revised Sexual Harassment Guidance: Harassment of Students by School Employees, Other Students, or Third Parties (11/02/2000) 65 Fed. Reg. 213. pp. 66091–66114.

Title VII of the Civil Rights Act, 42 U.S.C. 2000e et seq. (2008).

Title VII Guidelines on Discrimination Because of Sex, 29 C.F.R. 1604.11.

Title IX of the Education Act of 1974, 20 U.S.C. 1681 (2008).

7.15 Age Discrimination in Employment Act

—David Snyder
State University of New York College at Cortland

The Equal Employment Opportunity Commission (EEOC) reported that $82.8 million in damages were awarded in 2008 under the Age Discrimination in Employment Act (ADEA). The $82.8 million figure, which excludes monetary awards from litigation, represents the highest amount recovered from ADEA-related cases in a single year from 1992 to 2008. For 2008, that breaks down to approximately $122,124 awarded for each claim that was deemed to have "reasonable cause." The total damages derived from ADEA complaints in 2008 rose 124 percent from $66.8 million in 2007 (EEOC Website, http://www.eeoc.gov/stats/adea.html). This data does not include age discrimination actions based on other federal and state laws.Although not all age discrimination claims involve sport or recreation, there have been a number of age discrimination lawsuits initiated by coaches, and these cases appear to be on the rise. For example, in 2005, Ferne Labati, the former coach of the University of Miami's women's basketball team, filed a lawsuit against the university alleging age- and gender-based discrimination. Labati, who was 60 years old when she was fired, was replaced by a thirty-seven-year-old. She was inducted into the university's Sports Hall of Fame just 11 months before she was terminated. Another example is Don Moreau, the former baseball coach at Loyola University, New Orleans, who filed an age discrimination lawsuit against the university in 2003. Loyola claimed that Moreau, who had coached baseball at Loyola for 12 years, needed a college degree to be a full-time coach at Loyola. Moreau, who was 65 years old at the time he was fired, was replaced by a 33-year-old as head baseball coach.

In addition, the stakes in age discrimination cases are often high. In 2000, two former golf coaches at California State University at San Bernardino were initially awarded $1.2 million from a jury as part of an age discrimination case against their former employer. This amount was reduced to $750,000 on appeal. Two years after being fired as a sportscaster by ABC Sports in 1998, former Olympian Donna De Varona filed a $50 million unlawful termination lawsuit against her former employer alleging she was discriminated based on her age and gender. The case was later settled out of court. Former football referee Ben Dreith filed suit against the NFL alleging the league discriminated against him based on his age by refusing to allow him to officiate any playoff games, and by demoting him to line judge during the 1990–91 season (see the Supplemental CD). He also claimed the league retaliated against him for filing his ADEA claim by not renewing his contract. The case reportedly settled for six figures. (Epstein, 188-89) These examples, coupled with the legal costs to defend such cases, reflect the financial risk involved with age discrimination litigation.

With people living longer, healthier lives, our workforce is steadily growing older. This demographic shift has often come into direct conflict with the economic reality of reductions in the labor force and other cost-cutting measures. The tension between an aging society and these dynamic market forces, and the growing risk of liability in these cases make it vital for sport and recreation managers to have a clear understanding of the age discrimination laws.

FUNDAMENTAL CONCEPTS

Federal Legislation

The Age Discrimination in Employment Act of 1967 (ADEA)

The Age Discrimination in Employment Act protects employees and job applicants who are 40 years of age or older from employment discrimination based on age. The ADEA, which applies to employers with 20 or more employees, pertains to various terms and conditions of employment, including but not limited to the hiring process, compensation schemes, promotion decisions, job assignments, training opportunities, temporary lay-offs, and termination of employment.

Although the ADEA was modeled after Title VII, there are some noteworthy differences between the two statutes. One such distinction is that the definition of what constitutes an "employer" under the ADEA is broader than Title VII. Unlike Title VII, the ADEA does not exclude groups such as religious organizations or Native American tribes, among others, from being characterized as "employer" under the statute. The ADEA specifically defines an "employer" as "a person engaged in an industry affecting commerce who has twenty or more employees for each working day in each of 20 or more calendar weeks in the current or preceding calendar year" [29 U.S.C.A. § 630(b)].

There are some limitations to the scope of the ADEA. For example, certain employees that are vital to public safety and welfare, such as police officers, cannot seek protection under the ADEA. Employees under 40 years of age cannot seek relief under the ADEA, even if they are subject to discrimination in the workplace based on age.

Enforcement of the ADEA falls under the purview of the Equal Employment Opportunity Commission (EEOC). Code of Federal Regulations contains the procedures for charges made with the EEOC under the ADEA. (29 C.F.R. § 1625-27). A party alleging age discrimination under the ADEA is generally required to file a claim with the EEOC within 180 days from the date of the challenged conduct. [42 U.S.C. §§ 2000e-5(e)(1)]. However, that deadline may be extended if the claimant also has a claim under state law. A party who files a charge of age discrimination with the EEOC "may file a civil action at any time after 60 days have elapsed from the filing of the charge with the Commission" [29 C.F.R. § 1626.18 (b)].

Until recently, the only way to establish a claim under the ADEA was for the plaintiff to prove that age was the motivating factor for the challenged conduct. One theory of liability under the ADEA is for the plaintiff to prove **disparate treatment** by a direct showing that the employer intentionally discriminated or displayed discriminatory animus against the plaintiff solely because of the plaintiff's age. Another theory is that the defendant engaged in **systemic disparate treatment** by instituting widespread employment practices that displayed a pattern of discrimination based on age. In 2005, the U.S. Supreme Court substantially expanded the ADEA by also allowing claims based on **disparate impact** in *Smith v. City of Jackson, Mississippi*, 125 S. Ct. 1536 (2005) (see the Supplemental CD). In *City of Jackson*, the Court held that an employment practice that discriminates based on age could be considered unlawful under the ADEA, regardless of the discriminatory intent of the employer. Prior to the decision in *City of Jackson*, most federal courts had ruled that such disparate impact claims were not permitted. Now, under the authority of *City of Jackson*, seemingly "neutral" employer practices can be held to violate the ADEA if they result in a disparate impact on older workers. The plaintiff no longer has to establish that the employer intended to discriminate to prevail under the ADEA. To establish a prima facie case under the ADEA, the plaintiff must establish the following elements by a preponderance of the evidence:

1. The plaintiff is an employee or applicant for employment with the employer;

2. The employee is a member of the protected class (i.e., 40 years old or above);

3. The employer has twenty or more employees;

4. The plaintiff was qualified for the job (if an applicant for employment) or was performing the duties and responsibilities of the job satisfactorily. (if an employee);

5. The plaintiff suffered some adverse condition with respect to their employment (e.g., was not hired, was fired);

6. The employer hired someone outside the protected class (for job applicants) or replaced the plaintiff with someone outside the protected class (for employees).

In addition to these theories of liability, it is unlawful to retaliate against someone for filing an age discrimination charge, participating in an investigation, or testifying in a proceeding or lawsuit filed under the ADEA. The ADEA states, "It shall be unlawful for an employer to discriminate against any of his employees or applicants for employment, for an employment agency to discriminate against any individual, or for a labor organization to discriminate against any member thereof or applicant for membership, because such individual, member or applicant for membership has opposed any practice made unlawful by this section, or because such individual, member or applicant for membership has made a charge, testified, assisted, or participated in any manner in an investigation, proceeding, or litigation under this section" [29 U.S.C.A. § 623(d)]. The elements for a retaliation claim under the ADEA are identical to the filing of such a claim under Title VII.

It is also a violation of the ADEA to harass older workers or subject them to a hostile work environment (*Eggleston v. South Bend Community School Corporation*, 1994). Once again, the criteria for a harassment claim under the ADEA and Title VII are the same.

Once the plaintiff establishes a prima facie case under the ADEA, the burden shifts to the defendant to establish a defense by a preponderance of the evidence. One affirmative defense that can be asserted in ADEA cases is that *other reasonable factors besides age* prompted the employer's conduct. Another defense to a claim under the ADEA is to prove that a **bona fide occupational qualification (BFOQ)** exists by demonstrating that age is a legitimate factor to consider for the performance of that particular job (e.g., airline pilots, firefighters, police officers). Certain seniority systems may be free from ADEA attack, provided the scheme does not discriminate against older workers.

Assuming the employer is able to provide a legitimate, nondiscriminatory reason for the alleged discrimination, the burden then shifts back to the plaintiff to refute the defendant's purported rationale by showing that the justification offered is merely a **pretext** for actual discrimination. Plaintiffs typically attempt to establish pretext by offering evidence of pervasive bias against members of the protected class (older workers in this case) or by introducing into evidence data reflecting inequity or favoritism among certain classes of employees.

If the plaintiff prevails in age discrimination claim under the ADEA, the plaintiff is entitled to back pay for lost wages, injunctive and declaratory relief, and attorney's fees. [29 U.S.C. § 216(b)]. The plaintiff may also receive liquidated damages if the defendant's conduct is found to be willful. (29 U.S.C. § 626(b)). In addition, the court may, in its discretion, order that the plaintiff be reinstated or promoted or award the plaintiff front pay for loss of future wages (See *Moore v. The University of Notre Dame*, 1998).

Older Workers Benefit Protection Act (OWBPA)

In 1990, Congress amended the ADEA with the enactment of The Older Workers Benefit Protection Act (OWBPA), which specifically prohibits employers from denying benefits to older workers. However, under the OWBPA, an employer may reduce the benefit plans for older workers provided that the cost of such plans is the same as the cost of providing benefits to younger employees.

The OWBPA is also significant in that it imposes extremely stringent standards for settling a claim under the ADEA. There is no counterpart to these provisions in Title VII, and as a result, it is more difficult to settle an ADEA case.

In addition, the OWBPA contains very specific criteria that must be met for an employee to waive rights secured under the ADEA. To be valid, such a waiver must:

1. Be in writing;

2. Be clear and unambiguous;

3. Clearly make reference to ADEA rights or claims;

4. Only apply to current rights and claims. It cannot waive future rights or claims that might arise in the future;

5. Be in exchange for valuable consideration;

6. Contain a clause advising the employee to consult an attorney before signing the waiver;

7. Allow the employee twenty-one days to consider the waiver before it becomes effective;

8. Give the employee at least seven days to revoke the waiver after signing it.

State Legislation

In addition to federal law, most states have some type of law prohibiting age discrimination. Some state statutes provide different or greater protection than the ADEA, and therefore they may provide relief in circumstances where the ADEA does not apply. For example, some states allow age discrimination cases for workers younger than 40 years of age. Other states statues extend age discrimination protection to workplaces with fewer than twenty employees. In a few states, age discrimination can be a criminal offense.

In addition, states typically have their own administrative agencies that handle age discrimination claims based on state law, as well as their own deadlines for filing such claims. EEOC refers to such state agencies as **Fair Employment Practices Agencies (FEPAs).** The EEOC and the FEPAs have agreements that are designed to enable the state and federal agencies to work together efficiently and that allow for "dual filing" when a party has a claim based on both state and federal law. The general 180-day deadline for filing an ADEA claim with the EEOC is extended to 300 days if the charge also is covered by a state law.

For these reasons, it is important for the sport and recreation manager to be aware of the applicable state laws concerning age discrimination in addition to the pertinent federal legislation.

Alternative Legal Grounds for Relief

In addition to state and federal age discrimination laws, other areas of law may provide the basis for a claim in situations where an individual is discriminated against based on age. However, these are not considered true "age discrimination" cases because the cause of action is not based on a law that prohibits discrimination based on age. For example, Maurice Clarett's lawsuit against the NFL challenged the league rule making players ineligible for the draft until they were three seasons removed from their high school graduations. Although the impact of the league rule was to discriminate against Clarett based on his age, his suit was based on the claim that the league unreasonably restrained free trade in violation of antitrust law.

SIGNIFICANT CASE

One of the more publicized sport-related age discrimination cases involved the termination of Joe Moore as assistant football coach at Notre Dame University. Moore prevailed against Notre Dame on his age discrimination claim at trial and was awarded back pay and liquidated damages by the jury. After the trial, Moore moved to either be reinstated to his former position or awarded front pay in addition to the damages already awarded him by the jury. The portion of the decision dealing with Moore's request for attorney's fees and costs has been omitted.

JOSEPH R. MOORE V. UNIVERSITY OF NOTRE DAME

United States District Court for the Northern District of Indiana
22 F. Supp. 2d 896 (1998)

This cause is before this Court on Plaintiff's Motion for Award of Reinstatement/Front Pay and Plaintiff's Bill of Costs. Plaintiff, Joseph R. Moore (Moore) filed a claim in this Court against The University of Notre Dame (Notre Dame) alleging age discrimination, retaliation, and defamation. Only the age discrimination claim survived summary judgment. The case went to trial in Lafayette on July 9, 1998. On July 15, 1998, after four and one-half hours of deliberation, the Jury found that Notre Dame had violated the Age Discrimination in Employment Act (ADEA) and awarded Moore back pay in the amount of $42,935.28. Additionally, because the jury determined that Notre Dame's violation of ADEA was willful, Plaintiff also was awarded liquidated damages in the additional amount of $42,935.28. Judgment must and now does enter in favor of the plaintiff, Joseph E. Moore and against the defendant, Notre Dame in the amount of $85,870.56. Accordingly, the Court now considers Moore's post-trial motions.

* * *

I. RELIEF UNDER THE ADEA

The remedial scheme for a discriminatory discharge is designed to make a plaintiff who has been the victim of discrimination whole through the use of equitable remedies. *See Albemarle Paper Co. v. Moody*, 422 U.S. 405, 95 S. Ct. 2362, 45 L. Ed. 2d 280 (1975) (discussing equitable remedies for Title VII); *Straka v. Francis*, 867 F. Supp. 767 (N.D. Ill. 1994) (stating that ADEA and Title VII are treated similarly regarding available remedies). When confronted with a violation of the ADEA, a district court is authorized to afford relief by means of reinstatement, back pay, injunctive relief, declaratory judgment, and attorney's fees. 29U.S.C.§ 626(b); *McKennon v. Nashville Banner Pub'g Co.*, 513 U.S. 352, 357-58, 115 S. Ct. 879, 884, 130 L. Ed. 2d 852 (1995); *see also Lorillard v. Pons*, 434 U.S. 575, 584, 98 S. Ct. 866, 872, 55 L. Ed. 2d 40 (1978). Additionally, in the case of a willful violation of the Act, the ADEA authorizes an award of liquidated damages equal to the back pay award. 29 U.S.C. § 626(b).

* * *

Moore now asks the Court to reinstate him in his former coaching position, or to award five year's front pay in lieu of reinstatement. Notre Dame contends that Moore has received all relief to which he was entitled and therefore asks this Court to deny Moore's Motion for Reinstatement/Front Pay.

A. Reinstatement

Although reinstatement is the preferred remedy in a discrimination case, it is not always appropriate. The factors which should be considered when determining its propriety include, hostility in the past employment relationship and the absence of an available position for the plaintiff. Civil Rights Act of 1964, § 701 et seq., as amended, 42 U.S.C.A. § 2000e *et seq.; McKnight v. General Motors Corp.*, 973 F.2d 1366, 1370 (7th Cir. 1992); *Ward v. Tipton County Sheriff Dept.*, 937 F. Supp. 791 (S.D. Ind.1996). Additionally, under ADEA, when a period for reinstatement is relatively short, such that plaintiff is close to retirement, the strong preference in favor of reinstatement is neutralized by the increased certainty of potential loss of pay permitting consideration of a front pay award. *See McNeil v. Economics Laboratory, Inc.*, 800 F.2d 111, 118 (7th Cir. 1986), *cert. denied*, 481 U.S. 1041, 107 S. Ct. 1983, 95 L. Ed. 2d 823 (1987), overruled on other grounds by *Coston v. Plitt Theatres, Inc.*, 860 F.2d 834 (7th Cir. 1988). *See also, Chace v. Champion Spark Plug Co.*, 732 F. Supp. 605 (D. Md. 1990).

1. Hostility

The decision to reinstate a discriminatorily terminated employee is consigned to the sound discretion of the district court which should not grant reinstatement "where the result would be undue friction and controversy." *McKnight v. General Motors Corp.*, 908 F.2d 104, 115 (7th Cir. 1990); *Wilson v. AM General Corp.*, 979 F. Supp. 800 (N.D. Ind. 1997) (may consider friction that exists between employer and employee unrelated to discrimination). Evidence that hostility developed between the employer and employee during litigation may also be considered, but is not dispositive. *U.S. E.E.O.C. v. Century*

Broadcasting Corp., 957 F.2d 1446 (7th Cir. 1992); *Cassino v. Reichhold Chemicals, Inc.*, 817 F.2d 1338 (9th Cir. 1987).

In the present case, Moore's reinstatement would cause significant friction as well as disruption of the current football program. Moore and Davie, his direct supervisor, are no longer on speaking terms. During trial, sufficient evidence was presented to infer that Moore and Davie would be unable to engage in a workable relationship. Reinstatement in this instance is impracticable. Moreover, even if hostility and undue friction were not a problem, reinstatement is not appropriate in this case.

2. Available Position

The Seventh Circuit has also held that reinstatement can reasonably be denied when "someone else currently occupies the employee's former position." *Century Broadcasting*, 957 F.2d 1446 (*quoting Graefenhain v. Pabst Brewing Co.* 870 F.2d 1198, 1208 (7th Cir. 1989). Other Circuits hold similarly. *See e.g., Ray v. Iuka Special Mun. Separate School Dist.*, 51 F.3d 1246, 1254 (5th Cir. 1995); *Shore v. Federal Express Corp.*, 777 F.2d 1155, 1157-59 (6th Cir. 1985); *Spagnuolo v. Whirlpool Corp.*, 717 F.2d 114, 119-122 (4th Cir. 1983) (holding that reinstatement is not appropriate if it requires bumping or displacing innocent employee in favor of plaintiff). The law is clear. Even if this Court determined that reinstatement is warranted, it is not an appropriate remedy in this case as there is no available position to which Moore could return. Therefore, the Court turns to the more difficult issue of whether front-pay is warranted.

B. Front Pay

Plaintiff is incorrect in stating that "if the Court rejects Moore's request for reinstatement, it *must* award him front pay." (Pl.'s Mem. at 7) (emphasis added). Front pay is an available remedy under ADEA, however, such an award remains discretionary with court. *Williams v. Pharmacia Opthalmics, Inc.*, 926 F. Supp. 791 (N.D. Ind. 1996), *aff'd*, 137 F.3d 944 (7th Cir. 1997); *Downes v. Volkswagen of America, Inc.*, 41 F.3d 1132, 1141 (7th Cir. 1993); *Tennes v. Commonwealth of Massachusetts Dept. of Revenue*, 944 F.2d 372, 381 (7th Cir. 1991); *Drago v. Aetna Plywood, Inc.*, 1998 U.S. Dist. LEXIS 12249, No. 96C2398, 1998 WL 474100 (N.D. Ill. Aug. 3, 1998). The Seventh Circuit has defined front pay as "a lump sum . . . representing the discounted present value of the difference between the earnings (an employee) would have received in his old employment and the earnings he can be expected to receive in his present and future, and by hypothesis, inferior, employment. *Century Broadcasting*, 957 F.2d 1446, 1463 n.18 (quoting *McKnight*, 908 F.2d 104, 116). *See also, Downes*, 41 F.3d 1132, 1141, n. 8. Such a remedy may especially be indicated when the plaintiff has no reasonable prospect of obtaining comparable employment or when the time period for which front pay is to be awarded is relatively short. *Inks v. Healthcare Distributors of Indiana, Inc.*, 901 F. Supp. 1403 (N.D. Ind. 1995). *See e.g., Nelson v. Boatmen's*

Bancshares, Inc., 26 F.3d 796 (8th Cir. 1994) (front pay appropriate when employee is nearing retirement age); *Duke v. Uniroyal, Inc.*, 928 F.2d 1413 (4th Cir. 1991); *Linn v. Andover Newton Theological School, Inc.*, 874 F.2d 1 (1st Cir. 1989); *Stratton v. Department for the Aging for the City of New York*, 922 F. Supp. 857 (S.D. N.Y. 1996) (all holding similarly). The court determines the amount of front pay to award depending on whether:

1. the plaintiff has a reasonable prospect of obtaining comparable employment;

2. the time period for the award is relatively short;

3. the plaintiff intends to work or is physically capable of working; and

4. liquidated damages have been awarded.

Williams, 926 F. Supp. 791, 796 (finding an award of front pay in Title VII context proper and consistent with the 1991 amendments). Front pay is awarded for a reasonable period of time, until a date by which the plaintiff, using reasonable diligence, should have found comparable employment. *Hutchison v. Amateur Electronics Supply, Inc.*, 840 F. Supp. 612 (E.D. Wisc. 1993), *aff'd. in part, rev'd in part*, 42 F.3d 1037 at 1045 (7th Cir. 1994). Moreover, an award must be grounded in available facts, acceptable to a reasonable person and not highly speculative. *Downes*, 41 F.3d at 1142. It cannot be based simply on a plaintiff's own stated intentions with regard to how long he or she would have worked. *Pierce v. Atchison, Topeka & Santa Fe Ry. Co.*, 65 F.3d 562, 574 (7th Cir.1995).

Notre Dame contends that Moore is not entitled to front pay because (1) evidence acquired by Notre Dame after Moore's discharge would have led to his discharge based on legitimate, non-discriminatory reasons, (2) Moore's award of liquidated damages has already made him whole, and (3) Moore has failed to make reasonable efforts to mitigate his damages.

1. Award of Liquidated Damages

The fact that Moore is entitled to damages based on the jury's finding of a wilful violation does not conclusively preclude front pay. Front pay *may be* less appropriate when liquidated damages are awarded. *Id.* (emphasis added); *Hybert v. Hearst Corp.*, 900 F.2d 1050, 1056 (7th Cir. 1990) (liquidated damages are a relevant consideration in determining *whether and how much* front pay to award). Authority clearly states that liquidated damages is *one* factor to be considered in awarding front pay and does not stand for the proposition that front pay and liquidated damages may never be awarded to the same plaintiff. *Century Broadcasting*, 957 F.2d 1446, 1450; *McNeil*, 800 F.2d 111, 118; *Graefenhain*, 870 F.2d 1198, 1,205. Furthermore, an award of front pay, constituting an estimate of what the employee might have earned had he been reinstated at the conclusion of trial is necessarily speculative, this speculative aspect should not deter courts from fashioning awards that accomplish ADEA's goal of making a wronged employee whole. *Selgas v. American Airlines, Inc.,* 104 F.3d 9 (1st Cir. 1997), on remand 977 F. Supp. 100 (D. P.R 1997).

In the present case, Notre Dame argues that Moore's jury award of $42,935.28 and liquidated damages award of $42,935.28 makes him whole and that further compensation would "be a total award greater than the statute contemplates." *Avitia v. Metropolitan Club of Chicago, Inc.,* 49 F.3d 1219, 1232 (7th Cir. 1995). The Court disagrees. Moore's 1996–97 annual salary was $79,552.08. Assuming an annual increase of 4%, his 1997–98 salary would have been $82,734.16 and his 1998–99 salary $86,043.53. In addition to loss of salary, Moore also lost several benefits. It is unlikely he will be able to duplicate the benefits and prestige the Notre Dame position provided him. Moreover, as Moore is at or near retirement age, it is unlikely he will find comparable employment at the salary level he enjoyed while at Notre Dame. *Compare, Stratton,* 922 F. Supp. 857 (S.D. N.Y. 1996) (finding front pay appropriate in ADEA action, where it was clear from evidence presented at trial that employee, who was now 66 years of age, had no reasonable prospect of obtaining positions similar to that she previously held). The evidence showed that Moore had coached at Notre Dame for nine years and intended to continue in that position until retirement. Moore has been unable to replace his Notre Dame position with a comparable one. He is currently earning $46,600 and working three jobs. In this Court's opinion, the jury award has not "made him whole" and front pay may be appropriate.

2. After-Acquired Evidence

Notre Dame also asserts that Moore is not entitled to front pay because Notre Dame Administrators made it clear that had they known of Moore's alleged physical and verbal abuse of players, they would have terminated him immediately. Notre Dame argues that evidence of the alleged abuse was "after acquired" and therefore precludes both front pay and reinstatement.

What sets an after-acquired evidence case apart * * * is that the articulated "legitimate" reason for terminating the employee was non-existent at the time of the adverse decision and could not possibly have motivated the employer to the slightest degree. *Delli Santi v. CNA Ins. Companies,* 88 F.3d 192 (3d Cir. 1996). Furthermore, "Where an employer seeks to rely upon after-acquired evidence of wrongdoing, it must first establish that the wrongdoing was of such severity that the employee in fact would have been terminated on those grounds alone if the employer had known of it at the time of discharge." ADEA, 29 U.S.C. § 621 *et seq.*; *McKennon,* 513 U.S. 352, 115 S. Ct. 879, 130 L. Ed. 2d 852; *Moos v. Square D Co.,* 72 F.3d 39 (6th Cir. 1995); *Coleman v. Keebler Co.,* 997 F. Supp. 1102 (N.D. Ind. 1998); *Vandeventer v. Wabash Nat. Corp.,* 887 F. Supp. 1178 (N.D.

Ind. 1995). It is this Court's opinion that Notre Dames argument fails on both points.

* * *

First, the after-acquired evidence doctrine does not bar front pay to a discharged employee whose alleged wrongdoing was known to the employer at the time of the discharge and was asserted as being a reason for the discharge. *Delli Santi,* 88 F.3d 192, 205. It is this Court's opinion that Defendant's knowledge of Moore's coaching behavior does not fall within the ambit of after-acquired evidence as set forth in *McKennon.* Moore coached football at Notre Dame for nine years. Davie knew of, and in fact argued that Moore's behavior was one of the reasons for his termination. The record is replete with such evidence. (Trial Tr. July 10, 1998 p. 18, 19, 30-38). The jury apparently rejected this argument. Based on its defense at trial, Notre Dame cannot now claim that this "legitimate" reason was non-existent at the time of the adverse decision and could not possibly have motivated it to the slightest degree. *Delli Santi,* 88 F.3d 192, 205-06.

Notre Dame has also failed to establish that Moore's alleged wrongdoing was of such severity that he in fact would have been terminated on those grounds alone. Football is an aggressive sport. Coaching a winning team requires a degree of "killer instinct." Notre Dame's blanket assertion that if certain administrators had known of Moore's alleged abuse of players, Moore would have been immediately fired is insufficient to prove that such would have actually occurred. This assertion is nothing more than an excuse made after the fact. Additionally, this Court will not speculate, like defendant does, as to the reason the jury did not award a large amount of back pay. (Def.'s Mem. at 4). An award of back pay less than requested does not necessarily mean the jury concluded Moore would have been terminated for nondiscriminatory reasons and it does not therefore preclude front pay. *See Curtis v. Electronics & Space Corp.,* 113 F.3d 1498, 1504 (8th Cir. 1997); *Downes,* 41 F.3d 1132, 1143-44 (7th Cir. 1994). Accordingly, this Court finds Defendant's after-acquired evidence argument without merit.

3. Failure to Mitigate

Notre Dame finally argues that Moore is not entitled to front pay because he failed to undertake reasonable efforts to mitigate his damages. This Court disagrees. Generally, an ADEA plaintiff satisfies the mitigation of damages requirement that he use "reasonable diligence in attempting to secure employment" by demonstrating his commitment to seeking active employment and by remaining ready, willing and able to work. However, a plaintiff's duty to mitigate his damages is not met by using reasonable diligence to obtain any employment, rather the employment must be comparable employment. *Finch v. Hercules Inc.,* 941 F. Supp. 1395 (D. Del. 1996). The Seventh Circuit has defined "comparable work" as a position that affords "virtually identical promotional opportunities, compensation, job responsibilities, working conditions and status" as the previous position. *Best v. Shell Oil Co.*, 4 F. Supp. 2d 770 (N.D. Ill. 1998) (quoting *Hutchinson*, 42 F.3d 1037 at 1044). The goal of mitigation is to prevent the plaintiff from remaining idle and doing nothing. Furthermore, an employee is not required to go to heroic lengths in attempting to mitigate his damages, but only to take reasonable steps to do so. *Suggs v. ServiceMaster Educ. Food Management*, 72 F.3d 1228 (6th Cir. 1996); *Ford v. Nicks*, 866 F.2d 865 (6th Cir. 1989). Furthermore, a claimant has no obligation to accept lesser employment . . . or relocate to a new community. *See, e.g., Ford Motor Co. v. E.E.O.C.*, 458 U.S. 219, 231-32, 102 S. Ct. 3057, 3065-66, 73 L. Ed. 2d 721 (1982); *Coleman v. City of Omaha*, 714 F.2d 804, 808 (8th Cir. 1983); *Glass v. IDS Financial Services, Inc.*, 778 F. Supp. 1029 (D. Minn. 1991); *Raimondo v. AMAX, Inc.*, 843 F. Supp. 806 (D. Conn. 1984).

When evaluating the reasonableness and duration of a job search a court may consider the plaintiff's background and individual characteristics. *Rasimas v. Michigan Dep't of Mental Health*, 714 F.2d 614, 624 (6th Cir.1983) (for example, older claimants need not exert same effort as younger claimants); *Sellers v. Delgado College*, 902 F.2d 1189, 1193 (5th Cir. 1990). Moreover, it is the defendant's burden to prove that a plaintiff has failed to discharge his duty. *Smith v. Great American Restaurants, Inc.*, 969 F.2d 430 (7th Cir. 1992); *Padilla v. Metro-North Commuter R.R.*, 92 F.3d 117, 125 (2d Cir. 1996). In the present case, Notre Dame has not met this burden. Moore sought and obtained employment shortly after his discharge. He currently works at three different jobs. The fact that he did not accept a position at Cornell does not indicate a failure to mitigate. That position offered a $40,000 salary, significantly less than Moore's former salary, and involved a tenuous situation where the head coach was seeking other employment. Nor does the fact that Moore did not apply for certain positions mentioned by defendant indicate a failure to mitigate. *Compare Buchholz v. Symons Mfg. Co.*, 445 F. Supp. 706 (E.D. Wis. 1978) (62-year-old salesman, who was discharged in violation of ADEA was not required to relocate for three years of employment until planned retirement as a reasonable effort to mitigate damages). Moore is presently sixty-six years old. The options available to him are not as great as those available to someone younger. Moore has demonstrated his willingness to work, but, the chances of finding "comparable work" as defined by the Seventh Circuit, *supra*, are slim. It is this Court's opinion that Moore used reasonable diligence in attempting to obtain employment.

* * *

3. Summary
The purpose of front pay under the Age Discrimination in Employment Act is to ensure that a person who has been discriminated against on the basis of age is made whole, not to guarantee every claimant who cannot mitigate damages by finding comparable work an annuity to age 70. *Anastasio v. Schering Corp.*, 838 F.2d 701 (3d Cir. 1988). Furthermore, the risk of non-continuity of future employment in a "volatile" must be considered in determining an award of front pay, *Price v. Marshall Erdman & Assoc., Inc.*, 966 F.2d 320, 327 (7th Cir. 1992); 901 F. Supp. 1403, 1408, and the Court has considered this fact.

Defendant's argument that front pay is too speculative when the plaintiff's profession has a high turnover rate (Def.'s Mem. at 12) does not preclude a front-pay award. *See Century Broadcasting*, 957 F.2d 1446 (front pay improperly denied on grounds employment in industry was tenuous). In this case, such an award is not "highly speculative." The Court has solid evidence concerning Moore's annual salary and the number of years he hoped to continue his employment. While Moore asserts that five years front pay is warranted, this Court disagrees. The evidence presented at trial establishes that Moore expressed a desire to work two more years and then retire. There was no guarantee that Davie would remain at Notre Dame longer than his current contract or that Moore would indefinitely remain in Davie's employ. The evidence also suggests that Moore and Davie had philosophical differences which may have lead to a parting of the ways. With all evidence considered, the Court finds an award of two years front pay sufficient. The front pay is calculated as follows:

Had Moore remained at Notre Dame his total 1998 salary would have been $84,388.84. Subtracted from this amount is Moore's annual salary from his present employment. Moore testified that he currently earns $1,600 for his services as assistant football coach at Cathedral Preparatory School, $15,000 for his work with the Baltimore Ravens, and $30,000 from his work with Tollgrade Communications. His total current yearly earning amount is therefore $46,600. The difference between Moore's Notre Dame salary and his current salary is $37,788.84 per year. This amount is multiplied by a period of two years and yields a total of $75,577.68. Because the Court is not including an additional amount for lost benefits and is not factoring in any increase for the second year, no discounting of the front pay award is warranted. *See Stratton v. Dep't for the Aging for City of New York*, 132 F.3d 869, 882 (2d Cir. 1997); *see e.g. Gusman v. Unisys corp.*, 986 F.2d 1146, 1147-48 (7th Cir. 1993). Thus, the total front pay award equals $75,577.68 plus post judgment interest.

* * *

CONCLUSION

For the preceding reasons it is hereby ordered that Plaintiff's Motion for Reinstatement is DENIED. Plaintiff's Motion for Award of Front Pay is GRANTED "in part as modified herein". Plaintiff is awarded front pay in the amount of $75,577.68 plus post-judgment interest.

It is further ordered that Plaintiff's Motion for Costs and Fees is GRANTED. Plaintiff is awarded costs in the total amount of $9,672.45. Plaintiff is also awarded attorney fees and expenses in the total amount of $394,865.74.

Finally, pursuant to jury verdict, the Plaintiff is awarded $42,935.28 in back pay and an additional $42,935.28 in liquidated damages.

IT IS SO ORDERED.

CASES ON THE SUPPLEMENTAL CD

Dreith v. National Football League, 777 F. Supp, 832 (D. Colo. 1991). This case examines whether the NFL violated the Age Discrimination in Employment Act.

Shreve v. Cornell University, No. 84-CV-918, 1988 U.S. Dist. LEXIS 3109 (N.D.N.Y. 1988). This case examines whether the university's decision to not hire, retain as an assistant coach, or appoint as Assistant Director of Admissions was predicated on his age.

Smith v. City of Jackson, Mississippi, 125 S. Ct. 1536 (2005). This case examines some of the factors used by the Courts to determine if an individual was discriminated based on age.

QUESTIONS YOU SHOULD BE ABLE TO ANSWER

1. What sports-related situations are age discrimination cases likely to arise?

2. Is the ADEA a likely avenue of relief for professional athletes who are banned from participating in their sport because of their age? Give reasons to support your position.

3. What must an aggrieved plaintiff do under the ADEA before filing a federal law suit?

4. Defined and describe some of the main defenses that can be made in ADEA claims.

5. In *Moore v. The University of Notre Dame*, what was meant by "front pay?" Did the court award the plaintiff front pay in this case?

REFERENCES

Cases

Clarett v. National Football League, 306 F. Supp. 2d 379(S.D.N.Y. 2004), reversed, 369 F.3d 124 (2nd Cir. 2004), *cert. denied*, 125 S. Ct. 1728 (2005).

Eggleston v. South Bend Community School Corp., 858 F. Supp. 841 (N.D. Ind 1994).

Lane v. Colorado High School Activities Association, No. 96-Z-2143 (Colorado 1996).

Moore v. The University of Notre Dame, 22 F. Supp. 2d 896 (N.D. Ind. 1998).

Legislation

Age Discrimination in Employment Act, 29 U.S.C.A. §§ 621-634.

Age Discrimination Act of 1975, 29 U.S.C.A. §§ 6101-6107.

Websites

Equal Employment Opportunity Commission (EEOC): www.eeoc.gov

U.S. Department of Labor: www.dol.gov

7.16 Title I of the Americans with Disabilities Act

—**Mary A. Hums**
UNIVERSITY OF LOUISVILLE

What do the following athletes have in common: Magic Johnson (basketball), Tamika Catchings, (basketball), Natalie Du Toit (swimming), Oscar Pistorius (track and field), Marla Runyan (track and field), and Casey Martin (golf)? Each has some type of disability. Johnson is HIV-positive. Catchings is hearing impaired. Du Toit is a single below-the-knee amputee. Pistorius is a double below-the-knee amputee. Runyan is visually impaired. Martin has a circulatory disorder. Yet each has had a successful athletic career.

Events such as the Paralympic Games and the athletes with disabilities who compete in them are becoming more visible every day. But what about other people with disabilities who wish to work as sport and recreation managers in some segment of the sport and recreation industry? What barriers do they face and what kind of legal protections do they have against employment discrimination? In addition to addressing facility issues, the Americans with Disabilities Act (ADA) provides guidelines for employers when dealing with employees with disabilities. These guidelines help ensure equal opportunity for people with disabilities by opening up the definition of who is a "qualified individual" to people of all abilities.

FUNDAMENTAL CONCEPTS

The Americans with Disabilities Act of 1990 (ADA) is not limited to facility accessibility issues, but addresses employment issues as well. It is important to remember that the ADA covers the entire scope of the employment process. Title I of the ADA states "[N]o covered entity shall discriminate against a qualified individual with a disability because of the disability of such individual in regard to job application procedures, the hiring, advancement or discharge of employees, employee compensation, job training, and other terms, conditions, and privileges of employment" [42 U.S.C. 12112(a)]. According to Masteralexis and Wong (2008), "The sport industry is people intensive, so sport managers must have a working knowledge of how the law affects human resource management, particularly a basic knowledge of labor and employment laws," and this includes The Americans With Disabilities Act. This section focuses primarily on the question of reasonable accommodation. Before examining the ADA's application to sport organizations, some basic definitions must be established.

Employer

According to Title I, § 12111 [sec. 101] (5)(a) of the ADA, the term *employer* means "a person engaged in an industry affecting commerce who has 15 or more employees for each working day in each of 20 or more calendar weeks in the current or preceding calendar year, and any agent of such person." In *Jones v. Southeast Alabama Baseball Umpires Association* (1994), an umpire who wore a prosthetic leg had his request to work an increased number of varsity high school baseball games denied and proceeded to file an ADA claim. The Umpires' Association filed for summary judgment, claiming it did not fall under ADA coverage because it did not employ umpires for more than twenty weeks. Jones was able to show that because the Association assigned umpires during both the school year and for summer youth games, it actually employed umpires for approximately six months, and therefore the Association's request for summary judgment was denied.

Disability

Under the ADA, the term **disability** means (1) a physical or mental impairment that substantially limits one or more of the major life activities of such individual; (2) a record of such impairment; or (3) being regarded as having such an impairment [§ 12103 (Sec. 3)] (2). Although the ADA does not specifically define "major life activities," the Department of Health and Human Services defines it as "functions such as caring for one's self, performing manual tasks, walking, seeing, hearing, speaking, breathing, learning, and working" [45 C.F.R. 84.3(j)(2)(i)(1985)].

Qualified Individual with a Disability

According to Title I, § 12111 [Sec. 101] (8) of the ADA, a "qualified individual with a disability" means: "an individual who, with or without reasonable accommodation, can perform the essential functions of the employment position that such an individual holds or desires." In order to be qualified, a person must still meet certain prerequisites for the position. For example, a teacher who could not pass the required national teachers' examination could be considered not qualified for a teaching position (*Pandazides v. Virginia Board of Education*, 1992). In *Sawhill v. Medical College of Pennsylvania* (1996), the plaintiff, a licensed clinical pathologist, was told his termination was because he did not fit into his department's future plans, but later discovered his termination was related to his disability (clinical depression). The plaintiff alleged termination based on his disability violated the ADA. The defendant's motion to dismiss was denied. The term "qualified individual with a disability" does "not include any employee or applicant who is currently engaging in illegal use of drugs, when the covered entity acts on the basis of such use" (42 U.S.C. 12112(a)). In *Collings v. Longview Fibre Company* (1995), Collings and seven other employees alleged Longview Fibre wrongfully terminated them for their drug addiction disability in violation of the Americans with Disabilities Act. The employees were discharged because of their drug-related misconduct at work and not because of their alleged substance abuse disability. The regulations accompanying the ADA indicate that employers may discharge or deny employment to people illegally using drugs, and the courts have recognized a distinction between termination of employment because of misconduct and termination because of a disability.

Reasonable Accommodation/Undue Hardship

According to the Job Accommodation Network (n.d., p. 1): In relation to the ADA, reasonable accommodation is any modification or adjustment to a job or the work environment that will enable a qualified applicant or employee with a disability to participate in the application process or to perform essential job functions. Reasonable accommodation also includes adjustments to assure that a qualified individual with a disability has rights and privileges in employment equal to those of employees without disabilities.

A reasonable accommodation means making some modifications in the work environment that allows a person with a disability an equal employment opportunity. These accommodations take place in three aspects of employment (Colker & Milani, 2005):

- To ensure equal opportunity in the employment process;

- To enable a qualified individual with a disability to perform the essential functions of a job;

- To enable an employee with a disability to enjoy equal benefits and privileges of employment (p. 20).

It is good to ask the following questions when considering reasonable accommodations:

1. What limitations is the employee experiencing?

2. How do these limitations affect the employee and the employee's job performance?

3. What specific job tasks are problematic as a result of these limitations?

4. What accommodations are available to reduce or eliminate these problems? Are all possible resources being used to determine possible accommodations?

5. Has the employee with a disability been consulted regarding possible accommodations?

6. Once accommodations are in place, would it be useful to meet with the employee with a disability to evaluate the effectiveness of the accommodations and to determine whether additional accommodations are needed?

7. Do supervisory personnel and employees need training regarding disabilities? (Job Accommodation Network, 2009, p. 6).

To comply with the ADA, employers must make reasonable accommodations for their workers with disabilities. However, employers only need to do so if providing the reasonable accommodation does not result in undue hardship. According to Title I, § 12111 [sec. 101] (9) of the ADA, a "**reasonable accommodation**" may include:

> *Making existing facilities used by employees reasonably accessible to and usable by individuals with disabilities; and Job restructuring, part-time or modified work schedules, reassignment to a vacant position, acquisition or modification of equipment or devices, appropriate adjustment or modifications of examinations, training materials or policies, the provision of qualified readers or interpreters, and other similar accommodations for individuals with disabilities.*

When making reasonable accommodations, employers should consider using the following process (U.S. Department of Labor, 2003):

Step 1. Decide if the employee with a disability is qualified to perform the essential functions of the job with or without an accommodation.

Step 2. Identify the employee's workplace accommodation needs.

Step 3. Select and provide the accommodation that is most appropriate for the employee and employer.

Step 4. Check results by monitoring and evaluating the effectiveness of the accommodation

Step 5. Provide follow-up, if needed.

According to Title I, § 12111 [sec. 101] (10)(a) of the ADA, an **undue hardship** is "an action requiring significant difficulty or expense, when considered in light of the factors set forth in subparagraph (b)":

> *(b) In determining whether an accommodation would impose an undue hardship on a covered entity, factors to be considered include:*
>
> *(i) the nature and cost of the accommodation needed under this Act;*
>
> *(ii) the overall financial resources of the facility or facilities involved in the provision of reasonable accommodation; the number of persons employed at such a facility; the effect on expenses and resources, or the impact otherwise of such accommodation upon the operation of the facility;*
>
> *(iii) the overall financial resources of the covered entity; the overall size of the business of the covered entity with respect to the number of its employees; the number, type and location of its facilities; and*
>
> *(iv) the type of operation or operations of the covered entity, including the composition, structure, and functions of the workforce of such entity; the geographic separateness, administrative, or fiscal relationship of the facility or facilities in question to the covered entity.*

The courts have interpreted the meaning of reasonable accommodation and undue hardship differently in different cases (Churchill, 1995). Some reasonable accommodations include working at home for an employee who experiences pain while commuting (*Sargent v. Litton Systems*, 1994); taking a leave of absence for alcoholism treatment (*Schmidt v. Safeway*, 1994); eliminating heavy lifting and strenuous work (*Henchey v. Town of North Greenbush*, 1993); allowing a police officer to carry food, glucose, and an insulin injection kit (*Bombrys v. City of Toledo*, 1993); and transferring an employee to a city where better medical care was available (*Buckingham v. United States*, 1993).

There are instances, however, when the courts have indicated that the requested accommodations were unreasonable or would have resulted in undue hardship. Reasonable accommodation did not require allowing an employee who has unpredictable violent outbursts to remain in the workplace (*Mazzarella v. U.S. Postal Service*, 1993), accommodating frequent or unpredictable absences (*Jackson v. Veteran's Administration*, 1994), or assigning limited tasks that substantially reduce an employee's contribution to the company (*Russell v. Southeastern Pennsylvania Transportation Authority*, 1993).

Accommodations do not have to be expensive according to the Job Accommodation Network, a service of the Office of Disability Employment Policy of the U.S. Labor Department. When examining the average cost of workplace accommodations made between October 1992 and August 1999, 20 percent were cost-free, 51 percent cost $500 or less, 11 percent cost between $501 and $1000, 6 percent cost between $1001 and $2000, 8 percent cost between $2001 and $5000, and 4 percent cost more than $5000 (Job Accommodation Network, 1999). Some examples of accommodations and their cost are:

- A timer with an indicator light allowed a medical technician who was deaf to perform laboratory tests. Cost $27.00;

- A groundskeeper who had limited use of one arm was provided a detachable extension arm for a rake. This enabled him to grasp the handle on the extension with the impaired hand and control the rake with the functional arm. Cost $20.00;

- A desk layout was changed from the right to left side to enable a data entry operator who is visually impaired to perform her job. Cost $0;

- A blind receptionist was provided a light probe that allowed her to determine which lines on the switchboard were ringing, on hold, or in use. (A light-probe gives an audible signal when held over an illuminated source.) Cost $50.00 to $100.00;

- A person who had use of only one hand, working in a food service position could perform all tasks except opening cans. She was provided with a one-handed can opener. Cost $35.00 (Job Accommodations Network, 2006, Acquisition or Modification section, ¶ 12)

Providing reasonable accommodations for employees need not be excessively expensive or complicated. Working off EEOC guidance, here are examples of reasonable accommodations:

- Making existing facilities accessible

- Job restructuring

- Reassignment to a vacant position

- Part-time or modified schedules

- Acquiring or modifying equipment

- Changing the physical layout of the work area

- Removing requirements to stand when a job is performed

- Changing tests, training materials, or policies

- Providing readers or interpreters

On the other hand, these are examples of what EEOC says it may view as an unreasonable accommodation:

- Eliminating an essential job function

- Lowering production standards (after reasonable accommodations have been instituted)

- Having to provide personal-use items for daily activities (prosthetics, wheelchairs, hearing aids, etc.)

- Arrangements that conflict with the company's seniority system, regardless of whether it is a product of collective bargaining or simply of management decision (Schleifer, 2007, p. 1).

According to the Job Accommodation Network (2000), a variety of reasonable accommodations can be made for employees with disabilities. A carpentry supervisor who had no functional hearing was required (as part of his job) to order supplies from various vendors. A text telephone used in conjunction with the local relay service allowed the supervisor to make the necessary orders. A maintenance technician restricted from working in extreme temperatures was accommodated with a modified schedule not requiring her to work outside in these conditions. People with low vision who must access information from a computer screen have a variety of accommodation options available. Those who benefit from larger type might find screen magnification software helpful. The creative use of scheduling may be helpful in maximizing an employee's productivity while accommodating potential problems with fatigue related to an illness such as cancer or HIV. The use of flexible scheduling, longer rest breaks, frequent short breaks, part-time work, or self-pacing may be helpful. Allowing an employee to work from home may be another alternative to consider.

Americans with Disabilities Act Amendments Act of 2008

In September of 2008, President George W. Bush signed the Americans with Disabilities Act Amendments of 2008. These Amendments went into law on 1 January 2009. According to the Equal Employment Opportunity Commission (2009, ¶3), the Act retains the ADA's basic definition of "disability" as an impairment that substantially limits one or more major life activities, a record of such an impairment, or being regarded as having such an impairment. However, it changes the way that these statutory terms should be interpreted in several ways. Most significantly, the Act:

- Directs EEOC to revise that portion of its regulations defining the term "substantially limits";

- Expands the definition of "major life activities" by including two non-exhaustive lists:

  (1) The first list includes many activities that the EEOC has recognized (e.g., walking) as well as activities that EEOC has not specifically recognized (e.g., reading, bending, and communicating);

  (2) The second list includes major bodily functions (e.g., "functions of the immune system, normal cell growth, digestive, bowel, bladder, neurological, brain, respiratory, circulatory, endocrine, and reproductive functions");

- States that mitigating measures other than "ordinary eyeglasses or contact lenses" shall not be considered in assessing whether an individual has a disability;

- Clarifies that an impairment that is episodic or in remission is a disability if it would substantially limit a major life activity when active;

- Changes the definition of "regarded as" so that it no longer requires a showing that the employer perceived the individual to be substantially limited in a major life activity, and instead says that an applicant or employee is "regarded as" disabled if he or she is subject to an action prohibited by the ADA (e.g., failure to hire or termination) based on an impairment that is not transitory and minor;

- Provides that individuals covered only under the "regarded as" prong are not entitled to reasonable accommodation.

According to Prosser (n.d.), a number of Supreme Court cases in the 1990s and early 2000s weakened the opportunities for people with disabilities to demonstrate they were entitled to protection under the ADA. The Amendments Act has restored the ADA back to its initial intent. "Under the new amendments, effective January 1, 2009, the determination of whether a person has an impairment that substantially limits a major life activity, a "**disability**" in the legal sense under the ADA, must be made, with a few exceptions, ***without regard*** to the beneficial effects of a mitigating action, such as taking medication" (Prosser, n.d., p. 1). This legislation can help both employees and employers. Employees can more readily establish they have a disability, and employers can more clearly determine if one of their employees is disabled.

SIGNIFICANT CASE

This case offers a good example of the ADA in action. It also involves an illness we do not always think of as being a disability, alcoholism. We usually think of disability in terms of a mobility disability or perhaps a hearing or visual impairment.

MADDOX V. UNIVERSITY OF TENNESSEE

United States Court of Appeals for the Sixth Circuit
62 F.3d 843 (1995)

Opinion: Bailey Brown, Circuit Judge.

The plaintiff-appellant, Robert Maddox, a former assistant football coach at the University of Tennessee, brought suit against the school, its Board of Trustees, and its athletic director, Doug Dickey (collectively "UT"), under § 504 of the Rehabilitation Act of 1973, as amended, 29 U.S.C. § 701, et seq., and the Americans with Disabilities Act of 1990 ("ADA"), 42 U.S.C. § 12101, et seq., alleging discriminatory discharge on the basis of his disability, alcoholism. The district court granted UT's motion for summary judgment, concluding that Maddox was not terminated solely by reason of, or because of, his handicap, but rather, because of a well-publicized incident in which Maddox was arrested for driving under the influence of alcohol. Maddox appealed. We AFFIRM.

I. FACTS

On February 17, 1992, Doug Dickey, acting as UT's athletic director, extended to Maddox an offer of employment as an assistant football coach. The position did not carry tenure and was terminable at will in accordance with the policies of the Personnel Manual. As part of the hiring process, Maddox completed an application. On the line after "Describe any health problems or physical limitations, which . . . would limit your ability to perform the duties of the position for which you are applying," Maddox wrote "None." In response to the question "have you ever been arrested for a criminal offense of any kind?" Maddox replied "No." These responses were not accurate. According to what Maddox alleges in this lawsuit, he suffers from the disability of alcoholism. Also, Maddox was arrested three times before 1992, once for possession of a controlled substance, and twice for driving a motor vehicle under the influence of alcohol. As to the first answer, Maddox claims that it is in fact correct because "it has never affected my coaching ability . . . I never drank on the job." As to the second question, Maddox claims that another university employee, Bill Higdon, advised him not to include the information concerning his prior arrests on the application.

On May 26, 1992, after Maddox began working at UT, a Knoxville police officer arrested Maddox and charged him with driving under the influence of alcohol and public intoxication. According to newspaper reports, the accuracy of which is not contested, Maddox backed his car across a major public road at a high rate of speed, almost striking another vehicle. When stopped by the officer, Maddox was combative, his pants were unzipped, and he refused to take a breathalyzer. He also lied to the arresting officer, stating that he was unemployed. This incident was highly publicized, and UT was obviously embarrassed by the public exposure surrounding the event.

Maddox entered an alcohol rehabilitation program at a UT hospital after his arrest. UT first placed Maddox on paid administrative leave. In June 1992, however, Dickey and then Head Coach Johnny Majors determined that the allegations were accurate and jointly issued a letter notifying Maddox that his employment was being terminated. They testified that termination was necessary because of: (1) the criminal acts and misconduct of Maddox; (2) the bad publicity surrounding the arrest; and (3) the fact that Maddox was no longer qualified, in their minds, for the responsibilities associated with being an assistant coach. Both Dickey and Majors deny that they were aware that Maddox was an alcoholic or that Maddox's alcoholism played any part in the decision to discharge him. Nevertheless, Maddox brought this action alleging that the termination was discriminatory on the basis of his alcoholism in violation of his rights under the Rehabilitation Act and the ADA. UT responded by filing a motion for summary judgment which the district court granted. The court recognized that, under both statutes, a plaintiff must show that he was fired by reason of his disability. In the court's view, summary judgment was appropriate because Maddox could not establish the existence of a genuine issue of material fact with respect to whether he had been fired by reason of his status as an alcoholic rather than by reason of his criminal misconduct. Maddox now appeals.

II. ANALYSIS

1. Standard of Review

Review of a grant of summary judgment is de novo, utilizing the same test used by the district court to determine whether summary judgment is appropriate. A court shall render summary judgment when there is no genuine issue as to any material fact, the moving party is entitled to judgment as a matter of law, and reasonable minds could come to but one conclusion, and that conclusion is adverse to the party against whom the motion is made.

2. Maddox Was Not Terminated Because of His Disability

Maddox raises a number of issues on appeal which he contends show that the district court erred in granting summary judgment to the defendants. Maddox first alleges that the district court erred in analyzing his claim under the Rehabilitation Act. Section 504 of the Act provides, "no otherwise qualified individual with a disability . . . shall, solely by reason of her or his disability, be excluded from the participation in, be denied the benefits of, or be subject to discrimination under any program or activity receiving Federal financial assistance." 29 U.S.C. § 794(a). Thus, in order to establish a violation of the Rehabilitation Act, a plaintiff must show:

(1) The plaintiff is a "handicapped person" under the Act; (2) The plaintiff is "otherwise qualified" for participation in the program; (3) The plaintiff is being excluded from participation in, being denied the benefits of, or being subjected to discrimination under the program solely by reason of his handicap; and (4) The relevant program or activity is receiving Federal financial assistance.

It is not disputed in this case that UT constitutes a program receiving Federal financial assistance under the Act. Likewise, we assume, without deciding, that alcoholics may be "individuals with a disability" for purposes of the Act. . . . Thus, our analysis focuses on whether Maddox is "otherwise qualified" under the Act and whether he was discharged "solely by reason of" his disability. The burden of making these showings rests with Maddox.

In support of its motion for summary judgment, UT contended that both factors weighed in its favor. First, Dickey and Majors contended that they did not even know that Maddox was considered an alcoholic in making both the decision to hire and fire him. Moreover, they contended that Maddox was discharged, not because he was an alcoholic, but because of his criminal conduct and behavior and the significant amount of bad publicity surrounding him and the school. UT alternatively contended that Maddox is nevertheless not "otherwise qualified" to continue in the position of assistant football coach.

The district court granted UT's motion for summary judgment, specifically holding that UT did not discharge Maddox solely by reason of his disability. The court found it beyond dispute that Maddox's discharge resulted from his misconduct rather than his disability of alcoholism. The court noted,

It cannot be denied in this case, Mr. Maddox was charged with . . . [driving while under the influence and public intoxication] which would not be considered socially acceptable by any objective standard. The affidavit testimony of Mr. Dickey and Mr. Majors is clear on the point that it was this specific conduct, not any condition to which it might be related, which provoked the termination of Mr. Maddox's employment.

As a result, the court found it unnecessary to decide the alternative ground of whether Maddox was "otherwise qualified."

Maddox contends that the district court erred in distinguishing between discharge for misconduct and discharge solely by reason of his disability of alcoholism. Maddox claims that he has difficulty operating a motor vehicle while under the influence of alcohol and therefore he characterizes drunk driving as a causally connected manifestation of the disability of alcoholism. Thus, Maddox contends that because alcoholism caused the incident upon which UT claims to have based its decision to discharge him, UT in essence discharged him because of his disability of alcoholism. In support, Maddox relies on *Teahan v. Metro-North Commuter R.R. Co.*, 951 F.2d 511, 516-17 (2d Cir. 1991), cert. denied, 121 L. Ed. 2d 24, 113 S. Ct. 54 (1992), in which the Second Circuit held that a Rehabilitation Act plaintiff can show that he was fired "solely by reason of" his disability, or at least create a genuine issue of material fact, if he can show that he was fired for conduct that is "causally related" to his disability. In *Teahan*, the defendant company discharged the plaintiff because of his excessive absenteeism. The plaintiff responded by claiming that his absenteeism was caused by his alcoholism and therefore protected under the Rehabilitation Act. The district court disagreed and granted summary judgment for the employer because, the court found, Teahan was fired for his absenteeism and not because of his alcoholism. The Second Circuit reversed the district court's grant of summary judgment on appeal, however, rejecting the court's distinction between misconduct (absenteeism), and the disabling condition of alcoholism. The court presumed that Teahan's absenteeism resulted from his alcoholism and held that one's disability should not be distinguished from its consequences in determining whether he was fired "solely by reason" of his disability. *Id.* Thus, Maddox argues that, in the instant case, when UT acted on the basis of the conduct allegedly caused by the alcoholism, it was the same as if UT acted on the basis of alcoholism itself.

We disagree and hold that the district court correctly focused on the distinction between discharging someone for unacceptable misconduct and discharging someone because of the disability. As the district court noted, to hold otherwise, an employer would be forced to accommodate all behavior of an alcoholic which could in any way be related to the alcoholic's use of intoxicating beverages; behavior that would be intolerable if engaged in by a sober employee or, for that matter, an intoxicated but nonalcoholic employee.

Despite Teahan, a number of cases have considered the issue of misconduct as distinct from the status of the disability. In *Taub v. Frank*, 957 F.2d 8 (1st Cir. 1992), the plaintiff Taub, a heroin addict, brought suit against his former employer, the United States Postal Service, alleging discriminatory discharge under the Rehabilitation Act. The Post Office discharged Taub after he was arrested for possession of heroin for distribution. The district court granted the Post Office's motion for summary judgment and Taub appealed. The First Circuit affirmed and held that Taub could not prevail on his Rehabilitation Act claim because his discharge resulted from his misconduct, possession of heroin for distribution, rather than his disability of heroin addiction. The court reasoned that addiction-related criminal conduct is simply too attenuated to extend the Act's protection to Taub.

The conduct/disability distinction was also recognized by the Fourth Circuit in *Little v. F.B.I.*, 1 F.3d 255 (4th Cir. 1993). In *Little*, the F.B.I. discharged the plaintiff, known by his supervisors to be an alcoholic, after an incident in which he was intoxicated on duty. The district court granted summary judgment in favor of the F.B.I. on the basis that the plaintiff was no longer "otherwise qualified" to serve as an F.B.I. agent. The Fourth Circuit affirmed, noting as an additional basis that the plaintiff's employment was not terminated because of his handicap. The court noted, "based on no less authority than common sense, it is clear that an employer subject to the . . . [Rehabilitation] Act must be permitted to terminate its employees on account of egregious misconduct, irrespective of whether the employee is handicapped." *Id.*; see also *Landefeld v. Marion Gen. Hosp., Inc.*, 994 F.2d 1178, 1183 (6th Cir. 1993) (Nelson, J., concurring) ("The plaintiff was clearly suspended because of his intolerable conduct, and not solely because of his mental condition.")

Moreover, language within the respective statutes makes clear that such a distinction is warranted. Section 706(8)(c) of the Rehabilitation Act states:

"Individuals with a disability" does not include any individual who is an alcoholic whose current use of alcohol prevents such individual from performing the duties of the job in question or whose employment, by reason of such current alcohol abuse, would constitute a direct threat to property or the safety of others.

Likewise, the ADA specifically provides that an employer may hold an alcoholic employee to the same performance and behavior standards to which the employer holds other employees "even if any unsatisfactory performance is re-lated to the alcoholism of such employee." 42 U.S.C. § 12114(c)(4). These provisions clearly contemplate distinguishing the issue of misconduct from one's status as an alcoholic.

At bottom, we conclude that the analysis of the district court is more in keeping with the purposes and limitations of the respective Acts, and therefore, we decline to adopt the Second Circuit's reasoning in Teahan. Employers subject to the Rehabilitation Act and ADA must be permitted to take appropriate action with respect to an employee on account of egregious or criminal conduct, regardless of whether the employee is disabled. In the instant case, for example, while alcoholism might compel Maddox to drink, it did not compel him to operate a motor vehicle or engage in the other inappropriate conduct reported. Likewise, suppose an alcoholic becomes intoxicated and sexually assaults a coworker? We believe that it strains logic to conclude that such action could be protected under the Rehabilitation Act or the ADA merely because the actor has been diagnosed as an alcoholic and claims that such action was caused by his disability.

3. Pretext

Maddox alternatively contends that even if UT has successfully disclaimed reliance on his disability in making the employment decision, the district court nevertheless erred in determining that Maddox had produced no evidence that the reasons articulated by UT were a pretext for discrimination. A Rehabilitation Act plaintiff may demonstrate pretext by showing that the asserted reasons had no basis in fact, the reasons did not in fact motivate the discharge, or, if they were factors in the decision, they were jointly insufficient to motivate the discharge.

Maddox first alleges that Dickey and Majors knew that Maddox was an alcoholic. Setting aside for a moment the legal significance of this statement, it is not supported factually in the record.

Maddox also claims that he knew of other coaches in the football program who drank alcohol in public and who were arrested for DUI but who were not discharged. This point is also irrelevant. Whether Maddox had such knowledge is immaterial. There is no evidence in the record establishing that Majors or Dickey had knowledge of the public intoxication of any other coach, or failed to reprimand or terminate any coach who they knew to have engaged in such behavior.

Maddox finally contends that UT's conclusion that he is no longer qualified to be an assistant coach at UT is without merit. Maddox claims that his misconduct did not affect his "coaching" responsibilities because an assistant coach's duties are limited to the practice and playing fields, and do not comprise of serving as a counselor or mentor to the players or serving as a representative of the school. Maddox relies on the fact that none of these functions were explained to him in his formal job description.

We first note that this allegation seems more appropriate for determining whether he was "otherwise qualified" rather than whether he was discharged because of his disability. Nevertheless, Maddox's position is simply unrealistic. It is obvious that as a member of the football coaching staff, Maddox would be representing not only the team but also the university. As in the instant case, UT received full media coverage because of this "embarrassing" incident. The school falls out of favor with the public, and the reputation of the football program suffers. Likewise, to argue that football coaches today, with all the emphasis on the misuse of drugs and alcohol by athletes, are not "role models" and "mentors" simply ignores reality.

The district court's grant of summary judgment in favor of the defendants is AFFIRMED.

CASES ON THE SUPPLEMENTAL CD

McFadden v. Grasmick, 485 F. Supp. 2d 642 (2007). This case examines whether a wheelchair athlete should be allowed to compete with able bodied runners.

PGA Tour v. Martin, 532 U.S. 661 (2001). This case examines whether walking is an essential element in the game of golf.

This is the third case on the supplemental CD to be set after the PGA *Tour v. Martin* text.

Bowers v. The National Collegiate Athletic Association, 475 F.3d 524 (3rd Cir. 2007). This case examines the rights of college athletes under the Americans with Disabilities Act of 1990 (ADA) and the Rehabilitation Act of 1973.

QUESTIONS YOU SHOULD BE ABLE TO ANSWER

1. Define reasonable accommodation.

2. Give two examples of how you could make a reasonable accommodation for:

   a. An Assistant Athletic Director with a hearing impairment

   b. A Director of Marketing who is a single below the knee amputee

3. What is meant by a qualified person with a disability?

4. What criteria must a person meet to be a person with a disability? How has the Americans with Disabilities Act Amendments changed this?

5. Which of the following would be classified as an employer? Why or why not?

   a. A Major League Baseball team

   b. A two-week summer basketball camp

   c. A major metropolitan downtown YMCA

REFERENCES

Cases

Bombrys v. City of Toledo, 849 F. Supp. 1210 (N.D. Ohio 1993).

Buckingham v. United States, 998 F.2d 735 (9th Cir. 1993).

Collings v. Longview Fibre Company, 63 F.3d 828 (1995).

Henchey v. Town of North Greenbush, 831 F. Supp. 960 (N.D. N.Y. 1993).

Jackson v. Veterans' Administration, 22 F.3d 277 (11th Cir. 1994).

Jones v. Southeast Alabama Baseball Umpires Association, 864 F. Supp. 1135 (M.D. Ala. 1994).

Mazzarella v. U.S. Postal Service, 849 F. Supp. 89 (D. Mass. 1993).

Pandazides v. Virginia Board of Education, 804 F. Supp. 794 (1992).

Russell v. Southeastern Pennsylvania Transportation Authority, 2 A.D. Cas. [BNA] 1419 (E.D. Pa. 1993).

Sargent v. Litton Systems, 841 F. Supp. 956 (N.D. Cal. 1994).

Sawhill v. Medical College of Pennsylvania, 1996 U.S. Dist. LEXIS 4097.

Schmidt v. Safeway, 864 F. Supp. 991 (D. Ore. 1994).

Publications

Churchill, S. S. (1995, June). Reasonable accommodations in the workplace: A shared responsibility. *Massachusetts Law Review,* 73–83.

Colker, R., & Milani, A. A. (2005). *The law of disability discrimination handbook.* Newark, NJ: Lexis Nexis.

Equal Employment Opportunity Commission. (2009). Notice concerning the Americans with Disabilities Act Amendments of 2008. Retrieved March 30, 2009 from http://www.eeoc.gov/ada/amendments _notice.html

Hums, M. A. (1994). AIDS in the sport arena: After Magic Johnson, where do we go from here? *Journal of Legal Aspects of Sport, 4*(1), 59–65.

Hums, M. A., & Wolff, E. A. (2006, January). *Inclusion of athletes with disabilities: Connections and collaborations.* Presented at the Annual NAKPEHE Conference, San Diego, CA.

Job Accommodation Network. (1999). *Accommodation benefit/cost analysis.* Retrieved January 3, 2003 from http://www.jan.wvu.edu/media/Stats/BenCosts0799.html

Job Accommodation Network. (2000). *Home page.* Retrieved from http://www.jan.wvu.edu/

Job Accommodation Network. (n.d.). Frequently asked questions. Retrieved March 27, 2009 from http://www.jan.wvu.edu/links/faqs.htm#reas

Job Accommodation Network. (2006). Technical assistance manual: Title I of the ADA. Retrieved February 2, 2006 from http://www.jan.wvu.edu/links/ADAtam1.html#III

Job Accommodation Network. (2009). Occupation and industry series: Accommodating educators with disabilities. Retrieved March 27, 2009 from http://www.jan.wvu.edu/media/educators.pdf

Masteralexis, L. P., & Wong, G. (2008). Legal principles applied to sport management. In L.P. Masteralexis, C. A. Barr, & M. A. Hums, (pp. 80–108). Sudbury, MA: Jones & Bartlett Publishing.

Prosser, A. (n.d.). Americans with Disabilities Act: Big changes in 2009. Retrieved March 30, 2009 from http://fchr.state.fl.us/fchr/resources/commissioners_speak_out/americans_with_disabilities_act_big _changes_in_2009

Schleifer, J. (2009). Finally....a reasonable explanation of ADA reasonable accommodation.... Retrieved March 28, 2009 from http://hrdailyadvisor.blr.com/archive/2007/07/05/ADA_Americans_with _Disabilities_Act_reasonable_accommodation_undue_hardship_definitions.aspx

U.S. Department of Labor. (2003). *Workplace accommodation process.* [Electronic version]. Retrieved January 2, 2003 from http://www.dol.gov/odep/pubs/ek97/process.htm

Legislation

Americans with Disabilities Act of 1990, 42 U.S.C.A. § 12101 et seq. (West, 1993).

Americans with Disabilities Act Amendments of 2008. Public Law 110-325.

7.20 Intellectual Property Law

7.21 Copyright and Patent Law Copyright and Patent

—**Merry Moiseichik**
University of Arkansas

Copyright and patent are both forms of intellectual property. The United States Constitution grants Congress the power to enact laws governing patents and copyrights. Article 1, Section 8 of the United States Constitution states: Congress shall have the power . . . to promote the Progress of Science and useful Arts, by securing for limited Times to Authors and Inventors the exclusive Right to their respective Writings and Discoveries. . . .

Copyright law protects artistic endeavors while patent law safeguards inventions, designs, and ideas. The use and protection of intellectual property is becoming more important to the sport and recreation industry. For example copyright becomes an issue in designs of logos and stadiums, ownership of television and video game rights, and use of music in recreational settings. Since much of recreation and sport involve artistic endeavors, copyright plays a significant role. Patent protects inventions and processes and is important to the scientist who creates better equipment and methods for improving athletic action.

FUNDAMENTAL CONCEPTS

Copyright

The first section of this section will discuss copyright. Congress enacted the United States Copyright Act of 1909 to *protect the work of authors and other creative persons from the unauthorized use of their copyrighted materials and to provide a financial incentive* for artists to produce, thereby increasing the number of creative works available in society. This legislation was completely revised in 1976 to take into account changing technology, and to become more inclusive of the types of medium technology produced. In 1989 the United States became a member of the Berne Convention, where an international copyright treaty was created. This brought new revisions of the Copyright Act in 1990. The act was revised still again in 1994 because of the United States' entrance into the North American Free Trade Agreement and the passing of the Visual Artists Rights Act of 1990, and again in 1999 and 2002 to reflect changing technology and the Internet.

Copyright Protection

The purpose of copyright is to protect those who have put time and energy into some creative project. These creators deserve to reap the financial benefits of their work. The law is economically motivated, designed to protect the rights of those who provide the many creative endeavors we hear and see daily.

A copyright gives the owner of the work the exclusive right to copy, reproduce, distribute, publish, perform, or display the work. There are two fundamental criteria for copyright protection: (1) the work must be original, and (2) it must be in some tangible form that can be reproduced (17 U.S.C. § 102). Registration of a copyright is not required for protection, although no action for infringement can be instituted until the copyright has been registered (17 U.S.C. § 401). The protection exists as soon as the work is fixed in some tangible form, such as on paper, a video tape, a cassette tape, on canvas, and so forth. Copyright protection lasts 70 years beyond the death of the author or for 95 years for anonymous works or works made for hire (17 U.S.C. § 301). The federal government grants registration of a copyright, which provides procedural advantages in enforcing rights under law.

There are eight broad categories of copyright protection, including: (1) literary works; (2) musical works; (3) dramatic works; (4) pantomime and choreographic works; (5) pictorial, graphic, and sculptural works; (6) motion pictures and other audiovisual works; (7) sound recordings; and, (8) architectural works (17 U.S.C. § 102). Computer programs and video games and other technological protection has been added through the courts (*Apple Computer, Inc. v. Franklin Computer*, 1983; *Williams Electionics, Inc. v. Artic International, Inc*, 1982). It is the expression adopted by the programmer that is copyrightable, not the method of programming.

To appreciate what can be copyrighted, it is instructive to consider what cannot be. "In no case does copyright protection for an original work of authorship extend to any idea, procedure, process, system, method of operation, concept, principle, or discovery, regardless of the form in which it is described, explained, illustrated, or embodied in such work" (17 U.S.C. § 102). Government documents and works in the public domain do not have copyright protection either. Works in the public domain include those with expired copyrights and works where copyright has not been requested (17 U.S.C. § 105).

Works that do not hold originality cannot be considered for copyright (17 U.S.C. § 104). This would include standard works such as calendars, height and weight charts, tape measures, and lists of tables (Talab, 1986). This allows freedom to make use of these articles. The outline of a calendar cannot be copyrighted, but the format and the pictures that go with the calendar can be. This allows recreation or sport programs, for example, to use a common calendar and add their own dimensions including pictures, special events, and any additional information specific to their programs. Similarly, no copyright can be held for blank forms that are used to obtain information (17 U.S.C. § 201). Therefore, agencies can use anyone's accident report form or registration form as long as the forms do not include creative authorship but rather, just request information. They are designed to gather information and not to convey it.

While you can copyright the broadcasts, the underlying games cannot be copyrighted. The court in *Motorola*, 105 F.3d at 846, recognized the practical problems which would arise were it to be determined that a sporting event itself was copyrightable. For example: "If the inventor of the T-formation in football had been able to copyright it, the sport might have come to an end instead of prospering. Even where athletic preparation most resembles authorship—figure skating, gymnastics, and, some would uncharitably say, professional wrestling—a performer who conceives and executes a particularly graceful and difficult—or, in the case of wrestling, seemingly painful—acrobatic feat cannot copyright it without impairing the underlying competition in the future."

Works where authorship is small cannot hold a copyright (17 U.S.C. §102). This includes slogans, titles, names, variations, typographic ornamentation, lettering, or coloring. If slogans, titles, names, etc., were copyrighted, there would be a loss of freedom to speak. Such words like "uh huh" would then belong to certain companies like Pepsi, and with those words, Pepsi's right to control how they are used. These short sayings are protected by the trademark laws (see Section 7.22, *Principles of Trademark Law*).

Facts also cannot be copyrighted. Research data are facts. Any raw data collected can be used by anyone. In *Feist Publications v. Rural Telephone Service Co.* (1991), Feist Publications published a telephone book. They had done all the research to put it together. Rural Telephone Service used the Feist book and reorganized it using addresses as the listing. The court found that Feist had published facts. Rural Telephone used the facts, just in a different way. It was not infringement.

Rights of the Copyright Owner

A copyright gives its owner certain rights to the works, including: (1) the right to reproduction; (2) the right to preparation of derivative works including translation from language to language and from one form to another (i.e., from book to movie, from movie to play); (3) the right to public distribution; (4) the public performing rights, which include live renditions that are face to face, on recordings, broadcasts, and retransmissions by cable; (5) the right to the public display, specifically written or art work; and (6) to perform the copyrighted work publicly by means of a digital audio transmission (17 U.S.C. § 106). This section has been strengthened with the Visual Artists Rights Act of 1990 (VARA), which has become section 106A of the Copyright Act (17 U.S.C. § 106A). Among the rights afforded artists by this law is the right to prevent any intentional distortion, mutilation, or other modification of that work. This allows the artist to control the visual art work until his or her death. In *Phillips v. Pembroke Real Estate* (2003), a renowned sculptor brought suit against a manager of a public sculpture park on Boston Harbor. He was seeking preliminary injunction to prevent manager from modifying the park and from altering sculptures that he created specifically for the park. Pembroke, a Fidelity Investments company, leased the land upon which the Park was built from the Massachusetts Port Authority ("Massport"), had to approve changes to the design of the Park. The Boston Redevelopment Authority ("BRA") must also approve changes. The Park must be open to the public free of charge 24 hours a day. According to the *Boston Business Journal,* this is the only privately managed public park in the City of Boston. Permission had been granted to build an office building and a convention center in the park and move the sculpture to a different location. The artist stated that his design was created with the environment in mind and it would negatively affect the art if it were moved. An expert testified that if Phillips' sculpture was moved, it would impact his reputation as an artist because he would no longer have an important piece in an important location: his art will be "in exile." The court granted preliminary injunction even though delay on the project would cost $120,000.

Section 113 provides the rights of the owner of a building in which works of art are a part of a building. If the owner wants to remove the work, she must notify the artist. The artist may reject removal. The artist should keep their name and address registered with the copyright office for this purpose. For this reason, managers who wish to include artwork and murals in their buildings and parks should maintain copyright ownership as part of their contract.

Copyright Ownership

Who is the owner of the copyright? It vests initially in the author or creator of the work. However, in the case of a "work made for hire," it is the employer or person for whom the work was prepared that is the owner of the copyright. Section 201(b) of the Copyright Act provides that "the employer or other person for whom the work was prepared is considered the author for the purpose of this title, and, unless the parties have expressly agreed otherwise in a written instrument signed by them, owns all of the rights comprised in the copyright."

In *Baltimore Orioles v. Major League Baseball Players* (1986), the players claimed part ownership of the copyright to televised games since they were the ones being filmed and retained ownership in their own likenesses. The Seventh Circuit, however, found for the Orioles, based on the fact that the players were working for the club at the time of the game and the filming, and, therefore, the Orioles owned the copyright, not the players. This was likened to actors and actresses who do not own the copyright of the films in which they appear unless specifically stated in the contract. Even if the contract gives an actor a percentage of the film's profit, it does not mean that he or she owns a percentage of the copyright unless it is specifically stated.

Fair Use

An important section of the law for those who are not creators, but are users of copyrighted works, is the fair use section (17 U.S.C. § 107). This section was passed to strike a balance between the copyright monopoly and the greater interest of society (Hohensee, 1988). There are four factors to ascertain fair use: (1) the purpose and the character of use, whether it is for commercial or for nonprofit educational purposes; (2) the nature of the copyrighted work; (3) the amount and substantiality of the material used in comparison with the whole; and (4) the effect of the use on the potential market or value of the work (17 U.S.C. § 107).

Fair use allows for "criticism, comment, news reporting, teaching, scholarship or research." For example, Ted Giannoulas, the creator of the sports mascot—"the Chicken," was sued by the owners of Barney, a purple dinosaur in a children's TV show. The Chicken, as part of a pregame show, beat up on Barney. Barney owners said they did not approve of their character being used in that manner and it negatively affected the small children who loved Barney. The court ruled it was a parody and thus fair use (*Lyons Partnership, L.P. v. Giannoulas,* 1999).

A primary motivator for the passage of the fair use section was the use of copyrighted works for educational purposes. The educational fair use test is based on three rules: (1) brevity (using small parts of the whole); (2)

spontaneity (if there is time to request permission, it should be requested); and, (3) cumulative effect (how will it affect the creator?). The copying is not allowed when it replaces a book that would be purchased. Consumables are not allowed to be copied under any circumstances. Therefore coloring books, consumable material, cannot be copied for use in after school or day care programs.

In *Basic Books, Inc. v. Kinkos Graphics* (1991), the court considered whether the production of professors' course packets, which were a compilation of articles directly relating to one course, were a violation of copyright or educational fair use. The court found that Kinkos had violated the copyright laws in creating the packets. Kinkos' motivation was not educational, but to make a profit from the works of others, and, therefore, the educational fair use exemption did not apply. Kinkos advertised and did its best to get the business of professors.

Music and Performance

Musical scores that are performed by band and chorus should be purchased. However, there are guidelines in § 110 of the Copyright Act, similar to the educational fair use guidelines, to allow for music and dramatic performances by nonprofit agencies, religious institutions, or for educational uses. Performance of music is legal without paying royalties if it is not for profit and all money goes to charity. Music and dramatic works can be performed in classrooms, for religious assembly, and for transmission to the public, without any purpose of direct or indirect commercial advantage and without payment of any fee or other compensation for the performance to its performers, promoters, or organizers. There can be no direct or indirect admission charged unless the proceeds, after deducting the reasonable costs of producing the performance, are used exclusively for educational, religious, or charitable purposes and not for private financial gain (17 U.S.C. § 110). The 2002 amendments specifically discuss the transmission of these performances. It is not legal to make digital displays of these works unless they are specifically and only for registered students. They also cannot be transmitted or stored where public has access to them for any length of time other than what is absolutely necessary.

Section 110 does not include colleges and universities playing their pep music at games or for fraternities and sororities using music at parties, unless the function is to raise money for charity. Licenses must be secured from performance rights agencies. This exemption also does not include music played at conferences even though one may define that as an educational setting they charge an admission fee. For conferences, conventions, or workshops, special licenses must be purchased to allow the playing of background music, music at socials, or live performances. This license is purchased by the convention center or the conference directors and is negotiated based on the size of the conference, the use of the music, and number of conferees.

Public Performance Restrictions

According to the Copyright Act (17 U.S.C. § 101), a performance or display is public if it is open to the public or at any place where a substantial number of persons outside a normal circle of a family and its social acquaintances are gathered. This includes any place where people are not specifically invited and there is use of music or video displays. For public performances, a license must be obtained. This even includes dormitory public areas. Both in 1987 and in 1990 there was an attempt to seek an exemption for nursing homes and long-term care medical facilities so that these facilities could show movies without a license in their general living areas. The lobbying by the motion picture industry was so strong, however, that this exemption did not pass. Nursing homes, who often use videos as a leisure activity for their residents, must obtain a license to show them in their public areas even though they do not charge a fee for viewing and the people who would be watching live in the facility. Thus the same would be true for college dormitories, camps, day cares, and so on. In order to show a video in a public setting, one must have a license.

Music is also affected by public performance restrictions. Playing compact discs (CD), for example, in a public place is prohibited without a license. If a manager of a fitness center, for example, wants to play background music in the center and people paid to be members, the manager must obtain a license. If that same center has aerobic instructors who play CD's during exercises, the center must have a license, especially if there is profit. It is not the responsibility of the aerobics instructor to get the license, it is the responsibility of the center in which the class is being given. It is not particularly expensive and the amount is decided by the size of the facility, the amount of use, and the number of participants in the program. Cases involving copyright infringement for public performances of music include: *Tallyrand Music, Inc. v. Frank Stenko* (1990), involving background music played in a skating rink; *Broadcast Music, Inc. v. Melody Fair Enterprises, Inc.* (1990), involving a club where musical compositions were performed by live artists; *Tallyrand Music Inc. v. Charlie Club Inc.* (1990), where the health club's license covered music played in their restaurant and bar, but not for aerobics classes; and *Broadcast Music Inc. v. Blueberry Hill Family Restaurants, Inc.* (1995), where a restaurant chain operated jukeboxes that patrons played for free. Each of these defendants was found guilty of playing copyrighted music without a license and were fined significantly for the act.

Television and Radio Broadcasting

The Copyright Act protects any original works of authorship fixed in any tangible medium, including motion pictures and other audiovisual works. The broadcast, by radio or television, of a live sporting event is eligible for protection. The Act has become a significant source of protection for the major professional sport leagues to combat the unauthorized interception of commercial-free feeds of broadcast signals. For live transmissions "the first fixation of which is made simultaneously with its transmission, the copyright owner may, either before or after such fixation takes place, institute an action for infringement . . . if . . . the copyright owner (1) serves notice upon the infringer not less than 48 hours before such fixation . . . and (2) makes registration for the work . . . within three months after its first transmission" 17 U.S.C. § 411(b). In *Live Nation Motor Sports, Inc. v. Davis*, (2007) Davis was infringing on Live Nation Motor Sports, Inc. through his website by sending live audio feeds of motor cross events that were being produced live by Live Nation Motor Sports, Inc. for TV. Even though the transmission was live and therefore not yet fixed, it is copyrighted at the time of transmission as long as the formalities are followed.

A second issue has focused on sport bars where sport fans gather to watch satellite transmission of games that could only be seen through the use of satellite dish antenna systems. The professional sport leagues contend that the piracy of distant network satellite signals of games both devalues advertising revenues when patrons at sport bars watch contests commercial-free, and affects local ticket sales when a blacked-out game is broadcast in a local sport bar.

In 1976, Congress enacted 17 U.S.C. § 110(5), the "home-use" exemption, to limit the exclusive rights granted copyright owners under 17 U.S.C. § 106(4) to perform and publicly display their copyrighted work. Section 110(5) bars a finding of infringement when the transmission is received by equipment similar to the type "commonly used in private homes." In 1998, the "Fairness in Music Licensing Act of 1998" (17 U.S.C. § 110-5B) was incorporated into the Copyright Act to provide business establishments with the right to use radio, television, and cable transmission on a limited basis without infringement. The business establishments cannot charge for the programming and cannot provide retransmissions. Thus, the clause exempts commercial businesses that use standard radio or television equipment in their establishments to provide entertainment as long as they are not transmitting cable or some other pay-per-view transmission. Sport bars have attempted to use the "home-use" exemption to exempt their interception of satellite feeds by contending that satellite dish equipment is commonly used in private homes. Such arguments have been unsuccessful. Thus, sport bars or other public establishments desiring to transmit cable or pay-per-view broadcasts must have a license (*Cablevision Systems Corp. v. 45 Midland Enterprises, Inc.*, 1994; *National Football League v. McBee & Bruno's, Inc.*, 1986; *National Football League v. Play by Play Sports Bar, et al.*, 1995). The bars pay a premium for the transmission, as it is considered commercial use.

This "home-use" exemption clause does not include rebroadcasting. It is a copyright infringement to tape a copyrighted program and exhibit it at another time in a public setting without explicit permission from the producers. The broadcasting rights of time and place are reserved for the broadcasters. On the other hand, it is legal to tape a show for later viewing if it is done in the confines of a home with friends and family. This is considered time shifting and has been held legal in nonpublic settings (*Sony Corp. v. Universal Studios*, 1984). In *Sony Corp.*, Universal Studios attempted to enjoin the production of home-use videotape recorders, under the theory that the machines could be used for the unauthorized copying of movies owned by Universal Studios, to be viewed at a later time. In finding for Sony, the court found that in-home time shifting would not cause any actual harm to Universal Studios. The result in *Sony*, however, did not affect the right to time shift in public places, which remains a copyright violation. A sport bar, for example, cannot tape a game for later viewing in their establishment without infringing on copyright.

Internet

Internet is a major issue in copyright infringement as it has made pirating music etc. easily available to the general public. Starting with Napster, which was a website that allowed the downloading of music from the Internet without charge, there is an ongoing battle with copyright protection. Like *Sony Corp. v. Universal Studios,* Napster was providing the mechanism by which people could share files across the Internet. Although Napster was vicariously libel for copyright infringement as it provided the method, should have known copyright infringement was occurring, and was in direct supervision of the website. The court shut down the site (*A & M Records, Inc. v. Napster, Inc.*, 2002).

File sharing did not stop as more sophisticated software was developed. Direct file-to-file sharing occurs regularly. However, *Digital Millenium Copyright Act* of 1998 17 U.S.C. § 512a protects the Internet service providers as long as they do not get directly involved in the file sharing.

There are new hearings before Congress because of what the Digital Millenium Copyright Act did. Apparently to secure a compromise from the music industry to get the law passed, agreement was made that radio stations would pay the producers of the record companies when they played their music and not have to pay the artists as well. It was believed that the artists would earn their money by increased sales of records and tours because they will become known through their radio performances. However, the artists now say that the downloading of music from the Internet has lowered the sale of records and therefore a musician can never retire. They can only make their money touring to survive. The musicians are asking that the radio stations also pay the artists when playing their songs.

Such an interplay of the legislative system is why laws must be reviewed constantly. Unfortunately, we cannot see how a law will affect the various groups especially in the light of changing technology.

Patent

The U.S. Patent Law was passed in 1870 to "promote the progress of science and the useful arts." This law, too, changes with technology and court holdings that have broadened its scope to "anything under the sun that is made by man." (*Diamond v. Chakrabarty et al.*, 1980 at 150). Patent was revised the last time in 2002, which focused on changes in technology. While copyright's purpose is to advance creativity and the arts, patent law is designed to advance science and invention. To that end, a person can obtain a patent for "any new and useful process, machine, manufacture, or composition of matter, or any new and useful improvement" (35 U.S.C. § 101). A patent is not allowed for laws of nature, natural phenomena, and abstract ideas.

Patents, therefore, can be obtained for new sports equipment that would allow the user to hit harder or further or jump higher. Patents can also be obtained for designs. In sport, the shoe companies patent their new designs for shoes.

The invention must be newly created by the filer and useful for the patent to be granted. The purpose of the patent is to allow the holder of the patent to have a monopoly on the way the invention is used for a period of 20 years (35 U.S.C. § 154). That includes the right to "exclude others from making, using, offering for sale, or selling" the patented invention. This permits the holder to gain benefits encouraging further advancement.

Originally it was thought that patents were for inventions. As the courts have been more lenient in their interpretation of what could be patented there is lots of controversy. As the courts began allowing patents for business methods and mathematical formulas, doors have opened to a wide variety of patents and sport entrepreneurs have taken advantage of the climate. Dale Miller, for example, patented his grip on the golf club for his putt (Kukkonen, 1998). Nolan Ryan has patented a pitch (Smith, 1999). This trend creates questions as to what else will be patented in the near future. For example, if someone created a new football formation or a new method for moving a soccer ball, could this process be patented? With a patent, the creator would have complete control over who could use it, and when. Imagine if the Fosbury Flop in high jump had been patented (Wilson, 1997).

The problem with patenting sport moves is that it would be extremely difficult to enforce. Mr. Miller's grip can only be used by him and others who pay for the right. But, unless he is right there, how will he know a recreation golfer is using it? Such enforcement is more difficult than other, more tangible objects (Kukkonen, 1998). The second problem with such patents is that they will affect competition. When a player invents a new move that obviously creates advantage, the playing field is no longer level (Smith, 1999). Loren Weber, (2000) sees this to be especially inviting to those in extreme sports. Since the competitors are individuals using specially named moves, the moves would be easy to patent. Weber says they should be copyrighted and put on video to put it into tangible form.

The process issues for patent do not seem to have created problems. Patent cases in sports stem from various improvements in sports equipment and another company trying to use it without paying for the rights.

The following case examines the issues surrounding who owns the rights to copyright, the players who provide the entertainment or the owners and producers. The case explains how a game can be a copyrighted work and what constitutes copyright.

BALTIMORE ORIOLES, INC. V. M.L.B. PLAYERS ASSOCIATION
United States Court of Appeals for the Seventh Circuit
805 F.2d 663 (1986)

The primary issue involved in this appeal is whether major league baseball clubs own exclusive rights to the televised performances of major league baseball players during major league baseball games. For the reasons stated below, we will affirm in part, vacate in part, and remand for further proceedings.

This appeal arises out of a long-standing dispute between the Major League Baseball Clubs ("Clubs") and the Major League Baseball Players Association ("Players") regarding the ownership of the broadcast rights to the Players' performances during major league baseball games. After decades of negotiation concerning the allocation of revenues from telecasts of the games, the Players in May of 1982 sent letters to the Clubs, and to television and cable companies with which the Clubs had contracted, asserting that the telecasts were being made without the Players' consent and that they misappropriated the Players' property rights in their performances. The mailing of these letters led the parties to move their dispute from the bargaining table to the courtroom.

On June 14, 1982, the Clubs filed an action (entitled *Baltimore Orioles, Inc. v. Major League Baseball Players Association*, No. 82 C 3710) in the United States District Court for the Northern District of Illinois, in which they sought a declaratory judgment that the Clubs possessed an exclusive right to broadcast the games and owned exclusive rights to the telecasts.

* * *

The Clubs sought a declaratory judgment "that the telecasts of Major League Baseball games constitute copyrighted 'works made for hire' in which defendant and Major League Baseball players have no rights whatsoever." Baltimore Orioles Complaint, Prayer for Relief para. 1. The district court found that the Clubs, not the Players, owned a copyright in the telecasts as works made for hire and that the Clubs' copyright in the telecasts preempted the Players' rights of publicity in their performances. * * *

Our analysis begins by ascertaining whether the Clubs own a copyright in the telecasts of major league baseball games. In general, copyright in a work "vests initially in the author or authors of the work," 17 U.S.C. § 201(a); however, "in the case of a work made for hire, the employer or other person for whom the work was prepared is considered the author . . . and, unless the parties have expressly agreed otherwise in a written instrument signed by them, owns all of the rights comprised in the copyright." 17 U.S.C. § 201(b). A work made for hire is defined in pertinent part as "a work prepared by an employee within the scope of his or her employment." 17 U.S.C. § 101. Thus, an employer owns a copyright in a work if (1) the work satisfies the generally applicable requirements for copyrightability set forth in 17 U.S.C. § 102(a), (2) the work was prepared by an employee, (3) the work was prepared within the scope of the employee's employment, and (4) the parties have not expressly agreed otherwise in a signed, written instrument.

* * *

The district court concluded that the telecasts were copyrightable works. We agree. Section 102 sets forth three conditions for copyrightability: first, a work must be fixed in tangible form; second, the work must be an original work of authorship; and third, it must come within the subject matter of copyright. See 17 U.S.C. § 102(a). Although there may have been some question at one time as to whether simultaneously recorded live broadcasts were copyrightable, this is no longer the case. Section 101 expressly provides that "[a] work consisting of sounds, images, or both, that are being transmitted, is 'fixed' . . . if a fixation of the work is being made simultaneously with its transmission." Since the telecasts of the games are videotaped at the same time they are broadcast, the telecasts are fixed in tangible form. * * *

"The two fundamental criteria of copyright protection [are] . . . originality and fixation in tangible form." H.R. Rep. No. 1476, 94th Cong., 2d Sess. 51, reprinted in 1976 U.S. Code Cong. & Ad. News 5659, 5664. These requirements have been derived from the Constitution's limited grant of authority to the Congress "to promote the . . . useful Arts, by securing for limited times to Authors . . . the exclusive Right to their . . . Writings." U.S. Const. art. I, § 8, cl. 8; * * *.

Moreover, the telecasts are original works of authorship. The requirement of originality actually subsumes two separate conditions, i.e., the work must possess an independent origin and a minimal amount of creativity. * * * It is obvious that the telecasts are independent creations, rather than reproductions of earlier works.

It is important to distinguish among three separate concepts — originality, creativity, and novelty. A work is original if it is the independent creation of its author. A work is creative if it embodies some modest amount of intellectual labor. A work is novel if it differs from existing works in some relevant respect. For a work to be copyrightable, it must be original and creative, but need not be novel. (Thus, in contrast to patent law, a work that is independently produced by two separate authors may be copyrighted by both.) * * *

As for the telecasts' creativity, courts long have recognized that photographing a person or filming an event involves creative labor. * * * For example, one court held that the Zapruder film of the Kennedy assassination was copyrightable because it embodied many elements of creativity. Among other things, Zapruder selected the kind of camera (movies, not snapshots), the kind of film (color), the kind of lens (telephoto), the area in which the pictures were to be taken, the time they were to be taken, and (after testing several sites) the spot on which the camera would be operated.

Time Inc. v. Bernard Geis Associates, 293 F. Supp. 130, 143 (S.D.N.Y. 1968). The many decisions that must be made during the broadcast of a baseball game concerning camera angles, types of shots, the use of instant replays and split screens, and shot selection similarly supply the creativity required for the copyrightability of the telecasts. * * * ("When a football game is being covered by four television cameras, with a director guiding the activities of the four cameramen and choosing which of their electronic images are sent to the public and in which order, there is little doubt that what the cameramen and the director are doing constitutes 'authorship.'").

The Players argue that their performances are not copyrightable works because they lack sufficient artistic merit. We disagree. Only a modicum of creativity is required for a work to be copyrightable.

* * * Contrary to the Players' contentions, aesthetic merit is not necessary for copyrightability. * * * A recording of a performance generally includes creative contributions by both the director and other individuals responsible for recording the performance and by the performers whose performance is captured. * * * Judged by the above standard, the Players' performances possess the modest creativity required for copyrightability. As Justice Holmes once declared, "if . . . [certain works] command the interest of any public, they have a commercial value — it would be bold to say that they have not an aesthetic and educational value—and the taste of any public is not to be treated with contempt." *Bleistein v. Donaldson Lithographing Co.*, 188 U.S. 239, 252, 47 L. Ed. 460, 23 S. Ct. 298 (1903) (holding circus poster copyrightable). Courts thus should not gainsay the copyrightability of a work possessing great commercial value simply because the work's aesthetic or educational value is not readily apparent to a person trained in the law. That the Players' performances possess great commercial value indicates that the works embody the modicum of creativity required for copyrightability.

Moreover, even if the Players' performances were not sufficiently creative, the Players agree that the cameramen and director contribute creative labor to the telecasts. The work that is the subject of copyright is not merely the Players' performances, but rather the telecast of the Players' performances. The creative contribution of the cameramen and director alone suffices for the telecasts to be copyrightable.

Furthermore, the telecasts are audiovisual works, which under § 102 come within the subject matter of copyright. See 17 U.S.C. § 101 (definition of "audiovisual works"); * * * The telecasts are, therefore, copyrightable works.

8 Section 102(a) provides: Copyright protection subsists . . . in original works of authorship fixed in any tangible medium of expression, now known or later developed, from which they can be perceived, reproduced, or otherwise communicated, either directly or with the aid of a machine or device. Works of authorship include the following categories:

(1) literary works;

(2) musical works, including any accompanying words;

(3) dramatic works, including any accompanying music;

(4) pantomimes and choreographic works;

(5) pictorial, graphic, and sculptural works;

(6) motion pictures and other audiovisual works; and

(7) sound recordings.

17 U.S.C. § 102(a) (emphasis added). "Audiovisual works" are works that consist of a series of related images which are intrinsically intended to be shown by the use of machines or devices such as projectors, viewers, or electronic equipment, together with accompanying sounds, if any, regardless of the nature of the material objects, such as films or tapes, in which the works are embodied. 17 U.S.C. § 101.

b. Employer-employee relationship

With regard to the relationship between the Clubs and the Players, the district court found, and the Players do not dispute, that the Players are employees of their respective Clubs. We add only that this finding is consistent with the broad construction given to the term "employee" by courts applying the "work made for hire" doctrine. * * * (a person acting under another's direction and supervision is an employee for the purpose of the work made for hire doctrine * * *.

c. Scope of employment

The district court further found that the scope of the Players' employment encompassed the performance of major league baseball before "live and remote audiences." See Baltimore Orioles, 1985 Copyright L. Dec. at 19,731. On appeal the Players argue that there exist genuine issues of material fact as to whether the performance of baseball for televised audiences is within the scope of the Players' employment. Nevertheless, the Players failed to raise this contention in timely fashion. In their briefs and argument before the district court, the Players asserted several reasons that telecasts of major league baseball games might not be works made for hire. * * * * However, they never claimed that the performance of baseball before televised audiences was not within the scope of their employment. Indeed, the only issue as to which Players argued that there was a genuine issue of material fact concerned the parties' written agreements respecting ownership of the telecasts' copyright. * * * The Players, therefore, failed to preserve this argument.

Moreover, even on appeal, the Players do not identify any evidence that would create a genuine issue of material fact as to the scope of the Players' employment. In contrast to the Players' perfunctory claim that playing baseball for television audiences is not within the scope of their employment, see Appellant's Brief 29, the Clubs brought forth detailed evidence in support of their motion for summary judgment that the scope of the Players' employment encompassed performances before broadcast audiences. Because of the Players' failure to point to any evidence to the contrary, we would not reverse the district court's finding that the performance of baseball before remote audiences is within the Players' scope of employment even if the Players had preserved their contention. * * *

For example, the Clubs adduced evidence that the Players are acutely aware of the fact that major league baseball games are televised, and that the Players understand that television revenues have a bearing on the level of the salaries that they receive.

d. Written agreements

Because the Players are employees and their performances before broadcast audiences are within the scope of their employment, the telecasts of major league baseball games, which consist of the Players' performances, are works made for hire within the meaning of § 201(b). (the parties can change the statutory presumption concerning the ownership of a copyright in a work made for hire, but cannot vary the work's status as a work made for hire). Thus, in the absence of an agreement to the contrary, the Clubs

are presumed to own all of the rights encompassed in the telecasts of the games. The district court found that there was no written agreement that the Clubs would not own the copyright to the telecasts, and, therefore, that the copyright was owned by the Clubs. * * *

The provisions of the three written agreements on which the Players rely to establish a genuine issue of material fact are paragraph 3(c) of the Uniform Player's Contract, paragraph 7 of the Benefit Plan, and article X of the Basic Agreement. First, the Uniform Player's Contract is the standard form contract between individual players and their respective clubs. In 1947, the first year that the Clubs sold network television rights to major league baseball games, the following language was added to the contract:

The Player agrees that his picture may be taken for still photographs, motion pictures or television at such times as the Club may designate and that all rights in such pictures shall belong to the Club and may be used by the Club for publicity purposes in any manner it desires.

Uniform Player's Contract para. 3(c). The language of paragraph 3(c) has remained materially unchanged over the years.

Second, the Benefit Plan sets forth the particulars of the Players' pension fund. First entered into in 1967, the Benefit Plan arose in large part out of the parties' long-standing dispute as to the allocation of national television revenues to the pension fund. In negotiations over the 1969 Benefit Plan, the Players asserted their long-held claim that broadcasts of baseball games without their consent violated their rights of publicity in their performances. The Clubs, however, maintained that the Players had no rights whatsoever in the telecasts. The parties accordingly agreed to the following compromise provision:

The execution of this Agreement shall not be deemed to change any rights or obligations of the Clubs or the Players with respect to the funding of the Plan (except to the extent set forth in other Paragraphs of this Agreement) or with respect to radio and television, as such rights and obligations existed immediately after the execution of the Agreement Re Major League Baseball Players Benefit Plan of January 1, 1967.

1969 Benefit Plan para. 7. Identical provisions have been incorporated in every Benefit Plan negotiated since 1969.

Third, the Basic Agreement represents the collective bargaining agreement between the Players and the Clubs. The original Basic Agreement entered into in 1968 provided that grievances would be arbitrated by the Commissioner of Baseball. When the parties entered into the 1970 Basic Agreement, they agreed to arbitration of grievances by a tripartite panel, rather than by the Commissioner; however, the Clubs did not agree to submit to impartial arbitration those disputes concerning the right to broadcast major league baseball games. The parties thus agreed that:

Anything in the Grievance Procedure provided for in the Basic Agreement to the contrary notwithstanding, complaints or disputes as to any rights of the Players or the Clubs with respect to the sale or proceeds of sale of radio or television broadcasting rights in any baseball games by any kind or method of transmission, dissemination or reception shall not be subject to said Grievance Procedure. However, nothing herein or in the Grievance Procedure shall alter or abridge the rights of the parties, or any of them, to resort to a court of law for the resolution of such complaint or dispute. 1970 Basic Agreement art. X. This language has been included verbatim in each Basic Agreement entered into since 1970.

The Players contend that these three provisions create a genuine issue of material fact with respect to the parties' agreements concerning the ownership of the copyright to the telecasts. We disagree. Section 201(b) states that the employer owns the copyright in a work made for hire "unless the parties have expressly agreed otherwise in a written instrument signed by them." The requirement that an agreement altering the presumption that an employer owns the copyright in a work made for hire represents a substantial change in the "work made for hire" doctrine. Under prior law, "such an agreement could be either oral or implied." * * *However, § 201(b) requires that an agreement altering the statutory presumption be both written and express. * * *

In this case, the parties have not expressly agreed to rebut the statutory presumption that the Clubs own the copyright in the telecasts. Paragraph 3(c) of the Uniform Player's Contract does not declare that the copyright in the telecasts is owned by the Players, rather than by the Clubs. Instead, it merely grants the Clubs the rights to take the Players' pictures for still photographs, motion pictures, and television and to use the pictures for publicity purposes. A limitation on the Clubs' rights to televise the Players' performances perhaps might be implied by the grant of these particular rights; however, even if such an implied limitation were plausible, paragraph 3(c) nowhere contains an express statement that the Clubs do not own the copyright in the telecasts of the Players' performances.

The Players rely on the common law maxim of construction expressio unius est exclusio alterius, under which the expression of one right implies the exclusion of another right that is not expressed. This maxim is, however, inapplicable to ascertaining whether the parties have expressly agreed in a signed, written instrument that the Players own the copyright in the telecasts of the games.

Paragraph 7 of the Benefit Plan and Article X of the Basic Agreement similarly do not declare that the Players, rather than the Clubs, own the copyright in the telecasts. The two provisions simply preserved whatever rights in the telecasts that the parties might possess and reserved each party's right to have disputes concerning television rights

be resolved in court, rather than by arbitration. They nowhere state that either the Clubs or the Players own the copyright in the telecasts. These provisions thus do not represent an express agreement that the Players own the copyright in the telecasts. If anything, they reflect the parties' express disagreement as to the copyright's ownership.

The Players point to the absence of a provision expressly granting the Clubs the right to televise the games as support for their assertion that they have "reserved" their rights of publicity in their performances. Nonetheless, there is no need for such an express declaration because under § 201(b) the Clubs are presumed to own the copyright in the works produced by their employees unless the parties expressly agree otherwise in a signed, written instrument.

The Players also argue that these three provisions must be read in light of the agreements' collective bargaining history, and that the circumstances surrounding the agreements cannot be determined without a trial. We disagree. Under § 201(b), an agreement altering the statutory presumption that the employer owns the copyright in a work made for hire must be express. This is to say, the parties' agreement must appear on the face of the signed written instrument. Section 201(b) thus bars the use of parol evidence to imply a provision not found within the four corners of the parties' agreement. * * * Moreover, even if extrinsic evidence were admissible to explain an ambiguity in the parties' agreement, the provisions relied upon by the Players are unambiguous with respect to the ownership of the copyright in the telecasts. Since the contractual terms regarding television rights are clear, it is unnecessary to examine the parties' collective bargaining history to ascertain the meaning of the agreements.

The Players rely on labor law cases concerning the construction of collective bargaining agreements. Such cases, however, have no bearing on the consideration in a copyright case of the parties' agreements concerning the ownership of the copyright in a work made for hire. Congress considered incorporating in § 201(b) the "shop right" doctrine of patent law under which the employer would acquire the right to use the employee's work to the extent needed for the purposes of the employer's regular business, but the employee would retain all other rights so long as he or she refrained from authorizing competing uses. Congress rejected this change because it would create uncertainty as to the ownership of the copyright in a work made for hire. * * * In any event, the collective bargaining history behind the parties' agreements similarly reflects a sharp dispute as to the ownership of the television rights to the games. A fortiori, it cannot establish that the parties agreed that the Players would own the copyright in the televised broadcasts.

The Players further assert that the parties' traditional practice of devoting approximately one-third of the revenues derived from nationally televised broadcasts to the Players' pension fund establishes a genuine issue of material fact as to the ownership of the copyright in these telecasts. We disagree. The allocation of revenues from nationally televised broadcasts is determined by the parties' relative bargaining strength and ability. Depending on the Players' bargaining power, they can negotiate a greater or a lesser share of the national telecast revenues. Nevertheless, there is no relationship between the division of revenues from nationally televised broadcasts and the ownership of rights in those telecasts. For example, a motion picture star might negotiate to receive a certain number of "points" from a film's profits; however, that she shares in the film's profits does not mean that she owns some share of the copyright in the film. (Indeed, the producer most likely holds the copyright in the work.) Just as the ownership of points in a film's profits does not represent a proportionate ownership of the copyright in the film, the Players' receipt in the form of pension contributions of a certain fraction of the revenues from nationally televised broadcasts in no way suggests that they own any part of the copyright in the telecasts.

The Players do not claim that they traditionally have received some share of the revenues from locally televised broadcasts. Therefore, even under the Players' analysis, the division of revenues from national broadcasts does not create a genuine issue of material fact as to the ownership of the copyright in local telecasts. Moreover, the Clubs contest the assertion that they traditionally have devoted to the Players' pension fund approximately one-third of the revenues from nationally televised broadcasts. They argue that since it was first entered into in 1967, the Benefit Plan simply has provided for the Clubs to contribute to the pension plan a flat dollar amount from whatever source of revenue they choose, and never has required the Clubs to contribute any amount, let alone one-third, of the national telecast revenues. Nonetheless, as our subsequent discussion indicates, we need not resolve this dispute because it is not material to the ownership of the copyright in the national telecasts. * * *

We thus conclude that there are no genuine issues of material fact as to the ownership of the copyright in the telecasts, and that the parties did not expressly agree to rebut the statutory presumption that the employer owns the copyright in a work made for hire. We, therefore, hold that the Clubs own the copyright in telecasts of major league baseball games.

* * *

CASES ON THE SUPPLEMENTAL CD

Baltimore Orioles, Inc. v. M.L.B. Players Assoc., 805 F.2d 663 (1986). This case examines who owns the copyright to the game, players or team.

Emi April Music Inc. v. Know Group, LLC, 2006 U.S. Dist. LEXIS 80967. This case examines how a copyright infringement is handled and the kinds of punishments.

Incredible Technologies Inc. v. Virtual Technologies Inc., 400 F.3d 1007 (2005). This case examines what one has to prove to succeed in a copyright infringement case.

Phillips v. Pembroke Real Estate, Inc., 288 F.Supp.2d 89 (2003). This cases evaluates how the Visual Artist Rights Act is handled.

QUESTIONS YOU SHOULD BE ABLE TO ANSWER

1. What is the difference between a copyright and a patent?

2. For what can you get a copyright and what cannot carry a copyright?

3. Explain the difference between public and private and contrast how they are treated differently when playing music or watching videos.

4. What is meant by "fair use," and what rights and privileges does it confer?

5. Many musicians claim that the Internet may be the demise of music as a career as musician can no longer make a living through music. Discuss this statement in relation to the copyright law.

REFERENCES

Cases

A & M Records, Inc. v. Napster, Inc., 284 F.3d. 1091 (C.A. 9, 2002).

Apple Computer, Inc. v. Franklin Computer, Inc., 714 F2d 1240 (3rd. Cir. 1983).

Baltimore Orioles v. Major League Baseball Players, 805 F.2d 663 (7th Cir. 1986).

Basic Books, Inc. v. Kinkos Graphics Corp., 758 F. Supp. 1522 (S.D. N.Y. 1991).

Broadcast Music, Inc. v. Blueberry Hill Family Restaurants, Inc., 899 F. Supp. 474 (N.D. Nev, 1995).

Broadcast Music, Inc. v. Melody Fair Enterprises, Inc., 1990 WL 284743 (W.D. N.Y. 1990).

Cablevision Systems Corp. v. 45 Midland Enterprises, Inc., 858 F. Supp. 42 (S.D. N.Y. 1994).

Diamond v. Chakrabarty, et al., 447 U.S. 303 (1980).

Feist Publications v. Rural Telephone Service Co., 111 S.Ct. 1282 (1991).

In re Aimster Copyright Litigation, N.D. Ill. 2000 (Slip copy) 1-19.

Live Nation Motor Sports, Inc. v. Davis, 81 U.S.P.Q.2d (BNA) 1826 (2007).

Lyons Partnership, L.P. v. Giannoulas, 179 F.3d 384 (5th Cir. 1999).

National Basketball Association and NBA Properties, Inc. v. Motorola, Inc. DBA SportsTrax, 105 F.3d 841 (2nd Cir., 1997).

National Football League v. McBee & Bruno's, Inc., 792 F.2d 726 (8th Cir. 1986).

National Football League v. Play by Play Sports Bar, et al., 1995 WL 753840 (S.D. Tex. 1995).

Phillips v. Pembroke Real Estate, Inc., 288 F. Supp 2d 89 (D. Mass. 2003).

SONY Corp. v. Universal Studios, 104 S. Ct. 774 (1984).

Tallyrand Music Inc. v. Charlie Club Inc., 1990 WL 114561 (N.D. Ill. 1990).

Tallyrand Music Inc. v. Frank Stenko, 1990 WL 169163 (M.D. Pa. 1990).

Williams Electronic, Inc. v. Artic International, Inc., 685 F2d 870 (3rd Cir. 1982).

Publications

Digital Music Interoperability and availability. Hearing before Subcommittee on Courts, The Internet, and Intellectual Property of the Committee of the Judiciary, House of Representatives, 109th Cong., 1 (2005).

Gorman, R. A. (1990). Visual Artists Rights Act of 1990. *Journal of the Copyright Society of the U.S.A.*, 38, 233–241.

Hohenese, J. M. (1988). The Fair Use Doctrine in copyright: A growing concern for judge advocates. *Military Law Review*, 19, 155–197.

Kukkonen, C. A. (1998). Be a good sport and refrain from using my patented putt: Intellectual property protection for sports related movements. *Journal of the Patent and Trademark Office Society*, 80, 808.

Martin, S. M. (1992). Duplication of error. *Journal of Copyright Society of the U.S.A.*, 429, 429–525.

Patent Office Reform. Hearing before the Courts, The Internet, and Intellectual Propertyof the Committee of the Judiciary, House of Representatives, 109th Cong., 1 (2005).

Smith, J. A. (1999). It's your move—No it's not! The application of patent law to sports moves. *University of Colorado Law Review*, 70, 1051.

Spelman, K. C. (1999). Current developments in Copyright Law 1999. *Patents, Copyrights, Trademarks, and Literary Property Course Handbook Series, 567*, 31–113.

Weber, L. (2000). Something in the way she moves: The case for applying copyright protection to sports moves. *Columbia –VLA Journal of Law and the Arts, 23*, 317.

Wilson, D. C. (1997). The legal ramifications of saving face: An integrated analysis of intellectual property and sport. *Villanova Sports and Entertainment Law Journal, 4*, 227.

Yu, P. K. (2004). The escalating copyright wars. *Hofstra Law Review*, 907–957.

Legislation

Copyright Remedy Clarification Act, 104 U.S.C. 2749 (1990).

The 1976 Copyright Act 17 U.S.C. § 101 et seq. (2008).

Patents 35 U.S.C. § 101 et seq. (2008).

Visual Artists Rights Act of 1990, 104 U.S.C. 5128 (1990).

7.22 Principles of Trademark Law

—Paul M. Anderson
NATIONAL SPORTS LAW INSTITUTE OF MARQUETTE UNIVERSITY LAW SCHOOL

One of the most valuable assets a recreation or sport management organization is its name, logo, or some other defining characteristic that the public will recognize when viewing its products or services. These characteristics help promote the organization and help to sell its products and services. Because such identifying marks are so valuable, competitors will often engage in counterfeiting or other behavior that harms the value or association of these characteristics with the original organization. It has been estimated that U.S. companies lose at least $250 billion a year to counterfeiting behavior, whereas the worldwide impact has been estimated to be 5 to 7 percent of global merchandise trade, or the equivalent of $600 billion in lost sales. One of the strongest ways for an organization to protect itself is by seeking trademark protection for the organization's name, logo, or other defining symbols.

FUNDAMENTAL CONCEPTS

The purpose of trademark law is to protect the owner of a mark, and to prevent others from using the mark in a way that will cause consumer confusion. The Federal Trademark Act of 1946, known as the Lanham Act, governs the law of trademarks and their registration, and provides measures to protect a trademark from infringement.

According to the Act, a **trademark** is any word, name, symbol, or device, or any combination thereof, adopted or used by some entity to identify their goods and distinguish them from those manufactured or sold by others. A trademark: (1) identifies a seller's goods and distinguishes them from those sold by others, (2) signifies that goods come from one particular source, (3) indicates that products are of a certain quality, and (4) advertises, promotes and assists in selling the particular goods (McCarthy, 1991).

Trademarks can also be categorized by strength. The strongest marks are **arbitrary or fanciful marks** that bear no direct relationship to the product itself, such as "Adidas" for sports apparel, and "Ping" for golf clubs. These marks are inherently distinctive because they serve as an indicator of the source of the goods rather than describing the goods themselves.

Next are **suggestive marks** that hint at the characteristics of the goods or services, but require some consumer imagination to be understood as descriptive. For instance, although some consumers would understand a "Hot Pocket" to be a warm food item, it takes a bit of imagination to understand that the name stands for a meal wrapped in a flaky crust.

Descriptive marks identify a characteristic or quality of a good or service. For example, if a golf ball that produces a loud screeching sound when hit were named the "Screech Golf Ball," this name could be a descriptive trademark. These marks only receive trademark protection after they obtain "**secondary meaning**." Secondary meaning is obtained through widespread use and public recognition, so that the mark primarily indicates the source of the good or service instead of the good or service itself. For example, collegiate team logos and color schemes, although not in themselves inherently distinctive, obtain secondary meaning once they have been associated with the respective team or university by use in the marketplace.

Generic marks receive no trademark protection because they refer to the name or class of the good or service, and are so common or descriptive that they are not indicative of the source or sponsorship of the good or service. Some companies who originally adopt distinctive names or logos eventually lose their trademark rights in these same names or logos because they become so well known, such as *Kleenex* for facial tissue and *Jell-O* for gelatin.

The Lanham Act also protects service marks and collective marks. A **service mark** is a mark used in the sale of advertising or services to identify and distinguish the services of one entity from the services of others.

Whereas a trademark identifies the source and quality of a product, a service mark identifies the source and quality of an intangible service. The mark "NCAA," as it stands for events and services related to the National Collegiate Athletic Association, is a service mark. A **collective mark** is a trademark or service mark used by the members of a cooperative, association, or other collective organization to indicate membership in that organization. Examples of collective marks in sports include "NBA," "NFL" and "Big East."

Use and Registration

To create ownership rights in a trademark, the trademark owner must be the first to use the mark in trade and make continuous, uninterrupted use thereafter. Once the trademark is used, consumers can rely on it to identify and distinguish the owner's particular goods or services from those of others. Federal registration is not required to establish common law trademark rights, nor is it required to begin using a trademark. However, with registration, a trademark right extends to the use of the mark across the United States. Federal registration also provides constructive notice to others that the registrant owns the trademark and can exclusively use the mark. Every ten years the trademark can be reregistered to provide continuous protection.

Any sport or recreation organization that wants to ensure that its logo, design, or other insignia is not already registered as a trademark can search all federally registered trademarks online at http://tess2.uspto.gov/bin/gate.exe?f=tess&state=srvgcc.1.1. The following is information for the trademark *National Sports Law Institute of Marquette University Law School*

Word Mark	NATIONAL SPORTS LAW INSTITUTE MARQUETTE UNIVERSITY LAW SCHOOL
Goods and Services	IC 041. US 100 101 107. G & S: Educational services; namely, conducting educational and international classes, workshops, meetings and seminars in the field of sports law. FIRST USE: 20000531. FIRST USE IN COMMERCE: 20000531
Mark Drawing Code	(3) DESIGN PLUS WORDS, LETTERS, AND/OR NUMBERS
Design Search Code	05.15.02—Laurel leaves or branches (borders or frames); Wreaths 13.01.02—Blow torch; Propane torches; Torches; Welding torch 26.01.08—Circles having letters or numerals as a border; Circles having punctuation as a border; Letters, numerals or punctuation forming or bordering the perimeter of a circle
Serial Number	76133371
Filing Date	September 22, 2000
Published for Opposition	November 6, 2001
Registration Number	2533880
Registration Date	January 29, 2002
Owner	(REGISTRANT) Marquette University CORPORATION WISCONSIN 615 N. 11th Street Room 015 Milwaukee WISCONSIN 53233
Disclaimer	NO CLAIM IS MADE TO THE EXCLUSIVE RIGHT TO USE "SPORTS LAW INSTITUTE" APART FROM THE MARK AS SHOWN
Type of Mark	SERVICE MARK
Distinctiveness Limitation Statement	as to "NATIONAL SPORTS LAW INSTITUTE"

Infringement

Even if a recreation or sport management organization registers its trademarks, legal disputes may still arise when another organization develops a product that includes similar marks. The first organization can then sue the offending organization for trademark infringement.

To sustain a claim for trademark infringement under Section 1114(a) of the Lanham Act, the owner of the trademark must establish the following:

- First, that she has a protectable property right in the trademark. Use and registration can establish a valid protectable right in a particular trademark;

- Second, that the other party's use of a similar mark is likely to cause confusion, mistake, or deceive consumers as to who is the true source of the mark.

Courts will focus on any number of the following factors when evaluating whether an ordinary consumer will be confused, including:

1. Strength of the mark;

2. Similarity between the marks;

3. Similarity between the products and marketing channels used to sell them;

4. Likelihood that the trademark owner will expand their use of the mark on future products;

5. Evidence of actual confusion;

6. Defendant's "good faith" intent in adopting the mark;

7. Quality of the defendant's product;

8. Sophistication of the consumers.

Ignition Athletic Performance Group, LLC v. Hantz Soccer U.S.A., LLC (2007), involved a challenge by a Cincinnati-based sports training organization called "Ignition" to the use of "Ignition" as the name for a Major Indoor Soccer League team. The plaintiff's mark and logo were federally registered on March 5, 2006. The team name was not announced until April 19, 2006. In analyzing whether the team's use of "Ignition" created a likelihood of confusion, the court looked to many of the factors listed above, including the strength of the senior mark, the relatedness of the goods or services, the similarity of the marks, evidence of actual confusion, the marketing channels used, the likely degree of purchaser care, the intent of the team, and the likelihood of expansion of the product lines. The court found that all of these factors weighed against a likelihood of confusion, and that the public would not think that the Detroit indoor soccer team was affiliated with the Cincinnati area sports training company.

Counterfeiting

Another form of trademark infringement is **counterfeiting**, often known as piracy. Section 1127 of the Lanham Act defines a **counterfeit mark** as "a spurious mark that is identical with, or substantially indistinguishable from, a registered mark." Counterfeiting is an intentional effort to produce products that reproduce a genuine trademark without a license or permission. Organizations that attempt to counterfeit the trademarks of a recreation or sport management organization are subject to severe criminal and civil penalties.

Dilution

Dilution law protects the distinctive quality and selling power of a trademark, even if consumers are not actually confused by a non-trademark owner's use of the mark. The Federal Trademark Dilution Act of 1995 defines **dilution** as the lessening of the capacity of a famous mark to identify and distinguish goods or services, regardless of either the presence or absence of competition between the parties, or a likelihood of confusion, mistake, or deception.

In 1999, the record company Untertainment was about to release a rap album titled *SDE: Sports, Drugs, & Entertainment*. Along with the album, the company constructed a banner in New York City bearing the NBA trademark, while submitting the same advertisement to *Blaze* magazine. In the ad, the NBA player in the mark was holding a gun. After several residents complained to the NBA about their sponsorship of the ads, NBA Properties sued Untertainment, claiming trademark infringement and dilution. The court found that the advertisements would create a negative association with the NBA logo, and therefore, under the tarnishment theory of dilution, Untertainment was forced to stop using the advertisement (*NBA Properties, Inc. v. Untertainment Records LLC*, 1999).

Unfair Competition and False Advertising

Unfair competition refers to a broader area of law than trademark infringement. It can involve any activity where one party attempts to deceive or mislead consumers by using the trademarks of another party to give the consumer the mistaken belief that the products of the infringer are actually the products of the true trademark owner. Unfair competition claims can be brought under Section 1125(1)(a) of the Lanham Act, and provide a cause of action for false designation of origin alleging that an infringer has used the trademark rights of another to deceive consumers as to the affiliation, connection, or association of the infringer with the legitimate trademark owner, and Section 1125(1) (b), which provides a cause of action for false advertising alleging that another party has used commercial advertising or promotions to misrepresent the nature, characteristics, quality, or origin of their products.

Defenses

Often a recreation and sport management organization will fight an infringement claim by arguing that the plaintiff does not have any protectable rights in the trademark, or the defendant's use will not cause consumer confusion. In addition, the organization may claim the trademark has been abandoned, that the doctrine of laches applies, that it is disparaging, that the use was a fair use or parody, or that there has been no infringement due to the presence of certain disclaimers.

Laches

In certain circumstances if trademark owners have neglected to assert their trademark rights in a timely manner, the **doctrine of laches** may limit them from recovery, if such recovery would be prejudicial to the potential infringer. In a case dealing with the University of Pittsburgh, the university was barred from recovery for past infringement when it delayed objecting to the sale of unauthorized clothing and novelty items including its name and mascot for 36 years (*University of Pittsburgh v. Champion Products, Inc.*, 1982). However, the university was granted an injunction to stop future unauthorized use of its marks.

Abandonment

Although trademark rights can be renewed continuously through registration, a trademark owner must still actively use the mark for it to remain valid. Section 1127 of the Lanham Act defines **abandonment** as discontinued use of a trademark with the intent not to resume such use, or when any act or omission of the owner of a mark causes it to become the generic name for the goods in connection with which it is used. When a defendant asserts abandonment as a defense, the claim is that the mark has fallen into the public domain because of the plaintiff's lack of use and intent not to resume use. An abandoned mark may be claimed and used by the public at large.

Hawaii-Pacific registered the marks "Top Dawg" and "Lil Dawg" in the mid-1990s (*Hawaii-Pacific Apparel Group, Inc. v. Cleveland Browns Football Co. LLC*, 2006). In 1999, when Cleveland was awarded a new NFL franchise to replace the franchise that left and became the Baltimore Ravens, NFL Properties attempted to use the mark "Dawg Pound" to associate with the new Cleveland Browns franchise. Hawaii-Pacific contested the NFL's use of the mark claiming that it had abandoned the mark by not using it during the time when Cleveland did not have an NFL franchise. The court disagreed, finding that the NFL attempted to protect this mark during this time even though there was no Browns franchise from 1995 to 1999, and that the NFL was the senior user of the mark in the first place.

Fair Use or Parody

Section 1115(b)(4) of the Lanham Act provides that where a trademark is used fairly and in good faith only to describe the goods or services involved, there is no trademark infringement. For example, a television station's use of the term "Boston Marathon" to describe its unlicensed broadcast of the marathon was not found to be trademark infringement, even though another station was exclusively licensed to broadcast the event. The Court found that this use was merely descriptive of the event being broadcast and did not create viewer confusion (*WCVB-TV v. Boston Athletic Association*, 1991).

Courts have also held that parody of a trademark is not infringement. In *Cardtoons, L.C. v. Major League Baseball Players Association* (1996), the court found that parody baseball cards that included caricatures of baseball players along with some commentary did not create confusion regarding the source of the cards.

Disparaging Marks

Trademark protection can also be denied if a mark is shown to be immoral, deceptive, scandalous, or disparaging, under Section 1052(a) of the Lanham Act. In *Harjo, et al. v. Pro-Football, Inc.* (1999), Native Americans petitioned to cancel the trademark registrations for the marks "Washington Redskins" and "Redskins," both owned by Pro-Football, Inc., the owners of the NFL's Washington Redskins franchise. The Patent and Trademark Office initially granted the petition to cancel the marks. The team then sued for summary judgment to avoid the cancellation of the marks. The district court reversed, finding that the plaintiff presented insufficient evidence that the marks were disparaging to Native Americans and that the claim was barred by the doctrine of laches because there was a twenty-five-year delay in bringing the suit (2003).

Disclaimers

A potential trademark infringer may also argue that a conspicuously placed **disclaimer** alerting consumers that the product or service does not contain certain attributes or features, and that it is not from a certain source organization, absolves it from liability for infringement. In 1994, the University of Arkansas sued Razorback Sports and Physical Therapy Clinic for the use of the university's mark "Razorbacks" (*Board of Trustees of the University of Arkansas v. Professional Therapy Services*, 1995). Although the Clinic put a disclaimer on its stationary disclaiming any connection with the university, the court made clear that this did not help it avoid liability for possible trademark infringement.

Licensing

Merchandisers, manufacturers and sponsors often wish to associate themselves with a recreation or sport management organization. One way to do this is through the grant of a license. A **license** is a permit given by the trademark owner that allows another entity to associate their business and/or product with the name, goodwill, logos, symbols, emblems, and designs of the trademark owner. By paying some form of compensation, the company that receives the license (the licensee) can then use the trademark of the licensor to sell its own products. Problems occur when entities other than the licensee attempt to use the licensor's marks or when the licensor becomes unhappy with the licensee's use of the license.

Professional Sports. Most professional sports leagues have developed profitable licensing programs to capitalize on public demand for sports-related items with team and league affiliations. Each of the four major sports leagues (NFL, NBA, NHL, and MLB) have created separate properties divisions (i.e., NBA Properties) that deal with licensing of league and club trademarks to vendors who manufacture and sell products to consumers. The revenue realized from the sale of such licensed products is then divided among the teams within the league, normally on an equal basis.

The players associations also have formed separate entities that handle licensing issues for athletes (i.e., Players, Inc. for the NFL Players Association and the Players Choice Group Licensing Program for the MLB Players

Association). These entities provide marketing and licensing services to companies interested in using the names and likenesses of current and past players. Revenues are normally distributed among the players that make up the association on a pro rata basis.

Some players have even gone so far as to seek trademark protection for their own name and likeness. Brett Favre, former quarterback of the New York Jets and Green Bay Packer, has trademarked his name and image. Only companies given a license from Favre can use his name or likeness to sell their products.

The NCAA. The National Collegiate Athletic Association (NCAA) protects the intellectual property of the approximately 74 trademarks and service marks associated with the NCAA and its championships. In addition, approximately 300 schools license the use of their names and registered trademarks. Through its current licensing and marketing structure, the NCAA has approximately 45 merchandise licensees, 11 nonretail licensees, three corporate champions, and six corporate partners. These licensees may not use the NCAA's marks in advertising to promote their brands. Instead, the marks can only be used to promote the sale of licensed products. On the other hand, the corporate partners may associate their products and services directly with NCAA marks and championships and promote the corporate partner brand in keeping with strict NCAA guidelines (www.ncaa.org).

The Olympics. The International Olympic Committee (IOC) owns the familiar "Olympic Rings" logo and the right to use the mark all over the world. The U.S. Olympic Committee (USOC) owns the exclusive right to use and license the Olympic marks in the United States and vigorously protects the use of its protected marks and terminology. In addition, unauthorized use of the Olympic name or marks may also be held to violate the Ted Stevens Olympic and Amateur Sports Act.

In a recent case, the USOC sued a manufacturer of toy trucks that had applied for a trademark for its trucks bearing the mark "Pan-American" (*USOC v. Toy Truck Lines*, 2001). Originally, the Patent and Trademark Office allowed the registration even though the USOC had previously registered such marks as "Pan American Games" and "USA Pan Am Team." The appellate court reversed, noting that the Amateur Sports Act provides the USOC with a higher level of protection for its trademarks than other marks; therefore, the USOC prevailed in its opposition of the "Pan-American" mark.

The Internet

In the mid 1990s, as recreation and sport management organizations began to promote their products and services on the Internet, many found that someone else had already registered their preferred domain name. These "cybersquatters" register famous trademarks as domain names in the hopes of selling them to the famous entity for substantial profit.

In the fall of 1999, two measures were established to combat the now-widespread problem of cybersquatting. The Anti-Cybersquatting Consumer Protection Act (ACPA) amended the Lanham Act by creating a specific claim against cybersquatters. The Act outlawed the act of registering, with the bad-faith intent to profit, a domain name that is confusingly similar to a registered or unregistered mark or dilutes a famous mark. The Act allows a court to resolve domain name disputes even when the disputed owner of the name cannot be found or cannot be served in the United States.

A case dealing with a claim under the ACPA involved the NCAA, the Illinois High School Association (IHSA), and the domain name "marchmadness.com." The IHSA began using the phrase "March Madness" to refer to its boys' basketball tournaments in the 1940s. The NCAA's first use was in 1982, when CBS broadcaster Brent Musberger used the phrase to describe the NCAA men's basketball tournament. In the early 1990s both the IHSA and the NCAA claimed exclusive trademark rights to the phrase. After going through some initial litigation, the NCAA and IHSA agreed to work together to protect their rights. In 2000, they formed the March Madness Athletic Association (MMAA), and each retained a license to use the phrase in association with their tournaments. After falsely claiming association with the NCAA, Netfire acquired the domain name "marchmadness.com" in 1996. MMAA sued claiming that Netfire was engaging in cybersquatting in violation of the ACPA. Finding that Netfire acted with bad faith to profit from use of the trademarked phrase, and that the domain name was identical with or confusingly similar to the actual trademark, the court upheld the district court determination that Netfire violated the ACPA (*March Madness Athletic Association, LLC v. Netfire Inc.*, 2005).

In addition to the ACPA, trademark owners can submit their dispute to a form of alternative dispute resolution. The Uniform Dispute Resolution Process (UDRP) is administered by the Internet Corporation for Assigned Names and Numbers (ICANN). By using the UDRP, a trademark owner must allege that its mark is "identical or confusingly similar" to the mark used by the cybersquatter who has no legitimate rights or interests in the domain name, and that the cybersquatter registered and used the domain name in bad faith. In addition, a UDRP proceeding does not preclude a lawsuit under the ACPA.

In 2007, the NFL sued Peter Blucher, the owner of BluTech Tickets, who registered approximately fourteen domain names, all containing "www.superbowl," relating to various Super Bowl ticket, tour, and packaging sites for Super Bowls XLI through XLIV (*NFL v. Blucher*, 2007). The NFL owns four trademarks and over 50 foreign trademarks for "SUPER BOWL." Finding that each of the 14 disputed domain names were confusingly similar to the NFL's "SUPER BOWL" marks and that Blucher did not have legitimate interest in the domain names because all of the sites mislead visitors into thinking that there is an affiliation between Blucher and the NFL, the panel ordered that the domain names be transferred to the NFL.

Ambush Marketing

With rights fees for events such as the Super Bowl and Olympic Games costing several millions of dollars, official sponsors of these events want to ensure they are the only company given the exposure associated with the particular event. Still, companies that are not official sponsors want to create some association with these events to sell their products. **Ambush marketing** refers to the efforts of one company to weaken or attack a competitor's official association with a sports organization or event by using advertising and promotional campaigns designed to confuse consumers and to misrepresent the official sponsorship of the event. Recreation and sport management organizations are reluctant to challenge ambush marketing campaigns because there is little case law supporting them because corporations have successfully defended themselves with claims of commercial free speech. In addition, most ambush campaigns are short-lived, and courts support the use of disclaimers allowing ambush companies to make limited use of a registered trademark as long as they avoid creating consumer confusion.

Visa paid $20 million to the IOC for the right to act as the official credit card of the 1992 Olympic Games, and $40 million for worldwide marketing rights to the 1994 and 1996 Games. To counter Visa's advertisement of its wide acceptance at the Olympics, American Express bought substantial advertising time on major networks. Although American Express did not use the Olympic five-ring symbol or the word *Olympic*, it referred generically to "winter fun and games," depicted the French Alps, and stated, "In Spain, you won't need a Visa" in its advertisements. The IOC threatened to sue American Express for ambush marketing, asserting that American Express attempted to create the false impression that it was an Olympic sponsor, but no suit was ever filed.

Regardless of the limited success of ambush marketing claims, sport organizations can minimize the negative affects associated with these tactics by developing a comprehensive antiambush marketing plan. As part of this plan, official sponsors should monitor nonsponsor signage and advertisements to ensure that official event names, marks, and logos are not being used.

The following case illustrates how a court will examine likelihood of consumer confusion in a trademark infringement case. Of special note is the court's examination of the similarity of the marks and products and overlap in the geographical markets. The court discussed survey evidence used to demonstrate consumer confusion. The court also noted that even though the Colts did not use the contested mark, they did not abandon it over the intervening period of time.

INDIANAPOLIS COLTS, INC. V. METROPOLITAN BALTIMORE FOOTBALL CLUB

United States Court of Appeals for the Seventh Circuit
34 F.3d 410 (7th Cir. 1994)

POSNER, *Chief Judge.* The Indianapolis Colts and the National Football League, to which the Colts belong, brought suit for trademark infringement *(15 U.S.C. §§ 1051 et seq.)* against the Canadian Football League's new team in Baltimore, which wants to call itself the "Baltimore CFL Colts." (Four of the Canadian Football League's teams are American.) The plaintiffs obtained a preliminary injunction against the new team's using the name "Colts," or "Baltimore Colts," or "Baltimore CFL Colts," in connection with the playing of professional football, the broadcast of football games, or the sale of merchandise to football fans and other buyers. The ground for the injunction was that consumers of "Baltimore CFL Colts" merchandise are likely to think, mistakenly, that the new Baltimore team is an NFL team related in some fashion to the Indianapolis Colts, formerly the Baltimore Colts. From the order granting the injunction the new team and its owners appeal to us under *28 U.S.C. § 1292(a)(1).* Since the injunction was granted, the new team has played its first two games—without a name.

A bit of history is necessary to frame the dispute. In 1952, the National Football League permitted one of its teams, the Dallas Texans, which was bankrupt, to move to Baltimore, where it was renamed the "Baltimore Colts." Under that name it became one of the most illustrious teams in the history of professional football. In 1984, the team's owner, with the permission of the NFL, moved the team to Indianapolis, and it was renamed the "Indianapolis Colts." The move, sudden and secretive, outraged the citizens of Baltimore. The city instituted litigation in a futile effort to get the team back—even tried, unsuccessfully, to get the team back by condemnation under the city's power of eminent domain—and the Colts brought a countersuit that also failed. *Indianapolis Colts v. Mayor & City Council of Baltimore, 733 F.2d 484, 741 F.2d 954 (1984), 775 F.2d 177 (7th Cir. 1985).*

Nine years later, the Canadian Football League granted a franchise for a Baltimore team. Baltimoreans clamored for

naming the new team the "Baltimore Colts." And so it was named—until the NFL got wind of the name and threatened legal action. The name was then changed to "Baltimore CFL Colts" and publicity launched, merchandise licensed, and other steps taken in preparation for the commencement of play this summer.

* * *

The Baltimore team wanted to call itself the "Baltimore Colts." To improve its litigating posture (we assume), it has consented to insert "CFL" between "Baltimore" and "Colts." A glance at the merchandise in the record explains why this concession to an outraged NFL has been made so readily. On several of the items "CFL" appears in small or blurred letters. And since the Canadian Football League is not well known in the United States—and "CFL" has none of the instant recognition value of "NFL"—the inclusion of the acronym in the team's name might have little impact on potential buyers even if prominently displayed. Those who know football well know that the new "Baltimore Colts" are a new CFL team wholly unrelated to the old Baltimore Colts; know also that the rules of Canadian football are different from those of American football and that teams don't move from the NFL to the CFL as they might from one conference within the NFL to the other. But those who do *not* know these things—and we shall come shortly to the question whether there are many of these football illiterate—will not be warned off by the letters "CFL." The acronym is a red herring, and the real issue is whether the new Baltimore team can appropriate the name "Baltimore Colts." The entire thrust of the defendants' argument is that it can.

They make a tremendous to-do over the fact that the district judge found that the Indianapolis Colts abandoned the trademark "Baltimore Colts" when they moved to Indianapolis. Well, of course; they were no longer playing football under the name "Baltimore Colts," so could not have used the name as the team's trademark; they could have used it on merchandise but chose not to, until 1991 (another story—and not one we need tell). When a mark is abandoned, it returns to the public domain, and is appropriable anew—in principle. In practice, because "subsequent use of [an] abandoned mark may well evoke a continuing association with the prior use, those who make subsequent use may be required to take reasonable precautions to prevent confusion." 2 McCarthy, *supra*, § 17.01 [2], at p. 17-3. This precept is especially important where, as in this case, the former owner of the abandoned mark continues to market the same product or service under a similar name, though we cannot find any previous cases of this kind. No one questions the validity of "Indianapolis Colts" as the trademark of the NFL team that plays out of Indianapolis and was formerly known as the Baltimore Colts. If "Baltimore CFL Colts" is confusingly similar to "Indianapolis Colts" by virtue of the history of the Indianapolis team and the overlapping product and geographical markets served by it and by the new Baltimore team, the latter's use of the abandoned mark would infringe the Indianapolis Colts' new mark. The Colts' abandonment of a mark confusingly similar to their new mark neither broke the continuity of the team in its different locations—it was the same team, merely having a different home base and therefore a different geographical component in its name—nor entitled a third party to pick it up and use it to confuse Colts fans, and other actual or potential consumers of products and services marketed by the Colts or by other National Football League teams, with regard to the identity, sponsorship, or league affiliation of the third party, that is, the new Baltimore team.

* * *

Against this the defendants cite to us with great insistence *Major League Baseball Properties Inc. v. Sed Non Olet Denarius, Ltd.*, 817 F. Supp. 1103, 1128 (S.D.N.Y. 1993), which, over the objection of the Los Angeles Dodgers, allowed a restaurant in Brooklyn to use the name "Brooklyn Dodger" on the ground that "the 'Brooklyn Dodgers' was a non transportable cultural institution separate from the 'Los Angeles Dodgers.'" The defendants in our case argue that the sudden and greatly resented departure of the Baltimore Colts for Indianapolis made the name "Baltimore Colts" available to anyone who would continue the "nontransportable cultural institution" constituted by a football team located in the City of Baltimore. We think this argument very weak, and need not even try to distinguish *Sed Non Olet Denarius* since district court decisions are not authoritative in this or any court of appeals. *Colby v. J.C. Penney Co.*, 811 F.2d 1119, 1124 (7th Cir. 1987). If it were a Supreme Court decision it still would not help the defendants. The "Brooklyn Dodger" was not a baseball team, and there was no risk of confusion. The case might be relevant if the Indianapolis Colts were arguing not confusion but misappropriation: that they own the goodwill associated with the name "Baltimore Colts" and the new Baltimore team is trying to take it from them. Cf. *Quaker Oats Co. v. Mills Co.*, 134 F.2d 429, 432 (7th Cir. 1943).

They did make a claim of misappropriation in the district court, but that court rejected the claim and it has not been renewed on appeal. The only claim in our court is that a significant number of consumers will think the new Baltimore team the successor to, or alter ego of, or even the same team as the Baltimore Colts and therefore the Indianapolis Colts, which is the real successor. No one would think the Brooklyn Dodgers baseball team reincarnated in a restaurant.

* * *

. . . for if everyone *knows* there is no contractual or institutional continuity, no pedigree or line of descent, linking the Baltimore-Indianapolis Colts and the new CFL team that wants to call itself the "Baltimore Colts" (or, grudgingly, the "Baltimore CFL Colts"), then there is no harm, at least no harm for which the Lanham Act provides a remedy, in the new Baltimore team's appropriating the name "Baltimore Colts" to play under and sell merchandise under. If not everyone knows, there is harm. Some people who might otherwise watch the Indianapolis Colts (or some other NFL team, for remember that the NFL, representing all the teams, is a coplaintiff) on television may watch the Baltimore CFL Colts instead, thinking they are the "real" Baltimore Colts, and the NFL will lose revenue. A few (doubtless very few) people who might otherwise buy tickets to an NFL game may buy tickets to a Baltimore CFL Colts game instead. Some people who might otherwise buy merchandise stamped with the name "Indianapolis Colts" or the name of some other NFL team may buy merchandise stamped "Baltimore CFL Colts," thinking it a kin of the NFL's Baltimore Colts in the glory days of Johnny Unitas rather than a newly formed team that plays Canadian football in a Canadian football league. It would be naive to suppose that no consideration of such possibilities occurred to the owners of the new Baltimore team when they were choosing a name, though there is no evidence that it was the dominant or even a major consideration.

Confusion thus is possible, and may even have been desired; but is it likely? There is great variance in consumer competence, and it would be undesirable to impoverish the lexicon of trade names merely to protect the most gullible fringe of the consuming public. The Lanham Act does not cast the net of protection so wide. * * * The legal standard under the Act has been formulated variously, but the various formulations come down to whether it is likely that the challenged mark if permitted to be used by the defendant would cause the plaintiff to lose a substantial number of consumers. Pertinent to this determination is the similarity of the marks and of the parties' products, the knowledge of the average consumer of the product, the overlap in the parties' geographical markets, and the other factors that the cases consider. The aim is to strike a balance between, on the one hand, the interest of the seller of the new product, and of the consuming public, in an arresting, attractive, and informative name that will enable the new product to compete effectively against existing ones, and, on the other hand, the interest of existing sellers, and again of the consuming public, in consumers' being able to know exactly what they are buying without having to incur substantial costs of investigation or inquiry.

To help judges strike the balance, the parties to trademark disputes frequently as here hire professionals in marketing or applied statistics to conduct surveys of consumers. * * *

Both parties presented studies. The defendants' was prepared by Michael Rappeport and is summarized in a perfunctory affidavit by Dr. Rappeport to which the district judge gave little weight. That was a kindness. The heart of Rappeport's study was a survey that consisted of three loaded questions asked in one Baltimore mall.

* * *

The plaintiffs' study, conducted by Jacob Jacoby, was far more substantial and the district judge found it on the whole credible. The 28-page report with its numerous appendices has all the trappings of social scientific rigor. Interviewers showed several hundred consumers in 24 malls scattered around the country shirts and hats licensed by the defendants for sale to consumers. The shirts and hats have "Baltimore CFL Colts" stamped on them. The consumers were asked whether they were football fans, whether they watched football games on television, and whether they ever bought merchandise with a team name on it. Then they were asked, with reference to the "Baltimore CFL Colts" merchandise that they were shown, such questions as whether they knew what sport the team played, what teams it played against, what league the team was in, and whether the team or league needed someone's permission to use this name, and if so whose. If, for example, the respondent answered that the team had to get permission from the Canadian Football League, the interviewer was directed to ask the respondent whether the Canadian Football League had in turn to get permission from someone. There were other questions, none however obviously loaded, and a whole other survey, the purpose of which was to control for "noise," in which another group of mallgoers was asked the identical questions about a hypothetical team unappetizingly named the "Baltimore Horses." The idea was by comparing the answers of the two groups to see whether the source of confusion was the name "Baltimore Colts" or just the name "Baltimore," in which event the injunction would do no good since no one suggests that the new Baltimore team should be forbidden to use "Baltimore" in its name, provided the following word is not "Colts."

* * *

Jacoby's survey of consumers reactions to the "Baltimore CFL Colts" merchandise found rather astonishing levels of confusion not plausibly attributable to the presence of the name "Baltimore" alone, since "Baltimore Horses" engendered much less. * * * Among self-identified football fans, 64 percent thought that the "Baltimore CFL Colts" was either the old (NFL) Baltimore Colts or the Indianapolis Colts. But perhaps this result is not so astonishing. Although most American football fans have heard of Canadian football, many probably are unfamiliar with the acronym "CFL," and as we remarked earlier it is not a very conspicuous part of the team logo stamped on the merchandise. Among fans who watch football on television, 59 percent displayed the same confusion; and even among those who watch football on cable television, which attracts a more educated audience on average and actually carries CFL games, 58 percent were confused when shown the merchandise. Among the minority not confused about who the "Baltimore CFL Colts" are, a substantial minority, ranging from 21 to 34 percent depending on the precise sub-sample, thought the team somehow sponsored or authorized by the Indianapolis Colts or the National Football League.

* * *

But with all this granted, we cannot say that the district judge committed a clear error (the standard, *Scandia Down Corp. v. Euroquilt, Inc., 772 F.2d at 1427-28*) in crediting the major findings of the Jacoby study and inferring from it and the other evidence in the record that the defendants' use of the name "Baltimore CFL Colts" whether for the team or on merchandise was likely to confuse a substantial number of consumers. This mean[s]—given the defendants' failure to raise any issue concerning the respective irreparable harms from granting or denying the preliminary injunction—that the judge's finding concerning likelihood of confusion required that the injunction issue.

* * *

The defendants make some other arguments but they do not have sufficient merit to warrant discussion. The judgment of the district court granting the preliminary injunction is AFFIRMED.

NFLP, Inc. v. New York Football Giants, Inc., 637 F.Supp. 507 (D. NJ 1986). This case examines the leagues efforts to control its collective trademark rights.

University of Georgia Athletic Association v. Laite, 756 F.2d 1535 (11th Cir. 1985). This case focuses on factors used by the courts to determine the likelihood of confusion.

USOC v. Kayser-Roth Corporation, 2004 TTAB LEXIS 28. This case examines the court's discussion of intent to use a mark and how it relates to possible abandonment.

QUESTIONS YOU SHOULD BE ABLE TO ANSWER

1. Explain the functions of a trademark for a recreation and sport management organization.

2. What is the benefit of federally registering your organization's trademarks?

3. What must a trademark owner establish in order to show infringement by another organization?

4. If your recreation or sport management organization is accused of infringing another organization's trademarks, what defenses can you use to show that no infringement took place?

5. As a recreation or sport management organization, why would you want to provide other organizations with a license to use your trademark on their goods or services?

REFERENCES

Cases

Board of Trustees of the University of Arkansas v. Professional Therapy Services, 873 F. Supp. 1280, 1284 (W.D. Ark. 1995).

Cardtoons, L.C. v. Major League Baseball Players Association, 95 F.3d 959 (10th Cir. 1996).

Harjo, et al. v. Pro-Football, Inc., 50 U.S.P.Q. 1705 (1999), *rev'd, summary judgment granted in part, summary judgment denied in part*, 68 U.S.P.Q.2d 1225 (2003).

Hawaii-Pacific Apparel Group, Inc. v. Cleveland Browns Football Co. LLC, 418 F. Supp. 2d 501, 509 (S.D. N.Y. 2006).

Ignition Athletic Performance Group, LLC v. Hantz Soccer U.S.A., LLC, 245 Fed. Appx. 456 (6th Cir. 2007).

March Madness Athletic Association, LLC v. Netfire Inc., 120 Fed. Appx. 540 (5th Cir. 2005).

NBA Properties, Inc. v. Untertainment Records LLC, 1999 U.S. Dist. LEXIS 7780 (S.D. NY 1999).

NFL v. Blucher, Case No. D2007-1064 (WIPO Arbitration and Mediation Center, September 24, 2007).

United States Olympic Committee v. Toy Truck Lines, 237 F.3d 1331 (Fed. Cir. 2001).

University of Pittsburgh v. Champion Products, Inc., 686 F.2d 1040 (3rd Cir. 1982), *cert. denied* 495 U.S. 1087 (1982).

WCVB-TV v. Boston Athletic Association, 92 F.2d 42 (1st Cir. 1991).

Publications

International Chamber of Commerce (ICC). (2008, November 4). An ICC Initiative: BASCAP–Business action to stop counterfeiting and piracy. Report on BASCAP mission, achievements, work plan and membership. Retrieved February 11, 2009, from http://www.iccwbo.org/uploadedFiles/BASCAP/Statements/BASCAP%20Prospectus_081120(1).pdf

McCarthy, J. T. (1991). *McCarthy's desk encyclopedia of intellectual property*. Washington, DC: BNA Books.

Legislation

The Anti-Cybersquatting Consumer Protection Act, 15 U.S.C. § 1125(d) (1999).

The Federal Trademark Act, 15 U.S.C. §§ 1051-1127 (2002).

The Federal Trademark Dilution Act, 15 U.S.C. § 1125(c) (1995).

Ted Stevens Olympic and Amateur Sports Act, 36 U.S.C. §§ 220501-220529 (1998).

7.23 Image Rights

—**John T. Wolohan**
ITHACA COLLEGE

The term **image rights** relates to a person's name or likeness, such as photograph or other visual representation of the person. When examining the image rights of athletes and other celebrities, historically, the courts found that by seeking fame in their sport or other endeavor, the athletes or celebrities had forfeited their right of privacy. Courts in the past have ruled that the right of privacy was only available to private persons, and once someone, as result of their activities, became a public figure they lost their right of privacy (*O'Brien v. Pabst Sales Co*, 1941).

The courts began to move from this position in the 1950s, when in order to protect athletes and other celebrities against commercial misappropriation and prevent the unjust enrichment of others off a celebrity's reputation, the courts extended the right of privacy to include a **Right of Publicity**. In recognizing such a right, the Second Circuit Court of Appeals held that "in addition to and independent of that right of privacy (which in New York derives from statute), a man has a right in the publicity value of his photograph, . . . and that many prominent persons (especially actors and ball-players), far from having their feelings bruised through public exposure of their likenesses, would feel sorely deprived if they no longer received money for authorizing advertisements popularizing their countenances displayed in newspapers, magazines, busses, trains and subways. This right of publicity would usually yield them no money unless it could be made the subject of an exclusive grant which barred any other advertiser from using their pictures" (*Haelan Laboratories, Inc. v. Topps Chewing Gum, Inc.*, 1953).

Since the Second Circuit Court's decision in *Haelan Laboratories v. Topps*, in addition to protecting a person's name or likeness, some states have even begun to broaden the right of publicity by expanding the "traditional meaning of 'name and likeness' to include such things as nicknames, drawings, celebrity look-alikes or by including characteristics such as vocal idiosyncrasies within a more general formulation of identity" (Clay, 1994). For example, in *Motschenbacher v. R.J. Reynolds Tobacco Co.*, R.J. Reynolds produced some television ads "utilizing a stock color photograph depicting several racing cars on a race track" (*Motschenbacher v. R.J. Reynolds Tobacco Co.*). The drivers in the cars were not visible in the photo, and the cars had been altered, the numbers were changed, and a spoiler was added on which the company placed their product's name. In finding the ads violated Motschenbacher's, a well-known race car driver, right of publicity, the Ninth Circuit Court of Appeals held that even though the driver's personal likeness was unrecognizable, his identity could still be inferred by the distinctive decorations on his car (*Motschenbacher v. R.J. Reynolds Tobacco Co.*, 1974).

FUNDAMENTAL CONCEPTS

Right of Publicity

In 1960, William Prosser identified four distinct kinds of invasion of privacy. Although tied together by a common name, Prosser argued that the four different actions have almost nothing in common except that each represents an interference with an individual's right to privacy.

The four different types of interests are:

1. Intrusion upon an individual's seclusion or solitude, or into his or her private affairs;

2. Public disclosure of embarrassing private facts about an individual;

3. Publicity which places an individual in a false light in the public eye; and

4. Appropriation of an individual's name or likeness (Prosser, 1960).

It is the fourth type of privacy interest identified by Prosser, "appropriation of an individual's name or likeness" (Prosser, 1960), for the benefit of another, usually of a commercial nature, that the courts cite as the right of publicity.

Common Law Misappropriation

The courts have generally found that there are two forms of appropriation. The difference between the two is found not in the activity of the defendant, but in "the nature of the plaintiff's right and the nature of the resulting injury" (McCarthy, 2003). The first type of appropriation is the right of publicity, which is "in essence that the reaction of the public to name and likeness, which may be fortuitous or which may be managed or planned, endows the name and likeness of the person involved with commercially exploitable opportunities" (*Lugosi v. Universal Pictures*, 1979).

The other type of appropriation brings injury to the feelings, that concerns one's own peace of mind, and that is mental and subjective (*Stilson v. Reader's Digest Assn., Inc.*, 1972). The most common form of appropriation involves the use of a person's name or identity in the advertisement of another's products or services. To establish a cause of action for common law misappropriation in these situations, the courts have generally held that an individual must demonstrate the following four elements:

1. The defendant used the plaintiff's identity;

2. The appropriation of plaintiff's name or likeness provided the defendant some advantage, commercially or otherwise;

3. Lack of consent; and

4. Resulting injury (*Eastwood v. Superior Court*, 1983).

In determining whether there is a cause of action for common law misappropriation, one of the hardest questions for the court to answer is whether an individual's identity or likeness was even used. For example, in *Newcombe v. Adolf Coors Co.*, the Ninth Circuit Court of Appeal was asked to determine whether a beer ad featuring an old-time baseball game, showing a pitcher in a windup position, misappropriated Don Newcombe's image. Even though the player's uniforms did not depict an actual team, and the background did not depict an actual stadium, the Ninth Circuit Court ruled that the player's windup was so distinctive that it made the identity of the player readily identifiable (*Newcombe v. Adolf Coors Co.*, 1998).

Finally, it is important to note that although some states recognize a common law cause of action for the misappropriation of a person's name or likeness, it is not the law in every state. In fact, a number of states still do not recognize an individual's right of privacy or the common law misappropriation of an individual's name or likeness.

Statutory Protection

In addition to the common law, eighteen states have enacted legislation to protect individuals against misappropriation of their image or protect an individual's right of publicity. The eighteen states are California, Florida, Illinois, Indiana, Kentucky, Massachusetts, Nebraska, Nevada, New York, Ohio, Oklahoma, Rhode Island, Tennessee, Texas, Utah, Virginia, Washington, and Wisconsin. The statutory cause of action of misappropriation complements rather than codifies common law and occurs when the plaintiff can show that another "knowingly" used his or her "name, . . . photograph, or likeness, in any manner, on or in products, merchandise, or goods, or for purposes of advertising or selling, or soliciting purchases of, products, merchandise, goods or services, without prior consent" (*Montana v. San Jose Mercury News*, 1995).

A good example of the rights available under statutory law is *Ali v. Playgirl, Inc.* In their February 1978 issue, *Playgirl* printed a portrait of a nude black man in the corner of a boxing ring. The man is unmistakably recognizable as Muhammad Ali, former heavyweight boxing champion, and is accompanied by the phrase "the Greatest." In defense of their use, *Playgirl* argued that because Ali was a public figure, he waived his right of privacy and therefore they did not need his consent.

In examining Ali's rights under section 51 of the New York Civil Rights Law, the federal District Court held that it was clear that *Playgirl* used Ali's portrait or picture for the purpose of trade within the meaning of § 51 without his consent. Such use, the court held, amounted to a wrongful appropriation of the market value of Ali's likeness. As for *Playgirl*'s argument that the use was privileged, the court ruled that "the privilege of using a public figure's picture in connection with an item of news does not extend to commercialization of his personality" (*Ali v. Playgirl, Inc.*, 1978).

Another example is *John Doe, a/k/a Tony Twist, v. TCI Cablevision*. Tony Twist, a former professional hockey player in the National Hockey League, had a reputation as an enforcer on the ice. The creator of the comic book, *Spawn*, developed a villainous character in the book sharing his name. In trying to determine whether the use of a person's name and identity violated Twist's right to publicity, the Supreme Court of Missouri held that the threshold legal question is whether the use of a person's name and identity is "expressive," in which case it is fully protected, or "commercial," in which case it is generally not protected (*Doe, a/k/a Tony Twist, v. TCI Cablevision*, 2003). For instance, the court went on, "the use of a person's identity in news, entertainment, and creative works for the purpose of communicating information or expressive ideas about that person is protected "expressive" speech. On the other hand, the use of a person's identity for purely commercial purposes, like advertising goods or services or the use of a person's name or likeness on merchandise, is rarely protected (*Doe, a/k/a Tony Twist, v. TCI Cablevision*, 2003).

Intellectual Property Provisions

In addition to state law, federal law can also be an effective tool in defending a person's right of publicity. Federal law is especially important because the right of privacy is only available to individuals, and corporations and partnerships must rely on theories such as trademark law to prevent the unauthorized commercial use of their identity.

Federal Trademark Law (The Lanham Act)

Although mainly thought of as a means for manufacturers to identify their goods and distinguish them from those manufactured or sold by others, the Lanham Act also protects consumers and competitors from a wide variety of misrepresentations of products and services in commerce, including the unauthorized use of an individual's image rights. Therefore, although narrower in scope than the right of publicity or misappropriation, the federal Trademark Act can be a powerful tool in protecting an athlete's image rights. (See also Section 7.22, *Principles of Trademark Law*.)

False Endorsement Claims. Commonly referred to as "false endorsement claims," the Lanham Act bars the unauthorized commercial use of a celebrity's identity to help sell a defendant's goods or services when that use is likely to cause confusion among consumers as to the association, sponsorship, or approval of goods or services by another person (15 U.S.C. § 1125(a)). In deciding whether the unauthorized use of a celebrity's identity is likely to cause confusion in the mind of the consumers, the Ninth Circuit court has developed the following eight factor test. The factors are:

1. Strength of the plaintiff's mark;

2. Relatedness of the goods;

3. Similarity of the marks;

4. Evidence of actual confusion;

5. Marketing channels used;

6. Likely degree of purchaser care;

7. Defendant's intent in selecting the mark;

8. Likelihood of expansion of the product lines (*AMF, Inc. v. Sleekcraft Boats*, 1979).

One example of an athlete using trademark law to prohibit the use of his name is *Abdul-Jabar v. General Motors Corp.* Kareem Abdul-Jabar, a professional basketball player, sued General Motors after they used the name Lew Alcindor in a television commercial without his consent. Abdul-Jabar was born Lew Alcindor and used that name throughout his college and early professional career. He began using the name Abdul-Jabar in 1971, after he converted to the Muslim religion.

In overturning the lower court, the Ninth Circuit Court of Appeals held that the Lanham Act clearly prohibited "false endorsement" claims based on the unauthorized use of a celebrity's identity. As for General Motors' claims that Abdul-Jabar had abandoned the name Lew Alcindor, the Court refused to extend the abandonment defense under federal trademark law to cover a person's name. "One's birth name is an integral part of one's identity; it is not bestowed for commercial purposes, nor is it 'kept alive' through commercial use" (*Abdul-Jabar v. General Motors Corp.*, 1996). As for General Motors' defense that its use of the name Lew Alcindor was protected under the "fair use" doctrine, which protects the unauthorized use of a trademark when "the mark is used only to describe the goods or services of a party or their geographic origin," the Court found that there was a genuine issue as to whether the use of Abdul-Jabar's old name implied his endorsement or sponsorship. In support of its decision, the Court noted that because the "use of celebrity endorsements in television commercials is so well established . . . a jury might find an implied endorsement in General Motors' use of the celebrity's name in a commercial" (*Abdul-Jabar v. General Motors Corp.*, 1996).

However, it should be noted that under trademark law most personal names are not inherently distinctive terms and can only receive trademark protection after they obtain secondary meaning (McCarthy, 2003). To obtain secondary meaning, the name or mark must have widespread use and public recognition so that the mark primarily indicates the source of the good or service instead of the good or service itself. For example, *Hirsch v. S.C. Johnson & Son* involved the use of Hirsch's nickname, "Crazylegs," on a shaving gel. The Supreme Court of Wisconsin not only found that Hirsch had a common law right of publicity under Wisconsin law, but that the trial court also "failed to consider the common law of tradename infringement and that, [for there to be an infringement] under tradename law, there need be no evidence of the prior marketing of a product or service under the nickname 'Crazylegs'" (*Hirsch v. S.C. Johnson & Son*, 1979). All that was necessary, the court ruled, was that Hirsch "show that Crazylegs designated the plaintiff's vocation or occupation as a sports figure and that the use of the name on a shaving gel for women created a likelihood of confusion as a sponsorship" (*Hirsch v. S.C. Johnson & Son*).

Postmortem Rights

An area of growing importance involves the image rights of the dead. To illustrate how important this area is, Forbes reported that the top "13 Top-Earning Dead Celebrities" earned a combined $194 million in 2008. Topping the list were Elvis Presley who earned an estimated $52 million, and Charles Schultz who earned $33 million (Forbes.com).

In an effort to protect the estates of these celebrities, states have begun to recognize that the right of publicity in addition to being assignable and licensed could also be descendible. Probably the most cited case dealing with the postmortem right of publicity is *Lugosi v. Universal Pictures*. The widow and children of Bela Lugosi, a movie actor famous for his role as Dracula, brought suit against Universal to recover profits made by Universal in licensing of merchandise associated with the film. The family claimed that Universal had misappropriated property, Lugosi's image, they had inherited from Lugosi. In ruling for Universal, the California Supreme Court held that "the right to exploit name and likeness is personal to the artist and must be exercised, if at all, by him during his lifetime" (*Lugosi v. Universal Pictures*, 1979).

As a result of the court's decision in *Lugosi*, California passed Civil Code § 990, which prohibits the use of "a deceased personality's name, voice, signature, photograph, or likeness, in any manner, on or in products, merchandise, or goods, or for purposes of advertising or selling, . . . without prior consent . . . shall be liable for any damages sustained." Some states have followed California's lead in recognizing a right of publicity as a fully transferable and descendible property right. It is important to note, however, that not every state recognizes a postmortem right of publicity.

First Amendment Defenses

The First Amendment states, "Congress shall make no law respecting establishment of religion, or prohibiting the free exercise thereof; or abridging the freedom of speech, or of the press . . ." (U.S. CONST. Amendment I).

Because the intent of the First Amendment is to protect the dual freedoms of speech and the press, the courts will allow the "unauthorized use of an individual's name or likeness" when it is used for the "dissemination of ideas and information" or for other cultural purposes (McCarthy, 2003). However, if an individual's name or likeness is used for commercial purposes, the courts will not protect it. The four main First Amendment defenses involving image rights are: the newsworthiness doctrine; the incidental use exception; the parody defense; and artist expression.

Newsworthiness Doctrine

The newsworthiness doctrine permits the media to use the unauthorized likeness of celebrities or anyone of interest in connection with a news item about the person. The definition of "news" has been given a broad reading and includes matters of public concern and interest. One example of how the doctrine relates to athletes and their image rights is *Montana v. San Jose Mercury News*. Joe Montana sued the *San Jose Mercury News* newspaper for reproducing his name, photograph, and likeness in poster form and selling it to the general public without his consent. In ruling that the newspaper had the right to use Montana's image, the California Court of Appeal held that the newspaper accounts of Montana's performance in two Super Bowls and four championships constituted publication of matters in the public interest and was entitled to protection by the First Amendment of the United States Constitution. In particular, the Court of Appeal held that Montana's name and likeness appeared in the posters for the same reason they appeared on the original newspaper pages: because he was a major player in contemporaneous newsworthy sports events and therefore may be republished in another medium, without the person's written consent. (See also Section 3.13, *Other Intentional Torts*.)

The Incidental Use Exception

The courts have recognized an incidental use exception in cases where a newspaper or magazine has used, for advertising purposes, the image or photo of an athlete or other celebrity previously printed in a story, for advertisement. The advertisements, the courts have held, are simply "incidental" to the original, newsworthy publication. A good example is *Joe Namath v. Sports Illustrated*. Joe Namath sued *Sports Illustrated* after the magazine used his photograph in advertisements promoting subscriptions without his consent. The photograph used was originally used in the magazine in conjunction with an article published by *Sports Illustrated* concerning the 1969 Super Bowl game.

In holding that the publication and use of Namath's photo in the advertisements did not violate the law, the court held that the use of the photograph, originally used in conjunction with a news article, was merely incidental advertising of the magazine. In particular, the court noted that the reproduction was used to illustrate the quality and content of the magazine in which Namath had earlier been properly and fairly depicted and in no way indicated Namath's endorsement of the magazine.

Parody Defense

The First Amendment also allows for the use of parodies under certain circumstances. For example, parodies that use another person's image, when used in a traditionally noncommercial medium such as a newspaper, magazine, television program, book, or movie will likely be granted First Amendment protection. Parodies used in a commercial context, however, will generally not receive First Amendment protection. An example of the parody defense is *Cardtoons, L.C. v. Major League Baseball Players Association*. Cardtoons, a trading card company, designed "parody" trading cards of active major league baseball players. Cardtoons did not obtain either a license or consent from Major League Baseball Players Association (MLBPA). In ruling for MLBPA, the court stated that although parodies used in a traditionally noncommercial medium such as a newspaper, magazine, television program, book, or movie will likely be granted First Amendment protection, the primary purpose behind Cardtoons' parody is commercial. Commercial speech, the Court held, does not receive the same type of Constitutional protection. First Amendment rights end when Cardtoons preys on the MLBPA's names and likenesses for purely commercial purposes. Indeed, the court found that the only reason for using the players' likenesses and names was to entice the consumer to purchase the product.

Artistic Expression

Another area where the courts will allow the unauthorized use of another's trademark is when the mark is used in an artistic expression. For example, in *New York Racing Association v. Perlmutter Publishing*, the owner of a registered trademark asked the Court to consider whether Perlmutter Publishing's use of their trademark in paintings and other merchandise infringed on the New York Racing Authority's ("NYRA") trademarks. The court, in ruling against NYRA ruled that the inclusion of NYRA's trademarks on T-shirts and other merchandise would not cause confusion among the average consumers, who would realize that the shirts displayed reproductions. The court found that the evidence showed that defendants use the images to describe Saratoga horse racing and not as an indication of source. Finally, in finding that the paintings were permitted under the First Amendment, the court ruled that the paintings serve the artistically relevant purpose of accurately depicting that scene. The Lanham Act, therefore, does not apply because the interest in free expression outweighs the need to avoid consumer confusion (*New York Racing Association v. Perlmutter Publishing*, 1997).

SIGNIFICANT CASE

Although not a sport case, the Ninth Circuit Court's decision in *Vanna White v. Samsung Electronics* is important nonetheless because of its expansion of the traditional meaning of "name or likeness" under the Right of Publicity.

<hr>

VANNA WHITE V. SAMSUNG ELECTRONICS AMERICA
United States Court of Appeals for the Ninth Circuit
971 F.2d 1395 (1992)

<hr>

Plaintiff Vanna White is the hostess of "Wheel of Fortune," one of the most popular game shows in television history. An estimated forty million people watch the program daily. Capitalizing on the fame which her participation in the show has bestowed on her, White markets her identity to various advertisers.

The dispute in this case arose out of a series of advertisements prepared for Samsung by Deutsch. The series ran in at least half a dozen publications with widespread, and in some cases national, circulation. Each of the advertisements in the series followed the same theme. Each depicted a current item from popular culture and a Samsung electronic product. Each was set in the twenty-first century and conveyed the message that the Samsung product would still be in use by that time. By hypothesizing outrageous future outcomes for the cultural items, the ads created humorous effects. For example, one lampooned current popular notions of an unhealthy diet by depicting a raw steak with the caption: "Revealed to be health food. 2010 A.D." Another depicted irreverent "news"-show host Morton Downey Jr. in front of an American flag with the caption: "Presidential candidate. 2008 A.D."

The advertisement which prompted the current dispute was for Samsung video-cassette recorders (VCRs). The ad depicted a robot, dressed in a wig, gown, and jewelry which Deutsch consciously selected to resemble White's hair and dress. The robot was posed next to a game board which is instantly recognizable as the Wheel of Fortune game show set, in a stance for which White is famous. The caption of the ad read: "Longest-running game show. 2012 A.D." Defendants referred to the ad as the "Vanna White" ad. Unlike the other celebrities used in the campaign, White neither consented to the ads nor was she paid.

Following the circulation of the robot ad, White sued Samsung and Deutsch in federal district court under: (1) California Civil Code § 3344; (2) the California common law right of publicity; and (3) § 43(a) of the Lanham Act, 15 U.S.C. § 1125(a). The district court granted summary judgment against White on each of her claims. White now appeals.

I. Section 3344

White first argues that the district court erred in rejecting her claim under section 3344. Section 3344(a) provides, in pertinent part, that "any person who knowingly uses another's name, voice, signature, photograph, or likeness, in any manner, . . . for purposes of advertising or selling, . . . without such person's prior consent . . . shall be liable for any damages sustained by the person or persons injured as a result thereof."

White argues that the Samsung advertisement used her "likeness" in contravention of section 3344. In *Midler v. Ford Motor Co.*, 849 F.2d 460 (9th Cir. 1988), this court rejected Bette Midler's section 3344 claim concerning a Ford television commercial in which a Midler "sound-alike" sang a song which Midler had made famous. In rejecting Midler's claim, this court noted that "the defendants did not use Midler's name or anything else whose use is prohibited by the statute. The voice they used was [another person's], not hers. The term 'likeness' refers to a visual image not a vocal imitation." *Id.* at 463.

In this case, Samsung and Deutsch used a robot with mechanical features, and not, for example, a manikin molded to White's precise features. Without deciding for all purposes when a caricature or impressionistic resemblance might become a "likeness," we agree with the district court that the robot at issue here was not White's "likeness" within the meaning of section 3344. Accordingly, we affirm the court's dismissal of White's section 3344 claim.

II. Right of Publicity

White next argues that the district court erred in granting summary judgment to defendants on White's common law right of publicity claim. In *Eastwood v. Superior Court*, 149 Cal. App. 3d 409 , 198 Cal. Rptr. 342 (1983), the California court of appeal stated that the common law right of publicity cause of action "may be pleaded by alleging (1) the defendant's use of the plaintiff's identity; (2) the appropriation of plaintiff's name or likeness to defendant's advantage, commercially or otherwise; (3) lack of consent; and (4) resulting injury." *Id.* at 417 (citing Prosser, Law of Torts (4th ed. 1971) § 117, pp. 804–807). The district court dismissed White's claim for failure to satisfy Eastwood's second prong, reasoning that defendants had not appropriated White's "name or likeness" with their robot ad. We agree that the robot ad did not make use of White's name or likeness. However, the common law right of publicity is not so confined.

The Eastwood court did not hold that the right of publicity cause of action could be pleaded only by alleging an appropriation of name or likeness. Eastwood involved an unauthorized use of photographs of Clint Eastwood and of his name. Accordingly, the Eastwood court had no occasion to consider the extent beyond the use of name or likeness to which the right of publicity reaches. That court held only that the right of publicity cause of action "may be" pleaded by alleging appropriation of name or likeness, not that the action may be pleaded only in those terms.

The "name or likeness" formulation referred to in Eastwood originated not as an element of the right of publicity cause of action, but as a description of the types of cases in which the cause of action had been recognized. The source of this formulation is Prosser, Privacy, 48 Cal.L.Rev. 383, 401-07 (1960), one of the earliest and most enduring articulations of the common law right of publicity cause of action. In looking at the case law to that point, Prosser recognized that right of publicity cases involved one of two basic factual scenarios: name appropriation, and picture or other likeness appropriation. *Id.* at 401-02, nn.156-57.

Even though Prosser focused on appropriations of name or likeness in discussing the right of publicity, he noted that "it is not impossible that there might be appropriation of the plaintiff's identity, as by impersonation, without the use of either his name or his likeness, and that this would be an invasion of his right of privacy." *Id.* At 401, n.155. n1 At the time Prosser wrote, he noted however, that "no such case appears to have arisen." *Id.*

Since Prosser's early formulation, the case law has borne out his insight that the right of publicity is not limited to the appropriation of name or likeness. In *Motschenbacher v. R.J. Reynolds Tobacco Co.*, 498 F.2d 821 (9th Cir. 1974), the defendant had used a photograph of the plaintiff's race car in a television commercial. Although the plaintiff appeared driving the car in the photograph, his features were not visible. Even though the defendant had not appropriated the plaintiff's name or likeness, this court held that plaintiff's California right of publicity claim should reach the jury.

In Midler, this court held that, even though the defendants had not used Midler's name or likeness, Midler had stated a claim for violation of her California common law right of publicity because "the defendants . . . for their own profit in selling their product did appropriate part of her identity" by using a Midler sound-alike. *Id.* at 463-64.

In *Carson v. Here's Johnny Portable Toilets, Inc.*, 698 F.2d 831 (6th Cir. 1983), the defendant had marketed portable toilets under the brand name "Here's Johnny"—Johnny Carson's signature "Tonight Show" introduction—without Carson's permission. The district court had dismissed Carson's Michigan common law right of publicity claim because the defendants had not used Carson's "name or likeness." *Id.* at 835. In reversing the district court, the sixth circuit found "the district court's conception of the right of publicity . . . too narrow" and held that the right was implicated because the defendant had appropriated Carson's identity by using, inter alia, the phrase "Here's Johnny." *Id.* at 835-37.

These cases teach not only that the common law right of publicity reaches means of appropriation other than name or likeness, but that the specific means of appropriation are relevant only for determining whether the defendant has in fact appropriated the plaintiff's identity. The right of publicity does not require that appropriations of identity be accomplished through particular means to be actionable. It is noteworthy that the Midler and Carson defendants not only avoided using the plaintiff's name or likeness, but they also avoided appropriating the celebrity's voice, signature, and photograph. The photograph in Motschenbacher did include the plaintiff, but because the plaintiff was not visible the driver could have been an actor or dummy and the analysis in the case would have been the same.

Although the defendants in these cases avoided the most obvious means of appropriating the plaintiffs' identities, each of their actions directly implicated the commercial interests which the right of publicity is designed to protect. As the Carson court explained:

the right of publicity has developed to protect the commercial interest of celebrities in their identities. The theory of the right is that a celebrity's identity can be valuable in the promotion of products, and the celebrity has an interest that may be protected from the unauthorized commercial exploitation of that identity. . . . If the celebrity's identity is commercially exploited, there has been an invasion of his right whether or not his "name or likeness" is used.

Carson, 698 F.2d at 835. It is not important how the defendant has appropriated the plaintiff's identity, but whether the defendant has done so. Motschenbacher, Midler, and Carson teach the impossibility of treating the right of publicity as guarding only against a laundry list of specific means of appropriating identity. A rule which says that the right of publicity can be infringed only through the use of nine different methods of appropriating identity merely challenges the clever advertising strategist to come up with the tenth.

Indeed, if we treated the means of appropriation as dispositive in our analysis of the right of publicity, we would not only weaken the right but effectively eviscerate it. The right would fail to protect those plaintiffs most in need of its protection. Advertisers use celebrities to promote their products. The more popular the celebrity, the greater the number of people who recognize her, and the greater the visibility for the product. The identities of the most popular celebrities are not only the most attractive for advertisers, but also the easiest to evoke without resorting to obvious means such as name, likeness, or voice.

Consider a hypothetical advertisement which depicts a mechanical robot with male features, an African-American complexion, and a bald head. The robot is wearing black hightop Air Jordan basketball sneakers, and a red basketball uniform with black trim, baggy shorts, and the number 23 (though not revealing "Bulls" or "Jordan" lettering). The ad depicts the robot dunking a basketball one-handed, stiff-armed, legs extended like open scissors, and tongue hanging out. Now envision that this ad is run on television during professional basketball games. Considered individually, the robot's physical attributes, its dress, and its stance tell us little. Taken together, they lead to the only conclusion that any sports viewer who has registered a discernible pulse in the past five years would reach: the ad is about Michael Jordan.

Viewed separately, the individual aspects of the advertisement in the present case say little. Viewed together, they leave little doubt about the celebrity the ad is meant to depict. The female-shaped robot is wearing a long gown, blond wig, and large jewelry. Vanna White dresses exactly like this at times, but so do many other women. The robot is in the process of turning a block letter on a game-board. Vanna White dresses like this while turning letters on a game-board but perhaps similarly attired Scrabble-playing women do this as well. The robot is standing on what looks to be the Wheel of Fortune game show set. Vanna White dresses like this, turns letters, and does this on the Wheel of Fortune game show. She is the only one. Indeed, defendants themselves referred to their ad as the "Vanna White" ad. We are not surprised.

Television and other media create marketable celebrity identity value. Considerable energy and ingenuity are expended by those who have achieved celebrity value to exploit it for profit. The law protects the celebrity's sole right to exploit this value whether the celebrity has achieved her fame out of rare ability, dumb luck, or a combination thereof. We decline Samsung and Deutch's invitation to permit the evisceration of the common law right of publicity through means as facile as those in this case. Because White has alleged facts showing that Samsung and Deutsch had appropriated her identity, the district court erred by rejecting, on summary judgment, White's common law right of publicity claim.

III. THE LANHAM ACT

White's final argument is that the district court erred in denying her claim under § 43(a) of the Lanham Act, 15 U.S.C. § 1125(a). The version of section 43(a) applicable to this case provides, in pertinent part, that "any person who shall . . . use, in connection with any goods or services . . . any false description or representation . . . shall be liable to a civil action . . . by any person who believes that he is or is likely to be damaged by the use of any such false description or designation." 15 U.S.C. § 1125(a).

To prevail on her Lanham Act claim, White is required to show that in running the robot ad, Samsung and Deutsch created a likelihood of confusion over whether White was endorsing Samsung's VCRs.

This circuit recognizes several different multi-factor tests for determining whether a likelihood of confusion exists. None of these tests is correct to the exclusion of the others. Normally, in reviewing the district court's decision, this court will look to the particular test that the district court used. However, because the district court in this case apparently did not use any of the multi-factor tests in making its likelihood of confusion determination, and because this case involves an appeal from summary judgment and we review de novo the district court's determination, we will look for guidance to the 8-factor test enunciated in *AMF, Inc. v. Sleekcraft Boats*, 599 F.2d 341 (9th Cir. 1979). According to AMF, factors relevant to a likelihood of confusion include:

(1) strength of the plaintiff's mark;

(2) relatedness of the goods;

(3) similarity of the marks;

(4) evidence of actual confusion;

(5) marketing channels used;

(6) likely degree of purchaser care;

(7) defendant's intent in selecting the mark;

(8) likelihood of expansion of the product lines.

We turn now to consider White's claim in light of each factor.

In cases involving confusion over endorsement by a celebrity plaintiff, "mark" means the celebrity's persona. The "strength" of the mark refers to the level of recognition the celebrity enjoys among members of society. If Vanna White is unknown to the segment of the public at whom Samsung's robot ad was directed, then that segment could not be confused as to whether she was endorsing Samsung VCRs. Conversely, if White is well-known, this would allow the possibility of a likelihood of confusion. For the purposes of the Sleekcraft test, White's "mark," or celebrity identity, is strong.

In cases concerning confusion over celebrity endorsement, the plaintiff's "goods" concern the reasons for or source of the plaintiff's fame. Because White's fame is based on her televised performances, her "goods" are closely related to Samsung's VCRs. Indeed, the ad itself reinforced the relationship by informing its readers that they would be taping the "longest-running game show" on Samsung's VCRs well into the future.

The third factor, "similarity of the marks," both supports and contradicts a finding of likelihood of confusion. On the one hand, all of the aspects of the robot ad identify White; on the other, the figure is quite clearly a robot, not a human. This ambiguity means that we must look to the other factors for resolution.

The fourth factor does not favor White's claim because she has presented no evidence of actual confusion.

Fifth, however, White has appeared in the same stance as the robot from the ad in numerous magazines, including the covers of some. Magazines were used as the marketing channels for the robot ad. This factor cuts toward a likelihood of confusion.

Sixth, consumers are not likely to be particularly careful in determining who endorses VCRs, making confusion as to their endorsement more likely.

Concerning the seventh factor, "defendant's intent," the district court found that, in running the robot ad, the defendants had intended a spoof of the "Wheel of Fortune." The relevant question is whether the defendants "intended to profit by confusing consumers" concerning the endorsement of Samsung VCRs. Toho, 645 F.2d 788 (9th Cir. 1981). We do not disagree that defendants intended to spoof Vanna White and "Wheel of Fortune." That does not preclude, however, the possibility that defendants also intended to confuse consumers regarding endorsement. The robot ad was one of a series of ads run by defendants which followed the same theme. Another ad in the series depicted Morton Downey Jr. as a presidential candidate in the year 2008. Doubtless, defendants intended to spoof presidential elections and Mr. Downey through this ad. Consumers, however, would likely believe, and would be correct in so believing, that Mr. Downey was paid for his permission and was endorsing Samsung products. Looking at the series of advertisements as a whole, a jury could reasonably conclude that beneath the surface humor of the series lay an intent to persuade consumers that celebrity Vanna White, like celebrity Downey, was endorsing Samsung products.

Finally, the eighth factor, "likelihood of expansion of the product lines," does not appear apposite to a celebrity endorsement case such as this.

Application of the Sleekcraft factors to this case indicates that the district court erred in rejecting White's Lanham Act claim at the summary judgment stage. In so concluding, we emphasize two facts, however. First, construing the motion papers in White's favor, as we must, we hold only that White has raised a genuine issue of material fact concerning a likelihood of confusion as to her endorsement. *Cohen v. Paramount Pictures Corp.*, 845 F.2d 851, 852-53 (9th Cir. 1989). Whether White's Lanham Act claim should succeed is a matter for the jury. Second, we stress that we reach this conclusion in light of the peculiar facts of this case. In particular, we note that the robot ad identifies White and was part of a series of ads in which other celebrities participated and were paid for their endorsement of Samsung's products.

IV. The Parody Defense

In defense, defendants cite a number of cases for the proposition that their robot ad constituted protected speech. The only cases they cite which are even remotely relevant to this case are *Hustler Magazine v. Falwell*, 485 U.S. 46, 99 L. Ed. 2d 41 , 108 S. Ct. 876 (1988) and *L.L. Bean, Inc. v. Drake Publishers, Inc.*, 811 F.2d 26 (1st Cir. 1987). Those cases involved parodies of advertisements run for the purpose of poking fun at Jerry Falwell and L.L. Bean, respectively. This case involves a true advertisement run for the purpose of selling Samsung VCRs. The ad's spoof of Vanna White and Wheel of Fortune is subservient and only tangentially related to the ad's primary message: "buy Samsung VCRs." Defendants' parody arguments are better addressed to non-commercial parodies. The difference between a "parody" and a "knock-off" is the difference between fun and profit.

V. Conclusion

In remanding this case, we hold only that White has pleaded claims which can go to the jury for its decision.

CASES ON THE SUPPLEMENTAL CD

Namath v. Sports Illustrated, 371 N.Y.S.2d 10 (1975). The case examines whether a magazine can use a photograph, which was originally used by the magazine without objection, in advertisements promoting subscriptions to their magazine.

John Doe, a/k/a Tony Twist v. TCI Cablevision, 110 S.W.3d 363 (2003). The case examines whether the use of a fictional character named "Anthony 'Tony Twist' Twistelli" in the Spawn comic book violated Tony Twist's image rights, even though the characters bear no physical resemblance to each other and, aside from the common nickname, are similar only in that each can be characterized as having an "enforcer" or tough-guy persona.

Newcombe v. Adolf Coors Co., 157 F.3d 686 (9th Cir. 1998). The case examines whether an image in a magazine was the plaintiff and, it so, whether it violated the plaintiff's image rights.

QUESTIONS YOU SHOULD BE ABLE TO ANSWER

1. What are some of the laws available to protect the unauthorized use of your image?

2. Historically, the right of publicity only covered the use of a person's "name or likeness"; however, the courts have now expanded the right to include what else?

3. What are some of the specific uses of a person's image that are protected?

4. What are some of the First Amendment defenses available?

5. What are some of the specific uses of a person's image that are prohibited?

REFERENCES

Cases

Abdul-Jabar v. General Motors Corp., 85 F.3d 407 (9th Cir. 1996).

Ali v. Playgirl, Inc., 447 F.Supp. 723 (1978).

AMF, Inc. v. Sleekcraft Boats, 599 F.2d 341 (9th Cir. 1979).

Cardtoons, L.C. v. Major League Baseball Players Association, 838 F. Supp 1501 (N.D. Okla. 1993).

Eastwood v. Superior Court, 149 Cal. App. 3d 409, 198 Cal. Rptr. 342 (1983).

ETW Corp. v. Jireh Publishing, Inc., 99 F. Supp. 2d 829 (2000).

ETW Corp. v. Jireh Publishing, Inc., 332 F.3d 915 (6th Cir., 2003).

Haelan Laboratories, Inc. v. Topps Chewing Gum, Inc., 202 F.2d 866 (2nd. Cir. 1953).

Hirsch v. S.C. Johnson & Son, 280 N.W. 129 (Wis. 1979).

Joe Namath v. Sports Illustrated, 48 A.D.2d 487; 371 N.Y.S.2d 10 (1975).

John Doe, a/k/a Tony Twist, v. TCI Cablevision, 110 S.W.3d 363 (2003).

Lugosi v. Universal Pictures, 603 P.2d 425 (1979).

Montana v. San Jose Mercury News, 40 Cal. Rptr. 2d 639 (1995).

Motschenbacher v. R.J. Reynolds Tobacco Co., 498 F.2d 821 (1974).

Newcombe v. Adolf Coors Co., 157 F.3d 686 (9th Cir. 1998).

New York Racing Association v. Perlmutter Publishing, 959 F.Supp. 578 (1997).

O'Brien v. Pabst Sales Co., 124 F.2d 167 (1941).

Stilson v. Reader's Digest Assn., Inc., 28 Cal.App.3d 270, 273 (1972).

Publications

Clay, S. (1994). Starstruck: The overextension of celebrity publicity rights in state and federal courts. *Minnesota Law Review, 79*, 485–517.

McCarthy, J. T. (2004). *The rights of publicity and privacy* (3rd ed.). Deerfield IL: Clark Boardman Callaghan.

Prosser, W. (1960). Privacy. *California Law Review, 48*, 383–423.

Warren, S., & Brandeis, L. (1890). The right of privacy. *Harvard Law Review, 4*, 193–220.

Wolohan, J. T. (2005). Sports image rights in the United States. In I. S. Blackshaw & R. C. Siekmann (Eds.), *Sports Image Rights in Europe*. The Hague: T.M.C. Asser Press.

Legislation

California Civil Code § 990.

Lanham Act § 45, 15 U.S.C. § 1125(a).

Websites

Hoy, P. (2008, October 27). Top-Earning Dead Celebrities: It's still a bull market in the bone yard. Retrieved from http://www.forbes.com/2008/10/27/top-dead-celebrity-biz-media-deadcelebs08-cz_ph_1027celeb .html

7.30 Antitrust and Labor Law

7.31 Antitrust Law: Professional Sport Applications

—Lisa Pike Masteralexis
UNIVERSITY OF MASSACHUSETTS-AMHERST

Professional sport leagues' structure and labor management relations have been imprinted by antitrust cases. Professional sport leagues operate efficiently due to many restrictive practices. No other industry employs such restrictive rules and policies, and thus, the professional sport industry may be more likely to face antitrust challenges. Restraints on free agency and salary spending and restrictions on franchise ownership have opened leagues up to antitrust challenges by players, owners, prospective owners, competitor leagues, cities possessing franchises, cities seeking franchises, and media entities. The business of individual professional sport tours is not free from antitrust challenges often made over its governance and decision-making authority.

FUNDAMENTAL CONCEPTS

Antitrust Law

In 1890 Congress passed the Sherman Antitrust Act to break up business trusts and monopolies. Section 1 of the Act prohibits "every contract, combination . . . or conspiracy in restraint of trade or commerce among the several states [interstate commerce]" (15 U.S.C. §1), and section 2 makes it illegal, "to monopolize, attempt to monopolize, or combine or conspire . . . to monopolize" (15 U.S.C. § 2). Violators must pay treble damages, which by statute are three times the damage suffered.

The Sherman Act is dependent on judicial interpretation, as its vague language lends itself to different opinions as to the Act's intent and meaning (Roberts, 1990). Thus, the Supreme Court has adopted three approaches to determine violations of Section 1 of the Act. First, the Court has adopted a "rule of reason" defense that is founded on the notion that some restraints are necessary business practices. In other words, the Court weighs pro-competitive effects against the anti-competitive ones that lead to liability. The defense requires an inquiry as to the necessary business practices of the industry, and it must overcome the plaintiff's convictions that the defendant's conduct is unreasonable. This theory has been advanced in sport on many occasions due to the numerous and arguably necessary rules and restrictions generally required for competitive balance among the teams in the league. Such restrictions include player drafts; free agency restrictions; restraints on salary, franchise sale, ownership, and movement; franchise territorial restraints; and revenue sharing, among others, all of which can be justified as necessary for the proper operation of the leagues. Courts will, however, judge such restrictions on their reasonableness or fairness, balancing the business necessity against the degree of anticompetitive behavior of the practice.

The second approach is where the anticompetitive conduct is deemed **illegal per se**. *Illegal per se* activities are presumed to have no benefit to competition in the industry. Use of the *illegal per se* approach is limited and is applied in two situations: where the Court is examining agreements between traditional business competitions and where the Court is seeking to avoid a lengthy inquiry into an industry's business operations (Greenberg, 1993).

A third approach in which the Court focuses solely on the effect a challenged practice has on consumer welfare has also emerged (Roberts, 1990). This approach, however, has yet to be applied in cases in the professional sport industry. Roberts (1990) has argued that this consumer welfare standard may be very important for sport-related antitrust cases and, if applied, would likely limit a plaintiff's success as the plaintiff would be forced to demonstrate that league conduct injures consumer welfare. The success of this approach may vary, for instance, with restrictions in the player market harder to prove under this application than other aspects of the business of professional sport.

Antitrust Law Applied to Baseball

Baseball possesses a unique status in professional sport, as well as American business, by virtue of its **exemption from antitrust laws**. In a 1922 Supreme Court decision, *Federal Baseball Club of Baltimore, Inc. v. National League of Professional Baseball Clubs, et al.* (1922), the Court concluded that baseball was neither interstate nor commerce—two elements necessary for federal antitrust laws to apply. The Supreme Court viewed baseball as a professional service business presenting local exhibitions and thus, not commerce. Further, it found the travel of players across state lines was purely incidental to the game and not an essential element of the baseball business. Over time the exemption has faced attack and been amended by the Curt Flood Act, but *Federal Baseball* is still viewed as controlling.

In *Toolson v. New York Yankees* (1953), and in *Flood v. Kuhn* (1972), baseball players contended that the player reserve system violated federal antitrust laws. Under the reserve system teams could perpetually renew players, and without a free market, the players were forced to stay with those teams. In both decisions the Supreme Court reaffirmed baseball's exemption by shifting the burden to Congress to create legislation to abolish the exemption. *Flood* also encouraged baseball players to use labor relations rather than antitrust law to resolve their disputes over the reserve clause (See Supplemental CD). Incidentally, the Major League Baseball Players Association used labor arbitration to successfully challenge the player reserve system, ultimately limiting the reserve clause to a one-year renewal favoring the club (*In Re Twelve Clubs Comprising the National League and Twelve Clubs Comprising the American League and Major League Baseball Players Association*, 1975).

In 1998, Congress codified baseball's exemption through the Curt Flood Act (15 U.S.C. § 27). The Flood Act clarified the exemption by exempting the baseball business, but not the labor or employment of the major baseball players. The Act includes the following in the business of baseball: the minor leagues and minor league player reserve clause; the amateur draft; franchise expansion, location, or relocation; franchise ownership; marketing and sales of the entertainment product of baseball; and licensed properties.

This Act reversed a growing number of court decisions subjecting baseball's business practices to antitrust: *Butterworth v. National League of Professional Baseball Clubs*, 1994 (franchise relocation); *Fleer v. Topps Chewing Gum and Major League Baseball Ass'n*, 1981 (baseball card licensing); *Henderson Broadcasting Corp. v. Houston Sports*, 1982 (broadcasting); *Piazza v. Major League Baseball*, 1993 (court concludes baseball's exemption limited to reserve clause); *Postema v. National League of Professional Baseball Clubs*, 1992 (umpiring); and *Twin City Sportservice, Inc. v. Finley*, 1972 (concessions).

Antitrust Law Applied to Other Sports

Players, owners and prospective owners, and other competitors have challenged antitrust laws in other professional sports. *United States v. International Boxing Club* (1955), was the first case to subject professional sport to antitrust law. Soon after, the Supreme Court made football subject to antitrust. In *Radovich v. National Football League* (1957), a football player challenged a rule restricted his ability to sign a contract with a team other than the one that held his rights and that blacklisted him from signing as a player-coach with a team affiliated with the NFL. Radovich contended that the blacklist was a group boycott in restraint of trade. The trial and appellate courts dismissed Radovich's claims on the ground that football, like baseball, was exempt from antitrust law. The Supreme Court, however, reversed and held that due to the NFL's radio and television contracts, the NFL was engaged in interstate commerce and subject to the Sherman Act.

Single-Entity Status

In an attempt to gain Section 1 immunity, a number of new leagues have structured themselves as single entities with owners investing in the league, not teams, and the adoption of central operations for business and personnel decisions. The logic is that with centrally administered entities operated by owner–investors, there is a single entity, thus the league is unable to contract, combine, or conspire in restraint of trade in the manner that leagues made up of numerous individually owned teams might. Single-entity status for traditionally organized sports leagues has been rejected in the majority of cases (*Sullivan v. NFL*, 1994; *Los Angeles Mem'l Coliseum Comm'n v. NFL*, 1984; *NASL v. NFL*, 1982; *Smith v. Pro Football, Inc.*, 1978; *Mackey v. NFL*, 1976). Four cases, however, *Chicago Professional Sports Limited Partnership v. National Basketball Association* (1996), *Fraser v. Major League Soccer* (2000)(See Supplemental CD), and most recently, *American Needle, Inc. v. National Football League* (2008), and *Madison Square Garden v. National Hockey League* (2008), have been open to the use of the single entity defense after a case-by-case examination of the application of the single entity to sport league activity. The variety of activities of a sport league will likely lead courts to determine whether the league is engaging in behavior of a single entity or acting more like a joint venture. For instance, in the Chicago Bulls case, the Seventh Circuit Court of Appeals in the *Chicago Bulls* case determined that no case set forth a characterization on how a single entity is structured. Thus, it instructed that an analysis be done on a case-by-case or practice-by-practice basis. Under such an analysis, the court found it possible that the NBA could act as a single entity when imposing league-wide limitations on broadcasting through superstations, yet act as a joint venture when imposing restrictions on player mobility. The Seventh Circuit expressly withheld judgment as to whether the NBA was a single entity and remanded the case to district court for such a finding. The case, however, settled out of court in 1996. The *American Needle* case followed this logic, by applying the single entity to the leagues in areas involving licensing and broadcasting. However, in the Madison Square Garden case, the court determined it could not decide if the NHL was a single entity for purposes of its new media policy at the pleading stage. The court favored an examination in line with the *Chicago Bulls* analysis that required a factual examination as to whether new media strategy and practice could be determined centrally, such that competition was barred and individual clubs could be forced to comply with a central management system implementing a standard web page format.

In *Fraser*, the First Circuit Court of Appeals determined that Major League Soccer (MLS) was a single entity organized as a limited liability company made up of operator-investors who sacrificed local autonomy for centralized operations. Specifically, MLS owns all teams and their intellectual property rights, tickets, and broadcast rights. It sets team schedules, negotiates stadium leases and assumes related liabilities, pays the salaries of referees and other league personnel, and supplies certain equipment. *Fraser* makes clear that a sports league can be organized uniquely and avoid antitrust liability provided it is organized as a single entity from its inception, not as a result of revising or restructuring itself to avoid antitrust liability. Keep in mind that the single-entity defense will not affect the ability to sue leagues under § 2 *Monopolies*, it will only serve as an exemption of § 1, the clause generally used to challenge restrictive sport league practices.

Finally, a jury decision in August 2008 determined that the ATP Tour acted as a single economic entity and thus, did not violate section 1 of the Sherman Act when it downgraded the Hamburg tennis tournament from a top-tier to a second-tier event. The jury favored the argument proffered by defendants in their jury instructions that, "the ATP and its members function as a single business entity or single enterprise with respect to operating and participating in the ATP Tour, including with respect to the categorization of tournament members, the creation of an annual calendar, the setting of ranking points to be awarded for performance in different ATP events, and the adoption of rules pertaining to when and where player members shall play. . . . Defendants contend that the ATP and its members function as a single economic enterprise for the purpose of producing the ATP brand of professional tennis through the ATP World Tour and for the purpose of carrying out the core functions of a global professional tennis tour." (*Deutscher Tennis Bund v. ATP Tour*, 2008).

Antitrust Challenges by Competitor Leagues

Three Section 2 cases emerged to challenge competitor leagues over the practices of established leagues as monopolistic. Only one case, *Philadelphia World Hockey, Inc. v. Philadelphia Hockey Club, Inc.* (1972), was substantially successful for the plaintiff. There the World Hockey Association successfully argued that the NHL monopolized the labor pool of talented players through the use of their reserve system. The NHL's reserve system perpetually bound players to a team. The World Hockey Association successfully argued that the system restrained their ability to acquire marquee NHL players.

Two other cases brought by upstart competitors were not as successful. In *American Football League v. National Football League* (1963), the plaintiff was unable to prove that the NFL, by expanding into Dallas and Minneapolis, two cities the AFL was also considering for expansion, was monopolizing the market for professional football. In *United States Football League v. National Football League* (S.D.N.Y., 1986), a jury found that the NFL had monopolized the market for football in the United States, but only awarded nominal damages.

Antitrust Challenges by Prospective Team Owners and Team Owners

Individual franchise owners have challenged league rules, on the theory that rules diminish competition. Many league rules restrict opportunities of the individual in favor of the good of the league. Prospective team owners have brought antitrust challenges to league ownership restrictions that have kept them from becoming owners. The courts in *Levin v. National Basketball Association* (1974), and *Mid-South Grizzlies v. National Football League* (1983), upheld rules requiring three-fourths approval of league owners for transfer of ownership (*Levin*) and admission to the league (*Mid-South Grizzlies*). The most recent of these challenges, *Piazza v. Major League Baseball* (1993), involved potential owners prevented from purchasing and relocating the San Francisco Giants. The case settled out of court just after the *Piazza* court entered a declaratory judgment that the claim should not be dismissed due to baseball's antitrust exemption.

The most celebrated case of an owner challenging a restrictive franchise policy involved Raiders owner Al Davis in *Los Angeles Memorial Coliseum and the Los Angeles Raiders v. National Football League*, (1984). This case involved the Raiders' successful antitrust challenge to league restraints on franchise relocation in which the club convinced the court that the three-fourths vote needed for relocation into the Los Angeles market was unreasonable. At the time it was highly unusual for an owner to sue co-owners. However, a new breed of owners who have made large investments to purchase teams may be more willing to challenge league policies on antitrust grounds. Some owners such as Jerry Jones of the Cowboys and Bob Kraft of the Patriots do not believe they should share their stadium, marketing, and licensing revenues with others in the league. This represents a major shift from the "league-think" philosophy championed by former NFL Commissioner Pete Rozelle.

Other lawsuits filed by franchise owners involve challenges over the number of games telecast nationally on a superstation (*Chicago Bulls and WGN v. National Basketball Association*, 1996); ownership policies, such as restrictions against public ownership relocation (*Sullivan v. National Football League*, 1994, *VKK v. National Football League*, 1999); and marketing and revenue sharing (*Dallas Cowboys v. NFL Trust*, 1995).

Antitrust Challenges by Individual Athletes

Suspended athletes have used antitrust to challenge league actions. In *Molinas v. National Basketball Association* (1961), the plaintiff NBA player was suspended for wagering on games in which he was participating. Molinas's application for reinstatement with the league was rejected, and Molinas argued that the expulsion from the league restrained trade because he had no economic alternative to playing basketball in the NBA. The court upheld the suspension, finding that the restraint was a reasonable one, as the NBA had a legitimate interest in banning gambling.

Antitrust Exemption for Sport Broadcasting Contracts

In 1961 Congress exempted sports leagues' national television deals from antitrust liability (15 U.S.C. §§ 1291-1294). The statute grants professional leagues an exemption to pool their television rights to increase bargaining power when negotiating league-wide television packages.

Convergence of Labor and Antitrust Laws

Early on, employers used the Sherman Act against labor movements, claiming workers organizing boycotts or work stoppages were committing conspiracies in restraint of trade. Employers used injunctions to thwart labor activities and the threat of treble damages to chill the labor movement. In 1914 Congress enacted the Clayton Act to exempt organized labor acting in its own self-interest from antitrust liability. However, as organized labor soon discovered, the federal courts willingly continued to grant injunctions against labor activity. In response Congress passed the Norris-La Guardia Act in 1932; often called the Anti-injunction Act because it restricted the federal judiciary's power to grant injunctions against labor unions in labor disputes (see Section 7.33, *Labor Law: Professional Sports Applications*).

During the Term of the Collective Bargaining Agreement

Together the Clayton and Norris-La Guardia Acts created an antitrust exemption for unions acting in their own self-interest, but did not protect union-management actions, such as entering into collective bargaining agreements (CBAs). CBAs are contracts that contain restrictive provisions and as such could be deemed "contracts, combinations or conspiracies in restraint of trade." The U.S. Supreme Court addressed this issue in a number of nonsupport's cases involving multiemployer bargaining units and established the nonstatutory labor exemption to antitrust law (*Allen Bradley Co. v. Local Union No. 3, International Brotherhood of Electrical Workers*, 1945; *Local Union No. 189, Amalgamated Meat Cutters, and Butcher Workmen of North America, AFL-CIO v. Jewel Tea*, 1965; *United Mineworkers of America v. Pennington*, 1965; and *Connell Construction v. Plumbers*, 1975). The Court balanced the interests of antitrust law against labor law and implied the exemption from the labor statutes that set forth a national labor policy favoring free and private collective bargaining (*Brown v. Pro-Football*, 1996)(see Supplemental CD). A goal of federal labor policy is to bring labor and management together to negotiate a CBA that best suits their needs. The Court found that Congress did not intend for antitrust laws to subvert the goal of achieving labor peace through labor-management relations. The objective of the labor exemption is to protect those mandatory subjects agreed to through good faith bargaining from antitrust scrutiny by a party to the collective agreement. It would not be fair to agree to a restrictive practice, receive concessions in exchange for the agreement, and then turn around and sue a counterpart under antitrust law over the practice. The Supreme Court has established that terms negotiated between labor and management in their collective agreement, which outside a collective agreement would be subject to antitrust law, are in fact exempt from antitrust scrutiny, provided the defendant meets this test:

1. The injured party is a party to the collective bargaining agreement.

2. The subject contested on antitrust grounds is a mandatory subject for bargaining (hours, wages, and other terms and conditions of employment).

3. The collective bargaining agreement was reached through bona fide arms' length bargaining.

Scope of the Labor Exemption

A number of cases address the scope of the labor exemption in the professional sport industry. The league and union are protected from antitrust suits by the labor exemption for suits brought by players not in the league when a collective bargaining agreement with restrictive policies is negotiated (*Wood v. National Basketball Association*, 1987; *Clarett v. National Football League*, 2003). At the time restrictive provisions limit a players' earning capacity, a player is then in the league and must take the burdens of collective bargaining to receive the benefits. The same holds true for suits by former players who may disagree with a union's negotiating decisions and challenge restrictive practices agreed to in negotiation (*Reynolds v. National Football League*, 1978).

Courts have examined practices such as restrictions on free agency, the draft, and salary caps as mandatory subjects. As long as the restriction affects hours, wages, or terms and conditions of employment, courts have found the provisions to be mandatory subjects. For example, in *Mackey v. National Football League* (1976), the court found that although the Rozelle Rule did not directly deal with hours, wages, and terms and conditions of employment, its effect was to depress player salaries (wages), and thus it was deemed a mandatory subject.

Two cases, *Mackey v. National Football League* (1976), and *McCourt v. California Sports, Inc.* (1979), are useful in examining the concept of arms length bargaining. In *Mackey*, a number of former and current football players challenged the Rozelle Rule, a restriction on free agency that required teams signing free agents to pay compensation to the athlete's former team. The owners argued that the labor exemption applied. The court disagreed, finding that there was no bona fide arms length bargaining because the Rozelle Rule remained unchanged from the time it was unilaterally implemented in 1963. Further, there was no evidence that players agreed to the Rozelle Rule as a *quid pro quo* for better pension benefits and the right to individually negotiate their salaries (as was argued by the NFL's defense). In fact, the *Mackey* Court found that there was no direct bargaining on the Rozelle Rule. Contrast *Mackey* with *McCourt*, where the NHL's By-Law 9A, a similar free agent compensation structure, was subject to antitrust attack by Dale McCourt, a player named as compensation. The court found that the labor exemption protected the NHL because the players' association had bargained vigorously against By-Law 9A. The court stated that player benefits were bargained for in connection with the reserve system remaining unchanged, and the inclusion of the free agent compensation clause was not the result of collusion, but of good-faith bargaining.

Duration of the Labor Exemption

The labor exemption continues to protect parties from antitrust scrutiny after a collective bargaining agreement has expired. The subjects of a collective bargaining agreement survive its expiration because labor law requires parties to maintain the status quo and continue bargaining for a new agreement until impasse. Impasse occurs when there is a total breakdown in negotiations between union and management and often leads to a strike or a lockout. Like the subjects of the collective bargaining agreement, the labor exemption survives the agreement's expiration provided the parties maintain the status quo. If this were not the case, the players' association may have no incentive to bargain and opt to drag its feet in negotiations until the expiration of the agreement to seek treble damages through an antitrust suit, thereby increasing its leverage in labor negotiations. The duty to maintain the status quo only extends to impasse, and once an employer has bargained in good faith to impasse, the employer may unilaterally impose changes to the mandatory bargaining subjects without incurring antitrust liability, provided those changes are consistent with the latest proposals made to the union prior to impasse.

SIGNIFICANT CASE

In this case, a corporation that designed, manufactured and sold headwear carrying trademarked names and logos of NFL teams brought an antitrust suit against the NFL, its teams, their owners, and the competitor, Reebok, that had received exclusive licensing agreement for trademarked headwear and apparel. The Court of Appeals held that NFL teams were a single entity for purposes of antitrust laws, and therefore could not have conspired to restrict trade, and as a single entity for purposes of licensing, NFL teams were free to license their intellectual property on an exclusive basis.

AMERICAN NEEDLE INC. V. NATIONAL FOOTBALL LEAGUE

U.S. Court of Appeals for the Seventh Circuit
538 F.3d 736 (2008)

KANNE, Circuit Judge.

American Needle Inc. sued the National Football League (NFL), its member teams, and NFL Properties LLC (to whom we will collectively refer as "the NFL defendants"), along with Reebok International Ltd. ("Reebok"), alleging that the teams' exclusive licensing agreement with Reebok violated the Sherman Antitrust Act. *See* 15 U.S.C. §§ 1-2. The district court granted summary judgment to the NFL defendants. We affirm.

I. HISTORY

As the most successful and popular professional sports league in America today, the NFL needs little introduction. Indeed, the NFL has inspired countless hours of heated and in-depth discussion about the league's 88 years of professional-football history, including its great players, championship teams, and memorable games. But the only discussion the NFL inspires here involves aspects of the league that are not as well known: the league's corporate structure, and the nature of its relationships with its member teams and the entities charged with licensing those teams' intellectual property.

. . . [T]he NFL is an unincorporated association of 32 separately owned and operated football teams that collectively produce an annual season of over 250 interrelated football games. Each season culminates in a championship game-a game better known as the Super Bowl. As such, the product that the teams produce jointly-NFL football-requires extensive coordination and integration between the teams. After all, NFL football is produced only when two teams play a football game. Thus, although each team is a separate corporate entity or partnership unto itself, no team can produce a game-the product of NFL football-by itself, much less a full season of games or the Super Bowl. Likewise, the teams' individual success is necessarily linked to the success of the league as a whole; to put it another way, it makes little difference if a team wins the Super Bowl if no one cares about the Super Bowl.

Realizing that the success of the NFL as a whole was in their best interests, in the early 1960's the individual teams sought to collectively promote the NFL Brand-that is, the intellectual property of the NFL and its member teams-to compete against other forms of entertainment. With this promotional effort in mind, in 1963 the NFL teams formed NFL Properties: a separate corporate entity charged with (1) developing, licensing, and marketing the intellectual property the teams owned, such as their logos, trademarks, and other indicia; and (2) "conduct[ing] and engag[ing] in advertising campaigns and promotional ventures on behalf of the NFL and [its] member [teams]." Among other things, the NFL teams authorized NFL Properties to grant licenses to vendors so the vendors could use the teams' intellectual property to manufacture and sell various kinds of consumer products that bear the teams' logos and trademarks-products such as team jerseys, shirts, flags, and, as pertinent here, head-wear, like baseball caps and stocking hats.

For a while after its establishment, NFL Properties granted headwear licenses to a number of different vendors simultaneously; one of those vendors was American Needle, which held an NFL headwear license for over 20 years. But then in 2000, the NFL teams authorized NFL Properties to solicit bids from the vendors for an exclusive headwear license. Reebok won the bidding war, and in 2001 the NFL teams allowed NFL Properties to grant an exclusive license to Reebok for ten years. NFL Properties thus did not renew American Needle's headwear license, or the licenses of the other headwear vendors.

American Needle responded to the loss of its headwear license by filing an antitrust action against the NFL, NFL Properties, the individual NFL teams, and Reebok. As relevant here, American Needle claimed that the exclusive headwear licensing agreement between NFL Properties and Reebok violated § 1 of the Sherman Antitrust Act, which outlaws any "contract, combination . . . or conspiracy, in restraint of trade." 15 U.S.C. § 1. As American Needle saw it, because each of the individual teams separately owned their team logos and trademarks, their collective agreement to authorize NFL Properties to award the exclusive headwear license to Reebok was, in fact, a conspiracy to restrict other vendors' ability to obtain licenses for the teams' intellectual property. American Needle also contended that, by authorizing NFL Properties to award the license to Reebok, the NFL teams monopolized the NFL team licensing and product wholesale markets in violation of § 2 of the Sherman Antitrust Act. *See Id.* § 2.

One year after American Needle brought its suit, the NFL defendants filed a motion for summary judgment on the company's § 1 claim. The NFL defendants argued that, under the United States Supreme Court's decision in *Copperweld Corp. v. Independence Tube Corp.,* 467 U.S. 752 (1984), and its progeny, they were immune from liability under § 1. In *Copperweld,* the Supreme Court concluded that a parent corporation and its wholly owned subsidiary are a single entity for antitrust purposes. *Id.* at 771. The Court based its conclusion on its determination that the parent-subsidiary relationship did not yield the anti-competitive risks that the Sherman Antitrust Act was enacted to combat. *Id.* at 769, 771, 104 S.Ct. 2731. Specifically, the Court stated that agreements between companies are generally subject to § 1 review because they deprive the market of the independent sources of economic power that competition requires. *Id.* at 769, 104 S.Ct. 2731. But because the parent-subsidiary relationship is always "guided or determined not by two separate corporate consciousnesses, but one," the relationship does not deprive the market of any independent sources of economic power. *Id.* at 771, 104 S.Ct. 2731.

Federal courts in later cases extended the single-entity concept beyond the context of a parent-subsidiary relationship, stating that affiliated companies or individuals could also be considered a single entity in certain circumstances. *See, e.g., Jack Russell Terrier Network v. Am. Kennel Club, Inc.,* 407 F.3d 1027, 1035 (9th Cir. 2005); *Eleven Line, Inc. v. N. Tex. State Soccer Ass'n,* 213 F.3d 198, 205 (5th Cir. 2000); *Chi. Prof'l Sports Ltd. v. Nat'l Basketball Ass'n ("Bulls II"),* 95 F.3d 593, 597-600 (7th Cir. 1996); *City of Mt. Pleasant v. Associated Elec. Coop., Inc.,* 838 F.2d 268, 271, 276-77 (8th Cir. 1988). Relying on this gradual extension of *Copperweld,* the NFL defendants asserted that they functioned as a single entity when collectively promoting NFL football by licensing the NFL teams' intellectual property, and were thus immune from liability under § 1.

American Needle did not immediately oppose the NFL defendants' summary-judgment motion. Instead, the company moved for a continuance under Fed.R.Civ.P. 56(f) on the ground that it was "unable to present admissible evidence" to dispute the NFL defendants' single-entity defense. That evidence, American Needle stated, "was in the possession of the defendants." The company therefore asked the district court for the opportunity to take discovery regarding the NFL defendants' single-entity de-

fense and "a number of issues generally," and included a list of 51 discovery requests.

The NFL defendants, in turn, objected to American Needle's discovery requests on the ground that, as a whole, they were not limited to the single-entity issue. The NFL defendants, did, however, offer to produce a wide range of documents they considered to be related to their single-entity defense. The district court reserved judgment on the NFL defendants' objection, and urged American Needle to narrow its discovery requests. In response, American Needle made additional discovery requests that were even more extensive in scope and number than its original requests. The NFL defendants again objected, and the district court ruled that, until the NFL defendants' summary-judgment motion was resolved, discovery would be limited to the single-entity issue. The court then ordered the NFL defendants to produce all documents pertinent to their single-entity defense.

Discovery ensued. The NFL defendants abided by the district court's order and disclosed a voluminous amount of documents related to their single-entity defense. But when discovery concluded, American Needle filed a second Rule 56(f) motion. As it had done earlier, American Needle stated that it was "unable to present admissible evidence" to dispute the NFL defendants' single-entity defense because that evidence was "in the possession of the defendants." American Needle then listed 49 discovery requests it sought to have the NFL defendants complete; most of those requests were copied verbatim from the requests American Needle made earlier. The district court took American Needle's second Rule 56(f) motion under advisement, and ordered the company to respond to the merits of the NFL defendants' summary-judgment motion.

Shortly after briefing completed, the district court issued an order in which it both denied American Needle's Rule 56(f) motion, and granted the NFL defendants' motion for summary judgment on American Needle's § 1 claim. The district court determined that further discovery on the single-entity issue was unnecessary because "the facts that materially [bore] upon the [court's] decision[ ] [were] undisputed," and led "to the conclusion that the NFL and the teams act as a single entity in licensing their intellectual property." The court's conclusion was based on its determination that the NFL teams' collective-licensing agreement serves "to promote NFL football." And by promoting NFL football through collective licensing, the court continued, the NFL teams "act[ ] as an economic unit" in such a manner that "they should be deemed to be a single entity." The court therefore concluded that American Needle's § 1 claim failed as a matter of law because, under *Copperweld,* single entities cannot restrain trade in violation of the Sherman Antitrust Act. The court then sought supplemental briefing on whether its single-entity finding compelled the dismissal of American Needle's § 2 monopolization claim.

After the parties submitted their briefs addressing American Needle's § 2 monopolization claim, the court granted summary judgment to the NFL defendants. The court concluded that its earlier single-entity determination doomed American Needle's § 2 claim because, as a single entity, the NFL and its member teams could collectively license their intellectual property "to one or many without running afoul of the antitrust laws." This appeal followed.

II. ANALYSIS

American Needle attacks the district court's judgment by forwarding two arguments. First, American Needle contends that the district court incorrectly denied its Rule 56(f) motion before granting summary judgment to the NFL defendants on its § 1 claim. American Needle further asserts that the district court was wrong to grant the NFL defendants' motions for summary judgment on both its § 1 and § 2 monopolization claims. We address these arguments in turn.

A. The district court's denial of American Needle's Rule 56(f) motion

We first address the district court's denial of American Needle's Rule 56(f) motion, a decision that we review for abuse of discretion. *See Hammer v. Ashcroft*, 512 F.3d 961, 971 (7th Cir. 2008).

***

After American Needle submitted its second set of wide-ranging discovery requests, the district court ruled that discovery would be limited to only those documents pertaining to the NFL defendants' single-entity defense, and ordered the defendants to turn over all the documents related to their defense. And in its order rejecting American Needle's second Rule 56(f) motion, the court clearly explained that further discovery was unnecessary because "the facts that materially [bore] upon the [court's] decision[ ] [were] undisputed," and led "to the conclusion that the NFL and the teams act as a single entity in licensing their intellectual property."

In any event, American Needle fails to show that the district court was wrong to deny additional discovery. To succeed on its challenge, American Needle needs to identify the "specific evidence which [it] might have obtained from [the NFL defendants] that would create a genuine issue" as to the defendants' single-entity defense, and thus allow American Needle's § 1 claim to survive summary judgment. *Davis v. G.N. Mortgage Corp.*, 396 F.3d 869, 885 (7th Cir. 2005); *see also United States v. All Assets & Equip. of W. Side Bldg. Corp.*, 58 F.3d 1181, 1190-91 (7th Cir. 1995) (affirming district court's denial of defendants' request for additional discovery because request "lacked specificity concerning what information [the defendants] hoped to uncover and how it would refute [the claims brought against them]"). American Needle identifies no such evidence, however; instead, the company merely ex-

plains that further discovery was necessary because "the determination of the single entity question [sic] requires a fact intensive inquiry [sic]."

However, American Needle's point is irrelevant. Just because the resolution of the single-entity issue is "fact intensive" does not speak to whether additional discovery was necessary to uncover specific evidence; after all, the large number of documents American Needle obtained from the NFL defendants could have provided such a complete answer to the "fact-intensive" question as to render further discovery unnecessary. We thus cannot say that the district court abused its discretion by denying American Needle's Rule 56(f) motion. *See Davis*, 396 F.3d at 885; *All Assets & Equip.*, 58 F.3d at 1190-91.

B. The district court's grant of summary judgment to the NFL defendants

American Needle next challenges the district court's grant of summary judgment to the NFL defendants. We review the district court's grant of summary judgment *de novo*, taking the facts in the light most favorable to American Needle, the non-moving party. *See Foskett v. Great Wolf Resorts, Inc.*, 518 F.3d 518, 522 (7th Cir. 2008). And in so viewing the record, we will examine whether there is a genuine issue of material fact that precludes judgment as a matter of law. *See* Fed.R.Civ.P. 56(c); *Celotex Corp. v. Catrett*, 477 U.S. 317, 322-23 (1986); *Cady v. Sheahan*, 467 F.3d 1057, 1060-61 (7th Cir. 2006).

American Needle first contends that the district court erred by granting the NFL defendants' summary judgment on its § 1 claim. Specifically, American Needle argues that the district court incorrectly concluded that the NFL teams constitute a single entity under *Copperweld* when collectively licensing their intellectual property. American Needle's argument leads us into murky waters. We have yet to render a definitive opinion as to whether the teams of a professional sports league can be considered a single entity in light of *Copperweld*. The characteristics that sports leagues generally exhibit make the determination difficult; in some contexts, a league seems more aptly described as a single entity immune from antitrust scrutiny, while in others a league appears to be a joint venture between independently owned teams that is subject to review under § 1. *See Brown v. Pro Football, Inc.*, 518 U.S. 231, 248-49 (1996) ("[T]he clubs that make up a professional sports league are not completely independent economic competitors. . . . In the present context, however, that circumstance makes the league more like a single bargaining employer. . . ."); *Bulls II*, 95 F.3d at 597-99 ("To say that the league is 'more like a single bargaining employer' than a multi-employer unit is not to say that it necessarily is one, for every purpose."); *see also Super Sulky, Inc. v. U.S. Trotting Ass'n*, 174 F.3d 733, 741 (6th Cir. 1999) ("[T]he notion of concerted action liability in the field of professional sports is at best confusing."). For instance, from the perspective of fans, a professional sports league can be seen as "a single source" of entertainment that produces "one product," even though the league's member teams are distinguishable. *Bulls II,* 95 F.3d at 599. Yet at the same time, individuals seeking employment with any of the league's teams would view the league as a collection of loosely affiliated companies that all have the independent authority to hire and fire employees. *See Brown,* 518 U.S. at 249 (noting that professional football players "often negotiate their pay individually with their employers," NFL teams); *Bulls II,* 95 F.3d at 599 ("[F]rom the perspective of college basketball players who seek to sell their skills, the teams [in the National Basketball League (NBA)] are distinct . . .").

That being said, we have nevertheless embraced the possibility that a professional sports league *could* be considered a single entity under *Copperweld. Bulls II,* 95 F.3d at 598. *But see Fraser v. Major League Soccer, L.L.C.,* 284 F.3d 47, 55-56 (1st Cir. 2002) (citing *Sullivan v. Nat'l Football League,* 34 F.3d 1091, 1099 (1st Cir. 1994), to note that *Bulls II* has not yet been adopted by United States Court of Appeals for the First Circuit). But because of the many and conflicting characteristics that professional sports leagues generally exhibit, we have expressed skepticism that *Copperweld* could provide the definitive single-entity determination for all sports leagues alike. *See Id.* at 599-600. This skepticism, in turn, has led us to opine that the question of whether a professional sports league is a single entity should be addressed not only "one league at a time," but also "one facet of a league at a time." *Id.* at 600. Thus, in reviewing the district court's decision, we will limit our review to (1) the actions of the NFL, its members teams, and NFL Properties; and (2) the actions of the NFL and its member teams as they pertain to the teams' agreement to license their intellectual property collectively via NFL Properties.

With this compartmentalization of *Copperweld* in mind, we turn to American Needle's challenge to the district court's single-entity determination. According to American Needle, the district court applied the wrong legal standard when concluding that the NFL teams were a single entity. As American Needle sees it, the district court concluded "that the NFL [t]eams are a single entity because they 'act' as a single entity in licensing their intellectual property." American Needle asserts that this approach undercuts the Supreme Court's central teaching in *Copperweld:* that the Sherman Antitrust Act was designed to combat the deprivation of independent sources of economic power in the marketplace. *See* 467 U.S. at 469-71, 104 S.Ct. 2518.

Therefore, American Needle continues, instead of asking whether the NFL teams merely " 'act' " as a single entity, the district court should have inquired into whether the NFL teams' agreement to license their intellectual property collectively deprived the market of sources of economic power that control the intellectual property. That question, the company contends, can be answered by looking to whether the teams could compete against one another when licensing and marketing their intellectual property. If

so, American Needle posits, then it is the individual teams who actually control their intellectual property, meaning that they cannot be considered a single entity for the purposes of licensing their intellectual property.

We agree with American Needle that the Supreme Court in *Copperweld* was concerned about the anti-competitive effects that collective action might introduce into the market. *See Id.; Bulls II,* 95 F.3d at 598; *see also Spectrum Sports v. McQuillan,* 506 U.S. 447, 458-59 (1993) (discussing *Copperweld* in context of § 2 claim); *Goldwasser v. Ameritech Corp.,* 222 F.3d 390, 397 (7th Cir. 2000) (same). We further agree that when making a single-entity determination, courts must examine whether the conduct in question deprives the marketplace of the independent sources of economic control that competition assumes. *See Copperweld,* 467 U.S. at 769-71; *Bulls II,* 95 F.3d at 598; *Ball Mem'l Hosp., Inc. v. Mut. Hosp. Ins., Inc.,* 784 F.2d 1325, 1337 (7th Cir. 1986).

But we are not convinced that the NFL's single-entity status in the present context turns entirely on whether the league's member teams can compete with one another when licensing and marketing their intellectual property. American Needle's proposed approach is one step removed from saying that the NFL teams can be a single entity only if the teams have "a complete unity of interest" a legal proposition that we have rejected as "silly." *Bulls II,* 95 F.3d at 598. As we have explained, "*Copperweld* does not hold that only conflict-free enterprises may be treated as single entities"; "[e]ven a single firm contains many competing interests."*Id.* at 598 (discussing Robert G. Eccles, *Transfer Pricing as a Problem of Agency, in Principals and Agents: The Structure of Business* 151 (1985)). Thus, though the several NFL teams could have competing interests regarding the use of their intellectual property that could conceivably rise to the level of potential intra-league competition, those interests do not necessarily keep the teams from functioning as a single entity. *Id.* at 597-98. We therefore cannot fault the district court for not considering whether the NFL teams could compete against one another when licensing and marketing their intellectual property.

And with that said, American Needle's assertion that the NFL teams have deprived the market of independent sources of economic power unravels. Certainly the NFL teams can function only as one source of economic power when collectively producing NFL football. Asserting that a single football team could produce a football game is less of a legal argument than it is a Zen riddle: Who wins when a football team plays itself? *See Nat'l Collegiate Athletic Ass'n v. Bd. of Regents,* 468 U.S. 85, 101 (1984) (" '[Some] activities can only be carried out jointly. Perhaps the leading example is league sports. When a league of professional lacrosse teams is formed, it would be pointless to declare their cooperation illegal on the ground that there are no other professional lacrosse teams.' " (quoting Robert Bork, *The Antitrust Paradox* 278 (1978))); *Bulls II,*

95 F.3d at 599 ("[T]he NBA has no existence independent of sports. It makes professional basketball; only it can make 'NBA Basketball' games. . . ."). It thus follows that only one source of economic power controls the promotion of NFL football; it makes little sense to assert that each individual team has the authority, if not the responsibility, to promote the jointly produced NFL football. Indeed, the NFL defendants introduced uncontradicted evidence that the NFL teams share a vital economic interest in collectively promoting NFL football. After all, the league competes with other forms of entertainment for an audience of finite (if extremely large) size, and the loss of audience members to alternative forms of entertainment necessarily impacts the individual teams' success. *See Bulls II*, 95 F.3d at 597; *see also Brown*, 518 U.S. at 248 ("[T]he [teams] that make up a professional sports league are not completely independent economic competitors, as they depend upon a degree of cooperation for economic survival."); *Nat'l Football League v. N. Am. Soccer League*, 459 U.S. 1074, 1077 (1982) (Rehnquist, J., dissenting) ("The NFL . . . competes with other sports and other forms of entertainment in the entertainment market. Although individual NFL teams compete with one another on the playing field, they rarely compete in the market place.").

But most importantly, the record amply establishes that since 1963, the NFL teams have acted as one source of economic power-under the auspices of NFL Properties to license their intellectual property collectively and to promote NFL football. Tellingly, American Needle does not dispute that the NFL teams collectively license their intellectual property to promote NFL football; in fact, when opposing the NFL defendants' motion for summary judgment, American Needle relied on NFL Properties's Articles of Incorporation, which state that the teams formed NFL Properties "[t]o conduct and engage in advertising campaigns and promotional ventures on behalf of the [NFL] and the member [teams]." And our review of the record reveals no evidence that requires us to question the purpose of the teams' licensing agreement.

Simply put, nothing in § 1 prohibits the NFL teams from cooperating so the league can compete against other entertainment providers. Indeed, antitrust law encourages cooperation inside a business organization-such as, in this case, a professional sports league-to foster competition between that organization and its competitors. *See Bulls II*, 95 F.3d at 599. Viewed in this light, the NFL teams are best described as a single source of economic power when promoting NFL football through licensing the teams' intellectual property, and we thus cannot say that the district court was wrong to so conclude.

Moving on, the failure of American Needle's § 1 claim necessarily dooms its § 2 monopolization claim. As a single entity for the purpose of licensing, the NFL teams are free under § 2 to license their intellectual property on an exclusive basis, *see Cook Inc. v. Boston Scientific Corp.*, 333 F.3d 737, 740 (7th Cir. 2003), even if the teams opt to reduce the number of companies to whom they grant licenses, *see Bulls II*, 95 F.3d at 598 ("To say that participants in an organization may cooperate is to say that they may control what they make and how they sell it: the producers of Star Trek may decide to release two episodes a week and grant exclusive licenses to show them, even though this reduces the number of times episodes appear on TV in a given market. . . ."); Gregory J. Werden, *Antitrust Analysis of Joint Ventures: An Overview,* 66 Antitrust L.J. 701, 730-31 (1998) ("An antitrust claim based solely on a single firm's denial of a license to a trademark would readily be dismissed. . . ."). As such, American Needle has no colorable claim that the NFL teams and NFL Properties created a monopoly by awarding Reebok the exclusive headwear licensing contract. *See Cook Inc.*, 333 F.3d at 740 (discussing competitive effects of exclusive-licensing agreements); *Bulls II*, 95 F.3d at 598. The district court was therefore correct to grant summary judgment to the NFL defendants on American Needle's § 2 monopolization claim.

III. CONCLUSION

We AFFIRM the district court's judgment.

CASES ON THE SUPPLEMENTAL CD

Brown, v. Pro Football, Inc., d/b/a Washington Redskins, 518 U.S. 231 (1996). This case examines whether the NFL violated the Sherman Act, when they implemented unilateral changes after the parties had bargained to an impasse.

Flood v. Kuhn, 407 U.S. 258 (1972). This case examines whether the reserve clause in baseball was exempt Federal Antitrust law.

Fraser v. Major League Soccer, L.L.C., 284 F.3d 47 (2002). This case examines whether Major League Soccer was a single entity for antitrust purposes.

QUESTIONS YOU SHOULD BE ABLE TO ANSWER

1. Why is baseball exempt from antitrust law? Why does it continue to be exempt almost 90 years after the original decision granting the exemption by the U.S. Supreme Court?

2. What is the single entity defense and why is it so important to leagues and tours to be declared single entities?

3. Why would leagues want unions to protect themselves from antitrust challenges?

4. What must a league raise to exe rt the labor exemption defense?

5. Why are sports leagues "magnets" for antitrust litigation?

REFERENCES

Cases

Allen Bradley Co. v. Local Union No. 3, International Brotherhood of Electrical Workers, 325 U.S. 797 (1945).

American Football League v. National Football League, 323 F.2d 124 (4th Cir. 1963).

American Needle v. NFL, 538 F.3d 736 (7th Cir. 2008).

Brown v. Pro-Football, Inc., 518 U.S. 231 (1996).

Butterworth v. National League of Professional Baseball Clubs, 644 So.2d 1021 (Fla. 1994).

Chicago Bulls and WGN v. National Basketball Association, 95 F.3d 593 (7th Cir. 1996).

Chicago Professional Sports Limited Partnership v. National Basketball Association, 95 F.3d 593 (7th Cir. 1996).

Clarett v. National Football League, 306 F.Supp.2d 379 (S.D.N.Y. 2004).

Connell Construction v. Plumbers, 421 U.S. 616 (1975).

Dallas Cowboys v. NFL Trust, 94-C-9426 (N.D. Cal. 1995).

Deutscher Tennis Bund v. ATP Tour, 07-CV-00178, 2008 WL 3857712 (D.Del. 2008).

Federal Baseball Club of Baltimore, Inc. v. National League of Professional Baseball Clubs, et al., 259 U.S. 200 (1922).

Fleer v. Topps Chewing Gum and Major League Baseball Ass'n, 658 F.2d 139 (3rd Cir. 1981).

Flood v. Kuhn, 407 U.S. 258 (1972).

Fraser v. Major League Soccer, 97 F. Supp. 2d 130 (D. Mass. 2000).

Henderson Broadcasting Corp. v. Houston Sports, 541 F. Supp. 263 (S.D. Tex. 1982).

Levin v. National Basketball League, 385 F. Supp. 149 (S.D. N.Y. 1974).

Local Union No. 189, Amalgamated Meat Cutters, and Butcher Workmen of North America, AFL-CIO v. Jewel Tea, 381 U.S. 676 (1965).

Los Angeles Memorial Coliseum and the Los Angeles Raiders v. National Football League, 726 F.2d 1381 (9th Cir. 1984).

Mackey v. National Football League, 543 F.2d 606 (8th Cir. 1976).

Madison Square Garden v. National Hockey League, 2008 U.S. Dist. LEXIS 80474 (S.D.N.Y. 2008).

McCourt v. California Sports, Inc., 600 F.2d 1193 (6th Cir. 1979).

Mid-South Grizzlies v. National Football League, 550 F. Supp. 558 (E.D. Pa. 1982), *aff'd* 720 F.2d 772 (3rd Cir. 1983), *cert. denied,* 467 U.S. 1215 (1984).

Molinas v. National Basketball Association, 190 F. Supp. 241 (S.D. N.Y. 1961).

National Football League v. North American Soccer League, 459 U.S. 1074 (1982).

North American Soccer League v. NFL, 670 F.2d 1249 (2d Cir. 1982).

Philadelphia World Hockey, Inc. v. Philadelphia Hockey Club, Inc., 351 F. Supp. 462 (E.D. Pa. 1972).

Piazza v. Major League Baseball, 831 F. Supp 420 (E.D. Pa. 1993).

Postema v. National League of Professional Baseball Clubs, 799 F. Supp 1475 (S.D. N.Y. 1992).

Powell v. National Football League, 930 F.2d 1293 (8th Cir. 1989).

Radovich v. National Football League, 352 U.S. 445 (1957).

Reynolds v. National Football League, 584 F.2d 280 (8th Cir. 1978).

Smith v. Pro Football, Inc., 593 F.2d 1173 (D.C. Cir. 1978).

Sullivan v. National Football League, 34 F.3d 1091 (1st Cir. 1994).

Toolson v. New York Yankees, 346 U.S. 356 (1953).

Twin City Sportservice, Inc. v. Finley, 365 F. Supp 235 (N.D. Cal. 1972), *rev'd on other grounds,* 512 F.2d 1264 (9th Cir. 1975).

United Mineworkers of America v. Pennington, 381 U.S. 657 (1965).

United States v. International Boxing Club, 348 U.S. 236 (1955).

United States Football League v. National Football League, 644 F. Supp. 1040 (S.D. N.Y. 1986).

VKK v. National Football League, 55 F. Supp. 196 (S.D.N.Y. 1999).

Wood v. National Basketball Association, 809 F.2d 954 (2nd Cir. 1987).

Publications

Greenberg, M. J. (1993). *Sports law practice.* Charlottesville, VA: Michie Co.

Roberts, G. (1990). Antitrust issues in professional sports. In G. Uberstine (Ed.), *Law of professional and amateur sports* (pp. 19-1–19-54. Deerfield, IL: Clark Boardman Callaghan.

Legislation

The Clayton Act of 1914, 15 U.S.C. §§ 12–27 (1989).

The Curt Flood Act of 1998, 15 U.S.C. § 27 (1998).

National Labor Relations Act, 29 U.S.C. § 151-69 (1988).

The Sherman Antitrust Act of 1890, 15 U.S.C. § 1, et seq. (1989).

7.32 *Antitrust Law: Amateur Sport Applications*

—John T. Wolohan

ITHACA COLLEGE

Unlike professional sports organizations, the courts have afforded the NCAA and other amateur athletic organizations plenty of room under the antitrust laws to "retain a clear line of demarcation between intercollegiate athletics and professional sports" (*NCAA Manual, 2008-09*). Yet, even though the courts have been reluctant to apply the antitrust laws against athlete eligibility requirements and other rules regulating the relationship between member school, the NCAA and other amateur athletic organizations have faced a number of antitrust lawsuits involving the commercial relationships between member institutions and other organizations. These lawsuits, which range from the unlawful restraint of trade in the television market and the college basketball coaches' market to the unlawful use of their monopoly power to destroy another amateur athletic organization, will all be explored in the following section.

FUNDAMENTAL CONCEPTS

In reviewing Federal Antitrust challenges against the NCAA, the first question the courts must determine is which of the two major sections of the Sherman Act applies. The two sections of the Sherman Act are Section 1 (15 U.S.C. § 1); which prohibited restraints of trade or commerce, and Section 2 (15 U.S.C. § 2), which prohibits monopolies or attempted monopolies. Once the court determines what section of the Sherman Act applies, it must then determine whether the NCAA's rule or policy has a pro-competitive benefit to consumer (athletes and sports fans) or an anti-competitive effect.

Sherman Antitrust Act

Section 1 of the Sherman Act

Section 1 of the Sherman Act states that "[E]very contract, combination in the form of trust or otherwise, or conspiracy, in restraint of trade or commerce among the several States, or with foreign nations, is hereby declared to be illegal" (15 U.S.C. § 1).

As we will see below, it is important to note, that not every restraint of trade violates the antitrust law. Because nearly every contract that binds the parties to an agreed course of conduct "is a restraint of trade" of some sort, the Supreme Court has limited the restrictions contained in Section 1 to bar only "**unreasonable restraints of trade**" (*NCAA v. Board of Regents of University of Oklahoma*, 1984). Therefore In order to prevail on a Section 1 claim under the Sherman Act, the plaintiff must show that the defendant (1) participated in an agreement that restrained interstate trade or commerce; and (2) that the agreement unreasonably restrained trade in the relevant market.

Establishing a Section 1 Violation

In determining whether a defendant's conduct unreasonably restrains trade, the courts have developed three tests: the per se rule, the rule of reason, and the "quick look" rule of reason.

Per Se Rule. The **per se rule** condemns practices that are entirely void of redeeming competitive rationales and creates a presumption of a Sherman Antitrust Act violation for certain types of behavior. The reasoning behind the per se rule is that certain types of combinations or agreements are almost always antitrust violation, regardless of the intent of the participants or the justifications offered. As a result, the courts have refused to engage in a detailed (and costly) market and effects analysis of conduct that fits into a per se category because such a close look would almost never save the prohibited conduct from Section 1 condemnation. There are only a handful of categories that will trigger the per se rule. Some examples include: price fixing, resale price maintenance, and market allocations.

In the 1970s, the Supreme Court sharply altered its antitrust stance by either expressly overruling or limiting the application of the per se rule for most categories, therefore it is only applied in clear-cut cases (Weiler & Roberts, 1998).

Rule of Reason. The **rule of reason** analysis, on the other hand, requires the court to take a careful look at the markets and parties affected and whether the challenged restraint has a substantially adverse or anticompetitive effect on competition in the relevant product market.

The focus of the rule of reason inquiry is not so much the legal category in which the conduct falls, but rather the actual purpose and effects of the restraints, and how they affect competition. Under the rule of reason analysis, the court must perform a case-by-case economic and legal analysis, not only evaluating the restraint, but also the actual history and purpose behind the restraint and the effects of the practice and whether it "unreasonably" affects competition under the circumstances. Examples of contracts, combinations, or conspiracies that "**unreasonably**" restrain trade under Section 1 include price fixing, market allocation, group boycotts, and vertical territorial restrictions.

Since Section 1 only bars "unreasonable restraints of trade," an agreement to restrain trade may still survive scrutiny under Section 1 if the pro-competitive benefits of the restraint justify the anticompetitive effects. Justifications offered under the rule of reason may be considered only to the extent that they tend to show that, on balance, "the challenged restraint enhances competition" (*NCAA v. Board of Regents of University of Oklahoma*, 1984).

Finally, even if the defendant can show pro-competitive elements, the plaintiff may still show that the restraint is not reasonably necessary to achieve the stated objective. To prove this, the plaintiff may argue that the restraint does not further the stated objective or that there are less restrictive alternatives.

"Quick Look" Rule of Reason. When a practice has obvious anticompetitive effects, such as price fixing, the courts have developed a "quick look" rule of reason analysis which allows the courts to proceed directly to the question of whether the pro-competitive justifications advanced for the restraint outweigh the anticompetitive effects.

For example, in *Law v. National Collegiate Athletic Association* (1998), the court, using a quick look rule of reason analysis, found that the undisputed evidence supported a finding of anticompetitive effect. The NCAA adopted the Restricted Earnings Coach (REC) Rule to reduce the high cost of part-time coaches' salaries by limiting compensation to entry-level coaches to $16,000 per year. At trial, the NCAA did not dispute that the cost reduction had effectively reduced restricted-earnings coaches' salaries. Therefore, since the rule was successful in artificially lowering the price of coaching services, the court ruled that no further evidence or analysis was required to find market power to set prices. Thus, the district court did not need to resolve issues of fact pertaining to the definition of the relevant market to support its decision on summary judgment that the REC Rule is a naked price restraint.

Section 2 of the Sherman Act

Section 2 of the Sherman Act states that "[E]very person who shall monopolize, attempt to monopolize, or combine or conspire with any other person or persons, to monopolize any part of the trade or commerce among the several States, or with foreign nations, shall be deemed guilty of a felony . . ." (15 U.S.C. 2).

Establishing a Section 2 Violation

Unlike Section 1, which requires that at least two parties combine or conspire in restraint of trade, it is important to note that Section 2 of the Sherman Act can be triggered by a single party acting alone. In order to establish a violation under Section 2, the courts must prove two elements. First, the court will look to determine whether the company or organization possesses monopoly power in the relevant market. Monopoly power has traditionally been defined as "the power to control market prices or exclude competition (*U.S. v. E.I.duPont*

Nemours & Co., 1956). In addition to having the ability to control market prices or exclude competition, it is essential that the courts identify the relevant markets adversely affected by the anticompetitive actions. For example, while the NCAA may have a monopoly over college sports, it has very little control over professional sports. Therefore, the key to most Section 2 cases is the definition of the relevant market (See Section 7.31, *Antitrust Law: Professional Sport Applications*), for more examples of various monopoly markets). Once you have determined that a company or organization has a monopoly, the second question for the court, is whether the company or organization has unlawfully used their monopoly power to restrict competition.

The NCAA and Antitrust Law

The following section looks at just some of the antitrust lawsuits filed against the NCAA. In particular, the cases examine the difficulty the courts have in distinguishing between rules and regulations that are designed to protect the amateur nature of intercollegiate athletes and those that are commercial in nature.

Student-Athletes Eligibility

In *Banks v. NCAA* (1992), Braxston Banks, while still a college football player, entered his name into the professional draft. Banks, who was not drafted, brought suit against the NCAA seeking to have his eligibility to play intercollegiate football restored. Banks alleged that the NCAA's rules withdrawing an athlete's eligibility to participate in collegiate sports when the athlete chooses to enter a professional draft or engages an agent to help him secure a position with a professional team is an illegal restraint on trade or commerce in violation of the Sherman Antitrust Act.

The Seventh Circuit Court of Appeals, however, rejected Banks claim and held that he failed to allege an anticompetitive effect on a relevant market; at best, the court found that Banks had merely attempted to frame his complaint in antitrust language. Although Banks alleged a restraint on the market of college football players, college institutions that are members of the NCAA, and perhaps an NFL player recruitment market, the complaint failed to explain how these alleged restraints diminish competition in or among the markets. In other words, the court ruled, Banks merely claimed that there was an anticompetitive effect, but failed to explain what it was.

In *Hairston v. Pacific 10 Conference and NCAA* (1996), the PAC-10 after conducting an eight-month investigation into the allegations of recruiting improprieties, placed the University of Washington football team on probation for recruiting violations. The levied sanctions included, among other things, a two-year post-season bowl ban, a one-year television revenue ban, and a two-year probationary period.

A group of former and current football players at the university sued the conference, alleging that the sanctions violated the Sherman Antitrust Act. In rejecting the players' claim, the Court of Appeals held that the players failed to show that the penalties imposed by the PAC-10 constituted an unreasonable restraint of trade.

In *Smith v. NCAA* (1998), Renee Smith sued the NCAA, alleging that the NCAA's enforcement of a bylaw prohibiting her from participating in athletics while enrolled in a graduate program at an institution other than her undergraduate institution violated the Sherman Antitrust Act. The Court of Appeals held that as matter of first impression, the Sherman Act's restraint of trade provision did not apply to NCAA's promulgation of eligibility rules. Even if the Sherman Act was applicable, the court held, the challenged rule was not unlawful restraint of trade.

In *McCormack v. NCAA* (1988), a group of football players from Southern Methodist University sued the NCAA after the organization suspended the SMU football program for the entire 1987 season and imposed restrictions on it for the 1988 season. In particular, the athletes argued that the NCAA's restriction on compensation to football players constituted illegal price-fixing in violation of Section 1; and that the suspension of SMU constitutes a group boycott by other NCAA members in violation of Section 2.

In rejecting the players' claim, the court ruled that the Sherman Act does not forbid every combination or conspiracy in restraint of trade, only those that are unreasonable. Therefore, the essential inquiry under the rule-of-reason analysis, the court held, was whether the challenged restraint enhances competition. Applying this test, the court ruled that the NCAA's rules were reasonable and that the players had failed to allege any facts to the contrary.

In January 2008, the NCAA settled a federal antitrust suit filed on behalf of former NCAA athletes challenging the restricting a scholarship to the cost of tuition, books, housing and meals. Because of the billions of dollars the NCAA earned through broadcast and licensing deals, the athletes argued that such a rule was an unlawful restraint of trade. In the agreement, the NCAA agreed to make available $10 million of supplemental money above the standard athletic grant-in-aid to athletes who have competed in Division I-A football and in 16 Division I men's basketball conferences between Feb.17, 2002, and the present (Carey & Gardiner, 2008).

Television

In *NCAA v. Board of Regents of the University of Oklahoma* (1984), the U.S. Supreme Court ruled that the NCAA's plan for televising college football games of member institutions violated the Sherman Antitrust Act. The Supreme Court held that the plan on its face constituted a restraint on operation of a free market; that the relevant market was college football; and that the restraints were not justified on the basis of procompetitive effect, protecting live attendance, or maintaining competitive balance among amateur athletic teams.

Women's Athletics

From 1906 to 1980, the NCAA only sponsored men's intercollegiate athletic programs. In 1971, the Association for Intercollegiate Athletics for Women (AIAW) was organized to govern women's sports. By 1980–81, AIAW's membership had grown to 961 colleges and universities. In 1981, the NCAA introduced twenty-nine women's championships in twelve sports. During the same season, the AIAW suffered a significant drop in membership and participation in its events. The AIAW's loss in membership dues totaled $124,000, which represented approximately 22 percent of the dues collected the previous year. Forty-nine percent of those institutions leaving AIAW elected to join the NCAA. As a result of the membership loses, the National Broadcasting Company (NBC) decided not to exercise its exclusive television rights to telecast AIAW championships. In addition, the Eastman Kodak Company and the Broderick Company also sought to withdraw sponsorship of AIAW achievement awards. Because the AIAW's leadership expected these financial hardships only to worsen, it decided to close for business on June 30, 1982.

Claiming that the NCAA unlawfully used its monopoly power in men's college sports to facilitate its entry into women's college sports and to force AIAW out of existence, the AIAW sued the NCAA. In *Association for Intercollegiate Athletics for Women v. NCAA* (1984), the Court held that the AIAW failed to prove an illegal agreement between the NCAA and NBC to "tie" television rights to the NCAA's newly instituted women's basketball championship to NBC's contract with the NCAA and their men's basketball tournament. The court also held that the AIAW failed to prove specific intent necessary to sustain a claim of attempted monopoly. Even if the conduct of the NCAA was avowedly anticompetitive in purpose, the court found that the record did not support a finding that its effect on the AIAW was the result of anything but direct competition.

College Coaches

In an attempt to reduce the costs of intercollegiate athletics "without disturbing the competitive balance" among member institutions, the NCAA developed bylaws limiting the number of Division I basketball coaching staffs to four members, one head coach, two assistant coaches, and one entry-level coach called a "restricted-earnings" coach; and restricting the compensation of restricted-earnings coaches in all Division I sports other than football to a total of $12,000 for the academic year and $4,000 for the summer months had a clear anticompetitive effect in restricting salaries.

In *Law v. National Collegiate Athletic Association* (1998), the Bylaws were challenged by a group of restricted-earnings coaches under Section 1 of the Sherman Antitrust Act. In upholding the district court's decision, the Tenth Circuit Court of Appeals, using a "quick look" rule of reason analysis, found that the restricted-earnings coaches Rule was anticompetitive and had no procompetitive rationales and therefore was an unlawful restraint of trade. As a result, the court found the NCAA liable for nearly $22.3 million damages, which when trebled, made the NCAA potentially liable for approximately $67 million. The NCAA eventually settled the case for $54.5 million (Dauner, 2000).

In *Hennessey v. NCAA* (1977), a group of assistant football and basketball coaches challenged an NCAA bylaw limiting the number of assistant coaches member institutions could employ at any one time. In upholding the NCAA bylaw, the Fifth Circuit Court, after weighing the anticompetitive effects with the pro-competitive benefits, concluded that the coaches had failed to show that the bylaw was an unreasonable restraint of trade.

When trying to distinguish the precedents established in *Law v. NCAA* and *Hennessey*, there are two aspects the reader must keep in mind. First, it is important to note that Hennessey predates the Supreme Court's opinion in *NCAA v. Board of Regents of University of Oklahoma*, (1984). Second, the Hennessey court placed the burden of showing the unreasonableness of the coaching restriction on the plaintiff and then found that the coaches could not make such a showing because the rule had only recently been implemented. In Law, the plaintiff only had the burden of establishing the anticompetitive effect of the restraint at issue. Once the coaches met that burden, which the coaches did by showing the naked and effective price fixing character of the agreement, the burden shifted to the NCAA to justify the restraint as a "reasonable" one.

The following antitrust case establishes the precedent that even though the NCAA plays a vital role in protecting and preserving the nature of amateur athletics, when its regulations are purely commercial in nature, it will be held to same antitrust standards as other commercial businesses.

NCAA V. BOARD OF REGENTS OF THE UNIVERSITY OF OKLAHOMA

United States Supreme Court
468 U.S. 85 (1984)

Justice STEVENS delivered the opinion of the Court.

The University of Oklahoma and the University of Georgia contend that the National Collegiate Athletic Association has unreasonably restrained trade in the televising of college football games. After an extended trial, the District Court found that the NCAA had violated section 1 of the Sherman Act and granted injunctive relief. The Court of Appeals agreed that the statute had been violated but modified the remedy in some respects. We granted certiorari, and now affirm.

I.

The NCAA

Since its inception in 1905, the NCAA has played an important role in the regulation of amateur collegiate sports. It has adopted and promulgated playing rules, standards of amateurism, standards for academic eligibility, regulations concerning recruitment of athletes, and rules governing the size of athletic squads and coaching staffs. In some sports, such as baseball, swimming, basketball, wrestling, and track, it has sponsored and conducted national tournaments. It has not done so in the sport of football, however. With the exception of football, the NCAA has not undertaken any regulation of the televising of athletic events.

The NCAA has approximately 850 voting members. The regular members are classified into separate divisions to reflect differences in size and scope of their athletic programs. Division I includes 276 colleges with major athletic programs; in this group only 187 play intercollegiate football. Divisions II and III include approximately 500 colleges with less extensive athletic programs. Division I has been subdivided into Divisions I-A and I-AA for football.

Some years ago, five major conferences together with major football-playing independent institutions organized the College Football Association (CFA). The original purpose of the CFA was to promote the interests of major football-playing schools within the NCAA structure. The Universities of Oklahoma and Georgia, respondents in this Court, are members of the CFA.

* * *

The Current Plan

The plan adopted in 1981 for the 1982–1985 seasons is at issue in this case. This plan, like each of its predecessors, recites that it is intended to reduce, insofar as possible, the adverse effects of live television upon football game attendance. It provides that "all forms of television of the football games of NCAA member institutions during the Plan control periods shall be in accordance with this Plan." The plan recites that the television committee has awarded rights to negotiate and contract for the telecasting of college football games of members of the NCAA to two "carrying networks."

* * *

In separate agreements with each of the carrying networks, ABC and the Columbia Broadcasting System (CBS), the NCAA granted each the right to telecast the 14 live "exposures" described in the plan, in accordance with the "ground rules" set forth therein. Each of the networks agreed to pay a specified "minimum aggregate compensation to the participating NCAA member institutions" during the 4-year period in an amount that totaled $131,750,000. In essence the agreement authorized each network to negotiate directly with member schools for the right to televise their games. The agreement itself does not describe the method of computing the compensation for each game, but the practice that has developed over the years and that the District Court found would be followed under the current agreement involved the setting of a recommended fee by a representative of the NCAA for different types of telecasts, with national telecasts being the most valuable, regional telecasts being less valuable, and Division II or Division III games commanding a still lower price. The aggregate of all these payments presumably equals the total minimum aggregate compensation set forth in the basic agreement. Except for differences in payment between national and regional telecasts, and with respect to Division II and Division III games, the amount that any team receives does not change with the size of the viewing audience, the number of markets in which the game is telecast, or the particular characteristic of the game or the participating teams. Instead, the "ground rules" provide that the carrying networks make alternate selections of those games they wish to televise, and thereby obtain the exclusive right to submit a bid at an essentially fixed price to the institutions involved. See 546 F.Supp., at 1289-1293.

The plan also contains "appearance requirements" and "appearance limitations" which pertain to each of the 2-year periods that the plan is in effect. The basic requirement imposed on each of the two networks is that it must schedule appearances for at least 82 different member institutions during each 2-year period. Under the appearance limitations no member institution is eligible to appear on television more than a total of six times and more than four times nationally, with the appearances to be divided equally between the two carrying networks. See *Id.*, at 1293. The number of exposures specified in the contracts also sets an absolute maximum on the number of games that can be broadcast.

Thus, although the current plan is more elaborate than any of its predecessors, it retains the essential features of each of them. It limits the total amount of televised intercollegiate football and the number of games that any one team may televise. No member is permitted to make any sale of television rights except in accordance with the basic plan.

Background of this Controversy
Beginning in 1979 CFA members began to advocate that colleges with major football programs should have a greater voice in the formulation of football television policy than they had in the NCAA. CFA therefore investigated the possibility of negotiating a television agreement of its own, developed an independent plan, and obtained a contract offer from the National Broadcasting Co. (NBC). This contract, which it signed in August 1981, would have allowed a more liberal number of appearances for each institution, and would have increased the overall revenues realized by CFA members.

In response the NCAA publicly announced that it would take disciplinary action against any CFA member that complied with the CFA-NBC contract. The NCAA made it clear that sanctions would not be limited to the football programs of CFA members, but would apply to other sports as well. On September 8, 1981, respondents commenced this action in the United States District Court for the Western District of Oklahoma and obtained a preliminary injunction preventing the NCAA from initiating disciplinary proceedings or otherwise interfering with CFA's efforts to perform its agreement with NBC. Notwithstanding the entry of the injunction, most CFA members were unwilling to commit themselves to the new contractual arrangement with NBC in the face of the threatened sanctions and therefore the agreement was never consummated. See *Id.*, at 1286-1287.

* * *

II.

There can be no doubt that the challenged practices of the NCAA constitute a "restraint of trade" in the sense that they limit members' freedom to negotiate and enter into their own television contracts. In that sense, however, every contract is a restraint of trade, and as we have repeatedly recognized, the Sherman Act was intended to prohibit only unreasonable restraints of trade.

It is also undeniable that these practices share characteristics of restraints we have previously held unreasonable. The NCAA is an association of schools which compete against each other to attract television revenues, not to mention fans an athletes. As the District Court found, the policies of the NCAA with respect to television rights are ultimately controlled by the vote of member institutions. By participating in an association which prevents member institutions from competing against each other on the basis of price or kind of television rights that can be offered to broadcasters, the NCAA member institutions have created a horizontal restraint—an agreement among competitors on the way in which they will compete with one another. A restraint of this type has often been held to be unreasonable as a matter of law. Because it places a ceiling on the number of games member institutions may televise, the horizontal agreement places an artificial limit on the quantity of televised football that is available to broadcasters and consumers. By restraining the quantity of television rights available for sale, the challenged practices create a limitation on output; our cases have held that such limitations are unreasonable restraints of trade. Moreover, the District Court found that the minimum aggregate price in fact operates to preclude any price negotiation between broadcasters and institutions, thereby constituting horizontal price fixing, perhaps the paradigm of an unreasonable restraint of trade.

Horizontal price fixing and output limitation are ordinarily condemned as a matter of law under an "illegal per se" approach because the probability that these practices are anticompetitive is so high; a per se rule is applied when "the practice facially appears to be one that would always or almost always tend to restrict competition and decrease output." *Broadcast Music, Inc. v. Columbia Broadcasting System, Inc.*, 441 U.S. 1, 19-20 (1979). In such circumstances a restraint is presumed unreasonable without inquiry into the particular market context in which it is found. Nevertheless, we have decided that it would be inappropriate to apply a per se rule to this case. This decision is not based on a lack of judicial experience with this type of arrangement, on the fact that the NCAA is organized as a nonprofit entity, or on our respect for the NCAA's historic role in the preservation and encouragement of intercollegiate amateur athletics. Rather, what is critical is that this case involves an industry in which horizontal restraints on competition are essential if the product is to be available at all.

As Judge Bork has noted: "[Some] activities can only be carried out jointly. Perhaps the leading example is league sports. When a league of professional lacrosse teams is formed, it would be pointless to declare their cooperation illegal on the ground that there are no other professional lacrosse teams." R. Bork, The Antitrust Paradox 278 (1978). What the NCAA and its member institutions market in this case is competition itself—contests between competing institutions. Of course, this would be completely ineffective if there were no rules on which the competitors agreed to create and define the competition to be marketed. A myriad of rules affecting such matters as the size of the field, the number of players on a team, and the extent to which physical violence is to be encouraged or proscribed, all must be agreed upon, and all restrain the manner in which institutions compete. Moreover, the NCAA seeks to market a particular brand of football—college football. The identification of this "product" with an academic tradition differentiates college football from and makes it more popular than professional sports to which it might otherwise be comparable, such as, for example, minor league baseball. In order to preserve the character and quality of the "product," athletes must not be paid, must be required to attend class, and the like. And the integrity of the "product" cannot be preserved except by mutual agreement; if an institution adopted such restrictions unilaterally, its effectiveness as a competitor on the playing field might soon be destroyed. Thus, the NCAA plays a vital role in enabling college football to preserve its character, and as a result enables a product to be marketed which might otherwise be unavailable. In performing this role, its actions widen consumer choice—not only the choices available to sports fans but also those available to athletes—and hence can be viewed as procompetitive.

* * *

Respondents concede that the great majority of the NCAA's regulations enhance competition among member institutions. Thus, despite the fact that this case involves restraints on the ability of member institutions to compete in terms of price and output, a fair evaluation of their competitive character requires consideration of the NCAA's justifications for the restraints.

Our analysis of this case under the Rule of Reason, of course, does not change the ultimate focus of our inquiry. Both per se rules and the Rule of Reason are employed "to form a judgment about the competitive significance of the restraint." National Society of Professional Engineers v. United States, 435 U.S. 679, 692 (1978). A conclusion that a restraint of trade is unreasonable may be "based either (1) on the nature or character of the contracts, or (2) on surrounding circumstances giving rise to the inference or presumption that they were intended to restrain trade and enhance prices. Under either branch of the test, the inquiry is confined to a consideration of impact on competitive conditions."

Per se rules are invoked when surrounding circumstances make the likelihood of anticompetitive conduct so great as to render unjustified further examination of the challenged conduct. But whether the ultimate finding is the product of a presumption or actual market analysis, the essential inquiry remains the same—whether or not the challenged restraint enhances competition. Under the Sherman Act the criterion to be used in judging the validity of a restraint on trade is its impact on competition.

III.

Because it restrains price and output, the NCAA's television plan has a significant potential for anticompetitive effects. The findings of the District Court indicate that this potential has been realized. The District Court found that if member institutions were free to sell television rights, many more games would be shown on television, and that the NCAA's output restriction has the effect of raising the price the networks pay for television rights. Moreover, the court found that by fixing a price for television rights to all games, the NCAA creates a price structure that is unresponsive to viewer demand and unrelated to the prices that would prevail in a competitive market. And, of course, since as a practical matter all member institutions need NCAA approval, members have no real choice but to adhere to the NCAA's television controls.

The anticompetitive consequences of this arrangement are apparent. Individual competitors lose their freedom to compete. Price is higher and output lower than they would otherwise be, and both are unresponsive to consumer preference. This latter point is perhaps the most significant, since "Congress designed the Sherman Act as a 'consumer welfare prescription.'" Reiter v. Sonotone Corp., 442 U.S. 330, 343 (1979). A restraint that has the effect of reducing the importance of consumer preference in setting price and output is not consistent with this fundamental goal of anti-trust law. Restrictions on price and output are the paradigmatic examples of restraints of trade that the Sherman Act was intended to prohibit. See Standard Oil Co. v. United States, 221 U.S. 1, 52-60 (1911). At the same time, the television plan eliminates competitors from the market, since only those broadcasters able to bid on television rights covering the entire NCAA can compete. Thus, as the District Court found, many telecasts that would occur in a competitive market are foreclosed by the NCAA's plan.

Petitioner argues, however, that its television plan can have no significant anticompetitive effect since the record indicates that it has no market power—no ability to alter the interaction of supply and demand in the market. We must reject this argument for two reasons, one legal, one factual.

As a matter of law, the absence of proof of market power does not justify a naked restriction on price or output. To the contrary, when there is an agreement not to compete in terms of price or output, "no elaborate industry analysis is required to demonstrate the anticompetitive character of such an agreement." Professional Engineers, 435 U.S., at 692. Petitioner does not quarrel with the District Court's finding that price and output are not responsive to demand. Thus the plan is inconsistent with the Sherman Act's command that price and supply be responsive to consumer preference. We have never required proof of market power in such a case. This naked restraint on price and output requires some competitive justification even in the absence of a detailed market analysis.

As a factual matter, it is evident that petitioner does possess market power. The District Court employed the correct test for determining whether college football broadcasts constitute a separate market—whether there are other products that are reasonably substitutable for televised NCAA football games. Petitioner's argument that it cannot obtain competitive prices from broadcasters since advertisers, and hence broadcasters, can switch from college football to other types of programming simply ignores the findings of the District Court. It found that intercollegiate football telecasts generate an audience uniquely attractive to advertisers and that competitors are unable to offer programming that can attract a similar audience. These findings amply support its conclusion that the NCAA possesses market power. Indeed, the District Court's subsidiary finding that advertisers will pay a premium price per viewer to reach audiences watching college football because of their demographic characteristics is vivid evidence of the uniqueness of this product. Moreover, the District Court's market analysis is firmly supported by our decision in *International Boxing Club of New York, Inc. v. United States*, 358 U.S. 242 (1959), that championship boxing events are uniquely attractive to fans and hence constitute a market separate from that for nonchampionship events. See *Id.*, at 249-252. Thus, respondents have demonstrated that there is a separate market for telecasts of college football which "[rests] on generic qualities differentiating" viewers. *Times-Picayune Publishing Co. v. United States*, 345 U.S. 594, 613 (1953). It inexorably follows that if college football broadcasts be defined as a separate market—and we are convinced they are—then the NCAA's complete control over those broadcasts provides a solid basis for the District Court's conclusion that the NCAA possesses market power with respect to those broadcasts. "When a product is controlled by one interest, without substitutes available in the market, there is monopoly power."

Thus, the NCAA television plan on its face constitutes a restraint upon the operation of a free market, and the findings of the District Court establish that it has operated to raise prices and reduce output. Under the Rule of Reason, these hallmarks of anticompetitive behavior place upon petitioner a heavy burden of establishing an affirmative defense which competitively justifies this apparent deviation from the operations of a free market. See Professional Engineers, 435 U.S., at 692-696. We turn now to the NCAA's proffered justifications.

IV.

Relying on Broadcast Music, petitioner argues that its television plan constitutes a cooperative "joint venture" which assists in the marketing of broadcast rights and hence is procompetitive. . . . The essential contribution made by the NCAA's arrangement is to define the number of games that may be televised, to establish the price for each exposure, and to define the basic terms of each contract between the network and a home team. The NCAA does not, however, act as a selling agent for any school or for any conference of schools. The selection of individual games, and the negotiation of particular agreements, are matters left to the networks and the individual schools. Thus, the effect of the network plan is not to eliminate individual sales of broadcasts, since these still occur, albeit subject to fixed prices and output limitations. Unlike Broadcast Music's blanket license covering broadcast rights to a large number of individual compositions, here the same rights are still sold on an individual basis, only in a noncompetitive market.

The District Court did not find that the NCAA's television plan produced any procompetitive efficiencies which enhanced the competitiveness of college football television rights; to the contrary it concluded that NCAA football could be marketed just as effectively without the television plan. There is therefore no predicate in the findings for petitioner's efficiency justification. Indeed, petitioner's argument is refuted by the District Court's finding concerning price and output. If the NCAA's television plan produced procompetitive efficiencies, the plan would increase output and reduce the price of televised games. The District Court's contrary findings accordingly undermine petitioner's position. In light of these findings, it cannot be said that "the agreement on price is necessary to market the product at all." Broadcast Music, 441 U.S., at 23. In Broadcast Music, the availability of a package product that no individual could offer enhanced the total volume of music that was sold. Unlike this case, there was no limit of any kind placed on the volume that might be sold in the entire market and each individual remained free to sell his own music without restraint. Here production has been limited, not enhanced. No individual school is free to televise its own games without restraint. The NCAA's efficiency justification is not supported by the record.

Neither is the NCAA's television plan necessary to enable the NCAA to penetrate the market through an attractive package sale. Since broadcasting rights to college football constitute a unique product for which there is no ready substitute, there is no need for collective action in order to enable the product to compete against its nonexistent competitors. This is borne out by the District Court's finding that the NCAA's television plan reduces the volume of television rights sold.

V.

Throughout the history of its regulation of intercollegiate football telecasts, the NCAA has indicated its concern with protecting live attendance. This concern, it should be noted, is not with protecting live attendance at games which are shown on television; that type of interest is not at issue in this case. Rather, the concern is that fan interest in a televised game may adversely affect ticket sales for games that will not appear on television.

Although the NORC studies in the 1950's provided some support for the thesis that live attendance would suffer if unlimited television were permitted, the District Court found that there was no evidence to support that theory in today's market. Moreover, as the District Court found, the television plan has evolved in a manner inconsistent with its original design to protect gate attendance. Under the current plan, games are shown on television during all hours that college football games are played. The plan simply does not protect live attendance by ensuring that games will not be shown on television at the same time as live events.

There is, however, a more fundamental reason for rejecting this defense. The NCAA's argument that its television plan is necessary to protect live attendance is not based on a desire to maintain the integrity of college football as a distinct and attractive product, but rather on a fear that the product will not prove sufficiently attractive to draw live attendance when faced with competition from televised games. At bottom the NCAA's position is that ticket sales for most college games are unable to compete in a free market. The television plan protects ticket sales by limiting output—just as any monopolist increases revenues by reducing output. By seeking to insulate live ticket sales from the full spectrum of competition because of its assumption that the product itself is insufficiently attractive to consumers, petitioner forwards a justification that is inconsistent with the basic policy of the Sherman Act. "[The] Rule of Reason does not support a defense based on the assumption that competition itself is unreasonable."

VI.

Petitioner argues that the interest in maintaining a competitive balance among amateur athletic teams is legitimate and important and that it justifies the regulations challenged in this case. We agree with the first part of the argument but not the second.

Our decision not to apply a per se rule to this case rests in large part on our recognition that a certain degree of cooperation is necessary if the type of competition that petitioner and its member institutions seek to market is to be preserved. It is reasonable to assume that most of the regulatory controls of the NCAA are justifiable means of fostering competition among amateur athletic teams and therefore procompetitive because they enhance public interest in intercollegiate athletics. The specific restraints on football telecasts that are challenged in this case do not, however, fit into the same mold as do rules defining the conditions of the contest, the eligibility of participants, or the manner in which members of a joint enterprise shall share the responsibilities and the benefits of the total venture.

The NCAA does not claim that its television plan has equalized or is intended to equalize competition within any one league. The plan is nationwide in scope and there is no single league or tournament in which all college football teams compete. There is no evidence of any intent to equalize the strength of teams in Division I-A with those in Division II or Division III, and not even a colorable basis for giving colleges that have no football program at all a voice in the management of the revenues generated by the football programs at other schools. The interest in maintaining a competitive balance that is asserted by the NCAA as a justification for regulating all television of intercollegiate football is not related to any neutral standard or to any readily identifiable group of competitors.

The television plan is not even arguably tailored to serve such an interest. It does not regulate the amount of money that any college may spend on its football program, nor the way in which the colleges may use the revenues that are generated by their football programs, whether derived from the sale of television rights, the sale of tickets, or the sale of concessions or program advertising. The plan simply imposes a restriction on one source of revenue that is more important to some colleges than to others. There is no evidence that this restriction produces any greater measure of equality throughout the NCAA than would a restriction on alumni donations, tuition rates, or any other revenue-producing activity. At the same time, as the District Court found, the NCAA imposes a variety of other restrictions designed to preserve amateurism which are much better tailored to the goal of competitive balance than is the television plan, and which are "clearly sufficient" to preserve competitive balance to the extent it is within the NCAA's power to do so. And much more than speculation supported the District Court's findings on this score. No other NCAA sport employs a similar plan, and in particular the court found that in the most closely analogous sport, college basketball, competitive balance has been maintained without resort to a restrictive television plan.

Perhaps the most important reason for rejecting the argument that the interest in competitive balance is served by the television plan is the District Court's unambiguous and well-supported finding that many more games would be televised in a free market than under the NCAA plan. The hypothesis that legitimates the maintenance of competitive balance as a procompetitive justification under the Rule of Reason is that equal competition will maximize consumer demand for the product. The finding that consumption will materially increase if the controls are removed is a compelling demonstration that they do not in fact serve any such legitimate purpose.

VII.

The NCAA plays a critical role in the maintenance of a revered tradition of amateurism in college sports. There can be no question but that it needs ample latitude to play that role, or that the preservation of the student-athlete in higher education adds richness and diversity to intercollegiate athletics and is entirely consistent with the goals of the Sherman Act. But consistent with the Sherman Act, the role of the NCAA must be to preserve a tradition that might otherwise die; rules that restrict output are hardly consistent with this role. Today we hold only that the record supports the District Court's conclusion that by curtailing output and blunting the ability of member institutions to respond to consumer preference, the NCAA has restricted rather than enhanced the place of intercollegiate athletics in the Nation's life. Accordingly, the judgment of the Court of Appeals is Affirmed.

CASES ON THE SUPPLEMENTAL CD

Association for Intercollegiate Athletics for Women v. NCAA, 735 F.2d 577 (1984). The case examines whether the NCAA's move into women's athletics violated antitrust law.

Banks v. NCAA, 977 F.2d 1081 (7th Cir. 1992). The case examines the NCAA's rules on player eligibility and whether they restrain the trade of college athletes.

Law v. NCAA, 134 F.3d 1010 (10th Cir. 1998). This case examines the NCAA's rule on the salaries colleges could pay certain coaches and whether the rule violates antitrust laws.

QUESTIONS YOU SHOULD BE ABLE TO ANSWER

1. How do courts determine a restraint of trade under a Rule of Reason analysis?

2. When will the courts consider using a "quick look" rule of reason analysis?

3. How do you define monopoly power?

4. What are some of the cases in which the court will condemn a practice as void under the **per se rule**?

5. In evaluating NCAA rules and bylaws, what are some of the things the court look for when considering the reasonableness of the rule?

REFERENCES

Cases

Association for Intercollegiate Athletics for Women v. NCAA, 735 F.2d 577 (1984).

Banks v. NCAA, 977 F.2d 1081 (7th Cir. 1992).

Hairston v. Pacific 10 Conference, 101 F.3d 1315 (9th Cir. 1996).

Hennessey v. NCAA, 564 F.2d 1136 (5th Cir. 1977).

In Re NCAA I-A Walk-on Football Players Litigation, 398 F. Supp. 2d 1144 (2005).

Law v. NCAA, 134 F.3d 1010 (10th Cir. 1998).

McCormack, v. National Collegiate Athletic Association, 845 F.2d 1338 (1988).

NCAA v. Board of Regents of the University of Oklahoma, 468 U.S. 85 (1984).

Smith v. NCAA, 139 F.3d 180 (3rd Cir. 1998).

U.S. v. E.I.duPont Nemours & Co., 351 U.S. 377 (1956).

Worldwide Basketball and Sports Tours, Inc. v. NCAA, 273 F. Supp. 2d 933, 954-55 (S.D. Ohio 2003).

Publications

Carey, J., & Gardiner, A. (January 30, 2008). NCAA settles antitrust lawsuit; Football, basketball athletes due $10M. *USA Today*, p. 1C.

Dauner, J. T. (2000, June 14). Court hears payout arguments from restricted earnings coaches. *The Kansas City Star*, p. D4.

Mitten, M., Davis, T., Smith, R., & Berry, R. (2005). *Sports Law and Regulation: Cases, Materials and Problems.* New York, NY: Aspen Publishers.

NCAA Constitution, Art. 1.3.1 (NCAA Manual (2008–09).

Weiler, P. C., & Roberts, G. R. (1998). *Sports and the law.* St. Paul, MN: West Group.

Legislation

The Sherman Antitrust Act of 1890, 15 U.S.C.A. § 1-7.

The Clayton Act of 1914, 15 U.S.C.A. § 12-27.

7.33   Labor Law: Professional Sport Applications

—Lisa Pike Masteralexis
University of Massachusetts-Amherst

Labor law has been a critical component to the U.S. workforce as it has created structures for employees to bargain for safe and productive work environments. Labor laws, along with employment laws, delineate the conduct that is acceptable in the work environment. Labor laws exist on both state and federal levels. State labor laws apply to public entities, such as a city or state's sports authority or a state university athletic or recreation department. Federal labor laws apply to private employers engaged in a business involving interstate commerce, such as a professional sports league or an arena operated by a facility management company.

The National Labor Relations Act in particular sets forth the parameters of conduct by employers and employees in private-sector unionized workplaces through a process of collective bargaining that allows employees and employers to determine what issues must be resolved in their particular workplace and negotiate a contract for their workplace. As a manager in the sport industry, it is critical that management decisions are made with an eye toward the collective bargaining agreement and its rules, policies, and procedures, lest you find yourself facing a grievance and arbitration process.

FUNDAMENTAL CONCEPTS

Fair Labor Standards Act

The Fair Labor Standards Act (FLSA) establishes minimum hourly wages, overtime wages for work exceeding 40 hours, and child labor protections. It also requires employers keep records on those aspects. There are numerous exemptions from the overtime pay and/or the minimum wage provisions and some from the child labor provisions. Exemptions are narrowly construed against the employer asserting them. Consequently, employers and employees should always closely check the exact terms and conditions of an exemption in light of the employee's actual duties before assuming that the exemption might apply to an employee. The burden of proving the exemption rests with the employer. Exemptions likely to apply in the sport industry include those for individuals working in executive or administrative positions and those engaged in commissioned sales for the retail or service industry, of which sports and recreation are a part. "[A]n establishment which is an amusement or recreational establishment, if (1) it does not operate for more than seven months in any calendar year, or (2) during the preceding calendar year, its average receipts for any six months of such year were not more than 33-1/3 per centum of its average receipts for the other six months of such year" [FLSA, 29 USC § 213 (a)(3) (2005)] is also exempt from FLSA wage and overtime provisions.

National Labor Relations Act

The National Labor Relations Act of 1935 (NLRA) applies to private employers. It was enacted to "eliminate . . . or mitigate the causes of certain substantial obstructions to the free flow of commerce . . . by encouraging collective bargaining and by protecting the exercise by workers of full freedom of association, self-organization, and designation of representatives of their own choosing, for the purpose of negotiating the terms and conditions of their employment or other mutual aid or protection" (NLRA, § 151, 2005). The NLRA set forth employee rights to join or assist unions, engage in concerted activity for economic benefits and work protections, and the right to engage in collective bargaining. It applies to employees and employers in the private sector, drawing distinctions between employees for assignment to bargaining units, such that employees who are in the same bargaining unit need not do the exact same job, but must have common bargaining interests.

Through the NLRA Congress created the National Labor Relations Board (NLRB), because it believed a specialized agency charged with regulating labor relations was necessary. Congress also established the NLRB because it mistrusted the manner in which the federal courts handled labor cases, by often aligning with employers. The two primary activities of the NLRB are to conduct secret ballot union elections for certification and decertification and to prevent and remedy unfair labor practices.

Taft-Hartley Act of 1947

There is no doubt that the NLRA was pro-labor. A dozen years later the Taft-Hartley Act amended the NLRA to give balance to labor relations by focusing on rights of employers and non-union members. Among other things, Taft-Hartley amended the NLRA by granting the right of employees to choose to *not* join or assist unions, the right of employers to engage in lockouts, and also a provision that prohibits the union from discriminating against non-union members. Section 9 of the NLRA was amended to include among NLRB responsibilities the decertification of unions as well as certification of unions.

Employee Rights

NLRA § 7 established three significant employee rights:

1. the right to join or assist unions and the right not to join or assist unions;

2. the right to engage in collective bargaining through representative of own choosing; and

3. the right to engage in concerted activity for one's own mutual aid and protection (29 USCS § 157, 2005).

When employees want to join a union, they must petition the NLRB to conduct a secret ballot election under § 9 of the act to determine whether at least one-third of all employees are interested in conducting an election and whether the group is an appropriate unit to collectively bargain with the employer. The NLRB examines the community of interests of the group to determine if there is enough in common to make bargaining successful. **Community of interests** include: commonality of supervision, work rules, and personnel policies; shared work areas, similarity of job duties and working conditions; similarity of methods for evaluation; similarity in pay and benefits; integration and interdependence of operations; and history, if any, of collective bargaining between the parties (Feldacker, 2000; Gold, 1998).

In a case involving the North American Soccer League (NASL), the league challenged the NLRB's certification of all players into a national bargaining unit for purposes of collective bargaining (*North American Soccer League v. NLRB*, 1980). The NASL argued that employee units at the local team level were the appropriate bargaining unit. The NLRB disagreed, finding that where an employer has assumed sufficient control over the working conditions of employees of its franchisees, the NLRB may require employers to bargain jointly. The court agreed that labor relations were in fact conducted at a leaguewide level and not delegated to individual teams, and thus, the NLRB's designation was appropriate. From the union's perspective, if the NASL had successfully limited bargaining to the local level, employers could easily undermine solidarity by trading union supporters. Local units could also undermine the union's strike threat, such that if a team in Boston went on strike, the league could continue to play and give any team playing Boston a bye. By continuing without a franchise, the strike's force would be severely limited. With the shared revenue structures in place in most leagues, the Boston franchise could also still receive a cut of revenues from the league, severely disabling the leverage of the union.

Once a union is designated as an appropriate bargaining unit, elections are held, and a union is certified as the exclusive bargaining representative for employees, granting two important changes for employees. First, management then has a duty to bargain in good faith with the union and second, the union has a duty of fair representation for its employee members.

Duty to Engage in Collective Bargaining

Once a union is in existence, management *must* engage in collective bargaining over mandatory subjects of bargaining or risk being charged with an unfair labor practice under § 8 (a)(5) of the NLRA for failing to bargain in good faith (*NLRB v. Katz*, 1962). Mandatory subjects are hours, wages, and terms and conditions of employment. They are those things "plainly germane to the 'working environment' and not those 'managerial decisions which lie at the core of entrepreneurial control'" (*Ford Motor Co. v. NLRB* at 498, 1979). The result of good faith negotiations is to create a collective bargaining agreement (CBA). Wages are basically anything else that has monetary value including salaries, per diem, bonuses, severance and termination pay, and fringe benefits, such as health care, life or disability insurance. Hours provisions cover anything related to time spent at work. Terms and conditions of employment cover the majority of remaining provisions in one's work life, including job security, seniority, grievance and arbitration provisions, drug-testing provisions, safety concerns, and the like.

There are also permissive subjects for bargaining, over which management is not obligated to negotiate and the union cannot bargain to impasse. An example of a permissive subject might be if the National Basketball Players Association wanted its logo to appear in all NBA advertisements. An impasse is a stalemate in negotiations that often leads to a strike or a lockout. In collective bargaining relationships, unions often give up the right to strike in return for management giving up the right to lock employees out. Although there is a protected right for employees to engage in concerted activity, unions are allowed to bargain away this right, if the union members so choose. Another word on concerted activity is that it is a protected § 7 right, provided the behavior does not become violent.

Duty of Fair Representation

After certification by the NLRB, a union becomes the exclusive bargaining representative for *all* employees. The duty of fair representation requires that a union represent *all* employees fairly, even those employees who are not union members (*Steele v. Louisville & Nashville Railroad*, 1944). If the union does not represent employees fairly, it qualifies as an unfair labor practice under § 8(b) (1) (A) the section that prohibits interference with § 7 rights (*Miranda Fuel Co.*, 1962). Fair representation requires that unions must not discriminate or act in an arbitrary or bad faith manner (*Vaca v. Sipes*, 1967). Most duty of fair representation cases challenge decisions to pursue grievances on behalf of employees. In *Peterson v. Kennedy and the NFLPA*, the plaintiff NFL player sued his union for failing to fairly represent him when it erred in not filing his grievance in a timely manner (1985). The court held that because the union's conduct amounted to no more than negligence, it did not meet the standard required for a duty of fair representation case. The court emphasized that unions are not liable for good faith, nondiscriminatory errors of judgment made in interpreting CBAs, in processing grievances or representing them in the process, (*Id.*).

Unfair Labor Practices

Section 8 of the NLRA provides the enforcement mechanism by establishing employer and union unfair labor practices.

Employer Discrimination or Retaliation for Union Activity

It is an unfair labor practice for the employer to interfere with, restrain or coerce employees who are engaged in union activity [NLRA, § 8(a)(1)]. It is also an unfair labor practice to discriminate against employees for such activity and for showing support of the union [NLRA, § 8(a)(3)]. In theory, this is straightforward, but in practice, like all discrimination cases, its application is difficult. Often workplace discipline, demotion, or termination decisions arise from mixed motives—union animus by the employer combined with an employee's poor work performance or misconduct.

Duty to Bargain in Good Faith

Once a union is certified by the NLRB, management and union have a duty to bargain in good faith over hours, wages, and terms and conditions of employment. Either party can negotiate to impasse and decide whether to use their economic weapons of imposing a strike or a lockout. In practice, management may unilaterally implement its last best offer and still fulfill the duty to bargain in good faith (*Brown v. Pro Football*, 1996). Because there is no duty to bargain over permissive subjects, employers can unilaterally impose permissive and "management rights" subjects. Management rights subjects generally encompass managerial decisions that "lie at the core of entrepreneurial control" (*Ford Motor Co. v. NLRB* at 498, 1979). Management need not negotiate management rights, but it may have to negotiate their effect if they impact mandatory subjects for bargaining. For example, management need not negotiate with the union to relocate a sports franchise to a new city, but will have to negotiate with the players' union over such effects of the decision as how players will cover relocation costs from one city to the next.

Duty to bargain in good faith cases may arise in professional sports when the commissioner attempts to make a new rule that impacts mandatory subjects. For instance, in *National Football League Players Association v. National Labor Relations Board*, the NFLPA argued that the NFL commissioner's imposition of a rule and corresponding fines for players leaving the bench during fights without negotiating with the union was a refusal to bargain in good faith (1974). Often a conflict arises between the commissioner's best interest powers and the players' right to negotiate over mandatory subjects. Keep in mind that the *NFLPA v. NLRB* does not limit the NFL's ability to impose rules or fines for bench clearing, it simply requires that such rules be negotiated with the union.

Collective Bargaining Relationship

The CBA is a contract that expresses the final negotiations between management and union over the mandatory subjects of their business, and the collective bargaining relationship is an ongoing one. There may be a need for additional negotiations after that document is formed, that require union and management to continue to discuss or negotiate for other issues that affect mandatory subjects. Either side has the right to convince the other side to come back to the bargaining table to discuss or negotiate over a new or current term of employment.

Over the term of the collective bargaining relationship there is also considerable time spent by union and management in the administration of the collective bargaining agreement. An important component of the administration is the reliance on an arbitration process to resolve disputes. Arbitration is a less costly, more efficient alternative to the court system or to union striking or management locking employees out as a means of resolving disagreements. Arbitration clauses are common in labor agreements and create a mechanism for employees and employers to resolve disputes as to interpretations of the CBA or to resolve grievances challenging disciplinary action. There are two forms of arbitration: rights and interest. Rights arbitration is for disputes over the interpretation or application of the contract. Interest arbitration deals with disputes over the actual terms of contract, such as salary arbitration (*Silverman v. MLBPRC*, 1995). In salary arbitration for example, the contract provision delegates to the arbitrator(s) the power to determine the compensation term for a given player based on a salary dispute between the player and the team.

Despite the quality of negotiating or the clarity of expression in the CBA, disputes are bound to arise during the course of the agreement. Disputes can be lodged through a grievance process negotiated into the CBA. The road to an arbitration case starts with one party filing a grievance against the other. Unions will generally file these on behalf of their employees. The contract will set forth a process for resolving the disputes that leads up to the final, binding arbitration hearing. The Steelworkers Trilogy cases (*U.S. Steelworkers v. American Mfg. Co.*, 1960; *U.S. Steelworkers v. Warrior Gulf Co.*, 1960; *U.S. Steelworkers v. Enterprise Corp.*, 1960) established federal policy that an arbitrator's decision should not be the subject of judicial intervention provided that the arbitrator's award is based on the essence of the collective bargaining agreement. Thus, a court cannot substitute its decision for an arbitrator's if it does not agree with it. A court can only overturn a decision if the plaintiff can prove that the arbitrator has exceeded the scope of the authority granted in the CBA or by the parties or that the arbitrator has decided the grievance in an arbitrary or capricious manner.

A recent issue being addressed through collective bargaining is drug testing. Congress has threatened to impose uniform drug-testing policies for professional sports. Policies achieved through collective bargaining are more likely to be effective in protecting the rights and obligations of employees and employers. Through a bargaining process an employee's privacy rights, confidentiality of tests, medical concerns, the determination of what drugs to test for and what amounts of those drugs must be in one's system to be subject to suspension, concerns over "what else" the organization might discover in testing, the role of results and international competition, and the like will be negotiated to develop fair provisions. The bargaining table also provides a forum for the two sides to add educational and rehabilitative components. Further, union and management may negotiate testing policies and procedures in the context of other aspects of their employment relationship, such as disciplinary actions and arbitration provisions.

Professional Sport Labor Relations

Despite the NLRA's enactment in 1935, it took another thirty to forty years before the labor movement took hold in the sport industry. The first decision to enforce union certification in professional sports involved baseball umpires. In the *American League of Professional Baseball Clubs and the Association of National Baseball League Umpires* (1969), Major League Baseball challenged the NLRB's jurisdiction. MLB argued that because it was exempt from antitrust laws under the 1922 U.S. Supreme Court decision in *Federal Baseball,* then it should likewise be exempt from labor laws. Next MLB argued that it had an internal system of self-regulation creating no need for NLRB involvement. The NLRB disagreed, arguing that MLB's internal system would put the umpire before the Commissioner for a final resolution of disputes. The NLRB recognized that the system was designed by the employers, who also hire and manage the Commissioner. Without evidence of a neutral third party as the final arbiter, the NLRB noted that this case might just be the beginning of a whole host of employees who might seek NLRB assistance in the future including professional athletes, clubhouse attendants, front office staff, scouts, groundskeepers, and maintenance staff.

Today virtually all major league teams are unionized workplaces for professional athletes, but not for the other employees envisioned by that umpires case in 1969. The reasons for this are varied, and among them might be (1) the far fewer white-collar workers in unions, (2) the high turnover in front office and coaching positions, (3) the competition for jobs might deter people from working together in a union organizing movement, and (4) organizing front office staff or coaches on a national, multiemployer level like the professional athletes is challenging.

Unionized workplaces for professional athlete-employees are unique because the dynamics of the collective bargaining relationship make every negotiation a battle. The turnover rate for professional athletes is high due to their short careers. A majority of athletes lack job security, causing players to want to achieve the best deal possible in collective bargaining negotiations. With an average career length hovering around three years and most collective bargaining agreements having three- to six-year terms, unions are motivated to negotiate for the best contract possible. There is a great disparity between players' talent and thus, their need for the union. A superstar will have far different bargaining goals than a bench player. When negotiating for the collective interests of all players, players' unions must struggle to keep the superstars and average players equally satisfied. Without the solidarity of all players, a players' association loses its strength.

Players' associations are transnational employee bargaining units that negotiate with a transnational multiemployer bargaining unit. Players associations must constantly spread their message to new members. In spreading the message, the associations face logistical challenges of a large, diverse, geographically expansive bargaining unit. In the high-pressure world of professional team sports, the multiemployer bargaining team also faces challenges by having disparate bargaining priorities, such as large versus small market clubs; corporate versus family ownership; ownership stake in one club versus ownership stakes in a more diverse set of sport/entertainment business venture, such as those ownership groups that have cross-ownership in teams, media ventures, and/or facilities. Despite the very contentious labor struggles between owners and players, leagues do favor unionized workforces in professional sport for the labor exemption protection from antitrust liability that unions provide. The topic is discussed in greater detail in Section 7.31, *Antitrust Law: Professional Sport Applications.*

Palace Sports & Entertainment v. NLRB explores the concept of an employee's right to organize a union in the workplace. It also examines when an employer may terminate a union leader's employment in the workplace when the firing is allegedly made through mixed motives—alleged anti-union animus toward the employee and alleged employee misconduct.

PALACE SPORTS & ENTERTAINMENT, INC., D/B/A ST. PETE FORUM V. NATIONAL LABOR RELATIONS BOARD (NLRB)

United States Court of Appeals for the District of Columbia Circuit
411 F.3d 212 (2005)

I. BACKGROUND

Palace owns and operates various sports and entertainment arenas. In July 1999, the Company purchased the Ice Palace in Tampa, Florida, an arena which has since become known as the St. Pete Times Forum. Palace assumed various contractual obligations made by the previous owner, including a contract with SMG, a company whose employees maintained the facility and performed the work necessary to effectuate conversions of the arena floor. SMG had a labor contract with the Union.

When Palace purchased the Forum, it decided that it would take control over the maintenance and conversion operations itself instead of employing subcontractors like SMG. On June 30, 2001, when SMG's contracts with the Forum and the Union expired, Palace assumed the maintenance and conversion operations for the arena. The Company hired some of SMG's former employees, including Peter Mullins, a mechanical engineer who had been on the Union's negotiating committee while he was employed by SMG. After he was hired, Mullins and other pro-union employees began soliciting union authorization cards. The presence of this union activity at the Forum resulted in a number of incidents involving the management of the Company, which ultimately resulted in the filing of unfair labor practice charges in this case.

On June 27, 2001, the Company posted a policy prohibiting solicitation by one employee to another "while either is working." In response to some complaints from employees regarding solicitation on behalf of the Union, Palace vice president Sean Henry reviewed this no-solicitation policy with employees at a meeting on July 18. He informed the employees that solicitation in violation of the Company's policy could result in termination. During the course of the meeting, Henry effectively promulgated a rule prohibiting any conversation about the Union. Specifically, Henry told employees that they could "talk about virtually anything" so long as they did not solicit. But by "virtually anything" Henry excluded conversations about the union, because he viewed any discussion regarding the Union as Solicitation.

In mid-July, operations manager Carson Williams asked employee Thomas Roberts whether anyone had approached him "about the union organization process." After Roberts responded that nobody had, Williams said, "I know if anyone comes to you, you will let me know." Also in mid-July, employee George Freire spoke with a new employee and gave him a union authorization card. The next day, Williams told Freire "not to be discussing union issues on the clock or in the building."

Around November 20, 2001, Williams approached Roberts and told him that he "didn't like rumors" and wanted to clear one up. He said that he had heard that Roberts had gone to the NLRB to complain about him, and asked Roberts to explain his action. Roberts answered that he did not know what Williams was talking about, that he had not gone to the NLRB. Williams then conceded that it might have been another employee with the same name as Roberts who had complained to the NLRB, but that "it would all come out and once it did" Williams "would take care of it."

On June 18, 2002, Williams called Mullins to his office to fix a problem with the building's automation system. After the problem was corrected, Williams commented that he would be "lost" without Mullins, to which Mullins replied that he was not planning on going anywhere. Williams then told Mullins that if he "and the rest of the union supporters file for a new election, then you are going to be terminated." When Mullins responded that he could not be fired for "doing something legal," Williams stated that the Company would terminate the leader "and then the rest of you will get in line." Mullins asked Williams who had told him that, and Williams replied, "Sean Henry."

On July 11, 2002, less than a month after this conversation, employee James Carpenter arranged to speak with Henry to complain about Peter Mullins. According to Henry, Carpenter reported that Mullins would not leave him alone, that he "is always . . . talking to me and telling me the merits of the Union." Carpenter told Henry that initially this happened "three, four, five times a week," but that it was now "every time" he saw Mullins. Carpenter further noted that he had told Mullins to leave him alone "dozens of times."

Henry referred the matter to the Company's human resources director, Beth Fields, and, the next day, Henry, Fields, and Williams met with Carpenter. According to a memorandum summarizing this meeting, Carpenter reported being "harassed and solicited" by Mullins. He specifically reported the most recent incident, which had taken place in the employee break room at 7:30 a.m. on July 11, before Carpenter had clocked in but after Mullins began work at 7:00 a.m. Carpenter related that he and another employee went to the break room, where Mullins asked him why he would not join the Union. Carpenter explained that he liked working for Palace and that the Company had been good to him. Mullins told Carpenter that the Union could negotiate a better raise for him, but Carpenter responded that he was not interested and then left. Carpenter reported that Mullins was always "'antagonizing'" him about joining the Union and confronts him "at least 3–5 times per week," and that it was interfering with his work. Following this meeting, Carpenter prepared a written statement, dated July 17, 2002, in which he stated that, "for the past couple of weeks," he had been "stopped in the hallways" and "inside the breakroom" by Mullins "about having the union back into this building," and that he was "getting tired" of it. Carpenter's statement recounted the July 11 break room incident, adding that he told Mullins before walking away, "I don't want to hear about it anymore."

There is no evidence that Carpenter again complained about Mullins after July 11. On July 18, Fields, Henry, and Williams interviewed Mullins regarding Carpenter's complaints. Henry testified that, at that meeting, Mullins stated that he had no idea what Carpenter was talking about. Mullins asserted that Carpenter was already a member of the Union and that he talked to Carpenter about the Union only to answer Carpenter's questions. Henry also recalls that when he confronted Mullins with Carpenter's claim that he asked Mullins to stop "countless times," Mullins replied, "I don't recall him ever asking me to stop."

In his own testimony, Mullins claimed that he never initiated any conversations about the Union with Carpenter, but rather that Carpenter would bring up the subject and was "confused," "afraid that . . . he was going to lose his job if he supported the Union." Mullins maintained that he never intimidated or harassed Carpenter during these conversations. Regarding the specific incident on July 11, Mullins recalled that Carpenter "brought up the subject about how his father-in-law had told him that he didn't need a union." Mullins responded, "Well, James, you know, in a perfect world you don't need a union . . . [but we are] already making a lot less money since Palace . . .

eliminated the contract and, you know, we're not getting overtime after eight."

For his part, Carpenter testified that Mullins had spoken to him about bringing the Union back, and that he replied that he wanted to give the Company a chance. Mullins replied, "Okay." A couple of weeks later, Mullins spoke with him again, and he replied, "No. I don't want it yet." Carpenter testified that Mullins continued to approach him "on several occasions." He explained that when he was in the break room before clocking in and "when I'm going from one job to another job . . . he approaches me and stops and asks me about the Union." On those occasions, Carpenter told Mullins, "I don't want to discuss it right at this moment." Carpenter denied initiating the conversations as Mullins has claimed.

On July 25, 2002, Mullins was issued two disciplinary warnings. The first was a written warning for violating the Company's solicitation policy on July 11, 2002. The warning states that, while on work time, Mullins "asked an employee why he would not join a labor union." The second warning, a final written warning, was for violation of the Company's policy against harassment. It explains that "during the months of June and July 2002," Mullins harassed an employee "in various work areas at least 3 to 5 times a week even after the employee being harassed asked [Mullins] to stop. The employee states that [Mullins] has stopped him in his work area and in his words, 'intimidated' him about joining a labor union while he was on work time. The employee repeatedly asked [Mullins] to stop talking to him about joining a labor union, but [Mullins] continued."

On October 2, 2002, Carpenter signed a union authorization card. Mullins testified that Carpenter requested the card. Carpenter admitted signing the card, but denied requesting it. There is no evidence that Carpenter made any complaint on this occasion. About three weeks later, the Union filed a petition for a representation election.

On October 23, Mullins initiated a conversation with Alice Castillo, an employee of a vendor located in the Forum. The two were discussing a newspaper article regarding wages in Florida when the conversation turned to whether wages in Florida were lower than those paid in northern states. According to Castillo, she asked Mullins what wages were in other southern states like Alabama and Mississippi, in response to which Mullins loudly called her a "Yankee bitch." Mullins denies making the remark. Castillo prepared a statement for her supervisor recounting the incident that was ultimately forwarded to Palace officials.

Upon learning of the incident, Fields spoke with Castillo, who repeated her allegation regarding the incident and stated that "it had been going on for a long time and that she had just had enough." Mullins heard from a fellow employee that Castillo was upset with him over something, and went to her to apologize for anything he may have said that offended her.

On October 31, Henry, Fields, and Williams met with Mullins. Mullins stated that he did not recall calling Castillo a "Yankee bitch"; he also explained that he had apologized to her for anything he may have said. Fields testified that she believed Castillo, because Mullins had only stated that he "did not recall" making the offensive statement. On November 3, Mullins was discharged. Fields testified that the Company fired Mullins because he "made inappropriate comments and his conduct was inappropriate."

B. The NLRB's Decision

On the basis of the above evidence, a NLRB Administrative Law Judge ("ALJ") concluded that Palace violated § 8(a)(1) by: (1) prohibiting conversations about the Union while permitting conversations relating to other matters; (2) interrogating employees about their knowledge of employee interest in the Union and directing them to report the union activities of their coworkers; (3) interrogating employees about their communications with the NLRB and threatening reprisals if employees cooperated with the NLRB; and (4) threatening employees with discharge because of their support for the Union.

Considering next the disciplinary warnings issued to Mullins, the ALJ credited Mullins' version of the events on July 11 and, accordingly, found that he did not solicit Carpenter. The ALJ alternatively found that, even if Mullins did solicit Carpenter, Mullins did not violate the Company's solicitation policy, because Mullins talked with Carpenter while engaged in nonwork activity. With respect to the harassment warning, the ALJ credited Mullins' assertion that he never approached Carpenter and found that, even if he had, the encounters to which Carpenter testified did not constitute harassment. Finding that Mullins was disciplined while engaging in protected activity for misconduct he did not commit, the ALJ concluded that Palace violated § 8(a)(1). Without any further explanation, the ALJ found that Mullins was warned for engaging in union activity, and thus concluded that the warning also violated § 8(a)(3).

Turning to Mullins' conversation with Castillo, the ALJ credited Mullins' testimony that he did not make any offensive statement, finding that Castillo either misheard or misunderstood his remark. The ALJ noted, however, that because Mullins was not engaged in protected activity when he committed the alleged misconduct, * * * the Company was entitled to rely on its good-faith belief in Castillo's version of the incident.

Applying the *Wright Line* test for determining the relationship, if any, between employer action and protected employee conduct, the ALJ concluded that the General Counsel had carried his burden of showing that Mullins' union activity was a substantial and motivating factor in Palace's decision to discharge Mullins. The ALJ next considered whether the Company had carried its burden of showing that it would have taken the same disciplinary ac-

tion even in the absence of Mullins' protected activity. Evaluating the Company's written policies regarding "indecent conduct or language," as well as the only other documented incident in the record regarding such behavior, the ALJ found that Palace had not satisfied its burden. The ALJ accordingly concluded that Mullins' discharge violated § 8(a)(3).

* * * [T]he NLRB affirmed the ALJ's findings and conclusions. The NLRB, however, specifically addressed Mullins' discharge. The NLRB ostensibly applied the *Wright Line* framework, agreeing first with the ALJ that the General Counsel "made the required initial showing that Mullins' union activity was a substantial or motivating factor in his discharge." Proceeding to the question of whether Palace had established that it would have discharged Mullins even in the absence of his protected activity, the NLRB noted that the Company had argued that "Mullins' angry outburst at Castillo created sufficient concern for Title VII liability that it discharged him." The NLRB then concluded that Palace had "failed to show that it would have discharged Mullins even in the absence of his union activity in order to avoid the imposition of Title VII liability." * * *

In reaching this judgment, the NLRB suggested that it would have been "unreasonable" for Palace to discharge Mullins in order to avoid Title VII liability. The NLRB reasoned as follows:

> The Supreme Court has held that a single, isolated comment generally is not sufficient to justify the imposition of Title VII liability. Clark County Such. Dist. v. Breeden, 532 U.S. 268, 271 (2001). Moreover, even where an employee has been shown to have sexually harassed a co-worker, Title VII does not necessarily require the employee's discharge, so long as the employer takes reasonable action to protect the complainant from further harassment. Baskerville v. Mulligan International Co., 50 F.3d 428, 432 (7th Cir. 1995).

> Based on this understanding of Title VII law, the NLRB concluded:

> We recognize that employers have a legitimate interest in preventing workplace sexual harassment and a correlative obligation to respond when such incidents occur. In this case, however, we find that the [Company] has not established that it had reasonable grounds for determining that it had to remove or discipline Mullins in order to avoid liability under Title VII.

On this basis, the NLRB found that Palace's "asserted Title VII concerns" were perpetual. In light of these conclusions, the NLRB ordered Palace to cease and desist from engaging in the unlawful conduct it was found to have committed or, in any like manner, interfering with, restraining, or coercing employees in the exercise of their rights under the Act. The NLRB also ordered Palace to offer Mullins full reinstatement to his former job or a substantially equivalent position, make him whole for any loss of earnings or other benefits, and expunge any records of his disciplinary warnings and discharge.

II. ANALYSIS

* * *

B. The NLRB's Conclusion That the Warnings Were Unlawful

Palace challenges the NLRB's conclusion that it committed unfair labor practices in violation of § 8(a) (1) and (3) by issuing the disciplinary warnings to Mullins on July 25, 2002. Because we conclude that the NLRB's § 8(a) (1) finding is supported by substantial evidence, and because Palace offers no persuasive reason to believe that the additional finding under § 8(a) (3) had any material effect on the order, we have no occasion to address the latter finding. * * *

Section 8(a) (1) of the Act makes it an unfair labor practice for an employer "to interfere with, restrain, or coerce employees in the exercise of" their rights to organize, bargain collectively, and engage in concerted activities. 29 U.S.C. § 158(a) (1). * * * In this case, the NLRB found that the warnings violated § 8(a) (1) because Mullins did not in fact engage in the misconduct for which he was disciplined.

* * *

The NLRB, adopting the ALJ's credibility determinations, credited Mullins' testimony regarding his encounters with Carpenter in general, and their July 11 conversation in particular. Accordingly, the NLRB found that, on July 11, Mullins did not ask Carpenter "why he would not join a labor union." Rather, the NLRB accepted Mullins' account that Carpenter approached Mullins, mentioning that his father-in-law had told him that employees did not need a union, and that Mullins merely responded by giving reasons why the employees did need a union, referring to reductions in wages and benefits since the Company became their employer. The NLRB also accepted Mullins' claim that he never approached Carpenter to talk about the Union, but only discussed the subject when Carpenter brought it up.

In crediting Mullins, the NLRB observed that there was "no evidence contradicting" Mullins' assertion that Carpenter was already a union member, and also noted that Carpenter, though called as a witness by the Company, did not testify about the July 11 conversation, and thus failed to contradict Mullins' account of it. The NLRB further cited numerous inconsistencies in Carpenter's statements and concluded that the fact that Carpenter eventually signed a union authorization card in October 2002 "casts serious doubt upon [Carpenter's] assertion that he informed Mullins that he was not interested in the Union and supports Mullins' testimony that Carpenter was 'confused.'"

* * *

Moreover, the NLRB alternatively found that *even if* it were not to credit Mullins' testimony, Mullins' conduct nevertheless would not have constituted violations of Palace's solicitation and harassment policies. Regarding the warning for soliciting Carpenter on July 11, the NLRB concluded that even if Mullins had solicited Carpenter during their conversation, this would not have violated the solicitation policy because "he was engaged in a nonwork activity." * * *

With respect to the second warning, for harassment of Carpenter during June and July of 2002, the NLRB found that, even if Mullins did initiate conversations with Carpenter to the extent alleged by Carpenter, Carpenter's testimony before the NLRB did not establish that he was "harassed," "intimidated," or approached after telling Mullins to stop the conduct cited by the warning. This alternative finding is also supported by substantial evidence.

As the NLRB noted, Carpenter made it clear that he did not fear that Mullins would hurt him. Carpenter also testified that when Mullins approached him, Mullins never physically restrained him; Carpenter would simply tell Mullins that he did not want to discuss the matter and would walk away. Indeed, neither Carpenter nor any other witness cited any conduct by Mullins that could reasonably be thought to constitute "intimidation." Regarding the warning's only specific example of "harassment"—the continued solicitation of Carpenter after he asked Mullins to stop—the NLRB found that Carpenter made no such unequivocal request until July 11. * * * Accordingly, the NLRB reasonably found that Carpenter did not tell Mullins until July 11 not to talk to him about the Union. Thus, in light of Mullins' undisputed testimony that, after July 11, he did not speak to Carpenter again until October 2002 (when Carpenter signed the authorization card), substantial evidence supports the NLRB's finding that the harassment asserted as the ground for the second warning never occurred.

* * *

On this record, the NLRB reasonably concluded that Palace violated § 8(a) (1) of the Act by issuing the disciplinary warnings to Mullins.

C. The NLRB's Conclusion That the Discharge Was Unlawful

* * *

In addressing the § 8(a) (3) charge, the NLRB treated this case as one involving a question of "dual motivation," *i.e.*, a case in which the employer defends against a § 8(a) (3) charge by arguing that, even if an invalid reason might have played some part in the employer's motivation, the employer would have taken the same action against the employee for a permissible reason. The NLRB analyzes such claims under the framework set forth in *Wright Line*, 251 N.L.R.B. at 1089. * * * Under the *Wright Line* test, the general counsel must first show that the protected activity was a motivating factor in the adverse employment decision. If this prima facie showing is made, the burden shifts to the employer to demonstrate that it would have made the adverse decision even had the employee not engaged in protected activity.* * *

The ALJ clearly applied this framework in evaluating Mullins' discharge. After finding that the General Counsel had made out a prima facie showing, the ALJ proceeded to evaluate whether Palace had established that it would have discharged Mullins even in the absence of his protected activity. The ALJ noted that, although Palace characterized Mullins' remark as "sexual harassment," "there is no evidence of any sexual advance by Mullins." The ALJ then discussed the Company's written policies prohibiting "indecent conduct or language," noting that the policies include a progressive disciplinary system whereby "'termination is the *last step*'" in the disciplinary progression. Finally, the ALJ found that, in the only other comparable disciplinary incident in the record, another employee who used "vulgar and profane language towards customers" was only warned after his first offense. This employee was not fired until after a repeat offense. On this record, the ALJ held that the Company had not met its burden under *Wright Line*. *Id.*

The NLRB, at the outset of its decision, announced that it had "decided to affirm the judge's rulings, findings, and conclusions." The NLRB then went on to render its own opinion, employing a rationale to support the finding of a § 8(a) (3) violation that is entirely different from the rationale offered by the ALJ. It is therefore unclear whether the NLRB opinion is intended to supplement or displace the ALJ's rationale in sustaining the § 8(a) (3) charge. The NLRB agreed with the ALJ that the General Counsel had made out a prima facie case. That conclusion was justified: the ALJ found that Mullins' supervisors had threatened to fire him if the Union filed for a new election, and Mullins was indeed fired shortly after the Union filed. The NLRB also agreed that Palace had failed to establish that it would have discharged Mullins even in the absence of his union activity. However, in considering whether the Company had met its burden under *Wright Line*, the NLRB focused almost exclusively on Palace's claim that it would face potential liability under Title VII if it did not dismiss Mullins for his alleged offensive statement to Castillo.

In following this approach, the NLRB stated that the ALJ's decision rested on a finding that Palace "failed to show that it would have discharged Mullins even in the absence of his union activity *in order to avoid the imposition of Title VII liability*." *Id.* (emphasis added). The NLRB's characterization of the ALJ's decision is perplexing, because, although the ALJ did conclude that there was "no evidence of any sexual advance by Mullins," the ALJ's holding that Palace had violated § 8(a) (3) rested on findings that neither the Company's "progressive disciplinary system" nor the Company's handling of "other documented incidents

regarding indecent conduct or language" could explain Palace's decision to fire Mullins. The ALJ's analysis and concluding findings say nothing about Title VII. Indeed, there is *nothing* in the ALJ's opinion even to suggest that Palace argued that the employer fired Mullins in order to avoid the imposition of Title VII liability. And Palace does not contend here that this affirmative defense was specifically raised in the hearing before the ALJ.

Ignoring the ALJ's stated grounds for finding a § 8(a)(3) violation, the NLRB concluded that Palace had "not established that it had reasonable grounds for determining that it had to remove or discipline Mullins in order to avoid liability under Title VII." The basis for this conclusion was the NLRB's view that Title VII liability would not arise from Mullins' single, isolated remark.

The problem here is that, in focusing on Title VII, the NLRB misapplied **Wright Line**. The question under *Wright Line* is whether the Company has established in fact that it would have taken the same action in the absence of any anti-union animus. It is not whether the Company has established that its actions were "reasonable."* * *

As noted above, the NLRB stated that it meant to affirm the ALJ's rulings, findings, and conclusions. But the NLRB's *Wright Line* analysis focuses solely on the Title VII issue and never addresses the ALJ's evaluation of the Company's written policies and disciplinary practices. Therefore, we cannot be sure to what extent the NLRB meant to incorporate the ALJ's analysis in those respects while merely rejecting any implication in the ALJ's decision that sexual harassment arises only in connection with comments containing sexual advances.

* * * On remand, the NLRB should explain the precise reasoning on which it means to rest its conclusion that Mullins' discharge violated the Act. The NLRB should specifically state which portions of the ALJ's analysis it adopts and which parts it rejects. We also note that, although the ALJ appeared to evaluate Mullins' discharge solely under § 8(a)(3), using the *Wright Line* framework, *see Palace Sports & Entm't Inc.*, 342 N.L.R.B. No. 53, 2004 WL 1701333, at *23, the NLRB, without explanation, stated that it "agreed with the judge that [Palace] violated Section 8(a)(1) *and* (3) when it discharged employee Peter Mullins," *342 N.L.R.B. No. 53,* [WL] at *1 (emphasis added). It is unclear whether the NLRB really meant to find that Palace violated § 8(a) (1) when it fired Mullins and, if so, on what grounds. The NLRB can address this issue on remand.

III. CONCLUSION

For the foregoing reasons, we grant in part the NLRB's application for enforcement. We remand the case to the NLRB, however, for clarification of its conclusion that Palace violated the Act by discharging Mullins.

National Football League Players Association v. National Labor Relations Board, 503 F.2d 12 (1974). This case explores the duty to bargain in good faith over mandatory subjects for bargaining.

North American Soccer League v. National Labor Relations Board, 613 F. 2d. 1379 (5th Cir. 1980). This case explores the appropriate bargaining units in professional sports unions and when manage-ment has a duty to bargain with players versus its ability to change terms of conditions of employment unilaterally.

Silverman v. Major League Baseball Player Relations Committee, 880 F. Supp. 246 (1995). This case examines the parameters of an employer's ability to impose unilateral changers after impasse and after players have gone on strike.

QUESTIONS YOU SHOULD BE ABLE TO ANSWER

1. What are the mandatory subjects for bargaining? Give an example of each.

2. Why are provisions, such as drug testing, better addressed through collective bargaining than through an Act of Congress?

3. What are employee rights established by the National Labor Relations and the Taft Hartley Acts?

4. What are the unique aspects of professional sports labor relations?

5. What is the difference between rights and interest arbitration?

REFERENCES

Cases

Brown v. Pro Football, Inc., 518 U.S. 231 (1996).

Ford Motor Co. v. NLRB, 441 U.S. 488, 498 (1979).

Miranda Fuel Co., 140 NLRB 181 (1962).

National Football League Players Association v. National Labor Relations Board, 503 F.2d 12 (1974).

NLRB v. Katz, 369 U.S. 736 (1962).

North American Soccer League v. NLRB, 613 F. 2d. 1379 (5th Cir. 1980).

Palace Sports & Entertainment, 2005.

Peterson v. Kennedy and the NFLPA, 771 F.2d 1244 (1985).

Silverman v. Major League Baseball Player Relations Committee, 880 F. Supp. 246 (1995).

Steele v. Louisville & Nashville Railroad Co., 323 U.S. 192 (1944).

The American League of Professional Baseball Clubs and the Association of National Baseball League Umpires, 180 N.L.R.B. 190 (1969).

U.S. Steelworkers v. American Mfg. Co., 363 U.S. 564 (1960).

U.S. Steelworkers v. Warrior Gulf Co., 363 U.S. 574 (1960).

U.S. Steelworkers v. Enterprise Corp., 363 U.S. 593 (1960).

Vaca v. Sipes, 386 U.S. 171 (1967).

Publications

Feldacker, B. (2000). *Labor guide to labor law* (4th ed.). Upper Saddle River, NJ: Prentice Hall.

Gold, M. E. (1998). *An introduction to labor law* (2nd ed.). Ithaca, NY: ILR Press/Cornell University Press.

Legislation

Fair Labor Standards Act, 29 USCS § 201, et seq. (2005).

Labor Management Relations Act, 29 USCS § 141, et. seq. (2005).

National Labor Relations Act, 29 USCS § 151, et. seq. (2005).

7.40 *Sport Agent Legislation*

—John T. Wolohan

ITHACA COLLEGE

Although the creation of the modern sports agent is usually credited to Boston attorney Bob Woolf in the mid-1960s, individuals have been representing athletes as far back as the 1920s. One of the first sports agents was Charles "Cash & Carry" Pyle, who in 1925 reportedly negotiated a $3,000-per-game contract between Red Grange and the Chicago Bears (Shropshire & Davis, 2008). In truth, however, it was only the rare and special athlete that needed an agent before the 1970s. Before, 1976, most professional athletes were bound to their team through a reserve system and were left with few alternatives and little negotiating power. As a result, the only real contract negotiation in these circumstances was a matter of taking what was offered or refusing to play.

Beginning in the mid-1970s, due to court decisions, arbitration, collective bargaining, and in some instances, the emergence of competing professional leagues, players gained greater freedom and bargaining leverage to market themselves to the highest bidder. At this same time, large sums of money was coming into the leagues via increased television and radio rights. These events expanded media coverage,escalating rights fees paid by networks to leagues, and made professional sports more popular and profitable. As a result, team owners had more money to spend, albeit grudgingly, on attracted high quality and high priced players to their teams. With all the millions of dollars coming into professional sports, it became more and more essential for many athletes to seek the help of professional "sports agents" to maximize their salary and other compensation.

FUNDAMENTAL CONCEPTS

Although few would argue that the services of a competent agent can be extremely valuable for a professional athlete, the emergence of the sport agent in professional sports has not been without problems. For example, there is only a limited supply of quality athletes. In the four major sports in America, there are only a total of 4,200 athletes playing at the very top level. At the same time, there are over 1,600 registered agents in those same sports, of which, less than 50 percent of them actually have clients (Davis, 2006). The competition to secure a client has encouraged corruption and forced some agents to provide all types of illegal inducements to get an athlete to sign with them. The following section outlines some of the attempts by the state and federal governments and other various organizations to protect college and professional athletes, as well as colleges and universities, from actions of unscrupulous agents.

Sport Agent Legislation

Since 1981, there have been numerous attempts to regulate sport agents. Unfortunately, due to a variety of reasons, these attempts have mostly failed to stop the unethical, unscrupulous, and illegal conduct of sport agents.

State Legislative Efforts

In 1981, California became the first state to pass legislation regulating sport agents when it enacted the California Athlete Agents Act. Twenty-Eight (28) years later, the number of states regulating the activities of sport agents has grown to 41. However, instead of protecting the athletes from unethical and unscrupulous agents, the focus of current state sport agent statutes has shifted to addressing the economic damage an unscrupulous agent could cause for a college or university. This current legislative trend is characterized by provisions requiring notice to school and state before and/or after the signing of a representation contract, waiting periods for valid contracts, the creation of causes of action in favor of colleges and universities for agent misconduct resulting in damages, and an abandonment or modification of the onerous registration requirements common in earlier legislative schemes (Rodgers, 1988–89).

Uniform Athlete Agent Act

The most recent attempt by states to regulate the sport agent profession began in 1997, when the National Conference of Commissioners on Uniform State Laws (NCCUSL), at the request of several major universities and the NCAA, appointed a drafting committee to develop a uniform statute for regulating sport agents. The NCCUSL is a national association, which endeavors to promote the uniformity of state laws. For example, the NCCUSL is responsible for the drafting and development of the Uniform Commercial Code (UCC).

As a result of their work, the NCCUSL developed the **Uniform Athlete Agents Act (UAAA)** in the fall of 2000. The stated goal of the UAAA is the protection of student-athletes from unscrupulous agents. To achieve this goal, the UAAA contains a number of important provisions regulating the conduct between athletes and agents. For example, the UAAA requires an agent to provide important information, both professional and criminal in nature. This information enables student-athletes, their parents and family, and university personnel to better evaluate the prospective agent. The UAAA also requires that written notice be provided to institutions when a student-athlete signs an agency contract before their eligibility expires. In addition, the UAAA gives authority to the secretary of state to issue subpoenas that would enable the state to obtain relevant material that ensures compliance with the act. Finally, the UAAA provides for criminal, civil, and administrative penalties with enforcement at the state level (www.ncaa.org, 2009).

In addition, the UAAA also covers such key areas as agent registration requirement; liability insurance; notice to educational institution; student-athlete's right to cancel, and penalties. Perhaps the most important part of the UAAA is the section allowing an agent's valid certificate of registration from one state to be honored in all other states that have adopted the act. The success of the reciprocal registration process is contingent on states establishing a reasonable fee schedule, including lower registration fees for reciprocal applications and renewals. Thus, more agents are likely to register due to the efficiency of this process, its practical cost-saving implications for the agent, and the benefits of complying with a single set of regulations.

As of July 2009, the UAAA had been passed in thirty-eight (38) states and two territories. In addition, five states have laws dealing with agent behavior on the books that do not conform to the UAAA (see Table 7.40.1). However, some critics argued that the UAAA is more interested in protecting NCAA member institutions, than athletes. For example, the UAAA requires agents and student-athlete to notify the institution within seventy-two hours of the signing of a contract, or before the student-athlete's next scheduled athletics event, whichever occurs first. If a prospective student-athlete has signed a contract, the agent must notify the institution where the agent has reasonable grounds to believe the prospect will enroll. Finally, the act provides institutions with a right of action against the agent or former student–athlete for any damages caused by a violation of this act.

The UAAA has not been the panacea many anticipated, however. Since not every state has passed the Act, there is still a lack of uniformity, which in turn, has had an impact on the number of agents registering with the states. Therefore, it is not surprising that agents prone to abuse have ignored these statutory provisions and continued to conduct business as usual. In addition, differing state requirements have created an administrative nightmare for many honest agents doing business in several states. This, coupled with a perceived lack of enforcement, often encourages the breach of these provisions.

In addition, while states have at least made an attempt to control the corruption of agents, most states have made little or no attempt to stop incompetent sport agents. The only jurisdiction that currently requires agents to pass a competency examination as a prerequisite to licensure is Florida. The exam tests an agent's knowledge of Florida law and NCAA bylaws.

National Legislative Efforts

To correct some of the shortcomings of the state's efforts, some people have argued that federal sport agent legislation is needed. Federal legislation would address the jurisdictional ambiguities and substantive inconsistencies of existing state regulation, erase multiple application and fee requirements, and eliminate forum shopping by agents who attempt to avoid states that have legislation.

Table 7.40.1 States That Have Passed the UAAA, as of July 2009

Alabama	Indiana	Nevada	Tennessee
Arizona	Iowa	New Hampshire	Texas
Kansas	Nevada	New York	Utah
Arkansas	Kansas	North Carolina	Washington
Colorado	Kentucky	North Dakota	West Virginia
Connecticut	Louisiana	Oklahoma	Wisconsin
Delaware	Maryland	Oregon	Wyoming
Florida	Minnesota	Pennsylvania	
Georgia	Mississippi	Rhode Island	
Hawaii	Missouri	South Carolina	
Idaho	Nebraska	South Dakota	

States That Have Passed Non-UAAA Laws Designed to Regulate Athlete Agents

California	Michigan	Ohio

States That Currently Have No Existing Law Regulating Athlete Agents

Alaska	Massachusetts	New Mexico
Illinois	Montana	Vermont
Maine	New Jersey*	Virginia

*States with UAAA legislation in their legislative chambers.
Source: www.ncaa.org, 2009.

Although there had been earlier attempts to formally introduce legislation in Congress, it was not until September 2004 that Congress passed national legislation regulating the conduct of sports agents. Titled the **Sports Agent Responsibility and Trust Act (SPARTA)**, SPARTA was sponsored by Tom Osborne, a Republican from Nebraska and the former football coach at the University of Nebraska. Signed into law in October 2004, the new law prohibits agents from making false or misleading promises or providing gifts, cash, and anything else of monetary value to student-athletes or anyone associated with them. In addition, the act also requires agents to give students a written disclosure that they could lose their eligibility to play college sports by signing an agency contract and predating or postdating contracts. Finally, the act requires agents and athletes to notify their college athletic director within seventy-two hours of entering into a contract or before the student's next athletic event, whichever is earlier. Agents who fail to report the contract can be fined as much as $11,000 per day (15 U.S.C.A. 7801 *et. seq.*).

Individual states can also bring a civil action if the attorney general of a state has reason to believe that an interest of the residents of that state has been or is threatened or adversely affected by the engagement of any athlete agent. It should be noted that like the Uniform Athlete Agents Act, which SPARTA encourages every state to enact, the main goal of SPARTA is to protect the NCAA eligibility of student-athletes and universities. It does little to protect professional athletes who no longer attend college or have eligibility left.

Other Regulatory Efforts

Agent-specific legislation is not the only legal means used to regulate the conduct of athlete agents. Other common law or statutory remedies, although not specifically directed at agents, have been used to attempt to control their abusive conduct. For example, the common law civil remedies of breach of contract, misrepresentation, fraud, deceit, and negligence have been applied in cases of agent misconduct (Shropshire, 1989). In addition, various federal and state criminal statutes have been used, albeit with limited success, to attempt to criminally sanction agent misconduct. Sport agent Jim Abernethy, for example, who had signed and provided illegal payments to an athlete before his eligibility had expired, was indicted and convicted at trial on a charge of tampering with a sports contest in the state of Alabama. Abernethy's conviction was overturned on appeal when the Alabama Court of Criminal Appeals construed the Alabama tampering statute in a manner favorable to Abernethy and sport agents in general (Narayanan, 1990).

In addition, such organizations as the NCAA, professional sport players' associations, and the American Bar Association can also be used in regulating this relationship between athletes and agents.

The National Collegiate Athletic Association (NCAA)

By the mid-1970s, repeated instances of agent abuse prompted the NCAA to promulgate regulations in an attempt to limit the likelihood of an unscrupulous agent preying on a talented, young, and financially naive athlete (Wilde, 1992). NCAA Bylaw 12.3 prohibits "a student-athlete (any individual who currently participates in or who may be eligible in the future to participate in intercollegiate sport) may not agree verbally or in writing to be represented by an athlete agent in the present or in the future for the purpose of marketing the student-athlete's ability or reputation. If the student-athlete enters into such an agreement, the student-athlete is ineligible for intercollegiate competition" (*NCAA Manual*, 2008–09). In addition to sports agents, the NCAA Bylaws also prohibits athletes from accepting gift from runner (individuals who befriend student-athletes and frequently distribute impermissible benefits on behalf of sports agents) and financial advisors.

The problem with NCAA regulations, however, is that they do not directly apply to sport agents. NCAA rules and regulations are only applicable to student-athletes and the academic institutions in which the athletes are enrolled. Therefore, an agent can violate NCAA regulations without fear of NCAA sanctions, whereas the student-athlete with whom the agent dealt will likely lose his or her remaining eligibility, and the academic institution will be subject to sanctions (Fluhr, 1999).

In addition, as mentioned earlier, the NCAA worked with the National Conference of Commissioners on Uniform State Laws on the drafting of the UAAA. The NCAA now encourages each state to adopt the UAAA as a means of limiting the damage resulting from the impermissible and oftentimes illegal practices of some athlete agents.

Professional Team Sports Players' Associations

The power of the players' associations of the four major sports leagues to regulate sport agents derives from the National Labor Relations Act and other federal labor law. Essentially, the players' associations regulate agents by "requiring their members to hire regulated agents only, and by obtaining the agreement of teams to negotiate with regulated agents only" (Fluhr, 1999). The first professional team sport players' union to initiate a player-agent certification program was the National Football League Players' Association (NFLPA) in 1983. The 1982 collective bargaining agreement between the NFL and NFLPA had reserved the exclusive right for the NFLPA or "its agent" to negotiate individual NFL player contracts. The 1983 program was established to certify agents as "NFLPA Contract Advisors," who, under the program, are required to use a standard representation agreement, comply with certain limits on compensation for contractual negotiations, and attend periodic training seminars (Ring, 1987). Fines, suspensions, and/or revocations of licenses are among the penalties imposed for noncompliance.

Despite the program's intent to protect athletes from agent incompetence and corruption, several problems still persisted. First, the program, in its original form, did not address the corruption occurring in intercollegiate athletics. Only agents representing current NFL players were covered. Alerted to the potential for agent abuse of athletes who had yet to sign their first NFL contract, the program was amended to prohibit agents from communicating with a college football player who is ineligible to be drafted, including a player who has applied for early eligibility, until his name appears on the NFL's official list of draft-eligible players. Second, the plan was limited in scope. The plan regulated only "contract advisors" of NFL players, and its rules prohibit the charging of excessive fees for only contract negotiation and money-handling services. Agents providing other services could charge excessive fees and effectively evade the plan's restrictions (Dunn, 1988). Third, the plan was devoid of any specific criteria for granting or denying agent certification.

Since 1998, however, the NFLPA, by trying to enforce higher standards, has taken a more active role in policing agents. The union has rolled back the maximum percentage that agents can charge players to negotiate a contract from 4 percent to 3 percent (Freeman, 1998). In 1999, concerned about the quality of the agents representing its players, the NFLPA started testing anyone who registers to become a NFL player's agent. The test covered such areas as the collective bargaining agreement, salary cap issues, and free agency. Any agent who fails the test will not be certified (Freeman, 1998). The NFLPA also requires current agents to take that same test every year, and if they fail, those agents will be suspended and possibly decertified. Any NFL team that negotiates with an agent not sanctioned by the union is subject to a fine from the commissioner. The NFLPA's program, like the agent certification programs implemented by the other players' unions, also expects applicants to disclose their educational, professional, and employment background. However, none of the programs require any minimum levels of training or education as a condition for representing professional athletes.

In 1985, the Major League Baseball Players' Association (MLBPA) became the next union to adopt an agent certification plan. The National Basketball Players' Association (NBPA) followed the MLBPA in 1986, when it adopted its agent certification plan. The National Hockey League (NHL), which was the last union to start regulating agents, joined the other major sports leagues in 1996 when it drafted its agent certification program (Couch, 2000). In November 2004, Major League Soccer (MLS) and the players union included language in their collective bargaining agreement that allows the union to develop and implement an agent certification program. However, at the present time, no such program exists.

The general scheme in professional sports leagues is that only those agents registered with the unions can negotiate on behalf of the players. The unions also require annual registration and fees, annual attendance at seminars, a disciplinary system including an arbitration provision, and the ban on specific conflict of interest situations. Unfortunately, sanctions are rarely levied when the preceding policies are violated either due to lack of knowledge or improper enforcement techniques (Couch, 2000).

The American Bar Association (ABA)

While the ABA's Model Code of Professional Responsibility proposes standards of integrity and conduct for all attorneys and has been adopted in some form or another by many state bar associations, unfortunately, even though many sport agents are attorneys, the code has no effect on agents who are not lawyers. In addition, since there is no requirement that agents be attorneys, even if an attorney was disbarred from practicing law, he or she might still be able to represent athletes.

Financial Advisors

In addition to negotiating contracts, a number of agents and their firms act as financial advisor to their clients. In 2002, the National Football League Players Association (NFLPA), prompted by sports agent William "Tank" Black's conviction of fraud for stealing more than $11 million from players he once represented, became the first sports union to regulate anyone wishing to be a financial advisor to NFL players. To be eligible for the NFLPA's Financial Advisors Program, financial advisors must apply to the NFLPA and submit to annual background checks, developed in conjunction with the Securities and Exchange Commission.

While the NFLPA's list of financial advisors also includes a disclaimer, indicating that the advisers are neither endorsed nor recommended by the union, the NFLPA is currently involved in a lawsuit over one of the advisors formally on the list. In 2006, several current and former NFL players who had invested with Kirk Wright, a financial advisor approved by the NFLPA sued the NFL and the NFLPA after Wright defrauded the players of around $20 million. The players argued that the union improperly allowing Wright onto a list of financial advisers provided to members, even though liens had been filed against Wright (*Atwater v. The National Football League Players Association*, 2007).

Wright, who was eventually convicted in 2008 on 47 counts of mail fraud, securities fraud, and money laundering faced up to 710 years and $16 million in fines, hanged himself in prison (Tierney, 2008).

SIGNIFICANT CASE

The following case is perhaps the most famous case of agent abuse. In 1989, Norby Walters was sentenced to five years in prison; his conviction, however, was overturned and remanded for a new trial by the Seventh Circuit (913 F.2d 388). Walters subsequently pleaded guilty to federal mail fraud charges to avoid more serious racketeering and conspiracy charges. Walters' conviction, based on his plea, was also overturned by the Seventh Circuit (997 F.2d 1219). Although their unscrupulous conduct went unpunished by the courts, no case has been as responsible for focusing public awareness on the problems associated with the unscrupulous sport agents, and prompting the development of agent-specific legislation.

UNITED STATES V. WALTERS

United States Court of Appeals for the Seventh Circuit
997 F.2d 1219 (1993)

Opinion: Easterbrook, Circuit Judge.

Norby Walters, who represents entertainers, tried to move into the sports business. He signed 58 college football players to contracts while they were still playing. Walters offered cars and money to those who would agree to use him as their representative in dealing with professional teams. Sports agents receive a percentage of the players' income, so Walters would profit only to the extent he could negotiate contracts for his clients. The athletes' pro prospects depended on successful completion of their collegiate careers. To the NCAA, however, a student who signs a contract with an agent is a professional, ineligible to play on collegiate teams. To avoid jeopardizing his clients' careers, Walters dated the contracts after the end of their eligibility and locked them in a safe. He promised to lie to the universities in response to any inquiries. Walters inquired of sports lawyers at Shea & Gould whether this plan of operation would be lawful. The firm rendered an opinion that it would violate the NCAA's rules but not any statute.

Having recruited players willing to fool their universities and the NCAA, Walters discovered that they were equally willing to play false with him. Only 2 of the 58 players fulfilled their end of the bargain; the other 56 kept the cars and money, then signed with other agents. They relied on the fact that the contracts were locked away and dated in the future, and that Walters' business depended on continued secrecy, so he could not very well sue to enforce their promises. When the 56 would neither accept him as their representative nor return the payments, Walters resorted to threats. One player, Maurice Douglass, was told that his legs would be broken before the pro draft unless he repaid Walters' firm. A 75-page indictment charged Walters and his partner Lloyd Bloom with conspiracy, RICO violations (the predicate felony was extortion), and mail fraud. The fraud: causing the universities to pay scholarship funds to athletes who had become ineligible as a result of the agency contracts. The mail: each university required its athletes to verify their eligibility to play, then sent copies by mail to conferences such as the Big Ten.

After a month-long trial and a week of deliberations, the jury convicted Walters and Bloom. We reversed, holding that the district judge had erred in declining to instruct the jury that reliance on Shea & Gould's advice could prevent the formation of intent to defraud the universities. 913 F.2d 388, 391-92 (1990). Any dispute about the adequacy of Walters' disclosure to his lawyers and the bona fides of his reliance was for the jury, we concluded. Because Bloom declined to waive his own attorney-client privilege, we held that the defendants must be retried separately. *Id.* at 392-93. On remand, Walters asked the district court to dismiss the indictment, arguing that the evidence presented at trial is insufficient to support the convictions. After the judge denied this motion, . . . Walters agreed to enter a conditional Alford plea: he would plead guilty to mail fraud, conceding that the record of the first trial supplies a factual basis for a conviction while reserving his right to contest the sufficiency of that evidence. In return, the prosecutor agreed to dismiss the RICO and conspiracy charges and to return to Walters all property that had been forfeited as a result of his RICO conviction. Thus a case that began with a focus on extortion has become a straight mail fraud prosecution and may undergo yet another transformation. The prosecutor believes that Walters hampered the investigation preceding his indictment. . . . The plea agreement reserves the prosecutor's right to charge Walters with perjury and obstruction of justice if we should reverse the conviction for mail fraud.

"Whoever, having devised . . . any scheme or artifice to defraud, or for obtaining money or property by means of false or fraudulent pretenses, representations, or promises . . . places in any post office or authorized depository for mail matter, any matter or thing whatever to be sent or delivered by the Postal Service . . . or knowingly causes [such matter or thing] to be delivered by mail" commits the crime of mail fraud. 18 U.S.C. § 1341. Norby Walters did not mail anything or cause anyone else to do so (the universities were going to collect and mail the forms no matter what Walters did), but the Supreme Court has expanded the statute beyond its literal terms, holding that a mailing by a third party suffices if it is "incident to an essential part of the scheme." . . . While stating that such mailings can turn ordinary fraud into mail fraud, the Court has cautioned that the statute "does not purport to reach all frauds, but only those limited instances in which the use of the mails is a part of the execution of the fraud." . . . Everything thus turns on matters of degree. Did the schemers foresee that the mails would be used? Did the mailing advance the success of the scheme? Which parts of a scheme are "essential?" Such questions lack obviously right answers, so it is no surprise that each side to this case can cite several of our decisions in support. . . .

"The relevant question . . . is whether the mailing is part of the execution of the scheme as conceived by the perpetrator at the time." . . . Did the evidence establish that Walters conceived a scheme in which mailings played a role? We think not—indeed, that no reasonable juror could give an affirmative answer to this question. Walters hatched a scheme to make money by taking a percentage of athletes' pro contracts. To get clients he signed students while college eligibility remained, thus avoiding competition from ethical agents. To obtain big pro contracts for these clients he needed to keep the deals secret, so the athletes could finish their collegiate careers. Thus deceit was an ingredient of the plan. We may assume that Walters knew that the universities would ask athletes to verify that they were eligible to compete as amateurs. But what role do the mails play? The plan succeeds so long as the athletes conceal their contracts from their schools (and remain loyal to Walters). Forms verifying eligibility do not help the plan succeed; instead they create a risk that it will be discovered if a student should tell the truth. . . . And it is the forms, not their mailing to the Big Ten, that pose the risk. For all Walters cared, the forms could sit forever in cartons. Movement to someplace else was irrelevant. In Schmuck, where the fraud was selling cars with rolled-back odometers, the mailing was essential to obtain a new and apparently "clean" certificate of title; no certificates of title, no marketable cars, no hope for success. Even so, the Court divided five to four on the question whether the mailing was sufficiently integral to the scheme. A college's mailing to its conference has less to do with the plot's success than the mailings that transferred title in Schmuck.

To this the United States responds that the mailings were essential because, if a college had neglected to send the athletes' forms to the conference, the NCAA would have barred that college's team from competing. Lack of com-

petition would spoil the athletes' pro prospects. Thus the use of the mails was integral to the profits Walters hoped to reap, even though Walters would have been delighted had the colleges neither asked any questions of the athletes nor put the answers in the mail. Let us take this as sufficient under Schmuck (although we have our doubts). The question remains whether Walters caused the universities to use the mails. A person "knowingly causes" the use of the mails when he "acts with the knowledge that the use of the mails will follow in the ordinary course of business, or where such use can reasonably be foreseen." . . . The paradigm is insurance fraud. Perkins tells his auto insurer that his car has been stolen, when in fact it has been sold. The local employee mails the claim to the home office, which mails a check to Perkins. Such mailings in the ordinary course of business are foreseeable. Similarly, a judge who takes a bribe derived from the litigant's bail money causes the use of the mails when the ordinary course is to refund the bond by mail. . . . The prosecutor contends that the same approach covers Walters.

No evidence demonstrates that Walters actually knew that the colleges would mail the athletes' forms. The record is barely sufficient to establish that Walters knew of the forms' existence; it is silent about Walters' knowledge of the forms' disposition. . . . In the end, the prosecutor insists that the large size and interstate nature of the NCAA demonstrate that something would be dropped into the mails. To put this only slightly differently, the prosecutor submits that all frauds involving big organizations necessarily are mail frauds, because big organizations habitually mail things. No evidence put before the jury supports such a claim, and it is hardly appropriate for judicial notice in a criminal case.

There is a deeper problem with the theory of this prosecution. The United States tells us that the universities lost their scholarship money. Money is property; this aspect of the prosecution does not encounter a problem under *McNally v. United States*, 483 U.S. 350 (1987). Walters emphasizes that the universities put his 58 athletes on scholarship long before he met them and did not pay a penny more than they planned to do. But a jury could conclude that had Walters' clients told the truth, the colleges would have stopped their scholarships, thus saving money. So we must assume that the universities lost property by reason of Walters' deeds. Still, they were not out of pocket to Walters; he planned to profit by taking a percentage of the players' professional incomes, not of their scholarships. Section 1341 condemns "any scheme or artifice to defraud, or for obtaining money or property" (emphasis added). If the universities were the victims, how did he "obtain" their property?, Walters asks.

According to the United States, neither an actual nor a potential transfer of property from the victim to the defendant is essential. It is enough that the victim lose; what (if anything) the schemer hopes to gain plays no role in the definition of the offense. We asked the prosecutor at oral argument whether on this rationale practical jokes violate § 1341. A mails B an invitation to a surprise party for their mutual friend C. B drives his car to the place named in the invitation. But there is no party; the address is a vacant lot; B is the butt of a joke. The invitation came by post; the cost of gasoline means that B is out of pocket. The prosecutor said that this indeed violates § 1341, but that his office pledges to use prosecutorial discretion wisely. Many people will find this position unnerving (what if the prosecutor's policy changes, or A is politically unpopular and the prosecutor is looking for a way to nail him?). Others, who obey the law out of a sense of civic obligation rather than the fear of sanctions, will alter their conduct no matter what policy the prosecutor follows. Either way, the idea that practical jokes are federal felonies would make a joke of the Supreme Court's assurance that § 1341 does not cover the waterfront of deceit.

Practical jokes rarely come to the attention of federal prosecutors, but large organizations are more successful in gaining the attention of public officials. In this case the mail fraud statute has been invoked to shore up the rules of an influential private association. . . . The NCAA depresses athletes' income—restricting payments to the value of tuition, room, and board, while receiving services of substantially greater worth. The NCAA treats this as desirable preservation of amateur sports; a more jaundiced eye would see it as the use of monopsony power to obtain athletes' services for less than the competitive market price. Walters then is cast in the role of a cheater, increasing the payments to the student athletes. Like other cheaters, Walters found it convenient to hide his activities. If, as the prosecutor believes, his repertory included extortion, he has used methods that the law denies to persons fighting cartels, but for the moment we are concerned only with the deceit that caused the universities to pay stipends to "professional" athletes. For current purposes it matters not whether the NCAA actually monopsonizes the market for players; the point of this discussion is that the prosecutor's theory makes criminals of those who consciously cheat on the rules of a private organization, even if that organization is a cartel. We pursue this point because any theory that makes criminals of cheaters raises a red flag.

Cheaters are not self-conscious champions of the public weal. They are in it for profit, as rapacious and mendacious as those who hope to collect monopoly rents. Maybe more; often members of cartels believe that monopoly serves the public interest, and they take their stand on the platform of business ethics, . . . while cheaters' glasses have been washed with cynical acid. Only Adam Smith's invisible hand turns their self-seeking activities to public benefit. It is cause for regret if prosecutors, assuming that persons with low regard for honesty must be villains, use the criminal laws to suppress the competitive process that undermines cartels. Of course federal laws have been used to enforce cartels before; the Federal Maritime Commission is a cartel-enforcement device. Inconsistent federal laws also occur; the United States both subsidizes tobacco growers and discourages people from smoking. So if the United States simultaneously forbids cartels and forbids undermining cartels by cheating, we shall shrug our shoulders and enforce both laws, condemning practical jokes along the way. But what is it about § 1341 that labels as a crime all deceit that inflicts any loss on anyone? Firms often try to fool their competitors, surprising them with new products that enrich their treasuries at their rivals' expense. Is this mail fraud because large organizations inevitably use the mail? "Any scheme or artifice to defraud, or for obtaining money or property by means of false or fraudulent pretenses, representations, or promises" reads like a description of schemes to get money or property by fraud rather than methods of doing business that incidentally cause losses.

None of the Supreme Court's mail fraud cases deals with a scheme in which the defendant neither obtained nor tried to obtain the victim's property. . . . We have been unable to find any appellate cases squarely resolving the question whether the victim's loss must be an objective of the scheme rather than a byproduct of it, perhaps because prosecutions of the kind this case represents are so rare. According to the prosecutor, however, there have been such cases, and in this circuit. The United States contends that we have already held that a scheme producing an incidental loss violates § 1341. A representative sample of the cases the prosecutor cites shows that we have held no such thing.

Many of our cases ask whether a particular scheme deprived a victim of property. . . . They do so not with an emphasis on "deprive" but with an emphasis on "property"—which, until the enactment of 18 U.S.C. § 1346 after Walters' conduct, was essential to avoid the "intangible rights" doctrine that McNally jettisoned. No one doubted that the schemes were designed to enrich the perpetrators at the victims' expense; the only difficulty was the proper characterization of the deprivation. Not until today have we dealt with a scheme in which the defendants' profits were to come from legitimate transactions in the market, rather than at the expense of the victims. Both the "scheme or artifice to defraud" clause and the "obtaining money or property" clause of § 1343 contemplate a transfer of some kind. Accordingly, following both the language of § 1341 and the implication of Tanner, we hold that only a scheme to obtain money or other property from the victim by fraud violates § 1341. A deprivation is a necessary but not a sufficient condition of mail fraud. Losses that occur as byproducts of a deceitful scheme do not satisfy the statutory requirement.

Anticipating that we might come to this conclusion, the prosecutor contends that Walters is nonetheless guilty as an aider and abettor. If Walters did not defraud the universities, the argument goes, then the athletes did. Walters put them up to it and so is guilty under 18 U.S.C. § 2, the argument concludes. But the indictment charged a scheme by Walters to defraud; it did not depict Walters as an aide de camp in the students' scheme. The jury received a boilerplate § 2 instruction; this theory was not argued to the jury, or for that matter to the district court either before or after the remand. Independent problems dog this recasting of the scheme—not least the difficulty of believing that the students hatched a plot to employ fraud to receive scholarships that the universities had awarded them long before Walters arrived on the scene, and the lack of evidence that the students knew about or could foresee any mailings. Walters is by all accounts a nasty and untrustworthy fellow, but the prosecutor did not prove that his efforts to circumvent the NCAA's rules amounted to mail fraud.

REVERSED

CASES ON THE SUPPLEMENTAL CD

Brown v. Woolf, 554 F.Supp. 1206 (1983). The case looks at the fiduciary relationship between players and their agents.

Hillard and Taylor v. Black, 125 F. Supp. 2d 1071 (2000). The case looks at the fiduciary relationship between players and their agents and the agents' obligation to disclose certain facts.

United States of America v. Piggie, 303 F.3d 923 (8th Cir. 2002). The case looks at whether secretly paying high school athletes in violation of NCAA rules and then falsely certifying that they had not previously received payments, was a violation of criminal law.

QUESTIONS YOU SHOULD BE ABLE TO ANSWER

1. What were some of the events that brought about the need for professional sports agents?

2. What was the first state to pass legislation regulating sport agents?

3. What are some of the benefits of the Uniform Athlete Agents Act (UAAA)?

4. What are some of the negatives of the Uniform Athlete Agents Act (UAAA)?

5. What role should the professional sports leagues and their unions play in regulating an agent's relationship with college athletes?

REFERENCES

Cases

Atwater v. The National Football League Players Association, 2007 U.S. Dist. LEXIS 23371; 181 L.R.R.M. 2993.

Brown v. Woolf, 554 F.Supp. 1206 (1983).

Detroit Lions, Inc. v. Argovitz, 580 F.Supp. 542 (1984).

Hillard and Taylor v. Black, 125 F. Supp. 2d 1071 (2000).

Steinberg, Moorad & Dunn Inc., v. David Dunn, 136 Fed. Appx. 6; 2005 U.S. App. LEXIS 5162.

U.S. v. Piggie, 303 F.3d 923 (8th Cir. 2002).

U.S. v. Walters, 997 F.2d 1219 (7th Cir. 1993).

U.S. v. Walters and Bloom, 711 F. Supp. 1435 (N.D. Ill. 1989), *reversed and remanded*, 913 F.2d 388 (7th Cir. 1990).

Williams v. CWI, Inc., 777 F.Supp. 1006 (D.D.C. 1991).

Zinn v. Parrish, 644 F.2d 360 (7th Cir. 1981).

Publications

Couch, B. (2000). How agent competition and corruption affects sports and the athlete-agent relationship and what can be done to control it. *Seton Hall Journal of Sport Law, 10,* 111–137.

Davis, T. (2006). Regulating the Athlete-Agent Industry: Intended and Unintended Consequences. *Willamette Law Review, 42,* 781–827.

Dunn, D. (1988). Regulation of sports agents: Since at first it hasn't succeeded, try federal legislation. *The Hastings Law Journal, 39,* 1031–1078.

Fluhr, P. (1999). The regulation of sports agents and the quest for uniformity. *Sports Lawyers Journal, 6,* 1–25.

Freeman, M. (1998, July 26). Protecting players from their agents: Misconduct leaves N.F.L. Union fearful of incompetence and greed. *The New York Times,* sec. 8, p. 1, col. 1.

Mitten, M., Davis, T., Smith, R., & Berry, R. (2005). Sports Law and Regulations: Cases, Materials and Problems. New York, NY: Aspen Publishers.

Narayanan, A. (1990). Criminal liability of sports agents: Is it time to reline the playing field? *Loyola of Los Angeles Law Review, 24,* 273–316.

NCAA Constitution, Bylaw 12.3 NCAA Manual (2008–09).

Ring, B. (1987). An analysis of athlete agent certification and regulation: New incentives with old problems. *Loyola Entertainment Law Journal, 7,* 321–335.

Rodgers, J. (1988–89). States revamp defense against agents. *The Sports Lawyer, 6,* 1–7.

Shropshire, K. (1989). Athlete agent regulation: Proposed legislative revisions and the need for reforms beyond legislation. *Cardozo Arts & Entertainment Law Journal, 8,* 85–112.

Shropshire, K., & Davis, T. (2008). *The business of sport agents* (2nd ed.). Philadelphia, Pa: University of Pennsylvania Press.

Tierney, M. (2008, June 2). *After Financier's Death, Suit Against Union Lives On. The New York Times,* p. D 3.

Wilde, T. J. (1992). The regulation of sport agents. *Journal of Legal Aspects of Sport, 2,* 18–29.

Legislation

Sports Agent Responsibility and Trust Act, 15 U.S.C.A. 7801-7807 (2006), Pub. L. No. 108-304, 118 Stat. 1125 (2005).

Websites

Uniform Athlete Agents Act (UAAA) History and Status (n.d.). Retrieved from the National Collegiate Athletic Association Web site: http://www.ncaa.org/wps/ncaa?key=/ncaa/ncaa/legislation+and+governance/eligibility +and+recruiting/agents+and+amateurism/uaaa/history.html

INDEX OF CASES

Page references followed by n indicate material in notes, page references followed by t indicate material in tables, and page references followed by f indicate material in figures.

C

SUBJECT INDEX

Page references followed by n indicate material in notes, page references followed by t indicate material in tables, and page references followed by f indicate material in figures.

Crisis management manual, developing, 327–29
  activating the plan, 329–30
  crisis communication, proper, 330
  crisis response team, forming, 329
  debrief employees and others affected, 332
  media contact person, guidelines for, 331–32
  news media, dealing with, 330–31
  practicing the plan, 329
  response evaluation, 332
  surviving a crisis, 329
Crisis management plan (CMP), developing,
    327–29. *See also* Crisis management manual,
    developing
  case related to, 334–36
  communication issues, 328
  documentation, 328
  emergency equipment issues, 328
  facility issues, 328
  follow-up procedures, 329
  fundamental concepts of, 326
  personnel issues, 327–28
Cross-examination, 8
Cross liability insurance, 355
Crowd management, 338–50
  closed-circuit television (CCTV), 340, 344
  evaluation of, 339–40
  foreseeability in, 338–39
  importance of, 338–39
  orientation program, 344
  peer-group or T-shirt security, 343–44
  screeners/searchers, 343
  since September 11, 2001, 340–43
  ticket takers, 343
  ushers, 343
Crowd management plan, 343–45
  case related to, 346–48
  communication network, effective, 345
  crisis management and emergency action plan, 344
  fan ejections, 344
  implementing and evaluating, 345
  signage, effective, 345
  trained and competent staff, 343–44

D

Damage
  vs. damages, 47–48
  defined, 47
Damages
  vs. damage, 47–48
  in defamation cases, 229
  general, 229
  special, 229

Databases, 19
Declarations, 352
Dedication of land, 135
Deductible, insurance, 354–55
Defamation, 226–37
  case related to, 231–35
  damages, 229
  defenses, 229
  defined, 226
  elements of, 226–27
  First Amendment protections, 227–28
    limited-purpose public figures, 228
    private figures, 228
    public figures, 227–28
    status of the plaintiff, 228
  slander *vs.* libel, 227
Defamatory statement, 226
Defendant, defined, 6
Defenses based on contract law, 71–74
  age, 74n
  agreement to participate, 72
  equipment rental agreements, 72
  facility leases agreements, 72
  indemnification agreements, 73–74
  independent contract for services, 74
  informed consent, 71–72
  waivers, 71
Defenses, infringement, 623
Demurrer, 7
Deposition, 7, 9
Design defects, 190
Digests, 18–19, 22–23
Dilution, 622–23
D.I.M. process, 283–91
  avoidance/elimination, 286
  categories of risk, creating, 284–86, 285t
  identification stage, 284
  indemnification clauses, 287
  independent contractor, 287–88
  reduction, 288–89
  retention, 288
  transfer, 286–87
  treatment of risk, 286–87, 286t
Directors and officers liability insurance, 356
Disabilities, participants with, 505–16. *See also*
    Americans with Disabilities Act (ADA);
    Individuals with Disabilities Education Act
    (IDEA)
  Individuals with Disabilities Education Act
    (IDEA), 506–15
  Rehabilitation Act of 1973, 505–6
Disabled participants, supervising, 169

Hotels, 201–4
  guest privacy, 203
  guest property, protecting, 202–3
  overbooking, 202
  recreational facilities, 203–4
Human subject research, informed consent and, 107–8

I

Image rights, 632–43
  common law misappropriation, 633–34
    statutory protection, 633–34
  First Amendment defenses, 636–37
    artistic expression, 637
    incidental use exception, 636
    newsworthiness doctrine, 636
    parody defense, 636–37
  intellectual property provisions, 634–35
    Federal Trademark Law (The Lanham Act), 634–35
    postmortem rights, 635
  right of publicity, 632–33
Immunity, 80–94. *See also* Shared responsibility and statutory assumption of risk statutes; Volunteer immunity statutes
  in assault and battery, 220
  automated external defibrillator (AED) statutes, 88–89
  charitable, 81–82
  Federal Tort Claims Act, 80–81
  first aid statutes (Good Samaritan), 74–75, 87–88
  governmental, 80
  in hazing, 267
  legislation-based, 74–75
  recreational user statutes, 74–75, 82
  sovereign, 80
  for using automated external defibrillator (AED), 149
Implied contracts, 372
Implied primary assumption of risk, 70
Implied warranty of merchantability, 193
Incidental use exception, 636
Indemnification agreements
  in corporate liability, 58
  defenses based on contract law, 73–74
  D.I.M. process clauses, 287
  venue concerns, 399
Independent contractor
  vs. employee contracts, 388–89
  employment contracts *vs.* employee, 388–89
  insurance requirements, 357
  liability insurance coverage for, 358

for services, corporate liability and, 57–58, 74
  in transportation, 179–80
  workers' compensation for, 363–64
Index to Legal Periodicals (ILP), 17, 22
Indiana State University Sport Law Links, 21
Individual disparate treatment, 562–64
Individuals with Disabilities Education Act (IDEA), 506–15
  Ted Stevens Olympic and Amateur Sports Act and, 507–8
Informed consent, 107–11
  consent in, 107
  defined, 71–72
  disclosure in, 107
  human subject research, 107–8
  medicine, 107
  minor participants, 109, 113f, 114
  overview of, 107
  sport and fitness, 108–11
    administrative, 109
    content, 108–9
    documentation, 109
    illustrative informed consent, 110–11
Infringement, 622
Inherent relationship, as source of duty, 41–42
  in emergency care, 146
Inherent risks
  agreements to participate, 112–15
  assumption of risk, 69, 99, 115–16
  case related to, 117–19
  defined, 43–44
  express assumption of risk and, 70–71
  informed consent agreements, 107–11
Initial eligibility, determining, 475
Injunction, defined, 378
Injunctive relief, 420–21
  application of, 421
  case related to, 422–27
  permanent injunction, 420
  preliminary injunction, 420
  scope of, 421
  specific performance, 420–21
  temporary restraining order, 420
Insurance coverage in risk management plan, 314–15, 351–60. *See also* Insurance, types of
  additional insured endorsement, 358
  case related to, 359
  certificate of insurance, 358
  contractual agreement, 352–53
    conditions section, 353
    coverage's section, 352
    exclusions section, 352

Insurance coverage in risk management plan (*cont'd.*)
  declarations, 352
  definitions, 352
  endorsements, 352
  event policy, 358
  independent contractors, 358
  requiring insurance of other parties, 357–58
    Additional Insured Endorsement, 358
    certificate of insurance (ACORD form certificate), 358
    event policy, 358
    independent contractors, 358
  selecting the agent and carrier, 358
  typical financial risks, 354t
  understanding the policy, 351–53
Insurance Information Website, 21
Insurance, types of, 353–57
  employment practices liability, 355
  event insurance, 357
  general liability, 355
  liability protecting employees, 356
  motor vehicle, 356–57
  property, 353, 354–55
  umbrella liability, 356
  workers' compensation, 357
Integration clause, 102
Intellectual property law. *See also individual headings*
  copyright, 606–11, 613–19
  image rights, 632–43
  patent, 611–12
  trademark law, principles of, 620–31
  venue concerns, 397–98
Intellectual property provisions, 634–35
  Federal Trademark Law (The Lanham Act), 634–35
  postmortem rights, 635
Intentional actions, 250
Intentional infliction of emotional distress (IIED), 243–47
  case related to, 245–47
  claims of, 244
  elements of, 243–44
  negligent infliction of emotional distress, 244
Intentional torts, 216–49. *See also individual headings*
  assault and battery, 216–25
  breach of duty, 241–42
  defamation, 226–37
  intentional infliction of emotional distress, 243–47
  invasion of privacy, 238–41

Intercollegiate regulations of eligibility, 474–76
Internal Revenue Codes
  charitable exemption provision of, 559
  501(c) of Title 2, 530
  independent contractor *vs.* employee, 389
  subchapter C of, 30
  subchapter S of, 30–31
International Amateur Athletic Federation (IAAF), 5
International Association of Assembly Managers (IAAM), 333
International Council of Arbitration for Sport (ICAS), 411
International Health, Racquet & Sportsclub Association (IHRSA), 302, 304
International Olympic Committee (IOC), 406, 410–11
International sports
  disputes, 410–11
  due process in, 443–44
Internet
  sales, 204
  searches, 19–20
  trademark issues, 625–26
Internet Reference Desk Website, 20
Interrogatories, 9
Interstate and Foreign Travel (Travel Act), 254
Intervening act, 47
Intimate association, 529
Invasion of privacy, 238–41
  appropriation, 239–40
  false light intrusion, 241
  unreasonable disclosure of private facts, 240–41
    case related to, 245–47
    highly offensive, 241
    private *vs.* public facts, 240–41
  unreasonable intrusion on seclusion, 238–39
Involuntary manslaughter, 252
Involvement theories, 429

J

Joint and several liability doctrine, 56
Joint programming, 59
Joint ventures, 59
Journal of Legal Aspects of Sport, 18
Journal of Marketing & Public Policy, 18
Judgment proof, 221
Judicial review, 418–19
  alcohol and drugs, 419
  application, 418–19
  athletic associations, 419
  married students, 419
  scope of, 418

M

Mail fraud, 256–57
Malice, actual, 227
Malpractice insurance, 356
Manufacturing defects, 191
Maritime laws, 206–7
Marketing defects, 191
Mark's Sports Law News, 21
Marquette Law School, 21
Marquette Sports Law Review, 18
Married students, judicial review and, 419
Martindale-Hubbell, 17
Matter of common knowledge, 26
Media
  contact person, guidelines for, 331–32
  dealing with, 330–31
  insurance coverage for, 357
  venue concerns, 398–99
Mediation
  in alternative dispute resolution, 409
  in participant agreement, 99, 102
Medicine, informed consent and, 107
Memorandum of Understanding (MOA), 22
Mens rea, 250
Ministerial acts, 81
Minors
  agreement to participate and, 113f, 114
  informed consent and, 109
  supervising, 169
  waivers or release of liability and, 97–98, 99f
Miscellaneous private sites, 21
Misdemeanor, 250
Mismatching, 170
Misrepresentation of warranty, 193–94
Model Penal Code, 251
Model State Act, 82, 86
Modified comparative fault, 74
Motion for summary judgment, 7, 9, 10
Motion to intervene, 420
Motion to sever, 7
Motion to strike, 7
Motor sports, 91
Motor vehicle insurance, 356–57
Moving into the Future: National Physical Education Standards, 303
Mutual benefit nonprofit corporation, 31

N

National Association for Sport and Physical Education, 303
National Center for State Courts, 20

National Collegiate Athletic Association (NCAA)
  ADR applications used by, 410
  antitrust law, 659–67
    college coaches, 660–61
    student-athletes eligibility, 659–60
    television, 660
    women's athletics, 660
  application to/membership in, 430–31
  Catastrophic Injury Insurance Program, 364–65
  intellectual property rights, 625
  intercollegiate regulations, 475–76
    academic regulations, 475
    amateurism, 475–76
    longevity, 476
    transfer rules, 476
  overview of, 474–75
  sport agent legislation in, 684
National Conference of State Legislatures, 182
National Highway Traffic Safety Administration (NHTSA), 183
National Intramural-Recreational Sports Association (NIRSA), 147, 148
National Labor Relations Act of 1935 (NLRA), 669–70
National Labor Relations Board (NLRB), 3, 5
National Recreation and Park Association, 302
National Sport Law Institute publications, 21
National Standards for Sport Coaches, 303
National Strength & Conditioning Association (NSCA), 302, 303
National Therapeutic Recreation Society (NTRS), 302
National Transportation Safety Board (NTSB), 180
Negative easement, 136
Negligence
  action, 9
  comparative, 267
  criminal, 252
  defined, 40
  per se, 42
Negligence, defenses against, 66–120. *See also individual headings*
  based on common law, 67–71
  based on contract law, 71–74
  based on statutory law, 74–75
  immunity, 80–94
  inherent risks, agreements related to, 107–20
Negligence, elements of, 40–52
  breach of duty, 43–46
  case related to, 49–50

Preponderance of the evidence, 217n
Primary assumption of risk, 67–70, 68–69t
Principal, 207
Private carrier, 179
Private clubs in recreation and sport, 528–36
  Americans with Disabilities Act (ADA), 531
  case related to, 533–35
  Civil Rights Act of 1964, 529–31
  discrimination in, 528
    eradicating, suggestions for, 532
  freedom of association, 529
Private figures, 228
Private nuisance, 139–40
Private nuisances, 139–40
Private schools, separating from public schools,
    474
Privileged liability, 220
Probable consequences rule, 47
Procedural due process, 484–86
Procedural mistake, 8
Procedural noncompliance, 75
Product defects, categories of, 190–91
  design defects, 190
  manufacturing defects, 191
  marketing defects, 191
Products liability, 190–200. *See also* Product defects,
    categories of
  action and defenses, causes of, 191, 192t
  breach of warranty considerations, 193–94
    implied warranty of merchantability, 193
    misrepresentation of warranty, 193–94
    Uniform Commercial Code (UCC), 193
  case related to, 195–98
  risk-utility balancing test, 192–93
  strict liability considerations, 191–92
Professional and Amateur Sports Protection Act of
    1992, 254
Professional insurance, 356
Professional sports
  conduct issues in, 487–88
  labor relations, 673
  leagues, 432
  teams, emergency care for, 153–54
Program sponsorship, 59
Promissory estoppel, 375
Property damage insurance coverage, 356
Property insurance, 353, 354–55
  actual cash value insurance, 354
  basic coverage, 353
  broad coverage, 353
  building ordinance coverage, 355
  business income insurance, 354

coinsurance clause, 354
  deductible, 354–55
  extra expense insurance, 354
  replacement cost insurance, 354
  special form coverage, 353
Property interest, 441–42
Property law, 134–45
  nuisance law, 139–40
  real property, 134–37
  recreational user statutes, 137–39
Proximate cause, 46–47
Public access defibrillation (PAD) program, 304
Public and private schools, separating, 474
Public corporations, 31
Public figure, 227–28, 240
Public function theory, 428–29
Public invitees, 122
Publicly traded corporations, 31
Public nuisances, 139
Public policy, 96–97
Public trust doctrine, 136
Public *vs.* private schools in eligibility, 474
Punitive damages, 48, 220, 229, 377
Pure comparative fault, 74
Purposeful discrimination, 451

Q

Qualified or conditional privilege, 229

R

Racketeer-Influenced and Corrupt Organizations
    Act of 1970 (RICO), 254
Real property, 134–37
  acquiring, modes of, 134–36
  land use controls, 136–37
  rights of, 134
Reasonable foreseeability test, 252–53
Reassignment clause, 384
Reckless actions, 250
Reckless homicide, 252
Reckless manslaughter, 252
Reckless misconduct, 45
Recreational clubs and facilities, application to,
    429–30
Recreational user statutes, 82, 123
  cases related to, 76–77, 141–43
  characteristics of, 137–39
  legislation-based immunity, 74–75
  two-pronged analysis of applicability, 139
Recreation and sport management, 471–536. *See
    also individual headings*
  alternative dispute resolution in, 410

September 11, 2001, crowd management since (*cont'd.*)

operational procedures, changes in (*cont'd.*)

closed circuit television (CCTV), 341

evacuation, 341

physical security measures, 340

security systems, 341

searches and resulting legislation, 342–43

Seton Hall Journal of Sport Law, 18

Settlement, 8

Severability, 99

Sex crimes in hazing, 268–69

Sexual harassment, 573–86

employment practices liability insurance and, 355

in the schools, 576–78

coach/athlete sexual harassment, 577

peer sexual harassment in athletics, 577–78

sexually harassing behaviors, 574t

in the workplace, 573–76

affirmative defense, 575

hostile environment harassment, 574

quid pro quo harassment, 573–74

state legislative protection, 575–76

totality of the circumstances, 574–75

Shared responsibility and statutory assumption of risk statutes, 74–75, 89–93

defined, 89–90

equine liability statutes, 90

general recreation and sport immunity statutes, 92

hazardous recreational activity immunity statutes, 92–93

skating statutes, 91

ski operator immunity statutes, 90–91

statutes pertaining to other activities, 91–92

Shepardizing, 22–23

Shepard's Citations, 17–18, 22

Sherman Antitrust Act, 657–59

section 1 of, 657–59

violation of, establishing, 657–58

section 2 of, 658

violation of, establishing, 658–59

Signage, effective, 345

Simpson, O. J., 6

Single-entity status, 646

Skateboard parks, 91

Skating rinks, emergency care in, 153

Skating statutes, 91

Ski operator immunity statutes, 90–91

Slander, 227

Small businesses, workers' compensation for, 362

Snowmobile statutes, 91, 92

Society for the Study of the Legal Aspects of Sport and Physical Activity, 18

Sole proprietorships, 28

Southeastern Reporter, 8

Southern Reporter, 8

Southwestern Reporter, 8

Sovereign immunity, 71, 80

Special damages, 229

Special doctrines of contract law, 375

Special form coverage insurance, 353

Specific performance

for breach of contract, 378

injunction, 420–21

Sphere of control, 204

Sponsor, defined, 4

Sponsorship contracts, 395–96

Sport activities, emergency care in, 153

Sport agent legislation, 681–90

American Bar Association (ABA), 685

financial advisors, 685

fundamental concepts of, 681

National Collegiate Athletic Association (NCAA), 684

national legislative efforts, 682–83

other regulatory efforts, 683–84

professional team sport players' associations, 684–85

state legislative efforts, 681

Uniform Athlete Agents Act (UAAA), 682, 683t

Sport Agent Responsibility and Trust Act (SPARTA), 14

Sport and legislation, 537–690. *See also individual headings*

antitrust law, 644–68

federal statutes and discrimination, 538–605

intellectual property law, 606–43

labor law, in professional sport applications, 669–80

sport agent legislation, 681–90

Sport and Recreation Law Association, 21

Sport law blogs, 19–20, 21

Sport law, introduction to, 1–37

business structure and legal authority, 28–37

legal research, 13–27

legal system, 2–12

Sport Marketing Quarterly, 18

Sports Agent Responsibility and Trust Act, 14

Sports and Law: Contemporary Issues (Appenzeller), 17

Sports and the Law: Major Legal Cases (Quirk), 17

SportsBusiness Journal (Street and Smith), 18, 22

Sport-shooting statutes, 91, 92

Voidable contracts, 373
Voir dire, 7
Voluntary associations and eligibility issues, 471–82
  arbitrary and capricious standard, 472
  case related to, 477–81
  high school privilege, 473
  home-schooled eligibility, 473–74
  intercollegiate regulations, 474–76
  separating public and private schools, 474
  state or federal constitutional rights, 472–73
Voluntary assumption, as source of duty, 42
  in emergency care, 146
Voluntary consent, 70
Volunteer immunity statutes, 82–87
  legislation, 74–75, 83–85t
  recreation and sport volunteer, 86
  state volunteer immunity statutes, 82, 86
  Volunteer Protection Act (VPA), 86–87
Volunteer Protection Act (VPA), 86–87
Volunteers, workers' compensation for, 363

W

Waivers or release of liability, 58, 95–106
  in agreement to participate, 114
  case related to, 103–5
  defined, 71, 95
  format of, 98–99
  parental waiver, minors and, 97–98, 99f
  participant agreement, 99–102, 100–102f
  requirements for, 96–97
    consideration, 97
    parties to the contract, 97
    public policy, 96–97
  state, territory, and Washington, D.C. classifications, 96f
WESTLAW, 19

West's Key Number System, 22–23
Willful acts by an employee, 55–56
Willful and wanton misconduct, 45
Wire and mail fraud, 256–57
Wire Communications Act of 1961 (Wire Act), 254
Workers' compensation, 357, 361–70
  additional claims, 364
  additional coverage, consequences of, 364
  athletes, 364, 366–68
  case related to, 366–68
  eligibility requirements, 361–62
  employee benefits, 364
  independent contractors and, 363
  NCAA Catastrophic Injury Insurance Program, 364–65
  nonscholarship athletes, 364
  small businesses and, 362
  state legislature covering athletes, 363–64
  tax effect on school, 364
  transportation issues, 182–83
  volunteers and, 363
Work stoppage provision, 399
World Anti-Doping Agency (WADA), 411, 497–98
Writ of certiorari, 5
Wrongful death, 97, 217
Wrongful termination
  employment practices liability insurance and, 355
www.findlaw.com, 19, 22
www.law.com, 22

Y

Yahoo, 19
Youth sport programs, emergency care in, 150–51

Z

Zoning, 136–37